Charles H. Hession
Hyman Sardy
DEPARTMENT OF ECONOMICS, BROOKLYN COLLEGE

ASCENT TO AFFLUENCE
A HISTORY OF AMERICAN ECONOMIC DEVELOPMENT

ALLYN AND BACON, INC. BOSTON

Library of Congress Catalog Card Number: 69–15252

Printed in the United States of America

Third printing . . . August, 1971

PREFACE

In our fast-changing culture, new models in textbooks are as necessary as novel designs and improvements in automobiles or other industrial products that incorporate the latest technological improvements. Advances in knowledge, the ceaseless march of national and world events, and shifts in the focus of scholarly and public interest acutely indicate the need for innovation in the organization and content of such books, if they are to be up-to-date, effective teaching instruments. In our opinion, in no field is this more true today than in that of American economic history.

Although as producers of a new "model" textbook in this competitive area we are naturally partisans of change, we submit that there are substantial reasons for challenging the status quo. In the post-World War II period, an extraordinary number of new nations have come into existence; all have been faced with the difficult task of economic development. At the same time, some of the more advanced nations, such as the United States, have begun to grapple with the largely unanticipated costs and consequences of rapid, uncontrolled growth. These problems of development have led modern economists to return to the classical concern with the overall process of economic growth. Growth theories have multiplied, and the increased interest in the whole field has contributed, in turn, to the employment of the analytic approach to economic history, as contrasted with the merely descriptive method.

More recently, another interdisciplinary subject has evolved in the United States, known either somewhat ambiguously as the "new economic history," or perhaps more descriptively for some, as econometric history. This sophisticated, imaginative orientation to an old subject has stimulated a number of controversial studies, many of which have appeared only in the professional literature. During these same years, intellectual developments in the behavioral sciences, notably in psychology, sociology, and anthropology, have sparked interest and suggested new ways of analyzing the influence of culture, social structure, and personality on economic growth. Not all historians have been immune to the findings and implications of these disciplines for the study of their subject. The students of entrepreneurial history, in particular, have sought to employ some of the social science concepts in their work. However, much of this new work and outlook has not as yet been incorporated in the standard texts.

This book summarizes and embodies many of the most significant of the quantitative and qualitative studies of American economic development that have appeared in the post-1945 literature and relates them to the conventional body of knowledge in this field. Its treatment is distinctive because it emphasizes the analytic approach and seeks an understanding of American economic development in the light of some of the major theories of growth. We believe that it offers a more integrated picture of the process of economic growth than do other approaches. Rather than employing a topical organization, which tends to give the student separate stories about banking, agriculture, or international trade, et cetera, we have preferred to use the chronological method because it permits a more direct treatment of the interactions among the sectors of the economy in the process of growth. And we have not neglected the institutional framework of American economic development. This is so because we began this book in complete agreement with two economic historians who had written: "The ideal textbook for economic history would do more than use theory to analyze the process of economic growth, it would convey a strong sense of how and why economic institutions evolve and the cause for structural change. . . ."[1] Because of our acceptance of this point of view, we have sought throughout to demonstrate the relevance of the changing cultural context to the process of economic development. In doing so, we have drawn upon some of the important studies that reflect the newer work in the behavioral sciences.

There have been a number of recent publications, such as those of North, Hughes, and Vatter, which have provided precedents for a deliberately analytical approach to American economic history.[2] These books have demonstrated, we believe, the fruitfulness and general value of this type of treatment. In addition, the short but brilliant book of Bruchey has shown the importance of the American cultural background in the period before the Civil War for our growth as a nation.[3] We acknowledge our indebtedness to these pioneers of the discipline and our gratitude for the inspiration they have given us. In effect, we have brought together the contributions of these and other

---

[1] R. Fels and J. G. Williamson (Book Review), *The Journal of Economic History* (June, 1962), pp. 268–69.

[2] These books are, respectively, D. C. North, *The Economic Growth of the United States, 1790–1860* (Englewood Cliffs, N.J.: Prentice-Hall, Inc., 1961); J. Hughes, *The Vital Few* (Boston: Houghton Mifflin Co., 1966); and H. G. Vatter, *The U.S. Economy in the 1950's* (New York: W. W. Norton and Co., Inc., 1963).

[3] See S. Bruchey, *The Roots of American Economic Growth, 1607–1861* (New York: Harper and Row, Publishers, 1965).

eminent scholars in one book covering the whole of American economic development since colonial times. At the conclusion of such a work, one is very conscious of the reality of that academic "chain of being" that underlies most scholarly effort.

In the organization of this book, pedagogical considerations have been foremost in our minds. The primary evidence of this is found in the decision not to present summaries of the growth theories at the beginning of our treatment. Instead, they have been introduced serially in parts of the book where they have the most relevance and usefulness for the student's understanding of the subject. We should like to call attention to the fact that the structure of the book as a whole follows a systematic pattern. In each Part there is an Introduction that presents one or more theories of growth as a possible analytical framework for the understanding of the period in question. This Introduction is followed by chapters successively describing the main sectors of growth in the period, analyzing the applicability of the theory to the historical data, and interpreting the political and cultural processes accompanying the economic changes.

Whereas one or more theories of growth have been used as a frame of reference, we do not subscribe to a monistic explanation of the growth process. In fact, wherever possible we have pointed to the multiplicity of factors involved in social and economic causation. We believe that there are pedagogical advantages in examining the process of economic growth in terms of a given theoretical framework, as long as its limitations are recognized. The basic rationale for this type of approach lies in the desirability of interpreting historical events from the standpoint of a coherent theoretical position so that the student can see, despite the complex and massive character of historical phenomena, the essential structure of economic change and institutional development.

In writing this book we have benefited immeasurably from the criticisms of the following colleagues at Brooklyn College who read one or more chapters: Professors Thomas B. Birkenhead, Patricia Bowers, Abraham Hirsch, Norman Hubbard, Edward Marcus, Hans Trefousse, and Theresa Wolfson. Jerry Kurland and David Laibman have also been very helpful in the area of their expertise. Marie N. Hession read the entire manuscript and graciously provided assistance on substantive as well as literary matters. Susan Sardy gave us material as well as moral support. Mrs. Ann Feldstein conscientiously typed innumerable versions of the text. We are deeply obliged to all these understanding persons, but exonerate them completely from responsibility for any errors of commission or omission, which is solely ours.

Charles H. Hession
Hyman Sardy

CONTENTS

PART VII

The Organizational Revolution in American Economic and Political Life, 1897–1918

PART VIII

The Emergence and Development of the "Consumer Economy," 1919–1932

Chapter 1

BASIC CONCEPTS OF ECONOMIC DEVELOPMENT

THE HISTORICAL SIGNIFICANCE OF AMERICAN ECONOMIC DEVELOPMENT

The economic development of the United States has been a subject of wide interest for many years. The rise of the American nation from a status of political dependence and economic undevelopment to its present position as a world power has been dramatic and relatively swift. The extraordinary development of its economy has fascinated many people because of its inherent human interest and great significance for the welfare of man. In the aftermath of World War II many new nations emerged from the colonial state, and the study of economic development has become one of major importance. The analysis of the American case has taken on added significance because it is recognized, as one political sociologist has recently stated, that "The United States was the first major colony successfully to revolt against colonial rule. In this sense, the United States was the first 'new nation.' "[1]

During the almost two hundred years since the United States won independence from Great Britain, a remarkable metamorphosis has taken place in the American economy and way of life. In the not so accurate terminology of popular writers on economics, the change was from an economy of scarcity to one of potential abundance. In the more concrete, quantitative terms of the economist, the gross national product[2] (measured in constant 1929 dollars) increased from about $3 billion in 1839 to close to $250 billion in 1959. On a per capita basis, the gross national product over this span of years multiplied almost sevenfold. The annual rate of growth of output per capita over this period was 1.64 per cent. At such a rate of increase, output per capita doubled every 43 years. In the light of this rate of growth over so long a period, it is neither ethnocentric nor chauvinistic for one American economist to write, "Of all the major countries in the world, the United States presents the most dramatic example of the effects and potentialities of modern economic growth.

[1] S. M. Lipset, *The First New Nation* (New York: Basic Books, Inc., 1963), p. 2.
[2] The concept of national product and the methods of measuring it are discussed below, pp. 5–8.

The American achievement, accomplished in an environment favored by geographical, historical and political circumstances, has yet to be matched by any other nation."[3]

THE NATURE OF ECONOMIC DEVELOPMENT

To understand the evolution of the American economy, it is necessary to comprehend the basic concepts of economic development and the nature of the accompanying social and political processes. Although economists in developing their various theories of economic growth have often employed different terminology, there are a number of common, stock notions in the literature with which we need to be familiar. One of these, for example, is the simple distinction between growth or expansion and economic development. When we speak of economic development we do not have in mind simply a rise in total output over time that reflects or results from an increase in the labor force or from additional inputs of other factors of production. As will be noted in more detail below, most economists prefer to define economic development as involving a rise in output per capita. For that to take place, changes in the processes of production must occur; the factors of production (natural resources, labor, capital, and management) must be combined in new and more productive ways to increase output relative to population growth.

When we consider the vast changes that have occurred in the supply and cost of the various factors of production over the course of our nation's history, it is evident that for these factors to be used, or as the economist would say, allocated efficiently, they increasingly had to be mobile so that they could move from places and uses of relative surplus to those of deficit. For example, it should be clear that the combinations of the factors of production that are efficient when the process of economic development starts may not be the best attainable at a later stage when new types of plant and equipment have become available, or when more workers of given types have been trained. When this stage is reached, new techniques of production may become profitable; in more technical terms, production functions or the proportions with which the factors of production are combined vary with changes in the supply and demand and, therefore, with the changes in the cost of such factors. For this reason, if the full fruits of economic development are to be gained, resources—and that term includes human resources, people— have to adapt in time and place to the requirements of the economic process. This means that the people of a developing economy must accept change and innovation in the products they buy, the conditions of work, the policies of their governments, etc. Indeed, western man has discovered that the industrialization of a nation entails a revolution, almost a continuous revolution in

[3] R. T. Gill, *Economic Development: Past and Present* (Englewood Cliffs, N.J.: Prentice-Hall, Inc., 1963), p. 77.

the way of life of its people. Professor Duesenberry has summed up this fundamental point by insisting in a much-quoted article that the essence of the process of economic development is fluidity or flexibility in the techniques of production and resource allocation.[4] We see, then, that economic development is not a mere matter of quantitative expansion in the use of economic resources. It is true that new resources must be brought into efficient use if an economy is to grow at a maximal rate. But they must also be combined and recombined in new proportions as the available supply and demand for them changes, if optimal production is to be attained with a resulting increase in output per capita.

A more rigorous definition of economic development than we have presented thus far can be formulated. Whereas there are a number of alternative concepts of economic development, they all have certain universal factors in common. All definitions of economic development require an increase in either existing output or in the capacity to produce more. Unless the economy can produce more economic goods, or increase its productive capacity, a rise in the average plane of consumption will be impossible, except as a result of a reduction in the population. But societies that improve their levels of consumption or productive capacity as a consequence of a population decline are not generally considered as undergoing economic development, even though the average degree of material well-being may rise significantly. In short, it is contended that unless output is increased through greater productive effort, economic development has not taken place.

A convenient analytical tool that is useful in demonstrating certain essentials of economic development is the production possibility graph shown below (Chart 1). On this graph, the production of capital goods is measured along the y axis and the output of consumer goods along the x axis. The curve given by P_1P_2 is called the "production possibility frontier." At any point on this curve we can calculate the number of units of capital goods produced by drawing a horizontal line from that point to the y axis. To obtain the number of consumption goods produced at that point we would drop a vertical line to the x axis. Any point on the curve P_1P_2 represents a combination of the factors of production (land, labor, capital, and management) that are being used optimally. Any point between 0 and the curve, such as the point S, is a less efficient use of the factors of production. If the production possibility frontier can be moved from P_1P_2 to P_3P_4, then this pushing out of the curve represents economic development. Economic development can, therefore, be considered as an increase in the potential performance of the economy.

In connection with the production possibility curve, it should be noted that increases in the potential output of an economy may be considered economic development, even if the level of consumption is not altered immediately. Production of machines that will in turn make shoes constitutes an increase in the productive potential of a society and, therefore, exhibits growth. Conse-

---

[4] J. S. Duesenberry, "Some Aspects of the Theory of Economic Development," *Explorations in Entrepreneurial History* (December 15, 1950), pp. 68–69.

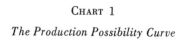

CHART 1

The Production Possibility Curve

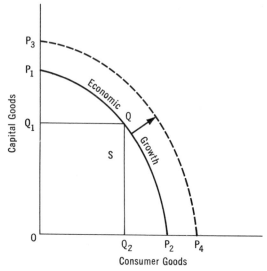

quently, such increases in capacity should be taken into account in measuring the latter.

An alternative concept of economic development to that described above is offered by James Knowles in a recent, provocative study.[5] In his view,

> Economic growth is an increase in the nation's capacity to produce goods, services, and leisure. It is, therefore, not synonymous with the idea of progress or with the more conventional concept of economic growth as an expansion of real per capita gross national product, or with other definitions of growth that have been used from time to time. . . . Progress relates to an increase in the welfare of the people of the nation while economic growth is an increase in the country's productive capacity, i.e., an increase in the nation's ability to provide the material means to satisfy the individual or collective desires for different kinds of goods and services, and thus, in the end, contribute to an increase in welfare. . . .[6]

Mr. Knowles stresses that economic growth as an end of national policy is an intermediate objective—

> it is a goal which the nation can seek in order to provide a material basis for progress or an increase in welfare. If the output of goods and services that results from the increased productive capacity of the economy is used widely, and in accordance with the desires of individuals and of the community as expressed

[5] Joint Economic Committee, 86th Congress, 2nd Session, Study of Employment, Growth and Price Levels, Study Paper No. 20, *The Potential Economic Growth in the United States*, by James W. Knowles (Washington, D.C.: U.S. Government Printing Office, 1960).

[6] *Ibid.*, p. 4.

through community and political channels, it can contribute to welfare and progress.[7]

Knowles' concept of economic growth suggests a useful distinction, that between the performance of the economy in any given period of time and its capability. Mention of performance brings to mind too the idea that economic growth cannot be considered apart from other social goals, such as individual freedom, democracy, price stability, equality of opportunity, sense of community, etc. Attainment of a high rate of economic growth may involve sacrifice of one or more of these goals. In other words, it may not be possible to achieve all these goals simultaneously, and in fact, many of these goals may be conflicting or mutually exclusive. An ordering of priorities among such goals will have to be made by society, and this ordering will inevitably involve value judgments that will in turn affect the growth of the economy.

THE ELEMENTS OF NATIONAL INCOME ACCOUNTING

Changes in an economy's output of goods and services are measured with the aid of a system known as national income accounting. In order to understand the elements of that system we must consider its five basic accounts. The product accounts are called Gross National Product (GNP) and Net National Product (NNP). The income accounts include National Income (NY), Personal Income (PY), and Disposable Income (DY).

Gross National Product measures the total amount of goods and services that are produced in a given year. It does not measure the accumulated wealth in the economy in that year or the stock of wealth in the economy; it is an estimate rather of the new flow of goods and services in a particular year. There are two methods of determining Gross National Product—the value added method and the final products approach. The latter approach requires that we ascertain the final selling price of a commodity or service to the consumer. The sum of these final prices will be the GNP. The value added method requires that we form a cumulative total of the value of a commodity or service as it goes through the successive stages of production. We must exclude the purchase price of the commodity as it goes from one stage of production to another and include in the total only the value added by that particular phase. In this manner, double-counting is avoided in ascertaining the value of a good or service. Chart 2 graphically summarizes the items included in the national income accounts; it will be helpful to the reader to refer to it as we describe the composition of the remaining four accounts.

Net National Product is GNP minus depreciation. The capital goods, i.e., the goods used to produce other goods, are subject to a certain amount of "wear and tear" and obsolescence in the course of the production process. This depreciation is called capital consumption; therefore, NNP can be de-

[7] *Ibid.*, p. 5.

CHART 2

National Income Measurements[a]

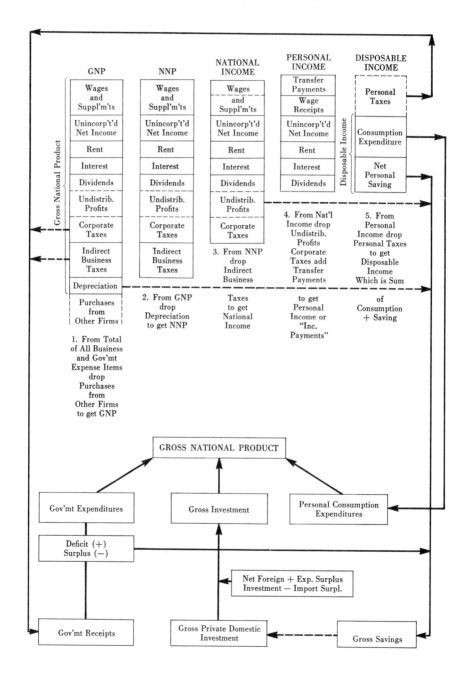

[a] Source: K. W. and L. L. Kapp, *A Graphic Approach to Economics*, Rev. Ed. (New York: H. Holt and Co., 1954), p. 73.

fined as GNP minus capital consumption or depreciation. These accounts, GNP and NNP, are termed product accounts because they measure the output of goods and services and not the returns to the factors of production.

The account that measures such factor income is called the National Income, and it is derived by deducting indirect business taxes from the NNP. Personal income is the money measurement of what the individuals or agents who comprise the factors of production receive as payment for their services. From National Income we subtract corporate savings (undistributed profits) and corporate taxes, and we add government transfer payments to individuals in order to obtain Personal Income. Before the recipients of such Personal Income can decide what to do with it, we must deduct the share that the government takes in the form of personal income taxes. The resultant figure is called Disposable Income, and as the chart shows, this is what is finally available for consumer expenditure or for saving.

For an economy to achieve economic development, it must have positive net investment. This means that a society must increase its capital stock and that capital formation must exceed capital consumption. Only by increasing the capital stock and human resources can the production possibility frontier be driven outward.

THE MEASUREMENT OF ECONOMIC GROWTH

There is one additional factor that must be considered before we can give economic growth a rigorous definition. Since all our measurements are in dollars or money, we must insist that comparisons can only be valid if the dollars have the same purchasing power over time. A constant dollar must be established for measuring purposes, if time series comparisons are to be meaningful. Constant value or real dollars are arrived at through the use of index numbers. By the use of such constant dollar procedures, distortions of output measures because of changes in the value of money can be avoided.

Although any definition of economic growth is not perfectly satisfactory for measuring the increase in the real value of goods and services, the one most economists prefer is the measure known as real per capita product or income. The movement of such a statistical series over time is widely used as a measure of economic growth. The series is formed by calculating the fraction $\frac{\text{(Real NNP (or NY) } t)}{\text{(size of population) } t}$ where the "t" stands for time period t. The percentage rate of change between this ratio at period t, $t + 1$ year, $t + 2$ years, etc. is a measure of the increases or decreases in the total real value of the goods and services produced.

Economic growth, as expressed in these terms, has to be understood as being subject to several important qualifications. It takes no account, for example, of changes in the amount of leisure available to a people over time. Furthermore, figures of this kind tell us nothing about the equality or inequality of the distribution of the increased income, and yet it may be more important to know for whom the increased goods and services have been produced than their total amount. In other words, since this type of statistic is an average, a society with a distorted distribution of income favoring the very rich may find that the improvement of the level of consumption for the masses is insignificant in spite of its achieved economic growth. Changes in the quality of goods and services over time are not recorded very accurately, if at all, in quantitative measures of this kind; if improvement in quality has actually occurred over the time period, their neglect will obviously tend to understate the degree of economic advance.

Finally, and perhaps this is the most important limitation, it must be recognized that statistics of Gross National Product for different countries or for one country over a long span of years ignore the non-economic aspects of the welfare of peoples. The culture of a people is a whole, and many of its intangible features defy measurement by statistics. We have to be very cautious, for example, about comparing the economic well-being of the American people in the colonial period with that of today in terms of national income data. The two periods are so different culturally that measuring economic welfare in quantitative terms is very much like Dr. Kinsey's much criticized study, *Sexual Behavior in the Human Male.* He analyzed sexual behavior only in so far as it could be measured, and undoubtedly left many of his readers with the impression that quantity rather than quality is what counts. In Economics as in a healthy sex life, the quality and context of the experience are all important.

ECONOMIC DEVELOPMENT AS A PROCESS OF
SOCIAL CHANGE

Economists and economic historians are in fairly general agreement that economic development is not an autonomous process, i.e., it is not a phenomenon that can be adequately analyzed and understood in purely economic terms. The basic reason for this is that economies are usually embedded in a culture of which they are an integral part, and in assessing the prospects for an economy's growth it is necessary to consider this broader cultural environment. Cultures and their associated social and political structures differ greatly in the degree to which they promote or inhibit economic growth. The modernization of what has been termed traditional or folk societies is often a very difficult and drawn-out process because of the close and subtle interrelationships between their economic practices and other cultural aspects. In studying the economic evolution of traditional and more advanced societies, social scientists and economists have conceptualized the sociological and psychological processes involved in such change in a variety of ways. The subject is so complex, difficult, and relatively new, at least for economists, that such differences in analysis are understandable. Thus, E. E. Hagen in a penetrating, original work conducts his analysis in terms of the categories of social structure, culture, and personality.[8] Talcott Parsons employs a "pattern variables" approach in such an effort.[9] Professor Hoselitz explores a number of taxonomic classifications of the patterns of economic growth.[10] For our purposes, it would seem best, however, to explain the influence of the cultural context of economic development in terms of a somewhat simpler framework than these authors employ and to demonstrate its meaning and usefulness by applying it to two contrasting phases of economic development. (It should be understood that we are not seeking to discover new principles or truth in this exercise, but rather simply familiarizing the reader with some basic concepts that will prove of value in our later analysis.)

We may begin by noting that if a society is to endure, it must have certain characteristics that have been termed "social imperatives."[11] These imperatives are essential because they promote orderly procedures in man's social relationships and serve to maintain and perpetuate his society. These universal components of all social systems are: groups, values, status, role, authority, and ideology. By *groups* we refer to "the formation of social entities within which there is a sense of commonality among members, a felt distinction between members and outsiders, and an internal structure. By *values* is meant those recognized qualities that persons in the society should possess and the symbolic representations by which these desirable qualities are given overt expression. The term *status* denotes the position of persons (and of groups) within the total configuration of the society, the standing of persons relative to other persons.[12] *Role* combines the attitude, behavior, and sentiments that are appropriate to particular statuses and are expected of those persons who hold them. *Authority* is the recognized relationship involving the legitimate power of decision-making over certain areas of the conduct and activities of other members of the society. *Ideology* is the system of beliefs that offers an understanding of the established social order: the intellectual and spiritual rationale for the social status quo."[13]

In describing the character of these social imperatives in the traditional society and in mature industrial society, by way of contrast, it must be kept in mind that we are employing "ideal types," in which the essential features of a

---

[8] E. E. Hagen, *On the Theory of Social Change* (Homewood, Ill.: The Dorsey Press, 1962).

[9] T. Parsons, *The Social System* (Glencoe, Ill.: The Free Press, 1951).

[10] B. F. Hoselitz, *Sociological Aspects of Economic Growth* (Glencoe, Ill.: The Free Press, 1960).

[11] See W. Goldschmidt, *Man's Way* (New York: Holt, Rinehart and Winston, 1959). This lucid exposition of anthropological concepts has provided the basis of much of our treatment of this subject.

[12] Goldschmidt's definition of status seems broad enough to embrace the concept of social stratification. Some sociologists would insist that the latter concept should have independent "status" as a social imperative. See, e.g., K. Davis and W. E. Moore, "Some Principles of Stratification," *American Sociological Review* (April, 1945), pp. 242–249.

[13] Goldschmidt, *op. cit.*, pp. 65–66.

society are singled out and described for analytical purposes. We do not pretend that these generalizations apply without modification to any particular phase of development in real events.

The traditional society, as Rostow defines it, is "one whose structure is developed within limited production functions, based on pre-Newtonian science and technology, and on pre-Newtonian attitudes toward the physical world."[14] In such a society, the relative ignorance of scientific law and technology sets a ceiling on the level of attainable output per head. As a consequence, whether we look at the dynasties of China, the ancient civilizations of the Middle East or of the Mediterranean, or the world of medieval Europe, we see that the bulk of the people are engaged in agriculture. And related to and growing out of this agricultural way of life is a hierarchical social structure in which family and clan connections play a large part. In some of these pre-industrial societies the family is of the extended type, embracing a large number of relatives and kinsmen, often living under one roof. The individual is often so submerged in and identified with the group that he does not have a sharp sense of individualism, such as later came to characterize capitalistic society. In such cultures also, as Parsons points out, the criteria employed in hiring people for work or in other economic transactions, tend to be "particularistic" ones, i.e., persons are dealt with in terms of who they are rather than on the basis of the norms of efficiency, of what they can do. In short, economic relationships and processes tend to be subordinated to familial, religious, or political considerations. The nature of the social groups and one's status in them tends to be radically different from what we have come to be familiar with in more advanced, industrial societies. Voluntary associations and special interest groups, such as our lobbies, etc., are conspicuous by their absence; one's status in the group tends to be a matter of ascription in terms of birth rather than one of achievement.

The value system of the traditional society is characterized by heavy reliance on custom, on what is sanctioned by magic, sacred lore, or religion. Often this is accompanied by a sort of "long-run fatalism," i.e., a view that individual effort cannot change the world and that one's heirs will live in a condition much the same as one's own.

The status and role systems of traditional societies tend also to be vastly different from those of industrial society. The emphasis on ascribed status tends to make the individual much more a prisoner of social role expectations. Though we cannot rule out the possibility as well as the actuality of individual deviation in such societies, it is likely to be less because of the close-knit character of the society, the relative lack of mobility, and the absence of alternative ways of life. The most striking example of such a rigid, hierarchical system of status is the institution of caste in India, which, despite legislative attack upon it, is still highly resistant to change.[15]

[14] W. W. Rostow, *The Stages of Economic Growth* (Cambridge: Cambridge University Press, 1960), p. 4.

[15] See K. W. Kapp, *Hindu Culture and Economic Planning* (New York: Asia Publishing House, 1963) *passim*.

Political authority too tends to have a very different character in traditional societies from that with which we are familiar in the modern world. Whereas political rule was often centralized in certain traditional societies, thereby transcending the self-sufficiency and power of the localities, the center of political authority tended to be in the hands of those who owned or controlled the land. Indeed, the centralization of political authority that took place in Western Europe during the Mercantilist era is regarded by economic historians as an indispensable antecedent of modern economic development. The fragmentation of political authority, such as existed in the period of the medieval baronies in Europe, made unified markets, standardized measures, and media of exchange an impossibility.

In the area of ideology or belief-systems as a whole, we find a vast gulf between the world of traditional societies and that of industrial nations. Whereas the culture of traditional societies tends to foster a view of the physical world and of the individual's relation to it which underwrites what is familiar or given by authority, political or ecclesiastical, industrial man comes to believe that his natural environment is modifiable through his own effort. The passivism of the traditional society gives way to an activism and confidence in man's power to transform nature. In place of the fixed horizons of traditional society, there must develop, as we have come to say, a "revolution of rising expectations." These changes in man's outlook upon nature, his fellow men, and himself which industrialization required, were the product of a long process of revolution and reform in political, religious, and scientific realms of thought.[16] The protracted nature of that process of release by which Western man won his freedom from the "limiting parameters of traditional society" testifies to the tenacious hold of ancient ideologies and belief-systems on the mind of man. The difficult struggle that the underdeveloped nations of the world today are having in overcoming the repressive influence of their cultural past is additional testimony to the grip of familiar ideas and the "conventional wisdom" upon man. A basic difficulty in overcoming the past is the fact that social life is not simply a conglomeration of separate institutions and social practices; it is rather a close web of culture, interdependent and interlocked, so that the individual cannot deviate from a single pattern of behavior without risking the loss of a whole world of values and associations.

In summary, the transition from a traditional to a modern industrial society requires a massive and far-reaching transformation in the cultural pattern of a people, in the social and political structure as well as in the economic processes, in intellectual preconceptions and in the expectations of man. Politically, such a change seems to demand that a new elite—a new leadership—arise with a faith in the possibility of modernization and a sense of ethical mission in carrying it out. Sociologically, this new elite must supplant the old holders of power, usually the landed aristocracy, and divert the society's surplus of income to the new, growing sectors of the economy. The

---

[16] Some of the theories of the institutional relationships and ideological change required for the development of capitalism in Western Europe and America will be considered below in the Introduction to Part I.

mass of the people, both in rural and in urban areas, must raise the level or horizon of their expectations; they must adapt themselves to a life of change and specialized function.[17]

A revolution of these proportions in the accustomed ways of a people inevitably involves much hardship and deprivation; it means not only estrangement from the familiar and the certain, but it disrupts vested interests and throws human beings into a maelstrom of social change. It demands very often that they live in a world not of their own making, but one that is more the product of technological and political-economic forces with which they have had no previous contact. It is significant that many nations in the past have not embarked upon this difficult course of modernization except in reaction to the threat of domination and humiliation by foreigners. In the history of Germany, Japan, and China, to mention only a few instances, we can clearly see the influence of what Rostow has termed "reactive nationalism" in their drive and determination to become industrialized. It will be interesting in reading the following chapters to assess what importance this factor had in the development of our own nation.

The complex interaction between the central core processes of economic development and the non-economic factors embodied in the social and political structure of a nation presents the economic historian with one of his most difficult problems of analysis. While history offers considerable evidence of the role that social and political changes have played in setting the stage for and ushering in economic change, the exact nature of these inter-relationships has often been a matter of dispute. They have very frequently been more the subject of theoretical inquiry than of definitive, factual study commanding a large degree of agreement. The reverse relationship, namely, the "feedback" from the economic processes to what Lowe terms the extra-systemic (non-economic) forces,[18] has been even more controversial. The Marxian version of economic determinism, in its vulgarized form, is perhaps the most extreme theory of this relationship. But whatever the difficulties in this phase of historical analysis, we cannot evade the subtle problems involved because, as we have contended above, the economic process, narrowly conceived, is invariably embedded in a cultural matrix. We may abstract from the latter for the purposes of pure theorizing about these economic processes, but if we would understand the functioning of an economy in all its actual complexity and response to historical factors, we cannot ignore its cultural context.

ECONOMIC HISTORY AND THE ROLE OF THEORY

Relatively speaking, economic history is a young discipline, particularly if we think of it as the systematic study of man's efforts to provide himself with goods and services. Only in the last hundred years or so have scholars sought

[17] Rostow, *The Stages of Economic Growth*, p. 26.
[18] A. Lowe, *On Economic Knowledge* (New York: Harper and Row, 1965), pp. 49–50, 89–92, and *passim*.

to organize the information on the history of man's economic endeavors, to subject it to research and analytical testing. Yet even in that short period of time the focus of analysis has shifted with the changing generations of historians, reflecting the specific concerns and policy problems of their times.[19] The present generation of economic historians has increasingly, but not wholly, concerned itself with the topic of economic development in its various processes and manifold consequences. There are dissenters from this concentration of interest, but on the whole it is recognized that the study of economic development provides a comprehensive and, in many cases, a most fruitful approach to the subject. ". . . This is because it serves, or should serve, not so much as a means to limit or restrict the historian's interests, but as a way of posing research questions to, and consequently ordering and organizing the enormous mass of facts and topics with which the student of economic history has to deal."[20]

This need to organize and order the data of history is central to the task of the historian. For contrary to some popular impressions, the historian is not an antiquarian interested in facts and events for themselves, but in so far as he aspires to be scientific in his work, he seeks to provide causal explanations for what has occurred in the past. He attempts to establish the connections among the events of history. And making these connections depends upon his ability to subsume or classify the data or events under "appropriate causal regularities." This means that historical "explanation depends upon the availability and proper use of theoretical generalizations. . . ."[21] Such a view of the economic historian's objectives and methods does not rule out the possibility of unique events or chance factors operating, but insists rather that in the field of economics we are interested in the systematic, repetitive aspects of economic behavior. From this standpoint, total explanation of the course of economic development is a goal sought for, but never fully attained. The economic historian, recognizing the contingencies of events, will be wise to seek limited generalizations about man's economic behavior.[22]

History, properly conceived, is not mere chronology or narrative. In so far as it seeks a causal explanation of the sequence of events, it must employ hypotheses and theories to guide its inquiry. The American philosopher, Morris R. Cohen, who was an acute student of scientific method, wrote, "Without an anticipatory idea or hypothesis we do not know what specific

[19] A famous British economic historian has written, "Ages read and write history by the light of their own knowledge and ideals, and they interpret it by their own experience. Although no conscientious scholar would deliberately write either 'proletarian' or 'bourgeois' economic history, only the most technical and therefore the least human history will fail to show some stamp not merely of the historian's age and philosophy but of his country and class or the country and class to which his sympathies principally go out." (J. H. Clapham in *The Encyclopedia of the Social Sciences*, Vol. 5, p. 320.)

[20] B. E. Supple, ed., *The Experience of Economic Growth, Case Studies in Economic History* (New York: Random House, 1965), p. 5.

[21] A. H. Conrad and J. R. Meyer, "Economic Theory, Statistical Inference, and Economic History," in their *The Economics of Slavery* (Chicago: Aldine Publishing Co., 1964), p. 14.

[22] See *ibid.*, pp. 15–17 for a more complete statement of this view.

facts to look for and cannot recognize what is relevant to the inquiry." Yet a good deal of historical investigation, based as it is upon a philosophy of radical empiricism, is carried on without regard for this need for hypotheses or theories. Very frequently such history involves implicit theorizing, employing a variety of unstated theories about the nature and dynamics of personality, the structure of society and the processes of economic and social change. But such theories are not better for being left implicit and unexamined; in fact, they are often questionable from the standpoint of modern knowledge about the nature of man and society.

In economic history the need for theories to suggest the interrelationships among the complex variables of changing economies is very real. One economic historian puts the matter well when he states, "Like the geologist, the economic historian must go about his work with his pockets full of hypotheses. For there is so much to do if we are ever to have a more complete understanding of the past that we cannot afford to waste our time collecting unimportant facts."[23]

In recent years American economic historians have devoted a good part of their attention to these problems of methodology and historiography. For example, since World War II in the field of entrepreneurial history, there have been important discussions of method and of possible uses of the other social sciences in inquiry.[24] In general, historians in the United States have been showing an increased interest in the findings of the behavioral sciences and the implications of such work for their own studies.[25]

An even more recent development in the United States has been the emergence of what is called the "New Economic History," or econometric history. This approach stresses a very sophisticated use of theory and quantitative economics to analyze and measure that which was previously considered unmeasurable. Some of the work of this new school of Cliometricians, as they have been called at Purdue University, will be examined below.[26]

In summary, we may say that practically all contemporary economic historians acknowledge the need for hypotheses and theories in historical analysis, but some wisely warn against the danger of such theoretical frameworks becoming intellectual straitjackets. Furthermore, at the present time no one theory or all-embracing set of hypotheses concerning economic development commands the general acceptance of economists or of economic historians. The current state of knowledge warrants no more than tentative

---

[23] E. A. J. Johnson, "New Tools for the Economic Historian," *The Journal of Economic History* (December 1941), p. 38.

[24] See *Change and the Entrepreneur* (Cambridge: Harvard University Press, 1949); T. C. Cochran, *The Inner Revolution, Essays on the Social Sciences in History* (New York: Harper and Row, A Harper Torchbook, 1964).

[25] See, for example, E. N. Saveth, ed., *American History and the Social Sciences* (Glencoe, Ill.: The Free Press, 1964); also *The Social Sciences in Historical Study: A Report of the Committee on Historiography*, Bulletin 64 (New York: Social Science Research Council, 1954). Another valuable reference on this subject is R. F. Berkhofer, *A Behavioral Approach to Historical Analysis* (Glencoe, Ill.: The Free Press, 1969).

[26] See pp. 439–440.

generalizations about the processes of economic development. It is for this reason that in the following chapters we have taken a pluralistic or eclectic approach in our use of economic theories. We have employed a variety of theoretical perspectives, applying them to the periods in our history to which they seem most relevant. We would have it understood that in considering a theory's usefulness or validity with respect to a single period, nothing is implied about the validity of such theories in other periods, other economies, or of their general acceptability. In some cases, as the reader will discover, we have used theoretical frameworks which upon investigation of the relevant American experience prove to be defective in the sense of giving us a deeper understanding of the period in question or explaining developments within it. In these cases, we would contend that an explicit theoretical framework is better than none at all. Indeed, there is a further advantage: in verifying and learning the limitations of a particular theory the student has an opportunity to experience vicariously the intellectual challenge of that kind of critical testing and debate that animates so much the life of scholarship.

Part 1

THE COLONIAL PERIOD AS CULTURAL PREPARATION FOR OUR INDEPENDENT ECONOMIC GROWTH

Introduction: Sociological Factors in Economic Growth

The American Colonists and the Spirit of Their Institutions

British Mercantilism, the Revolution, and Our Colonial Heritage

The Making and Adoption of the Constitution

INTRODUCTION: SOCIOLOGICAL FACTORS
IN ECONOMIC GROWTH

The colonial period of American life, just as any historical subject, can be studied from a variety of perspectives. In this section we shall be primarily concerned with how the experience of the American people during that period fostered those institutions, human values and attitudes that aided and promoted our subsequent economic growth as an independent nation. We need first, perhaps, to be clear about the phrase "cultural preparation" in our title. The adjective "cultural" refers in our usage to the anthropological concept of culture as meaning a complex of the institutions, social values and attitudes of a people that constitutes their "way of life." The term "preparation" is used in the usual sense of that word.

The influence of culture on the character of the American colonists was stressed in a notable way by that keen observer of that time, Crèvecoeur, in his *Letters from an American Farmer*, when he wrote: "What then is the American, this new man?" Remarking that the colonist was usually a European, or a descendant of a European, he went on to say, *"He* is an American, who, leaving behind him all his ancient prejudices and manners, receives new ones from the new mode of life he has embraced, the new government he obeys, and the new rank he holds. He becomes an American by being received in the broad lap of our great *Alma Mater.* Here individuals of all nations are melted into a new race of men, whose labors and prosperity will one day cause great changes in the world. Americans are the western pilgrims, who are carrying along with them that great mass of arts, sciences, vigor and industry which began long since in the east; they will finish the great circle. . . ."[1]

Crèvecoeur's famous observation on the social character of the American colonists, as he knew them in the late colonial period, contains several elements. It will be noticed that he stresses the break with their European past and the influence of the new physical and social environment that they have "embraced." But somewhat inconsistently, it would seem, he mentions toward the end of the passage that they carried along with them a great cultural heritage of "arts, sciences, vigor and industry." He does not examine at the point of the quotation from his book the nature of the colonists' cultural heritage, but of course we know much about that from other sources and studies. Since Crèvecoeur's remarks raise, in a provocative way, the question of the precise relationship between a people's culture and economic development, it will be worthwhile for us to examine briefly some of the literature on this subject.

[1] J. H. St. John de Crèvecoeur, *Letters from an American Farmer* (New York: E. P. Dutton and Co., Inc., 1957), p. 39.

One of the most famous theses with respect to the relationship between religion as an element of culture and economic development was advanced by a German sociologist and economic historian, Max Weber, in his influential book, *The Protestant Ethic and the Spirit of Capitalism* (1904). Weber

Max Weber (1864–1920) was a German sociologist and economic historian. He taught at Freiberg, Munich, and Heidelberg Universities. He was a pioneer in the use of an interdisciplinary approach to social phenomena.

Keystone Press Agency, Inc.

argued in this work that Protestantism, and especially Calvinism, had provided an indispensable psychological impetus to the growth of western capitalism. He stressed two factors as producing this result: (1) the doctrine of the "calling," which meant that a Christian's primary responsibility was to do his best in whatever station or occupation he had in life rather than to withdraw from the world and devote himself in a monastic fashion to God; (2) Calvin's doctrine of predestination, which stressed that his followers "rationalize" their lives in a way most conducive to economic development. In understanding these doctrines, it is important to note that the early Protestants were opposed to the sale of indulgences by the Roman Catholic Church as well as to the idea that "good works" alone could purchase salvation. Calvin argued instead that the decision as to who were the "elect" (that is, saved) had already been made by God and that no amount of good works on earth could affect that decision. This left the ordinary believer of these doctrines with no more than the practical problem as to whether he was one of the elect or not. Only by trying in every particular way to be like one of the Biblical elect would the faithful get rid of the fear of eternal damnation. Thus, the average Calvinist had to behave well in every respect, not as a "technical means of purchasing salvation, but of getting rid of the fear of damnation. . . ." "In practice," says Weber,

> this means that God helps those who help themselves. Thus the Calvinist, as it is sometimes put, himself creates his own salvation or, as would be more correct, the conviction of it. But this creation cannot, as in Catholicism, consist of a gradual accumulation of individual good works to one's credit, but rather

of a systematic self-control which at every moment stands before the inexorable alternative, chosen or damned.[2]

Calvin's doctrine of predestination was interpreted by later preachers to mean that the "chosen" could gain a sign of their being saved from their prosperity in this world. The Calvinist's close, rational scrutiny of his conduct and the emphasis on his doing his duty in his particular station in life destroyed the leisureliness, in Weber's opinion, that had characterized economic life up to that time. Weber insisted that he was not denying the role of acquisitiveness in previous economic life, the *sacra auri fames* (the accursed lust for gold), but held that the Protestant quest for profit was subjectively characterized by an intensity and anxiety not previously known because of the theological views of this sect. "The entrepreneur worked harder—in fact he could not relax for a moment. The Protestant labor force he recruited worked harder, and none of them could enjoy the increased fruit of their labors for fear of losing the conviction that they were saved. So profits and savings were available to be plowed back into further expansion of business which in itself was a serious calling ordained by God."[3] Psychologically, it is important to note that Weber was in effect offering a psychodynamic theory of social behavior before Freud's doctrines had been publicized to any important degree.

The late Professor Richard Tawney developed the Weberian thesis, with some modifications, in its historical setting in his *Religion and the Rise of Capitalism.*[4] He concluded also that it was Calvin's teachings rather than Luther's that gave the greatest encouragement to the capitalistic spirit. The Puritans, Tawney tells us, disciplined, rationalized, and systematized their lives. They narrowed their interest to the serious business of salvation and profits; they simplified their dress, their speech, their church services. Images and art, sport and recreation, were taboo. Their moral self-sufficiency strengthened their will, but at the same time it tended to weaken their sense of social solidarity. The Puritans, says Tawney, were not notable for their charity. From their idealization of personal responsibility they drew "a theory of individual rights, which secularized and generalized, was to be among the most potent explosives the world has ever known."[5]

Werner Sombart, a German economist, wrote a famous book in the early years of this century in which he insisted that capitalism embodied a definite spirit that had not existed previously.[6] Sombart stressed the rationalistic character of capitalism, but attributed its origins not to the Reformation, but to the role of the Jews and Catholics in the emergence of the new economic

---

[2] M. Weber, *Protestantism and the Spirit of Capitalism*, pp. 338–339.

[3] D. C. McClelland, *The Achieving Society* (Princeton: D. Van Nostrand Co., Inc., 1961), p. 48.

[4] Richard Tawney, *Religion and the Rise of Capitalism* (New York: Penguin Books, 1947).

[5] *Ibid.*, p. 191.

[6] Werner Sombart, *Modern Capitalism* (Leipzig: Duncker and Humblot, 1902).

order. Catholicism, according to Sombart, was important because it preached abstinence, rationalism, and discipline, all necessary conditions for a growing capitalism. The Jews, as outcasts in the medieval Christian world, developed the acquisitive art and especially became adept as money-lenders.

As this brief reference to Sombart's work suggests, the Weber-Tawney thesis concerning the relationship between religion and the rise of capitalism has been a subject of almost continuous academic controversy.[7] Many historians regard it as altogether too one-sided in its failure to recognize the influence of capitalistic development upon religion and its disregard of other factors in the evolution of western capitalism, such as the rise of the national state, the influence of the new interest in science and humanism that came with the Renaissance, the direct effect of the Reformation itself on economic enterprise, etc.[8] While disagreement on this subject among scholars is still rife, there would seem to be sufficient warrant for this cautious statement by a capable student of economic development: "It is fairly generally agreed today that the Protestant ethic was *one* element in the *acceleration* of capitalistic development."[9]

David C. McClelland and his associates in their recent work on the achievement motive have shifted the whole discussion of the Protestant ethic to a more sophisticated, psychological level.[10] Indeed, to McClelland, the connection first seen by Max Weber between the Protestant ethic and the rise of the entrepreneurial spirit now appears as a special case, by no means limited to Protestantism, representative of a general increase in achievement motivation produced by an ideological change. By the achievement motive is meant such things as striving to improve oneself, to work hard, and excel. McClelland sees this achievement motive as being more important than the so-called profit motive; profit merely provides a conventional method of measuring achievement. McClelland and his co-workers find a close relationship between achievement motivation and the existence of creative enterprisers in an economy. In seeking to discover how Protestantism encouraged this entrepreneurial spirit, they have come to place much emphasis on early childhood training in independence and self-mastery (self-reliance). Some early studies along this line seemed to indicate that there were statistically significant differences with respect to these traits between children raised in Protestant, Jewish, and Roman Catholic homes, with the higher scores being reported for the first two groups. (That is to say, parents of these religious backgrounds tended to require independence and self-reliance of their children at an earlier

---

[7] See, for example, H. M. Robertson, *Aspects of the Rise of Economic Individualism,* and P. C. G. Walker, "Capitalism and the Reformation," *Economic History Review* (November 1937); also G. Kolko, "Max Weber on America: Theory and Evidence," *History and Theory,* Vol. I (1961), pp. 243–260.

[8] See, for example, H. Heaton, *Economic History of Europe* (New York: 1948), Chaps. XI–XX.

[9] B. Higgins, *Economic Development* (New York: W. W. Norton & Co., Inc., 1959), p. 222. Our italics.

[10] McClelland, *The Achieving Society, op. cit.*

age than the latter.) Later findings led McClelland to revise his conclusion to this effect: ". . . we can reasonably infer that the lower-class Catholics are less influenced by the American achievement ethic, but that middle-class Catholics have assimilated it to the point where they are indistinguishable from other groups."[11] McClelland sees optimistic implications in his study of the achievement motive in society. If it does nothing else, he writes, "perhaps it will serve to redress the balance a little, to see man as a *creator* of his environment, as well as a creature of it . . . History must be written again, as it was in the 19th century, at least partly in terms of national characters in terms of what a people is trying to do or is most concerned with."[12]

While the psychologist McClelland has been invading economics in pursuit of the complexities of the achievement motive, an economist, Everret E. Hagen, has published a book on the theory of social change in which he makes a bold foray into the domain of the behavioral sciences in the endeavor to understand the dynamics of economic growth.[13] Hagen bases his treatment of social change upon a complex analysis of human needs or motivations. He emphasizes the effect of what he terms "withdrawal of status respect" on the submerged and underprivileged in a traditional society and examines how their reaction to such treatment by their superiors affects social change and economic growth. Such withdrawal of respect, writes Hagen, causes conflict within the individuals who are subject to it. Following a typology of individual adaptation suggested by R. K. Merton, Hagen argues that the alienated individuals may either retreat into *anomie* (normlessness), engage in a ritual-like conformity, become innovators, or rebel in some other way in order to assert their own identity or purposes in life. Immigrant groups or those alienated for other reasons who are relatively blocked off from the sanctioned channels of achievement in the traditional society may find an outlet for their creative needs in the assertion of their economic prowess or in technological innovation. So, groups that may have practiced retreatism or ritualism over several generations may under favorable social circumstances turn to creative innovational activities. While generally such personality changes require a long period, even centuries, to work themselves out, Hagen states that after the end of colonial rule, economic growth may begin in some instances without so long a period of adaptation. "Rather quickly, say in the period between infancy and maturity of one generation, creativity may emerge out of retreatism on a fairly large scale, and the creative individuals may see in economic prowess their best opportunity to prove their worth."[14]

Hagen offers a most interesting modification of the Weberian thesis. He contends that the English Nonconformists who played so prominent a role in the Industrial Revolution owed their entrepreneurial and innovative achieve-

---

[11] McClelland, *The Achieving Society*, p. 359.
[12] *Ibid.*, p. 392.
[13] E. E. Hagen, *On the Theory of Social Change* (Homewood, Illinois: The Dorsey Press, 1962).
[14] *Ibid.*, p. 429.

ments not to Calvinist dogma, but that rather their religious and economic non-conformity were co-results of a third factor, their independence or psychological need for autonomy. "I suggest that the innovators were men who felt strongly a compulsion to understand the problems about them through the exercise of their own capacities. This high need achievement and need autonomy operated in their confrontation with the spiritual aspects of life as well as with the material and political. Their nonconformity in religion and in economic activity were common results of their personality traits."[15]

Hagen analyzes perceptively the impact of colonialism upon economic growth, but unfortunately for us, does not comment on our period of colonialism under British rule. He stresses the adverse psychological effects on the colonialists of the derogation of their culture by their rulers and points out how such subject peoples may turn to retreatism as a defense or in more extreme cases of exploitation to ritualism or to the messianic appeals of native leaders.

While many of the insights contained in these theories of Weber, McClelland, and Hagen are relevant to later phases of American economic development, it will be helpful to keep them in mind as we review the motives of the American colonists in migrating to the New World and the manner of their coming here.

[15] *Ibid.*, p. 297.

Chapter 2

THE AMERICAN COLONISTS AND THE SPIRIT OF THEIR INSTITUTIONS

THE MIGRATION OF THE AMERICAN COLONISTS

The colonization of the New World was a vast economic task requiring large sums of capital, an adequate supply of settlers, and the leadership and managerial skill equal to the challenge. England's colonial secret, as the Beards aptly characterize it in their magisterial work, *The Rise of American Civilization,*[1] was that she had more of these essentials for successful colonization than her rivals. She had broken with the old feudal order first and was rapidly accumulating the capital, the labor, and the organization and administrative genius necessary to carry out this great business enterprise. Furthermore, political and religious changes had occurred in England, even more so than in the continental countries of Europe, which profoundly stimulated colonial expansion.

One of the most difficult problems the English faced in colonizing America was that of recruiting the necessary labor. The Indians, being largely nomadic and unskilled in the European trades, were unsuitable for producing the products in which the promoters of colonies were interested. The cost of equipping the settlers came to no small sum. They had to be transported three thousand miles across the sea and supplied with clothing, tools, arms, and ammunition. Moreover, food had to be supplied until a settlement could be made self-sustaining. The cost of transporting and settling a colonial family probably amounted to several hundred dollars.

There were three classes in England who could be considered potentially interested in colonization. First, there were the fairly well-to-do members of the middle class who were willing to migrate and able to pay their own expenses. Secondly, there was a group of nobles and rich merchants and other people who had funds to invest in the colonies, but who did not wish them-

[1] Revised College Edition, 2 vols. in one (New York: The Macmillan Co., 1935), Chapter 1. This well-written chapter provides a fascinating analysis of the subject that the scope of the present book does not permit us to undertake.

selves to migrate. Thirdly, there was the mass of workers, farm tenants, paupers, and unemployed who could either be compelled to migrate or convinced that they would be better off in America, but who lacked the means of paying for their transportation. Since the first group mentioned were not sufficiently numerous to settle a colony, the problem was essentially this: How could the poor who were willing but unable to migrate be financed by the more prosperous who were willing to invest but not to go themselves?

This problem was solved in several different ways. One took the form of establishing chartered companies, such as those in Virginia and Massachusetts, in which the funds provided by the investors were used to equip, transport, and maintain the colonists. The settlers of these corporate efforts were usually people who were willing to undergo the hardships of migrating to a primitive frontier because of religious reasons; such was the case, for example, with the Pilgrims who settled at Plymouth and later the Puritans who migrated *en masse* to the Massachusetts Bay Colony. These separatist communities did not fit in well with the plans of British businessmen or proprietors who hoped to make quick profits out of their land grants. The reason was that these dissenting groups wished to cut themselves off from Europe and establish communities that would be as self-sufficient as possible. They did not suit the British government well either because they offered it little prospect of compensation for the expenses of military defense and the public works needed by the colonists. Because of these shortcomings in the group method of settlement, the British joint-stock companies and the proprietors of the colonies were forced to devise other methods of recruiting a labor supply.

The most common means of bringing settlers over was the indentured-servant system. This was a practice that had a long history in England. For many years in the past, minors had been apprenticed by their parents or guardians to work for a master for a specified period of years or until they were adults. Under the labor contract, or indenture, as it was called, the immigrant agreed to a period of temporary servitude, usually three to seven years, in exchange for his transportation, maintenance, and compensation at the end of his period of service. These so-called "freedom dues," which were established by law and custom, generally consisted of working tools and clothing and, in some cases, land. The immigrants who came to the colonies in this way were known as redemptioners. In general, it is estimated that the indentured servant system financed the transportation of more than one half of the colonial immigrants to America. It is said by good authority that a majority of the Scottish, Scotch-Irish, Irish, German, and Swiss immigrants came to this country as indentured workmen; Pennsylvania received the greater part of this immigration. It was not uncommon for Philadelphia newspapers to advertise such workmen, as did this one in 1729:

> Lately arrived from London, a parcel of very likely English servants, men and women, several of them tradesmen; to be sold reasonable and time allowed for

payment. By Charles Read of Phila., or Capt. John Ball, on board his ship, at Anthony Millkinson's Wharf.[2]

While most of the indentured servants came here of their own free will, there were some people who were transported abroad by force. The English recruiting agents who canvassed the inland towns and villages were often unscrupulous. After securing the signature of immigrants on an indenture, they would sometimes imprison them aboard ship to prevent their breaking the contract before sailing. This practice apparently led some of these agents actually to "spirit away" drunkards and even children to transport them to the New World.[3]

In addition to those who were thus tricked into migration, there was a small but important group consisting of convicts who were sentenced to servitude in the colonies, their services being bought by promoters or prosperous settlers. Parliament in 1662 and 1717 specifically provided for such disposal of convicts. Under the first act, "rogues, vagabonds and sturdy beggars" could, if judged incorrigible, be deported. The second law authorized the transportation of persons convicted of even lesser crimes. Some of "His Majesty's Seven Year Passengers" undoubtedly pursued unlawful careers in America after their period of servitude. Others apparently reformed in the new environment; one source tells us that in Maryland, on the eve of the Revolution, most of the school teachers were transported convicts. Altogether, it is estimated that about 50,000 convicts were transported to America, of which 20,000 went to Maryland.[4] The majority of these convicts were unskilled workers, not noted for their industry or obedience. Despite the heavy import duties imposed on them by some of the colonies—laws which, by the way, were disallowed by the Crown because it favored wholesale dumping of convicts—convicts continued to be brought in throughout the colonial period. Poor farmers and frontiersmen who could not afford slaves apparently found these convicts a cheap source of labor. Johnson and Kroos argue that some of these exconvicts "imparted drive and dynamism to the economy. They became masters at risk taking, and in competition with them, the instinctively more conservative were compelled to become more venturesome in their business activities."[5]

Another method of inducing people to migrate to the colonies was the "headright" system. This took several forms. In some cases, for example, joint stock companies or proprietors granted land to prosperous people who were willing to bring colonists to America or finance their transportation. For each "head" so transported, payment was made in land of so many acres. By this

[2] V. L. Parrington, *Main Currents in American Thought,* Vol. I: *The Colonial Mind* (New York: Harcourt, Brace & Co., 1927), p. 134.

[3] See A. E. Smith, "Indentured Servants: New Light on Some of America's 'First' Families," *Journal of Economic History,* Vol. II (May, 1942), pp. 40–53.

[4] R. B. Morris, "Production During the Colonial Period," *The Growth of the American Economy,* ed. by H. F. Williamson (Englewood Cliffs, N.J.: Prentice-Hall, Inc., 1946), p. 52.

[5] E. A. J. Johnson and H. Kroos, *The American Economy* (Englewood Cliffs, N.J.: Prentice-Hall, Inc., 1960), p. 123.

means many wealthy Britishers came into possession of estates of large proportions. Then, again, the headright system was often related to that of indenture. Servants were compensated after the end of their servitude with tracts of land, and in this manner many small farmers were led to take up what was often marginal land in the outlying, more inaccessible parts of the colonies. Another group who were enticed by the headright system were those who could finance their own transportation and were granted land by proprietors or others in order to induce them to migrate. While the headright system did bring many people to America, it was marred by corruption and sharp dealing; indeed, it gave such encouragement to land jobbery that it has been spoken of as "a training school for land speculators." In this way it encouraged in some Americans an almost obsessive interest in getting rich fast, with little regard to the means employed.

A large number of the "first Americans" to come to these shores did not come of their own free will. We refer, of course, to the Negro slaves. History has it that the first were brought into the colonies in 1619 by a Dutch privateer. They were used on the tobacco farms of Virginia; this was the beginning of Negro slavery in the English mainland colonies. Actually, the practice did not become more widespread until later in the seventeenth century. After 1660 the belief developed in Great Britain that the country was being depopulated by the migration, voluntary or forced, of so many people to the colonies. The government, therefore, looked with favor upon the slave trade as a means of providing the colonists with a labor supply. In 1662 the Royal African Company, an English joint stock company, broke the Dutch monopoly in the slave trade and thereafter increasing numbers of slaves were brought to the colonies. It was the practice at that time to "season" the slaves in the British West Indies for three years before bringing them over to the mainland. Their numbers at first were not large. Virginia's slave population in 1690 was about 4,000; in the colonies as a whole there were over 20,000 slaves in 1700. After that date their numbers grew more rapidly and the slave trade flourished. In the years from 1715 to 1750 the imports averaged 2,500 a year, but by the 1760's, 7,500 were being brought in. At the time of the Revolution there were about 450,000 Negro slaves in the colonies.

By the end of British rule every colony had its slaves. They worked in cities as well as in the country, in shops and mills as well as in the fields. Their numbers, of course, were greatest in the southern colonies. In Virginia, for example, probably about half of the population in 1760 consisted of slaves. In South Carolina by 1730, they already outnumbered the whites, and thirty years later two-thirds of the population of that colony was Negro. Slaves were numerous in these colonies in the seventeenth century because they were widely used in growing such crops as tobacco, rice, and indigo. In the following century cotton and sugar were also grown with their aid. That it was profitable, on the whole, to use them in this way is shown by the rising price of slaves. The average price in 1650 was £20 a head, in 1700 £25, and by the eve of the Revolution £50 to £80 a head.

Many white colonists found the use of slaves profitable and advantageous;

moreover, slaves were preferable to convicts and had advantages over indentured servants. The slaves were well-suited in the eyes of their owners for the
many tasks to be performed throughout the year on southern plantations.
They were capable of being taught various skills, valuable in the shop and
home, as well as doing the arduous, relatively unskilled work in the fields.
While only the Quakers as a religious group opposed the practice of slavery,
there were many other enlightened people who saw its economic disadvantages
to society. It was obvious, even to the great planter William Byrd of Virginia,
that when Negro slaves came to constitute the bulk of the working population,
the willingness of the whites to work was weakened. Manual labor, as with the
ancient Greeks, came to be associated with the status of the slave and was
therefore depreciated. Apart from the moral aspect of the practice, and we do
not wish to seem to condone the brutal and brutalizing slave trade, it must be
recognized that the Negro slaves made a considerable contribution to American economic development during the colonial period and indeed up to the
time of their emancipation. They provided a large part of the sheer manpower
required to turn the raw resources of a new country into valuable export
commodities or into capital goods of various kinds. The slaves built many of
the houses, barns, roads, levees, and other forms of fixed capital so badly
needed in an underdeveloped country in its early years. No one can calculate
with any certainty whether this labor, if it had been hired on a free basis,
would have promoted a more rapid rate of economic growth, but there can be
no dispute that as slave labor it made a massive contribution to our growth
then and later.

COLONIAL POPULATION GROWTH IN RELATION
TO NATURAL RESOURCES

The growth of the American colonies, measured in terms of population, was
relatively slow at first. The best available estimates set forth in Table 1
below, show that there were only 250,000 people in the colonies by 1700. By
1770 their estimated number was slightly over two million and even by 1775
there were only 2,500,000 inhabitants. We can appreciate the fact that the
colonies were not densely populated when we realized that in one year we
add more than that number to our present population. The line of geographic settlement moved only slowly westward as the population increased.
By 1700 the settlements generally extended to the fall line.[6] By 1750 they had
reached well into the Piedmont region and within two decades hardy settlers
and pioneers were crossing the Appalachian mountain barrier.

Most of the increase in population after the first settlements was mainly
through natural growth. Benjamin Franklin in 1775 thought that only 80,000
out of about one million had braved the Atlantic. The dangers of crossing

---

[6] In physiographic terms, the fall line marks the line of waterfalls along the Atlantic
coast at the points where the harder rocky terrain gives way to the sandy coastal plain.

undoubtedly deterred many, and the high mortality among those who essayed it tended to keep the number of immigrants relatively low. The substantial natural increase was the result, of course, of the large families of the time; it is estimated that the population doubled about every 23 years, despite the extremely high infant mortality rate (40 per cent of the infants of that time died in their first year). Geographically considered, this population was mainly rural. There were no really large cities, in our sense of the term. For example, in 1754, Philadelphia was the largest with 10,000 inhabitants, followed by Boston with 7,000, and New York City with 5,000. These latter cities were large, however, with respect to contemporary standards.

TABLE 1

The Growth of Colonial Population (estimated)[a]

1660	75,058
1670	111,935
1700	250,000
1720	466,185
1740	905,563
1760	1,593,625
1770	2,148,076

[a] Source: *Historical Statistics of the United States, Colonial Times to 1957* (Washington, D.C.: U.S. Government Printing Office, 1958), p. 756.

The ethnic composition of the colonies, as our discussion of the background of the immigrants might suggest, showed a remarkable degree of homogeneity. The majority of the people were of English descent; the three main exceptions were the Negro slaves, the Germans, often referred to as the Pennsylvania Dutch, and the Scotch-Irish. In general, the colonial population was predominantly WASP: white, Anglo-Saxon, and Protestant.

The land to which the colonists came, in Crèvecoeur's pleasant phrase, "the broad lap of our Alma Mater," was, on the whole, a hospitable one. While the Pilgrims had to endure the rigors of the New England winter, the middle colonies enjoyed a more moderate climate, and the southern ones, a mild one. "The effect of the American scene upon the European newcomer," writes Nettels, "was to invite him to remain and to enable him to obtain a foothold. . . ."[7] In general, the climate was appealing. John Smith wrote, in praise of Virginia, "Heaven and earth never agreed better to frame a place for man's habitation." The coastline that the colonists first discerned from their ships was generally covered with a dense forest extending down to the edge of the water. And this was the case from Maine to the Carolinas. This virgin forest, with its profusion of species, offered the settler a source of cheap fuel and lumber for his houses, barns, tools, and furniture. To the European of

[7] C. P. Nettels, *The Roots of American Civilization* (New York: F. S. Crofts and Co., 1938), p. 146.

that day this abundance of lumber was indeed a treasure, for wood had the function in their technology, which iron and steel have in ours.

The native food products of America were also a boon to the settlers. The variety of fish, wild game, berries, and nuts, many of them new to these Europeans, was a source of delight as well as of nutrition. The Indians, we know, also introduced them to many new cultivated crops—corn, pumpkins, squash, cucumbers, and melons—which added to the variety of their diet. The land and the climate were suitable to the growth of the common English grains. The cattle that the settlers brought over from Holland, Sweden, England, and Germany, as they sought to improve their breeds, multiplied rapidly, and grew to "a far greater bulk of body" than in their native lands. Transplanted fruit trees flourished in many of the orchards of the New World.

Of course the areas settled were not all of equal fertility. The New Englanders in time found much of their soil to be rocky and unsuitable for cultivation, but they discovered a compensation in the abundance of fish in nearby waters and on the Grand Banks and in the value of their region's forest products. The middle region was favored with soils that enabled it to become the "bread colonies"; the southern had soils and climate suitable for growing that "brown gold," tobacco, as well as such valuable staples as cotton, rice, and sugar.

Nature even smiled upon the colonists' efforts with respect to the Atlantic coastline, marked as it was by numerous inlets and harbors and traversed, particularly in the middle and southern colonies, by rivers that linked the coastal plain with the seaports. To these advantages, modern geographers point out, was added the fact that there is a steep temperature gradient from Maine to Florida, which produces a variety of climates and products—a situation very favorable to an inter-regional division of labor and trade. But more of this later.

The significance of these rich natural resources of the colonies cannot be grasped unless seen in relation to the population and its density. While the wealth of the whole of the continent was not available for use and exploitation by the colonists (Indians and natural barriers barred them from much of it), the population per square mile was low, as compared to European conditions. This very favorable man-land ratio had a profound and far-reaching effect upon the institutions that were transplanted to these English colonies from the Old World, as well as upon the character of the colonists themselves.

THE ADAPTATION OF COLONIAL INSTITUTIONS
TO THEIR ENVIRONMENT

The manorial organization of English society was already in a state of decay when the American colonies were being settled. Although the greatest period of the enclosures was still ahead, Englishmen in the sixteenth century were already commuting labor services, renting land for money, and acquiring free legal title to their farms. The conditions in the colonies and especially the great abundance of land greatly encouraged this process and laid a firm basis for the institutions of individual enterprise and private property in land. After Sir Walter Raleigh's ill-fated effort to settle a colony at Roanoke had shown the weaknesses of individual effort in so costly and risky a venture as colonization, it was almost inevitable that the task would be attempted by the joint-stock companies of the time. But the original corporate settlements in Virginia and at Plymouth, although they were more successful in raising the necessary capital, likewise failed at first to enlist the full energies of the settlers. The promoters of both colonies devised plans whereby the settlers labored as servants of their respective companies. The product of their labor went into the company storehouse, from which they drew food and clothing. Any surplus production belonged to the company to augment its profits. It is true that both the Virginia and Plymouth promoters had provided that after a seven-year term all improved land and other property was to be divided among the company's investors in accordance with their share ownership (the actual settlers had been allowed shares in the enterprise).

Still, even for this short period these plans did not work well. In Virginia the settlers "loafed on the job," since they knew that they would be taken care of in any case. Likewise, at Plymouth there was much dissatisfaction with community control of production; bachelors felt that they were supporting unjustly the families of married men and in general, the more industrious resented the principle of equal shares. As a consequence, these collective plans of organization were soon abandoned, in Virginia in 1614–18 and at Plymouth in 1623–24. Steps were taken in both colonies, which resulted in the transfer of the land from the companies to the individual settlers. This introduction of private landowning was a great landmark in American history because it influenced profoundly the subsequent course of our economic development. The Englishmen of the time in America demanded the change because land had become the basis of social status in their society. Further-more, as Nettels says, "When the early settlers saw such great stretches of idle land about them they were not satisfied to work as employees or tenants of English companies. Only with individual ownership did the colonist feel the spur to industry necessary in subduing a hostile wilderness."[8] This trend to private ownership in land was accelerated in America because certain colo-nies, such as Pennsylvania, liberally offered freehold grants of land to induce settlement and the others, in competition, were forced to follow. So it was that private property in land steadily became typical in all the colonies, and the rental of land was regarded as but the transition to ultimate private owner-ship.

The new owners of these lands had, of course, the right to sell its produce for what they wished, and they soon demanded that those who bought or sold to them should not be permitted to practice monopoly and thus deprive them

[8] C. P. Nettels, *The Roots of American Civilization*, p. 224.

of the advantages of their ownership. Consequently, the adoption of private landholding was soon followed by the abolition of corporate trading monopolies. Their place after 1624 in both colonies was taken by private traders and partnerships, which competed with one another for the patronage of the farmers.

Medieval institutions, someone has written, like plants when transplanted, soon withered away in the environment of the New World. Nowhere was this tendency better illustrated than in some of the proprietary colonies where efforts were made to introduce semi-feudal schemes of land tenure. In Maryland Sir George Calvert sought to establish a great family estate and planned to have other members of the British aristocracy set up manors there. But Lord Baltimore soon authorized his brother, who was the first governor of the colony, to grant "headrights" to new settlers and others in order to speed up its settlement. These grantees later found it profitable to sell their holdings, and so Maryland ultimately became a colony of small and medium-sized farms.

In the Carolinas there was a much more fantastic effort made to graft the ideas and institutions of the Old World upon the New. When Charles II was restored to the British throne in 1660 he granted to eight of his favorites and supporters a great province, known as Carolina, stretching from the Atlantic to the Pacific, which they were to rule as they pleased subject to the laws of England and with the consent of a local assembly. One of the royal favorites, Lord Ashley Cooper, later the Earl of Shaftesbury, hired John Locke, the famous political philosopher and Whig pamphleteer, to draft a constitution for this imperial estate. Locke drew up an elaborate charter of feudal government, with a hierarchy of a titled nobility and with provision for manors and baronies to be tilled by hereditary serfs bound to the soil. This curious constitution with its high-sounding title was ratified by the proprietors and declared in force, but "it could no more be realized in Carolina," write the Beards, "than in the moon. Its interest today lies in the fact that it reveals the type of society which the Whigs, the most liberal of the governing classes in England, would have established in America if they had not been defeated by the irrepressible and stubborn realities of life on the frontier." The settlers who flocked into the Carolinas engaged in a long series of disputes with their governors over paper money and other issues, so that in 1729, the weary proprietors were willing to have their colonies become royal provinces. The only remnant and reminder of the antique form of government were the quitrents, which the colonies continued to oppose even after they had come under the direct rule of the Crown.

The stresses and strains produced by the new conditions of life upon the inherited religious and economic ideology of the colonists were clearly evident also in the early years of the Massachusetts Bay Colony. One sees there the inevitable modification of the conventional stock of ideas and practices, such as occurred elsewhere in the colonies. At Plymouth the Pilgrims returned, not merely to medieval social ethics and practices, but went back still further to the teachings of the early Church fathers. These very strict Puritans believed that economic life could only be purified by returning to the rules and customs of the Church before it had become a great institution. Their experiment with common ownership was in accordance with the tradition that the early Christians had lived together and "had all things in common except their wives."[9] Their effort to do this was a distinct failure. Governor Bradford in 1623 roundly condemned the collective mode of production and allotted separate tracts of land to each family to cultivate. From that time on private property became "a fundamental cornerstone of the American economy."

Calvinist ethics and the practices of the merchants clashed almost from the beginnings of the Massachusetts Bay Colony. In the early settlement years there were marked shortages of provisions, which the Company was unable to overcome. Manufactured goods likewise became unobtainable so that the settlers came to know how indispensable were such things as a pound of nails, a yard of cloth, or an iron cauldron. It was during this period of scarcity and consequent inflation that the first Puritan import merchants established themselves. To understand how conflict developed between them and the other settlers we must realize that these merchants had very different social origins from the majority of the colonists. Whereas the latter were mainly rural Englishmen—gentlemen, independent farmers, tenants, or laborers—with the very conservative attitudes and desires of such people, the merchants were usually natives of London or the surrounding port towns who were largely bustling, self-made men. Their life patterns, writes Bailyn, were "characterized by geographical and social mobility."[10] While the Calvinist doctrines of "just price" and prohibition of usury (as then taught)[11] made sense and suggested security and status to most of the settlers, to many of the merchants they were intolerable restrictions. ". . . Freed from the complexities and competition of the Old World cities and trained in some aspect of the production and distribution of goods, the merchants experienced a release of energies in America which frequently struck the Puritan leaders as brashness and insubordination. . . ."[12]

It was in these circumstances that an episode occurred that, as described by Bailyn, vividly reveals the clash between the Puritan morality and the emerging ethics of the merchant group. It involved one Robert Keayne, a typical self-made merchant of London who had migrated to the colony in 1635. Keayne had started as a butcher's son and had risen through apprenticeship to become a prominent merchant taylor. When he came to Boston, he brought with him a substantial estate of two or three thousand pounds and promptly established

[9] E. A. J. Johnson, *American Economic Thought in the Seventeenth Century* (London: P. S. King, 1932), Chap. XII.

[10] B. Bailyn, *The New England Merchants in the Seventeenth Century* (Cambridge: Harvard University Press, 1955), p. 39.

[11] For the modifications that took place in Calvinistic doctrines, see Tawney, *Religion and the Rise of Capitalism;* also Bailyn, cited above, pp. 20–23.

[12] *Ibid.*, pp. 39–40.

himself as a retailer of imported manufactures. During the next four years, taking advantage of the inflation, he sold many sorely-needed goods to his fellow immigrants for whatever he could get. Keayne's troubles started over the sale of a mere bag of nails at what he claimed was a reasonable price. Once this charge had been made, a veritable barrage of denunciation descended upon him for over-charging for "great gold buttons, a bridle, and a skein of thread." He was tried before the highest court in the colony, convicted, and fined no less than £200. Actually, Keayne felt that he got off lightly because many of the people would have fined him much more and subjected him to corporal punishment into the bargain.

But Keayne's tribulations were not done. Only the civil sword had struck. The church elders took up the matter, examined the charges, and gave him a severe admonition ". . . in the Name of the Church for selling his wares at excessive Rates, to the dishonor of God's name, the Offence of the Generall Cort, and the Publique scandall of the Country." Though he escaped excommunication, Keayne had to make a "penetenciall acknowledgment" of his sin to regain full membership in the church.

The merchants' dilemma in these circumstances was very real. The settlers, already inclined to regard middlemen as parasites, and not being able to understand or control the workings of the economy, tended to attribute the inflation and shortage of goods to human malevolence. The merchants, on the other hand, finding evidence in the social teachings of Calvin for their practices and their diligence and frugality, regarded their detractors as the sinful ones. ". . . From the same texts the Puritan magistrates and the merchants read different lessons.

The former learned the overwhelming importance of the organic society which subordinated the individual to the general good. Keayne learned the righteousness of those individual qualities whose secondary but attractive virtue it was to aid in the fight for success in business. . . ."[13]

The later growth of the New England economy, spurred on by these very ambitious merchants, carried them still farther away from their old Calvinist moorings. With the passage of the years, the restoration of the monarchy, there was a "declension" of religious fervor, which weakened the influence of the church's teachings on business. The Puritan divines denounced the new, more luxurious way of life and the decline of the old virtues. But their efforts were largely to no avail. "In the larger port towns of provincial New England, particularly those in continuous contact with Europe, the business community represented the spirit of a new age. Its guiding principles were not social stability, order, and the discipline of the senses, but mobility, growth, and the enjoyment of life. Citizens of an international trading world as well of New England colonies, the merchants took the pattern for their conduct not from the Bible or from parental teachings but from their picture of life in Restora-

[13] *Ibid.,* p. 43.

tion England. To the watchmen of the holy citadel nothing could have been more insidious."[14]

Actually, in performing their trading functions the merchants robbed the commonwealths of that isolation and close-knit community life that the Puritan leaders knew served to maintain godliness and the observance of Calvin's strict doctrines. But the merchants' avid pursuit of profits brought them into contact with alien norms, and the rigor of their austere faith was sapped. The later generations of merchants had not only a broader view of British commerce and affairs, but they were also not bound as closely by their church's doctrines. Indeed, by the third generation, some, having grown rich, were going Anglican or marrying into families of that faith.

THE SOCIAL CHARACTER OF THE COLONISTS

In analyzing the character and values of the colonists, we must keep constantly in mind the nature of the work or occupations in which most of them were engaged. For men's daily employment and the manner in which they are raised for adult life are mighty molders of character. The colonists, we know, despite the attention we have devoted to the merchants, were predominantly engaged in agriculture and in the extractive industries, such as lumbering, fishing, and trapping. To survive as a society they had to develop in themselves those values and attitudes that would be functional for the daily tasks of such industries, and inculcate them in their children.[15] What were these values and how did the colonists develop them in the successive generations?

Crèvecoeur, the Frenchman turned American, provides us with some revealing facts about such matters in his justly famous *Letters*. Though written some years before 1782, and inclined to picture the American in the best light, nevertheless they give us an incomparable glimpse of the everyday life of that era. Crèvecoeur writes of an agrarian America, "We are all tillers of the earth, from Nova Scotia to West Florida." In the third Letter, he sets himself the task of explaining how many Americans, formerly poor "wretches" in Europe, practically without a country, had become men and citizens in this society. "By what invisible power," he asks, "has this surprising metamorphosis been performed?" And he answers, "By that of the laws and that of their industry."[16] Our indulgent laws, he explains, protect them and they receive ample rewards for their labors; these accumulated rewards enable them to buy land and those lands confer on them the title of Freemen. As to

---

[14] *Ibid.*, p. 139.

[15] See E. Fromm, *Escape From Freedom* (New York: Rinehart and Co., 1941) (Appendix) for an instructive discussion of the relationships between socialization (social learning) and the tasks of a society.

[16] Crèvecoeur, *Letters from an American Farmer* (New York: E. P. Dutton and Co., Inc., 1957), p. 38.

their motivation, he observes that the Americans of his day were all animated with a spirit unfettered and unrestrained, because each person works for himself, for self-interest; here and elsewhere in his *Letters*, Crèvecoeur stresses the Smithean doctrine. Enumerating the traits of his countrymen, he recites industry, good living, selfishness, litigiousness, country politics, the pride of freemen, and their religious indifference. Perhaps the last characteristic needs some explaining, in the light of what we have said above about the strictness of New England religion. In general, Crèvecoeur contends that in the late colonial period about which he was writing, religious zeal had cooled and the various sects were more tolerant of each other. He attributes this waning of religious enthusiasm to the mixing of the sects and to the fact that, although parents instructed their children in religion as well as they could, their instructions were feeble compared to those given in Europe. "Their children will therefore grow up less zealous and more indifferent in matters of religion than their parents. . . ."[17]

In his *Sketches of Eighteenth Century America*,[18] Crèvecoeur describes most vividly the hardships of the self-sufficient farmer and the values that his way of life fostered. In an essay entitled "A Snow Storm as It Affects the American Farmer," he gives an inimitable picture of the foresight, the prudence and the economy such a farmer needed to live through the winter, cut off for long periods of time even from neighbors, with his wife, children, and livestock. He extols the usefulness of an industrious wife, the *"aurum potabile"* of an American farmer. "For such is our lot; if we are blessed with a good wife, we may boast of living better than any people of the same rank on the globe." He stresses too the colonist's need for ingenuity: "The philosopher's stone of an American farmer is to do everything within his own family; to trouble his neighbors by borrowing as little as possible; to abstain from buying European commodities. He that follows that golden rule and has a good wife is almost sure of succeeding."[19] He finds most of his contemporaries to be innovative. "The European," he exults, no sooner breathes our air than he forms schemes and he says that he himself took "delight in inventing and executing machines which simplify my wife's labor." He strains our credulity certainly, however, when as an instance of his own ingenuity he claims to have read by the light of a firefly.[20]

We get a valuable insight into the quality of morality in everyday colonial life and the reasons for the colonist's "litigiousness" in this observation: ". . . He sells for good that which he knows to be indifferent because he also knows that the ashes he has collected, the wheat he has taken in may not be so good or so clean as it was asserted. Fearful of fraud in all his transactions, he arms himself, therefore, with it. Strict integrity is not much wanted, as each is

[17] *Ibid.*, p. 46.
[18] *Sketches of Eighteenth Century America*, edited by H. L. Bourdin, et al. (New Haven: Yale University Press, 1925).
[19] *Ibid.*, p. 104.
[20] *Letters from an American Farmer*, p. 107.

on his guard in his daily intercourse, and this mode of thinking and acting becomes habitual."[21]

Crèvecoeur offers us a priceless vignette of how the Quakers of Nantucket Island raised their children. Writing like a modern anthropologist, he says, "The easiest way of becoming acquainted with the modes of thinking, the rules of conduct, and the prevailing manners of any people, is to examine what sort of education they give their children: how they treat them at home, and what they are taught in their places of public worship. . . ."[22] He goes on to describe the imperturbable gravity of the parents and how they early inure the young to a principle of subordination. The children are "held by an uniform silk cord, which unites softness and strength." Perfect equanimity prevails in most of their families and they soon acquire a taste for simplicity, neatness, frugality, and a fondness and appetite for commerce. In their meetinghouses, they are taught the simple tenets of their sect: "tenets as fit to render men sober, industrious, just and merciful, as those delivered in the most magnificent churches and cathedrals. . . ."[23] Leaving school at twelve, they serve early apprenticeships in the cooper's trade (barrelmaking) or on board a ship and "after having performed several such voyages, and perfected themselves in this business, they are fit either for the counting house or the chase."[24]

That Crèvecoeur's praise of the New England fishermen was justified and not unrecognized by others, we might cite Edmund Burke's eloquent speech to Parliament, in which he warned against treating the Americans as puny children and bade them "look at the manner in which the people of New England have of late carried on the whale fishery. Whilst we follow them among the tumbling mountains of ice and behold them penetrating into the deepest frozen recesses of Hudson's Bay and Davis's Straits, whilst we are looking for them beneath the Arctic Circle, we hear that they have pierced the opposite region of polar cold, that they are at the antipodes, and engaged under the frozen serpent of the South. . . . No sea but what is vexed by their fisheries . . . No climate that is not a witness to their toils. Neither the perseverance of Holland, nor the activity of France, nor the dexterous and firm sagacity of English enterprise ever carried this most perilous mode of hard industry to the extent to which it has been pushed by this recent people; a people who are still, as it were, but in the gristle and not yet hardened into the bone of manhood."[25]

Many authorities and contemporary observers of colonial life other than Crèvecoeur could be cited on this subject of the colonists' character, but in

---

[21] *Sketches*, pp. 77–78.

[22] *Letters from an American Farmer*, p. 108.

[23] *Ibid.*, p. 109.

[24] *Ibid.*, p. 110. An invaluable source on parent-child relations and family life generally among the Puritans is E. S. Morgan, *The Puritan Family*, new ed. (New York: Harper & Row, 1966), *passim*.

[25] Beards, *The Rise of American Civilization*, pp. 92–93 with certain modifications by the authors.

general, they only bear out and confirm what he tells us. For example, Professor Nettels emphasizes the point that one of the most important forces shaping colonial life was the determination of the people not to relapse into a primitive mode of existence but to maintain a European standard of living such as they had known personally or by hearsay. But to do this, unremitting labor was necessary. "To the mass of the farmers and workers life meant incessant toil; similarly, members of the upper class, possessed of relatively small fortunes, could achieve superiority in society only by that vigilant attention to the details of business through which the accumulation of capital was effected. . . ."[26] Many writers comment, of course, on the stern moral code, especially of the Puritans, noting also how in certain respects it served a functional purpose. A. W. Calhoun, for example, writes, "Puritan emphasis on sexual restraint was of a piece with the general gospel of frugality so appropriate among a people trying to accumulate capital in an age of deficit."[27] John Adams, writing to his wife in 1774, reminds us of Crèvecoeur's remarks: ". . . make your children *hardy, active,* and *industrious;* for strength, activity and industry will be their only resource and dependence."

THE COLONIAL VALUE SYSTEM

In general, two views of life prevailed and struggled for mastery in the colonial era. One, the materialistic outlook, was a belief that life evolved in reaction to the external forces of environment and social organization. Only man through his own efforts could lighten the burdens of his labor on earth. The second, the religious or spiritual conception, held that man moved in response to the divine will. Divine revelation and inspiration were to be his guide; he must conform to the divine will as revealed in the Scriptures. Nor was man a mere physical mechanism, in this view, but made in the image of God, with an immortal soul and the hope of eternal life.[28] There was a good deal of diversity in colonial religion, both with respect to individuals and among social classes. And then as now, religious precepts were often more observed in the breach than in the performance; but withal, it was a much more religious culture than prevails today, at least so far as organized ritual and observance were concerned. But as Nettels says, "Despite the religious inheritance of the colonists, their preoccupation with practical concerns, their day-long labor in field and shop, and the necessity of subduing nature in order to mitigate the rigors of life: all these influences strengthened the materialistic conception of life. New Englanders gained a reputation as shrewd traders and investors; travelers in the middle colonies noted that the religious impulse was at a low ebb (Christian sects tended to "wear themselves out"; "religious

[26] Nettels, *The Roots of American Civilization*, p. 449.
[27] *Ibid.,* p. 450.
[28] *Ibid.,* p. 452–53.

indifference becomes prevalent"). Jernegan says that the "main energies and thoughts" of most of the southern planters "were centered on material gains."[29]

Indeed, it is very instructive and significant so far as colonial values are concerned that Max Weber in his analysis of the Protestant ethic and capitalism cited Benjamin Franklin's maxims and way of life as epitomizing the capitalistic spirit. Nettels says as much in an admirable summary: "The colonial outlook may be described as an expression of a middle class psychology which exalted industry and thrift and which exposed both a core of utilitarianism overlaid with religious tradition and a spirit of individualism, tempered by cooperation and association. . . ."[30]

Colonial society, though it was characterized by much competition and class conflict over economic matters, was held together by adequate integrating influences. Foremost among these cohesive forces were religious toleration, the shared values of industry and thrift, the widespread ownership of land, and the apparent greater degree of social mobility as compared with Europe. This prevailing sense of social integration and harmony was expressed in the literature of the time, which suggests an unfailing serenity, zest for life, and faith in progress. John Adams was probably by no means unique in his sentiment, written in 1765, in which he said: "I always consider the settlement of America with reverence and wonder, as the opening of a grand scheme and design in Providence for the illumination and the emancipation of the slavish part of mankind all over the earth." Crèvecoeur voices a similar sense of optimism and of American mission, when he confidently asserts, ". . . we are the most perfect society now existing in the world. . . ."

THE COLONIAL SOCIAL STRUCTURE AND CLASS CONFLICTS

As the colonial economy grew and matured, a class system made its appearance largely as a result of the unequal holdings of land and of other privileges, economic and political. Three broad classes may be distinguished as making up the social structure.[31] During the seventeenth century a colonial upper class had taken form, although this incipient aristocracy was numerically weak. It consisted of the largest landowners, the most wealthy merchants, and the royal and proprietary governors. It distinguished itself from its inferiors by its ostentatious way of living, its leisurely pursuits, its dress, and its religion (predominantly Anglican). The middle class, which was much larger, comprised professional men, lesser merchants, landowning farmers, artisans, ship captains, and storekeepers. In general, such people did not possess sufficient wealth to exempt them altogether from toil. This middle class imitated the manners of the upper class and strove to enter its rather restricted

---

[29] *Ibid.*, p. 454.

[30] *Ibid.*, p. 460.

[31] Much reliance has been placed on the work of C. P. Nettels, *The Roots of American Civilization*, Chaps. 12 and 13.

ranks. The lower class was composed in the main of indentured servants and Negro slaves.

While the colonies undoubtedly consisted of a class society, the class structure differed in certain notable ways from that of contemporary Europe. The colonies did not produce a class of serfs bound to the soil with a hereditary nobility "lording" it over them. On the other hand, Negro slavery became a peculiarly American institution the baneful effects of which were to be felt for several centuries. Perhaps the most distinctive feature of the colonial social class structure was its greater flexibility or, to be more precise, the greater degree of social mobility that was possible in moving from one class to another. One could rise, it seems, from the lower to the middle class relatively easily, but the movement from there to the upper class was much more difficult.

The conflict among these social classes in the colonies centered mainly on who should control the land and its products. Another constant source of friction was the subject of money and its control. In the seventeenth century, the upper and lower middle classes clashed over the issue of land in legal combat, and on other occasions, in open warfare. The two most serious conflicts of the latter sort were Bacon's rebellion in Virginia (1675) and Leisler's rebellion in New York in 1689. Nathaniel Bacon led the yeomanry of the backwoods country of Virginia against England's control of the tobacco trade and the low prices that prevailed; they were opposed too to an inequitable tax system—a poll tax—and complained that they were being given inadequate protection against the Indians. Governor Berkeley, who was interested in the fur trade, did not heed the colonists on this and other questions. At the height of the revolt, however, Bacon suddenly died and the rebellion was suppressed. Leisler's revolt in New York was directed essentially at a monopoly by the New York merchants of the wheat and flour trade. Aroused by the Glorious Revolution in Great Britain the previous year, the small farmers and city workers denounced the regulation passed by the councils of the colony that made the town of New York a depot for all trade and required that flour be bolted or sifted in no other place. Leisler and his followers took over the control of the colony in May, 1689, and ruled it for nearly two years. This rebellion was then put down and Leisler himself was hung. But a victory of a sort was achieved; in 1691 the elected assembly was restored, and four years later the small farmers of New York abolished the flour monopoly of New York.

In the adjoining province of New Jersey also, conflict took place in the seventeenth century over the payment of quitrents and the commercial regulations of New York. In South Carolina, a revolt took place against Locke's Fundamental Constitutions, which as we have seen, would have established a medieval aristocracy in the colony. In the eighteenth century, struggles over land and the currency continued in New England, the Carolinas, and in other sections between the tidewater and the back country. These cleavages in the colonial communities over domestic issues contributed to the coming of the War of Independence, which is, in part, the subject of the next chapter.

Chapter 3

BRITISH MERCANTILISM, THE REVOLUTION, AND OUR COLONIAL HERITAGE

THE FIRST SUCCESSFUL COLONIAL REVOLUTION

The American Revolution has been described as "the first successful colonial revolution in history."[1] It is not our intention in this chapter to evaluate the correctness of this statement so far as the primacy of our domestic revolt in time is concerned, but rather to investigate how those human qualities and social institutions that came into existence during the preceding years of colonial rule contributed to the coming of the Revolution and its successful completion.

Americans are very likely to have a distorted view of their colonial ancestors because of a character trait that has been delightfully termed "our infracaninophilism," i.e., our liking for the underdog. Picturing ourselves as the colonial underdogs we are possibly inclined to exaggerate the might, the tyranny, and the incarnate evil of George III and the whole British establishment at the time of the Revolution. What needs to be done to correct such a misconception is to note the human values that 150 years of British rule had nurtured in these colonials without minimizing the superior economic might of the Empire. The preceding chapter would suggest that we agree with Professor Gipson when he says, "colonials in 1763 were, by and large, self-confident, resourceful, energetic, and positive, and they displayed a forthrightness born of these qualities."[2] The American colonies in 1763 were arriving not only at economic maturity, but at political maturity as well. "It may be questioned," writes Gipson, "whether in any part of the world, including Great Britain, there was to be found so high a percentage of the inhabitants versed in the art of government. Though most of this political activity took place on the level of local government, and while the right of franchise was strictly limited in most of the colonies, American colonials by

---

[1] H. Aptheker, *The American Revolution* (New York: International Publishers, 1960), p. 23.

[2] L. H. Gipson, *The Coming of the Revolution, 1683–1775* (New York: Harper and Bros., 1954), p. 11.

and large had a degree of awareness respecting matters of public interest and a degree of understanding of the problems of statecraft that would have been a matter of surprise to most of the peoples of continental Europe. . . ."[3] What were the factors in the nature and administration of the old mercantile system that had contributed to this high degree of economic and political maturity of the colonists that led them to revolt? In asking this question, we are implying that the British mercantilist regulations had an important role in bringing about the Revolution. We shall see that the colonists had other grievances as well as those about the mercantile system, but the latter played so direct a role in the immediate events leading up to the break with England that we shall consider them first.

THE OLD AND THE NEW COLONIAL SYSTEMS

The old colonial system refers to the Navigation Acts and the accompanying legislation that Great Britain had in force up to 1763. The foundation stone of the old commercial system was the Navigation Act of 1660. This law confined the carrying trade entirely to English and colonial shipping. We have noted too how the "enumeration" system of this Act channeled the export of certain colonial products (tobacco, sugar, raw cotton, indigo, ginger, fustick, and other dye-stuffs) through British ports before they could be sold elsewhere. The list of such enumerated commodities was extended in the eighteenth century to include naval stores (1704), molasses and rice (1706), copper ore, beaver, and other furs (1722). The Staple Act of 1663 required the importation of most colonial imports via British ports, with certain specified exceptions. The laws regulating certain colonial manufactures were also an important part of the old colonial system.

Still another integral part of the system was the Molasses Act of 1733. This law imposed a prohibitive tax of 6d. a gallon on molasses imported from the foreign West Indies into the colonies. The New Englanders preferred to buy their molasses from these foreign possessions because their molasses was cheaper than that produced in the British islands. France, as a wine-drinking nation, had little use for molasses; therefore, since the supply of this commodity in the French islands was greater than the demand, the price tended to be depressed. The colonists' trade with these islands was obviously a violation both of the letter and the spirit of Britain's mercantilistic policy, but fortunately for them the duty was rarely collected. If it had been, it would have taken all the profit out of the rum-making business, the export of which had become so important in balancing their trade with England.

In assessing the impact of these laws on the colonists, it is important to note that their basic economic conditions (the relative lack of capital, the shortage

3 *Ibid.*, p. 27.

of labor, and the inaccessibility of markets) tended to make the extractive industries more attractive to them than manufacturing. In addition, these laws gave certain of their industries a preferred position in the Empire and granted others bounties or financial aid. Finally, one should not ignore the military and naval security that the British gave the colonists and their close relationship to the structure and objectives of the old commercial system. There is much support, therefore, for Professor Gipson's view that "while it is true that much has been written against the system, it is difficult to visualize one that would under given conditions have been better adapted to serve the end of preserving and nurturing the colonies embraced within the old British Empire before 1763. That they themselves were among its chief beneficiaries can hardly be questioned in view of the impressive evidence of their unprecedented development in the course of the eighteenth century."[4]

To understand the train of revolutionary events that Great Britain's revision of the old colonial system brought on, we must appreciate fully the consequences of the end of the so-called French and Indian War. This badly named war, which determined nothing less than the future of the whole North American continent, had been fought by the British at a staggering cost to themselves. Though one of the main objects of the war had been to protect the colonists, some of the latter had engaged in the shameful business of trading with the enemy on a large scale from practically the beginning of hostilities. Pitt, the Prime Minister of Great Britain, himself declared that this "dangerous and ignominious Trade" had sustained and protracted the long and expensive war. Even before 1763 the British government took steps to tighten up the administration of the customs system and thus stop the smuggling; it pressed for a renewal of the "writs of assistance," which authorized a court officer to accompany customs officials in the search for smuggled goods. Some Massachusetts merchants opposed the issuance of these writs in 1761; it was on that occasion that James Otis made his famous speech attacking the writs and denying their constitutionality in the colonies. "Then and there," wrote John Adams who was present, "the child Independence was born."

The war disturbed the harmony of imperial relations in another way as well. Its great cost had resulted in a doubling of the British national debt from £72 million to £140 million. In order to defray the cost of defending the enlarged Empire, the Tories under the new Prime Minister, George Grenville, who took office in 1763, decided to tighten up the colonial administration and to drop the policy of "salutary neglect" that had been followed in many of the preceding years. One of the first steps in this direction was the Royal Proclamation of 1763. This proclamation carried out a pledge that the Crown had made to the Indians in the midst of the previous war to respect their

---

[4] Gipson, pp. 26–27. Schlesinger also found British mercantilism down to 1763 to be noninjurious to colonial interests. A. M. Schlesinger, *Colonial Merchants and the American Revolution, 1763–1776* (New York: Facsimile Library, Inc., 1939). See also O. M. Dickerson, *The Navigation Acts and the American Revolution* (Philadelphia: University of Pennsylvania Press, 1951).

claims to the lands west of the Appalachians and not to dispose of them without their consent. The Indians were suspicious of the British, and the two-years War of Pontiac's Conspiracy had already begun. The Proclamation, in effect, made the territory beyond the Alleghenies an Indian reservation. Fur trading in that area was prohibited except by royal license. This legislation was a blow to the land promoters in the colonies, many of them southern plantation owners who looked to the profits of land speculation to offset their losses in tobacco. Those who were engaged in the fur trade were also, of course, disappointed.

Grenville had decided to station 10,000 troops in the colonies to protect them from the Indians and to keep the subdued French under control. Experience had shown that the colonists themselves were either unwilling to serve or unsuited to such garrison duty. In order to meet the cost of maintaining these troops, the British administrators asked Parliament to pass two tax laws, which it was estimated would yield about one-third of the needed revenue. The first law, the Sugar Act of 1764, was a revision of the old Molasses Act of 1733, which had levied a duty on imported molasses of 6d. a gallon. The latter legislation had been poorly enforced; in fact, colonial customs as a whole were yielding only £1,000–£2,000 a year, yet it was costing from £7,000–£8,000 to collect this sum. The new Sugar Act cut the molasses duty in half, raised the levy on sugar from the foreign West Indies, and prohibited altogether the importation of foreign-made rum. Finally, high duties were imposed on wines directly imported, and substantial duties were placed on coffee, indigo, and pimento. New and severe regulations were made for the enforcement of this Act. This legislation, which struck at the vital and profitable trade with the foreign West Indies, created consternation in New England; both fair traders and smuggling merchants claimed injury. It was with this Act in mind that Samuel Adams was later to declare, "I know not why we should blush to confess that molasses was an essential ingredient in American independence."

But to add to the colonists' sense of grievance, the sugar tax, according to the 1764 statute, had to be paid in specie, despite the fact that the Currency Act of the same year extended the ban on New England bills of credit to all the colonies. Many colonists wondered where they would obtain the specie to pay such taxes, if they could not use paper money for their domestic transactions. Petitions and memorials were forwarded to Parliament. Benjamin Franklin complained that "on a slight complaint of a few Virginia merchants, nine colonies have been restrained from making paper money, become absolutely necessary to their internal commerce from the constant remittance of their gold and silver to Britain."

While the protest was still great, Parliament passed the second tax measure, the Stamp Act, with little debate or opposition. Modelled after stamp duties that had been in force for many years in Britain, the new duties required the colonists to pay taxes through stamps on legal documents such as bills, notes, bonds, deeds, mortgages, licenses to practice law or to sell liquor, as well as on newspapers, pamphlets, college diplomas, and playing cards—a queer assort-ment, indeed. If the protest against the first law was thought great, there was a veritable storm of denunciation of this one, largely because it was an internal tax (i.e., levied on domestic transactions of the colonists rather than on their foreign trade), and it affected almost every class, but especially printers and lawyers—both vociferous, articulate groups. There was widespread nullifica-tion and disregard of the new law and considerable mob violence and terrori-zation of those who sought to enforce it. The Stamp Act of Congress, held in New York in October, 1765, protested against the principle of the law. But more important was the passive resistance that the merchants of New York, Massachusetts, Rhode Island, and Philadelphia turned to in the form of agreements not to import from the mother country. The year before, non-consumption had been tried, particularly in Massachusetts. Merchants had agreed not to wear laces and ruffles, to have less ostentatious funerals, con-sume no lamb, and the New Yorkers agreed to drink no beer. Even the Yale men generously agreed to abstain from the use of foreign liquors.

The first non-importation agreement was relatively weak; New York and Providence merchants took advantage of their fellow businessmen, thus diminishing its effect.[5] Nevertheless, British exports declined from £1,925,564 in 1764 to £1,580,324 in 1765. The protests and petitions finally led Parlia-ment to repeal the Stamp Act in 1766, thanks in part to an effective plea by Franklin. But to protest and emphasize its sovereignty, Parliament at the same time passed the Declaratory Act, asserting its authority to bind the colonies "in all cases whatever." The new molasses duty, which was enacted in this same year, was reduced to one penny per gallon and as such was clearly a tariff for revenue.

Charles Townshend, who became Acting Prime Minister in the following year (1767), sought to meet the Crown's revenue problem by imposing import duties on wine, glass, oil, paper, red and white lead, painters' colors, and tea. These were articles of general consumption, and since the duties were external, they could not be objected to by the colonists as an innovation. The law also stipulated that the revenue so raised was to be used to pay judges and other civil officers, thereby freeing them from dependence on rebellious colonial legislatures. Again, this new legislation elicited protest and produced a second non-importation agreement among nine of the colonies to boycott English goods. The merchants now favored this form of passive resistance rather than the direct action they had instigated before. This boycott was very effective in New England and the middle colonies, but soon broke down in the plantation provinces. In the latter, the Scottish and English merchants, as well as other factions, had opposed such action from the beginning; the boycott was largely forced on them by radical planters and small farmers and mechanics. The trade of the South with Great Britain actually increased in 1769.

---

[5] A. M. Schlesinger, *Colonial Merchants and the American Revolution*, is excellent on the non-importation agreements of this period.

However, at this time a period of relative tranquillity had settled over the colonies. Most of the objectionable Townshend duties had been repealed in 1770, and now for three years a period of greater prosperity set in. The New York merchants led in the break away from non-importation. But the peace was of short duration. It was broken by Parliament's passage of the short-sighted Tea Act of 1773, which sought to aid the financially ailing East Indies Company. Up to that time, tea had been imported into the colonies by jobbers, who purchased from English wholesalers, who in turn bought from this Company, which held the monopoly of the business in India. This, at least, was the marketing system in use for the legal sale of the product, although a considerable amount of the commodity was brought in illegally without payment of any import duty. Parliament now tried to aid the English joint stock company by allowing it to sell 17 million pounds of tea directly in America through its own branches and with a large refund (drawback) of the duty on much of the tea it held in storage. This change in marketing practices threatened the status and livelihood of the colonial middlemen who handled the product, and in addition, the duty-free tea would be able to undersell even the smuggled product of which there was a good deal. The colonial merchants direly predicted that such a monopoly was only the beginning, and John Dickinson pointed to the abject condition of the East Indians. The merchants, shrewd propagandists, emphasized the hygienic argument against drinking tea, proving that "spasms, vapors, hypochondrias, apoplexies of the serious kind, palsies, dropsies, rheumatisms, consumptions, low nervous military and tetechial fevers" were all due to the drinking of this favorite beverage. The town of Hinsdale raised the embarrassing question as to the hygienic value of rum, but apparently received no satisfactory answer. As for the East Indies Company, the remainder of the familiar story is soon told. Shipments of the hated tea had been consigned to New York, Philadelphia, Charleston, and Boston, but only at the southern port was it permitted, after heated debate, to be landed. When the impasse between the obdurate Governor at Boston and the aroused populace over the landing of the tea could not be broken, Samuel Adams' "Mohawks" made tea, as the saying has it, for all the codfish on the banks of Newfoundland; the Boston tea party of December 16, 1773 was a decisive event in the hectic sequence of events that was rushing the colonies toward outright revolution. But soon, the good people of Annapolis "out-Bostoned the Bostonians"; they burned the "Peggy Stuart" rather than permit tea to land.

To preserve imperial dignity, Parliament now passed what the colonists branded as "The Intolerable Acts." These numbered five: (1) the Boston Port Bill removed all the custom houses and blockaded the harbor, with the aim of stopping all landing and shipping of goods until reparation was made to the East Indies Company. (2) Town meetings were to be held only with the permission of the Governor, and jurors were to be chosen by sheriffs, agents of the Governor, instead of in a town meeting. (3) The Governor was to appoint and remove judges and could send a person accused of a capital crime to trial in a sister colony or in England. (4) The Quartering Act renewed a law that made inns, alehouses, or other inhabited buildings subject to use for the housing of troops. (5) The Quebec Act annexed the territory beyond the Alleghenies and north of the Ohio River to the province of Quebec and recognized Catholicism as the established church in Quebec. This Act in effect abrogated the claims of Virginia, Massachusetts, and Connecticut to the lands west of the Alleghenies, while its religious provisions were regarded by New Englanders and others as a threat to Protestantism.

In the fall of that same year, 1774, the first Continental Congress, attended by delegates from all the colonies except Georgia, drew up a Declaration of American Rights. Many merchants grew apprehensive at the revolutionary turn of events; nevertheless, most of them participated in the formation of the Continental Association, whose members now imposed the third non-importation agreement on the trade with Britain. Under the influence of this boycott, which was more effectively enforced than the other two, English imports fell from over two and a half million pounds in 1774 to a mere £201,000 in 1775. Again Parliament was flooded with petitions, but this time it did not yield. In fact, it imposed even more restrictive and punitive measures on the colonists, forbidding them to trade with any other part of the world except Great Britain and the British West Indies and banning fishing on the Grand Banks of Newfoundland. The colonies and the mother country had come to an irreconcilable parting of the ways and soon the shots at Lexington and Concord were to mark the beginning of the War for Independence.

What were the background factors that contributed to this conflict between an imperial power and its colonies, when their relations prior to 1763 had been on the whole harmonious and mutually beneficial? One of the most important of such factors was the depression that characterized many of the years after the close of the French and Indian War. This long period of poor business was not conducive to the comprehensive revision of the old colonial policy undertaken by the British government at that time. The shrinkage of trade in the colonies and the poor agricultural conditions in Great Britain during many of the inter-war years probably interfered greatly with the development of a spirit of mutual accommodation during that transition. Strangely enough also, the removal of the Spanish from Florida and the French as a military threat to the colonists led the colonists to reassess their self-interest in the matter of the mercantilist regulations. There was a growing conviction on the part of many colonists that the disadvantages of remaining in a subordinate position within the Empire outweighed the advantages. Their revenue and regulatory measures, which had been accepted before 1760 with some equanimity, were now deemed intolerable. With the change in the relative status of the great European powers in North America, there was a growth of American nationalism and a sense of self-sufficiency that made the old status of a colony too restraining for many. Furthermore, there was an evolution in the political thinking of the colonists toward self-determination, which the mother country was not prepared to accept or understand. When they migrated to the colonies, the Englishmen among them knew that they went "with all the first great privileges of Englishmen on their backs," and as their controversies with the mother country developed, they were quick in adapting the natural rights philosophy of the Revolution of 1688 to their own needs. Their skill in political debate made them a match for their contemporaries in Britain, especially in view of the fact that while England had a constitution, a constitution for the empire as distinguished from the realm had never been worked out.[6] The rupture of the old British Empire, says Gipson on the basis of his long and scholarly study of imperial relations, "had its source fundamentally in the fact that America embodied a mature and powerful English-speaking community with a mind of its own and a future that it considered peculiarly its own. British statesmen as a group were responsible for the breach, to the extent of their failure to realize that the old system of imperial control was no longer applicable to a society so highly cultivated, so extended, and so numerous. American radicals were responsible for it to the extent of their failure in turn to realize that their own violent words and acts were provocative of coercion rather than conciliation. . . ."[7]

ECONOMIC ENTERPRISE DURING THE REVOLUTION

In looking at what went on behind the shifting battlelines of the long and often desultory Revolutionary War, we must remember that fortunately it was not a period capable of the total, destructive war that modern man can wage. Agriculture, in which most of the people were engaged, was not injured greatly by the military campaigns. After 1776 New England was affected hardly at all by the war, and southern farmers were not disturbed by the British and Indian raids until 1780. Many farmers prospered because of the needs of the armies for wool and other supplies. The plantation owners of the South suffered because of the British blockade and the actions of privateers; toward the end of the hostilities many of their slaves were carried off by the invading British army. By the end of the war, depreciated paper money helped many farmers pay off their debts in New York and other colonies. In general, agricultural conditions varied according to the fortunes of war and the special marketing problems it created.

Household manufactures were little affected by the war, whereas the production of goods needed by the military showed some increase; this was

---

[6] C. H. Van Tyne, *Causes of the War of Independence* (Boston: Houghton Mifflin, Inc., 1922).

[7] Gipson, *The Coming of the Revolution*, pp. 232–33. Clinton Rossiter in his *Seedtime of the Republic* (New York: Harcourt, Brace & World, Inc., 1953) perceptively writes, "Despite all the shouting about English rights and ways, the colonial mind was growing steadily less English and more American. By the standards of the Old World, it was a mind not especially attractive, not least because it was setting out at last to find standards of its own."

especially true of iron products, gunpowder, nails, and some textiles. Numerous bounties and other forms of financial aid were offered to stimulate manufactures, but in many cases these were not effective. The army had to rely largely on imports for uniforms.

The fisheries were almost destroyed by the British, and their interference with ocean shipping crippled the trade with the West Indies; the colonists' supply of sugar and molasses was cut off, with the result that the production of rum fell off. The colonists turned to drinking whiskey instead; this was one of the minor revolutions caused by the war. Merchants and ship captains turned to privateering, and many new fortunes were made in this way as well as by carrying on an illicit trade with the British West Indies. Elias Derby of Salem is said to have made more than four hundred captures, becoming thereby one of the richest merchants in New England.

The war in general encouraged a gainful and speculative business spirit in the new states. There was "the transfer of some wealth into the hands of a small but vigorous set of newcomers, invariably young in years and national in viewpoint, . . ." The country "was not left in the deplorable economic state frequently attributed to it. . . ."[8] Robert Treat Paine wrote from Boston in 1777, "The course of the war has thrown property into channels, where before it never was, and has increased little streams to over-flowing rivers: and what is worse, in some respects by a method that has drained the sources of some as much as it has replenished others. Rich and numerous prizes, and the putting 600 or 700 per cent on goods bought in peacetime, are the grand engines. Money in large sums, thrown into their hands by these means, enables them to roll the snowball of monopoly and forestalling."[9] Loyalists spoke of "base fellows" elevated to "honors and great wealth."

The war had an educational value for many merchants. It encouraged the business group idea and gave them invaluable experience in cooperation. The provisioning of the army led to larger and more complex business associations than those of the colonial period. A number of the successful army contractors became "big business men" in the postwar period; William Duer of New York was an outstanding example of a man who took this road to riches. The war also widened the commercial horizons of Americans, freeing them, for a time, from dependence on British firms. These new contacts "fostered a spirit of independence; the rigorous activities of war had a toughening effect, inuring shippers to a way of life in which hazard, struggle and danger were ever-present. Experience and skill gained in the hard school of conflict, an increased knowledge of the intricacies of foreign business and finance, and a

[8] R. A. East, *Business Enterprise in the American Revolutionary Era* (New York: Columbia University Press, 1938), pp. 237–38. On this subject see also C. L. VerSteeg, "The American Revolution Considered as an Economic Movement," *Huntington Library Quarterly* (August, 1957), pp. 316–372, reproduced in S. Coben and F. G. Hill, *American Economic History*, Essays in Interpretation (Philadelphia: J. B. Lippincott, 1966), pp. 125–134.

[9] Quoted in East, *Business Enterprise in the Revolutionary Era*, pp. 213–214.

quickened spirit of adventure equipped American merchants, after the war, to engage in a world-wide trade, in the face of uncertainty, hardship and peril."[10]

FINANCING THE REVOLUTION

Next to the battlefield where their reverses were many and the prospect of ultimate triumph often dim, the American cause came closest to defeat in the matter of financing the new government and its prosecution of the war. The reasons for this weakness are fairly clear. As colonists, the Americans were a tax-hating people, and the Continental Congress was slow to develop the financial machinery and administration necessary to raise the needed funds. Three methods were available to the Congress in the financing of the war: (1) issuance of bills of credit; (2) taxation; (3) borrowing. Within a week after the battle of Bunker Hill, Congress authorized an issue of two million dollars of bills of credit. These issues were to be redeemed by the states in stated amounts between 1779 and 1782. By November, 1779, forty of such emissions of bills of credit were authorized, totalling more than 241 millions of dollars. The amounts by years were as follows:

> 1775— $6,000,000; 1776— $19,000,000; 1777—$13,000,000;
> 1778—$63,000,000; 1779—$140,052,480.

The states were to be responsible for the redemption of these later issues also, but they themselves put out $290,524,776 of paper notes.

The inflation caused by the issuance of the Continental currency and the excessive wartime demand for goods and profiteering caused a good deal of social strife in the new nation. There was much denunciation of those who refused to receive these bills and futile efforts to halt the rise of prices by the calling of "price conventions." Depreciation became very rapid in 1778 and 1779. By November of the latter year, the value of this currency in specie was 38½ to 1; by 1781, it was 100 to 1 and later it became 1,000 to 1. It was under these conditions of hyper-inflation that barbershops were papered with the despised currency, and sailors had suits of clothes made from it. The expression "not worth a continental" dates from this first experience of the American nation with an inflated currency.

Before the war ended, the currency situation materially improved, largely because hard money was received from the British and French for army supplies, and specie was obtained also from foreign loans and from trade with continental Europe and the foreign West Indies. There was a bright side to the new nation's experience with the Continental currency and its ultimate collapse. It served an educational purpose in that the merchants' opposition to currency inflation was strengthened, and the need to safeguard against it by

[10] C. P. Nettels, *The Emergence of a National Economy, 1775–1815* (New York: Holt, Rinehart & Winston, 1962), p. 22.

Constitutional provision was emphasized. The Revolution also stressed the necessity of a stable and uniform hard money supply. Robert Morris proposed a plan for a national coinage system based on the decimal principle, and Jefferson was already studying the problem.[11]

Concerning the financing of the Revolution, the question of whether paper money was necessary has often been asked. At the time there was much criticism of the Continental Congress for resorting, in effect, to a forced loan via inflation to finance the prosecution of the war. But in retrospect there would seem to have been several extenuating circumstances that explain the action of that body. For one, borrowing from abroad was impossible at any early date because of the poor credit of the new government. Borrowing from the people at home was largely prevented by the absence of free capital, though Robert Morris late in the war raised some money in this way. As to taxation, Congress did not have the power to tax under the Articles of Confederation, and the states were extremely jealous of their sovereignty where taxation was concerned. It is significant that attempts to secure a national tax in 1781 and 1783 were both failures. A 5 per cent import duty was proposed in the first year as a means of raising some revenue. Under the then existing Articles of Confederation, unanimous consent was required for an amendment to make possible the new tax. However, Rhode Island stubbornly refused her consent, stating through her representatives that "She considered it the most precious jewel of her sovereignty that no state be called upon to open its purse but by the authority of the State and by her own officers." A similar plan of taxation failed in 1783 because of the refusal of New York State to give its approval.

The financial problems facing the new United States were indeed great. Paper money was being demanded by the debtors and the ignorant, yet the successive issues were sending prices soaring and compounding the difficulties of private citizens and the government alike. The tax machinery available to the Congress was but poorly developed. It relied upon a system of requisitions from the states, but the latter did not meet the demands made upon them even in paper money. Between 1777 and 1779, Congress requisitioned $95 million in paper money, but received only $54,667,000. Specie requisitions produced even worse results: Congress demanded $10,642,988 from the states and received only $1,592,222. Requisitions were also made in kind for corn, beef, pork, rum, etc., and there too great waste and inefficiency prevailed in the handling of these transactions.

Robert Morris, the financier of the Revolution, raised $11.5 million (specie value) in domestic loans, but welcome as this aid was, it was a small part of the total expenditures of the American government. He found that the government's credit was so weak that an interest rate of 4 per cent on its loan certificates was too low; he had to raise it to 6 per cent to borrow the

---

[11] E. B. Greene, *The Revolutionary Generation* (New York: The Macmillan Co., 1943), pp. 262, 274.

necessary funds. The foreign loans that the new nation was able to obtain were secured mainly from France. Between 1777 and 1783, Congress borrowed $7,830,517; of that amount, $6,352,500 came from a French government loan, $1,304,000 was raised by a private loan negotiated in Holland, and the Spanish government loaned us $174,017. Most of the money borrowed from France, incidentally, was spent there for supplies. The French government also spent $6 million on her army and navy, which aided us materially in bringing the war to a successful conclusion. Dutch bankers did not lend us any money until 1782, by which time victory was assured.

In summation, it may be noted that the direct money cost of the Revolution is estimated in specie to have been $135 million. Against this total we may place the federal debt in 1789, which stood at $42,413,000, and state debts, which aggregated $18,271,786. The difference between the total direct cost as stated and the total debts of over $60 million may be considered as paid for by taxation, depreciated paper money, and other sources of revenue.

THE ECONOMIC AND SOCIAL CONSEQUENCES OF
THE REVOLUTION

The Revolution contributed to a reconstruction of the American social structure and its underlying property system, which was indispensable to the future growth of the economy. In the Introduction to this section the point was made that economic growth depends upon a certain fluidity or mobility of the factors of production so that they may be combined in the most efficient way. Prior to the Revolution vast tracts of vacant land in the colonies were held by the Crown, proprietors, and wealthy individuals under a form of tenure that was monarchical and feudal in principle. These land magnates were entitled to exact yearly quitrents from settlers who bought or otherwise acquired the land. Generally speaking, the existence of these vast landed estates was not conducive to their rapid development and settlement. One of the paramount questions posed by the Revolution was whether feudal land law or the system of freehold tenure should prevail in the eastern states. The feudal principle was doomed as a result of the break-up and sale of many of the great landed estates. In 1777, the Continental Congress recommended that the states confiscate and sell loyalist property; the proceeds could be invested in Continental loan certificates. Pennsylvania took over the ungranted land of the Penns and gave them £130,000, though the lands were supposed to be worth £1 million. New Hampshire confiscated 28 estates, including the extensive holdings of Governor Wentworth. Massachusetts seized the Pepperell estate containing 30 miles of Maine coast land. New York realized more than three million dollars from the sale of the acres confiscated from 59 Loyalists, including the Johnson, Philips, and Morris estates. This land was sold in small parcels or given to soldiers; such redistribution of land ownership contributed to greater economic equality, but this tendency was partially offset by a new concentration of property brought about by wealthy speculators. In other states, too, the sale of land at low prices, the granting of land bounties to soldiers, and the legalizing of squatters' claims enlarged the number of small landholders and established firmly the principle of freehold tenure and the democratic ideals of yeoman and pioneers.[12]

Another feudal remnant abolished by the Revolution was the hated quitrents. These payments, as the name suggests, when made by tenants freed them from all other services. Actually since such services had long been abandoned, the quitrents were no more than a tax. They were particularly annoying in Maryland and North Carolina, where the proprietors had realized in a single year, 1774, a total of $100,000. The Revolution simply voided the obligation of paying them. Still another feudal vestige that fell before the sweeping revolutionary reform were the ancient practices of primogeniture and entail. By 1786, every state but two had abolished entail; within five more years, primogeniture was abolished. The abandonment of both these institutions greatly increased the sale and alienation of property so essential to capitalistic economic development. These measures, as Jefferson said so well, "laid the axe to the root of pseudo-aristocracy."

The Revolutionary War years saw significant changes in other social institutions in the states.[13] Public sentiment developed against slavery. Congress itself agreed not to import or deal in slaves throughout the war. By 1786, Delaware, Virginia, Maryland, South and North Carolina had passed laws prohibiting the importation of slaves. The New England states as well as New York and Pennsylvania provided for abolition or gradual abolition of slavery by the end of the century. Prison reform was begun, and at least two of the states relaxed the provisions of their harsh penal codes. Even religion felt the influence of the war. Separate American branches of the Methodist and Episcopalian churches were organized, and more important, the principle of separation of church and state was promoted. By 1786, the church had been disestablished in every state of the Union except Massachusetts, New Hampshire, and Connecticut. The radicals in some states, such as Pennsylvania, were successful in having "bills of rights" included in the state constitutions.

THE COLONIAL AND REVOLUTIONARY HERITAGE

The colonial and revolutionary years, it is clear, served as a long period of cultural and psychological preparation for our subsequent autonomous economic development. The mobile men and women who emigrated to the colonies and raised families truly produced, as Crèvecoeur contended, a new

---

[12] C. P. Nettels, *The Emergence of a National Economy*, pp. 138–146.

[13] The classic study of this subject is J. F. Jameson, *The American Revolution Considered as a Social Movement* (Princeton, N.J.: Princeton University Press, 1926).

variant of western man. This was so for a number of reasons. Colonial culture in America, though its economy was largely a satellite of the British, developed a social structure that gave more opportunity for enterprise and upward social mobility than that of contemporary European societies. The withering away of feudal institutions in the colonial environment and the eventual abolition of their remnants during and after the Revolution moved the society's pattern variables, in Parson's terms, closer to universalistic norms in the selection process for economic roles; the roles themselves became functionally more specific, and persons were evaluated in their performance of these roles more in terms of their achievement than on the basis of their social status. In short, American society moved further away from those practices that had been handed down from the traditional, late folk community of medieval times, and moved toward adoption of customs and values better adapted to a capitalistic society based on free contract and individual enterprise. Certain strategically placed elements of colonial society, especially the merchant class of New England, reflected in their character and values the strong influence of Calvinistic theology, which imparted to them not only a pronounced individualism but an almost obsessive concern with the rational ordering of their lives for the purpose of economic advancement. So it was that such colonists acquired a propensity to save and an experience in business investment, both of which were highly functional and beneficial for capitalistic economic growth.

Over the years of colonial rule the Americans did not develop, as did the people of British India in later years, a static, dependent outlook on the world. Partly because Britain was heavily involved in wars with continental powers and hence did not administer the American colonies with any great degree of strictness, and partly because as Englishmen the colonists claimed the rights deriving from their heritage of freedom, the Americans grew up, we might say, with strong egos, with a collective self-image of confidence and assurance. Their experience in conquering a wilderness, in braving the seas, in developing an extensive commerce strengthened this characteristic and further encouraged their self-reliance, independence, and willingness to assume business risks.

During the Revolutionary years these traits were given further development and testing and underwent some modifications. The "new men" who rose in business during that period, replacing in part the Tories who emigrated, undertook larger group ventures. The political leaders, many of whom had long training in local "grassroots" government, gained invaluable experience in directing the affairs of a nation at war. The merchants who prospered during the Revolution later exercised a powerful influence in national politics. The political figures themselves developed a national outlook with the aid of the strong figure of Washington as a symbol of unity. In short, the colonial and Revolutionary period saw the emergence of a mature economic and political elite who were ready and able to assume the responsibilities of independence. As Adam Smith wrote in 1776 with rare prophetic vision: "From

shopkeepers, tradesmen and attorneys, they are become statesmen and legislators and are employed in contriving a new form of government for an
extensive empire which, they flatter themselves, will become and indeed seems
very likely to become, one of the greatest and most formidable that ever was
in the world."

The drafting and adoption of the Constitution, which was to become the
legal charter and political framework of the new American economy, were so
largely the product of the experience of these colonial and Revolutionary
years as well as of the immediate social conflicts and problems of the Critical
Period that we shall consider these topics in the following chapter as part of
this section.

Chapter 4

THE MAKING AND ADOPTION
OF THE CONSTITUTION

THE CONSTITUTIONAL CRISIS

The immediate post-Revolutionary years saw the re-emergence of a problem that had confounded the British and indeed brought on the Revolution itself; the organization of government for a large area composed of diversified interests and the reconciliation of the need for central authority with the claims of local governments for some degree of autonomy. The solution to this problem, the federal system worked out by the Constitutional Convention, was a major innovation in the art and science of government. The delegates to that Convention drew upon a storehouse of wisdom and experience in the art of self-government accumulated over the long years of colonial rule and revolutionary disorder; they were sustained, too, by the heritage of humanism that the American enlightenment embodied. And like the early humanists they were confronted with the task of reconciling speculative thought on the nature of man with the immediate problem of creating a new political order. They did their work so well that to this day some observers see our nation as one conceived in genius, yet almost ever since persisting in mediocrity. It is the purpose of this chapter to analyze the social context in which this great political achievement was accomplished and to indicate some of its contributions to our economic growth.

The political and economic difficulties experienced by the new nation after the Revolution were not, at least in hindsight, surprising or unexpected. In adopting the Articles of Confederation in 1781 the states had relinquished as little of their sovereignty as possible; they had established a government with the very minimum of powers to govern. There was neither an executive nor a judiciary. Congress had no power to tax, but could merely apportion the amount of money it needed among the states according to population and wait for them to collect it. It could not levy an import duty, whereas the states were permitted to impose them on each other's products. The Congress had to share with the states the power to issue money, and under the Articles there were no safeguards for private property or for the observance of the obligations of contracts. Government was hampered by provisions of unusual rigidity, such as the requirement that Congress pass no law in conflict with state law, or that unanimous consent was necessary for any amendment of the Articles.

The not-so-United States had limped through the Revolution under the Articles. But the circumstances after the war revealed even more strikingly their dire limitations. The nation had to rebuild an economy disrupted by its war efforts. This task was vastly complicated by the huge buying spree that Americans went on after the close of hostilities. They had been used to British goods and styles, and the British merchants, anxious to regain their patronage and to stifle American industry in its cradle, shipped unusually large amounts of merchandise here and granted liberal terms of credit. As a consequence, the United States in 1784 imported five times as much from England as it had exported to it. At the same time, trade with the West Indies, which had formerly been a major source of indirect returns for the American merchants, was severely curtailed. The British government almost immediately after the signing of the Treaty of Paris excluded American shipping from its West Indian Islands and prohibited them from importing fish and meat from the United States. France was more liberal in regulating her West Indian possessions trade with the Americans; they were permitted to import all American produce except wheat and flour. As a consequence, we carried on a flourishing trade with the French islands in the post-war years, but the exclusion of American fish from the British islands resulted in a surplus in the French ones, with the result that prices were badly depressed. The Spanish and Portuguese, strict Mercantilists as ever, absolutely refused to permit any foreign merchants or vessels to engage in direct trade with their colonies. Even the trade with the Mediterranean countries was brought to a standstill by the exorbitant demands of the Barbary pirates for tribute. These restrictions on our export trade were also reflected in the decline in our earnings from shipping and from the slave trade.

The huge surplus of imports into the United States and the immediate post-war boom soon led to depression, as people refused to pay the high prices asked for merchandise and merchants found themselves overextended. The depression and the concomitant deflation of prices led the various states to pass tariff laws in an effort to protect their young industries from British competition. Between 1780 and 1789, Pennsylvania enacted 15 tariff acts; Virginia, 12; Massachusetts, New York, and Maryland, 7; etc. These individual state efforts to protect themselves against the deflation were largely futile, as the British goods entered via the free or cheapest port. In the midst of the growing depression, commercial war broke out among the states. New York placed high import duties on British goods, Connecticut and New Jersey lowered theirs. New York in retaliation then taxed the products of these states brought to New York City. New Jersey replied to this act by placing a tax of £30 per month on the lighthouse at Sandy Hook, which was so essential for the navigation of the New Yorkers' ships. Furthermore, the states found themselves at loggerheads at this time over boundary disputes. Pennsylvania people attacked Connecticut settlers in the Wyoming Valley; Connecticut and New York disputed their rights in what is now Vermont.

The finances and currency of the nation were in a chaotic state during this so-called "critical period." The depreciated Continental and statepaper monies were disappearing. Business was again being done in terms of English, French, Spanish, and Portuguese coins, and confusion reigned. Lacking available currency, the people in some sections were resorting to barter. There were three banks in the United States at this time: the Bank of North America at Philadelphia, the Bank of New York at New York City, and the Bank of Massachusetts at Boston. The notes of these banks provided a medium of exchange for the merchants of these cities, but they did not circulate very far beyond their limits. Under these circumstances, farmers were attracted, as they had been in colonial times, by paper money issues or proposals for land banks. New Issues of paper money were authorized in seven states: Rhode Island, New York, Pennsylvania, New Jersey, the Carolinas, and Georgia. The reasons for the resort to paper money varied from state to state, and often the support for it was very broad and not limited only to debtor farmers[1]; to many creditors, however, it undoubtedly recalled the disastrous inflation of Continental currency days.

The fiscal condition of the central government in 1786 was desperately serious. Its total debt, foreign and domestic, had amounted in 1784 to $39,323,000, and the yearly interest on this sum came to $1,850,000. Its total income, on the other hand, in 1785 and 1786 came to about $1,100,000—an annual average of $555,000. Thus, its income fell short of the interest on the national debt by about $1,320,000 a year. As a result, the national debt was growing, so that by 1790 it reached an estimated total of $52,788,000—an increase of over $13 million since 1784.[2] The financial difficulties of the Congress, including its inability to pay the troops, produced a near mutiny in the army. The officers of the army, while still mobilized at Newburgh, New York, threatened to use force to coerce the states to pay them, and somewhat later a band of mutinous and drunken troops actually marched on the Continental Congress sitting in Independence Hall and demanded their pay; that body was forced to flee unceremoniously to Princeton.

The shortage of currency, the depressed prices of commodities, and the mounting real burden of taxes and interest on farmers' mortgages brought the interests of debtors and creditors into conflict. Struggles took place in more than one state between these interests, but of all the conflicts, the one most disturbing to men of property and supporters of civic order was Shay's Rebellion in Massachusetts. The farmers in the middle and western parts of that state found themselves in a sorry plight in 1786. With prices depressed, they

[1] New light on the motives for the issuance of paper money in Rhode Island and other states is shed by the extraordinary work of F. McDonald, *We the People* (Chicago: University of Chicago Press, 1958), *passim* and pp. 321ff.

[2] C. P. Nettels, *The Emergence of a National Economy, 1775–1815* (New York: Holt, Rinehart, & Winston, 1962), p. 94.

found that the mortgages and other debts that they had contracted at inflated levels were now impossible to bear, and many of them were being evicted from their homes and farms for non-payment of debts. The legislature, in fact, had levied new taxes to redeem notes given to soldiers for back pay, but had adjourned without giving relief by authorizing the issuance of more paper money or permitting debts to be paid in horses and cows, as the farmers demanded. Meeting first at Worcester, the armed debtors under Daniel Shays, a former captain in the Continental Army, prevented the court from sitting at Northfield and Springfield. Later, Shays, with a thousand men under his command, moved on the federal arsenal at the latter town, but was repulsed and captured by an army of forty-four hundred men, a force financed by the wealthy merchants of Boston. The leaders of the outbreak were condemned to be executed for treason, but John Hancock, the newly elected governor, pardoned them. The wealthy feared that populism was on the march and told of mass meetings at which cries of "no taxation" and "common property" were heard. George Washington's concern at these events led him to write, "There are combustibles in every state which a spark might set fire to—I feel—infinitely more than I can express to you, for the disorders in these states. Good God! Who, besides a Tory, could have foreseen, or a Briton, predicted them?"

Discouraging and disturbing as these events were at home, there was little in the foreign relations of the new nation to provide a basis for optimism or confidence in its future. Seeking markets for its ships and products, Congress sent John Adams to Great Britain in 1785 to negotiate a trade treaty. But he found the British adamant in their refusal to grant any worthwhile concessions to the United States, primarily because they thought that we would buy from them in any case. At the same time we could not bring political pressure on them to grant such concessions because of the disunity and conflict among the States on commercial matters. Adams concluded that favorable terms for trade could only be obtained by granting Congress full and exclusive power over foreign trade for bargaining purposes. He and Jefferson met similar rebuffs in their negotiations with the Barbary pirates of North Africa. John Jay, Secretary for Foreign Affairs, found that the Spanish also refused to permit us to export to the Spanish colonies or to Spain itself and, most objectionable of all to many southerners and westerners, denied the free navigation of the Mississippi. Jay, in his report to Congress on the failure of his mission, emphasized the weaknesses of the Union under the Articles of Confederation. He said that the United States, "unblessed with an efficient government, destitute of funds, and without public credit, either at home or abroad," must "be obliged to wait in patience for better days or plunge into an unpopular and dangerous war, with very little prospect of terminating it by a peace, either advantageous or glorious." He concluded that the "seriously delicate" situation of the Union "both at home and abroad" would continue until a "vigorous national government" could be established.[3]

[3] C. P. Nettels, *The Emergence of a National Economy*, p. 69.

THE MAKERS OF THE CONSTITUTION AND THEIR MOTIVES

Americans are familiar with the fact that commissioners from Virginia and Maryland met at Mount Vernon in an attempt to reach an agreement on the navigation of the Potomac, and that the result of the meeting was that the Annapolis Convention was called the following year to "consider how far a uniform system in their commercial relations may be necessary to their common interest and their permanent harmony." They recall too that not enough delegates arrived for the Annapolis confab, and at that point Alexander Hamilton, a delegate from New York, issued a ringing call for a general constitutional convention, to be held the next year at Philadelphia, "for the sole and express purpose of revising the Articles." While these external facts about the origin of this famed Convention and its handiwork, the Constitution, are matters of common knowledge and agreement, there is much more dispute about the motives of the Founding Fathers. Charles A. Beard in 1913 in his celebrated pioneer study, *An Economic Interpretation of the Constitution of the United States*, contended that the Constitution was "an economic document drawn with superb skill by men whose property interests were immediately at stake; and as such it appealed directly and unerringly to identical interests in the country at large."[4] He went on to argue that the Constitution was based "upon the concept that the fundamental private rights of property are anterior to government and morally beyond the reach of popular majorities."[5]

Beard believed that previous interpretations of the Constitution had placed too much emphasis on abstract principles of political science and had been too prone to view the Constitution as the work of the whole people. Believing that history could profitably be interpreted in terms of the contending economic interests in society, Beard prefaces his analysis of the Constitution with a survey of the economic interests in the nation as of 1787. He first notes that there were four completely disenfranchised groups at that time—slaves, indentured servants, disqualified white males, and women. He then divided the property holding groups into two major classes, realty and personalty. The real property interests, he contended, could be considered as consisting of three sub-groups: (1) the small farmers of the hinterland who were largely debtors; (2) the manorial lords of the Hudson River Valley who, Beard felt, were adversely affected by the Constitution and therefore opposed its adoption;[6] (3) the slaveholding planters of the South, who favored the Constitu-

---

[4] Charles A. Beard, *An Economic Interpretation of the Constitution of the United States* (New York: Macmillan Company, 1913), p. 188.

[5] *Ibid.*, p. 324.

[6] The Hudson River lords were a power in state politics and had used their position to shift the burden of taxation from the land to imports. The Constitution deprived states of the power to levy import duties. This would probably mean that the burden of state taxes

tion as a whole, according to Beard, because they were not adversely affected by it. While the Constitution subjected the planters to "regulation devised immediately in behalf of northern interests," there were several "overbalancing compensations" for the planters.

Beard divided the personal property interests of 1787 into four major classes: (1) the money-lenders, who are seen by Beard as threatened by stay laws (moratoria on the foreclosing of property), inflation, and lack of protection of their investment in manufactures (they could not obtain the passage of a protective tariff law under the Articles) and in western land or in shipping; (2) holders of state and Continental securities. With the latter selling at from one-sixth to one-twentieth of their par value, holders of such securities, Beard alleges, had much to gain from the establishment of a strong central government that could honor its debts; (3) manufacturing and shipping interests, who were concerned with protection or subsidies for their industries; (4) speculators in western lands.

Beard proceeded in a subsequent chapter of his work to analyze the property holdings of the fifty-five delegates to the Constitutional Convention. Twelve of the states sent delegates; agrarian Rhode Island alone refused to send any. Beard thinks it significant that none of the fiery radicals of the pre-Revolutionary era was present, such as Jefferson, Adams, or Tom Paine. Patrick Henry stayed away because, as he said, he "smelt a rat." In general, of the 55 members of the Convention, Beard says that not one represented in his own interest the small farming or mechanic classes. His analysis revealed the following distribution of economic interests among the delegates:

> 14—speculative interest in land
> 24—money-lenders
> 40—holders of public securities
> 11—mercantile, manufacturing and shipping interests
> 15—slaveholders

Beard's classifying of forty of the delegates as holders of public securities was based on the manuscript records of the Loan of 1790, which he had unearthed in the basement of the U.S. Treasury. He assumed that those delegates whose names appeared on the funding books of the federal government in 1790 were public creditors at the time of the Convention. "It is hardly to be supposed," he writes, "that many of them would sink to the level of mere speculators." From his analysis Beard concluded that "The overwhelming majority of members, at least five-sixths, were immediately, directly, and personally interested in the outcome of their labors at Philadelphia, and were to a greater or

---

would fall upon the land owned by the manor lords. In the introduction to the 1935 edition of his book, Beard revised his position on this subject somewhat. He cites T. C. Cochran as contending that some of the lords held public securities and were thus in favor of a stronger national government that could pay the interest and principal on its obligations. (C. A. Beard, *An Economic Interpretation* . . . , p. xv.)

lesser extent economic beneficiaries from the adoption of the Constitution."[7] Another conclusion that emerged from his study was that the personal property interests really constituted the dynamic element in the movement for the Constitution.

In a later chapter of his influential work Beard surveyed the political doctrines of the members of the Convention, largely on the basis of their remarks on the floor of that assemblage. He cited the anti-democratic remarks of Randolph, Hamilton, Gerry, and Gouveneour Morris and highlighted the philosophy of economic interests of James Madison in Federalist Paper No. 10 as giving us the best exposition of the political science of the Constitution. From this material and from his analysis of the Constitution itself, he concluded that that document was constructed on two fundamental principles, the one positive, the other negative. As to the former, we have a government endowed with certain positive powers, but so constructed to break the force of majority rule and prevent invasions of the property rights of minorities. The system of checks and balances in the Constitution is seen as designed to do just this. Suffrage restrictions, bicameralism, the executive veto, judicial review—all these are pictured as safeguards against the dangers of populist and debtor legislation. The negative principle in the Constitution is considered by Beard to consist of those restrictions on the state legislatures that had vigorously attacked capital during the critical, uncertain years under the Articles. We defer consideration of these provisions until later in this chapter.

Beard's interpretation of the motives of the Founding Fathers was accepted by many historians, especially the authors of college texts, until relatively recently.[8] Professors Brown and McDonald have independently written two well-documented critiques of the Beardian thesis.[9] We shall summarize some of their main points of criticism with respect to the Constitutional Convention here and consider their analysis of the context over ratification below. Brown attacks Beard's interpretation with respect to the disenfranchisement of the "mass of men" in 1787, arguing that the Constitution had widespread popular support. Many of the points of his criticism are more powerfully argued in McDonald's remarkable work. Beard acknowledged that his pages were

[7] Beard, *An Economic Interpretation of the Constitution of the United States,* p. 149. Beard explicitly denied that he was charging the members of the Convention with writing the Constitution for their personal benefit. Though his manner of expression frequently conveys the former impression, he insisted that he was analyzing their holdings to determine whether because of their experience with certain forms of property they could be considered as representatives of holders of such property in general (*Ibid.,* p. 73). Marxists have frequently charged Beard with a crass economic determinism that neglects the relationships between interests, class, and ideology.

[8] R. E. Brown, *Charles Beard and the Constitution* (Princeton, N.J.: Princeton University Press, 1956), *passim.*

[9] Brown and McDonald, *We The People, op. cit.,* Criticisms along the lines of Brown and McDonald's work have appeared earlier, e.g., cf. E. S. Corwin's article in *History Teachers' Magazine* (February, 1914), pp. 65–66 and the balanced views of B. and L. P. Mitchell, *American Economic History* (Boston: Houghton Mifflin Co., 1947), p. 231ff. and H. S. Commager, "The Constitution: Was It An Economic Document?," *American Heritage, The Magazine of History* (December, 1958), pp. 58–61, 100–3.

"frankly fragmentary," and that he left it to others to fill in the details; this young scholar, by arduous effort and analysis, has done just that. He finds that the most common and important property holdings of the delegates were not, as Beard claimed, mercantile, manufacturing, or public security investments, but agricultural property. He shows that the delegates at the Convention hardly behaved as a consolidated economic group whose property interests were immediately at stake. Fully a fourth of them had voted for paper-money and debtor-relief laws in their state legislatures. Further, the seven opponents of the Constitution held two and a half times as much in securities per capita as the 39 proto-Federalists. McDonald's position here seems to be that Beard's analysis is over-simple and does not do justice to the complexity of the motivations of the participants. He admits that an economic interpretation "renders intelligible many of the forces at work in the making of the Constitution," but that it is far from adequate because countless non-economic factors must be taken into consideration.

THE RATIFICATION OF THE CONSTITUTION

Professor Beard emphasizes the unseemly haste with which the supporters of the proposed Constitution went about seeking its ratification. He goes out of his way to cite a remark of a fellow political scientist to the effect that the method adopted for ratifying the Constitution, if followed by a Napoleon, would have been spoken of as *coup d'etat*. He refers to the provision the Constitutional Convention had made for ratification by nine states rather than for unanimous approval. He stresses the haste in the election of delegates to the state conventions and contends that the delegates to the ratifying conventions were elected by probably not more than one-sixth of the adult male population. Standing in opposition to the approval of the new charter of government, according to Beard, were four main groups: the small farmers, the town mechanics, the petty traders, and the politicians at the state capitols who feared that they would lose in power and preferment as a result of the establishment of a federal type of government. The struggle, we know, was particularly intense in New Hampshire, Massachusetts, and New York. The popular vote in the latter state was originally adverse to the Constitution. Governor Clinton and Melancthon Smith controlled 46 votes, mostly from the interior of the state, against the 19 from New York City and its environs, which were for the Constitution. The day was finally won for its supporters, thanks to the threat of the City of New York to secede if the Constitution were not ratified, to the influence of the Federalist papers, and to the strenuous argumentative and political efforts of Hamilton, Livingstone, Jay, and others who, on the last vote in the Convention, converted a minority of 27 into a majority of three.

Two states refused to ratify the Constitution until after the new government had already been established; these were Rhode Island and North Carolina. Some of the doubtful states had, in fact, demanded a Bill of Rights as the price for their approval. So, in 1789, the first Congress approved the first ten Amendments, despite the fact that two years previously the Philadelphia Convention had unanimously voted down a bill of rights.

In his interpretation of these events, Beard held that "in the ratification, it became manifest that the line of cleavage for and against the Constitution was between substantial personalty interests on the one hand and the small farming and debtor interests on the other."[10] Beard's implication that the Constitution was repugnant to the farmers is hard to reconcile with the fact that in such agricultural states as Delaware, Georgia, and New Jersey, each of the conventions ratified it unanimously, and in agricultural Connecticut and Maryland it was approved by votes of more than three to one. McDonald's detailed analysis of the ratification process in these and other states demonstrates that the issues were more complex than allowed for in Beard's monistic explanation.

Beard's second contention, so far as the contest over ratification is concerned, was that public securities were the dynamic element among the personal property interests in bringing about the ratification of the Constitution. In his words: "Inasmuch as so many leaders in the movement for ratification were large security holders, and inasmuch as securities constituted such a large proportion of personalty, this economic interest must have formed a very considerable dynamic element, if not the preponderant element, in bringing about the adoption of the new system." McDonald's exhaustive analysis of the votes of the ratifying conventions in the various states completely demolishes this proposition of the Beardian thesis. He shows, for example, that in the states that unanimously approved the Constitution (Delaware, New Jersey, and Georgia), security-holders were a distinct minority among its supporters, and in three states (Pennsylvania, South Carolina, and New York), a considerably larger percentage of the delegates opposing ratification held Federal securities than was true of those supporting the Constitution. In other states there was no correlation of any significance between security-holding and the attitude displayed toward the Constitution. Not only, then, were there some holders of public securities among the opponents of the Constitution, but contrary to Beard's contention, they were as numerous as the security-holders among its supporters. "Beard's essential error," concludes McDonald, was in attempting to formulate a single set of generalizations that would apply to all the states. Any such effort is necessarily futile, for the various interest groups operated under different conditions in the several states, and their attitudes toward the Constitution varied with the internal conditions in their states."[12]

---

[10] C. A. Beard, *An Economic Interpretation of the Constitution of the United States*, p. 325.

[11] Beard, *op. cit.*, p. 29.

[12] McDonald, *We The People, op. cit.*, p. 357.

McDonald's criticism of Beard's famous work, *An Economic Interpretation of the Constitution,* is itself sub-titled *The Economic Origins of the Constitution.* Some may see in this an inexplicable paradox, but an answer is readily found in the former's remark that "economic factors were by no means without influence in the making of the Constitution."[13] The question, he asks himself, is whether these factors can be reorganized in such a way as to reduce them to an economic interpretative system or set of systems that will make the contests over ratification intelligible. In other words, McDonald, like Marx, does not believe that merely to call attention to the role of economic factors in history is adequate; everything depends upon the way in which the so-called economic interpretation is carried out. In two brilliant concluding chapters, McDonald explores four possible economic interpretations of the Constitution, other than Beard's. While we cannot enter into the details of these explorations here, it may be of interest to cite the situation existing in 1787 so far as economic interest groups were concerned, as McDonald perceives it in contrast to Beard's views outlined earlier. It is interesting psychologically to note that in analyzing the economic interests of the 1780's, McDonald believes they can be seen in "sharper focus" if they are considered as activities of men, while Beard prefers to classify them as forms of property. In other words, McDonald stresses the occupations and professions by which men earned a living or acquired wealth, and finds that practically all free Americans of that day fell into one or more broad occupational classes: farmers, nonagrarian producers, commercial groups, and professional men. After analyzing the respective interests of these classes and their subdivision and of the various forms of capital, he presents a much more complex situation than Beard portrayed. "There were in the United States in 1787 at least twenty basic occupational groups having distinctly different economic characteristics and needs, and there were six basic forms of capital in addition to capital incidental to occupational activity. Most of the occupational groups and all the forms of capital may be divided into two to seventy-five subdivisions. Of the grand total of major economic interest groups and forms of investment, about 30 per cent were affected by the Constitution directly and immediately in a favorable way, and about 15 per cent were directly and immediately affected in an unfavorable way. The remaining 55 per cent were either not directly affected at all or were affected in indefinite, indecisive or unpredictable ways."[14] McDonald goes on to point out that even among the important groups affected favorably by the Constitution there were numerous internal conflicts of interest, so that it is not possible, theoretically, to state a single set of alignments among such interests on the issue of ratification.

McDonald analyzes the struggle over the ratification of the Constitution as a single national contest and as thirteen contests in the various states. The only hypothesis that seems to him to be meaningful when the contest is viewed

[13] *Ibid.,* p. 358.
[14] *Ibid.,* p. 398.

as a single contest is that the Constitution was the expression of the prevailing ideology of the socially desirable or normal relationship between government and the economy. He finds that this prevailing ideology in the states was a mercantilistic one, with each state molding its policy to fit its own local requirements. Hence, he says, the general mold of opinion in America at that time did not imply national mercantilism, but a group of local mercantilisms. Americans were accustomed to fairly extensive governmental interference in their economic lives in the form of these various mercantilistic policies, but they feared the centralization of power in a government removed from local supervision and control. McDonald's analysis takes an incomprehensible and, we believe, an erroneous position at this point, for he holds, on the one hand, that the "one radical feature of the Constitution was that it created a general government to replace the Congress of the Confederation"[15] and thereby shifted the equilibrium of the federal system that Americans had known. On the other hand, he contends that the Constitution did not create a new system of political economy, partly because the people of the states assumed that they would retain control over those matters that were not the concern of all the states.[16] There are possibly semantic difficulties in our understanding of McDonald's ideas, but it does seem that he does not sufficiently recognize the extent to which the economic provisions of the Constitution were a break with custom, indeed a great political innovation that moved the country toward a more nationalistic application of mercantilism than it had known up to that time. This was its challenge and one of the reasons that it stirred up the controversy that it did. It is appropriate for us at this point to consider these economic provisions of the Constitution and the influence of that document and the framework of government it established on the contemporary economic life and on the subsequent economic growth of the nation.

THE CONSTITUTION AND AMERICAN ECONOMIC GROWTH

The men who favored "a more perfect union" at the Constitutional Convention have been termed "nationalists" or "federalists," though the former word more aptly describes their philosophy. They were those who were not content with merely amending the Articles of Confederation, but believed that a new, strong national government should be established. Their ideas were expressed in the opening statements of the Virginia Plan, which was advocated by the larger states: "That a union of the States merely federal will not accomplish the object proposed . . . namely, common defence, security of liberty, and general welfare . . . That a *national* government ought to be established, consisting of a supreme Legislative, Executive and Judiciary."[17]

---

15 *Ibid.*, p. 416.
16 *Ibid.*, pp. 410–11.
17 As quoted in B. and L. P. Mitchell, *American Economic History*, p. 236.

While some of the features of the Virginia Plan were modified to meet the objections of the small states that backed the New Jersey Plan, the objectives of the Constitution, as written, largely reflect the objectives of the nationalists. What were these objectives? First, the original aim of these nationalists was to provide for the payment of the wartime debts of the Union in specie. Secondly, they sought to revise and prevent the states from passing the kind of laws that threatened to disrupt the national economy that had begun to emerge during the Revolution. Expressed more positively, they desired to direct the development of the economy along national lines; to accomplish this, they sharply reduced the economic powers of the states and conferred many new ones upon the central government.[18]

The provisions of this nature are found in Article I, sections 8–10 of the Constitution. There we find that Congress is given "the power to lay and collect taxes, duties, imposts and excises, to pay the debts and provide for the common defense and general welfare of the United States. . . ." We notice that payment of the debts is mentioned as one of the first uses of the taxing power. This purpose is made even more explicit in the first clause of Article VI, which states: "All debts contracted and engagements entered into, before the adoption of the Constitution, shall be as valid against the United States under this Constitution, as under the Confederation." The supporters of these provisions believed that by giving the public securities a durable value, they would in effect increase the supply of money and thereby give a stimulus to production and exchange.[19]

One of the most dangerous developments of the post-Revolutionary years was the tendency of the several states to levy imposts on each other's products, thereby threatening the free flow of what interstate commerce there was. Without uniform commercial regulations and the power to formulate such for the nation as a whole, the country's ambassadors and law-makers found themselves handicapped in bargaining over trade matters with foreign countries and without the power to take reprisal against discriminatory foreign legislation. It was to remedy these defects of the Articles that the Constitution provided that the states should give up the right to levy duties on imports and Congress was granted the exclusive right to regulate foreign and interstate commerce. These provisions in effect made possible the establishment of a single, national trading area, a condition that was essential if the nation was to have the extensive markets needed for large-scale production. Furthering this objective as well as offering protection to the creditor class was the provision granting Congress the power to establish uniform laws on the subject of bankruptcies. Likewise, in order to encourage business in the national trading area, the Constitution provided for a single postal system and

---

[18] Nettels, *The Emergence of a National Economy*, pp. 90–92.

[19] Hamilton in particular argued that a national debt well provided for and in the hands of the rich would serve as collateral in loan transactions and, by providing a relatively safe investment, would enable capitalists to invest the remainder of their funds in more speculative enterprises.

a common standard of weights and measures. Power was granted Congress too to adopt a national patent and copyright system so that the inventive and artistic genius of the nation might be encouraged without the complication of having to comply with the diverse laws of thirteen states. Immigration of artisans and others who might be useful in the development of economic projects was facilitated by a clause giving Congress the power to establish a "uniform rule of naturalization"; thus immigrants also would not be forced to comply with the possible conflicts among the various state laws.

The Constitution made provision for the settlement, government, and defense of the West by giving Congress the power "to dispose of and make all needful rules and regulations respecting the territory . . . belonging to the United States." This was a feature appealing greatly to those who had plans for land speculation in the trans-Appalachian West. The clauses giving Congress the right to raise and support armies and a navy and to call forth the militia were obviously of importance to such interests because they provided the means to meet Indian uprisings as well as such internal insurrections as Shays' Rebellion. The provisions in the Constitution that no state should pass a law giving liberty to a fugitive slave, that Congress was not to interfere with the slave trade, external or internal, for twenty years, and the "three-fifths rule" in the representation of the South in the Congress—all were very favorable to the planter interests. Protection was also offered in direct or indirect forms to manufacturing, maritime, and agricultural groups. Propertied interests were thus not only explicitly taken care of, but safeguards were provided against hostile legislation by the states. Section 10 of Article 1 placed fetters on such state action: "No state shall enter into any treaty, alliance or confederation; grant letters of margue or reprisal; coin money; emit bills of credit; make anything but gold and silver coin a tender in payment of debts; pass any bill of attainder, ex-post facto law, or law impairing the obligation of contracts, or grant any title of nobility." This sweeping ban on the types of state laws that had caused fright and uncertainty among the creditor class was to prove a bulwark against anti-capitalistic governmental action. While the Constitution was to afford even greater protection to property and risk-taking enterprise in later years with the extension of the corporate privilege and the interpretations of the fifth and fourteenth amendments with their "due process clauses," for its day it was an unprecedented and most explicit charter and political and legal framework for business enterprise. By granting such strong protection to property and enterprise, it provided a most congenial and favorable atmosphere for the risk-taking and innovation that are indispensable to vigorous economic growth. The Founding Fathers in meeting the political and economic exigencies of their day so boldly drew upon a cultural heritage especially favorable to the spirit of individual enterprise. Theirs was a creed that emphasized, as J. E. Sawyer points out, certain special lines of thought within the European heritage—"notably Puritanism, Lockian individualism, Newtonian ideas of the working of automatic harmonies, the late Enlightenment's faith in the inexorable relation of reason and individual effort to human progress." Not only was this creed "designed to fortify creative and aggressive entrepreneurship, but it was," he says, "at a moment of unusual clarity and simplicity . . . crystallized and codified in the basic symbols and laws of the Republic. . . ."[20]

---

[20] W. Miller, ed., *Men In Business* (Cambridge, Massachusetts: Harvard University Press, 1952), p. 21.

Part 2

THE RISE OF AN INDEPENDENT AMERICAN CAPITALISM, 1789–1814

Introduction: Adam Smith's Vision of the Growth Process

The Directions of American Economic Growth, 1789–1814

Establishing the Pre-Conditions for a More Specialized Market Economy

The Political Economy of Jeffersonian Agrarianism

INTRODUCTION: ADAM SMITH'S VISION OF
THE GROWTH PROCESS

The year 1776 saw the publication of two documents that had a revolutionary influence upon the course of world history. These were the Declaration of Independence and Adam Smith's great work on political economy, *An Inquiry into the Nature and Causes of the Wealth of Nations*. The appearance of these two remarkable publications in the same year was more than historical coincidence. Both documents reflected the ferment of social change and the demand for political and economic liberty that agitated some parts of the Western world in the late eighteenth century. Our interest in this Introduction is primarily in Smith's work as the first statement of what has come to be known as the classical theory of economic growth.[1]

Adam Smith (1723–1790), the great Scottish economist, was educated at Glasgow and Oxford Universities. He became professor of moral philosophy at the former institution in 1752. In 1778 he was appointed commissioner of customs for Scotland.

A. M. Kelley Publishing Company

At the time Adam Smith wrote, the Industrial Revolution had not yet transformed economic life in Great Britain, but markets were widening, new opportunities were opening up for the small merchant capitalists, if they could but escape from the restrictions of mercantilism. Actually, for a century before Smith condemned the old mercantile system, individuals in that country were violating its regulations, just as in America colonial merchants were smuggling goods past the British customs officials in defiance of the law.

---

[1] A. Lowe, "The Classical Theory of Economic Growth," *Social Research*, Vol. 21 (1954), pp. 127–158; J. J. Spengler, "Adam Smith's Theory of Economic Growth," *Southern Economic Journal*, Vol. 25 (1959), pp. 397–415; G. M. Meier and R. E. Baldwin, *Economic Development* (New York: John Wiley and Sons, 1957), Chap. 1.

Adam Smith defended the cause of these small, enterprising merchants, and in his famous book made out a classic case against the increasingly archaic restraints of the old system.[2]

In place of the planned economy of mercantilism, Smith advocated what he called "the obvious and simple system of natural liberty." This emphasis on natural liberty is important in understanding Smith's views because it reflects his acceptance of the widely held eighteenth century doctrine of natural law. This doctrine maintained that there is a set of rules or rights having to do with social morality, known to men through "reason" or moral intuition, which are superior in authority to that of the commands of kings or of customary legal or moral regulations that contravene them. Smith applied this natural law doctrine to economics, arguing the right of every man to pursue his self-interest. This freedom of self-interested individuals in combining the factors of production in the manner that will make for the largest profit was the secret of production and of the wealth of nations. Better still, Smith demonstrated that if the proper initial political decisions were made, the economic machine would operate in a self-correcting way in accordance with "laws" that almost had the certainty and order that Newton had discovered in the physical world.

Smith's achievement in formulating such a theory of economic growth was particularly opportune because it occurred when Great Britain was on the eve of the transition from pre-industrial to industrial capitalism. His work "reveals the political and social as well as economic foundations on which traditional theory rests"[3] and makes clear the delicate inter-relationships among these factors.

While Smith's work has been the subject of study for centuries, only recently have economic scholars distilled the essential elements of his model of economic growth from the widely scattered passages in his *magnum opus*. Lowe, for example, has presented an admirable analysis of the "constants" and variables of the Smithian system, which depicts the economy growing cumulatively, once development has been started under the benign auspices of natural liberty. Beginning with the institutional constants, we note that Smith posits a competitive market place with a constitutional government concerned mainly with the maintenance of law and order, the preservation of personal liberty, freedom of contract and private property. Accepting too the class character of society as the background of the economy he is describing, Smith explicitly postulated the social mobility of the factors of production and assumed as well a certain "technical mobility" in the sense that enterprises were small and the factors of production relatively replaceable for one another. Supporting all this are the basic organizational principles of the division of labor and free exchange.

[2] E. Ginzberg, *The House of Adam Smith* (New York: Columbia University Press, 1934).

[3] Lowe, "The Classical Theory of Economic Growth," p. 167; see also his *On Economic Knowledge* (New York: Harper and Row, 1965), pp. 168–179. The description of elements of the Smithian model in the following pages relies heavily upon Lowe's analysis.

The working of these fundamental institutions reflects certain psychological "constants" in Smith's model, such as the human "propensity to truck, barter and exchange," the urge to procreate, and "the desire of bettering our conditions." A most important assumption of Smith's theory, which goes far to account for his optimistic vision of the beneficent working of the free enterprise system, is the idea of constant returns on natural resources. That is to say, additional land could be brought into production *ad infinitum* without any decline in fertility.

Given the fact that it is in the nature of the economic process that production tends to drain off and deplete the productive factors, what prevents a free enterprise system from running down in accordance with a principle analogous to the law of entropy in physics? Smith contends in effect that there are three fundamental laws of long-term motion that assure the reproduction of these factors on an increasing scale, despite their being used up in the current cycle of production. He believed that although the "demand for men, like that for any commodity, necessarily regulates the production of men," real wages can and do rise so long as the national product increases and there is a rising wages fund.[4] The latter variable in turn depends upon a law of capital accumulation. So long as people can better their condition by saving and investing their funds in industry for a profit, increased opportunities for employment are created. As Smith says, "Every increase or diminution of capital, therefore, naturally tends to increase or diminish the real quantity of industry, the number of productive hands, and consequently the exchangeable value of the annual produce of the land and labour of the country, the real wealth and revenue of its inhabitants."[5]

The growth of capital (out of profits) and the increase of real wages depends upon a rise in productivity, and this, the most strategic variable in the whole system, depends upon the progressive "division of labor" that Smith described so vividly in his opening chapter on pin manufacture. But productivity and division of labor do not rise spontaneously; they are dependent on a prior increase in aggregate demand, or as Smith expressed it in a famous dictum, the division of labor is limited by the extent of the market. This is Smith's third law of the dynamic movement of the economy: the rate of increase in aggregate demand governs the rate of increase in productivity.

So long as a nation then can assure an increase in aggregate demand and maintains the institutional constants described above, it can anticipate a cumulative process of economic growth. As Professor Schumpeter wrote concerning Smith's picture of the process of economic development, "The

[4] The wage fund was that portion of the circulating capital that the classical economists assumed to be available for the payment of the workers in an economy. They thought of it as a fixed sum so that as the labor force grew, each individual in it would receive a decreasing share.

[5] Adam Smith, *The Wealth of Nations* (New York: E. P. Dutton and Co., 1910), p. 321.

economy grows like a tree. This process is no doubt exposed to disturbances by external factors that are not economic, or not strictly so, but in itself it proceeds, steadily, continuously. Each situation grows out of the preceding one in an uniquely determined way, and the individuals whose acts combine to produce each situation count individually for no more than do the individual cells of a tree."[6]

Smith looked to the powerful motive of self-interest to energize economic growth because, as he said, it is "the uniform, constant and uninterrupted effort of every man to better his own condition." Each individual, he held, is a better judge of how to spend his own time and labor than any statesman or mercantilist bureaucrat could be. And since the wealth of a nation is simply the sum total of the income of the individuals who comprise it, it followed that the economic good of the nation would be best promoted by allowing each person to seek his own interest. Indeed, self-interest was already at work in the British economy; Smith wrote, "It is not from the benevolence of the butcher, brewer, or the baker, that we expect our dinner, but from their regard to their own interest. We address ourselves, not to their humanity but to their self-love, and never talk to them of our own necessities but of their advantages. . . ." What was needed in his day, he believed, was to give self-interest greater scope and freedom of action.

Smith contended that the potent force of self-interest could be held in check by the influence of "the invisible hand" of competition. Individuals seek their own self-interest, but in doing so they create a competition in which each will check the other, and their activities consequently will be harnessed for the social good. Greater freedom of enterprise and competition thus enabled Smith to endorse what the French economists of the time called *laissez faire*. But he was far from being a doctrinaire believer in that famous policy.[7] As Professor Viner has written, "He did not believe that laissez faire was always good, or always bad. It depended on circumstances; . . ." And the circumstances were such that with English government in the hands of an aristocratic clique, often corrupt, cynical, biased, and uninformed in its judgment, it seemed to Smith that the evils of unrestrained selfishness might be better than the evils of incompetent rule. At times he expresses a deep pessimism about the future of society as when he writes, ". . . The violence and injustice of the rulers of mankind is an ancient evil, for which, I am afraid, the nature of human affairs can scarce admit of remedy."[8]

According to the Scottish economist, the state or the sovereign has only three duties to attend to; ". . . first, the duty of protecting the society from the violence and invasion of other independent societies; secondly, . . . the

---

[6] J. Schumpeter, "Theoretical Problems," *Journal of Economic History*, Supplement VII (1947), pp. 6–7.

[7] See especially the classic discussion in J. Viner, "Adam Smith and Laissez Faire," in his *The Long View and the Short* (Glencoe, Ill.: The Free Press, 1958), pp. 231ff.

[8] Adam Smith, *Wealth of Nations*, Canaan Edition, I (New York: The Modern Library, 1937), p. 457.

duty of establishing an exact administration of justice; and thirdly, the duty of erecting and maintaining certain public works and certain public institutions, which it can never be for the interest of any individual, or small number of individuals, to erect and maintain; because the profit could never repay the expense to any individual or small number of individuals, though it may frequently do much more than repay it to a great society."[9] Smith nowhere gives a complete list of the public works proper to government, but he refers to highways, bridges, canals, and harbors. In general, Smith judges the propriety of government participation in commerce and industry in terms of whether the state can derive a net income from it. Thus, he approves of government operation of the post office and of the coining of money; on the whole, however, he disapproves of government ventures into business because the state is a poor trader and a worse manager. On the other hand, Smith supported government provision of education for the people because he was concerned about the detrimental effects of extreme specialization of labor upon them. Contrary to the general view of him, Smith saw a wide and elastic range of activity for government and was inclined to extend it farther, if its standards of competence could be raised.

Smith took a most optimistic view of Britain's American colonies; just as China was the prime example of a stagnant society, America represented the progressive state *par excellence*. He pointed to the high and rising wages earned in America and suggested, in fact, that Britain might convert her "project of an empire" into a federated organization in which America would be an equal partner. He saw America, indeed, overtaking Britain in wealth and population, saying: "Such has hitherto been the rapid progress of that country in wealth, population and improvement, that in the course of a little more than a century, perhaps, the produce of American might exceed that of British taxation. The seat of empire would then naturally remove itself to that part of the empire which contributed most to the general defense and support of the whole."[10] The accuracy of Smith's forecast as to the future of America is another evidence of his remarkable insight into the nature of the economic process.

Reference was made above to Smith's dictum that the division of labor is limited by the extent of the market. This theorem of the Smithian economics is extremely relevant to the analysis of the early years of the Republic with which we deal in the following three chapters. It is especially important in analyzing the developments in the export sector of the American economy that underwent an extraordinary growth during the years 1793–1807. Prior to those years the American economy labored under some of the handicaps which are common to the underdeveloped nations of today. One of these is that the domestic market of underdeveloped countries is often small, scattered, and predominantly rural. The people of such countries are apt to be highly

9 *Ibid.*, II, 185.
10 *Wealth of Nations*, p. 590.

self-sufficient economically. These conditions, it is obvious, are not favorable to the development of specialization and the division of labor. Increase in export trade, under these circumstances, may provide a most valuable stimulus to the expansion of the domestic market, to growth in money income, and to a wider division of labor. Indeed, some economists regard a successful export sector as the most common initiating factor in the early stages of the growth of market economies.[11]

In the following chapters we shall have an opportunity to examine the relevance and validity of Adam Smith's theory of economic growth in terms of the economic experience of the young Republic. We shall probe into the effects of the expanding export trade upon the division of labor and its limits and other such matters. But one remaining prefatory remark needs to be made before we begin such an analysis. We need to emphasize that an analytical framework for the study of this early period of our national economic growth must take cognizance of the fact that the nation then was definitely not a closed economy, but rather heavily dependent on the tides of international commerce and exogenous factors generally. Culturally, of course, our dependence upon the societies of Western Europe and especially Great Britain was even more pronounced during these formative years. In the case of technological progress in particular, we were, on the whole, followers rather than leaders. Samuel Slater was one of the first Americans to adapt the technological innovations of Western Europe to his pecuniary advantage and the nation's ultimate benefit. Even where our innovations were of an indigenous character, Professor North points out, "The most striking aspect of many of them was they emerged in the context of a mounting problem, reflecting the search for alternative uses of existing sunk capital or the rising price of a resource or productive factor, especially labor. Whether it was Eli Whitney's cotton gin—certainly the major domestic innovation for the economy's growth during the period—or the labor-saving devices which impressed British investigators of American manufacturing in the 1850's, they clearly owed their origins to the deliberate search for solutions to economic problems, particularly in the export sector."[12]

Theoretical and factual considerations of this kind make it inappropriate to give domestic innovations the primary role in the dynamic evolution of the economy during this period that they seem to deserve in later years. In this period, as Schumpeter himself admitted, ". . . external factors obviously dominate the picture. . . .[13] In the following analysis of the economic growth of these years, the temporal divisions employed reflect this predomi-

---

[11] D. C. North, *The Economic Growth of the United States, 1790–1869* (Englewood Cliffs, N.J.: Prentice-Hall, Inc., 1961), p. 2; A. J. Youngson, in *Possibilities of Economic Progress* (Cambridge: The University Press, 1959), p. 311 states, "It is scarcely an exaggeration to call this (export trade) the traditional first major step in economic development."

[12] *Ibid.*, p. 8.

[13] Schumpeter, *Business Cycles*, Vol. I (New York: McGraw-Hill Book Co., 1939), p. 287.

nance of external or exogenous influences. Thus, for example, while the availability of statistics for the decennial censuses might incline us to terminate this period as of 1820, recognition of the external factors at work has led us to prefer ending our treatment in 1814 with the close of the Napoleonic Wars and the conclusion of our own hostilities with Great Britain.

Chapter 5

THE DIRECTIONS OF AMERICAN ECONOMIC GROWTH, 1789–1814

THE UNITED STATES IN 1789

The new, infant Republic over which George Washington assumed the Presidency on April 30, 1789 was faced with many complex economic problems, both domestic and foreign. While the adoption of the Constitution resolved the political crisis that had weakened the nation under the older form of government, much remained to be done in establishing the financial foundations of the nation and in lifting it out of the economic doldrums it had experienced during the Critical Period. Compared to the European nations, the United States at that time ranked among the smaller countries of the world; the number of its inhabitants was slightly larger than that of Portugal, the Netherlands, or Sweden, but it ranked far below that of the larger European nations from whom it sought recognition. The census of 1790 showed a population total of close to four million (3,930,000 to be exact), of which about 700,000 were slaves. Most Americans at that time lived in rural areas; only slightly more than 200,000 people were designated as urban dwellers. No city had a population of more than 50,000, and there were only six towns with 8,000 or more inhabitants. While it is difficult to say precisely what proportion of the population produced for the market or were themselves customers, it is clear that a large percentage of the people were not involved in a market economy or were related to it only peripherally. The high cost of land transportation restricted the movement of bulky goods to short distances. All these factors limited the size of the domestic markets and made household manufacturing the most feasible and predominant method of making goods.

The conditions under which our foreign trade and shipping were carried on were hardly more satisfactory. Independence meant that we no longer received favored treatment from Great Britain, and at the same time our trade was hampered and restricted by the mercantilist measures of other European countries. The valuable trade with the West Indies was denied us as well as commerce with the North American colonies. Our ships were subject to discriminatory duties in their direct trade with these countries with the result that foreign bottoms carried a substantial percentage of our overseas trade.

With the West Indian trade barred to them, enterprising Yankee merchants opened up new fields of commerce in China and the East Indies. Elias Derby's *Grand Turk* began the trade with Canton as early as 1785, and a few years later Captain Gray's *Columbia* established the famous Northwest trade in which furs secured on the Pacific coast were exchanged for Chinese tea. But despite these innovating voyages of our merchants, the economic position of the carrying trade and exports showed no significant improvement over the years 1790-1792. Jefferson, Secretary of State, wrote a long report in the latter year in which he catalogued the many obstacles still faced by our foreign commerce.

In 1783, the Earl of Sheffield had minimized the damage to Great Britain caused by American independence and wrote slightingly of our economic prospects as follows: " . . . Great Britain will lose few of the advantages she possessed before these States became independent, and with prudent management she will have as much of their trade as it will be her interest to wish for, without any expense for civil establishment or protection. The States will suffer,—they have lost much by separation. . . ."[1]

Ten years after this prediction, its accuracy seemed to have been borne out by events. The prospects for the economic growth of the United States were darkened by the fact that the domestic markets were small and scattered, and foreign trade gave little hope of substantial expansion. But the outbreak of the wars of the French Revolution in 1793 suddenly opened up the empires of Europe for our traders and ship captains and inaugurated a period of rapid commercial expansion. The importance of external events, such as these, makes it possible and appropriate to divide the analysis of these years into three distinct phases: (1) the period from the ratification of the Constitution to 1793; (2) 1793-1807, the latter being the year that Jefferson's Embargo went into effect; (3) 1808–1814, the latter year marking the conclusion of the Second War with Great Britain with the signing of the Treaty of Ghent.

AN OVERALL VIEW OF THE NATION'S EXPANSION IN THE YEARS 1789–1814

Before turning to such a detailed analysis of these subdivisions, it will pay us to survey the aggregate growth of the economy over these years. Aggregate growth, we have observed in Chapter 1, is best measured in terms of the statistics of national income or gross national product. Unfortunately, such an approach is badly hampered for these years by the dearth of reliable data. The available statistical material for a national income series are "extremely

---

[1] Sheffield, *Observations on the Commerce of the American States, 1783* as quoted in G. S. Callendar, *Selections from The Economic History of the United States, 1765–1860* (Boston: Ginn and Co., 1909), p. 210.

fragmentary." Even the figures of the U.S. Census before the Civil War are of little use because of inaccuracy and inadequate reporting. The most well-known effort at construction of national income estimates for these years is that of Robert F. Martin.[2] His figures for the years under study are reproduced in Table 1.

TABLE 1

Total and Per Capita Realized National Income, 1799–1819
(adjusted for changes in the cost of living)

Year	Total	Per Capita
	(Millions of dollars)	
1799	$1,115	$216
1809	1,441	204
1819	1,625	173

Martin's estimates have been the subject of much criticism because of their alleged inadequacy and because, surprisingly enough, they indicate a decline in real income per capita from 1799 right down to 1839; indeed, his figure for per capita real national income does not exceed that of 1799 until 1849!

Several inherent limitations in Martin's data should be noted immediately. The phrase "realized income" in Table 1 refers to cash income actually received from the sale of goods and services in the market. Yet in these early decades a great many goods and services originated in the home and therefore did not enter the exchange economy. Further, it is to be noted that the decennial years of 1809 and 1819 were years of business depression, and this fact weakens the comparability of the data.

Simon Kuznets has pointed to serious weaknesses in Martin's estimates and argues that both industry and agriculture during the years 1800 to 1840 were both characterized by a moderate degree of growth.[3] Other students have demonstrated the limitations in Martin's original data and have rejected Kuznets' attempt at rectification of his estimates.[4] Professor North has indicated his belief that Martin's high relative figure for 1799 is correct, adding "if not for 1799 then at least for 1806–1807." He says that "The answer to this lengthy controversy which Martin initiated is not that individual well-being was declining from 1799 to 1829 but that the brief period 1793–1807 was an

---

[2] R. F. Martin, *National Income in the United States, 1799–1938*, National Industrial Conference Board, N.I.C.B., Studies 241, 1939.

[3] S. Kuznets, "Long-Term Changes in the National Income of the United States of America from 1805 to 1950," in *Income and Wealth of the United States*, Income and Wealth Series II (The Johns Hopkins Press, 1952), pp. 221–241; also "National Income Estimates for the United States prior to 1870," *Journal of Economic History* (Spring, 1952).

[4] See W. N. Parker and F. Whaternby, "The Growth of Output before 1840," *Trends of the American Economy in the Nineteenth Century*, Studies in Income and Wealth, Vol. 24 (Princeton, N.J.: Princeton University Press, 1960), pp. 191–212.

extraordinary and unique era which raised per capita real incomes far above the previous or subsequent years."[5]

While recognizing the very real weaknesses in Martin's estimates of change in the total real income for these years, it may be instructive, nevertheless, to examine his figures for the shifts shown in the relative importance of the different sectors of the economy during this period. Table 2 provides information of this nature for the years 1799–1819.

TABLE 2

Private Production Income by Sector of Origin, Decades, 1799–1819
(current dollar figures in millions) [a]

Sector	1799	Per Cent	1809	Per Cent	1819	Per Cent
Agriculture	$264	40%	$306	34%	$294	34%
Mining and quarrying	1		2		2	
Manufacturing	32	5	55	6	64	7
Construction	53	8	72	8	58	7
Transportation and communication	160	24	236	26	176	21
Trade	35	5	41	5	55	6
Service	64	10	110	12	132	15
Miscellaneous[b]	59	9	79	9	74	9
Total	$668	100%	$901	100%	$855	100%

[a] Source: Martin, *op. cit.*, p. 58.
[b] Including finance.
The sector, "electric light, power and gas" has been dropped from the above table. In the original, it was indicated that it was the source of less than $500,000 or 1 per cent for each of three years shown.

Perhaps we need to reiterate that the figures in this table are based only on incomes realized from the sale of goods and services in the market and further remind the reader that 1819 was a depression year. The salient feature of this table is, of course, the evident importance of agriculture and transportation and communication as the largest sectors in the economy in both 1799 and 1819; in the former year, they accounted for just under two-thirds of the total income, and by 1819 they still comprised 55 per cent of the total. The growth in the importance of manufacturing, service, and the financial sectors of the economy are developments we will examine in more detail shortly.

The overall pace of the nation's development in this period was closely tied to foreign events and to the fluctuations especially in our foreign trade and shipping. The secular expansion revealed in some of the figures of the preceding table was interrupted and reversed several times as the commercial and military policies of England and France changed with dizzying speed. Before 1793, to be sure, the most important developments affecting the future growth

[5] North, *The Economic Growth of the United States* (Englewood Cliffs, N.J.: Prentice-Hall, Inc., 1961), pp. 10–11, footnote 10.

of the economy occurred at home. These were the financial policies of
Alexander Hamilton, which resulted in the funding of the American foreign
and domestic debts, the establishment of a monetary system, and the creation
of the First Bank of the United States. These fundamental monetary and fiscal
measures established the financial foundations of our subsequent economic
growth.[6] The years from 1793 to 1808 were a period of unusual prosperity,
though they too were interrupted by two periods of peace—1797–1798 and the
Peace of Amiens, 1801–1803. The sharp downturn in the earnings of our
merchant marine brought about by this Treaty are clearly evident in Chart I
below. The renewal of hostilities in 1803 between the two great European
powers caused another surge in the growth of our exports and shipping
earnings, which continued until 1808. The intensification of the European
conflict led Napoleon to promulgate the Berlin decree whereby he sought to
establish a blockade of Britain; this policy made every American ship entering that country subject to capture by the French. Britain, in retaliation,
issued her Orders in Council of November, 1807, which prohibited trade
between the United States and Europe. In the face of harassment and seizure
of our ships, Jefferson in a desperate effort to preserve our neutrality had
Congress pass the Embargo Act in December, 1807. This drastic measure, in
effect, closed down our foreign trade. The economic distress resulting from it
was so great that the government was forced to repeal it and substitute the
Non-Intercourse Act of March, 1809. Under the latter law, trade was permitted with all countries except France and England. Despite this relaxation
in the regulation of our foreign trade, the value of our exports never fully
recovered to the pre-Embargo level (See Chart I below). With the outbreak of
the War of 1812, the British imposed a very effective blockade of our ports
with the consequence that the earnings of the American carrying trade
suffered another disastrous slump. But there was a silver lining to this cloud
over our foreign trade during America's "second war for independence"; we
turned in these years to increased manufacture of textiles and thus laid a basis
for future manufacturing growth.

THE MAJOR SECTORS OF ECONOMIC EXPANSION

FOREIGN TRADE. Although the statistical data on our foreign economic
relations for these years are almost as unsatisfactory as those on our domestic
growth the scholarly investigations by D. C. North of the nation's balance of
payments in the pre–Civil War period have recently provided invaluable new
information on this aspect of our economic development. North's figures show,
of course, that our economic expansion during the years 1793–1807 was
heavily dependent on the growth of international trade and shipping. Between
1793 and 1801, he finds, "there was almost a five-fold increase in the value of

[6] See the following chapter for a discussion of these measures.

our exports and in net earnings from the carrying trade."[7] The value of our exports and the earnings of the carrying trade fluctuated considerably in these years, reaching a peak in 1807. North vividly shows that the expansion of our exports in those years was primarily a consequence of the development of the re-export trade. Domestic exports doubled between 1790 and 1807, but re-exports grew from $300,000 in 1790 to $59,643,558 in the latter year! These re-exports consisted largely of tropical and semi-tropical products such as sugar, coffee, cocoa, tea, and pepper, which were imported into the United States. Duties were paid on them, but upon re-export the importer was granted a "drawback" of almost all the amount paid. Re-exports also consisted of European manufactures moving to colonial ports via this country. Our neutrality during the long-drawn-out period of European hostilities enabled us to prosper at a most opportune time. Foreign demand was so great that export prices as a whole more than doubled between 1794 and 1799 as did ocean freight rates. The gyrations in the value of our total exports and re-exports are shown in Chart 1. The net earnings of the U.S. carrying trade for these and subsequent years are graphically shown in Chart 2.

[7] North, *The Economic Growth of the United States*, p. 25.

CHART 1

Value of Exports and Re-exports from the U.S. 1790–1815

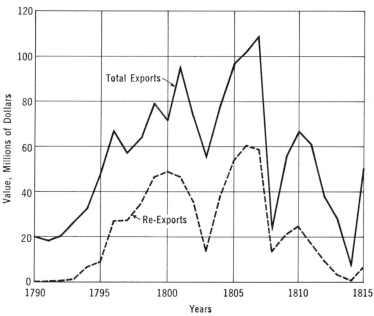

Reproduced from D. C. North, *The Economic Growth of the United States, 1890–1860* (Englewood Cliffs, N.J.: Prentice-Hall, Inc., 1961), p. 26, with the permission of the publisher.

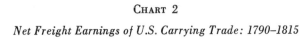

CHART 2

Net Freight Earnings of U.S. Carrying Trade: 1790–1815

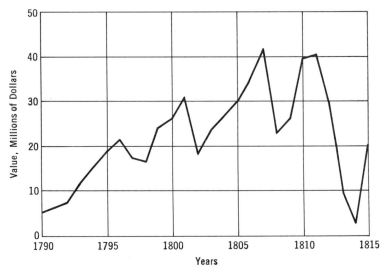

Reproduced from D. C. North, *The Economic Growth of the United States, 1790–1860* (Englewood Cliffs, N.J.: Prentice-Hall, Inc., 1961), p. 28, with the permission of the publisher.

Apart from re-exports, there were significant shifts in the export of our domestic products. Foodstuffs, especially wheat and flour, were generally in great foreign demand either because of the closing-off of a traditional source of supply or because of crop failures. In addition, forest products were in increased demand, whereas tobacco and rice, staples of the old export trade, made less conspicuous gains. The greatest contributor of all, however, to the expansion in the value of our domestic exports was cotton. "From 1791 to 1807 exports originating in the United States increased by approximately $30 million, and cotton accounted for almost half of this total ($14,232,000.)"[8] By 1807 Great Britain was obtaining over 60 per cent of its raw cotton for its growing textile industry from this country; needless to say, this change reflected a major agricultural transformation in the American South.

The prosperity of the years 1793 to 1807 generated a large increase in the value of imports. The nation's propensity to import was so great that imports grew even faster than exports, resulting in an import balance of trade in every year except 1811 and 1813. While much of our imports were subsequently re-exported, the statistics show that imports for consumption in 1807 were almost four times their value in 1790.[9] The earnings of the carrying trade fortunately enabled the young nation to maintain this luxurious style of life

[8] *Ibid.*, p. 40.
[9] *Ibid.*, p. 28.

without parting with much of its specie to settle the balance of payments. We were favored also in this respect by the fact that the terms of trade, so far as they can be calculated, seem to have been to our advantage during much of this period.[10]

SHIPBUILDING.   This industry was the principal one directly stimulated by the expansion of the carrying trade and the rise in ocean freight rates between 1793 and 1807. Shipbuilding was going full blast at Philadelphia, Boston, and New York during most of these years. Our tonnage of ships grew from 335,070 to over a million between 1790 and the latter years. Pitkin, an early historian of the period, says, "the increase of American tonnage, during the period under review, has no parallel in the commercial annals of the world."[11] The proportion of the foreign trade carried in our own ships during these years mounted from 54 per cent in 1789 to 92 per cent in 1807.[12] Our comparative advantage in shipbuilding was such that about one out of every five ships built in these years is estimated to have been sold abroad.

This hectic expansion came to a sudden end in 1808. The Embargo of that year and the War of 1812 brought about drastic reductions in shipbuilding activity with output slumping to one-quarter or less of what it had been at previous peaks of construction.

DOMESTIC COMMERCE AND TRANSPORTATION.   The growth of the cities that were the centers of the shipping and foreign trade and the auxiliary businesses that sprang up to serve them created an increased demand for foodstuffs to feed the swelling urban population. But widening the market area around such cities was at first a difficult problem because the roads were poor and the existing means of overland transport very expensive. It was said as of 1790 that a ton of goods could be brought 3,000 miles from Europe for nine dollars, but it could not be carried on land for that price for more than thirty miles.

It was conditions such as these that led to the wide demand for turnpikes. Indeed, there was such a craze for their construction that historians have referred to the period as the "turnpike era." The mania started with the construction of the pike from Philadelphia to Lancaster, a distance of 62 miles. The state of Pennsylvania had chartered a private company to build and operate this road, and when it was completed in 1794 it made a return of some 15 per cent yearly from the tolls. The success of the Lancaster Pike soon led many to seek to imitate it. As McMaster wrote, within a few years "a sum almost equal to the domestic debt at the close of the Revolution was volun-

---

[10] *Ibid.*, p. 31. The "terms of trade" are the amount of goods a nation has to export to obtain a given quantity of imports.

[11] T. Pitkin, *A Statistical Survey of the Commerce of the United States* (New York: A. M. Kelley, 1967), p. 425.

[12] U.S. Dept. of Commerce, *Historical Statistics of the United States, 1789–1945*, p. 216.

tarily invested by the people in the stock of turnpike companies."[13] These roads were usually financed by private, state, town, or county subscriptions or from the proceeds of lotteries. The mania was so great that in the next thirty years New England had chartered more than 180 such companies and Pennsylvania, 86. New York invested more heavily in turnpikes than any other state. By 1811, it had chartered 137 companies, and they had built 1400 miles of road.

But the turnpikes were not the answer to the nation's need for good transportation. The tolls were usually high, thus limiting the transport of heavy articles such as flour and grain to short distances. As late as 1817, it was said that wheat grown in western New York could not be profitably sent to New York City. Transport via turnpike cost $100 per ton, three times the market value of wheat, six times the value of oats, and far in excess of the value of cured provisions. The high tolls led many to use so-called "shunpikes," alternative routes on which no charge was imposed, so that in the later years of this period many of the turnpikes proved to be financial failures.

In these years, work was begun on "the one major developmental enterprise of the time to be constructed directly by the federal government."[14] This was the Cumberland or National Road, which had as its aim to breach the Appalachian barrier and enable the farmers of the Ohio valley to reach Eastern markets. Congress in 1806 passed the act, which was approved by President Jefferson, providing for the construction of the road from Cumberland, Maryland to Wheeling, West Virginia. Work was started in 1811 under the direction of the War Department, but it was not completed through to the latter town until 1817. This great thoroughfare, following the general route of historic Braddock's Road, in time became an important artery for trade, travel, and the mails. Two years after the first surveys were authorized for the National Road, Albert Gallatin, as Secretary of the Treasury, submitted to the Senate his far-sighted Report on Roads and Canals in which he outlined a comprehensive national plan of internal improvements. But very few of Gallatin's proposals were carried out in this period, and the question of internal improvements continued to divide the nation on constitutional and sectional issues down to and beyond Jackson's administration.[15]

In view of the transportation obstacles we have described, it is understandable that most of the internal trade in this period was local, consisting of exchange between the seaboard cities and other towns and their hinterland. The interregional trade was limited, at least so far as overland transport was concerned, to "a trickle of high value goods" and to the driving of livestock eastward across the Appalachian mountains. There are few statistics available on this overland traffic for these years; practically the only data we have is on the tonnage of ships engaged in the coastwise and internal trade; these show a

[13] J. B. McMaster, *History of the People of the United States*, Vol. 3, 1892–1919 (New York: D. Appleton-Century Co., Inc.), p. 463.

[14] C. Goodrich, *Government Promotion of American Canals and Railroads, 1800–1890* (New York: Columbia University Press, 1960), p. 19.

[15] See Chapters 7 and 10 below.

steady, three-fold growth from 1790 right down to the end of the period. Traffic on the Mississippi in these years was mainly downstream because steamboats were not as yet used on the River and upriver movement was slow and expensive. Still, the figures show that the value of goods arriving at New Orleans between 1799 and 1807 rose from $1 million to over $5 million.[16]

AGRICULTURE. While agriculture, as indicated above, was the occupation of the great majority of our people in these years, no accurate figures on production are available because there were no censuses of agriculture in the years 1800–1830. From export statistics we know of the importance of wheat and other grains in the Middle Atlantic and New England states. The growth of the cities and other urban areas were providing markets for the products of the surrounding farms, but much of this trade was impeded by poor transportation.

One of the most significant developments of this period, so far as agriculture was concerned, was the movement into the trans-Appalachian West. Agricultural expansion into the Northwest territory was slow at first; land speculators and hostile Indians turned migration more largely to Kentucky and the Southwest. By 1800, as Table 3 shows, Kentucky had over 220,000 inhabitants while the whole Northwest could boast of only about 50,000.

TABLE 3

Population of the Western States and Territories, 1790–1810[a]

State	1790	1800	1810
Kentucky	73,677	220,955	406,511
Tennessee	35,691	105,602	261,727
Ohio		45,365	230,760
Indiana		5,641	24,520
Illinois			12,282
Mississippi		8,850	40,352
Louisiana (Missouri)			20,845
Territory of Orleans (Louisiana)			76,556
Michigan			4,762

[a] Source: E. R. Johnson et al., *History of Domestic and Foreign Commerce of the United States* (Washington, D.C.: Carnegie Institution, 1915), p. 209, Table 12.

Agriculture in these new areas and in many of the older, more settled communities was in the process of transition from a subsistence basis to a cash, market-oriented type of farming. Nevertheless, the growth of productivity in farming as a whole seems to have been very slow in the first two decades of the nineteenth century.[17] As Bidwell and Falconer state, however, "The first four decades of the nineteenth century were characterized by

[16] North, *The Economic Growth of the United States*, pp. 34–35.
[17] M. W. Towne and W. D. Rasmusen, "Farm Gross Product and Gross Investment in the Nineteenth Century," in *Trends in the American Economy in the Nineteenth Century*, p. 269.

important beginnings in agricultural progress, rather than by striking or revolutionary accomplishments. It was a period of preparation both in the technical and in the business sides of farming—preparation for subsequent progress and expansion."[18] The beginnings these authors refer to include the publication of the first farm journal, which started in 1810, and the holding of the first "cattle show" or fair in 1807. One of the leaders in this type of work was Elkanah Watson, a retired merchant who was interested in improving the quality of American wool. He not only organized this first country fair, but started the Berkshire Agricultural Society in 1810, which was the first of the many such societies to be formed in the United States.

In the South, after 1793, Eli Whitney's cotton gin revolutionized southern agriculture because it permitted the profitable growing of the upland variety of cotton, which could be grown more widely than the long staple type. As a consequence, cotton growing spread into North Carolina, southeastern Virginia, and across the mountains into Tennessee in these years. Soon it was pushing into the rich alluvial land of Alabama and Mississippi. The production of the crop increased from an average annual output of less than 2 million pounds in 1790 to 80 million pounds for the years 1811–1815. Tobacco and rice, on the other hand, made less spectacular gains in these years; the former crop, faced with the exhaustion of the Tidewater plantations, was increasingly being grown in the Piedmont region of Maryland, Virginia, and North Carolina. In addition to these cash crops, southern farmers grew considerable quantities of corn, wheat, rye, and oats as well as vegetables and fruits. Most of these products were not marketed. Rather, entire regions of the South depended on the sale of single crops, such as cotton or tobacco, for their cash income.

MANUFACTURING.   The history of manufacturing in this period logically starts with the "Report on the Subject of Manufactures," which Alexander Hamilton submitted to Congress in 1791. Putting the best face upon a condition that was hardly encouraging, Hamilton described 17 small "industries," which, he said, "had grown up and flourished with a rapidity which surprises, affording an encouraging assurance of success in future attempts." But Hamilton's optimism was hardly justified by the developments of the following decade. While Samuel Slater, an English emigrant who had worked as an apprentice in one of Arkwright's factories, had smuggled the Industrial Revolution into America by setting up the first successful Arkwright mill at Pawtucket, Rhode Island, in 1790, only two other textile factories were started in the 1790's. Slater had been induced to come to America by bounties offered by Almy and Brown, two merchant capitalists of Providence, who wished to assure themselves of a supply of cloth for their trade. Slater himself built a mill of his own in 1799 and accumulated considerable property in the 40 years after his arrival, but in 1829, through the failure of a neighbor, he was forced to pass the last few years of his life struggling to pay his debts.

[18] P. W. Bidwell and J. I. Falconer, *History of Agriculture in the Northern United States, 1620–1860* (Washington: Carnegie Institution, 1925).

The fact was that the growth of manufacturing was extremely slow in these early years; eleven years after the establishment of the first cotton mill by Slater, there were only eight cotton factories in the United States. However, the rise in the price of manufactured goods brought on by the Embargo gave a sharp impetus to the establishment of cotton mills. By the end of 1809, 87 additional mills had been built, and the number of spindles had increased from 8,000 in 1808 to 31,000 at the end of the following year. By 1815 their number was 130,000.

Among the notable developments in the early history of this industry was the establishment by Francis C. Lowell of the Boston Manufacturing Company. This company was indeed a pioneer; in fact, it has been credited with being the "first complete factory in the world." Lowell not only organized his company as a corporation, which was a novelty for a manufacturing enterprise in that period, but he revolutionized the business by combining power loom weaving with spinning under one roof. He even instituted a crude cost accounting system and by concentrating on the manufacture of coarse sheeting, put the hand weavers out of business and operated one of the most profitable businesses for many years.

One industry that made extraordinary progress even before the War of 1812 was the manufacture of firearms. Here a group of mechanical geniuses, men like Eli Whitney, Simeon North, and Asa Waters, all New Englanders, introduced the technique of interchangeable parts in the manufacture of firearms for the first time. Recognizing the need to make the nation completely free of reliance on foreign arms, Congress in 1792 authorized the creation of two national armories at Springfield, Mass. and Harpers Ferry, Va. and generously subsidized private contractors to make pistols, muskets, and rifles for the Government. Connecticut clockmakers, such as Eli Terry and Seth Thomas, were soon applying the interchangeable part system to the making of their product. Thus, the urgencies of war and the high prices and scarcities it created served to stimulate the enterprise of the young nation in manufacturing.

BANKING AND FINANCE. When the Constitution went into effect in 1789 there were but three banks in existence to meet the nation's financial needs. The Bank of North America had been organized in 1781 primarily to meet the needs of the Continental government for short-term financing. The Banks of Massachusetts and of New York, both started in 1784, were designed to serve both private and governmental needs. The success of these banks, Hamilton's Report on a National Bank, and the general optimism in the country after 1793 stimulated a flood of bank-chartering. By 1801, 30 state-chartered banks were in existence with a capital of $12 million. Ten years later, there were 88 such state banks and between 1811 and 1815, after the closing of the First Bank of the United States, 120 new state banks were organized. Such in summary was the hectic growth of private banks organized in this period to make a profit on the circulation of their bank notes. We do not need to recount here the graft and corruption that surrounded the chartering of many of these state banks nor to describe the laxity practiced in their extension of loans. Suffice it to say, as our later analysis will suggest, that as a whole the private banking of this period, with some notable exceptions, was somewhat of a drag on an economy that was growing with considerable rapidity and tending to burst its mercantile seams.

REGIONAL DIFFERENCES IN ECONOMIC EXPANSION

As one might surmise from the preceding sketch of the expansion of the different sectors of the economy in these years, all the regions of the new Republic did not benefit alike. The Northeast and especially the great port cities of New York, Philadelphia, Baltimore, and Boston experienced the greatest expansion. Their growth in the census years of 1790, 1800, and 1810 is set forth in Table 4 below. The population of these and other smaller cities were obviously swelling in response to the growth of the foreign and domestic commerce in which they specialized and of the auxiliary and locally situated industries and services serving them and their people. The census of 1810

TABLE 4

Population of Leading Atlantic Ports, 1790 to 1810[a]

City	1790	1800	1810
Baltimore	13,503	26,114	35,583
Boston	18,038	24,937	33,250
New York	33,131	60,489	96,373
Philadelphia	45,520	69,403	91,874

[a] Source: Reproduced from North, *Economic Growth, op. cit.,* Table 5 on p. 49.

revealed the growing urbanization of the society; 7.3 per cent of the population were shown to be living in urban areas in the latter year compared to 5.1 per cent in 1790. The Republic of the Federalists was becoming more urban, distasteful as that was to some diehard followers of Jefferson and Madison, in response to the increased diversification of the economy.

Such a trend was not so clearly discernible in the South. That region was undergoing a difficult process of adjustment in this period as it shifted from general agriculture into a more specialized, commercial cultivation of cotton. Its principal cotton port, Charleston, did not grow nearly as rapidly as the major urban centers of the Northeast; its population rose from 18,000 in 1790 to 24,000 in 1810. New Orleans alone underwent a considerable population growth in these years, but this was largely due to its role as entrepôt of the Mississippi River commerce rather than to the influence of the cotton trade. The spread of the cotton plantation type of culture, with its peculiar income and social structure of slave and master, was not inducing the kind of urbanization that was already beginning to transform the life of northern society in these years. The causes and consequences of this momentous, disparate development will claim our attention in the following chapter.

Many Americans in the trans-Appalachian west, as the preceding material has indicated, were in the first part of this period virtually cut off from the market economy. Their exports and imports to or from the stream of domestic and world commerce were channeled through the Mississippi or dribbled in painfully small amounts and at great cost across the mountain barrier separating them from the East. The Warhawks, as their representatives in Congress were called, made their political influence felt in the nation's involvement in the second war with Great Britain. In the years to follow, they were to make their economic demands for integration with the rest of the nation's economy known in no uncertain terms.

We turn now from this preliminary sketch of the pace and pattern of our early economic development to examine in more detail the dynamic, interdependent processes by which it was brought about.

Chapter 6

ESTABLISHING THE PRE-CONDITIONS FOR A MORE SPECIALIZED MARKET ECONOMY

THE HAMILTONIAN VISION AND PROGRAM

The trade and business of American merchants at the outset of the United States' existence as a nation were hampered not only by the adverse trade regulations of foreign governments, but also by the inadequate means of overland transport, the disorganized currency, and the low state to which the nation's finances and public credit had sunk under the Confederation. As partisans and supporters of the Constitution, many of the merchant class looked to the new government to rectify the disordered state of the country's finances and to improve its prospects for prosperity and growth. They found a statesman and a spokesman of such views in the new Secretary of the Treasury, Alexander Hamilton.

The nation's need for revenue under the Constitution was so pressing that the matter was taken up even before the inauguration of Washington as President. James Madison introduced a bill, modelled on that of 1783, which became law after seven weeks of sectional debate. This first important piece of legislation enacted by Congress provided specific duties on over 30 kinds of commodities; the ad valorem rates varied from 7½ per cent to 15 per cent. It is estimated that the average rate of duty under this tariff, reducing everything to an ad valorem basis, was 8½ per cent. In addition, aid in the form of preferential taxes was given to American shipping. Goods imported in ships built or owned by Americans were allowed a drawback of 10 per cent. On the other hand, a tonnage tax of fifty cents a ton was imposed on foreign vessels using American ports. The main objective of the new law was not to restrict foreign goods and ships but to produce a revenue, and in this it was successful.

Hamilton was not appointed as Secretary of the Treasury by Washington until September of 1789, after he had considered Robert Morris, who was his first choice for this important post. The nation was fortunate in the President's selection, for his appointee proved to be an official of uncommon energy and ability. Recent re-appraisals and interpretations of Hamilton's life and work have given us a renewed appreciation of the boldness and breadth of his vision. We realize, as Broadus Mitchell has written, that ". . . His Treasury proposals had deeper motives than the fiscal and the monetary; . . . he was devising not simply an exchequer, but a proliferating economy."[1]

In analyzing Hamilton's various measures, it is well to have in mind his basic economic presuppositions, for his proposals were not isolated and independent of each other, but rather integral pieces of a larger design. Hamilton had read the work of some of the mercantilists and of Adam Smith, but, being an eclectic and empiricist, he was willing to challenge the applicability of the new doctrine of *laissez faire* and to insist instead that economic truth was relative to time and place. Having seen in the West Indies the disadvantage of a country's being dependent on a single commodity for its export trade and impressed with the importance of a strong economy for national defense in an era of war, he argued for a diversified, balanced economy and was ready to employ governmental action to achieve it.

> If anything, Hamilton was more the prophet and practitioner of government than he was the patron of finance, trade and manufactures. In a young country, of enormous potential resources, but sparsely populated, overwhelmingly agricultural and extractive in its pursuits, and fractioned into conflicting political and economic divisions, organization became his dearest object. Public action must come before private. Capital could be secured and varied enterprise stimulated by the fostering care of federal government. He knew that what we call national wealth, in its origin and maintenance, is not material (land, labor, capital, consumption goods), but is exceedingly immaterial. It is capacity for economic processes. This means cooperation under conditions of self-discipline, safety of persons and property, and stability.[2]

Hamilton understood and was influenced by *The Wealth of Nations*, but he was even more impressed by the fact that British manufactures had been promoted by the "fostering care" of the British government; that the "judicious and unremitting vigilance" of the Dutch government had transformed a small country into one of the greatest commercial nations in the world; and that the "Great Colbert" had brought France to a high level of industrial prosperity. Unlike Adam Smith, Hamilton had not lost his faith in the ability of the government to guide the national economy; indeed, in certain ways he considered the wisdom of the government to be superior to that of individuals in the economic realm.

Hamilton, living at a later period than Smith and aware of the progress of technology and its implications for national power, embraced the Industrial Revolution. He sought to equip America, as rapidly as possible, with the industrial power that was a prerequisite of national advance. Hamilton did

---

[1] B. Mitchell, *Alexander Hamilton, The National Adventure, 1788–1804* (New York: The Macmillan Co., 1962), Vol. 2, p. 90.

[2] B. Mitchell, "Alexander Hamilton as Finance Minister," in A. S. Eisenstadt, *American History, Recent Interpretations* (New York: Thomas Y. Crowell Co., 1962), Book I, p. 232.

not reject the whole of *The Wealth of Nations* because he found *laissez faire* unsuited to the needs of the United States. In fact, there were many points of agreement between the American statesman and the Scottish economist. "Both men, for example, held the same objective in view—national prosperity and power. They agreed that hampering impediments ought to be removed in order that individual initiative and the competitive spirit could enjoy free play. They regarded production as the key to national wealth; they recognized self-interest to be the main spring of human conduct; and they took a skeptical view of all philosophies that credited mankind with a highly developed sense of social responsibility. They were agreed that avarice, far from being a deadly sin, was an integral part of the order of nature. In this respect it might be said of Hamilton, as it was said of Adam Smith, that he supposed "there was Scotsman inside every man.""[3]

Hamilton's first major endeavor as Secretary of the Treasury was his Report on the Public Credit, which he submitted to Congress in January of 1790. Its aim was the recovery of the financial solvency of the nation. The nation's credit or ability to borrow could not be established until provision had been made for its existing debt. The nation's finances, which Hamilton undertook to set straight, were as a contemporary said, a "deep, dark and dreary chaos." The domestic debt consisted of a mass of virtually worthless paper money, loan office certificates, IOU's signed by the Quartermaster, lottery prizes, certificates given to soldiers and officers in lieu of pay, Treasury certificates, and various other evidences of debt. The Continental Congress had hardly overlooked a single means of going into debt known to the governments of that time, and "it enjoyed the unenviable distinction of having more creditors than any other government in the world."[4]

When Hamilton assumed his new post, the total debt of the nation stood at slightly over $50 million. Foreign claims, principal and interest, came close to $12 million, and the domestic debt was estimated to be slightly over $27 million, not including $13 million in accrued interest.

When there were those who considered the nation's debt as an albatross hung about its neck and urged that it should be repudiated, Hamilton saw the debt as a means of invigorating the national economy. He stated that the proper funding of the debt would render it a national blessing. If the "dead corpse" of the public credit was to be resurrected, it would only be accomplished, according to Hamilton, by the strict observance of financial integrity and good faith on the part of the government. Not only must the nation justify the confidence of its creditors, but support of the public credit would serve other "great and invaluable ends." These were "to promote the increasing respectability of the American name;. . . to restore landed property to its due value; to furnish new resources, both to agriculture and to commerce; to cement more closely the union of the States; to add to their security against

---

[3] J. C. Miller, *Alexander Hamilton, Portrait in Paradox* (New York: Harper and Row, 1959), p. 293.

[4] *Ibid.*, p. 230.

foreign attack; to establish public order on the basis of an upright and liberal policy. . . ."[5]

Hamilton stressed that a well funded national debt would serve to augment the money supply in that it would serve as collateral in the making of loans. An enlarged monetary media would thus lower the rate of interest, give vigor to commercial enterprise as well as energy to manufactures and trade. Hamilton's conception of the dynamic possibilities of the national debt, though not original with him, strikes a modern note to present-day studies of public finance. He "perceived the connection between national income and national debt and he recognized that there was no more certain way of disposing of the national debt than by stimulating the productive forces of the country."[6]

Hamilton, it must be understood, was not inimical toward the men who were engaged in engrossing the national debt into their hands through buying it up at low prices. He regarded public creditors, generally speaking, as practical and enlightened men who would accept terms that would not strain the nation's resources. Furthermore, basing himself upon British example, he believed that strengthening the position of those men who had disposable capital would serve the national interest. As David Hume had noted, capital was of little value to the economy "if it is dispersed into numberless hands, which either squander it in idle show and magnificence, or employ it in the purchase of the common necessaries of life." The "improvident majority" could not provide the capital necessary for the support of the state and the furthering of economic enterprise.[7] Hamilton's objective, it has been said, was to bind the speculators and investors to the national government by durable ties of "Ambition and Avarice."

The Report on Public Credit divides into three parts: (1) the reasons for supporting the public credit; (2) the means of providing for the various classes of claimants; (3) the choice of the sources of revenue. Having dealt with the first aspect, we can turn now to its second and third parts.

The new Secretary of the Treasury, in summing up the debt of the United States, found that the foreign and domestic debt, with arrears of interest, came to over $54 million. To this was to be added the war debts of the states, which he estimated at $25 million. The grand total of over $79 million would require annual interest payments of more than $4.5 million, allowing 4 per cent on the arrears of interest. Even after it was funded, the national debt on a per capita basis came to $20, a staggering sum for the times.

Hamilton in his Report boldly called for the recognition and consolidation of all the elements of this debt, national and state. In funding the old evidences of debt, he proposed a new loan to the full amount of the debt, which enabled him to cut the interest rate roughly from 6 to 4½ per cent. The creditors were assured that instead of annual appropriations by the legislature for debt retirement, permanent appropriations would inviolably be made for

[5] B. Mitchell, *Alexander Hamilton*, II, p. 48.
[6] J. C. Miller, *Alexander Hamilton, Portrait in Paradox*, p. 253.
[7] *Ibid.*, p. 233.

the payment of interest and principal. Five choices were offered the creditors as to the method of their conversion payment, any one of which they were privileged to accept.

Delicate and politically "loaded" questions had to be faced by the Secretary with regard to the handling of the different types of debt. The foreign debt offered the least trouble. In his Report, Hamilton had written, "It is agreed on all hands . . . that the foreign debt ought to be provided for according to the precise terms of the contracts relating to it. It is to be regretted that there is not the same unanimity of sentiment concerning the domestic debt as on the other." The dispute over the domestic debt revolved around the question as to whether it should be paid at face value, as Hamilton advocated. Those opposing this policy held that the loans having created these debts had been made during the war at inflated values. Further, many of the original holders of these debts had sold them at $\frac{1}{20}$ to $\frac{1}{6}$ of their face value to speculators. Madison, to Hamilton's dismay, came out in opposition to non-discrimination; he made an eloquent speech denouncing it and dwelling upon the plight of the widows, orphans, and ex-soldiers who had been defrauded by the speculators. He proposed, instead, that the government discriminate between the original holders and secondary holders of the debt. He would pay the first group face value and the others market value.

Hamilton rejected this doctrine of discrimination on two grounds: (1) it would be a breach of contract; (2) it would be a violation of the rights of a fair purchaser. In the long debate over Hamilton's first report, one of the most significant in the nation's early history, the Secretary's position on this point was upheld by the House. But there was the still more controversial question of the assumption of the states' debts by the federal government. Here, Hamilton argued that one plan of finance would be simpler than thirteen; that the states might adopt confusing and oppressive forms of taxation; and that, since the states could not levy import duties, it was only fair to the creditors of the states that the federal government assume them. But the rub was that some states, such as Virginia, had already paid off most of their debts, while others, notably South Carolina and Massachusetts, had not and therefore would be greatly benefitted. The debate on assumption dragged on into the summer; the funding aspect was separated from assumption, voted on, and the bill sent to the Senate. Hamilton's gamble seemed to have been lost, but then, being a practical politician, he made his famous bargain with Jefferson to locate the national capital on the banks of the Potomac. The necessary southern votes were obtained to approve assumption. Hamilton's friends remonstrated with him over this kind of expedient behavior, but he replied that "The funding system, including the assumption is the primary national object; all subordinate points which oppose it must be sacrificed; . . ." As Professor Miller has written, to secure that point, "Hamilton probably would have been willing to put the national capital in an even hotter spot than the Potomac in mid-August."[8]

[8] J. C. Miller, *Alexander Hamilton, Portrait in Paradox*, p. 251.

The third part of Hamilton's Report dealt with the proposed revenues for servicing the debt and covering the other expenses of the Government. Interest on the whole debt, plus $600,000 for the ordinary operations of the government, brought the total to over $2,800,000. This sum could be covered, Hamilton suggested, by the existing duties on imports and tonnage, with additional duties, which he outlined, on wines, spirits, tea, and coffee. The taxes on whiskey proved, we know, to be very unpopular, especially in western Pennsylvania where the so-called Whiskey Rebellion broke out in 1794.

But the success of this part of Hamilton's financial program as a whole is undoubted. His funding system caused large sums of European capital to be added to the active stock of the United States. After the outbreak of the French Revolution, large sums of European capital took refuge in this country. By the end of 1794, the United States had the highest credit rating in Europe and Talleyrand told his friends that the bonds of the United States were "safe and free from reverses. They have funded in such a sound manner and the prosperity of this country is growing so rapidly that there can be no doubt of their solvency." In May, 1795, foreigners held over $20 million of the domestic debt of the United States and six years later, over $33 million.

"Finally," as one eminent biographer of Hamilton points out, "the funding system provided the means of creating wealth. Every three months, almost a million dollars was pumped into the· national economy; and this money, drawn from the taxpayers of the United States, made possible capitalistic enterprise on a scale hitherto unknown in the republic. And the fact that the money thus extracted from the taxpayers was concentrated in comparatively few hands accelerated the growth of capitalism: it made available for purposes of investment and exchange a sum estimated at ten times the amount of all the specie circulating in the country. Thus Hamilton activated the springs of national credit and a torrent began to roar down the dry creek bed."[9]

Hamilton's second report to the Congress, that on a National Bank, which he sent to the House in December of 1790, was the outgrowth of his experience in administering the nation's finances and of his own practical knowledge of banking; he had been one of the founders of the Bank of New York. He regarded a national bank as "an indispensable engine in the administration of the finances." In urging such an institution upon the country, Hamilton was undoubtedly greatly influenced in this, as in much else, by the example of Great Britain. He attributed the wealth and national power of that country to the excellence of its institutions; and of these, the Bank of England was probably one of the most important, in his eyes. Though a privately owned bank, this body performed such a number of monetary and fiscal functions for the state that Adam Smith described it as "a great engine of state." Hamilton hoped perhaps to establish a similar arrangement in the United States and thus supply the nation with a dependable circulating medium. Despite Hamilton's fears of paper money "issued by the mere authority of government," he seems to have been influenced by John Law's view that the way to stimulate a

[9] *Ibid.*, pp. 253–54.

sluggish economy was to increase the quantity of the circulating medium; a controlled inflation, in fact, would be of immense benefit to an economy that had just undergone a destructive deflation.[10]

Hamilton proposed that the Bank of the United States should be a mixed institution, with the government as a partner, but the ownership and management predominantly private. He fixed the capital of this new Bank at $10 million; this was a considerable sum in view of the fact that the combined capital of three existing state banks was little more than $2 million. Eight million of the ten million dollar capitalization was to be privately subscribed, with the government being allowed ten years to pay in its $2 million share. The shareholders were allowed to pay one-quarter of their subscription in specie and the remaining three-quarters in government bonds. (This provision, it hardly needs mentioning, would tend to raise the price of government securities, an objective that Hamilton certainly had in mind.)

The Bank was authorized to issue notes secured by the Bank's capital, ⅘ of which could consist of government securities and the rest of gold and silver. The Bank was also intended to serve as a bank of deposit, a fiscal agent of the government, and as a source of credit. Among other provisions there were such salutary regulations as follows: its debts could not be larger than its capital stock; it could not purchase any public debt whatsoever; the rate of interest on loans could not exceed 6 per cent; the Secretary of the Treasury could call for reports as often as once a week.

Hamilton's proposal for a national bank did not immediately arouse the storm of controversy in the Congress such as had broken out over the funding system. Madison and others spoke against the proposal, but the House passed the bill easily on a vote cast on strictly sectional lines. Washington asked his Attorney General and Jefferson for legal opinions, which turned out to be negative, and then informed Hamilton that unless he could convince him to the contrary, he would be forced to veto the measure. Hamilton, dumbfounded at the President's attitude, is reported to have spent the greater part of a night preparing his opinion, in which he made a historic argument for the doctrine of implied powers. The Bank, he contended, was a necessary and proper means of facilitating the regulation of commerce and of providing for the public credit and national defense. Though not entirely convinced by Hamilton's state paper, Washington signed the Bank bill into law.

The Bank's early years were marked by the speculative fever that surrounded the initial sale of its shares and by the controversy over whether it should open branches in states already having banks. Though Hamilton was not sympathetic to the state banks, he favored them in handling the government's business and thus, ironically enough, strengthened the very force that was ultimately to bring about the demise of the federally-chartered institution. The First Bank proved itself in the succeeding years to be a great asset to the

[10] S. McKee, ed., *Papers on Public Credit, Commerce and Finance* (New York: Columbia University Press, 1934), pp. 55, 66, 92.

nation; indeed, it was termed by one admirer "the mainspring and regulator of the whole American business world." It increased and stabilized the supply of the circulating medium, made credit more available, and aided the federal government immensely in its fiscal operations. Financially, the Bank was a great success also. The Government received a handsome annual dividend of 8⅜ per cent on its investment, and the high dividends paid to its private shareholders made it second only to the funding system in promoting the development of a moneyed class. Its very success in this respect, as a "potent instrument of capitalism," earned it the enmity of many southerners and others who feared a moneyed aristocracy.

A less controversial aspect of Hamilton's policies was his report on the establishment of a mint, which was submitted to the House of Representatives in January, 1791, having been ordered by that body nine months before. In preparing this difficult report, Hamilton showed his usual care, studying numerous European works on coinage and exchange. At the time both the people and the legislators seemed to favor a silver standard; Hamilton, however, believed that a single monetary standard would lead to a scanty circulation of money, whereas a bimetallic one would make for more abundant money and thus serve as a tonic to the economy. He therefore recommended a bimetallic standard at a mint ratio of 15 to 1; the dollar should contain 24¾ grains of pure gold or 371¼ grains of pure silver. In this report, he also recommended the coinage of ten-dollar and one-dollar gold pieces, one-dollar and ten-cent silver pieces, and one-cent and one-half cent copper pieces. (The dollar had been established as the money unit and a decimal system of coinage adopted by a prior Congress; Hamilton simply took over these features of the older legislation.) The mint ratio of 15 to 1 established by the Mint Act of 1792 slightly overvalued silver, so it was that metal that was principally brought to the mint. This was in the form of Spanish milled dollars since no silver mines existed in the United States at that time. These foreign coins were 2 per cent heavier than our silver dollar, creating very real possibilities of profit in their conversion. Thus, that perennial problem of a bimetallic standard of maintaining a parity between the mint and market ratios for the two metals resulted at the very beginning of our monetary history in a *de facto* silver standard.

Hamilton's Report on Manufactures, the broadest of all his reports to Congress, though it did not result in much specific legislation, nevertheless marks him, as one of his recent biographers states, as "the earliest American economic planner and one of the first in any country. . . ."[11] This historic report is the more remarkable because during its preparation Hamilton was having an affair with one Maria Reynolds; the anxiety he must have felt as a result of the blackmail involving him with this wanton woman would have completely distracted lesser men, but not Alexander Hamilton.[12]

[11] B. Mitchell, *Alexander Hamilton*, II, p. 142.
[12] See *Ibid.*, p. 399 for a thorough discussion of this incident.

In January of 1791, the House of Representatives had requested him to prepare a plan "for the encouragement and promotion of such manufactures as will tend to render the United States independent of other nations for essentials, particularly for military supplies." The ambitious Secretary, as was his wont, gave the broadest possible interpretation to this directive and submitted in December a comprehensive survey of manufactures in the United States, the obstacles they faced, and a disquisition on how they might be promoted. He prepared three drafts of the report, drawing upon information compiled by the Assistant Secretary of the Treasury, Tench Coxe, and data supplied by other Treasury agents on the progress of manufactures in their localities.

When Hamilton prepared his Report, the American people had already started numerous small manufactures, especially of a domestic nature. These had been established during the Revolutionary War and in its aftermath when the nation could not establish trade relations with the rest of the world that would permit it to pay for imports of manufactures with exports of its own produce.[13] Hamilton stated that his purpose was "to cherish and bring to maturity this precious embryo." For the fact was that the nation was overwhelmingly engaged in agricultural and other extractive pursuits. "Despite the progress made in manufacturing, Hamilton considered the economy of the United States (at that time) to be in a dangerous state of imbalance. The preponderance of agriculture impressed him as a source of weakness: by pursuing agriculture as single-mindedly as did Americans, Hamilton feared that they were perpetuating the very conditions from which they had sought to escape by declaring their independence—a colonial inferiority and dependence upon the more industrialized countries of Europe. National wealth and power, he perceived, were passing rapidly into the hands of those countries that devoted their energies to commerce and manufacturing: here, he believed was the wave of the future upon which nations would rise to greatness. Those that chose to ride agriculture would end, he suspected, by sinking into the status of second-rate powers."[14]

Hamilton espoused the view he did because, despite the publication of Smith's *Wealth of Nations* with its advocacy of free international trade, the great powers of the world still adhered to mercantilist policies and sought to exclude the trade of the foreigner. The prospect was that the United States would experience increasing difficulty in selling its agricultural products abroad.

Hamilton began his brief for manufacturing by stating that the expediency of encouraging manufactures in the United States "appears at this time to be pretty generally admitted." Nevertheless, he reviewed the arguments, many of them still popular, which were advanced against this policy. These were four in number: (1) "Agriculture is the most beneficial and productive object of

---

[13] G. S. Callender, *Selections from the Economic History of the United States* (Boston: Ginn and Co., 1909), p. 443.

[14] Miller, *Alexander Hamilton, Portrait in Paradox*, p. 284.

human industry." Here, Hamilton argued against Smith and others who had advanced theoretical analyses to support this view that no one had made a comparison "upon sufficient data, properly ascertained and analyzed" to prove this contention. Such particular studies as he had been able to make persuaded him "that the net produce of capital engaged in manufacturing enterprises is greater than that of capital engaged in agriculture."[15] (2) "To endeavor, by the extraordinary patronage of government, to accelerate the growth of manufactures, is . . . by force of art, to transfer the natural current of industry from a more to a less beneficial channel." (3) The United States had peculiar disabilities for manufacturing, such as a sparse population, and lack of skilled labor and capital. (4) Promotion of manufactures would sacrifice the community's interest to that of an industrial class.

Hamilton met these latter arguments by conceding their theoretical plausibility, but holding that practically they were not convincing. The conditions they assumed—for example, that all nations would practice free trade—did not exist. He asserted, on the contrary, that diversification of economic effort was in the national interest. Manufactures would further the division of labor and the use of machinery, give employment to those without work, promote emigration from other countries, furnish scope for diversity of talents, open new fields of enterprise, and create a steady demand at home for the surplus produce of our farms.

The political case advanced by Hamilton for a more balanced economy had two aspects. The union of the sections composing the Republic would be cemented by encouraging industry in the one (the North) and agriculture in the other (the South). "Mutual wants," he later told Talleyrand, "constitute one of the strongest links of political connection. . . ."[16] Secondly, in a world in which war might involve a nation, however peace-loving, the United States was particularly vulnerable because of its dependence upon foreign supplies and the possibility that it would be cut off by an enemy possessing superior sea power. To Hamilton, the United States in a world of warring states could not afford to remain a backward nation. To these political points, Hamilton added an economic one of compelling force. He contended that even in peacetime the nation had suffered from a chronic shortage of sterling exchange because the northern states bought more than they sold to Great Britain. The drainage of specie overseas as a result of its unfavorable balance of payments tended to defeat the nation's efforts to put its finances upon a stable basis.

Hamilton believed that the times were especially auspicious to encourage manufacturing. Thanks to his funding of the debt and the speculation that had developed in national and state securities, the nation had received a considerable influx of foreign capital. Rather than have this surplus capital dissipated in reckless speculation or in the purchase of foreign luxuries, he would direct

[15] Quoted in J. C. Miller, *Alexander Hamilton*, p. 285.
[16] *Ibid.*, p. 286.

it into investment in manufactures. Hamilton had noted among the characteristics of his contemporaries "a certain fermentation of mind, a certain activity
of speculation and enterprise which, if properly directed, may be made
subservient to useful purposes but which, if left entirely to itself, may be
attended with pernicious effects."[17] He did not have, it is obvious, that
sublime confidence in the beneficence of the "invisible hand" of self-interest
and competition displayed by Adam Smith. He would have government direct
the money-making instinct of the capitalists into channels that would be most
advantageous to the national welfare.

To accomplish these objectives, Hamilton recommended that Congress
provide money for bounties, premiums, and other financial aids to industry.
Though Hamilton's name has been most frequently associated with protective
tariffs, actually he preferred bounties as being more positive and direct than
import duties. Ideally, the revenue from a duty on foreign manufactures
should be appropriated as a bounty to encourage the production of the
product at home. When such "infant industries" have been established, the
bounties should be withdrawn. Hamilton admitted that initially bounties and
tariffs would raise prices, but in the long run by stimulating competition at
home they would result in a permanent reduction of them. He recommended
that a commission be established to allocate the bounties and other aids to
industry; he thought that the nation could make itself most readily self-
sufficient in such products as iron, nails, firearms, ardent spirits, and malt
liquor. The production of cotton and woolen cloth could be encouraged later.

Hamilton carefully considered the obstacles to the development of manufacturing in the United States at that time; these were mainly the shortage of
skilled labor and the scarcity of capital. He saw the first being overcome by
the employment of women and children, the arrival of skilled immigrants, and
the employment of machinery. Following the thinking of Adam Smith and
Tench Coxe, Hamilton believed that machinery was a prime means of introducing manufactures into a sparsely settled country. He believed that machinery would "prodigiously lessen the necessity for manual labor" and that with
the water-power available in the United States and marked mechanical
aptitude of the American people, we could become one of the most advanced
industrial nations.

The supply of capital for manufacturing would be provided, according to
Hamilton, by the establishment of banks, the investment of funds from
abroad, the funding of the public debt, and by the security offered by protective tariffs. He also recommended, as essential to the development of manufactures, the improvement of such means of internal transport as roads and
canals, citing Adam Smith on the subject in the course of his argument. He
wished that the national government could "lend its direct aid on a comprehensive plan" of internal improvements.

Such was the vision of this extraordinary man, this ardent nationalist and
promoter of the progress of his adopted country, who prided himself that he
"thought continentally" rather than in provincial or sectional terms. Para-

doxically, as one of his most capable recent biographers points out, "While he spoke the language of conservatism, Hamilton in fact undertook to revolutionize the economic and political life of the United States. His dream was the transformation of the republic into a highly centralized nation in which manufacturing, commerce and agriculture were made to serve the purposes of an overriding nationalism. Far from envisaging the federal government as a guarantor of the existing order, he intended it to play a decisive part in shaping a progressive national economy. No man in the United States had less love for the *status quo* or less reverence for many of the accepted values of the Americans of his generation than did Hamilton; and no man did more to alter fundamentally their existing institutions and way of life."[17]

While Hamilton favored a centralized government, a favorable balance of trade, and economic unification of the nation, he was far from being an unadulterated mercantilist. He did not hold a beggar-your-neighbor philosophy; nor did he make a fetish of national self-sufficiency or measure the wealth of a nation in terms of the quantity of precious metals it acquired. His criterion of national wealth was rather productive capacity and, being an empirical thinker rather than a pure theorist, he subjected all ideas to the test of whether they were applicable to the conditions and needs of the United States. He concluded that the theory of *laissez faire* failed to pass such a test because, although attractive as an ideal, it ran counter to one of the strongest forces then current in the world—nationalism.

Actually, Hamilton's plans for the United States were in a sense an application of Adam Smith's concept of a world in which each country produced that for which it was best fitted. However, instead of dealing with nations, Hamilton's proposals had to do with sections. Further, just as Smith's principles tended to make Great Britain "the workshop of the world," Hamilton's measures would make the North the workshop of the union. Such an outcome, Hamilton argued, would not be prejudicial to either section because "the aggregate prosperity of manufactures and the aggregate prosperity of agriculture are intimately connected"—a phrase Hamilton quoted directly from *The Wealth of Nations*.[18]

Hamilton's employment of the concept of a balanced economy here and in other parts of his famous *Report* should be noted because of its relation to the much discussed subject of balanced economic growth in our time. In the passage just quoted, Hamilton is using the concept of balance in the sense of an accomplished state of affairs, not as a description of an ongoing process or as a prescription for overcoming the deadlock in an economy's growth because of the lack of markets. Hamilton's zeal for promoting manufactures grew out of his belief that the nation's over-reliance on agriculture was dangerous because of foreign restrictions on American agricultural exports. But Hamilton did not fully comprehend the degree and scope of economic

17 J. C. Miller, *Alexander Hamilton, Portrait in Paradox*, pp. 289–290.
18 *Ibid.*, p. 293.

imbalance he would have to create to achieve his ideal of a more balanced, diversified economic structure. Certainly, the dynamic Secretary of the Treasury did not anticipate the political imbalances that his proposals soon provoked. So far as the constitutionality of aid to manufactures was concerned, Hamilton believed that there was ample warrant in the "common defense and general welfare" clause of the Constitution to justify the program he recommended to Congress. This clause, he maintained, endowed Congress with powers separate and distinct from the enumerated ones and was in no way restricted by the enumeration. But to Madison and Jefferson, one of the most disturbing features of the Report of Manufactures was the indication it offered that Hamilton was prepared to interpret the Constitution in this broad way; they refused to accept the idea that "Mr. Hamilton and the Constitution are synonymous terms."

But the obstacles in the way of Hamilton's economic planning were more than constitutional ones. As a matter of fact, even before the publication of his Report on Manufactures, Hamilton had participated in the formation of a manufacturing enterprise, which was to acquaint him with the many difficulties such enterprise faced in this country. He was of the opinion that manufactures would not flourish unless they were undertaken on a much larger scale than had been the practice and by corporations with very much larger capital funds than had been customary. Together with certain other promoters, some of them outright speculators, Hamilton now put his ideas to the test. In the late summer of 1791, he drew up the prospectus of the Society for Useful Manufactures, a corporation capitalized for $1 million—a sum larger than the total capitalization of all the existing joint-stock manufacturing companies in the nation. The capital of this company was to consist, in accordance with Hamilton's plans, mainly of government bonds and shares of the Bank of the United States. Thus, this multiple-purpose project would bolster the securities of the government and attach its stockholders to the support of the federal government. The prospectus of the new venture stated that it would engage in making paper and pasteboard, sailcloth and other carpets, hats, women's shoes, pottery, brass and iron ware, and the printing of cotton and linen goods.

A site was selected at the falls of the Passaic River in New Jersey, and with the help of Governor Paterson, the state legislature issued a charter to the new company in November, 1791, which provided it virtually with all the powers that Hamilton had requested. The S.U.M., as it was called, was granted a perpetual monopoly, tax exemption for a stated number of years, and control of waterpower at Passaic. In honor of the Governor, whose aid was indispensable in launching the venture, the town was named Paterson.

Through the sales efforts of that extraordinary promoter and speculator, William Duer, who was the Governor of the Society, some $600,000 of the company's stock were quickly sold, some $25,000 of the total being subscribed by Dutch bankers. Hamilton had believed that manufactures would succeed in the United States only by taking advantage of the latest labor-saving machinery. Accordingly, the Society allocated part of its capital for the importation of machinery and skilled workmen from Europe. Hamilton himself, overburdened as he was with the responsibilities of office, made crucial selections of certain managers of the enterprise, some of whom proved to be either incapable or unreliable. The fortunes of the new company were quickly jeopardized by the financial panic of 1791–92, which involved Duer and other stockholders in the company; the Society suffered a grievous loss when they went bankrupt.

The company was managed in a most desultory way for the next three years, confronted as it was by its inability to secure enough foreign artisans, by frequent changes of plans, lack of working capital, and indifferent management. By 1795, the Society's directors abandoned their attempt to create an industrial empire in New Jersey. Hamilton's plan to build an industrial center there would probably have failed for reasons other than those bringing about its downfall; its success presupposed a more highly developed system of transportation and a more reliable supply of skilled labor than existed. Furthermore, Hamilton had obviously overreached himself in trying to manage and direct this complex operation at the same time that he was at the center of the nation's economic and political affairs. Successful manufacturing enterprise demanded more specialized and constant attention to its manifold problems than these early financial promoters were able or willing to give it.

Hamilton's efforts to promote manufacturing had rested on the assumption that the European market for American raw products would undergo a decline. But instead, with the outbreak of war between England and France early in 1793, the demand for our agricultural products expanded enormously. This expansion did not similarly encourage the growth of American manufactures; rather, by interrupting the flow of European capital and labor to our shores and by opening up enticing business opportunities in agriculture and shipping, it deflected the growth of the economy into other channels than manufacturing, at least temporarily. Hamilton's national planning was not comprehensive enough to anticipate the influence of international events as powerful as these.

Nor was he able to predict the consequences of so revolutionary a technological development as Eli Whitney's invention of the cotton gin in 1793. This invention gave Negro slavery a new lease on life, and by permitting the southern planters to shift to the cultivation of the short-staple, upland cotton, opened up markets in Europe that proved to be even more important to the South than its trade with the North. Hamilton looked to trade and commerce between an industrial North and agricultural South to create that mutual dependence that would cement their political union. He did not foresee that complex parallelogram of forces, stemming from the Industrial Revolution abroad as well as at home, which was to bring the Cotton Kingdom into being and contribute to the "irrepressible conflict."

Nevertheless, though some of Hamilton's plans did not come to fruition, he made an enormous contribution to our future economic development. While he showed a tendency to seek to transplant certain British institutions, such as the Bank of England, to the very different cultural environment of the United States, on the whole his thinking stressed a pragmatic, empirical approach that served to protect us from the doctrinaire theories of European philosophy. Institutionally, he contributed greatly to strengthening the social infrastructure of the American economy at a crucial period; his efforts in establishing the national credit, in creating a capital market, and, most important, in approaching economic questions in continental rather than in local or sectional terms, were truly those of a master nation-builder. His interventionist economics foreshadowed the mixed economy and policies of our own day. "Thus," as Broadus Mitchell has written, "Hamilton lives in the present, and for the future. Particularly new nations asserting their independence and looking to development may take lessons from him."[19]

THE GOLDEN YEARS OF NEUTRALITY

The beginning of the Napoleonic wars in 1793 inaugurated a new era in the development of the American economy. Whereas the most important developments for the future growth of the nation before 1793 had been the domestic policies of the Washington-Hamilton regime, from that date down to 1807 the economy's fate was tied to the fluctuations in international trade and shipping. Domestic politics too felt the strong repercussions of the momentous events occurring in Europe in those years. Prosperity in the nation was closely related to the ups and downs in the European struggle; it was interrupted in 1797–98 and again during the twenty month Peace of Amiens, 1801–1803.

The European wars opened up trade opportunities denied Americans because of the inability of the new nation to negotiate commercial treaties with the powerful governments of the world. With the British Navy pretty much in control of the seas, French ships ran a great risk in making the long voyage from the West Indies to the continent. The French threw open the long haul to us, but though the English tried at first to interfere with this traffic, they finally permitted it under the "broken voyage" doctrine. Under this system, a Yankee ship could load sugar and coffee at Haiti, bring it to New York, unload it, and pay the customs duty. Then the cargo would be reloaded, most of the duties refunded, and the ship would sail as a "neutral" to a French port without fear of seizure. French goods were brought to the West Indies in the same way via New York or other eastern ports. So our trade was swollen with the volume of these re-exports with the handsome profits they involved. Other rich opportunities were to be found in tramp voyages all over the world, which the belligerents were not able to engage in. In these years New England merchants sent their ships into ports their fathers had never

[19] Mitchell, *Alexander Hamilton*, II, p. 546.

known in Asia Minor, South America, and other remote parts of the world. Boston, Salem, and other New England shipping centers flourished, and their merchants built mansions, churches, and other buildings with remarkable style and elegance.[20]

The expansion induced by this advance in the export sector of the economy has been analyzed in terms of its effects on the growth of subsidiary, complementary, and residentiary types of economic activity.[21] The principal subsidiary industry was shipbuilding. Profits of maritime commerce were so large that vessels were able to pay for themselves in a voyage or two with the result that shipbuilding boomed; our tonnage of ships built doubled and trebled over the pre-war level. Likewise, such ship-fitting trades as sail-making and ropeworks expanded rapidly.

Other complementary industries that developed to serve the carrying trade during these years were such firms as commission merchants, brokers, banks, marine insurance companies, warehousing and docking organizations, etc. Not all of the banks formed or expanded during these years grew out of foreign trade, but it was a major factor in the expansion of many of them. The capital facilities and the business experience built into these new organizations were to provide a strong basis for the later development of the economy.

The residentiary industries referred to above were those manufacturing and service trades that grew up in these years to serve the people who increasingly congregated in the growing cities of the Northeast. The increased demand for food for this expanding urban population, in turn, contributed to a widening of the market areas around the cities and to efforts to reduce the cost of internal transport. The amazing "turnpike craze" discussed above can be seen as a response to the latter need.[22]

The expansionary consequences of the growth of the carrying and export trades did not make themselves equally evident in all sections of the nation. Though the South during these years was undergoing a great revolution in its agriculture with the spread of cotton cultivation, the income earned in this activity did not have the multiplier type of effect in anything like the same degree as the income earned in the Northeast from the export trade. Southern cities, with the exception of New Orleans, did not grow substantially in population during this period. Part of the explanation for this difference in economic response to the additional income in the two sections lies in the nature of cotton growing and of the income and social structure resulting from the plantation culture. The slaves and the low-income whites did not provide a growing market for food raised by independent farmers such as was the case in the North. Furthermore, a good deal of the income from cotton and cash crops flowed out of the South in payment for such items as services

---

[20] S. E. Morison, *The Maritime History of Massachusetts* (Boston: Houghton Mifflin Co., 1921), Chap. 9.

[21] North, *The Economic Growth of the United States*, pp. 49ff.

[22] *Ibid.*, p. 51.

rendered by others, food for slaves and planters, and import of such manufactured goods that could not be produced on the plantation. In short, even in these years conditions were developing to produce an economic dualism in the nation that would make the South peculiarly dependent upon other sections of the nation.

FISCAL AFFAIRS OF THE NEW NATION

The financial policies of Hamilton were a focus of much partisan debate in the first years of Washington's administration; they continued to provide a source of controversy in the remaining years of the century to the suspicious Republicans. An understanding of these matters is essential for a grasp of the politics of the period as well as for the light they shed on the growth of the economy during the nation's first decade.

The customs and tonnage duties imposed by the Act of 1789 were the principal source of the government's revenue in the first two years of its life. Customs duties, reflecting the increase in imports during these generally prosperous years, rose from $4,399,000 in 1791 to over $9,000,000 in 1800. But despite the increase in these and other revenues, the Federalists found expenditures exceeding their anticipations. The Indian War in the Northwest in 1790, the Whiskey Rebellion of 1794, and the strained relations in later years with Britain and France led to steadily mounting military expenditures. The following table presents a condensed comparison of the federal government's annual receipts and expenditures during the years 1791–1801:

TABLE 1

Revenues and Expenditures of the Federal Government, 1791–1801[a]

Year	Customs	Total Revenues	Total Expenditures
	(In millions of dollars)		
1791	$4.4	$4.4	$3.1
1792	3.4	3.7	6.2
1793	4.2	4.6	3.8
1794	4.8	5.4	6.2
1795	5.6	6.1	7.3
1796	6.5	8.4	5.8
1797	7.5	8.6	6.0
1798	7.1	7.9	7.6
1799	6.6	7.5	9.2
1800	9.1	10.8	10.8
1801	10.7	12.9	9.3

[a] Source: D. R. Dewey, *Financial History of the United States* (New York: Longmans, Green and Co., 1931) p. 112. Reprinted by permission of David McKay Company, Inc., New York, New York.

As a consequence of this need of additional revenue, Hamilton recommended an extension of import duties and the imposition of new excises on the consumption of luxuries. Immediately, a bitter opposition to these measures made its appearance both in Congress and without. It was argued that the proposed taxes were direct taxes, and the excise on whiskey, in particular, was a discriminating tax on one of the necessities of life. But the need for additional revenue was so pressing that the opposition was overcome; in March, 1791, Congress imposed a tax of 11 cents on low-proof liquors made from imported materials and a tax of 9–25 cents per gallon on spirits distilled from domestic grain.

Despite the successive rate reductions made in the tax, hostility to it was very great, especially in the agricultural regions of the middle and southern states. The backwoods farmers of the Alleghenies contended that the only form in which they could get their bulky corn to market was distilled spirits. Attempts to enforce the law in western Pennsylvania in 1794 led to sudden revolt—the Whiskey Rebellion. Urged on by Hamilton, Washington promptly sent a force of troops against the rebels, and they were easily quelled.

The revenue from the whiskey tax fell far below expectations (in 1794 it produced under $275,000), so Congress in that same year, at Hamilton's recommendation, imposed duties on carriages, the refining of sugar, the manufacture of snuff, and the sale of slaves at auction. In 1797 stamp taxes were imposed on legal documents and bank notes.

The representatives of the southern states, the Jefferson Republicans, led by Albert Gallatin of Pennsylvania, maintained a steady criticism of these federal excises, arguing that they bore disproportionately on them. They advocated instead a federal "direct" tax, which, under the Constitution, would be so apportioned as to shift the burden of taxation to the northern states. This agitation for a direct tax finally led to the passage of a measure in 1798 that apportioned a levy of some $2 million among the states, the tax to take the form of progressive rates on houses and a flat rate of 50 cents per head on slaves between the ages of twelve and fifty. This tax proved also to be a disappointment both in its yield and in the tedious procedures involved in its collection.

The federal debt, long a sore point with the economical Republicans, actually increased over the years of the Federalist administration of Washington and Adams. Hamilton had anticipated that the debt of $75 million would be steadily, if slowly, retired out of the surpluses of receipts over expenditures. But, because of higher expenditures than he had counted on, the debt stood at $83 million in 1801, some $7.5 million greater than it had been ten years earlier. The Jefferson Republicans, far from agreeing with Hamilton that a public debt could be a national blessing, regarded it as a "moral canker." Unless avoided, they believed, it would commit the nation to "the English career of debt, corruption and rottenness, closing with revolution." Actually, the Republicans would seem to have greatly exaggerated the burdensomeness of the debt at that time for it was far from crushing. After Hamilton's funding, the per capita debt of the nation stood at $20 with per capita interest payments of $1 annually. This contrasted with the British debt in the same year of some $200 per capita, requiring an annual per capita payment of $8 in interest.[23] Such comparisons did not quiet the Republicans or answer their doubts about the soundness of Hamilton's fiscal policy because they held an altogether different view of the consequences of a public debt. To them it was a dead weight upon the economy, an impediment to the productivity of the nation because it was so largely expended for military purposes, and a basis for that "moneyed aristocracy," which they so feared. Sooner than they realized, however, they were to be given an opportunity to put their own ideas, fiscal and otherwise, into practice in the administration of the affairs of the developing nation. Perhaps it would be appropriate here to note some of the events contributing to the Revolution of 1800 that brought Thomas Jefferson to the Presidency, to the testing time of his principles.

One hardly needs to point out that the party spirit and "factionalism," which had broken out over the merits and consequences of Hamilton's measures and which divided Americans into Federalists and Republicans, was gravely aggravated by those political earthquakes, the French Revolution and the wars let loose by it. This political controversy became even deeper when American commercial interests became involved in the war between France and England cn the high seas. With English commanders seizing American ships or impressing sailors or French privateers preying on American commerce with England, the Federalists could see every wrong committed by the French, the Republicans every wrong of the English. Federalist merchants saw the issue as England, law and order, versus France, Jacobinism and terror. The rash acts and highhanded conduct of Citizen Genet, the first minister of the new French Republic to the United States, further heightened tensions and deepened the gulf between political partisans.

Washington, seeking to escape entanglement in the European imbroglio, sent John Jay to Great Britain to negotiate the unsettled questions left over from the Treaty of Paris as well as the issues of impressment of our sailors, the British refusal to surrender forts and trading posts on our soil, and other equally delicate matters. Jay, who dealt with the wily Grenville, brought back a treaty that satisfied no one. The southerners were particularly incensed by the clause that bound the United States to pay the long-standing claims of British creditors, three-fourths of which were owed by them; on the other hand, there was no redress for the slaves carried away by British soldiers. Jefferson denounced the treaty as an infamous alliance between the "Anglomen" in the United States and the English. Southern planters vowed that the hated treaty would be repudiated. The President, however, anxious to preserve the peace, sent the treaty for ratification to the Senate, where it passed by a bare two-thirds vote. Washington's signing of it was the most unpopular act

[23] A. Balinky, *Albert Gallatin* (New Brunswick, N.J.: Rutgers University Press, 1958), p. 37.

of his life, and he ended his second term under a storm of criticism and abuse.

The administration of John Adams was even more dominated by the European war than that of his predecessor. His efforts to maintain peace and neutrality encountered even greater difficulties than those faced by Washington. For example, the French Directory, believing that the Jay Treaty was a violation of the Franco-American pacts of 1778 and that it augured an Anglo-American alliance, directed their navy to attack American shipping. By June, 1797 over three hundred American ships and their cargoes had been seized. Later, Adams sent a peace mission to France only to have them humiliated by the blackmail of Talleyrand's agents, as revealed in the XYZ papers. Congress, including many Republicans, were incensed by the affair and quickly planned retaliation. It abrogated the treaties of 1778, ordered the construction of new naval vessels, authorized the President to issue letters of marque and reprisal against France, and provided for an army of 10,000 men. The United States entered into a quasi-war with France, without declaration, in the course of which the remaining French commerce in the West Indies was destroyed. Hamilton, who was pressing for a declaration of war, broke even more decisively with the President over this matter.

The Federalists, strengthened by the war furor and their victories in the Congressional elections of 1798–1799, now committed a fatal error. They hurriedly passed four acts in 1798 known as the Alien and Sedition Acts. The alien acts, aimed at French agents and their Irish sympathizers, gave the President the power in time of war to expel or imprison such alien enemies. It, however, was not enforced. The Sedition Act, which made it a crime to write or publish "any false, scandalous or malicious" statements concerning the President or either House of Congress or bring them into "contempt or disrepute," was enforced, and it aroused a storm of indignation. Republican editors found themselves jailed or fined; others who had made contemptuous remarks about the President were convicted of sedition. Hamilton and John Marshall had advised against the passage of such a law, but it was too late. The law proved to be a boomerang. Madison and Jefferson respectively drew up the Virginia and Kentucky resolutions, asserting the states' rights theory of government and declaring that if the federal government assumed undelegated authority, its acts were null and void.

The Virginia and Kentucky resolutions, the waning of the enthusiasm for war, the unpopularity of the new taxes, factional fights within the party, all served to weaken the party of the "rich and well born." The Republicans carried the elections of 1800, thanks to the well organized party of Jefferson, but the choice between him and Aaron Burr for the Presidency had to be made by the House. After thirty-five ballots, Hamilton used his influence to make possible the election of his great antagonist, at the same time deepening the enmity of the man who was to end his life. A new era, that of Jeffersonian democracy, had begun.

Chapter 7

THE POLITICAL ECONOMY
OF JEFFERSONIAN AGRARIANISM

THE ECONOMIC PHILOSOPHY OF JEFFERSON

As contrasted with the economic philosophy of Adam Smith, Jefferson was much more an admirer of the ideas of the French physiocrats. To him, as to them, the farmer was the most productive member of society, and in addition, Jefferson regarded agrarian people as the most virtuous, politically. His ideal society was a democracy of small landowning farmers. He believed that the true wealth of a nation lay in its soil, and further that agriculture develops and maintains in man those virtues most desirable in a democracy. "Those who labor in the earth," exclaimed Jefferson, "are the chosen people of God, if ever He has a chosen people, whose breasts He has made his peculiar deposit for substantial and genuine virtue. . . ." It is the independence of the farmer, his secure economic basis, his freedom from the caprice of customers, which guarantee and nourish his political virtue. The other classes that grow up with the advance of the industrial arts, the merchants, artisans are dependent in one way or another. And "dependence," says Jefferson, begets subservience and venality, suffocates the germ of virtue, and prepares fit tools for the designs of ambition. . . ."[1]

To Jefferson, then, it followed that while we had free land to settle, it was preferable that Americans should be farmers rather than citizens occupied at a workbench. Our workshops should remain in Europe. For, as he expressed it in a much quoted passage, ". . . The mobs of great cities add just so much to the support of pure government, as sores do to the strength of the human body. It is the manners and spirit of a people which preserve a republic in vigor. . . ."[2] In another place, he wrote, ". . . When we get piled upon one another in large cities, as in Europe, we shall become as corrupt as in Europe, and go to eating one another as they do there."[3]

[1] C. A. Beard, *Economic Origins of Jeffersonian Democracy* (New York: The Macmillan Co., 1936), pp. 423–424.
[2] *Ibid.*, p. 425.
[3] *Ibid.*, p. 426.

But Jefferson recognized that pragmatic realism demanded some modification of his theoretical views. If he could indulge his own theory, he would prefer his countrymen to practice neither commerce nor navigation. He frankly admitted, ". . . But this is theory only, and a theory which the servants of America are not at liberty to follow. Our people have a decided taste for navigation and commerce. They take this from their mother country; and their servants are in duty bound to calculate all their measures on this datum."[4]

Jefferson's compromise with commerce was a qualified one. He accepted the necessity of domestic trade as a means by which agricultural surpluses could be marketed, but he could never bring himself to grant the importance of the carrying trade. He had two great fears concerning the development of this type of activity. The first was that the growth of such commerce would tend to convert this great agricultural country into "a city of Amsterdam—a mere headquarters for carrying on the commerce of all nations with one another." Such a result had no attractions for Jefferson for it would mean a departure from the virtuous independence of the cultivator of the soil. The second threat of foreign commerce, as Jefferson saw it, was the danger of foreign entanglements. "Foreign commerce," he held, "would bring the United States into collision with others in every sea and will force the United States into every war of the European powers."[5] And Jefferson, as the nation was soon to see, had a passion for peace and an utter detestation for the entangling alliances, which, he believed, led to war.

In summary, then, the Republican economic philosophy stressed the need to limit the government's role in any premature development of the United States as a leading commercial and industrial power. It preferred to place reliance on natural self-interest in the development of the nation. In a letter written to John Jay in 1809, Jefferson spoke of "an equilibrium of agriculture, manufacturing and commerce as essential to independence." After the experience of the Embargo, he was willing to concede the need for some manufacturing. But he meant "manufacturing for our own consumption of what we raise, the raw materials and no more; commerce sufficient to carry the surplus produce of agriculture, beyond our own consumption . . . and no more." These, he argued, "are the true limits of manufacturing and commerce. To go beyond them is to increase our dependence upon foreign nations and our liability to war."[6]

Given these economic views, it is not surprising that the Republicans advocated politically a reduction in the positive role played by the federal government during the preceding administrations. According to their ideals,

[4] As quoted in A. Balinky, *Albert Gallatin: Fiscal Theories and Policies* (New Brunswick, N.J.: Rutgers University Press, 1958), p. 19.

[5] *Ibid.*, p. 20.

[6] In A. E. Bergh, ed., *Writings of Jefferson*, XII, p. 271 as quoted in Balinsky, p. 22.

the federal government should limit its functions to three essentials: the maintenance of domestic order, the defense of the country from foreign aggression, and the enforcement of voluntary contracts. Apart from Jefferson's precept of humanitarianism, the Republican political philosophy was that of the "night watchman" state of classical theory.[7]

In broad outline, the views of Albert Gallatin were very similar to those of the more articulate Jefferson. Any differences that existed among them were minor and did not come into prominence until late in the former's term as Secretary of the Treasury. Like the President, Gallatin detested most the extension of the power of the federal government. He had been drawn into politics originally out of his conviction that the Constitution had made the central government too powerful. If he had had his way, there would be only a single house in the legislature with very limited powers, free from corruption, very little capacity for violence, and with as little debt, navy, and taxes as could be managed. Only this type of government, Gallatin insisted, would make the United States "a happy and not a powerful nation, or at least no way powerful except for self-defense."[8] Rather than encouraging industrial and commercial development, Gallatin would maintain a *laissez faire* government and preserve America's isolationism from the wars and intrigues of Europe.

In broad perspective, Jeffersonian agrarianism did not involve any revolutionary principles such as abandonment of the property requirements on voting or office-holding; it did not urge any fundamental alterations in the Constitution such as would make more direct government by the people possible. As Beard states, Jeffersonian Democracy "simply meant the possession of the federal government by the agrarian masses led by an aristocracy of slaveowning planters, and the theoretical repudiation of the right to use the Government for the benefit of any capitalistic groups, fiscal, banking or manufacturing."[9] The reader will note the qualification, "theoretical," in the last sentence, for the swift and unanticipated course of events forced the Republicans, once they had gained power, to make many compromises with their theoretical principles. Jefferson rationalized about the matter early in his administration in a letter to DuPont de Nemours: ". . . When this government was first established, it was possible to have kept it going on true principles, but the contracted, English, half-lettered ideas of Hamilton destroyed that hope in the bud. We can pay off his debts in 15 years: but we can never get rid of his financial system. It mortifies me to be strengthening principles which I deem radically vicious, but this vice is entailed on us by the first error . . . What is practicable must often control what is pure theory."[10]

---

[7] *Op. cit.*, p. 22.

[8] *Ibid.*, p. 24.

[9] C. A. Beard, *Economic Origins of Jefferson Democracy*, p. 467.

[10] *Ibid.*, pp. 436–7.

THE GOLDEN YEARS, 1801–1807

It was this same practicalism, in fact, which had gained Jefferson the Presidency at the time of the stalemate in the voting with Burr. Hamilton, in deciding to throw his support to the Virginian, remarked that Jefferson was a practical man unwilling to sacrifice his immediate political advantage for a remote ideal. In his conciliatory inaugural address, behind the splendid prose, we can clearly see that Hamilton was not to be disappointed. The new President promised "A wise and frugal government, which shall restrain men from injuring one another, which shall leave them otherwise free to regulate their own pursuits of industry and improvement, and shall not take from the mouth of labor the bread it has earned. This is the sum of good government, and this is necessary to close the circle of our felicities."[11] Following these "glittering platitudes" suggesting *laissez faire* and limited government, Jefferson was quick to guarantee "the honest payment of our debts and sacred preservation of the public faith; encouragement of agriculture, and of commerce as its handmaid." Thus, the much maligned funding system was to be retained after all, despite the dire predictions of the Federalists. When the President held out the olive branch, saying "We are all Republicans, we are all Federalists," the latter took him to mean that there would be no revolutionary changes in the government. Hamilton, indeed, rejoiced that the speech represented a "candid" retraction of past misapprehensions, and a pledge to the community, that the new President will not lend himself to dangerous innovations, but in essential points will tread in the steps of his predecessors." In some respects the worst fears of the Federalists were to be realized. For what Jefferson did was not to undermine the financial structures and arrangements that they had built up, but to steal their very political principles. By the end of his second term, he left them only their morbid fears of democracy, their Francophobia and hatred of dissent, and appropriated their nationalism and belief in positive government.[12]

One of the first efforts of the new administration was in the field of finance because the Republicans believed that the Federalists had built up a wholly unnecessary fiscal machine that threatened the nation's welfare and freedom. Economy was the keynote of Gallatin's administration of the Treasury. The army, he believed, should be cut to a minimum and the expenditures of the navy drastically curtailed. The debt of some $80 million, which he took over from the previous administration, should be retired as soon as possible. Upon assuming his position, Gallatin had written Jefferson, "The reduction of the public debt was certainly the principal object in bringing me into office."

[11] *Ibid.*, p. 440.
[12] J. C. Miller, *Alexander Hamilton, Portrait in Paradox*, p. 539.

In understanding Gallatin's financial policies, it must be stressed that the federal public debt was the focal point of his reforms. Though from the standpoint of modern fiscal theory we would not regard the national debt inherited from the Federalists as excessively burdensome, to him it was an "unmitigated evil." His objections to a public debt rested on several grounds. Most fundamental of these was his belief that government expenditures, especially when based on borrowing, involve a destruction of national capital. He believed this because of his attitude toward the various categories of public expenditure. Spending for military purposes he regarded as totally destructive. As for the civil expenditures of government, since he held with the early classical economists that productivity consisted only of the creation of material goods, these were simply unproductive. The only category of government expenditure he considered productive, in fact, was that on internal improvements, such as roads, canals, etc., but the government had not as yet entered this field. Apart from these financial considerations, Gallatin was prone like a good Genevan to moralize against any form of expenditure that was not paid for out of current income. Furthermore, he did not make any distinction between private and public borrowing, holding that in either case it arose from past extravagance. The higher interest payments that a public debt involved would necessitate heavier taxes upon the industrious for the advantage of the idle, if they did not lead the government to abandon the practice of taxation altogether. In short, to Gallatin a public debt of whatever sort was an abomination, a "moral canker" to be avoided at all costs. His fixation on debt reduction was to involve him ultimately in an inflexible fiscal policy that nearly proved disastrous for the nation.[13]

In the years 1802–08 Gallatin realized his objective of reducing the public debt even beyond his expectations. By the close of the latter year, the unredeemed portion of the debt stood at $57 million as against $80 million upon his assuming the office. By January, 1809 Gallatin calculated that almost $34 million of the debt would be redeemed, and the interest charges on the unredeemed part would be down to $4.6 million annually instead of the $8 million formerly devoted to this purpose. All the more impressive was the fact that included in the $57 million total was some $11,250,000, which had been borrowed in 1803 to cover the greater part of the price of the Louisiana Purchase. How had this "miracle" of Republican finance been accomplished?

In planning the finances of Jefferson's first administration, Gallatin sought to achieve his objective of debt reduction by a spartan program of economy. As it turned out, however, the savings he was able to make on the civil expenditures of the government were minor; economies on the army came to an annual average of $321,348 over the years 1801–08 as compared with comparable figures of the Federalists for this purpose over the years 1789–

[13] These observations rest mainly on the penetrating analysis in Balinsky, *Albert Gallatin*, Chap. 3.

01. And as for the navy, which Gallatin was constantly looking to for economies, its expenditures climbed from $915,000 in 1802 to $1,722,000 by 1807. Gallatin's hopes for economy in that department were defeated by the natural resistance of some of its leaders to retrenchment, to Jefferson's foolhardy insistence on building small gunboats to defend the nation, and most important, by the outbreak of the Mediterranean war against the Barbary pirates in 1804. Clearly, economies on expenditures were not the explanation of Gallatin's financial miracle.

The answer or at least the greatest part of the explanation was on the revenue side of the government's operations during these years. Gallatin had estimated that the total average annual revenue for the years 1802–08 would amount to $10 million without the internal taxes (which the Republicans had more or less pledged themselves to repeal) and $10.6 million with them. The government's total expenditures (debt included) over these years averaged $13.5 million annually; this is a measure of the failure of Gallatin's economy efforts in the period. But the actual annual revenue of the government climbed from $12,662,000 in 1802 to $17 million in 1807. The average annual revenue of the government was $14 million, or $4 million more than Gallatin had expected. The reason for this, of course, was the sensational increase in the nation's volume of imports from a value of $76.3 million in 1802 to a peak of $138.5 million in 1807. It was this unplanned and unprecedented increase in the nation's foreign trade and the revenue it yielded that was mainly responsible for the "golden age" of Republican finance.

Gallatin's policies had, in fact, made the nation's exchequer extremely dependent on the revenue from import duties. On becoming President, Jefferson recommended the repeal of all internal taxes, and the Republicans, who regarded these taxes as oppressive, unequal, unfair, odious, and hard to collect, were quick to oblige. In April, 1802 the President signed the bill repealing the entire internal tax system; Gallatin thereby lost an estimated $650,000 in revenue and was left only with $450,000 in land-sale and postal revenue, apart from the income from tonnage and custom duties. Gallatin showed concern about the immediate loss of revenue due to the repeal of the internal taxes, but he was largely unaware of the need for a permanent revenue, which would not fluctuate with the course of foreign affairs and trade. His optimism with regard to adequacy of the government's revenue was to be short-lived. In 1803 the purchase of Louisiana, the reduction in the impost duties following upon the temporary peace in Europe the year before, and the intensification of the war with the Barbary States caused the government's revenue to fall about $1 million short of its expectations. Gallatin met the government's need for additional revenue by proposing that Congress increase the *ad valorem* import duties by 2½ per cent, which it promptly did. The Revenue Act of 1804, incorporating these changes, earmarked the total revenue from these increases in imposts for the prosecution of the Barbary War, hence these moneys became known as the "Mediterranean Fund." By this device, Gallatin was able to maintain the fiction that he had held down the expenditures of the navy, a subterfuge that he would have been quick to criticize if it had been resorted to by Hamilton.

The renewal of hostilities in Europe in 1803 caused a resumption of the foreign trade boom and with it a rise in the government's revenue. Its total income rose from $10.6 million in 1803 to a peak of $17 million by 1808. The development of a substantial annual surplus in the government's accounts toward the end of this period led the President and his followers to press for a repeal of the salt tax, which yielded an average annual revenue of $500,000. Gallatin again rather reluctantly consented; the tax was abolished in 1807 and so the Treasury was made still more dependent on external duties. Gallatin's failure to develop a permanent, diversified system of revenues in this period was to prove a serious liability to the nation in the trying years of embargo, non-intercourse, and war, which followed. In not constructing a more elastic revenue system, he made the nation's income overwhelmingly dependent on the volume of foreign trade, which events were destined to contract and shrink with far-reaching results.

JEFFERSON AND THE EMBARGO

The life and death struggle between the two great imperial powers of Europe grew more intense as Jefferson's second term drew to its close. By his victory at Austerlitz in 1805 Napoleon had made himself master of the Continent, while the British by annihilating the united fleets of France and Spain at Trafalgar, put themselves in a position to impose a tight blockade on all the principal ports of the French empire. In the early years of this struggle, American merchants as well as politicians were willing to tolerate a certain amount of interference and annoyance with their trade and shipping as a necessary price for the commercial advantages of neutrality. But as the great conflict approached its climax, neutral rights were more frequently and more flagrantly violated. The number of sailors who were impressed increased, more ports were closed to our shipping, and insults to the flag on the high seas multiplied. The capture of the frigate *Chesapeake* by the British man-of-war *Leopard* in June of 1807 was a striking demonstration of the intensified belligerence of the warring powers against the United States. The two military antagonists resented the prosperity of the neutral United States. France and England had gone to war over the carrying trade of the world only to discover that we were running away with it.

Events were now quickly to put an end to our period of profitable neutrality. Napoleon, in retaliation against the British blockade, now devised his so-called Continental System under which, on November 21, 1806, he issued the celebrated Berlin Decree, which placed the British Isles under blockade. The British, in turn, about a year later issued their Orders in Council, declaring that no neutral vessel might trade at any port of France or her allies without first stopping and paying duties at an English port. Napoleon answered this action with his Milan Decree of December, 1807, which stated that any vessel submitting to British search or touched at a British port or that of her allies was liable to seizure. Napoleon's decrees, owing to the destruction of the French fleet, were largely a paper blockade. But, nevertheless, these edicts of the two warring powers, if enforced, were a threat to most of the foreign commerce of the United States. Though often evaded and but poorly enforced, these orders and decrees resulted in the capture of 1600 American ships and the destruction of $60 million in property.

The United States was faced under these circumstances with a harsh dilemma, either to wage war against either one or both of these powers (and thanks to Gallatin's program of economy, we were frightfully unprepared for such a course) or to adopt a policy of complete submission. Jefferson, ardent pacifist that he was, sought a middle course in terms of what he termed "peaceable coercion." His idea was that if England and France could attempt an economic boycott, why couldn't we? "Our commerce is so valuable to them," he wrote, "that they will be glad to purchase it, when the only price we ask is to do us justice." With this in mind, Congress early in 1806 passed the Non-Importation Act, which provided that certain goods could not be imported from Great Britain after November of that year. Meanwhile, James Monroe and William Pinckney, who had been sent on a diplomatic mission to England to secure our rights, returned with such an unsatisfactory treaty that Jefferson refused to submit it to the Senate. Instead, on his advice, Congress in December, 1807 passed the Embargo Act, which prohibited all American vessels from sailing to foreign ports, all foreign vessels from taking out cargoes, and required all coasting vessels to post heavy bond to land their cargoes in the United States. Jefferson showed great political courage in espousing this economic and "moral equivalent for war," for his closest advisers, such as Gallatin, advised him against it. The latter, for example, spoke against it, saying: "In every point of view, privation, suffering, revenue, effect on the enemy, politics at home, etc., I prefer war to a permanent embargo. Governmental prohibitions always do more mischief than had been calculated, and it is not without much hesitation that a statesman should hazard to regulate the concerns of individuals."

Gallatin's worst fears about the adverse economic effects of the embargo were soon demonstrated which, as Justice Story, a one-time advocate of the policy, said "had prostrated the whole commerce of America." Exports in 1808 fell to one-fifth of the total of the preceding year, from $108 million to $22.4 million, and our imports were more than cut in half in the same period, falling from $138.5 million to $57 million. McMaster estimates that 55,000 sailors and 100,000 mechanics were thrown out of work for a year by the embargo; he graphically described its general effects as follows:

"The newspapers were full of insolvent-debtor notices. All over the country, the court-house doors, the tavern doors, the post-offices, the crossroads posts, were covered with advertisements of sheriffs' sales. In the cities, the jails were not large enough to hold the debtors. At New York during 1809 thirteen hundred men were imprisoned for no other crime than being ruined by the embargo. A traveler who saw the city in this day of distress assures us that it looked like a town ravaged by pestilence. The counting-houses were shut or advertised to let. The coffee-houses were almost empty. The streets along the water-side were almost deserted. The ships were dismantled; their decks were cleared, their hatches were batten down."[14]

The embargo hit Massachusetts especially hard, and some of the seaport towns, such as Salem, Newburyport, and Plymouth, never recovered. In the South, tidewater Virginia and Maryland suffered greatly from the curtailment of the export of their crops, and their decline dates from this period. The ultimate damage felt by the former state was greater than that of New England, but it was surprisingly loyal to its chief, Jefferson.

The decline in foreign trade as a result of the embargo quickly produced a crisis in the government's finances. By 1809, when its effects were fully evident, total revenue was reduced from its 1808 peak of $17 million to $7.7 million. Apart from the surplus of $17 million, which it had accumulated in the years between 1801 and 1807, the Treasury suddenly found itself in the worst position it had been since 1789. From 1809 to the declaration of war against Great Britain, the government's expenditures exceeded its revenues, as Table 1 shows. Gallatin's over-reliance on the revenue from foreign trade was amply demonstrated during these years.

TABLE 1

Revenues and Expenditures of the United States, at Close of Years 1809–1811[a] (millions of dollars)

Year	Total Expenditures	Total Revenue	Deficit
1809	$13,870	$ 7,700	$6,170
1810	13,300	9,300	4,000
1811	18,600	14,400	4,200

[a] Source: Balinky, *Albert Gallatin, op. cit.*, p. 159. First appeared in *American State Papers, Finance* (Washington, D.C.: U.S. Printing Office, 1832, V. II, pp. 919-920). The expenditure figures in the above table include provision for debt service in the years indicated.

Gallatin's obsession with reduction of the federal debt and his insistence on economy, though he did not succeed in keeping military and naval expenditures down to the level he desired, did result in a failure to provide the nation with an adequate national defense at a critical time. While other factors played a part, his reluctance to build up our military and naval forces to a

[14] J. B. McMaster, *A History of the People of the United States from the Revolution to the Civil War*, 8 vols. (New York: Appleton-Century-Crofts, Inc., 1892–1919), III, p. 415.

state of adequacy left Jefferson no other alternative than his effort at peaceful coercion.

Meanwhile, to return to the embargo, the opposition to it mounted to a thunderous pitch. Though coastwise trade was a source of considerable evasion—ships were "accidentally" blown off their course and wound up at European ports—and goods reached Great Britain by smuggling through Canada and Florida, the economic hardships of the nation were great. Resolutions against the embargo came from a hundred towns, and the tide of opposition in Congress mounted. The fact was that the obstacles to the success of the embargo were psychological as well as economic. Americans were called upon to play a passive role while their pocketbooks were being touched. As Sears put it, we "were pitted against Europe, but the struggle was negative—a test not of aggression, but of endurance. This in itself was a handicap, since the usual incitements to emotional patriotism were absent . . . The rich merchant, who would have willingly given his son for his country, scorned a country which asked only for his moneybags."[15] Economically, the embargo to some New England merchants was bad because it ran counter to *laissez faire*, to the doctrines of Smithianismus. Josiah Quincy expressed this view when he said: "This is the misfortune of the policy of the embargo, that you undertake to do what laws never did do—what they never can do. You undertake to protect better the property of the individual than his own personal interest would enable him to protect it. .The interests which society has in the property of the merchant are much better secured by his own prudence and understanding of his business, than by any general law."[16] Those who were of the opinion of Quincy would simply let the risks of trade under the British orders in council reflect themselves in the marine insurance rates; those who found the latter too high would not undertake the voyage; those who calculated otherwise, would. Senator Giles of Virginia gave the administration's reply to arguments such as Quincy's when he said: "Sir, if we repeal the embargo laws without any substitute, and agree to trade under the British Orders in Council, what would be the premium of insurance on our national character and national independence? Sir, six per cent would not insure them."[17]

The presidential election of 1808 came while the opposition to the embargo was rapidly mounting. Jefferson was now being reviled for his policy; letters were written to him addressed, "You Infernal Villain," and one demanded that he support an orphan made penniless by the embargo. Despite the hue and cry, the Republican Congress in January, 1809 passed the Force Act, which authorized federal officials without warrants to seize goods if they suspected that their destinations were foreign ports. At this, even Jefferson's followers in New England predicted civil war. Under the irresistible pressure, enough

[15] L. M. Sears, *Jefferson and the Embargo* (Durham, N.C.: Duke University Press, 1927), pp. 73–74.
[16] *Ibid.*, pp. 161–162.
[17] *Ibid.*, p. 248.

Republicans broke with the administration to vote with the opposition to repeal the Embargo Act, and Jefferson, three days before he retired from office, sadly signed the bill. In its place the Congress passed the Non-intercourse Act, which prohibited trade only with Great Britain and France and their possessions.

The embargo did not have the success its advocates had hoped it would for a number of reasons apart from those already noted. For one thing, the working class of England upon whom the embargo bore with greatest weight were unrepresented in Parliament, so they could not make their influence felt. Furthermore, during the embargo the revolution in Spain opened up new ports in South America to British merchants, and this commerce compensated for the loss of American export trade. Table 2 clearly shows the shift in trade that took place during these years. British imports from the United States were likewise replaced in part by goods bought in other countries. British imports from the United States in the year of the embargo fell £4,779,424, but gains in other directions enabled the British to end the year with a net loss of only £668,633.

TABLE 2

Foreign Trade of Great Britain, 1806–1808[a]

Year	Exports to U.S.A.	Exports to South America	Total
1806	£ 12,389,488	£ 10,877,968	£ 38,732,730
1807	11,846,513	10,439,423	35,412,867
1809	5,241,739	16,591,871	35,007,501

[a] Source: L. M. Sears, *Jefferson and the Embargo, op. cit.*, p. 296.

Under the non-intercourse policy there was a partial revival of foreign trade and a corresponding easing of the government's fiscal problems. Exports increased from $22.5 million in 1808 to $52 million in 1808 and $67 million in 1810, while imports climbed from $57 million in 1808 to $85.4 million in 1810. The government's revenue closely reflected this improvement in business by rising from $717 million in 1809 to $14.4 million in 1810. This was more or less what Gallatin had hoped for in supporting the non-intercourse policy. The revival of foreign trade would raise his impost revenue, and by practicing rigid economy so far as government expenditures were concerned, he hoped to be able to restore the government's finances to something approximating their old happy state. But his hopes for great economies, as in the earlier years of his administration, were not completely fulfilled. The annual revenue of the government between 1809 and 1811 averaged only $10 million, and annual expenditures rose to an average level of $6.5 million. Gallatin returned to his old policy of reducing the national debt with the aid of his surpluses, but he did not succeed in this objective in the years 1810–12 as handsomely as he had done earlier. Nevertheless, by the latter year the debt stood at $45.2 million, close to one-half of what it had been at the beginning of his Treasury service. Gallatin wanted to postpone any involvement in war until the debt had been nearly paid off. He concentrated on that aim and did not devise an interim system of finance, but counted on being able to formulate a system of war finance when that dreaded eventuality would arrive. This approach to the matter proved to be one of the serious mistakes of his financial administration.

The failure of the embargo and the continuance of war in Europe made more military preparations necessary, and Congress therefore approved new appropriations for the fortification of ports and harbors, more gunboats were purchased, and the regular army was expanded. Yet, as one able student of Gallatin's policies writes, "Congress appropriated just enough money to prevent the realization of Gallatin's financial plans but not enough to prepare the nation adequately in the event of war."[18] In the face of conditions that had revolutionized and destroyed the adequacy of his fiscal system, Gallatin had not moved away from his cherished notions of orthodox finance. The only basic change he had made during the unsettled years of 1808–11 was to work out a theory of war finance. But as long as the nation was at peace, however precarious it was, he was content, even determined to cling to his old policies of debt reduction, economy, and sole reliance on the revenue from import duties. The costs of that course of action were only to become painfully evident during the financially disastrous years of the War of 1812.

THE WAR OF 1812

The War of 1812 imposed a great financial burden on the new nation. Actually, the federal government's annual expenditures more than quadrupled as a result of the war; its outlays rose from $8.1 million in 1811 to $32.9 million in 1815. As the prospect of war became more imminent, Gallatin developed the theory of war finance for which he was famous. This consisted of borrowing to meet the extraordinary expenses of war and levying taxes to meet the ordinary cost of government, plus interest charges on the new and old debt. Gallatin espoused this theory because of his belief that war would greatly disrupt the maritime and internal commerce of the nation and that new taxes should not be imposed to further aggravate matters.

When the war did come, the conditions the Secretary of the Treasury faced were rather different than he had anticipated in the earliest formulation of his theory. Altogether, during the years of 1812–16 some $86.5 million were issued in short and long-term loans, and at the end of the war the government's permanent debt was $68 million larger than it had been at the beginning. While the first loan was successful, successive issues had to be sold at

18 Balinky, *Albert Gallatin*, pp. 162–3.

heavy discounts to induce buying. The government's credit grew progressively worse during much of the war, for Congress was very tardy in legislating adequate taxation to service the ever-larger loans; foreign borrowers were slow to come to our aid; the Federalists wouldn't open their moneybags; and with the depreciation in the value of money, the government received only a fraction of the face value of the loans. A House Ways and Means Committee in 1830 estimated that for over $80 million in loans, the Treasury received about $34 million as measured in specie.

The basic reason for this disastrous fiscal policy was Gallatin's vacillation about asking Congress to levy internal taxes and the reluctance of that body to do so. It was not until the summer of 1813 that the sheer impossibility of further borrowing led Congress to reimpose the much hated internal taxes. A direct tax was laid upon slaves and dwellings and excises were imposed on pleasure carriages, sugar refining, and the distillation of spirits. Taxes were placed too upon auctions and financial instruments, and retailers of liquors were required to purchase licenses. Congress called these "war taxes" and stipulated that they should be repealed within one year after its conclusion. Some of the basic figures of war-time revenue and expenditure are set out in Table 3.

TABLE 3

Revenue and Expenditures of the U.S. Government, 1812–15[a]

Year	Total Revenue	Customs	Internal Revenue	Direct Tax	Expenditures	Deficit
		(In millions of dollars)				
1812	$ 9.8	$ 8.9	—	—	$20.2	$10.4
1813	14.3	13.2	—	—	31.6	17.3
1814	11.1	6.0	1.6	2.2	34.7	23.6
1815	15.6	7.3	4.7	2.1	32.9	17.3

Source: D. R. Dewey, *Financial History of the United States, op. cit.*, p. 142. Reprinted by permission of David McKay Company, Inc., New York, New York, Miscellaneous receipts are omitted from the above.

The government's credit reached its nadir in the fall of 1814 when the Treasury was practically empty and Gallatin reported to James Monroe that no loans could be obtained in Europe. The two basic reasons for this deplorable state of the nation's finances was that Congress had taxed "too little and too late," and Federalist opposition to the war had impeded sound borrowing. Second in importance was the closing of the Bank of the United States in 1811, which left the government without a fiscal agent to facilitate its borrowing and left it a victim to the depreciated notes of the state banks. During the war there was no shortage of these latter institutions; Gallatin stated that no fewer than 120 of them were organized between 1811 and 1815. Their bank note circulation rose from $28 million to $45.5 million between these two years. The nation, then, did not suffer from an inadequacy of currency, but rather from its grave shortcomings in quality. Many of the southern and western banks did not redeem their notes in specie and of those which did, they circulated at par only in restricted localities. During these war years the nation did not have a national currency, but rather a bewildering mass of local currencies that could only be accepted in business with the aid of "bank note lists," which indicated their varying values. This jerry-built system of banking collapsed in 1814. When the British captured Washington in August of that year, the Baltimore banks suspended specie payments, then Philadelphia institutions closed their doors, and finally New York banks stopped payment. Only the New England banks with their more conservative policies and more adequate specie reserves were able to continue to honor their notes. The nation's system of private finance was as disorganized and as weak as its public finances. The termination of the war late that year came none too soon.

THE JEFFERSONIAN IDEOLOGY MODIFIED

As we have seen, one of the principal economic reactions to the embargo and the War of 1812 was the beginning of manufacturing activity. As early as 1810, Gallatin in his Report on Manufactures claimed that we were self-sufficient in the production of manufactures of wood, leather, soap and tallow candles, spermaceti oil, flaxseed oil, coarse earthenware, snuff, chocolate, hair powder, and mustard. He went on to contend that we produced the greater part of our needs for iron and manufactures of iron, of cotton, woolen, and flax products, hats, paper and printed books, spiritous liquors, gunpowder, window glass, jewelry and clocks, straw bonnets, and several manufactures of hemp and lead. This variegated list of oddly assorted products suggests that the Secretary was hard pressed to compile an impressive list for his report. For, indeed, as subsequent events were to show, many of these manufactures had sprung up to fill the need created by the decline of imports during the embargo and later during the war. Prices rose for these scarce commodities, and capital and labor were partially diverted from shipbuilding and maritime activity to these new fields of activity. Gallatin in his Report of 1810 actually contended that some of the principal obstacles to manufacturing had been removed, in the following, rather cautious language:

> The most prominent of those causes are the abundance of land compared with the population, the high price of labor, and the want of sufficient capital. The superior attractions of agricultural pursuits, the great extension of American commerce during the late European Wars, and the continuance of habits after the causes which produced them have ceased to exist, may also be enumerated. Several of these obstacles have been removed or lessened. The cheapness of provisions had always, to a certain extent, counterbalanced the high price of manual labor; and this is now, in many important branches, nearly superseded by the introduction of machinery; a great American capital has been acquired

during the last twenty years; and the injurious violations of the Neutral commerce of the United States, by forcing industry and capital into other channels, have broken inveterate habits, and given a general impulse, to which must be ascribed the great increase of manufactures during the last two years.[19]

While Gallatin's statement about the diversion of capital and labor into manufacturing during this period was undoubtedly correct, he was altogether too sanguine about the other impediments to manufacturing still existing, such as inadequate land transportation and lack of power to drive machinery. The developments after the War of 1812 were to reveal many of the shortcomings of American manufacturing of that date.

One of the most interesting changes that took place as a result of the nation's experiment with manufacturing during these trying years was the shift in Jefferson's thinking about industry. In his *Notes on Virginia*, the great Virginian had expressed a very hostile view of manufacturing and of cities in which such activity was carried on. But the experience of the war and Jefferson's patriotic concern for the nation's survival led him to a partial revision of his ideology. Writing to Benjamin Austin in 1816, he stated that we could no longer depend on England for manufactures, as he had contended in the *Notes*. The reason, he said, was that in the 1780's, when he composed the *Notes*, the suppliers of raw materials to manufacturing nations were welcomed as customers in a friendly and peaceful way. But since then, he went on to state,

> . . . We have experienced what we did not then believe, that there exists both profligacy and power enough to exclude us from the field of interchange with other nations: that to be independent for the comforts of life we must fabricate them ourselves. We must now place the manufacturer by the side of the agriculturalist. . . . Shall we make our own comforts, or go without them, at the will of a foreign nation? He, therefore, who is now against domestic manufacture, must be for reducing us either to dependence on that foreign nation, or to be clothed in skins, and to live like wild beasts in dens and caverns. I am not one of these; experience has taught me that manufactures are now as necessary to our independence as to our comfort."[20]

The general weakness in the Jeffersonian ideology as it related to economic development was no where better demonstrated than in connection with Gallatin's Report on Roads and Canals, which, unfortunately, never saw realization of its plans while he was in office. The background of this statesmanlike Report was in the sizeable surplus that the government was enjoying toward the end of Jefferson's second term because of the prosperity growing out of our neutral status in the great European War. Jefferson urged spending

[19] *American State Papers, Finance,* II (Washington, D.C.: U.S. Government Printing Office, 1815), p. 426.

[20] *The Writings of Thomas Jefferson,* edited by P. L. Ford (New York: G. P. Putnam's Sons, 1892–1899, 1904), XI, 503–4 as quoted in M. and L. White, *The Intellectual versus the City* (Cambridge, Mass.: Harvard University Press and the M.I.T. Press, 1902), p. 18.

part of this surplus on a program of internal improvements, and in accordance with the ideas of his leader, Gallatin spent a year preparing the aforementioned Report, which was submitted to the Senate in April, 1808. His plan called for a ten-year program of road and canal construction at a total cost of $20 million, to be spent at the rate of $2 million a year out of the surplus in the Treasury. This far-sighted plan, which anticipated by many years projects later completed, urged the construction of a great turnpike from Maine to Georgia, of canals connecting the Hudson and Lake Ontario, others connecting other eastern cities with the hinterland, improvement of rivers, etc. It was a great vision of economic development and national planning, but it had to be "shelved" because with the coming of the Embargo the decline of the government's revenue made it impractical to carry out.

This unhappy development was not the product merely of national misfortune, but rather a consequence of Gallatin's inflexible system of fiscal policy. By making the government's revenue so heavily dependent on tariff imposts and tonnage duties, Gallatin failed to work out a permanent, diversified and stable source of income. This failure meant that, by necessity, a decline in foreign trade would mean a reduction of governmental income and the curtailment of any program dependent upon it.

Furthermore, as Balinky has pointed out,

> "The Republican revenue system was largely anachronistic. Being agrarians, Republicans tied their entire revenue system to the fortunes of foreign trade—the very economic pursuit that they were unwilling to support. At the same time that they took measures to reduce foreign trade (in an effort to solve other problems—the embargo), they permitted themselves to depend almost entirely on the revenue proceeds from that trade. One may well question the wisdom of rejecting an alliance between the mercantile classes and the government while depending upon mercantile success as the sole source of revenue."[21]

The Jeffersonian philosophy as spelled out by Gallatin in terms of fiscal policy had other serious defects. The latter's phobia about public debt and his insistence upon an annually balanced budget had most serious economic consequences. Gallatin wished to promote private capital investment to spur the growth of the nation, but his

> desire for the productive investment of existing capital was actually undermined by his approach to the debt question. Capital could be most profitably employed in mercantile activity in the short run and industrial activity in the longer run. The American economy, being young, needed certain forms of governmental protection and encouragement. Because of the peculiar circumstances of the Napoleonic Wars and America's commercial role in them, governmental participation in assuring freedom of the seas, freedom of entry into world ports, etc. was essential. Various forms of government aid and direction also were necessary toward encouraging the longer-run development of industry. To help assure profitable and stable opportunities for private investment (a goal which Gallatin favored) government could easily have been

[21] Balinky, *Albert Gallatin*, p. 228.

justified in assuming a certain debt obligation to the extent that the costs of such a program could not be met entirely out of current revenue.[22]

Gallatin's fiscal philosophy did not take sufficient account of the fact that the nation was still young and that certain initial costs of securing political and economic independence had to be met, even if by borrowing. Gallatin's virtues were those of moderation, temperateness, and honesty, but the birth of a nation requires in addition those qualities of boldness of action, decisiveness, and a talent for innovation that dogma, fiscal or otherwise, seldom encourages. The years of Jefferson's administration, despite the fears voiced at his inaugural, were largely a period of consolidation, so far as fiscal and economic matters were concerned, after the bold innovations of Hamilton. In the years after the War of 1812, the function of governmental innovation was more largely assumed by the separate states in partnership with the enterprise and ingenuity of their citizens.

[22] *Ibid.*, p. 225.

Part 3

THE GROWING INTEGRATION
OF THE ECONOMY, 1815–1843

Introduction: The Staple and Innovational
Theories of Growth

Basic Economic Changes in the Years
1815–1843

The Role of Staple Exports and Creative
Entrepreneurship in the Economy's
Growth

The Ethos and Politics of the Age
of the Common Man

INTRODUCTION: THE STAPLE AND INNOVATIONAL THEORIES OF GROWTH

In this part of our study we consider two theories of economic growth: the staple theory and that of creative entrepreneurship and innovation. While analysis of two theories in a section is a departure from our usual practice, the greater plausibility of this approach for this particular period of our economic history seems to warrant such a treatment.

The so-called staple theory of economic growth was largely the innovation of the late Harold Innis, a brilliant Canadian professor of economic history who employed the concept in a broad way in his historical studies of the cod fisheries and the fur trade.[1] While students of Canadian economic history dispute its relevance to their economy today, the theory seems to be particularly applicable to the process of growth in a new country. It must be emphasized that the staple theory is not a general theory of economic growth, but rather one useful in interpreting economic growth in such "empty" lands as the United States and the British dominions in their early years when there was a favorable man-land ratio and few cultural traditions inhibiting growth.

Harold A. Innis (1894–1952) was born at Otterville, Ontario, Canada. He studied at McMaster University and the University of Chicago where he received the doctorate in 1920. Thereafter he taught at the University of Toronto where he became full professor in 1936.

---

[1] See his *The Fur Trade in Canada: An Introduction to Canadian Economic History* (Toronto, University of Toronto Press, 1930; 2nd edition, 1956); *The Cod Fisheries: The History of an International Economy* (Toronto, University of Toronto Press, 1940; 2nd edition, 1954). The American economic historian, Guy S. Callender, also stressed the importance of international trade in staples in the economic growth of the United States. (See G. S. Callender, *Selections from the Economic History of the United States, 1765–1860* (Boston: Ginn and Co., 1909). R. E. Baldwin offered an incisive interpretation of the impact of staple production on an economy in his article, "Patterns of Development in Newly Settled Regions," *Manchester School of Economic and Social Studies,* XXIV (May, 1956), pp. 161–79.

The basic assumption of the staple theory—so called because staple exports are the leading sector of the economy—is that they set the pace for economic growth.[2] Because of the usual limited domestic market and the peculiar proportions of the factors of production in the new land—a surplus of land relative to labor and capital—there is a comparative advantage in the intensive production of staples. Economic development tends then to take the form of a process of diversification around the export base. The key idea of a staple theory, therefore, is the spread effects of the export sector, i.e., the impact of the export trade on the rest of the domestic economy and society.

The chief determinants of the spread effects of the export staple—given the resource base of the new country and the environment of the rest of the world—is the character of the staple or staples being exported and, more especially, its technology, which tends to determine the production function of the industry. The latter in turn defines the degree of substitutability of one factor of production for another and the nature, if any, of the economies of large-scale production.

With a given production function for the export staple, one can infer that there will be a certain demand for the various factors of production and, possibly, for certain intermediate inputs of goods; there will also be the possibility of further processing of the staple commodity. From the resulting pattern of production, there will be an associated distribution of income.

The above factors influence the range of investment opportunities in the domestic economy and the degree of diversification around the export base. Let us follow a typical sequence of change in this staple model. A rise in the demand for the staple will induce an increase in its supply and a consequent rise in income in the export sector. The spending of this income will create investment opportunities in other sectors, both domestic and foreign. The impact of these income flows may be further explained in terms of the combined multiplier-accelerator principles.[3] Further, the inducement to domestic investment stemming from the expansion of the export sector can be analyzed in terms of Hirschman's so-called linkage effects: backward linkage, forward linkage, and final demand linkage.[4]

Backward linkage is a measure of the inducement to invest in the domestic production of goods, including capital goods, to supply the expanding export sector. The most important example of backward linkage is the building of transportation facilities to collect and distribute the export staples. Such building may generate additional spread effects.

Forward linkage is a measure of the inducement to invest in industries using the export commodity. Examples would be investment in warehouses

[2] This summary of the theory relies heavily on M. H. Watkins, "A Staple Theory of Economic Growth," *The Canadian Journal of Economics and Political Science* (May, 1963), pp. 141–158.

[3] See below, pp. 169 (footnote 12), 660, 700.

[4] A. O. Hirschman, *The Strategy of Economic Development* (New Haven: Yale University Press, 1958), Chap. 6; Watkins, *op. cit.*, p. 145.

and in facilities for processing or manufacturing finished goods from the export-staple.

Final demand linkage is a measure of the inducement to invest in domestic industries that produce consumer goods for the people engaged in the export sector of the economy. The extent of such induced final demand will depend on the absolute size of the export sector. Some of the income generated in the export sector may be lost through "leakages" in the form of payments to foreign factors of production who remit their income abroad, wages paid to migratory labor, etc.

The average level of income in the export sector will be greatly influenced by the fertility of the land, assuming that other factors of production can be imported. The distribution of income in the export sector will depend on the nature of the production function of the staple commodity. Professor Baldwin has described two polar models in this connection—the plantation-grown crop, with its unequal distribution of income, and the relatively equal distribution of the family farm crop. He has pointed out that if the export commodity can be efficiently produced on family-sized farms with relatively smaller amounts of labor than would be necessary for plantation-type agriculture, there would be a more equitable distribution of incomes and a consequent demand for a broad range of goods and services. Such demand would create what the economist calls *induced investment* in other lines of industry. If, in contrast, the export commodity is produced on large plantations with slave labor, there will tend to be an extremely unequal distribution of income. The slaves would probably live on practically a subsistence basis, while the plantation owners would very likely import many luxury goods. These conditions, it is clear, would not tend to induce as much investment outside the export sector as in the first instance. Furthermore, it is likely that there would be very different attitudes toward investment in knowledge and in the education of the people in the two cases described, with all the possible effects on subsequent economic growth.

Other factors affecting final demand linkage include the questions as to whether the export generated incomes are spent on home-produced goods or imports, on subsistence goods, or luxuries. Generally speaking, the higher the marginal propensity to import, the lower will be the final demand linkage. Furthermore, "final demand linkage will tend to be higher, the higher the average level of income and the more equal its distribution. . . ."[5] Equal distribution of income reduces the likelihood of large-scale import of luxury goods and, on the other hand, enhances the likelihood of a mass market for more standardized goods.

Analysis of the linkages above has assumed that the additional investment is induced by the expansion in demand created by the growing export sector. Whether these potential investment opportunities will in fact be exploited depends much on the quality of entrepreneurship and, more specifically, its

[5] Watkins, *op. cit.*, p. 146.

ability to perceive and exploit new market opportunities. Professor Schumpeter's theory of creative entrepreneurship, outlined later in this Introduction, is very relevant here.

But even where the supply and quality of entrepreneurs are adequate, their collective effectiveness will depend on the availability of labor and capital (foreign or domestic), the richness of the country's natural resources, and the international environment that prevails when the new country undertakes development. The difficulty in generalizing about these factors should not lead us to underrate their importance. For example, the resource base of a nation may be bad at the outset of its development, but it may be improved by new discoveries, changing technology, etc. New countries seeking to grow via the staple route may be greatly aided by their favorable man-land ratio and by the absence of inhibiting cultural traditions. ". . . The fact that new countries do not start their development with population pressing against scarce resources gives them an enormous advantage over the typical under-developed country. Specifically, they have neither a large subsistence agricultural sector severely limiting markets for domestic industry, nor a pool of cheap labor permitting industrialization to proceed with only limited impact on the incomes of much of the population. Subsequent population growth, in part by immigration, means that the size of population is closely related to economic opportunity at a relatively high standard of living. The second feature, the lack of traditions, means that institutions and values must be formed anew, and although there will be a substantial carry-over from the old world, the process will be selective and those transferred are likely to take a form more favorable to economic growth."[6]

The growth path of the staple economy will depend much upon its ability to import scarce factors of production. Once the export sector starts growing, the spread effects may result in driving up the prices of the production factors in other sectors. However, if the supply of foreign factors of production (say capital or labor) is elastic, this tendency may be averted or postponed. Such a process is alleged to explain the prolonged booms that have characterized the growth of some staple economies.

Sustained growth for the staple economy requires an ability to shift resources as market demand changes. This is so because diminishing returns in exploiting the export commodity may ultimately drive up its costs; adverse shifts in demand and new sources of supply make reliance on one commodity dangerous. The greatest hazard is the development by staple exporters, particularly those in political control, of an "export mentality" (e.g., the "sugar mentality" of pre-Castro Cuba) with the result that the economy gets caught in a "staple trap." If such pitfalls are avoided through the staple or staples generating strong linkage effects creatively developed, then the "staple economy" may grow and diversify to the point where such a characterization

---

6 Watkins, *op. cit.*, pp. 149, 150.

will no longer be justified. Such growth and development in a staple economy depend vitally upon what Schumpeter termed "creative entrepreneurship"; his theory of economic growth logically deserves our attention at this point.

The theory of economic growth associated with Joseph A. Schumpeter was first presented in his brilliant book, *The Theory of Economic Development* (1911), written in German when he was only 28 years old.[7] The author further extended and illustrated his ideas in his massive work on *Business Cycles,* published in 1939.[8] Schumpeter's theory of enterpreneurship and of innovation is so important and relevant to the early as well as later phases of our economic growth that we need to grasp the essentials of his "vision" of the capitalistic process.

Joseph A. Schumpeter (1883–1950), late Professor of Economics at Harvard University, was one of the great modern economists. Before joining the Harvard faculty he was successively a lawyer, Finance Minister of Austria, and professor of economics at Graz, Bonn, and Tokyo Universities.

Wide World Photos

Schumpeter insisted that capitalism had to be analyzed in dynamic, evolutionary terms. "Capitalist reality is first and last a process of change," he wrote. In his *Theory of Economic Development,* it is true, he begins his exposition with a description of the economy in terms of the circular flow of goods and money in stationary equilibrium. In this hypothetical model, all economic activity is essentially repetitive, following the course of familiar routine, under conditions of pure competition. As Clemence and Doody describe it, ". . . Every firm in the system is in perfect competitive equilibrium, with its costs consisting of wages and rents, exactly equal to its receipts. Prices everywhere are equated to average costs; profits are zero; profit

[7] (Cambridge: Harvard University Press, 1934.) Besides the works cited above, he is best known for his provocative *Capitalism, Socialism and Democracy* (New York: Harper and Bros., Rev. 1947) and his scholarly *The History of Economic Analysis* (New York: Oxford University Press, 1954).

[8] (New York: McGraw-Hill Book Co., Inc., 1939) 2 vols.

opportunities are non-existent; interest rates are zero; and there is no involuntary unemployment of resources. Every household, like every firm, is in full long-run equilibrium, with receipts equal to expenditures, and with a budgetary pattern that cannot, under existing circumstances, be advantageously altered."[9] In this simple model of the economy, changes are continuous and gradual; economic life runs on in channels that are essentially the same year after year—"similar to the circulation of blood in an animal organism."

But the changes that most interested Schumpeter and that propel the economy to new levels of income and output are what he terms developmental ones. They are usually discontinuous and impart a spasmodic pattern of growth to the economy. These developmental changes are caused by "autonomous" investment, which arises out of innovations, to be contrasted with "induced" investment, which is stimulated by the resulting increases in income, sales, or profits. By the term "innovation," Schumpeter meant, in general, any change in a production function, i.e., the proportions in which the factors of production are combined. Economic development, he insisted, in contrast to mere routine growth, "consists primarily in employing resources in a different way, in doing new things with them, irrespective of whether those resources increase or not. . . ." "Development in our sense," he wrote in another place, "is a distinct phenomenon, entirely foreign to what may be observed in the circular flow or in the tendency toward equilibrium. It is spontaneous and discontinuous change in the channels of the flow, disturbances of equilibrium which forever alters and displaces the equilibrium state previously existing. . . ."[10]

Schumpeter recognized five major forms of innovation: "(1) The introduction of a new good—that is, one with which consumers are not yet familiar or of a new quality of a good. (2) The introduction of a new method of production, that is, one not yet tested by experience in the branch of manufacture concerned, which need by no means be founded upon a discovery scientifically new, and can also exist in a new way of handling a commodity commercially. (3) The opening up of a new market, that is, a market into which the particular branch of manufacture of the country in question has not previously entered, whether or not this market existed before. (4) The conquest of a new source of supply of raw materials, or half-manufactured goods, again irrespective of whether this source already exists or whether it has first to be created. (5) The carrying out of a new organization of any industry, like the creation of a monopoly position (for example, through trustification) or the breaking up of a monopoly position."[11]

Schumpeter, it will be noted, did not consider population growth as a major economic force in his system; he preferred to regard it as a dependent

[9] R. V. Clemence and F. S. Doody, *The Schumpeterian System* (Cambridge, Mass.: Addison-Wesley Press, Inc., 1950), p. 9.

[10] J. Schumpeter, *Theory of Economic Development*, p. 64.

[11] *Ibid.*, p. 66.

variable in the growth process. He treated population change this way also because of his distinction between growth and development. True development required qualitative change. He expressed his view on this as follows:

> "By development, therefore, we shall understand only such changes in economic life as are not forced upon it from without but arise by their own initiative from within. . . . Nor will the mere growth of the economy, as shown by the growth of the population and wealth, be designated here as a process of development. For it calls forth no qualitatively new phenomena, but only processes of adaption of the same kind as the changes in the natural data. Since we wish to direct our attention to other phenomena, we shall regard such increases as changes in data."[12]

Innovations, it is obvious, are of different kinds and varying degrees of importance. Schumpeter tended in the elaboration of his theoretical model to center attention on those innovations that involved the founding of new firms and the rise of new men to business leadership. These creative entrepreneurs are the prime movers of economic change in the Schumpeterian vision of the capitalistic process. As he said, the mechanisms of economic change in capitalist society pivot on entrepreneurial activity. The entrepreneur is the person who sees an opportunity for introducing a new technique, a new commodity, or a new form of business organization. He raises capital to launch the enterprise, assembles the factors of production, and sets the organization going. Schumpeter sees these creative entrepreneurs as social deviants, egocentric, untraditional, and ambitious. They are motivated by more than pecuniary considerations; Schumpeter's description of them recalls McClelland's power and achievement motives.

> First of all, there is the dream and will to found a private kingdom, usually, though not necessarily, also a dynasty. The modern world really does not know any such positions, but what may be attained by industrial and commercial success is still the nearest approach to medieval lordship possible to modern man. . . .
> Then there is the will to conquer; the impulse to fight, to prove oneself superior to others, to succeed for the sake, not for the fruits of success, but of success itself. From this aspect, economic action becomes akin to sport—there are financial races, or rather boxing-matches. . . .
> Finally, there is the joy of creating, of getting things done, or simply exercising one's energy and ingenuity.[13]

The innovations that spur economic development are seen by Schumpeter as being carried out when the economy is in the neighborhood of equilibrium, e.g., the early stages of recovery. The innovators may undertake the construction of a new plant or equipment to capitalize on their new product or process, often inaugurating a whole new industry in so doing. They are lured on by the prospect of monopoly profits growing out of their headstart or the novelty of their product or achievement. Soon they are followed by a host of imitators or

---

[12] *Ibid.*, p. 63.
[13] *Ibid.*, p. 93.

routineers, as Schumpeter termed them, who cause a secondary wave of expansion, employment and credit creation. Schumpeter indeed argues that even the primary wave of investment is financed largely by the new credit created by the banks rather than an increase in current (*ex ante*) savings, so that the new and induced investment generates a marked upswing in business activity. Old industries are forced to adapt themselves to the changed pattern of demand and those that are not are quickly destroyed. Thus, Schumpeter visualizes capitalism as growing and flourishing in "the perennial gale of creative destruction" in which new industries rise in the process of destroying others that do not meet the demands of consumers or achieve the technological efficiency of the creative entrepreneurs and their new enterprises. Schumpeter champions this dynamic competition, belittling the price competition of the orthodox model:

> But in capitalist reality as distinguished from its textbook picture, it is not that kind of competition [i.e., price competition] which counts but the competition from the new commodity, the new technology, the new source of supply, the new type of organization (the largest-scale unit of control, for instance)—competition which commands a decisive cost or quality advantage and which strikes not at the margins of the profits and outputs of the existing firms but at their foundations and their very lives. This kind of competition is as much more effective than the other as a bombardment is in comparison with forcing a door, and so much more important that it becomes a matter of comparative indifference whether competition in the ordinary sense functions more or less promptly; the powerful lever that in the long run expands output and brings down prices is in any case made of other stuff.[14]

In the Schumpeterian system, different types of innovation tend to produce different types of business cycles. In his work on the latter subject, Schumpeter employed a three-cycle schema, seeking to relate the 44 month Kitchins, the eight or nine year Juglars, and the fifty year "long waves" of Kondratieff. Thus, in this view the sweep of each longer wave provides neighborhoods of equilibrium for the wave of the next lower order. This feature of Schumpeter's system has been much criticized as too rigid and mechanical; the very existence of the Kondratieff type of fluctuations has been seriously questioned and others have complained of the neglect of evidence for a construction and a transport-building cycle.[15] While agreement among economists does not exist on these matters, there would appear to be more acceptance of Schumpeter's insistence on the cyclical character of capitalistic progress. As Schumpeter himself wrote, "Analyzing business cycles means neither more nor less than analyzing the economic process of the capitalist era. . . . Cycles are not, like

---

[14] J. Schumpeter, *Capitalism, Socialism and Democracy* (New York: Harper and Bros., 1947), pp. 84–5.

[15] See Clemence and Doody, *op. cit.*, Chaps. 9 and 10, for a concise statement of these criticisms. The authors of this handy volume are perhaps too favorably disposed toward Schumpeter's work. They state in their general appraisal that "the goal of the Schumpeterian System is the explanation of the process of capitalist economic development. Few models have been constructed with so broad an end in view, and the Schumpeterian System comes closer than any other to achieving it (p. 98).

tonsils, separable things that might be treated by themselves, but are, like the beat of the heart, of the essence of the organism that displays them. . . ."[16]

Schumpeter emphasized that his model of economic growth rested on institutional conditions which "may turn out to belong to an epoch that is rapidly passing." He assumes not only the general features of capitalist society, such as private property and individual initiative, but definite types of both. He presupposes not only money, banks, and banking credit, but also certain attitudes, moral codes, and traditions, especially the spirit of the industrial bourgeoisie and the motivations peculiar to it. Thus, Schumpeter deliberately limited the applicability of his model to the historical epoch prior to what he referred to as the period of Trustified Capitalism.

In the last book he wrote, Schumpeter provided a fascinating sketch of the possible decay of capitalist civilization, tracing the decline of the entrepreneurial economy to its very success. In his view the development of large-scale, bureaucratized enterprise was likely to bring about the obsolescence of the entrepreneurial function. Entrepreneurs, like generals in a society perfectly sure of permanent peace, would become useless; innovation, he held, is being reduced to routine, economic progress tends to become depersonalized and automatized. "Bureau and committee work tends to replace individual action." At the same time, the advance of capitalistic progress destroys the protecting strata of a politically capable land-holding class and encourages a rationalist social atmosphere hostile and critical of the whole scheme of bourgeoisie values. "Thus, the modern corporation," he wrote, "although the product of the capitalist process, socializes the bourgeoisie mind; it relentlessly narrows the scope of capitalist motivation; not only that, it will eventually kill its roots." This process, he believed, was being abetted by the disintegration of the bourgeoisie family, which had given the classic entrepreneur an incentive to work and save for future generations. A champion of capitalist change and innovation, Schumpeter died in the midst of a vast social transformation that he feared was making his carefully worked-out system archaic and irrelevant to the contemporary scene.

[16] *Business Cycles*, vol. 1, p. v.

Chapter 8

BASIC ECONOMIC CHANGES
IN THE YEARS 1815–1843

THE UNITED STATES IN THE ATLANTIC ECONOMY, 1815

Historians have often stated that the year 1820 was a major turning point in the history of the United States; they have stressed that at about that year the nation for the first time turned its face away from Europe and pointed it westward. While it is undoubtedly true that many Americans began to take part in the great trek westward in the years after the depression of 1819, analysis of the deeper economic forces molding American development in this period reveals that the massive changes that occurred have to be seen in the broader context of the Atlantic economy of which we were still a part.[1] Perhaps the best way for us to appreciate this point is to consider briefly the broad outlines of the American economy in 1815 and then take note of the major economic changes during the period 1815–43 that were stimulated by such "exogenous" factors. Actually, our interpretation of the process of economic change in this period embraces both external international forces as well as those internal institutional and innovational developments that determined and shaped the actual organization of economic activity.

The United States in 1815 was predominantly an agricultural country. While manufacturing had made a bold beginning during the recent unpleasantness with the British, the economy was principally an extractive-commercial one in fundamental character. The population of some 8,400,000 was over twice that of 1790, but only about one fourth of that to be reached by the eve of the Civil War. The Americans of that day lived mainly in rural areas; 93 per cent of the people lived on farms or in small towns. There were only thirteen cities having a population of more than 8,000 in 1820, and these communities were very uneven in size. In fact, more than half of the total urban population was concentrated in the six largest cities: New York, Philadelphia, Baltimore, Boston, New Orleans and Charleston.[2] These cities

[1] This point of view is capably maintained by Professor Douglass C. North in his original volume, *The Economic Growth of the United States, 1790–1860* (Englewood Cliffs, N.J.: Prentice-Hall, Inc., 1961). Chap. 7.

[2] G. R. Taylor, *The Transportation Revolution, 1815–1860* (New York: Holt, Rinehart and Winston, 1951), p. 16.

were great seaports and in them much of the commerce of the nation was carried on. The leading citizens of these cities were the merchant capitalists through whose counting houses and warehouses moved merchandise from all over the world to the homes of the aspiring and seemingly insatiable Americans. Life in early nineteenth century America had a seaward orientation, for despite the building of turnpikes and other roads in the years after the Revolution, the sea still remained the chief highway for the transport of goods and passengers. While travel overland was possible, its high cost and slowness were a major barrier to economic development.

Part of the difficulty in developing better transportation was to be found in the natural topography of the nation. As clearly pointed out by Harvey H. Segal in a recent monograph on canals,

> . . . The Appalachian mountain barrier was the principal impediment to the rapid development of the American economy in the early decades of the nineteenth century. Until it was effectively breached, the economy was spatially and functionally compartmentalized. In the eastern seaboard sector, which was endowed with good harbors and a number of navigable rivers, economic development, as measured by the growth of real income per head, was probably proceeding at a moderate rate, stimulated by the rising volume of commodity exports to Europe and South America and the growth of manufacturing activities. But beyond the mountain barrier there was virtual stagnation as manifested by lightly populated though fertile lands, the widespread persistence of subsistence farming, a very low volume of regional exports and unfavorable terms of trade with the east.[3]

> The economic difficulties of the west, as its more reflective inhabitants realized, stemmed proximately from an inability to realize a great wealth potential through the disposition of the region's surplus. At the root of the problem was the high cost of transportation, which in turn acted to depress economic activity. As a consequence, a superabundant supply depressed agricultural prices in the west; and, without access to eastern markets, where prices were considerably higher, there was little incentive to shift from subsistence farming to the production of cash crops.

> The lack of efficient interregional transportation also inhibited economic development in the east. Without transport improvements its domestic market was severely limited—not only by the high costs of shipping products to the west but also by the low level of per capita income in the trans-Appalachian area. By impeding interregional trade the mountain barrier thus imposed a low ceiling upon the growth potential of the American economy. So long as it remained unbroken the country would be divided into two rather distinct economic regions, tenuously linked by an uneconomical, triangular trade via the Mississippi and the Atlantic coast.[4]

The seriousness of the Appalachian mountain barrier to the nation's economic development lay in part in the fact that by 1815 population growth

---

[3] The phrase "terms of trade" refers to the relative cost to an individual or a region of acquiring the goods of another. Measured in real terms, it tells us how much of one's good we must give to acquire that of another.

[4] C. Goodrich, *Canals and American Economic Development* (New York: Columbia University Press, 1961), pp. 221–22.

west of the mountains had become substantial. By 1820, the census reported that there were 2,419,369 people living in the Mississippi valley. These westerners were scattered over a wide area and lived either outside the market economy or at best peripherally to it. They were served with a wide variety of merchandise by the merchants of the small towns or by the itinerant peddlers of the day. It was a striking fact that this vast population of more than two million people supported almost no urban area of any size, with the exception of Cincinnati and New Orleans, which were the only trans-Appalachian cities in 1820 among the list of the thirteen largest. In 1815, the integration of this vast inland empire of the West into the American economy awaited the coming of the Transportation Revolution and the development of markets to absorb its many products.

THE RE-ALLOCATION OF RESOURCES

The manner and speed with which the great structural transformations in the American economy occurred in the 1820's and 1830's can hardly be indicated by statistics. In fact, as we have observed in reviewing the preceding period, the available statistics for these early years of our nation's history are woefully inadequate and, at the same time, surprising. Martin's national income series (the only one available) shows real per capita income declining down to 1829 and not recovering to the 1799 level until 1849. (Table 1)

TABLE 1

Total and Realized National Income, 1819–1839[a]
(adjusted for changes in the cost of living)

Year	Total	Per Capita
	(Millions of dollars)	
1819	1,625	173
1829	2,057	164
1839	3,295	198

[a] Source: R. F. Martin, *National Income in the United States, 1799–1938.*

Agriculture continued to be the leading source of private income in these years with transport and communication and the service trades providing the next largest share, as shown in Table 2. Manufacturing continued to grow also as a source of income for Americans, increasing from 7.5% in 1819 to 10.3% in 1839. As indicated earlier, these percentages must be accepted with some reservation because of the weakness of the underlying statistical data.

TABLE 2

Percentage Distribution of Realized Private Production Income
by Sector of Origin, 1819–1839[a]
(*in percentages*)

	1819	1829	1839
Agriculture	34.4%	34.7%	34.6%
Mining and Quarrying	0.2	0.3	0.3
Manufacturing	7.5	10.3	10.3
Construction	6.8	7.0	6.0
Transportation and Communication	20.6	15.1	17.6
Trade	6.4	6.4	8.6
Service	15.4	17.2	14.1
Miscellaneous, incl. Finance	8.7	8.9	8.6

[a] Source: R. F. Martin, *National Income in the United States, 1799–1938*, pp. 60–61.

Furthermore, we would remind the reader that these figures reflect the distribution of realized income only, i.e., that obtained from the sale of goods or services in the market. A much larger percentage of Americans were engaged in farming in these years than the above percentages suggest; many of them were subsistence farmers whose real "income" is not reflected in such a tabulation.

Martin's total and per capita estimates of national income have been challenged as to their adequacy and accuracy by the distinguished economic statistician, Simon Kuznets.[5] While Martin's statistics are undoubtedly weak, Kuznets' own contention that there was a rising real per capita income over this period as a whole seems equally dubious.[6] His criticism rests upon the assumption of a constant, or rising, level of productivity in agriculture during this period. We cannot examine the data on this matter at this point, but suffice it to say that this view, in the light of the available evidence, seems questionable.[7] It is true that in these years of numerous innovations and remarkable mobility of people and capital that we would expect productivity to rise. But as Samuel Rezneck remarks about this tendency in the reverse direction, "It was one of the paradoxes of U.S. economic development that the very expansion of the frontier and occupation of new land was perhaps a retarding factor in economic growth during the early period. Capital and labor were drawn off into regions not easily accessible, and were not immediately translated into increased output and productivity. The chief lure was the

[5] S. Kuznets, "National Income Estimates for the United States prior to 1870," *Journal of Economic History* (Spring, 1952).

[6] The controversy is capably reviewed in the paper by W. N. Parker and F. Whatenvy, "The Growth of Output before 1840," *Trends in the American Economy in the Nineteenth Century* (Princeton: Princeton University Press, 1960), pp. 206–212.

[7] *Ibid.*, for the reasons for questioning the validity of Kuznets' view.

appreciation of land values, which did not immediately or always materialize."[8]

The changes in agriculture in this period, the decline of the Old South, the large pockets of inefficient subsistence agriculture created after the 1820's as machine and factory production undermined household industry, all these developments militated against rising productivity in agriculture. In this period, in short, there were the beginnings of change in agricultural techniques, in regional specialization, in improved transportation and enlarged markets, but they were only to bear fruit in the form of increased productivity and accelerated economic growth in the years after 1843. In these years the sections were being woven into huge interdependent units of economic specialization; while these disruptive processes were at work, economic efficiency was not appreciably enhanced.

THE LEADING SECTORS OF GROWTH—THE STAPLE CROPS

Professor North has advanced the thesis that the economic growth of these years took place in the form of long surges of expansion followed by periods of slower growth, which seem to be related to the fluctuations in the price of certain key staples, mainly cotton and wheat.[9] North elaborates on his view as follows:

> It was cotton which was the most important influence in the growth in the market size and the consequent expansion of the economy: the slow development of the 1820's, the accelerated growth in the 1830's. In this period of rapid growth, it was cotton that initiated the concomitant expansion in income, in the size of domestic markets, and creation of the social overhead investment (in the course of its role in the marketing of cotton) in the Northeast which were to facilitate the subsequent rapid growth of manufactures. Cotton also accounted for the accelerated pace of westward migration as well as for the movement of people out of self-sufficiency into the market economy.[10]

North does not contend that cotton was the only expansive force in the economy during this period, but he does regard it as "the major independent influence on the evolving pattern of interregional trade."[11]

The validity of North's contention about the dynamic importance of cotton in the economy's growth during this period may be judged in the light of a variety of pertinent statistics. Evaluated in terms of physical output, the production of lint cotton expanded 350 per cent over the years 1820–1840 compared to an increase of 80 per cent for wheat and 77 per cent for corn for the same years. Roughly, during this same period, the dollar value of agricul-

---

[8] *Ibid.*, p. 214.

[9] For an early statement of this view by North see his essay, "International Capital Flows and the Development of the American West," *The Journal of Economic History* (December, 1956), pp. 493–505; also his *The Economic Growth of the U.S.*, p. 66ff.

[10] North, *The Economic Growth*, p. 68.

[11] *Ibid.*

tural output as a whole, as estimated by Martin, grew 85 per cent.[12] Analyzed in terms of its share of the national income, the "direct income from the cotton trade was probably no more than 6 per cent of any plausible estimate of national income which we might employ," but would be appreciably higher if we included the income generated in the transport, financing, and marketing of that staple. But the truly strategic significance of cotton is only seen when we consider its place in the foreign trade of the nation. In 1815 it must be realized that the previous sources of expansion, the re-export, the carrying trade, and manufactures, were declining in the face of increased competition from abroad. Cotton, on the other hand, was experiencing a remarkable growth in demand, both domestic and foreign. Cotton exports mounted steadily to supply the needs of the textile mills of Great Britain and continental factories, as the Industrial Revolution gained momentum in Europe; toward the end of this period the value of cotton exports amounted to over half the total value of all our exports.

Eli Whitney's great invention, the cotton gin, which made its appearance in 1793, made possible the growth of upland short staple cotton, a variety that could be grown over a much larger part of the South. As prices for the staple periodically rose and fell in the expansions that culminated in 1819 and 1836, there occurred huge booms in the sale of public lands, as speculators and planters sought profits in the appreciation of farm values. It will be noticed in Chart 1 that the secular trend of cotton prices over these years was downward; this was because, even though the foreign and domestic demand for the commodity was growing enormously, the supply grew even more rapidly. Before the end of the 1830's the new South in such states as Alabama and Mississippi were producing more cotton than their Southeastern neighbors.

In the West also the lure of new lands and the possibility of speculative profits led to an amazing surge of population and the rapid admission of new states into the Union in these years. The rich soil of the Mississippi Valley drew many Americans westward, as they followed the pattern of settle and sell, settle and sell. One traveller, Morris Birbeck, in 1817 remarked that "Old America seems to be breaking up and moving westward." Twenty years later, the movement was so fast that the trail of westward expansion had crossed the Mississippi and was occupying the first tier of states on the west side. As a popular song of the period put it:

> Come all ye Yankee farmers who wish to change your lot,
> Who've spunk enough to travel beyond your native spot,
> Come follow me and settle in Michigan-i-a,
> Yea, yea, yea, in Michigan-i-a![13]

Other settlers were venturing into southern Wisconsin and Minnesota and "Ioway, Ioway, that's where the tall corn grows!" In an incredibly short

[12] The foregoing percentages are calculated from National Bureau of Economic Research, *Trends in the American Economy in the Nineteenth Century*, pp. 193, 294, 308.

[13] S. E. Morison and H. S. Commager, *The Growth of the American Republic*, Vol. 1 (New York: Oxford University Press, 1937), p. 393.

CHART 1

Public Land Sales and Cotton Prices: 1814–1860

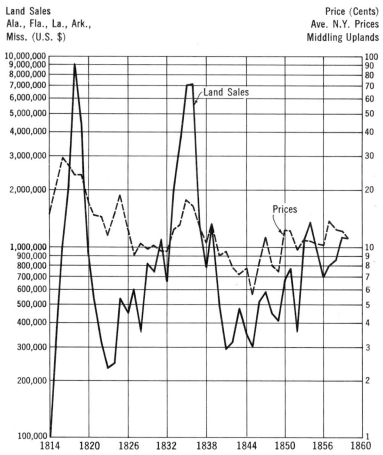

Land Sales
Ala., Fla., La., Ark.,
Miss. (U.S. $)

Price (Cents)
Ave. N.Y. Prices
Middling Uplands

Reproduced from D. C. North, *The Economic Growth of the United States,
1790–1860*, p. 124. By permission of Prentice-Hall, Inc., Englewood Cliffs, New
Jersey.

period, these new states were being admitted into the Union; Indiana in 1816,
Illinois in 1818, Missouri, 1821, and Michigan in 1837. To the south, Stephen
F. Austin and other adventurers were moving into the area of what was to
become Texas in 1821; by 1837, President Jackson had recognized the Lone
Star Republic.

In the western and northern states of this period, corn was by far the most
important crop. While we have estimates of production prior to 1839, the
census data of that year are much more reliable. They indicate an output of
close to 378 million bushels, with Tennessee, Kentucky, and Virginia being the
leading producers in that year. Ten years later, Ohio had jumped into the lead

with Kentucky and Illinois following in that order; total output of the crop had increased to 592 million bushels by that year. Much of this corn was not sold for cash; the farmers of this period, particularly in the Northwest, turned the hogs and cattle into the corn fields and let the animals harvest the crop.

The main cash crop grown by northern farmers in these years was wheat. In 1839, about 50 per cent of the output of close to 85 million bushels was produced by Ohio, Pennsylvania, and New York. As in the case of corn, the centers of production of this crop were shifting westward in this period; but in 1849, Pennsylvania, Ohio, and New York (in that order) were still the leading producers. Leadership in production did not shift to the mid-western states until the 1850's, when the canals began to move the grains east and the eastern farms, which had been gradually losing out to the more productive soil of the west, were turned to other uses. By 1840 many New Englanders were using western flour; with good reason, for whereas Wisconsin wheat farms were yielding 25 bushels to the acre, those in New England were capable of only 10 to 12 bushels.

Other grain crops were produced on northern farms in these years, such as oats, rye, barley, flax, and buckwheat. Of these, oats was by far the most important, but most of it too was harvested by the livestock.

The farm economy of the nation, as is evident from the preceding statistics showing the leading regions of production, was undergoing a basic transformation as farmers shifted to the production of those commodities for which they had the greatest comparative advantage. The opening up of new lands, the shifts of population, and the development of better means of transportation that changed the access of the different regions to markets were drastically altering the relative advantages of the different states as producers of the great American staples.

Prior to the building of the Erie Canal, the produce of the Northwest reached the South by being transported down the Ohio River and its tributaries to the Mississippi and New Orleans, where after being reloaded, it would be carried to other parts of the region. A curious triangular trade had been built up along this route in which grain, hogs and other products of the West were carried to New Orleans, the boat sold, and the merchants would travel around to Philadelphia, Baltimore, and other northern ports and carry manufactured goods, principally fineries, over the Allegheny Mountains to begin the cycle again. The limitations of this method of marketing the West's products tended to restrict their supply and, as we have noted earlier, retarded the development of the region.

THE TRANSPORTATION INDUSTRY

The lack of an efficient means of up-river navigation was nowhere more clearly seen than on the Mississippi River and its tributaries. The journey up this long river in the days before steam was so difficult that the upstream

traffic was about one-tenth of that going down the river. A trip from New
Orleans to Pittsburg took four months or more and required a crew of strong
men to use every conceivable means of propelling a craft upstream.

The steamboat was the first technological innovation to break the geographical isolation of the upper Mississippi Valley and by greatly reducing
transport costs both up and down the river, "gave the first great impetus to
western growth."[14] After Robert Fulton had successfully steamed up the
Hudson in the *Clermont* in 1807, the steamboat was rapidly introduced on the
great rivers and lakes of the West. Fulton and Robert Livingston, his partner,
sought to monopolize the steam navigation of New York waters, but an
unrelenting rival by the name of Thomas Gibbons challenged them, and
finally, in 1824, the Supreme Court in the famous decision of *Gibbons vs.
Ogden* held that the monopoly was invalid because of Congress' plenary power
to regulate interstate commerce.

The Fulton-Livingston group tried, equally unsuccessfully, to maintain a
monopoly of steamboat traffic on the Mississippi, but westerners refused to be
bound by monopoly grants, and by 1817 the legal obstacles were removed and
the flamboyant age of the steamboat on our western rivers had begun.
Steamdriven vessels were to become "the most important factor in the great
industrial development of the Mississippi Valley from 1815 to 1860 and in no
other part of the nation or the world were so many steamboats built and
operated. In 1817, 17 steamboats with a total tonnage of 3,300 operated on
western rivers; by 1845, there were no fewer than 557 with a tonnage of
98,200."[15]

The steamboat did not completely displace other river craft, but rather
stimulated and facilitated their operation. However much ridiculed by deep-
sea sailors, the lightly constructed, shallow draft steamboat was ingeniously
designed to navigate in shallow water. Indeed, western boatmen, in characteristic American fashion, boasted that they needed only a heavy dew to navigate
their stately craft. The saga of the steamboat with its colorful pilots, gamblers,
racers, explosions, and the queer tricks of the Father of Waters was im-
mortally described by Mark Twain in his delightful *Life on the Mississippi*.

The "canal era" began with the opening of the Erie Canal in 1825—a
major landmark in the nation's growth. In the opinion of one student, "Its
opening, indeed, may be regarded as the most decisive single event in the
history of American transportation."[16]

The Erie was started as a result of the strenuous rivalry of the Northeastern
seaports to capture the trade of the rich hinterland behind the Appalachian
barrier. The possibilities of aiding the development of the nation by internal

[14] G. R. Taylor, *The Transportation Revolution, 1815–1860* (New York: Rinehart and
Co., 1951), p. 159.

[15] L. C. Hunter, *Steamboats on the Western Rivers* (Cambridge: Harvard University
Press, 1949), p. 33.

[16] C. Goodrich, *Government Promotion of American Canals and Railroads, 1800–1890*
(New York: Columbia University Press, 1960), p. 55.

improvements had been proposed by John Quincy Adams, Secretary Gallatin in his remarkable *Report on Roads and Canals*,[17] and by other men of vision, but no project as large as this had been carried out in the nation. Indeed, with the exception of the Languedoc Canal in France in the seventeenth century, "no one in the western world had ever built a lock-canal one tenth the size of the Erie; and most of the European canals had been dug through regions fully settled and cleared. The remarkable fact is that a population of little more than a million took on an expected burden of $5–6 million in order to build an immensely long canal through a sparsely settled wilderness without the aid of a single experienced engineer. . . ."[18]

Under the inspired leadership of DeWitt Clinton, New York State pushed through the completion of this first grand trunk canal in the nation after eight years of labor over a distance of 363 miles. It cost some 7 million dollars, but during the first nine months of its operation tolls exceeded 8.5 million dollars. By 1882, when tolls were abolished on the Canal, the Erie had collected $120 million. During its construction, cities outside New York had shown no anxiety but rather expressed their ridicule, but when, upon completion, its success was soon demonstrated, there was a veritable mania to imitate the great innovation. Between 1815 and 1860, some $195 million was spent on canal construction, of which sum $121 million was spent by state government and $74 million by private companies.[19] Down to 1890, Carter Goodrich has estimated, Americans built some 4,000 miles of canals, nearly twice the mileage of the renowned British system.

Philadelphia tried to match its arch rival's system by building the Mainline Canal to Pittsburgh. But the Allegheny Mountains made necessary portage of its canal boats over heights as great as 2,000 feet, whereas the maximum elevation encountered over New York's water-level route was about 500 feet. This handicap could never be overcome; the Mainline was a dismal financial failure. Boston planned a canal to the Hudson River, but here too topographical conditions made it impracticable. In the following years, the New England capital suffered a serious loss of trade. Baltimore's project, the Chesapeake and Ohio Canal Co., was stymied by sectional conflicts over terminals. As a result, the Baltimore and Ohio Railroad was started instead by Maryland in 1828. Of the four interregional canals designed to link the eastern seaboard with the trans-Appalachian west, the Erie alone was successful.

The canals built in the middle west during these years had as their prime aim the connecting of the Great Lakes with the Ohio River, thus making possible a continuous inland waterway from New York to New Orleans. Thus,

[17] See Chapter 2 of Goodrich's work for a most interesting description of this famous report.

[18] C. Goodrich, ed., *Canals and American Economic Development* (New York: Columbia University Press, 1961), p. 65.

[19] This is the estimate of Jerome Cranmer in his paper, "Canal Investment, 1815–1860," in National Bureau of Economic Research, *Trends in the American Economy in the 19th Century*, p. 558.

the Ohio and Erie Canal connecting Cleveland and Portsmouth was completed in 1833. The Miami and Erie joined Toledo and Cincinnati in 1829. The Wabash and Erie ran from Toledo to Evansville and was finished in 1843. The Illinois and Michigan Canal was started in 1836 and not completed until 1848. The routes of some of these canals are shown in the map below.

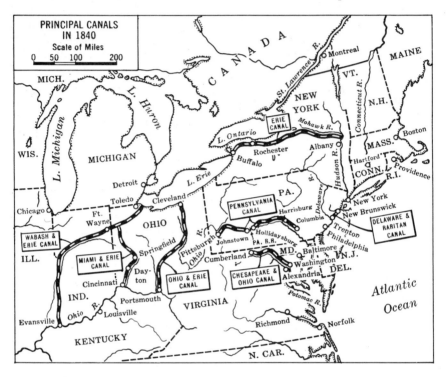

Map of Principal Canals in 1840 from *American Economic History*, 5th Edition, by Harold Underwood Faulkner (Harper and Row, 1943).

The canals of this period were largely financed by state borrowing, and the cycles of investment in them are closely related to the fluctuations in business activity that we shall examine later in this chapter. Suffice it to say that when the total of state debts reached a near-peak of $170 million in 1838, $60 million of this is estimated to have been for canals; the rest was invested in banks, railroads, and roads. Although more than a fifth of the total investment in canals represented failures, the system as a whole in the United States, in the opinion of a recent student, was successful in terms of the customary tests of benefit-cost analysis.[20] We shall study the direct and indirect effects of the canals upon American economic growth in more detail in the next chapter.

[20] Harvey H. Segal in Goodrich, ed., *Canals and American Economic Development*, p. 247.

THE MERCHANT MARINE

In those years ocean shipping was another growth industry; indeed, the earlier part of the period has often been characterized as "the golden age of the United States merchant marine." By 1826, in fact, the proportion of American carriage in foreign trade reached 92.5 per cent, a larger percentage than had been attained before or since.

The first important marine innovation after the War of 1812 was the trans-Atlantic packet line. Up to that time, there had been two types of vessels engaged in our foreign trade: tramp ships and regular traders. The first, as the term suggests, followed no fixed route or schedule and in sailing from port to port, would accept any available cargo. The latter, usually larger than the tramps, customarily traded between a fixed number of predetermined ports. Increasingly during this period these ships, which were usually owned by the more important merchants, acted as common carriers. They carried most of the passengers and the mail because the unpredictable schedules of the tramp vessels made them unsuitable for these purposes.

The novelty of the packet lines lay in the fact that they not only operated on regular routes, but they sailed on definite time schedules upon which shippers could depend. The Black Ball Line inaugurated the packet service in 1818 when the *James Madison* sailed from New York for Liverpool and, slightly later, the *Courier* left Liverpool for New York. For four years, this pioneer line had no competitors, but with improving business in 1822 there was a host of imitators of the idea. The packet lines soon had the cream of the trans-Atlantic business, such as the mails, most of the passengers, and the best-paying freight, such as goods having high value in small bulk. They also carried much bulky freight, such as cotton, flour, and tobacco. By 1845 no fewer than 52 trans-Atlantic packets were sailing from New York. Other eastern and southern ports tried to establish such services, but generally they were no match for the aggressive New Yorkers. Many packet lines also operated in the coastwise trade during this period. Most of the vessels engaged in this trade were small, except for the large square-riggers, which plied between New York and the cotton ports.

After about 1825 there was a noticeable tendency for the ships, the square-riggers as well as the packets, to be built larger, with sharper lines, and more sail. The growing concentration of trade in the major ports, the increased role of these ships as common carriers of bulky products, such as cotton, and the demand for speed and better passenger accommodations on the Atlantic voyage —all these factors were behind the growing size of ships. Curiously enough, though the *Savannah* was the first steamship to cross the Atlantic in 1819, economic and technical difficulties hampered the steam-driven vessel in its competition with the increasingly efficient sailing vessels. While better progress was made by steamships on shorter sea voyages in these years, it was not until 1838 that steamship service was established on the Atlantic, and another decade passed before its rapid growth took place. The net earnings of the U.S. shipping as a whole as well as the earnings of foreign ships carrying U.S. imports in these years are shown in Chart 2.

CHART 2

Net U.S. Shipping Earnings and Earnings of Foreign Ships Carrying U.S. Imports: 1815–1860
(in Millions of Dollars)

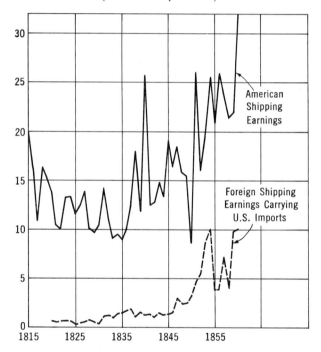

Reproduced from D. C. North, *The Economic Growth of the United States, 1790–1860* (Englewood Cliffs, N.J.: Prentice-Hall, Inc., 1961), p. 78, with the permission of the publisher.

FOREIGN TRADE AND DOMESTIC COMMERCE

The poor quality of statistical data, especially on interregional trade during this period, makes comparison of the volume and value of foreign trade and domestic commerce a subject for estimation rather than for precise measurement. Still the general direction of the trend seems fairly clear. The foreign trade of the nation reached extraordinary heights, as we have seen, during the years of our neutrality in the European Wars. For the immediate post-war period, 1816–1820, the total foreign trade of the United States averaged $186 million a year. While we have no comparable statistics for domestic commerce for these years, we do know that Secretary of the Treasury Walker estimated in 1846 that the value of American production, "interchanged among the several states of the Union," was worth at least $500 million. In comparison, the total foreign trade of the United States for that year was reported to be $277 million and for the five years 1832–36 it averaged $226 million.[21] In brief, these and other data for the period suggest that the nation in these years was transacting a volume of domestic commerce that was gradually exceeding the volume and value of its foreign trade.

The causes for this remarkable expansion in the nation's internal commerce during this period were many, but most fundamental was the fact that with increasing geographical specialization the basis of domestic trade was correspondingly enlarged. As Southern planters devoted increased amounts of their productive resources to the growth of cotton and other export crops, they came to rely upon other regions of the nation for commodities that they could not produce so advantageously. The West shipped them foodstuffs while the Northeast provided banking, insurance, brokerage, and transport services and supplied both Western and Southern farmers with goods of its own manufacture or with imports.

The quantitative indices of the growth of this interregional trade are incomplete, but some measures are available. We see the value of receipts of produce from the interior at New Orleans growing sixfold from 1815–16 to 1843–44; the tonnage moving over the Erie Canal from the Western states to tidewater swells almost sixfold between 1836 and 1843; the tonnage of vessels in the Atlantic coasting trade practically doubled over these same years.[22]

The foreign trade of the United States underwent important shifts in its composition during this period. The re-export trade, which had been so important in earlier years, grew in value from a low of $6.5 million in 1815 to approximately $24 million in 1825. After that date, it suffered an irregular decline so that New York merchants who had done the bulk of the business found themselves tied more closely to the cotton trade. While it lasted, Americans handled a great variety of products—tropical and semi-tropical products from the West Indies and Central and South America, Canadian wheat, Far Eastern goods, etc., not to overlook British cotton textiles and other manufactures, which were the most important items of all. Until the 1830's Americans re-exported a great quantity of British cotton textiles, but after that date they increasingly exported large quantities of cheap domestic cotton cloth.

American commodity exports were the leading earners of foreign exchange in these years, with raw cotton accounting for more than one half of the total value of our exports. The total value of exports rose from $52.5 million in 1815 to a high of $124 million in 1836, before receding to a depression low of

[21] Taylor, *The Transportation Revolution, 1815–1860*, Table 4 of Appendix A, p. 445.
[22] North, *The Economic Growth of the United States*, pp. 104–112 and Appendix II for charts exhibiting the interregional flows during this period.

$83 million in 1843. The immense importance of raw cotton exports in our foreign trade can be seen in the fact that their value in 1840 was close to $64 million, compared to a value of $3.5 million for manufactured cotton (the leading export of manufactured products) and of $31 million for manufactures of all kinds.[23] Wheat and tobacco were important exports during the early part of this period, but later they declined, largely because of competition from other sources of supply.

MANUFACTURING

The statistics of Tables 2 and 3 presented earlier in this chapter reveal that, relatively, manufacturing was one of the fastest growing sectors of the economy during these years. Viewed from another perspective, that of comparison with the rate of population growth over a somewhat longer period than we are analyzing in this section, we find that whereas population of the United States increased less than four times between 1815 and 1860, the value of manufactured products grew about eightfold and their volume nearly twelvefold.[24] But these statistics can be misleading if we do not take careful account of the qualitative character of "manufacturing" in these years. At the beginning of the period, the bulk of manufactured products was accounted for by what Professor Taylor terms "the household-handicraft-mill complex." Household manufacturing was, in fact, the chief form of industry in these postwar years. As a result of the embargo and the war with Britain, household manufacture of textiles, according to one estimate, went from $38 million in 1810 to $120 million in 1816. As much as two-thirds of the clothing worn in the United States in these years was made in the home.

This household manufacture was supplemented typically, particularly in the more populous eastern sections of the nation, by the handiwork of a wide variety of craftsmen, such as cobblers, blacksmiths, hatters, tailors, weavers, etc. The less settled parts of the country were served by travelling journeymen who utilized the raw materials supplied by the customer in making goods to order. The more successful of these craftsmen often set up shop in the larger towns and cities, hired apprentices, and made products for general sale as well as for specific order. Many of these communities had long been supplied also by small gristmills and sawmills, which typically utilized local materials to meet the needs of consumers in very restricted local markets. While there were merchant mills and furnaces favored by cheap water transportation that carried on production on a larger scale, these were the exception rather than the rule. The limitations of the existing means of overland transportation

---

[23] *Ibid.*, p. 233; Taylor, *The Transportation Revolution*, p. 189; *Historical Statistics of the United States, 1789–1945*, p. 247.

[24] Taylor, *The Transportation Revolution*, p. 207.

narrowed the geographical scope of most enterprises of this kind and consequently forced them to operate on a small scale of production. The revolution
in transportation, which was so marked in these years, remade the market
environment of most of the existing manufacturing activity and led to a
fundamental transformation of its character and scope. The transition from
household manufactures to other, more market-oriented modes of production
became especially marked after 1830. But the changeover was neither orderly
nor uniform; rates of change differed from industry to industry. In general,
the demand for more manufactured goods was met in one of three ways:
increased shop production occurred as in the famous Danbury, Connecticut
hat shops, which gradually became bigger until the factory system began to
appear in the 1850's. Secondly, increased demand led in some lines such as
shoes, textiles, and men's clothing, to the rise of the domestic or putting-out
system. In this mode of production, a merchant or master craftsman supplied
the raw materials to workers in their homes, often women and children, and
after they had performed some operation on the material, he would collect it
and send it on to market. Lastly, there was the spread of the factory system
as markets widened and the volume of demand increased. It is to be noted,
however, that the initial result of this widening of markets was to modify and
enlarge production, not to cause the immediate adoption of the factory system
in any uniform way.

In boot and shoe manufacture, where the domestic system had perhaps its
most significant development, expanding demand led at first to a dispersal of
some of the manufacturing functions to the homes of workers where a pool of
part-time and under-employed, cheap labor could be obtained. Similar considerations led to the use of the domestic system in the weaving of cotton and
woolen cloths and the making of men's clothing, buttons, horse whips, sus-
penders, and straw and palm-leaf hats.

These years witnessed many significant beginnings of the factory system
and its spread in cotton textiles from the crude, pioneer efforts of a Samuel
Slater, but they did not see the full development of this marvelously efficient
method of production. The cotton textile industry ranked first during most of
these years among all American industries in terms of value added by
manufacture and as the example *par excellence* of the factory system. After
weathering the hard times of the immediate post-war years, the industry,
according to the Census of 1820, had 250,000 spindles in operation. Between
that year and 1831, the number of spindles quadrupled and factory looms
increased tenfold. In the vanguard of this growth were the enterprises established at Waltham, Lowell, and Chicopee, Massachusetts and other New
England towns by Francis Cabot Lowell and a group of fellow Bostonians.
The daring innovations of this great entrepreneur will be examined in more
detail in the following chapter; suffice it to say here that by 1850 it has been
estimated that the group of businessmen who exploited his "breakthrough" in
cotton textile manufacturing, famous as the Boston Associates, alone produced
about one-fifth of the total output of cotton cloth in the nation. Their success

in the use of the factory system accelerated its wide adoption in textiles and many other industries.

The factory system replaced the household method of manufacturing in many other lines after about 1830 as the relative efficiency of power-driven machinery and the newly-found virtues of the corporate form of organization in raising capital were increasingly recognized. Its growing dominance was often relatively gradual and unspectacular and its spread was very uneven, depending as it did on the possibilities of technological development, the need for standardized products, the varying possibilities of profit, and the availability of capital. In addition to cotton textiles, the factory system was of growing importance in such industries as woolen manufactures, carpets, boots and shoes, iron products, flour milling products, men's clothing, etc. Still we should not exaggerate this pre-Civil War development of the factory system. Compared to the post-war growth, the increase in capital invested in manufacturing from approximately $100 million in 1828 to $300 million ten years later was but an auspicious beginning.

FINANCE, PRIVATE AND PUBLIC

The expansion of banking facilities was one of the major phenomena of these years. As the statistics of Table 3 demonstrate, the growth of the nation's banks, their deposits and loans and discounts, would seem to have more than kept pace with its extraordinary expansion. Still, as we shall see, the adequacy both in terms of quantity and quality of the circulating medium and of the bank credit extended was one of the principal foci of political controversy in the hectic, Jacksonian era.

The state banks played a critical role in financing the land speculation, which was so conspicuous a feature of the economic growth of this period. These banks, like the insurance companies, roads, and canals built in these years, constituted indispensable social overhead capital so necessary for

TABLE 3

Outline of Banking Development, 1820–1843[a]

Year	Number of Banks	Loans and Discounts (In units of $1 million)	Deposits
1820	307	——	$ 31.2
1830	329	$159.8	55.6
1834	506	324.1	102.3
1837	788	525.1	189.8
1843	691	254.5	77.6

[a] Source: U.S. Bureau of the Census, *Historical Statistics of the United States, 1789–1945* (Washington, D.C.: Government Printing Office, 1949), pp. 261, 263.

further development. Not to be overlooked also were the Anglo-American merchant bankers who supplied so much of the credit for the extensive import trade in these years.[25] Eight large English houses dominated this business, including such famous banks as Baring Brothers and Company, W. and J. Brown and Company, and Rothschild and Sons. These banks extended lines or "letters" of credit to American importers. The English exporters could then draw drafts payable in sterling upon the American importers, send them to one of these banks in their own country and upon acceptance, such bankers' acceptances were readily discounted. Meanwhile, the invoice and bills of lading for such shipments were sent to the bank's agency in America, for delivery to the importer. Payment would be made directly to the agency of the English bank in this country, a purely domestic transaction. The sterling balances so accumulated could later be transferred to the parent house in England. We have sketched the procedures of this method of import financing because of its great importance in the international trade of that day.

Among the many other functions performed by these bankers, not the least was their role as intermediaries in the flow of long-term capital to the United States in this period. Our earlier description of canal and railroad construction in these years has emphasized the part played by state governments in this expansion. Much of the capital needed for such activities came from abroad. It has been estimated that nearly one-half of the state bonds issued between 1818 and 1828 made their way, directly or indirectly, to Europe. Another estimate tells us that $300 million of foreign capital was loaned to the United States between 1815 and 1840. These English banks and some new American "investment houses" such as Thomas Biddle and Company, Astor and Sons, Brown Brothers and Company, which made their appearance in these years, underwrote the securities for these ventures, selling them at home or abroad.

Underlying and, indeed, making possible this huge import of foreign capital were our exports of the staple crops, principally cotton and wheat. During most of this period the balance of trade of the United States was usually unfavorable. In the most expansive phases of the economy's growth during this period, as in 1815–18 and 1831–39, the terms of trade became extremely favorable and at such times there was an increased capital inflow.[26] Professor North's investigations make it clear that international capital movements were not the cause or initiating factor in the periodic surges in expansion in these years, but they did play "a vital role in making possible each expansion and in influencing its duration and character. The importance of foreign capital lay in directing real resources into transportation and plantation expansion and sustaining this expansion by making possible an import surplus."[27]

[25] R. W. Hidy, "The Organization and Functions of Anglo-American Merchant Bankers, 1815–1860, *Journal of Economic History*, Supplement I (1941), pp. 53–66.
[26] North, *The Economic Growth of the United States*, pp. 91, 94.
[27] D. C. North, "International Capital Flows and the Development of the American West," *The Journal of Economic History* (December, 1956), as reproduced in H. N. Scheiber, *United States Economic History* (New York: Alfred A. Knopf, 1964), pp. 173–4.

What, in effect, North's analysis indicates is that if we as a nation had to wait until we had accumulated the necessary capital for these internal improvements, our growth would have been so much slower. As it was, by exporting the staple crops on as large a scale as we did and earning foreign exchange in other ways, the nation was able to effect huge amounts of capital formation without greater restrictions or retrenchment on domestic consumption.

As later treatment will disclose, fundamental institutional changes were occurring that made possible the raising of the larger sums of capital. Notable among these was the increased use of the corporate form of business enterprise and the steps taken toward the close of this period to facilitate the chartering of such organizations. We refer in the latter to the passage of the general incorporation act in Connecticut in 1837, which provided a precedent for many other states. Actually, in these years corporations were used to organize railroads, canals, banks, and other public utility enterprises. Other than these, their use was still extremely limited. "The shares of an industrial corporation appeared on an exchange in 1827, but this was an isolated exception, well ahead of its time. . . ."[28] The shares of six manufacturing corporations were traded in on the Boston exchange in 1830, another indication of the relative infrequency with which industrial corporations tapped the capital market for funds. Industrial capital had to grow in large part in these years through self-accretion. Callendar contended that so much of the available capital in the United States was in the hands of small savers, who sought security, that there was a dearth of speculative venture capital and hence the need to rely on public securities or the securities of corporations that were guaranteed or assisted by the government.[29]

The growing needs of the new nation for capital were reflected in the increased importance of New York City as a financial center. During the 1820's, in fact, New York City displaced Philadelphia as the country's leading capital market. Security trading increased so much in Manhattan that a second exchange, the New Board of Brokers, was established. The rivalry between these two financial centers played a part, as we shall see, in the struggle over the re-chartering of the Second Bank of the United States.

The fiscal operations of government, federal, state, and local, had varying effects on the growth of the economy in these years, but aside from expenditures on internal improvements, their direct impact on business was not too large because of the relatively small scale of governmental activity. Martin's statistics on the income realized from government show the amounts ranging from $17 million in 1819 to $39 million in 1839; in percentage terms, the income realized from government in these years was no more than 1.9–2.4 per

[28] W. J. Shultz and M. R. Caine, *Financial Development of the United States* (Englewood Cliffs, N.J.: Prentice-Hall, Inc., 1937), p. 192.

[29] G. S. Callendar, "The Early Transportation and Banking Enterprises of the States in Relation to the Growth of Corporations," *Quarterly Journal of Economics*, XVII (1903), pp. 11–162, as reproduced in J. T. Lambie and R. V. Clemence, *Economic Change in America* (Harrisburg, Pa.: The Stackpole Co., 1954), p. 551.

cent of the total realized national income.[30] However, the effect of government upon enterprise and economic growth cannot be limited simply to analysis of government as a source of income; while governments in this period did not assume the entrepreneurial role, the state governments in particular pursued promotive policies that were of great importance in establishing the foundations and conditions for economic growth.

The recovery from the depression of 1819 enabled most of the states to establish a satisfactory equilibrium in their finances. In the prosperous years leading up to the boom of 1836, many of them borrowed on long term to finance internal improvements; it has been estimated that the state governments as a whole borrowed $175 million between 1820 and 1837. With the collapse of prosperity in the latter year, many of them defaulted on their interest payments and some even repudiated their debts.

The pattern of federal finance in these years contrasted rather markedly with that of the state governments. As Chart 3 shows, the federal government enjoyed substantial surpluses in its accounts after 1821 (1824 was an exception), until the depression of 1837 resulted in six annual deficits before the upturn came in 1844. The deficits of these and earlier years were not the result of deliberate policy so much as the consequence of the cyclical fluctuations in business activity. The administrations in power in these years did not pursue compensatory fiscal policies, but rather by their financial practices and efforts to achieve budgetary balances, often aggravated the booms and intensified the depressions.

In 1817, the federal government had $120 million of federal debt outstanding. By 1828, half of this total had been retired and four years later the federal debt was cleared off entirely. The causes and consequences of this remarkable achievement will be analyzed below.[31]

CYCLICAL FLUCTUATIONS IN THE GROWTH OF THE ECONOMY

The economic growth of the nation during these years was far from being steady and progressive. It consisted rather of surges of expansion and accelerated movement, followed by periods of depression and retarded growth. On the whole, the depressions of this period were more serious and prolonged than those of the preceding years in the nation's history. Seemingly, as the economy became more complex and interdependent, both interregionally and internationally, it became subject to a larger number of disruptive forces.

The readjustment to the end of the War of 1812 in the years 1816–18 led to conditions of mixed prosperity and depression. Domestic manufacturing such

[30] R. F. Martin, *National Income in the United States, 1799–1938* (New York: National Industrial Conference Board, 1939), p. 87.
[31] See pp. 188, 212.

Chart 3

Federal Expenditures, Receipts and Surplus (+) or Deficit (−)
for the Years, 1815–1844[a]
(In millions of dollars)

a Source: U.S. Bureau of the Census, *Historical Statistics of the*
United States, 1789–1945, pp. 297–301.
b Totals will not always add up because the data have not been
rounded.

as had grown up during the years of the embargo and the war was subject to a
"shakedown" in which only the efficient survived. In agriculture, on the other
hand, the huge demand for our staples abroad, partly owing to the progress of
the Industrial Revolution in Great Britain and poor crops in Europe generally,
led to the settlement of huge areas of land in the West and South, accompanied by liberal credit policies to finance their development. This land
"boom," characterized by the speculative fever and excessive expectations that
mark most periods of this kind, collapsed in 1818–19 with the decline in the
prices for manufactured goods, cotton, and other staples. The ensuing depression lasted until 1821 in the Northeast and until 1823 in the West and South.

The economy grew relatively slowly in the 1820's, picked up speed in the 1830's and then went on another speculative spree of investment in land in 1836–37. Financial panic hit the nation in 1837, and then severe depression set in again in 1839, which lasted until 1843. This depression was one of the most severe and protracted in our pre-Civil War history. The cyclical fluctuations of this period pose difficult problems in analysis, for they are compounded of both domestic and external factors so far as causation is concerned. A most interesting question has to do with their relation to the so-called "long swings," which a number of economists have noted in the economic growth of the nation. This and other similar questions will be our main concern in the analysis of the following chapter.

Chapter 9

THE ROLE OF STAPLE EXPORTS AND CREATIVE ENTREPRENEURSHIP IN THE ECONOMY'S GROWTH

THE STAPLE THEORY AND ECONOMIC GROWTH

In the Introduction to this Part, the staple theory was described and it was stated that the key idea of this theory is the spread effects of the export sector; i.e., the impact of the export trade on the rest of the domestic economy and society. The organization of this chapter will be centered on the testing of this hypothesis and that of Schumpeter's theory of creative entrepreneurship as explanatory frameworks for understanding the developments of the period. Given the limited space of a single chapter, the treatment will, of necessity, be brief; it is to be hoped that the reader will be led to make additional inquiries into neglected aspects of the subject.

As the Introduction states, "The chief determinants of the spread effects of the export staple—given the resource base of the new country and the environment of the rest of the world—is the character of the staple or staples being exported and, more especially, its technology, which tends to determine the production function of the industry." Since we have already examined the relative importance of cotton in the economy's growth in this period in the preceding chapter, we can proceed to examine the economic and social structure that grew out of its technology and mode of production and compare it with those of grain production in the West during the same years.[1]

One of the principal facts to keep in mind in comparing these two regions is the tremendous comparative advantage in cotton growing in the South because this factor, apart from slavery itself, greatly influenced the structure and the utilization of the factors within the region. While this comparative advantage varied with changes in the prices and costs of cotton production

[1] North, *The Economic Growth of the United States, 1790–1860.* Chaps. 10 and 11 present a cogent analysis in outline form of these matters; see also P. W. Gates, *The Farmer's Age; Agriculture, 1815–1860* (New York: Holt, Rinehart and Winston, 1960), Chaps. 7–9; K. Stampp, *The Peculiar Institution: Slavery in the Ante-Bellum South* (New York: Knopf, 1956).

and the prices of alternative products, it was only in the depths of the depression of 1839–43 that cotton prices were so low that a planter might consider shifting his capital and labor to other uses. Cotton production was not only the most efficient use of the region's resources as a whole, but more important, it yielded a return upon capital throughout most of this period, which attracted funds from the old South, the Northeast, and Europe.[2]

In fact, the alternative uses for resources in the South were limited. Rice and sugar could only be planted with profit in certain areas, and when tobacco production declined, states such as Virginia and North Carolina found it difficult to discover profitable alternatives other than cotton. Likewise, South Carolina, which continually lost slaves and capital to the new western states of the Cotton Belt, faced a serious problem of adjustment because of the lack of substitutes for cotton.[3]

The growth and cultivation of cotton had special requirements that gave the plantation system based on slavery an unusual advantage in this period. Cotton was a crop requiring much labor for hoeing, chopping, and picking; it was, in other words, labor intensive, and employed relatively little inanimate capital. On the other hand, it entailed an extensive use of land, and as its production moved west in these years, the plantations became larger. Yields were higher and production costs lower in the Southwest as compared with the old South. The optimum combination of factors demanded large amounts of labor and land; in other words, there were substantial economies of scale. For example, whereas the average size farm in the United States in 1850 was 203 acres, in Mississippi and Alabama the average sizes were 309 and 289 acres, respectively, and in Texas the average was 942 acres. The plantations were large in the more fertile regions; in the rich black belt of south central Alabama, the average size of farms ranged as high as 770 acres. Alabama boasted 696 plantations of 1,000 acres or more, and over 2,000 between 500 and 1,000 acres.[4] The scale of operations was increasing, especially in the Southwest, and the big planters were making it harder and harder for their smaller rivals to compete profitably. Stampp writes, "The planters who owned more than thirty slaves were the ones who achieved maximum efficiency, the most complex economic organization, and the highest degree of specialization within their labor forces. Slightly less than half of the slaves belonged to the approximately twenty-five thousand masters operating plantations of these dimensions. . . ."[5] Some of the largest plantation owners had over 1,000 slaves, though since supervision became difficult when the number exceeded 100 or 125 on any one plantation, so large a number would be spread over several plantations.

[2] A. H. Conrad and J. R. Meyers, "The Economics of Slavery in the Ante-Bellum South, *Journal of Political Economy* (April, 1958), pp. 95–130.

[3] A. G. Smith, Jr., *Economic Readjustment of an Old Cotton State, South Carolina, 1820–1860* (Columbia, S.C.: University of South Carolina Press, 1958).

[4] Gates, *The Farmer's Age . . .* , p. 147.

[5] Stampp, *The Peculiar Institution*, p. 38.

The marketing of the cotton and the other staple crops of the South was such that it required relatively small amounts of capital for social overhead purposes and brought little in the way of distributive industries into existence. The abundance of navigable rivers simplified the transportation problems of the larger planters and those who were not located on rivers had usually only short hauls by wagon to reach a port. The crop was handled by the numerous "factors" who had their main offices in New York or other northern cities; they served as intermediaries between the planters and the "outside world." They sold the planter's crop for a commission and bought the necessary consumption goods for him on credit. As for the other services of banking and insurance, the earlier development of these activities in the Northeast gave the northerners insuperable advantages in the way of experience and connections with bankers abroad, etc., compared to would-be southern rivals.

Another basic factor that hampered the development of direct trade on the part of southern merchants with Great Britain and Europe was the economics of water transportation, as it had developed up to that time. Cotton as a cargo occupied a great deal of shipping space, far more than the return cargoes of manufactured goods coming from Great Britain, with the consequence that the freight rates on the latter were extremely low. This structure of rates gave little protection to possible southern efforts at manufacturing, and more important, the unbalanced route structure made New York and other northern cities more desirable as ports of call for the ships coming from the Old World than the southern ports. The earlier headstart of New York in trade and its access to the commerce of the whole country assured shippers of more cargo on the western voyage by making it their destination rather than a southern port. The European merchandise destined for the South, therefore, was channeled through northern ports and then re-shipped to the South; likewise, for the reasons indicated the South's raw cotton was usually shipped via New York or other northern ports to its European purchasers. This pattern of trade and transportation tied the South to a heavy dependence upon the services of the businessmen of the Northeast and, correspondingly, discouraged more autonomous activity of this nature in its own region.[6]

The supply of slaves was vital for the preservation of the plantation system. Indeed, Conrad and Meyer have argued that the production of slaves as an intermediate good was an essential feature of the plantation system. As they conclude, "Slavery was profitable to the whole South, the continuing demand for labor in the Cotton Belt ensuring returns to the breeding operation on the less productive land in the seaboard and border states. The breeding returns were necessary, however, to make the plantation operations on the poorer lands as profitable as alternative contemporary economic activities in the United States. . . ."[7] While Ulrich Phillips and others have argued that the

[6] North, "Ocean Freight Rates and Economic Development, 1750–1913," *Journal of Economic History* (December, 1958), pp. 537–555.

[7] A. H. Conrad and J. R. Meyer, *The Economics of Slavery* (Chicago: Aldine Publishing Co., 1964), p. 82.

plantation system had an "irresistible tendency to overvalue and overcapitalize" its slave supply, citing the tendency of the falling prices of cotton and the increased price of slaves to converge (see Chapter 15, Chart 1), Conrad and Meyer hold that the rise in the price of a prime field hand from $600 to $1800 represented a rational increased capitalization of the value of slaves. They point out that Phillips' approach neglects the change in the productivity of the slaves. Their data show that the crop value per slave rose from $14.68 in 1802 to $101.09 in 1860. Furthermore, when one divides the crop value per slave by the corresponding price of slaves over these years, there is no evidence of a decline; rather, the productivity of the slave, measured in these terms, seems to have at least doubled.

The plantation system and the unequal distribution of income it promoted had very serious consequences also for the economic growth of the South on the demand side. The poverty of the slaves, subsistence farmers, and poor whites created a condition of insufficient aggregate demand in the region, which inhibited industrialization and agricultural diversification. Thus, by way of demonstrating this effect, Genovese points out that ". . . The slaveholding farms and plantations in Mississippi annually spent about thirty or thirty-five dollars per person for food and supplies; non-slaveholders spent about twenty-five dollars per person. In Georgia, slaveholding farms and plantations spent about twenty-five dollars per person, and non-slaveholders were just about self-sufficient. In contrast, Philip Foner reports that contemporary newspapers and other sources indicate that the small farmers who made up the great majority of the rural population of the West accumulated store bills of from one hundred to six hundred dollars. . . ."[8]

Plantation slavery in this view so limited the mass purchasing power of the South that it could not sustain much industry. This effect is manifested also in the remarkable lack of urbanization in the South in these years and a corresponding low level of development of such a residentiary industry as retailing. With the exception of Baltimore and New Orleans, the slave states had no large cities and only three with a population of more than 15,000 (Mobile, Charleston, and Savannah). The urban population of the lower South in 1860 was only 7 per cent of the total population, whereas in New England the percentage was 37 per cent; in the Middle Atlantic states, including Ohio, 35 per cent; and in Indiana, Illinois, Michigan, and Wisconsin, 14 per cent. The retarding effects of this plantation culture of the South upon the development of a local service industry such as retailing is evident in the fact that in an enumeration of retail stores by states in the 1840 census, most of the southern states were at the bottom of the list of stores per thousand of population.[9]

Finally, but even more suggestive of the retarded and retarding economic

[8] E. D. Genovese, "The Significance of the Slave Plantation for Southern Economic Development," *The Journal of Southern History* (November, 1963), pp. 422–37 as reproduced in H. N. Scheiber, *United States Economic History* (New York: Knopf, 1964), p. 158.

[9] North, *The Economic Growth of the United States*, p. 132.

environment of the South, was the slow development of public education. In 1840 the ratio of pupils in school to the white population was one-third of that in the non-slaveholding states. Illiteracy was equally greater in the South than in the states having free labor.

The West in these years presented a very different economic pattern from that which we have described for the South. It was a less homogeneous region than the latter, being subject to more rapid change and having a wider variety of activities within its bounds. The pattern of settlement was widely dispersed, as the settlers staked claims over large areas, first along the watercourses of the main streams, then in the interior, and lastly on the limitless prairies. After thirty or forty years of settlement, the dominant figure was that of the middling farmer, the owner of a hundred or two-hundred acre farm and of a substantial frame house. His total worth was between five and ten thousand dollars. His property might include an orchard, sheep, cows, horses, hogs, oxen, and domestic fowl. Typically, he fattened his pork on his own corn, made his own cider, killed his beef, and raised grain crops for his own use. In this period, however, the shift from self-sufficient farming to a market-oriented agriculture was occurring, as improved transportation lowered freight costs and made markets in the East and Europe more accessible.

The farming practiced in most of the West during these years made extensive use of land. Since land was cheap and labor and capital dear, the farmer usually followed an exploitative style of farming. Though there were exceptions, many followed a one crop system without fertilization or crop rotation. Central to an understanding of the farming of this period and later is the fact that many farmers were as much interested in capital gains from the sale of their farms as they were in the growing crops. The growth of population, the exploitative nature of the farming and above all the restless, mobile nature of the Americans of that day made the quest of unearned increment on the land an irresistible urge.

The labor required to clear this land, to cultivate, harvest, and market its crop was almost literally back-breaking. In the age before the extensive use of farm implements and machinery, the crop, say, of wheat, was frequently hand sown, reaped with a cradle, and threshed out with a flail or tramped out by horses or oxen, and the grain separated from the chaff by the age-old method of tossing it into the wind. The transportation problems of these farmers in the years before canals and railroads were equally staggering. A bushel of wheat weighs 60 pounds, so the load that could be carried by horse or slow-moving oxen over trails or unimproved roads was not large. Fodder had to be provided for the animals by carrying it or purchasing it along the way. In the 1820's and 30's, farmers in central Indiana hauled loads of wheat 75 miles to the Ohio River, the trip going and coming taking about ten days. In states farther west, such as Minnesota, the distance to market was often far greater than this. These conditions of difficult transport made investment in the social overhead capital of roads, canals, and railroads a "must" in many communities of the West and Northeast.

Until the new methods of transport overcame this marketing problem there was nothing for isolated farmers and townspeople to do but to process their surplus local products. So it was that numerous subsidiary industries grew up to convert wheat and corn into flour, cornmeal, bacon, ham, salt pork, and, of course, whiskey. The reader of biographies of Mark Twain will recall the vivid description of the many local trades of this kind that flourished in Hannibal, Missouri in the pre-Civil War period. There was hardly a county in many western states that did not have a local distillery or brewery to utilize the grain that farmers could not otherwise dispose of; and as one historian perceptively notes, much of the whiskey produced in the smaller plants was consumed locally.[10]

The economic consequences of the western pattern of land ownership were far different from those of the South. For one, it resulted in a more even distribution of income than existed in the slave states, and this, in turn, made possible sufficient aggregate demand to support a wide variety of small town, residentiary industry. Service trades and retail distribution, printing and publishing, metal fabrication and wood products, etc., developed in response to this widespread consumer demand as the acquisitive and achievement-minded westerners sought ways to improve themselves.

Not the least of the consequences was the fact that with the improvement of their economic status, or in anticipation of it, westerners showed an early willingness to finance public education and training. The statistics on schools, literacy, and tax money devoted to public education for these years demonstrate the great lead the West was gaining over the South in these respects. As Professor North succinctly expresses it, "The Westerner looked upon education as a capital investment with a high rate of return. . . ."[11]

Generalizing from the differences noted above in the economic structures of the West and South, we can see that the economic development of a region depends greatly upon the use made of the income it derives from its export goods. In the case of the West, a multiplier-accelerator process was set in motion in which the initial, autonomous investment in the growth of the export staple induced additional consumption spending by means of the multiplier process. The rise in the level of output that resulted from the original increment in investment spending and the induced consumption spending probably induced additional investment spending via the accelerator.[12] Indeed, this powerful combination of the multiplier and accelerator processes contributing to the growth of the West also played a part in the

[10] P. W. Gates, *The Farmer's Age*, p. 162.

[11] North, *The Economic Growth of the U.S.*, p. 155.

[12] For a definition of the multiplier and acceleration principles and analysis of their interaction, see, e.g., W. C. Peterson, *Income, Employment and Economic Growth* (New York: W. W. Norton and Co., Inc., 1962), pp. 225–232; advanced students will wish to study P. A. Samuelson's article, "Interactions between the Multiplier Analysis and the Principle of Acceleration," *The Review of Economics and Statistics* (May, 1939), reprinted in American Economic Association, *Readings in Business Cycle Theory* (Philadelphia: The Blakiston Co., 1944), pp. 261–269.

unstable pattern of its growth. In the South, on the other hand, the income from the region's export staples tended to flow out in the purchase of goods and services from outsiders rather than stimulating local subsidiary and residentiary industries. In the former region, the export base was widened and the size of the domestic market enlarged, whereas in the South there was relatively little such diversification of the export base, and the lopsided income distribution tended to promote luxury spending by the planter class rather than a broad increase in mass consumption. These divergent economic processes were to have momentous social and political consequences.

THE DEVELOPING ECONOMY OF THE NORTHEAST

Thus far in our analysis of the dynamic growth of the economy in this period the emphasis has fallen on the role of staple exports such as raw cotton and wheat in influencing the economic structures of the South and West, respectively. The Northeast's development in these years must also be seen as taking place in the context of the Atlantic economy, for its economic structure too was shaped by the products its inhabitants produced, the trade they engaged in, as well as by other factors. But it is quite clear that a staple theory alone, however modified or elaborated, is not sufficient to explain the course of this region's growth. We propose to test Schumpeter's hypothesis concerning creative entrepreneurship and innovation as a supplement to what the staple theory would suggest as the main explanation of the economic growth during these years.

Schumpeter in his sketchy comments on the economic history of this period indicated that he regarded water-power development, improved means of transportation, such as the turnpikes and the canals, and shipbuilding as "the backbone of the strictly industrial component" of the prosperity phase in these years. Writing of the Erie Canal, he added, "The truly revolutionary effect of this on physical production, prices, and location—an ideal instance by which to illustrate the nature and *modus operandi* of innovation, in particular the way in which innovation produces prosperity and depression—is luckily so obvious and its quantitative importance so palpable that we need not stay to prove it. . . ."[13] While these comments have a measure of truth, and we shall examine further the effects of the canals on the economy's growth, it seems that Schumpeter passed over many other forms of innovation and of creative entrepreneurship that played an essential part in the economic development of the period.

In the preceding period we have seen that the Northeast had acquired a commanding headstart in shipping, banking, and the export and import trades

---

[13] J. A. Schumpeter, *Business Cycles* (New York: McGraw-Hill Book Co., 1939), Vol. 1, p. 291.

over other sections of the nation; these established lines of business continued to influence the course and pace of the region's growth after the War of 1812. But the rivalry of the merchant groups of the different ports for the trade of the hinterland grew more intense after the war. New York City, though it was already in the lead as a seaport, thanks in part to its natural advantages as a harbor, now took steps destined to put it far in front of such rivals as Philadelphia, Baltimore, Boston, and other ports. Its citizens displayed "an aggressive energy" in the immediate post-war years, which ensured its continued lead over its rivals. R. G. Albion points to four measures that contributed to this result: (1) establishment of an attractive auction system for disposing of imports; (2) organization of regular transatlantic packet service; (3) development of the coastwise trade, especially the bringing of southern cotton to New York for export; and (4) the building of the Erie Canal.[14]

Creative entrepreneurship of a high order was responsible for most of these accomplishments. The "aggressive energy" referred to was largely the result of the invasion of New York City by Yankees from New England, especially from Connecticut. These hard-driving men, many of them self-made, played a leading role in the rise of New York to commercial supremacy even before the Erie Canal was opened.[15]

The auction system, the first innovation referred to above, served as an effective means of disposing of the goods that the British "dumped" on these shores after the War of 1812. The New York merchants had the Albany legislature pass a law in 1817 that made their auctions more attractive than those held elsewhere. As a consequence, the back-country merchants showed such a preference for buying "bargains" at the auctions on Pearl Street that for a considerable time the regular merchants in other ports could not compete.

New York's second innovation, the transatlantic packet, was the inspiration of a Yorkshire woolen importer, Jeremiah Thompson, who had migrated to this country to carry on his business; he and some other New York merchants inaugurated the celebrated "Black Ball Line" in 1818. Some years before, Thompson had played a prominent part in establishing the so-called "cotton triangle." In this trade pattern, cotton, instead of being transported directly to Europe from the South, was brought to New York City, trans-shipped, and then carried to Britain; on the return voyage European goods reached the South *via* New York rather than going direct to a cotton port. Albion, the historian of New York port, writes, ". . . The New Yorkers dragged the trade between the South and Europe 200 miles out of its normal course in order that they might exact their lucrative toll from it and secure eastbound

14 G. R. Taylor, *The Transportation Revolution, 1815–1860* (New York: Holt, Rinehart and Winston, 1951), p. 7.

15 R. G. Albion, *The Rise of New York Port* (New York: Charles Scribner's Sons, 1939), Chap. 12; D. M. Ellis, "The Yankee Invasion of New York, 1783–1850," *New York History*, 32:3 (January, 1951).

voyages for their ocean packets."[16] When the southerners finally realized what was happening, they claimed that the New Yorkers and other northerners were getting forty cents of every dollar paid for southern cotton. By 1822, it is clear, cotton was by far the most valuable of New York's exports, comprising 40 per cent of the total value of the port's outgoing trade.

The Erie Canal, that remarkable "act of faith" by the Empire State's leaders, may be seen as the work of creative entrepreneurship in government. "Clinton's Big Ditch" owed its successful completion more to this far-sighted governor of the state than to any other single person. Its imitators, as Schumpeter suggests, offer an excellent illustration of the pattern he thought fundamental to economic growth, though it is to be noted that it was the only successful canal of the four interregional projects initially designed to link the eastern seaboard with the trans-Appalachian West. The others functioned mainly as interregional carriers or feeders for the trunk canals. But it is not our intention here to investigate the financial success of the canals or to analyze their significance as a form of governmental enterprise. It suits our purpose more to consider the developmental impact of the canals in long run terms, leaving the question of their role in the business fluctuations of the period to a later section. Harvey Segal's research offers a most interesting theoretical and empirical study of this subject; we shall outline the highlights of his work in what follows.[17] Segal begins by assuming that the construction of the canals led to a drastic reduction in transport costs and then postulates the economic changes as "a series of virtually linear sequences" between two conceptually distinct regions, the East and the West. The first consequence of the construction of a successful interregional canal is that it enabled the West to dispose of its agricultural surplus in the higher price markets of the East, thus narrowing the price differentials between the domestic markets. Such a development would not only improve the West's terms of trade, but would facilitate the shift from subsistence farming to the production of cash crops. This, in turn, would tend to raise the region's level of income per capita and its ability to purchase imports from the East.

In the East the transport innovation would contribute to a widening of its market as a result of the lowering of freight costs and the rising level of per capita income in the West, inducing also a higher level of eastern investment. Real incomes in the East would be expected to rise also with the availability of cheaper western farm products. Thus, in effect, there may result a cumulative

[16] R. G. Albion, *Square Riggers on Schedule* (Princeton: Princeton University Press, 1938), p. 50. E. D. Genovese challenges Albion's interpretation in his "The Significance of the Slave Plantation for Southern Economic Development," reprinted in H. N. Scheiber, *United States Economic History* (New York: Knopf, 1964), p. 151. Genovese argues that "if the ships carrying cotton had sailed from Southern ports direct to Europe and back, they would have to return in ballast. New York's domination of the South's export trade was, therefore, not accidental. . . ."

[17] H. E. Segal, "Canals and Economic Development," Chap. 5 in C. Goodrich, et al., *Canals and American Economic Development* (New York: Columbia University Press, 1961).

process of multiplier-accelerator effects, which raises the level of economic activity in both regions.

Another sequence Segal sees resulting from canals as a transport innovation is the promotion of western settlement, the stimulation of the growth of urban centers, and a tendency to higher land values in the region served by the canals. He notes also that construction operations would be likely to provide a new source of employment and money income in the backward areas through which the canals were built. And lastly, he envisages the development along the route of the canal of industries dependent for their growth on external transport economies, such as farming or non-agricultural activity, which may be stimulated by the growth of population and income in the vicinity of the canal.

Turning from theoretical analysis to the far more difficult task of measuring the impact of the canals upon the nation's economic growth, Segal first notes the decline in overland transport costs that resulted from their construction. In the case of the Erie, the average rate for freight shipments between Buffalo and New York via wagon and the Hudson River was 19.12 cents per ton-mile in 1817. After the completion of the Canal in the years 1830–50, the average rate fell to only 1.68 cents per ton-mile, leading the author to conclude that "In their impact upon transport costs the canals proved to be a far more radical innovation than the railroads which superseded them. . . ."[18] However, offsetting this great advantage in economy was the fact that the canals were slower, required much handling of merchandise in trans-shipment at terminal points, and were closed, for the most part, in the winter.

The Erie Canal's impact is judged next in terms of the growth of tonnage from the western states to tidewater. This traffic, mostly farm products, grew from 54,000 tons in 1836 to a peak of nearly 1.9 million tons in 1860, a thirty-sevenfold increase! Comparing this growth of tonnage from the West over the Erie Canal, with the increase in national commodity output, as computed by R. E. Gallman, Segal found that until 1849, when the railroad competition became strong, shipments from the West over this Canal increased far more rapidly than the national output.

The population growth in such states as Ohio, Indiana, Illinois, and Michigan grew in total from .8 to 18.2 per cent of the nation's total over the years from 1820 to 1850. While all of this increased settlement in this vast region cannot be attributed to the canals, a strong case can be made for the view that they played an important role in the settlement of the old Northwest.

One index of the widening of the market resulting from the opening of the Erie was the increase in the value of the merchandise shipped to the western states over this route; its total rose from less than $10 million in 1836 to a peak of $94 million in 1853. Even more significant for regional development was the redistribution of trade in favor of the northeastern, or Erie Canal, route. Prior to the opening of the Erie, the bulk of western exports were

[18] Segal, *op. cit.*, p. 228.

shipped southward on the Ohio and Mississippi rivers for trans-shipment at New Orleans. As Table 1 clearly shows, while the absolute volume of shipments on all routes increased rapidly between 1835 and 1853, the northeastern route gained markedly at the expense of the alternative routes.

TABLE 1

*Distribution of the Commodity Trade of the Northwest
by Shipping Routes, 1835–53[a]
Percentage of Total Trade Shipped by*

	Northeastern Route (via Lake Erie and Erie Canal	Southern Route (Down the Mississippi River)	Eastern Route (via the Penn. Mainline, Pittsburgh Turnpike, or the Cumberland Road)	Total
1835	23.7%	62.2%	14.1%	100.0%
1839	38.2	45.4	16.4	100.0
1844	44.1	43.9	12.0	100.0
1849	52.7	38.4	8.9	100.0
1853	62.2	28.9	8.9	100.0

[a] Source: as reproduced in Goodrich, *op. cit.*, p. 231. Percentage computed from tonnage data presented in Abraham H. Sadive, *Transport Improvement and the Appalachian Barrier: a Case Study in Economic Innovation* (unpublished Ph.D. dissertation, Harvard University, 1950, p. 197)

While data on the effects of canals on regional terms of trade are not available, except for the Cincinnati area, Berry's study of price movements there suggests that with other factors, the transport innovations contributed to an improvement of that region's terms of trade. There is also evidence to support the view that the urban growth of such cities as Buffalo, Cleveland, Syracuse, Rochester, Toledo, Chicago, and Peoria was stimulated by their canal connections.

The income effects of construction operations are more noticeable when considered from the state and local level rather than from a national vantage point. For example, while the ratios of canal investment to total income in such populated states as New York and Pennsylvania were not high, they were much higher in more sparsely settled states such as Ohio, Indiana, and Illinois. If information was available on a county basis, it seems very likely that it would show that income in the backward areas was increased substantially as a result of canal construction.

The stimulus to interregional trade provided by the canals is reflected in the growth of industrial activity and employment in such states as New York and Pennsylvania. Between 1820 and 1840, manufacturing employment more than doubled in these states. While this is a crude measure, it seems very unlikely whether this degree of expansion could have taken place without the large quantities of anthracite coal that the canals made available at reduced prices. (Before

1845 the coal canals transported more than 80 per cent of Pennsylvania's annual production of anthracite.) "By making it possible to transport coal at a rate of less than one cent per ton-mile by the 1840's, the canals stimulated the growth of eastern cities and made a significant contribution to the growth of the iron and steel industry."[19]

Another measure of the influence of the canals on economic improvement is its effect on land values. In the case of the Erie, the fourteen counties bordering on that Canal showed an increase of 91 per cent in the value of land and its improvements between 1820 and 1846, whereas the real value of property in the non-canal counties, excluding Manhattan and Brooklyn, increased by only 52 per cent; property values in the state as a whole during this period increased by 66 per cent. Similarly, employment in manufacturing and commerce grew more rapidly in the years 1820–40 in fourteen counties bordering on the Canal than in any other county category.

The canals, when appraised from the standpoint of their financial profitability, were not, with certain notable exceptions, outstandingly successful; in fact, there were a number of costly failures, which in the aggregate represented more than a fifth of the total investment. Still when we consider that while the wagon rates in the period 1837–46 averaged about 25 cents contrasted to two cents per ton-mile for the canals, and that the latter tended to stimulate traffic that otherwise would not have been transported at all, it seems clear that the canals produced benefits exceeding their cost by a substantial margin. Indeed, a benefit-cost analysis does not take full account of the indirect, developmental effects of the canals on economic growth.

> . . . By accelerating the growth of interregional trade between the north Atlantic seaboard and the territory of the old Northwest, the Erie Canal and its tributaries played a vital role in extending and integrating spatially separated markets. Had there been no canals, the expansion of industrial activity in the East would have been inhibited by reliance on a much narrower domestic market and by the high costs of foodstuffs produced on inferior land; and the effective development of the West, which depended on a substantial outflow of agricultural products, could not have occurred until the coming of the railroads. By connecting the two regions, the canals initiated a sequence of cumulative impacts that promoted a rapid rate of economic growth.[20]

Indeed, the extent and character of the effects of the canals upon our nation's economic growth in this period was so great that it seems strained and inadequate to regard them as backward links growing out of the growth of our staple exports; though, of course, related to that trade, they seem in their own right to have been true innovations, the product of the imagination and vision of the creative innovators of the period. Certainly, it would seem true that however powerful the influence of the staple exports on the timing and pace of the economy's development in this period, the contours of our domestic growth, the channels and regions through which development took

[19] *Op. cit.*, p. 234.
[20] Segal in Goodrich, *Canals and Economic Development*, p. 240.

place, were profoundly affected by the human response to the entrepreneurial problems and opportunities that this nation's growth produced in such epic proportions.

MANUFACTURING DEVELOPMENT AND
THE GROWTH OF MARKETS

The sketch of manufacturing development in the preceding chapter has already emphasized the growth in the size of the market as a factor contributing to the rise of the factory system and of specialization generally. Expressed in terms of linkage theory, the growing income or induced final demand created by the export of staples to other regions or nations provided the markets for factory products, and the decline of freight costs increasingly made possible the localization of such industry in specialized centers. Whereas there continued for some time to be a good deal of resource-oriented, local production in various parts of the West and other sections of the country, manufacturing on a large scale became concentrated in those localities having access to national markets and possessing the quantity and quality of productive factors that made for efficient, low-cost production. The localization of a large part of this modern type of manufacturing in the Northeast built upon the groundwork laid in the years before the War of 1812. It was aided by the region's earlier urban growth, the social overhead capital in the form of transport facilities, banks, etc., which had grown up to serve foreign trade, and by the growth of its supply of labor and entrepreneurial talent.

It is to be noted that manufacturing developed first in those industries in which imports had been largest, partly because of the demonstrated existence of a market and of a distribution system to dispose of the product. This has been the case not only in the United States, but in many developing nations today, as Hirschman has pointed out.[21] Textiles have been favorite industries for new industrial nations in part because of their important linkages with other products. With the growth in the demand for our domestic textiles, backward linkage was established with the textile machinery industry, as the textile mills gave up their own machine manufacturing and relied upon specialized manufacturers. The textile machine industry in turn developed important linkage effects with iron casting, machine tools, and metal working in general. In this process, skills and training were acquired that were later effectively transferred to other industries. G. S. Gibb has pointed to this important relationship in our formative industrial years in these words:

> The manufacture of cloth was America's greatest industry. For a considerable part of the 1813–53 period the manufacture of textile machinery appears to have been America's greatest heavy goods industry, occupying the primary

---

[21] A. O. Hirschman, *The Strategy of Economic Development* (New Haven: Yale University Press, 1958), Chap. 7.

position in point of size and value of product among all the industries which fabricated metal. Size, however, is not the most critical measure of importance. From the textile mills and the textile machine shops came the men who supplied most of the tools for the American Industrial Revolution. From these mills and shops sprang directly the machine tool and the locomotive industries together with a host of less basic metal fabricating trades. The part played by the textile machinery industry in fostering American metal working skills in the early nineteenth century was a crucial one.[22]

Forward linkage from the cotton and woolen textile industries into final consumer goods contributed to the spread of manufacturing in the Northeast, especially after the introduction of the sewing machine. The diversified manufacturing industry that grew up in centers outside of New England, such as that in the Middle Atlantic states, had started originally as a locally oriented enterprise, but with the widening of markets and improved transportation, it gradually expanded to serve larger areas. New York and Philadelphia particularly were the centers for manufacture of growing quantities of men's clothing, refined sugar, boots and shoes, bakery products, furniture, machinery, and newspapers. As this list suggests, these products were produced for the growing markets being provided by urban development in this period. To provide perspective on this dynamic phase of the economy, it is worthwhile to compare the relative value of manufacturing products in the different sections of the nation as of 1860 (Table 2).

TABLE 2

Manufacturing by Sections of the United States, 1860[a]

Section	Number of Establishments	Capital Invested[b] (In millions of $)	Annual Value of Products[b] (In millions of $)
New England	20,671	$ 257	$ 223
Middle	53,287	435	358
Western	36,785	194	385
Southern	20,631	96	156
Pacific	8,777	23	71
Territories	282	4	4
Total	140,433	$1,010	$1,886

[a] Source: Eighth Census of the United States; Manufactures, p. 725. Adapted from Table in Taylor, *The Transportation Revolution, 1815–1860* (New York: Holt, Rinehart and Winston), p. 247.

[b] The figures in these columns have been rounded off, consequently totals will show discrepancies.

The Boston Manufacturing Company, started by Francis Lowell, one of the most creative entrepreneurs of this period, grew rapidly in these years, especially after the introduction of the power loom in the 1830's. The concentration

[22] C. S. Gibb, *The Saco-Lowell Shops, Textile Machinery Building in New England, 1813–1849* (Cambridge: Harvard University Press, 1950), p. 168.

on mass production of coarse cotton fabrics enabled this company to meet British competition. Other companies modelled on the Waltham enterprise were established in these years in other parts of New England by the Boston Associates. Their success was so great that by 1850 these companies alone accounted for approximately one-fifth of the total output of cloth in the nation.[23]

The quality of America's entrepreneurial skill and innovational talents were evident in the widespread technical developments of these years: in machine tools, waterpower development, spinning machinery, power looms, and other fields of technology. Where Americans did not innovate, they were quick to borrow the innovations of foreigners and improve on them. Such was the case in the iron industry, where after 1815 the rolling process of making bars was introduced from Great Britain, as was the puddling process. This latter process permitted large-scale operations and the use of coal rather than charcoal as fuel; it contributed greatly to the centralization of the whole iron industry. The use of coal in the blast furnace was delayed until after 1840 in this country because American iron workers found charcoal iron to be more malleable and better suited to their needs.

Manufacturing progress was aided by the concomitant developments in the Northeast during these years, such as the decline of agriculture and the consequent willingness of many New England girls to enter the New England factories in order to supplement their family's incomes. The advantages American industry had in these years were more than the brilliance of its entrepreneurs or the ingenuity of its inventors. As was pointed out above, "Important innovations developed in every industry, frequently in small shops and firms at the hands of mechanics with little or no formal scientific training."[24] This widespread aptitude for innovation and its possible sources was commented on by a contemporary as follows:

> From the habits of early life and the diffusion of knowledge by free schools there exists generally among the mechanics of New England a vivacity in inquiring into first principles of the science to which they are practically devoted. They thus frequently acquire a theoretical knowledge of the processes of the useful arts, which the English laborers may commonly be found to possess after a long apprenticeship and life of patient toil.[25]

Manufacturing development as a whole in these years was not attributable to one or two strategic industries, but to "the general improvement of factor endowments for manufacturing. . . ."[26] Given the stimulus of the widening of markets, which came with improved transportation, American entrepreneurship and labor had a drive and interest in labor-saving methods and a sense of moral improvement via industry that worked wonders. With a social en-

[23] Taylor, *Transportation Revolution*, p. 231.
[24] North, *The Economic Growth of the U.S.*, p. 173.
[25] Z. Allen, *Science of Mechanics* (Providence: Hutchens and Corey, 1829), p. 349 as quoted in North, *The Economic Growth of the U.S.*, p. 173–4.
[26] North, *The Economic Growth of the U.S.*, p. 174.

vironment that did not put the seal of approval on the familiar and the customary, but rather encouraged innovation and "projects," Americans had a culture highly congenial to the advance of machine industry.

REGIONAL INTERDEPENDENCE AND
THE GROWTH OF SPECIALIZATION

The improvement of transportation and the consequent widening of the market not only revolutionized manufacturing in this period, but it transformed the relations of the nation's regions to each other. Louis B. Schmidt has given us a striking summary of this mutual interdependence in these words:

> The rise of internal commerce after 1815 made possible a territorial division of labor between the three great sections of the Union—the West, the South and the East. The markets which were developed for various products opened the way for the division of labor where it had been practically unknown before. Each section tended to devote itself more exclusively to the production of those commodities for which it was best able to provide. There was fostered a mutual economic dependence between sections and the establishment of predominant types of industry in each which were in turn dependent on foreign commerce. The South was thereby enabled to devote itself in particular to the production of a few plantation staples contributing a large and growing surplus for the foreign markets and depending on the West for a large part of its food supply and on the East for the bulk of its manufactured goods and very largely for the conduct of its commerce and banking. The East was devoted chiefly to manufacturing and commerce, supplying the products of its industries as well as the imports and much of the capital for the West and the South while it became to an increasing extent dependent on the food and fibers of these two sections. The West became a surplus grain- and livestock-producing kingdom, supplying the growing deficits of the South and the East.[27]

So it was that in these years the domestic market increasingly became national in its dimensions. And the increased specialization that this trend promoted in turn raised the productivity of the economy as a whole. The importance of a growing national market for our economic growth cannot be overstressed, for this American "common market" was to nineteenth century America what the European common market is to twentieth century Europe.[28]

One of the most important consequences of the growing integration of the economy and the increased volume of business it made possible was the decline of the old sedentary merchant and his replacement by more specialized operators. Though banking and finance had become a separate calling by 1815, this field was further differentiated in these years with the development

---

[27] L. B. Schmidt, "Internal Commerce and the Development of a National Economy before 1860," *Journal of Political Economy* (December, 1939), p. 811.

[28] S. Bruchey, *The Roots of American Economic Growth, 1607–1861* (New York: Harper and Row, 1965), p. 91.

of commercial banks, savings banks, insurance companies, and stock exchanges. The rise of factories led to a more definite separation of the marketing function from manufacturing, and in transportation likewise the moving of goods became the responsibility more and more of specialized common carriers. In commerce, the distinction in function as well as in name between wholesalers and retailers became more common; specialized operators, such as commission merchants or factors dealing only in a narrow class of commodities, became more numerous, as did brokers who brought buyers and sellers together, and retailers who operated speciality shops in the cities. In the rural areas, the general store carrying a wide array of goods was still the most common type of establishment.

STAPLE EXPORTS AND INNOVATIONS IN RELATION TO THE CYCLICAL FLUCTUATIONS OF THE PERIOD

The broad features of the cyclical fluctuations of the economy in this period have been described at the close of the preceding chapter. What part did the changing demand and supply of our staple exports play in these recurrent fluctuations? Does the Schumpeterian theory of innovations provide us with the key to their fundamental causes and timing? These are some of the questions we shall examine in this section; in doing so we shall be studying, of course, the dynamic functioning of the whole economy over time so that many of the elements of our previous analysis will have to be kept in mind if we are to grasp the nature of these complex movements of an ever more interdependent economy.

The severity of the depressions of these years raises the question at the outset of our analysis of the possible relationships between the business cycles of this period and the so-called "long swings."[29] M. Abramowitz has assembled evidence supporting the view that swings or waves of this sort characterized the economic growth of the nation between 1815 and 1870. He has

---

[29] The long swing hypothesis is that economic growth moves in recurrent waves of acceleration and retardation with a period of 15 to 20 years. Simon Kuznets first noted them in his study, *Secular Movements in Production and Prices* (New York: Houghton Mifflin, 1930) and Arthur F. Burns also in his *Production Trends in the United States* (New York: National Bureau of Economic Research, 1934). The length of the long wave seems to be related to the long gestation period of such heavy investment projects as construction; several investigators have found evidence in the statistical series of this activity of a cycle approximating 18 years. See J. S. Duesenberry, *Business Cycles and Economic Growth* (New York: McGraw-Hill Book Co., 1958) Chap. 7. Long waves characterize not only construction, but all activities in which people have to commit themselves over long periods of time—e.g., the founding of new businesses, the settlement of land, the movement of people from one country to another, etc. [M. Abramowitz, "Long Swings in United States Economic Growth," 38th Annual Report of the National Bureau of Economic Research (New York: National Bureau of Economic Research, 1958), pp. 47–56.] See also S. Kuznets, "Long Swings in Population Growth and Related Economic Variables," in S. Kuznets, *Economic Growth and Structure* (New York: W. W. Norton and Co., Inc., 1965), pp. 328ff.

offered the following rough chronology of long swings in the rate of growth of the economy for these years:

Peak	1814–15
Trough	1819
Peak	1833–34
Trough	1839
Peak	1846–50
Trough	1858

As to the relation between these long swings and business cycles, we may note that A. F. Burns found that each retardation in the secular rate of growth since 1870 was marked by a business depression of unusual severity. This also seems to be the case with the pre–Civil War swings. The retardation that began about 1815 was accompanied by a depression in 1816, which passed into the severe depression of 1819–20. Similarly, the retardation beginning in 1833–34 was marked by the panic of 1837, and generally depressed business conditions lasted until 1843. We cannot undertake to assess the validity of the long swing hypothesis as applied to the business fluctuations of this period; it must suffice for our purposes to note the putative relationship of these swings to the shorter cycles and especially the severity of those of 1819 and 1839. The theory does suggest also the temporal limits of the periods of expansion in this and other time spans.

In seeking to understand the cyclical movements of the economy in these years, one must not forget that our expansion was taking place within the broader context of the Atlantic economy. The economy moved forward in huge surges of expansion, followed by periods of contraction and then gradually by another expansion, usually ending in a boom. These movements were often initiated and sustained by a rise in the prices of certain key commodities such as raw cotton or grain. The higher prices induced a shift of resources into new areas of production, but commonly there was a lag before production added to the supply with all the possibility of speculative overdoing and excess output. Professor North has elucidated this process of periodic expansion and contraction very vividly.[30] He stresses that behind the irregular pattern of economic development was the shape of the supply curve of cotton or wheat and the way in which the curve shifted. When cotton prices were high, large amounts of land were purchased from the government to grow the crop. But clearing the land, preparing the soil, and growing it took time. (North finds that there was a lag of approximately four years between a peak in land sales and a large increase in cotton production.) Once this new land was producing, the supply curve shifted very sharply to the right. So long as demand remained about the same, such a shift would mean a decline in price. During a period of depressed prices for cotton, a good deal of the land would be devoted to alternative uses, such as growing food for slaves or fodder for the livestock. In effect, such land represented unused capacity for cotton growing,

---

[30] North, *The Economic Growth of the U.S.*, pp. 71–74.

and the slightest increase in the price of the staple could and usually did, lead to shifting of some of this land back into cotton production. Such a practice was possible and rational on those plantations where slaves were raised as an intermediate good. The result of these characteristics of production is that the supply curve of cotton had a shape such as that shown in Chart 1.

CHART 1

Shape of Supply Curve of Cotton

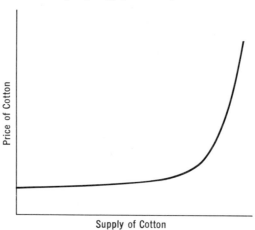

Supply of Cotton

Reproduced from D. C. North, *The Economic Growth of the United States, 1790–1860,* © Copyright 1961, Englewood Cliffs, N.J.: Prentice-Hall, Inc.

The graph shows that the curve is relatively horizontal (i.e., elastic) up to the point where it bends sharply upward. This elastic part of the curve represents the responsiveness of supply to change in price over the range of output, which included all the land cleared and ready for producing cotton. So long as there was much unused cotton land, in other words, the production would be very responsive to even slight increases in price. But when all the available land that had been cleared and prepared, etc., had been brought into use, a further increase in demand would result in substantial price increases because the supply curve in that range of output becomes very inelastic. These characteristics of the supply curve of cotton go far to explain the boom and bust pattern in the sales of land and in the prices of that commodity.

A similar pattern, with some important modifications, applied to the growing of wheat and corn in the West. There too land sales tended in these years to parallel the prices of these staples. But there was an important difference in the West. Transportation was the limiting factor in increasing the supply of wheat or corn in that region. Once the land accessible to water transportation was taken up, the rise in prices would bring into cultivation land further from cheap transportation. This limit on the production of wheat and corn probably encouraged a boom in land sales and strengthened the agitation for new investment in transport facilities. But construction of canals and railroads took time, and when the additional production of staples that they had made possible became available, there was usually a big shift to the right in their supplies, producing again the familiar boom-bust cycle.

Now that we have considered some of the fundamental economic processes underlying the business cycles of this period, we can turn to examine the factors influencing the timing of these cyclical movements.

The period immediately following the War of 1812 was one of difficult economic readjustment, especially in New England. With wartime restrictions removed, Americans were eager to buy the foreign goods they had been denied by the blockade. Foreign manufacturers, especially the British, were ready to meet this demand, and they exported huge quantities of goods from their accumulated stocks to this country. This flood of imports made the going difficult for many of the marginal American textile, iron, and other producers, but the more efficient survived to go on to further expansion. Incidentally, the agitation of these infant industries for protection led to the passage of the Tariff Act of 1816, which is often said to mark the establishment of the protective principle in the United States. While its rates were not high, the average increase being about 20 per cent above the level of 1789, the protective purpose of this legislation was clear. New England was distressed at this time also by the decline in freight rates and in the formerly lucrative re-export trade, though the latter revived somewhat later.

While business conditions were mixed in the Northeast in the years 1816–18, a boom of remarkable proportions spread over the South and West. The pent-up demand for wheat and flour, tobacco, and cotton caused the prices of these exports to rise more than 50 per cent between 1815 and 1818. These high prices encouraged a massive surge of planters into Alabama and of other farmers into the western areas suitable for growing wheat and tobacco. The expansion of cotton production in the new South provided in turn a rich market for such Western products as corn, flour, meat, and whiskey. The sections acted and reacted to each other; prosperity spiralled into a boom.

The capital to finance this boom in the West and South came mainly from the liberal extension of credit by state banks, whose note issues rose by more than 50 per cent from 1815 to 1816 and by British exporters who largely financed the import surplus of this period. Specie payments had been resumed in February, 1817, but this did not curb the mounting note circulation of the state banks. Nor did the Second Bank of the United States, which began operations early in 1817, do much to check the credit expansion; rather it actually augmented the inflationary pressure by an excessive increase in its note circulation and loans.[31]

[31] W. B. Smith, *Economic Aspects of the Second Bank of the United States* (Cambridge: Harvard University Press, 1953), Chap. 7; also L. M. Schur, "The Second Bank of the United States and the Inflation after the War of 1812," *Journal of Political Economy* (April, 1960), pp. 118–134.

These were prosperous years indeed for many Americans, for the terms of trade (the export prices for their products relative to what they paid for imports) were very much in their favor, but unfortunately, they did not last very long. With the return of good crops in Europe in late 1818, the British markets for our exports collapsed, and grain prices plummeted downward. To make matters worse, Britain herself now fell into a major financial crisis that led her banks and business houses to curtail their loans and demand payment on those overdue. Cotton and tobacco prices slumped badly, the former falling from a peak of 35 cents a pound in 1818 to a low of 8½ cents by March of 1823. Credit extended on the basis of high prices for these staples now became suspect; banks cut back on their loans, specie flowed out of the country, and the nation experienced the most severe panic since the establishment of banks in the late eighteenth century. Many state banks failed, and the Bank of the United States avoided bankruptcy only by contracting its loans, though that, of course, only aggravated the general financial deflation.

The depression hit the South and the West the hardest. Sales of land stopped, and to prevent widespread foreclosures, debt moratoria were declared in several states, and in others seizure of property for non-payment was prohibited. Many communities were without an adequate medium of exchange, but through barter, self-sufficient farming, and household manufacturing, the most pressing needs of the people were met. Adjustment to these hard conditions of depression was especially difficult in the old South, because many of its plantations could not operate profitably with cotton selling for 9 cents a pound. This section entered a period of slow decline, which was "cushioned" only by its sale of slaves to the new South and by later recoveries in the price of cotton. The losses suffered in the South and West as a result of the contraction of credit in these years bred a hatred toward banks, especially toward the Bank of the United States, which was to have serious political consequences in the next decade.

The impact of the depression on "mechanics" in the form of unemployment is not fully known. The estimates of unemployment range from 40,000 to 100,000, but these figures are not very satisfactory because the concept of unemployment in a handicraft economy such as that of 1820 was not very definite. Many self-employed artisans probably suffered greatly from involuntary part-time unemployment.[32]

The recovery from the depression took place in the Northeast in 1821 and two years later in the South and West when staples rose in price. The expansion of the economy during the decade of the twenties was relatively slow, but with short interruptions in 1834 and 1837–38, accelerated in the thirties, reached boom proportions in 1836–37, and then sank into one of the most severe depressions in our history from 1839 to 1843.

The slow pace of the economy in the 1820's was due to the mixed state of business activity in those years. The Northeast was going through a painful

---

[32] Taylor, *The Transportation Revolution*, p. 338.

transformation in which manufacturing was growing, while shipping and foreign commerce were in a state of relative decline. The South also was experiencing the adjustments alluded to above. Only in the West was there much vitality as the increasing interdependence of the sections provided investment opportunities in towns, cities, and in building the facilities necessary to move and store the region's growing wealth.

One striking fact about the economy's performance in the years 1823–33 was the general downward drift in the prices of consumer goods, despite the fact that labor and capital were being devoted heavily to long-term capital projects, such as canals. Apparently, the increased productivity of the newly settled land, the advances in manufacturing, and the improvements in transportation tended to keep prices low. The existence of unemployed and under-employed resources in the later 1820's probably also acted as a damper on price rises. Still another factor in the nation's favor at that time was the import surplus of consumer and capital goods, which made it possible to carry out large-scale investment projects without diverting domestic resources from consumer goods production and thus raising their price.[33]

In the thirties the pace of the economy quickened as the prices of cotton and grain rose, reaching a peak in 1836, and there developed a terrific speculative boom in land sales. A close correlation can be seen between the price of cotton and the volume of land sales in the five southern states of Alabama, Louisiana, Mississippi, Arkansas, and Florida, as shown in Chart 2. A roughly similar situation developed in the West somewhat earlier, starting after 1827, and reached an equally dramatic culmination in the huge land spree of 1836–37. (See Chart 3.)

The speculation in land and commodities in these hectic years was stimulated by a vast monetary expansion. The money supply (bank notes and deposits) increased by 55 per cent in the years 1834–39. This credit inflation was promoted in part by the closing of the Second Bank of the United States in 1832 and by the extraordinary number of state banks that were chartered to fill its place. Their number increased from 506 in 1834 to 988 in 1837; the bank note circulation soared in these same years from $95 million to $149 million. The Bank of the United States, rechartered under Pennsylvania law and led by the erratic Nicholas Biddle, contributed its part to the excessive extension of credit and reckless speculation in these years. The eagerness with which British investors bought up state bonds fueled the boom also; the total foreign indebtedness of the United States rose from $85 million in the 1820's to more than $297 million in 1839.

The investment in canal construction formed an integral part of the land and commodity-price boom in these years. The investigations of Harvey Segal show that while canal construction accounted for but 5½ per cent of the total non-agricultural employment in ten canal-building states and that canal invest-

[33] D. C. North, "International Capital Flows and the Development of the West," *The Journal of Economic History* (December, 1956), pp. 493–505.

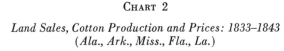

CHART 2

Land Sales, Cotton Production and Prices: 1833–1843
(Ala., Ark., Miss., Fla., La.)

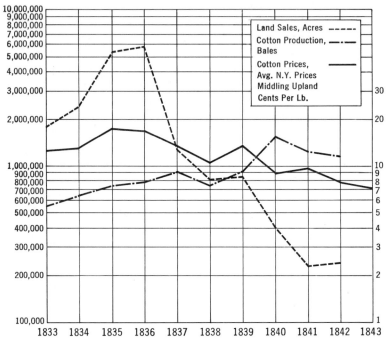

Reproduced from D. C. North, *The Economic Growth of the United States,*
1790–1860 (Englewood Cliffs, N.J.: Prentice-Hall, Inc., 1961), p. 74, with the
permission of the publisher.

ment in 1839 came to only 1 per cent of the total value added by commodity
production in that year, the building of the canals intensified the boom and
exacerbated the ensuing depression of 1839–43. He argues that canal construction, by transferring funds to the western banks having notoriously low reserve ratios, led to an inflation of credit, which in turn fed the boom in land
sales. He concludes that the first and third cycles of canal construction, which
preceded and followed that of 1838–44, had a neutral effect on general economic activity; the second cycle "clearly accentuated economic instability" in
these years.[34]

Fundamentally, the economic situation in 1837 grew increasingly dangerous because with the economy at full employment, the spread of the craze
for internal improvements necessitated a shift of labor out of agriculture and
other activities into construction. The latter activity increased aggregate consumer demand without adding much to the supply of consumer goods; the
result was rising prices, which the import surplus from abroad could only

[34] Goodrich, *Canals and American Economic Development,* pp. 206–7.

CHART 3

Land Sales in Seven Western States: 1815–1860
(Ohio, Ill., Ind., Mich., Iowa, Wis., Mo.)

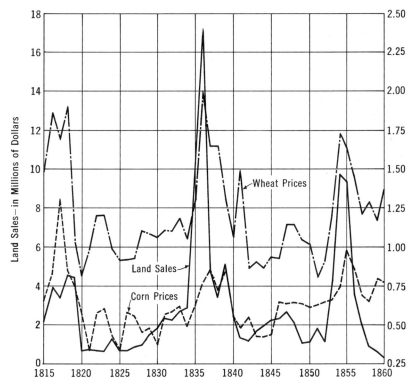

Reprinted from A. H. Cole, "Cyclical and Sectional Variations in the Sale of
Public Lands, 1816–1860," in the *Review of Economics and Statistics*, IX, No. 1
(January, 1927), p. 52.

Reproduced from D. C. North, *The Economic Growth of the United States, 1790–
1860* (Englewood Cliffs, N.J.: Prentice-Hall, Inc., 1961).

partially offset. Despite the crash that followed, the American economy's resources in terms of land settlement and transportation facilities were substantially augmented by the real expansion that took place in these years.

The coming of the financial crisis in 1837 was complicated by many
factors.[35] Earlier, we referred to the inflation caused by the distribution of
the federal government's deposits among the state banks and how this contributed to the so-called bank "madness" in certain sections of the country.
Riots are said to have occurred when the subscription books of these banks
were opened; one person advertised for "a man with pugilistic ability to enter
bank stock subscriptions." The craze for internal improvements had an irra-

[35] See R. C. McGrane, *The Panic of 1837* (Chicago: University of Chicago Press,
1924) for an interesting analysis of the causes of this depression.

tional character also that is hard to believe. For example, the first session of the Michigan legislature, sitting in 1837, the year the state was admitted to the Union, voted construction of 543 miles of highway, 557 miles of railway, 231 canals, and 321 improvements of rivers. As Shultz and Caine have written,

> "State capitalism" became the current doctrine. States were frankly urged to borrow, and to invest their borrowings in profit-producing capital enterprises. Not only was it expected that the dividends from these enterprises would exceed the interest on the borrowed funds, but they would also provide the state governments with an investment income sufficient to cover current expenditures. Alabama established the Bank of Alabama and then, in 1836, abolished the state tax system; bank stock dividends, it was thought, would provide the state governments with all the necessary revenue.[36]

It is important too to understand how the liberal extension of bank credit created a vicious circle between this factor and the federal government's sale of land. Generally, the purchasers of such land borrowed the purchase price from the local banks in the form of bank notes. These bank notes were then deposited by the government with a local bank, as often as not with the very institution that had issued them, and was credited with a specie deposit. (The latter practice was necessary under a Treasury ruling.) As land sales mounted in 1835 and 1836, an unhealthy situation developed; the specie deposits credited to the government threatened to become larger than the entire specie holdings of the western banks.

At the same time, the receipts from public land sales had created such a large surplus revenue that Congress had passed the Surplus Distribution Act in June of 1836. This law called for a deposit with the states of any surplus revenue of over $5 million on January 1, 1937 in proportion to the states' representation in Congress; actually, the deposit took the form of a loan, though it was understood that it would never be repaid. On the first day of 1837, there was a $42 million surplus in the Treasury so that $37 million was available for deposit with the states. $28 million of this amount had been deposited in three installments, but before the fourth installment was paid, the Treasury itself was in financial difficulties.

The distribution of the federal government's surplus caused a sequence of troubles and adverse reactions. In order to shift the government's deposits in accordance with the law, the western banks had to have ample specie reserves. In fact, at the time many had very low reserves because of their very liberal extension of credit on land sales. It was in part to correct this situation that President Jackson in July, 1836, issued the famous Specie Circular. It required that government land offices accept only gold and silver in payment for federal land, with the one exception that resident buyers could pay in bank notes over a four month period. The effects of this edict were immediate: it cut short the credit sales of land and it threw doubt upon the note issues of the

---

[36] W. J. Shultz and M. R. Caine, *Financial Development of the United States* (Englewood Cliffs, N.J.: Prentice-Hall, Inc., 1937), p. 220.

state banks. Further, the distribution of the surplus forced the state depositary banks to contract their loans; many of them had made large extensions, often for investment capital purposes, in the belief that these government funds would be theirs for an indefinite period.

Another major factor precipitating the financial crisis was the credit contraction caused by the Bank of England raising its discount rate, first to 4½ per cent, and then to 5 per cent in 1836. In 1834 the United States had passed the Gold Act, which changed the mint ratio to 16 ounces of silver for 1 ounce of gold; this ratio stimulated the gold flow in this direction. Actually at the time, the balance of payments was in our favor, but not in trade. Three English banks were making large commercial loans in this country during 1836, the total of which was conservatively estimated to be approximately $100 million. This large advance of credit grew out of the huge volume of imports that the prospering Americans were consuming. But now with the tightening of credit at home, these banks found themselves unable to rediscount the bills drawn upon them by southern cotton brokers and commission merchants against the 1836 crop. Foreign banks began to call for specie, causing a run on the banks and resulting in the suspension of specie payments. Specie was in fact, at the height of the crisis, being drawn out of the eastern banks in two directions; some of it was going abroad and the rest was being drawn out by western banks. Commercial paper rates soared. Popular uneasiness mounted during the winter of 1836 and then in the spring a group of New Orleans cotton houses failed. This news caused near panic in New York City with the result that a series of bank runs started. Finally, on May 10, 1837, the New York banks were forced to suspend specie payments; within two weeks other banks were forced to do likewise.

Economic activity was hit hardest in New York City and New Orleans, where failures and unemployment mounted in the spring and summer of 1837, but western farming continued to be fairly prosperous. British credit expanded again in 1837–38, and her investors continued to purchase large amounts of the bond issues of the American states, which had continued with their programs of internal improvements. But the recovery did not last. British credit tightened again in 1839, specie began to flow abroad, and then with the closing of the Bank of the United States, which under its Pennsylvania charter had engaged excessively in cotton speculation, another series of bank failures started that ushered in a depression that lasted until 1843. "The difference between 1837 and 1839 was that the former panic had centered around temporary maladjustments in internal monetary affairs and external influences, while these monetary and external influences in the latter period were combined with the real effects of a decade of uninhibited expansion of productive capacity which necessarily entailed a long period of readjustment.[37]

The deflation caused by this depression shrank prices and values to a fraction of what they had been at the peak of prosperity. Farm prices were

---

[37] North, *The Economic Growth of the U.S.*, pp. 201–2.

especially hard hit, falling by more than 50 per cent between 1839 and
1843.[38] The amount of public land sold in 1842 fell to but 6 per cent of its
level in 1836. Real estate values evaporated, especially in the West; in Chicago, land values in 1842 were 14 per cent of what they had been six years
earlier. Railroad stocks declined a little more than 50 per cent.

The working class was also injured badly by this depression. The suspension of public works, which became general in 1840, meant unemployment for
many, and as we would expect, the investment multiplier went into reverse, so
that unemployment spread to other lines as income shrank. The relief provided for the casualties of the depression was very haphazard; many cities
simply opened soup houses to feed the poverty stricken, but otherwise nothing
substantial was done to alleviate their lot. Under these conditions, unions
practically disappeared. Indeed, the New York *Journal of Commerce* advised
employers to "employ no men who do not forever abjure the unions. . . .
Now is the time to deliver mechanics and their families from the cruel oppression of the unions. . . . To work only 10 hours in summer and 8 hours in
winter is to waste life. No man can prosper who does not abandon such
rules."[39]

One of the most serious consequences of the depression was the default and
repudiation of state debts, which followed in the wake of the depression. As
we have seen, many of the states continued their ambitious programs of internal improvements in the years 1838–40. New York, for example, in 1838
authorized a loan of $4 million to continue enlargements on the Erie Canal.
The result was that the confidence of the money lenders was destroyed; the
state 6 per cent bonds fell from 120 in 1833 to 80 in 1842. As economic
conditions worsened in 1841 and 1842, no fewer than eight states defaulted on
their interest payments on outstanding bond issues. Mississippi, Florida, and
Michigan more or less directly repudiated their obligations. Pennsylvania,
Maryland, Indiana, Illinois, Arkansas, and Louisiana announced their inability to repay. The indignation, especially of the British, at this evidence of
American lack of financial responsibility was intense; even the poet Words-
worth and the minister, the Rev. Sidney Smith, were led to revile us in
poetry. A more serious aspect was that as a result of the repudiation, British
capital turned away from America temporarily, but by the end of the decade
the high return on American issues was too alluring to be resisted.

Domestically, the depression stimulated a number of important reforms in
our economic and political practices. Actually, the depression had no sooner
set in than various special interest groups began to use it as an argument for
their particular panaceas. For one thing, there developed a strong movement
to revise state constitutions in the direction of curbing the economic powers of
the legislatures by requiring state-wide referenda before the state could undertake new obligations. Stringent rules were imposed too upon the legislatures'
incorporation of banks and other enterprises. In New York State, the famous

[38] W. B. Smith and A. H. Cole, *Fluctuations in American Business, 1790–1860* (Cambridge: Harvard University Press, 1935), p. 65.
[39] *New York Journal of Commerce* (September 20, 1836), p. 1.

free banking law of 1838 was passed. Under its terms anyone complying with the statutory provisions was free to open a bank; no special charter had to be authorized by the legislature as had been the case before. This law provided for new security for the note issues of these "free" banks. The state comptroller was authorized to issue the notes upon receipt of an equivalent in either (1) federal bonds, New York State obligations, or bonds of any other approved state; or (2) New York State real estate mortgages to twice the value of the notes issued. In addition, this law required banks to keep a specie reserve of 12.5 per cent against their note issues, although this salutary provision was later repealed. The New York law became something of a model of good banking; sixteen states adopted its system in whole or in part. And the national banking system later adopted the idea of bond backing for currency under the Act of 1862.

The harassed businessmen in these depression years were given some relief by the passage of the Bankruptcy Act of 1841, which Congress passed to aid business debtors. Under its terms, some 28,000 debtors freed themselves of half a billion dollars of debt by paying about 10 cents on the dollar. Another federal law permitted merchants to postpone payment of custom bonds. But apart from such relief measures, President Van Buren's sole remedy for the depression was the Independent Treasury plan. While this subject will be considered from a political point of view in the next chapter, we may simply take note of its economic character here. The basic idea of the subtreasury plan was to separate the operations of the United States Treasury completely from dependence upon private banks. Subtreasuries were established in six leading cities, and they alone could receive or pay out public funds. All receipts and disbursements of these offices had to be made in gold or silver coins or treasury notes. In short, the Independent Treasury plan was the Jacksonians' "hard money" system by which they hoped to avoid the economic and political consequences of the government being served by private banks. While the System worked well during the Mexican War and enabled the nation to avoid a serious inflation or banking crisis at that time, it had an intrinsic flaw that later led to its abandonment.

During the long years of the depression, other changes were taking place that were contributing to long-run growth. As Schumpeter had contended, depressions had a positive side; the decline of prices and profits put a premium on efficiency, for only through increasing productivity could the superior firms survive. In these years, we can see these processes very much at work. For example, in the shoe industry the manufacture of that product in factories was proceeding apace, as the less efficient merchant employers failed in great numbers. Technical improvements under the pressure of falling prices were occurring also in such industries as woolen manufacture, brass works, and others. On the farm, too, there was a striving for greater efficiency. There was an increased interest in farm exhibits and in agricultural societies. In South Carolina, for long a hard pressed state in competition with the fertile acres of the new South, there developed a trend toward greater diversification.

We shall close this chapter by summarizing what our analysis suggests concerning the validity of the two theories of economic growth that we have proposed as having peculiar relevance for this period. Given the international context in which the economy operated, the staple theory offers a most useful explanation of the pace and timing of the fluctuations of the American economy in these years. Taken together with the theory of linkages and the analysis of the cultural as well as the natural endowments of the economy's regions, it provides a suggestive picture of how such an economy diversified and grew in efficiency and productivity as the widening of the market made for increased regional specialization and functional types of division of labor. We would emphasize, however, that the retrospective view of history should not lead us to any mechanistic interpretation of the role of staple exports in the American economy or any other. The export sector of a growing economy provides challenges and opportunities, but as we have seen, whether such challenges are taken up and exploited depends very much on the human factor as well as on the natural resources available for exploitation. That human factor was very evident in these years in the role of creative entrepreneurship in spotting the opportunities for growth and assuming the risks of innovation. Nor does Schumpeter's theory of innovation provide us with an all-sufficient key to the growth of these years; we have seen that the industries he singled out as the leading sectors of innovation and growth in this period are very much subject to dispute. But the usefulness of his theory, not the specific application that he gave it in these years, as a supplementary explanation of the processes of growth, of the establishment of the linkages, would seem to be demonstrated in the preceding pages. The Schumpeterian vision of the process of economic growth also requires supplementation if we are to understand the cultural factors that contribute to or detract from creative entrepreneurship. In the following chapter we shall examine the changing social milieu of entrepreneurship, seeking to discern the influence of the social structure and governmental policy and practice upon that elusive but essential ingredient of economic growth.

Chapter 10

THE ETHOS AND POLITICS
OF THE AGE OF
THE COMMON MAN

ON TOCQUEVILLE'S IMAGE OF JACKSONIAN AMERICA

Tocqueville's classic work, *Democracy in America*, has seldom been used as a commentary on Jacksonian America, which he visited in the years 1831–32. Yet, as Marvin Meyers has contended in a brilliant essay, "His work offers just what is most needed by the student of Jacksonian times: an integrative view of society and culture, grounded in experience."[1] In the opening part of this chapter we seek to summarize the great Frenchman's view of American social structure and character, using for the purpose the categories of social analysis discussed in Chapter 1. This treatment of America's social structure and character will serve as background for our analysis of the political and economic changes of these times.

Tocqueville states at the outset of his book that nothing impressed him more than "the general equality of conditions" that prevailed in America, and he went on to say that this equality of conditions was "the fundamental fact from which all others seem to be derived, and the central point at which all my observations constantly terminated."[2] This levelling condition produced a phenomenon that Tocqueville was the first to term "individualism," and in a striking passage he describes what an individualistic society implied to one who had been brought up in the older, hierarchical society of Europe.

---

[1] M. Meyers, *The Jacksonian Persuasion* (Stanford: Stanford University Press, 1957), p. 24. Alexis Tocqueville was the scion of a French family of nobility who travelled in the United States in the years 1831–32, studying the American penal system and taking notes for his incomparable commentary. His monumental work, published in 1835 and 1840 in four volumes, has been called "the most illuminating commentary on American character and institutions ever penned by a foreigner." [H. S. Commager in his edition of *Democracy in America* (New York: Oxford University Press, 1947), p. xi; quotations below are from this edition.] If the passage above reminds one of the descriptions of our so-called "mass society" of the type described in Riesman's *The Lonely Crowd*, or C. W. Mills' *White Collar*, it should be noted that Tocqueville, along with Goethe, Burkhardt, Nietzsche and others, has been regarded as one of the prophets of the mass age. On this, see J. P. Mayer, *Prophet of the Mass Age* (Gloucester, Mass.: P. Smith, 1939).

[2] Commager, *Democracy in America*, the author's preface to the first part, p. 3.

Among democratic nations new families are constantly springing up, others are constantly falling away, and all that remain change their condition; the woof of time is every instant broken and the track of generations effaced. Those who went before are soon forgotten; of those who come after, no one has any idea: the interest of man is confined to those in close propinquity to himself. As each class gradually approaches others and mingles with them, its members become undifferentiated and lose their class identity for each other. Aristocracy has made a chain of all the members of the community, from the peasant to the king; democracy breaks that chain and severs every link of it . . .

Thus not only does democracy make every man forget his ancestors, but it hides his descendants and separates his contemporaries from him; it throws him back forever upon himself and thus threatens in the end to confine him entirely within the solitude of his own heart.[3]

Tocqueville's primary theoretical problem, as Meyers has noted, was "to discover how equality, the primal active element, can constitute a social system, democracy."[4] In other words, what would hold together a conglomeration of striving, atomistic individuals and establish a sense of community and viable nationhood? Tocqueville emphasizes his view that the Americans of Jackson's day were primarily interested in the acquisition of wealth. He says so in innumerable places: "The passions which agitate the Americans most deeply are not their political but their commercial passions. . . ." "That love of prosperity and that spirit of enterprise which seem to be the distinctive characteristic of the race." "Americans are the most cold and calculating, the most unmilitary and the most prosaic of all the peoples of the earth." Equality, he says in another place, "tends to isolate them [men] from each other, to concentrate every man's attention upon himself; and it lays open the soul to an inordinate love of material gratification. . . ." "The first of all distinctions in America is money."[5] Tocqueville speaks of American cupidity, willingness to defraud, and bad faith.

Living in a rich continent ("The valley of the Mississippi," writes Tocqueville, "is the most magnificent dwelling place prepared by God for man's abode . . ."), he describes Americans as ceaselessly and avidly seeking "the booty" which fortune and the land afforded. Their constant migration, "a continuous removal of the human race," seems to him to be without parallel since "those irruptions which caused the fall of the Roman Empire." He describes their mobile, rootless, anxious way of life in unforgettable terms:

In the United States a man builds a house in which to spend his old age, and he sells it before the roof is on; he plants a garden and lets it just as the trees are coming into bearing; he brings a field into tillage and leaves other men to gather the crops; he embraces a profession and gives it up; he settles in a place, which he soon afterward leaves to carry his changeable longings elsewhere. If his private affairs leave him any leisure, he instantly plunges into the vortex of politics; and if at the end of a year of unremitting labor he finds a

[3] *Ibid.*, p. 312.
[4] Meyers, *The Jacksonian Persuasion*, p. 26.
[5] Commager, *Democracy in America*, pp. 258, 416, 433–55.

few days' vacation, his eager curiosity whirls him over the vast extent of the United States, and he will travel fifteen hundred miles in a few days to shake off his happiness. Death at length overtakes him, but it is not before he is weary of his bootless chase of that complete felicity which is forever on the wing.[6]

As to the social character of Americans, Tocqueville found the people of Jackson's day rather serious and repressed. The reason for this in his view was the anxiety and singleness of purpose with which these self-made Americans sought wealth. ". . . A man who raises himself by degrees to wealth and power, contracts in the course of this protracted labor, habits of prudence and restraint which he cannot afterward shake off. A man cannot enlarge his mind as he would his house. . . ."[7] In addition to their soberness and lack of humor, Tocqueville noted a certain insensibility to the wonders of inanimate nature, and a proneness to religious insanity. As to the last, it must be remembered that Tocqueville saw the United States when religious revivalism was at its height; he believed that when the people became tired or depressed with their incessant pursuit of fortune, they turned with an equal manic fervor to religion.

In their economic life, Americans, valuing education and having a lively faith in the perfectibility of man, tend to "consider society as a body in a state of improvement, humanity as a changing scene, in which nothing is, or ought to be permanent; and they admit that what appears to them to be good today may be superseded by something better tomorrow."[8] In short, Americans were inclined to take change and innovation for granted. And in seizing the rich opportunities that their changing economic condition offered, Americans more and more turned to associated effort, to forming corporations and other joint ventures for profit or otherwise. "Americans of all ages, all conditions, and all dispositions, constantly form associations. . . . Wherever, at the head of some new undertaking, you see the Government in France, or a man of rank in England, in the United States you will be sure to find an association." Tocqueville marvelled at the uses Americans were making of the corporation; he thought of it as "potential mass energy, actually released and organized for work."[9]

In describing the status system, such as it was, in this open, individualistic society of Jackson's day, Tocqueville noted that all honest occupations were honorable; everyone worked for money, even the President. The rich as well as the poor strive, for the former feel "the most imperious of all necessities, that of not sinking in the world." These individualistic citizens in their competitive striving for success are influenced in their various social roles by the tyranny of public opinion, by the belief that the majority can do no

[6] *Ibid.*, pp. 344–55.
[7] *Ibid.*, p. 426.
[8] *Ibid.*, p. 226.
[9] G. W. Pierson, *Tocqueville and Beaumont in America* (New York: Oxford University Press, 1938), p. 607.

wrong. The individual submerged in a mass of equals senses his own insignificance and weakness. On the whole, Tocqueville found that the distinctions of rank in civil society in the United States were slight, though Americans, while boasting of equality, were prone to make exceptions for themselves and sought to trace their lineage to the first founders of the nation.

But how could a society composed of such individualistic, self-concerned persons endure as a democracy? Part of the answer was, as Tocqueville expressed it, that Americans had arrived at a state of democracy without having to endure a democratic revolution; they were "born equal" instead of having become so. He was inclined to believe also that Americans with a continent to exploit and with no formidable enemies had rationalized their fortunate situation into the political doctrine of individualism. In addition, there were certain institutions that gave powerful support to the maintenance of democracy. The decentralized form of their government, the institutions of a free judiciary and a free press, the jury system, all gave the people experience and practice in the difficult art of self-government. The American faith in education tended too to make the people relatively enlightened. Their practice of a moralistic religion served to curb excess and act as a restraint on the commercial passions. Thus, while Tocqueville saw powerful centrifugal forces at work in America, he concluded that democracy in the New World worked and that the United States was destined with Russia to sway the future of half the world.

SOCIAL MOBILITY AND THE INDUSTRIAL REVOLUTION

While Tocqueville showed brilliant insight into many aspects of American culture in Jacksonian times, he does seem to attribute too much of the nation's character and ethos in that period to the general principle of equality and not enough to the peculiar historic situation in which Americans found themselves. True, he noted the ceaseless change that characterized America, but he saw this, as we have seen, as a manifestation of the American character and pursuit of wealth. He failed to see the economic changes that were ushering America into a market society: the accelerating Industrial Revolution abroad with its immense demand for our staples; the Transportation Revolution here in the United States; the movement of the nation toward regional specialization and a common national market for its products producing unprecedented opportunities for social advancement for the common man. Indeed, the suddenness and pace of social change in Jacksonian times were such as to create a state of *anomie* or confusion about social and moral norms. Bray Hammond has expressed this aspect of Jacksonian America so well that his remarks deserve quotation:

During the half century that ended with General Jackson's election, America underwent changes perhaps the most radical and sweeping it has ever undergone in so short a time. It passed the climacteric separating a modern industrial economy from an older one of handicraft; it passed from colonial weakness through bare independence to actual power and from an unjostled rural culture to the complexities of populousness, sectionalism, urban slums, mechanized industry, and monetary credit. Men who spent their childhood in a thin line of sea-board colonies, close even in their little cities to the edge of the western continental wilderness, spent their late years in a tamed and wealthy land spread already to the Missouri and about to extend beyond it. They lived to ride on railways and steamships, to use the products of steam-driven machinery, to dwell in metropolitan centers, and to feel within their grasp and the grasp of their sons more potential and accessible wealth than had ever before excited the enterprise of man.[10]

The rising level of aspiration in America in these years was powerfully stimulated by the construction and completion of the Erie Canal. As Lee Benson shrewdly suggests, the phenomenal success of New York's Canal, even before it was completed, seemed to galvanize the economy. "Inspired by the Erie, men all over the country now saw opportunities where before they had seen obstacles."[11] Psychologically, this is often the effect of the achievement of the path-breaker whether he be an innovating businessman or a runner breaking the four-minute mile; the possibility of achievement is a matter of perception and that is usually subtly influenced by group norms. Once a "break-through" occurs, reality and what is considered possible are drastically altered.

American confidence and determination were supported not only by achievements such as the Erie Canal but by a strong nationalistic feeling that nature and Providence itself were on the side of Americans in their rivalry with decadent Europe. The agrarian mind was prone to see Nature's nobleman in the plain, practical, and relatively unlettered American and to feel that he was more than a match for the more civilized European. The young nation bolstered its security and self-esteem by finding God's special favor behind almost every passing event and by believing that its destiny was in His care.[12]

Nationalistic and moral elements of this kind seem to have motivated some of the principal founders of manufacturing in the highly patriotic period after the War of 1812. As one acute student of this subject reminds us, these pioneers of manufacturing were "convinced, on the whole, of an identity between moral and material progress. These industrialists were men with a reforming sense of mission who, while not averse to profits, were conscious of making a patriotic contribution and of trying to establish a pattern in manufacturing for their nation."[13] Some of the early New England manufac-

---

[10] B. Hammond, *Banks and Politics in America* (Princeton: Princeton University Press, 1957), p. 326.

[11] L. Benson, *The Concept of Jacksonian Democracy* (Princeton: Princeton University Press, 1961), p. 13.

[12] J. W. Ward, *Andrew Jackson, Symbol for an Age* (New York: Oxford University Press, 1955), *passim*.

[13] C. L. Sanford, "The Intellectual Origins and New-Worldliness of American Industry," *Journal of Economic History* (March, 1958), pp. 1–16.

turers disliked the industrial system of Europe and regarded it as symptomatic of the Old World's moral degradation. Like the ideological Jeffersonians, they cherished the countryside and saw the city as a place of luxury and moral decline. To men such as these, "Manufacturing was not evil; it was productive of positive good in rescuing labor from indolence, drunkenness, pauperism, vice and in initiating habits of industry, learning and religious piety." This sense of moral mission and "reactive nationalism" in excelling the British and Europeans generally in manufacturing was an intangible that exercised an immeasurable but important influence on American attitudes through much of the nineteenth century. Some foreign observers of the American scene believed that some of its effects could still be seen in the mid-twentieth century.[14]

It is little wonder, given this climate of opinion and belief and these prospects and tokens of economic achievement, that this was the dawn of the age of the "self-made" man. *Niles Weekly Register* at the beginning of the period in 1815 observed that America was characterized by "the almost universal ambition to get forward." It pointed out that in the United States "one half of our wealthy men, over 45 years of age, were once common day-laborers or journeymen, or otherwise very humble in their circumstances when they began the world."[15] At the very end of the period, in 1844, we find a contemporary declaring,

> Ours is a country where men start from an humble origin . . . and where they can attain to the most elevated positions, or acquire a large amount of wealth, according to the pursuits they elect for themselves. No exclusive privileges of birth, no entailment of estates, no civil or political disqualifications, stand in their path; but one has as good a chance as another, according to his talents, prudence and personal exertions. This is a country of self-made men, than which nothing better could be said of any state of society.[16]

It is quite evident that the rapid growth of cities in the West in this period facilitated very much this process of upward social mobility. With their more complex division of labor, these new municipalities needed many specialized talents. "The professional classes were one of the great beneficiaries of post-war urban expansion. As the cities grew, the need for specialized skills multiplied, and in the twenties doctors, lawyers, ministers, teachers, and

---

[14] A visiting productivity team from Great Britain in 1953 concluded as follows: " 'The real secret of American productivity is that American society is imbued through and through with the desirability, the rightness, the morality of production. Men serve God in America, in all seriousness and sincerity, through striving for economic efficiency.' The importance of this 'psychic factor' of moral justification is that it concentrates energy, initiative, and dedication to the pursuit of the profit incentive without a crippling inner guilt. . . . These industrialists' hearts and minds were shaped in large part by the myth of a moral America" [*ibid.* p. 16, quoting G. Hutton, in the London *Economist*, reprinted in the New York *Herald Tribune* (July 20, 1953)].

[15] *Niles Weekly Register* (December 2, 1813), pp. 238–39.

[16] Calvin Colton, *Junius Tracts*, no. vii (New York), p. 15, as quoted in the epigraph in C. R. Fish, *The Rise of the Common Man, 1830–1850* (New York: The Macmillan Co., 1950).

editors flocked to western communities."[17] Wage earners as well as professionals grew in numbers and influence in these bustling, growing centers. With
urban development came the beginnings of social stratification. The early
settlers brought ideas of social distinction with them from further east and
their children maintained and elaborated on the pattern of social status. The
idea of equality was not as powerful and as widely accepted in the towns as it
was in the countryside. In fact, one student of the urban frontier tells us, "by
1830 classes were becoming increasingly aware of their separateness and
status. . . ."[18]

While we do not have as much historical evidence on social mobility in this
period as we would like, the available data do indicate that it was relatively
easier for farmers and workmen to rise in the social scale than at any time in
our history before or since. Still, according to the research of the late
C. Wright Mills, the majority of successful businessmen derived from upper and
upper-middle class homes or were the sons of businessmen, professionals, or
civil servants. "The best statistical chance of becoming a member of the
business elite . . . was to be born into it."[19] The fluidity of the social structure and the opportunities for advancement in it is indicated by the variety of
careers and occupational roles that the more ambitious seem to have had in a
lifetime. Thus one is struck in the description of the men around President
Andrew Jackson by their successive careers—farmer, land speculator, merchant, banker, railway-builder, newspaper publisher, etc. Jackson himself
illustrated this kind of occupational mobility, having been planter, soldier,
lawyer, legislator, jurist, merchant, and land speculator, and finally President.[20] It is significant that the phrase itself, "self-made man," is credited to
that arch proponent of Whig economics, Henry Clay, in a speech in Congress
in 1832, though, ironically enough, it was in the course of a plea for a
paternalistic tariff.[21] Equally significant, psychologically, is the recurrent
element of envy and resentment as well as signs of a sense of insecurity and
inferiority that Hammond discerns in many of President Jackson's associates.
As he says, a nation of democrats were tired of being governed by gentlemen
from Virginia and Massachusetts, however well, and they showed their
resentment toward the "aristocrats" in many overt and latent forms. Torn as
they were between their simple agrarian world of the Old Republic and their
vision of the affluence of a business society still in the making, they exhibited

[17] R. C. Wade, *The Urban Frontier, The Rise of Western Cities, 1790–1830* (Cambridge: Harvard University Press, 1950), p. 210. Chapter 7 of this book is especially good
on the changing social structure of the western communities in this period.
[18] *Ibid.*, p. 229.
[19] "The American Business Elite: A Collective Portrait," *Tasks of Economic History*
(December, 1945), pp. 28–39; see also S. M. Lipset and R. Bendix, *Social Mobility in
Industrial Society* (Berkeley: University of California Press, 1962), Chap. IV.
[20] See Chap. 12 in *Hammond, Banks and Politics in America*, for an excellent portrait
of the men around the President.
[21] Ward, *Andrew Jackson*, p. 174 and footnote 21.

many symptoms of ambivalence and guilt feelings in their attacks upon the old social and political order.[22]

LABOR'S AWAKENING

While the Astors were amassing their millions in New York real estate, and thousands of other "go-ahead Americans" were pursuing the main chance in their various ways, the working poor were growing more restive in the eastern cities. The working men in such cities as Philadelphia, New York, and Boston formed political parties in 1827 and 1828 to protest their conditions of life and to obtain redress. This movement coincided with the campaign to elect Andrew Jackson as President, but it had deep, independent roots in the conditions of life of the workingmen of that time. Some historians regard this politico-economic development as the true beginnings of the trade union movement in the United States. The workers' complaints at that time arose out of their feeling that they and their children were deprived of the right to "life, liberty and the pursuit of happiness," which were being exercised so flamboyantly by their more prosperous fellow citizens. The workers of this time tended to see their conflict not so much as one between employer and employee, but rather between rich and poor. Their gospel was the Declaration of Independence, and they rallied to the cause of those who assured them of their rights and, particularly, of their opportunity for economic advancement and improvement.

What the workers of this period, around 1827–28, found most galling and degrading was the denial to the children of the poor of the opportunity for a free education. While most of New England at this time had free, tax-supported schools, such populous states as New York and Pennsylvania still had private schools only. The poor had to send their children to charity schools, if they attended at all. As a matter of fact, in 1829 the Public School Society of New York City estimated that some 24,200 children between the ages of five and fifteen were not attending any school whatsoever. At the same time, 10,000 were in charity schools and 17,500 in private schools, so that nearly as many were not in school as were in attendance. Similarly, in Pennsylvania in 1837 it was estimated that 250,000 out of 400,000 children were not in any school. One of the major reasons for this deplorable situation was that the long hours of work of the children of the poor precluded the possi-

---

[22] M. Meyers in *The Jacksonian Persuasion*, Chap. 6, "The Judges and the Judged," catches some aspects of the hypocrisy and ambivalence of Jackson's day, but misinterprets it, we feel. Hammond states the matter more accurately when he says, ". . . But the preoccupations of *laissez faire* were in fact materialistic. It was the device of men who wished to make money. They clothed their new aspirations in the familiar, idealistic language of the religious and agrarian traditions in which they had been reared. There was no other period in American history, one would hope, when language was more idealistic, endeavor more materialistic, and the tone of public life more hypocritical than during the Jacksonian revolution." (*Banks and Politics in America*, p. 365.)

bility of their gaining an education. A vigilance committee of a group of
Paterson, New Jersey strikers pathetically expressed their plight as follows:

> Scarcely time allowed them to take their scanty meals, they retire to their beds
> at night worn down and exhausted with excessive labor—hence they are
> deprived of any privilege except working, eating and sleeping. Is it to be
> wondered at, that our country has become the great theater of mobs, yea, we
> may say murderers too, when we remember that the poor and their children in
> manufacturing towns and districts are kept in ignorance and regarded but little
> superior to the beasts which perish.[23]

Many of the reforms that the Workingmen's Party of this period advocated,
such as free education, were taken up by more conservative parties and in
time became law. Thanks to the vision of such humanitarian leaders as Horace
Mann of Massachusetts, Henry Barnard of Connecticut, DeWitt Clinton of
New York, and others, the opposition to free public education, which was
considerable, was overcome. But without the support of the urban workingmen, it is doubtful whether the free school movement would have achieved its
goal as quickly as it did. Public education was adopted in Pennsylvania in
1834, in New York City in 1842, and in New York State by 1849. By the eve
of the Civil War, most states in the North had adopted a tax-supported school
program.

Another of the reforms that labor agitated for in these years had to do with
imprisonment for debt. At that time, many workers were languishing in jail
for failure to pay trifling debts. For example, the Boston Prison Discipline
Society estimated that 75,000 persons were annually imprisoned for non-
payment of debts in the United States, and in more than half of these cases
the sum was less than twenty dollars. The burden of the existing laws on the
subject fell most heavily upon the working classes, especially the unemployed.
To make matters worse, the jails were usually crowded and terribly un-
sanitary.

Still another grievance of the workers was the militia system, which called
for periodical drills and parades. All men of military age had to appear,
providing themselves with arms and other equipment at their own expense.
Failure to do so made one subject to fines or imprisonment. Here, again, there
was discrimination. The rich could pay the fines, the poor, unable to do so,
more often went to jail.

Finally, the workers agitated against monopolies, especially banks, which
many of them felt contributed to the high cost of living because of their
excessive issuance of banknotes. In the later years of this period many
workers espoused the Jacksonian cause of "free banking" believing that it
would facilitate their own entry into business in good petty bourgeois style. Of
this, we shall have more to say below in our analysis of the political struggle
over the Second Bank of the United States.

---

[23] Quoted in J. R. Commons *et al., History of Labour in the United States,* Vol I (New
York: The Macmillan Co., 1936), p. 183.

Following this early stirring of organized labor on the eve of Jackson's first election, the movement did not progress further until the next great upsurge in the years 1833–37. The inflation accompanying the hectic speculation and land boom of those years increased the cost of living and led to the formation of new unions. In Philadelphia, for example, the workingmen's societies grew in number from 21 in 1833 to 53 in 1836; in New York City, their number rose from 29 to 52 over the same years. Significantly, organization was successful first in the skilled trades, among the plasterers, bricklayers, "segar" makers, and plumbers. The Female Improvement Society included the tailoresses, seamstresses, binders, folders and milliners. City centrals or trades' unions were also established in large numbers; there were at least 13 in the nation by 1836. Even a National Trades' Union was set up in 1834 "to advance the moral and intellectual condition and pecuniary interests of the laboring classes," but it was merely an agitational and advisory convention; organized labor had to wait until after the Civil War for a general organization of labor on a national scale. Five separate crafts, however, were organized on a national basis during this period—the cordwainers (shoemakers), printers, combmakers, carpenters, and hand-loom weavers. The resort to national organization on the part of these groups was the result of the widening of the market that the Transportation Revolution was bringing about. With it came increased inter-city competition, so the unions sought to standardize wages and conditions of apprenticeship at this time.

Apart from the craft unions, there was even an industrial union established in these years. The New England Association of Farmers, Mechanics and Other Workmen was started in 1831 as a result of a fight for the ten-hour day. Still, its immature nature as a union was shown by the fact that small employers were allowed to join; class lines were not sharply drawn, the psychology of petty bourgeois thought persisted. Employers turned to organization also in this period in order to combat unionism, eight such associations being formed in New York City alone.

Labor unions were subjected to legal attack as well as other tactics of opposition in these years. Another wave of conspiracy cases was brought against organized labor; there were eight such trials in the years 1829–42. Yet this time there were only two convictions. The usual arguments against restraint of trade were heard, injury to business being alone sufficient to convict. Nationalistic sentiment was appealed to by contending that the members of the unions were foreigners. But despite the uphill legal battle faced by labor, one great victory was earned. In 1842, the Massachusetts Supreme Court held in the historic case of *Commonwealth* vs. *Hunt* that unions were legal for the first time, establishing a precedent that has been followed ever since. Chief Justice Shaw in his opinion even upheld, in effect, the strike for the closed shop.

But legal victories were of little avail to organized labor in these years of deep depression. As was noted earlier, the onset of the business slump of 1837 had led to a widespread collapse of unions. The result was that labor increasingly turned to politics for redress of its wrongs. In New York City, the Equal

Rights Party, or the "Loco Focos," as its members were derisively called, had challenged the rule of Tammany Hall (the official Democratic organization in Manhattan) as early as 1835. Its agitation was directed against banks and chartered monopolistic combinations in business generally, among other grievances. In 1837, this party actually succeeded in defeating the Tammany candidate for Mayor. But "The Tiger," alerted to the danger, absorbed its new rival in the next election. It was from this time that Tammany Hall began organizing the labor vote.

One of the most popular demands of labor toward the end of the 1830's was for a shorter working day. Political demand by the workers for a ten-hour day finally led to its adoption first by the federal government; President Van Buren put it into effect in the Navy Yards in 1840. The agitation for this reform was strongest in New England, but at the level of state government labor suffered many disappointments. For example, New Hampshire passed a ten-hour law in 1847 with a clause exempting special contracts; the latter provision proved to be the "joker" since many employers claimed such exemption. Other laws of this nature had a similar result, as was the case in Pennsylvania. In Massachusetts, the corporations seem to have bought up the legislators to win their opposition to such legislation. In that state employers brazenly posted notices on their factory gates: "Whoever votes the Ben Butler ten-hour ticket on Monday next will be discharged." As a consequence of these pressures and other tactics, the United States on the eve of the Civil War had still an 11½-hour day in most of its manufacturing activity. For the most part, labor still had to be effectively organized and long, bitter, and bloody struggles had to be waged in the latter half of the century before that goal was accomplished.

THE POLITICS OF BANKING

The most violent political controversy in this era was not over labor, but, surprisingly enough, over the more mundane and much more complex subjects of banking and monopoly. In a period of expansive economic growth such as this, the pace and direction of the economy's development and those of individual and sectional interests were vitally affected by the availability of bank credit. Furthermore, banking practice and theory were in a very primitive, changing state in these years so that even apart from conflict of economic interests, there was much room for differences of opinion. As a matter of fact, after decades of study of the struggle over the renewal of the charter of the Second Bank of the United States, historians have only recently come to appreciate some of the more intricate economic and political issues involved in that famous conflict.[24]

[24] Bray Hammond, in his monumental study, *Banks and Politics in America,* has done more than any other recent scholar to shed new light on this subject and the all-important political and cultural context of the controversy. In the following pages we draw heavily upon the insights of this magnificent study.

One of these neglected aspects needing emphasis if we are to understand the struggle over "The Monster," as the Jacksonians termed the federal bank, has to do with the economic nature of frontier farming. One is inclined to think that pioneering on the frontier required mainly large amounts of labor and fortitude in meeting the hardships of that life. But we are now coming to see that to develop that type of land, say in the Ohio Valley in these years, and bring it into cultivation required more cash than most farmers realized. In the seventeenth and eighteenth centuries the needs of a frontier family could be met mainly by labor on the land; there was relatively little that he needed or could buy. But in these years, with the growth of settlement and the advance of agricultural techniques, larger amounts of cash were needed for equipment and livestock than had hitherto been the case. On all frontiers, the cost of pioneering is apt to exceed expectations, but in the West in such states as Ohio, Kentucky, Tennessee, and elsewhere this was very much the case in the years after the depression of 1819. The illusion of cheap land made the dearth of capital even worse, and for years the agrarian distress and foreclosures of farms made these questions burning political issues. The bitterness of being forced off the land after years of hard labor in developing it without much return and being compelled to start all over again further westward was intense. In times of prosperity and rising prices, on the other hand, the banks could not advance enough credit to satisfy the dreams of these land-hungry, speculating Americans. The troubles of the Second Bank cannot be comprehended unless we keep in mind the acquisitive, expansive psychology of many Americans in this period.

The Second Bank of the United States had started under favorable enough auspices in 1816. Even the former enemies of a federal bank had come to recognize its value during the years of financial disorganization in the War of 1812; Henry Clay and John Calhoun had reversed their previous stands on the question, and some of the private banks had recognized its function in the economy.

The Second Bank itself was mainly a private bank endowed with governmental functions. Of its $35 million of capital, four-fifths was privately subscribed, and one-fifth was provided by the federal government. Its management consisted of twenty-five directors, five of whom were appointed by the President. Under the provisions of its charter, foreign stockholders could not vote either in person or by proxy. Another provision required that both the Bank's notes and deposits were to be paid in specie. Indeed, there was a 12 per cent penalty imposed on the Bank if it failed to pay claims upon it in specie; this proved to be one of the most salutary features of the Bank's charter. Finally, the promoters of the Bank had been required to pay the government a bonus of $1.5 million for its charter; offsetting this was the fact that the deposits of the United States in the Bank did not receive interest.

In its functioning, the Second Bank had to provide the services of a central bank at a time when this term, let alone the theory of the subject, was hardly recognized. In effect, the Bank served as "the balance wheel" of the financial system. By its practice of returning the note issues of the private banks to them for redemption, it provided an over-all regulation of the supply of money and restrained the expansion of bank credit. It governed the foreign exchanges and safeguarded the money market from the disturbing influences of the Treasury's operations. It facilitated the payments on balance of inter-regional and international trade and acted as well as the government's fiscal agent. In addition, and this was to be one of the principal sore spots and causes of complaint, the Bank through its branches in twenty states and the District of Columbia competed directly with private banks in lending and note issue. In the West this type of operation served to supplement the inadequate banking facilities of the region, but in the East there was less need for this, and consequently it drew the censure of the private commercial banks, which felt that they were sufficient and resented the Bank's competition. (Today, fortu-nately, for the most part the Federal Reserve as a central bank does not compete directly with the member banks, but acts rather as a bank of last resort and as a bankers' bank.) This feature of the Second Bank's operation and its general regulatory function made it objectionable to many "get-rich quick" Americans; they wanted bank credit to finance their ambitious schemes, and the Second Bank, on the whole, could not be expansive enough to suit their purposes. Many of them did not appreciate the need for any regulation of bank credit as a whole, and complained that it was oppressive and that it drained the wealth from the newer sections of the nation into the rich East.

In its first years under the new charter, the Bank's management was marked by laxity and gross corruption. Captain William Jones, its first president, was hardly qualified for the difficult post, and he surrounded himself with specu-lators and others who were not scrupulous about how they got rich. Loans were made on unpaid stock of the Bank, and dividends declared even on shares that were not fully paid up, in violation of the charter. Then, to make matters worse, the president and cashier of the Baltimore branch, which had the most grandiose ideas of all, defrauded the Bank of $1,600,000. In the midst of all this the Bank was extending credit freely and adding to the speculative boom of 1819. When the crash came, the Bank had to curtail credit drastically to save itself and thus made the deflation worse than it might otherwise have been.

Even before these disastrous events, the tide of opposition toward the Bank had been rising in the states. Early in 1818 the state of Maryland imposed a tax of $15,000 a year on all branches or banks in the state that were not chartered by its legislature. The Bank refused to pay, and having lost its case in the state courts, it appealed to the federal Supreme Court. This case, *McCul-loch* vs. *Maryland*, was of great importance because at the time, a host of other states, such as Tennessee, Georgia, North Carolina, Kentucky, and Ohio, were levying similar punitive taxes on the Bank. In his decision, Chief Justice Marshall struck down these efforts to hamstring the Bank by his "loose con-struction" interpretation, relying on the doctrine of implied powers in the Con-stitution to uphold the Bank's functioning.[25] Meanwhile, the Bank was being

---

[25] *McCulloch* vs. *Maryland*, 4 Wheaton 420 (U.S. 1819). A key sentence in this famous decision runs, "Let the end be legitimate, let it be within the scope of the Constitution,

flouted and resisted by banks in Ohio and Georgia, some of which refused to pay the debit balances due it. In Illinois the legislature imposed a flat prohibition on the opening of branches in the state. But here too, the Supreme Court sustained the Bank's position, permitting it to operate until the ultimate confrontation between Nicholas Biddle and President Jackson.[26]

THE JACKSONIAN ASSAULT ON THE BANK

Nicholas Biddle, the scion of a wealthy, aristocratic Philadelphia family, a man of letters as well as of affairs, had been appointed a director of the Bank during the difficult times of 1819. When he assumed the presidency of that institution four years later, he was taking command of what was then the largest corporation in America and one of the largest in the entire world. Quick, precocious, talented, he soon brought the Bank under effective control and guided it successfully until the first administration of General Jackson. When he came into conflict with the Jacksonians, however, his naiveté, tactlessness, and political immaturity were his undoing, even if he could have won the President over to his view of the need for a central bank, which is very questionable, indeed.

The President in his very first message to Congress suggested his opposition to the Bank, saying in part, "Both the constitutionality and the expediency of the law creating this bank are well questioned by a large proportion of our fellow citizens; and it must be admitted by all, that it has failed in the great end of establishing a uniform and sound currency." Old Hickory's notions of banking were exceedingly crude; in the same year he had written Biddle, "I do not dislike your Bank any more than all other banks. But ever since I read the history of the South Sea bubble I have been afraid of banks." He had a vague agrarian prejudice against banks, especially those in Philadelphia where years before he had suffered a grave financial setback at the hands of a speculating merchant. The President's views, an amalgam of agrarianism and Jeffersonianism, tended to fade into *laissez faire*. As a self-made man and a rugged individualist, he paid his debts and he expected others to pay theirs. He was the champion of the common man, but more often than not, this new common man was manufacturer, banker, builder, and promoter. He was espousing the cause of the "active and enterprising" against the "wealthier classes"; the conflict he symbolized was between "those who already were rich and those who sought to become rich."[27]

---

and all means which are appropriate, which are plainly adapted to that end, which are not prohibited but consist with the letter and spirit of the Constitution, are constitutional."

[26] *Osborn* vs. *Bank of the United States*, 9 Wheaton 737 (U.S. 1824) ; *Bank of the U.S.* vs. *Planters Bank*, 9 Wheaton 904 (U.S. 1824).

[27] Hammond, *Banks and Politics in America*, p. 349; see also J. W. Ward, *Andrew Jackson.*

The House Committee on Ways and Means and the Senate Finance Committee submitted reports on the President's message that practically refuted all of his main points with regard to the Bank's constitutionality, its expediency, and the wisdom of founding an alternative institution based upon the credit and revenues of the government. Jackson took a somewhat milder tone on the Bank in his messages of 1830 and 1831, but then Henry Clay pressed Biddle to make the Bank the chief issue in the election of the following year. To force the issue, a recharter bill was introduced in Congress in the spring of that year; it passed both houses with moderate majorities, but died at the hands of the President's veto. In his veto message, Jackson declared the Bank unconstitutional; he contended that it was largely owned by foreigners; that the few American-held shares were concentrated in the hands of a small number of eastern individuals; that the annuity the bank paid was much too small. The battle lines in this titanic struggle were drawn, but the outcome was certain. Biddle had expanded the Bank's operations in the West and South immensely between 1829 and 1832; in the fall of 1831, he tried to put the brakes on credit, contending that he had to do so to prepare for a shift in the government's deposits. The cry went up from the West and South of "financial strangulation" by the "Monster."

Jackson's triumph in the election of 1832 sealed the fate of the Bank; he received 219 electoral votes to 67 for all the other candidates, Clay winning but 49. We need not give a detailed account of the familiar sequel: of the President's difficulty in finding a Secretary of the Treasury who would remove the government's deposits from the Bank; of his hesitation when Roger Taney, a consistent foe of the Bank, was ready to do his bidding because he feared that it would give Biddle an excuse for contracting the Bank's credit. Biddle did contract the Bank's credit drastically in anticipation of the closing, causing a considerable deflation, but he seems to have overshot the mark. His actions proved to be something of a boomerang in that even its friends turned upon it. Admitting defeat, Biddle obtained a new charter in Pennsylvania, and the Bank entered upon a speculative period of loaning money on stocks, contributing to the inflation that burst in 1837; it was finally forced to suspend payments on its notes during the depression years and in the subsequent liquidation; though it paid its creditors, its stockholders received nothing on their shares. Nicholas Biddle lost his fortune and the Jackson men were able to feel that their suspicion and hatred of the Philadelphian had been confirmed by events. But the distribution of the government's funds to the private banks swelled their reserves and contributed to the runaway inflation of the years 1833–37.

The ideology and rhetoric of the Jacksonians were filled with terms of abuse such as "oppression," "money power," "aristocracy," "monopoly," but as Hammond argues, in adapting the phraseology of agrarian idealism to money-making, the creed of the earlier generation became the cant of the later. Nor did they see any difference between the principle of freedom in an age of agrarianism and in one of business enterprise.

. . . Notwithstanding their language, therefore, the Jacksonians' destruction of the Bank of the United States was in no sense a blow at capitalism or property or the "money power." It was a blow at an older set of capitalists by a newer, more numerous set. It was incident to the democratization of business, the diffusion of enterprise among the mass of people, and the transfer of economic primacy from an old and conservative merchant class to a newer, more aggressive, and more numerous body of business men and speculators of all sorts.[28]

Behind the popular rhetoric were not only the pressures of aspiring Americans for greater scope for their enterprise but the even more powerful influence of sectional rivalry. New York State and its leading city, growing rapidly at the expense of its eastern rivals, had an important part behind the scenes in the destruction of the Bank of the United States. New York Democrats, such as Governor Van Buren and others, held leading positions in the administration of President Jackson. The state and New York City banks, recently greatly strengthened by the adoption of the Safety Fund system,[29] resented the regulatory powers which the Philadelphia bank had over their affairs. The revenues of the port of New York which were larger than those of all other American ports combined had to be deposited in the Wall Street office of the Bank and thereby came under the control of directors who were mostly Philadelphians. This practice rankled the pride of the New Yorkers, but they could not secure relief from the tyranny of Chestnut Street by a direct attack on the Bank. Their assault had to take the form of a popular crusade against privilege—a struggle of the "people" against the "money power." Van Buren, a close adviser to the President, had the skill and charm of a master politician to carry this off. Even Nicholas Biddle did not detect the enmity of the New York bankers until early 1833 when he wrote, "It is a mere contest between Mr. Van Buren's government bank and the present institution—between Chestnut Street and Wall Street—between a Faro Bank and a National Bank." The agrarian and state bank opposition to a federal bank were of long standing, but the enmity of the New Yorkers, moved as they were by covetousness and rivalry, was "the decisive new ingredient" in the Jacksonian attack upon the Bank of the United States.

Summarizing, we can note with Hammond the five important elements that in his view made the Jacksonian assault an effective one: "These were Wall Street's jealousy of Chestnut Street, the businessman's dislike of the federal Bank's restraint upon bank credit, the politician's resentment at the Bank's interference with states' rights, popular identification of the Bank with the aristocracy of business, and the direction of agrarian antipathy away from banks in general to the federal Bank in particular. . . ."[30] This combination

---

[28] Hammond, *Banks and Politics in America*, p. 229.

[29] The Safety Fund system was a state-wide insurance of bank notes and, as later turned out, of deposit liabilities established in 1829. The member banks, which were limited in number, were required to pay ½ per cent of their capital into the Fund for six years. These banks were subjected also to periodic inspection by three bank commissioners, the first such supervisory authority established over banks in the states. See Hammond, *op. cit.*, pp. 556–563.

[30] *Ibid.*, p. 329.

of forces ended an effort at central banking that was ahead of its times; it was not until the nation adopted the Federal Reserve system was it to have a regulation of money and credit as potentially effective as the Bank of the United States.

FREE BANKING AND GENERAL INCORPORATION

"There is perhaps no business," said Roger B. Taney, Andrew Jackson's devoted aide, "which yields a profit so certain and so liberal as the business of banking and exchange; and it is proper that it should be open, as far as practicable, to the most free competition and its advantages shared by all classes of society."[31]

The culmination toward which the Jacksonian monetary philosophy tended came to realization with the passage of free banking laws in Michigan and New York in 1837 and 1838, respectively. In the past the privilege of operating a bank could be obtained only by passage of a specific legislative act. Now under these laws anyone was free to engage in banking so long as he complied with the general conditions provided in these statutes. One had to have the necessary money to start and meet certain other formalities, but otherwise banking was considered like trade in a commodity.

Free banking was, in essence, the application of *laissez faire* to the business of credit. Considering the dangers in such a course, one may wonder how it came to be accepted. Part of the answer is that it resulted from a curious combination of forces. On the one hand, there was the Loco Foco view that all banks should be abolished; on the other, there were those imbued with the spirit of enterprise who felt that their number should be increased and entry into the business facilitated. In opposition stood the supporters of the already chartered banks; for example, in New York, the bulk of the Jacksonian Democrats. When the depression of 1837 caused these banks to suspend payments, the demand for free banking became irresistible. Governor Marcy asked the Whig-dominated legislature to enact a free banking law such as the previous Democratic legislature had rejected. It was passed, becoming the second such law in the nation, the new state of Michigan having adopted a similar law the year before. The New York statute contained a provision that the notes of such banks be backed by government bonds equal in value to the notes issued, and it required such banks to keep a 12½ per cent reserve behind their banknotes. These were innovations in banking practice that were to be imitated more widely later.

The benefits of free banking, however popular, were very controversial. To its critics democratic banking opened the way to inflation and a flood of depreciated banknotes and a long history of bank failures. Its supporters pointed to the stimulus given enterprise by the democratization of the privi-

[31] *Ibid.*, p. 741.

lege. Certainly, there can be no question that the ambitious Americans of that time took advantage of their opportunities. In New York state, for example, within the first three years of the law's existence the number of banks doubled. In Michigan, within a year of the law's passage, more than forty banks were established under its terms. But, alas, within two years more than forty were in receivership. Free banking, which in time become general in the United States, has not always been synonymous with stable, well-regulated banking. The need for regulation and responsibility in banking came to be recognized much later than the freedom of starting a bank.

Jacksonian democracy assailed the Bank of the United States as only the most obnoxious of the species of privileged corporations. It feared monopolies in their various forms, and as in these years of lusty economic expansion corporations became more numerous, there were increased reasons for protest. Thus, Daniel Raymond, the lawyer-economist, wrote in 1820: "The very object of the act of incorporation is to produce inequality, either in rights, or in the division of property. *Prima facie*, therefore, all money corporations are detrimental to national wealth. They are always created for the benefit of the rich, and never for the poor. . . ."[32] In the corporation lies the possibility of anonymity and therefore the evasion of that individual moral responsibility that the Jacksonians were so fond of emphasizing. "As Directors of a company," wrote William Gouge, "men will sanction actions of which they would scorn to be guilty in their private capacity. A crime which would press heavily on the conscience of one man, becomes quite endurable when divided among many."[33] This type of fear and denunciation of corporations was strongest in the West, but as time passed and the need for corporations became more evident, the Jacksonians turned to making corporations safe for democracy rather than abolishing them. Indeed, with the restriction of the functions of government, such as was implied in Jackson's Maysville veto, there was a need for corporate enterprise and for such a privilege as limited liability. These objectives could only be obtained through changes in the process of corporate formation.

Connecticut led the way in this reform in 1837 by passing the first general incorporation law in the United States. Actually New York state had moved in this direction as early as 1811, but popular distrust of corporations delayed widespread action along these lines for a quarter of a century. After 1837 the adoption of such law was so common that by the 1850's most of the important manufacturing states had passed such legislation. While most enterprises continued to be organized in the individual or partnership form, these laws facilitated the formation of railroad corporations and other types of enterprise in the following years.

---

[32] D. Raymond, *Thoughts on Political Economy* (Baltimore, Fielding Lucas, Jr., 1820), p. 427, quoted in Taylor, *Transportation Revolution* (New York: Rinehart, 1951), p. 242.
[33] A. M. Schlesinger, Jr., *The Age of Jackson* (Boston: Little, Brown and Co., 1950), p. 335.

General incorporation laws reflected the Jacksonian stress on the need to democratize enterprise, to give wider economic opportunity to all. "By opening the process of incorporation to all comers who could meet state requirements, legislators progressively sundered the concept of the corporate form of business from its association with monopoly privilege and for many decades made it an element in the growth of free enterprise—a contribution to the development of American business that can hardly be overestimated."[34]

The philosophy of free, competitive enterprise as against the maintenance of corporate monopoly privilege was forcefully asserted by Justice Taney in the Charles River Bridge case in 1837.[35] This bridge had been erected by Harvard College and some prominent Bostonians in the 1780's under a Massachusetts charter. With the growth of population and business, traffic over it mounted with the result that the value of its stock skyrocketed. Believing that a new bridge was badly needed, the state legislature in 1828 chartered another, the Warren Bridge, to be constructed close to the older one. The proprietors of the latter, anxious to protect the value of their stock, sought to stop the construction of the new bridge. In the ensuing lawsuit they were represented by four distinguished lawyers, among them Daniel Webster, who argued that the legislative grant to the original company was a contract and that the state should not violate the bridge franchise by allowing another company to compete for the traffic.

Judge Taney's majority opinion, which reflected the view of the five Jacksonian appointees to the Supreme Court, was a historic plea for the public interest and free competition as against the case for entrenched monopoly. The rights of property, Taney conceded, should be "sacredly guarded," but "we must not forget that the community also have rights, and that the happiness and well being of every citizen depends upon their faithful preservation." The State, he argued, could not be supposed to have surrendered "its power of improvement and public accommodation in a great and important line of travel along which a vast number of its citizens must daily pass." And in a country like ours, he went on to state, "free, active and enterprising, continually advancing in numbers and wealth new channels of communication are daily found necessary, both for travel and trade, and are essential to the comfort, convenience and prosperity of the people."

To the conservative lawyers such as Kent and Story, Taney's opinion appeared as another "manifesto of anarchy," as bad as Jackson's bank veto message. Actually, however, as one student of the Supreme Court has observed, it gave encouragement to "all businessmen who contemplated investments of capital in new corporate enterprise and who were relieved against claims of monopoly concealed in ambiguous clauses of old charters."[36] In

---

[34] R. Hofstadter, *The American Political Tradition* (New York: A. A. Knopf, Inc., 1948), p. 63.

[35] *Charles River Bridge* vs. *Warren Bridge et al.* 11 Pet. 420.

[36] C. Warren, *The Supreme Court in United States History* (Boston: Little, Brown and Co., 1935), Vol. 2, p. 24.

court decisions after this Justice Taney continued to give strong support to corporate development and free enterprise.

GOVERNMENT AND ECONOMIC GROWTH

Our study of Schumpeter's theory of economic growth has not taken explicit account of the influence of government upon the process of innovation. In the first part of this chapter we have taken note of the influence of the culture and social structure of the United States in these years upon the supply of entrepreneurs and innovators; in this section we need to examine more closely the effect of governmental policies (other than those already discussed) upon economic growth in this period.

In analyzing the role of government in the Jacksonian era, it is especially important to differentiate sharply between federal and state activity because, on the whole, while the federal government's promotional role was a declining one, the state governments assumed extraordinary burdens in these years.[37]

When viewed from the standpoint of the sources of realized income, the contribution of both the federal and state governments was not large. Martin's data show that in 1819 Americans realized some $17 million of income from government, or 1.9 per cent of their total realized income and in 1839, some $39 million, or 2.4 per cent of the total income of that year.[38] Yet such an aggregative approach to the subject ignores the possible "leverage effects" that governmental policy may have had on private economic activity; the mere presence of government may stimulate economic activity that appears, on the surface, to be wholly autonomous and private.[39]

The fiscal operations of the government in general were on such a small scale as not to exert a large influence upon the normal operations of the rest of the economy. Total expenditures of the government at Washington typically remained under $20 million annually in the years up to 1837 and in that year they reached $37 million. In the following nine years they averaged below $30 million. The federal government's financial position in most of these years was an easy one; in the years 1816–36 there was a deficit in only three years and in most of the period the annual surplus amounted to many millions. The contribution of the state governments to the income of the people both in its direct and indirect forms varied from time to time and from region to region, depending on the extent of the state's participation in the economy. Harvey

---

[37] S. Bruchey, *The Roots of American Economic Growth, 1607–1861* (New York: Harper and Row, 1965), pp. 124–128.

[38] R. F. Martin, *National Income in the United States, 1799–1938* (New York: National Industrial Conference Board, 1939), p. 87.

[39] H. W. Broude, "The Role of the State in American Economic Development, 1820–1890," in H. G. J. Aitken, ed., *The State and Economic Growth* (New York: Social Science Research Council, 1959), pp. 4–25.

Segal's studies of canal construction show us that in specific areas the state governments could contribute a substantial share to a locality's income.[40]

The bulk of the federal government's revenue in these years came from public land sales and the duties on imports. Chart 1 shows the fluctuations in these two major sources of revenue over the years 1815–43.

CHART 1

Receipts of the Federal Government, 1815–1860

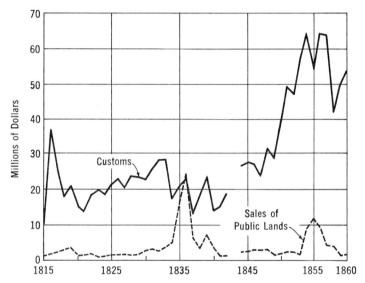

Reproduced from G. R. Taylor, *The Transportation Revolution, 1815–1860* (New York: Holt, Rinehart and Winston, 1951), p. 356, with permission of the publisher. First appeared in the *Annual Report of the Secretary of the Treasury*, 1932, pp. 362-363.

In view of the importance of agriculture in the economy of this period it is logical enough for us to consider initially federal land policies as they relate to economic growth. The main features of the land laws of these years are summarized in Table 1. As can be seen from this table, after 1820 the emphasis in our federal land policy shifted from revenue to stress the quick settlement of the land. As the representatives of the new western states became more numerous in Congress, the land laws became more liberal. The credit system had been started in 1796 and was increasingly liberalized until it broke down in the speculative boom of 1819. As a consequence, Congress in the following year abolished the credit feature and lowered the price to $1.25 per acre. A would-be farmer could purchase a farm from the government for as

[40] C. Goodrich, et al., *Canals and American Economic Development* (New York: Columbia University Press, 1961).

little as $100 after that. In addition, relief laws were passed to aid farmers who had purchased more land on credit than they could afford.

TABLE 1

*The Essentials of Government Land Policy
in the United States,* 1785–1832[a]

Act	Minimum Unit in Acres	Minimum Auction Price per Acre	Terms of Sale
1785	640	$1.00	Cash, ½ by township; ½ by sections
1796	640	2.00	½ cash, ½ credit, 1 year
1800	320	2.00	¼ cash; ¼ 2 years; ¼ 3 years; ¼ 4 years
1804	160	2.00	Same as in 1800
1820	80	1.25	Cash
1832	40	1.25	Cash

[a] Source: H. F. Williamson, ed., *The Growth of the American Economy* (Englewood Cliffs, N.J.: Prentice-Hall, Inc., 1946), p. 104.

Despite the low price at which the government was selling land, there were many who could not buy it; these people settled on land that was as yet unsurveyed. As "squatters" they contended that the actual settlers who had improved the land were entitled to make the first bid for it when it was put up for auction. Under their pressure Congress granted partial preemption rights to such squatters in a series of acts passed between 1832 and 1840. Then, in 1841, Congress passed Henry Clay's permanent preemption law, which gave the actual settler a right to buy the land on which he had a claim at the minimum price in advance of the auction.

The federal government's land policy was a subject of constant controversy in these years. In retrospect, we may ask to what extent it contributed to the nation's economic growth in this period. Generally, it is agreed that it had the merit of getting the land quickly settled and distributed among a large number of people, though not all of them lived on the land. With the improvements in farm technology and transportation and the development of regional specialization in this and the following periods, the pattern of land ownership that the federal government's policy fostered made possible a veritable agricultural revolution. This development was an indispensable step in the nation's progress toward an industrialized economy and higher levels of consumption and welfare.

Still, there are those who would point to the shortcomings in the policy we followed in the disposition of the public domain in these years. They criticize its encouragement of excessive land speculation and point to the adverse social consequences of the latter on the nation. The extent of land speculation at the height of the booms in this period was remarkable. One expert on the subject states that "Between 1835 and 1837, 38,000,000 acres of public land were sold, 29,000,000 of which were acquired for speculation. . . ."[41] While the speculators were very important in securing internal improvements from the federal and state governments and in that way spurred some desirable economic growth, they contributed, on the other hand, to the development of land tenancy by the usurious rates of interest that they charged the poorer settlers and by other devious practices. Professor Gates provides us with this damaging appraisal of their role:

> Speculator ownership and tenancy did not always result in the best use of the land. It has already been seen that speculator ownership forced widespread dispersion of the population and placed heavy tax burdens upon farmers whose improved lands could be more heavily assessed than the speculators' unimproved land. Furthermore, speculators were slow to pay taxes. They resisted increased levies, secured injunctions against expenditures for buildings and roads, and sometimes simply refused to pay taxes. Heavy interest penalties and tax titles did not trouble them particularly since they knew they could later make a compromise settlement with the hard-pressed county boards, or could have the tax titles set aside by the courts. All this meant that the tillers of the soil, if they were to enjoy the benefits of schools, roads and local railroads had to dig down into their own jeans more deeply because the speculators were not carrying their share of the burden. Taxes continued to climb and rarely or never declined, even in a period of depression . . . Heavy tax burdens forced farm practices which depleted the soil, produced erosion and diminished land values.[42]

Thus, while our federal land policies in this period made for rapid economic growth, they also contributed to periodic instability in the economy and a good deal of inequity in the process.

The protective tariff in these years was the subject of varying degrees of controversy, sectional and otherwise, depending upon the level of the rates and, should we say, upon the participants' state of ignorance. The first tariff of this period, that of 1816, represented a reduction from the high levels of protection prevailing during the War, but it was still protectionist in intent and effect. The act provided for a general rate of about 20 per cent on dutiable goods, somewhat higher levies on cotton and woolen cloth, but it was not opposed violently in the South; even John C. Calhoun voted for it.

The tariff bill of 1820, carrying increases on the rates on woolens, cotton goods, iron, and hemp, was intended to protect the hard-pressed small manufacturers who had sprung up during the years of the embargo and the war. It created more sectional differences. This proposed law was notable too for the fact that for the first time popular support for a tariff came from the working class and others who were badly injured by the depression of 1819. The home markets argument now made its appearance, Henry Clay contending that a

---

[41] P. W. Gates, "The Role of the Land Speculator in Western Development," *The Pennsylvania Magazine of History and Biography* (July, 1942), as reproduced in G. D. Nash, ed., *Issues in American Economic History* (Boston: D. C. Heath and Co., 1964), p. 187.

[42] *Ibid.*, p. 192.

prosperous working class would provide markets for the products of our farms. For the first time too a group of "home-grown" economists and publicists, men such as Daniel Raymond, Hezekiah Niles, and Matthew Carey, attacked the free trade principles of Adam Smith and argued the case for protectionism as a cure for unemployment. The tariff bill of 1820 failed passage in the Senate by one vote; the weakness of the protectionist cause at this time is usually attributed to the divided state of the New England mind, the shipbuilders, distillers, and woolen interests opposing higher duties.

The Act of 1824 pushed the rates up to a level of between 25 and 40 per cent, particularly for such products as wool, iron, hemp, and cotton goods. Still the woolen manufacturers were not satisfied and pressed for revision, but despite the fact that they now had Daniel Webster on their side, Vice-President Calhoun defeated the Mallery bill with his deciding vote. There followed the political farce of the "tariff of abominations" in 1828, which the Jackson men hoped would defeat Adams for the Presidency; as John Randolph of Virginia sarcastically said, "the bill referred to manufactures of no sort or kind, except the manufacture of the President of the United States." The Jackson supporters had loaded the bill with abnormally high duties on raw materials and ship supplies needed by New England manufacturers and merchants, but to their surprise, the woolen interests favored the bill, despite the hardships it imposed on others, and it passed. This law was the high-water mark of pre-Civil War protective legislation, carrying the level of the average duty to 50 per cent.

The tariff Act of 1832 reduced the level of the rates to about that of 1824 (an average of 33 per cent on dutiable imports), but this was not satisfactory to Southerners and particularly to the South Carolinians who were being hard pressed by the new cotton regions. South Carolina led in the nullification movement by declaring the tariffs of 1828 and 1832 "null and void and no law, nor binding upon this state, its officers or its citizens." President Jackson met this emergency with force and statesmanship. With Henry Clay's aid, he had enacted the Compromise Tariff of 1833, which provided for a gradual reduction of all tariff duties to 20 per cent by 1842. The Force bill, another Jacksonian measure, gave the President the power to use the Army and Navy to collect duties, if judicial processes were obstructed. South Carolina repealed the nullification ordinance, but saved face by declaring the Force Act null and void; however, there was no longer any need for the latter. A crisis in sectional relations had been met and passed—until another day.

The reductions provided for in the tariff law of 1833 were duly carried out until with the onset of the depression in 1839 a popular demand for remedial legislation led to substantially higher rates under the provisions of the Act of 1842. This short-lived law was later revised downward with the return of the Democrats to power and the enactment of the Walker Tariff of 1846.

The influence of the various tariff laws on the nation's economic development in this period is exceedingly difficult to determine, and most students have been careful in drawing conclusions on the subject. However, one highly respected economic historian has made this general observation on tariffs before 1860: "It is not going too far to say that no important feature in our economic development during that period can be attributed unmistakably to tariff legislation. No important industries can be said to have been created or prevented from growth by that legislation. Other influences determined the main features of development, and the tariff policy did nothing more than modify them a little, where it had any effect at all."[43] The tariff was a prominent subject of political debate during these years, but the main lines of the nation's economic development seem to have been attributable much more to other policies, private and public.

THE POLITICS OF DEPRESSION

One of the most amusing and yet significant developments in the political history of this period was the so-called Whig counter-transformation, which followed the depression of 1837. With the coming of that depression, the Whigs finally had an issue, and the political tide turned almost immediately. In 1837 and in the interim elections the Whigs scored important victories. Then, in 1840, they rode into office with their log-cabin campaign for General William Harrison, the hero of Tippecanoe. It was a perfect case of the opposition imitating the political innovations of the Jacksonians and by stealing their thunder, the slogans and the rhetoric of democracy, beating them at their own game.

The Whigs took up the tactics of the despised Democrats. They reviled President Van Buren as an aristocrat, given to high living and lordly manners. They pictured him as one who put cologne on his whiskers, ate from gold plate, "laced himself in corsets such as the women in town wear and if possible tighter than the best of them." General Harrison, on the other hand, was the noble Roman of the West who lived in a hut, worked with his own hands, etc. One of the assets of General Harrison was that his political views were as unknown as Jackson's had been when he came to office. Nicholas Biddle, not otherwise known for his political savvy, shrewdly advised: "If General Harrison is taken up as a candidate, it will be on account of the past. . . . Let him say not one single word about his principles, or his creed—let him say nothing—promise nothing. Let no Committee, no convention—no town meeting ever extract from him a single word about what he thinks now or will do hereafter. Let the use of pen and ink be wholly forbidden."[44]

It is not our intention to pursue further the changes in political tactics that

[43] Substantially similar conclusions were drawn by the late Professor Taussig in his famous *The Tariff History of the United States*, 8th Ed. (New York: G. P. Putnam's Sons, 1931).

[44] C. A. and M. Beard, *The Rise of American Civilization* (New York: The Macmillan Co., 1935), Vol. 1, p. 576.

accompanied the depression, but we might briefly consider the ideological ferment of the 1840's, which has led some historians to dub it the "hot-air decade." In an age buffeted by change, the strains produced by the long depression of 1837 served, it would seem, to aggravate the tendency for Americans to turn to religion, reforms, and "isms" with a vengeance. The temper of the age was certainly a reforming one, as Emerson wrote to Carlyle: "We are all a little wild here with numberless projects of social reform; not a reading man but has a draft of a new community in his waistcoat pocket." The columns of a newspaper might announce for Monday night a meeting of the anti-slavery society; Tuesday night, the temperance society; Wednesday night, the graham bread society; Thursday night, a phrenological lecture; Friday night, an address against capital punishment; Saturday night, the Association for Universal Reform."

Prominent among these movements of the 1840's was the Associationism of Fourier, which Albert Brisbane sought to popularize, the famous experiment at Brook Farm, and the agrarianism of George H. Evans, which stood for equal, individual, and inalienable landholdings. Some of these reforms and panaceas have been regarded as protests and reactions to the spread of the new industrialism; all of them testify in some way or another to the fact that this was an age of such turbulent change that Americans were led to seek new answers to the perennial problems of social life. Certainly, this period was constructive in further shaping the American political, social, and institutional framework so that it promoted the impulses to expansion in the economy and prepared it for what Rostow terms the "take-off" to sustained economic growth.[45] Still, the human costs involved in so rapid a transformation of the nation's economic and social life should not be overlooked. It was something of this that Albert Gallatin probably had in mind when he wrote to an old friend toward the end of Andrew Jackson's administration:

> The energy of this nation is not to be controlled; it is at present exclusively applied to the acquisition of wealth and to improvements of stupendous magnitude. Whatever has that tendency, and of course an immoderate expansion of credit, receives favor. The apparent prosperity and the progress of cultivation, population, commerce and improvement are beyond expectation. But it seems to me as if general demoralization was the consequence; I doubt whether general happiness is increased; and I would have preferred a gradual, slower, and more secure progress. I am, however, an old man, and the young generation has a right to govern itself. . . .[46]

---

[45] Many of the political and sociological changes that Rostow regards as a necessary precondition for the take-off occurred in this period. See W. W. Rostow, *The Stages of Economic Growth* (Cambridge: Cambridge University Press, 1960), p. 26.

[46] As quoted in Hammond, *Banks and Politics in America*, p. 9.

Part 4

THE ACCELERATION OF GROWTH AND CAPITAL FORMATION, 1844–1857

INTRODUCTION: THE TAKE-OFF STAGE

The changes that took place in the United States during the period 1844–57 were remarkable when one considers the relative speed with which they occurred. One might well wonder whether it is possible for any theory of economic growth to provide a framework wide enough to encompass the diverse developments occurring in the social, political, and economic life of the nation. It might be pertinent to ask whether the developments had a common cause that accelerated change of such a widespread nature. Our question indicates that the requirements we place on a theory of economic growth, adequate enough to explain this period in United States economic history, are complex indeed.

In light of these requirements for such a comprehensive theory we find that the work of Walt Whitman Rostow provides a model for interpreting the dynamics of the period 1844–57. Professor Rostow first presented his ideas on economic growth in *The Process of Economic Growth*[1] published in 1953. The concept of the "take-off" first appeared in an article in the *Economic Journal* in March, 1956.[2] In 1961 an elaboration of his earlier thesis appeared in the book, *The Stages of Economic Growth*.[3]

Essentially, Professor Rostow perceives economic growth taking place in a series of five chronological stages. We have discussed the first two stages, the traditional society and preconditions for take-off, in an earlier section. The third, or take-off stage, and its analysis, provide a framework within which we may consider the economic growth of the United States from 1844–57. Rostow defines this take-off stage as a series of related conditions, all of which are necessary for rapid growth. These are:

1. A rise in the rate of productive investment from five per cent or less to ten per cent of national income . . . [That is the fraction

$$\frac{\text{total productive investment}}{\text{Net National Product}} \geqq 10\%]$$

2. The development of one or more substantial manufacturing sectors, with a high rate of growth;
3. The existence or quick emergence of a political, social and institutional framework which exploits the impulses to expansion in the modern sector

[1] W. W. Rostow, *The Process of Economic Growth* (Oxford: Oxford University Press, 1953).

[2] W. W. Rostow, "The Take-Off into Self-Sustained Growth," *Economic Journal* (March, 1956).

[3] W. W. Rostow, *The Stages of Economic Growth* (Cambridge: Cambridge University Press, 1961). In this treatment of Rostow's work we will not discuss the internal consistency of the theory; however, students interested in a mathematically rigorous exposition are encouraged to consult S. C. Tsaing "A Model of Economic Growth in Rostovian Stages," *Econometrica*, Vol. 32, No. 4 (October, 1964), pp. 619–651.

Walt Whitman Rostow was born in Brooklyn, N.Y. in 1916. He was educated at Yale and Oxford Universities. He taught economic history at the Massachusetts Institute of Technology as well as at Oxford and Cambridge Universities. From 1961 to 1966, he was Chairman of the Policy Planning Council of the U.S. Department of State. During 1966–1969 he was Special Assistant to the President. Currently, he is teaching at the University of Texas.

World Wide Photos

and the potential external economy effects of the take-off, and gives to growth an ongoing character.[4]

Rostow points out that if we take the marginal capital to output ratio $(\Delta K/\Delta O)$ for the economy, at an early stage of development, as being 3.5 to 1, a *prima facie* case can be made for the need to fulfill this investment requirement. If population were to rise by 1–1.5% we would need 3.5 $(\Delta K/\Delta O)$ times that increase as our productive investment (or from 3.5% to 5.5% of NNP as regular investment), just to maintain the same level of per capita NNP. In addition, if an increase in NNP of 2% per annum is also desired then we need an additional 7% as productive investment, and total capital formation would range from 10.5% to 12.5%. Clearly, it is necessary to increase investment from 5% to 10% per annum if a 2% growth rate is desired in the face of a population rise of 1–1½%. At a 2% rate of growth in NNP, compounded annually, the economy would double every 35 years, and at best this would be considered a slow rate of development. (This investment criterion, condition number one, has been described as the "Arthur Lewis condition" after its author, a well-known growth theorist.)

This condition is not so difficult to attain as it might look at first glance because autonomous investment increases of 10% or more would be accelerated by the increased income, which in turn would increase consumption and provide more opportunities to invest. This cycle of increased investment, which leads to increased income, increased consumption, and then increased autonomous investment again, could then take on an explosive character, lifting the economy into a cumulative process of economic growth and expansion at accelerated rates. This kind of cyclical effect would give economic growth a self-sustaining quality that would provide the minimum effort leading to a take-off into rapid economic development.

[4] Rostow, *The Stages of Economic Growth*, p. 39.

Rostow's condition number two requires the existence of one or more sectors in manufacturing that will accelerate growth. These sectors are defined as industrial complexes with the following characteristics:

1. They produce a product or products that enlarge effective demand and serve as the basis for a rapid rate of growth in output.
2. They create new production functions and an expansion of capacity in manufacturing that will then show increased productivity of new investment inputs.
3. They exhibit a high rate of plough-back of the profits by the entrepreneurs and a desire by management in these sectors to supply investment funds to other industries as well.
4. Expansion of manufacturing sectors leads to a chain reaction in other industries. This in turn encourages technical transformations and the potential for new production functions in other areas of a progressive nature.

The notion that particular sectors of the economy have different growth rates is indicated by a careful examination of characteristic number one. The sectors in the economy, as categorized by Rostow, are contained in three classes. The first class, called primary growth sectors, are areas within which many economies of scale occur. These primary growth sectors permit innovation or exploitation and set off a high rate of growth elsewhere. In direct response to the high growth rate in the primary growth sectors, the supplementary growth sectors initiate a rapid rate of economic expansion. Finally, as a result of the rapid advance in primary and supplementary growth sectors, total real income, production, and productivity increase. The industries that derive economic benefit from the overall growth of these variables are called derived growth sectors.

The following is a hypothetical example of the interaction of these sectors in an economy. Given: some innovation in the production of fuel (e.g., a pill, which when dropped into a bucket of water would supply high energy rocket fuel). The industry devoted to the production of such pills would be a leading growth sector. If, as a result of the innovation there was an increase in the production of rockets because the fuel was so abundant, the rocket-producing industries would be labelled the supplementary growth sector. Increase in the production of rockets and pills would increase the number of employed persons, while decreasing unemployment, thus causing an increase in real income and output. If some of the increased income was used to increase the demand for housing, the housing industry would be called a derived growth sector.

The conditions within the firm that encourage increasing returns to scale are usually due to changes in the quantity of the factors of production; land, labor, management, and capital. The specific mixture of these factors of production, and the relationship of these inputs to output, defines the production function. In characteristic number two, Rostow is suggesting that the production functions in primary growth industries are such that by adding more factor inputs, output will rise faster than input increases. In all industries as the size of the individual plant or producing unit increases up to a point, the efficiency of production rises. This is the definition of increasing returns to scale. At some point the increases in input will be equal to the increases in output and this is called constant returns to scale. Finally, at a later point increases in input may yield proportionately lower output. This is termed decreasing returns to scale.

There are several advantages to an economy whose producing units are enjoying increasing returns to scale. Larger plants can hire better managers, utilize labor more effectively by encouraging specialization, institute quality controls, and invest in research and development. In addition they can use specialized equipment, purchase raw materials at quantity discounts, utilize wastes to form by-products and reduce per unit selling costs. There are also diseconomies of scale (higher possible costs because of increased plant size), such as increases in salaries because of the employment of excessive management and vulnerability to depressions. However, Rostow believes that in the take-off stage the economies will be greater than the diseconomies.

In capitalistic enterprise, there are four major sources of financial funds: equity investment, borrowing, internal fund generation (i.e., depreciation), and retention of profits. The latter, commonly referred to as the plough-back of profits, is generally high when there is an expectation and realization of increased rates of return on capital investment. A rising demand for domestically manufactured consumer goods places an increased proportion of income in the hands of entrepreneurs who are anxious to use this income and other funds in order to raise their production and to benefit from the high prices arising from expanded consumption. Under these conditions there is a substantial degree of plough-back of profits and good investment opportunities in other industries. In this connection Rostow cites the use of the income derived from foreign trade that is often diverted from the income earning sector and used for the importation of capital equipment. This imported capital equipment is usually scarce in an economy undergoing take-off because agricultural and primary commodities are the major goods produced efficiently and exported. Thus, the importation of capital goods allows for the development of infant industries, which might not exist because of lack of capital, and permits diversification of the economy, enabling it to avoid the staple trap.

In characteristic four of the leading sectors, Rostow is arguing that as a result of the expansion of these growth sectors, there would be an inducement to invest in other areas that would create the financial backing for innovations. These innovations would encourage technical changes, which might create new products, make older products more efficient to produce, or create new demands that would encourage further expansion.

Condition number three, which requires entrepreneurs to exploit impulses to expand, results from what economists call the external economy effect. An external economy is defined as a development that occurs outside a firm enabling it to produce its product more cheaply. For example, an increase in the size of automobile plants that would allow an increase in the scale of steel firms, reducing the average total cost of steel, would be an external economy effect to the automobile industry.

External economies of scale are the result of a variety of forces such as the availability of cheaper and better trained labor, more efficient communications, and more accessible markets. Productivity factors in one firm are improved by expansion in other firms when this phenomenon occurs. Cheaper raw materials and lowered overhead costs for utilities may also be deemed external economies. In short, external economies of scale could be defined as an increased demand for an industry's product, which results in a movement to lower positions of the firm's cost curves, which is caused by external factors.

External economies are usually accompanied by what is called "indivisibilities" in the supply of the factors of production or in demand. The former phrase refers to productive factors that cannot be utilized in small, discrete amounts, but must be employed in relatively large units or not at all. Thus, there is often an indivisibility in the supply of social overhead capital (a lumpiness of such capital) which precludes small, incremental efforts and requires instead a big project. Indivisibility of demand means that certain goods must be used together with others if their utilities are to be enjoyed (complementarity of demand).

The indivisibilities of investment in social overhead capital may be illustrated as follows: Investment in a socially desirable project A (which would be to the immediate benefit of a private entrepreneur) requires investment in equally socially desirable project B. An example is a dam in a river in a primitive part of a country that has no access roads to the proposed dam site. Investment in the dam would necessitate the investment in the roads as well. In short, there is no feasible way to break up the investment into smaller parts.

Realization that these indivisibilities might accompany external economies has led economists to suggest two alternate strategies of growth. One group of economists claims that since there are indivisibilities in the growth process, a synchronized application of investment funds must be administered to a wide range of the economy if rapid growth is to be promoted. The application of investment funds to a broad spectrum of the economy in order to stimulate economic growth is called the strategy of balanced growth. On the other hand, some economists believe that a narrower use of investment funds in industries having high growth impact is necessary. This has been termed the strategy of unbalanced growth.

The existence, or quick emergence, of a political, social and institutional framework that takes advantage of the external economies, the impulses to expand, differentiates Rostow's theory from that of Hagan.[5] Rostow requires that these conditions occur rapidly in the leading sectors. His treatise argues that war might be a method chosen to accelerate this process.

The three afore-mentioned conditions are not only necessary, but must be satisfied for the take-off to occur. Rostow's description of the first take-off (that of Great Britain) emphasizes this and defines the "demonstration effect"

---

[5] See above, pp. 23–24.

as the mechanism by which other nations have met the requirements for this minimum effort. He suggests that the first take-off in Britain was a result of a specific set of circumstances. In his words,

> It is, essentially, that, in the late eighteenth century, while many parts of Western Europe were caught up in a version of the preconditions process, only in Britain were the necessary and sufficient conditions fulfilled for a take-off. This combination of necessary and sufficient conditions for take-off in Great Britain was the result of the convergence of a number of quite independent circumstances, a kind of statistical accident of history which, once having occurred, was irreversible, like the loss of innocence.[6]

Rostow believes that the transmission of this demonstration of economic growth led other nations to emulate Great Britain's take-off.

When discussing the American take-off, Rostow states:

> The American take-off is here viewed as the upshot of two different periods of expansion: the first, that of the 1840's, marked by railway and manufacturing development, mainly confined to the East—this occurred while the West and South digested the extensive agricultural expansion of the previous decade; the second, the great railway push into the Middle West during the 1850's, marked by a heavy inflow of foreign capital. By the opening of the Civil War the American economy of North and West, with real momentum in its heavy-industry sector, is judged to have taken off.[7]

In short, Rostow's view suggests that the railways were a primary growth sector that had supplementary growth sector effects on the manufacture of iron, coal, and steel. The derived growth effects of the latter industries resulted in the momentum to take-off in other branches of the economy.

In a wider sense we can interpret the take-off stage as the underlying structure of an industrial revolution. This revolution is a conflict between people who hold a traditional view of economic society and those who seek to modernize the economy. The victory is won by new institutions of government, society, and economics. The victory may come in forms as bloody as warfare or as evolutionary as the gradual accommodation of diverse points of view. Thus, we may enter the laboratory of economics—history—to examine the usefulness of Rostow's ideas.

---

[6] W. W. Rostow, *The Stages of Economic Growth*, p. 31.
[7] *Ibid.*, p. 38.

Chapter 11

LEADING SECTORS IN THE TAKE-OFF STAGE, 1844–1857

THE RESUMPTION OF THE ECONOMY'S
FORWARD MOVEMENT

The major economic event of the year 1843 was the emergence of the United States from the long depression that had stalled its economy for six years. Statistically, the evidence is clear that the economy's upward movement resumed in that year, gained momentum, and assumed boom proportions in the fifties. The decade 1844–54 was one of unusual growth; Gallman's figures show manufacturing output increasing in those years by 69 per cent, a rate only slightly exceeded in the decade 1874–84.[1] Secular evidence of this growth can be seen also in the increase of the nation's population from 17 million in 1840 to more than 31 million by 1860. The line of westward settlement continued toward the Rocky Mountains, and in the later years of the period, the population movement eastward from the Pacific began.

The ethnic composition of the nation's population was changing rapidly, as new immigrants arrived at an accelerated pace. The number of these newcomers rose from a low of 72,000 in 1843 to a high of 428,000 in 1854. Whereas one million immigrants had come to the United States between 1790 and 1845, three million did so in the years 1845 to 1855. During the years 1843–44 alone, immigration from Ireland and Germany doubled, bringing in many farmers and mechanics and thus increasing the labor supply.

On the political front during this period, significant events were taking place: the annexation of Texas in 1845, the acquisition of the Oregon territory in the following year and of California and the Southwest in 1848, and the Gadsen Purchase of 1853. The continental boundaries of the nation were being rounded out, and vast new areas, rich in resources, were being opened up for exploitation and development. On the other hand, the nation's unity and stability were being increasingly threatened by the sectional differences over the institution of slavery.

[1] R. E. Gallman, "Commodity Output, 1839–1899," *Trends in the American Economy in the Nineteenth Century* (New York: National Bureau of Economic Research, Princeton University Press, 1960), Table 3.

This period saw a remarkable rise in the population of the nation's cities. Indeed, "the rate of urban growth in the United States reached its highest level in the twenty years before 1861."[2] Urban concentration was occurring at a more rapid rate than overall population growth. New York City's population trebled in these years, and Philadelphia's increased in nearly that proportion (166 per cent). By 1860, the former had more than one million inhabitants, and the latter had nearly 600,000. Boston and Baltimore also increased in numbers at a growth rate exceeding that of the nation. The rapid pace of urbanization reflected the growth of industry and commerce, the high native birth rate, and the flood of immigration.

Another indication of the nation's growing economic maturity was the advance of the railroad network during this period. From less than 3,000 miles in 1840, the railways expanded to more than 30,000 miles of track by 1860. Whereas the roads built before 1840 were largely in the East, in these years there was a rapid building of lines into the Midwest. The importance of the railroad as a factor in the economic growth of this period and subsequent decades of the nineteenth century is evidenced by the emphasis laid upon it by a number of economists. In Professor Schumpeter's analysis, for example, 1843 marks the beginning of the second Kondratieff (long cycle), which extends to 1897. This noted economist liked to refer to this whole span of years as being dominated by the "railroadization of the United States," and it is to be observed that in this same period there was a vast amount of railroad construction in Great Britain, France, and Germany as well.[3]

The integration of the market economy, which as we have seen in the preceding chapters was one of the great accomplishments of the years 1815–43, was carried a step further by a number of astounding inventions and innovations in the field of communications. Samuel B. Morse invented a practical telegraph in 1837, and six years later Congress appropriated $30,000 for the construction of the first telegraph lines from Baltimore to Washington, D.C. Ten years later, in 1853, an enterprising Rochester lawyer, Hiram Sibley, formed Western Union. By 1861 the telegraph lines of that company had reached the Pacific, and a total of 50,000 miles of telegraph line were in operation.

The merchant marine flourished also in this period. The years after 1845 were the era of the famous American clipper ships. Shipbuilding was carried on at a high rate from 1848 to 1858, with 400,000 tons of ships being constructed, on the average, in a year. These clipper ships were especially used for the California and Far Eastern trade. One reason for the increased ocean traffic to the West was to carry the forty-niners to California. Another factor in the prosperity of the shipping industry in these years was war; the wars

[2] G. R. Taylor, "American Urban Growth Preceding the Railway Age," *The Journal of Economic History* (September, 1967), p. 309.

[3] J. A. Schumpeter, *Business Cycles*, Vol. I (New York: McGraw-Hill Book Co., 1939), pp. 325ff.

between Great Britain and China in 1840–42 and 1855–60 threw part of the China carrying trade into American hands. The Crimean War of 1855 also provided a stimulus to our merchant marine because of the increased attention we gave to markets abandoned by other nations.

But in general, the most spectacular strides in economic growth were being made in agriculture, manufacturing, construction, and mining. Only the development of the railroad played as important a role in our economic development as did these industries. Farming continued to be the leading occupation of most people and contributed most to the nation's gross national product. Of the total value added in 1839, 70 per cent was derived from agriculture. The growth rate of the manufacturing sector in the period 1839–59 exceeds Rostow's required growth rate of from 5 to 10 per cent. Chart 1 provides good visual indication of the varying rates of growth in the different sectors of the economy. At this point it will be useful to examine the specific industries composing the leading sectors and to consider the historical factors that gave them a strategic role in the take-off process.

CHART 1

Value Added by Selected Industries in Current Prices 1839–1850

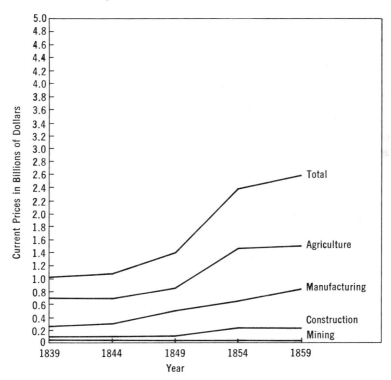

Source: *Historical Statistics of the United States*, pg. 139.

AGRICULTURE AS A LEADING SECTOR

While the statistics of growth for agriculture in the period 1844–57 show the dramatic expansion of this sector of the economy, the life of the average farmer during this time was far from easy. A minimum of forty acres of land was usually required if the farmer was to provide his family with a means of livelihood. To obtain these forty acres, a would-be farmer had to pay between one and two dollars an acre, or about $60 for the minumum acreage. Since there was a distinct preference by farmers for timber-covered land in the earlier period of the nation's history, by 1840 most of the desirable land of this type had been purchased. It was necessary, therefore, for many farmers to move westward. In general, many had to move so far west that they were in the open, prairie country of the Middle West. Prairie farming posed new and difficult problems for the settler. One of the most important was that the prairie sod was hard and resistant to cultivation. Clearing and breaking up this land required about $1.50 an acre in labor and materials. In computing the total investment involved, an additional $60 must be included to represent the farmer's equity in his property. If he chose to fence in his forty acres with lumber, the cost would be between $200 and $300. (Later on, Osage Orange hedge, developed by J. D. Turner of Illinois College, which was an inexpensive fencing material, could be used.) The supplies necessary to build a good farmhouse of lumber might cost an additional $500. Since water was not always immediately available, the farmer would often have to drive a well into the water table and use a windmill to drive the pumps that provided the precious fluid. The approximate cost of this equipment might be about $100. Initial seed and livestock purchases required additional working capital. Thus, an average farmer needed an investment of about one thousand dollars to begin his operations. Having made this substantial investment, he could look forward to working from sunrise to sunset for an annual income of much less than $1,000.[4]

Considering the enormous human effort involved in such an undertaking and the low rate of return, it is remarkable that such a high rate of growth was achieved. Even more astonishing was the fact that when the farmer did have excess capital funds he usually used it to expand his land holdings. A good part of the explanation for this seemingly irrational behavior lies in the fact that the American farmer was an optimist; he looked forward to an appreciation in the value of his land with the process of settlement and thought of the possible capital gains to be made from its sale. As was later said of him, he usually had one eye on his crop and the other on the "For Sale" sign.

---

[4] C. H. Danhof, "Farm-Making Costs and the 'Safety-Valve,' 1850–1860," *Journal of Political Economy* (June, 1941).

While the above description and calculation of possible costs is generally representative of the problems of the midwestern farmer in this period, it must be recognized that wide differences existed, depending on the region in which the farmers resided. In those years, the pattern of regional specialization in agriculture was undergoing marked change, as methods of transportation improved and new markets opened up. The corn, hog, and wheat belts, for example, were moving west. While corn was widely grown in the nation, by 1859 the supremacy in the production of this grain was held by Illinois, Ohio, and Missouri, in that order. The corn belt is traditionally the center of hog production so that we are not surprised to see that in that same year, Indiana and Illinois were the leading producers of pigs. The old "razor-back" type of hog was giving way to a better variety grown and fattened on the corn farms of the Midwest. At that time, before the day of the refrigerator car, it was common to drive the hogs over the Allegheny Mountains to such markets as Philadelphia, Baltimore, or New York. Cincinnati was the "Porkopolis" of the nation rather than Chicago, whose fame in this line was still in the future.

Wheat production was undergoing a marked transformation in these years also, so far as its regional location was concerned. Wheat has always been a frontier crop *par excellence* because it is less perishable than corn and its higher value, compared to its weight and volume, and easy transportability makes it ideal for remote, frontier regions. For these reasons, among others, the farmers who pushed into the upper Mississippi Valley were quick to take up its production. And so, though in 1849, Pennsylvania, Ohio, and New York were the leading states in the production of wheat, by 1859 Illinois, Indiana, and Wisconsin were first. (See map.)

The pattern of regional specialization in agriculture was clearly discernible in other fields as well. In dairy products, New York was the leader, as of 1859, producing nearly half of the nation's output of cheese and one-quarter of its butter. In sheep-raising, between 1830 and 1840, Ohio was the leading center; after 1850, sheep-raising moved still farther west.

This regional specialization in agriculture grew out of the desire of farmers to grow the products upon which they could make the largest profit, and it has been traditionally explained in terms of the principle of comparative advantage. The mechanism that leads sections to specialize in order to gain the benefits of interregional trade would work in the following way. Let us consider the interregional trade between the South and the Northeast in two commodities: corn and cotton. If we postulate that it takes one worker one man-year of labor to produce 4 bales of cotton or 2,000 bushels of corn in the South or 1 bale of cotton or 1,000 bushels of corn in the Northeast, we can see that farmers in the South can clearly produce more cotton and corn than workers in the Northeast. The South has an *absolute* productive advantage in the production of both commodities. But whereas workers in the South can produce four times as much cotton as the Northeast, they can produce only twice as much corn. By using all its labor resources in the production of

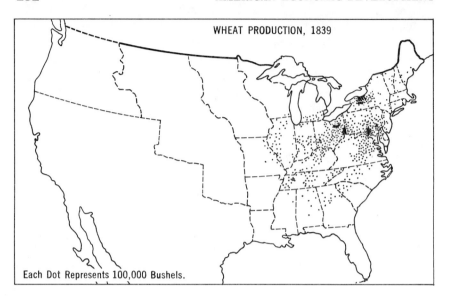

WHEAT PRODUCTION, 1839

Each Dot Represents 100,000 Bushels.

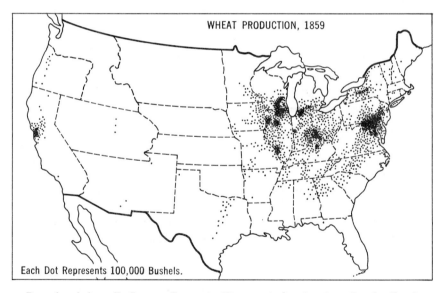

WHEAT PRODUCTION, 1859

Each Dot Represents 100,000 Bushels.

Reproduced from E. Bogart, *Economic History of the American People* (London: Longmans Green & Co., Ltd.), pp. 285–86. Reprinted by permission of the David McKay Company, Inc.

cotton and employing the labor of the man-year now released from the production of corn, the South might now realize up to 8,000 bushels of corn in exchange for its output of cotton. The Northeast would produce 2,000 bushels of corn and could receive up to 4 bales of cotton in trade with the South. Both regions would thereby gain by concentrating on the production of goods in which they had the greatest comparative advantage.

Whereas the model is valid under certain conditions,[5] we are not suggesting that all these conditions existed in the United States during the period 1844–57. Specialization was beneficial in agriculture because of the reason cited in the above example together with others that are more complex than the model indicates. Specialization in other areas did not take place when some of these complex conditions were not present. For example, large parts of the Middle West in these years remained self-sufficient in agriculture and other industries because of the inadequacy of interregional transportation.

FARMING AS A COMMERCIAL ENTERPRISE

Prior to the War of 1812, there was a foreign market for such staples as cotton, tobacco, wheat, and flour, but the domestic demand was so weak that a good deal of farming was of the self-sufficient variety. After the war, with the growth of American towns and cities, subsistence farming in the neighborhood of these markets began to decline as commercial opportunities for the sale of farm products opened up. Momentum was given to this development by the agricultural organizations that had been originally founded to disseminate information about these new markets and improved production techniques. The methods and benefits of scientific farming had been explored earlier, in the eighteenth century, by Englishmen such as Jethro Tull, Charles Townsend, Arthur Young, and others. This information appealed to the educated and wealthy farmers. Agricultural journals such as *The American Farmer* began to make these people aware of the demand for farm products in the industrialized Northeast and in the countries of Europe that needed raw materials. As was noted earlier, by 1820 the British cotton market was consuming more than half of the entire cotton crop of the South. In the next twenty years foreign nations demanded increased quantities of such crops as tobacco, wheat, corn, potatoes, and other vegetables. The foreign demand for beef, poultry, pork, and dairy products had also increased.

This increased commercial demand for these farm products led their growers to take more interest in cash crops, and in order to meet the demand they began to take careful stock of the state of their agricultural technology. It was at this point that the interaction of the agricultural and industrial sectors formed a leading link relationship. The farmer produced more surplus, thus making it possible to release labor from agriculture and make it available for use in manufacturing. The increased mechanization of production techniques helped to provide the food needed to sustain the newly created labor force in the cities. This need for improved farming methods in turn caused an increase in the demand for agricultural capital goods.

[5] For a detailed discussion of the theory of comparative advantage and its assumptions, see J. Viner, *Studies in International Trade Theory* (New York: Harper and Row, 1937). The reader who is interested in the limitations of this theory might also consider S. E. Harris, *International and Interregional Economics* (New York: McGraw-Hill, 1957).

FARM TECHNOLOGY AND RISING
AGRICULTURAL PRODUCTIVITY

The first major need in the development of agricultural technology was the improvement of land utilization. Because land was cheap under the federal policies in force during this period, farmers had paid little attention to good land utilization. But by 1820 a good deal of the acreage in northeastern United States was no longer prime farm land, and much of it had deteriorated into the category of the truly marginal. In the effort to counteract this condition, the farmers of this section turned to crop rotation and greater use of fertilizers during the 1820's and 1830's. In place of the weed fallow technique, more and more farmers began to use nitrogen fixing crops as a regular rotational device.[6] By 1840, fertilization and crop rotation were widespread in the region. However, these conservation measures were "too little and too late" because by that year the center of production of many of the most profitable crops had moved to the Midwest and the South. Fortunately, the farmers of the former region had learned a lesson from the soil butchery that had been practiced in the East; they avoided it not only for this reason but also because the high capital cost of the land they cultivated made such a policy irrational.

The second major need of American agriculture in this period was to improve the breed of livestock and raise the quality of the crops so that more power could be obtained from work animals and larger yields secured. Our livestock breeders turned to Europe for a more economical species of animal. In cattle the Herefords, Durhams, Jersey, and Holstein cows replaced the older breeds. European hogs were substituted for American razorbacks. Horses from Scotland, France, and the Lowlands were imported to take the place of oxen, the principal source of farm power prior to 1840. Better breeds of sheep, mules, and poultry were also imported in order to increase the hardiness of livestock being grown commercially in the United States.

The field crops developed in the United States in earlier years were hardier than most European species. The mere application of the more intensive continental methods of tillage was sufficient to increase crop output at an almost exponential rate of growth.

Of all the technical developments in the agricultural sector, none was more productive of a leading link effect than the invention of farm tools. In our earlier discussion of Schumpeterian theory (Introduction to Part 3), it was pointed out that the innovator has had a tremendous role in the dynamic

---

[6] Leo Rogin's study, *Introduction of Farm Machinery in its Relation to the Productivity of Labor in Agriculture in the United States during the Nineteenth Century* (Berkeley, Calif.: University of California Press, 1931), describes the technology of agriculture as it was practiced in that century.

development of our economic system. Innovations, we have learned, provide an impetus to autonomous investment and thereby help to accelerate the rate of economic growth. Probably no sector of the American economy benefitted as much from innovation as that which occurred in agriculture in these years. The list of innovators in agricultural technology is long. Thomas Jefferson, Charles Newbold, Jethro Tull, John Deere, Jethro Wood, and others made significant contributions to the evolutionary development of the plow. Cyrus McCormick and Obed Hussey invented the reaper, while Hiram and John Pitts devised a thresher. It was essentially the plow, the cradle, the reaper, and the thresher that were responsible for the major productivity increases in agriculture in these years.

John Deere, who developed a steel plow with interchangeable parts, established a factory for the manufacture of this valuable implement in Moline, Illinois in 1847. An average of about 8,000 plows per year were turned out for the period 1847–58. Cyrus H. McCormick sold 4,500 reapers between the years 1840 and 1850. Five hundred more reapers were sold by Hussey. The production of this kind of farm equipment required steel and other manufactured goods; in other words, a derived demand was created for the latter. Most important of all, the pioneering work in the invention of these tools led to a cycle of further experimentation with the result that better equipment was developed. The cumulative expansionary effects of these innovations on agricultural output and productivity can best be illustrated by the developments in the principal agricultural regions of the United States.

THE NORTHEAST

In these years, a tremendous agricultural upheaval occurred in the northeastern section of the nation. During the early colonial period, the Northeast had fed the local population from small, 150-acre farms, producing such commodities as wheat, rye, oats, barley, buckwheat, potatoes, pumpkins, peas, and beans. The region was self-sufficient agriculturally and was able to produce enough commercial crops to feed the urban areas of Boston, New York, and Philadelphia. But after 1820, insects such as the Hessian fly and plant diseases reduced the wheat crop at the very time that competition from the more fertile acres of the West was increasing. The center of wheat production moved westward, and the northeastern farmer increasingly turned to livestock production. Wool, a commodity required by the manufacturing mills that had sprung up throughout the region, became a good agricultural investment. But the requirements of sheep raising, in terms of land, rather quickly became prohibitive, and beef production became more profitable. Along with the production of beef there was an increased output of dairy products. As the urban areas grew, the demand for dairy goods dominated the New England agricultural market. Specialization in the production of these products led to the demise of the self-sufficient farm by 1860. Cows and heifers kept for milk rose from 6,385 in 1850 to 8,586 in 1860. Butter production increased substantially between 1849 and 1859 in the region; indeed, much of the increase in the national output of this commodity over these years can be accounted for by the growth of intensive dairy farming in the Northeast.

Lumber was another major product of the Northeast, and many farmers of the region were engaged in lumbering as well. Over half of all the lumber produced in the nation during this period came from the Northeast. Timber production was growing by leaps and bounds. Output and price trends for this period tell much of the story, as can be seen in Table 1.

TABLE 1

Lumber Production and Prices in the United States, 1799–1859[a]

Year	Total Production (in board feet per capita)	Per Cent Increase from Previous Period	Wholesale Price Index	Per Cent Increase or Decrease from Previous Period
1799	300	—	23	—
1809	400	33%	26	11%
1819	550	14	28	11
1829	850	15	28	0
1839	1604	88	45	61
1849	5392	236	40	−13
1859	8029	49	46	15

[a] Source: U.S. Bureau of the Census: *Historical Statistics of the United States, Colonial Times to 1957*, p. 312.

As the Northeast became an area of dairy farming and lumbering, the need for a large labor supply to till the largely marginal soil disappeared; the result was a surplus of labor that looked for employment in the industrial sector or in other agricultural regions of the nation. Many displaced New England and New York farmers moved west rather than add to the number of workers who were seeking employment in the industrial sector.

THE WEST

If we examine the development of agriculture in the West in these years, we see a situation largely the reverse of that in the Northeast, for much that the latter lost was gained by the West. The West became the chief source of grain such as wheat, barley, corn, and oats, with wheat ranking as the most important cash crop. Quantitatively, more corn was produced than wheat or any other grain, but this product was valuable mainly when converted into whiskey or pork. The livestock industry, important from the time of earliest western settlement centered in this area also, with beef cattle, pigs, and other meat animals being the principal products. Fruit, hemp, flax, and tobacco were other important crops raised in this area during the period 1844–57. Examination of the production figures for grains provides some insight into the rate of growth in this area; the pertinent statistics are set forth in Table 2.

TABLE 2

Grain Production in the United States, Selected Years, 1839–59[a]
(All figures in 1,000 bushels)

Year	Corn	Wheat	Oats	Barley
1839	377,532	84,823	123,071	4,162
1849	592,071	100,486	146,584	5,167
1859	838,793	173,105	172,643	15,826

[a] Source: U.S. Bureau of the Census, *Historical Statistics of the United States, 1879–1945,* pp. 106–107.

Because of the considerable amount of labor required to grow these crops, and its relative shortage in this region, farmers sought mechanical innovations to improve acreage yields. It is no wonder, therefore, that the value of farm implements and machinery in the United States jumped from $152 million in 1850 to $246 million in 1860. Fertilizer consumption in the same period jumped from 53,000 short tons to 164,000 short tons, an increase of over 200 per cent. Man-hours per 100 bushels of wheat dropped from 233 in 1840 to 200 in 1860, while the yield per acre actually increased by one bushel. In corn-growing, the picture was much the same. In 1840, 276 man-hours were needed to produce 100 bushels of corn, while only 230 man-hours sufficed to produce the same quantity in 1860. Yield per acre was up one half bushel as well over the same period. Thus, we see that regional specialization, new machines, better management, and innovation had made the West one of the most efficient agricultural regions in the history of the world as early as 1860.

THE SOUTH

The agriculture of the South was very different from that of the other regions in products, techniques of cultivation, and organization.[7] There were four major commercial crops in this region: cotton, tobacco, sugar cane, and rice. All these crops made high nitrogen demands of the soil and all required intensive labor under the existing state of technology.

The major innovational breakthrough for southern agriculture in this

[7] A leading work on this subject is L. C. Gray, *History of Agriculture in the Southern United States to 1860,* Vols. I and II (Magnolia, Mass.: Peter Smith, 1958).

period was the invention of the cotton gin in 1793. Tobacco continued to be the South's leading export and cash crop until 1803, but after that year cotton reigned as the region's leading product. Tobacco must be grown with intense care so that insect pests of one kind or another can be eliminated. In this period it was rare for more than fifteen acres of a farm to be devoted to tobacco growing. After a tobacco harvest it often took five or six years to replace the minerals lost from the soil. Slave labor was extensively used to produce this commodity, but its use presented major difficulties. First, the slaves were not well motivated to work the long, hard hours that tobacco cultivation required; secondly, the slaves were not trained for the technical problems that the growth of this product entailed; and, finally, since specialization was not practiced in growing this crop, the slave was required to learn more techniques than he could possibly master.

In cotton production, the problems posed by nature and the use of slave labor were much the same. Land was cheap, and as a consequence, the planters and small farmers did not pay careful attention to its cultivation or to its conservation. When the land was no longer productive, farmers moved on to more fertile areas. The complications and consequences of this exploitative attitude toward the land will be examined further in connection with the coming of the Civil War.[8]

Rice and sugar were also important cash crops. Their production was limited by the scarcity of the land suitable for their cultivation; rice was grown on the tidelands of South Carolina and Georgia, and the commercial production of sugar was largely limited to the Gulf coast area of Louisiana. The large labor requirements of this crop and the expensive equipment needed for sugar refining tended to limit the number of plantations engaged in its cultivation.

The South produced many other agricultural commodities in the antebellum period, but most of them were not cash crops. Corn, for example, was actually the leading crop of the South in that period in terms of value and the acreage harvested. It provided food for slaves, livestock, and was also consumed by the whites in many forms, not the least being whiskey. But little of the crop was sold for cash. Instead, as we have seen, the destiny of most of the South from 1843 to 1857 was tied to the fluctuations of the commodity markets for tobacco, cotton, or sugar; in this respect, their situation was much like that of the contemporary undeveloped societies that produce and rely upon a single commodity for their income. This lack of diversification in southern commercial farming was tied up, as we shall see, with the region's relative backwardness in general economic development.[9]

Considered as whole, it is clear that agriculture had a leading link effect on the American economy during the years 1844–57, as shown by the increase in the value of farmlands and the buildings thereon in this period. The

---

[8] See pp. 345–346 below for further analysis of these matters.
[9] See below, p. 359 for further discussion of this topic.

available statistics show an increase in this type of investment from $11.14 per acre in 1850 to $16.32 in 1860. This capital expansion of the nation's farms undoubtedly increased the demand for manufactured goods. The total value of agricultural gross output rose from $757 million in 1840 to $904 million in 1850 and finally to $1,579 million in 1860. This immense increase in output had to be largely financed by credit, and so the financial sector of the economy was another direct beneficiary of agricultural expansion in this period.

LEADING MANUFACTURING SECTORS OF THE ECONOMY

While agriculture was still the principal source of income and employment for the majority of Americans in this period, manufacturing also emerged as a leading sector of the rapidly evolving economy. This fact is evident in the mere increase in the number of those so engaged; the number of establishments in manufacturing showed an increase of about 15 per cent in the years 1849–59. Progress was very fast, particularly in the manufacture of steel, railroad equipment, fabrics, and in mining and the generation of power. But in this sector too, there were major differences in the rate of manufacturing development. The South, for example, accounted for less than 10 per cent of the production of iron and steel. While that region was one of the first in the nation to use railroads, it produced practically no railroad equipment. It did make a beginning in these years in the manufacture of cotton textiles, but its progress in this field was greatly overshadowed by the advances made by the northern mills. In mining also, the southern branch of the industry was not an important source of supply nor did it contribute as much income as that generated in other parts of the nation. In the production of power, the South still lagged behind the growth of the rest of the nation. Each of these industries had a leading link effect on the American economy that was to a large degree absent in the South. Because of this factor there were substantial differences in the character of overall economic growth in the South as compared with that in the Northeast and West.

THE IRON AND STEEL INDUSTRY

The development of the iron industry from colonial times to about 1840 had been somewhat retarded.[10] While, as we have seen, the American industry in the late colonial period was in some respects ahead of the British, technical developments were slow to appear in the early nineteenth century. The two

[10] An excellent study of this industry is P. Temin, *Iron and Steel in Nineteenth Century America, An Economic Inquiry* (Boston, Mass.: M. I. T. Press, 1964).

principal types of iron in use were cast and wrought iron. Iron-making was geographically scattered and carried on in small local forges and bloomeries; still, the iron deposits in eastern Pennsylvania made it a leading center, and there were other establishments in northern New Jersey, southern New York, and around Boston, Massachusetts, all of which depended on charcoal as a smelting fuel.

In 1840 the pig iron production of the 804 firms in operation amounted to 283,000 short tons. In the course of the next decade, the number of firms producing this product fell to 404 (as of 1850), but their output rose to 564,000 short tons. An industry estimate of 1856 put production at 813,000 short tons and four years later the census of 1860 showed production to be 988,000 short tons. The industry's rate of growth from decade to decade was approximately 40 per cent, and as can be seen from the statistics cited above, there was a decided trend toward economic concentration in the industry.

In this period iron and steel were mainly used in the production of armament, rails, nails, farm tools, carriages, wire, and machines. In 1840 the manufacture of cast and bar iron employed 30,497 workers and represented an investment of $20.5 million. The industry was the nation's third largest employer of labor, with only cotton textiles and construction having a larger work force. In terms of invested capital, it also stood in third place, the investment in textiles and construction alone exceeding it. By 1850 the capital value of all the iron works, foundries, forges, furnaces, and rolling mills exceeded $59 million and the industry employed over 50,000 workers.

The iron industry had so large a labor force partly because it employed the technique known as the puddling process. A resumé of the technical developments in the industry in the nineteenth century will be helpful in understanding the place of this process in its growth. Prior to 1784, both in this country and abroad, it was the practice of the ironmakers to hammer the impurities out of the "bloom" by hand. In that year an Englishman by the name of Henry Cort developed a process in which the molten iron was passed into a furnace with an iron oxide lining. The puddler who stirred the hot metal fluid with long bars caused the oxygen in the lining and the carbon in the iron to unite and escape as either carbon monoxide or carbon dioxide. Puddling was an important technical advance in the industry because it greatly increased productivity, but such was the resistance to new techniques that it was not introduced in the United States until about 1840. Meanwhile, other technological developments were occurring here which markedly increased the efficiency of the American industry. In 1833 a Rev. Frederick W. Geissenhainer, a Lutheran minister, discovered and patented a method of using anthracite coal instead of charcoal in the smelting of iron ore. The following year the hot blast oven, using anthracite, revolutionized the industry and made it possible to secure higher temperatures, expand capacity, and economize on fuel. After about 1840 this "anthracite iron" largely supplanted the charcoal variety in the American market; the English iron manufacturers, lacking adequate charcoal or anthracite, had already turned to the use of coke in their smelting operations.

One of the major factors underlying the growth of our domestic iron and steel industry was the tariff imposed during this period on European iron and steel. The United States could not compete with British iron because of the widespread use of coke in that country in contrast to our own use of the more expensive charcoal. However, the high tariff on foreign iron prevented it from capturing the American market. Also, the tremendous demand for iron because of the expansion of the railroads created a price level for the commodity that was so profitable that it drew new producers into the industry and caused those who were already producing iron to expand their production. Despite the progress made in the production of cast and wrought iron, these metals did not adequately meet the needs of our growing industries. Cast iron was brittle and wrought iron was very malleable and tended to wear out fast; our machine-using industries and the railroads desperately needed good, cheap steel. It was not until the close of this period, in 1856, to be exact, that the innovation appeared that made the production of high grade steel in large quantities and at a sufficiently low cost a feasible economic project.

The development of the technique for producing cheap and efficient steel provides an interesting historical example of coincidence in invention. In Great Britain around 1841, Henry Bessemer had experimented with a technique of passing a current of air over molten iron in a specially built converter in order to decarbonize the metal. In 1845, William Kelly of Eddyville, Kentucky, a manufacturer of kettles for boiling sugar cane, developed a blast furnace to accomplish the very same result in exactly the same way. Bessemer and Kelly each patented his process in his own country in 1856. Meanwhile, another Englishman, Robert Mushet, had obtained a patent for the use of spiegeleisen (an alloy of manganese and carbon) in steel-making. In the protracted patent litigation that followed, Kelly claimed that Bessemer had learned of his technique through English workmen who had been at the Kelly iron works. He was never able to substantiate his allegation. The outcome of the whole dispute was that Bessemer finally bought Kelly's claim on the process and paid Mushet a stipend for his contribution. Behind this seemingly remarkable instance of simultaneity in the process of discovery is the old saw about necessity being "the mother of invention." In this case, of course, the necessity arose out of the growing demand for steel in the industrial world.

THE EARLY DEVELOPMENT OF THE RAILROADS

As stated above, the railroads, one of the "growth industries" of this period, was a major consumer of iron and steel. It would seem appropriate, therefore, on this ground alone to examine the economic revolution of this dynamic industry. In addition, it is to be noted that Rostow and others contend that the railroads served the function of being a primary sector in the development of the American economy.[11]

Railroads make their appearance on the nineteenth century scene in a quite precocious manner. As early as 1815 the New Jersey state legislature granted the first railroad charter. Unfortunately, it expired before the state's Surveyor-General, John Stevens, could ever build a railroad. Ten years later Stevens built a pioneer locomotive powered by a single cylinder steam engine mounted across a track with a rack that could be meshed with a steam-driven gear. This crude locomotive was given its first experimental run on a half-mile track in Hoboken, New Jersey. Stevens had modelled his machine on the technology of the steam engine previously invented by the Scotsman, James Watt, and on the tram road pioneered by Silas Whitney of Boston (1807) and Richard Trevithick of Wales (1804). Actually, the first major success in steam locomotion was achieved by George Stephenson in 1825, when he ran Locomotive No. 1 between Stockton and Darlington in England. In 1829, Stephenson developed a new locomotive called *The Rocket* and won an open contest sponsored by the Liverpool-Manchester Railway. In the United States at the same time Horatio Allen tested his English-built locomotive *Stourbridge Lion* on a two mile track.

Perhaps the most colorful event in the early history of the railroad was the development of Peter Cooper's *Tom Thumb,* which made a successful run from Baltimore to Ellicott Mills, Maryland in 1830. The well-known story of the race of Peter Cooper's engine with a horse-drawn rail car and its subsequent defeat needs no retelling. However, it is often overlooked that the publicity and the performance of the *Tom Thumb* created a strong sentiment favoring the locomotive in this country. Soon, in perfect accord with Schumpeter's theory of the routineers following the innovator, other ventures were undertaken. In 1830 *The Best Friend of Charleston* set out on Christmas day with its train of cars in the first regular service to be offered in the United States. By the very next year, South Carolina, New York, and Maryland all had regular service lines. In that same year Robert L. Stevens developed the T-rails, which are used by all railroads today.

While the early efforts of these pioneers were primitive and cumbersome, in less than ten years a more sophisticated technology in railroading began to develop. After experimenting with wooden and stone rails, the railroads substituted iron rails in 1844 and they soon became standard; they permitted heavier loads and the attainment of faster speeds. Likewise, the different gauge tracks, which had caused much annoyance and inconvenience at first, were replaced in the 1850's when the modern standard gauge of 4 feet, 8½

---

[11] An outstanding study of railroads during the nineteenth century contends that they did not exercise a leading link effect. However, there is much controversy over the methodology used to arrive at this conclusion. See R. W. Fogel, *Railroads and American Economic Growth: Essays in Economic History* (Baltimore: The Johns Hopkins Press, 1964). For a good counter-argument, see A. Fishlow, *American Railroads and the Transformation of the Ante-Bellum Economy* (Cambridge: Harvard University Press, 1966); also for further discussion of the Fogel thesis, see below, pp. 439–440.

inches was widely adopted. Meanwhile the stage coach, which had been taken over as the passenger vehicle on the railroads, was being adapted and modified to the needs of the new mode of transport. One "peculiarly American device" was the "cow-catcher" to push off the animals that favored the rails as a place to nap.

Not the least of the resistances to be overcome by the railroad as an innovation was the popular mistrust, prejudice, and ignorance of the new form of transportation. Some ministers, it is said, denounced the railroads as being contrary to the divine will; other opponents said that the noise of the locomotives would stop hens from laying eggs, while wiseacres contended that man could not live a moment going at the unheard-of speed of 30 miles an hour.[12] The most serious opposition came from those who had a vested interest in the older means of transport, such as tavern-keepers or investors who benefitted from the canals or turnpikes. In New York State, for example, the canal interest was so great that up to 1844, no New York railroad was permitted to carry freight; it was not until 1851 that this ban was completely lifted.

In the early years, the first use generally of the railroads was as connecting links, carrying passengers to other systems of transportation, providing a subject for curiosity, and in other cases, transporting coal to seaboard. By the 1840's freight service had surpassed passenger service as the chief source of railroad revenue. The railroads soon became an important rival of the canals for traffic, but in the length of their mileage they quickly outdistanced the older form of transportation, especially after 1840. (See Table 3)

TABLE 3

Mileage of Railroads and Canals in the United States,
Selected Years, 1830–1860[a]

Year	Canals	Railroads
1830	1,277	73
1840	3,326	3,328
1850	3,698	8,879
1860	—	30,636

[a] Source: G. R. Taylor, *The Transportation Revolution,*
1815–1860 (New York: Rinehart, 1951), p. 79. Reprinted
from Annual Report of the Secretary of the Treasury, 1932,
pp. 362–363.

[12] Such critics contended that the speed of the railroads would contribute to giddiness and personal instability. An amusing example of the type of satire that some newspapers used against the early railroads is found in the following: "Twenty miles an hour, sir! Why you will not be able to keep an apprentice boy at his work! Every Saturday evening he must have a trip to Ohio to spend a Sunday with his sweetheart. It will encourage flightiness of the intellect. All conceptions will be exaggerated by the magnificent notions of distance. Only a 100 miles off? Tut, nonsense, I'll step across, madam, and bring you your fan." Quoted by B. J. Stern, "Resistances to the Adoption of Technological Innovations," in National Resources Committee, *Technological Trends and National Policy* (Washington, D.C.: U.S. Government Printing Office, 1937), p. 42.

Cootner has identified four distinct spurts in rail construction before the Civil War and the factors with which they were associated as follows:[13]

Phase I   (1827–34) in the eastern seaboard—increased demand for coal, the more rapid intercity passenger facilities, and the intensified rivalry among cities produced this first expansion.

Phase II (1834–41)—rail construction shifted to the old Southwest and Midwest in response to the westward movement of the cotton and wheat belts.

Phase III (1841–48)—confined to the New England and the Mid-Atlantic states and related to their industrial expansion.

Phase IV (1848–60)—northern wheat and southern cotton provided the impetus to the geographical shift in rail construction in this last phase.

In spite of their rapid growth in terms of mileage constructed, the railroads were unduly retarded during the 1840's and much of the 1850's by the prevailing promotional practices. In those years the development of a railroad was usually carried out by a rail promoter. Such an individual was not generally interested in the long term prospects of railroading and thus geared his promotion to selling short lines to relatively small communities as prestige items as much as a means of transportation. In New York, for example, roads were built between Albany and Schenectady, Schenectady and Utica, Utica and Syracuse, Syracuse and Auburn, and Mohawk and Hudson. These local roads did not constitute a "trunk line" (i.e., one connecting major cities) until the entrepreneurial talent of Erastus Corning forged them into one system, the New York Central Railway, in 1853. At about the same time two other trunk lines were formed by the consolidation of various small lines traversing the Alleghenies: the Pennsylvania Railroad, connecting Harrisburg and Pittsburgh (1852), and the Baltimore and Ohio, linking Baltimore to Wheeling, Virginia (1853). Before the end of the 1850's there were seven such trunk lines in operation in the nation.

Extension of the railroads into the Middle West with its greater distances required faster and more powerful equipment than had been used in the East. Again, the advancing art of rail technology responded dramatically to the need. By 1850 superb, new locomotives such as the Rock Island Lines' *Rocket*, the *Camelback*, and the *Pioneer* had made their appearance. These powerful machines were efficient, effective, and inexpensive to operate, and railroad expansion began to boom. As the tracks were laid, the frontier was pushed westward. Despite this advance of the railroads into the Middle West in these years, there was little rail construction west of the Mississippi prior to the Civil War. The building of the trans-continental lines was to be one of the major accomplishments of the post-war period.

It is important to note that very often the railroads were extended into undeveloped areas before settlement had taken place. Following their con-

[13] P. H. Cootner, "The Role of the Railroad in U.S. Economic Growth," *The Journal of Economic History* (December, 1963), pp. 477–521. This provocative article is based on the author's unpublished thesis, *Transport Innovation and Economic Development, the Case of the U.S. Steam Railroads, 1826–1886* (Mass. Institute of Technology, 1953).

struction came settlers ready to take advantage of the economical transportation already in their locality. Extending the railroads into the Middle West in itself moved labor in that direction. Railroad wages were relatively high, about $25 a month for laying track as compared with an average wage during the 1850's of about $20 per month. But there were more basic economic factors than these inducing this massive railroad construction into the Middle West in the years from 1848 to 1860. A major one was the vast increase in the flow of American wheat into the export market after the repeal of the British Corn Laws in 1846.

Cootner, whom we have cited above on this subject, explains what happened thus: "The western states as a whole shipped only one million bushels (wheat and flour equivalent) through the Erie Canal in 1835; 7.5 million in 1841; and 8.6 million bushels in 1848. Railroad construction in the 1840's was more the effect of this outpouring than the stimulus for it."[14] The remarkable increase in the quantity of United States' export of foodstuffs between 1841 and 1861 can be seen in Table 4.

TABLE 4

United States' Exports of Selected Foodstuffs[a]
(In millions of units)

(Annual Averages)	Total Wheat and Flour (bushels)	United Kingdom Only All Grain and Flour (bushels)
1841	6.5	1.3
1846–50	10.8	15.4
1851–55	17.6	12.2
1861	—	43.2
1856–60	—	14.1

[a] Source: P. H. Cootner, "The Role of the Railroad in U.S. Economic Growth," *The Journal of Economic History* (December, 1963), p. 497.

The impact of these changes on United States' railroads has been described as follows:

> These huge shipments from the West for export immediately pointed up a bottleneck in the transport system—the Erie Canal. Since that artery was closed in the winter, the huge shipments had to be made in the seven warmer months. When the volume of shipments soared in 1847, the freight charge on a barrel of flour from Buffalo to Albany rose to $1.12 from a charge of $.45 prior to the repeal of the Corn Laws. The railroads leaped into the breach. . . .[15]

We have here another striking illustration of the stimulative spread effects deriving from increased export of staple commodities and of backward linkage in the form of railroad construction.[16] It is to be noted also that the

[14] *Ibid.*, p. 495.
[15] *Ibid.*, p. 497.
[16] See above, p. 134.

Middle West in these years was developing products other than agricultural ones that needed to be shipped, such as lead from Missouri, Michigan copper, iron from around Pittsburgh and later from the Lake Superior region, and lumber. These products not only provided traffic for the new railroads, but they frequently resulted in what North has termed subsidiary industries engaged in processing these raw materials into finished goods.[17]

The economic expansion and capital investment attendant upon this rapid regional growth was fortunately supported by far-sighted governmental policies that encouraged and even subsidized the key industries. In 1850, for example, President Millard Fillmore signed the First Land Grant Act, which was to play a large part in the Middle West's development and the opening up of its rich, virgin lands. One of the first beneficiaries of this Act was the Illinois Central Railroad, which built a 700-mile road connecting Dubuque, Iowa and Chicago and Cairo, Illinois. The grant consisted of alternate sections of land in a belt six miles wide on either side of the railroad. Where land had already been taken up by settlers, the railroad companies were given compensatory acreage nine miles from the track. The amount that was granted by the federal government to the states for transfer to private companies came to 3,750,000 acres. Much of the leadership in the Congressional debate over the passage of this Act was provided by Senator Stephen A. Douglas of Illinois.

The Land Grant Act made the problem of obtaining a railroad right of way a minor consideration in the total investment decision. Along with the liberal land grant the federal government made railroad building lucrative by offering contracts to carry the mails and government freight. Refuse lands that were swampy or overflowing with water were conveyed to the states by Congress for internal improvement purposes. Until about 1857 land grants were easily obtainable from the federal government for railroad construction. The liberal land grant system adopted by Congress was mainly motivated by the need to improve communication between the East and the West, especially after the discovery of gold in California in 1849. The vision of a trans-continental railroad captured the mind of many a Congressman in the pre-Civil War years, but it was not to become a reality until after the sectional struggle.

The nation's accomplishment in the field of railroading in these years is revealed in the regional distribution of the mileage. By the 1850's, the New England states had developed extensive railroad systems. The South, on the other hand, was slow in building railroads, but it is to be noted that on a percentage basis the increase in that region's mileage during this period was greater than in the Northeast or West. Part of the reason for the smaller absolute mileage of railroads in the South was that the region had been able in the past to ship many of its commodities to market by water. Demand for the services of the railroad in the Northeast was much greater because of the location of that region's manufacturing centers; in many instances the latter

---

[17] North, *The Economic Growth of the United States,* p. 154. North has provided a masterly, concise analysis of western economic development in Chaps. 11 and 15 of this book.

could not employ cheap water transportation. The movement of raw materials and finished goods to and from these factories had to be accomplished overland. The canals had made some contribution to the solution of the problem. But the railroads were found to be more flexible as to location, and slowly they began to capture the canal traffic because of their greater convenience, speed, and economy.

THE STRUCTURE OF THE MANUFACTURING SECTOR

In appraising and determining the leading sectors of the economy in this period, it would seem sensible to consider first the industries that ranked highest in terms of value added. In Table 5 we have such a list of industries presented on that basis as of 1860. Examination of this table shows that these

TABLE 5

Leading Manufacturing Industries of the United States, 1860[a]

	Number of Employees	Value of Product (in thousands of dollars)	Value Added by Manufacture (thousands of dollars)	Rank by Value Added
Cotton goods	114,955	$107,338	$54,671	1
Lumber	75,595	104,928	53,570	2
Boots and shoes	123,026	91,889	49,161	3
Flour and meal	27,682	248,580	40,083	4
Men's clothing	114,800	80,831	36,381	5
Iron (all kinds)	48,075	73,175	35,689	6
Machinery	41,223	52,010	32,566	7
Woolen goods	40,595	60,685	25,032	8
Carriages and wagons	37,102	35,558	23,655	9
Leather	22,679	67,306	22,786	10

[a] Source: R. M. Robertson, *History of the American Economy* (New York: Harcourt, Brace & Co., 1955). L. M. Hacker, *The Triumph of American Capitalism* (New York: Columbia University Press, 1940, 1947).

industries were primarily of two types: first, those engaged in the processing of such raw materials as lumber or grain and, secondly, those with relatively low capital requirements (cotton goods, boots and shoes, men's clothing, leather, and woolen goods). The former were the type of manufactures developed in the West, whereas the latter tended to be concentrated geographically in the Northeast.[18] Some of these industries had important links, as we

[18] North, "Industrialization in the United States—1815–1860," in W. W. Rostow, ed., *The Economics of Take-Off into Sustained Growth* (New York: St. Martin's Press, 1963), p. 49.

shall see, to other industries and importantly affected their development. Furthermore, the localization of these industries meant that there was a need for an increasing amount of transportation to move raw materials to processing centers and to ship manufactured goods from the Northeast to other parts of the nation. The "industrialization of a region means the development of manufacturing for a larger market than the particular geographical area" in which the industry happens to be located; in other words, it implies the localization of industry. But industries engaged in processing a single raw material may not develop into an industrial region in the correct meaning of that phrase. If they are tied to a wasting resource or one subject to diminishing returns, they may never transcend this limitation. And if they are of a nature that induces little subsidiary or complementary industry, the region in which they are located will probably never experience the sustained expansion and diversification that we associate with industrialization.[19]

This industrialization process was more conspicuous in this period in the Northeast than in the West or South. Indeed, by 1860 the former region provided 71 per cent of the nation's manufacturing employment. The four leading manufacturing states, as of that date, were New York, Pennsylvania, Massachusetts, and Ohio, to list them in descending rank. Boots and shoes, cotton and woolen goods were manufactured chiefly in New England. Pennsylvania was already the leading producer of iron and coal. New York was a center for the manufacture of flour, men's clothing, refined sugar, and leather. Animal products, agricultural implements, and machinery were the major products of Ohio.

The localization of manufacturing industry, which was developing in this period, and the increased volume of products produced by the factories, farms, and mines of the growing nation created an increasingly difficult transportation problem. Its magnitude can be seen in a single statistic. In 1853, $94 million of manufactured products were shipped from New York to the western states by canal. The west-bound freight included products such as dry goods, boots and shoes, nails, rails, hardware, machinery, paper, coffee, tea, tobacco, fish, and large quantities of furniture. The freight moving eastward included pork, beef, wheat, and lumber. The shipment of these goods placed a great strain on the transportation facilities that existed in the early part of the period. Freight rates were relatively high because the demand for transport was in excess of the supply at the prevailing rates. It was this imbalance between the supply and demand for speedy, efficient transport that encouraged the development of new trunk line railroads. The profit conditions in this sector were favorable for such expansion; in short, we have a clear case of what the economist calls induced investment.

The shifting role of the different sectors in the economy's expansion in this period is concealed in the aggregative statistics of gross national product and national income. Still, we know from a number of economic indicators that

---

[19] *Ibid.*, p. 47.

the pace of the overall movement and of these different sectors was not steady, but revealed the familiar cyclical pattern of "boom and bust," expansion and contraction. Stimulated by the rising demand for cereals at home and aboard, western settlement and increased agricultural production characterized the years from 1843 to 1848. In the East, manufacturing expansion provided a major impetus to general prosperity. The South did not experience recovery until 1845 when rising prices lifted the pall of depression. Exogenous factors played a large part in the fluctuations of the economy in the period 1843–49, the most notable being the Irish potato famine and the repeal of the Corn Laws. 1847–48 witnessed a slowing of the economic expansion, largely as a result of European turmoil, but the recession was largely limited to the Northeast. By 1849, the acceleration of business activity was evident in all sections of the nation: railroad building went on at a feverish pace in the West, eastern manufacturing continued its lusty growth, the "gold rush" to California favored economic expansion there, and southern and western agriculture responded to the gradually rising prices of the 1850's, which were interrupted only in 1851 and 1854. The latter year brought severe recession to the West, but recovery was rapid and the boom continued until the downturn of 1857. This bare recital of the gyrations of the economy in this period is offered merely to suggest the need of analyzing these movements in greater detail in the next chapter. Such analysis, it is suggested, may be useful in understanding the role of the different sectors in the economy's growth and, in particular, determining the validity and usefulness of Rostow's concept of the "take-off." A close study of the depression of 1857 may provide insight into his contention that the railroads played a major part in the American take-off.

Chapter 12

THE ACCELERATION OF PRODUCTIVE INVESTMENT

"THE TAKE-OFF INTO SUSTAINED CONTROVERSY"

The Rostow hypothesis of a take-off stage leading to sustained economic growth has generated a remarkable amount of scholarly controversy at home and abroad. One witty reviewer of a volume containing an excellent sample of the professional disagreements on this subject recently characterized it by the phrase quoted above.[1] While disputes among scholars are likely to have a variety of causes, personal and otherwise, there would seem to be two basic reasons for the seemingly interminable and indecisive nature of this particular disagreement. One is a conceptual difficulty and the other has to do with the inadequacy of the statistical data necessary to test the hypothesis. Since this chapter is devoted mainly to verifying or disconfirming the principal elements of the take-off thesis as systematically as possible in terms of the American experience, we need to take account of these methodological problems at the very start of the analysis.

Rostow, it will be recalled, defines the take-off as a period of "decisive," "rapid," and "radical" structural change in the economy, which makes further economic growth more or less automatic. In other terms, we might say that the take-off implies that a critical level or "threshold" must be achieved for an economy to develop a self-contained momentum to grow. Once the "minimum effort" necessary to reach this level has been made, the society will automatically be driven to higher levels of income and wealth by the endogenous (internal) factors in its economy.

[1] H. Rosovsky's review of *The Economics of Take-Off into Sustained Growth*, edited by W. W. Rostow (New York: St. Martin's Press, 1963), in the *Journal of Economic History* (June, 1965), pp. 271ff. Reviews of Rostow, *The Stages of Economic Growth*, will be found in *American Economic Review* (December, 1960), p. 550 (by W. N. Parker); A. K. Cairncross, *The Economic History Review* (April, 1961), p. 450; P. Baran and E. J. Hobsbawm, "The Stages of Economic Growth," *Kyklos*, XIV, No. 2, 1961; D. C. North, "A Note on Professor Rostow's 'Take-Off' into Self-Sustained Growth," *The Manchester School* (January, 1958); Goran Ohlin, "Reflections on the Rostow Doctrine," *Economic Development and Cultural Change* (July, 1961); G. L. S. Shackle, "The Stages of Economic Growth," *Political Studies* (February, 1962). An interesting Russian review is Iu. Semenov, "The Theory of 'The Stages of Economic Growth,'" *Mirovaia ekonomika i mezhdunarodnye* (1963), No. 6, reproduced in *Problems of Economics* (June, 1964), Vol. vii, No. 2.

According to Rostow, the key elements in this minimum effort are to be found in the behavior of investment and manufacturing. It is asserted that once an economy achieves a rise in the rate of its productive investment from, say, 5 per cent or less to over 10 per cent of national income (or net national product) and a burgeoning manufacturing sector, a self-sustaining cycle will form to drive it to higher levels of well-being. However, in order to accomplish this it is a necessary prerequisite to have social and political institutions that will exploit "the impulses to expansion."[2] In short, the take-off involves a limited number of rapidly expanding primary industries whose "expansion and technical transformation induce a chain of requirements for increased capacity and the potentiality for new production functions" in secondary and derived growth sectors of the economy.

Conceptually, some of Rostow's critics are annoyed by his failure to define certain key terms. Thus, Fogel writes,

> Yet, despite the colorful language used to describe it, the exact nature of this crucial structural transformation never becomes very clear in *The Stages of Economic Growth.* One perceives a series of adumbrations rather than a clearly specified theory. What precisely does "industrialization taking hold" mean? How far must industrialization proceed before it is adjudged to have "taken hold"? What is a "decisive" breakthrough for the "forces of modernization"? How does one recognize it? Exactly what does one mean by the structure of the economy? And how far does structural change have to go before it is "better viewed" as a change "in kind" rather than "merely in degree"?[3]

Such ambiguity of central terms can be seen also in such phrases as "substantial manufacturing" or "high rate of growth."

Another powerful critic, Professor Kuznets, contends that "any sequence of stages, even if offered as a suggestive rather than a substantive scheme," must meet some minimum requirements—if it is to be taken seriously."[4] Rostow's theory, he holds, is too vague in differentiating between the pre-condition stage and the take-off stage. He argues that Rostow does not provide any solid ground upon which to discuss the analytical relation between the take-off stage and the preceding and the succeeding stage. Fuzziness in delimiting the take-off stage and in formulating its distinctive characteristics does make for difficulty in using empirical data to prove or disprove this theory. It leads one to make subjective judgments as to what exactly Rostow means when he refers to certain concepts. A good example of this is to be seen in Professor Kuznets'

---

[2] Rostow, *The Stages of Economic Growth,* p. 39.

[3] R. W. Fogel, *Railroads and American Economic Growth: Essays in Econometric History* (Baltimore: The Johns Hopkins Press, 1964), p. 113. The authors do not agree with all of Fogel's criticisms along this line. While the phrase "structure of the economy" is notoriously a "weasel" expression, Fogel has little trouble in taking the one that seems most plausible in the context and in general usage and subjecting it to analysis. Some, but not all of Rostow's fuzziness in the use of terms, stems from the arbitrary judgments he had to make in delineating historical phenomena that have a large degree of continuity, but that he needed to differentiate in terms of time periods.

[4] S. Kuznets, "Notes on the Take-Off," in *The Economics of Take-Off into Sustained Growth,* pp. 23–24.

objection to Rostow's use of the term automatic or self-sustained growth. In Kuznets' view all growth is to some degree self-sustaining and self-limiting; the latter is so in the sense that growth may lead to a decline in incentive, may be checked by scarcity of irreplaceable natural resources, or may strengthen vested interests who resist growth in other sectors. Kuznets, therefore, expressed the wish to know how the growth after the take-off differs from the non-self-sustained growth before the take-off. Rostow, in reply, practically concedes the validity of the criticism when he states that self-sustained growth still requires the repetition of the take-off process. That is, a society that wishes to continue to grow must repeat the often painful process of introducing new production functions as the old leading sectors of its economy decelerate. There is nothing automatic, says Rostow, about the inner mechanism of self-sustained growth. "But the deeper fundamentals required for an effective take-off (the acceptance of the Newtonian outlook, with its world of modern science and technology) appear, on present evidence, sufficiently powerful to make growth an ongoing process, on long term. . . ."[5]

The second difficulty in testing the Rostow hypothesis is that there is simply an insufficiency of reliable statistical data for that period of American history to which the hypothesis has application. This lack encourages speculative analyses and elaborate statistical inferences to make up for the gaps in the available information, but both of these efforts often leave much to be desired. Granted that the data necessary for the validation of the Rostow hypothesis are deficient, we should not use this weakness of the data as a means of discounting the concept itself. It is foolish to confuse inadequacy of the data with inadequacy of the hypothesis.

The shortcomings of the Rostow hypothesis, as originally stated, both with respect to conceptual rigor and empirical support, have led some economists to reject it altogether as being totally disproved and discredited. The present authors believe that it is unwise at the present time to take an "all-or-none" or "either-or" approach to the evaluation of the validity of this particular hypothesis. Rostow, it must be remembered, developed the take-off hypothesis as part of a broad schema of economic development with a good deal of polemical response in his formulation to the communist challenge.[6] In some ways his definition of the period of the take-off and its principal characteristics was influenced by his conception of the later stage, the drive to maturity. The capital-orientation of this latter stage leads Rostow to give investment and the capital goods industries a leading role in the take-off stage. While there is much in Rostow's "preliminary hypothesis" about which we too have reservations, new knowledge and insight may be gained into the process of economic

5 W. W. Rostow, "Leading Sectors and the Take-Off," *The Economics of Take-Off into Sustained Growth*, pp. 9, 11.
    6 Note the book's subtitle, *A Non-Communist Manifesto*, and Chapter 10, in which it is argued that Marxism is a disease of the transition from traditional to modern status. According to Rostow, societies in the pre-conditions stage of confusion are "peculiarly vulnerable to such a [communist] seizure of power" (*The Stages of Economic Growth*, p. 163).

growth by making a discriminating appraisal of its different elements rather than rejecting it out of hand. Whatever the final verdict on the original version of his take-off hypothesis, Rostow has stimulated all of us into re-examining our own ideas. As Trevor-Roper put it, "There are times when a new error is more lifegiving than an old truth. . . ."[7] It is in this spirit that we turn to the task of analyzing the take-off hypothesis in terms of the American experience.

CONTINUITY VERSUS DISCONTINUITY IN AMERICAN ECONOMIC GROWTH

The take-off hypothesis alleges that the American economy went into a spurt in the decade or two after take-off that carried it to sustained growth. What evidence is there for such a *saltum,* or discontinuity, in the processes of American economic growth in these years? Unfortunately, the statistical series on national income for the pre-Civil War years are so deficient that we cannot answer this question as definitively as we would like. Martin's national income figures, which are reproduced in Table 1, show substantial increases in total and per capita national income for the years 1839–59 as contrasted particularly with the declining per capita trend for the years 1799–1829.[8]

The data of Robert Gallman on commodity output for the years 1839–99, part of which are presented in Table 2, also show a jump in national product in the years 1839–59. Real product per capita rose in the years 1844–54 at a rate greater than the long term trend. Manufactures grew especially rapidly in the years between 1839 and 1859, their share of the total commodity output increasing from 17 per cent to 32 per cent.

[7] History, *Professional and Lay* (Oxford: Oxford University Press, 1957), p. 22, as quoted in Rosovsky, *op. cit.,* p. 275. Our own doubts about the Rostow schema as a whole are very fundamental. (1) His model abstracts from the historical context of development and tends too strongly to view each nation in isolation from others. Kuznets argues that any specific country has to be "looked at in terms of the timing of its entry into modern economic growth, the state of knowledge at the time, and the country's own historical heritage." (W. W. Rostow, *The Economics of Take-Off* . . ., p. 397); (2) Rostow's model ignores the level of capital investment already attained in the economy and focuses only on the coefficient of investment (net investment divided by NNP), even though the latter is inevitably influenced by the former; (3) Rostow flirts with the idea of regional take-offs within a nation, but does not develop this approach as a possible alternative to his leading sectors approach; (4) Essentially, Rostow conceives the take-off as a process of development in Schumpeterian terms (new production functions, innovations, etc.), while his critics persist in measuring growth phenomena rather than development in the strict sense of that distinction. An excellent antidote to the Rostow stages approach will be found in the little book of the brilliant Brazilian economist, C. Furtado, *Development and Underdevelopment,* translated by R. W. DeAguiar and E. C. Drysdale (Berkeley: University of California Press, 1964), *passim.*

[8] In the book *Trends and Structure in the American Economy* (London: Bowes & Bowes, 1952), p. 222, Professor Simon Kuznets reports that the Martin estimates rest upon a tenuous basis. He points out that the accuracy of the Martin data is open to question.

TABLE 1

Total and Per Capita National Income in the United States, 1829–59[a]

Year	National Income (Millions of $)	Percentage Change (Per decade)	Per Capita Income (Current prices)	Per Capita Income (In 1929 prices)
1829	975	11.3%	78	171
1839	1,631	67.3	98	206
1849	2,420	48.4	107	244
1859	4,311	78.1	140	308

    [a] R. F. Martin, *National Income in the United States, 1799–1938* (New York: National Industrial Conference Board, 1939), p. 79. Percentages calculated by the authors.

Studies of Andreano, Goldsmith, and Lebergott also suggest that there was an "upward break" in the secular rate of growth of the national product around the end of the third decade and the beginning of the fourth in the last century.[9] On the other hand, Professor North contends that "it is the decade of the 1830's . . . which gives clear evidence of an acceleration in the growth of manufacturing throughout the Northeast. . . ." His view is that the rate of

TABLE 2

Total and Per Capita Output in the United States, 1839–59[a]
In Absolute and Decennial Rates of Change

Figures:

Year	Output (mill.)	Population (thousands)	Output per Capita	Output per Worker
1839	$1,094	17,120	$64	$244
1844	1,374	20,182	68	—
1849	1,657	23,261	71	268
1854	2,317	27,386	85	—
1859	2,686	31,513	85	330

Averages:[b]   *Decennial Rates of Change*
(Per cent)

1839–99	49	28	16	16
1839–44	57	36	16	—
1869–99	54	24	24	21

    [a] Adapted from R. E. Gallman, "Commodity Output, 1839–1899," in William N. Parker, ed., *Trends in the American Economy in the Nineteenth Century*, p. 16. © Copyright 1960 by Princeton University Press for the National Bureau of Economic Research.
    [b] Geometric means calculated from terminal year values.

    [9] See R. L. Andreano, "Trends and Variations in Economic Welfare in the United States before the Civil War," *New Views on American Economic Development* (Cambridge, Mass.: Schenkman Publishing Co., 1965), pp. 131–167; R. Goldsmith, "Long Period Growth in Income and Product, 1839–1960," in *Ibid.*, pp. 337–361; S. Lebergott, *Labor Force Mobility and Unemployment, 1800–1960*, in *Ibid.*, pp. 362–371. See also R. E. Gallman, "Estimates of American National Product Made before the Civil War," in *Ibid.*, pp. 168–186.

growth of the American economy accelerated "somewhere between 1815 and 1860." To quote him further: "While the initial impetus took place in the 1830's, the manufacturing base broadened and the pace was still further accelerated during the expansion that followed the depression of 1839–43. . . ."[10]

Part of the disagreement in assigning an approximate date for the so-called take-off arises from differences among economic historians in emphasizing sectional as opposed to national growth. Thus, Professor North emphasizes the leading role of the textile industry of New England in the acceleration of manufacturing growth and its remarkable development in the years after 1815. Yet, Rostow also in a not-to-be-overlooked footnote in *The Stages of Economic Growth* had written: "If we are prepared to treat New England of the first half of the nineteenth century as a separable economy, its take-off into sustained growth can be allocated to the period, roughly, 1820–1850, and, again, a disproportionately large cotton textile industry based substantially on exports (that is, from New England to the rest of the United States) is the regional foundation for sustained growth."[11] Rostow, emphasizing "momemtum in its heavy-industry" as being central to the take-off process, placed the date of that phase of growth later than North.

With the exception noted, there would seem to be considerable agreement that there was something of a discontinuity, a breakthrough, or a take-off, in the industrialization of the United States in the period of the two decades preceding the Civil War. However, it would not seem correct to overdramatize or exaggerate the element of discontinuity even in that period; the aeronautical metaphor of take-off tends perhaps to do this, and in this respect it is objectionable. As one careful student of this period has said, ". . . One impressive feature of nineteenth-century United States economic growth is precisely its apparent continuity in such spheres as technological progress, internal migration, commercial activity, etc."[12] But the question still remains, is Rostow right with respect to the reasons he assigns for the industrial transformation that occurred in those years? By way of an answer to that question, we turn next to examine the behavior of investment in that period to see whether it conformed to the first condition for take-off, i.e., a rise in the rate of productive investment from 5 per cent or less to 10 per cent or more of national income.

[10] D. C. North, "Industrialization in the United States (1815–1860)" in Rostow, ed., *The Economics of Take-Off into Sustained Growth*, pp. 45, 46.

[11] Rostow, *The Stages of Economic Growth*, footnote, p. 55.

[12] A. Fishlow, *American Railroads and the Transformation of the Ante-Bellum Economy* (Cambridge, Mass.: Harvard University Press, 1965), p. 12, footnote 21. In his volume, *The Economic History of the United States, 1790–1860*, North had written, " . . . Economic growth during the long swing 1823–1839 had set the scene for an industrial society by widening the market. Manufacturing growth throughout the Northeast in the 1830's gave evidence that this development was under way. *But it was during the 1840's and early 1850's that the pace of industrialization accelerated to the degree that the Northeast could unequivocally be called a manufacturing region. . . .*" (Our italics, p. 204 of *Ibid.*)

THE BEHAVIOR OF INVESTMENT

The calculation of the size and relative proportions of capital formation in the United States before the Civil War is of necessity a matter of estimation; the figures cited below, therefore, are subject to all the reservations that have been made previously about such statistics. Gallman's most recent figures of this kind show that the share of capital formation, both gross and net, in real national product was relatively high in the ante-bellum period.[13] Net capital formation by 1843 was apparently already higher as a percentage of net national product than the 5 per cent or less that Rostow cites as characteristic of a non-industrialized economy. As can be seen from the data presented in Table 3, the shares of gross capital formation in GNP underwent a "marked

TABLE 3

Shares of Capital Formation in Gross National Product,
1860 Prices, 1834–44 through 1899–1908[a]
(In percentages)

	Shares of Capital Formation[b] in			
Decades	GNP I	GNP II	GNP*	GNP* II
1834–43	9	16	10	16
1839–48	11	14	11	14
1844–53	13	14	13	15
1849–58	14	16	15	17
1859–69		Data not available		
1869–78	22	24	23	24
1874–83	21	22	21	22
1879–88	22	23	23	24
1884–93	26	26	27	27
1889–98	28	28	28	28
1894–1903	27	27	26	26
1899–1908	28	28	27	28

[a] Source: R. E. Gallman, "Gross National Product in the United States, 1834–1909," in *Output, Employment and Productivity in the United States after 1800*, Studies in Income and Wealth, Vol. 30, published by the National Bureau of Economic Research (New York: Columbia University Press, 1966), p. 11.
[b] Gallman computed four variants of the share of capital formation in product. The first (in column 2 above) shows the share of domestic savings in product. The second and fourth estimates are calculated from capital formation and product data which *include* value added by home manufactures and the value of farm improvements made with farm materials. The shares shown under GNP I and GNP* are based on data which *exclude* value added by home manufacturing and the value of farm improvements made with farm construction materials.

[13] R. E. Gallman, "Gross National Product in the United States, 1834–1909," in *Output, Employment and Productivity in the United States after 1800*, National Bureau of Economic Research, Inc., Studies in Income and Wealth, Vol. 30 (New York: Columbia University Press, 1966), p. 23 and *passim*.

long-term increase" between 1834–43 and 1899–1908, but the precise timing and duration of that increase has not as yet been definitely established.

It can be seen from the table that gross capital formation more than doubled in the case of two of the estimates between 1834–43 and the latter years of the nineteenth century. The inclusion of data, which include home manufacturing and the value of farm improvements made with farm materials (columns 3 and 5 in the table), result in less than doubling of the capital formation share over that period. Net capital formation estimates are difficult to make because we do not have capital consumption figures for the pre-war years. Gallman, assuming that capital consumption accounted for one-third of gross capital formation, has concluded that "the share of net capital formation (including inventory changes) in net product ran between 9 and 14 per cent before the Civil War. . . ."[14]

If we take Gallman's single-year estimates for gross capital formation, deduct one-third for capital consumption, and place the resulting net capital formation figures against his estimates of gross national product for the same years, we find that net capital formation more than doubled in absolute terms between 1839 and 1859. (See Table 4 below.) Gallman provides no estimates of net national product for this period, but if we calculate the share of net capital formation (derived in the manner described above) in GNP, produc-

TABLE 4

Gross National Product, Gross and Net Capital Formation,
and Percentage of Latter to Former, Single-Year
and Overlapping Decade Averages, 1834–1859[a]
1860 Prices (In billions of dollars)

Year of Decade	Gross National Product	Gross Capital Formation	Net Capital Formation[b]	Net Capital Formation as % of GNP
1839	$1.62	$.200	$.14	8.6%
1844	1.97	.194	.124	6.3
1849	2.32	.258	.17	7.3
1854	3.53	.542	.36	10.2
1859	4.17	.532	.35	8.5
1834–43	1.56	.141		
1839–48	1.94	.216		
1844–53	2.54	.319		
1849–58	3.30	.474		

[a] Excludes the value of improvements made to farm land with farm construction materials, value added by home manufacturing, and changes in inventories.

[b] Calculated by the authors from the Gallman data by deducting one-third of gross capital formation to allow for capital consumption.

Source: Gallman, "Gross National Product, etc." In *Output, Employment . . . after 1800, op. cit.,* pp. 26, 34.

[14] *Ibid.,* p. 14.

tive net investment does not double *in percentage terms* between 1839 and 1859.

A similar calculation, using Martin's data on national income and Seaman's on domestic product for the years 1839, 1849, and 1859, likewise shows no tendency for net capital formation to increase as a percentage of these estimates of the aggregate production of the nation. (See Table 5.)

TABLE 5

Net Capital Formation, National Income, and Domestic Product Estimates for the United States for the Years 1839, 1849, and 1859[a]
(In millions of dollars)

Year	Net Capital Formation (In 1860 Prices)	National Income (In Current Prices)	Domestic Product (Current Prices)	NCF as % of National Income	NCF as % of Domestic Product
1839	$140	$1,577	$1,040	8.9%	13%
1849	170	2,326	1,485	7.3	11
1859	350	4,098	2,630	8.5	13

[a] Sources: Net capital formation data from Gallman, "Gross National Product, etc." in *Output, Employment . . . After 1800, op. cit.,* p. 34, with deduction of ⅓ for capital consumption as explained in text above; Martin data from *Historical Statistics of the United States, 1789–1945, op. cit.,* p. 14; Seaman data from R. E. Gallman, "Estimates of American National Product Made Before the Civil War," in Andreano, *New Views of American Economic Development, op. cit.,* p. 171.

In conclusion, it is apparent that the available statistical data are far from satisfactory for the purposes of verifying empirically Rostow's first condition of take-off. Nevertheless, the best existing estimates indicate that in the years 1839–59 net capital formation was already higher at the beginning of the period than the 5 per cent figure advanced by Rostow.[15] The reason for this is reasonably clear: the United States before 1843, when the nation was in a preconditions period, had reached a level of development in manufacturing, agriculture, and social overhead development that made for a higher percentage of net capital formation than Rostow had assumed as typical for undeveloped economies. It is evident also from the statistics of Tables 3–5 that there was considerable acceleration in the nation's rate of capital formation in absolute terms, but, percentagewise, it does not seem that a doubling of the savings or investment ratio occurred in the years 1843–60. In fairness to Rostow, however, it should be noted that he has stated that "when he had first

[15] Rostow took the 5 per cent figure from a classic article by W. Arthur Lewis, "Economic Development with Unlimited Supplies of Labor," *Manchester School* (May, 1954) in which the latter wrote, "The central problem in the theory of economic growth is to understand the process by which a community is converted from being a 5 per cent to a 12 per cent saver—with all the changes in attitudes, in institutions and in techniques which accompany this conversion." See the latter's *The Theory of Economic Growth* (London: Oxford University Press, 1955), p. 226 for the same statement.

discussed the rise of net investment from 5 to 10 per cent of national income, he had said that 'pure Arthur Lewis' behavior was not to be expected because of differences in the rate of population increase, in the scale of social overhead requirements, etc. He therefore did not expect to find rigid behaviour of precisely this kind. . . ."[16] Reactions to this qualification on the first condition of the Rostow hypothesis will probably vary. Some will say that it is equivocation and destroys any possibility of verifying the condition statistically; others may defend it, admitting that the first condition as originally stated by Rostow was altogether too rigorously defined.

THE SUPPLY OF LOANABLE FUNDS

Regardless of whether we think Rostow's first condition was satisfied or not, there can be no gainsaying the fact that there was an enormous amount of capital investment in the American economy during the years 1844–57. One index of this remarkable capital expansion was the fact that by 1860 there was more than two billion dollars of corporate securities outstanding in the nation;[17] and that sum did not reflect the vast amount of capital investment in agriculture and other fields where the corporate device was not employed to raise capital. What were the principal sources of loanable funds and what economic institutions were developed in this period to mobilize the people's savings and provide credit to make this capital investment possible? We turn first to the latter part of this question.

The limited liability corporation was one such institution that flourished and increased in numbers in these years to meet the increased capital needs of the economy. The general incorporation statutes passed in a number of states after 1837 greatly facilitated the formation of corporations, and their number showed a sizable increase. (See Chart 1.) The railroads with their huge capital requirements and risks were of necessity organized on a corporate basis. And the new canals, banks, and insurance companies of this period also resulted in a corresponding increase in the corporate population.

The mutual savings banks, which had been first organized in the preceding period, provided additional supplies of accumulated savings for investment during these years. Prior to 1837, these institutions had invested their funds mainly in bank stocks. But during the 1840's and 1850's, they increasingly placed their depositors' funds in state and local bonds and in real estate mortgages. By so doing they made a major contribution to the financing of metropolitan growth, which, as we have seen, was so notable a feature of the period. The extent of their financial support can be seen roughly in the fact that by 1860 there were 278 such institutions and they had assets of almost

---

[16] See W. W. Rostow, ed., *The Economics of Take-Off into Sustained Growth*, p. 320.

[17] W. J. Shultz and M. R. Caine, *Financial Development of the United States* (Englewood Cliffs, N.J.: Prentice-Hall, Inc., 1937), p. 239.

CHART 1

Business Incorporations, Eight States, 1800–1875
2-item Centered Moving Averages of Annual Data

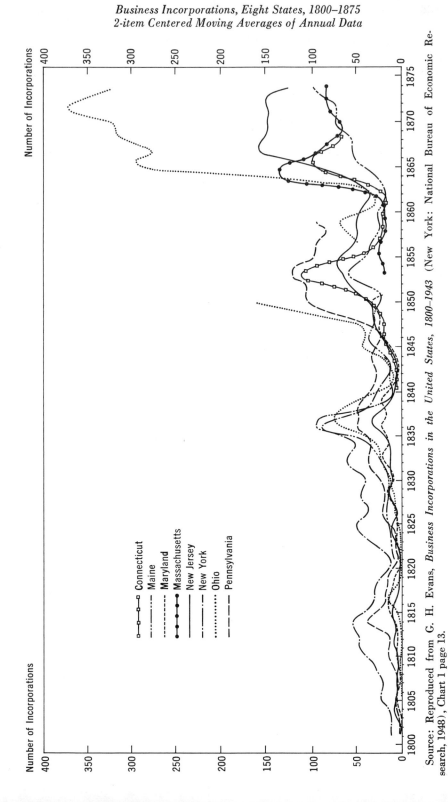

Connecticut
Maine
Maryland
Massachusetts
New Jersey
New York
Ohio
Pennsylvania

Source: Reproduced from G. H. Evans, *Business Incorporations in the United States, 1800–1943* (New York: National Bureau of Economic Research, 1948), Chart 1 page 13.

$150 million. However, while the savings banks were an important means of marshalling capital in the Northeast, they were not established in the South or in the states west of Pennsylvania; they consequently did not finance urban growth in those regions nor did they contribute to the mobility of capital among the states.

The insurance companies, which had first developed in the United States about the end of the eighteenth century, had increasing funds available for investment in this period. By 1841 there were 131 mutual and stock fire and marine insurance companies, and a number of companies were writing life insurance policies. In the following years these companies grew and invested their swelling funds in securities, collateral loans, and real estate mortgages. By 1860 it is estimated that fire and marine insurance policies totalled some $3,000 million and life insurance policies about $200 million. These sums were not available for investment, but rather the amounts derived from premiums on the face value of the policies, a much smaller figure. Trust companies to invest and protect legacies left to widows, orphans, and others legally incompetent to act for themselves were being organized in these years also; the first and largest of these institutions was the Massachusetts Hospital Life Insurance Company, organized in 1823.

While these particular financial intermediaries for the collection and investment of funds were important, their contribution to the supply of long-term finance in this period should not be exaggerated; their greatest era of growth lay ahead of them. This was also the case with regard to the organized capital markets, the security exchanges. It is true that in this period, New York City outdistanced Boston, Philadelphia, and other cities as a center for security transactions; the collapse of the Second Bank of the United States in 1842 doomed Chestnut Street as a rival of Wall Street and the availability of large bank balances in the latter center to supply "call money" for stock speculation assured the New York stock exchange the financial leadership of the nation. Still, in terms of contemporary standards, the trading was as yet limited. In these years Boston was still the leading capital market for industrials. In 1835 there were no industrial companies listed on the New York exchange, and even in 1856 there were only twenty. Most manufacturing enterprises were unincorporated, so the trading was confined to governmental, railroad, bank, and public utility issues. In 1857, a record day on the New York exchange meant a turnover of 71,000 shares. From the modern perspective, Wall Street had not as yet "taken-off," but it was enjoying a lusty preconditions period.

On this last topic and the one to which we next address ourselves, the commercial banks, we shall borrow a text from Rostow: ". . . Virtually without exception, the take-off periods have been marked by the extension of banking institutions which expanded the supply of working capital; and in most cases also by an expansion in the range of long-range financing done by a central, formally organized capital market."[18] As the statistics of Table 6

---

[18] "The Take-Off into Self-Sustained Growth," *Economic Journal* (March, 1956), p. 39.

plainly show, the commercial banking system more than doubled in the number of its institutions and the amount of its loans in the years 1844–60. After the financial debacle of 1837, the banking system was slowly repaired, aided by increased supervision by the state governments. Some of the states,

TABLE 6

Commercial Banking Development in the United States, Selected Years,
1844–60[a]
(In millions of dollars)

Year	Number of Banks	Capital	Loans	Individual Deposits	Note Circulation	Specie
1844	696	$210.9	$264.9	$ 84.6	$ 75.2	$49.9
1848	751	204.8	344.5	103.2	128.5	46.3
1850	824	217.3	364.2	109.6	131.4	45.4
1855	1,307	332.2	576.1	190.4	187.0	53.9
1860	1,562	421.9	691.9	253.8	207.1	83.6

[a] Source: 37th Congress, 3rd Sess., House of Representatives, *Ex. Document No. 25,* p. 210.

whose citizens had been injured by the banking excesses of the years before 1837 and the subsequent collapse, outlawed banking by statute and constitutional provision in the 1840's and early '50's. But most of these anti-bank laws were repealed soon after their passage, and such states usually adopted regulated "free banking" systems such as that of New York. On the whole, the banking system in this period was stronger and better developed than that which had existed prior to 1837.

The insatiable demand for capital in the growing sections of the nation tended to encourage inflationary banking policies. Underdeveloped nations often seek to expand their capital plant faster than voluntary saving will permit; ultra-liberal credit extension is one way to accomplish this. In this period, when credit was given by the issuance of banknotes rather than the creation of demand deposits, many loans were made for long term capital purposes, even though that involved the danger of a loss of liquidity by the lending bank. In this way, a considerable but undetermined amount of capital formation was accomplished through the operation of the commercial banking system rather than as the result of individual saving.

Rostow has asserted that foreign borrowing was a major source of funds in the American take-off. Professor North has contested this, stating that in the 1840's expansion in the East was accomplished without any significant capital imports.[19] In fact, capital was returning to Europe during most of that

[19] D. C. North, "A Note on Professor Rostow's 'Take-Off into Sustained Economic Growth,'" *Manchester School of Economic and Social Studies* (January, 1958), pp. 68–75. North states that "the total capital imports for the entire period 1847–1860 were very modest." (*Ibid.,* p. 68.)

decade. Foreigners did not return to the capital market of the United States until the 1850's. The crash of the British railway boom in 1847 turned the flow of British capital in our direction. It has been estimated that $300 million of new foreign capital entered this country between 1850 and 1857; most of these funds were invested in railroads, but foreign investors also invested in federal, state, and local bonds, bank shares, and, to a much slighter degree, in industrial issues. An interesting statement of the extent of foreign ownership of American securities, as of 1853, is presented in Table 7.

TABLE 7

American Securities Owned Abroad in 1853[a]
(In millions of dollars)

Issued by	Total Outstanding	Foreign-owned	Per cent Foreign-owned
United States	$ 58.2	$ 27	46%
States	190.7	110.9	58
Counties and cities	93.2	21.4	23
Railroad bonds	170.1	43.9	26
Railroad stocks	309.8	8	3
Banks and insurance	279.5	7	3
Canals and navigation	58	2.5	4
Miscellaneous	18.7	1	6
Total	1,178.6	222	18

[a] Reproduced in M. Myers, *The New York Money Market* (New York: Columbia University Press, 1931), Vol. 1, p. 36.

Much less disputable is the role the Anglo-American merchant bankers played in the financing of American short and long term credit needs. These were a small group of banking firms, principally located in London, who performed a variety of functions for American business in this period. They served as commission merchants, buying and selling for their clients; they granted short-term credit to American importers and exporters, accepting commercial drafts and foreign bills of exchange; they sold the securities of American banks, railroads, and manufacturing companies abroad. The leading firm of this type was Baring Brothers, but there were others who were also very important—N. M. Rothschild and Sons, Thomas Wilson and Co., Timothy Wiggin and Co., etc.[20]

Despite the increased capital supply, both domestic and foreign, and the larger commercial banking facilities of this period, discount rates on short term loans were amazingly high; in New York City, they ranged from 6 to 15 per cent and higher, despite the constantly increasing gold supply after 1849. Money was tight in most years of the 1850's in practically all sectors of the

[20] A classic treatment is L. H. Jenks, *The Migration of British Capital to 1875* (New York: A. A. Knopf, Inc., 1927), Chap. III.

economy; suppliers of loanable funds were able to charge premium rates.[21] All this suggests that our economic growth was so rapid in that decade that swelling credit from home and abroad could not satisfy our needs.

LEADING SECTORS AND THE TAKE-OFF

The second condition required for take-off is "the development of one or more substantial manufacturing sectors, with a high rate of growth." The basic argument is that the rapid growth of such a manufacturing sector provides a powerful and essential engine of economic transformation. This so-called "leading sectors" argument requires the emergence of primary growth sectors with possibilities for innovation or exploitation of newly profitable or hitherto unexplored resources.

The essential requirements for such a leading sector are:

1. An enlarged demand for the product of such a sector.
2. The introduction into these sectors of new production functions as well as an expansion of capacity.
3. A high rate of plough-back of profits by entrepreneurs in the primary and supplementary growth sectors that are expanding, and a society capable of generating the capital initially required to detonate the take-off in key sectors.

Rostow's view is that to understand economic growth it is necessary to break down large aggregates such as consumption and investment and to investigate "the consequences of growth in particular sectors of the economy." In the American case, he sees our take-off as "the upshot of two different periods of expansion: the first, that of the 1840's, marked by railway and manufacturing development" in the East; "the second, the great railway push into the Middle West during the 1850's. . . ." The railroads were "decisive" in the American take-off, according to Rostow; they were the primary growth sector that imparted their primary and secondary impulses to the economy and produced a transformation in its structure. What evidence is there that there was a marked change in the structural make-up (i.e., the relative composition of its sectors) in the years 1843–60?

Assuming that Rostow means by "structural change" a change in the percentage distribution of output among the various industries making up the economy, we can use Gallman's data on commodity output to determine the nature and extent of such sectoral shifts. Table 8 presents a percentage distribution of the value added in commodity production in the United States for selected years in the period 1839–59 (in constant dollars). We see that there was a rapid increase in manufacturing's share of commodity output in those years and a steady decline in that of agriculture. While critics of Rostow

---

[21] See L. Davis, "Mrs. Vatter on Industrial Borrowing, A Reply," *Journal of Economic History*, Vol. 21 (June, 1961), p. 226.

TABLE 8

Percentage Distribution of Value Added in Commodity Production—
Gallman's Constant Dollar Series, 1839–59[a]

Year	Agriculture	Mining	Manufacturing	Construction (Variant A)
1839	71.9%	0.7%	17.4%	10.1%
1844	68.7	1.0	21.1	9.2
1849	59.7	1.1	29.5	9.8
1854	56.8	1.1	29.2	12.9
1859	55.5	1.2	32.0	11.2

[a] Source: Gallman, "Commodity Output," p. 43 *op. cit.*

often minimize the significance of these figures, they clearly indicate that by 1860 the manufacturing base had been greatly broadened as compared to that of the pre-1843 years. North himself has said that "The most striking contrast between the 1840 census figures on manufactures and the 1860 figures is not so much the rapid growth of output as the spread of manufacturing into new industries."[22] The extent of that development is reflected in the increase in the aggregate value of manufactures from $484 million in 1840 to $1,886 million in 1860. In the final decade before the Civil War output soared in a number of industrial lines: cotton textile output increased 77 per cent, wool textile production increased 42 per cent, hosiery goods, 608 per cent, carpets by 45 per cent, men's clothing 55 per cent, and boot and shoe production increased 70 per cent.[23] Furthermore, manufacturing activity in the 1850's became more active in regions other than the Northeast, so that if one stresses the acceleration in the rate of industrial growth of more than regional significance there is warrant for singling out the 1843–60 period as a crucial one. In those years the scale of productive activity reached a "critical level" and changes occurred that led to a massive and progressive structural transformation in the economy.

Another indication of the unusual industrial growth during this period is the rise of commodity output per capita and the increased productivity of the average worker. Table 2 above shows the former rising $14 per capita between 1849 and 1854, and the jump in output per worker is much larger in the period 1849–59 than in the preceding ten years.

These signs of increased acceleration in industrial growth in this period and especially in the years 1849–57 do not dispose of the question as to whether railroads were the "leading sector" in this so-called take-off. That issue, as one judicious student of the matter has stated it, is "whether railroads first set in motion the forces culminating in the economic development of the decade (i.e., the 1850's), or whether arising in response to profitable situations they

[22] D. C. North, "Industrialization in the United States (1815–60)" in *The Economics of Take-Off* . . . p. 62.
[23] *Ibid.*, p. 45.

played a more passive role."[24] The underlying hypothesis of those who have argued for a leading role for the railroads has usually been the notion that the railroads were constructed ahead of demand and that they therefore gave rise to new, autonomous investment that spurred the growth of the economy. The influential analyses of Schumpeter and Jenks and the later pioneering studies of Carter Goodrich lent force and vitality to this interpretation.[25] Yet Fishlow, in a recent, incisive analysis, has shown quite conclusively that railroads of this period in the mid-West were not constructed ahead of demand, but rather extended out progressively from more to less densely settled areas.[26] The "pattern of sequential construction" followed was conducive to a satisfactory rate of return on capital and made external governmental subsidies less necessary. Local funds rather than federal or state assistance played the most important role in encouraging railroad building in this period; the use of the former is consistent with the interpretation that the roads were mainly subsidized by already settled towns and counties seeking the "social return" from such transportation investment. Furthermore, construction ahead of demand is insufficient as an explanation because "railroad promotion in already settled areas sparked anticipatory population movement to less settled areas. As a consequence, demand was already there when the railroads were ultimately built farther west. In a larger sense, therefore, railroads *were* a leading factor. . . ."[27] But this is not to say that they were the leading sector in the overall growth of the economy in this period.

In examining the American economy of these years for evidence of leading sectors it is necessary to go back to Rostow's so-called "preconditions stage" of economic growth to find some of the basic stimuli to take-off. Paradoxically, it is in the agricultural sector in which we discover both the major obstacle and stimulus to the beginning of accelerated economic growth. The obstacle that agriculture presented to the possible industrialization of the United States was not so much the sociological impediment involved in overcoming the resistances of a traditional society, but rather the economic problem of transcending the high attraction of continuing to be a profitable supplier of foodstuffs and raw materials. What weakened the lure of such a role for the United States and moved the nation toward industrialization in such rapid fashion?

The embargo and the War of 1812 had earlier encouraged the growth of a domestic textile industry. Now, in the 1840's it would appear to have been the repeal of the British Corn Laws and crop failures abroad (particularly in Ireland) that enlarged the market for our agricultural products and contributed to higher prices for our major export staples. It is important to note too

---

[24] Fishlow, *American Railroads* . . . , p. 203.

[25] See Schumpeter, *Business Cycles* (New York: McGraw-Hill, 1939), Vol. 1, p. 303; L. H. Jenks, "Railroads as an Economic Force in American Development," *Journal of Economic History*, IV (1944), pp. 1–20; C. Goodrich, *Government Promotion of American Canals and Railroads* (New York: Columbia University Press, 1960).

[26] A. Fishlow, *American Railroads* . . . , Chap. IV.

[27] *Ibid.*, p. 165.

that these higher prices were attained at a time when improved agricultural machinery was coming into use and facilitating increased production. The enormous increases in the production and export of such crops as wheat and cotton (described in Chapter 11) in turn induced investment in railroad construction.[28] In the complex process of interaction and dynamic sequences, which is the essence of economic growth, the railroads built, especially in the 1850's, opened up vast new lands for cultivation in the West and thereby made it possible for them to market their products profitably.

In the East, industrialization in the 1840's does not seem to have been so dependent upon the construction of the railroads. While theoretical analysis of the effects of the external economies created by railroads might suggest that a strong forward linkage existed between the railroads as a leading sector and manufactures, close historical study does not support this causal relationship. Cootner in fact concluded on the basis of his studies that causality ran in the opposite direction: in the East, industrial requirements in the 1840's determined the pace of railroad construction.[29] But Fishlow, in a closely-knit historical analysis finds that the assumption that the railroads were built in that region primarily to serve manufacturing or mining needs is defective and that in considerable part they were constructed rather to serve broader commercial functions, including the transport of passengers.[30]

The indispensability of rail transportation for our pre-war industrial expansion is contradicted, of course, by the substantial development that took place prior to the rail age. The growth of the textile industry in the 1820's is evidence enough that the railroad was not a necessary factor in its inception. With the other modes of transport that were available and usually cheaper than rail, no real or absolute constraint on industrial development was removed by the railroad expansion of the 1840's. This is in line with what we would expect. Actually, distribution costs were a small fraction of total expenditure of industrialists so that it is possible to explain the industrial expansion in terms of other factors. Thus, the "industrial breakthrough" of that period seems to be independent of the railroad; in Fishlow's words, ". . . There is little reason to suppose that the rapid rise of ante-bellum

[28] It is instructive to note that at the Konstanz conference on the take-off, which took place subsequent to the publication of *The Stages of Economic Growth*, Rostow argued that the economic expansion in the decisive decade of the American take-off (the 1850's) was "triggered" by the transport requirements for exploiting the grain fields of the West. "The first phase of accelerated industrialization was, to a degree, a by-product of an agricultural revolution." "The rising world grain prices of the 1850's . . . made the massive laying of rail lines attractive. . . ." (*The Economics of Take-off* . . . , p. 14). This line of analysis, which is not to be found in the sections on the take-off in *The Stages* would seem to demote the railroads from the rank of the "leading sector" in both the temporal and causal connotations of that phrase. As far as causality goes, it brings Rostow's position much closer to that argued for by North and others who have consistently rejected the thesis that the railroads were the leading sector in the economic growth of this period.

[29] See P. H. Cootner, "The Role of the Railroads in U.S. Economic Growth," *Journal of Economic History* (December, 1963), pp. 477–521.

[30] Fishlow, *American Railroads* . . . , Chap. VI.

manufacturing in the 1840's evoked, except in a general way, the construction of railroads, or that it depended crucially upon completion of the rail network. . . ."[31] Rather than leading economic development in that decade, the construction of the railroads seems to have been a response to the general expansion of the economy. In the 1850's they played a more positive role in extending western agriculture and in redirecting the flow of interregional trade. The railroads did not forge a national market in the ante-bellum years, but they did bind the East and West together more closely and served to expand their trade with each other while the direct trade of the latter with the South dwindled relatively.

THE BACKWARD LINKAGES OF THE RAILROADS

The backward linkage effects of the railroads is a central aspect of Rostow's conception of the take-off. As he himself put it, " . . . perhaps most important for the take-off itself, the development of railways has led to the development of modern coal, iron, and engineering industries. In many countries the growth of modern basic industrial sectors can be traced in the most direct way to the requirements for building and, especially, for maintaining substantial railway systems."[32] This demand side of the railroads' expansion in this period has been a source of disagreement partly because of the limitations of the available quantitative data. There can be little dispute, however, as to the importance of railroad expenditure in the aggregate. On the eve of the Civil War, the railroads were second in size only to the whole agricultural sector. On their accounting, they were "the first billion dollar, nonagricultural enterprise in the United States." According to the 1860 census, the total cost of construction of the American railroads was $1,152 million. In the same year, according to the same source, the capital investment in all manufacturing was $1,010 million.[33] The railroads were truly the giant corporations of that era, over-shadowing in size the more than 2 million farms and dwarfing even the Second Bank of the United States and most manufacturing enterprise.

Railroad capital expenditure, as Table 9 shows, was a sizeable fraction of total capital formation in most years of this period, and its volatility had large actual and potential effects on total demand, especially in the 1850's. From 1834 to 1858 railroad investment never fell much below 10 per cent of total capital formation and in the years 1849–58 it amounted, on Fishlow's accounting, to more than 15 per cent of investment outlay. Further, according to the same author, "by 1859, the combined income flow emanating from

---

[31] *Ibid.*, p. 260.

[32] Rostow, *The Stages of Economic Growth*, p. 55.

[33] U.S. Bureau of the Census, Preliminary Report on the Eighth Census (Washington, 1862), pp. 227–231, cited in Fishlow, *American Railroads* . . . , p. 100, footnote 4.

TABLE 9

*Railroad Capital Formation in Relation to Gross Capital Formation
before 1860 (In millions of dollars and per cent)* [a]
(In 1860 dollars)

Year or Annual Average	Railroad Gross Investment	Gross Capital Formation	Railroad Investment as % of Gross Capital Formation
1839	$ 17.0	$200	8.5%
1844	8.5	194	4.4
1849	39.4	258	15.3
1854	103.6	542	19.1
1859	60.4	532	11.4

[a] Source: Adapted from A. Fishlow, *American Railroads and the Transformation of the Ante-Bellum Economy* (Cambridge: Harvard University Press, 1965), p. 101. See the author's Appendix B for the methods used in deriving these estimates.

the railroad sector was perhaps 3 per cent of annual product in that year, equivalent to the sum of the value added of the cotton, iron, and machinery industries."[34]

By the 1850's the railroads' investment and its fluctuation were exerting a marked leverage upon the movement of the economy. Two aspects of rail investment tended to give it unusual influence: one was the industry's high capital-output ratio (roughly five times that in manufacturing) and borrowing-expenditure ratio and the second, its high debt-equity ratio, particularly in the 1850's. Both of these factors tended to give railroad investment an unusual capacity for stimulating the economy's rate of growth, thus permitting its promoters to generate the savings necessary to realize their investment plans.[35] It is for these reasons that it can be contended that the railroads' expenditures were critical in the cycle of 1849–58.

So much for the possible effect of railroad expenditures in general upon the economy. How did the railroads affect specific demands for such raw materials as iron, coal, machinery, etc.? This question has been the subject of much scholarly dispute, partially because of the inadequacy of the statistics. Fogel and North, on the basis of careful studies, concluded that the influence of the railroad industry on the pre-war pig iron industry was minor. Fogel found that the demand for railroad iron in the decade ending in 1849 was 10

[34] *Ibid.*, p. 103.

[35] Fishlow invokes a multiplier-accelerator model of income determination to explain this point, saying " . . . Within the context of a multiplier-accelerator model of income determination (that is, demand determined), an excess of planned investment over planned savings results in an increase of income sufficient to generate the necessary savings. Thus anything that increases the gap, such as increased capital requirements or greater resort to borrowing, will increase the rate of growth." (Fishlow, *American Railroads* . . . , p. 117.) He argues further that the railroads were able to induce a substantial inflow of foreign capital in the 1850's the effect of which was to augment the total savings available to the nation. For these reasons he thinks that "railroad investment must be regarded as less than perfectly replaced by other expenditure, and hence at least partially contributing to the realized rate of growth by the 1850's."

per cent of the consumption of domestic crude iron; North, while noting that railroads provided "the most important single demand from industry," argues that it was "dwarfed by the value added of the polyglot classification of iron castings . . . Indeed, the value added to stove making alone was equal to that of iron rails."[36] Fishlow, in a more recent study, offers an expenditure analysis of the railroads for rails and finds that there was more than a doubling of domestic pig iron requirements for that product by the end of the 1850's, whereas Fogel had found a gain of only 40 per cent by his method of estimation. In the years 1849–54, imports of rails from Britain met 80 per cent of our domestic needs, but after that period the American producers gained a larger share of the market; on the average in the years 1856–60 railway demand absorbed more than 15 per cent of American pig iron production (on the basis of Fogel's figures) or 21 per cent, on Fishlow's. The railroad demand for rails had an important qualitative effect as well; the rail mills could use anthracite pig more efficiently than other users, and this encouraged the crucial shift from charcoal to anthracite and, ultimately, to coke iron. "The rail mills were the largest in the country and in the technological van. . . ."[37] These considerations underscore the importance of the backward linkage of the railroads to the iron industry, a relationship to become more marked in the post-war years.

The railroads' demand for machinery does not seem to sustain Rostow's statement that the railways "brought to life" the machinery industry. In 1860 the value of locomotive production was less than $5 million, while the value of the aggregate production of the machinery sector totaled more than $52 million. Nor can one accept the view that the railroads brought into being specialized engineering firms for the first time because such concerns had earlier built stationary steam engines for a variety of uses. The railroads' development of repair shops was a far more potent effect because this disseminated mechanical skills so necessary to an industrial society. The side effects of maintaining these numerous machine shops to keep the iron horse and its appurtenances in working order were not limited to one region, as was the case with textile machinery, but extended throughout the nation.

The railroads' derived demand for coal was not large; on one estimate, the direct railway requirements came to a mere 2 per cent of total coal consumption in 1859. If indirect needs in the form of coal used in fabricating iron for the railroads is included, the total comes to about 5 per cent. The demand of this industry for lumber, contrary to common impression, was likewise not very large—about 3–4 per cent of total lumber production in the 1840's and 10 per cent in the next decade.[38]

In general, the backward linkage effects of the railroads became substantial

---

[36] North, "Industrialization in the United States," in *The Economics of Take-Off*, p. 53; Fogel, *Railroads and American Economic Growth*, p. 233.

[37] See Fishlow, *American Railroads* . . . , pp. 132–149, for a lucid treatment of this controversial subject.

[38] *Ibid.*, pp. 156–159.

and even decisive in some lines of industrial activity by the 1850's, partly because of the industry's high capital-output ratio. On the other hand, iron and coal production had developed rapidly in the 1840's quite independently of railroad demands. In this sense, Rostow would seem to be partially in error when he ties the industrial take-off to the effects solely of the railroads' expansion. The derived demands of that sector were insignificant in the 1840's, but they had more positive effects in the following decade when railroad investment increased. A monistic, one-factor explanation of economic growth is hazardous and unlikely to be correct because "the process of economic development is too complex, and also too diversified, to permit of unequivocal prime movers. . . ."[39] In the next section, we shall see more clearly the international factors at work in the dynamic expansion of the American economy during these two remarkable decades.

THE INTERNATIONAL CONTEXT OF
ACCELERATED ECONOMIC GROWTH

The take-off thesis places great emphasis on the "dynamics of railroadization" in explaining the acceleration of economic growth and industrialization in this period. But one cannot disregard the fact that agriculture was still very important in the pre-war years; in fact, about three-fifths of the value added in commodity production was in the agricultural sector, and according to Martin's national income data, over 30 per cent of the income generated originated there.[40] Now most of the commercial agriculture in those years was oriented in part to the international markets for its products. While the expansion of the American economy was not as dependent on the export of a single farm staple as it had been in the preceding period, some of its principal agricultural commodities were still in the "orbit" of the larger Atlantic economy and felt very strongly the changes that occurred there. The pace of our westward expansion in these years was profoundly affected by the demand for foodstuffs in Europe and in the industrializing Northeast. Furthermore, the international movement of labor and capital in these years had important effects on the performance of the economy.[41]

After the long depression of 1839–43, recovery was slow, but our agriculture received a mighty impetus as a result of the repeal of the Corn Laws and the Irish famine. There was an increased demand for wheat and corn, their prices rose, and this in turn led to a new wave of settlement in the West and

---

[39] *Ibid.*, p. 204.

[40] See Gallman, "Commodity Output, 1839–1899," in Parker, *Trends in the American Economy in the Nineteenth Century* (Princeton, N.J.; Princeton University Press, 1960), p. 43, and *Historical Statistics of the United States* (1949), p. 14.

[41] An admirable, concise analysis of this phase of American economic development will be found in D. C. North, *The Economic Growth of the United States*, Chaps. 8 and 15.

increased interest in transportation improvements. The demand for and speculation in land assumed boom proportions in the West in the 1850's. The
favorable movement of farm prices encouraged bank credit expansion and to
the capital provided by domestic sources there was added the funds attracted
from abroad.

The volume and value of foreign trade increased substantially in the years
after 1843. The value of our exports multiplied almost threefold in the period
under discussion, but imports grew so rapidly after 1849 that the nation had a
deficit trade balance in the '50's. (Compare Chart 2.) More than two-thirds of
our exports were classified as crude materials, with raw cotton accounting for
over half of the annual value of United States exports down to the Civil War.
The traditional exports, tobacco, rice, lumber, and potash showed no tendency
to grow, while there was a modest increase in the export of manufactured
goods. Our lag in the latter respect is not surprising because our comparative
advantage still lay in land-intensive types of activity rather than in those
involving great utilization of capital and labor.

CHART 2

Value of Imports and Exports of the United States: 1815–1860
(Figures from "U.S. Balance of Payments, 1790–1860.")

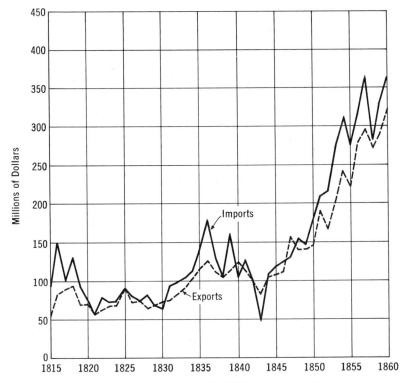

Source: D. C. North, *Economic Growth of U.S., op. cit.,* p. 84.

Our imports consisted mainly of textiles, manufactures of iron, and such tropical foodstuffs as sugar, coffee, tea, and cocoa, most of which could not be efficiently produced in this country. The rising volume of imports reflected the improving plane of consumption and the prosperity that characterized most of the 1850's. The United States could afford this growing import surplus because of the compensating movement of other items in its balance of payments; these were "invisible items," gold movements and capital flows. Our earnings from shipping and the funds brought in by immigrants were the principal credits of an invisible nature. Offsetting them were immigrant remittances and the excess of tourists' expenditures.

For the quarter century prior to 1848, the United States had imported more specie in most years than we exported, but all that changed with the California gold discoveries. After that historic event most of the gold mined in that state was exported, and in effect, it was this gold credit, plus the earnings of our merchant marine, that paid for the large surplus of imports.[42] (See Chart 3.) Capital inflow during this period underwent marked changes. After the debacle on state debts during the depression of 1837, aggregate foreign indebtedness declined by over $100 million. But when the railroad boom of 1849–57 got under way, European investors (first the Germans and later the British again) returned to investing in our railroad securities. North estimates that foreign investors purchased between $150 and $200 million of railroad securities during that period. This capital inflow, though not as important relatively as that of the 1830's, was important because it permitted us to enjoy a high level of importation without suffering a deterioration in the external value of the dollar (i.e., in foreign exchange rates). During the period of 1850–57 there was probably a substantial diversion of resources from consumer goods production into construction of canals and railroads. If the United States had not been able to finance the large imports of consumer and capital goods, we might have experienced a rapid inflation in the price level. As it was, the consumer price level displayed a decided downward trend in the years after 1837.[43]

Since the great immigration in the period from 1845–55 is the subject of further analysis in the next chapter, we need only note here that it too eased the strain of economic readjustment in this period of rapid capital formation. The immigrants, especially the Irish, provided a new source of labor for the growing textile factories of New England, and they also supplied the manpower for the arduous task of railroad construction.

---

[42] The standard treatment of our balance of payments for this period is D. C. North, "The United States Balance of Payments, 1790–1860," in Parker, *Trends in the American Economy in the Nineteenth Century*, pp. 573–627. An earlier classic study is C. J. Bullock, J. H. Williams, and R. S. Tucker, "The Balance of Trade of the United States," *Review of Economic Statistics*, preliminary Vol. 1 (July, 1919); see also J. G. Williamson, *American Growth and the Balance of Payments, 1820–1913* (Chapel Hill, North Carolina: University of North Carolina Press, 1964).

[43] See testimony of Ethel B. Hoover in *Historical and Comparative Rates of Production, Productivity and Prices*, Part II (1959), p. 39.

CHART 3

*United States Trade Balance, Specie Balance, and Service and
Other Items Balance, Excluding Interest, 1820–1860*

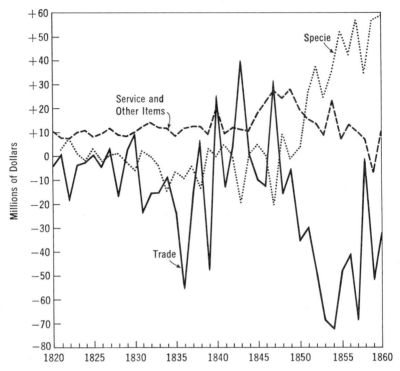

Source: Reproduced from W. N. Parker, ed., *Trends in the American Economy in the
Nineteenth Century* (Princeton, N.J.: Princeton University Press, 1960), p. 583.

THE ROLE OF FINANCIAL INSTITUTIONS

The part played by the expanding commercial banks and the financial
intermediaries in the acceleration of the nation's economic growth in this
period has been touched upon above. We have noted that the banknotes of the
1840's and 1850's possessed much greater stability of value than their predecessors of earlier years, thanks to greater regulation by the states. But it would
not do to leave the impression that the financial system was perfectly adjusted
to the commercial needs of the day. For one thing, the very number and
variety of state banknote issues and the widespread counterfeiting of such
paper money created a serious problem for businessmen. For example, bogus
money became so serious that in 1853 the banks themselves formed an
Association for the Prevention of Counterfeiting. The hand-to-hand currency
was complicated too by the various unauthorized issues of paper money in
circulation. The promissory notes, issued by construction companies, had to be

accepted at fluctuating discounts; in addition, there were the "shinplasters" of private merchants. It is no wonder that it has often been said that business was done in spite of the chaos in the currency.

This monetary confusion was further aggravated when gold started to flow in large quantities from the mines of California. With the increased production of gold, the market ratio between silver and gold departed still further from the mint ratio; the old familiar problem posed by Gresham's Law again confronted the nation. By 1851, the specie value of the American silver dollar in relation to the gold dollar had become $1.04½. Silver dollars disappeared from circulation, as the cheap money (gold) drove out of use the dear money (silver). Fractional silver also disappeared. "By the close of 1851, the lack of 'small change' was demoralizing the retail trade of the country."[44] To ease the situation, some New England banks issued notes for odd amounts—$1.25, $1.37½, etc. Foreign silver coins came into use to make up the shortage, and businessmen issued shinplasters for fractional amounts. The problem, fortunately, was finally solved when Congress, after debating the matter for two years, passed the Subsidiary Coinage Act of 1853. This law cut the silver content of all coins from the half dollar down by about 7 per cent. Furthermore, this subsidiary coinage was made legal tender only for amounts up to five dollars. The new coins provided for by this Act were promptly minted, and since their bullion value was less than their mint value, they stayed in circulation.

Government finances during these years were handled by the so-called Independent Treasury System. President Van Buren, a Jacksonian Democrat, had established this system in 1840. The Whigs, fighting to establish another United States Bank, shelved it the following year, but it was re-established in 1846 on practically the same basis as provided for in the 1840 law. This legislation authorized the Treasury to keep its cash balances in its subtreasury offices instead of depositing them in private banks. Payments to the Treasury could be made only in specie or in treasury notes. Payments by the government could be made only in cash or, after 1853, by drafts on bullion held at the mint. This was a "hard money" system in which the government kept its cash in its own vaults. It divorced the finances of the federal government completely from the banking system of the country; its backers argued that in the future no financial crisis could tie up federal funds.

It is true that this system aided the government at Washington in financing the relatively light expenditures for the Mexican War. It permitted the federal government too to survive the panic of 1857 without embarrassment, while the state governments with deposits in state banks could not draw out their specie. But there was a fatal flaw in the Independent Treasury system, which in more difficult times could have caused considerable trouble. The danger in the system was that during a time of surplus revenue for the federal government—when its income was exceeding its expenditures, as in the 1850's—it

---

[44] W. J. Shultz and M. R. Caine, *Financial Development of the United States*, p. 255.

might lead to a contraction of the currency available for business because of the accumulation of specie in the Treasury vaults. Students of finance have pointed out that if such a system was not to have adverse effects upon business, there was a necessity for a careful adjustment of government revenues to expenditures. The Independent Treasury system was in fact an anomaly in an economy that was becoming more interdependent and more complex in its fluctuations and movements. It did not provide the direction and control of a real central bank to the banking system, and during the Civil War certain of its provisions were so restrictive that they were suspended by Congress.

But we anticipate later events; let us return to examine the course of business activity and its fluctuations prior to 1857. The recovery that occurred in 1843 slowly grew and by the later years of that decade was in full swing. The tightening of credit, which reflected the serious cyclical downturn in England in 1848, did not have appreciable effects here, and when in the following year gold was discovered in California, the boom was truly on. This cyclical expansion was marked by the usual increase in land sales, following rising prices, a high level of internal and international migration, and a considerable capital inflow. Railroad investment especially grew phenomenally in the years 1849–54. Over that period it rose from $37 million to $111 million and resulted in doubling the mileage of the nation's rail network. By 1854 the demand of the railroad promoters for capital was outrunning the supply; rising interest rates curtailed some projects, but the prosperity of the nation continued until it came to a sudden halt with the panic of 1857. An examination of the causes of the depression that followed sheds a revealing sidelight on the role of the railroads in the functioning of the economy at that time.

THE DEPRESSION OF 1857 AND RAILROAD INVESTMENT

The depression of 1857 has customarily been viewed by economic historians as being commercial in character and international in origin. Professor Taylor emphasizes its similarity to previous cyclical reversals, and Van Vleck, who has studied the subject most recently, says, "fundamentally the causes of the panic of 1857 were not localized in the United States. . . . Indeed, anyone who endeavors to explain the panic of 1857 as something divorced and independent of what was transpiring in the Old World will be largely wasting his time."[45] The chronology of that panic lends some surface plausibility to this view. A financial depression set in first in Europe in the summer of that year; security prices fell here and then in August the New York branch of the Ohio Life Insurance and Trust Co. (a bank of deposit despite its title) failed. The panic was underway. Country banks started a "run" on New York City

[45] G. R. Taylor, *The Transportation Revolution, 1815–1860* (New York: Holt, Rinehart and Winston, 1951), pp. 345–51; G. W. Van Vleck, *The Panic of 1857* (New York: Columbia University Press, 1951), p. 105.

banks and within two months had withdrawn $25 million. Call loans in New York went to 20 per cent; western banks went down like houses of cards. In September, the Philadelphia and Baltimore banks began to fail, and in the following month, the New York banks, with the exception of the Chemical Bank, suspended specie payment. Railroad security prices fell sharply, and the Illinois Central, the New York and Erie, and the Michigan Central declared bankruptcy. This relatively short, sharp depression seems to have been shortened by the continued flow of gold from California. That this downturn in business was not too prolonged or severe can be seen clearly from the statistics of domestic and foreign trade in Table 10.

TABLE 10

Indices of the Volume of Trade in the United States, 1849–60[a]
(No base years shown)

Year	Domestic Trade	Foreign Trade (Imports and exports)
1849	94	88
1850	88	97
1851	93	97
1852	94	98
1853	101	108
1854	106	102
1855	108	102
1856	104	114
1857	97	102
1858	91	96
1859	98	104
1860	114	91

[a] Source: W. B. Smith and A. H. Cole, *Fluctuations in American Business, 1790–1860* (Cambridge: Harvard University Press, 1935), p. 104. © Copyright renewed in 1963 by W. B. Smith and A. H. Cole.

Fishlow has argued that the panic inaugurating the depression of 1857 was "merely a final overt symptom of an already pervasive weakness." His analysis leads him to conclude that the turning point in business activity had come much earlier, in 1854, when railroad investment peaked out. When that occurred, "the economy could not manage more than temporary escape. . . ." A number of series show turning points much earlier than 1857: domestic trade, as can be seen from Table 10, reached a peak in 1855; land sales also were at a maximum in 1854–55; migration to the West and immigration had turned down before 1857. Commodity prices continued to rise, and the volume of foreign trade soared in 1856; these developments probably prevented the underlying weakness in domestic business from manifesting itself sooner. These lines of analysis lead Fishlow to conclude that "railroad expenditures led and thus helped to generate a significant downturn in the 1850's. . . ." He adds: "From the broader perspective of aggregate activity, the downturn of the 1850's seems to represent the first *industrial* boom in the United States; a cyclical fluctuation primarily associated with the pattern of real nonagricultural investment and independent of the fortunes of cotton. . . ."[46] If this view is accepted, it would mean that, though the railroads in themselves were not sufficient to generate Rostow's take-off, they had come to play such a crucial role in the economy's growth by the 1850's that a decline in their rate of investment was important enough to precipitate a "letdown" in the pace of growth of the whole economy. Such a conclusion will have to be incorporated or rejected, as the case may be, in the economic historian's final evaluation of the validity of the take-off hypothesis.

As a form of social overhead capital, the railroads were a potent historical force in the decade preceding the Civil War. Their impact on the economy came at a time when it was moving into sustained, long term growth. Its economic influence was as great as it was because it had a composite character: it affected both the supply and demand conditions of the evolving system.

> What made the innovation so beneficial in fact was the specific American historical context. At every turn the circumstances of the American success were a far cry from the initial conditions in the low income countries today. The extensive role of private investment bespeaks a responsiveness to market forces, a pool of local capital, a foresight—properties that go far to explain the substantial gains reaped from lower cost transportation. The concentration of those benefits in agriculture, moreover, testifies to an economy with abundant fertile land, farmers that were profit motivated and market oriented, and a population that was geographically mobile. . . .[47]

In the following chapter we examine the political and sociological changes in the period, which continued to foster these cultural values as well as the institutions that were so conducive to the acceleration of the nation's economic growth.

[46] Fishlow, *American Railroads* . . . , pp. 114–115.
[47] *Ibid.*, p. 311.

Chapter 13

THE POLITICAL AND SOCIAL CONDITIONS OF ACCELERATED ECONOMIC GROWTH

THE THIRD CONDITION OF TAKE-OFF

According to Rostow, the third condition for economic take-off is the existence or quick emergence of "a political, social and institutional framework which exploits the impulses to expansion in the modern sector and the potential external economy effects of the take-off and gives to growth an ongoing character."[1] In this chapter we shall examine the extent to which these conditions were realized in the years 1844–57, though our analysis will not be confined wholly to Rostow's emphasis. To Rostow, the third condition implies "a considerable capability to mobilize capital from domestic sources"; that aspect of the matter has been dealt with above.[2] In addition, the Rostovian take-off "requires the existence and the successful activity of some group in the society which is prepared to accept innovations."[3] That requirement, we have seen, was amply satisfied in the United States for many years prior to 1843, but we shall be interested to document the further flourishing of the spirit of enterprise and innovation in this dynamic period of our history. It is clear that in the main Rostow regards the United States as one of those fortunate countries where the problem of entrepreneurship has not been a serious one. In "a limited group of wealthy agricultural nations whose populations derived by emigration mainly from western Europe," he says, "the problem of take-off was primarily economic; and when economic incentives for industrialization emerged commercial and banking groups moved over easily into industrial entrepreneurship. . . ." That statement is a fairly accurate description of what happened in the United States, so far as the shift of individual businessmen from mercantile to industrial pursuits was concerned. But, the larger dimensions of the transformation that converted the nation from a primarily agricultural to an industrial one and that had some of

[1] Rostow, *The Stages of Economic Growth* (Cambridge: Cambridge University Press, 1961), p. 39.
[2] See pp. 259–264.
[3] *Ibid.*, p. 50.

its most notable beginnings in the '40's and '50's do reveal a good deal of strife and struggle, both social and spiritual. Perhaps we can grasp some of the possible causes of the stresses and strains in American society in these years by reference to one final quotation from Rostow in which he attempts to put the take-off in historical perspective:

> In non-economic terms, the take-off usually witnesses a definitive social, political and cultural victory of those who would modernize the economy over those who would either cling to the traditional society or seek other goals; but— because nationalism can be a social solvent as well as a diversionary force—the victory can assume forms of mutual accommodation, rather than the destruction of the traditional groups by the more modern; . . .[4]

In this and in Chapter 16 of the following Part we shall be examining the delicate political compromises by which a "mutual accommodation" was sought between the industrializing sections of the North and the more traditional, agrarian culture of the South. From one perspective, it can be argued that the definitive victory of the modernizers over the traditionalists was not to be achieved in the take-off period proper (as defined by Rostow), but in the even more revolutionary years of the Civil War and Reconstruction period.

THE ENTERPRISING AND INNOVATING AMERICANS

In this period as in the earlier years of the Jacksonian era, the social structure enabled many Americans to fulfill their aspirations for improved economic and social status.[5] The revival of business from the long depression of 1837, the boom conditions in various fields of enterprise, the opening up of vast new resources for exploitation, and the dynamic technological change of the time provided numerous opportunities for the aspiring to "better themselves." Perhaps the most important factor promoting upward social mobility, in addition to those cited, was the industrialization of the economy. Sociological study has revealed that rapid upward mobility usually accompanies the expansion of an urban industrial economy;[6] the United States in this period

---

[4] *Ibid.*, p. 58.

[5] Actually, very little scientific study of social mobility in the United States has been done by historians. One authority on the subject, Oscar Handlin, states, "Historians have taken for granted the fluidity of American society and have often ascribed to it a uniqueness as compared with other societies; but they have done so on the basis of general impressions rather than systematically organized data. . . ." [O. and M. Handlin, "Mobility," in E. N. Saveth, ed., *American History and the Social Sciences* (London: The Free Press of Glencoe, Collier-Macmillan, Ltd., 1964), p. 219.]

[6] Greater social mobility in large urban centers is due to the fact that such communities develop a greater degree of specialization and a more complex division of labor than small towns. Furthermore, it seems that there are a greater number of non-manual positions in the labor force of the large city than in a small community. The large population and economic growth in cities in the nineteenth century meant too that there were many more new positions to be filled in such centers than in demographically stable communities. Lastly, it is to be noted that the relatively low birth rates in cities as contrasted with small, rural areas and especially the low reproduction rates of those in the higher socio-

was not an exception to this generalization. Various notables of the time alluded in their speeches to the opportunities that America offered for economic and social advancement. Thus, Daniel Webster celebrated a society in which every man could become a landed yeoman, and Edward Everett, another great orator of the day, exclaimed that "the wheel of fortune [in the United States] is in constant operation, and the poor in one generation furnish the rich of the next."[7]

Many Americans in this period as in the earlier years showed an interest and aptitude for innovations, particularly technological ones. "Invention seemed an American pastime." Yet, it was more than that, it was a business. "The hope of fortune, the ambition of growing rich lured the inventor on."[8] This period, as another historian says, was "The Era of the Thousand-and-One Beginnings."[9] It saw the development of the mechanical harvester by Cyrus McCormick and numerous other farm implements that increased agricultural productivity; it witnessed the invention of the Morse telegraph, Goodyear's process for vulcanizing rubber, Elias Howe's sewing machine, and countless other devices of varying importance.

This innovative talent in production was so striking and it led to such a distinctive pattern of producing manufactured goods that Europeans by the 1850's were referring to the "American system of manufacturing." " . . . Centering in southern New England and in the light metal working industries, notably in firearms, clocks, watches, locks, and tools of various kinds, and then spreading into neighboring states and a broadening range of industries, there came into being the basic elements and patterns of modern mass manufacturing: that is, the principles and practice of quantity manufacture of standardized products characterized by interchangeable parts and the use of a growing array of machine tools and specialized jigs and fixtures, along with power, to substitute simplified and, as far as possible, mechanized operations for the craftsman's arts. . . ."[10] Altogether, there were more than twenty industries in which an "American system of manufacturing" was recognized at the industrial exhibitions held by the western nations in the years between 1851 and 1867. European observers often scoffed at the crudity or light construction of American products, but they could not conceal their admiration for their effectiveness, simplicity, and originality, and especially for their cheapness and volume output.

The Crystal Palace Exhibition at London in 1851 made the world aware of

---

economic strata create greater opportunities for upward social mobility in the city than in the small town. See S. M. Lipset and R. Bendix, *Social Mobility in Industrial Society* (Berkeley: University of California Press, 1962), pp. 217–219.

[7] Saveth, *American History and the Social Sciences*, p. 218.

[8] A. Nevins, *Ordeal of the Union: A House Dividing, 1852–57*, Vol. 2 (New York: C. Scribner's and Sons, 1949), pp. 251–252.

[9] J. Chamberlain, *The Enterprising Americans* (New York: Harper and Row, 1963), p. 8.

[10] J. K. Sawyer, "The Social Basis of the American System of Manufacturing," *Journal of Economic History* (December, 1954), p. 369.

the remarkable strides that had been taken in American manufacturing since the founding of the nation. A variety of products from armaments to clocks impressed observers by their ingenuity and effectiveness. In 1854, a British commission studying the American techniques concluded that Britain would do well to "imitate" them. In general, Europeans were impressed by several key aspects of American manufacturing techniques. First, they noticed that American factory managers were frequently dissatisfied with the degree of labor-saving attained by machinery; they observed the avidity with which new ideas were accepted and improved upon. Secondly, they noted that American workmen were continuously devising new improvements on existing equipment. Third, the conditions of work were regarded as relatively clean, wholesome, healthful, and fair by comparison with European standards. Finally, they conceded that the American workmen had a superior education and they were not hampered in their advance by a rigid apprenticeship system. Part of their education was "on-the job" training, which encouraged invention and innovation. Practical insight into mechanics, physics, and chemistry were gained by experimentation in an empirical and eclectic manner. The feeling of the European was that the American was prepared to go beyond master work to creative and inventive utilization of the resources at his command.

This surprising level of manufacturing development took place before massive capital formation had been achieved in the American economy and before the laying of a national rail network made possible the continental, mass market of today. In fact, certain elements of the American pattern of production were worked out in small New England towns whose entrepreneurs had to sell their products in thin and scattered markets. How did the relatively underdeveloped United States overleap the more mature economies of Western Europe in achieving this distinctive pattern of manufacturing and marketing? Part of the answer is found, of course, in the factors usually cited—the high cost of labor and shortage of skills, the improving transportation system and the expanding markets this created for cheap manufactures, the advantage of our "late start" in industrial development, etc. But these economic factors do not seem adequate to account fully for the phenomenal American development. The emphasis placed by European industrial commissions and by numerous foreign travellers on certain non-economic elements seems warranted. These include such things as: ". . . the nature and diffusion of education in America; the absence of rigidities and restraints of class and craft; the freedom from hereditary definitions of the tasks or hardened ways of going about them; the high focus on personal advancement and drives to higher material welfare; and the mobility, flexibility, adaptability of Americans and their boundless belief in progress. . . ."[11]

The quality of the labor force in the Northeast can be attributed in part to the spread of the idea of free public education in these years. Earlier in the

[11] *Ibid.*, p. 376.

century the United States was really educationally underdeveloped. Though the principle of the free school was incorporated in the Indiana constitution as early as 1816, in most states communities were slow to tax themselves for this purpose. The rich were able to send their children to private schools, but most of the poor received inadequate or no education at all. Slowly the value of schooling came to be recognized. One favorable development in this direction was the introduction of the Lancasterian system of instruction, so called after the English educator Joseph Lancaster. His monitorial method employed the advanced pupils as teachers; it was first employed in New York in 1806. Despite its defects, this system was economical and it demonstrated that schools could be operated at a moderate cost.

Another movement that promoted an increase in the number and quality of schools was the educational reform advocating free compulsory education. In the fifties, largely because of the pioneering efforts of such educators as Horace Mann, Henry Barnard, and others, the idea of the free public school began to gain wider acceptance. While the number of such elementary and free public high schools was limited geographically, being more developed in the Northeast and the West than in the South on the eve of the Civil War, such "investment in human capital" was to grow more rapidly in the post-war era. But even before the sectional conflict, visiting British observers noted its beneficial effects on our industrial efficiency, remarking in their reports that the compulsory educational system "lays the foundation for that wide-spread intelligence which prevails amongst the factory operatives of the United States. . . ."[12]

THE TECHNOLOGICAL IMPULSES TO EXPANSION

Rostow's conception of the take-off, we have seen, embraces the idea that the impulses to expansion in the modern sector (railroading and related industries) will spread to other fields and give the economy a dynamic character. We can see this happening very clearly in the iron and steel industry in the 1850's. Consider briefly the history of the Cooper-Hewitt Iron Company by way of illustration.[13] Abram Hewitt and the venerable Peter Cooper had started iron production at Trenton, New Jersey in 1845; they took ore from the Jersey hills, converted it to pig iron in their blast furnaces at Phillipsburg, and transported the cast iron to Trenton by canal and rail where it was rolled into a variety of products. By the middle fifties their Trenton mills were the largest in the country, but they had to meet stiff competition from the British and from the new mills springing up in the Ohio Valley. In 1853, for example,

[12] Quoted in S. Bruchey, *The Roots of American Economic Growth* (New York: Harper and Row, 1965), p. 179. Pages 178–193 of this book are excellent on the topic of education; we have relied heavily on it in these two paragraphs.

[13] For the detailed story of this historic company, see A. Nevins, *Abram S. Hewitt: With Some Account of Peter Cooper* (New York: Harper and Bros., 1935), *passim*.

the Cambria Iron Works had opened at Johnstown, Pa. and in the same year Jones and Laughlin began production at Pittsburgh. When competition first became cut-throat in 1848–49, the versatile Cooper-Hewitt Co. turned to the production of wire, which was in great demand for the construction of tele-graph lines, bridges, etc. Its sales of iron to John A. Roebling made that company a leader in its field. Later, when the boom of 1850–53 gave way to depression, the Trenton Iron Works shifted to the output of structural beams for building construction. This was a great innovation for its time. The first complete cast-iron building in the world had only been erected in 1850, but cast iron proved to be too thick and heavy to be satisfactory. With others the Cooper-Hewitt firm experimented with wrought iron for this purpose and in 1854 their wrought-iron beams were used in the construction of the Cooper Union building in New York City. Later these beams were used in the new building of Harper Brothers, the publishers, after their old structure had been destroyed by fire in 1853. This was the first large fire-proof building for commercial purposes, and soon there were many imitators. By 1856, Cooper-Hewitt beams were being used in more than a hundred federal and state buildings.

In the late summer of 1856, Americans first heard of the new Bessemer process of producing steel without fuel. By December of that same year the Cooper-Hewitt firm was experimenting with the new technique, but their first efforts were not successful. Most American and British ores were not imme-diately adaptable to the revolutionary method; mechanical and chemical ad-justments had to be made, so the Bessemer method did not come into wide use in the United States until after the Civil War. This bit of history, nevertheless, illustrates further the alertness of one company to technological innovation. This case could be multiplied many times to show how innovations and other impulses to expansion were quickly taken advantage of in the iron and other industries of the nation during this period.

The external economies that Rostow conceives as important in giving the take-off a dynamic character were very evident in the iron industry. A pro-ducers' good industry is in a position to have such effects because it is vertically related to other industries in preceding and succeeding stages of production. An innovation in iron production is likely to change, either quantitatively or qualitatively, the demand for goods at the preceding stage or the supply to a following stage. If the innovation makes mass production possible, say, in the iron industry, it is likely to make similar innovations economical in those industries that supply the iron-makers (because of the increased demand for their product) and also in those industries using iron (because of iron's increased supply and reduced price). These relationships are not a matter of speculation, but have actually characterized the Industrial Revolution since its beginning.

> . . . In terms of *quantity*, lower-priced iron made the wider use of machinery possible, which allowed the development of large-scale machine tools, and this

reduced the price of machinery still more. The resulting lower price of blast-furnace and rolling-mill machinery once more lowered the price of iron. In terms of *quality*, superior grades of iron or steel made possible degrees of machine-tool precision that allowed the construction of entirely new types of machines which could themselves be improved by novel alloys. . . . "[14]

Influences of this kind had been evident in the iron and engineering industries of Great Britain since the eighteenth century, but they did not become conspicuous in the United States until the 1840's. In the earlier years the market for iron was largely confined to country blacksmiths; most machinery was constructed of wood and powered by water-wheels; and machine-tool innovations were being made principally in the firearms industry, though the technique of interchangeable parts had already spread to other fields. By the 1850's, the interrelatedness of innovations was more noticeable, because of the expansion of the railroads, the introduction of iron turbines, the Corliss steam engine, and the application of standardized manufacturing methods to new products. "The interrelatedness of innovation in key industries by 1850 set the basis for an accelerated pace of mutually reenforcing changes. . . ."[15] This stepped-up tempo of technological change continued throughout the remainder of the nineteenth century, but, actually, in the opinion of some observers it was not as rapid as it might have been on the basis of technology alone. Inter-industry innovation was retarded in this earlier period because entrepreneurs were not organized to act on interrelated projects and usually were uninformed about matters in industries other than their own.[16]

In appraising the quality of American entrepreneurship in this period it is well to keep in mind the economic factors that fostered innovations and not to exaggerate the contribution of cultural factors to the dynamism of American business leadership. The United States had many advantages in technological competition with the older countries of Europe. As a matter of fact, in many lines of industry, the European capacity for fundamental invention was superior to the Americans'; the latter's genius frequently lay in application, and they borrowed heavily from the foreigners, especially during the first half of the nineteenth century. The Americans had the advantage of a late start in the Industrial Revolution; they often could borrow the latest technique of

[14] W. P. Strassmann, *Risk and Technological Innovation* (Ithaca, N.Y.: Cornell University Press, 1959), p. 206.

[15] *Ibid.*, p. 208.

[16] This view is advanced by Professor Strassmann in *Risk and Technological Innovation*, pp. 208–210. Professor John E. Sawyer has suggested that the individualistic decision-making of American entrepreneurs tended to speed up economic development, compared to what it would have been if subject to centralized control. In his view "American entrepreneurs tended to overestimate the returns and underestimate the difficulties of their projects. But these errors were frequently matched by similar errors in complementary projects, and all the errors collectively generated the conditions for realizing the original visions. . . ." See J. E. Sawyer, "Entrepreneurship in Periods of Rapid Growth: The United States in the 19th Century," *Entrepreneurship and Economic Growth* (papers presented at a conference sponsored jointly by the Committee on Economic Growth of the Social Science Research Council and the Harvard University Research Center in Entrepreneurial History, Cambridge, Mass., 1954, pp. 1–7).

the Europeans or leap ahead to a more integrated use of known technical ideas. They did not suffer from a legacy of established plant and deeply-ingrained traditions of craftmanship. The peculiar factor-endowment of the United States, especially the shortage of skilled labor in the first forty years of the nineteenth century, encouraged mechanization and the development of labor-saving devices. The mechanization of industry, in turn, gave scope for the development of mechanical skills and stimulated the training of specialists, such as engineers and administrators, who could supervise the capital-inten-sive methods of manufacture. Furthermore, when communication improved as a result of the transportation revolution, the labor and product markets be-came less imperfect, and businessmen faced severe penalties for not adopting the more capital-intensive techniques that were coming into use.[17] While it is clear that there were many factors favoring technological innovation and mechanization in these years, it would be incorrect to suggest that innovators and enterprising Americans had an easy path. Entrepreneurs, even in the rapidly growing railroad industry, often encountered failure as well as success.

GOVERNMENT AND ECONOMIC GROWTH

Despite the important functions of government in economic development in these years, the percentage of national income that originated in that sector was small. From Table 1 it can be seen that the percentage of total realized national income originating in the government sector during the "take-off period" was less than 2½ per cent, and that it remained relatively constant over the span of years covered. However, a large part of that income was

TABLE 1

Realized Income from Government, by Kind, in the United States, 1839–59[a]
(In millions of dollars)

Year	Realized Income from Government	Percentage of Total Realized National Income	Production Income from Government	Other Income from Government
1839	$ 39	2.4%	$ 37	$2
1849	58	2.4	57	1
1859	101	2.3	100	1

[a] Source: R. F. Martin, *National Income in the United States, 1799–1938* (New York: National Industrial Conference Board, 1939), p. 87.

[17] For a perceptive comparison of American and British technology and a keen analysis of the factors encouraging labor-saving inventions in the former, see H. J. Habakkuk, *American and British Technology in the Nineteenth Century* (Cambridge: Cambridge University Press, 1962), *passim.*

production income, which means that its monetary impact must have been greater than the absolute amount suggests. Another statistical authority reports that in 1850 the government's share of physical structures was roughly 2.9 per cent of reproducible wealth—real wealth (in current prices).[18] The government's ownership of equipment probably totalled an additional ½ per cent. In terms of aggregate national income, therefore, the role of government in the economy of this period would appear to have been relatively modest. Since it is generally agreed that the federal government did not play a substantial direct part in the economic activity of those times, we must next consider the functions assumed by the state and local governments.

Much of the state and local governments' expenditures went for the traditional services that were expected from the state. For example, expenditures on police and fire departments had been a function of local government since the founding of the Republic. However, spending on water supply, sewerage, sidewalks, bridges, and roads were areas in which the precedent for government involvement was not always clear. This kind of government activity, though quite positive, was in keeping with the conventional general view of government's functions in a free enterprise system. The creation by government of this type of social overhead capital had as its predominant objective access to and communication with the market; it did not envision or support active government participation in the market itself.

Some of the indirect activity of the federal government in these years was beneficial to business or at least created a favorable industrial climate; examples would be such legislation as the Land Grant Act of 1850, some of the tariff laws, and the underwriting of scientific expeditions, all of which were of assistance to some specific economic interests, though often opposed by others. In these instances the use of the government's economic power was subtle and yet was often as important as direct intervention in the market. The Land Grant Act of 1850 provided for the grant of 3,750,000 acres to the states of Illinois, Mississippi, and Alabama for retransfer to the railroads so that a "great national thoroughfare" could be built.[19] Without the grant of this land the states would have been hard pressed to raise the tremendous amount of capital necessary for such a vital communication system. In the opinion of some Americans, the use of the protective tariff to transfer income from the one-crop agriculture of the South to the industrialized Northeast had the effect of enabling the nation as a whole to avoid the "staple trap," which might have had serious retarding effects on economic development. The pathfinding expeditions and surveys financed by Congress opened up vast undeveloped areas for settlement by providing knowledge of the economic potential of the western areas and communication between them and the rest of the country. Five

[18] R. W. Goldsmith, "The Growth of Reproducible Wealth of the United States of America from 1805 to 1950, *Income and Wealth Series II* (Cambridge, England: Bowes and Bowes, 1952).

[19] A classic work is P. W. Gates, *The Illinois Central Railroad and Its Colonization Work* (Cambridge: Harvard University Press, 1934).

surveys of land between the thirty-second and forty-ninth parallels were made between 1853 and 1855. The data collected later proved useful for railroading and mining in these vast, relatively unexplored lands.[20]

Finally, there was direct action on the part of government in the market itself. Before World War II many historians, focusing unduly on the federal government, presented the view that government's role in the ante-bellum economy was a minor one in accordance with the tradition of *laissez faire*. But this *"laissez faire* cliché" has been completely demolished as the result of more recent work, which has emphasized the vital promotional and developmental activities of the state and local governments.[21] Instead of the interpretation that the economy's growth was mainly the work of private enterprise there emerged another in which

> the elected public official replaced the individual enterpriser as the key figure in the release of capitalist energy; the public treasury, rather than private saving, became the major source of venture capital, and community purpose outweighed personal ambition in the selection of large goals for local economies. "Mixed" enterprise was the customary organization for important innovations, and government everywhere undertook the role put on it by the people, that of planner, promoter, investor, and regulator.[22]

The mixed enterprise referred to in this quotation involved a "mixing" or joining of private and public capital in the same venture with boards of directors composed of private individuals and public officials as well. Louis Hartz who made a pioneer study of the subject in Pennsylvania writes of the background of such enterprise as follows:

> Originating in the banking field in the late eighteenth century, it (the mixed private and public corporation) flourished with increasing strength for half a century eventually being extended to transportation and embracing various types of enterprise there. In 1844 over 150 mixed corporations were currently listed in the official records of Pennsylvania, with public investments ranging from a few shares of stock to several thousand. It is hard to view such a policy as an incidental phase of state action worthy only of marginal notice.[23]

In order to understand the reasons for the emergence of this "sturdy tradition of public responsibility for economic growth," we need to realize that the alternative of federal planning of internal improvements had been practically foreclosed by the course of events. Gallatin's ten-year plan of federal support for internal improvements had been a casualty of the War of 1812; the

---

[20] The work of the Army engineers in this field is described in F. G. Hill, *Roads, Rails and Waterways: The Army Engineers and Early Transportation* (Norman: University of Oklahoma Press, 1957).

[21] The recent literature is capably summarized by R. A. Lively, "The American System: A Review Article," *The Business History Review* (March, 1955), pp. 81–96. The modern view was stressed early in this century by G. S. Callendar in "The Early Transportation and Banking Enterprises of the States in Relation to the Growth of Corporations," *Quarterly Journal of Economics*, XVII (1902–03), pp. 111–162.

[22] Lively, *op. cit.*, p. 82.

[23] L. Hartz, *Economic Policy and Democratic Thought: Pennsylvania, 1776–1860* (Cambridge: Harvard University Press, 1948), p. 290.

Secretary had said himself that direct appropriations for such purposes could not be considered because of the state of the nation's finances. Under Madison and Monroe's administrations internal improvements by the national government were blocked by Presidential vetoes and constitutional objections. Under the Presidency of John Quincy Adams there was more vigorous action on such undertakings, and four of the canals that were part of Gallatin's original plan received Congressional appropriations. But the election of Andrew Jackson to the Presidency decisively changed the prospects for federal support of internal improvements. On May 27, 1830 his veto of the Maysville Road bill, which proposed a subscription of $150,000 to the stock of a private company to build a 60-mile turnpike within the single state of Kentucky, signalled the change in policy. It is true that, as its critics claimed, the Maysville project did not meet the specifications of Gallatin's plan; but even those doing so fared no better. Subsequently, the federal government withdrew its participation in the Chesapeake and Ohio Canal, one of the largest federal undertakings, and Congress refused all further aid to such ventures. Jackson's administration marked the end of the era of national projects.[24]

The defeat of the idea of national planning for internal improvements left the task to the states, local government, and private enterprise. The financial capacity of the latter fell far short of the capital needed to build canals, railroads, and roads, so the expedient of the mixed enterprise was employed. The competition between the cities for the growing mercantile trade caused the municipalities to enter into more and more mixed enterprises with private management; a sort of "metropolitan mercantilism" developed. But the aim of these undertakings was neither the establishment of an all-powerful "commonwealth," as the Handlins defined it,[25] nor permanent government ownership and operation. The objective of such mixed enterprises was more compatible with orthodox capitalist purpose; as Milton Heath describes it, ". . . the public function was viewed as an initial, developmental one. After enterprises became established on a profitable basis, city governments tended to transfer their investments to new projects, and so, normally, a transition from public or quasi-public to private ownership and operation took place."[26]

Heath, in an important study of railroad construction in the South, has dissected the pattern of finance, construction, and the government's role in these efforts.[27] By 1861 the federal, state, municipal, and county governments had invested roughly $71 million in private railroads in the Southeast. In the

[24] C. Goodrich, *Government Promotion of American Canals and Railroads*, p. 42. This work has an excellent summary of the era of national projects in its Chap. 2.

[25] O. and M. F. Handlin, *Commonwealth: A Study of the Role of Government in the American Economy, Massachusetts, 1774–1861* (New York: New York University Press, 1947).

[26] M. S. Heath, "Public Railroad Construction and the Development of Private Enterprise in the South before 1861, *Journal of Economic History*, X, Supplement (1950), p. 49. We draw upon this study in the next few paragraphs. See also M. Heath, *Constructive Liberalism: The Role of the State in Economic Development in Georgia to 1860* (Cambridge, Mass.: Harvard University Press, 1954).

[27] *Ibid.*

Gulf states the figure was approximately $31 million, while the state governments in the interior of the South invested about $53 million. The total government investment in the South totalled over $144 million. State governments supplied well over 56 per cent of the contribution of the public sector, while the federal government provided less than 5 per cent.

An important element in the development of these mixed enterprises was the entrepreneurial leadership that it created. A group of men who were leaders in business, or the professions such as education or the church, usually allied itself with the officials of the city to provide the managerial talent needed. As one commentator says, "As an early American institution . . . the [mixed] corporation was a public school for enterprise. Its graduates were never very loyal, but they were no less obligated to it for their experience with major engineering projects, their knowledge of managerial problems, and their skill at gathering and handling large capital. . . ."[28] In these endeavors the decisions about the use of public property, credit, and the taxing power were made by the community in a democratic fashion. In short, the managerial group did not behave like an oligarchy; it did not abuse its powers, and it used public resources only when private funds proved to be inadequate.

Throughout the South in these years, there was a shortage of liquid capital because the major types of business organization were proprietorships and partnerships, and such firms could not raise the large sums required for internal improvements. As a matter of fact, the very lag in the development of private corporations created an atmosphere more favorable to the use of the mixed corporation. In general, reliance on the device of mixed enterprise was in keeping with the prevalent attitude toward business organizations.

Management of these mixed enterprises in the South tended to be rational and prudent in the sense that efficient solutions were sought to the community's transportation problems; this was so because their officials were conscious of the public trust they bore. Efficiency in management and the allocation of resources was especially needed because the natural barriers of the topography often made roads and waterways inferior to the railroad as a means of communication. There was a necessity, in short, to transfer spending on internal improvements from the former to the latter, and this was attempted. Yet the riskiness of the railroad ventures discouraged private investment in them; public support of such endeavors was indispensable because it reduced the uncertainties and provided the requisite funds. Furthermore, such public money could be raised at lower rates of interest than private capital had to pay; this meant, of course, that the mixed corporation had lower carrying charges on its outstanding debt than a private borrower.

It is to be noted that in addition to fostering and supporting internal improvements, some of the western states employed the mixed corporation to revitalize their banking system.[29] A prototype of this kind of bank was set up

[28] Lively, "The American System . . ." p. 92.
[29] B. Hammond, "Banking in the Early West: Monopoly, Prohibition and Laissez Faire," *Journal of Economic History* (May, 1948), pp. 1–25.

in Indiana in 1834. The state subscribed half the capital, chose its president and most of the board of directors, and half of all the branch directors. It was the only bank permitted in the state, and it was allowed to have a maximum of seventeen branches. A central office had the function of clearing all branch transactions and examining each branch twice a year.

This bank had as a major objective the provision of credit to farmers so that agricultural output could be brought to market. To accomplish this purpose it issued short term loans so that it was always prepared to meet its liabilities. As more and more of the marketing function was shifted to merchants and exporters, the Indiana banks found themselves lending increased amounts to such borrowers. On the whole, they followed conservative practices and proved successful in providing the capital needed for a rapid industrialization.

In general, it is clear that the quasi-public enterprises of various types organized in this period fulfilled the roles and efficiently carried out the tasks that a relatively immature private sector was not yet able to perform. Their achievements along these lines reflected the general political maturity displayed by many American communities in facing the problems of the "take-off period." As Goodrich has said, ". . . Those who are planning the programs of the developing nations would be fortunate indeed if they could enlist in their effort the civic spirit that led so many American communities to make sacrifices to obtain their canals and railroads. . . ." And he added in a comment that is very relevant to the question of how well Americans in this period satisfied Rostow's third condition of take-off: "The provision of public overhead capital will not promote development in any country unless the advantages it offers are seized, by private or governmental means, with somewhat the same vigor with which American farmers and merchants and manufacturers made use of the opportunities created by the Erie Canal."[30]

While agriculture was undergoing sweeping changes, and the business economy was being transformed by the accelerated rate of economic growth, significant changes were occurring also in the life of the workingmen in the cities. How were they affected by the alleged "take-off" process and how did the cost of labor influence the pace of capital investment in the new machinery of industry? These aspects of the changing American scene next deserve our attention.

ORGANIZED LABOR AND IMMIGRATION

The union movement in the United States made a slow recovery after its practical destruction in the long depression following 1837. For some time after 1840 it remained weak, and such unions as existed were mainly local organizations. In the "hot air decade" of the forties, labor was diverted from trade union's modern objectives by such movements as associationism, agrar-

---

[30] Goodrich, *Government Promotion of American Canals and Railroads*, p. 297.

ianism, and producer and consumer cooperation. Associationism was Albert Brisbane's popularization of the doctrines of the utopian socialist Charles Fourier. It sought to establish cooperative communities in the form of phalanxes to escape the evils of industrial capitalism. But associationism had a colorful, short life; its most successful attempt, that of the North American Phalanx near Red Bank, New Jersey, lasted only twelve years. Shortage of capital, internal dissension, and the hostility of the outside world, which often levelled charges of "free love" and atheism against the cooperators, proved their undoing.

Agrarianism was a doctrine preached by George H. Evans, editor of the *Working Man's Advocate,* in opposition to associationism. Basing his philosophy on the idea of natural rights, Evans insisted that landholdings should be equal, individual, and inalienable. He believed, in short, that the salvation of the wage earner lay in becoming an owner of land, a farmer. His agitation was important in bringing about the adoption of the Homestead Act during the Civil War, but even that legislation did not carry out the broad principles of his program.

Producer cooperatives arose in the depressed and troubled years of the 1840's when unemployed or striking workers in their desperation turned to self-employment. The iron molders, tailors, and bakers were the principal groups to experiment with this type of cooperation. German immigrants were especially attracted to producer cooperation. But these efforts were almost uniformly failures for a variety of reasons: lack of capital to do business on a large scale; lack of business ability; dishonesty among the members; and the opposition of employers. Advocates of producer cooperation often failed in getting the protection of the law; for example, they had difficulty securing corporate charters for their enterprises. In addition, they faced the opposition of the clergy. Some Catholic churchmen criticized the small cooperative workshops because they were "the first steps to Socialism."

On the whole, the consumer cooperatives, especially in New England, had greater success than the projects of producer cooperation. The former started in 1845 under conditions of depression and unemployment similar to those that gave birth to the famous Rochdale movement in Great Britain. The American cooperatives did not follow the famous principles of the British organization and, perhaps significantly, never attained anything like its success.

With the revival of business in the fifties and the turning away from the Utopian plans of the intellectuals, a new trade unionism came into existence. This was a craft unionism with the "pure and simple" business union approach. National organizations of much greater effectiveness than those of the thirties were started. By 1865, to include the Civil War years that also gave an impetus to the movement, there were no fewer than eleven national organizations of workers. They included such bodies as the typographical union, the stone-cutters' union, the hat finishers, the Molders International Union, and the National Union of Machinists and Blacksmiths (both founded in 1857).

This new labor movement emancipated the worker from the tradition of "community of interest" between employer and employee, which had been emphasized in the years before 1837. It became trade conscious rather than reformist. Still it would not be accurate to exaggerate the extent and influence of trade unions in that day. In fact, one student concludes his survey of such organizations on this pessimistic note, "The labor movement in America finished the period 1840–60 as it began—practically in nothingness."[31]

The most important factor influencing the general condition of labor in these years was the huge immigration. The extent of the immigration and the national origins and occupational distribution of the immigrants for the years 1820–55 can be seen from Chart 1 and Table 2. During the period of the

CHART 1

Immigration to the United States: 1815–1860[a]

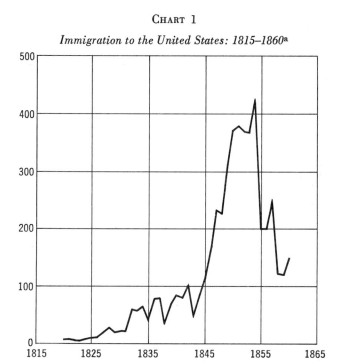

Source: Reproduced from D. C. North, *The Economic Growth of the United States, 1709–1860.* © Copyright 1961 by Prentice-Hall, Inc., Englewood Cliffs, N.J.

"take-off" the United States reached a high in immigration of close to 428,000 in 1854. This was eight times as many immigrants as in the year previous to the take-off, 1843. These immigrants drastically changed the geographic distribution of the population partly because many of them moved westward immediately after their arrival in the United States. Prior to the "take-off,"

[31] N. J. Ware, *The Industrial Worker, 1840–1860* (New York: Houghton Mifflin, 1924), p. 240

Table 2

Immigrant Origins and Occupational Distribution
for the United States, 1820–55[a]

| Year | Total | Alien Arrivals | | | Occupation as Percentage of Total Arrivals | | |
		Irish	English	German	Labor	Merchants	Mechanics & Farmers
1820	8385	3974	1782	948	9%	25%	31%
1	9127	3388	1036	365	8	27	31
2	6911	2421	856	139	9	31	24
3	6354	1908	851	179	8	33	27
4	7912	2606	713	224	8	38	24
5	10199	5857	1002	448	10	29	32
6	10837	6032	1459	495	11	29	29
7	18875	10971	2521	425	18	21	31
8	27382	14047	2735	1806	21	19	31
9	22520	8331	2149	582	20	28	22
1830	23322	3105	733	1972	12	25	41*
1	22633	7639	251	2395	10	27	44
2	53179	16665	944	10168	13	18	46**
3	58640	8648	2966	6823	13	15	33
4	65365	33724	1129	17654	14	14	51***
5	45374	29350	468	8245	15	20	55
6	76242	43156	420	20139	29	11	55
7	79340	39810	896	23036	28	12	55
8	38914	17860	157	11369	18	20	55
9	68069	34172	62	19794	22	16	58
1840	84066	41704	318	28581	22	12	63
1	80289	53723	147	13727	28	13	55
2	104565	71542	1743	18287	33	10	53
3	52496	24542	3517	11432	23	14	57
4	78615	46460	1357	19226	29	12	54
5	114371	61942	1710	33138	32	10	56
6	154416	70626	2854	57010	28	6	62
7	234968	124880	3476	73444	32	4	62
8	226527	142631	4455	58014	43	3	52
9	297024	207162	6036	60062	45	3	50
1850	310004	169533	5276	63168	38	5	54
1	379466	266257	5306	71322	48	7	42
2	371603	161351	30007	143575	44	7	48
3	368645	165130	28867	140653	48	7	42
4	427833	105931	48901	206054	37	7	53
5	200877	51877	38871	66219	39	13	45

* Large per cent not stated this year   ** Missing quarter
*** Large per cent not stated this year

[a] Source: Bromwell, William J., *History of Immigration to the United States* (New York: Redfield, 1856), as reproduced in North, *The Economic Growth, op. cit.*, p. 98.

the South and West were approximately equal in population. After the end of
this period the West's population was almost as large as that of the Northeast
and much larger than the South's. (See Table 3.)

TABLE 3

United States Population Distribution by Regions
1810–60

Year	South*		West*		Northeast*		Total U.S. Population (does not include territories)
	Population	% of Total Pop.	Population	% of Total Pop.	Population	% of Total Pop.	
1810	2,314,556	32.1	961,407	13.3	3,939,895	54.6	7,215,858
1820	2,918,198	30.4	1,845,863	19.2	4,836,722	50.4	9,600,783
1830	3,774,405	29.4	2,980,294	23.2	6,066,169	47.3	12,820,868
1840	4,749,875	27.9	4,960,580	29.1	7,309,186	42.9	17,019,641
1850	6,271,237	27.2	7,494,608	32.5	9,301,417	40.3	23,067,262
1860	7,993,531	25.6	11,796,680	37.8	11,393,533	36.5	31,183,744

* South—Alabama, Arkansas, Florida, Georgia, Louisiana, Mississippi, North Carolina,
South Carolina, Texas and Virginia; West—Illinois, Indiana, Iowa, Kansas, Kentucky,
Michigan, Minnesota, Missouri, Nebraska, Ohio, Tennessee, Wisconsin, California,
Nevada and Oregon; Northeast—Connecticut, Delaware, Maine, Maryland, Massachusetts,
New Hampshire, New Jersey, New York, Pennsylvania, Rhode Island and Vermont.

Source: U.S. Census Bureau, *A Compendium of the Ninth Census, June 1, 1870,* by
Francis A. Walker, Superintendent of Census (Washington: Government Printing Office,
1872), pp. 8–9.

The ethnic composition of these immigrants also had important influences
on the nation and its way of life. Many of them were from western Europe,
particularly from Ireland, England, and Germany. The Irish potato famine
caused more than 100,000 persons per year to emigrate from that country to
the United States in the years 1847–54. While the predominant occupations of
the immigrants in this period were those of farmers and mechanics, the trend
in the number who were laborers was startling. Prior to 1825 under 10 per
cent of all immigrants were laborers. From 1825 to the Civil War the trend
was on the upswing and averaged in the period under study approximately 50
per cent. Whereas prior to the "take-off" a large number of merchants came to
the United States, during the period 1844–57 an average of under 10 per cent
was in this category as compared with a pre-1843 figure of 20 per cent.

In the light of such demographic trends it is not surprising that some of the
new immigrants had a strong influence on American ideology and particularly
on the trade union movement. In the countries they had come from, a greater
proportion of the population had been employed as laborers and some had
previous experience with trade unions and their objectives. This was true
especially of the Germans and the English; it was not the case with most of
the Irish because they came in the main from the rural areas of that country.

Just as some of the immigrants affected American attitudes on trade unionism, the immigrants were in turn influenced by the existing American
ideology. Many progressed from wage earning to the ownership of property
and farming. In this connection, one of the questions that has concerned
historians over the years is whether the condition of labor in this country was
greatly improved by the existence of an open frontier.

The idea that the free land of the frontier acted as a "safety valve" for
industrial labor has had a long history in America. Long before the historian
Frederick Jackson Turner tacitly accepted the validity of the theory,[32] there
were Americans who believed that the frontier performed this salutary function. The agrarians of the 1840's, led by George Henry Evans, lauded the
virtues of the safety valve they were trying to bring into existence. In the
Working Man's Advocate of July, 1844, they asserted "the right of the people
to the soil" and claimed:

> That once effected, let an outlet be formed that will carry off our super-
> abundant labor to the salubrious and fertile West. In those regions thousands,
> and tens of thousands, who are now languishing in hopeless poverty, will find a
> certain and speedy independence. The labor market will thus be eased of the
> present disturbing competition; and those who remain, as well as those who
> emigrate, will have the opportunity of realizing a comfortable living.[33]

Turner himself made only incidental use of the safety-valve theory as an
illustration of his general interpretation of the influence of the West on American society. Some of his followers, however, made a fetish of the idea and
continued to argue that the frontier with its cheap land acted as a safety valve
to siphon off the unemployed or discontented laborers in the industrial
Northeast. There have been several variations on this theme, but we shall
concern ourselves only with the view that wage earners could escape the pressures and hardships of the industrial system by moving to the frontier.[34]

Even brief consideration of the theory makes it evident that it rests upon
some questionable assumptions, namely, that workers were residentially mobile and were capable of making the necessary occupational shift from industrial labor to farming. Implicit also in the theory is the notion that wages in
the Northeast were partly determined by the competition with the opportunities on the frontier and that they were sufficiently high to finance the average
worker's movement from the eastern cities to the West. While the assumption
that American labor has shown a high degree of residential mobility has been
generally recognized, there is doubt that such mobility was always toward the
frontier. On the contrary, the spectacular growth of urban population in this
period suggests that the general movement was more one from the farm to the

---

[32] F. J. Turner, *The Frontier in American History* (New York: Henry Holt, 1921), pp.
259, 275.

[33] Quoted in J. R. Commons et al., eds., *A Documentary History of American Industrial
Society*, Vol. 7 (Cleveland: A. H. Clark, 1910), p. 301.

[34] F. A. Shannon, "A Post Mortem on the Labor Safety-Valve Theory," *Agricultural
History*, 22 (1948), pp. 32–38.

city than the reverse. Indeed, one student states that "there is a substantial body of facts to support an argument for the city safety valve for rural discontent. . . ."[35] Wage laborers who came to the northeastern cities in these years tended to stay there. The reasons are not difficult to understand. To make a farm on the prairie or to purchase and operate an established western one required in the 1850's about $1,000 in capital. The wages of unskilled labor in the East at that time were less than $1.00 per day; they were probably close to $.80 per day. Annual incomes were less than $300 and only extraordinary frugality would permit savings, say, of $50 per year on such an income. The acquisition of $1,000 by an eastern mechanic therefore assumes long and steady employment, regular savings, and successful investment, and even then such a sum would not be accumulated until middle or old age.

The idea that workers could go west and start farming had validity only, if at all, in the years before 1830 when agriculture was more self-sufficient and pre-commercial. As it became market-focused and capital-using, it was often subject to depression at the very time unemployment existed in the East. It was therefore not very attractive as a refuge when extreme "hard times" existed.

The only variation of the safety-valve theory with plausibility is the one stressing that the West provided an alternative opportunity for those eastern farmers who could not compete with the fertile West. Rather than crowding into eastern cities, many of these marginal farmers sought a new life in the West and by so doing reduced the supply of wage labor in the urban areas below what it otherwise would have been. This tendency may have had some effect upon eastern wage rates, but it was probably offset by the large number of foreign immigrants who were drawn to this country by the apparent opportunities in agriculture, but who became wage earners in the cities instead.[36]

The large immigration of these years, especially of the Irish, had momentous consequences for the future of the factory system in the Northeast. Increasingly, Irish factory hands took the place of girls in the New England mills; this was noticeably so after the depression of 1847 and they came to constitute a permanent labor force. With the low rural standard of living they had experienced in famine- and oppression-ridden Ireland, they were willing to work for low wages and were hard to organize in labor unions. In the cities, the poorest of them often lived under conditions of unbelievable squalor and misery. Their homes were frequently in cellars where they slept six to eight in a bed, with no sanitation to speak of. For example, in 1850 one in thirty of the population of New York City was said to be living underground in unimaginable conditions. In some cases, with two to four families in a room, lodgers were taken in!

[35] *Ibid.*, p. 35.
[36] See C. H. Danhof, "Economic Validity of the Safety-Valve Doctrine," *The Journal of Economic History*, Vol. 1 (1941), pp. 96–106. We have drawn heavily on this excellent article in the above paragraphs. See also C. Goodrich and S. Davison, "The Wage-Earner in the Western Movement," *Political Science Quarterly* (March, 1936), pp. 61–116.

The lowest standards of living were found in the boarding and lodging cellars.

> In some of these there were three classes of boarders. The first class paid $.37 a week for board and lodging, sleeping on straw thrown loose over the floor and eating at what was called the "first table." The second class paid $.18¾ a week, slept on the bare floor, and ate at the "second table." The third class paid $.09 a week, slept on the floor on sufferance, being turned out when the second class boarders were available, and ate at the "third table." These cellars were generally bare of furniture except for one or two benches and a long table. The marketing was done by children who were sent out to beg for food, or by professional beggar-women with whom the boarding house keeper made contracts. All the baskets were brought in at a certain hour, the boarders assembled, and the whole mass was thrown upon the table. The first class boarders had the first picking, the rest took what was left as unceremoniously as could be imagined.[37]

In general, the accelerating industrialism of these years did not strengthen the sense of community among urban Americans. On the contrary, the mechanization of work displaced many of the skilled artisans or threw them into harsh competition with the new immigrants or with cheap female labor. Very often their discontent found expression in racial and antiCatholic rioting or nativist politics. All the while, the rapid transition from the pre-industrial town to the industrial big city was destroying the informal neighborhood street life that the people had known in the eighteenth century. As yet the urban melting pot did not create segregated slums for the whites; the black population, however, was still confined to ghettoes. Most of the white immigrants were scattered through the various wards of the cities and were integrated with much tension and violence into the heterogeneous neighborhoods. There, people of diverse occupations, nationality, and religion lived side by side.

One noticeable reaction to the loss of the old style of sociability and informal community was the formation of numerous associations. Americans joined clubs, lodges, fire companies, or gangs of all kinds. The political leaders of the day organized the ethnic groups into neighborhood clubs and parishes; they sponsored picnics and dances. These activities provided the people with small-scale ties and loyalties that seemingly served to counteract feelings of personal isolation and mass anomie. However beneficial these various associations were for the individuals who joined them, they still did not meet important public needs. They did not effectively nourish the growth of community in a broad, comprehensive way. As a consequence, municipal government, too often corrupt, pinch-penny, and unresponsive, failed to solve the mounting problems of America's industrial cities. As one student of pre-war city life concludes, ". . . The big city of 1860 had regained public order, but as a meaningful democratic society it was out of control."[38]

---

[37] Ware, *The Industrial Worker*, p. 16.
[38] S. B. Warner, Jr., *The Private City, Philadelphia in Three Periods of Its Growth* (Philadelphia: University of Pennsylvania Press, 1968), p. 157. Chaps. 3–7 of this work provide an excellent analysis of the impact of early industrialization on an American city;

The paucity and inadequacy of the available data have made the calculation of the trend of real wages in the first half of the nineteenth century "probably impossible." The best estimates we have are no better than "careful guesswork." One older study, that of A. H. Hansen, indicates that real wages rose somewhat in the forties, but that the rising cost of living in the fifties negated whatever gains the workers made.[39] Chart 2 shows this deterioration in the 1850's in terms of an index of purchasing power.

CHART 2

The Trend of Real Wages in the United States,
1840–1860ᵃ (1913 = 100)

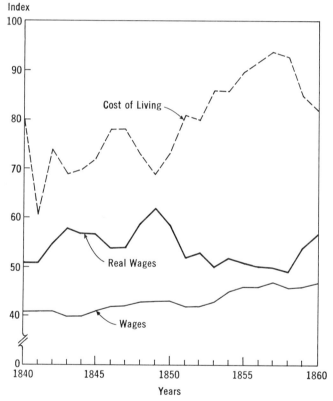

ᵃ Source: A. H. Hansen, "Factors Affecting the Trend of Real Wages," *American Economic Review*, March, 1925, p. 32.

---

we have drawn upon this book for much of the above. For the subject in general, see W. A. Sullivan, *The Industrial Worker in Pennsylvania, 1800–1840* (Harrisburg, Pa.: Pennsylvania Historical and Museum Commission, 1955).

[39] A. H. Hansen, "Factors Affecting the Trend of Real Wages, *American Economic Review* (March, 1925), pp. 27–42; on this subject see also S. Lebergott, "Wage Trends, 1800–1900," in Gallman, *Trends in the American Economy in the Nineteenth Century* (Princeton, N.J.: Princeton University Press, 1960), p. 493; on changes in the levels of living generally in the ante-bellum period, see R. L. Andreano, *New Views of American Economic Development* (Cambridge: Schenkman Publishing Co., Inc., 1965), pp. 131–167.

The cost and availability of labor to the employers of this period had important effects on a subject discussed earlier, the rate of technological innovation. Generally, it has been held that the scarcity and, hence, dearness of labor and the relative inelasticity of its supply in pre-Civil War America stimulated the development of labor-saving machinery.

> In the early decades of the century the principal effect of labour-scarcity in America was probably to induce American manufacturers to adopt labour-saving methods invented in other countries earlier and more extensively than they were adopted in their country of origin. . . . And already in the early nineteenth century there were a number of important American inventions induced directly by the search for labour-saving methods and these became increasingly common as time went on.[40]

This feature of the country's factor endowment is seen as one of the basic elements in its early development of the technique of interchangeable parts (the American system).[41]

The relatively high level of American wages in the early part of the nineteenth century was explained by most commentators in terms of the abundance and accessibility of land and the high productivity of American agriculture. The heavy immigration of the 1840's and 1850's narrowed the differential in unit labor costs between the United States and England and reduced the disparity in the inelasticity of labor-supply between them, but it did not eliminate entirely the American employment of more capital-intensive methods of manufacture. In fact, it has been argued that even in the latter half of the nineteenth century, despite additional immigration, the availability of cheap, unskilled labor and the relative scarcity and militancy of the skilled workers tended to promote mechanization.[42]

British observers, in commenting on American technology in the years before the Civil War, often stated that our technology was more labor-saving than their own. It would seem more accurate to say that it was the factor proportions within the same technology that varied between the two countries.[43] With the interest rate in the United States at a higher level than in Britain during the first half of the nineteenth century, we should have used less machinery than the British, if we were using the same technology. Actually, we probably did so in the sense that our machines were more flimsy, less carefully made, and more quickly discarded than those of the British. In addition, we operated our machinery more rapidly and for longer hours than

---

[40] Habakkuk, *American and British Technology in the Nineteenth Century*, p. 50. This work contains an excellent analysis of this whole subject.

[41] *Ibid.*, p. 104.

[42] B. Thomas, *Migration and Economic Growth* (Cambridge: Cambridge University Press, 1954), pp. 158, 165, as quoted in Habakkuk, *American and British Technology* . . . , p. 128.

[43] On the ambiguities in the British discussion of American technology, see P. Temin, "Labor Scarcity and the Problem of American Industrial Efficiency in the 1850's," *Journal of Economic History* (September, 1966), pp. 277–298; on this subject, see also W. Rothbard, "Causes of the Superior Efficiency of the U.S.A. Industry as Compared with British Industry," *Economic Journal* (September, 1966), pp. 383–390.

the British. The optimistic Americans preferred to run their machines hard and scrap them early, counting on purchasing new, more efficient machinery to replace those which were obsolete or worn out. These business practices were, nevertheless, favorable to our economic growth. They resulted in an American capital stock that was younger than that of the English and one that embodied more up-to-date technical knowledge. Thus, in this instance the American climate of entrepreneurial opinion, pervaded by an expectation of rapid technological change, tended itself to fulfill what it expected.

In the midst of this technological change, Americans were confronted also with new political ideas and conflicting views as to how the national government could best promote economic growth. We need to examine next how these national policies and programs affected the prospects and achievements of accelerated economic growth.

NATIONAL PARTY POLITICS AND ECONOMIC GROWTH

Americans in the 1840's believed, on the whole, that national problems could be solved by using national institutions, particularly their political parties, for this purpose. By the opening of that critical decade, the electorate was divided into two stable political parties—the Democrats and the Whigs. This stability extended below the national level, as evidenced by the fact that there were two strong parties in the eight regional areas of the United States.[44] While some historians have seen the party conflicts of the Jacksonian era as being merely struggles for control of the government and patronage, others have concluded that the divisions between the two main parties were real and long standing. In this latter view, the leaders of both parties were concerned with economic growth and generally believed that the government—federal as well as state and local—had a vital role in the operation of the American economy. However, these party chiefs often sought the passage of legislation that would benefit and promote the economic growth of different groups in the society. As one student says, the issues of economic policy "were not whether the government had or had not a role in the economy, but, what was to be the character of its role, what agencies were to exercise it, who was to control it, and in whose interests it was to operate."[45]

The Democrats first presented a national party platform in 1840, the Whigs in 1844. While both these party programs reflected middle-class norms and ideals and represented politically a nation predominantly middle-class, there were significant differences between them. The Democrats feared a powerful central government. They wanted the government to maintain the framework of the system, such as the institution of money and the rule of law, preserve

[44] J. H. Silbey, *The Shrine of Party* (Pittsburgh: University of Pittsburgh Press, 1967), p. 19. This study is a model of modern political history.

[45] O. Handlin, "Laissez-Faire Thought in Massachusetts, 1799–1869," *Tasks of Economic History*, III (December, 1943), p. 65, as quoted in *Ibid.*, p. 27.

competition by acting against monopolies and removing governmental aids to special privilege. Programatically, the Democrats opposed a national bank and wanted a tariff for revenue rather than for protection. They favored a small, well-run, efficient government. Such a program, they claimed, would permit the full development of the nation for it would guarantee the free play of natural economic forces.

The Whigs, on the other hand, had a rather different conception of the federal government's role in a time of change and economic expansion. They would have the federal government "exert a beneficent, paternal, fostering care upon the Industry and Prosperity of the People."[46] Consistent with this philosophy, they stressed the importance of financial institutions in a period of rapid economic development. Specifically, they endorsed and fought for a government-sponsored national bank. They urged protective tariffs and insisted that they benefitted not just one section of the country but the whole people. The Whigs differed with the Democrats on land policy also; they wanted the proceeds from land sales to be distributed to the states, whereas the Democrats opposed this, fearing that it would necessitate an increase in the tariff to offset the loss of revenue. The Whigs approved of federal aid for internal improvements, arguing that if a project benefited all the people the government should finance it. The Democrats, on the contrary, in their platforms from 1840 onward resolved "that the Constitution does not confer upon the general government the power to commence and carry on a general system of internal improvements." These were the major policy issues on which the two parties differed; but other differences emerged between them as time passed. For instance, in 1841, when the Whigs came to power, they advocated a federal bankruptcy law and wanted the national government to assume state debts. The Democrats opposed both proposals.

A persistent exponent of Whig-like ideas in these years was Henry C. Carey, the son of the publisher, Matthew Carey. The younger Carey as an economist and publicist rejected the Ricardian economics and argued, particularly after 1847, that "the great progressive forces [in the economy] were corporations, bank notes, and a proper tariff."[47] The idol of the iron manufacturers of Pennsylvania, Carey was quoted by innumerable Congressmen, and businessmen were willing to subsidize the reprinting of his writings. Without doubt, Carey was an important economist for a nation in the process of accelerated economic growth because of his emphasis on dynamic factors in economic development.

However rational the Whig principles, the implementation of their ideas in national politics was hardly a success. Henry Clay, the party's leader in Congress, saw his program for a national bank, a higher tariff, and for distribution of the revenue from land sales defeated by President Tyler's

---

[46] The *Whig Almanac* as quoted in Silbey, *The Shrine of Party*, p. 28.

[47] J. Dorfman, *The Economic Mind in American Civilization, 1606–1865*, Vol. 2 (New York: Augustus M. Kelley, 1966), p. 804; the best analysis of Carey's thought is A. D. H. Kaplan, *Henry Charles Carey, A Study in American Economic Thought* (Johns Hopkins University Studies in History and Political Science), Series XLIX, No. 4.

vetoes. And when the Democrats returned to power under the Presidency of James K. Polk in 1845, the Whigs were doomed to further frustration and defeat. The New Jacksonians aligned themselves more clearly with southern interests than had been the case in the 1830's. The passage of the Walker Tariff of 1846, the reinstitution of the Independent Treasury system, and the new President's relentless veto of river and harbor bills passed by Congress, all testified to his opposition to Whig ideas and, in particular, to internal improvements at national expense.

In the 'fifties, the existing national parties, riven by factionalism and sectionalism, moved toward distintegration. The Free Soil movement of 1848, the heightening of antislavery sentiment, the disappointment of the Whig hopes, the emergence of the Know-Nothing Party and other dissidents, all pointed toward the decline of truly national party organizations and the appearance of sectional ones. That finally occurred in 1854 when the passage of the fateful Kansas-Nebraska Act crystallized the nation's parties into new forms; the establishment of the Republican Party in that year was the outcome of these powerful divisive forces.[48]

Before this process of deterioration in party structure had fully set in, the nation had been caught up in a fever of expansionism in the forties. This expansionist movement must be considered in relation to the acceleration of the nation's economic growth after 1843.

THE SPIRIT OF MANIFEST DESTINY

In speculating on the relationship between his stages of growth theory and war, Rostow has advanced the view that a particular type of war has arisen from the dynamics of the preconditions period: regional aggression.[49] Modifying the timing of this phenomenon, he argues in a later passage of the same work that the new nations in the "late preconditions or early take-off periods" are likely to turn to external objectives, often out of a desire to promote cohesion in their young societies or to avoid the concrete and frequently divisive tasks of modernization. In his words:

> Historically, it has proved extremely tempting for a part of the new nationalism to be diverted to external objectives, notably if these objectives looked to be accessible at little real cost or risk. These early aggressive exercises were generally limited in objective, aimed at territories close to the new nation's own borders. . . .[50]

While we shall not attempt to test the validity of this particular Rostovian hypothesis, it is perhaps worthwhile to keep it in mind as we examine the foreign policy of the United States in the expansionist decade of the forties.

The years 1844–57 certainly witnessed an extraordinary geographical ex-

[48] For further discussion of the disruption of the national parties on the eve of the Civil War, see Chap. 16 below.
[49] Rostow, *The Stages of Economic Growth*, Chap. 8.
[50] *Ibid.*, p. 113.

pansion of the United States. During that time the land area of the nation increased 69 per cent over what it had been in the initial year as a result of the annexation of Texas, the vast cessions of land growing out of the Mexican War, and the settlement of our dispute with the British over Oregon. The Gadsden Purchase of 1853 added much less to the size of the country than these other acquisitions, but it gave us a valuable route for a transcontinental railroad. The extent of these territorial acquisitions is conveniently summarized in Table 4.

TABLE 4

Territorial Expansion of the United States,
1845–60[a]

Year	Acquisition in Square Miles		Total Area of the United States in Square Miles
1845	Texas	390,144	2,178,150
1846	Oregon	285,580	2,463,730
1848	Mexican Cession	529,017	2,992,747
1853	Gadsden Purchase	29,640	3,022,387

[a] Source: U.S. Bureau of the Census, *Historical Statistics of the United States, 1789–1945* (Washington, D.C.: U.S. Government Printing Office), p. 25.

In the 1840's the direction of American life underwent a significant shift. As the nation painfully emerged from the long depression, it turned away from the old Jacksonian ideas to new objectives and ideals; it gazed more and more intently on the West and Southwest, and sought its Manifest Destiny in expansionism.[51] Incidentally, this phrase, which sums up so well the concept of expansion, was first used by a Democratic editor, John L. O'Sullivan, in 1845.

The ideas and forces behind this expansion had been germinating for some time before they reached a new intensity in this decade. They had been evident in the purchase of Louisiana, the acquisition of Florida from Spain, and in the early attempts to purchase Texas from Mexico. Back of this imperial drive was national pride and belief in American potentialities. There was some fear of the foreign interests on the American borders. Land hunger played a part, as the frontier, swelled by farmers and planters seeking additional or more fertile acres to cultivate, pushed westward. And in the thrust to the Pacific there was the consciousness of ports, commerce, and whale fisheries—the rich trade opportunities available to the enterprising on all sides of that vast ocean.

President Tyler had pressed a vigorous expansionist policy in supporting

[51] An important study of expansionism is A. K. Weinberg, *Manifest Destiny: A Study of Nationalist Expansionism in American History* (Baltimore: Johns Hopkins Press, 1935); see also R. Van Alstyne, *The Rising American Empire* (New York: Oxford University Press, 1960).

the annexation of Texas, but his successor in the White House clearly outdid him in this respect. President Polk devoted a major part of his inaugural address to foreign policy, strongly endorsing the annexation of Texas and declaring that the United States' title to the Oregon country was "clear and unquestionable."

The friction between the United States and Great Britain over the latter territory was easily developed because of past hostilities with the mother country. Many Americans had patriotically kept alive the 1776 and 1812 quarrels. Furthermore, the United States was in debt at the time to British bondholders for about $150 million, and creditors have seldom been loved by the debtor. To these causes of animosity toward Britain, the Oregon problem added the important factor of substantial American economic interest in the territory. By 1845 over five thousand American pioneers had settled in that region, mainly in the Willamette Valley. In addition, there were northeastern mercantile interests who wanted the valuable Columbia River and Puget Sound ports for the trade with the Orient. Combined with the expansionist sentiment of the western states, these groups now clamored for an end of joint occupation and extension of America's claim to the entire region right up to the southern limits of the Alaska Panhandle. The cry was "Fifty-four forty or fight." But, despite a good deal of American bluff and "brinksmanship," or its equivalent, a compromise on the forty-ninth parallel was reached. The United States was already at war with Mexico; the President feared that an extreme position would risk a split in his party, and furthermore, he was aware that ports on the Pacific were more important than territory, and a bigger prize was in the offing—California—if the British could be kept out of that area.

The second important controversy the United States faced in the 1840's was the dispute with Mexico. The Texas border problem had been festering since the middle of the previous decade. By that time some 35,000 Americans were living in Texas, despite a requirement that they become Mexican citizens and Roman Catholics. Mexican-American relations had become strained because of several past incidents. First, there was the massacre of the Alamo and Goliad garrisons during the Texan War for Independence. Secondly, Mexico's refusal to agree to the Rio Grande as the border between the two countries was a source of conflict. And, thirdly, the United States had large monetary claims on debts owed us by Mexico. California, over which the Mexicans had tenuous control, was already prized for its fertile farm land and its magnificent harbors. The fear that it would fall into the hands of a government stronger than that of the Mexicans stimulated the American desire for its possession.

When the Slidell mission to purchase New Mexico and California had failed, and Mexican troops, by crossing the Rio Grande and killing some Americans, had conveniently provided an act of aggression, the United States went to war with Mexico on May 13, 1846. The House of Representatives passed a bill authorizing the President to call up 50,000 volunteers and to use $10 million to finance military operations.

The Mexican War became in time a very unpopular war with some Americans. At its outset, John Quincy Adams had voted against it, terming it "a most unrighteous war," and millions of other Americans came to consider it a war of aggression on the United States' part. But, when peace came on July 4, 1848, the fruits of the military victory were clear—rich territories, strategic additions to the nation's western and southwestern borders, and a substantial increment to its national income—the news of the bonanza at Sutter's millrace was beginning to spread toward the close of the treaty ratification proceedings ending the war.

This war cost the nation some 13,000 deaths and close to $98 million in expenditure. Its full cost did not become evident until it was seen how it contributed to increased sectional strife, the disruption of the major parties, and the beginning of the strains that culminated in the Civil War. Ralph Waldo Emerson in 1848 had stated, "The United States will conquer Mexico, but it will be as the man who swallows the arsenic which brings him down in turn. Mexico will poison us."[52] Emerson's prophecy was to be borne out thirteen years later at Fort Sumter.

Meanwhile, in the 1850's the growth of California stimulated the nation's expansion as no other section of the West. It bought a growing volume of goods and services from the East and its chief export, gold, which increased throughout the decade, permitted the nation to enjoy a large import surplus of consumer and capital goods. On Wall Street, the brokers and speculators were fascinated by the tales from the West. "Most investors believed that the bull market [of the fifties] was founded on a storehouse of California gold, when it actually rested on promissory notes, commercial paper, and questionable railroad securities. But the gold shares did provide glamour for the market. Bullion shipments from California reached New York monthly, and the brokers and their customers would often meet the ships and wait for the unloading. They would rush back to Wall Street in time for the evening auction, and bid prices up to new highs."[53] The United States was indeed a fabulous country in this period of accelerated economic growth.

[52] B. De Voto, *The Year of Decision* (Boston, 1943), p. 492, as quoted in G. G. Van Deusen, *The Jacksonian Era, 1828–1848* (New York: Harper and Row, 1959).

[53] R. Sobel, *The Big Board, A History of the New York Stock Market* (New York: The Free Press, 1965), pp. 55–56.

Part 5

DUALISTIC TENDENCIES IN PEACE AND WAR, 1858–1865

Introduction: Theories of Economic and Sociological Dualism

Dualistic Development in the American Economy Before and During the Civil War

Forces Underlying the Sectional Divergence in Economic Development

The Process of Sectional Polarization: Political and Sociological Aspects

INTRODUCTION:
THEORIES OF ECONOMIC AND
SOCIOLOGICAL DUALISM

In recent years economists have devoted considerable attention and study to the inequalities in economic development among nations and among the different regions within a single nation. Very often they have found even within one country evidences of industrialization or modernization alongside a very backward, undeveloped sector. This co-existence has frequently puzzled government officials and frustrated plans for general economic advancement. The theories of dualistic development that have been advanced to explain such disparate economic growth within a nation have possible usefulness in explaining the divergent character of economic and social evolution in the North and South prior to the Civil War. Such theories may also have some relevance to the relative performance of the economies of the two sections during that bloody struggle. As a background for testing these general propositions, we outline in this Introduction one of the principal theories of this type.

J. H. Boeke, a Dutch economist who was one of the first to write on dual economies, argued that it was possible to characterize any society, in the economic sense, by "the social spirit, the organizational forms and the techniques dominating it." On the basis of this approach, he went on to define social dualism as "the clashing of an imported social system with an indigenous social system of another style."[1] Most frequently, Boeke claimed, the imported social system is high capitalism, but it may be socialism or communism, or a blending of them. The economic theory of such a dualistic, heterogeneous society, he further contended, must itself be dualistic and consider specifically the behavior of a precapitalistic, capitalistic, or socialistic society, and the interactions between them.

Boeke's work has given us a starting definition of a dualistic economy, but we need a fuller description of the different characteristics of the two sectors of such an economy. Professor Leibenstein has presented the contrasting features of a progressive and of an underdeveloped economy in "ideal type" form.[2] He pictures the latter economy as being primarily agricultural, using little capital per person on small landholdings. Its transportation system is poor and its internal markets undeveloped. Demographically, it has high

---

[1] J. H. Boeke, *Economics and Economic Policy of Dual Societies* (Haarlem: H. D. Tjeenk Willink, 1953), p. 5. Boeke's observations on this subject were drawn from his experience as a Netherlands East Indies civil servant before the people of that region gained their independence; he was also professor of eastern economics at Leiden University for many years. A persuasive critique of Boeke's dualistic theory will be found in B. Higgins, *Economic Development, Principles and Policies* (New York: W. W. Norton and Co., 1959), pp. 274–293.

[2] See H. Leibenstein, *Economic Backwardness and Economic Growth* (New York: John Wiley and Sons, 1957), pp. 40–41.

fertility and mortality rates and suffers from inadequate nutrition, poor public health practices, and rural overcrowding. Culturally, such a society is described as having inadequate educational facilities and a high degree of illiteracy; child labor is prevalent. In its social structure, a middle class is absent or very weak. Women tend to have an inferior status, and slavery may be practiced. The technology of such an economy is generally crude, and much of the social behavior is determined by tradition.

In contrast, the progressive economy is oriented mainly to manufacturing industry, and it has a dynamic and sophisticated technology and transport system. Productivity is high both in agriculture and manufacturing because capital intensive methods are employed.[3] Whereas the typical undeveloped economy exports foodstuffs and raw materials, the progressive one tends to export highly fabricated goods. In this urbanized economy, birth and death rates are lower than in the backward society. There is provision of a minimum education for all; child labor hardly exists. A large and powerful middle class is to be found, and women generally have a high social status. Slavery is absent because of its inefficiency. In this type of economy, a "conformity to dynamic behavior patterns" is said to prevail.

Actually, the mere listing of these alleged characteristics of the two sectors of a dual economy is far from satisfactory for a full understanding of these phenomena. It runs the risk of suggesting that the relationship and the characteristics are static and fixed, when what is wanted is some conception of the process that fosters these polarizing tendencies. Fortunately, this approach has been attempted by the brilliant Swedish economist, Gunnar Myrdal, in his well-known book, *Rich Lands and Poor*.[4] This author has presented a "theory of regional polarization" that is so imaginative and challenging and contains so many important concepts of economic development that we shall describe it in some detail.[5]

Myrdal's formulation of a theory of this kind was stimulated by his great dissatisfaction with the orthodox theory of international trade and its underlying assumptions. This theory, he contends, has "developed in the direction of stressing ever more the idea that trade initiated a tendency toward a gradual equalization of factor prices and incomes among nations."[6] Yet, he

---

[3] By the phrase "capital intensive goods" the economist means those commodities in whose production a high proportion of capital is used, relative to the other factors of production.

[4] Subtitle, *The Road to World Prosperity* (New York: Harper and Bros., 1957). This book was published in England in the same year under the title of *Economic Theory and Under-Developed Regions*.

[5] Myrdal is represented as proposing a theory of regional polarization by A. H. Conrad and J. R. Meyer in their *The Economics of Slavery* (Chicago, Ill.: Aldine Publishing Co., 1964), p. 225. As Conrad and Meyer note, a similar view has been advanced by Raul Prebisch. For the latter's position, see UN Economic Commission for Asia and the Far East, *The Economic Development of Latin America and Some of Its Problems* (New York, 1949), pp. 1–3. Prebisch's argument is summarized in Higgins, *Economic Development . . .*, pp. 366–368.

[6] Myrdal, *Rich Lands and Poor*, p. 152.

and others fail to see any such tendency; rather they are impressed with the growing income inequality among the advanced trading nations and those of the so-called underdeveloped world. He attributes this failure of the conventional theory to explain the international facts of life to its assumption, among other factors, of the false and unrealistic analogy of stable equilibrium. This assumption, which, he points out, dominates so much of the established

Gunnar Myrdal was born in Sweden in 1898. He became professor of economics at the University of Stockholm in 1931. Apart from public service in Sweden, he was executive secretary of the United Nations Economic Commission for Europe in the years 1947–57.

American Swedish News Exchange

theory, implies the belief that "normally a change will call forth as reaction secondary changes with an opposite direction." He also assails the restriction of the analysis in the theory of international trade to economic factors; he contends that the non-economic factors in such an analysis cannot be taken as given and static.[7] And furthermore, when the latter react, they normally do so in a disequilibrating way. In general, then, Myrdal insists that the theory of international trade as well as economic theory in general were not developed to "comprehend the reality of great and growing economic inequalities and of the dynamic processes of underdevelopment and development."

In place of the rejected theory, Myrdal boldly presents the elements of a more adequate general theory based on the idea of circular causation of a cumulative process. It is his conviction that "this idea contains *in nuce* the approach to a more realistic analysis of social change—indeed a vision of the general theory of underdevelopment and development which we are all yearning for." These notions, Myrdal further believes, should be the main hy-

[7] Myrdal says further on this point: "To define a certain set of phenomena as the 'economic factors,' while keeping other things outside the analysis, is a procedure closely related to the stable equilibrium approach. For it is precisely in the realm of those 'noneconomic factors,' which the theory of international trade usually takes as given and static, that the equilibrium assumption is most unrealistic and where, instead, circular causation is the rule" (*Ibid.*, p. 157).

pothesis when studying economic underdevelopment and development, though
he admits that his "sketch" or outline "hardly gives more than a vision of
what has to be accomplished before we can really talk about a general theory
for the economic process."[8]

Myrdal begins his own theorizing about social processes with the idea that
"in the normal case" there is no tendency toward automatic self-stabilization
in the social system. . . . The system is by itself not moving toward any sort
of balance between forces but is constantly on the move away from such a
situation. In the normal case a change does not call forth countervailing
changes but, instead, supporting changes, which move the system in the same
direction as the first change but much further. Because of such circular causation a social process tends to become cumulative and often to gather speed at
an accelerating rate."[9]

The concept of circular causation can perhaps be best explained in terms of
the vicious circles of development or underdevelopment that Myrdal has had
so important a part in popularizing. He explains the concept of circular
causation most clearly by means of the illustration of the vicious circle of
poverty and disease. ". . . Men and women were sick because they were
poor; they became poorer because they were sick, and sicker because they
were poorer."[10] Myrdal acknowledges that these cumulative social processes
can be stopped or counterbalanced, but he denies that the balance so established is a natural outcome of the forces within the system or that it is
stable.

Myrdal conceives of social processes as being subject to two types of influences—"market forces and [governmental] policies." Unhampered market
forces, he contends, tend toward regional inequalities, because of the cumulative processes (vicious or virtuous) they set off in the economy. This is
especially true, in his view, in undeveloped societies with weak "spread
effects," where the competitive forces of the market may contribute to these
regional inequalities, while at the same time the latter will be discouraging
economic development and weakening the power basis for egalitarian policies
of the government. (In this sentence, we have used one of Myrdal's favorite
concepts, the "spread effects"; these are the stimulating effects of expansionary momentum, which, acting cumulatively, move the growing sector of the
economy toward higher levels of development. Opposing them are his so-
called "backwash effects"—the unfavorable, cumulative depressing consequences of economic change.)

Let us see how Myrdal's "simple model of circular causation with cumulative effects" operates by considering a hypothetical example. We should
preface this illustration by noting that the Myrdal economic process may be
started by any one of a variety of exogenous forces—war, invention, a
population boom, the advantages of a good geographical location, favorable
terms of trade, etc. In our example, we have, say, a southern town that has

developed from the need for field workers to harvest cotton. The townspeople are engaged in providing the consumer goods and services needed by the cotton pickers. After many years the soil becomes depleted of its minerals. The cotton crop becomes marginal; cheaper and better cotton is grown elsewhere. Some workers now become unemployed. Finding little opportunity to employ themselves elsewhere in the community, they decide to move, perhaps to a better cotton-growing area. As a result of the loss of this group's jobs and the resulting decline in income, the demand for goods and services in the community will decline. Decreased demand will reduce income and cause unemployment in all sorts of other businesses that had depended for their survival on the sale of commodities and services to the now unemployed persons. At this point the well-known multiplier process has been triggered downward. The situation begins to deteriorate further into a vicious cycle as more workers leave, causing more unemployment for those who had previously served them. This cumulative, circular process may continue downward until some outside force enters the picture to reverse it.

Thus, while one locality may be undergoing a downward, cumulative spiral, other parts of the nation may be experiencing a marked expansion because of a new discovery, a new invention, or some foreign interference. The younger people in the disintegrating community are likely to migrate to the rapidly developing areas. In the backwash of the expansion of these rapidly developing areas the older section may find their younger people being lured away and all their old and infirm inhabitants remaining. This will further aggravate the situation since local taxes must be raised to care for the welfare of this increasingly indigent population (the backwash effect). At the same time, the rapidly developing centers may shortly develop a high population density, and as a result, suburbs may grow up around them to house those who cannot or will not tolerate a highly crowded environment. This tendency for economic growth to proliferate or spread out over a wider area is the now familiar "spread effect."

Our illustration should make it clear that expansion in one locality may have "backwash effects" on others. Myrdal himself states very confidently, ". . . More specifically the movements of labor, capital goods and services do not by themselves counteract the natural tendency to regional inequality. By themselves, migration, capital movements and trade are rather the media through which the cumulative process evolves—upward in the lucky regions and downward in the unlucky ones. In general, if they have positive results for the former, their effects on the latter are negative."[11] Migration of labor, being selective, will tend to have cumulative effects favoring the growing

[11] *Ibid.*, p. 27. Myrdal takes note of qualifications of this argument in another section of his book. He recognizes that counteracting changes, such as "external dis-economies," higher wages in the advanced sector, a loss of entrepreneurial spirit and willingness to take risks in a quasi-monopolistic setting, etc., may weaken or stop the cumulative processes altogether. Nevertheless, he comes down on the side of cumulative rather than counteracting forces. ". . . I believe that when main trends over somewhat longer periods are under consideration the changes will in the main support each other and thus tend to be cumulative in their net effects." (*Ibid.*, pp. 35–37.)

region at the expense of the lagging ones. Similarly, Myrdal thinks, capital movements will tend to have the effect of increasing inequality. Investment in the expanding region will increase incomes, savings will rise, making possible a second round of investment and increased employment, etc. Trade too often operates with a bias in favor of the progressive region and against the poorer one. The former, with their larger plants (increasing returns to scale), may thwart the development of competing industries in the backward sections. The poorer regions, concentrating perhaps on primary staples, may confront inelastic demand in the export market, a slow growth in demand, and excessive price fluctuations. So he concludes, "On the international as on the national level trade does not by itself necessarily work for equality. It may, on the contrary, have strong backwash effects on the undeveloped countries" (and, we may add, undeveloped regions).

> A widening of markets often strengthens in the first instance the rich and progressive countries whose manufacturing industries have the lead and are already fortified by the surrounding external economies, while the underdeveloped countries are in continuous danger of seeing even what they have of industry and handicrafts priced out by cheap imports from the industrial countries, if they do not protect them.[12]

Citing a United Nations study, which found that disparities of income are much wider in poorer countries than in the richer ones, Myrdal, speculating on the causes of this tendency, argues that the higher the level of development in a country, the stronger the spread effects will be. Development brings better transportation, communication, education; all of which strengthen the centrifugal forces of expansion. Conversely, in the underdeveloped countries and regions, the spread effects tend to be weak. As the old adage has it, "Nothing succeeds like success." Failure breeds failure; "poverty becomes its own cause."

Myrdal briefly considers the effects of short run, cyclical changes on these longer, cumulative economic processes. He hazards the suggestion that "A boom will probably always increase the strength of the spread effects. A depression will have the opposite result."[13] He urges more research on the consequences of business cycles for economic development generally, and more especially, for its differential effects on localities and regions.

The economic impact of colonialism is dealt with briefly but trenchantly in Myrdal's analysis of regional polarization. Among other points, he argues that enforced dependency, while it had certain advantages for the dependent country in the short run, causes at the end of the process considerable economic disadvantage. This was usually the case, he maintains, because the colonial relationship "tends to worsen its [i.e., the dependent country's] terms of trade by restricting artificially the scope of the markets where it buys and sells." The metropolitan country has a self-evident interest in monopolizing

---

[12] *Ibid.*, pp. 51–52.
[13] *Ibid.*, p. 38.

the export and import trade of the dependent country. This "enforced bilateralism," however, inevitably militates against balanced economic development for the dependency. In addition, the segregation usually followed in the social relationships between the peoples of the dependent country and those of the colonial power hampers the transfer of culture, including in the latter both technical skills and the entrepreneurial spirit, to the native population. It is for these reasons, he asserts, that the economic ventures of colonialism remain enclaves in the native economy with extremely weak or negative spread effects. We have noted Myrdal's observations on the economic consequences of colonialism not for their bearing on that problem in the world at large but for their relevance to the colonial structure that underlay the plantation economy of the American South; and, need we add, for the effect of that dependency's capacity for balanced economic development.

Myrdal's generalizations on the role of the non-economic factors in economic development lead him to suggest that these too may operate in a cumulative direction. Not only may the poor or deteriorating regions fail to keep up their public utilities, such as roads, railways, etc., but their inhabitants may become, because of inadequate medical care and education, less healthy and efficient.

> The people living there would on the average be believers in the more primitive variants of religion, sanctioning traditional mores by taboos and functional magic, and they would be more superstitious and less rational generally. Their entire systems of valuations would take on such an imprint of poverty and backwardness that they would become even less susceptible to the experimental and ambitious aspirations of a developing society.[14]

Myrdal does not enter the difficult terrain of social psycho-pathology, but we do have some studies that suggest how declining regions develop collective fixations and other defense mechanisms to rationalize their deteriorating status relative to that of those in the expanding sector of the economy.[15] The extension of the concepts of spread and backwash effects to the psycho-social realm opens up vast, unexplored regions for social analysis.

Myrdal is equally imaginative and challenging in treating the role of the state in general economic development. Here he uses the term "state" to include "all organized interferences with the market forces." He goes on to observe that

> The traditional role of the "state" in this inclusive sense was mainly to serve as a means for supporting the cumulative process tending toward inequality. It was the economically advancing and wealthier regions and social groups which were the more active and effective in organizing their efforts, and they usually had the resources to stop organizational efforts by the others. And so the

---

[14] *Ibid.*, p. 30.

[15] See, for an enlightening analysis of this kind, A. J. Vidich and J. Bensman, *Small Town in Mass Society* (Garden City, N.Y.: Doubleday and Co., Inc., 1960), esp. Chap. 11; also R. Hofstadter, *The Paranoid Style in American Politics* (New York: Alfred Knopf, Inc., 1965), and Erich Fromm, *Escape From Freedom* (New York: Farrar and Rinehart, 1941).

"state"—which stands here for organized society—usually became their tool in advancing their interests.[16]

While this is a very broad and controversial concept of the state, it enables Myrdal to develop the idea that the preindustrial state was in general an "oppressor state" and that with the industrial revolution and the spread effects it had in certain advancing countries there emerged the liberal state with its emphasis on equality of opportunity. With the rising level of economic development there has been a movement toward a "welfare state," though this trend has been subject to numerous detours and deviations historically. In advancing economies committed to a democratic philosophy and policies there have been successive interferences with market forces, designed to improve what the classical economists called "the quality of the factors of production" and seeking also to prevent any region, industry, or social group from lagging behind in its development. Thus, Myrdal describes the circular process in the relationship of economic advance to political development in these terms:

> Economic progress has supported the spread effects of expansionary momentum, hampered the trend toward inequalities, and thus also solidified the basis for democracy. It has at the same time created the easier conditions for mutual generosity which made the enactment of the equalizing state policies more possible. In its turn the greater equality of circumstances in these countries has sustained economic progress.[17]

We are not interested in evaluating the validity of the general statements Myrdal makes in this sketch of politico-economic development in the western world, but wish rather to call attention to his emphasis on the circular causation between the democratic process and economic progress. He expresses this connection rather cloudily as follows:

> Thus policies for national integration, including regional equalization, themselves represent only a phase of the cumulative social process of economic development—though this process has to be conceived of as a higher order since it includes, in addition to the evolution of the market forces, people's political attitudes, interferences by the state and, in fact, the entire political process. In these countries social and economic reforms now develop further by their own momentum as almost incidental to economic progress—which has been, and continues to be, in part due to their results.[18]

Myrdal has not sought to trace out the inter-relationships between the political life of a backward region or country and the backwash effects he alleges it experiences in its trade and commerce with the progressive entity. But the implications of his analysis for such a situation are clear: if economic progress generates tendencies toward a freer, more democratic and humanitarian society, economic retrogression or stagnation may promote a more restrictive, repressive, and authoritarian regime. Myrdal, we think, would heavily underscore the "may." He is too sophisticated a social scientist and

[16] Myrdal, *Rich Lands and Poor*, p. 42.
[17] *Ibid.*, p. 47.
[18] *Ibid.*, pp. 47–48.

too non-doctrinaire to defend a crude economic determinism. In any case, he has left the complexities of this particular relationship for others to unravel.[19] Considering the wealth of provocative ideas and concepts concerning the process of politico-economic development he has given us in his little book, we should be content enough.

In the following chapters of this Part, we shall explore the usefulness particularly of Myrdal's conception of the dualistic process of development as a theoretical frame and perspective for analyzing the economies of the North and South on the eve of the Civil War. We shall seek to test some of its concepts and key processes also with respect to the economic and political developments during the war years themselves.

---

[19] In his monumental work, *An American Dilemma, The Negro Problem and Modern Democracy* (New York: Harper and Bros., 1944), *passim,* Myrdal in a sense touched upon some elements of this problem insofar as he analyzed the relationship between Negro poverty, one result of the South's economic backwardness, and white prejudice, and demonstrated the circular causation involved therein. See also his remarks on this in *Rich Lands and Poor,* pp. 14–18.

Chapter 14

DUALISTIC DEVELOPMENT IN THE AMERICAN ECONOMY BEFORE AND DURING THE CIVIL WAR

The fault of the Free States in the eyes of the South is not one that can be atoned for by any yielding of special points here and there . . . Their crime is the census of 1860. Their increase in numbers, wealth, and power is a standing aggression. It would not be enough to please the Southern States that we should stop asking them to abolish slavery,—what they demand of us is nothing less than that we should abolish the spirit of the age.[1]

James Russell Lowell

The wealth of the South is permanent and real, that of the North fugitive and fictitious.[2]

J. D. B. DeBow

SECTIONAL ECONOMIC PROGRESS ON THE
EVE OF THE CIVIL WAR

The economic development of the United States went forward in giant strides during the 1850's, as industrialization proceeded in the Northeast, agriculture expanded in the rich North Central area, and the South's cotton production soared in response to the ever-increasing demands of factories in the Northeast and Europe. The seven years of general prosperity after 1850 allayed somewhat the political unease over the slavery dispute. Even after business turned downward again in 1857 in a relatively short, sharp depression, the revival enabled many Americans to concentrate on making money rather than on arguing over the longstanding controversy between the sections, which was to lead to the "irrepressible conflict." The indices of the nation's economic expansion were there for all to see: in the seven years 1850–57, both exports and imports trebled; the American merchant marine came to outnumber the ships of Great Britain during this great era of the

---

[1] "The Question of the Hour," *Atlantic Monthly* (1861), p. 120, quoted in A. C. Cole, *The Irrepressible Conflict, 1850–1865* (New York: The Macmillan Company, 1934), v.

[2] *DeBow's Review*, XXIII (1857), p. 592, quoted in *Ibid.*, p. 33.

clipper ship; capital investment in manufacturing by 1860 had doubled the level of a decade before; and lastly, contributing mightily to this economic surge of growth was the tripling of the nation's railroad lines, the spanning of the continent by the telegraph (accomplished in October, 1861), the laying of the trans-Atlantic Ocean cable, and the continued growth of that profession so dear to the heart of one Sam Clemens, steamboating. The pace of the vast transportation and communication revolution that was knitting the nation together was strikingly illustrated in the colorful but brief history of the pony express. This innovation in express mail was started in April, 1860 by the reputable freighting firm of Russell, Majors, and Waddell. Riders on hardy Indian horses dashed over the Plains between St. Joseph and Sacramento on a ten-day schedule. But then, in October, 1861, the Pacific telegraph from New York to San Francisco began operation. In that same month, the firm of Russell *et al.*, now bankrupt, discontinued the pony express.

In these years of the fifties, while the Northeast and West boomed, the South was also able to claim its share of the prosperity. The southern farmer and plantation owner enjoyed higher prices than they had received for their crops in the 1840's; the doubling of southern agricultural output, which took place in the decade of the fifties, meant a larger total income for the region. The general prosperity of the cotton economy was reflected in the rising price of slaves during these years, indicating that the expansion of plantation culture in the Deep South and the new areas of the Southwest Central states (Louisiana, Texas, Arkansas, and Oklahoma) was pressing upon the available supply, causing the price of this factor of production to rise. Yet there were disturbing trends in southern agriculture in this decade also. A comparison of the censuses for 1850 and 1860 revealed that the agriculture of the South as a whole was less diversified in the latter year than ten years before. While the population of the South increased 23.9 per cent between 1850 and 1860, the annual production of cotton doubled and that of tobacco more than doubled. Over the same period, the per capita production of Indian corn fell from 32.75 bushels in 1850 to 31 bushels in 1860.[3] Homage to King Cotton and other export staples was resulting in a less diversified agriculture.

There was notable progress in other lines of economic activity in the South in these years. For example, the South had but 2,936 miles of railroad in 1850, but in the following decade it more than quadrupled its mileage to 8,838. On a percentage basis, this was a faster rate of growth than in the North; the New England and Middle states just about doubled their mileage in this period, raising their total from 5,709 to 10,365 miles. The western states and territories were achieving the fastest rate of railroad expansion in these terms; their total mileage went from 1,276 to 11,400 in the same decade.[4] The expansion of the South's rail system in the fifties was a con-

---

[3] R. R. Russel, *Economic Aspects of Southern Sectionalism, 1840–61* (Urbana, Ill.: University of Illinois, 1924), p. 203.

[4] R. Andreano, ed., *The Economic Impact of the American Civil War* (Cambridge, Mass.: Schenkman Publishing Co., 1962), p. 190.

siderable accomplishment, considering the difficulties the region experienced in raising capital. Northern and English investors were averse to buying southern rail bonds, thus it was necessary to sell securities at home. As a consequence of the capital shortage, the southern railroads were cheaply built and poorly equipped. The traffic on many of them proved to be light and dividends were small, but the situation was improving by 1860.

Manufacturing had made a modest start in the South during the 1840's when the depressed price of cotton and other commodities led certain men to advocate greater diversification of industry. The movement to bring the spindles to the cotton led first to the establishment of cotton manufacturing. By 1840 the value of product of cotton factories in the region was $1,912,215 and it trebled during the next decade to $5,665,362; in the fifties the rate of increase fell to 43 per cent, the value of product in 1860 totalling $8,145,067. The region's relatively small proportion of the nation's output of that commodity is shown in the fact that in the latter year the U.S. value of product for cotton textiles was $115,681,774.

Manufacturing developed also as a consequence of the building of railroads. Machine and repair shops were established; some rolling mills were erected, and a small number of railroad cars were built. For example, the Tredegar locomotive works at Richmond made 19 of the 470 locomotives built in the United States in 1860. However, most manufacturing in the South in the antebellum period was based on processing of the region's primary staples, such as flour, meal, lumber, tobacco, and turpentine. These five items accounted for one-half of the total value of product of all southern manufactures and an equal proportion of the capital invested.[5]

An overall picture of southern manufacture relative to that of the nation is gained from the following statistics: the capital invested in southern manufactures was 13.6 per cent of the capital so invested in the nation in 1840, 10.4 per cent in 1850, and 9.5 per cent in 1860. Whereas the number of employees in manufacturing in the North in the latter year was over 1,200,000, the South had only 110,000 persons so engaged.

In general, we can say that while the South was not in the throes of an industrial revolution on the eve of the Civil War, neither was it stagnant. In fact, in the depression of 1857 the South fared relatively well. In the first place, it was not as hard hit by the downturn as the West and North, and it recovered rapidly, thanks to high prices and large crops. In 1858 to 1860, the South had a larger proportion of the nation's specie in its banks than it ever had before.[6] Still, the financial crash of 1857 demonstrated again to the southerners their financial dependence upon New York City. The South was pictured in some newspapers that year as being on the eve of a "great flood-tide of prosperity." "And yet—and yet—almost in the twinkling of an eye,

---

[5] Russel, *Economic Aspects of Southern Sectionalism* . . . , p. 228.
[6] *Ibid.*, p. 205.

with the suddenness of an earthquake, as unexpectedly as a stroke of lightning from a cloudless sky, cotton was struck down, and became almost unsalable in the Southern market," lamented one journal.[7]

DEVELOPMENT AND UNDERDEVELOPMENT

Despite the growth in absolute terms in many aspects of the South's economy, what rankled many of its leaders was this dependence upon the North, the relative disparity in its development, and the sense that their region was not growing in proportion to its potentialities. In general, many of them "felt that they did not enjoy the prosperity and were not making the material progress that the South's natural resources and their own efforts entitled them to expect." This feeling was "greatly augmented because a political struggle between the sections, over slavery especially, called sharp attention to the relationship between material progress and political power."[8] Let us examine some of the principal indications of the disparity in the rate of growth of the two regions.

One manifestation of the divergence in the regional growth rates was the unequal increase in population in the years before the War. In 1860, the total population of the United States was 31.5 million. Of that number, 20.3 million resided in the Northeast, north central, and western states; the remainder, 11.2 million, were inhabitants of the South.[9] Between 1840 and 1860, the former group of states increased in numbers some 95 per cent, while the population of the South was growing 61 per cent. Another way to show the change is to compare the distribution of the total population by region in percentage terms as in Table 1:

TABLE 1

Distribution of U.S. Population by Region, 1800–60[a]
Per Cent of Population in

Year	Continental United States	North- east	South	North Central	West
1800	100.0%	50.0%	50.0%	—	—
1820	100.0	45.4	45.4	9.2%	—
1840	100.0	39.6	40.7	19.8	—
1860	100.0	33.8	35.4	29.0	1.9%

[a] Adapted from P. B. Kenen, "A Statistical Survey of Basic Trends," in S. E. Harris, ed., *American Economic History, op. cit.,* p. 68.

[7] *Hunt's Merchants' Magazine,* XLII, p. 315, quoted in *Ibid.,* pp. 102–103.
[8] Russel, *Economic Aspects of Southern Sectionalism . . . ,* p. 289.
[9] U.S. Bureau of the Census, *Historical Statistics of the U.S., 1789–1945* (Washington, D.C.: U.S. Printing Office, 1949), pp. 25–27.

One can see that whereas the two sections, the Northeast and the South, were an equal proportion of the total population in 1800, by 1860 the addition of the people living in the North Central and western states to those of the Northeast gave the latter grouping a great predominance in numbers. This trend and what it portended for their section in political terms was not lost upon many southern leaders. The political equilibrium of the nation, so delicately achieved over the years by negotiation and compromise, was being threatened in a most drastic manner by the geographical shifts in population. Still, this was but an inevitable accompaniment of economic change and development in the nation.

There were other differences in the distribution of population in the two regions that became more pronounced as time passed. The South's economy was largely a rural one, and the population was relatively widely dispersed and sparse in many sections;[10] the Northeast, on the other hand, was moving toward urbanization, and local towns and villages were growing up in the West also as it developed. Urbanization was slow in coming to the South. Aside from such ports as New Orleans, Charleston, Savannah, or Mobile, which had grown up largely to serve the cotton trade, there were few other large cities in the region.

Table 2, which presents the fifteen leading cities in the United States in

TABLE 2

Fifteen Leading Cities in the United States, Ranked by Size of Population in 1860[a]

City	Rank	Population	Per Cent of Population Engaged in Manufacturing
New York	1	1,080,330	9.5%
Philadelphia	2	565,529	17.5
Baltimore	3	212,418	8.0
Boston	4	177,840	10.8
New Orleans	5	168,675	3.0
Cincinnati	6	161,044	18.3
St. Louis	7	160,773	5.8
Chicago	8	109,260	4.9
Buffalo	9	81,129	6.9
Newark	10	71,941	26.2
Louisville	11	68,033	9.8
Albany	12	62,367	9.3
Washington	13	61,122	3.9
San Francisco	14	56,802	2.6
Providence	15	50,666	22.0

[a] Source: U.S. Bureau of the Census, *Historical Statistics of the United States.*

[10] The distribution of population in the South was quite irregular. In 1860, the density of population per square mile ranged from 56.26 in Maryland to only 2.39 in Florida and 2.27 in Texas. [E. Q. Hawk, *Economic History of the South* (Englewood Cliffs, N.J.: Prentice-Hall, Inc., 1934), p. 227.]

1860 in the order of their size, shows the concentration in the North of growing cities; the only truly southern city on this list was New Orleans, though Baltimore and Louisville had a southern character. New Orleans was the only city in the table that became part of the Confederacy. Altogether, there were some 27 cities in the South with a population exceeding 4,000. These cities were either seaports, river ports, or state capitals. The percentage of people living in these cities was 7.8 of the entire region, whereas in the New England and Middle Atlantic states the urban population was about 35 per cent of the total population; in the West North Central states the corresponding figure was over 10 per cent and rising. Part of the reason for the South's lag in urbanization was that most of the immigrants who came to the United States in the ante-bellum period settled in the North or West; the South received only about 13 per cent of the total in the pre-war period.

Still another aspect of the divergent economic trends of the two sections that was tied up, as we shall see, with the growing urbanization of the North was the distribution of the nation's foreign trade. Our earlier study has shown that in the late ante-bellum period the South was furnishing two-thirds of the nation's exports, yet she received *directly* only one-tenth of its imports. The remainder of the goods the South imported from abroad came to her by way of northern seaports. In 1807, the direct imports of Charleston, S.C. were said to have amounted to several million; by 1833 they had shrunk to one-half million. A similar reduction was believed to have taken place in Virginia.[11] This routing of the region's trade to the North contributed to the decline of its shipping and import trade and became a source of great grievance and resentment to many leading southerners. (The causes of this development will be considered in the next chapter.)

The statistics we have on the distribution of personal income for these years are not as reliable as those of population, but if we analyze them with the caution their compilers urge upon us they are very revealing. The careful statistical analysis of Professor Easterlin gives us the estimates of personal income per capita in the principal regions as percentages of the United States average in the years 1840 and 1860 (Table 3). Thus, at a glance we can see the regional trends in relative per capita income. If a region's rate of growth was above the national average, relative per capita income would rise; if it was less than the national average, it would fall.

Commenting upon the data of this table, Professor Easterlin finds the difference in the relative rate of growth of the Northeast and the South "most significant." He states his belief that these figures indicate that "the income gap between Northeast and South was greater in 1860 than in 1840." And he adds,

. . . This conclusion implies a relative deterioration in the income position not only of the total Southern population but of the favored white population as well. Moreover . . . it is likely that the figures understate the widening of the

---

[11] Russel, *Economic Aspects of Southern Sectionalism* . . ., p. 19.

relative income gap. It should be emphasized, however, that our comparison deals only with *relative* income. In absolute terms, per capita income in the South probably rose between 1840 and 1860, and perhaps substantially. . . .[12]

TABLE 3

Personal Income per Capita in Each Region as Percentage of United States Average, 1840–60[a]

Regions	1840	1860
United States	100	100
Northeast	135	139
New England	132	143
Middle Atlantic	136	137
North Central	68	68
East North Central	67	69
West North Central	75	66
South	76	72
South Atlantic	70	65
East South Atlantic	73	68
West South Central	144	115

[a] Adapted from R. A. Easterlin, "Regional Income Trends, 1840–1950," in S. E. Harris, *American Economic History* (New York: McGraw-Hill Book Co., 1961), p. 528.

The trend in a region's share in total income depends on the trend in per capita income and on the change in the region's proportion of the national population. When account is taken of these two elements together, estimates such as those presented in Table 4 can be arrived at. This table shows the per cent distribution of personal income by region of the United States for 1840 and 1860, again as computed by Professor Easterlin. What is striking is that it shows the share of the Northeast declining in relative terms, as the North Central and western states gained in their share of the total personal income. The South's share, a smaller one to begin with, also falls, with a larger decrease in the South Atlantic states being offset somewhat by the rise in the Southwest Central states. It must be noted, by the way, that the definition of the South in this and the preceding table differs from the states included in the Confederacy (West Virginia and Kentucky were not members), but in Professor Easterlin's opinion this variation is not enough to affect the major findings of the analysis.[13]

[12] The understatement referred to results from the omission in the income estimates of compensation derived from service activities (such as finance and real estate), personal and professional services, and government. Because of the importance of some of these activities in the Northeast relative to the other parts of the nation, there is probably an understatement of the relative growth of per capita income in that section. It should be noted also that these estimates make no allowance for differences in the cost of living; it is believed by Easterlin on the basis of limited information that adjustment for these differences would not alter the major pattern revealed in the above statistics. Furthermore, these estimates take no account of income received "in kind," nor do they reveal differences in the level or trend in the distribution of income between rich and poor.

[13] R. A. Easterlin, "Regional Income Trends, 1840–1950," in S. E. Harris, ed., *American Economic History* (New York: McGraw-Hill Book Co., 1961), p. 546, footnote 6. Easterlin

TABLE 4

*Per Cent Distribution of Total Personal Income in the
United States, 1840 and 1860*[a]

Region	1840	1860
United States	100%	100%
Northeast	58	50
New England	17	14
Middle Atlantic	41	36
North Central	13	20
East North Central	12	15
West North Central	2	4
South	29	26
South Atlantic	14	9
East South Central	11	9
West South Central	4	8
West	—	4

[a] Adapted from Easterlin, *op. cit.*, in Harris, *ibid.*, p. 535. Totals may not add up because of rounding off percentages in calculation.

In concluding this evaluation of the pre-war progress of the two sections, we should note the findings of another recent study by a very capable scholar. Professor Williamson, employing Easterlin's data, concludes that the economic growth of the United States "traces out a 'classic' pattern of regional inequality. . . . Regional divergence of income growth in the United States was the case *prior* to the Civil War; the tendency toward increasing North-South dualism is evident, although not striking, between 1840 and 1860. . . ."[14]

In the crucial decade of the 1850's, the southern level of income in absolute terms was probably rising; yet in relative terms, the income gap between the Northeast and the South was widening. In understanding the causes of secession, it seems important to stress the latter trend because we have innumerable evidences of growing discontent among southerners over this divergence in the development of the two sections. One historian tells us, "During this period the people of the South, generally, were aware of a disparity between the North and South to the advantage of the former in material development—population, wealth, commerce, industry, financial strength, distribution of the comforts and conveniences of life. . . ."[15] Let us note how this perceived lag in the South's development relative to the North was expressed by some inhabi-

tells us that his income averages for the South include the slave population. He adds, ". . . If the slaves and their income (estimated at subsistence) are eliminated, one finds that the income of the white population in the South exceeded the national average and compared favorably with that in the Northeast. . . ." (*Ibid.*, p. 527.) One must keep in mind, however, that such regional averages do not reveal the range of income between rich and poor; income inequalities of this type were probably greater in the South than in the North in this period.

[14] Williamson, "Regional Inequality and the Process of National Development," *Economic Development and Cultural Change*, Vol. 13, No. 4, Part 2 (July, 1965), p. 23.

[15] Russel, *Economic Aspects of Southern Sectionalism* . . . , p. 289.

tants of the former section in the years before the war. By 1837 many
planters, editors, and politicians were concerned over "southern decline,"
growing out of the concentration of their import business in the North. They
wished to institute direct trade with Europe to break their commercial dependence upon northern merchants. This was one of the major objectives of
the commercial conventions held in the South in the pre-war years. The call of
the first such convention, which met at Augusta, Georgia, in August, 1837,
stated that the virtual monopoly of southern commerce had "either directly or
indirectly made the whole of the North and Northwest what they are." The
conveners of this meeting did not use the language of spread and backwash
effects, but had their own vivid metaphor: Because of that monopoly, they
said, "the one people has risen like the rocket, and the other has fallen like its
stick—their positions must have been reversed, if the southern people had
maintained their foreign trade."[16]

Later in the pre-war period the southerners gave attention to proposals for
diversification of their agriculture and the development of manufactures to
free them from their dependence on the North and West. These discussions
made people more aware of the disparity in the industrial development of the
two sections. And this knowledge humiliated some of them and made the more
loyal and progressive of them desirous of promoting the economic development of their section.

> It was galling to their pride that their section should be languishing and
> dependent. They wanted a denser population, cities, towns, railroads, develop-
> ment of natural resources, and the social benefits which they believed would
> follow material development. They wished to prove by the actual accomplish-
> ment that, contrary to the contentions of its Northern and British antagonists,
> cities, commerce, manufactures, and the "arts of living" could flourish in a
> slave society. . . .[17]

Apart from "southern decline," the other aspect of their condition found
intolerable by southerners was their dependence upon the more developed
regions of the nation. Listen to R. W. Roper, a rich planter, who in 1844 came
out for encouragement of manufactures and commerce: "As long as we are
tributaries, dependent on foreign labor and skill for food, clothing, and countless necessaries of life, we are in thralldom."[18] In that same year, Senator
McDuffie of South Carolina in a speech against the Tariff of 1842 warned the
protectionists that there was a point beyond which oppression would not be
borne, "even by the most enslaved community in the world." Six years later,
Senator Rhett, the secessionist successor to Calhoun, told the Senate, "The
South is nothing else now, but the very best colony of the North any people
ever possessed."

The feeling and vehemence of a large group in the South on this matter of

[16] *Niles Register*, LV, 42, quoted in *Ibid.*, p. 21.
[17] *Ibid.*, p. 98.
[18] *Ibid.*, p. 40.

dependence and "commercial vassalage" is illustrated best perhaps by this "typical quotation" from an Alabama newspaper, as of 1851:

> At present the North fattens and grows rich upon the South. We depend upon it for our entire supplies. We purchase all our luxuries and necessaries from the North. . . . With us, every branch and pursuit in life, every trade, profession, and occupation, is dependent upon the North; for instance, the Northerners abuse and denounce slavery and slaveholders, yet our slaves are clothed with Northern manufactured goods, have Northern hats and shoes, work with Northern hoes, ploughs, and other implements, are chastized with a Northern-made instrument, are working for Northern more than Southern profit. The slaveholder dresses in Northern goods, rides in a Northern saddle, . . . sports his Northern carriage, patronizes Northern newspapers, drinks Northern liquors, reads Northern books, spends his money at Northern water-places. . . . The aggressive acts upon his rights and his property arouse his resentment— and on Northern-made paper, with a Northern pen, with Northern ink, he resolves and resolves in regard to his rights! . . .[19]

We shall not anticipate our later analysis to show how these sentiments evolved from "calculating the value of [remaining in] the Union" to outright advocacy of secession. It is clear from this and other evidence that the prosperity of the 1850's shared in by the South cannot be thought to have fundamentally reduced the southern sense of falling behind in the matter of material progress as compared with the developing North. Nor can the rise in the region's absolute level of income in the pre-war years justify the view that its economy was viable. Much of that expansion in production and income, as we shall explain in the next chapter, represented primarily economic growth in quantitative terms, not balanced development containing the potentialities for further self-sustaining economic evolution. As Professor Genovese has said with respect to the growth of southern manufactures in the ante-bellum years, ". . . industry made some progress; industrialization, understood as a self-propelling process, did not."[20]

THE TWO REGIONAL ECONOMIES ON THE EVE OF THE CONFLICT

General William T. Sherman was once quoted as saying to a southern friend before the war, "The North can make a steam engine, locomotive or railway car; hardly a yard of cloth or a pair of shoes can you make. You are rushing into war with one of the most powerful, ingeniously mechanical and determined people on earth." The General knew whereof he spoke. Consider the economic potential of the two antagonists. In 1860, the South had the following assets: a total population of some nine million, composed of 5,477,-000 whites, about 3,500,000 slaves and 130,000 free Negroes; total assets of

[19] *Ibid.*, p. 48.
[20] E. D. Genovese, *The Political Economy of Slavery* (New York: Pantheon Books, 1965), p. 246.

$4,220,755,000, of which the value of the slaves were estimated to be $1.5 billion; $1.4 billion in real estate; one half billion in money loaned at interest and $94 million in bank stocks. Aside from cotton, the South could consider itself economically self-sufficient in foodstuffs, lumber, cloth, and some minerals. Manufactured items had to be imported from abroad and, of the strategic war materials, only steel and small arms were in adequate supply. The South's railroad system of 9,000 miles was in bad repair, and connections were lacking between some of its major cities. In short, the South had enough resources to wage a war of short duration. If, however, the war lasted more than a year, the Confederacy would obviously be in difficulty with respect to strategic goods.

On the other hand, the North held over 75 per cent of the nation's wealth; it had a population of 22 million persons, 81 per cent of the manufacturing plants, 70 per cent of the nation's railroad mileage, 67 per cent of the improved farm lands, 74 per cent of the bank deposits. In addition, the North had sufficient skilled labor and capital to expand its lead over the less developed section even more. At the outbreak of the war, the northern economy was depressed and therefore possessed unemployed factors of production that would augment output as its economy was brought to full employment. The North also had a fund of intangibles in the way of technical know-how, entrepreneurial drive and administrative skill, which even Great Britain, the "workshop of the world," could scarcely match. Ideologically, it conceived itself as defending a system of free labor against a slave-based society that was becoming an anachronism in the civilized world.

The South, in contrast to the diversified, better balanced economy of the North, put its faith in almost a single commodity as the basis of its economic strength and political power. The world's need for cotton was the foundation of her confidence in the outcome of any military clash with the North. Senator Hammond of South Carolina said in a famous speech in 1858: "Without firing a gun, without drawing a sword, should they make war on us, we would bring the whole world to our feet. . . . What would happen if no cotton was furnished for three years? I will not stop to depict what every one can imagine, but this is certain: England would topple headlong and carry the whole civilized world with her save the South. No, you dare not to make war on cotton. No Power on the earth dares to make war on it. Cotton is King."[21] Two years later he wrote in the same vein: "cotton, rice, tobacco and naval stores command the world; and we have the sense to know it, and are sufficiently Teutonic to carry it out successfully. The North without us would be a motherless calf, bleating about, and die of mange and starvation."[22] Delusions such as these were fairly widespread among southern leaders on the eve of the tragic conflict.

[21] Quoted by J. A. B. Scherer, *Cotton as a World Power* (New York: Fredrick A. Stokes Company, 1916), p. 239.

[22] Quoted by S. E. Morison and H. S. Commager, *The Growth of the American Republic* (New York: Oxford University Press, 1937), Vol. 1, p. 536.

When war came, the South believed that several factors in the situation would lead the North to accept its secession from the Union. First, it counted on the North's need for cotton exports, which had for long offset the huge volume of American imports. Secondly, the southerners were of the opinion that the British would recognize the Confederacy because of their reliance on cotton to sustain their growing textile industry. Finally, it was the South's belief that the logistical problems involved in supplying northern troops on southern soil would be insurmountable. Within a year after the onset of hostilities, the South found that these factors were either reversed or offset by others. An oversupply of cotton in Britain in 1861 led to a major decline in the demand for southern cotton. A serious shortage of wheat in the British Isles created a strong demand for the North's grain, which forced Britain into a position of neutrality. The Union blockade of southern ports prevented any sizeable amount of products from leaving the Confederacy. The North picked up a brisk domestic war trade, which compensated for the loss of its commerce in cotton. Finally, the South found that much of the fighting was taking place in the border states and some even in Union territory, which gave the northern troops an advantage in terms of logistics and morale.

REGIONAL DIVERGENCE IN ECONOMIC DEVELOPMENT IN THE CIVIL WAR YEARS

The foregoing analysis has provided evidence of a divergence in income equality between the North and South in the years between 1840 and 1860. We now turn to consider the effect of the war itself upon the income levels and development of the two sections. The reader may be inclined to think this unnecessary in the light of the South's defeat and the "triumph of business" in the North, but there are reasons for not prejudging the effects of war upon an economy. Historians have found the general subject of that relationship to be a very complex one; furthermore, some wars have strengthened the forces making for regional convergence in incomes.[23] Our questions, then, are these: What was the effect of the Civil War upon the whole nation and its major sections? Did the independence and national sovereignty sought by the South lead to some degree of economic growth in that region in the war years? Did the war further promote the process of industrialization in the North?

The conventional interpretation of the economic impact of the Civil War upon the American economy offered for some years by historians was that it promoted and accelerated economic development in the United States. The Beards saw it as the "second American Revolution, a social war . . . making vast changes in the arrangement of the classes, in the accumulation and distribution of wealth, in the course of industrial development." Arthur

---

[23] See Williamson, "Regional Inequality . . .," p. 23 where it is observed that World War II "tended to strengthen the secular forces [in the United States] toward [regional] convergence."

Schlesinger, Sr. wrote of it as having "the effect of a hothouse." Another popular text writer argued that "In the North it speeded the Industrial Revolution and the development of capitalism by the prosperity which it brought to industry." An erudite British political scientist as late as 1960 told the readers of *Harper's* that the War between the States "made 'the take-off' (to use Professor W. W. Rostow's brilliant metaphor) come sooner."[24]

In a now classic article published in 1960, Professor Cochran, using new statistical evidence on long-run indexes of industrial production, has shown instead that if we conceive of the process of industrialization in strictly production terms, then "on balance for the more important [statistical] series the trend is toward retardation in rates of growth rather than toward acceleration. . . ."[25] For example, using statistics on total commodity output compiled by Gallman, he cites the value added by manufacture in terms of constant dollars of the purchasing power of 1879 as follows:[26]

1839–49	–	157%
1849–59	–	76
1859–69	–	25
1869–79	–	82
1879–89	–	112

Cochran concluded, on the basis of these statistics, that as compared with the two decades before and after the war, the rate of increase in manufacturing as a whole was interrupted rather than accelerated by the sectional conflict.

Pig-iron production is certainly one of the most significant indexes of nineteenth century industrial growth. When we take the percentage increase in total production of that commodity at five year intervals from 1850, we find the following: 1850–55—24 per cent; 1855–60—17 per cent; 1860–65—1 per cent; 1865–70—100 per cent. Here, again, we see production of this vital commodity in industrialization falling to its lowest level in the quinquennium ending in 1865. Similarly, reviewing the trends in the production of other key products, Cochran found that the war did not markedly affect the rate of growth of bituminous coal; it seems to have caused copper production (cited by three other historians as having benefitted from the war) to nosedive from a 1,000 per cent increase in the decade 1850–60 to 18 per cent in the years 1860–65, and then rise again by 48 per cent in the five years after the military struggle. Railroad track laid fell to a low level during the war years—there was only a 15 per cent increase in 1860–65, contrasted with a 200 per cent increase per decade in the twenty years before the war and an average rate of 75 per cent in the next two decades. The story is similar in cotton textiles, "the most representative consumer-goods industry in the nineteenth century": the number of bales consumed

---

[24] T. C. Cochran, "Did the Civil War Retard Industrialization?" *Mississippi Valley Historical Review* (September, 1961), reprinted in R. Andreano, ed., *The Economic Impact of the American Civil War*, pp. 148–160.

[25] Cochran in Andreano, *The Economic Impact* . . . , p. 149.

[26] *Historical Statistics* (1960 Edition), p. 402.

in the United States rose 143 per cent between 1840–50, 47 per cent in
1850–60, and then fell 6 per cent in the Civil War decade. Offsetting the
decline in cotton textiles, wool consumption for manufacturing more than
doubled during the War. Among other statistical series, Cochran discovered
that immigration was discouraged by the war and civilian construction slowed
down. "Collectively," Cochran summarized, "these statistical estimates support a conclusion that the Civil War retarded American industrial growth.
. . . "[27]

More recent study of economic change in the Civil War era suggests that
Cochran's reliance on aggregative data may have misled him on essential
points in his analysis.[28] Professor Gallman on whose aggregative data
Cochran partly relied has indicated that there was perhaps a "sharp structural
shift toward industry in general [in the decade 1859–69] and within industry
toward heavy industry, for subsequent growth in the 1870's and 1880's when
growth of production was notably rapid." Gallman notes that in the decade
1859–69 there was a very pronounced shift in the structure of the labor
force toward manufacturing industry, more so than in others. Further,
within industrial production there was a "sharp shift toward heavy industry—
especially toward iron and steel, but toward machinery, too. . . . "[29]

The aggregative approach would seem to have very serious deficiencies in
measuring the impact of the Civil War upon the economy. The secession of the
South from the Union separated a region from the national economy that
accounted for approximately 26 per cent of the total personal income of the
United States in 1860, according to Easterlin's estimates. (See Table 4 above,
p. 325.) While we cannot assume that the loss of that share of total personal
income through secession of the South was felt in that proportion by northern
industry, the figure does suggest the potential magnitude of the dislocation the
economy must have suffered. Aggregative statistical analysis, using national
decennial data for 1859 and 1869, conceals rather than reveals the readjustments and shifts in markets and production that were inescapable during the
war. Furthermore, the year 1869 (four years after the close of the war)
because of the cyclical changes taking place during it is not exactly an ideal
one for measuring the changes generated by the military conflict. It is for
reasons of this nature that we find ourselves in agreement with the conclusion
of Professor Scheiber in a perceptive article: " . . . Given the disruptive
effects of the war, the devastation of the South, and prolonged southern

---

[27] Cochran in Andreano, *The Economic Impact of the American Civil War* . . . , p.
154.

[28] See D. T. Gilchrist and W. D. Lewis, eds., *Economic Change in the Civil War Era*,
Proceedings of a Conference on American Economic Institutional Change, 1850–1873, and
the Impact of the Civil War, held March 12–14 (1964) (Greenville, Del.: Eleutherian
Mills-Hagley Foundation, 1965); for a valuable appraisal of this conference, see H. N.
Scheiber, "Economic Change in the Civil War Era: An Analysis of Recent Studies," *Civil
War History* (December, 1965), pp. 396–411. This essay provides an excellent review of
the controversy on this subject.

[29] Gilchrist and Lewis, *Economic Change in the Civil War Era*, p. 160.

failure to share in industrialization, we must ask whether the growth record of the 1860's was truly a significant retardation (as Cochran avers) or rather a remarkable rate of increase in regions outside the South and a reenforcement of longer-term trend? . . ."[30]

What is certainly evident from our brief review of the war's impact on our industrialization is that Professor Cochran was very wise and circumspect in putting the title of his provocative article in the form of a question. The subject, with all the statistical difficulties that it presents for the historian, is one that requires much further research and investigation.

THE NORTHERN ECONOMY DURING THE WAR

If we look at the relative progress of different industries in the North during the war years, we find some explanation for the alleged retardation in the nation's economic expansion. Our analysis of the growth of the North and South thus far has suggested in a preliminary way that their relationship increasingly was a complementary one, with the commercial and farming sections of the former providing the latter with goods and services and the plantation economy shipping its valuable staples through northern ports to be distributed over the world. Naturally, the coming of the war dealt a devastating blow to this trading relationship. The breaking of these commercial ties with the South meant huge losses for northern merchants; it has been estimated that the South's debts to them amounted to about $300 million. The first reaction, therefore, to the war was depression. Even before the outbreak of hostilities, the general uncertainty of business led to retrenchment. Northern banks suspended specie payment in December, 1860. Indeed, in the ensuing contraction, there was a larger number of commercial failures among northern concerns than in the panic years of 1857.

As the war progressed with its mounting demands for food, and the nations of Europe turned to the American granary, great prosperity was created for northern and western agriculture. Eighteen fifty-nine had been an excellent crop year, but the production of wheat, for example, in every year of the war exceeded its previous level of output. Indeed, our huge exports of wheat to England helped to keep that country neutral. There were poor crops in England and Europe generally in the years 1860–62, and a corresponding increased demand for our grain. The extent of our increase in export of wheat can be seen in the following figures: For the ten years before 1861, the United States sent 20 million bushels of wheat to foreign countries annually; in 1861, we exported 60 million.

How was this vast increase in farm output in the West and North possible with so many of the men in the Union forces? Three wartime developments

[30] Scheiber, "Economic Change in the Civil War Era . . . ," p. 411.

saved the harvests:[31] (1) There was an increased use of labor-saving machinery. "The War suddenly popularized methods of cultivation in which the agricultural papers had striven in vain for a decade to arouse interest." Reapers, mowers, horse-rakes, and the steel ploughs so necessary to cut through the tough prairie sod made their appearance in much larger numbers. (2) Women took the place of men in the fields. Travellers wrote of seeing more women driving teams on the road and at work in the fields than men. (3) There was a continued influx of new settlers. Large numbers of the immigrants went straight west to Wisconsin, Illinois, or other western states. Others fled from the border states where the fighting was intense to the West. And many eastern farmers, unable to meet the competition from the more fertile acres of the West, added to the exodus. The decline in the rural sections of New York State during these years was alarming to many of its inhabitants. This vast relocation of American farmers and farming is another illustration of Myrdal's spread and backwash effects; the rapid expansion of western agriculture constituted the spread, leaving in its backwash many eastern farmers who could not match the productivity of the new farms of the West. Many of them, as a consequence, abandoned their farms and moved toward the frontier.

The general agricultural prosperity of the West was due not only to the demands of close to a million men who were in the Union Army, but to the increasing population of the country as a whole. (The estimated population of the United States increased from 32.3 million in 1861 to 35.7 million in 1865.) Another factor contributing to the farm prosperity was the general economic buoyancy in the North during the war. The high prices that came from the issuance of the greenbacks and the Union's deficit financing were also, of course, stimulating to the farm economy of the North.

The Civil War was, in many respects, the first modern war in terms of its scale both in the employment of men and material. Karl Marx so described it in a vivid article that he wrote for the Vienna paper, *Die Presse*, in March of 1862:

> From whatever standpoint one regards it, the American Civil War presents a spectacle without parallel in the annals of military history. The vast extent of the disputed territory; the far-flung front of the lines of operation; the numerical strength of the hostile armies, the creation of which drew barely any support from a prior organizational basis; the fabulous costs of these armies; the manner of leading them and the general tactical and strategical principles in accordance with which the war is waged, are all new in the eyes of the European observer.[32]

We have quoted Marx on the Civil War because his article suggests the magnitude of the logistical task of mobilizing the resources to produce and

---

[31] E. D. Fite, *Social and Industrial Conditions in the North during the Civil War* (New York: The Macmillan Company, 1910).

[32] K. Marx and F. Engels, *The Civil War in the United States* (New York: International Publishers, Inc., 1937), p. 164.

supply such large numbers of men as were involved on both sides. It is obvious that the successful waging of a war of the dimensions of the War Between the States not only demanded some degree of industrialization, but required also the skills necessary to mobilize and deploy masses of men on the home front as well as on the moving lines of battle. The Civil War was not a total war in the sense that the entire economy of the North was geared to winning it, as has been the case in the World Wars of the twentieth century, but it did pose unprecedented problems of military procurement.

The War Department of the Union government sought to meet the needs of the men in the field by contracting with private business firms for the necessary supplies. The governors of some of the states were also involved in dealings with these contractors to provision the soldiers of their militia. The resulting competition was not conducive to efficiency, to say the least. The swindling and profiteering that resulted from the lax contract system made the "shoddy aristocracy" a term of public contempt. Shoddy was a coarse compound made up of the refuse and sweepings of the shops that was made into a semblance of cloth. Blankets or uniforms made from this stuff often disintegrated when exposed to the elements. The *nouveau riche* class of arms contractors, coal suppliers, railroad magnates, and other operators were all labelled by the public as "shoddy." This kind of business was very profitable to those engaged in it. "New England factories often declared dividends of from 10 to 40 per cent on watered stock, while the soldiers were picking feathers out of their woolen overcoats."[33]

In general, the effect of the war upon northern manufacturing was highly selective or uneven. Manufacturers of woolen cloth, leather products, some iron and steel items, agricultural machinery, and shoes, among others, prospered, but the cotton textile and railroad industries, so important before the war, lagged in their growth.

In mining and the other extractive industries, there was no more than ordinary progress. The petroleum industry had made its debut at Titusville, Pa. in 1859, but coal oil was more widely used during the war. Silver from the Comstock Lode, discovered in 1859 in Nevada, added greatly to the volume of precious metals flowing from the Colorado Territory and from Montana and Idaho to the East.

Technological advance was not especially outstanding during these years. There were no major improvements or inventions such as had sparked economic progress before the war. Instead, there were a variety of novelties adding to the convenience of life—clothes wringers, automatic fans, passenger elevators, fountain pens, knitting machines were among the novelties of the war era. The number of patents filed at the Patent Office rose, but at a much slower pace than before the war. From 1861 to 1864, the number of patents

[33] On the contract system in the North, see F. A. Shannon, *The Organization and Administration of the Union Army, 1861–65*, 2 vols. (Cleveland: The Arthur H. Clark Co., 1928); another excellent study is R. V. Bruce, *Lincoln and the Tools of War* (Indianapolis, Bobbs-Merrill, 1956).

issued annually increased less than 50 per cent, whereas for the five years before the war their number had doubled. Even in the field of armament, where one would expect considerable technical advance, innovations were not conspicuous. Both the Union and Confederacy continued to use the muzzle loading rifle; the Gatling gun, the forerunner of the machine gun, had been patented in 1862, but the Union Army did not use it until late in the war. Though there were no major technical "break-throughs," as we would say today, the state of the industrial arts in many fields continued to make steady progress; the conflict on the battlefield did not halt all progress in the arts of peace.

THE SOUTH BEHIND THE LINES

The secessionist states faced insuperable problems in trying to meet the demands of the war. In contrast to the North, they did not start with much in the way of established manufacturing industry, so they had to undertake the difficult task of creating new industrial capacity to meet their needs. The Confederate government encouraged private enterprises for this purpose by making loans, and it started government-owned plants as well. The separate states also sought to spur manufacturing activity, but the results were often disappointing. Basically, these efforts were hampered by the lack of skilled workers, ample machine shops, and raw materials. Still it is important to note some of the "war babies" that came into existence to meet the South's needs for military supplies. The production of iron for ships and guns was begun on a mass scale in Selma, Alabama; Charlotte, North Carolina; and in the famed Tredegar Iron Works at Richmond, Virginia. Garment manufacture was greatly expanded in some of the larger southern towns, using the women workers skilled in this line. Shoes were made in large quantities by the Quartermaster Department at Richmond as well. The needs of the civilian market also led to production of textiles, leather, saddles, paper, sewing machines, and liquor in a number of scattered enterprises. But many of these manufacturing plants ultimately were destroyed by the advancing Union army as part of its strategy of economic warfare. Nevertheless, while most of these infant industries of the South did not survive the destruction of the war, the "know-how" and experience in these areas were to play some role in the reconstruction of the South.

The critical needs of the Confederate Army in the field often went unfilled because of the shortages caused by the inexperience of southern industrialists or by the lack of adequate distribution facilities. Gross errors occurred in the production of weapons. Skilled workers, who were few in number, were either drafted or moved from firm to firm by labor raids. Since skilled labor was needed for the production of many goods, women, children, and slaves were taught machine operation. The result of this use of a marginal labor supply was frequent breakdowns in equipment. When such occurred, it was nearly impossible to replace the broken parts because the machine producers were frequently outside the South and practically impossible to reach through the northern blockade.

By 1863, Confederate recruits were expected to enter outfitted for service in the Army. They could expect no issuance of a uniform, weapons, or food. As soldiers, they were expected to forage for themselves. In an attempt to alleviate such scarcities as these, the South turned to setting price ceilings and using other price stabilization measures. But the prices usually proved unrealistic, and the black market flourished. The South, by 1864, no longer had the implements to wage war and was reduced to the use of primitive weapons. It was defeated as much or more by its weakness in logistics as by the defeats it suffered on the battlefield.

In order to supply its army, the Confederate government found it necessary to resort to a system of impressment of those goods deemed essential for the prosecution of the war. Impressment officers seized huge quantities of goods, which often rotted in warehouses because of the difficulty of directing them to their appropriate destinations. The Confederate leaders at Montgomery claimed that droughts, poor transportation facilities, the Union armies, and the blockade were to be blamed for the scarcity of goods. Such explanations, however, left the civilian population largely unconvinced.

In agriculture, the war forced the South, of course, to shift from cotton growing to food production because the blockade increasingly destroyed the market for the staple. This conversion was successfully made in many instances, but because of poor transportation facilities or hoarding, food supplies were often inadequate; the Army's shortages were chronic.

The production of cotton fell from a peak of 4,491,000 bales in 1861 to 299,000 by 1864. (English imports of cotton from the United States plummeted from 819.5 million pounds in 1861 to 6.4 million pounds in 1863. The United Kingdom's *total* imports, however, did not show nearly so great a reduction; the Kingdom was able to offset the loss of American cotton in considerable part by imports from Egypt and the East Indies.[34]) The agricultural sector of the southern economy was largely liquidated during the war. In addition to the cutback in cotton we have noted, the raising of horses, cows, swine, mules, oxen, and cattle fell to new lows. The southern agricultural economy was totally disrupted and heavily damaged.

The region's railroads, too, suffered extensively from the war. The northern armies seized about one-third of the mileage, destroying track and rolling stock and any conceivable asset. By the end of the fighting, the rest of the South's railway system was practically junk because provision had not been made for repair and replacement of worn-out facilities.

The devastation wrought by the long struggle was truly staggering. One-third of the South's livestock was destroyed. By 1865 farm machinery was

---

[34] For these statistics, see Andreano, *The Economic Impact* . . . , p. 198.

only about one-half of pre-war levels. The value of farms was reduced to about 60 per cent of their pre-war level. The banks of the South, which had an aggregate capital in 1860 of $51 million had been reduced to a total of $15 million. With over 60 per cent of its economy wiped out, the South at the end of the war had to feed essentially the same number of persons as in 1860. In per capita terms, the region's income fell to well under $100. It is little wonder that Professor Easterlin's studies of regional income show "the sharpest increase in regional inequality" between the North and South and occurring between 1860 and 1880, the period covering the Civil War and Reconstruction.[35] If the South had been the underdeveloped section of a dual economy in 1860, it was destined to remain in a similar state in the long post-war period in part because of the huge losses caused by the war.

---

[35] Williamson, "Regional Inequality . . .," p. 23. Easterlin's estimates of personal income per capita show the South's percentage falling from 72 in 1860 to 51 in 1880, while the Northeast rises from 139 to 141 and the North Central states from 68 to 98 over the same period of time. (Harris, *American Economic History*, p. 528.)

Chapter 15

FORCES UNDERLYING THE SECTIONAL DIVERGENCE IN ECONOMIC DEVELOPMENT

THE QUESTION OF DUALISM IN AMERICAN ECONOMIC DEVELOPMENT

In evaluating the validity of Myrdal's concept of economic dualism as applied to the American experience, the first question that arises is whether the conception of dualism is relevant and appropriate in an analysis of the ante-bellum economy. Is it a valid category as applied to a relatively advanced economy such as that of the United States? In connection with the latter query, we might note that students of the theory of dualism have seen it as existing in varying degree in all economies.[1] As to its existence in the United States and in particular in the pre-war economy, there have been two schools of thought. One group of scholars, more or less following Lewis Gray's theory of the origin of the plantation, describes the southern economy as planter capitalism. Gray had defined the southern plantation as a "capitalistic type of agricultural organization in which a considerable number of unfree laborers were employed under a unified direction and control in the production of a staple crop."[2] Since "the plantation system produced for a distant market, responded to supply and demand, invested capital in land and slaves, and operated with funds borrowed from banks and factors,"[3] it was as capitalistic as the operations of the northern merchants. In this view, consequently, there would not seem to be much basis for an analysis along dualistic lines.[4] The other view holds that the southern plantation economy had such distinctive

---

[1] B. Higgins, *Economic Development* (New York: W. W. Norton, 1959), p. 285; J. H. Boeke, *Economics and Economic Policy of Dual Societies* (Haarlem: H. D. Tjeenk Willink, 1953), *passim.*

[2] *History of Agriculture in the Southern United States to 1860* (Gloucester, Mass., 1958), Vol. 1, p. 302.

[3] Genovese, *The Political Economy of Slavery* (New York: Pantheon Books, 1965), p. 14.

[4] For a strong statement of this point of view, see T. P. Govan, "Was the Old South Different?" *Journal of Southern History* (November, 1955), pp. 447–455.

features that a dualistic approach to an understanding of American economic development in this period is justified.[5]

Historically, it is true that the southern plantation developed in the context of international capitalism and it grew and adjusted to many features of its capitalistic environment in the United States. However, it is questionable whether the presence of various commercial features such as profits, banks, etc., justifies viewing "planter capitalism" as having the same essential dynamics as industrial capitalism. To do so is to ignore the fact that the southern plantation system as an economic enterprise was deeply imbedded in a culture very different from the social framework surrounding the commercial and nascent industrial capitalism of the North.

> . . . The plantation society that began as an appendage of British capitalism ended as a powerful, largely autonomous civilization with aristocratic pretensions and possibilities, although it remained tied to the capitalist world by bonds of commodity production. The essential element in this distinct civilization was the slaveholders' domination, made possible by their command of labor. Slavery provided the basis for a special Southern economic and social life, special problems and tensions, and special laws of development.[6]

The plantation economy had many pseudo-capitalist features, such as a merchant class, some industrialists, and banks, but the operations of these groups were so subordinated in their practices, values, and attitudes to those of the dominant, slave-holding class that this type of economy functioned as a dynamic whole in a manner very different from the industrial capitalism of the North or the small farmer capitalism of the West. It is not too strong a statement to say that

> The planters were not mere capitalists; they were pre-capitalist, quasi-aristocratic landowners who had to adjust their economy and ways of thinking to a capitalist world market. Their society, in its spirit and its fundamental direction, represented the antithesis of capitalism, however many compromises it had to make. . . . The essential features of Southern particularity, as well of Southern backwardness, can be traced to the relationship of master to slave.[7]

Not to be forgotten in any comparison or contrast of the "capitalistic" economies of the two regions in the pre-war period was the fact that many of the southern yeomen and "poor whites" or hillbillies were living on a subsistence basis. In that respect, the South and the growing money economy of

---

[5] Supporters of this approach, among others, include A. H. Conrad and J. R. Meyer, *The Economics of Slavery* (Chicago: Aldine Publishing Co., 1964), pp. 230–231, J. G. Williamson, "Regional Inequality and the Process of National Development," *Economic Development and Cultural Change*, Vol. XIII, No. 4, Part II (July, 1965), p. 23 and D. F. Dowd (see *The Economics of Slavery, op. cit.*, pp. 93–97).

[6] Genovese, *The Political Economy of Slavery*, pp. 15–16.

[7] *Ibid.*, p. 23. Professor Dowd had earlier stated very cogently the relationship between slavery and rational capitalism: ". . . The 'available productive surplus from slavery' could not exist apart from the social milieu required for the maintenance of slavery. If profits were made from the slave system, it was at a price: the domination of Southern society by the slave issue. This in turn meant the suppression of that kind of rationality which has been, for better or for worse, associated with the development of industrial capitalism." (Conrad and Meyer, *The Economics of Slavery*, pp. 94–95.)

the North presented the elements of dualism in a guise very similar to that found in other underdeveloped parts of the world and for the explanation of which the dualistic theory was first formulated. The question, indeed, might be posed as to why the poor whites of the South who were living on this degraded, subsistence basis, as Hinton R. Helper showed so vividly in his book *The Impending Crisis of the South* (1857), were not drawn more rapidly into the market economy in which the plantations operated. This way of looking at the subject presents the issue of dualism as one internal to the southern economy. If more southerners than Helper had done so, perhaps the sad history of the South would have been different. But to understand why they didn't as a whole and just what that internal dualism portended we need to look more closely at the cultural context of the plantation system. We need to employ the anthropologist's concepts of culture and social structure to appreciate the differences between the subcultures of the ante-bellum South and those of the North and West.

THE SLAVE-PLANTATION CULTURE

The plantation system of agriculture in the South was the major economic and social institution of a very distinctive culture. The white man who grew up in that society and who was ambitious socially, economically, or politically sought to acquire slaves and establish a plantation. This way of life had been started in the South during colonial times when many younger sons of middle or upper class background found themselves either because of politics or ill luck drawn to America. They brought with them the ideal of English country life in which the owners of broad acres constituted the dominant class in government and in society. So it was that the descendants of these early colonial planters who had inherited or acquired plantations themselves strove to maintain the aristocratic way of life. They laid far more stress on family, land, agreeable manners, and political power than on the mere accumulation of wealth. In their long days on the plantation they sought to cherish social life as an art.

> . . . Theirs was an aristocratic, antibourgeois spirit with values and mores emphasizing family and status, a strong code of honor, and aspirations to luxury, ease, and accomplishment. In the planters' community paternalism provided the standard of human relationships, and politics and statecraft were the duties and responsibilities of gentlemen. The gentleman lived for politics, not, like the bourgeois politician, off politics.[8]

The southern planter was acquisitive, but his acquisitiveness was directed toward ends peculiar to a slave society: the accumulation of slaves and the achievement of military and political status. For his was a status or hierarchical society in contrast to the contractual society of the North or West.

[8] Genovese, *The Political Economy of Slavery*, p. 28.

The maintenance of his status as a plantation owner required a style of life that exuded authority and gained respect. In ideal type terms, his relations to his inferiors were patriarchal and paternalistic rather than the more impersonal, cash nexus relationships of advanced industrial capitalism. (In modern sociological terminology, we would say that the planter's culture tended to be a particularistic one, especially in his dealings within the plantation.[9] The slaves were his people, these men were his foremen, etc., and he did not regard them wholly as interchangeable entities; this is in contrast to the norms of an advanced capitalistic society, which tends to stress universalistic values of impersonal efficiency and ignores the specific or status kinship relationship of the participants in the employment contract.) Likewise, the attitudes of the southern planters with regard to spending and saving often differed markedly from the more middle class orientation of businessmen or farmers in the North. One Mississippian summed up the difference between the two when he said: "The Northerner loves to make money, the Southerner to spend it."

The southern gentleman with his broad acres, his slaves, refined manners, and political power was the culture hero of this society, not the businessman. His ideals dominated southern life. "To become a large planter was the aspiration of every ambitious youth. Some nursed this ambition in the squalor of humble hill-country cabins, others in the luxury of comfortable city homes, while the elect awaited their inevitable inheritance on their paternal estates. . . ."[10] Even the rough, new planters of the western part of the Cotton Kingdom, the "Southern Yankees," aped the style and manners of the Virginia gentleman; only in their primitive acquisitiveness did they differ from their models. But while many aspired to this seignorial style of life, relatively few achieved the powerful status of slaveholder. Actually, most of the larger planters in the Old South probably had inherited their estates rather than acquiring them; though the inheritors often added to the size of their holdings, both of land and of slaves, in their lifetime.

THE SOCIAL STRUCTURE OF THE PLANTATION SOCIETY

The slave society of the ante-bellum South rested upon a caste system composed of the subjugated Negro slaves, who numbered 3,950,511 out of a total Negro population of over four million, as of 1860. The owners of slaves in the South in the same year numbered 383,635 out of approximately 1,400,000 white families; the total white population of the South at that time was somewhat more than seven million (7,033,973, according to the Census). Of course, many whites owned no slaves at all. The distribution of slave ownership in terms of the number of slaves owned in the South as of 1860 is

[9] For these sociological concepts, see T. Parsons, *The Social System* (Glencoe, Ill.: Free Press, 1951).

[10] A. C. Cole, *The Irrepressible Conflict, 1850–1865* (New York: The Macmillan Co., 1934), pp. 34–35.

presented in Table 1. If we define the status of a plantation owner as requiring the ownership of at least 20 field hands, then only 46,274 slaveholders so qualified. The majority of slaveholders, it can be seen from the table, held less than 10 slaves; these slaveholders were not planters in the general sense of the term, but middle class farmers — who often worked in the fields beside their slaves.

TABLE 1

Number of Slaveholders by Class in the South, 1860[a]

Over 1,000 slaves	1
500–1,000 slaves	13
100–500 slaves	2,278
50–100 slaves	8,366
20–50 slaves	35,616
10–20 slaves	61,682
1–9 slaves	275,679
Total slaveholders	383,635

[a] Source: U.S. Census, *Agriculture of the United States in 1860*, p. 247.

The hierarchal status society of the South had the form of a pyramid in terms of the number of people in the different classes. At the top of the pyramid stood the plantation aristocrats, the owners of 200 or more slaves; there were only 300 planters in this class. Next came the middle class, made up of smaller slaveholding planters, professional men, tradesmen, and skilled mechanics. Below them were the yeomen, vastly greater in numbers than the large planters, but insignificant in their political power. These were the small farmers who lived on the hilly fringes of the Black Belt where they raised a variety of crops and lived on "hog and hominy." They strove to become slaveholders and when they did so they were extremely proud. Far below these independent farmers were the "poor whites," proud but ignorant people who usually consumed more than they produced. They were the chronically unemployed; their numbers ran into the hundreds of thousands, but the exact total is difficult to estimate. Underneath all these classes, of course, were the Negroes, slave or free.

Apart from the occasional slave uprisings, the most important of which was the Nat Turner rebellion of 1831, the southern slave society was surprisingly stable. Even though the slave system raised ever higher barriers to whites who might aspire to be owners, and the number of the poor white class grew, there was little disposition to challenge the established order. Hinton Helper in 1857 challenged "the lords of the lash" and assailed them as the foes "of all non-slaveholding whites, whose freedom is merely nominal, and whose unparalleled illiteracy and degradation is purposely and fiendishly perpetrated." But Helper failed to arouse the white masses. The "chief paradox of the Southern social system" was that, despite their exploitation and poverty, so many white people were drawn into some sort of active support of the "peculiar institution."[11]

THE PECULIARITY OF AMERICAN SLAVERY

In studying slavery in the American South, it is especially important to view the institution in its cultural context. Chattel slavery in this country before the Civil War was in many fundamental respects unique, *sui generis*. As compared, for example, with slavery in Latin America, the American species of bondage was in many of its features harsher and more uncompromising than in Brazil or Spanish America.[12] In the latter, as a whole, the remnants of feudalism protected the slave; in the United States, on the other hand, the weakness of certain countervailing institutions as against the pressures of plantation capitalism tended to reduce the African to the actual status of a commodity, a "piece of mere property." Part of the reason for this was that when Virginia was settled the English middle class was in the process of reducing the power of those institutions, such as the crown and the church, which most directly limited the drive toward personal success and upward mobility. The capitalist planter in the English colonies who came through the hard times of 1660–80 found that he had to operate on a large scale and with complete control of his labor supply. It was in this situation that the legal status of the American slave was fixed.[13] The master had to have absolute power over the slave's body, and the law developed in such a way as to give it to him in most essential respects. As contrasted with the white servant, the Negro's state had been more and more depressed to a state of perpetual slavery. This fact was finally recognized by the legislatures of Maryland and Virginia, which definitively established the Negro slave's legal status. According to a Maryland law of 1663, "All Negroes or other slaves within the province, and all Negroes and other slaves to be hereafter imported into the province, shall serve *durante vita*; and all children born of any Negro or other slave, shall be slaves as their fathers were for the term of their lives."[14]

Under this legal interpretation the master was given almost unlimited power

---

[11] A. C. Cole, *The Irrepressible Conflict*, p. 38.

[12] See the brilliant study by Stanley M. Elkins, *Slavery, A Problem in American Institutional and Intellectual Life* (New York: Grosset and Dunlap, 1963). Elkin shows in a striking way the value of an interdisciplinary approach to this subject; we have relied heavily on his treatment in much of the above. For a position critical of the Tannenbaum-Elkins view, see D. B. Davis, *The Problem of Slavery in Western Culture* (Ithaca, N.Y.: Cornell University Press, 1966). On Elkins' thesis, see E. D. Genovese, "Rebelliousness and Docility in the Negro Slave: A Critique of the Elkins' Thesis," *Civil War History* (December, 1967), pp. 293–314.

[13] See on this, O. and M. F. Handlin, "Origins of the Southern Labor System," *William and Mary Quarterly*, 3rd Series (April, 1950), pp. 199–222.

[14] J. C. Hurd, *The Law of Freedom and Bondage in the United States* (Boston: Little, Brown and Co., 1958), quoted in Elkins, *Slavery . . .*, p. 40.

to use physical discipline to control the slave. The condition of the bondsman's soul—a subject of concern in the Spanish colonies—was here very quickly disregarded. Conversion to Christianity made no difference in the slave's status. The slave's family life or his marriage had no legal or moral recognition. As against the pressures of profitable management and consideration of the interests of the slave:

> . . . there were no counter-weights: those interests were unsupported by any social pressures from the outside; they were cherished by no customary feudal immunities; they were no concern of the government (the king's main interest was in tobacco revenue) ; they could not be sustained by the church, for the church had little enough power and influence among its own white constituencies, to say nothing of the suspicion its ministers aroused at every proposal to enlarge the church's work among the blacks. The local planter class controlled all those public concerns that most affected the daily life of the colony, and it was thus only in matters of the broadest and most general policy that this planter domination was in any way touched by bureaucratic decisions made in London. The emergent institution of slavery was in effect unchallenged by any other institutions.[15]

In Brazil and Spanish America, the status of the slave was not nearly as precise or as irrevocable as it was in the American colonies. His servitude was not for life and "for all generations." In fact, the presumption was, in cases of doubt, that a colored person was considered to be free rather than a slave. The slave's moral and familial life was given legal and religious sanction and support. Manumission was recognized by the state and the church and the freedman had no difficulty in taking his place in free society. Finally, it should be noted that when general emancipation took place in these Latin American countries, it occurred "without violence, without bloodshed, and without civil war."[16]

This sketch of slavery in the different societies of America demonstrates one basic point: "The presence or absence of other powerful institutions in society made an immense difference in the character of slavery itself. . . ."[17] In the United States, slavery operated as a "closed" system in the sense that there were few if any institutions that mediated between the coercive, overwhelming power of the plantation system and the personality of the slave. The latter adapted to the pressures and expectations of this system in such a way as to produce a recognizable personality type.[18] The stereotype of the irresponsible, childish Negro had its origins in the demands and conditions of an institution

---

[15] Elkin, *Slavery* . . . , pp. 50–51.

[16] F. Tannenbaum, *Slave and Citizen, The Negro in the Americas* (New York: Knopf, 1947), p. 106 quoted in *ibid.* For a contrary view of the duration of slavery in Latin America, see D. B. Davis, *The Problem of Slavery in Western Culture* (Ithaca, N.Y.: Cornell University Press, 1966), p. 226, footnote 2.

[17] *Ibid.*, p. 81. The point involved here is widely accepted in modern sociology and anthropology, namely, that an institution can only be understood in its whole cultural context. See, for a memorable analysis of this, R. Benedict, *Patterns of Culture* (Boston: Houghton Mifflin Co., 1934).

[18] On this and the subject of the next sentence, see Elkin, *Slavery*, Chap. 3.

that have been likened to those of the Nazi concentration camp. Of course, in its historical evolution the American plantation developed traditions and mores differing from those of the early colonial plantations. There were also considerable variations among slaveholders in their treatment of chattels, but historically it is known that the system became more repressive when the challenge to its existence became real. Some aspects of this development will be dealt with in the following chapter.

THE ECONOMICS OF SLAVERY

Negro slaves were used in the production of four staple crops of the South—cotton, sugar cane, rice, and tobacco—but since cotton was, in income terms, the most important for the region, we shall restrict our treatment to it. The cultivation requirements and the production functions that were possible in its growth and harvesting made slave labor particularly suitable. Cotton required a large amount of simple, routine labor in preparation of the seedbed, planting, weeding, cultivating, and picking. This labor was spread over most of the months of the year, and it could be easily supervised. When not so occupied the slaves were used in clearing new lands, building fences, and making general repairs. Since a slave could usually cultivate a greater cotton acreage than he could pick, it was common to use him in growing corn also. In 1850 it was the practice on many plantations to have the average field worker tend ten acres of cotton and ten acres of corn.

Cotton was grown on farms operated by small farmers or yeomen and on plantations of varying size. U. B. Phillips, a famous student of slavery, suggested that a plantation should be defined as a unit that required a minimum of 20 field hands since this was the smallest number of slaves for which it was profitable to hire an overseer. If we employ the figure of 20 acres as the amount of arable land a slave could cultivate, then practical plantation management would require not less than 400 acres. If, in addition, we allow for waste land and forest, it can be seen that the smallest plantation would be likely to amount to 700 or 800 acres. Actually, many plantations were much larger than this; in the cane-growing region of Louisiana, for example, there were plantations of from 20,000 to 400,000 acres cultivated by hundreds of slaves.

In cotton growing, the large plantations using slave labor increasingly ousted the white yeoman farmers. Under the practices of cultivation used in the early nineteenth century, which were aptly described as "soil mining," little attention was paid to fertilizer or improving the soil. With cheap land and a slave labor supply, it paid the plantation owners to practice extensive farming. They bought up big tracts and when the soil was depleted (the sandy coastal plain had poor soil to begin with; it was highly leached by heavy rainfall), the big planters purchased new land from the small, free farmers or moved on to the more fertile lands of the Southwest. The rich, virgin soils of Alabama's Black Belt and the river bottom lands of Mississippi could produce much higher yields—over 500 pounds an acre—than the land in the eastern, coastal states. By 1860, Mississippi, Alabama, and Louisiana raised over half of the total crop of the nation. (See map.)

The shifts in the location of the cotton-growing areas growing out of the comparative advantage of the crop in different places caused serious problems of economic adjustment. One can see in these movements the familiar spread and backwash effects that Myrdal speaks of. For example, when cotton growing spread into the Piedmont region of Georgia and the Carolinas in the years from 1795 to 1819, the old Dominion, Virginia, and Maryland became high cost regions. Their exhausted soils could not compete so well with the new lands enjoying the spread effects of expansion. But then after 1819, with the fall in cotton prices after that year, and the opening of the fertile lands of the Southwest, South Carolina began to feel the backwash of this new western expansion.[19] The familiar symptoms of a declining area caught up in regional competition made their appearance: population migration and loss of capital. Between 1820 and 1860 the state lost more than 200,000 whites and 170,000 slaves through emigration; the former figure was probably nearly half of those born in the state after 1800. In 1849 Governor Hammond estimated that the value of property and cash assets that had been removed from the state since 1820 was $90 million, though this figure may be high. This export of capital and the failure of the planters to diversify are thought to have perpetuated the plight of the "poor whites," thus further intensifying the relatively slow development of the state. With slower economic growth and expansion elsewhere, South Carolina experienced a loss of political influence as well. In the years from 1810 to 1840 the state had nine Congressmen, from 3.1 to 4.9 per cent of the total number of representatives in the lower House. By 1860, she was entitled to only four Congressmen and they constituted a mere 1.7 per cent of the total in Washington. The politicians and many of the people of the Palmetto State did not take kindly to this relative loss of economic and political power; Charleston did not relish being outstripped by other cities of the Atlantic seaboard. There was probably a strong sense of being displaced, and all the resentment that usually goes with that experience.

With the growth in the production of cotton and other staples in which slave labor was used, and the end of legal importation of slaves in 1808, there was a marked tendency for the price of slaves to rise. About 1790 the price of a prime field hand was $200–300; by 1830 it had risen to approximately $800 and in 1850 to $1,200. Ten years later the prices of slaves ranged from $1,200 to $2,000. The rising trend in slave prices after 1850 reflected the shortage of the supply relative to the growing demand. Despite the natural increase in the slave population between 1790 and 1860, which was more than

---

[19] A. G. Smith, Jr., *Economic Readjustment of an Old Cotton State, South Carolina, 1820–1860* (Columbia, S.C.: University of South Carolina Press, 1958), *passim*.

MAP

*Geographic Expansion of Cotton Production in the United States,
1821 and 1859*[a]

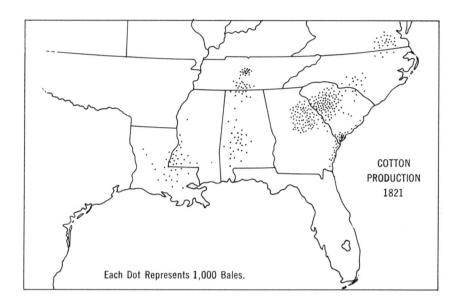

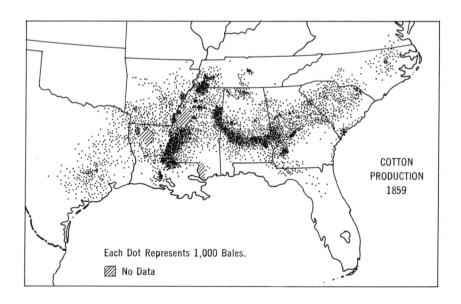

Source: L. C. Gray, *History of Agriculture in the Southern United States to 1860* (Washington,
D.C.: Carnegie Institution, 1933), pp. 684 and 891.

3,256,000, and the 270,000 estimated to have been smuggled in after 1808, the price of prime field hands continued to rise. This mounting cost of slaves put the small slaveholders under a great handicap. There had developed in the border states of the South, particularly Maryland, Virginia, and the Carolinas, a practice of selling their surplus slaves to the deep South. During the 1850's alone, it is estimated that 50,000 to 80,000 slaves were moved from the surplus area to the lower South. A conflict of interest arose between the two regions over the re-opening of the slave trade late in the pre-bellum period; the plantation owners of the deep South favored it, on the whole, while the Border states naturally opposed. At the last of the southern commercial conventions in 1859, the advocates of re-opening the African slave trade won the day, but before much was done along that line, the War Between the States had begun.

The economic problems of the South and the region's sense of losing ground to the advancing North and West led to a search for solutions. Among those much discussed was the need for agricultural reform and, in particular, for crop diversification. These efforts were, on the whole, a failure. Reform was achieved in only a few localities below Virginia. The planters generally did not show great interest in the subject. The number of agricultural societies and periodicals in the South were significantly lower, even in relative terms, than in the North. "In general, Southern agricultural societies were dominated by planters who were more interested in social activities than practical affairs and who preferred raising race horses to raising work animals."[19]

The expansion of the cotton growing region into the Southwest and the political conflicts in the 1850's between the supporters of slavery and its opponents led some to believe that slavery was doomed because of the scarcity of new land. For example, Marx was of the opinion that the confinement of the system to its boundaries as of 1850 would be its undoing. More recent study of this question suggests, however, that there was still plenty of land for additional farms and cotton plantations. There was still a great deal of unimproved land in the Southwest Central states, which have since been developed for cotton growing and were available for settlement in 1860. Rather than a shortage of land, the main threat to the spread of the slavocracy was the underemployment of its labor supply and the scarcity of capital.

The profitability of slavery has been a standard topic for discussion and debate for many years. Historians such as U. B. Phillips and C. W. Ramsdell argued that slavery was so inefficient that, given time, it would topple of its own weight. L. C. Gray and, more recently, Kenneth Stampp have rejected this view, holding that southern agriculture was at least as profitable as most business enterprises. The orthodox arguments for holding that slavery was unprofitable included the following:

> (i) slaves are notoriously inefficient and unwilling workers; (ii) slave property, unlike wage labor, must be supported in the years before and after the

[19] Genovese, *Political Economy of Slavery*, p. 128.

slave is economically productive; (iii) slaveholding absorbed plantation earnings; (iv) slave economies are constantly threatened by decline because they cannot in general maintain the number of slaves; (v) capitalization of the labor force inhibits the efficient allocation of labor.[20]

We shall not consider these arguments in detail here, but rather refer to a treatment of the subject that raised it to a new plane of analytical rigor. Conrad and Meyer did this by attempting to measure the profitability of slavery according to economic, as opposed to accounting, concepts.[21] They defined slavery as having two production functions—one relating the inputs of slaves (and the materials required to maintain them) to produce cotton, and the other having to do with the production of the slaves themselves. They sought to compare the marginal efficiency of slave capital to the rate of interest currently available in American capital markets. Their approach was essentially one of trying to measure the profitability of the system as a whole rather than the profit to be made by individual slaveholders. After calculating the parameters in their production functions, they concluded that slavery was about as remunerative as alternative profit opportunities available to the slaveholder. "The breeding returns were necessary, however, to make the plantation operations on the poorer land as profitable as alternative contemporary economic activity in the United States."[22]

In reaching their conclusions, Conrad and Meyer show that the view advanced by Ulrich B. Phillips and others, that the planters' profits were being squeezed by the rising price of slaves and the secular decline in the price of cotton in the pre-war years was fallacious. (See Chart 1.) That view altogether ignored the increase in the productivity of cotton production. Chart 1 shows that there was almost a fivefold growth in productivity (value of cotton output per head) between 1815 and 1860.

These authors concluded, therefore, that rather than being "on its last legs, slavery in the immediate ante bellum years was . . . an economically viable institution in virtually all areas of the South as long as the slaves could be expeditiously and economically transferred from one sector to another."[23]

[20] A. H. Conrad and J. R. Meyer, *The Economics of Slavery* (Chicago: Aldine Publishing Co., 1964), p. 67. The authors identify the supporters of these arguments respectively as (i) J. E. Cairnes, *The Slave Power* (New York: Follet Foster and Co., 1863), pp. 44–50; F. L. Olmstead, *The Cotton Kingdom* (New York: Mason Bros., 1861), pp. 100–110 (1953 Ed., New York: A. A. Knopf); W. Lewis, *Theory of Economic Growth* (Homewood, Ill.: Richard D. Irwin, Inc., 1955), pp. 107–8; (ii) U. B. Phillips, *Life and Labor in the Old South* (Boston: Little, Brown and Co., 1935), pp. 174–175; (iii) U. B. Phillips, "The Economic Cost of Slaveholding in the Cotton-Belt," *Political Science Quarterly*, XX (1905), 257–275; (iv) Lewis, *op. cit.*, pp. 111–113; (v) J. S. Duesenberry, "Some Aspects of the Theory of Economic Development," *Explorations in Entrepreneurial History*, III (1950), 9. The authors add: "This is, of course, intended only as a list of examples, chosen on the grounds that they are particularly well stated." (*Ibid.*, p. 111.)

[21] "The Economics of Slavery in the Ante Bellum South," *Journal of Political Economy* (April, 1958), pp. 95–122 (reproduced in *The Economics of Slavery*, pp. 43–92).

[22] *Ibid.*, p. 82.

[23] *Ibid.*, p. 66.

CHART 1

Slave Population and Prices and the Value of Cotton Production, 1802–60

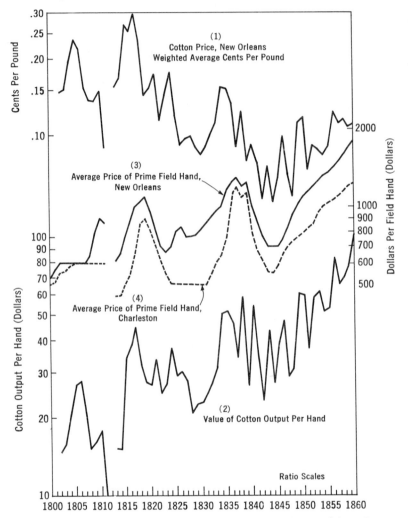

Source: Estimated visually from graph in U. B. Phillips, *Life and Labor in the Old South*, p. 177.

The Conrad and Meyer approach to the profitability of slavery has, however, a serious limitation, and some of the incidental remarks of these authors on the indirect effects of slavery are not substantiated by evidence. They concern themselves with the profitability of slavery as a business and relatively ignore the effects of this type of enterprise on the southern economy as a whole.[24] We shall explore some of these indirect effects below.[25]

All the above has had to do with the production economics of cotton

[24] This view was challenged by E. D. Genovese in his "The Significance of the Slave Plantation for Southern Economic Development," *Journal of Southern History* (Novem-

growing under slavery, but we need to understand also the distribution or marketing methods used by the southern planters. They had come to depend since colonial times on the so-called factor system. These factors who usually had their base in New York served not only as merchants but as bankers and brokers as well. They advanced long-term credit to the planters during the growing season and took a crop lien as collateral. They sold the crop on a commission basis and also bought, for a fee, any merchandise they might want. This system often led the planters to overproduce because they were pressed by the factors to grow enough to cover their debts. The wholly dependent relationship did much to foster the reliance on a single cash crop, monoculture, which stood in the way of a more diversified, better balanced agriculture. Indeed, the cotton planters in the pre-war years, were, as a whole, caught in the "staple trap."[26] Its nature, as applied to South Carolina before the War, has been described as follows:

> Basically, the State was caught in a trap with regard to attempts to alter the structure of the economy. As long as cotton could be produced at a profit, however modest that profit might be, the advantages of growing cotton seemed to be greater than those for any other crop. An allied factor was that in times past it had presented the best chance to make a fortune, which was the case with no other crop except rice and indigo. There was consequently an inclination to continue to plant cotton with the thought ever in mind of the grower that "next year" would bring his long awaited success.[27]

THE POLARIZING TENDENCIES AT WORK

In explaining the relative inequality of income and development between the North and South in the pre-war years, we shall consider the applicability of Myrdal's theory of regional polarization. We might begin by recalling his observation that "the movements of labor, capital, goods and services do not by themselves counteract the natural tendency to regional inequality. By themselves, migration, capital movements and trade are rather the media through which the cumulative process evolves—upward in the lucky regions and downward in the unlucky ones. In general, if they have positive effects for the former, their effects on the latter are negative."[28] Myrdal's vision of the developmental process conceives of expansion in one locality (spread effects) having backwash effects in other localities. Let us see how far such a theory will take us in explaining the disparity in the regional development of the North and South before the war.

Certainly it would be agreed that the northern complex of an expanding

---

ber, 1962), pp. 422–437 (reproduced in his *The Political Economy of Slavery*, pp. 157–179). Also see H. D. Woodman, "The Profitability of Slavery: A Historical Perennial," *The Journal of Southern History* (August, 1963), pp. 303–325.

[25] See below, pp. 357–360.

[26] See above, p. 136.

[27] A. G. Smith, Jr., *Economic Readjustment of an Old Cotton State, op. cit.*, p. 59.

[28] Myrdal, *Rich Lands and Poor*, p. 27.

agriculture, booming commerce and finance, and rapid manufacturing development enjoyed many of the benefits of Myrdal's spread effects. This is best illustrated in the remarkable rise of the commerce of the port of New York City and its related residentiary and supplementary industries. In the years 1815–25, New York gained a headstart on the other Atlantic port cities that put most of them, including the southern ones, very much in a shadow. In Myrdal's terms, New York's expansion created backwash effects, particularly for certain southern ports and localities.

> . . . New York alone [of the Atlantic ports] struck while the iron was hot, to make the streams of commerce flow to its wharves. It drew to itself the three major trade routes—from Europe, from the Southern ports, and from the West. Without producing many of the important articles of commerce itself, New York made itself into an entrepot where goods of every sort from every place were exchanged and the New Yorkers grew rich from the profits, commissions, freights, and other excuses for levying toll upon that volume of business. . . .[29]

In 1822, in less than ten months New York packet service to Liverpool underwent a fourfold expansion. The population of the Empire City grew more than eightfold between 1810 and 1860; its exports multiplied by fourteen times and its imports grew from $23 million to $248 million over the years 1815–60.[30] With this growth in the volume of their business, New York mercantile and banking houses gained substantial internal and external economies of scale that enabled them to extend credit to southern factors for as long as twelve months, a term of loan that few competitors could match.

The impact of New York's expansion on the other Atlantic and Gulf ports varied; some were definitely left behind; others, such as New Orleans, continued to grow, but more slowly than might otherwise have been the case. Charleston, South Carolina, was one city whose foreign commerce suffered severely. In the eighteenth century, that city had enjoyed an important foreign trade. On the eve of the Revolution, in fact, it stood third among American ports and had a greater volume of business than New York. In those days it received its imports directly from Europe without the aid of northern merchants. But in the years after 1819, Charleston's imports shrank from an average of $2 million annually during the years 1821–25 to $1.4 million between 1856–60. Her exports by 1856–60 (annual average) were less than double what they had been in the years 1816–20. The number of ships engaged in foreign trade owned by Charlestonians was about the same in 1854 as it had been in 1838, and many of these were built in northern ports.[31] In the early 1850's two efforts were made to establish direct trade with Amsterdam and Brussels, but when these ventures failed, Charleston fell back into its

[29] Albion, *Rise of New York Port*, p. 10.

[30] *Ibid.*, pp. 390–391, 419.

[31] *Ibid.*, also J. G. Van Deusen, *Economic Bases of Disunion in South Carolina*, Columbia University Series in History, Economics and Public Law, No. 305 (New York: Columbia University Press, 1928), pp. 183, 185, 204, 209. On Charleston as a port before the Revolution, see L. Sellers, *Charleston Business on the Eve of the American Revolution* (Chapel Hill: University of North Carolina Press, 1934), *passim.*

usual routine of relying on northern shipping and merchants for much of her foreign trade.

The South's general dependence on the North became a matter of concern by 1837 when the first of the southern commercial conventions met at Augusta, Georgia. The solutions most frequently offered, apart from establishing direct trade with Europe, were discriminatory taxation of northern products, agricultural diversification, and promotion of local manufactures. As we have noted earlier there had been some development of cotton textile production and processing of staples in the South, the former occurring during the hard times of 1840–50. But starting in the latter year and extending to 1854, cotton manufacturers, both North and South, were in a profit squeeze—the price of the raw material was rising at the same time that the prices of finished textiles were falling in response to increased supply; Great Britain, after the Tariff Act of 1846, had shipped more textiles here, and northern output had greatly increased. The low returns on capital in southern industry after 1852 discouraged further investment; there was little interest in cotton manufacturing until almost the eve of the war.

Southern producers of this and other products faced fundamental difficulties. Apart from insufficient capital and the disadvantage of a late start, the great weakness was lack of southern patronage. The low cost of manufacturing in the North, the wider range of goods to be found in New York, and their established quality—having come "from New York" they were known to possess merit[32]—all these factors reflecting the backwash effects of the North's earlier industrial expansion made southern diverification into manufacturing exceedingly difficult. In addition, there was opposition to manufacturing in influential quarters from such men as Cheves, McDuffie, and Calhoun. The opponents of manufacturing thought that it would mean developing free labor with possible adverse effects on slavery; it would lead to demands for protection that would compromise the free trade philosophy of many southerners.

The South's efforts to escape her "economic vassalage" to the North through developing local manufacturing were not eminently successful, though some significant starts had been made. South Carolinians were especially bitter because they suffered from backwash effects in agriculture as well as in commerce and manufacturing.

> Again and again attempts had been made to establish the economic independence of the state. Almost universally such attempts had met with failure. Steamship lines to Europe failed for lack of business. Southern manufactures failed for want of patronage. Southern mechanics starved for want of employment. Some of her railroads failed because of conflict of local selfish interests. Those which did succeed did not accomplish the object of making Charleston an European port. Northern steamship lines had extended southward and used the railroads concentrating upon Charleston as feeders to carry the commerce to New York. Each succeeding failure only increased the bitterness which South Carolina felt toward her successful rivals.[33]

[32] Van Deusen, *Economic Bases of Disunion in South Carolina*, p. 214; see also Russel, *Economic Aspects of Southern Sectionalism, 1840–61*, pp. 60–1.

[33] Van Deusen, *Economic Bases . . .*, p. 329.

As the turbulent fifties drew to their close and the sectional conflict became more intense, sentiments such as those uttered by one southern editor in October, 1859, were more frequently heard: "So long as the Union lasts, Charleston and Savannah will be mere suburbs of New York and Boston. For our cities to be independent in trade, they must be independent politically of the North."[34]

To many such southerners, trade in itself did not promote their region's development; it had, rather, increased its economic dependence on an ever more powerful North. In their opinion, it had had this effect not only because of what Myrdal termed backwash effects, but because the trade with the North since the passage of the first protective tariff and the establishment of bounties for the fisheries had been inequitable and worked to the detriment of the South. The northern manufacturer, they pointed out, enjoyed free trade with the South, but under the successive tariff laws the South was not able to import without paying tariff duties that added considerably to its cost of living. At the same time southern exports were jeopardized because her European customers were often debarred from the American market by the nation's prohibitive import duties. Threatened by inadequate dollar exchange, such nations were stimulated to look elsewhere for supplies of raw cotton. Furthermore, the shares contributed in the form of tariff revenue to the federal government by the North and South were altogether disproportionate, to the South's great disadvantage. And the monies so raised were spent on fortifications, lighthouses, and internal improvements in proportions considered to be most discriminatory and unjust to their region.

In the 1850's calculating the value of the Union became popular among southern disunionists. It became common also to compute the "tribute" in the way of profit that northern business levied on the South. Thus, one capable southern partisan calculated "the annual load which Southern industry is required to carry," apart from the $60 million that he alleged the North drew from the earnings of the other sections. These profits were approximated as follows:[35]

Bounties to fisheries, per annum	$ 1,500,000
Customs per annum, disbursed at the North	40,000,000
Profits of Manufacturers	30,000,000
" Importers	16,000,000
" Shipping, imports and exports	40,000,000
" on Travellers	60,000,000
" of Teachers, and others, at the South, sent North	5,000,000
" Agents, brokers, commissions, etc.	10,000,000
" Capital drawn from the South	30,000,000
Total from these sources	$231,500,000

[34] *Mercury* (October 3, 1959), quoted in *ibid.*, p. 218.
[35] T. P. Kettel, *Southern Wealth and Northern Profits* (New York: G. W. and J. A. Wood, 1860), p. 127.

Myrdal has argued that the movement of capital does not by itself counteract the tendency to regional inequality; instead, he says, it has the effect of increasing it.

> . . . In the centers of expansion increased demand will spur investment, which in turn will increase incomes and demand and cause a second round of investment, and so on. . . . Studies in many countries have shown how the banking system, if not regulated to act differently, tends to become an instrument for siphoning off the savings from the poorer regions to the richer and more progressive ones where returns on capital are high and secure.[36]

This trend toward regional inequality is exactly what many southerners believed was happening to the South. They saw the polarizing forces causing capital to accumulate in the North and become scarce in the South. Kettel explicitly recognized a cumulative tendency in the movement of capital in these words: ". . . The heavy drain of capital . . . prevents an accumulation at the South, and promotes it effectively at the North, where every such accumulation only accelerates the drain. . . ."[37] It is to be noted that this view saw the polarizing tendency working both ways in a circular fashion as Myrdal suggests: the economic dependency of the South fostered the expansion of the North, the expansion of the North made the South further dependent. It is also relevant to the Myrdal thesis, of course, to observe that many southerners described their relationship to the North as being a colonial one, with all that implied politically for a people who had rebelled against such a status in its earlier history.

Myrdal contends that population movement also contributes as a polarizing force to regional inequality. "The localities and regions where economic activity is expanding will attract net immigration from other parts of the country. As migration is always selective, at least with respect to the migrant's age, this movement by itself tends to favor the rapidly growing communities and disfavor the others"[38]

Southerners realized that the movement of population before the war was working to their disadvantage and to the favor of the North, but they tended very often to rationalize the significance of this particular polarizing tendency. We can see this psychological inclination to distort reality and to put a better face upon the threatening situation in Kettel's treatment of population, written in 1860. "In estimating the relative growth of the three sections [i.e. North, South, and West], population and its movement have a very important influence upon the result. The South has depended only on its own natural increase of whites and blacks; while the North and West have had immense accessions of men and capital from abroad to stimulate their industry."[39] Kettel presents a table showing the nativity of the white population and the movement from section to section and from abroad for 1850 (Table 2) :

---

[36] Myrdal, *Rich Lands and Poor*, p. 28.
[37] Kettel, *Southern Wealth and Northern Profits*, p. 127.
[38] Myrdal, *Rich Lands and Poor*, p. 27.
[39] Kettel, *Southern Wealth and Northern Profits*, p. 99.

TABLE 2

United States' White Population—1850[a]

	Living South	Living North	Living West	Total
Born South	5,510,687	69,501	660,142	6,240,330
" North	337,765	6,941,510	1,090,814	8,370,089
" West	57,296	19,696	3,060,177	3,137,169
" Abroad	316,670	1,292,241	601,928	2,210,839
Total	6,222,418	8,342,938	5,413,059	19,958,427

a Source: T. P. Kettel, *Southern Wealth and Northern Profits*, p. 101. The figures of this table are based on the U.S. census of 1850.

Kettel very realistically notes the favorable effects of the population and capital movement from abroad on the North, but then minimizes the importance of the former in the following fashion:

> . . . The—in round numbers—two millions of foreigners living at the North and West, at the date of the census, according to the estimates of the Emigrant Commissioners, brought into the country $200,000,000 in capital, which was applied by them in prosecuting that productive industry which, in its results, so largely swells the sum total of Northern prosperity. This is an element in which the South has not participated. It is sometimes alleged that the reason the South does not get its share of the immigration is that, slavery is objected to by the new-comers; that is, however, a superficial reason, since they can know little of the institution, or of the blacks, until they arrive here. The true reason is, probably, that they follow the parallels of latitude to which they have become accustomed, as do the emigrants from the Northern States. . . .[40]

Analysis of the figures of Table 2 shows the much larger number of immigrants from abroad who settled in the North and West rather than in the South as of 1850 (1,894,169 versus 316,670). They show too that as of that date 729,643 southerners had migrated to the North or West, while there were only 711,731 persons born in the North or West who went South. It is clear from these data, as Kettel admits, that the South "mainly depended upon its own resources for increase of [white] population, since it has lost more to the North than it has gained thence and from abroad." He then tries to demonstrate that the North had lost more of its native population by migration than the South with the following calculation:[41]

	North	South
Born	8,370,089	6,240,330
Living	6,941,510	5,510,687
Emigrated, 17%	1,428,579	729,643, or 12%

40 *Ibid.*, p. 101. Kettel ignores the fact that the general lack of economic opportunity for persons of small means in the South may have deterred many immigrants from moving to that region. For a view of this subject generally contrary to that of the text, see W. L. Miller, "Slavery and the Population of the South," *Southern Economic Journal* (July, 1961), pp. 46–54.

41 *Ibid.*, p. 103.

What he does to secure this favorable comparison for the South, of course, is
to avoid an analysis of migration for the North and West *combined*. When we
do this with the statistics of 1850 we find the following:

Whites Living North and West as of 1850

North	8,342,938	Living North and West	15,755,997
West	5,413,059	Born North and West	11,507,258
Total	15,755,997	Immigration	4,248,739

The latter calculation reveals that the North and West had added close to 37
per cent of their original inhabitants to the total 1850 population by immigration. Kettel, however, again sought to diminish the importance of the growing
West and the migration from the South with the following defensive argument:

> If this very clear reasoning is true of the South, whence less than 12 per cent of
> the population has migrated, what inference is to be drawn from the fact that
> 17 per cent of those born at the great, opulent, free North have emigrated? Is
> it slavery, or the want of it? If this fact of migration proves anything, is it that
> the poor whites are better off at the South than at the North, since they show
> less disposition to avail themselves of the promise of the West—a promise
> which, as yet, is very far from being fulfilled. . . .[42]

The speciousness of Kettel's reasoning was dramatically refuted by the figures
of the 1860 census, which showed that the West had had a population increase
of 4,133,279 over that of 1850, an increase of 75 per cent compared to an
increase of about 23 per cent for the northeastern states and 24 per cent for
the South. Thus, the dynamics of population movement and growth in these
pre-war years were operating steadily to the relative disadvantage of the
South. Among others who noticed this striking demographic fact was the then
relatively obscure correspondent of the Vienna *Die Presse*, Karl Marx, who
shrewdly observed in 1861 that the conflict between the North and South was
finally "brought to a head by the weight thrown into the scales by the extraordinary development of the Northwestern states.[43]

CULTURAL BARRIERS TO INDUSTRIALIZATION
IN THE SLAVE SOUTH

Myrdal's theory of regional polarization explains some of the factors that
were creating a disparity in the economic development of the North and South
before the war, but it does not wholly account for the failure of industrialization as a self-sustaining process to develop in the latter region. Manufacturing
did make an appearance in cotton textiles and in certain processing industries,
but as a whole industrialization seems to have been retarded. What were the
reasons for this? Our interest at this point is not in the economic obstacles so

[42] *Ibid.*, p. 103.
[43] K. Marx and F. Engels, *The Civil War in the United States* (New York: International Publishers, 1937), p. 226.

much as in those ideological and cultural factors which impeded industrialization.[44]

A broad social science approach to this problem is necessary because the slaveholders were not interested in maintaining an economic system only, but a whole cultural and political way of life. The planters generally viewed the desirability of industrialization not from the perspective of rational profit-making but from the particular cultural outlook they had as the aristocrats of the social order and the masters of southern political power. Together with the latter went certain values, attitudes, and interests that could not be reconciled with simple bourgeois profit-making. Thus, maintenance and advancement of one's status as a planter fostered investment in land and slaves; the more of the latter one had, the higher one's social position in the community. But this often meant that the planters lacked liquid capital to invest in other projects, however profitable they might be. Amos Lawrence, the famous northern textile manufacturer, noticed this, saying, "Though there are many rich men in the large cotton-growing States, the number of moneyed men is very small, and they are not usually the projectors of new enterprises. The planters are generally in debt, more or less. . . ."[45]

Prejudice existed toward manufactures in this aristocratic social order because manual labor, and especially mechanical labor, was considered to be degrading and beneath the dignity of white men. We have here the same attitude toward labor that was manifested in the ancient slave societies. Southern industrialists were often confronted with a shortage of skilled labor among whites because of this feeling that working in a factory would involve loss of caste. Many planters feared too that employment of Negro slaves in factories would have subversive tendencies. "Whenever a slave is made a mechanic," declaimed James Hammond in 1849, "he is more than half freed, and soon becomes, as we too well know, and all history attests, with rare exceptions, the most corrupt and turbulent of his class."[46] The employment of the poor whites in manufacturing was inhibited by the use of slaves, for generally the whites would not work side by side in competition with the Negroes.

The southern planters were very ambivalent about manufactures and manufacturers. While some of them had substantial investments in manufacturing, or were related to the industrial entrepreneurs through marriage, they tended to dislike industrialism and cities, possibly because they sensed that manufactures would generate ideas unassimilable to their way of life. They were willing to invest for a quick gain or to obtain the processed goods their plantations needed, but they did not give the type of subsidy and support to industrialism that was characteristic of the North. The truth was that the

[44] For an excellent, up-to-date treatment of this subject, see Genovese, *The Political Economy of Slavery*, esp. Chaps. 1, 8, and 9.

[45] Quoted in *ibid.*, p. 190.

[46] *DeBow's Review* (June, 1850), p. 518.

manufacturers needed the planters, but the planters did not have to depend on local manufacturers. They could and often did give their business to outsiders. The plantations did not generate the market demand for local manufactures as did the freehold farms of the North and West.[47] The restricted markets of the South did not permit the development there of firms of sufficient scale to compete with those of the North, which served markets of much greater geographical scope and of higher income. In turn, the discouragement of manufacturing and its relatively meager growth hindered urbanization, without which it was impossible to promote a general and more diversified agriculture. Without markets for cash crops in the cities, the agitation for diversification could only mean a return to self-sufficiency and a subsistence economy rather than a market-oriented one.

Another serious consequence of the southern political and social structure was the neglect of the education of the common people. While the South had a considerable number of colleges and private academies and denominational schools for the sons and daughters of the rich, it lagged badly behind the North and West in the development of a public school system. Jefferson himself had unsuccessfully sought the establishment of a tax-supported system of public education as early as 1779, but state and local support for such schools was very meager in the pre-war years. Public schools were regarded as being maintained for paupers, and men of property were not disposed to tax themselves for their benefit. C. G. Memminger wrote of the situation in South Carolina: "The mechanic and moving elements of society—those who work the actual machinery of the body politic and are its stay and support—these exhibit few of the results of education."[48] That this condition was quite general is evident from the statistics of education and literacy. In 1840 the ratio of pupils to white population was 5.72 per cent in the slaveholding states and 18.41 per cent in the non-slaveholding ones. Illiteracy among the white population in the same year was 7.46 per cent in the slaveholding states and 2.13 per cent in states not having slaves.[49] While northern education was steadily growing more democratic, and some wise voices in the South were deploring the neglect of the common schools, there were others who adamantly opposed the very idea of public education, as witness this letter written to A. H. Stephens in 1860:

> You are aware that the people at the North are all *educated* by government, and where educated they expect to *live* upon government, either town, county, city, state, or national, and *they will do it*. . . . This idea of educating everybody is taking root in the South, our people are beginning to demand taxes for the education of the masses, there is to be no more ignorant after this generation according to the new philosophy, upon the idea that its [sic] easier to build schoolhouses than jails and colleges than state prisons, but there never

[47] See above, p. 167.

[48] *Charleston Courier* (January 12, 1857), quoted in A. Nevins, *Ordeal of the Union*, Vol. 2 (New York: Charles Scribners' Sons, 1947), p. 548.

[49] D. C. North, *Economic Growth of the United States*, p. 133.

was a greater error upon earth, we can build the latter much cheaper and they are decidedly more useful. . . .[50]

Some industrialists urged that the southern whites should be educated so that they could hold superior jobs to those of the slaves or free Negroes. But even these pleas for a discriminatory type of public education were not heeded by the planter class. The industrialists were weak politically and had to accommodate themselves to the planter regime. The planters themselves were faced with an insoluble dilemma. "Rural slaveholders had to view industrialization with either slave labor or free with misgivings. They needed more local manufacturing to supply the needs of the plantations and to guarantee the economic and military power of their states, but could not afford to permit too much. . . . In the end, they could take no step along the industrial road without exposing themselves to perils so grave as to endanger their existence as a class."[51]

INDUSTRIAL MOBILIZATION FOR WAR IN THE TWO SECTIONS

The secession of the slaveholding states from the Union ended for the duration of the war the direct polarization effects we have described above, but it did not, of course, dissipate or obliterate the accumulated cultural and economic differences between the sections. These continued to affect profoundly the manner in which the two sections went about mobilizing their resources for the military struggle. The disruption of the pre-war channels of trade and economic relationship of the sections caused some economic activities to shrink and contract, while the prospect of war orders and the needs created by a greater degree of economic independence created new opportunities for investment. In the South and to a lesser degree perhaps in the North, these beneficial effects were offset by the belief that the war would be short, then by the belief of the southerners that the blockade would be lifted, and, finally, by the fact that inflation diverted business activity into speculative trading in commodities and tended to discourage long term investment. Unfortunately, statisticians have not been able to estimate regional income and its components for the war years so that we are forced to rely on a more or less speculative reconstruction of how the overall economic readjustments to the conflict and mobilization were made.

When we consider the great dependence of the South on its staple crops, and especially on King Cotton, it can be appreciated that the policy that the Confederate government adopted toward it once hostilities broke out was crucial to the maintenance of the region's income and employment. The cotton planters sought from the very beginning to have the government buy up the whole crop and use it as a basis for domestic credit and currency or to ship it

---

[50] Quoted in Nevins, *Ordeal of the Union*, Vol. 2, pp. 549–550.
[51] Genovese, *The Political Economy of Slavery*, p. 235.

abroad to establish foreign credits before the northern blockade became too tight. A number of the South's civil and military leaders supported such a policy, but Secretary of the Treasury Memminger saw objections to it. He argued that it would be discriminatory to buy cotton and not other crops; he lacked the money for such a great outlay as would be required; it would be state socialism and, in any case, unconstitutional. He reminded the proponents of this policy that the large amounts of cotton they suggested be purchased did not exist because the crop of 1860–61 had been exported before the Confederacy was set up. Furthermore, even if it existed, where were the ships to transport it?

Instead of this policy, the Confederacy discouraged the export of cotton while the blockade was easy to run, and did not purchase even a part of the crop. When we recall that the cotton crop harvested fell from 4.5 million bales in 1861 to less than 50,000 in 1863, we cannot help but believe that there was validity in the cotton planters' plea for a subsidy from the government. It is generally agreed that the wealthy planters lost in income relative to other classes during the war. We get some suggestion of the multiplier effects of the decline in their income and investment from a letter written to the editor of the New Orleans *Delta* in the fall of 1861:

> If the planters are prohibited from sending their cotton to market until the blockade is raised, and they are to receive no money in the meantime, how are they to get along? Their Negroes must have shoes and winter clothing; their families must have something; their country store debts must be paid, else the country merchants cannot pay their debts to the wholesale city merchants. Therefore, they can get no goods, and the whole business of the country is completely broken up.[52]

Instead of imaginatively using its greatest asset, cotton, in fighting the war, the Confederacy was forced to turn to a program of crop diversification to survive and then, when these crops were badly distributed and the monetary system in a shambles because of inflation, to turn to barter and local self-sufficiency. The Confederate Congress in April, 1862, passed a law allowing the people who promised to invest the proceeds in government bonds to sell cotton and other farm products at agreed upon prices. This was a step in the direction of the cotton purchase program originally advocated by some, but it came late, after the blockade was already tightening. The imperfect records show that throughout the war the government bought at least 474,471 bales. It was again a matter of "too little, too late." The southern leaders were to learn that they could not fight a war on the basis of "government as usual," but before they did, the South was in a state of economic collapse.

If we turn briefly again to consider the North's adjustment to the outbreak of war, we are struck by the favorable accommodation it made to the loss of the valuable southern trade. Apart from the $300 million in southern debts

---

[52] Quoted in E. M. Lerner, "Money, Prices, and Wages in the Confederacy, 1861–65," in Andreano, *The Economic Impact of the American Civil War* (Cambridge: Schenkman Publishing Co., 1962), footnote 23, p. 35.

outstanding at the time of Fort Sumter, the loss of which caused a short panic in the North, there was the heavy decline in the merchandise export trade and the accelerated collapse of the American merchant marine. The extent of the former can be seen in the statistics of Table 3.

TABLE 3

Exports of U.S. Merchandise by Economic Class, 1860–66[a]
(In thousands of dollars)

	Total	Crude Materials	Crude Foodstuffs	Manufactured Foodstuffs	Semi-Manufactures	Finished Manu-factures
1860	$316,242	$216,998	$12,166	$38,625	$12,642	$35,811
1861	204,900	58,463	48,796	53,736	8,401	35,504
1862	179,644	18,456	55,893	70,250	8,126	26,918
1863	186,004	29,950	45,166	66,048	11,393	33,447
1864	143,504	28,870	24,519	54,909	9,861	25,345
1865	136,940	34,213	13,975	47,981	10,650	30,121

[a] Source: U.S. Census, *Historical Statistics of the United States, 1789–1945*, p. 247.

This loss of over $100 million in export trade, and the virtual cessation of foreign investment in the United States during the war should have exercised a strong deflationary effect on the economy of the North. It did not apparently have so serious an effect because it was compensated for in part by a remarkable expansion of interregional trade between the Northeast and the West. This was reflected in the traffic on such railroads as the Erie and the Pennsylvania, which increased as much as 100 per cent during the war years, and on the Erie Canal, which carried one million more tons of freight in the middle of the war than it had in any previous year.[53] In connection with this great outpouring of the agricultural wealth of the West, which played so important a part in keeping the British neutral, we should note the part played by the mechanization of farming—another evidence that technological dynamism in the North was strong, while southern agriculture continued to employ less advanced methods.

In the mobilization of industry to meet wartime demand, the South was handicapped by the small industrial base with which it started. While Josiah Gorgas, head of the Ordnance Bureau of the War Department, accomplished wonders in the provision of munitions for the Army in gray, he had less success in meeting the needs of both civilian and the military for food, clothing, and other necessities. The Army drained 40 per cent of white men from the labor force, and even skilled labor was conscripted, causing shortages and interruptions in production. This over-mobilization created bottlenecks in production; it was necessary in the later years of the war to delegate troops to

[53] E. D. Fite, *Social and Industrial Conditions in the North during the Civil War* (New York: The Macmillan Co., 1910), pp. 43–44, 46.

work in the factories.[54] The shortcomings of southern mobilization were seen also in the reluctance or outright refusal of planters to allow their slaves to be used on military projects. Under the Impressment Act of March, 1863, slaves were used to work on fortifications; the government paid the owners $30 a month for each slave and, in case of death, his full value. Payment was slow and the owners complained of mistreatment, etc. This behavior by the planters led the poor non-slaveholders to complain that the struggle was "a rich man's war and a poor man's fight." The one redeeming feature of southern mobilization would seem to be that there was less graft in contracting for the Army as compared with conditions in the North.

The slackness in the South's mobilization efforts were exhibited as well in its operation of the railroads. Its leaders did not realize until it was too late how important the railroads were to success in war. The *laissez faire* philosophy and the stress on constitutionalism militated against government seizure. It was not until May, 1863 that a law was passed that gave the government the means to compel efficient operation of the 1,113 small lines in the region. But this law was not properly utilized by President Davis, and so it was not until a few months from the end of the war that the Confederate Congress gave the Secretary of War adequate powers over the railroads. This had been done much earlier in the North. The South was handicapped by a fatal dilemma that it never resolved during the long struggle: "strong government and great material sacrifice on the part of its citizens were necessary to win independence, yet the traditions and the whole political theory of the South were against a strongly centralized government and interference with property rights."[55]

WAR FINANCE—NORTH AND SOUTH

In comparing the financial policies of the two antagonists in the Civil War, it is wise to take a tolerant attitude on the subject because, from our present standpoint, so little was known of the causes of inflation. The nation, both North and South, was unaccustomed to heavy taxation, and the urgencies of the situation were great. Neither government, that of the Union nor the Confederacy, had a Secretary of the Treasury who was eminently qualified for the difficult problems of that office in wartime. Still, in the case of the South, it is well to remember the conclusion of one careful student of the Civil War who wrote that "the Confederacy had begun to crumble, or to break down *within*, long before the military situation appeared to be desperate."[56] The South's

[54] Lerner, in Andreano, *The Economic Impact of the American Civil War*, p. 19.

[55] C. Eaton, *A History of the Southern Confederacy* (New York: The Macmillan Co., 1959), p. 248.

[56] Quoted in *ibid.*, p. 233. C. W. Ramsdell in his book *Behind the Lines in the Southern Confederacy* (Baton Rouge, La.: Louisiana State University Press, 1944), vii, expresses the belief that "the greatest single weakness of the Confederacy was its handling of finances."

mishandling of her finances contributed significantly to this economic disintegration.

The inflation that occurred in both sections in this war is a matter of common knowledge; in the case of the South, its wartime currency has at times been a topic for comedians. When we compare the two phenomena, we find that the inflation that occurred in the North, according to the Aldrich Report, resulted in a little more than a doubling of the price level, whereas in the South the general price index increased twenty-eight fold from the first quarter of 1861 to January, 1864. In the one case, we can speak of inflation, in the other, we are justified in referring to hyperinflation. Table 4 presents the most reliable indexes of inflation in the two sections.

TABLE 4

Indices of Commodity Prices in the North and South,
1860–65[a]

	Prices in Currency in the North (1860 = 100)	Commodity Prices in the South (Jan. 1861 = 100)	
1860	100		
1861	100.6	January	100
		April	100
		June	108
		October	135
1862	117.8	January	191
		April	279
		June	328
		October	522
1863	148.6	January	756
		April	1,168
		June	1,296
		October	1,858
1864	190.5	January	2,776
1865	216.8		—

[a] Sources: The "Aldrich Report," Senate Reports, 52nd Congress, 2nd Session, 1892–93 (Special Session, March 4, 1893) Vol. III, Part I; E. M. Lerner, "Money, Prices and Wages in the Confederacy, 1861–65," in Andreano, *The Economic Impact . . .*, p. 21.

The austerity with which Secretary Memminger began his term of office as the Confederate Treasurer is illustrated by the story told of his starting operations in an unswept room in Montgomery, Alabama, which was later furnished out of his own funds. Memminger proposed a tax program suitable for a nation at peace—a few minor taxes, a small bond issue, and the establishment of a uniform paper currency. When the war came with its tremendous expenditures, he began issuing paper money (Treasury notes) to pay debts, while Congress debated revenue measures. In August he issued $100 million more in such notes and $100 million in bonds. By the end of 1861 over $311 million were issued and in the following years the amounts issued mounted: 1862—$268 million; 1863—$517 million; 1864—$456 million, bringing the total to close to $1,555 million by the end of the war.

The bonds referred to were issued under the so-called Produce Loan Act of 1861. Under this law the people were permitted to buy these 8 per cent bonds in return for pledges of agricultural commodities. The effort to collect these pledges dragged on until 1864, when it was calculated that over $34 million had been so offered. But more than $11 million of this amount could not be collected because the people refused to redeem their pledges. Under this law the Congress acquired vast stores of cotton, sugar, rice, tobacco, and wheat. However, only a small proportion of this stock could be shipped to Europe for cash or credit because of the Union blockade. This domestic loan, therefore, could not be considered a great success.

As the war progressed, Memminger tried to persuade the Confederate Congress to impose heavy taxes, but the war was half over before it passed a realistic tax law. By that time there were strong demands for taxation. Under the April, 1863 law, excise, license, income, sales, and property taxes were levied. There was also a 10 per cent tax, payable in kind, levied on a list of agricultural commodities. Such a tax was necessary because the spiral of inflation was making payments in currency meaningless. Despite the numerous taxes, the Confederacy raised only $207 million in taxes throughout its existence, or about 1 per cent of its total income. The South also tried to raise money by floating a foreign loan. A French banker, Emile Erlanger, in 1863 undertook to underwrite $15 million in 7 per cent bonds, to be backed by cotton. But the bonds did not sell well in Europe, their price declined heavily, so that the southern government only cleared about $2.5 million in cash from this loan.

With other alternatives cut off, the Confederate government continued to operate the printing presses, turning out its fiat currency by the millions, while prices skyrocketed. The supply was augmented by the paper money issues of the states and those of cities, railroads, and insurance companies. The rise in prices was not due only to the redundant currency; the general price index rose 28 times, but the stock of money over the same period rose elevenfold.[57] Part of the inflation was caused by the increased velocity of circulation and the shortages of commodities. In February, 1864, at Secretary Memminger's suggestion, the southern Congress passed a law requiring people to exchange $100 bills for long-term bonds bearing 4 per cent interest, or suffer a loss of one-third of their value after a certain date. Holders of smaller denominations were required to convert into bonds or accept new currency at the rate of three old dollars for two of the new money. This legislation resulted in a considerable contraction of the currency and a temporary, sharp drop in prices. But there was no lasting relief from

[57] Lerner in Andreano, *The Economic Impact* . . . , p. 20.

the rampant inflation. With defeat imminent and the economy disorganized, the currency continued to decline in value; the "flight from the currency" continued until it became entirely worthless with the surrender of the Confederate armies. A recapitulation of the South's finances has concluded that the total debt at the end of the war came to $2,345 million in Confederate currency, or $572 million in gold. On a per capita basis, this would indicate that the financial sacrifice of the southern people was over twice as great as that of the North.

The North's problems in financing the war were not as insoluble as those of the South because of its more diversified economy, its more adequate tax base, and its better credit, which enabled it to borrow more effectively. Yet it too faced many difficulties in meeting the extraordinary costs of war. For one, it lacked many of the necessary tools of financing. The revenue system in the past had relied mainly on customs and sales of public land, and it could not be expanded quickly. The methods of borrowing were defective; the government had no central bank that could act as its fiscal agent, nor was there any central direction or control of the banking business. There were 1,600 state banks, each issuing banknotes, which in total came to 7,000 varieties, with more than half of them being counterfeit. Under these circumstances, the Treasury and the Congress had to rely on interim financing, on every available way of raising money.

Lincoln's Secretary of the Treasury at the outset of the war was Salmon P. Chase of Ohio. His appointment to that post was based on political expediency; he had relatively little experience in finance. He was a staunch opponent of slavery, but on questions of finance he was basically a Jacksonian Democrat. As such, he was considered a hard money man and more sympathetic to state than to national banking. Upon assuming office, Chase found the Union in a weakened financial state. The Treasury had had three years of deficits and was experiencing difficulty in borrowing money. The national debt stood at $75 million—a large sum for those days—and soon the government was spending more than a million a day. Chase and his predecessor had relied on borrowing, which was none too successful, until Congress met in special session in July, 1861 to find the revenues to finance the war. Chase in his recommendations proposed to follow the tradition of war finance laid down by Gallatin fifty years before: "Finance your war costs on borrowed funds, and increase your taxes only for the purpose of covering service on the newly incurred debt." He estimated the government's expenditures for the fiscal year begining July 1, 1861 at $318.5 million and suggested that one-quarter of this amount, or $80 million, be raised by taxes and the rest by borrowing. His estimates of revenue and expenditure proved to be far from accurate and his proposals for taxation (mainly for increased duties on tea, coffee, sugar, and other articles) woefully inadequate.

In August of the same year, so insistent were the financial demands of the Union, Congress imposed a $20 million direct tax on property, adopted a 3 per cent income tax on all 1861 incomes over $800, and raised the customs duties again. At this same time Congress authorized the Secretary of the Treasury to deviate from the principles of the Independent Treasury system by depositing government funds in such specie-paying banks as he might select. Chase, being a supporter of the Independent Treasury idea, did not go along with the latter action; he insisted instead that the subtreasuries continue to deal in specie only. Soon he was forced to ask the private banks to make a $150 million loan to the government, to be paid in specie. The banks at that time had only $63 million of specie, and they were fearful that such a transfer would lead the public to question the redeemability of their notes. They reluctantly agreed to his plan, hoping that the specie would quickly flow back to their coffers. But in the meantime, the Union's diplomatic and military situation worsened, expenditures mounted and revenue lagged, with the result that there was a great increase in hoarding. This contributed to the suspension of specie payments by the private banks of the nation on December 30, 1861 and similar action by the government a day later. Gold was still needed by individuals to pay international obligations and customs duties and for the federal government to pay interest on its bonds. A gold market, such as a commodity exchange, was, therefore, opened at New York on January 13, 1862 where gold could be purchased for paper money by individuals and the government.

These critical events were the background of the issuance of the famous greenbacks. The idea was not Chase's, but rather was first advanced by Representative E. G. Spaulding of New York, a member of the Ways and Means Committee, who introduced a bill for the issue of Treasury notes to be made legal tender in the payment of all debts.[58] He believed that the Treasury's plight was so serious that its funds would be exhausted in thirty days. Taxes could not be quickly raised, and the government bond market was so weak that a new loan could not be considered. Therefore, Spaulding argued that there was no alternative, that necessity demanded a government issue of Treasury notes, not redeemable in specie. There was a strenuous debate on the proposal, but it carried the day when Secretary Chase himself, originally said to be opposed, stated in a letter to the House Ways and Means Committee that because of the government's financial difficulties he believed that "it had become necessary that we should resort to the issue of the United States notes." The Legal Tender Act of February, 1862 authorized the issue of $150 million of such notes with the provision that they were to be convertible at par into the 5–20 interest-bearing bonds. These greenbacks, as they came to be called, were made legal tender for all private and public debts, except payment of custom duties and payment of interest on United States bonds and notes. Two subsequent issues of Treasury notes brought the total in July, 1864, to $450 million.

Almost from the beginning of their issue the greenbacks went to a 2 per cent

[58] On Chase's position, see I. Unger, *The Greenback Era. A Social and Political History of American Finance, 1865–1879* (Princeton, N.J.: Princeton University Press, 1964), Chap. 3.

discount. Before the end of 1862, their value had fallen by one-quarter, and in July, 1864, they were selling at 35 cents on the dollar. This was their low point; by the spring of 1865, they were back to 65 cents. Why did the greenbacks depreciate in value? What part did they play in the price inflation reflected in the statistics of Table 4 above? Some economists, such as the late Wesley C. Mitchell and Davis R. Dewey, attributed this price inflation almost entirely to the greenbacks, but some contemporary economists believe this to be an erroneous view.[59] ". . . Even if greenbacks had not been issued and bonds had been sold at whatever price they would bring in the market, inflation would have taken place. It would have merely taken another form —that of monetization of the debt through the issue of bank currency or the creation of bank credit. . . . Once the government was forced to rely on credit, the exact form of credit expansion was not so important as assumed by some historians."[60] The reason for not considering these issues of greenbacks the sole cause of the price inflation is that from the standpoint of modern income-expenditure theory, several factors were at work to produce this result. The immediate cause of the rise in prices and incomes was the diversion of resources to war use, creating relative shortages of civilian goods, once the economy was fully employed. At the same time the government's spending out of borrowed funds increased aggregate demand relative to the supply of goods and services coming on the market. Short term variations in the value of the greenbacks were affected by the military news, the fluctuations of imports payable in gold, and the government's gold payments on its outstanding bonds. Hoarding of gold on receipt of bad news caused its price in terms of paper money to rise, and conversely, good news caused the price of gold to drop in anticipation of ultimate parity between the paper money and the monetary metal.[61]

The depreciation of the greenbacks created a serious problem in the fractional currency system of the North. There was a sort of "currency vacuum" between the one-cent piece and the one-dollar banknote. This was because

---

[59] See W. C. Mitchell, *Gold, Prices, and Wages under the Greenback Standard* (Berkeley: University of California Press, 1908), p. 249; also D. R. Dewey, *Financial History of the United States*, 12th ed. (New York: Longmans, Green and Co., 1934), p. 293.

[60] P. Studenski and H. E. Kroos, *Financial History of the United States* (New York: McGraw-Hill Book Co., 1952), pp. 147–148.

[61] In an interesting analysis comparing inflation in the Civil War, World Wars I and II, Milton Friedman contends that monetary inflation was more effectively curbed in the former than in the first World War. He states that "the major factor that explained the relative income increases in the three wars was not the extent of money creation by the government . . . , but the expansion ratio of the banking system. In the Civil War the total supply of money—currency plus deposits—increased about $1.50 for each $1.00 of money created directly by the government; in the first World War, it increased nearly $8.00; in the second World War, $5.50." Paradoxically, in Friedman's view, the lack of a central banking system which might have raised the expansionary power of the greenbacks tended to curb the extent of the Civil War inflation. [M. Friedman, "Prices, Income, and Monetary Changes in Three Wartime Periods." *American Economic Review* (May, 1952), pp. 612ff.]

under the Coinage Act of 1853, a dollar in subsidiary coins was worth 97 cents in gold. When the greenbacks depreciated to less than 97 cents in gold, Gresham's law went into action. Holders of half dollars, quarters, or dimes began to hoard them, passing the cheap, depreciated money, greenbacks, in exchange rather than the relatively more valuable coin. "In the midst of a war boom, the American people had no money that would buy them street car rides, drinks of beer, or haircuts."[62] All sorts of substitutes made their appearance. Dollar banknotes were cut into halves and quarters. Banks issued notes for odd amounts. Towns and cities issued small change notes. Even postage stamps were used. Special stamps, after the postal authorities could no longer handle the volume of business in the regular ones, ungummed and printed on both sides, were issued. By May, 1863, over twenty million dollars of such stamps were in circulation. Finally, the federal government issued fractional paper notes—5, 10, 25, and 50 cents—to take the place of the postage currency.

As the intensity of the war increased and expenditures mounted, the "inflationary gap" created by the policy of deficit financing was contributing mightily to the price inflation. (The expenditures and revenues of the Union government are presented in Table 5; the sizeable annual additions to the public debt, which had a great inflationary potential, are especially to be noted.) Fortunately, Congress at last acted by passing the Revenue Act of July, 1862.

TABLE 5

Expenditures and Revenues of the Union, 1861–65[a]
(In millions of dollars)

Year	Expenditures	Revenues	Additions to the Public Debt
1861	$ 66.5	—	—
1862	474.8	$ 52.0	$432.4
1863	714.7	112.7	595.4
1864	865.3	264.6	695.9
1865	1,297.6	333.7	871.6

[a] Source: U.S. Bureau of the Census, *Historical Statistics of the United States, 1789–1945*, pp. 297, 300.

This act levied taxes on almost everything—higher custom duties, a direct tax, income taxes, which toward the end of the war were producing one-third of the total internal revenue, sumptuary excises on liquor and tobacco, a gross receipts tax, i.e., a form of general sales tax, inheritance taxes, and licenses. Despite widespread evasion of some of these taxes, especially the whiskey and income levies, they brought in considerable revenue and also curbed consumer demand. Whereas taxes only accounted for 10 per cent of the expenditures of 1862, they paid 25 per cent of the expenditures of 1864 and 1865. It was

[62] Shultz and Caine, *Financial Development of the United States*, p. 327.

estimated that the consumption of such items as coffee, sugar, textiles, and shoes declined as much as 50 per cent between 1860 and 1865.[63] This reduction of consumer demand by fiscal policy was necessary if some control was to be exercised over inflation. No effort at retraining inflation by direct price control was attempted by the Union government, so that fiscal action was all the more needed.

Part of the excess purchasing power was mopped up too by the numerous bond issues the government resorted to. The bond drive undertaken by Jay Cooke in 1862–64 in which he sold $362 million of bonds by an extensive promotional and educational campaign was especially noteworthy.[64] The Third and Fourth Loan Acts of 1863–64, which authorized additional issues of millions of dollars of bonds, were not so successful as Cooke's original efforts. The relative failure of these loans compelled the Treasury to resume issuing one, two, and three-year notes, all of which were very inflationary in their effects.

One of Secretary Chase's accomplishments was the passage in February, 1863 of the National Banking Act, a measure long overdue. This law was a "war baby" in the sense that one of the reasons for passing it was that it created a demand for the government's bonds. Under their federal charters as provided by this law, the member banks were required to purchase federal bonds to the extent of one-third of their capital stock. They were permitted to issue national bank notes up to 90 per cent of the par or market value of the deposited bonds. In addition, these new national banks could be used as depositories for government funds, on condition that they were secured by United States bonds.

Under this banking law a twenty-year charter could be obtained from the Comptroller of the Currency by five or more persons. The latter would have to start with a minumum capital of $50,000 in a community of 6,000, the amount ranging up to $200,000 in a city of 50,000 or more. National banks in so-called reserve cities had to keep a 25 per cent reserve in lawful money against their deposits. Those in other cities were permitted to keep one-half of their 25 per cent reserve on deposit in New York City. Country banks had to maintain a 15 per cent reserve, $\frac{3}{5}$ of which could be deposited in a city bank. The banks of the North were very slow at first to join the new system, despite the 2 per cent discriminatory tax on state bank notes. When this tax was raised to 10 per cent in March, 1865, effective the following year, many of them were forced to join. Thus, this banking and currency reform was not fully realized until after the war. While it was a notable improvement over the old system, particularly in providing a more uniform currency, it had serious defects that were to harm the nation's economy in later years.

In summary, we see that in finance as well as in economic mobilization generally the more developed section was able to marshal and control its

[63] P. Studenski and H. E. Kroos, *Financial History of the United States*, p. 153.
[64] On Jay Cooke's role in the Civil War, see H. Larson, *Jay Cooke, Private Banker* (Cambridge: Harvard University Press, 1936).

resources to overcome secession and preserve the national union. In the South, the failure on the home front that preceded the military collapse was the result of the divergence in regional economic development, with the lagging section being unable to sustain the heroic efforts of its badly supplied forces in the field. Our analysis has shown too how the polarizing tendencies in the economic relationships between the two great sections contributed to the coming of the war. These forces, however, were far from sufficient in themselves to explain the origins of that historic conflict. In the next chapter, we shall consider further the non-economic elements behind the momentous sectional schism.

Chapter 16

THE PROCESS OF SECTIONAL POLARIZATION: POLITICAL AND SOCIOLOGICAL ASPECTS

The cumulative processes toward regional inequality work through many causal chains usually not accounted for in our theoretical analysis of the play of market forces . . . the term [backwash effects] refers to the total cumulated effects resulting from the process of circular causation between all the factors, "non-economic" as well as "economic."

G. Myrdal, *Rich Lands and Poor*

THE ROLE OF NON-ECONOMIC FACTORS IN MYRDAL'S THEORY OF DUALISM

Myrdal, as the above quotation and the Introduction to this Part make clear, contends that the non-economic factors are "among the main vehicles for the circular causation in the cumulative processes of economic change. . . ." He describes some of the non-economic symptoms of backwardness, such as poor health, inadequate education, primitive religion and susceptibility to superstitions, and relative lack of "the experimental and ambitious aspirations of a developing society." He states too that "these frustrating effects of poverty, *operating through other media than those analyzed by traditional economic theory*, are interlocked in circular causation, the one with the others and all with the biases I referred to in the working of migration, capital movements and trade. . . ."[1] Apart from stressing the circular, cumulative relationship of these factors to the economic ones, Myrdal does not analyze these "other media" with the aid of sociological or psychological concepts. He does consider the role of the state and presents a sketch of the development in the richer countries from the "oppressor state" to the "welfare state." He tells us that "it should not be overlooked that even in the poorest and least progressive countries policy actions were all the time taken by the state to counteract the tendencies toward inequality." Furthermore, he says,

[1] *Rich Lands and Poor* (New York: Harper, 1958), p. 30 (our italics).

"The underprivileged groups pressed for greater equality. From time imme-morial, history records uprisings of the poor against the rich, the exploited countryside against the city, the peasants against the landlord. When success-ful, these revolts by the underprivileged received the sanction of the state."[2]

We have reviewed these remarks of Myrdal on the role of the non-eco-nomic factors in economic development as a preliminary to testing the useful-ness and validity of this aspect of his theory of regional dualism and polariza-tion. He has given us very few specific hypotheses or corollaries of his theory to evaluate. His main emphasis, as we understand him, is that the interaction between the developing and the backward region is not limited to economic factors, but that the polarization process embraces important non-economic elements as well. It is this fascinating aspect of his theory that we wish to test in terms of the ante-bellum history of the relations between the North and the South. Such an undertaking is a large analytical order, and we shall conse-quently be forced to limit ourselves only to some main points in the complex and controversial terrain of that part of our development as a nation.

The "irrepressible conflict" between the two sections evolved in the mind of some with all the inevitability of a Greek tragedy; to others, it appeared as a "needless war." Whatever view one takes of that dubious question of the inevitability of the war, it is clear that the forces uniting the American people were overwhelmed by polarizing tendencies that led to disunion and armed struggle between the sections. In the preceding chapter we examined the economic factors that led to sectional inequality in income and to a feeling on the part of many southerners that they were a colonial dependency of the North. We did not offer that analysis as the supposed economic cause of the Civil War because such a monistic explanation does not do justice to the complexity of factors that resulted in the sectional struggle. In considering the non-economic factors in the process of that polarization of the sections that ultimately led to the armed conflict, we seek to present a more holistic and more acceptable understanding of the causes of that great upheaval.

THE CULTURAL CONTEXT OF THE SECTIONAL CONFLICT

In explaining the coming of the Civil War, historians have been accustomed to describing the "clash of cultures" and the divisive elements generally that separated the sections. But, as David Donald has recently suggested, it is equally important to take account of the massive social change that swept over the nation as a whole in the pre-war years.[3] We have previously described

[2] *Ibid.*, pp. 43, 46.

[3] See his Oxford lecture, *An Excess of Democracy: The American Civil War and the Social Process*, reproduced in D. Donald, *Lincoln Reconsidered*, 2nd Ed. (New York: Knopf, 1966), pp. 209–235. We have drawn upon this stimulating essay for many of the points below. While we do not agree with all that Donald says and implies in his analysis, his emphasis on the unrestrained social change as being a major background factor

many of these changes, but it is worthwhile to consider them again from the standpoint of their bearing on the sectional strife and national instability. First, there was the rapidity of these social changes—a pace so fast that they practically forced each generation to start anew. In the Northeast the rise of the city greatly disturbed the slow course of societal evolution, confronting thousands for the first time with the experience of pioneering in a new, relatively raw and competitive environment. In the South the old states of the eastern coast were thrown into competition with the rich alluvial lands of the Gulf coast, and they were forced to make difficult readjustments. In the Middle and Far West, the wealth of the prairies as farm country and the lure of gold in California led hundreds of thousands to migrate in an often frantic search for a quick fortune. In short, in these years "all sections of the United States were being transformed with such rapidity that stability and security were everywhere vanishing values; nowhere could a father safely predict what kind of world his son would grow up in."[4]

The very richness of the American land called for a people to develop it. Immigrants marvelled at the opportunities and entered avidly into the scramble to become rich. "Not everybody got rich, of course, but everybody aspired to do so." The land, the water power, the minerals, all were ruthlessly exploited.

With this swift change and promise of fortune, there was an extraordinary degree of upward social mobility. We do not have to accept the Horatio Alger legend, but a number of studies have shown that vertical mobility was, perhaps, as readily achieved in that period as in any other in our history.[5] It is not surprising that these upward bound Americans were devoted believers in the idea of progress. Their supreme confidence in America's future and their own encouraged them to speculate, to take a flier into the unknown rather than settling for the "sure thing." We have numerous instances in these new communities, in which sudden wealth could be won, of what Durkheim termed *anomie*—a loss of standards or social norms.

Even the family itself and its time-worn relationships were disrupted by the mobility of the population. In New England, where many of the males had migrated west, there was a surplus of females so that many women could not find partners in marriage. If they were of the lower class, they went to work to support themselves; if they were from the upper class, they had to turn to charity work or other humanitarian endeavor. In the West, on the other hand, women were scarce relative to men; they could much more easily marry, but when they did, they were not always willing to carry out the conventional

---

making for social instability and division is correct, in our opinion. Economic changes which tended to integrate the market economy and promote regional specialization (see above, pp. 196–197, 218) went forward at such a tempo as to threaten social disorganization and personality disorientation.

[4] Donald, *Lincoln Reconsidered*, p. 217.

[5] For example, see C. W. Mills, "The American Business Elite: A Collective Portrait," *The Journal of Economic History* (December, 1945), pp. 20–44.

notion of simply being subordinate to their husbands. The children in this society of relative abundance were an economic asset to their parents. They were treated well by their parents and given great freedom. European travellers in this country were almost uniformly surprised at the "uncurbed egotism of the American child." Reading these descriptions of early nineteenth century youth makes some of the children of today's affluence look like ninnies. "The lad of fourteen . . . struts and swaggers and smokes his cigar and drinks rum; treads on the toes of his grandfather, swears at his mother and sister, and vows that he will run away . . . the children govern the parents."[6]

Shrewd commentators on the American scene, such as Tocqueville, were struck by the rebellion against authority in all its forms. The church, formerly a powerful institution of social cohesion, had been disestablished and numerous sects had sprung up, fragmenting the Christian community. The squires and landed aristocrats had been displaced by a new, pushing bourgeosie. In government too, there had been a decline in the powers of the federal authority from the days of Washington to those of Buchanan. The state governments, though they often sought to promote private enterprise, became subject to the pressure of selfish groups or exercised merely the negative role of the Watchman—protector of property and guardian of fair play. While the central authority of government was being weakened, there was a steady movement toward extension of the franchise. With the necessity of appealing to a broad electorate, the parties began to play down the issues and to take their stand on broad evasive platforms. Candidates were selected because of their appeal to this mass public rather than for their demonstrated statesmanship. Ex-generals or candidates who had been born in a log cabin, regardless of their other qualifications for office, had preferment. This state of political and social life was so strange to Tocqueville that he had to invent a new term, "individualism," to describe it. He noted the institutions that tended to counteract the instability of this majoritarian form of democracy, but he also saw the dangers of "atomism packed tight." He warned that "men living in democratic countries eagerly lay hold of general ideas because they have but little leisure."[7] Lincoln too tried to counteract the majoritarianism of his day by stressing the Declaration of Independence, with its emphasis on the rights of the individual and of minorities.

In the midst of this convulsive change, with many of its institutions disorganized, the nation was faced by a series of complex, controversial questions growing out of its swift physical expansion. The annexation of Texas, the Mexican War, and the settlement of California and Oregon posed complex questions that tended to divide the sections. Yet, at this very time, "The permanent revolution that was America had freed its citizens from the bonds of prescription and custom but had left them leaderless. Inevitably the reverse

[6] Donald, *Lincoln Reconsidered*, p. 225.
[7] A. de Tocqueville, *Democracy In America* (New York: Knopf, 1946), p. 257.

side of the coin of individualism is labeled conformity. Huddling together in their loneliness, they sought only to escape from their freedom. Fads, fashions, and crazes swept the country. Religious revivalism reached a new peak in the 1850's. Hysterical fears and paranoid suspicions marked this shift of Americans to 'other-directedness.' Never was there a field so fertile for the propagandist, the agitator, the extremist."[8]

THE LIFE STYLE AND CHANGING VALUES
OF THE SOUTHERN PLANTER

The study of the relationship between character and culture is as yet a relatively new field of investigation for social scientists. While anthropologists have analyzed basic personality in primitive societies and in some modern ones, and some work has been done on the social character of American whites and Negroes, psychological study of, say, the southern planter of the pre-war era has barely begun. Historians have given us some biographical portraits that are of use, and considerable work has been done on the culture and social thought of the slave South. We need to review some of this work in order to obtain an understanding of the social character and life style of the ante-bellum planter class. That this is difficult to do, considering the rapidity of social change in that period, the heterogeneity of the class itself, and its wide geographical distribution over a large area, goes without saying. Still, there is reason to believe that a generic picture can be drawn of the chief features of the planter personality in that era. Wilbur J. Cash has presented a pioneering effort in his impressionistic, but penetrating study, *The Mind of the South*, and others have added significant details to the emerging portrait.[9]

The planter, whether Tidewater aristocrat or the new slaveholder of the Gulf coast, lived in a predominantly agrarian society. He owned and managed a plantation that could often be made into a fairly self-sufficient world, relatively tranquil and removed from the bustling city life of the North. His was a society with a more traditional, paternalistic character and atmosphere, which derived many of its basic features from the presence of the slaves and of the master-servant relationship. This institution tended to give the South, as we have seen, a more clearly defined class structure, and it served to preserve a sort of "vestigial feudalism." There was a strong emphasis on kinship ties among the whites and a glorification of the family as an institution.

Slavery helped to establish a type of civilization where habits of command and release from physical labor enabled the landed gentry to cultivate notions

---

[8] Donald, *Lincoln Reconsidered*, pp. 229–230.

[9] W. J. Cash, *The Mind of the South*, Book I (New York: Knopf, 1941), W. R. Taylor, *Cavalier and Yankee*, The Old South and American National Character (New York: George Braziller, 1961), T. J. Wertenbacker, *Patrician and Plebeian in Virginia* (New York: Russell & Russel, 1958). For a summary of some of this work, see A. Nevins, *Ordeal of the Union*, Vol. II (New York: Charles Scribners' Sons, 1947), pp. 537–554.

of chivalry, polished manners, elevated standards of scholarship, and individual refinement. This was the classic picture of the southern gentleman, an aristocrat of the old school. Yet, as Cash, Taylor, and others have shown, the development of the cotton kingdom and its spread westward after 1820 made the figure of the Virginia planter an atypical one. The new breed was often a back country farmer, or his descendant, who struck out for the frontier and hit it rich. This type of planter, after the 1840's, seems to have outnumbered the old southern planters in the new regions. These Cotton Snobs, as D. R. Hundley called them, were more largely self-made men. They lacked the polish and many of the values of the older aristocracy, though they often continued to imitate some of the manners of the old style of life. As the sectional tensions increased in the pre-war years, the political elite of the South were increasingly drawn from this non-aristocratic group of men. Yancey, Jefferson Davis, A. H. Stephens, Wigfall, and Reagan, were not of the old aristocracy. Even Calhoun himself, who represented the interests of the new planter class, was the son of a plain, slaveless farmer of middle South Carolina.

The world of the plantation was one of the socializing influences that shaped and molded the personality of the planter. The physical environment of the South was another—as Cash vividly describes it, a "sort of cosmic conspiracy against reality in favor of romance."

> . . . The country is one of extravagant colors, of proliferating foliage and bloom, of flooding yellow sunlight, and above all perhaps of haze. Pale blue fogs hang above the valleys in the morning, the atmosphere smokes faintly at midday, and through the long afternoons cloud-stacks tower from the horizon and the earth-heat quivers upward through the iridescent air, blurring every outline and rendering every object vague and problematical. I know that winter comes to the land, certainly. I know there are days when the color and haze are stripped away and the real stands up in drab and depressing harshness. But these things pass and are forgotten.
>
> The dominant mood, the mood that lingers in the memory, is one of well-nigh drunken reverie—of a hush that seems all the deeper for the far-away mourning of the hounds and the far-away crying of the doves—of such sweet and inexorable opiates as the rich odors of hot earth and pinewood and the perfume of the magnolia in bloom—a soft languor creeping through the blood and mounting surely to the brain. . . . It is a mood, in sum, in which directed thinking is all but impossible, a mood in which the mind yields almost perforce to drift and in which the imagination holds unchecked sway, a mood in which nothing any more seems improbable save the puny inadequateness of fact, nothing incredible save the bareness of truth.[10]

In this world of the rich Southland and of the plantation, the planter had "freedom from labor beyond the wildest dream of the European peasant and the New England farmer." The white men below the planter in this lush country also felt a reduced fear of want. They seldom needed to fear hunger; there was always the possibility of possession of some sort of land that would provide subsistence, if nothing else. In addition, the plantation with its impo-

---

[10] Cash, *The Mind of the South*, Book I, p. 46.

sition of the manual labor on a slave class tended to divorce individual pride from the idea of effort and achievement. These social conditions fostered a tendency toward unreality, toward romanticism, and a more unrestrained, hedonistic enjoyment of life.

> . . . In every rank men lolled much on their verandas or under their oaks, sat much on fences, dreaming. In every rank they exhibited a striking tendency to build up legends about themselves and to translate these legends into explosive action—to perform with a high, histrionic flourish, and to strive for celebrity as the dashing blade. In every rank they were much concerned with seeing the ponies run, with hearing the band, with making love, with dancing, with extravagant play. . . .[11]

This pattern of plantation culture, with its thin distribution of the population over large areas of countryside, its weak development of local government, tended to perpetuate the attitudes of the backwoods—its individualism and its disdain for all but the minimum of law and order. In addition, the Jeffersonian tradition of the South was such as to strengthen the *laissez faire* attitude. This was a setting ideally suited to foster an intense individualism, an emphasis on attitudes that were highly oriented toward the personal and assertion of the self. The fictions that grew up in this milieu and were absorbed from the traditions of the Virginia gentleman made every planter a gentleman, stressed his chivalry and sense of honor and *noblesse oblige*. But in all too many cases, much of this was external; the manners were put on, the culture artificial because it did not emanate from the inner man. Many of the new planters did not have the experience or the assurance that old wealth gives. Their manner smacked of condescension and was often overbearing, especially toward those who seemed to doubt their aristocratic claims. Their high conception of their honor made them particularly susceptible to offense, and this led very frequently to violence, to defense of wounded pride. The code duello was an anachronism in nineteenth century America, but the southern gentlemen adhered to it, nevertheless. And this sensitivity to status and honor, and the violence that went with it, was extended to the larger society because the social example of the planters taught that it was the correct, the only decent way to maintain face. Slavery too, despite the instances of affection and concern on the part of some planters for their slaves, tended to stimulate in the coarser masters their potentiality for sadism and violence and cruelty.[12] But this harsh reality of slavery, its brutality and degradation of the human spirit, was subtly covered over by the South's capacity for sentimentality. The South was peculiarly affected by Victorian sentimentality "with its false feeling, its excessive nicety, its will to the denial of the ugly" partly, perhaps, because of its romanticism and also because of its deep need to answer the critical Yankees and to place a veil over the questionable aspects of domestic life on the plantation.

[11] *Ibid.*, pp. 50–51.
[12] On this aspect of slavery, see J. H. Franklin, *The Militant South, 1800–1861* (Cambridge: Harvard University Press, 1956).

Another striking feature of the pre-war southern culture was its passion for rhetoric, for the oratory of the spell-binder and declaimer. The origin of this cultural trait was probably to be found in the paternalism of plantation society, with its great differences in culture and education. The poor, common white early fell into the habit of looking to the planter for leadership and opinion, especially in politics. So with the love of rhetoric went a love of politics—a field in which the articulate could impress their fellows and put down those who challenged their position.

> Thus the politics of the Old South was a theater for the play of the purely personal, the purely romantic, and the purely hedonistic. It was the arena wherein one great champion confronted another or a dozen, and sought to outdo them in rhetoric and splendid gesturing. It swept back the loneliness of the land, it brought men together under torches, it filled them with the contagious power of the crowd, it unleashed emotion and set it to leaping and dancing, it caught the meanest man up out of his own tiny legend into the gorgeous fabric of the legend of this or that great hero.[13]

It is consistent with these tendencies that, despite the hedonism in the planter way of life, it moved away from Anglicanism toward the sterner variety of Protestantism, the faith of the Methodists, Baptists, and Presbyterians. These sects with their revivalist religion achieved their greatest success in the first half of the nineteenth century in the South. They seemed to fit the emotional needs of its people better for a more anthropomorphic God, a Jehovah of the Old Testament—"a personal God, a God for the individualist, a God whose representatives were not silken priests but preachers risen from the people themselves." Furthermore, as the northern criticism of the "peculiar institution" increased, there was a tendency for southern religion to move toward a thorough-going Calvinism. Instead of free will determining man's destiny, everything in this dispensation became His responsibility and this was likewise true of slavery. If it was to be changed, it would be through His will or that of his servants, the ministers. The South's pre-war culture, it will be perceived, moved toward some sort of integration, in the cultural anthropologist's conception, at least.[14] Everything was of a piece, or tended to be so; in William Graham Sumner's terms, there was a strain toward consistency in the mores. Its religion tended toward a character that in some significant ways projected its own highly personal, emotional needs as well as those of the social order at large. The other worldiness of the evangelistic sects conduced to the complacency of both the masses and the master class.

Thus the planter and his people were in many ways the captives of their culture. Their ethnocentrism and chauvinism were gravely aggravated by the challenges of the abolitionists who accused them of personal sin and self-righteousness in maintaining slavery; but under attack most of the planters were far from able to assess their culture and its most cherished domestic institution with any degree of objectivity.

[13] W. J. Cash, *The Mind of the South*, pp. 52–53.

[14] The concept of cultural integration to which reference is made in the text is discussed in R. Benedict, *The Patterns of Culture* (Boston: Houghton Mifflin Co., 1934).

. . . The individualistic outlook, the lack of class pressure from below, their positions as captains against the Yankee, the whole paternalistic pattern in fact, the complete otherworldliness of the prevailing religious feeling, and in the *noveaux*, the very conviction that they were already fully developed aristocrats—all this, combining with their natural unrealism of temperament, bred in them a thoroughgoing self-satisfaction, the most complete blindness to the true facts of their world.[15]

By 1830 many southern values were out of step with the humanitarianism, which was sweeping the western world. The South, in order to maintain its values in a rapidly changing civilization, saw no alternative between cutting itself off from the world or cutting its economic throat and abandoning its life style.

NORTHERN INDIVIDUALISM AND THE BREAKDOWN
OF INSTITUTIONAL LIFE

The people of the North, on the other hand, believed that they were the exponents of a triumphant, moral democracy that was at last coming into its own. They had prospered as freehold farmers or as enterprising merchants, and some of them were becoming "merchant princes" in the growing cities. Small manufacturing enterprises had grown into corporations of considerable size. The settlers of the West, mainly recruited from the farmer, hard-working artisan, and peasant classes of Europe or from abandoned eastern regions, were supremely self-reliant and confident of the future. Land ownership, accumulation of wealth, and the enjoyment of freedom were their primary goals. With the influx of population from Europe they had no need for slave labor. Indeed, many of them looked askance even on the free Negro and supported the goal of "free soil" in the hope of establishing white societies on it.[16] On the whole, economic opportunism, hard work, and material gain so preoccupied them that they had little time for or understanding of a genteel life style.

By the eve of the Civil War, the North had become accustomed to the existence of bustling, growing cities alongside the old rural way of life. In these cities the dominant characteristic seemed to be incessant change. Change and progress became the slogans of the urban areas, which were burgeoning throughout the section. These values created such a dynamic environment that those who preferred the status quo were left behind in society. Indeed, as a result of this emphasis on change and success many of the religious and

---

[15] W. J. Cash, *The Mind of the South*, pp. 77–78.

[16] On this subject, see C. V. Woodward, "The Antislavery Myth," *American Scholar*, XXXI, 1962, pp. 312–328; also L. Litwack, *North of Freedom* (Chicago: University of Chicago Press, 1961). ". . . White supremacy was a national, not a regional credo, and politicians of the Democratic, Whig and the Republican parties openly and repeatedly expressed their allegiance to the doctrine. To do otherwise was to risk political suicide. . . ." [Woodward, "The Antislavery Myth," *American Scholar*, XXXI (1962), p. 316.]

political ideas of the past were abandoned; to many of the older landed and merchant elite a gross economic materialism was filling the vacuum in morality. ". . . What motives could be offered to Americans for acting collectively, rather than selfishly? This question preoccupied the twenties and thirties with an intensity which scarcely slackened. A strong sense of mutuality was clearly lacking in an age characterized by social atomism and high mobility. . . ."[17]

If the backwash effects of economic expansion were producing cultural retardation and myopia in the South, the spread effects of unrestrained growth under the auspices of Jacksonian democracy were creating serious strains in the social order of the North. That syndrome of values that some critical southerners referred to as "the Progress" seemed to be generating some very peculiar notions among the people. The economic individualism stimulated by the Jacksonian attack on political and economic privilege gathered such momentum that many Americans came to believe that they could dispense with institutions altogether. "Institutions," wrote Wendell Phillips, the great abolitionist orator, "as we are accustomed to call them, are but pasteboard, and intended to be, against the thought of the street."[18] The conception spread that if man could be aroused and uplifted, most of the traditional agencies of authority could be discarded to make way for man himself in his natural perfection. He would be free for the first time in history to throw off the burden of class, oppressive government, and outworn religion. The very dynamism of this northern society was seen as a source of stability. Traditional guarantees of social order had become superfluous.

> . . . Its religion was so dynamic that it needed no church; its wealth and opportunities were so boundless that a center of financial power could lose its meaning; and in its need for politicians and lawyers by the thousands it could do without a governing class and ignore many an ancient tradition of bench and bar. Thus for the American of that day it was the very success of his society—of capitalism, of religious liberalism and political democracy—that made it unnecessary for him to be concerned with institutions. . . . He was able to imagine that "stability" resided not in social organization but in "human nature." He no longer appeared to draw from society his traditions, his culture, and all his aspirations; indeed, he, the transcendent individual—the new symbol of virtue—now "confronted" society; he challenged it as something of a conspiracy to rob him of his birthright. Miraculously, all society then sprang to his aid in the celebration of that conceit.[19]

[17] W. R. Taylor, *Cavalier and Yankee* (New York: G. Braziller, 1961), p. 109. This question of the basis of community in a rapidly changing democracy had intrigued Tocqueville. He asked himself what held America together. He wrote: "Up to the present, it can't be said that the Americans have a national character, unless it's that of having none. Here there are no common memories, no national roots. What can be then the only tie which unites the different parts of this vast body? L'interet?" (G. W. Pierson, *Tocqueville and Beaumont in America* (New York: Oxford University Press, 1938), p. 114.

[18] *Speeches, Lectures and Letters*, First Series (Boston, 1902), p. 264, quoted in G. M. Frederickson, *The Inner Civil War* (New York: Harper and Row, 1965), p. 7.

[19] Elkins, *Slavery* (Chicago: University of Chicago Press, 1959), pp. 32–33.

Unfortunately, one of the forces powerfully strengthening that conceit was the body of ideas that emerged in New England in the 1830's known as Transcendentalism. Its leader was Ralph Waldo Emerson, and he influenced a large group of scholars, ministers, and intellectuals in the following decades. Emerson preached, in effect, a radical individualism, a "self-reliance," which minimized and even scorned institutions as such. True individuality could be reached only by turning away from all forms, institutions, and traditions. He approved the reformers of his day, many of whom were very critical of the new industrialism, egalitarianism, and anti-intellectualism that the age of Jackson had promoted in various ways.[20] Emerson's belief in intuition as the origin of truth offered the solitary man direct access to God or "the Over-soul." So he understood those reformers who withdrew their tender consciences from social organizations and who with him believed in the intuition that the "human spirit is equal to all emergencies, alone." Some of Emerson's contemporaries, such as George Ripley, William Henry Channing, and Theodore Parker, rejected his withdrawal from society to practice "self-culture." They believed that the intellectual who withdrew from the corrupt institutions had the responsibility to reform society. On the whole, however, the effect of Transcendentalism was not to transcend or revolt against its age, but to accentuate some of its most marked propensities—"its anti-institutionalism, its individual perfectionism, its abstraction, and its guilt and reforming zeal."[21]

THE POLARIZATION OF THE POLITICAL
CONFLICT OVER SLAVERY

The conflict over slavery was the subject of sharp negotiation and shrewd compromise over many decades after the adoption of the Constitution. In drafting the nation's governmental charter in 1787 the Founding Fathers gave the slave owners protection in return for favors to northern commerce and industry. A treaty of peace was struck, in effect, between the commercial and the planting states, and in the immediately following years the same process of accommodation was achieved: the Northwest territory was dedicated to freedom and the region below the Ohio opened to slavery.

The question arose again a quarter of a century later when the Missouri territory applied for admission to the Union with slavery. It had been practiced there since the early days of French settlement. When the issue came up for debate in the House of Representatives in 1819, Tallmadge of New York sought to amend the bill by providing that further introduction of slaves into

[20] On these topics, see A. M. Schlesinger, Jr., *The Age of Jackson* (Boston: Little Brown, 1945), Chap. 29; on anti-intellectualism during that period, see R. Hofstadter, *Anti-Intellectualism In America* (New York: Knopf, 1963), pp. 155–171.

[21] Elkins, *Slavery*, p. 158. Elkins' whole brilliant interpretation of the relation of the American intellectual to slavery and his comparative analysis of the British and American movements are essential reading here.

Missouri be prohibited and that all children born of slaves there be free at the age of twenty-five years.

Immediately there was a deadlock. The South, having half the Senators, could block passage of this plan for restricting slavery, and the North, with a majority in the House, could keep Missouri out of the Union. A long and stormy debate took place that caused Jefferson to fear for the safety of the nation. But the Compromise of 1820 resolved the conflict by admitting Missouri as a slave state and Maine, separated from the parent state of Massachusetts, as a free state. Further, it was agreed that the rest of the vast Louisiana territory north of the parallel of 36°30' should be free, and the smaller portion south of that line should be open to slavery. The extremists of either side were not satisfied with this adjustment, old John Randolph speaking of it as "a dirty bargain," but conciliation had won out—the perilous balance of power between the sections was maintained.

The next serious collision between the sections came more than a decade later over the tariff, a perennial bone of contention. The Tariff of 1832 antagonized South Carolina so much that it was led to declare that law null and void and it prepared to leave the Union. But again, compromise as in the Tariff Law of 1833 and Jackson's readiness to use force against this threat of secession saved the day.

Relative peace prevailed, at least in the halls of Congress, for close to twenty years before the next crisis erupted. In the meantime, the abolitionists were increasing the vigor of their attack upon slavery, but politically their efforts yielded little results. The combination of southern Democrats with their northern supporters was too powerful for the reformers. The abolitionists, demanding immediate, uncompensated emancipation of the slaves, were circulating their literature through the mails and submitting anti-slavery petitions to Congress. These petitions usually asked for the abolition of slavery in the District of Columbia, and opposed the admission of Arkansas as a slave state and the annexation of Texas. In 1836 Pickney of South Carolina introduced resolutions in Congress aimed at preventing this antislavery agitation of the northern petitioners. They stated that "all petitions, memorials, resolutions, propositions or papers relating, in any way, or to any extent whatever to the subject of slavery, shall, without being either printed or referred be laid upon the table, and that no further action whatever shall be thereon."[22] After the passage of this "gag resolution," Theodore Weld and other abolitionists redoubled their campaign to secure petitions. They contended that such rules that had been reenacted session by session until 1840 when they were made a standing rule of the House, were a denial of the constitutional right of petition. While previously many northerners had been unsympathetic to the abolitionists, now thousands felt that "if the issue of the question was to be . . . 'Slavery or the right of petition,' they had but one course to pursue,

---

[22] See W. B. Hesseltine, *Tragic Conflict* (New York: G. Braziller, 1962); also S. F. Bemis, *John Quincy Adams and the Union* (New York: Knopf, 1949).

however unpleasant it might be."[23] Many joined the American Anti-Slavery Society simply out of support for this cherished freedom. Actually, the gag rules were designed to expedite the House's business. They simply provided that petitions for the same purpose received thereafter were to be tabled without debate. But the public did not understand such parliamentary technicalities; thousands of women were enrolled in the crusade as part of the women's right movement; Congress was inundated with petitions. Under pressure, the House in December, 1844, rescinded the gag rule on the ground that the right to petition Congress could not be denied. The public misunderstood the right to petition, but the abolitionists had availed themselves of a priceless opportunity to agitate the whole nation on the question.

The sectional conflict flared again with the annexation of Texas, the War with Mexico, and the acquisition of territory stretching to the Pacific. Again the issue was the status of slavery in these areas and the impact on the balance of political power in Congress. In 1846, a Democratic Representative from Pennsylvania introduced a resolution that slavery should be entirely excluded from any territories acquired in the struggle—this was the famous Wilmot Proviso. Some southern Senators threatened disunion if it was passed. But it was voted down, though charges and countercharges were hurled by sectional spokesmen that the Mexican War was "a slave owners' scheme" to gain more land for the extension of slavery.

With the end of that war, it was simply necessary to provide for the governance of the newly acquired territories. Again, a great controversy erupted in 1849 over the question of the status of slavery in this vast new land. California had asked for admission to the Union as a free state. After a momentous debate in which the old masters Calhoun, Webster, and Clay participated, the latter was successful in engineering another sectional compromise. Utah and New Mexico were formally organized as territories, with the question of slavery to be determined by their constitutions at the time of their admission as states. In return for this concession to the South, California was admitted as a free state. The slave trade was abolished in the District of Columbia, but offsetting this was the passage of a drastic Fugitive Slave Law, which was to be enforced by federal officers. Thus, though there was much criticism of this settlement in the nation, the tenuous equilibrium of power was maintained—there were an even fifteen states on either side.

But not for long. While the election of Franklin Pierce, the Democratic candidate, as President in 1852 seemed to put the stamp of finality on the compromise, that same year saw the publication of *Uncle Tom's Cabin;* resistance to the newly enacted Fugitive Slave Law became marked; proposals to annex Cuba and for the granting of free homesteads out of land in the public domain were advanced; all these contentious matters kept the sectional feel-

[23] Barnes, *The Antislavery Impulse* (New York: Harcourt, Brace and World, 1933), p. 111; Chaps. 11–13 of this work are excellent on the subject. See also R. B. Nye, *Fettered Freedom; Civil Liberties and the Slavery Controversy* (East Lansing: Michigan State College Press, 1949).

ing alive. The conflict reached a new high with the debate over the Kansas-Nebraska Act of 1854.

This controversial law, the inspiration of which some laid to Stephen A. Douglas's desire to be President (although that is only one interpretation), repealed the pact that had served to preserve the Union for three decades—the Missouri Compromise of 1820. The law provided that the two new territories of Kansas and Nebraska, when they were admitted to the Union, might come in, with or without slavery, as their constitutions might provide. Since these territories lay north of the Missouri Compromise line, the provision set at nought the basic principle of that Act. In fact, Congress expressly declared that its provisions were null and void, being contrary to the principle of non-interference with slavery in the territories.[24] This law not only contributed to a polarizing of sentiment over the slavery question, it brought about a sudden realignment of factions and parties that did much to accelerate the coming of war. In the very year of its passage, the Whigs and Democrats came together at Ripon, Wisconsin and agreed that a new party must be formed, if the bill was adopted. In that year a number of fusion groups, combining independent Democrats, northern Whigs, and free soilers, came into existence—the Republican Party was born. In the midst of this disintegration of the parties, there emerged still another, the Know-Nothings, or Native Americans, who posed a further threat to the peace and stability of the nation.

Mass meetings, fiery sermons from the pulpit, flaming editorials, and burning of public figures in effigy now became almost daily events. In 1855, Kansas became the scene of armed conflict as partisans of slavery and freedom clashed in the effort to dominate the politics of that territory. Senator Sumner the following year aroused the nation with his powerful speech, "The Crime against Kansas," in which he harshly indicted the slavery party. Two days later a relative of one of the southern Senators attacked in that speech, Representative Preston Brooks, beat the Massachusetts Senator senseless with a heavy cane.

The following year the Supreme Court further intensified the conflict with its decision in the Dred Scott case. In a divided opinion, Justice Taney held for the majority that Scott, a Negro who had been taken from Missouri into a free territory, was still a slave and that the Missouri Compromise was null and void because Congress could not constitutionally abolish slavery in the territories. Pro-slavery supporters hailed the decision, while free soilers and Republicans could not restrain themselves over it; even Lincoln, usually calm and sober about such matters, showed his resentment at this ruling. Still another log was thrown on the fire of sectional animosity with the publication in the same year of Hinton R. Helper's *Impending Crisis of the South.* Helper showed how slavery was retarding the economic development of the South and the

---

[24] For a thorough treatment of the background and consequences of this law, see A. Nevins, *Ordeal of the Union*, Vol. II (New York: Scribners, 1947), pp. 94–121, 311ff. See also on this Act, R. F. Nichols, "The Kansas-Nebraska Act: A Century of Historiography," *Mississippi Valley Historical Review*, XLIII (1959), pp. 187–212.

improvement of the economic status of both whites and Negroes. His analysis was hailed by many in the North, but condemned and banned in the South as abusive and inflammatory.

The spiralling wave of emotionalism came to a climax in 1859 with John Brown's raid on the arsenal at Harper's Ferry, Virginia, in an attempt to start a slave rebellion and thus bring about emancipation. Brown and his confederates were caught, and he was quickly executed for treason under the state's laws. This incident rocked a nation that was already panicky, in the South over rumored slave revolts and in the North over the riots that sometimes accompanied the seizure of bondsmen under the Fugitive Slave Act. It gravely contributed to polarization of attitudes over the conflict and to stereotyping by each section of the other. "Republicans were all John Browns to the Southerners," Professor Dumond observes, "and slaveholders were all Simon Legrees to the Northerners."[25] Harper's Ferry fatally strengthened the hands of the extremists and revolutionists in the North and South and correspondingly weakened and discredited the influence of the moderates.

> The crisis psychology of 1859 persisted and deepened in the fateful year of 1860 into a pathological condition of mind in which delusions of persecution and impending disaster flourished. Out of Texas came wild rumors of incendiary fires, abolitionists plotting with slaves, and impending insurrection on a vast scale. Rumors of large stocks of strychnine in the possession of slaves and of plans for well-poisoning were widely believed, though unproved. . . .
> In the course of the crisis each of the antagonists, according to the immemorial pattern, had become convinced of the depravity and diabolism of the other. Each believed itself persecuted, menaced. . . . Paranoia continued to induce counter-paranoia, each antagonist infecting the other reciprocally, until the vicious spiral ended in war.[26]

This phenomenon, it need hardly be noted, is a striking instance of what Myrdal would term the circular causation of social change.

Before ending this review of some of the developments in the mounting polarization of the political conflict over slavery and the resulting disruption of the parties, we need to remind ourselves that right down to the firing on Fort Sumter and even into the war years, there were moderates and Unionists on both sides who resisted the arguments of the hard line extremists. There were many Whigs in the New York business community and elsewhere who sought to avoid the "irrepressible conflict."[27] But offsetting such efforts in the pre-war years were powerful forces arraying individuals and groups on either side of the sectional schism. Elkins, in a provocative analysis, argues that

[25] Quoted by C. V. Woodward in "John Brown's Private War," as reproduced in N. Kiell, *Psychological Studies of Famous Americans, The Civil War Era* (New York: Twayne Publishers, Inc., 1964), p. 56. Woodward remarks concerning Dumond's statement, "As a matter of fact Northern conservatives and unionists staged huge anti-Brown demonstrations that equalled or outdid those staged by the Brown partisans." (*Ibid.*)

[26] N. Kiell, *Psychological Studies of Famous Americans*, p. 62.

[27] See, e.g., P. Foner, *Business and Slavery* (Chapel Hill: University of North Carolina Press, 1941), *passim.*

that process was nothing less than the very democratization, North and South, of the controversy over slavery. The tragic flaw in an otherwise singularly favored society was the absence of mechanisms for checking such a development—the absence of mechanisms which might permit a range of alternatives in sentiment and idea to be crystallized and maintained and which might prevent the development of a lowest common denominator of feeling in each section, widely enough shared as to provide a democratic ground for war.[28]

Elkins seeks to show in the study cited that antislavery became less and less institutional (ie.., concerned with concrete patterns of behavior) as it became more and more democratized. In his view, antislavery moved from colonization of the ex-slaves as a solution, to philosophical abolitionism (slavery an evil that cannot be removed immediately, but must be reformed), to immediate emancipation gradually accomplished, to immediate and unqualified emancipation, Garrison's doctrine. The penultimate stage, immediate emancipation gradually carried out, came to mean in the minds of one group (the followers of Theodore Weld) immediate repentance of sin. This formula was very close to Garrison's, and finally, unqualified emancipation was abandoned by the Weld group in favor of unconditional immediatism. Garrisonianism had conquered the opposing antislavery factions and that meant, according to Elkins, that the slavery problem would henceforth be apprehended only in terms of the intellectual categories of anti-institutionalism, individualism, abstraction, and guilt.[29] What this led to can be illustrated by the ante-bellum debate over the nature of the Negro character. Slaveholders often argued that the Negroes suffered from an innate racial inferiority, while the abolitionists typically maintained the innate human perfectibility of the enslaved people. Such a debate, by abstracting from the cultural and institutional context influencing the Negro, virtually ignored those vitally important elements. A debate on such terms could never really be resolved.

Thus, as the antislavery movement became less and less institutional and more moralistic in its arguments, it became at the same time broader and more widely shared.[30] The assaults made on freedom of speech, freedom of assembly, and of the press by the opponents of the abolitionists widened the number of those generally involved in the struggle. Secondly, as we have seen, the ancient right of petition was involved, and this implicated indirectly many more in abolitionism's crusade. Third, the underground railroad involved a certain number who were sympathizers with the antislavery cause, but not necessarily abolitionists. (Incidentally, we now know that the number of those who were active in the U.G.R.R. was formerly greatly exaggerated.)[31] Fourth, the issue that had the greatest appeal—"free soil"—was "an antislavery position so widely shared that by 1860 it could command political

---

[28] Elkins, *Slavery*, p. 178.

[29] Elkins, *Slavery*, p. 189.

[30] Elkins, *Slavery*, p. 185ff. In his emphasis on the democratization of the slavery controversy Elkins is demonstrating a principle very familiar to students of modern propaganda, namely, the importance of broadening the group alleged to be under attack.

[31] See L. Gara, *The Liberty Line* (Lexington: University of Kentucky Press, 1961).

majorities in every Northern state but one. It was with this issue that the democratization of antislavery had become complete."[32] By democratization Elkins refers to the broadening or widening of antislavery sentiment and action; his use of the term, "democratization" of the controversy is apt to cause semantic confusion. Yet, we have summarized this part of Elkins' analysis because of its relevance to the polarization process as it affected slavery and the conflict between the sections. His stress on the forces broadening the sectional conflict is important and should not be disregarded because of differences over the nature of these developments.

POLARIZATION OF THE CONFLICT ON THE IDEOLOGICAL LEVEL

Though the abolitionists stirred the nation with their attacks on the slaveholders and the "peculiar" institution, they did not secure as many supporters as one might think. At the height of their movement, there were 2,000 antislavery societies with 200,000 members. The Liberty Party, which was backed by the abolitionists in 1844, could muster only 65,000 votes out of the total of two and a half million cast. The fact was that the opposition to slavery in the North was broken into innumerable factions; furthermore, the abolitionists antagonized many by their fanaticism. In addition, many of the lower class immigrants feared the competition of the Negroes as workers. White supremacy, it must be realized, was not just a southern credo in the ante-bellum period, but a national one. The Democratic, the Whig, and the Republican parties openly and repeatedly stated their allegiance to that doctrine. To do otherwise was to risk political suicide.[33]

In the fifties, the ideological war over slavery intensified. Harriet Beecher Stowe's novel reached hundreds of thousands and stirred intense southern resentment for its attack on the region's morals. Within three years of its publication, fourteen pro-slavery novels appeared by way of answer; one was entitled "Uncle Robin in his Cabin in Virginia and Tom without One in Boston." But even before this rash of southern novels appeared, the section's writers and intellectuals had begun to develop a political, ethical, religious, and philosophical justification for slavery. To understand that ideological defense, we must appreciate the South's painful inner conflict over slavery. For nowhere was this conflict more evident than in the elaborate body of theory by which the section's leaders tried to prove the beneficence of its peculiar social system.[34]

[32] Elkins, *Slavery*, p. 189.
[33] C. V. Woodward, "The Antislavery Myth," *American Scholar*, XXXI, 1962, p. 316.
[34] One of the best essays on this subject is that of C. G. Sellers, Jr., "The Travail of Slavery," in *The Southerner as American*, edited by Sellers (Chapel Hill: University of North Carolina Press, 1960), Chapter 3; see also C. Eaton, *Freedom of Thought in*

The conflict in the South's mind stemmed from its old devotion to liberty and the Union and the clash of those loyalties with the demands of slavery. The nullifiers and the radical sectionalists had transformed the old emphasis on the natural rights of men to a new stress on state's rights, but the old liberal principles could not be easily discarded. For many southerners had been staunch supporters of the Declaration of Independence, which they identified with Jefferson, and there had been a considerable antislavery movement in the section during the Revolutionary years and after. But now with the western world turning away from slavery and northern abolitionists denouncing it as a sin, the South's inner anxiety grew. The necessity to justify slavery, coupled with the white South's inability to escape its inherited liberalism or the common humanity it shared with the slaves, inspired "a mixture of pain and wild hyperbole."[35]

The ambivalence toward the slave was reflected in law, religion, and in the slaveholder's personal dealings with his bondsmen. Humanity and the profit motive were forever struggling against each other in the plantation owner's mind. The guilt feelings this engendered go far to explain the belligerent dogmatism of the South in the critical fifties. Social psychologists tell us that value conflicts, especially when they create the kind of institutional instability arising out of the ambiguities of southern slavery, make a society ready to follow the advocates of irrational, aggressive policies. The defense mechanisms to which southern thought resorted were numerous—denial of reality, rationalization, scape-goating (the overseers and slave traders served in this role), etc.—and all testify to the pathological state of the southern mind in the prewar decade. From Calhoun's assertion on the Senate floor in the mid-thirties that slavery was "a great good" to the defense of inequality and the elaboration of the ideal of a Greek democracy, and Hammond's picture of slavery as an eleemosynary institution, there is evidence of massive rationalization and fantasy-building.

In a sin-conscious society such as pre-war America, the abolitionists' indictment of the slaveholders in moral and religious terms was psychologically threatening. Duff Green, Calhoun's editorial mouthpiece, had warned him that the principal danger of abolitionism was its influence upon "the consciences and fears of the slaveholders themselves." It threatened, he said, to diffuse among our own people "a morbid sensitivity on the question of slavery." The

---

the *Old South*, 2nd Ed. (Durham, N.C.: Duke University Press, 1940) and W. S. Jenkins, *Pro-Slavery Thought in the Old South* (Chapel Hill: University of North Carolina Press, 1935).

[35] L. Hartz, *The Liberal Tradition in America: An Interpretation of American Political Thought since the Revolution* (New York: Harcourt, Brace, 1955), p. 145. Sellers has written: ". . . No picture of the Old South as a section confident and united in its dedication to a neo-feudal social order, and no explanation of the Civil War as a conflict between 'two civilizations,' can encompass the complexity and the pathos of the ante-bellum reality. No analysis that misses the inner turmoil of the ante-bellum Southerner can do justice to the central tragedy of the Southern experience." (Sellers in *The Southerner as American*, p. 40.)

pathological violence of the southerners to northern criticism in the fifties indicated that this had occurred. One New Orleans editor in the secession crisis wrote, "The South has been moved to resistance chiefly. . . by the popular dogma in the free states that slavery is a crime in the sight of GOD. The South, in the eyes of the North, is degraded and unworthy, because of the institution of servitude."[36] In these tragic developments we can see the circular, cumulative movements of events and ideas, of fears and fantasies, to which Myrdal alludes in his theory of regional polarization and the role of non-economic factors in the process.

Actually, the process of regional polarization had gone so far that by 1857 South and North were

> rapidly becoming separate peoples. The major Protestant sects had broken in twain; one major party, the Whigs, had first split in half and then disappeared; press, pulpit, and education all showed a deepening cleavage. With every passing year, the fundamental assumptions, tastes, and cultural aims of the two sections became more divergent. As tension grew, militant elements on both sides resented the presence of "outsiders"; Southerners were exposed to insult at Northern resorts, while the Yankees in the South were compelled to explain their business to a more and more suspicious population. . . .
>
> This schism in culture struck into the very substance of national life. Differences of thought, taste, and ideals gravely accentuated the misunderstandings caused by the basic economic and social differences between a free labor system and a slave labor system, between a semi-industrialized economy of high productiveness and an agrarian economy of low productiveness. An atmosphere was created in which emotions grew feverish; in which every episode became a crisis, every jar a shock.[37]

THE SECESSION CRISIS

In the midst of the social disorganization induced in both sections by the rapid geographic and economic expansion of the nation, there is evidence that the political machinery and its leaders were sadly lacking in the capacity required to meet the challenges. The situation was that described by Machiavelli—the "confusion of a growing state." "The baffling problem was not how to maintain a balance among states but how to preserve a balance among a number of emotional units or attitudes. It was this that proved beyond the political capacity of the time." There was a need, in other words, not only to accommodate the conflicting demands of sections, politically and in economic terms, but to maintain the Union in the face of a complex cultural pluralism. The divisive attitudes—in Roy Nichols' terms, notably metropolitanism, ter-

---

[36] D. L. Dumond, ed., *Southern Editorials on Secession* (Ann Arbor: University of Michigan Press, 1931), pp. 315–316.

[37] A. Nevins, *Ordeal of the Union, A House Dividing, 1852–1857*, Vol. II (New York: Charles Scribner's Sons, 1947), pp. 553–554.

ritorialism, southernism, New Englandism, and antislaverism—proved to be more powerful and dynamic than the cohesive ideas of nationalism, regionalism, and democracy.[38] The Democratic Party, the inheritor of Jackson's revolution and the developer of mass organization and party politics as we know it, was growing old; its formulae for holding the Union together, negativism and *laissez faire* on most domestic issues and expansionism in foreign policy, were about played out. And now there emerged a party with a positive program and a new style. The Republicans denounced the southern domination of the Democratic organization and boldly espoused liberty, "free soil," and a program of promotional benefits and subsidies for private enterprise. Under Freemont in 1856 they came within thirty-five electoral votes of capturing the Presidency.

The Democrats in power under Buchanan were beset by patronage problems, fraud, corruption, and the dilemma of "bleeding Kansas." In 1858, the party lost control of the House of Representatives and in the following year disintegrated completely when the southern Democrats walked out of the Charleston convention because of their bitter opposition to Douglas and his doctrine of popular sovereignty. The Douglasites nominated the Little Giant for the Presidency and Benjamin Fitzpatrick as his running mate; the bolters, meeting also in Baltimore, nominated John C. Breckenridge and Joseph Lane as their candidates for the nation's two highest offices. In retrospect, it can be seen that that step—the polarization of the Democratic Party—was the prelude to the dissolution of the Union and the coming of Civil War because it made possible the election of Lincoln. The split in the Democratic ranks enabled the "prairie dark horse" to be elected as a minority President in 1860. ". . . The breakup of the Democratic party and the beginning of armed conflict were almost simultaneous; they were intimately related phenomena. The shattering of the party of Jackson was the bursting of a dike which unloosened an engulfing flood."[39]

Various southern leaders had warned before the election that their states would secede if Lincoln was elected. When that event occurred, popular sentiment in South Carolina was overwhelmingly in favor of secession. In December, 1860, the fire-eaters of that state had their way—the state's convention unanimously voted an ordinance of secession and by February of the following year, a month before Lincoln's election, six additional states of the lower South had seceded from the Union. Despite strenuous efforts to compromise the sectional conflict, the drift to war continued. Douglas, who had played a prominent part in such efforts, suddenly died, Lincoln abandoned conciliation and sent re-enforcements to the besieged Fort Sumter, whereupon the Confederates fired on it, forcing the garrison to surrender. The Rebellion, as Unionists called the war, had begun.

[38] R. F. Nichols, *The Disruption of American Democracy* (New York: The Macmillan Co., 1948), pp. 21ff.
[39] A. Nevins, *Ordeal of the Union* . . . , p. 513.

SOCIAL AND POLITICAL CHANGE DURING THE WAR

While aggregative statistical data seem to suggest retardation of industrial growth in the Civil War years, there are those who contend that qualitative institutional and additudinal changes took place during that period that were of immense importance for the nation's subsequent economic growth.[40] The distinguished historian, Allan Nevins, believes that the war gave a distinct lift to the entrepreneurial spirit: "One of the most significant facts of the era was the sudden and complete release of organizing energy in the nation. . . ."[41] Nevins contends that there was an emergence of a number of bold captains of industry in this period, some of whom had learned "lessons of command and organization" in the Army and others who had learned such lessons in supplying the Union forces. Northerners, he says, were learning entirely new lessons of resourcefulness, initiative, and organization during the War. ". . . Parallel with the waste and sorrows of war ran a stimulation of individual initiative, a challenge to large-scale planning, and an encouragement of cooperative effort, which in combination with new agencies for developing national resources amounted to a great release of creative energy. . . ."[42] General Francis A. Walker, whose service in the war as a staff officer had taught him the importance of handling the mass detail of army organization pointed to even broader value changes in America as a result of the war. He stated that the war had produced "a vast change in popular sentiments and ideals, as it showed how much nobler are strength of will, firmness of purpose, resolution to endure, and capacity for action than are the qualities of the speech-maker and the fine writer, which the nation had once agreed chiefly to admire."[43] Walker saw the war as contributing to an intellectual revolution in that the nation turned away from the Transcendentalism and sentimentalism of the early nineteenth century to a more active, pragmatic confrontation of reality.

The war gave a stimulus to large-scale production and the consolidation of business. The Quartermaster of the Union Army, though he recognized the wisdom of scattering orders as widely as possible, found that many of the

[40] At the 1964 conference on economic change in the years 1850–1873 sponsored by the Eleutherian Mills-Hagley Foundation [see *Economic Change in the Civil War Era* (Greenville, Del.: Eleutherian Mills-Hagley Foundation, 1964)], the preponderant opinion of the principal speakers was that, "aside from commercial banking, the Civil War appears not to have started or created any significant new patterns of economic institutional change." There was, however, some dissent from this view and one speaker pointed out that very little attention had been paid to the personal factor in economic change during this "relatively unexplored period of American economic development." (*Op. cit.*, pp. 152–155, 172–174.)

[41] A. Nevins, *The War for the Union* (New York: Charles Scribner's Sons, 1960), Vol. II, p. 510.

[42] *Ibid.*, p. 483.

[43] G. M. Fredrickson, *The Inner Civil War* (New York: Harper and Row, 1965), p. 223.

small firms were inexpert or unreliable. He had to adjust to "an increasingly concentrated economy. It was the big horse dealer, the big tent-maker, the big ambulance supplier, who increasingly got the orders, for in the emergent industrial America the big establishments usually showed more efficiency. . . .''[44]

Another factor favoring the consolidation of business was the wartime tax system. The general sales tax of 6 per cent favored the integrated firm over the highly specialized one because the former had to pay the tax but once, while less integrated concerns paid such levies at every transfer of ownership. This tendency toward consolidation was especially noteworthy in the field of street railways. The military use of the railroads during the war also provided a stimulus to consolidation. The Union Army often connected short lines, converting them into "through" routes; financial consolidation usually followed.

Cooperative activities among independent business concerns were encouraged by the war. Many businessmen started trade associations to protest against internal taxes or to suggest fiscal changes. The National Association of Wool Growers, the New England Association of Cotton Manufacturers, and the American Iron and Steel Institute were all formed at this time largely to influence tariff legislation. One historian of the period sums up the trend of the times this way:

> Never in the history of the country up to that time had there been such a strong tendency toward united and harmonious action on the part of the employing classes, whether this resulted in a complete merging of one company into another or looser and more temporary organizations to consider the subject of prices, internal taxes, the tariff, or wages; never had there been such an incentive to consolidation and union. . . . There was a definite turning away from the independent, self-reliant localism and small units of the past, a decided right-about toward centralization.[45]

The organization of labor was also stimulated by the inflation of the war years. The rise in the cost of living was outstripping wages. As previous statistics suggested, prices advanced as much as 100 per cent during the entire war period, while wages increased 50 to 60 per cent. Though family income was sometimes supplemented by military wages and soldiers' bounties, real wages would seem to have declined. The wages of women were especially low, the seamstresses making army clothing being particularly exploited by contractors. The fact was that the labor supply was being added to by considerable immigration; the contract labor system, whereby workers agreed to repay the cost of their transport out of future wages, was a boon to employers. No fewer than 800,000 immigrants entered the country during the five years of the war. Under these conditions, the organization of labor grew active, though such efforts were often met with lockouts and blacklists by employers. Nevertheless, during the war many local unions and at least ten national

[44] A. Nevins, *The War for the Union*, Vol. 2, p. 472.
[45] E. Fite, *Social and Economic Conditions in the North during the Civil War* (New York: P. Smith, 1920), pp. 168–169.

organizations sprang into existence. In 1863, for example, the first of the
great railroad brotherhoods, the Brotherhood of Locomotive Engineers, was
formed. Union organization was so successful in the war and immediate post-
war years that by 1870 there were no less than thirty-two national trade
unions.

But the changes occurring in the relationship of government to business and
in the climate of enterprise itself during the war years were the most significant developments. The inflation, which was not of the runaway variety,
proved to be very stimulating to speculative enterprise and probably shifted
funds into the hands of those with a high propensity to invest, if not in the
war years proper, then after the close of the hostilities. ". . . On the great
crest of inflation," says Professor Sharkey, "thousands of businesses saw the
light of day and thrived. The entrepreneur flourished, but meanwhile the
creditor interest languished, as debts were repaid in money of constantly
diminishing value."[46] Meanwhile, the legislative program of Lincoln's administrations constituted a veritable "new deal" for business. Legislation that impa-
tient business and farmer interests had been futilely seeking under Democratic
administrations for years was now passed in the absence of the southern
legislators from Congress. The first Morill Tariff was adopted even before
Lincoln's inauguration. In successive laws passed in 1862 and 1864 Congress
gained additional revenue, but it also granted increased protection to many
articles that could be produced at home and greatly reduced the free list.
Manufacturers, says Stanwood of the 1864 Law, "had only to declare what rate
of duty they deemed essential, and that rate was accorded to them."[47] At the
end of the war some rates were 100 per cent *ad valorem*; the average level of
duties was about 47 per cent, more than double the average level of the 1857
Act.

The transcontinental railroad, which had been debated for years before the
war, came closer to realization with Lincoln's signing of the Pacific railway
bills of 1862 and 1864 providing for the construction of such a road by two
corporations—the Union Pacific and the Central Pacific—with liberal land
grants as an inducement. The Homestead Act of 1862 also fulfilled a pledge
the Republicans had made to the farmers who had been disappointed with
Buchanan's veto of similar legislation. It gave a quarter section of unoccupied
land to homesteaders on payment of nominal fees after five years of actual
residence on the land. This historic act was to play a significant part in the
settlement of the Far West during the remainder of the century, but it did not
achieve all the economic objectives that its proponents had anticipated. Of
great importance also was the Morill Land Grant Act of 1862, which provided
for the establishment of "agricultural and mechanical colleges"—in the states
through the device of federal land grants. By its terms each state was granted
30,000 acres of public land for each Senator or Representative in Congress.

[46] Gilchrist and David, *Economic Change in the Civil War Era*, p. 30.
[47] E. Stanwood, *American Tariff Controversies in the Nineetenth Century*, II (Boston,
Houghton Mifflin, 1928), pp. 129–130.

This law, which had also been delayed in its adoption by southern Democrats and a Presidential veto, greatly stimulated the states' efforts in the field of higher education. The Contract Labor Law of 1864 was intended to compensate for the alleged shortage of labor in the nation, but many industrialists who have traditionally been believed to have been supporters of this legislation were not enthusiastic about it. Many of them disliked contract labor because it was generally unskilled, difficult to train, and prone to trade-unionism.[48]

The Republican legislation of the war years was not extensive, but the spirit that the war boom and a supportive administration generated among the farmers and the entrepreneurial class was a most significant development in our political and economic history. Louis Hartz sees it as bringing about the ideological democratization of economic power in the sense that the Republicans were able to steal the Jacksonian thunder and give economic power an egalitarian cast. Under its religion of opportunity, every man had the right to enter, or at least to dream of entering, the Whig elite. The Republicans, he contends, succeeded under Lincoln in appropriating the Jeffersonian and Jacksonian symbolism.

> . . . That symbolism had assailed the state for granting the corporate charter and thus interfering with individual enterprise. Now, with the reliance on the state diminished, the capture of this symbolism was facilitated. The granting of the corporate charter could be confused with corporate regulation, the corporation could be confused with the individual, and Jackson could be turned inside out. The antagonism of state and individual, originally created to disadvantage the corporation, could be twisted to its defense. Down to the present day it is the genius of this achievement to convert the ideological Jeffersonian into his own worst enemy.[49]

Underlying this transformation in ideology was the fact that business enterprise with the aid of state capital had grown strong. It was now able "to stand on its own feet," and therefore in these years began to advance the philosophy of *laissez faire* more vigorously.

Indeed, the war not only strengthened nationalism and gave the *coup de grace* to the Jeffersonian philosophy of government, it changed the intellectual landscape in even more fundamental ways. Samuel Fowler, writing in October, 1865, presciently noted that "The Civil War has changed the current of our ideas, and crowded into a few years the emotions of a lifetime, has in measure given to the preceding years of our history the character of a remote state of political existence."[50] In no field was this more true than in the matter of humanitarianism and radical reform. The triumph of Unionism and nationalism led to a point of view that made obsolete the anti-institutional views of the abolitionists. The war had thwarted the movement for "humanitarian democracy" and strengthened the progress of secularism, which was

[48] See C. Erickson, *American Industry and the European Immigrant, 1860–1885* (Cambridge: Harvard University Press, 1957), pp. 7, 63.

[49] Gilchrist and David, *Economic Change in the Civil War Era, op. cit.*, p. 90.

[50] S. Fowler, "The Political Opinions of Thomas Jefferson," *North American Review*, CI (October, 1965), pp. 313–334, cited in Frederickson, *The Inner Civil War*, p. 184.

already beginning to feel the impact of the new scientific ideas, especially of Darwinism. The harsh discipline of the war, curiously enough, contributed in the post-war years to the acceptance of Social Darwinism even by the old-line aristocrats who were not especially friendly to business.

> . . . The wartime sense of the inevitability of mass suffering had prepared many people to adopt a callous view of the troubles of the poor, in the belief that progress comes only at a great human cost. Those who had stoically accepted the massive toll of dead and wounded, who had shown an "heroic" willingness to send brothers and husbands to their deaths, were fully prepared for the almost pitiless approach to poverty revealed in the new charity movements.[51]

The war seems to have led some to reject the utopian idealism of the antebellum variety and turned them to a more conservative, realistic, or practical approach to reform. Fortunately, too, some of the war generation saw the possibility that "science, organization and planning could be enlisted on the side of humanitarian reform."

But, as we shall see in the following chapters, most of the hopes for the reformation of American society by the discipline of war proved to be illusory. Instead of purging the nation once and for all of self-seeking, materialism, and corruption, the war opened the floodgates for the "greatest tide of personal and political selfishness the nation had ever seen. . . ."[52]

[51] Frederickson, *The Inner Civil War*, p. 215.
[52] *Ibid.*, p. 183.

Part 6

THE DRIVE TO INDUSTRIAL MATURITY, 1866–1896

Introduction: The Marxian Theory of
Capitalist Development

The Unstable Process of Capital
Formation and Growth

Capital Accumulation and Innovation—
Their Impact on Business Organization
and Economic Fluctuations

Political and Social Change in an Era
of Rapid Capital Growth

INTRODUCTION: THE MARXIAN THEORY
OF CAPITALIST DEVELOPMENT

> . . . It is in the drive to maturity that societies have behaved in the most Marxist way, but each in terms of its own culture, social structure, and political process; for growing societies, even growing capitalist societies, have differed radically in these respects. . . .[1]

It is our purpose in this part of our work to review the main elements of Karl Marx's theory of capitalist development and, having done so, to consider to what degree, if at all, the American economy behaved in these years "in the most Marxist way." In doing so we shall test the general validity and usefulness of this theory of economic growth as applied to the American case and analyze how the American milieu modified the Marxian prognosis of capitalism's development.

Rostow uses the phrase "drive to maturity" to "characterize the period when a society has effectively applied the range of (then) modern technology to the bulk of its resources."[2] In other words, this is the period when the process of capital formation, which was accelerated with the attainment of take-off, is carried through and the economy reaches a new level of productivity. We are not using the term to describe a stage in the economic development of the United States because if we accept a stages theory of growth *a la* Rostow then we prejudge and, in effect, beg the question of the applicability of the Marxian model. Marx's conception of the history of capitalism sees it as a continuous process of dynamic change; in this respect his treatment differs from that of Rostow.[3]

In considering the "drive to maturity" that took place in the years 1866–96, a period that witnessed a most dramatic development of our productive potential, it might be well at the outset to recall that Marx himself had a profound appreciation of the great productive role of the bourgeoisie in carrying out what he called the "historical task" of creating a productive apparatus that

---

[1] W. W. Rostow, *The Stages of Economic Growth* (New York: Cambridge University Press, 1960), p. 152.

[2] *Ibid.*, p. 59.

[3] In Rostow's theory of economic development the drive to maturity is alleged to take in the neighborhood of sixty years or so after take-off. Given his dating of these events, the year 1900 would roughly mark the symbolic time of achievement of technological maturity for the United States. According to Rostow, the process of the drive to maturity has within it the seeds of its own modification, which tend to bring it to a close. The economic, political, and sociological developments he cites as contributing to this result would seem to make 1908 or 1916 better terminal dates for the completion of the drive to maturity. However, since the continuity of historical development is such that the dating of processes of this kind is at best arbitrary and merely suggestive, we have employed a different scheme of periodization from that used by Rostow. Our treatment of this phase of the drive to maturity ends with the year 1896; in the following Part we consider some of the historical changes that tended to make this period a transitional phase to another "stage" of our development.

would be adequate for a higher form of human civilization. In the Communist Manifesto, Marx and Engels wrote:

> The bourgeoisie, during its rule of scarce one hundred years, has created more massive and more colossal productive forces than have all preceding generations together. Subjection of Nature's forces to man, machinery, application of chemistry to industry and agriculture, steam-navigation, railways, electric telegraphs, clearing of whole continents for cultivation, canalization of rivers, whole populations conjured out of the ground—what earlier century had even a presentiment that such productive forces slumbered in the lap of social labor?[4]

Marx largely wrote his three-volume work, *Capital,* in the British Museum while in political exile from his native Germany.[5] It is a treatise that has had an extraordinary influence on the political and economic systems of many nations of the world, and still stands as one of the most significant studies in the field of the theory of economic growth. In his work Marx set himself the analytical task of laying bare the "laws of motion" of capitalist society. In doing this, he had to develop a long-run theory of economic growth. This theory took its point of departure from the ideas of the classical school of economic thought. Marx differed, however, from the theory of the classical economists in that he regarded capitalism as but a stage in the history of civilization and sought to demonstrate the forces that would bring about its ultimate collapse.

Karl Marx (1818–83) was born in the German Rhineland, the son of a Jewish lawyer. He studied law at Bonn and Berlin, but took a PhD. degree in philosophy at Jena (1842). In the nineteenth century he became the chief theorist of modern socialism.

A. M. Kelly Publishing Co.

In presenting a summary of Marx's theory of economic development, it is hardly possible to portray adequately the broader philosophical suppositions

---

[4] K. Marx and F. Engels, "The Communist Manifesto," in *Capital,* edited by M. Eastman (New York: The Modern Library, 1932), p. 326.

[5] The first volume of this work appeared in 1867; the second and third were not published until after Marx's death, which occurred in 1883.

of his thought. In rejecting Hegel's idealistic dialectic, Marx developed a materialist theory of historical change that basically affected his entire system and in particular his economic analysis of capitalist development.[6] In short, Marx found the motive power of social change not in ideas, but in the material conditions of economic life and in the conflict of social classes. Hegel had seen history evolving as a result of the dialectical struggle of ideas—one idea, say that of slavery, is seen as a thesis that calls forth its opposite, its antithesis, freedom, and out of their conflict there emerges a synthesis. Marx turned right side up what he had found "standing on its head" in Hegel and presented history as a dialectical clash and evolution of material forces.

Marx distinguished four social systems in history. There were (1) primitive communism; (2) the ancient slave states; (3) feudalism; and (4) capitalism. In his analysis the key to these systems lies in their human institutions, which were determined basically by the mode of production and ownership of the means of production prevailing at the time. The mode of production as such embraces such social features as: (1) the organization of labor; (2) the geographic environment and the technological use of this environment; and (3) the technological and scientific level generally. Further, every mode of production has its own particular set of human relations that determine the nature of the class structure and of social existence generally in a society.

According to Marx, past and present societies have consisted of two basic classes: the dominating and directing class and the toiling, oppressed class. Evolution in society occurs because production relations and class structure, along with their accompanying cultural superstructure, lag behind the natural forces of production. This lag sharpens the conflicts between the classes in a society. Since the abused class under capitalism is by far the largest, and since its labor is responsible for the creation of economic goods, its victory, according to Marx, is assured. As a result, a new social order emerges, bringing with it new ideas and institutions. While these are the basic asumptions of Marx's analysis, it is necessary to pursue his analytical reasoning further in order to see how growth and development are accomplished. To do this it is necessary to begin with an explanation of the Marxian theory of value.

Let us consider the following Marxian example: A person produces a commodity (C); this commodity is produced to obtain money (M). This money is desirable only because it enables the seller to obtain a commodity of use to him. Hence, we have two kinds of value: value in exchange and use value. In our example, the exchange value of commodity (C) is equal to the exchange value of the other commodity. However, the usefulness or utility of the first commodity to its producer or seller is not the same as that for the second commodity. This utility value is different from the exchange value since the second commodity was more desirable than the first to the producer, even though they both sold at the same price.

[6] See M. M. Bober, *Karl Marx's Interpretation of History*, 2nd ed. (Cambridge: Harvard University Press, 1948).

Central to the Marxian analysis is the theory of surplus value. Marx contended that the value of the embodied labor in commodities is the determinant of their exchange value.[7] Labor, in turn, has two aspects: the first is its exchange value and the second is its use value. The capitalist purchases abstract labor power and pays the necessary exchange value (subsistence). In "consuming" labor power the capitalist obtains its use value, which is greater than the exchange value of labor power. The abilities of labor produce an output in excess of what is necessary for its own subsistence; this is the source of surplus value. In a capitalist system this surplus is the aim of profit-making. The capitalist goes to the market with money (M) and purchases a commodity—labor—and the other means of production. This commodity is transformed by production and its product is sold at M′. If profit is to be made, then M′ must be greater than M. The difference between M and M′ is called surplus value (s)—the capitalist's profit.[8]

From this example Marx argued that the value of any commodity is based on and can be decomposed into three parts. The first part is called constant capital and is equal to the value of the machines and materials used in the production process. The second part is called variable capital; its value is equal to the new labor costs or wages. The third part is called surplus value. It is the difference between the cost of sustaining the workers employed in the production processes plus constant capital consumed and the selling price of the commodity they produce. Therefore, the value of a commodity is equal to the sum of constant capital, variable capital, and the surplus value.

The rate of exploitation of labor can now be defined as the ratio of the surplus value (the output of labor that was taken by the capitalist) to the variable capital (the current labor used to produce the product.)

Although the absolute amount of surplus value will be dependent on labor productivity, labor utilization, and commodity output, Marx assumed that the rate of surplus value moves toward equality across all branches of industry. This assumption is necessary to the Marxian theory of growth because of the assertion that labor is homogeneous, transferable, and mobile and that all firms use only socially necessary labor. Marx postulates the existence of a "reserve army" consisting of unemployed workers who, by actively competing for employment, exercise a continuous downward pressure on the wage level. This causes the worker to be paid only a subsistence income. To understand the development and existence of the reserve army, it is necessary to consider the Marxian law of accumulation.

In the Marxian view, capital accumulation is the driving force of capitalism. Saving and investment of such funds in plant and equipment are essential for the individual capitalist's survival; he has no choice about the matter because of the unrelenting competition of his rivals. Part and parcel of the historic motive of capitalist accumulation is the increasing use of constant

[7] Students of Economics will recognize this as the labor theory of value.
[8] Profits, as Marx employs the term, embrace rent, interest, and proprietary income.

capital in relation to variable capital. This allows the individual producer to accomplish production with less than the socially necessary labor time. Marx, instead of relying on the population theory of Malthus to derive an Iron Law of Wages, chose to develop the theory of technological unemployment as the cause of the reduction in the wage level. He explains technological unemployment in terms of the concept of the "organic composition of capital" and in so doing lays the foundation for the first of the three business cycle theories that he advanced.

The organic composition of capital is a measure of the extent to which labor is furnished with materials, instruments, and machinery in the production process. It is defined as the ratio of constant capital to variable capital. If we define the capitalists' profits as the ratio of surplus value to total capital $(c + v)$, then we can define profits in terms of the organic composition of capital. Namely, the profit of the capitalist is equal to the rate of surplus value times one minus the organic composition of capital.[9] As the organic composition of capital increases, the reserve army will grow and the addition to the number of those unemployed will create competition for jobs, driving the wage level to "subsistence."

Marx realized that the process of capitalist accumulation can create new markets which results in a depletion of the reserve army, with a concomitant rise in the wage level. The capitalists, when faced with an increasing wage level in spite of technological unemployment, would have to take a cut in their surplus value. They would then be forced to react by withdrawing capital from investment and, thus, precipitate a crisis.

Crises and technological unemployment are the two capitalist mechanisms for replenishing the reserve army whenever it has been reduced to dangerously low levels. Thus, unlike the classicists, who tried to explain crises away, Marx makes them a fundamental part of his system. (Furthermore, in the Marxian system, the role of technological advancement is not the mere cause of the finite postponement of the stationary state of the classicists, but is the necessary cause for the continued existence of surplus value—the basis of the capitalist system.) The concept of the way the reserve army is formed is what economists have referred to as Marx's Law of Population.[10]

While the Marxian theory of economic growth presented a horrendous picture of the future of the working classes, who had nothing but unemployment and exploitation to look forward to, the prospects of the capitalists were also bleak. In Marx's words:

> . . . there is periodically a production of too many means of production and necessities of life to permit of their serving as means for exploitation of the laborers at a certain rate of profit. . . . In fact, the development of the productive power of labor creates in the falling rate of profit a law which turns into an

[9] This is written symbolically as $P = s\,(1 - Q)$, where P is profit, s is the rate of surplus value and Q is the organic composition of capital.

[10] A. Lowe, *On Economic Knowledge* (New York: Harper and Row, 1965), pp. 183–184.

antagonism of this mode of production at a certain point and requires for its defeat periodical crises.[11]

We must ask, what in the Marxian system leads to the Law of the Falling Rate of Profit? The answer brings us to another Marxian law, the Law of the Rising Organic Composition of Capital. As was previously stated, the rate of surplus value in Marx's economics was thought to be constant. If the organic composition of capital rises, then profits should show a decline. Why should there be a rise in the organic composition of capital? The capitalist who introduces machinery raises the productivity of his labor force. Thus, a larger proportion of the working day is devoted to the creation of surplus value because the worker will now reproduce the value of his own wage in a shorter period of time. As the new technology spreads, however, the socially necessary labor time for production of the commodity falls. Competition will therefore bring market price into line with the lower value of the product, reducing the ratio of surplus value (s) to the total capital advanced $(c + v)$. In order to keep surplus value high and constant, the capitalist introduces capital equipment, which then in the long run serves to drive his profits down. Thus, it can be shown that the capitalist is faced with a fundamental contradiction: If he tries to maintain or increase surplus value by introducing machines, his profits will ultimately fall because of the rise of the organic composition of capital. If, on the other hand, he chooses to hold back on the use of machines, he will emerge as a high cost producer as others adopt the new technology and lower the socially necessary labor time required for production.

The causes of crises in Marx form what modern economists call the theory of business cycles. In fact, as has been pointed out, there are several alternative business cycle theories in Marx's work. The three underlying causes of crises are given as:

1. crises arising from the falling rate of profit,
2. crises arising from disproportionality in production,
3. crises arising from underconsumption.[12]

The crises arising from the first cause listed above have been discussed in connection with the contradictory alternatives available to the capitalist. As to the second cause of crises, we need to note that disproportionality in Marx means overproduction of specific goods. This disproportionality occurs because the capitalists' knowledge of the market is incomplete and limited. Because capitalists act independently, each produces what he can sell at the market price, creating an overproduction. In short, the case for dispropor-

[11] K. Marx, *Capital: A Critique of Political Economy* (Chicago: Charles H. Kerr and Co., 1909), Vol. III, p. 303.

[12] There is no agreement among economists about the underconsumption theory in Marx. J. Hobson based his important work on *Imperialism* on this theory and in Vol. III of *Capital* (Charles H. Kerr, Co., 1909) on pages 286-7, 303 and 568 Marx seems to present an underconsumption analysis of crises. However, in Vol. III, page 475, he refutes an underconsumption theory by stating that "it is a tautology to say crises are caused by lack of consumers."

tionality rests on the fact that the seller in a freely competitive market has knowledge of the demand curve but not of the supply curve. Since demand is fixed and known to him, he attempts to obtain the largest portion of the market that he can. With all sellers behaving this way oversupply results. While this conception of the business cycle is intriguing, Marx did not develop it systematically or fully. The normal method under capitalism of resolving the disequilibrium between supply and demand is to allow prices to fluctuate to a level where equilibrium is re-established (and in that way to sell the over-production at a lower price). However, an oversupply can lead to unem-ployment as inventories increase and current production is cut back. If un-employment does result, then there will be an increase in the reserve army and wages will move to subsistence levels. Only the capitalist has the power to purchase the oversupply; but because of the falling profit rate growing out of the rise in the organic composition of capital he would in fact decrease his investment, thus making the prices of the commodities unstable until crisis reduces their value.

The capitalist, trapped by the imperative need for capital accumulation, cannot extricate himself from the dynamics of the system. Because he has driven down wages by the introduction of capital in the production process, the rate of growth of consumption is less than the rate of growth in the means of production. These technological instruments and mass production tech-niques in turn will cause the rate of growth of the means of production to fall relative to the rate of the output of consumer goods. In other words, the introduction of more efficient machinery permits an increase in production without a corresponding addition to purchasing power in the form of wages. As a consequence, the rate of growth of consumption will be less than the rate of growth of consumer goods' production. Stagnation and crises are, therefore, inevitable under capitalism.

The Marxian case for the existence of crises under capitalism has been made. An examination of the consequences of these crises is now in order. Again, turning to Marx:

> With the fall of the rate of profit grows the lowest limit of capital required in the hands of the individual capitalist for the productive employment of labor, required both for the exploitation of labor and for bringing the consumed labor time within the labor time necessary for the production of commodities, the limits of the average social labor time required for the production of commod-ities. Simultaneously, with it grows concentration, because there comes a time where large capital with a small rate of profit accumulates faster than small capital with a large rate of profit.[13]

The implications of these developments for the capitalist, particularly the small enterpriser, are all too clear. A crisis will cause the small capitalist to be destroyed because his rate of profit, although large, cannot attain a mini-mum absolute level to achieve accumulation. The small capitalist falls victim

[13] Marx, *Capital*, p. 166.

to short periods of disequilibrium between supply and demand, and when he overproduces his lack of capital resources prevents him from withstanding the crisis, and he fails. To sustain himself he now becomes a member of the working class to be exploited by the surviving capitalists. As Marx succinctly and harshly put it, "One capitalist always kills many."

The overproduction of consumer goods and the consequent decline in the number of capitalists because of crises would have three distinct effects. First, it would tend to enlarge the working classes and shrink the capitalist class. Second, the remaining capitalists would search for new markets. Third, the crises would tend to increase in intensity, magnitude, and frequency. The first effect is a result of capitalists being driven out of business and forced to join the ranks of the workers. The increase in the number of the workers will tend to drive wages toward the subsistence level. Hence, there is an increase in the number of workers who must endure poverty and misery because they do not own capital.

The second result refers to the international aspects of capitalism. Marx postulated that the overproduction of the capitalist countries would lead them to search for foreign markets. Capital invested in foreign trade would yield a higher rate of profit than domestic investment because it would compete with less highly developed resources and facilities. Investment in foreign markets would produce higher levels of surplus value because of the existence of slavery and forms of feudalism in these backward societies.

These Marxian ideas on the role of foreign trade in capitalism were later enlarged on by the English economist John Hobson, who argued that the underconsumption and overproduction in the developed nations would force them to search for colonies to act as captive markets for capitalistic over-production. Thus, we see that the origins of imperialism in its theoretical form were first developed by Marx.

An examination of the third result sheds light upon the future of capitalism and its prospects for economic growth. As machinery is used to replace labor, commodities are cheapened, and large concentrations of capital drive out smaller concentrations. This leads toward the centralization and concentration of capital because of the advantages of size (the economies of scale) and the competition among producers. A consequence of this centralization is that, as the mass of capital in a single ownership grows, fewer and fewer laborers are employed by it. The growth of monopoly capital reduces the demand for labor. This reduction in the demand for labor decreases wages and hence effective demand to the "subsistence" level. Larger units of capital are left, and they become involved in recurrent crises in order to restore the value of capital. Larger capital units require larger investments that must be dis-counted over time. This drive for profits to retrieve investments leads to the rising organic composition of capital and hence to a lower profit rate; crises recur more frequently. The prospect of increasingly severe depressions in shorter time periods becomes the crisis of capitalism.

Professor Fellner has pointed out some of the implications of this Marxian vision of the capitalist process very well.[14] According to Fellner, technological innovations in the Marxian system do not play the role of an offset to diminishing returns from capital. "This is because technological progress here [i.e., in Marx] is considered inseparable from processes by which it is accompanied and by which it is set in motion, processes which Marx expected to lead to a downtrend in profit rates as well as to very unfavorable wage trends."[15]

Fellner expresses the central hypothesis of the Marxian model of capitalistic growth and breakdown as holding that "more plentiful innovating activity is associated:

(1) with a greater relative labor-saving effect of the innovations and a more rapid increase in monopoly power, so that wage rates fall.

(2) with an accelerated increase in K/L [the Capital-Labor ratio] and K/R [the Capital-Resources ratio], so that rates of return to investors, too, become reduced."[16] In short, according to Fellner's interpretation of Marx, "Workers do not benefit from accelerated technological progress because a higher labor-saving effect and an increase in monopoly power 'come in a package' with increased technological progress; and investors do not benefit from rapid technological progress because an excessive rate of capital formation is induced by it."[17]

There has been much confusion about Marx's law of the "immiseration of the proletariat" due in part to his revision of ideas on this subject in the course of his life. In his later works (i.e., after the Communist Manifesto), Marx did not hold to an "iron law" or subsistence theory of wages. There is no secular tendency for wages to fall to subsistence; rather wages tend to fall to that level, but the content of this subsistence changes, consisting of "natural wants" and so-called "necessary wants," i.e., those established as "the product of historical development." Marx's notion of the worker living at subsistence does not preclude increases in real wages. Once a higher standard of living becomes established, it becomes the new subsistence level. While Marx implied that labor's relative share of the national income would fall over time, he never denied that real wages could rise under capitalism. Marx wrote not of material poverty but of "pauperization," of the growing "misery" and "mental degradation" of the working class. One passage runs: "in proportion as capital accumulates, the lot of the laborer, be his payments high or low, must grow worse."[18] Marx is presumably referring to the fact that mechanization sometimes destroys skills and contributes to the alienation of the worker from his work. Under capitalism, he argues, the worker "does not fulfill himself in his work, but denies himself" and "has a feeling of misery."

---

[14] W. Fellner, "Marxian Hypotheses and Observable Trends under Capitalism: A Modernised Interpretation," *Economic Journal* (March, 1957), p. 16 seq.

[15] *Ibid.*, p. 16. Fellner presumably refers to the process of capital accumulation.

[16] Fellner, "Marxian Hypothesis . . .," pp. 19–20.

[17] *Ibid.*, pp. 19–20.

[18] K. Marx, *Capital*, Vol. I, pp. 708–709.

This misery becomes progressively worse because with the development of capitalism the working class is increasingly estranged "from the intellectual potentialities of the labour-process. . . ." In his view, this is a fundamental deprivation that cannot be rectified by higher wages.[19] Furthermore, it still remains true that the failure of wages to rise with the productivity of labor contributes, in the Marxian analysis, to what is known as the absolute impoverishment of the worker.

While it is not an essential part of the Marxian theory of economic growth, it is important for our purposes to summarize the Marx-Engels theory of the state. In their view, the state is a public organization possessing a legal monopoly of the use of force. Such an institution, in this conception, is necessary in a society divided into classes with conflicting interests. In order to preserve social order and avoid the Hobbesian "war of each against all," there is a need for the capitalist state. Engels provided the most authoritative Marxian statement on this subject in these terms:

> The state is the result of the desire to keep down class conflicts. But having arisen amid these conflicts, it is as a rule the state of the most powerful economic class that by force of its economic supremacy becomes also the ruling political class and thus acquires new means of subduing and exploiting the oppressed masses. . . . The modern representative state is the tool of the capitalist exploiters of wage labor. At certain periods it occurs exceptionally that the struggling classes balance each other so nearly that the public power gains a certain degree of independence by posing as the mediator between them. . . ."[20]

As the instrument of the ruling class, the capitalist state would tend to be conservative and regard its principal function as the protection of the economic and social order in the interest of the dominant, ruling class. Lenin spoke of the state as "the executive arm of the ruling class."

The Marxian prognosis of the development of capitalism saw class conflict intensifying as the concentration of capital and the deteriorating condition of labor produced a gulf between the capitalists and the workers. Marx graphically depicted the eschatology, the last days of capitalism, as follows:

> Hand in hand with this centralization, or this expropriation of many capitalists by a few, develops . . . the entanglement of all nations in the net of the world market, and with this, the international character of the capitalist regime. Along with the constantly diminishing number of the magnates of capital, who usurp and monopolize all advantages of this process of transformation, grows the mass of the revolt of the working class, a class always increasing in numbers, and disciplined, united, organized by the very mechanism of the process of capitalist production itself. The monopoly of capital becomes a fetter upon the mode of production, which has sprung up and flourished along with it. Centralization of the means of production and socialization of labor at last

[19] T. Sowell, "Marx's Increasing Misery Doctrine," *American Economic Review* (March, 1960), pp. 111–120. We have drawn heavily on this excellent source for the above.

[20] F. Engels, *The Origin of the Family, Private Property and the State* (Chicago: Chas. Kerr and Co., 1902), pp. 208–209.

reach a point where they become incompatible with their capitalist integument. This integument bursts. The knell of capitalist private property sounds. The expropriators are expropriated.[21]

We see in this passage and in other phases of Marx's work one of its most striking and distinctive features, as contrasted with the ideas of the classical economists. He links the institutional and psychological conditions, which the latter had treated as constants with the cyclical process itself.[22] Thus, the structure of business enterprise, the organization of workers, their state of class consciousness, etc., are all connected quite explicitly with the progressively more unstable operation of the capitalistic system. This linkage of short-term fluctuations of the system with the secular developments in its institutional framework gave the Marxian synthesis a conceptual breadth and grandeur that had great intellectual appeal. It carried economic determinism to new lengths; in this lay both its tremendous insight and its gravest weakness.

In the opening sentences of this Introduction, we have quoted Professor Rostow's opinion to the effect that "in the drive to maturity . . . societies have behaved in the most Marxist way" with due allowance being made for their cultural, social, and political differences. We have sketched out some of the key propositions of the Marxian theory of economic growth in order to put some content into that rather opaque phrase, "the most Marxist way." As we have seen, Marx's theory is a very comprehensive one, embracing numerous economic, sociological, and political aspects of capitalism's development. Of necessity, we shall be able to consider only a few of its features in relation to the American experience in the years 1866–96. The following hypotheses of the Marxian system will be given explicit consideration in Chapters 18 and 19 more or less in the order in which they are listed:

1. Technological innovations in the process of capital accumulation tend to be so labor-saving and contribute so much relatively to a rapid increase in monopoly power that wage rates fall. Further, these innovations cause such an accelerated increase in capital/labor and capital/resources ratios, that profits are reduced.
2. Business depressions will become greater in amplitude and more frequent as capitalism develops.
3. As the economy matures, production will become more concentrated so far as ownership is concerned—the "law," or shall we more cautiously term it, the hypothesis of the increasing centralization of production.
4. Class conflict will grow more intense, as the "old" middle class of small independent shopkeepers, professionals, merchants, and farmers is de-

[21] *Capital*, Vol. I, p. 722.

[22] This aspect of Marx's work is treated most percipiently by Adolph Lowe in his *On Economic Knowledge*, Chap. 7. Schumpeter, of course, recognized this aspect of Marx's achievement, saying ". . . In his general schema of thought, development was not what it was with all the other economists of that period, an appendix to economic statics, but the central theme. And he concentrated his analytical powers on the task of showing how the economic progress, changing by virtue of its own inherent logic, incessantly changes the social framework—the whole society in fact." (J. A. Schumpeter, *History of Economic Analysis*, p. 573.)

stroyed, and society will be increasingly polarized into two opposing classes of the big bourgeoisie and the proletariat. Coincident with the latter, the class consciousness of the workers will grow, and they will organize to overthrow capitalism.

5. As economic concentration grows, the working class will face increasingly miserable conditions—the theory of increasing "misery."

6. The struggle for world markets among the more mature capitalist nations will intensify, giving rise to imperialist wars to offset the falling rate of profit at home.

Chapter 17

THE UNSTABLE PROCESS OF CAPITAL FORMATION AND GROWTH

THE TRANSFORMATION IN THE ECONOMIC STRUCTURE OF PRODUCTION

Historians have been accustomed to consider the post-Civil War years in the United States as witnessing a great transition from an agricultural to an industrial era. In the years 1866–1896 manufacturing rose to an unchallenged predominance over agriculture. In fact, by 1894 the United States was the leading manufacturing nation of the world. This development was of such momentous consequence for the nation economically, politically, and culturally that we need to examine its dimensions.

Agriculture's share in the national income for the decade 1869–78 was 27.5 per cent of the total, whereas manufacturing's divison was 17.1 per cent (computed in constant prices). For the decade 1889–98, agriculture's percentage had fallen to 18.4 per cent, while manufacturing's share had risen to 18.8 per cent.[1]

The shift in terms of employment of the labor force was not as dramatic. In 1870, 6,730,000 persons were gainfully employed in agriculture out of a labor force of close to thirteen million, with only 2,130,000 engaged in manufacturing. By 1900, the agricultural workers still comprised over one-third of the total labor force (10.9 million out of a total of 29 million), while the number of workers in manufacturing rose to over six million.[2]

In short, over these years a basic structural change took place in the economy; it shifted from one dependent on primary goods to one relying much more on industrial goods for employment. Such a change is typical of nations undergoing the industrialization process. The increased productivity of agriculture in effect released workers who could be absorbed in manu-

[1] S. Kuznets, *National Income, A Summary of Findings* (New York: National Bureau of Economic Research, 1946), Table 13 on p. 43.

[2] Department of Commerce, *Historical Statistics of the United States, 1789–1945* (Washington: U.S. Government Printing Office, 1947), p. 64.

facturing and other pursuits. This process was facilitated in the United States by the massive immigration of the period; more than twelve million immigrants came to this country in these years, though not all of them were employed in manufacturing industry.

Measurement of the tremendous expansion of the economy in this period is best expressed in terms of the changes in gross national product, total and per capita. Table 1 shows that the total GNP grew more than threefold over these years, while the per capita GNP nearly doubled, going from $223 for 1869–73 to $434 for 1892–96 (figures in 1929 prices).

TABLE 1

Gross National Product in the United States, 1869–96
Total and Per Capita in 1929 Prices[a]

Annual Average of Years	Total (Billions)	Per Capita (Dollars)
1869–73	$ 9.1	$223
1872–76	11.2	254
1877–81	16.1	327
1882–86	20.7	374
1887–91	24.0	388
1889–93[b]	27.3	424
1892–96[b]	29.6	434

[a] Source: U.S. Bureau of the Census, *Historical Statistics of the United States, Colonial Times to 1957*, p. 139.

[b] Figures for these years are based on the Department of Commerce concept of national income; all previous data are based on the Kuznet's concept.

REGIONAL AND OTHER DIFFERENCES
IN INCOME DISTRIBUTION

The increases in gross national product and income were not, of course, equal throughout the nation over these years. The regional income figures cited below are based only on commodity production in each area; further they relate only to money income rather than to real income differences; they do not include certain forms of income "in kind," such as food and fuel produced on farms. Finally, we should remind our readers of the dangers in equating income changes wholly to changes in economic well-being. For example, the figures to be cited do not take account of changes in the distribution of income between rich and poor, nor do they make any allowances for changes in leisure. In short, these data are at best only very rough indicators of regional differences in the growth of economic welfare, but they are exceedingly interesting for what they reveal, nevertheless.

With these cautions in mind, we present Easterlin's data on personal income per capita in each region as a percentage of the national average for the years 1840–1900. These relative income figures were obtained by dividing the regional per capita income figure by the national average for the indicated date.

TABLE 2

Personal Income Per Capita in Each Region as a Percentage of the United States Average, 1840–1900[a]

Regions[b]	1840	1860	1880	1900
United States	100	100	100	100
Northeast	133	139	141	137
New England	132	143	141	134
Middle Atlantic	136	137	141	139
North Central	68	68	98	103
East North	67	69	102	106
West North Central	75	66	90	72
South	76	72	51	51
South Atlantic	70	65	45	45
East South Central	73	68	51	49
West South Central	144	115	60	61
West			190	163
Mountain			168	139
Pacific			204	163

[a] Source: Adapted from R. A. Easterlin, "Regional Income Trends, 1840–1950." in S. E. Harris, ed.. *American Economic History, op. cit.,* p. 528.

[b] The regions and geographical divisions of the United States are as defined by the U.S. Bureau of the Census, except as stated in R. A. Easterlin, "Regional Income Trends, 1840–1950," in Harris, *op. cit.,* footnotes to Table 1 on p. 528.

Following the figures from decade to decade, we can gain some impression of the trends in regional income, though we must allow for variations within the decennial years. The major tendencies are quickly apparent. The Northeast throughout these years was one of the high-income regions; its average incomes were as much as one-third or more above the average. The North Central states were almost one-third below the national average in personal income per capita in the years 1840 and 1860, and they rose to around the national level in 1880 and as of 1900. We see a decline in the South's relative income between 1840 and 1860; at the latter date it was more than one-quarter less than the national average. The drastic decline to nearly one-half of the national level by 1880 is "an impressive memorial of the economic cost to the South of the Civil War and its aftermath." The high relative income for the West, nearly 70 per cent higher for the Mountain states than the national average and over 100 per cent higher for the Pacific states, is somewhat surprising until we realize that the West in 1880–1900 period had a high proportion of its income from non-agricultural activity, such as mining, and that the high ratio of single males and of workers to dependents generally would seem to account for the differences noted.

Apart from these regional differences, other significant variations occurred among industries with regard to per capita incomes. For example, in 1880, income per worker in agriculture amounted to only $252, which was less than one-half the corresponding figure for non-agricultural workers, $572. Twenty years later this differential had widened even further, with the farm worker receiving $260 to the industrial workers' $622. This relative loss of ground in purchasing power among the rural populations goes far to explain the general discontent among farmers in the last quarter of the nineteenth century.

While there is evidence of a rise in real income per capita in this period as a whole, there are also striking figures suggesting that the distribution of personal incomes became more unequal. The data are not satisfactory, but they tend to support the opinion so dramatically presented in Henry George's *Progress and Poverty* (1879), that amidst the growing riches, poverty had persisted and even increased. James Bryce, the perceptive British commentator on the American scene, in his *The American Commonwealth* (1888) noted the existence of poverty beside "many large fortunes, and a greater number of gigantic fortunes than in any other country in the world." He expected the growth of such fortunes and of inequality to continue and probably even to increase. The nation was stunned at the size of some of the larger accumulations. Thus, Commodore Vanderbilt when he died in 1877 left a fortune of $100 million. Andrew Carnegie, it has been calculated, had a personal paper gain in 1900 of $23 million as his share of the $40 million in profits made by his company. The gap between the incomes of the rich and poor was made wider in these years by the fact that the former's incomes were not subject to income tax. Many of the millionaires' incomes consequently dwarfed the annual wage of four or five hundred dollars for the average workman.[3]

The most reliable evidence that we have of an increase in income inequality in these years is found in the work of Simon Kuznets, who has argued that inequality probably increased in the last three decades of the nineteenth century.[4] Kuznets infers this partly from such factors as: (1) the relatively high level of unemployment at the end of the nineties (the unemployed were over 12 per cent of the total labor force in 1889–98 and about 10 per cent in the years 1894–1903), (2) the increased inequality between farm and non-agricultural incomes, and (3) the trend toward industrial combination in this period with the result that substantial capital gains must have gone to people who were already at or near the top of the income pyramid. Kuznets notes too that there was an apparent rise in the savings-income ratio in the last quarter

---

[3] Paul Douglas estimated the average yearly wage of industrial wage earners in 1900 to be $490. [See *Real Wages in the United States, 1890–1926* (Boston: Houghton Mifflin, 1930).]

[4] S. Kuznets, "Proportion of Capital Formation to National Product," *American Economic Review* (May, 1952), p. 522.

of the nineteenth century, and this probably reflected the trend toward increased inequality of incomes. He is of the opinion that this relatively high propensity to save was a major factor in accounting for the rather remarkable pace of capital formation in this period.

TRENDS IN CAPITAL FORMATION

"Accumulate, accumulate! That is Moses and the prophets!"[5] wrote Marx in *Das Kapital*, stating that this was the formula by which classical Political Economy expressed the historical mission of the bourgeosie under capitalism. American capitalists in the years between the end of the Civil War and the close of the century appear to have heeded the classical prescription faithfully. In fact, savings and investment took place at a higher relative level in the United States after 1865 than ever before or since. Gross capital expenditures averaged more than 30 per cent of total output during the years 1869 to 1899.

In reviewing the available statistics on capital formation, we need to be clear about definitions of the concept. There are significant variations in the usage of the term. For example, to Marx, capital accumulation meant employing surplus-value as capital, reconverting it into capital. Kuznets, as a statistician, gives us a more specific statement of what he means by capital formation. "By capital formation," he writes, "we mean diversion of part of the current product for use as capital, that is, goods to produce other goods or income. Specifically, it is defined here to include current construction, flow of producers' durable equipment to users, net additions to inventories of business units and other agencies (but not households) and . . . net changes in claims against foreign countries." Gross capital formation is the sum of these four components. Net capital formation is the latter sum, minus the allowance for capital consumption (depreciation and depletion).[6]

Savings—defined as the difference between current net output and consumption—are the source of capital formation. Whether accounted for by individuals, corporations, or the government, they make possible the acquisition of those capital goods, such as land, buildings, machinery, and other equipment without which modern production is impossible. With these definitions in mind, we can turn to the Kuznets' estimates of net capital formation, expressed as percentages of national income, in Table 3. The table shows that the rate of net capital formation was especially high in the years 1884–93 and 1889–98. The table is so constructed that we can see that when net capital formation was relatively high, as in the years just cited, the flow of goods to consumers was correspondingly reduced, demonstrating that capital formation

[5] *Capital* (New York: The Modern Library), p. 652.
[6] S. Kuznets, *Capital in the American Economy* (New York: National Bureau of Economic Research, 1961), pp. 389, 16 and 17.

must often be at the expense of current consumption. If the table were extended past the dates indicated to the 1920's, it would show that there was a fairly steady decline in net capital formation as a percentage of national income. In the years 1919–28 it averaged 11.4 per cent of the latter. In absolute terms, of course, the total annual value of net capital formation in the more recent periods is larger than in the earlier ones.

TABLE 3

National Income, Percentage Distribution between Flow of Goods to Consumers and Net Capital Formation, 1869–1903[a]
(Computed on the basis of constant 1929 prices)

Decade	Flow of Goods to Consumers	Net Capital Formation
1869–78	86.3%	13.7%
1874–83	85.6	14.4
1879–88	85.4	14.6
1884–93	83.9	16.1
1889–98	83.8	16.2
1894–03	85.2	14.8

[a] Source: Adapted from S. Kuznets, *National Income, A Summary of Findings* (New York: National Bureau of Economic Research, 1964), p. 53. © Copyright 1946 by National Bureau of Economic Research.

What was the meaning and significance of the high rate of capital formation for the Americans who lived and worked in this period? It meant primarily that workers had more tools to work with, families had residences, the community had other needed buildings, and all were provided with more roads, bridges, inventories, and other capital goods. It made possible the increases in the gross national product we have recorded in Table 1. Indeed, as Kuznets well says, the growth in GNP was both "cause and effect of the growth in capital formation. It was cause in that increased product made possible a larger diversion to capital stock, and it was effect in that the growing volume of capital formation and the growing stock of capital permitted higher total output per worker and per capita."[7] In Table 4, we can see in quantitative terms to what degree this was true.

If we express some of the figures of this table in percentage terms, we observe in an even more vivid way the remarkable changes that occurred. Namely, note that while the population was growing 87 per cent between 1869 and 1899, the capital stock accumulated by a magnificent 322 per cent over the same period. One can see the results of this disparate growth in the two variables in the rise of the capital stock per capita; it more than doubled over these years. A worker who, on the average, had $3,520 in capital goods to help him in

[7] S. Kuznets, *Capital in the American Economy*, p. 395.

TABLE 4

Growth in Gross Capital Stock in Relation to Population
and Labor Force, 1869–99[a] (*In 1929 prices*)

Years	Total Gross Capital Stock (In Billions of dollars)	Population (Millions)	Labor Force (Millions)	Gross Capital Stock per cap. (In Thousands of dollars)	Gross Capital Stock per member of the Labor Force (In Thousands of dollars)
1869	$ 45	40.0	12.8	$1.12	$3.52
1879	71	49.7	17.0	1.42	4.16
1889	116	62.5	22.3	1.86	5.22
1899	190	75.1	28.5	2.53	6.66

[a] Source: S. Kuznets, *Capital in the American Economy, op. cit.,* Table 3,, p. 64.

production in 1869 had almost twice that amount of capital for this purpose in 1899.

The massive capital formation of this period can be seen in its effects on the so-called capital-output ratio. [This ratio is the relationship between the capital stock at a given time (the numerator) and the annual output from that capital (the denominator).] Thus, in the railroad industry in 1882 the capital-output ratio was 15.0, meaning that for every dollar's worth of annual output, there were $15 of accumulated investment in road and equipment. This high ratio existed in railroads at that time because of the indivisibility (lumpiness) of railroad capital and the long planning horizon typically envisaged by railroad builders; in other words, they built far in advance of demand. In the course of time, the capital-output ratio fell in railroads, declining to 6.5 by 1900 and reaching 3.6 in 1920.[8]

The heavy investment in productive equipment tended to enhance the efficiency of the workers. We can see this effect in the growth of productivity; output of all commodities per man-hour increased 64 per cent between 1869–70 and 1899–1900.[9]

The relative importance of the different sectors in the process of capital formation during this period is made clear by the statistics of Table 5. This table shows the distribution of the capital stock of the nation, as estimated by Kuznets, as of June 1, 1880 and as of the same date in 1900, plus the net capital formation in the intervening years, for four major sectors as percentages of the totals.

It is evident from the table that the regulated industries, which included steam railroads, were by far the most capital intensive at the beginning of the period. During the years 1880–1900 over 80 per cent of the net capital forma-

[8] M. J. Ulmer, "Trends and Cycles in Capital Formation by U.S. Railroads," 1870–1950, Occasional Paper No. 43 of the National Bureau of Economic Research, 1954, p. 25.
[9] P. B. Kenen in S. E. Harris, *American Economic History* (New York: McGraw-Hill, 1961), p. 72.

TABLE 5

*Distribution of Capital Stock and Capital Formation,
in Percentages, 1880–1900*[a]

	Agricul- ture	Mining	Manu- facturing	Regulated Industries
Capital stock, June 1, 1880	31.9%	1.8%	9.1%	57.2%
Net capital formation, June 1, 1880–June 1, 1900	12.0	6.5	31.4	50.1
Capital stock, June 1, 1900	22.5	4.0	19.6	53.9

[a] Source: S. Kuznets, *Capital in the American Economy, op. cit.*, Table 27, p. 198. Kuznets states that the estimates of this table accounted for about 80% of the total net value of construction and equipment in the business sector, excluding nonfarm residential construction and that owned by governments and nonprofit organizations (*ibid.*, p. 200).

tion in the business sector of the economy took place in the manufacturing and the regulated industries. Apart from the regulated industries, in which railroads were primary, the capital formation was especially massive in the manufacturing sector.

In the early years of this period, capital formation in the railroad industry was an especially high percentage of the total in the nation and then declined quite steadily. As Table 6 indicates, in the years 1870–79, it was as much as 20 per cent of the total and then tapered off in the remaining decades of the century.

TABLE 6

*Railroad Gross Capital Formation as a Percentage of
Total U.S. Gross Capital Formation, 1870–1949*[a]

Decade	Per cent
1870–79	20.4
1880–89	15.6
1890–99	7.5
1900–09	7.8
1910–19	7.3
1920–29	5.3
1930–39	3.5
1940–49	2.1

[a] Source: M. J. Ulmer, "Trends and Cycles in Capital Formation by U.S. Railroads, *op cit.*, p. 11. © Copyright 1954 by National Bureau of Economic Research.

We gain some appreciation of the changing relative importance of the steam railroads in the nation's capital formation from the further fact that in the decade of 1880–90, they seemed to have accounted for more than 80 per cent of the change in the value of the reproducible wealth of the transportation and other public utilities, but in the next decade their share of the same had declined to about one-third of the total and, in fact, the electric railways (tramways) slightly outspent them for this purpose.[10]

A major element in capital formation which we have not yet taken into account is construction. And yet, construction in the most inclusive sense (i.e., embracing business, residential, and government building) amounted to almost 64 per cent of the total capital formation in the years 1869–98.[11] The business expenditure for buildings, etc. has been included in the figures already cited on capital formation, but there remain the categories of nonfarm residential construction and the building done by government. In the period 1869–98, the former amounted to 40 per cent of gross construction and government construction was 6.8 per cent of the total. The fluctuations in urban residential construction, which one can see involved substantial sums, seem to have been subject to long swings that approximated in timing and duration the long swings in the additions to the total population. The timing of the long swings in railroad capital expenditures are also similar to that of the long swings in population increases. This association in timing of these different series is not proof of causation, but these statistical facts have to be kept in mind, nevertheless, in any attempt to understand the cyclical history of these years.[12]

LEADING INDUSTRIES OF THE PERIOD

What specific industries stood out in the maturation of the American industrial economy during this period? In the thirty years after 1870, Americans settled more land than they had during the previous three hundred years. They constructed four new transcontinental railways to form iron links with the Pacific. The mining industry boomed, extending the "last frontier" into such states as Nevada, Arizona, New Mexico, Colorado, Idaho, Montana, and last, but not least, California. Great fortunes were made in the burgeoning cattle industry and on bonanza wheat farms. These activities were geared for agricultural production as corporations had organized for industrial production. We have already noted the broad dimensions of the advance in manufacturing that enabled it to displace agriculture as the leader in relative output. But the farms of America were producing vast quantities of staples for domestic and foreign consumption in these years; so much, indeed, that over-production was an almost constant complaint.

The expansion of American agriculture into the Great Plains and the Far West and the closer gearing of our farms and cattle ranges to the demands of the foreign market were dominating developments in these years. The staple

---

[10] S. Kuznets, *Capital in the American Economy*, Table R-35, p. 611.
[11] S. Kuznets, *Capital in the American Economy*, p. 146.
[12] *Ibid.*, pp. 328–332. For the definition and timing of "long swings," see pp. 180–181.

crops of the North and West grew in output after the war, but agriculture did not enjoy prosperity in the years 1870–73, and the early years of the depression after the latter date were a period of great loss for the farmers. Starting in 1877, however, exports of farm products began a great increase, which was to bring larger profits to agriculture and the railroads. A series of crop failures in western Europe led to a huge increase in our exports of wheat. Argentina was not as yet a factor to be reckoned with in the world's wheat trade. And so the fertile West responded to the world's need with a succession of record-breaking crops. "The total yield of all cereals increased from a little more than 1.5 billion bushels in 1873 to more than 2.4 billion in 1879." Our farms were able to produce these huge crops because of the abundance of labor and the continued improvement of farm machinery. In the late years of the 1870's, the heavy gang plow, the spring-toothed harrow, the McCormick self-rake harvester, and the hay-loader were widely employed. On the great wheat farms of the Northwest, the steam combine was already coming into use.

In the Far West, in Oregon and Washington, the number of farms more than doubled in the 1870's, and the value of livestock more than trebled. With the opening of vast new lands and under the impact of farm mechanization, wheat production, for example, soared from 169 million bushels in 1866 to over 522 million thirty years later. The output of corn almost quadrupled from 730 million bushels in 1866 to 2,671 million in 1899. Cotton production went from 2–2.5 million bales in average output in the years 1866–69 to an annual average for the years 1896–99 of 9.5 million bales. While the large internal growth of population consumed even bigger amounts of farm products (the population grew some 97 per cent between 1870 and 1900), an increasing share found its way into foreign markets, as American exports swelled.

While these tremendous gains in farm output were being made by the nation as a whole, the South in the early years of this period was making a slow recovery from the devastation wrought by the war. Cotton production slowly increased, but it did not exceed the bumper crop of 1859 until 1878. The rice industry of South Carolina and Georgia all but disappeared because of the war, and the sugar industry of Louisiana was badly hurt. In 1870 the tobacco crop of Virginia was only one-third that of 1860, and corn and wheat production about one-half that of the pre-war year. The disruption caused by the Reconstruction period and the low prices of the 1870's retarded the recovery of the South as an agricultural region. In later years, while its crop production soared, its exports were subject to severe fluctuations of foreign trade, and there was much complaint of low prices.

The mining industry, which we recall had started in a big way before the Civil War in California and in the "rush" of the silver miners, the "fifty-niners," to "Pike's Peak or Bust," attained new records of output in these years. The "boom towns" that sprang up in the Far West in such places as Alder Gulch, Virginia City, Helena, Aurora, and Golden Hill poured a stream of gold and silver into the East. The Comstock Lode in Nevada alone produced $340 million worth of silver in the years from 1860 to 1890. The reader will note from Table 7 that the production of all these minerals did not expand; gold output declined for most of the period, whereas silver's output skyrocketed. The consequence of this disparate behavior was to take form in a

TABLE 7

Production of Chief Metals in the United States, Selected Years, 1866–1896[a]

Year	Gold (Millions of fine oz.)	Silver (Millions of fine oz.)	Copper (Short tons)	Lead (Short tons)
1866	2.5	7.7	——	——
1870	2.4	12.3	14,112	17,830
1880	1.7	30.3	30,240	95,725
1890	1.5	32.8	129,882	157,844
1896	2.5	58.8	230,931	207,370

[a] Source: *Historical Statistics of the United States, 1789–1945*, pp. 151–152.

famous chapter in the nation's financial history.[13] But, generally speaking, the expansion of mineral production gave rise to new opportunities for investment and provided traffic for the growing rail system. In time, however, the mad, individualistic rush for mineral wealth ran up against the quartz veins of ore; the placer mining of the lone prospector gave way to quartz mining, which could alone be financed by corporations. With that development, many of the miners became day laborers working for a wage.

The cattle kingdom was extending its dusty sway during these years also. 1867 marks the beginning of the so-called "long drive." Thousands of head of cattle were driven north from Texas to such cities as Dodge City, Kansas, or later to Ogallala, Nebraska or to Miles City, Montana—these were "cow towns" on the railway lines from which the cattle were shipped east for slaughtering. In the early part of this period there occurred the invasion of the Great Plains, "the Great American Desert," by the cattlemen. Between 1866 and 1888, some six million cattle were driven up to winter on the High Plains. All this expansion of a vital industry was made possible by the opening of the public domain under the Homestead Act, the elimination of the Indians and the buffaloes, the spread of the rail network, and the decline of the cattle industry in the Middle West and the East. A strategic innovation of which Gustavus F. Swift and his brother and others soon took advantage was the refrigerator car (invented in 1875). It made possible shipments of fresh western meat to the eastern cities. On this basis there grew up in the 1880's and '90's the great integrated packing concerns with their plants and warehouses enabling them to serve not only the East but the world.

[13] See below, pp. 460, 492–493.

Important as these industries were, they could not compare to the railroad as the pace-setter for the economy in much of this period. This was the Age of the Railroad, and Schumpeter has gained the agreement of most historians in referring to this era as witnessing the "railroadization of the United States."[14] Our railroad mileage expanded from about 35,000 miles in 1865 to 198,964 in 1900 (see Maps 1 and 2). Thus, over this span of years while the population was growing 114 per cent, railroad mileage increased 468 per cent! The railroad industry's construction advanced in towering waves, surging forward in certain years and relapsing drastically in others and causing widespread repercussions on the whole economy. The fact was that "by 1870 railroads were no longer the lusty infants among American industries. They resembled more closely the vigorous adolescent—the pace of whose future growth was to be more fitful and more sensitive to environmental changes and, because of its greater size, readier still to effect the environment."[15]

Contemporaries recognized the railroad in the late nineteenth century as being one of the great shaping influences of the post-Civil War era. Henry Adams, for one, saw the task of railroad construction as being so big as to require the energies of a whole generation. For, as he said,

> it required all the new machinery to be created—capital, banks, mines, furnaces, shops, powerhouses, technical knowledge, mechanical population, together with a steady remodelling of social and political habits, ideas and institutions to fit the new scale and the new conditions. The generation between 1865 and 1895 was already mortgaged to the railways, and no one knew it better than the generation itself.[16]

Though factory production in the United States had started before the Civil War, the achievement of large-scale industrialization on anything like a scale approximating that of today was a post-bellum development. Between 1865 and 1900, the population increased 114 per cent; by comparison, over nearly the same years, from 1869 to 1900, the value of manufactured product rose 281 per cent. Together with this quantitative expansion came a radical change in the nature of the leading industries. In 1859, there were, as shown in Table 8, about 140,000 manufacturing establishments in the United States, employing over 1,300,000 workers. They were estimated to have an aggregate capital investment of slightly over $1 billion and produced almost $2 billion in value of product. By 1899, the number of establishments had grown more than threefold to 512,000, the number of employees had multiplied by almost five, there was nearly ten times as much capital, and the value of the gross product was 6½ times what it had been at the earlier date. Mass production had come

[14] J. Schumpeter, *Business Cycles*, Vol. 1 (New York: McGraw-Hill, 1939), p. 325; the impact of the railroad as an economic innovation is masterfully treated in L. H. Jenks, "Railroads as an Economic Force in American Development," *The Journal of Economic History*, IV (March, 1944), pp. 1–20.

[15] M. Ulmer, *Trends and Cycles* . . . , p. 27.

[16] Henry Adams, *The Education of Henry Adams* (New York: Houghton-Mifflin, 1931), p. 240.

MAP 1

The American Railroad System—1870

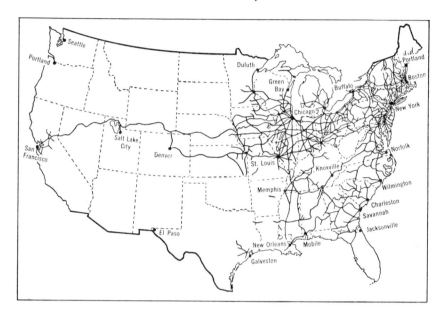

MAP 2

The American Railroad System—1900

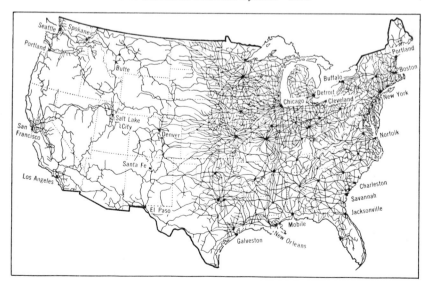

From Fite and Reese, *An Economic History of the United States, op. cit.,* p. 327.

TABLE 8

Growth of Manufacturing in the United States, 1859–1899[a]

Year	Establishments Number of (Thousands)	Wage earners (Thousands)	Amount of Capital (In Billions of Dollars)	Value of Products (In Billions of Dollars)
1859	140	1,311	$1.0	$ 1.9
1869	252	2,054	1.7	3.4
1879	254	2,733	2.8	5.4
1889	355	4,252	6.5	9.4
1899	512	5,306	9.8	13.0

[a] Source: U.S. Bureau of the Census, *Historical Statistics of the United States, 1789–1945*, p. 179.

of age in the United States; this could be seen in the character of the leading industries as of the two dates. In 1859, as Table 9 indicates, the ten leading industries were dominated by those providing consumer goods for the nation, such as food and clothing. By 1899, of the ten leading industries four were producing capital goods.

TABLE 9

*The Leading Manufacturing Industries, 1859 and 1899,
Ranked in Terms of Value Added*[a]

Rank	1859	1899
1	Cotton textiles	Foundry and machine products
2	Lumber	Lumber
3	Boots and shoes	Printing and publishing
4	Iron	Iron and steel
5	Flour milling	Malt liquors
6	Men's clothing	Tobacco
7	Gold mining	Cotton goods
8	Steam engines	Men's clothing
9	Woolen goods	Bakery products
10	Leather	Cars and general railroad construction

[a] Source: *U.S. Census of Manufactures* in *Historical Statistics of the U.S., op. cit.*

One of the most crucial industrial developments of these years was the remarkable expansion of the iron and steel industry. Pig iron production increased rapidly after 1860, doubling between that date and 1870 and doubling again in the next decade. At this rate of advance, by 1900 the United States was producing more than one-third of the world's production. But even more important was the sensational growth of steel production, for by the late sixties the Age of Steel had begun. By 1867 Bessemer steel was in commercial production, and thereafter its output soared. Steel rails were replacing wrought iron ones in the 1870's and 1880's and spurred by the voracious demand of the railways, steel became a "feast and famine" industry subject to all the gyrations of railroad expansion. Actually, in the years after the Civil War, the industry operated behind a very high tariff (almost 100 per cent *ad valorem* on some products, such as rails in 1881), and men like Carnegie and others were able to make net profits of 100 per cent a year and more on their capital investments. Imports of steel rails were only large in the boom years when the domestic industry could not meet the demand. In the quarter century following the Civil War, over one-third of rolled iron and steel products in the United States took the form of rails.[17] On some products the percentage was much higher. In the railroad boom of the early 1880's, rails accounted for over 90 per cent of rolled steel production. This growing demand had its effects on the improving technology of the industry. One of the most important of these developments was the rise of the coke industry. While coke had been used in smelting iron before the war, in the seventies Henry Clay Frick began converting coal into coke on a large scale. As a consequence, the Connellsville coal fields of southwestern Pennsylvania became famous as the source of coke for steel production.

By the late eighties the demand of the railroad industry for steel was flattening out; the steel men turned to other diversified markets, such as the growing one for structural steel in the expanding cities and in the needs of industry generally, both at home and abroad. Andrew Carnegie shifted his Homestead Mill from rails to structural products in 1887, a significant indication of the changing composition of steel demand. During these years another innovation in the dynamic steel industry was radically changing the technology of production. The open-hearth method, which had been invented in 1867, gradually began to replace Bessemer steel as its costs approached that of the older product, and it became known that better quality control could be maintained in its manufacture. By the year 1900 the quantity of open-hearth steel made was only one half that of Bessemer production, but by 1907 they were "neck and neck" in output, and thereafter the former progressively displaced the latter.

In this "heroic age of American enterprise," as Allan Nevins has termed it, many other manufacturing industries were booming. The mineral fuel industries took on new importance as the nation's need for energy mounted. The output of coal, whose production amounted to slightly more than 13 million tons in 1866, multiplied tenfold within the next thirty years. By the end of the

---

[17] P. Temin, *Iron and Steel in Nineteenth Century America* (Cambridge: The MIT Press, 1964), pp. 3–4. Temin writes: "Steel was used almost exclusively for rails in the years of its initial great expansion, and rails were the first major product to be composed almost entirely of steel. This was accomplished in the 1870's, and when the price of steel rails fell below the price of iron rails in 1883, iron rails ceased to appear on the market except for specialized uses, such as light street rails." (*Ibid.*, p. 221.) Fogel notes that rail production in 1872 was "about 35 per cent of weight of pig iron production" and in 1882 steel rails came to 75 per cent of all rolled steel. [R. W. Fogel, *Railroads and American Economic Growth* (Baltimore: Johns Hopkins Press, 1964), p. 130.]

century the United States was producing more coal than any other nation; by that time it was actually producing close to one-third of the world's production.

The rise of the petroleum industry in these years is, of course, one of the great sagas of American enterprise. Before Colonel Edwin Drake drilled the first well at Titusville in western Pennsylvania in 1859, petroleum was a curiosity and at most a nostrum of the patent medicine man. From the two thousand barrels the industry produced in that year its output gushed to over 60 million barrels in 1896. Petroleum became not only a major illuminant, practically driving whale oil and candles from the market, but soon became indispensable as a lubricant and as a source of innumerable by-products. Its use as a fuel in the form of gasoline came only in the latter years of this period when the motor vehicle first made its timid debut. The construction of the refining facilities, the tank cars, and pipe lines of this industry, which even before the end of the century was a great exporter of its products, called for vast enterprise. John D. Rockefeller, Sr. and his associates early assumed the lead in this field and set a pattern of "trustification" of industry, which was widely copied in other fields.

The farm implement industry grew very fast in these years with the opening up of the new western lands, which lent themselves so well to mechanized farming. The total value of the industry's product went from $246 million in 1860 to $761 million in 1900. This output included a host of new improvements: the new iron mold boards for plows, the twine binder, sulky and gang plows, and better harvesting and threshing equipment. On some of the large farms, steam plows were tried, but they proved too cumbersome and costly to operate; threshing by steam was more successful. At the turn of the century, it was estimated that a well-managed farm required about $785 worth of machinery. These mechanized farm aids greatly reduced the time needed for preparation of the soil and harvesting of the crop and thereby increased greatly productivity in man-hours. For example, the test time required to grow a bushel of wheat fell from 32.8 minutes in 1830 to 2.2 minutes in 1900. These gains in productivity were due not only to better and more machinery, but also to the use of more fertilizer, better tillage, and the development of improved strains of crops and livestock. Both the state and the national government were active in the post-Civil War years in promoting agriculture.

Many other manufacturing industries assumed a mass production scale in these years, as Table 9 suggests. The transformation of local markets into national ones brought about by the completion of the great continental rail networks, the rapid growth of the cities, and the agglomeration of people in them, natives and immigrants alike, created a mass market such as had never been known before. This immense common market of the continental United States was unique at the time as the largest area in the world unrestricted by trade barriers, taxes, or tariffs. At the same time, American manufacturers were protected from outside competition by unusually high protective tariffs on their own products. Their customers, living in a society with a relatively open class structure, were extraordinarily eager to buy the goods and services that they associated with a higher standard of living.

There is another industry that we should not overlook in this survey of manufacturing developments, because while its growth in this period was but a portent of the vast future that lay before it, it was supremely important. This was electric power. We are told that the census of 1880 did not even mention the use of electrical power in industry, and yet by 1900 electricity and steam supplied about equal percentages of the nation's power. Thomas Edison invented a method of illumination by electricity in 1876, but the high cost of transmitting this type of energy over long-distance lines impeded its growth for a while. George Westinghouse built a transformer that solved this problem, and by 1879–80 cities were lighting their streets with electricity. This was done at first with arc lights, but after Edison patented his incandescent lamp in 1880, the latter quickly displaced the older method of electric illumination. Edison also developed the idea of the central power station and improved the dynamo; about this same time the development of alternating current made it possible to establish a system type of illumination. The new source of power was used first for lighting; the cotton textile industry turned to it in the 1880's, and gradually as this clean, flexible kind of energy became available its use widened. This great innovation was soon to lay a basis for new capital intensive industries, such as the public utilities and street railways, and provide the outlets for substantial new investment after the recovery from the depression of 1893.

CAPITAL ACCUMULATION AND FINANCIAL INSTITUTIONS

Where were the capital funds obtained to make possible the massive capital formation of these years? In answering this question, it will be helpful to keep in mind these five sources of money capital: (1) undistributed earnings; (2) allowances for depreciation; (3) short-term borrowing from banks and individuals; (4) long-term borrowing by selling bonds or mortgaging property; (5) the sale of equity securities. The first two methods are usually spoken of as "internal financing"; the last three are often referred to as "external financing."

In the early part of this period, say until the 1880's, much of the capital that went into agriculture, cattle-raising, and mining was self-created in the sense that the farmer converted the labor of himself and his family into improving the land and buildings on it. Money was needed, of course, to purchase mechanical equipment, seed, fertilizer, etc. In industry also, once established, the successful private entrepreneurs and partnerships were accustomed to plough back their earnings into new plants and equipment. The initial capital for such enterprises had to be raised, however, by borrowing or the sale of securities. The securities of most industrial companies in this period were closely held, and there was no opportunity to trade in them on the stock exchanges.

In the case of the railroads, this was not true; railroad shares were sold on a large and small scale by investment bankers. Since the railroads were widely regarded at first as panaceas, state and local governments and their residents purchased their shares with great enthusiasm. Foreigners bought the bonds and shares of our railroads in large numbers. ". . . Between 1863 and 1873 some $1,300,000,000 of American securities were bought abroad. . . ." In this early period, the foreign investors preferred to invest in government securities; very often Americans sold their government bonds to foreigners and invested in railroads.

Beginning in the 1880's, when the concentration of railroad and industrial capital accelerated, incorporation of enterprise became more general, and external financing was frequently resorted to. Capital for manufacturing establishments began to be drawn through the capital market, though "industrials" were still considered highly speculative as compared to railroad shares. In these years the industrial combines were growing internally, so there was much self-financing. With the resumption of financial expansion after the depression of 1873 and the elimination of the uncertainty concerning specie payment, railroad finance became more frenzied and "stock watering" more common. Between 1880 and 1890 the par value of railroad securities increased by $4 billion. The retirement of the federal debt during the 1880's released a billion dollars for private investment and, in addition, with the recovery of business after 1879, European investors resumed their large-scale participation in purchasing our capital issues. Federal, state, and local bonds were purchased in these years mainly by American banks and other financial institutions. The Europeans had to content themselves with railroad bonds and, to a lesser degree, with railway and industrial shares. Altogether, it is believed that in the years from 1879 to 1890, Europeans purchased over $1.8 billion of American securities. "It is estimated that during the 1880's Europe contributed over two-fifths of the capital that went into American railroad building."[18]

In the cities where population was growing so stupendously, capital formation in the form of business and residential structures was increasingly financed by the swelling funds of a variety of financial institutions. As the prosperous middle class saved, the assets of savings banks, trust, and insurance companies expanded and became available for investment in real estate mortgages, which they preferred over less secure uses of their funds (see Table 10).

The commercial banking system of the nation underwent significant changes in the post-bellum years. Banks increased in size and numbers, checkbook money tended to replace banknotes, and the structure of the banking system changed. At first, national banks tended to outnumber the state institu-

---

[18] Shultz and Caine, *Financial Development of the United States* (Englewood Cliffs, N.J.: Prentice-Hall, Inc., 1937), p. 390.

TABLE 10

Assets of Selected Financial Institutions, 1865–1900[a]
(In Billions of Dollars)

Year	Savings Banks Assets	Trust Companies Assets	Life Insurance Companies Assets	Assets Total
1865	$ .2	—	$ .1	$ .3
1875	.9	$ .1	.4	1.4
1890	1.7	.5	.8	3.0
1900	2.6	1.4	1.7	5.7

[a] Source: A. B. Hepburn, *A History of Currency in the United States* (New York: The Macmillan Co., 1915), pp. 330, 341, 435; Institute of Life Insurance, *1956 Life Insurance Fact Book* (New York, 1956), p. 60.

tions, as the latter were subject to a 10 per cent discriminatory tax on their notes under an 1866 law. By 1870, almost 90 per cent of the nation's banks had federal charters. However, with the growth of the checkbook money and the existence of less stringent state regulation, there was a resurgence in the number of state banks, as shown in Table 11. The national banks continued to be the larger institutions, with more assets per bank, and with greater influence on the flow of credit. The state banks, which were permitted to engage in branch banking and to make loans on real estate, were usually to be found in the rural areas of the nation.

These rural banks as well as many urban ones in the South and West made it the practice to keep a fraction of their reserves with correspondent banks in New York City, where such funds were in turn invested in the call money market to finance stock purchases. This centralization of the reserves of the nation's smaller banks was profitable to the bankers, but it tended to make the banking system as a whole unstable. In the fall and spring of the year when the rural banks needed to finance the operations of their local customers, their withdrawal of these funds from New York would cause "call money" rates to skyrocket. This stringency of credit at such times often served to accentuate monetary instability and contributed to financial panics. This shortcoming of the national banking system caused the nation serious financial harm before it was eliminated by the adoption of the Federal Reserve System.

Another development in commercial banking in these years was the increased acceptance of the "real-bills" doctrine. Prior to the Civil War many bank loans had been made on a long-term basis with the result that they frequently financed the acquisition of fixed assets and became "frozen." In order to avoid this, commercial bankers in the post-bellum period came increasingly to insist on short-term paper based on self-liquidating loans. This practice assured safety, but some believe that it did so at the expense of restricting the rate of economic development. Further, as a consequence, the volume of bank credit became wholly dependent on the state of mercantile prosperity and varied widely with the expectations and confidence of business. This feature of the banking system was aggravated also by the absence of a central bank. These deficiencies of the banking system contributed seriously to the political discontent of the farmers and others in this period.

TABLE 11

Growth of State and National Banks, Selected Years,
1860–96[a]

Year	Number of State Banks	Assets of State Banks (Millions)	Number of National Banks	Assets of National Banks (Millions)
1860	1,562	$1,000	—	—
1866	297	197	1,634	$1,476
1870	325	215	1,612	1,566
1880	1,279	1,363	2,076	2,035
1890	4,717	3,296	3,484	3,062
1896	5,780	4,200	3,689	3,536

[a] Source: *Historical Statistics of the United States, 1789–1945*, pp. 264–265.

THE CHANGING ROLE OF FOREIGN TRADE
AND FINANCE IN THE ECONOMY

With the rapid industrialization of the United States in the post-war years, the foreign trade of the nation expanded in dollar volume and underwent significant change. Foreign trade showed a greater percentage increase, in fact, than the national income over the years of this period. In absolute terms the total dollar value of foreign trade more than doubled, going from $782 million in 1866 to $1,661 million in 1896. Exports as a percentage of the output of goods destined for domestic consumption seemed to have declined slightly from 1869 to 1896.[19] North states that while the United States was growing more rapidly than the rest of the world in the years 1860–1914, our share of world trade remained stable at about 10 per cent.[20] Foreign trade was not as large a proportion of the American economy in these years as it had been in the early nineteenth century, but its impact and especially its influence on the short-run fluctuations of the economy cannot be accurately gauged by aggregative analysis. Indeed, as will be developed below, changes in our exports played strategic roles at the turning points in several of the business cycles of this period. Furthermore, with the United States tied into the international economy through its adherence to the gold standard, fluctuations in foreign exchange rates and the international flow of gold had sub-

[19] See raw data in Kuznets, *Capital in the American Economy*, p. 553.
[20] D. C. North, "The United States in the International Economy, 1790–1950," in S. E. Harris, ed., *American Economic History*, p. 199.

stantial effects upon the monetary stability of the nation, most noticeably in the 1890's.

More important than the growth of foreign trade was the shift in our trade balance. From 1866–75, the United States had its usual unfavorable balance of trade, with the exception of the year 1874. But then from 1876 to 1898 we had a favorable balance of merchandise trade, except for 1888, 1889, and 1893. By 1893 American foreign trade exceeded that of every country in the world except England. And influential business and political groups had come to conclude by that year that expanding foreign trade was essential for the prosperity of the nation.[21]

The export trade not only enabled the United States to dispose of its mounting surplus of agricultural staples, but it also offered markets for its growing manufacturing output. In addition, these exports provided the indispensable foreign exchange with which the nation paid the interest charges on the large and increasing amount of foreign investment. In the years 1874 to 1895, it has been calculated that the United States paid out $870 million, or an annual average of $39.5 million, in interest on foreign investments. These "invisible" items of interest payments and the cost of the services rendered to us by foreign shipping and banking agencies were covered by our huge exports.

The industrialization of the economy was reflected very clearly in the changing composition of foreign trade. In the pre-Civil War period, our foreign trade consisted mainly of export of raw materials and import of manufactured goods. But with the growing maturity of the economy, there was a fundamental shift in the composition of our exports and imports. As shown in Chart 1, crude materials and foodstuffs declined from 24 per cent of our total exports in 1866–70 to 14 per cent in the years 1896–1900, while manufactured and semi-manufactured goods declined from 67 per cent of the total to 45 per cent over the same period. These trends continued into the twentieth century. Imports, on the other hand, showed a reverse trend—our imports of manufactured and semi-manufactured goods increased from 25 per cent of the total to 45 per cent over the same period; imports of crude materials and foodstuffs fell percentagewise over the course of these years.

The figures we have cited above have dealt only with the balance of trade. To understand how we balanced our accounts with other trading nations in these years, it is necessary to consider the balance of international payments. This statement attempts to measure, in terms of dollars, the total inpayments and outpayments of the United States in a stated period of time. In Table 12 we present a comparison of the balance of international payments of the United States for two periods, 1850–73 and 1874–95. "Exports" in the table cover all sources of U.S. claims against foreign countries and "imports" represent the sources of foreign claims against the United States.

[21] On this subject, see the important study by W. La Feber, *The New Empire* (Ithaca, New York: Cornell University Press, 1963), p. 18 and Chap. IV especially.

CHART 1

Percentage Composition of United States Exports and Imports
by Economic Classes, Yearly Averages for 1866–70
and 1896–1900[a]

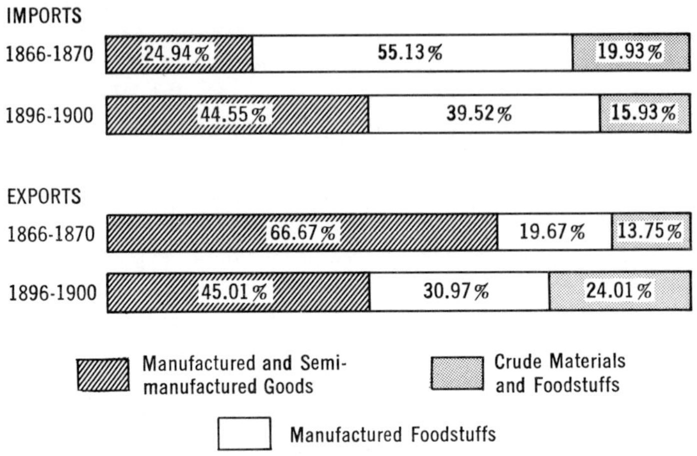

IMPORTS

1866-1870 | 24.94% | 55.13% | 19.93%

1896-1900 | 44.55% | 39.52% | 15.93%

EXPORTS

1866-1870 | 66.67% | 19.67% | 13.75%

1896-1900 | 45.01% | 30.97% | 24.01%

| Manufactured and Semi-manufactured Goods | Crude Materials and Foodstuffs |
| Manufactured Foodstuffs |

[a] Source: Fite and Reese, *An Economic History of the United States*, 2nd Ed. © Copyright 1959 by Houghton Mifflin Co., Boston. Reprinted by permission of the publisher.

TABLE 12

Balance of International Payments of the United States,
1850–73 and 1874–95[a]
(In billions of dollars, rounded to nearest 100 million)

Items	1850–73		1874–95	
	Exports	Imports	Exports	Imports
Merchandise	$ 6.6	$ 8.1	$17.2	$14.7
Investments of capital	1.0	—	1.0	—
Tourists' expenditures	—	0.6	—	0.8
Payments on investments	—	0.9	—	1.9
Specie	1.4	0.3	0.8	0.7
Shipping freights	0.6	0.4	0.1	0.7
Immigrants' funds	0.3	—	—	0.4
Insurance, financing	—	—	—	—
Sale of ships	0.1	—	—	—
Total	10.0	10.4	19.2	19.2

[a] Source: C. J. Bullock, J. Williams, and R. Tucker, "The Balance of Trade of the United States," *The Review of Economic Statistics* (July, 1919), pp. 223, 227.

As we have previously observed, there was a large flow of foreign capital into the United States during this period. Total foreign investment is estimated to have increased from $1.5 billion in 1873 to about $3.4 billion in

1897. While this inflow of foreign capital was taking place, the United States was beginning to be a capital exporter; by 1897, American investments abroad are calculated to have reached $685 million, so at that time we were still a debtor nation to the extent of having net liabilities of some $2,710 million.[22]

By far the most important "import" of the United States economy in these years was people. The millions who crossed the oceans in pursuit of better economic opportunity and escape from a restricting class structure or a hateful political system made an immense contribution to the growth of the economy in this period. Professor North has said, "Immigration played by far the most important role of any external influence in United States economic development. . . ." Since most of the immigrants came as adults, and in this period over 60 per cent were males, they made a substantial addition to the labor force, especially to the unskilled occupations. (As of 1910, foreign-born whites composed 20.5 per cent of male workers in all industries.)[23] The Handlins, who have made intensive studies of the subject, claim that "the more characteristic economic contribution of the immigrants" lay in the creation of reserves of cheap unskilled labor and an expanding consumer market, rather than the qualitative contribution they made to the development of the arts and professions in the United States.[24] Thus, while in the short run immigration created many problems of adjustment for both natives and newcomers alike, "in the long run it was a vital contribution to economic growth and to the vitality of American political democracy."[25]

THE CYCLICAL CHARACTER OF THE
NATION'S ECONOMIC GROWTH

The economic growth of the nation in this period was very unstable. At the end of the Civil War, a recession set in, which resulted in a mild depression in 1866 and a full-fledged one in 1867. In 1873, another depression began, which was one of the longest in our history, ending in 1879 to be succeeded by another cycle of depression that extended over the years 1883–85. The recovery from the latter reached a peak in 1887, only to be followed by another sinking-spell that bottomed out in 1891. Some regard this depression as

[22] The international financial position of the United States for this period is authoritatively analyzed in M. Simon, "The United States Balance of Payments, 1861–1900," in *Trends in the American Economy in the Nineteenth Century*, Studies in Income and Wealth, XXIV (New York: National Bureau of Economic Research, Inc., 1960), pp. 629–715.

[23] E. W. Gilboy and E. M. Hoover, "Population and Immigration," in S. E. Harris, ed., *American Economic History*, p. 270.

[24] O. and M. Handlin, "The United States," *Positive Contributions by Immigrants* (UNESCO, 1955), p. 21.

[25] D. C. North, "The United States in the International Economy, 1790–1950," in Harris, *American Economic History*, p. 200.

extending throughout the nineties to 1897, while others contend that a new, severe depression started in 1893 with the financial panic of that year. In all, one can count eight downturns and eight recoveries in a period of thirty years. Sixteen of these thirty years have been characterized as periods in whole or part of depression and twelve as years of prosperity; the other two were years of revival or recession. The monthly reference dates of the National Bureau of Economic Research for the business cycles of this period and the respective duration of the latter are set forth in Table 13.

TABLE 13

Business Cycles and Their Duration, 1867–97[a]

Business Cycle			Duration in Months		
Trough	Peak	Trough	Expansion	Contraction	Full Cycle
Dec., 1867	June, 1869	Dec., 1870	18	18	36
Dec., 1870	Oct., 1873	Mar., 1879	34	65	99
Mar., 1879	Mar., 1882	May, 1885	36	38	74
May, 1885	Mar., 1887	Apr., 1888	22	13	35
Apr., 1888	July, 1890	May, 1891	27	10	37
May, 1891	Jan., 1893	June, 1894	20	17	37
June, 1894	Dec., 1895	June, 1897	18	18	36

[a] Source: A. F. Burns and W. C. Mitchell, *Measuring Business Cycles* (New York: National Bureau of Economic Research, 1946), p. 78.

Two of the depressions of this period were unusually severe. The one beginning in 1873 was very long, and the 1893 contraction was of great amplitude. Both these depressions were marked by considerable industrial conflict and political tension. Yet, despite the instability of the economic process in these years, the nation's growth as a whole was remarkable. This is one of the paradoxes of the period that we shall seek to resolve as we test the relevance and relative validity of the Marxian hypotheses concerning capitalistic growth in the light of the American experience during these turbulent years.

Chapter 18

CAPITAL ACCUMULATION AND INNOVATION—THEIR IMPACT ON BUSINESS ORGANIZATION AND ECONOMIC FLUCTUATIONS

The old nations of the earth creep on at a snail's pace; the Republic thunders past with the rush of the express.

Andrew Carnegie, *Triumphant Democracy* (1886)

How did it happen that in the United States, where relatively, that is in comparison with civilized Europe, the land was accessible to the great mass of the people and to a certain degree (again relatively) still is, capitalist economy and the corresponding enslavement of the working class have developed more *rapidly* and *shamelessly* than in any other country.

Karl Marx in a letter to Friedrich Sorge (1881)

INNOVATIONS AND ECONOMIC GROWTH

A close reading of the above quotations reveals that both authors who were at odds on so many other points of economics were in agreement on the fact that the United States was expanding faster than other countries in the post-Civil War years. More recent students of the subject tend to find that, with some exceptions, this was so. For example, one study shows the industrial output of the United States growing at an annual rate of 4.3 per cent for the years 1860–80, compared to 2.4 per cent for the United Kingdom, 2.4 per cent for France, and 2.7 per cent for Germany; the world rate for this same period was estimated to be 3.2 per cent.[1] In the years 1880–1900, Germany's annual rate of 5.3 per cent exceeded our 4.5 per cent, but the latter rate was more than double that of the United Kingdom for the same period.

[1] S. J. Patel, "Rates of Industrial Growth in the Last Century," *Economic Development and Cultural Change* (April, 1961), pp. 316–330; also cf. Joint Economic Committee, 86th Congress, 1st Sess., Hearings on Employment, Growth and Price Levels, Part 2—*Historical and Comparative Rates of Production, Productivity, and Prices* (Washington: Government Printing Office, 1959), p. 246. Professor Goldsmith in his testimony before this Committee stated that what was extraordinary about our annual average growth of 1⅝% over a century or 120 years was its persistence over so long a period.

The growth of the United States in this period was not steady, but came in spurts. If we examine Kuznets' data on net national product, the percentage changes from decade to overlapping decade show that there were three periods of relatively faster growth: the decades of 1874–83, 1879–88, and 1894–1903.[2] In analytical terms, the growth of real income is a function of several factors, such as the rate of capital accumulation, innovation, the organization and efficiency of the labor force, the capability of management, etc. Changes in any one of these factors may affect the capital-output ratio. But usually, periods of rapid expansion in real income have been associated with accelerated capital formation, especially if the innovations have been of a capital-using rather than a capital-saving variety. The stimulus to increases in real income derive from the multiplier effect of new investment.

The transcontinental railroads were a major innovation of a capital-using type in this period. Constructed usually on a speculative basis, long in advance of the market demand for their services, they had a marked effect on the growth of the economy, especially until the early 1880's, both because of the autonomous investment they represented and the investment they induced. As a major form of social overhead capital, the railroads had the character of "linked innovations." As one specialist on the subject states, ". . . The development of a transcontinental railroad system was itself the initial link in a chain of innovations leading to the opening of new regions, to the appearance of new products, and new alignments of industry and distribution. . . ."[3]

The financial history of the railroads in the post-bellum period is one of the most colorful chapters in the history of American business. The frenzied speculation, the numerous bankruptcies, and political corruption that accompanied the process of their construction have been retold many times, but despite all this, the railroads were built. By 1910, sufficient traffic had been developed to make them "blue-chip" investments on Wall Street.

Before the Civil War, the railroad frontier had crossed the Mississippi and had pressed into the first tier of states beyond. The Union Pacific had been chartered in 1862, but construction during the war was slow; after its close, spurred on by generous subsidy from the federal government, the lines of the Central Pacific and the Union met at Promontory Point, Utah, in May, 1869. Thereafter, four other transcontinental trunk lines were built, and vast amounts of road were constructed in the East, West, and South to fill out the rail network. The breathtaking pace of the railroad construction in the nation in these years is reflected in Chart 1, which shows the net annual change in railroad mileage on a semi-logarithmic scale; the steep slope of the graph in the 1860's and early 1880's suggests the rapidity with which mileage was being added to the rail system in those years.

The rate of construction was especially hectic in the immediate post-war

---

[2] Cf. B. Weber and S. J. Handfield-Jones, "Variations in the Rate of Economic Growth in the U.S.A., 1869–1939," *Oxford Economic Papers* (June, 1954), pp. 101–132.

[3] M. J. Ulmer, *Capital in Transportation, Communications, and Public Utilities* (Princeton: Princeton University Press, 1960), p. 4.

CHART 1

Net Annual Change in U.S. Railroad
Mileage, 1831–1916[a]

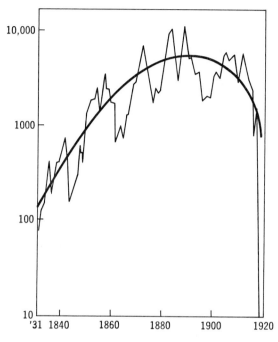

Source: Reproduced by permission from *The Journal
of Economic History*, IV (March, 1944), p. 5.

years. More than 7,400 miles were built in 1872 alone; this was more than
was built in any subsequent year. As one historian says, ". . . Never was an
economy of such magnitude knit together so quickly and so securely as the
economy of the United States during the first few years after the end of the
Civil War."[4]

Actually, the mere physical construction of the transcontinental lines did
not automatically give the nation a unified rail network. There was a need for
standardization of gauges, which was not achieved wholly until the middle
1880's; bridges had to be built, through bills of lading developed, freight rate
classification zones established, and much else done in the way of innovation
and administration before a national rail network could be completed. Vital to
this development were such innovations as George Westinghouse's airbrake,
worked out between 1866 and 1868, which made possible longer trains; the
Janney automatic coupler, invented in 1871, which was in use by 1889; and
the electric block signals, first introduced on the New Haven in 1866, which
proved invaluable in reducing accidents.

[4] L. J. Arrington, "The Transcontinental Railroad and Mormon Economic Policy," *The
Pacific Historical Review* (May, 1951), p. 143.

These improvements in the technology of the railroads, together with the rate wars among them, resulted in substantial reductions in commodity rates during this period. (Part of the explanation for the decline in these rates was the general deflation of prices over these years, but it does not completely account for the reductions made.) For example, the average cost of commodity transportation by railroad dropped from 1.925 cents per ton-mile in 1867 to 0.839 cents in 1895—a reduction of more than 50 per cent. The Chicago to New York rate for 100 pounds of wheat fell from 65 to 20 cents in the years 1866–97. These savings in rail costs constituted important external economies for the farmers and businessmen in other industries that used the railroads. They also had far-reaching effects on the pattern of regional specialization in the nation's production of its principal agricultural staples as well as on the location of its manufacturing and mining activities. By lowering the cost of transport, the railroads widened the market and opened up new economic space for many products, thereby stimulating the necessary investment that their production required.

At the start of the nineteenth century many sections of the country, we have seen, were agriculturally self-sufficient. By 1890 the North Atlantic, South Atlantic, and South Central regions embracing 25 states and 60 per cent of the nation's population had become deficit areas for many agricultural products, chiefly foodstuffs. The North Atlantic region, including New England and the Middle Atlantic states, in that year produced only 36 per cent of the wheat they required to feed the population, 45 per cent of their corn requirements, and 33 per cent and 27 per cent, respectively, of the beef and pork they needed. In contrast, the North Central states by 1890 were producing 71 per cent of the nation's cereals and were also the chief centers of cattle and swine production. The size of their surplus of wheat was tremendous. It has been estimated that the 440 million bushels they produced in 1890–91 was enough to feed four times the number of the region's inhabitants. Not only did the excess go to feed the East and the South, but one-third of it was exported to feed the nations of Europe and South America.[5]

The developmental impact of the railroad on American economic growth has been the subject of considerable study in recent years. Professor Jenks, basing his analysis on Schumpeter's theory of innovations, concluded in part that ". . . The early persistent succession of fresh waves of railway construction arising largely in the development of new areas in the American West and South, must be regarded as one of the basic phenomena in the total economic growth of the United States. . . ."[6] He pointed out, among other things, that "historically, the very existence of most American communities and regions, of particular farms and industrial aggregates, was made possible by the

[5] R. W. Fogel, *Railroads and American Economic Growth* (Baltimore, Md.: Johns Hopkins Press, 1964), pp. 17–18.

[6] Jenks, "Railroads as an Economic Force in American Development" (J. T. Lambie and R. V. Clemence) *Economic Change in America* (Harrisburg, Pa.: The Stackpole Co., 1954), pp. 54–55.

railroad." He called attention to the polarizing tendency of railroads, i.e., that the supply of traffic did not distribute itself at random along the lines of the railroads, but tended rather to locate about line terminals and traffic intersections.[7] This tendency of railroads is thought to have contributed to the growth of large urban conglomerations around the terminals of railroads.[8] Jenks cites the external economies that large firms can realize by availing themselves of rail transport, saying, ". . . Such phenomena as the ecological structure of wholesale trade, the localization and concentration of primary processing establishments and the vertical integration of production units in spite of their geographical separation are thus functionally related to railroad transportation service. . . ."[9]

More recently, Professor Rostow's views on the role of the railroad in the "take-off" have stimulated a large body of literature controverting his position. Perhaps the most significant of these writings has been that of Fogel, who has boldly challenged the "axiom of indispensability" of the railroad to the nation's economic growth.[10] Deploring the lack of empirical data proffered by those who accept this "axiomatic truth" of the "Gilded Age," he employs the technique of linear programming to measure the social saving attributable to the railroad, computing the loss that would have resulted had there been no interregional or intraregional distribution of agricultural products by that form of transport. Fogel's underlying supposition is that if the railroads did not perform this function, other alternative modes of transportation would have done so, without a large loss in social terms. He found, after an ingenious quantitative analysis, that the total social savings provided by the railroad in the shipment of farm products came to only $\frac{6}{10}$ of 1 per cent of the gross national product in 1890. The loss, if there had been no intraregional transport of farm products by railroad, he estimated to be between 2.1 per cent and 2.7 per cent of the 1890 GNP, though it would be smaller if possible waterways were built, etc. Extending the same principle to all commodities, Fogel calculated that the total social saving attributable to the railroad was 4.7 per cent of the gross national product in 1890, but this latter estimate did not rest upon detailed analysis. Expressed in per capita

---

[7] J. E. Holmstrom, *Railways and Roads in Pioneer Development Overseas* (London: P. S. King and Son, 1934).

[8] Jenks in *Economic Change in America*, p. 63.

[9] *Ibid.*

[10] R. W. Fogel, *Railroads and American Economic Growth, passim.* Fogel's provocative book tends to merge the issue of the railroad's role in the Rostovian "take-off" with the larger issue of the rails' effect on the economy in the *whole* of the nineteenth century. Albert Fishlow in his *American Railroads and the Transformation of the Ante-Bellum Economy* (Cambridge, Mass.: Harvard University Press, 1965) deals solely with this more limited thesis. He finds that the direct and indirect effects of the railroads in the antebellum period suggest a total social rate of return well above 20 per cent, and perhaps close to 30 per cent. (*Ibid.*, p. 305.) Fishlow states that "in the absence of railroads a concerted program of canal and road investment might have reduced the effects still further as Professor Fogel has alleged. Still, from the standpoint of historical fact, it was the railroad that actually brought the lowered transport costs and the induced sequences, and these must be credited to it." (*Ibid.*, p. 306.)

terms, the decline in potential income would have been about $3.40 out of the 1890 income per person of $190. In general, he concluded that "the railroad was undoubtedly the most efficient form of transportation available to the nation. But the combination of wagon and water transportation could have provided a relatively good substitute for the fabled iron horse."[11]

Fogel's aggregative type of analysis of the primary effects of the railroads did not involve an equally rigorous statistical examination of their derived effects, such as those produced by the external economies cited above. He assumes that these "disembodied" effects would have followed from the savings in transport cost induced by any innovation by approximately the amount attributed to the railroads. There is a question as to whether the non-rail modes of transport could have produced the external economies over as extensive a territory as the railroads. For example, in an earlier study Fogel cogently showed that the average annual social rate of return on the Union Pacific Railroad was 29.9 per cent for the decade 1870–79.[12] His maps of possible waterways in the later study show no project for a transcontinental canal with anything like so high a rate of return. An aggregative analysis that neglects the historical, sequential character of decision-making may too readily assume that one growth path for the economy is as good as another.[13]

Whatever view one may have about the role of railroads in the economy throughout the nineteenth century, there is little dispute that by the 1880's the industry's growth was showing signs of retardation (note the logistic character of the curve in Chart 1 above). Hansen, who early called attention to its effects on the economy generally, wrote:

> New railroad mileage experienced a rapidly rising trend from the middle forties to the decade of the seventies, and thereafter flattened out with, however, a major spurt in the middle eighties, and eventually in the nineties sharply declined. . . .
> . . . The mere slowing down in the *rate* of growth caused an absolute decline in the volume of new investment required in the plant and equipment of subsidiary industries, such as iron and steel, which manufactured the materials that went into railroad construction. . . .[14]

While the railroad industry was slowing down in terms of the new investment opportunities it provided, other sectors of the economy began to grow in the nineties, thanks to the innovations in such fields as street railways, electric

---

[11] Fogel, *Railroads and American Economic Growth*, p. 219.

[12] R. W. Fogel, *The Union Pacific Railroad* (Baltimore, Md.: The Johns Hopkins Press, 1960), (Johns Hopkins University Studies in Historical and Political Science, Series LXXVIII, No. 2), pp. 101–102.

[13] For a sharp critique of Fogel's latter volume, see S. Lebergott, "U.S. Transport Advance and Externalities," *The Journal of Economic History* (December, 1966), p. 437ff.; also see G. R. Taylor's review in the *American Economic Review* (September, 1965), pp. 890–892; on the method of econometric history, see F. Redlich, " 'New' and Traditional Approaches to Economic History and Their Interdependence," *The Journal of Economic History* (December, 1965), p. 480ff.

[14] A. H. Hansen, *Fiscal Policy and Business Cycles* (New York: Norton, 1941), pp. 39–40 (Hansen's italics).

light and power, and the telephone industry. The rate of new capital formation on steam railroads declined over $2 billion from the decade of the 1880's to the nineties, but these three latter fields almost made up the difference.[15] Expansion in other sectors such as mining was also substantial in this period. The great Mesabi iron ranges were developed to meet the mounting appetite of the steel industry, new pipelines were built to carry the oil and natural gas to the cities where residential construction over the entire decade of the nineties showed no relapse from the ten years before. Beyond the turn of the century, there were other great innovations, such as the widespread introduction of electric power for industrial and domestic use, the automobile, and the myriad products of the chemical industry, which were to provide powerful stimuli to the nation's further economic growth.

THE MARXIAN MECHANISM OF INNOVATION RE-EXAMINED

Marx's vision of the process of economic growth under capitalism embraced the idea of innovations. He saw, as Schumpeter has pointed out, that the process of capitalistic industrial growth would not be peaceful and gradual, nor would the economy expand in a steady manner. Rather it would be incessantly revolutionized from within by new enterprise—new commodities or new methods of production—and the competitors of the innovators would be forced to accumulate to keep up with such technological progress or be eliminated. Schumpeter went on to say, "Now Marx saw this process of industrial change more clearly and he realized its pivotal importance more fully than any other economist of his time. This does not mean that he understood its nature or correctly analyzed its mechanism. . . ."[16] Is Schumpeter right in this criticism of Marx? How does the latter conceive of the mechanism of innovation?

Marx took account of innovations and indeed spoke of the super-profits that the innovating capitalist would temporarily earn, but to him the main source of profit is derived from surplus-value. Innovation as a process is subordinated to capital accumulation.[17] Marx's theory holds in general that capital

[15] Kuznets, *Capital in the American Economy* (New York: National Bureau of Economic Research, 1961), p. 611.

[16] Schumpeter, *Capitalism, Socialism and Democracy* (New York: Harper and Bros., 1942), p. 32.

[17] The restricted view of innovation held by Marx is revealed by P. M. Sweezy in "Schumpeter's Theory of Innovations," *Review of Economics and Statistics* (February, 1943), reproduced in *The Present as History* (Monthly Review Press, 1953), pp. 274–282 by the same author. Sweezy writes: ". . . We may instead regard the typical innovator as the tool of the social relations in which he is enmeshed and which force him to innovate on pain of elimination. This approach implies a different view of profits and accumulation from that of Professor Schumpeter. For him profits result from the innovating process, and hence accumulation is a derivative phenomenon. The alternative view maintains that profits exist in a society with a capitalist class structure even in the absence of innovation. . . ." (P. 282 of *ibid.*)

will accumulate at so fast a rate that there will be a tendency toward a falling rate of profit. However, individual capitalists can seek to counteract this tendency by installing improvements and introducing innovations that will reduce costs or create new sources of profit. But Marx believed that in attempting to escape from this contradiction of the system the innovations made by the capitalists as a whole would tend to induce an excessive rate of capital formation, with adverse effects on the profit rate.

Without debating the abstract merits of the Marxian formulation of the innovation process, let us test it empirically in the light of economic trends in the United States in the late nineteenth century. To do this, note that one inference from the Marxian analysis would be that the rate of innovation will not be adequate to raise the total output of the economy as fast as capital accumulates. In technical terms, this would mean that the capital-output ratio would exhibit an upward secular trend. But the statistics available on this subject do not support such a hypothesis. "At least in the United States," writes Fellner, "the capital-output ratio seems to have declined over a period including several decades, that is the average productivity of capital seems to have risen. . . ."[18] Kuznets' estimates of capital-output ratios show them declining in the United States from 1880 to 1900 and from that year to 1922 and 1948, though the sector ratios reveal wide variation from the average, depending on the sector of the economy; the ratio of net capital formation to changes in net product tended to rise from the period 1869–88 to 1909–28, but then declined.[19]

Two British students, reviewing the long-run trend of the capital coefficient (the marginal capital-output ratio) in the American economy over the years 1879 to 1939, come to similar conclusions. They find that innovations and improvements "appear to have been powerful enough to maintain in the long run a stable capital coefficient in both the United Kingdom and the U.S.A."[20] In short, on the basis of these studies, the failure of average productivity to decline, and especially the tendency for average productivity to rise, points to the quantitative sufficiency of innovation to offset the tendency toward diminishing returns from capital. Another competent student of Marxian economics, J. M. Gillman, has analyzed the law of the falling rate of profit, using the Marxian categories as applied to the American experience since 1849.[21] On a flow basis in which depreciation is taken to be constant capital consumed, he discovered that, rather than falling, the rate of profit exhibited a slowly rising tendency over the years 1849–1939. On a stock basis, in which

---

[18] Fellner in *Economic Journal* (March, 1957), p. 23.

[19] S. Kuznets, *Capital in the American Economy*, pp. 80, 82, 199.

[20] B. Weber and S. J. Handfield-Jones, "Variations in the Rate of Economic Growth of the U.S.A., 1869–1939," *Oxford Economic Papers* (June, 1954), pp. 101–132 as reproduced in B. Supple, *The Experience of Economic Growth* (New York: Random House, 1963), p. 314. See also J. Steindl, *Maturity and Stagnation in American Capitalism* (Oxford, Eng.: B. Blackwell, 1952), pp. 191, 235–236, which reaches conclusions similar to Fellner's.

[21] J. M. Gillman, *The Falling Rate of Profit* (London: Dennis Dobson, 1957), pp. 38–39, 57 and Appendix 3.

constant capital was taken to be the value of fixed capital investment, the law was confirmed, except after 1919 it apparently ceased to operate. The law, this author concluded, has to be reformulated to conform to the new facts of American capitalism.

Another body of evidence on the question of the trend of profit rates is that of the Cowles Commission study of earning yields of common-stocks and railroad bonds, which is reproduced in Table 1. From this table one can see that the yield of common stocks for all types of shares declined in the latter

TABLE 1

Yields of Bonds and Common Shares in the U.S., 1871–1928[a]

	Yield: Railroad Bonds	Earnings-Yields[a] on Common Shares			
		All Shares	Industrials	Railroads	Utilities
1871–78	6.59%	8.83%	10.50%	8.79%	9.65%
1874–83	6.00	8.38	11.78	8.22	9.71
1879–88	5.34	7.00	12.20	6.88	8.02
1884–93	4.93	5.98	9.13	5.71	6.01
1889–98	4.64	5.75	10.32	5.20	6.80
1894–1903	4.27	6.44	11.35	5.81	6.18
1899–1908	4.04	7.48	11.91	6.71	5.69
1904–13	4.11	7.50	10.47	6.60	7.14
1909–18	4.35	9.83	13.07	7.90	8.48
1914–23	4.77	10.60	12.31	9.40	10.01
1919–28	4.80	9.09	8.51	10.08	10.10

[a] Source: Adapted from J. Steindl, *Maturity and Stagnation in American Capitalism* (Oxford, Eng.: B. Blackwell, 1952), p. 151.

part of the nineteenth century, but turned upward again in the present century and, indeed, exceeded the earlier level of returns in the years 1909–28. The yield of industrial shares demonstrated overall an upward trend. The common shares of both railroads and public utilities showed declines in the later decades of the last century, but also exhibited a reversal of trend in the present century. It would be difficult to substantiate the Marxian law over the whole period covered by this table with these statistics.

Generalizing from the above, we are led to the conclusion that Marx's manner of conceiving the *mechanism* by which innovations work under capitalism was too narrow and did not allow enough for their stimulating effects on the whole economy. He envisioned innovation largely as a response to the threatening forces of capital accumulation and competition; he emphasized those technological innovations that tend to raise the ratio of constant capital to labor and output, but in mature capitalism capital-saving innovations are also very important. Product and organizational innovations do not increase the organic composition of capital, but rather serve to widen the market for its output. In other words, Marx's way of conceptualizing the innovation process did not bring out its creative aspects in the sense that major, strategic innovations may open up new economic space in which the economy can grow. This is probably what Schumpeter had in mind when he wrote, ". . . With him [i.e., Marx] that mechanism [of innovation] resolves itself into mere mechanics of masses of capital. He had no adequate theory of enterprise and his failure to distinguish the entrepreneur from the capitalist, together with a faulty theoretical technique, accounts for many cases of *non sequitur* and for many other mistakes. . . ."[22] The American economy behaved "in the most Marxist way" in the years 1866–96 in the sense that it was a period of rapid capital accumulation, but the trends that Marx discerned in that process were not imminent and irreversible forces. They did not have the adverse effects on the long-run profit rate that he envisioned because innovation and creative entrepreneurship in its various forms either increased productivity or opened up new markets for the products of capital and labor.

THE LONG WAVE OF FALLING PRICES

Marx believed that as capitalism matured business depressions would increase in amplitude and frequency. In order to test whether this prediction was confirmed by the events of this period we need to consider first what has been called the "long wave depression" of those years. This term refers to the protracted price deflation and depression that characterized most of the 32 years from the end of the Civil War to 1897. This period of falling prices was an international phenomenon and in this country was marked by considerable political and social unrest. The decline in prices was accompanied, as we have previously noted, by three severe cyclical depressions, those of 1873–79, 1882–85, and 1893–97. If one compares these depressions of the 32 years 1866–96 with those of the succeeding 32, the former appear to be longer and more severe than the short depressions of 1907–08, 1913–14, and 1920–21. We need to examine the depressions of the years 1873–96 to find out whether they were as severe as they were for the reasons he stressed. Marx, after all, could be right, but for the wrong reasons!

In general, economists have explained the long decline in prices after the Civil War either in terms of monetary factors or real ones. Originally, there was much emphasis on the lag of gold production relative to the needs of trade for a monetary medium. In other words, it was believed that since the money supply was not growing rapidly enough, prices fell. Explanations in real terms have stressed overproduction, excess capital, and lack of investment opportunities. In what follows, we shall consider the monetary explanations first and consider later the evidences of overproduction. The monetary history

---

[22] *Capitalism, Socialism, and Democracy*, p. 32. On the erroneous concept of entrepreneurship in Marx and other classical economists, see F. Redlich, "Toward the Understanding of an Unfortunate Legacy," *Kyklos*, Vol. 19, No. 4 (1966), pp. 7, 9, 18.

of this long period falls conveniently into two phases: (1) the greenback period from 1865–79; and (2) the era of silver agitation from 1879–96. We treat them below in that order.

The period from 1866 to the resumption of gold payments in 1879 is one of unusual interest for the student of economic growth. During the Civil War, as we have seen, the price level had more than doubled. If the United States was to return to the gold standard, its inflated level of prices had to be brought into line with its chief trading partners. Otherwise, resumption of gold payments would not be permanent. During the fourteen years after the war the price level fell to half its initial level, yet economic growth proceeded at a very fast pace. This whole phenomenon casts doubt on the proposition that secular price deflation and rapid economic growth are incompatible.[23]

In order to determine the relationship between the supply of money and economic growth in these years, we need to begin with what economists call the "stock of money." In 1867, the first year for which we have good statistics on the post-war monetary situation, this stock of money consisted of a variety of forms of currency and of bank deposits (see Table 2). The public's stock of

TABLE 2

Currency and Commercial Bank Deposits Held by the Public,
June 10, 1867[a]
(Millions of dollars)

Currency:		
Gold coin	$ 48	
Gold certificates	19	
State banknotes	4	
National banknotes	280	
U.S. Notes (greenbacks)	319	
Subsidiary silver	7	
Fractional currency	16	
Other U.S. currency	124	
Total currency		$ 570
Adjusted commercial bank deposits:		
National	411	
State and private	280	
Total bank deposits		691
Total currency and deposits		1,261

[a] Source: Adapted from Friedman and Schwartz, *A Monetary History of the United States, 1867–1960*, p. 17. Footnotes omitted. Reprinted by permission of Princeton University Press.

money consisted at that time of more bank deposits than currency; the ratio was about $1.20 of bank deposits for each dollar of currency. In the years 1867–72, with the rapid growth of commercial banking, the ratio of deposits

[23] M. Friedman and A. J. Schwartz, *A Monetary History of the United States, 1867–1960* (Princeton, N.J.: Princeton University Press, 1963), p. 15. We have drawn heavily upon this important work.

to currency rose to two to one. It hovered around that level until 1880 and then began a rise that carried it up to $12 of deposits for each dollar of currency in 1929.

Most of the items composing the currency held by the public are familiar to the reader. The only item, perhaps, which calls for explanation is "other U.S. currency." This included various Civil War issues that circulated as currency, such as the unusual interest-bearing legal tender notes, government-demand notes and other non-legal tender obligations. In addition to the amounts shown in the table, the banks held $247 million in currency and the Treasury, $162 million, plus $33 million of deposits in national banks.

The United States in these years had, in effect, a dual monetary standard; the greenback was the official one and the gold dollar, the unofficial. The price of one in terms of the other was determined in the free market for gold or British sterling. Gold was used mainly for foreign transactions and for paying customs duties; in addition, the federal government paid all the interest and principal payments on its debt in gold at the pre-war value. The only part of the country that was on a specie basis was the West Coast; the remainder of the nation did business in terms of greenbacks. If gold was offered in payment, it was valued at its current market premium in greenbacks. In June, 1867, the date of Table 2, that premium was about $1.383 in greenbacks.[24]

The money stock, as defined above, first fell after the Civil War until January, 1868, when it rose until it reached peaks in 1873 and 1875, and then declined about 9 per cent to a low in early 1879. By the latter year, its level was only 17 per cent above that of 1867 (see Chart 2). Meanwhile, wholesale prices were falling sharply, with the exception of the short period after December, 1870, when the money stock was rising. The decline in prices was especially severe during the depression years 1873–79. Over the whole period, 1867–79, the money stock rose 1.1 per cent per year, but prices declined 3.5 per cent per year. How can we explain these paradoxical movements? While there are serious limitations in the available statistics and indices for this period, the explanation of this discrepancy is to be found either in a rise in output during the period or by a rise in the money balances the public held relative to output, i.e., a decline in velocity. Friedman and Schwartz estimate that of the 4.6 per cent to be explained, 1 per cent can be attributed to a decline in the velocity of money, so that leaves 3.6 per cent as traceable to a rise in output.[25] From what we know of the increases in population and economic growth in these years, this does not seem unreasonable. In short, what seems to have happened was that "an unusually rapid rise in output converted an unusually slow rate of rise in the stock of money into a rapid decline in prices." This drastic deflation produced serious strains among the various groups of American society; indeed, the political agitation for the expansion of the currency persisted throughout the last three decades of the

[24] Friedman and Schwartz, *A Monetary History* . . . , p. 26.
[25] Friedman and Schwartz, *A Monetary History* . . . , p. 34.

CHART 2

Money Stock, Income, Prices, and Velocity, in Reference
Cycle Expansions and Contractions, 1867–79

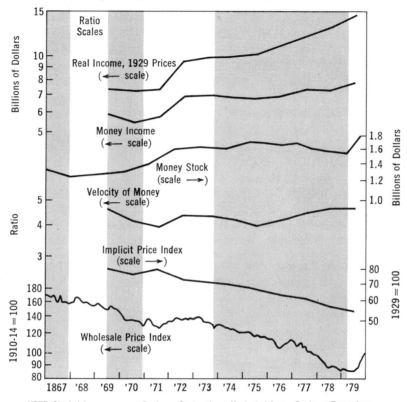

NOTE: Shaded Areas represent Business Contractions; Unshaded Areas, Business Expansions.

Reproduced from M. Friedman and A. Schwartz, *A Monetary History of the United States, 1867–1960* (Princeton, N.J.: Princeton University Press, 1963), p. 30, with the permission of the publisher.

century as a consequence.[26] But there was one major compensation: the 50 per cent deflation of prices in the years 1865–79 not only did not cause complete economic stagnation, but it produced a rapid rise in real income. The movement of some of the key economic variables between 1869 and 1879 is presented in Table 3. While some of the estimates for this period are "highly tenuous," the Friedman-Schwartz analysis tends to confirm the extraordinarily rapid rate of growth in output which they reveal.

The above figures throw an interesting light on the economics of resumption of specie payments that took place, according to the terms of the Resumption Act of 1875, on January 1, 1879 at the pre-war parity. (The

[26] See below, Chapter 19, pp. 479–481 for further discussion of the political aspects of these matters.

TABLE 3

Key Economic Variables in 1869 and 1879[a]

	Value of Indicated Variable		Rate of Change (Per cent per year)
	1869	1879	
Stock of money, valued in greenbacks, middle of the year ($ billion)	1,298	1,698	2.7%
Net national product, current prices ($ billion)	5.82	7.89	3.0
Net national product, 1929 prices ($ billion)	7.36	14.52	6.8
Implicit price index (1929 = 100)	79.1	54.3	−3.8
Velocity of money	4.48	4.65	0.4
Population at midyear (millions)	39.1	49.2	2.3
Net national product per capita, 1929 prices (dollars)	188	295	4.5

[a] Source: Friedman and Schwartz, *A Monetary History of the United States, 1867–1960*, p. 37. Reprinted by permission of Princeton University Press.

Secretary of the Treasury was authorized by that Act to use surplus revenue and to sell bonds in order to accumulate a gold reserve.) Before the Civil War the exchange rate between the U.S. dollar and the British pound was around $4.86; the actual rates varied between the so-called "gold points," depending on the demand and supply of foreign exchange. To get back to the pre-war parity meant that the greenback price of the pound sterling had to fall until the exchange rates were within the range set by the gold points. The basic requirement for this to happen was that U.S. prices in greenbacks bear about the same relation to prices in Great Britain in pound sterling as U.S. prices did before suspension of gold payments. Now prices in Great Britain in 1879 were 15 per cent lower than they had been in 1861, whereas in the United States in 1865, wholesale prices, according to the Warren-Pearson monthly index, were slightly double the 1861 level. To achieve resumption at the pre-war parity, therefore, the American prices had to fall to less than half the latter level, and this is exactly what they did. By December, 1878, the price index, which had averaged 185 for 1865, was 86, and resumption was accomplished without incident, despite the heated controversy preceding it. Basically, as Friedman and Schwartz point out in their monumental monograph, "The primary factor producing the decline in prices that made resumption possible was, therefore, the rapid growth in real income—the economy grew up to its money stock."[27]

In the years from 1879 to 1896, wholesale prices continued to decline secularly, but at a much slower rate than in the preceding period. Prices fell at the rate of over 1 per cent per year, while the increase in the stock of money

[27] Friedman and Schwartz, *A Monetary History* . . . , p. 81.

averaged an increase of about 6 per cent per year over this period. The
variations in the money stock, income, prices, and the velocity of money are
illustrated in Chart 3. The rate of growth of the money stock was very
uneven; in the years 1879–81, it rose over 19 per cent per year, but in the
years from 1892 to 1897 it was practically zero. The composition of the
money stock underwent important changes in these years; Chart 4 shows the

CHART 3

Money Stock, Income, Prices, and Velocity in Reference
Cycle Expansions and Contractions, 1879–1914

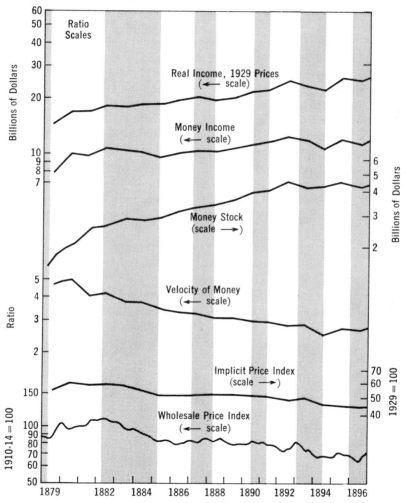

NOTE: Shaded Areas represent Business Contractions; Unshaded Areas, Business Expansions.

Reproduced from M. Friedman and A. Schwartz, *A Monetary History of the United
States, 1867–1960* (Princeton, N.J.: Princeton University Press, 1963), p. 94, with the
permission of the publisher.

fluctuations in its principal components. It can be seen that silver made little contribution to the total amount of the currency until 1886. Overall, the total of silver and Treasury notes of 1890 in circulation grew some $500 million, which reflects the power of the silver forces in these years. On the other hand, it is to be noted that the amount of national banknotes was shrinking, as the retirement of the government bonds upon which they were based forced contraction. The volume of bank deposits grew rapidly, as the commercial banking system expanded. Total deposits rose from $758 million in 1866 to $5,486 million in 1896; by the latter year, the public held more than $4 for each dollar of currency, compared to a 22 to 1 ratio in the earlier year. The rate of increase in the money stock varied considerably with the fluctuations in the economy. During this period, with the United States on the gold standard, the stock of money could no longer be controlled wholly by domestic considerations. With fixed exchange rates, the money stock was now controlled primarily by external influences. This was demonstrated most vividly during the disturbed years from 1891 to 1897 when the threat of silver legislation caused flights of capital and gold from the United States, with adverse effects on the size of the money stock. The details of these difficulties will be treated below; the politics of the subject receives attention in the next chapter.

Now that we have reviewed the factors bearing on the money supply, we can sum up the analysis and move on to other aspects. Despite the huge amount of research that has been done on the subject, economists are still at odds over the question as to whether a lagging money supply caused the secular decline of prices in the "Great Depression" of the last century. Rostow has attacked the monetary explanation for the long-wave depression in Britain by pointing out that the behavior of interest rates in the 1870's and 1880's was inconsistent (they declined) with the alleged shortage of gold.[28] The Friedman-Schwartz analysis seems to support a modified quantity theory view in the sense that it holds, particularly for the years 1867–79, that the money supply was not increasing as fast as output, with the result that the latter depressed prices. For the years after 1879, it points to the relatively slow growth in the stock of money and the adverse effects caused by the uncertainty over the nation's maintenance of the gold standard.

As to the view that real forces in the form of overproduction were more important than monetary ones in depressing prices, we need only point out that the Friedman-Schwartz data lend support to this as well. The massive increase in agricultural output (farm production doubled between 1866 and 1878) exerted strong deflationary pressure on prices. The increased supply of wheat coming from such countries as Russia, India, Egypt, and later Argentina after the early 1880's added greatly to the pressure on the price of this important staple. The effect of this international competition in the wheat market was especially evident after 1893. As Rothstein points out, ". . .

---

[28] W. W. Rostow, *The British Economy in the Nineteenth Century* (Oxford: Clarendon Press, 1948), pp. 145–160.

CHART 4

Composition of High-Powered Money, 1879–97

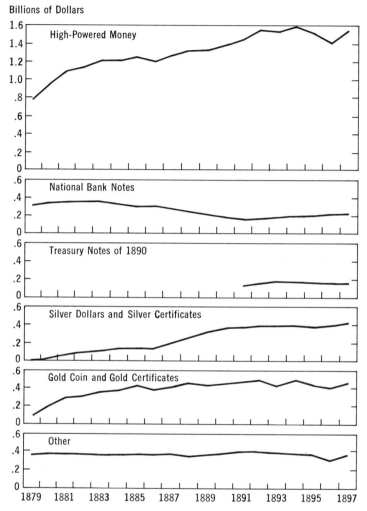

Billions of Dollars

Reproduced from M. Friedman and A. Schwartz, *A Monetary History of the United States, 1867–1960* (Princeton, N.J.: Princeton University Press, 1963), p. 129, with the permission of the publisher.

During most of the preceding seasons a bountiful crop in one region of the world had been offset by rather poor harvests in another, but from 1893 to 1895 all the major exporting nations enjoyed plentiful yields."[29] The result

[29] M. Rothstein, "America in the International Rivalry for the British Wheat Market, 1860–1914," *The Mississippi Valley Historical Review* (December, 1860), pp. 401–418, as reproduced in Scheiber, *United States Economic History* (New York: A. A. Knopf, 1964), p. 292.

on wheat prices was disastrous; they plunged to the level of from 48 to 53 cents per bushel during these three years, lower than they had been in decades.

Excess capacity relative to the demand also had depressing effects on prices in this period in railroading, manufacturing, and other fields. The effects of this weakness in industrial prices on the combination movement will be discussed below.[30] At this point, we can close our discussion of the 1873–96 long wave with the conclusion that both monetary and real factors combined to produce that particular secular decline in wholesale prices.

THE QUESTION OF THE INCREASING
SEVERITY OF CYCLICAL CRISES

Marx's thesis of the increasing severity of depressions under capitalism is theoretically interrelated with his vision of the drive of that system toward unlimited capital accumulation with the resultant tendency toward a declining rate of profits. The endless accumulation of capital under the conditions of capitalist production, given the need for proportionality between capital accumulation and ultimate consumer potentials, leads to the falling rate of profit.[31] The latter becomes, as Marxists are accustomed to say, a precipitating agent of crises. In the *Communist Manifesto*, Marx wrote that capitalism gets over its periodic crises by "paving the way for more extensive and more destructive crises, and by diminishing the means whereby crises are prevented." From the above and our remarks in the Introduction, it must be clear that Marx did not present a fully worked out theory of business cycles; he had a conception of their basic underlying cause, but did not concern himself, as do modern students of business cycles, with the mechanics of these economic fluctuations, their turning points, etc. Furthermore, he deals more with what we have come to call major cycles rather than with the shorter, minor cycles often associated with fluctuations in inventories. In what follows we shall test the Marxian thesis in relation to the major contractions of this period and of the succeeding years.

In Table 4 we present the main contractions of the years 1854–1954, ranked according to their duration and amplitude. In this table the shortest durations and amplitudes as computed by the National Bureau of Economic Research are given a rank of 1, the next a rank of 2, etc. We have computed a rough index of "severity" by multiplying the respective ranks of duration and

---

[30] On excess capacity and its effects on prices in the fields mentioned, see R. Ginger, *Age of Excess* (New York: The Macmillan Co., 1965), pp. 53–55.

[31] Marx stated the conflict between proportionality and the falling rate of profit as follows:

"The stupendous productive power developing under the capitalist mode of production relatively to population, and the increase . . . of capital values, which grow more rapidly than the population, contradict the basis, which, compared to the expanding wealth, is ever narrowing and for which this immense productive power works, and the conditions, under which capital augments its value. This [he concluded] is the cause of crises." (*Capital*, Vol. III, pp. 312–13.)

amplitude of each of these contractions. On the basis of the calculation used, the higher the index, the more severe the contractions.

TABLE 4

Ranks of the Duration and Amplitude of Cyclical Contractions in the United States, 1854–1954[a]

Peak	Trough	Rank of Durations	Rank of Amplitudes	Index of Severity (Duration rank × amplitude rank)
June, 1857	Dec., 1858	7	11	77
Oct., 1860	June, 1861	1	6	6
Apr., 1865	Dec., 1867	10	4	40
June, 1869	Dec., 1870	7	1	7
Oct., 1873	Mar., 1879	13	16	208
Mar., 1882	May, 1885	11	17	187
Mar., 1887	Apr., 1888	4	3	12
July, 1890	May, 1891	2	9	18
Jan., 1893	June, 1894	6	19	114
Dec., 1895	June, 1897	7	15	105
June, 1899	Dec., 1900	7	8	56
Sept., 1902	Aug., 1904	8	8	64
May, 1907	June, 1908	4	18	72
Jan., 1910	Jan., 1912	9	5	45
Jan., 1913	Dec., 1914	8	14	112
Aug., 1918	Apr., 1919	1	13	13
Jan., 1920	July, 1921	7	20	140
May, 1923	July, 1924	5	12	60
Oct., 1926	Nov., 1927	4	2	8
June, 1929	Mar., 1933	12	23	536
May, 1937	June, 1938	4	22	88
Feb., 1945	Oct., 1945	1	21	21
Nov., 1948	Oct., 1949	3	10	30
July, 1953	Aug., 1954	4	7	28

[a] Source: Adapted from A. Achinstein, "Economic Fluctuations," in Harris, *American Economic History*, p. 168. © Copyright 1961 by McGraw-Hill Book Company, New York. Reprinted by permission of the publisher. The reference dates and the durations and amplitudes of the contractions are those determined by the National Bureau of Economic Research. See A. F. Burns and W. C. Mitchell, *Measuring Business Cycles* (New York: National Bureau of Economic Research, 1946), *passim*.

Table 4 shows that the contractions of 1873–79, 1882–85, and 1893–97 were longer than all the contractions between 1854 and 1873 and also longer than those that followed 1897, with the exception of the "great depression" of the 1930's. The trend of wholesale prices seems to have an important bearing on the length of business contractions. The studies of Wesley C. Mitchell on business cycles in the United States, Great Britain, Germany, and France have shown that business contractions tend to be long when the trend of wholesale prices is downward and short when it is upward. Comparing the relative

duration of prosperity and depression in periods of rising and falling prices in
the United States over the years 1790–1920, Mitchell concluded that the ratio
of the duration of prosperity to depression was 2.9 to 1 in periods of rising
prices, while it was only .85 to 1 in periods of a falling price trend.[32] The
depressions that occurred between 1897 and 1920 did not get progressively
longer. The major contractions that followed immediately after 1897 during
the rising price trend of the years 1897–1919 were, in fact, of moderate
length. (The short recessions of the 1920's would be regarded as parts of
minor cycles.) In general, in the light of these data and on the basis of duration alone, Marx's prediction had some truth for the late nineteenth century
during the long wave of falling prices, but over a longer time period extending into the present century, his hypothesis was not sustained by the facts of
the American experience.

Marx's hypothesis, of course, was not concerned only with the duration of
depressions, but with their amplitude as well. From Table 4 it can be seen that
the contractions of 1873–79 and 1882–85 were exceedingly severe and that if
we add together the indices for the contractions beginning in January, 1893
and December, 1895, there is some tendency toward increasing severity over
time for the period under study. However, if we extend the period of the
analysis into the present century, it is difficult to demonstrate the thesis of
increasing severity, except by ignoring the moderate downturns in 1907–08
and 1913–14. Gillman has made a comparison of the relative severity of the
major depressions before World War I with those after that war.[33] He found
that by the four measures he used, all three post-World War I major depressions (those of 1920–22, 1930–36, and 1937–40) were more severe than any
of the four major depressions that occurred before that war. He conveniently
omits, however, the depressions of 1907–08 and 1913–14 in his analysis. In
general, Marx's prediction of increasing severity (embracing both length and
amplitude in that concept) seems to have had more of a semblance of validity
in the period of the "drive toward maturity" than in the years since the turn
of the century. What explains Marx's relative success in predicting a recurrence of severe depressions in the latter part of the nineteenth century? Marx's
theory of capitalist crises emphasizes the rising organic composition of capital
over time, which, aggravated by the competitive struggle to survive, leads to
periodic excess capacity and glut, with a falling profit rate. In the next section
we shall examine the main features of the major cycles of that period in order
to test this hypothesis. We begin with the post-war recession.

The nation faced a difficult task of economic readjustment after the cessation of hostilities. The federal government had a budget deficit of almost one
billion dollars in the fiscal year 1865, equal to perhaps one-seventh of the

[32] W. C. Mitchell, *Business Cycles* (New York: National Bureau of Economic Research, 1927), p. 411; A. Achinstein, "Economic Fluctuations," in S. E. Harris, ed.,
American Economic History (New York: McGraw-Hill Book Co., 1961), p. 172.

[33] Gillman, *The Falling Rate of Profit*, pp. 114–123; see also A. R. Eckler, "A Measure
of the Severity of Depressions," *Review of Economic Statistics* (May, 1933), pp. 75–81.

national income, and this dropped to less than zero in 1866. The deflationary effect of this fiscal change was compounded by the drop in wholesale prices in anticipation of a return to sound finance. Monetary pressures existed as well. During the immediate post-war years the currency was being contracted in accordance with Secretary McCulloch's plan of retiring a certain amount of greenbacks each month, in the hope that resumption of specie payments could ultimately be achieved.[34] During this same period, one and a half million men were being added to the labor force as a result of the demobilization of the armies and the cutback in military production. At about the same time, a stream of 300,000 immigrants flooded into the nation in each of the fiscal years 1866 and 1867. One would have expected a severe depression, but the recession was relatively mild. The reasons for this were primarily that balancing the budget merely removed inflationary forces with the result that prices fell in response to an increase in output; secondly, the decline in business activity caused by these post-war strains on the economy was offset by increased investment in building and railroad construction.

Indeed, beginning in the early part of 1868 an extraordinary expansion started, which continued with only a short interruption in 1869–71 until 1873. The short panic that occurred in the fall of 1869 resulted from the attempt of Jay Gould and Jim Fisk to corner the gold market.[35] Inventory accumulation stopped, and as a consequence the nation experienced another mild recession. The contraction was moderate because it was bucking against a huge expansion in railroads and the building industry; by the second quarter of 1871, recovery was under way. The prosperity that followed in the years 1871–73 extended the nation's industrial capacity far beyond its needs. The overexpansion was most marked in the railroad sector of the economy. Between 1865 and 1873 the railroad mileage increased from 35,085 to 70,651 miles; in this short period of eight years it nearly doubled. The construction of the Union Pacific and the grants of land by the federal government created a veritable railroad mania. Railroads were built in the West far in excess of immediate need. By 1873, 22,885 miles had been built in that section, amounting to more than 32 per cent of all the roads in the nation. Indeed, by that year the West had more railroad mileage than the East and had almost the same amount of capital investment in the industry. While the roads in the East were earning an average return of 6 per cent, that of the western railways

[34] Critics complained that the monetary contraction was a cause of poor business. Congressional opposition to this plan of gradual contraction of the greenbacks led to an act in February, 1868 that prohibited further retirement of these notes; by that time their amount had been reduced to $356 million.

[35] Gould argued that a higher price for gold would make for higher farm prices and the latter would, in turn, contribute to larger traffic for the railroads. His plan of cornering the gold supply depended upon the government not selling from its stock. President Grant, after much hesitation, gave Secretary of the Treasury Boutwell the order to sell, but not before the price of gold had been run up from 130 to 162. Stock prices pushed up during Gould's maneuver fell drastically in the panic of "Black Friday," September 23, 1869. Gould had gotten out in time; he had sold his gold upon the very crest of the buying wave.

was a bare 2 per cent. In 1872 only 100 of some 364 railroads paid dividends. The boom in railroads and construction created secondary expansions in such industries as iron and steel, and as the West was being opened up rapidly for settlement, agricultural output also soared. The influence of the railroad boom on the economy's overall expansion in this period is widely recognized: ". . . In the light of the capital intensity of railroad expansion, the high propensity to borrow, and the tendency to build ahead of demand, the impact of railroad investment upon the parameters of the multiplier-accelerator relationships in the postwar decade cannot be reasonably questioned."[36] The optimism of the boom was pervasive; by 1873 there were "unmistakable signs of over-expansion" in industry and agriculture as well as in transportation.

The long depression that set in with the banking panic in the fall of 1873 started with the failure of Jay Cooke and Co. Cooke, the "financier of the Civil War," was one of the most over-extended businessmen when the financial strains first manifested themselves. He had undertaken the financing of the Northern Pacific Railroad which, though chartered in 1864, had only 519 miles of road in operation in 1873. Promoting the "Banana Belt," as it was called, with all the hoopla for which he was famous, Cooke was still unable to sell $100 million worth of bonds to carry out this herculean project. His failure caused banks to call in loans and panicky depositors demanded cash. A partial suspension of bank operations followed for eleven days at the very time that farmers needed credit to harvest and market their crops. The financial panic soon led to a rush for liquidity; bank deposits fell, payrolls could not be met, and unemployment spread.

Apart from the over-expansion, what had caused this boom to come to so sudden an end? An immediate cause was tight money, but there were other important factors in the background that made the economy vulnerable to depression. The low rate of return on railroad bonds, the high risks involved in domestic investments and the rise of the farm and labor movements created an atmosphere not conducive to investment. These causes were coupled with unsound banking practices, political corruption (e.g., the disclosures concerning the Credit Mobilier, the Erie Ring, and "Boss" Tweed), and a government policy of complete *laissez faire* that further aggravated the economic situation.

The depression that followed took a heavy toll of marginal competitors, as Marx had stressed. In 1873 alone over 5,000 mercantile firms failed, and the number increased steadily until 1878, when 10,478 closed their doors. Railroad securities and the iron industry were especially affected. By 1876 railroad bonds totalling more than $789 million were in default. The price of pig iron fell from $53 in 1872 to $6.50 in 1878; many of the rolling mills and more than half of the industry's furnaces were closed the entire year. Nevertheless, although this depression was the longest in the history of American business cycles, in terms of output it was relatively mild. Thanks to the reduction in prices, per capita real income in 1879 was actually one-third

---

[36] A. H. Conrad, "Income Growth and Structural Change," in Harris, *American Economic History*, p. 50.

higher than it had been ten years before. Exaggerated reports held that there were three million mechanics out of work, but modern students are inclined to think that this figure is much too high. Workers in the construction and railroad industries were undoubtedly hard hit by unemployment, but in other lines the decline in wage rates seems to have resulted in some re-employment of workers. The flexibility of prices in this period also served to encourage recovery. The low prices of American farm staples stimulated our exports. Bumper crops throughout the period gave a strong impetus to renewed expansion of the economy. In the light of these facts, the question might well be asked, "Why did this depression last so long?"

The major reasons for this depression's length was the fact that investment opportunities had become more limited because of capital's preference for relatively liquid and non-risky projects. The high liquidity preference resulted from the weaknesses in the banking situation, and the degree of risk had to be kept low because of the instability of aggregate demand in the purchase of non-essential items. Railroad building and construction were long term, risky enterprises, and hence, investment dollars shunned these sectors of the economy. The decline in the price level also created adverse expectations, contributing to the unfavorable investment climate.

Long term investment prospects had strengthened by 1878. The return to the gold standard as of January 1, 1879 contributed to renewed confidence in the investment community. Good crop yields in 1878–79, coupled with poor crop yields in Europe, created a favorable export situation for the United States. Funds from abroad sought investment outlets here. Railroads and construction were obvious sectors of expansion because these fields had become hard pressed for capital funds and now they showed a higher rate of return. Rising population and a wave of immigration increased the need for expansion in the consumer goods sector as well. Recovery occurred in 1879 and lasted approximately three years until 1881.

Perhaps the single most important cause of the renewed prosperity was the return to the gold standard. The security of a stable monetary system encouraged a relatively liberal extension of credit. With funds available for investment, the neglected opportunities of the seventies were rediscovered and exploited. The falling rate of interest caused by the abundance of loanable funds made the flotation of bonds more feasible than in the preceding years. In addition, the supply of loanable funds was now augmented as the federal government used its surplus revenue to retire the national debt, thus making more money available for business investment.

In the cycle of 1879–85, railroad construction again led in the upswing. The number of miles built rose from 2,665 in 1878 to 11,569 in 1882. While we have no reliable figures on annual railroad investment, it was evidently "large enough to dominate the picture." The leverage effects of the multiplier-accelerator deriving from the railroads' expansion in this boom were substantial. Several of the main lines whose construction had been stopped by the panic of 1873 were pushed to completion. The Northern Pacific was completed in 1883. The Southern Pacific made a junction with the Texas and Pacific and the Santa Fe in 1881, and four years later the line was extended to San Diego. In addition, the rail network in the East and South was filled in by the construction of numerous feeder and branch lines. Most of this work was done not by new firms, but by the established companies. Irrational optimism and speculation again accompanied the boom. The railroad boom in turn caused a spree of over-building and expansion in other backward linkages, such as steel. One business journal summed it up thus: "We built 28,554 miles of new road in 1880, 1881, 1882. . . . This stimulated overproduction in all the industries contributing to, or allied with, railroad property, which in turn affected every other branch of business in the same way."[37]

Though overshadowed by the railroads, investment in construction was a major factor in the upswing also. The number of building permits increased $2\frac{1}{2}$ times between 1879 and 1883. Full employment seems to have been pretty well achieved, despite the large immigration of the period. There was a brief check to the expansion in the middle of 1881, which eventually turned into a gradual transition from prosperity to depression. Even in 1882 the downturn was not severe enough to cause great concern. The basic situation in many industries had become weaker. Railroads and steel were the first industries to be adversely affected. Rate wars, fraudulent management, mismanagement, and the increased risk of investment created an unfavorable situation in the former field. Sources of funds for railroads became so tight that by 1883 the industry was virtually starved financially. The slowdown in railroad construction had a marked secondary effect on the steel industry; the prices of steel rails dropped from $71 in 1883 to $35 per ton in 1885. Unemployment in these industries contributed to the downward acceleration of the cyclical process.

Business failures and foreclosed loans increased as inventories of unsold goods piled up. In 1884, a financial panic developed as the investment house of Grant and Ward failed, taking with it the Marine National Banks, the Metropolitan, and the Second National Banks. The federal government's silver policy at this time contributed to the financial uncertainty because it was using high-priced silver to clear foreign balances. Foreigners, feeling that the United States was insolvent, sold their American investments and took gold from the country. A widespread fear of devaluation and the accompanying gold drain renewed the anxiety of many over the stability of the dollar.

The trough of this cycle came in May, 1885. The contraction had come to an end largely because of an increase in autonomous investment in construction. Easier money conditions and a tendency for consumption to fall at a slower rate than income also contributed to the upturn. The railroads, though not the leaders in the recovery, now proceeded to expand feeder and complementary lines. The iron and steel industry again reaped the benefit of this

---

[37] Quoted by the *London Economist* (March 3, 1880), as cited in R. Fels, *American Business Cycles, 1865–1897* (Chapel Hill, N.C.: University of North Carolina Press, 1959), p. 122.

construction, and its output climbed to new records. This upswing continued, with interruptions in 1888 and 1890, until 1893. The revival was characterized, however, by an incomplete recovery in some sectors of the economy. While railroad profits were, on the whole, higher, the expansion of the industry was not up to previous levels. In short, this upswing was really not marked by a speculative boom; there was none of the exuberance and recklessness evident in the earlier booms of the seventies and eighties.

In order to understand the monetary difficulties that grew more acute in the following years of the decade, we need to re-examine the international economic position of the nation at this juncture. The important role foreign investment had played in the process of capital formation in the post-Civil War years has already been emphasized. By the late 1880's, for example, it is estimated that a billion dollars of American securities were sold abroad, an average of $200 million a year. In 1890, the British banking houses, faced with severe strain because of the Argentine revolution, were compelled to liquidate a large amount of their American securities; the failure of Baring Brothers of London started a chain of events that produced a drastic reversal in the flow of capital into the United States. The monetary disturbances caused by these developments were intensified by the Sherman Silver Purchase Act of 1890. This law initiated a period of more than six years of distrust of American money and was an important but partial cause of the reversal of the capital inflow into the United States.

The depression probably would have started soon after the British crisis, but the coincidence of good crops here and poor ones abroad in 1891–92 staved off the readjustment. In the preceding expansion, the railroads had not provided the driving force as they had done earlier. By 1892 many of the leading railways were not too profitable, and in the steel industry the obsolescent firms were having difficulty competing with the new capacity that had been installed in the previous five years. The depression started in January, 1893, months before the panic broke out. The decline in railroad investment in 1892 seems to have played a major role in the downturn and in the incomplete recovery in 1895.[38] But cutbacks in investment in manufacturing and especially in the producer durable lines were also of major importance.

The pyrotechnical stage of the contraction began with the failure of the Philadelphia and Reading Railroad in February, 1893, followed by numerous suspensions of banks and bankruptcies of iron and steel companies. The number of commercial houses failing was three times that of 1873. By 1894, 156 railroads with a capitalization of $2.5 billion were in the hands of the receivers. Over the years 1893–97 more than 800 banks failed. The consequent deflation of credit and reductions of output caused unemployment to mount; at its worst, unemployment was estimated to be 20 per cent of the labor force and over the course of the five years from 1893–98, unemployment in manufacturing and transportation amounted to over 9 per cent of the

[38] C. Hoffman, "The Depression of the Nineties," *The Journal of Economic History* (June, 1956), pp. 137–164 is excellent on all phases of this major downturn in business.

employable workers. Wage cuts led to strikes and violence, making this depression one of the most serious from the standpoint of industrial unrest and labor hardship.

The only sectors of the economy that showed a contracyclical tendency toward expansion were the booming street railways and some forms of construction, though they only mildly counterbalanced declining investment in railroads, manufacturing, and agriculture. Complicating the whole complex situation was the operation of the Sherman Silver Purchase Act and the resulting threat to the nation's maintenance of the gold standard. This law compelled the Secretary of the Treasury to purchase 4.5 million ounces of silver a month and to issue in payment Treasury notes with full legal tender power; these notes were redeemable in gold as well as silver coin. During the operation of the law until it was repealed in November, 1893, close to $156 million of Treasury notes were issued. The relationship of these notes to the effort to maintain the gold reserve will soon become evident.

The gold reserve behind the dollar was not a precise sum, nor was it segregated in the accounts of the Treasury. The public and tradition had put the safe minumum at $100 million. The gold reserve started falling in 1890, and by June, 1893, it was below the accepted minimum. There were several reasons for the gold outflow at this time: the British financial crisis had led to considerable repatriation of foreign investment; the decline in American exports and the tendency of our imports to fall by a smaller percentage created an unfavorable trade balance; and the uncertainty over monetary policy contributed to a flight of capital. Of these factors our unfavorable merchandise trade balance was most important. These factors in conjunction created such a demand for sterling exchange that its rate was forced above the export point. With the gold reserve sagging, partly because holders of the Treasury notes could demand redemption in gold, Cleveland, upon his election in 1892, called Congress into special session. The Sherman Act was repealed, but not without a hard fight on the part of the silverites. Still the gold reserve continued to fall. Secretary of the Treasury Carlisle sold four separate issues of bonds to bolster the reserve. These issues were only a partial success because their purchasers withdrew gold from the Treasury in order to pay for their bonds; this was called "the nightmare of the endless chain."[39] By February, 1895, the gold reserve was $41 million. In desperation, President Cleveland negotiated a private contract with a banking syndicate headed by J. P. Morgan and August Belmont. Under the terms of this agreement the bankers agreed to deliver to the Treasury $65 million of gold in exchange for $62 million of 4 per cent bonds at 1.04. The syndicate also agreed to obtain at least one-half of the gold from abroad; they would get none from the Treasury itself, and they undertook to protect the Treasury from withdrawals of gold during the period of the contract. To succeed, the bankers in effect had to peg

[39] A. F. Noyes, *Forty Years of American Finance: A Short Financial History of the Government and People of the United States since the Civil War, 1865–1907* (New York: G. P. Putnam's Sons, 1909), p. 232.

the price of sterling exchange; they did so for a while by partly cornering the market for foreign exchange. But then a New York coffee importer with powerful European connections offered sterling at $4.89. Next, it presented $1 million legal tender notes to the Treasury for redemption. The reserve started falling again. Within five weeks, it fell from its summer maximum of $107 million to $63 million; the syndicate had failed. The only recourse the Treasury now had was to try another sale of bonds to the public; of the $100 million of this loan, $40 million was secured by the redemption of notes. But by this time the floating supply of government notes that could be redeemed was materially reduced; the loan was a success, the Treasury was "out of the woods," the gold standard was safe until the election of 1896, when Bryan made his unsuccessful bid for the Presidency on a platform of bimetallism at a ratio of 16 to 1.

Conservative opinion attributed the continuance of the depression after the repeal of the Sherman Act to the uncertainty over money and the resulting withdrawal of foreign capital from this country. But modern scholarship is inclined to think that this oversimplifies the forces at work. Hoffman writes:

> . . . Actually neither mass repatriation of new foreign investments occurred before, or during the depression. . . . This falling off in foreign investment may have reflected "lack of confidence" in the economy of the United States because of its silver policy. . . . But a more plausible explanation is that the decline was related to a general reduction in European investment owing to the depression abroad which reached its low in 1895 in France, Germany, and England. Europeans continued investing in the United States and did not repatriate en masse.[40]

The economy staged a partial recovery in 1895, but the continued outflow of gold and the war scare over the Venezuela boundary dispute were negative factors. Actually, domestic investment in the railroads, steel, and other industries seems to have lagged, and this contributed to the economy's relative stagnation. Table 5, which presents estimates of the major changes in the components of the gross national product for these years, suggests very definitely that the 1895 recovery was based on inventory accumulation. What is striking in the figures for these turbulent years is the continued rise of consumption expenditures, the marked depression in capital investment in fixed forms (investment in fixed capital, according to these estimates, did not exceed the level of 1892 until 1902), and the gyrations in inventories and net foreign investment. This table beautifully suggests the cross currents and uncertainties that prevailed in the not-so-gay nineties.

The federal government under President Cleveland did relatively little to moderate the depression. The budget had a deficit of from $30 to $60 million a year during the depression, but the circumstances were such that these deficits probably had a deflationary effect. The government borrowed to finance the deficit and to build up the gold reserve; the net effect was to

---

[40] Hoffman, *The Journal of Economic History* (June, 1956), p. 156.

TABLE 5

Changes in Major Components of Gross National Product, 1892–97[a]
(Millions of 1929 dollars)

Year	Total GNP	Consumption Expenditures	Investment in New Construction and Equipment	Change in Business Inventories	Net Foreign Investment	Gov't. Purchases
1892	$30,010	$20,157	$7,488	$566	$−110	$1,909
1893	28,569	20,256	6,219	201	− 83	1,976
1894	27,756	19,659	5,887	180	4	2,026
1895	31,082	22,119	6,404	788	−278	2,049
1896	30,444	23,056	5,734	354	195	2,105
1897	33,327	23,794	6,197	799	313	2,224

[a] Source: Kendrick, *Productivity Trends in the United States, op. cit.*, Table A–IIa, p. 293. The figures are based on the Commerce concept, derived from Kuznets' estimates. © Copyright 1961 by Princeton University Press for the National Bureau of Economic Research.

withdraw cash from circulation. Everything considered, despite the mythology concerning the causes of this depression, it was not brought about solely by the monetary or fiscal policies of the government. It was more the result of a variety of powerful real economic forces, complicated by questionable monetary and fiscal policies. When at last McKinley was elected President, and the maintenance of the gold standard was assured, the United States was pulled out of the stagnation by another coincidence of good crops here and poor ones elsewhere. Our exports zoomed, the Dingley Tariff Act of 1897 gave an added stimulus to the protected industries, and the gold discoveries in Alaska and South Africa opportunely added to the money stock of the gold standard countries. The nation gratefully turned away from one of its most serious depressions to enjoy another period of boom and prosperity.

In concluding this survey of the cyclical fluctuations of the period, we may raise again the question of the relevance and validity of the Marxian conception of capitalist crises and their causes, as applied particularly to the depressions of this period. Generally speaking, Marx's approach to these phenomena, stressing excessive and irregular capital formation and falling profits, was supported by much of the cyclical behavior in the United States in these years, especially by the fluctuations in the 1870's and 1880's. Excess capacity resulting from hectic, unplanned capital accumulation was a notable factor contributing to these major depressions. Marx's vision of the capitalistic process had a peculiar relevance during the drive to maturity. However, his theory also had serious limitations: (1) The depression of 1893 is not adequately explained as the result of excess capital formation, unless one stresses the overbuilding of railroads by the British in the Argentine and the spread to the United States of the financial difficulties growing out of that episode. In this country, it was more the lack of adequate investment opportunities or of opportunities for innovation in the nineties, as Hansen and

Schumpeter respectively contended, plus the adverse balance of payments developments, which explain the onset of that particular depression.[41] (2) The Marxian system does not adequately account for the startling rate of economic growth in this period. The developments in railroads, manufacturing, and finance created external economies that carried the economy to a new plateau not fully explicable by the Marxian theory of exploitation. These external and internal economies of scale acted to reduce prices and to create higher levels of consumption as wages went up relative to costs of commodities. Businessmen began to shift from a cost orientation to sales maximization in order to exploit the emerging consumer market for goods. These were developments that the Marxian system, as then formulated, did not anticipate.[42] (3) It may be questioned whether the Marxian system sufficiently appreciated the effects of the growth in real income on Americans who were eager for social mobility and the higher standard of living associated therewith. These are queries having to do with wages and living conditions that we will consider further in the next chapter.

THE INCREASING CONCENTRATION
OF BUSINESS ENTERPRISE

The tying together of the nation by rail lines and the development of wider markets gave a great impetus in the post-war years to the combination movement in business. The railroad itself had promoted the use of the corporate form of enterprise, and in this period we have the continuation of the merger and consolidation of rail lines that had begun before the war. The heavy capital needs of railroads and the lack of regulation of their financing gave enormous opportunities for unscrupulous profit-making. In the scramble on the part of get-rich-quick Americans to control these strategic lines of transportation, none was more notorious than the activities of the Erie Ring— Daniel Drew, Jim Fisk, and Jay Gould, the three who controlled the railroad by that name in the years 1864 to 1872. Through their illegal, financial skulduggery, they made its history one of the most lurid in the annals of railroading.[43] The political corruption and economic mismanagement of which this group of financial freebooters were guilty calls to mind Marx's dire

---

[41] Cf. on this, Fels, *American Business Cycles*, pp. 213–219.

[42] We think it significant that Gillman as a Marxist sees the necessity of reformulating the Marxian law of falling profits to take account of the "unproductive expenditures" for sales efforts and advertising expense. See Gillman, *op. cit.*, p. 66ff. For a more recent effort along these lines, see P. Baran and P. M. Sweezy, *Monopoly Capital: An Essay on the American Economic and Social Order* (New York: Monthly Review Press, 1966), *passim.*

[43] E. C. Kirkland, *Industry Comes of Age* (New York: Holt, Rinehart and Winston, 1961), pp. 55–56; the classic account is found in C. F. Adams, Jr. and H. Adams, *Chapters of Erie and Other Essays* (New York: H. Holt and Co., 1886).

prediction of the effects of railways on capitalistic society. In a letter written in 1879, he argued that the railways as the "crowning work" of modern capitalistic industry had given impetus never before suspected to the *concentration of capital* and also to the accelerated and immensely enlarged *cosmopolitan activity of loanable capital*, thus embracing the whole world in a network of financial swindling and mutual indebtedness, the capitalist form of "international" brotherhood. He went on to say that in such nations "the railway creation has accelerated the social and political disintegration, as in the more advanced states it has hastened the final development and therefore the final change, of capitalistic production. . . ."[44]

The railroads had peculiarities as economic enterprises, which caused great difficulties in rate-making. They usually had monopolies on certain traffic and competed at other points—in short, they were examples of what modern economists call monopolistic competition. In addition, railroads had relatively large overhead or fixed costs, and this type of cost condition, given the nature of the demand for their services, tended to produce "cut-throat competition"—i.e., sale of their services at less than the average total cost of rendering the same. The economics of overhead costs also tend, as one famous study of the subject puts it, to make "discrimination" the "secret of business efficiency."[45] In overhead costs, therefore, lies much of the explanation of the rate wars in the 1870's and 1880's among the railroads and of their strenuous efforts to abate them by pooling traffic and other forms of cooperation. Thus, for example, one of the first great railroad pools was that among the three roads competing for the Chicago–Council Bluffs traffic in 1870. Though pools were widely advocated by their evangelist, Albert Fink, as the solution of the problem of excess competition, they were so easy to evade and so impossible to enforce under common law that they were superseded by interlocking stockholdings (communities of interest) and holding companies as more effective means of control.

Another famous incident graphically illustrates the economics of overhead cost. The railroads serving the nascent petroleum industry in western Pennsylvania sought in 1871–72 to moderate competition among themselves by regularizing or evening the traffic. They established the South Improvement Company for this purpose, and the principal refiners undertook to ship their oil in accordance with the percentages the railroad had agreed on. In return for performing this function, the refiners were to receive rebates as high as 50 per cent on their freight charges and drawbacks on all shipments made by those outside the agreement. This famous "arrangement," which had to be discarded by the railroads and the participating refiners because of the hostility it caused, shows the extent to which the railroads were willing to go to

---

[44] *K. Marx and F. Engels Correspondence, 1846–1895* (New York: International Publishers, 1934), pp. 358–359. (Italics in original.)

[45] J. M. Clark, *Studies in the Economics of Overhead Costs* (Chicago: University of Chicago Press, 1931), *passim*.

reduce the uncertainty involved in operating competitively under the economics of overhead costs.

In the post-war years and particularly after 1873, cooperation and combination became much more prominent in industry. With the high rate of capital formation in manufacturing, the shifts in industrial location induced by railroad building, and the improving productivity caused by advances in technology, there were frequent complaints of overproduction and excess capacity.[46] This condition, taken together with the higher fixed costs associated with capital-intensive methods of manufacture, was aggravated by the long periods of abnormally low demand during the depressions of these years. The price-cutting and the uncertainties induced by all-out competition led many businessmen in these years to seek an escape from such rivalry through cooperation, and when that failed, through outright combination of enterprises. Andrew Carnegie gave an exposition of the genesis of these forms of combination. After noting a tendency for capacity to exceed demand because of the apparent ease with which people could enter profitable lines, driving prices below cost, Carnegie observed,

> . . . Political economy says that here the trouble will end. Goods will not be produced at less than cost. This was true when Adam Smith wrote, but it is not quite true to-day. . . . As manufacturing is carried on to-day, in enormous establishments with five or ten millions of dollars of capital invested, and with thousands of workers, it costs the manufacturer much less to run at a loss per ton or per year than to check his production. Stoppage would be serious indeed. The condition of cheap manufacture is running full. Twenty sources of expense are *fixed charges*, many of which stoppage would only increase. Therefore the article is produced for months and, in some cases I have known, for years, not only without profit or without interest on capital, but to the impairment of the capital invested. . . . While continuing to produce may be costly, the manufacturer knows too well that stoppage would be ruin. . . .[47]

Carnegie pictures the manufacturers turning to trusts, syndicates, anything to stop the destructive competition among themselves, though he is skeptical that they will be effective if they raise prices above the level of "legitimate profits," because the great law of competition and survival of the fittest will lead to their undoing.

Businessmen sought to moderate or control competition first by entering into "gentlemen's agreements," i.e., simple agreements on prices. Such pacts were particularly common during the years from 1865 to 1875; they were to be found in such industries as anthracite coal, gun powder, salt manufacture, and others. These agreements were hard to maintain, however, because too frequently many of the participants were not gentlemen, but sought to evade

[46] See the evidences of excess capacity cited by Victor S. Clark in *History of Manufactures in the United States, 1860–1893* (New York: McGraw-Hill Book Co., 1929), pp. 164, 169, 170, 174. Professor Ray Ginger argues cogently in his *Age of Excess* (New York: The Macmillan Co., 1965), pp. 53–55, 157–160 that "from 1873 to 1898 excess capacity in the American economy was chronic and it affected virtually every industry. . . ."

[47] A. Carnegie, "The Bugaboo of Trusts," *North American Review*, Vol. 148 (February, 1889), as quoted in Clark, *History of Manufactures*, p. 174.

their terms at the expense of the others; further, these often unwritten understandings could not be enforced in a court of law. And so the unstable agreement gave way to the more stable pool. This latter form of business cooperation started before the depression of 1873; the Michigan Salt Association and the Chicago-Omaha railroad pools were early specimens. When the slump of the seventies set in, many American businessmen resorted to pools, whereas in Europe, especially in Germany, a legalized pool—the cartel—was increasingly employed to control competition. In the pool the independent member firms divided up their markets territorially, or assigned production quotas to each other, and even, in some cases, made complex arrangements for the sharing of income. Unfortunately for the businessmen, however, the pool, too, had its shortcomings. Its short duration often led to fierce conflicts and disagreements on market shares and quotas when it expired, and more serious, it was held by the courts to be illegal under the common law as a restraint of trade.

The difficulties in controlling competition were compounded by the fact that manufacturing in the early years of this period was dominated by individualistic entrepreneurs, so-called "captains of industry" who were not easily persuaded to cooperate with others. While we know that, contrary to the folklore on the subject, many of the businessmen of the post-war generation came from business or professional homes, there were a large number who were distinctly "self-made men," with all the drive and achievement motivation usually associated with that type.[48] Andrew Carnegie was a prime example of this class of competitive capitalist; his remarkable career and his philosophy of business tell us much about the period.[49]

Carnegie came to this country from Scotland as an immigrant boy of thirteen. Serving successively as messenger, telegrapher, and then assistant to the superintendent of the Pennsylvania Railroad, he entered the iron industry in 1863, and within a relatively few years, he and his partners owned one of the leading companies in the field. Carnegie surrounded himself with some of the best managerial talent in the business, pioneered in the introduction of the Bessemer method of steel production, and carried the idea of vertical integration of steelmaking to the highest degree attained in his day. As a competitor, Carnegie was fierce and ruthless. Since his company was a closed corporation and he could defer dividends when necessary, he was able to slash prices right and left, regardless of the consequences for his rivals. During depressions he bought out competitors and built new plants. "Build your plants in periods of depression," he wrote, "you can do it cheaply and thus be able to undersell your competitors when prosperity returns."

---

[48] F. W. Gregory and I. D. Neu, "The American Industrial Elite in the 1870's," in W. Miller, ed., *Men in Business* (Cambridge, Mass.: Harvard University Press, 1952), pp. 193–211.

[49] The standard biography of Carnegie is that of B. J. Hendrick, *The Life of Andrew Carnegie* (Garden City, N.Y.: Doubleday, 1932), 2 vols. A recent work is by L. Hacker, *The World of Andrew Carnegie, 1865–1901* (Philadelphia: J. P. Lippincott, 1968).

During periods of slack business, Carnegie did not seek to stabilize prices, but instead went after new orders by making drastic price cuts.

"The advantage of Carnegie management," says his official biographer, "was that, even at reduced prices, a profit could still be made, and decreased operations were regarded as preferable to suspended operations. Carnegie was the bull in the china shop of the other steelmakers. To their overtures to him to join their pools and maintain prices he replied only with disdain and sarcasm. "Consolidation sounds so much like consolation. I suppose it is like Mesopotamia in effect, a very comforting word." Then having ruined his rivals by his cutthroat methods, he would rub it in by quoting his favorite poets, Burns or Shakespeare, to them: "First in your right hand carry gentle peace but after Peace is gone, the worst policy in the world is 'gentle war.' "[50]

As a result of such methods and the seemingly unlimited demand of the nation for steel, the Carnegie industrial empire grew at a fabulous rate. In 1887 its profits were close to $3,500,000. By 1900, the last year of the firm's independent existence, its profits attained the unheard-of figure of $40,000,-000.

Carnegie, as is well known, was accustomed to defend his practices and those of his contemporaries in terms of the doctrines of Herbert Spencer, the English philosopher. Spencer had gained a tremendous following among conservative Americans in the late nineteenth century by arguing that competition was the law of nature and that, in the end, it was a beneficent force. We find Carnegie, for example, expounding the Spencerian philosophy in these words:

> . . . while the law [of competition] may be sometimes hard for the individual, it is best for the race, because it ensures the survival of the fittest in every department. We accept and welcome, therefore, as conditions to which we must accommodate ourselves, great inequality of environment, the concentration of business, industrial and commercial, in the hands of a few, and the law of competition between these, as being not only beneficial, but essential for the future progress of the race.[51]

Returning to the evolution of the forms of industrial combination, we find that after the pool the next great development was the trust. This corporate device emerged from the activities of another prominent captain of industry of this period, John D. Rockefeller, Sr. This calculating, shrewd man was the son of an itinerant trader and medicine vendor of Richford, New York. When his family fell upon adversity through the indiscretions of the father, John, as the eldest son, had to assume a good deal of responsibility. Rather quickly his precise, analytical way won him success in a Cleveland business office, then in the produce business, and ultimately as head of the world's largest oil manufactory—and this while he was still less than thirty. Allan Nevins has pictured him in his adulthood as a person of precise, analytical mind, ab-

---

[50] Quoted in B. J. Hendrick, *The Life of Andrew Carnegie*, Vol. 2, pp. 50, 115.
[51] Andrew Carnegie, "Wealth," in G. Kennedy, ed., *Democracy and the Gospel of Wealth* (Boston: D. C. Heath and Co., 1949), p. 2.

sorbed in work and business, alert to innovations and the main chance, in short, "a very acquisitive member of a very acquisitive society."[52]

Young Rockefeller had turned his attention to oil after the Civil War. But the hectic, disorganized part of that industry, oil production, had no appeal for his rational, systematic mind. So he entered the refining end of the business. He quickly saw that to survive and grow he would need to gain rebates from the railroads. (This was a fairly general practice in those days, but Rockefeller improved on it.) At that time there was no accepted code or public authority to govern rates. At the suggestion of his attorney, Samuel Dodd, Rockefeller now centralized the competing activities of some forty-odd companies by employing an old legal device, the trust, but with a new twist. The shareholders of the combining companies were given trustee certificates, which entitled them to their pro-rata share of profits, but not the right to vote. Control was centralized in a board of nine trustees, namely, Rockefeller and his chief associates. Shortly after the signing of this agreement, the trustees incorporated the Standard Oil Company of New Jersey. The latter Company then purchased from the trust its refineries, shipping facilities, and other factories in New Jersey. Through means such as this Rockefeller had by 1878 brought about 90 per cent of the refining capacity of the country under his management. With such economic power he was in a position to play one railroad against another, which he promptly proceeded to do. His rebates were enormous and the profits of his trust equally large, though it must be said in fairness that Rockefeller's management was superior to that of most of his rivals. He integrated production in a way that was altogether radical for his time. He made his own oil barrels and the sulphuric acid needed for refining; he owned his own warehouses; he was the first to ship by tank car; and he was thoroughgoing in the utilization of the by-products, which many of his rivals were disposing of as waste.

The Rockefeller enterprise in these years was also able to establish a dominant position in the pipeline transport of oil. In the 1870's it waged a successful struggle against the Pennsylvania Railroad, which had entered this business. Thereafter, it substantially defeated the efforts of the independent refiners to free themselves from dependence on its transport facilities.[53] Controlling the bottleneck of this growing industry, Standard was able to choke off competition on the Atlantic seaboard. The Pure Oil Company, which had its own pipe lines, was the only company able to withstand such competitive methods. Standard Oil's profits were large; in the years from 1882 to 1896 they were reported to be about 19 per cent per year.

The great success of the trust in oil soon led to its imitation in other fields.

[52] A. Nevins, *John D. Rockefeller, The Heroic Age of American Enterprise* (New York: Scribner's, 1940), Vol. 1, p. 77.

[53] R. W. Hidy and M. E. Hidy, *History of Standard Oil Company (New Jersey): Pioneering in Big Business, 1882–1911* (New York: Harper and Bros., 1955), p. 20; A. Nevins, *Study in Power: John D. Rockefeller, Industrialist and Philanthropist* (New York: Charles Scribner's Sons, 1953), Vol. I, pp. 182–183, 231–249.

The cottonseed oil trust was formed in 1884, the linseed oil trust the next year. In 1887, trusts were established in whiskey, lead, sugar and other industries. In the 1880's, contemporaries said that America was being "trustified." Rockefeller was quoted as saying, ". . . The day of combinations is here to stay. Individualism has gone, never to return."

Actually, the trust form of combination did not have a very long life, though several of them, besides the Standard Oil trust, were highly successful. Louisiana brought the first action against a trust when it prosecuted the cottonseed oil trust in 1887. But the suits that established the unlawfulness of the trusts were those brought under the common law by the Attorneys General of New York and Ohio against certain constituent members of the sugar and Standard Oil trusts, respectively. In 1890, the courts of these states held in effect that the transfer of the stockholders' rights of control to trustees was *ultra vires* (beyond the powers) of their corporate charters and the states' incorporation laws.[54] It was the intention of those prosecuting these suits that they would bring about the end of monopolistic combinations and a return of free competition in the industries affected. If so, their expectations were not fulfilled, for in 1889 the state of New Jersey very opportunely amended its incorporation law to permit one corporation to hold stock in another; thus, the way was prepared for the holding company.[55]

Though some important holding companies were formed between 1889 and 1893, the first trust movement came pretty much to a close with the onset of the depression of 1893. In the meantime, the Congress had passed the Sherman Antitrust Act in 1890, strengthening the general common law condemnation of combinations in restraint of trade and monopolies. The first test of this famous law as applied to business came before the Supreme Court in the case of the *United States* vs. *E. C. Knight Co.*, decided in January, 1895.[56] The legal issue in this case was whether the acquisition of the stock of four Pennsylvania sugar refiners by the American Sugar Refining Co., giving the trust control of 95 per cent of the sugar refining capacity of the nation, violated the new antitrust Act. The majority opinion of the Court held that it did not, largely on the ground that the power of the Congress was limited to regulating commerce among the several states or with foreign nations. Manufacturing sugar, the Court reasoned, was not commerce in the constitutional sense. As a consequence of this decision, businessmen came to view the federal law as relatively innocuous so far as combines were concerned. With the states confronting greater frustration in enforcing their statutes, the way was ultimately clear, after the election of McKinley and the passage of the high tariff law of 1897, for a far larger combination movement.

The first official survey of industrial combinations in the United States was made in connection with the manufacturing census of 1900. That census

---

[54] 24 N.E. 834 (1890) and 30 N.E. 279 (1892).

[55] H. R. Seager and C. A. Gulick, Jr., *Trust and Corporation Problems* (New York: Harper and Bros., 1929), p. 55.

[56] 156 U.S. 1 (1895).

showed that in the previous year there were in active operation some 185 manufacturing combinations with a combined capital outstanding (including $216 million in bonds) of over $3,093 million. The total capital invested in manufacturing in the same year was $8,975 million, so that, on this basis, the trusts controlled approximately one-third of the manufacturing capital of the nation.[57] In this census there were only 73 trusts out of the 185 whose capitalization equalled or exceeded $10 million, and of these, only 18 were organized before 1897. These statistics make it clear that the trust "movement" of the 1880's was a minor affair compared to the massive consolidation process that engulfed American business after 1897.

We shall not attempt to answer the complex question whether competition declined and monopoly increased in the various industries of the American economy over the years of this period. It is obvious, however, that compensating forces were at work: while some firms were entrenching themselves in monopoly or quasi-monopoly positions, others were eager to breach the walls of monopoly, and most important, the spread of the railroad network continually weakened local, geographical monopolies and widened the scope of competition. We do wish to note, in concluding this chapter, that Marx's prediction of increasing concentration of capitalistic enterprise was confirmed by the bare facts of this period of our industrial history and was to be borne out even more convincingly in the period to follow. Marx's powers of prognostication on this score did not rest on clairvoyance or on his technically deficient labor theory of value, but on his more exact specification of the institutionalist features of capitalism and his prescient comprehension of some of its vital processes.[58] Marx was truly the prophet of the advent of big business and the organizational society; in the United States that aspect of his vision of the future of capitalism was to be strikingly corroborated.

[57] Seager and Gulick, p. 60. See also R. L. Nelson, *Merger Movements in American Industry, 1895–1956* (Princeton: Princeton University Press, 1959).

[58] On this, see the brilliant article by the late Oscar Lange, "Marxian Economics and Modern Economic Theory," *Review of Economic Studies* (June, 1935). Marx appreciated the economics of overhead costs and saw their implications for competition and concentration. See *Capital*, Vol. III. W. Leontiff in his essay, "The Significance of Marxian Economics for Present-Day Economic Theory," *American Economic Review Supplement*, Vol. XXVIII, No. 1 (March, 1938), reprinted in *Essays in Economics* by the same author (New York: Oxford University Press, 1966), pp. 72–3, contends that Marx was "the great character reader of the capitalist system . . ." Leontiff qualifies his agreement with Lange as follows: "Neither his analytical accomplishments [i.e. Marx's] nor the purported methodological superiority can explain the Marxian record of correct prognostications. His strength lies in realistic, empirical knowledge of the capitalist system." (*Ibid.*, p. 82.)

Chapter 19

POLITICAL AND SOCIAL CHANGE IN AN ERA OF RAPID CAPITAL GROWTH

THE SIGNIFICANCE OF THE SECOND AMERICAN REVOLUTION

In their famous interpretation of American history, Charles and Mary Beard contend that the social, economic, and political changes during the Civil War and Reconstruction periods were so profound and cataclysmic as to merit the characterization of being a "Second American Revolution." The War between the States, they wrote, was "a social war, ending in the unquestioned establishment of a new power in the government, making vast changes in the arrangement of classes, in the accumulation and distribution of wealth, in the course of industrial development, and in the Constitution inherited from the Fathers." Neither accident nor rhetoric, they argued, should be allowed to obscure the fundamental nature of that struggle.

> If the operations by which the middle classes of England broke the power of the king and the aristocracy are to be known collectively as the Puritan Revolution, if the series of acts by which the bourgeois and the peasants of France overthrew the king, nobility, and clergy is to be called the French Revolution, then accuracy compels us to characterize by the same term the social cataclysm in which capitalists, laborers, and farmers of the North and West drove from power in the national government the planting aristocracy of the South. Viewed under the light of universal history, the fighting was a fleeting incident; the social revolution was the essential, portentous outcome.[1]

Though historians have modified some of the elements of the Beardian interpretation, many still agree with its overall dimensions and its analysis of the essential significance of those momentous periods in the life of the nation. With the qualifications to be noted below, the Republican Party was the dynamic political organization that sponsored and enacted many of the policies of these years, policies that accelerated the hegemony of business enterprise over the declining agrarian interests of the South and West: increased tariff protection, the establishment of the National Banking System,

[1] C. A. Beard and M. R. Beard, *The Rise of American Civilization*, rev. ed. 2 vols. in 1 (New York: The Macmillan Co., 1935), pp. 53–54.

and the issuance of the national banknotes, together with a prohibitive tax on state banknotes; federal subsidies for internal improvements, especially railroads; sale of mineral and timber resources on the public domain to private interests on such liberal terms as to lead one later critic of these policies to write of them as "the great barbecue";[2] lastly, the passage of the Public Credit Act of 1869, which assured federal bondholders, many of whom had purchased these securities with depreciated greenbacks, that they would be paid in gold.

The political situation was a complex one when the 39th Congress assembled in December, 1865, more than seven months after the assassination of Lincoln and the assumption of the Presidency by Andrew Johnson. There were four roughly defined groups at the beginning of the session: the small, disorganized Democratic minority; a band of conservative Republicans; a faction of radical Republicans, a minority within their own party; and a group of moderate Republicans—the largest group in that Congress. The first two groups supported the President, while the radical Republicans, originally skeptical about the new President, more and more became his chief antagonist. The moderate Republicans wavered between the radical and conservative camps at first, but the President's uncompromising, tactless behavior finally forced them into an alliance with the radicals. As a result, by the summer of 1866 the radicals, with their new allies, had control of Congress and were in a position to repudiate the President's Reconstruction program and formulate their own.[3]

The radicals wanted the process of Reconstruction in the South to be slow and complicated. They saw that the quick return of the seceded states to the Union would threaten the legislative program carried out during the war years. This was especially possible because the freeing of the slaves increased the southern representation in the Congress and in the electoral college; with Negroes free and the three-fifths provision no longer in force, the southern states were to have twelve additional representatives for their Negro population in 1870. For a variety of reasons, the radicals also wanted to extend political and civil rights to the Negroes. None of these goals interested the President; indeed, he regarded most of them as evils. We pass over the details of the historic, but futile effort to impeach the President to consider the more complex question of the motives of the radical Republicans. Such typical radicals as Representative Thaddeus Stevens, Senator Charles Sumner, and others have often been pictured as wishing to impose a Carthaginian peace upon the South. They have been described in such a way as to suggest that they had almost a conspiracy with a solid group of capitalists to use the Negroes and Reconstruction as "a smokescreen to conceal a carefully planned program of economic aggrandisement." But revisionist historians have recently shown

[2] V. L. Parrington, *Main Currents in American Thought*, Vol. III (New York: Harcourt, Brace & Co., 1927), p. 23.

[3] K. M. Stampp, *The Era of Reconstruction, 1865–1877* (New York: A. A. Knopf, 1965), pp. 83–84.

that the radicals were far from united on economic policy; for example, Representative Stevens favored a high protective tariff and inflation, while Charles Sumner favored tariff reduction and specie resumption. New England Republicans looked with favor upon tariff reduction, whereas western radicals supported protectionism.[4]

Further, a strict economic interpretation ignores the idealism that some of the politicians and businessmen of that era brought to business activity. "Most of the radicals," writes Stampp, "who were committed to a high tariff, the national banking system, and subsidies to the railroads seemed to believe quite sincerely that these measures were designed to benefit and enrich not just special interest groups but the country as a whole. Public lands and mineral and timber resources could almost be given away to private entrepreneurs, because there was a general belief then that America's resources were inexhaustible and that this was the best way to put them to productive use."[5] The radical Republicans carried out a program of political reconstruction in the South that was not as repressive and corrupt as historians formerly contended.[6] They secured written guarantees of the Negroes' civil and political rights and gave much needed relief to the distressed through the Freedmen's Bureau. But they never achieved land reform or other basic institutional changes that would have given the Negro a more solid economic foundation for his political life.

As early as August, 1868, death and retirement were weakening the leadership of the radical group of Republicans. Northern businessmen, who had originally supported President Johnson's program, had turned in disillusionment to the radicals. They wanted conditions that would favor northern economic penetration and investment in the South, but the violence and financial instability that accompanied the radical regimes there distressed them. By 1870 northern journals of business opinion were demanding the end of radical Reconstruction; it seemed that only southern conservatives, some of whom were being converted to the gospel of a "New South," could restore

---

[4] See, especially, R. P. Sharkey, *Money, Class and Party*, The Johns Hopkins University Studies in Historical and Political Science, Series LXXVII, No. 2 (Baltimore: The Hopkins Press, 1959), *passim;* Irwin Unger, *The Greenback Era, A Social and Political History of American Finance, 1865–1879* (Princeton, N.J.: Princeton University Press, 1964) ; S. Coben, "Northeastern Business and Radical Reconstruction: A Re-examination," *Mississippi Valley Historical Review*, XLVI (June, 1959), 67–90, reprinted in S. Coben and F. G. Hill, *American Economic History, Essays in Interpretation* (Philadelphia: J. P. Lippincott, 1966), pp. 434–454.

[5] Stampp, *The Era of Reconstruction*, p. 107.

[6] The First Reconstruction Act of March, 1867 stipulated the following: (1) No legal government existed in any southern state except Tennessee; (2) The remaining ten southern states were divided into five military districts and placed under military commanders; (3) This military regime was not to be lifted until a constitutional convention, chosen by universal male suffrage, set up governments based on Negroes and whites; such state legislatures had to ratify the Fourteenth Amendment. On Reconstruction, see J. G. Randall, *The Civil War and Reconstruction* (Boston: D. C. Heath, 1953) ; see also Stampp, *The Era of Reconstruction;* J. H. Franklin, *Reconstruction: After the Civil War* (Chicago: University of Chicago Press, 1961) ; E. L. McKitrick, *Andrew Johnson and Reconstruction* (Chicago: University of Chicago Press, 1960).

order and political stability in that region. Northerners in general were growing indifferent to the Reconstruction issue; "waving the bloody shirt" had reached the point of diminishing returns. Most northern voters were unmoved by charges of the disloyalty of southern whites or of reports about outrages against southern Negroes.

When the depression of 1873 set in, Republicans became more concerned with the long stagnation of business and the exposure of the scandals in the Grant administration than they were with Reconstruction. The revelation of the "saturnalia of plunder" in the federal government—the Credit Mobilier scandal, the "salary grab," the corruption in the War, Navy, Interior, and Treasury departments—badly shook public confidence in President Grant's administration. That great military hero even made Henry Adams doubt the validity of the theory of evolution:

> The idea that, as society grew older, it grew one-sided, upset evolution, and made of education a fraud. That, two thousand years after Alexander the Great and Julius Caesar, a man like Grant should be called—and should actually and truly be—the highest product of the most advanced civilization, made evolution ludicrous. One must be as commonplace as Grant's own commonplaces to maintain such absurdity. The progress of evolution from President Washington to President Grant was alone evidence enough to upset Darwin.[7]

The corruption, we know, during that "nadir of national disgrace" was by no means confined to the federal government. State governments were being run by bribed legislatures, as the shocking activities of Gould and Vanderbilt in New York revealed. In Iowa, Minnesota, and California, it was charged that the legislatures were controlled by the railroads—and the charges were not hard to substantiate. Cities were at the mercy of such venal politicians as "Boss Tweed" who cost New York City no less than $100 million. Philadelphia was being exploited by its Gas Ring, which was no less thorough than Tammany in New York. And in business, embezzlement, stock-watering, wildcat investment schemes, and railway wrecking were very common. The United States during the Civil War and the immediate post-war years seemed to be suffering from *anomie*, a disruption of its moral norms and standards. Walt Whitman showed his concern over the materialism of the nation in that period in his *Democratic Vistas*. In terms of modern social psychology we might say that in the "public-be-damned" era after the Civil War the social situation in which the businessmen operated was relatively unstructured. Social norms appropriate to the new conditions of national economic life had not as yet been established. The creation of wider, more impersonal markets as a result of the completion of the national rail network and the vast possibilities for profit existing in reorganizing business to take advantage of improving technology made for a very fluid, open environment for the profit seeker. The triumph of business over the southern aristocracy in the War Between the

---

[7] H. Adams, *The Education of Henry Adams; An Autobiography* (Boston: Houghton, Mifflin Co., 1918), p. 286.

States removed from the Congress for many years a group that had checked the ambitions and dreams of the industrial capitalists. The inflation that accompanied the war gave unprecedented opportunities to the irresponsible businessman. The complacency of the citizenry, its ignorance of the new methods of business operation, and its fatuous belief in the inexhaustibility of our natural resources set the stage for unrestrained profit-seeking and exploitation of the public. Rapid industrialization, like all uncontrolled social change, is frequently accompanied by unanticipated social disorganization; the Civil War and its aftermath offer a prime example of this type of social phenomenon.[8]

The long depression of 1873, the collapse of farm prices, and the decay in public and private morals not only caused northerners to lose interest in Reconstruction, but seems also to have weakened their faith in the Republican Party. In 1874 the Republicans lost control of the House of Representatives— their first national defeat since the Civil War. In the meantime, southerners in Mississippi and other states were resorting to increased violence to keep the Negroes from voting Republican. President Grant, in the state and Presidential elections of 1876, did nothing to check this illegal intimidation of voters. As a consequence, the Democrats regained control in many southern states. In 1876, indeed, in order to assure the peaceful inauguration of Rutherford B. Hayes, the Republicans entered into the sectional compromise of 1877, under which they agreed to remove the remaining federal troops from the South, and to deal fairly with southerners in the distribution of patronage and the voting of internal improvements. In return, the Southerners acquiesced in the inauguration of Hayes and promised to deal fairly with the Negroes. This compromise marked the end of radical Reconstruction. As for the Negroes, since the basic socioeconomic pattern of relations had not been destroyed, they were only half emancipated. In place of the ante-bellum plantation system, they worked as share-croppers under the vicious crop lien system. Despite the Fourteenth and Fifteenth Amendments, they were denied equal civil and political rights; the courts invalidated some of the basic protective legislation of the previous years, and in 1896 the Supreme Court with the "separate but equal doctrine" sanctioned the practice of social segregation. In place of slavery, the Negro lived under a caste system, which reduced him to second-class citizenship. The Republican Party, which had been the dynamic force behind the early legislative achievements in behalf of the Negro, increasingly retrenched and consolidated its position rather than breaking new ground. The fact was that the Republicans no longer needed the votes of southern Negroes. The party during the War and after had won the firm support of the dominant interests in the states of the old Northwest, a region that had previously backed agrarianism and copperheadism. The war and the laws passed during and after had made these states staunchly Republican. The

[8] On the impact of industrialization on social organization, see B. Berelson and G. A. Steiner, *Human Behavior, An Inventory of Scientific Findings* (New York: Harcourt, Brace and World, Inc., 1964), p. 399.

spread of the industrial revolution into the trans-Appalachian area and the growth of such industrial centers as Detroit, Cleveland, and Chicago led the business interests there to identify with those of the Northeast. ". . . With the decline of the idealism and the disappearance of the realistic political and economic considerations that had supported it, radical reconstruction came to an end."[9]

THE CHANGING CULTURE AND SOCIAL STRUCTURE

The Civil War and Reconstruction have been seen by the Beard school of historiography as causing a great revolution in the culture and social structure of the United States as well as in its economy. In this view, the civil conflict and its aftermath served to transfer the sovereignty in the nation from a landed and mercantile aristocracy to the eager hands of the new captains of industry. As Parrington expressed it:

> With the substitution of the captain of industry for the plantation master as the custodian of society, the age of aristocracy was at an end and the age of the middle class was established. A new culture, created by the machine and answering the needs of capitalism, was to dispossess the old culture with its lingering concern for distinction and its love of standards—a culture that should eventually suffice the needs of a brisk city world of machine activities. But that would take time. In the meanwhile—in the confused interregnum between reigns—America would be little more than a welter of crude energy, a raw unlovely society where the strife of competition with its prodigal waste testified to the shortcomings of an age in process of transition. . . .[10]

It will be noted that Parrington speaks of an "interregnum"; he implies that the new industrial elite did not immediately take command—this is more in harmony with contemporary historical understanding of the relative power of the principal economic interests in the complex political situation of the post-war era.[11] The fact was that with the growth of the West and the ethnic revolution caused by immigration, the political influence of the merchants of New England and the Middle Atlantic states waned, but it was not completely destroyed. The balance of political power was changing because many of the new industrial capitalists lived in the trans-Allegheny region. The growth in the political power of that area was to change the course of Reconstruction and affect subsequent national policies in a decisive way.

The generation of industrial leaders who came of age during or after the Civil War were endowed with strong achievement motives; in everyday terms, they were often pushing, pugnacious, and sometimes crude. Where did they get these qualities? Study of the social origins of the industrial elite of that

---

[9] Stampp, *The Era of Reconstruction*, p. 213. We have relied heavily upon the revisionist interpretation of this volume for some of the points made above.

[10] Parrington, *Main Currents*, Vol. III, p. 4.

[11] For example, see I. Unger, *The Greenback Era* (Princeton, N.J.: Princeton University Press, 1964), *passim*.

time reveals that, contrary to the rags-to-riches myth, most of them came from business and professional homes.[12] Still, it is notable that there were more farm boys among the railroad and steel leaders of the 1870's than there had been in the leadership of that older industry, textiles. Though many of the new captains of industry began life with decided advantages, there were enough self-made men among them to give substance to the Algerine myth. Further-more, the statistics of the study cited above shows clearly that many more of the railroad and steel leaders came from small towns than had been true of the textile men, confirming Allan Nevins' observation that in the 1870's, "the cities were full of wealthy newcomers of rural antecedents. . . ."[13] These were the men "on the make" who made the industrial history of the post-war years so colorful and dynamic. In their grotesque individualism, they were tough-minded, had "stout nippers," and "fought their way encased in rhinoc-eros hides." Some of them were "robber barons," but others were boldly adventurous and creative, "vital with the untamed energy of a new land."[14] With the passing of the years, particularly with the prosperity of the 1880's, the masters of the new corporations increasingly outdistanced the old mer-chant and professional classes in power and prestige. Many of the latter became the so-called Mugwumps, who criticized the actions of the industrial-ists from the sidelines and urged tariff and civil service reform almost as panaceas. The power of the new capitalist class was described in 1888 by James Bryce: ". . . How much capacity and energy, how much wealth and influence there is in the hands of this small class everybody knows! It includes the best executive ability of the country, and far more ability than is devoted to the public service of the state." Bryce goes on to observe that the indus-trialists' interest in politics was limited to using it for their own purposes, and especially in "resisting the attacks with which they are threatened. . . ."[15] So many of these powerful millionaires were, in fact, elected to the Senate in the 1880's and 1890's that it became known as "the Millionaires' Club." William

[12] Gregory and Neu in *Men in Business* edited by W. Miller (Cambridge: Harvard University Press, 1952), p. 202. This study does not disclose as well as it might the trans-Allegheny origins of many industrial leaders of this period. By using the census region, "Middle Atlantic," it does not differentiate between those born east and west of the Alleghenies in that region. (See Table 1, p. 197 of *Ibid.*) Furthermore, Gregory and Neu seem to resist the indications of their own data, as to the size of birthplace of the 1870 leaders. They stress that "half of the industrial leaders of 1870–79 were born in places with more than 2500 persons," but ignore the majority of the railroad and steel leaders who were shown to be born in communities of that size. By concentrating on the totals and ignoring the facts revealed by their data as to the size of birthplace of the railroad and steel leaders, they tend to confirm William Miller's findings in "The Business Elite in Business Bureaucracies" (See *Men in Business, op. cit.*, pp. 286–305), but they slight other interesting implications of their data.

[13] A. Nevins, *The Emergence of Modern America, 1865–1878* (New York: The Mac-millan Co., 1932), p. 75.

[14] Parrington, *Main Currents in American Thought*, Vol. III, pp. 1–13. It is interesting to note that Parrington, as critical as he was of the business leaders of the Gilded Age, saw their creative side.

[15] J. Bryce, *The American Commonwealth* (New York: Capricorn Books, G. P. Put-nam's Sons, 1959) (originally published in 1888), Vol. 2, p. 320.

Allen White, writing about 1889, said that a United States Senator had come to represent "something more than a state, more even than a region. He represented principalities and powers in business."[16] Many of the new rich of industry also lived in a lavish style in the Gilded Age, sporting their wealth in vast estates at Newport and other resorts, putting the older wealth in a shadow.

With the dissolution of the power of the southern planter aristocracy as a result of the Civil War and radical Reconstruction, the independent farmers of the nation were the sole agricultural interest left to oppose the growing power of the industrial capitalists. But they found themselves living in an economy and a world that "they hadn't made" and that often worked greatly to their loss and disadvantage. As commercial farmers, they were increasingly selling their cash crops in world markets reached by the spreading rail network and an intricate system of middlemen and buying manufactured goods from urban industries; they were daily becoming more dependent on the working of a complex industrial culture over which they had relatively little influence.[17] As a group they did not realize that the more industrialism advanced, the more their collective fortunes became affected by forces beyond their control. The technology of this industrial culture when applied in the form of farm machinery to the fertile acres of the West added tremendously to the productive capacity of agriculture at the same time that the new methods of transportation were enabling farmers of other nations to compete in the world market. Our American farmers were selling their products under conditions approximating pure competition and buying most of the goods they needed in markets that were either imperfectly competitive or monopolistically controlled. The complaint of the farmers about overproduction and falling prices was not limited in the years 1873–96 to the United States. As Lee Benson observes, the opening of the continental interiors to agricultural exploitation after 1870 created farm discontent on both sides of the Atlantic. "The Communication Revolution," he writes, produced "an international agrarian market, an international agrarian depression, and as a climax, international agrarian discontent."[18]

The workers also faced difficult adjustments in the new, raw industrial culture of the post-Civil War years. During that conflict, thanks to full employment and high profits, trade unionism had boomed because employers did not want to interrupt lucrative production by opposing labor's demands. But at the end of the war, with its demobilization of hundreds of thousands of men, falling prices, and the recession of 1868–69, employer resistance

[16] W. A. White, *Masks in a Pageant* (New York: The Macmillan Co., 1930), p. 79.

[17] On this aspect of agriculture's plight, see T. Saloutos, "The Agricultural Problem and Nineteenth Century Industrialism," reprinted in J. T. Lambie and R. V. Clemence, *Economic Change in America*, pp. 313–340; on this subject see also, W. F. Owen, "The Double Developmental Squeeze on Agriculture," *American Economic Review* (March, 1966), pp. 43–70.

[18] L. Benson, *Turner and Beard: American Historical Writing Reconsidered* (Glencoe, Ill.: Free Press, 1960), p. 48.

stiffened. Labor's strikes ended disastrously, and its leaders, men such as Andrew Cameron of the Chicago Trades Assembly and William Sylvis, president of the Iron Molders' International Union, turned to reformism. With the coming of the depression of 1873, the trade union movement almost completely disintegrated; the number of national trade unions fell from 30 to 8 or 9 by 1877; the membership in the following year was estimated at a mere 50,000. It is in the light of such disasters that we must see labor's subsequent history. Its leaders turned to consumers' and producers' cooperation and then to politics and greenbackism because they thought it was futile to attempt to soften capitalism by trade union activities alone. The nature of this trend and its success will be dealt with below.

CAPITAL ACCUMULATION AND THE MONEY QUESTION

The controversy over the contraction of the greenbacks, resumption, and the national banks dominated much of post-Civil War politics and gave rise to one of the most colorful third parties in our history. In the minds of many there was a close relation in those years between the supply of money, the interest rate, and the pace of capital formation. Whereas classical economic doctrine taught that only real savings made possible capital formation, there was now a revival of the mercantilist idea that the money supply affected the rate of interest and that cheap money would speed the process of capital accumulation. One of the most vigorous proponents of this theory was Henry C. Carey, who was already urging the benefits of an enlarged money supply in the late 1850's: "The larger the quantity of gold sent to the chief manufacturing centers of the earth the lower will be the rate of interest there—the greater will be the facilities for constructing new roads and mills—and the more rapid those exchanges from hand to hand which constitute commerce and for the making of which money is so absolutely indispensable."[19] Carey and his disciples were especially influential among the ironmasters of Pennsylvania, though belief in soft money was also held by promoters and industrialists in other lines. ". . . Soft money became the hallmark of industrialists, promoters, and speculators because they believed it would encourage continued economic buoyancy and meet the needs of a capital-scarce nation."[20] Opposed to the industrialists on this issue were the hard money interests, including the Protestant divines, the college professors, the genteel reformers of the middle and upper classes, respectable journalists, eastern merchants, and commercial bankers. These were the hard money men who, though "they

[19] H. C. Carey, *Principles of Social Science* (Philadelphia: J. B. Lippincott Co., 1888), II, p. 325, quoted in Unger, *The Greenback Era*, p. 52. Carey would seem to qualify as one of Keynes' "brave army of heretics" on the basis of his rejection of the Ricardian theory of interest.

[20] Unger, *The Greenback Era*, p. 59.

were politically weaker than in the days when a gentleman sat in the President's mansion, . . . were to prove capable still, through the potent moral and intellectual force of puritan New England, of confounding the massed power of the new leaders of Industrial America."[21]

The farmers did not espouse greenbackism until 1873. After the Grange had first directed the farmers' protests at the railroads and middlemen, when the depression of that year set in, the midwestern farmers began to attack the national banking system. This agricultural greenbackism was nourished by the pre-war philosophy of agrarianism, which pictured the farmer as one of the producing "industrial classes," long exploited by the monopolistic "money power." Thus, the national banks became the symbolic enemy of the post-war farmer. From complaints about the failure of the national banking system to provide cheap farm credit, the movement more and more denounced the "money lenders" and "usurers," finding in the money system the source of all the farmer's ills.

Organized labor's support of greenbackism traces back to labor's defeats after the war when some of its leaders became converts to the abstract monetary philosophy of Edward Kellogg and Alexander Campbell. Kellogg, an obscure New York dry goods merchant, had reached the conclusion before the war that scarcity of money and high interest rates discouraged enterprise and retarded economic growth. He conceived the idea of a federal "Safety Fund," which would issue government notes at 3 per cent on mortgages and commercial paper; this practice would, he believed, serve to establish a limit on the interest rate charged. Campbell, a manufacturer and promoter, modified Kellogg's ideas in the post-war period, substituting for the Safety Fund a government bond paying 3 per cent interest and interconvertible with the greenbacks. This ingenious arrangement would provide a flexible medium of circulation that would automatically prevent both inflation and contraction. Basically, the most rational argument of the labor greenbackers was that high interest rates reduced employers' profits and therefore led to low wages. But beyond this they told the workers that they were being exploited by "unproductive capital" and "irresponsible banking associations." In short, they returned to the old Jacksonian fear of the "money power," the aristocracy of untaxed wealth. Actually, to the self-made intellectual who led the movement, these ideas amounted to almost a secular religion, the introduction of which would quickly end the bitter strife between capital and labor. The popularity

---

[21] *Ibid.*, p. 162. Unger's splendid study argues that five elements, not just economic factors, influenced men on the Reconstruction money question: (1) acquisitiveness; (2) the factor of accident and personal idiosyncrasy; (3) the political forces; (4) prestige drives, social anxieties, and class frustration; (5) accepted values, such as those emanating from religion and the intellectual milieu. ". . . Men brought to the financial question, as to all complex public issues, a wide range of attitudes, moral postures, and preconceptions deeply rooted in the past. These not only shaped responses through direct confrontation; *they often determined what was perceived.*" (*Ibid.*, p. 25.) The latter is a major principle of modern social psychology: concepts tend to shape perception.

of these monetary solutions in the post-war years testifies to the amazing appeal of ideology and the significant role of persuasive personalities in the making of history. Some will see in the movement also a remarkable anticipation in some ways of the Keynesian thinking of our own time.

Politically, the greenback movement had a relatively short life. The workers first protested against the contraction of the greenbacks during the post-war depression of 1868–69. Even before this, in 1867, the National Labor Union had given its support to Campbell's "True American System." In the Presidential election year of 1872, a National Labor Reform Party was formed to press the greenback issue, but its candidate received less than 30,000 votes. By the next Presidential election, more farmers were drawn to the movement; in that year the octogenarian Peter Cooper of New York was nominated as the Party's standard-bearer on a platform that pledged repeal of the Specie Resumption Act of 1875 and the suppression of the national banknotes. Greenbackism reached its high water mark in 1878, when one million votes were cast for its candidates and fourteen Greenback candidates went to Congress. Two years later, however, General James B. Weaver received only a little over 300,000 votes (or about 3 per cent of the total cast) for President, despite his vigorous campaigning. The reasons for his poor showing were obvious; crops were good and the farmers' income large. After 1880, the Greenback Party rapidly disintegrated; it appeared in the field for the last time in 1884, when it merged with the Anti-Monopolists.

THE FARMERS TURN TO POLITICS

While we have taken note of the impact of the industrial culture generally on farming, we have not analyzed certain peculiarities of agriculture in the great open spaces of the West being developed during these years. This was a region of rich natural resources and a relatively scattered population; an agriculture had to be practiced that was labor extensive. At the same time there was a great need for fencing and barbed wire, deep wells and windmills, seeds, and new techniques of agricultural science if the Plains were to be cultivated. In short, there was a necessity for a more mechanized, capital intensive type of farming than had been practiced in the East or South. This meant that commercialized farming needed considerable monetary capital before it could be undertaken, and yet the pecuniary results were wholly dependent on the price fluctuations on the world commodity markets. Given the increasingly complex context of American agriculture, its great dependence on industry and finance, it is not surprising that the farmer was prone to explain his difficulties in terms of single factors. Further, given the American tradition of individualism in a society in which business and labor were rapidly turning to collective action to survive, the farmers were slow to organize; they were caught in the snare of their cherished, traditional independence.

Thus, while corporations and labor unions had been established before the Civil War, farmers were not successfully organized on a national basis until Oliver Hudson Kelley formed the Patrons of Husbandry as a secret order in 1867. The aim of the new Granges, as they were familiarly known, was to improve the condition of the farmers by encouraging intellectual and social intercourse among them. Kelley had been a Mason, and he believed that farmers could be helped by mutual assistance such as that fraternal order practiced. The growth of the new organization was slow during its first four years, but in 1870–71, "now advertised as vigorously as if it were a patent medicine," it appealed to the farmers' pocketbooks with such slogans as "Down with Monopolies" and "Cooperation." It began to spread like wildfire in the South and West in 1872, and in the following year, when depression set in, the farmers turned on their erstwhile saviors, the railroads, complaining first of high rates and then, after 1875, of rate discrimination. The farmers, not understanding the economics of imperfect competition under which the railroads operated, did not approve of their charging high rates for short hauls to intermediate points where they had a monopoly and lower ones on long shipments to so-called common points where the railroads had to meet competition. They resented also discrimination among persons, charging that the owners of large farms and ranches were favored. Private grain commission men were alleged to receive special rates, while the farm cooperatives were weakened by poor service.

The political parties that were formed "outside the gate" (i.e., after the Grange meetings) in some eleven states agitated for regulation of the railroads and warehouses. Illinois passed the first of these Granger laws in 1869, and soon similar laws were enacted in Minnesota, Iowa, and Wisconsin. The railroads obstructed the regulatory efforts of these early commissions, and the latter were often lacking in technical expertise. Nevertheless, out of the experience emerged one permanent gain—recognition of the right of a state to regulate a business that is public in nature, though privately owned and managed. In *Munn* vs. *Illinois* (1877), the Supreme Court declared that a state had the power to regulate business affected by a public interest. Ten years later, however, this dictum of the Court was reversed in *Wabash, St. Louis and Pacific Railroad* vs. *Illinois* (1886); this decision destroyed the effectiveness of state laws and made national regulation of the railroads imperative.

The enactment of the Interstate Commerce Act the following year was a major landmark in the development of government regulation of business in this country. Though the law was not to become truly effective until nearly twenty years later, its passage reflected the power of the agricultural interest and that of the small businessmen who joined with it in support of the law.[22]

[22] On the latter, see L. Benson, *Merchants, Farmers and Railroads: Railroad Regulation and New York Politics, 1850–1877* (Cambridge: Harvard University Press, 1955).

THE WORKERS IN A RAPIDLY INDUSTRIALIZING SOCETY

In this section we shall consider the relative validity of the Marxian theses regarding class consciousness and class conflict under capitalism as they apply to the workers in this turbulent period of our history. We have already described the disastrous effects of the depression of 1873 upon the labor movement and alluded to the consequent turn of labor leaders to greenback politics and consumer cooperation. Another indication of the lengths to which depression and the prevailing condition of labor pushed the workers of this time was the famous incident of the Molly Maguires. The collapse of unionism in the anthracite coal industry during the '73 depression intensified the murderous activities of this secret ring among members of the Ancient Order of Hibernians in eastern Pennsylvania. They retaliated against oppressive foremen by masquerading as women and assassinating their unsuspecting victims. Finally caught through the espionage activities of a Pinkerton detective who joined the organization to discover the culprits, fourteen of these miners were sent to prison and ten executed. Information subsequently came to light revealing that the Pinkerton agents had instigated some of these crimes to provide the coal operators with the evidence they needed to wipe out the Molly Maguires and thus destroy the union.[23]

When the labor movement revived after the end of the depression of the 1870's, it took a very significant form in the shape of the famous Knights of Labor. This labor organization had started as a secret society in 1869; its guiding spirit in its formative years was Uriah S. Stephens, a Philadelphia garment cutter. The Knights advocated what we today call industrial unionism; it urged "one big union" for all. Indeed, its relative lack of class consciousness in the Marxian sense can be seen in the fact that it admitted everyone who labored with hand or brain, except bankers, stockbrokers, lawyers, gamblers, and dealers in intoxicating liquors. In philosophy, the Knights were reformist and even utopian. They looked forward to the ultimate abolition of the wage system through producers' and consumers' cooperation. They urged land reform, particularly reserving the land for the actual settlers and not giving "another acre for railroads or speculators." They backed more education, wanted to prohibit the employment of children in workshops, mines, and factories before the age of fourteen, and wished to see a Bureau of Labor Statistics established in the federal government. One of their most important planks was currency reform; they urged their members "to prevail upon governments to establish a purely national circulating medium, based upon the faith and resources of the nation, and issued directly to the people, without the intervention of any system of banking corporations,

[23] An excellent study is W. G. Broehl, Jr., *The Molly Maguires* (Cambridge: Harvard University Press, 1964).

which money shall be a legal tender in payment of all debts." They were for arbitration rather than strikes, and advocated equal pay for equal work for both sexes, and the reduction of the hours of labor to eight.

Actually, the growth of the Knights at first was very slow. In 1881, more than ten years after their founding, they had less than 20,000 members. Then, in 1883 they received their first favorable publicity through the telegraphers' strike against the Western Union, which was at that time controlled by the ubiquitous Jay Gould. With the coming of the depression of 1884–85, unskilled workers began to join in large numbers, and then in the latter year, the union, with the support of the skilled trainmen, won an important strike against the Wabash Railroad and the Missouri, Kansas, and Texas. The public gained an exaggerated opinion of the power of the Knights; unskilled workers flocked into the order and membership soared from 104,000 in July, 1885 to 702,924 a year later. This unusual development is referred to in labor history as The Great Upheaval of 1886. Part of this sensational build-up in membership was in preparation for the general strike for the eight-hour day that various labor groups planned for May 1, 1886. While the national trade unions backed the eight-hour strike, Terence Powderly, the long-time leader of the Knights, issued a secret circular against it. A few days after the appointed day for the strike there occurred the Haymarket explosion in Chicago, of which we shall have more to say. The eight-hour movement almost immediately collapsed, and the Knights of Labor was struck a fatal blow. Though there was no substance to the charges, people associated it with the violence at Haymarket. Workers turned to the more conservative American Federation of Labor unions. In fact, the decline of the Knights was attributable in part to its questionable philosophy. It saw no disharmony between wage earners and employers; it sought rather to unite them both against the "money power." Furthermore, it assumed that the viewpoint and interest of all workers were identical, ignoring the differences between the skilled and the unskilled. Lastly, there are many who trace its failure to defective leadership; in the words of one critic, "The Knights of Labor was essentially an assembly of wind-bags. . . ."[24]

Even before their decline the Knights were involved in a jurisdictional struggle with the craft unions. They sought to use the trade unions as a lever to raise the status of the unskilled, and as part of that strategy they began to absorb that type of union. The latter protested and in 1881 formed a loose organization known as the Federation of Organized Trades and Labor Unions of the United States and Canada. The Knights at the height of their power rejected an overture of the trade unions for a "treaty of peace," and as a result the revolting trade unions met at Columbus, Ohio in December, 1886 and formed the American Federation of Labor.

The new Federation was just that, highly decentralized, with the autonomy of each constituent international union strictly recognized. Under the crafty

[24] L. Adamic, *Dynamite, The Story of Class Violence in America* (New York: The Viking Press, 1931), p. 52.

and relatively conservative leadership of Samuel Gompers, its president from its founding to 1924, except for one year, 1895, the A.F. of L. practiced a pragmatic, opportunistic type of "business unionism" with a strong stress on the "bread and butter issues"; it avoided political entanglements and commitments. Its early years after its formation were rather quiet, but when the terrible trial of the depression of 1893 came along it managed to weather the storm, despite some severe setbacks in industrial disputes. When the economic weather finally cleared in 1897, the A.F. of L. had a membership close to what it had been in 1893—275,000. The Federation was as yet relatively weak, but this was a signal accomplishment—the first time that the labor movement had come through a severe depression without being destroyed or suffering a great reduction in membership. Gompers attributed the Federation's survival to the high dues that enabled the unions to pay out unemployment benefits during the hard years of depression and thus retain members.

During the trying years of the 1890's Gompers had to meet attacks from within as well as from without his organization. The socialists, led by Daniel DeLeon of the Socialist Labor Party, were demanding political action. De-Leon, a master of invective, denounced the A.F. of L. as a "cross between a wind bag and a rope of sand"; the trade union officials, he said, were simply "labor fakirs." The socialist program presented at the 1893 convention of the A.F. of L. called not only for municipal ownership of public utilities and nationalization of railroads, telegraph, telephone, and the mines, but for "collective ownership by the people of all means of production and distribution." Gompers marshalled sufficient votes at the Federation's 1894 convention to defeat this program, but only after a bitter fight that lasted five days. The socialists retaliated against him; they had their revenge in the presidential elections that same year. They joined with the free silverites and the populists to elect John McBride of the United Mine Workers the president of the Federation, thus breaking Gompers' rule temporarily.[25]

In reviewing the evidences of class conflict and class consciousness in this troubled era of the drive to industrial maturity, it might be well at the outset to define the somewhat ambiguous Marxian concept of class consciousness. As Professor Williams has shown, class consciousness may be taken to mean several things.[26] It may refer to: (1) recognition of differences of income,

[25] For the early history of the A.F. of L. see Lewis L. Lorwin, *The American Federation of Labor; History, Policies and Prospects* (Washington, D.C.: The Brookings Institution, 1933) for an excellent more recent treatment, see P. Taft, *The A.F. of L. in the Time of Gompers* (New York: Harper & Row, 1957).

[26] R. M. Williams, Jr., *American Society, A Sociological Interpretation* (New York: Knopf, 1952), pp. 115–125. Williams says at one point in this cogent analysis of the subject: ". . . Similarity or identity of objective economic and political interests does not in itself necessarily lead to class consciousness, class identification, or class action. Full awareness of class interests, in this sense, is a highly sophisticated response, greatly dependent upon the perpetuation of a particular situation over such a period of time that an 'explanatory' ideology can be developed, communicated and widely accepted among people in similar political and economic circumstances. If there is to be collective class action oriented to class interests, it is of decisive importance, furthermore, that class be perceived as part of a *definite system of power*. Otherwise, similarity of condition may

wealth, power, or authority; (2) awareness of classes and status groups; (3) psychological identification with one's class; (4) existence of militant class ideologies, which define classes as struggle groups. The latter emphasis is central to the Marxian concept of class.

The rapid industrialization of the economy in these years, the huge influx of immigrant labor, and the hectic pace of urbanization created many opportunities for economic exploitation and resulted in much personal and social disorganization. The huge disparities in wealth and power that accompanied the process of industrialization saw large corporations displace the independent craftsman; mechanization of production reduced or eliminated the skills of numerous others. The strains and discontent caused by these massive social changes became most intolerable during the periods of depressed business and unemployment with their threat to the existence of the nascent trade unions. The first nation-wide series of strikes came in 1877 significantly enough on the railroads, in an industry national in its scope and operated by some of its most powerful corporations. It came too near the bottom, as we know, of one of the longest depressions in our history, just a year after the celebration of the nation's centennial when orators had said much about how much bigger, more populous, and stronger it was than it had been in Washington's day. But the orators of that day did not say much about the latent social discontent, the "mob-in-being" that was becoming increasingly frustrated in many of the cities served by the shiny, new railroads. As one perceptive student of this urban unrest tells us,

> . . . The elements of social upheaval were not evenly spread over the land, but instead were bunched together in the great cities. There one found what might be called the "mob-in-being": thousands of people massed together as never before, not by sympathy or excitement, but simply by the terms of their life. Whenever quitting time poured thousands into the streets, whenever warm weather emptied the tenements onto sidewalks and front stoops, there stood the mob, ready-made. Working on the minds of these people were the dishonesty and cynicism of politics, the injustice of law and courts, the weakness of law enforcement. They knew death as a daily acquaintance and violence as the normal response to frustration. They brooded on the oppression of labor, the arrogance of capital, the wild inequality of fortune, the misery of tenement life, the fear and hunger and degradation of hard times. The makings of a grand social bonfire were heaped high. Beneath them, like shavings, were scattered the tramps, bitter, desperate, standing to lose nothing but life and counting that small loss. And everywhere ran the volatile children and teen-agers, eager for excitement, full of dime-novel yarns, acting on pure impulse, ready like so much kerosene to take fire at the drop of a spark.[27]

The spark in this case was the 10 per cent reduction in wages that the Pennsylvania Railroad announced as effective on June 1, 1877. The first

---

lead to amorphous 'movements,' made up of many isolated and limited struggles between classes, but not to a unitary class consciousness, nor to the Marxian class struggle." (*Ibid.*, p. 123.)

[27] R. V. Bruce, *1877: Year of Violence* (Indianapolis, Ind.: Bobbs-Merrill Co., 1959), p. 27.

outbreak against this wage-cut occurred on the Baltimore and Ohio at Martinsburg, W. Va. and then spread rapidly to Pittsburgh, Toledo, Louisville, Chicago, St. Louis, and San Francisco—it was truly the first nation-wide strike. The railroad workers at this time were not fully organized, but the pent-up frustrations of the unemployed led to mob violence against the railroads on an extraordinary scale. Thousands of rolling stock were burned, whole depots set afire, and widespread looting and killing occurred. The local militia usually proved ineffective and at the behest of the frantic railroad officials President Hayes ordered federal troops to quell the disturbances—the first major intervention by the President in this way in our national history. While the strikes were largely a failure, they put an end to the deflation of railway wages and gave a greater impetus to union organization, especially of the unskilled. On the other hand, seemingly as a consequence, the courts became more reactionary in the treatment of labor, and it was notable that a number of cities thereafter built strong armories to cope with possible future riots.

The next famous episode of industrial violence was the Haymarket explosion of May 4, 1886, which grew out of a lockout at the McCormick Reaper works in Chicago. In the course of that dispute four strikers were killed by the police. In protest against this act, the members of a group of anarchists (the so-called Black International headed by Johann Most, a German refugee) called for a public meeting at which a bomb was thrown that killed several policemen; the police answered with gunfire, which resulted in the death of four more workers and the wounding of 200. A wave of public hysteria against anarchist societies followed, stimulated in part by the police. In this atmosphere a trial was held resulting in the conviction of seven of the alleged anarchist leaders. Four of these men were hanged and three were pardoned through the intervention of Governor Altgeld.

As Table 1 shows, the amount of labor unrest and strikes rose as the nation moved into the nineties, with its long, harrowing depression. Even before the depression started, a bitter dispute broke out at the Homestead, Pennsylvania plant of the Carnegie Steel works over the Company's reduction of wages. The weak Amalgamated Association of Iron and Steel Workers resisted the cut, but Henry Clay Frick, board chairman, was adamant in his stand and extremely hostile to unions. He attempted to bring 300 Pinkerton detectives into the plant under cover of night, but they were detected and a pitched battle occurred in which three Pinkertons and seven workers were killed. The state militia was called in, and the lockout dragged on for five months while non-union labor took the places of union workers; workers were evicted from their rented homes, and the Company undertook a costly legal prosecution of the union. The result was that the strike failed, the union was broken, and independent labor organization eliminated from the industry for years.

The year 1894 was, as Table 1 shows, a year of numerous strikes, but in contrast to those of 1886, they were defensive ones and resulted in greater failures for organized labor. The United Mine Workers failed first, and then there came the heaviest blow of all—the Pullman defeat. Pullman was the

TABLE 1

Number of Work Stoppages and Workers Involved in the United States, 1881–97[a]

Year	Number of Stoppages	Workers Involved (Thousands)	Year	Number of Stoppages	Workers Involved (Thousands)
1881	477	130	1890	1,897	373
1882	476	159	1891	1,786	330
1883	506	170	1892	1,359	239
1884	485	165	1893	1,375	288
1885	695	258	1894	1,404	690
1886	1,572	610	1895	1,255	407
1887	1,503	439	1896	1,066	249
1888	946	163	1897	1,110	416
1889	1,111	260			

[a] U.S. Bureau of the Census, *Historical Statistics of the United States, 1789–1945*, p. 73.

"model" company town maintained by the railroad coach builder near Chicago. Heavy wage cuts of 25–40 per cent in 1893, high rents, and other employer abuses made the paternalism of the Company intolerable to the workers, especially when they knew that dividends of 8–9 per cent continued to be paid. In June, 1893, Eugene Debs, resigning as secretary of the Brotherhood of Locomotive Firemen, had begun organizing an industrial union among railroad workers; he found the Pullman men good union prospects, and 4,000 of them were soon members. Indeed, in an amazingly short time Debs built up a large union of 150,000 members, and in May, 1894 a strike was started against Pullman. That Company stubbornly refused to arbitrate with the consequence that a sympathetic railway strike developed in the form of a boycott of the Pullman cars by railmen. The Railroad Brotherhoods opposed this effort, and their members acted as strikebreakers. The movement of the federal mail at Chicago was involved with the result that Cleveland's Attorney General sent federal troops to that city over the protest of Governor Altgeld. Chicago was an armed camp, with 12,000 troops on the scene. Rioting took place in which 25 were killed and some 60 injured; property damage was estimated to run to $80 million. Ultimately, federal intervention won the day for the employers. An injunction prohibited anyone from interfering with the mails or interstate commerce. Debs and other leaders of the union were arrested for conspiracy in restraint of interstate commerce and he later served one year in prison for violation of the newly enacted Sherman Antitrust Act. The leaders of the union were blacklisted by the railroads and in a short time one of the largest trade unions in American history up to that date had been destroyed.

This brief review of some of the famous labor disputes of this period suggests in some degree the suffering and discontent among the workers. The long hours of labor,[28] the lack of protection against accidents and other hazards of employment, the ever-present threat of lay-off, the bias of the courts against labor, the discrimination often practiced against Negroes and other ethnic minorities, and the vast disparity in power between the corporate employer and the unorganized worker were the sources of many grievances. But despite these provocations, the majority of the discontented were not radical. A militant class consciousness did not develop among most of the workers. Though socialism found followers in this period among the working class, its appeal was predominantly to the recent immigrants. Socialism itself was weakened by factionalism between the Lasalleans, who urged political action, and the Marxians, who believed that the movement would be advanced best through working within the trade unions. Another factor handicapping the latter group was its ideological rigidity. The Socialist Labor Party, the leading Marxist organization (formed in 1876), was so doctrinaire that Engels himself in 1894 said that it "managed to reduce the Marxian theory of development to a rigid orthodoxy," which the workers were expected to "gulp down as an article of faith at once and without development."[29]

A number of factors, indeed, were responsible for reducing class consciousness in its militant forms and class conflict generally. One of the most important of these was the rising level of real wages over the years 1860–90. The most recent study that we have of this subject concludes that real annual earnings in manufacturing increased 46 per cent over this span of years, with the greatest gain being made in the 1880's when capital formation and productivity increase were showing the largest gains of any of the decennial decades for the period.[30] As Table 2 shows, the cost of living was declining after 1870 and in 1890 was about 2 per cent less than it had been in 1860. Those workers, therefore, who were fortunate to escape unemployment were benefitting from an improvement in their real income. Needless to say, there were considerable wage differences among the regions and different occupations and establishments, but the average condition was one of improvement, especially in the decade of the 1880's.

Another more intangible factor in alleviating discontent, though not less important for that, was the prospect and achievement by large numbers of upward social mobility. Although comprehensive statistics on this matter are difficult to compile and historians reject the crude Horatio Alger myth as to the origins of the business leadership of the period, there are many indications

---

[28] In 1890 the average workday in manufacturing was ten hours; the reduction in the length of the workday over the years 1860–90 seems to have been very small, not more than 7 per cent.

[29] Engels to F. A. Sorge, May 12, 1894, quoted in K. Marx and F. Engels, *Letters to Americans, 1848–1895; A Selection* (New York: International Publishers, 1953), p. 263. For the early history of socialism in the United States, see H. H. Quint, *The Forging of American Socialism: Origins of the Modern Movement* (Columbia: University of South Carolina Press, 1953); or D. A. Shannon, *The Socialist Party of America: A History* (New York: Macmillan, 1955).

[30] C. D. Long, *Wages and Earnings in the United States, 1860–1890* (Princeton, N.J.: Princeton University Press, 1960), pp. 68, 109, 115.

TABLE 2

Real Average Annual Earnings in U.S. Manufacturing, 1860–90[a]

	1860	1870	1880	1890
Money annual earnings (dollars)	297	384	345	427
Consumer price index	100	144	109.5	98.5
Real annual earnings: 1860 dollars	297	267	315	434
Indexes: 1860 = 100				
Real annual earnings	100	90	106	146
Real daily wages (Aldrich data)	100	107	118	150
Real daily wages (Weeks-Bulletin 18)	100	103	122	154

[a] Source: C. D. Long, *Wages and Earnings in the United States, 1860–1890* (Princeton, N.J.: Princeton University Press, 1960), p. 68. © Copyright 1960 by Princeton University Press for the National Bureau of Economic Research.

for these years that numerous Americans, many of them of relatively recent foreign origin, moved up the social ladder.[31] For those who didn't there was always the hope that their children would get ahead. American economic and political behavior at least until 1892 must be understood against this background of upward mobility.

While there was a great deal of distress among those growing staple crops such as cotton and wheat during many of the years of this period, farmers in the Northeast engaged in dairy farming, hog raising, or food production for the growing cities often prospered. But the greatest opportunity for success and advancement were in the growing towns and cities of the nation. Professor Shannon estimates that for every industrial worker who became a successful farmer, twenty farm boys became urbanites. He concludes that "the rise of the city in the nineteenth century was a safety valve for rural discontent."[32] Urban discontent in the East was moderated by the vast demand for capital, manufactured goods, and services by the rapidly growing cities and towns of the Middle and Far West. The progressive development of such new regions with their vast opportunities for autonomous investment of a "once-and-for-all" character in such things as railroads, roads, buildings, etc., has been termed "sequential growth."[33] This process whereby backward and forward linkages (in Hirshman's terms) were established between growing towns and cities and the surrounding farming regions is one that makes

[31] For several striking examples, see the provocative book of Ray Ginger, *Age of Excess* (New York: The Macmillan Co., 1965), Chap. 5.

[32] F. A. Shannon, "A Post-Mortem on the Safety-Valve Theory," *Agricultural History* 19 (1945), pp. 31–37.

[33] G. S. Murphy and Zellner, "Sequential Growth, the Labor Safety Valve Doctrine and the Development of American Unionism," *The Journal of Economic History* (Sept., 1959), pp. 402–421. Murphy and Zellner carry their thesis to questionable extremes with regard to the effect of sequential growth upon labor unions and liberal labor legislation. For a needed corrective, see the critique of A. C. Bolino in *The Journal of Economic History* (June, 1960) and the authors' rejoinder in *Idem.* (March, 1961).

Turner's frontier concept a meaningful hypothesis for the explanation of the remarkable growth of this period. It especially makes the so-called "safety-valve" doctrine, as so modified, a more plausible explanation of certain features of American cultural history.

Thus, there is much support for the view, as one historian expresses it, that "in most American cities from 1877 to 1893, the entire social structure was moving upward rapidly. Even the very bottom, occupied mainly by immigrants in slums, was yet higher than the environments left behind in Europe. . . ."[34] Yet, such a process of unrestrained and uncontrolled technological and social change, though it benefitted many, caused widespread suffering for those who could not adjust to the bewildering demands of the new industrial discipline. The swift pace of industrialization and capital formation, though it raised the material standard of living, seemed to contribute seriously as a side effect to the insidious ailment of alienation. The mechanization of work, the growth of a more impersonal urban way of life, and the steady substitution of the pecuniary calculus and the "cash nexus" for more personal involvement, concern, and community with others were some of the key elements in the process. For example, those craftsmen, such as the molders, whose jobs were destroyed by mechanization, and the millions of others whose work was reduced to a monotonous routine by the same process probably experienced some degree of alienation. (On the credit side, however, there were new skills created by the progress of technology.) Even some of those who succeeded in the individualistic quest for middle-class success experienced some degree of estrangement from those they had left behind. The hectic pursuit of money and status in the crowded cities and the estrangement of people from one another caused a perceptible decline in the sense of community. The growth of extremes of wealth and poverty, the appearance of what Disraeli called the "two nations," and the neglect of the working class by organized Protestantism all made their contribution to this phenomenon. The immigrants, uprooted from their ancient cultures and cast into the slums of the great American cities, would seem to have been prime victims of alienation. But very often they avoided it, thanks either to the close ethnic communities of which they were a part, the aid and assistance given by the politicians and ward bosses who thus served as substitute relief agencies, or the immigrants' own hopes for a better future. Alienation was a growing reality for many Americans in the "Gilded Age," and it grew more acute when depression spread unemployment and social strife after 1893. Americans were beginning to learn that a market society did not automatically create a sense of community nor did the growth of national wealth assure a feeling of self-fulfillment in work and life. In this respect the American experience of these years confirmed the sociological insight of Marx so far as this aspect of capitalist development was concerned.

[34] Ginger, *Age of Excess*, p. 93.

THE AMBIGUOUS ROLE OF GOVERNMENT

Despite the stresses and strains in the society and the suffering of many citizens in these years, the federal government played practically a minimal role in economic affairs. State and local legislatures continued to favor and protect business interests, but at the federal level there prevailed what one writer calls the "politics of complacency." One reason for this was that in the political structure of the United States in the post-Civil War years, with its decentralization of power and with a party system in which control rested in the hands of local and state politicians, presidential government was minimized. This was the era of Congressional government in which powerful bosses and czars determined what legislation was passed; innumerable interest groups pressured and lobbied for political favor and the politicians served as brokers for their conflicting clients. Furthermore, in the latter part of the century there developed a conservative belief that government should have but a peripheral role in economic matters. Many businessmen, educators, and ministers held that the proper function of government was to preserve law and order and not to intervene or interfere with the iron law of supply and demand. *Laissez faire* in this sense was rationalized by some in terms of the popular ideas of Herbert Spencer, the British philosopher, who argued that competitive individualism promoted the best interests of society because it conduced to the "survival of the fittest." This adaptation of Darwin's theory of biology to the very different realm of the social world became a powerful rationale for the maintenance of the status quo in the United States, with all its gross inequalities in wealth, power, and individual welfare. Thus, during the depression of 1893, after decades of special privilege legislation, Governor Flower of New York rejected a demand for public works to alleviate unemployment by saying, ". . . in this country firm lines separate our political ideas from those of European countries. . . . In America the people support the government; it is not the province of the government to support the people."[35]

The agenda of government was largely limited to those projects which special interests were powerful enough to sponsor and have passed. Thus, the long agitation for free silver owed part of its force to the support of powerful mining interests in the Far West. At the bottom of the depression of 1873, "Silver Dick" Bland of Missouri introduced a bill in the House calling for free and unlimited coinage of silver. His bill was passed by that body, but in the Senate a limit was placed upon the volume of silver to be coined. Under the Bland-Allison Act of 1878, the Secretary of the Treasury had to buy not less than $2 million nor more than $4 million of the white metal and coin it into dollars. Under this law the minimum amount of silver was purchased each

[35] Quoted in S. Rezneck, "Unemployment, Unrest and Relief in the United States during the Depression of 1893–97," *Journal of Political Economy* (August, 1953), p. 332.

month; the currency of the nation was not increased greatly under this legislation, because, among other things, the "cartwheels" (large silver dollars) were
not popular. In 1886, Congress authorized the issuance of silver certificates in
payment for the metal brought to the Treasury. By 1890, with wholesale farm
prices continuing to fall and with the agitation for free silver still strong, the
silver advocates were able to secure far more favorable action for their cause.
Under the Sherman Silver Purchase Act of 1890 the Secretary of the Treasury
was required to purchase 4.5 million ounces of silver a month and issue in
payment Treasury notes of full legal tender power. (These notes were made
redeemable in gold and silver coin and contributed, as we have already shown,
to the "nightmare of the endless chain" of redemption in Cleveland's second
term.[36]) The sequel to this silver legislation—the decline of the gold reserve
—has already been recounted; the disruption it brought about, though we can
hardly consider it the cause of the depression of 1893, beautifully illustrated
the evil of special interest legislation in an economy that had no mechanisms
or policies for cyclical stabilization.

Tariff legislation was, of course, the most striking example of the predominance of special interests in law-making and of the corruption of the political
process. Only a few examples need be given to illustrate this truth. The Act of
1883 was the first effort at general revision of the import duties since the Civil
War. In the preceding ten years, other issues, principally the currency, had
commanded public attention. But, with the return of prosperity in 1879, the
Treasury began to run a surplus of about $100 million annually. Tariff
revenue had to be cut, so the Republican Congress in 1882 decided to "take
the tariff out of politics." President Arthur appointed a Tariff Commission,
headed by a Mr. John Hayes, secretary of the Wool Manufacturers Association; representation was given also to iron, sugar, and other interests. The
bills presented in the House and Senate carried moderate reductions; it was
necessary to take the bills to a conference to settle the differences. Amazingly,
the conference committee reconciled the two versions not by splitting the
differences on key schedules, but by raising the rates to a higher figure than
had been previously proposed! The resulting Act lowered the rates on some
items, such as wool and pig iron, but raised it on others, for example, iron
ore. The law came to be regarded as just a sop to the public demand for
reduction. Mr. Hayes, after passage of the Act, wrote: "Reduction in itself was
by no means desirable to us; it was a concession to public sentiment, a
bending of the top and branches to the wind of public opinion to save the
trunk of the protective system. . . . We wanted the tariff to be made by our
friends."[37]

Another attempt was made during Cleveland's first term to reform the
tariff, but the Mills bill passed by the Democratic House was seriously
modified in a protective direction in the Senate. President Harrison's victory

[37] F. W. Taussig, *Tariff History of the United States* (New York: G. P. Putnam's Sons,
1931), p. 249, footnote 7.

in the 1888 election was taken by the Republicans as a mandate for a higher tariff, and indeed, the McKinley Act of 1890 brought about a radical upward revision of the rates. The wool, iron, steel, and other favored interests were well taken care of; the rates on pig iron, steel, and copper were lowered so little as to be practically prohibitory, considering the lowered cost of production in this country. The surplus revenue of some $50–60 million was reduced by eliminating the duty of two cents per pound on raw sugar; a bounty of two cents per pound was given to domestic sugar producers. The law was made palatable to the farming interests by including reciprocity provisions whereby the United States was given the power to impose duties on certain imports if the exporting countries levied unjust or unreasonable duties on the agricultural or other products of the United States. Under these provisions reciprocity treaties were negotiated with England, Spain, and a number of South American countries, but they expired in 1894 with the adoption of the tariff law of that year. The higher prices seemingly caused by the McKinley Act led to large Republican losses in 1890 and 1891 and paved the way for the return to the Presidency of Grover Cleveland. Yet he too failed for a second time to obtain needed reform in the tariff. The Wilson-Gorman Act of 1894, which he allowed to become law without signing it, achieved no deep-reaching change in the character of our tariff legislation. The Democrats wanted to put a number of raw materials on the free list in the hope of reducing the cost of living, but the protectionists in the Senate succeeded in getting rates on most of these commodities that were about one-half of those of the McKinley Tariff. Sugar was a major focus of interest, but in the end the Sugar Trust prevailed, gaining a 40 per cent *ad valorem* duty on raw sugar, thanks to political campaign contributions and unsavory speculation in sugar stocks by Senators on the inside. This law carried a provision for an income tax of 2 per cent on all incomes above $4,000, but it was struck down as unconstitutional by a 5–4 decision of the Supreme Court.[38] The timing of the Tariff Act of 1894 was unfortunate for the Democrats. The intensification of the depression led a gullible public, following *post hoc propter hoc* reasoning, to believe that low duties would convert prosperity into depression like magic.

The political charade over the tariff was resumed with McKinley's victory over Bryan. Again, the election was claimed to be a mandate from the people, even though bimetallism had been the main issue. A Republican Congress passed the Dingley Act of 1897—a law that carried the highest duties in the history of the nation and remained in force for twelve years, another record.

The tariff legislation of these years was perhaps as important for its aggregative effects as for its impact on particular industries. Tariff duties and excises, which were the main source of the federal government's revenue, contributed to a high propensity to save in that they did not fall most heavily on the well-to-do; they were rather regressive taxes that hit the low-income groups the hardest. But in addition, the high tariff schedules of these years

---

[38] *Pollock* vs. *Farmers' Loan and Trust Co.*, 157 U.S. 429; 158 U.S. 601 (1895).

piled up surpluses averaging over $100 million annually from 1881 to 1890. These federal surpluses at a time when productive capacity tended to outrun demand contributed to the deflationary forces at work. It is little wonder that Congressmen, anxious to avoid reducing the tariff, spent millions on pensions for Civil War veterans and in 1890 discovered another way to reduce the surplus—build battleships.[39] The dilemmas of a Congress having no knowledge of Keynesian economics and faced with an economy prone to marked departures from full employment equilibrium were very real.

Regulation of the railroads was a subject the Congress had been debating since 1867; the number of bills designed for this purpose increased each year, and in 1884 the leadership of both major parties promised some form of interstate control of the rail lines. The Supreme Court's decision in the Wabash case, which struck down all regulation by states of interstate commerce, made some action imperative.[40] The Cullom Committee, after holding hearings throughout the country on the subject in 1886, reported: "It is the deliberate judgment of the Committee that upon no public question are the people so nearly unanimous as upon the proposition that Congress should undertake in some way the regulation of interstate commerce." The law Congress passed the following year was a conservative, compromise measure, based on the English law of 1854. It provided that railroad charges should be "reasonable and just"; that special rates and rebates were illegal and there should be no discrimination. Charging more for a short haul than a long one, when the conditions were substantially the same, and pooling operations were condemned. This law was passed in response to the pressures of the farmers and small merchants; even the railroads desired it because they feared state regulation with all its confusion and bungling. As Richard Olney, later Cleveland's Attorney General, and a leading railroad lawyer wrote, it "satisfies the popular clamor for a government supervision of railroads, at the same time that supervision is almost entirely nominal." In the twenty years after its passage, the law was little more than that. Cleveland's appointees were nearly all friendly to the railroads, and the latter's appeal of their cases to the Supreme Court resulted almost always in victories for their interests. A major blow at effective regulation was struck in the Maximum Freight Rate decision (1897), in which the Court denied the Commission authority to set a maximum rate. The Commission was almost completely frustrated, but the principle of regulation in the public interest had been established; its more effective implementation was to be accomplished in the next century.

The story was very much the same with regard to antitrust legislation. When the Granger and other protests against monopoly reached a peak in the late 1880's, the states were the first to take action. No fewer than fifteen states, with Kansas in the lead, passed such laws in 1889 and 1890, with some banning monopoly in their constitutions. But these state laws against com-

[39] Ginger, *Age of Excess*, p. 183.
[40] *Wabash, St. Louis and Pacific Railroad* vs. *Illinois,* 118 U.S. 557 (1886).

binations were almost uniformly ineffective, largely because of the failure to enforce them and even more because most states felt that they should not sacrifice themselves to solve what was essentially a national problem.

The federal legislators in enacting the Sherman Act in 1890 sought to establish in effect a common law for the United States as a whole; they drafted a statute with provisions almost as broad as those of a constitution, condemning contracts and combinations in restraint of trade and attempts to monopolize in very broad language. The Department of Justice, which had the responsibility for the enforcement of the new law, did not have a very creditable record in the first decade of its existence; its attorneys lost their cases against the Sugar Trust, the Whiskey Trust, and the Cash Register combine. The Supreme Court's decision in the E. C. Knight case (1895), involving the American Sugar Refining Co., held that a combination of *manufactures* did not constitute an illegal restraint upon interstate commerce.[41] This narrow interpretation assured businessmen that the law was a nullity, and ambitious corporate promoters soon launched one of the largest merger movements in our history.

Ironically enough, the Justice Department had more success in enforcing the law's provisions against a labor leader than it had in its prosecutions of business.[42] But here again, a legal framework for the social control of business had been established by Congress' action. Despite the law's disappointing first decade, it was to gain new life and meaning through more vigorous enforcement in the following decade. To many, the capacity of democratic government for effective control of capitalistic enterprise had not been demonstrated by these puny first efforts. But the capability or possibility of governmental action in behalf of the public interest had been established; this development in itself suggested that American government could not be considered merely as the executive arm of the ruling class, as the Marxian diagnosis contended. The agrarian-labor uprising, known as the Populist movement, which erupted in these years was to play an important part in changing the dominant ideology behind governmental action in the future.

THE POPULIST MOVEMENT AND THE ELECTION OF 1896

The political tornado that swept out of the Middle Border and the southern states in the late 1880's and early 1890's was a phenomenon long in the making. It had its origins in the disadvantaged position of individualistic agriculture in a rapidly concentrating, corporate society and all the abuses of power which that predicament encouraged. More directly, so far as the western farmers were concerned, its background was to be found in the great speculative land boom on the Great Plains in the years 1880–87, which

41 156 U.S. 1.
42 *In re Debs*, 158 U.S. 564 (1895).

carried settlement west of the 20-inch rainfall line during the humid phase of the weather cycle. When a ten-year drought descended upon the area in 1888, destroying investment in crops, ranches, and farms, blasting hopes of a better life, the over-mortgaged farmers of the region faced catastrophe.[43] It is little wonder that Kansas became the "mother of radicalism" with its "sockless" Jerry Simpson, its "hell-raising" Mary Lease, and other equally colorful figures. Many of the farmers of the West and South, even before the hard times of the late 1880's, had organized themselves into a new organization, the Farmers' Alliance. After futilely trying to solve their problems through cooperative buying and selling, these farm groups turned to the achievement of more specific objectives, having to do with marketing and transportation problems and the supply of money. Under the latter head, they supported what was known as the subtreasury scheme, whereby the U.S. Treasury would establish warehouses in each county where farmers could store their crops and receive paper money up to 80 per cent of the value of such collateral.

With the intensification of the farm crisis, the Alliance men joined with the Knights of Labor and other reformers in forming a People's Party in Kansas in 1890. Two years later this new third party was put on a national basis at St. Louis; a platform was drawn up and James B. Weaver of Iowa was nominated for President. The Populists advocated free and unlimited coinage of silver; a national currency to be issued by the government only as provided in the subtreasury plan, or "a better system"; a circulating medium of not less than $50 per capita; a graduated income tax; postal savings banks; prohibition of alien land ownership, and government ownership and operation of railroads, telegraph, and telephones. In the 1892 election, the Populists had considerable success, rolling up over 1 million votes for their Presidential candidate as well as electing ten Congressmen, 5 Senators, and 1500 local officers of government. In the off-year of 1894, the Populist vote was 42 per cent higher than it had been in 1892.

It has been common in some analyses of Populism to regard it as a reactionary, last gasp of middle-class agrarianism against the dominance of monopoly capitalism. But some historians now contend that Populism was not a retrogressive movement; it sought to use modern technology rather than shun it; it established alliances with workers and did not make a fetish of smallness in business.[44] While one of its leaders, Henry Demarest Lloyd, was a socialist, neither the Populists nor the Farmers' Alliance men were doctrinaire socialists. ". . . They were, rather, angry agrarian capitalists who found themselves unprotected by government from exploitation by the railroads. They responded with a pragmatic demand for government ownership, a

---

[43] The classic account is J. D. Hicks, *The Populist Revolt* (Minneapolis: University of Minnesota Press, 1931) ; another excellent treatment of the movement in the South is C. V. Woodward, *Tom Watson: Agrarian Rebel* (New York: The Macmillan Co., 1938).

[44] For a challenging protest of the conventional view of Populism, see N. Pollack, *The Populist Response to Industrial America* (Cambridge, Mass.: Harvard University Press, 1962), *passim*.

demand that made many of them uncomfortable but which persisted until federal regulation became a meaningful reality in the twentieth century."[45] Lloyd advocated government ownership in order to establish a different economic and social order. But most of the Populists backed it as a specific remedy for the abuses of transportation monopoly; they were not ready to jettison private enterprise completely. The Populists were radical, but not that radical. In many ways, the Populists regarded theirs as a class movement in which the farmers and the workers had a common bond because they were in the same material position in industrial society.

"Populism," writes Professor Pollack, "criticized industrial America for creating not only poverty but a new man—alienated man. . . ." He quotes a *Farmers' Alliance* editorial as saying,

> The materialism of today does all the time segregate human lives. . . . Take a man for instance, who labors hard from fourteen to sixteen hours a day to obtain the bare necessities of life. He eats his bacon and potatoes in a place which might rather be called a den than a home; and then, worn down, lies down the sleeps. . . . He is brutalized both morally and physically. He has no ideas, only propensities. He has no beliefs, only instincts. He does not, often cannot, read. . . . His contact with other people is only the relation of servant to master, of a machine to its director. . . . How can you reach this man, how kindle the divine spark which is torpid in his soul, when he knows that it is greed that enforces the material labor that is crushing him down, when he feels that it is the wage system that is stealing the fruits of his toil and abasing and enslaving him.[46]

Some of the Populists, Pollack shows, attacked industrial capitalism not just on economic, but also humanistic grounds. ". . . Its critique was neither partial nor superficial; higher crop prices and lower interest rates were not the answer. The issue at stake was nothing less than human dignity. And for Populism this permitted but one conclusion: Industrial America must be altered in a truly democratic direction. Technology must be harnessed for human uses, not for creating the surplus worker."[47]

As the depression of 1893 deepened and unemployment mounted, there were many such surplus workers. The number of tramps multiplied, and the tramp problem became almost a national concern. Unrest in the cities became so acute by 1894 that strikes involving hundreds of thousands of men broke out. The greatest of these was the Pullman strike at Chicago, which seemed to threaten the civil order itself. The militia was called out in twenty states. In the spring a number of "industrial armies," the most famous of which was Jacob Coxey's, began to march on Washington to demand relief. When Coxey's army reached the capital, its leader was arrested and his followers were beaten and trampled upon by the mounted police. Coxey was urging a scheme for financing public works to ease the hardship of unemploy-

---

[45] R. F. Durden, *The Climax of Populism; The Election of 1896* (Lexington, Ky.: University of Kentucky Press, 1965), p. 3.

[46] Pollack, *The Populist Response to Industrial America*, pp. 25, 26.

[47] *Ibid.*, p. 143.

ment, an idea that we now view as not very radical. To the conventional defender of law and order in his day, he was a menace and an enemy of society. The fact was that the industrial disturbances, the agitation and violence of these years greatly frightened the upper classes of that day and led them to anticipate the worst. "We are on the eve of a very dark night," Frances L. Stetson wrote President Cleveland in 1894, "unless a return of commercial prosperity relieves popular discontent." One railway editor gloomily opined, "It is probably safe to say that in no civilized country in this century, not actually in the throes of war or open insurrection, has society been so disorganized as it was in the United States during the first half of 1894; never was human life held so cheap; never did the constituted authorities appear so incompetent to enforce respect for the law."[48]

The fears of the elite for the stability of the American social order and the return of prosperity were intensified in 1896 by the fusion of the Democrats and the Populists in support of the candidacy of William Jennings Bryan for the Presidency. The nomination of the Great Commoner by both these organizations revolutionized the Democratic Party and party lines generally and greatly enhanced the political cause of free silver. The Gold Democrats who bolted their Party foresaw grave possibilities in all this. One of them, J. Sterling Morton, Cleveland's Secretary of Agriculture, wrote: "In the white-heat frenzy which the proletariats have worked up under the leadership of Bryan—who, as a sort of Peter the Hermit, has proved himself to be a competent leader of the commune—there is nothing which happened during the French Revolutions and Communes which cannot happen here." And Morton concluded that "nothing which ever happened during the worst periods of any French Revolution would be impossible under the direful catastrophe of Bryan's election."[49]

To some Populists also Bryan's nomination by their Party was a disaster. They disliked to see their broad program subordinated so much to the single issue of silver. Henry Demarest Lloyd, the leader of the socialist minority in the party, bitterly denounced the free silver movement as "a fake." Lloyd refused to support Bryan and voted for the Socialist Labor candidate instead. However, to many other Populists silver was simply a symbol—a common denominator issue—which represented many of the other grievances of the farmers and workers under the existing economic order. They did not regard silver and currency reform as the only issues, but simply as the first step toward many other necessary social changes.

In his strenuous barnstorming of the nation, Bryan waged an unusual campaign, one that foreshadowed some of the political techniques of later years, but Mark Hanna, the Republican national chairman, was likewise an innovator. The skill, organization, and system with which he conducted McKinley's campaign, plus the millions of dollars that business corporations

---

[48] H. P. Robinson, editor of the *Railroad Age*, in the *Forum* (January, 1895), p. 523.
[49] Pollack, *The Populist Response to Industrial America*, p. 130.

and the independent rich contributed to the effort, were remarkable for their day. The defenselessness of many of the unorganized workers to employer pressure and intimidation and the failure of many farmers to vote for Bryan were also influential in affecting the outcome. The "Popocrat" candidate polled only about a half million votes less than his Republican rival, but the electoral margin of the winner was much more decisive—271 to 176.[50] On hearing the election results, Hanna telegraphed the "advance agent of prosperity," the new President, "God's in his Heaven, all's right with the world!" His sentiments were undoubtedly shared by many formerly fearful Republicans who now believed that the Republic had been saved.

The return of prosperity after 1897, the increase in the world's production of gold, the Spanish-American War and the ensuing imperialism, all tended to kill Populism on the national scene. These changed circumstances of the last years of the old century had forced the Populists "to close their academy," but in retrospect, it is clear that before they did they had furnished many Americans, leaders as well as led, with an invaluable education in the need for expanded governmental action to cope with the legacy of economic ills created by mature industrialism. Many of the reforms of later years during the New Freedom and New Deal owed their origin to ideas that had germinated during the Populist era.

THE LURE OF IMPERIALISM

The crowded years of the late nineteenth century saw the United States enter the arena of world politics and economics in a new and more vigorous way. This development poses for us the question of the validity of the Marxian interpretation of imperialism with respect to these tendencies; space will hardly permit us to answer the questions involved here with completeness, but some elements of such an analysis may be indicated. Certainly, it is agreed that in its early history the United States had periodically shown an aggressiveness in foreign affairs. Various statesmen espoused policies of manifest destiny; Secretary of State Seward in Lincoln's administration was especially an advocate of a program of expansion. During the Civil War and the Reconstruction period there was a lull in this type of activity. However, in the 1880's there was again a noticeable increase in talk of the nation's manifest destiny. John Fiske, the American popularizer of Herbert Spencer's philosophy, advanced this thesis in numerous speeches throughout the country. The Rev. Josiah Strong, a Congregationalist minister, asserted that the Anglo-Saxon was divinely commissioned to be his brother's keeper. And perhaps most importantly, Captain Alfred Thayer Mahan, the president of the Naval War

---

[50] It has been estimated that a change of 14,000 votes, distributed in six states, would have produced a clear Democratic-Populist victory. (M. Josephson, *The Politicos, 1865–1896* (New York: Harcourt, Brace and Co., 1938), pp. 706–707.

College, in his books and articles persuaded many of the elite that trade and the naval power to protect it were the basis of national power.

The immediate events that involved us in the war with Spain over Cuba started with the insurrection of 1895 on that tormented island. The complex of factors leading to our declaration of war in 1898 were many and have been often recounted—the role of the "yellow press," the pressures of the political situation upon McKinley, and the emotional mood of public opinion after the tensions of 1893, among others.[51] Yet, while these factors have their place in any complete understanding of the events that led us to acquire an overseas empire, they must be seen in the context of the years 1895–98 and of the whole tendency of American foreign policy after the 1850's.[52] The fact was that American business in the 1880's and after was pushing aggressively into foreign markets and coming into intensified competition with European and other nations for the available world business.[53] The increasing productive capacity of the American economy, coupled with the depressions of the 1880's and 1890's with their accompanying violence and social unrest, led many businessmen and politicians to conclude that foreign markets had to be found to avoid economic collapse and social disorder.

Such a policy of commercial expansion—not of colonialism in the form of territorial acquisition—was seen by several leading politicians as the cure for the depression and the attendant labor troubles. One of these was Walter Q. Gresham, Cleveland's Secretary of State in 1893–95. He opposed the annexation of Hawaii, but not economic expansion through promotion of our exports. This point of view seemed very persuasive because it was believed that American agricultural exports were declining in relative terms, and if our balance of payments and gold problem were to be solved, the nation would have to export more industrial goods. This opinion became more pronounced after the repeal of the Silver Purchase Act. The Cleveland administration and the so-called "goldbugs" had argued at the time that the depression was not due to lack of money, but to overproduction. The glut of goods, it was seen, could be overcome either through a redistribution of incomes internally or through finding additional foreign markets. The inclination of some of the nation's most influential political leaders and businessmen to choose the second alternative had an important effect upon the subsequent course of American foreign policy.

The direction of our foreign policy in the 1890's cannot be understood

[51] On these topics, the following are indispensable: J. W. Pratt, *Expansionists of 1898: The Acquisition of Hawaii and the Spanish Islands* (Baltimore, Md.: The Johns Hopkins Press, 1936); W. Millis, *The Martial Spirit: A Study of Our War with Spain* (Boston: Houghton Mifflin Co., 1931); R. Hofstadter, "Manifest Destiny and the Philippines," in Aaron, ed. *America in Crisis; Fourteen Critical Episodes in American History* (New York: Knopf, 1952); E. R. May, *Imperial Democracy: The Emergence of America as a Great Power* (New York: Harcourt, Brace and World, Inc., 1961).

[52] W. LaFeber, *The New Empire: An Interpretation of American Expansion, 1860–1898* (Ithaca, N.Y.: Cornell University Press, 1963), p. 285.

[53] May, *Imperial Democracy*, p. 9.

without a grasp of our developing interest in Asia in the preceding decade. The early colonial trade and missionary activity in the Orient had waned during the middle of the century, but in the 1880's our industrialists began to think again of Asia's millions as potential customers. After the Sino-Japanese War, our exports to China and Japan more than doubled in a few years, and the belief became widespread in business circles that the Asiatic market had at last become a reality. However, American interest in an "open door" to this vast Asiatic market was suddenly threatened when the Germans in late 1897 seized the key port of Kiaochow in the Shantung Peninsula. The following March the Czar of Russia took control of Port Arthur and Talienwan, so important for trade with Manchuria and North China. Even the British entered the scramble for territory by seizing Wei-Hai-Wei. The United States seemed to stand alone in pressing for the principle of equal opportunity in foreign trade. These developments have to be appreciated to understand the change that swept over political and business leaders after the Spanish-American War, leading them to support annexation of the Philippines, Guam and Puerto Rico, whereas formerly many were opposed to such a policy. The dominant view was that these territories had to be annexed to provide strategic bases so that the United States could compete successfully with European competitors in Latin America and Asia. On the basis of this Mahanite doctrine, Hawaii, whose annexation had been rejected by Cleveland, was added to the territories of the United States by Congress even before the war with Spain. The other bases, seen as a protection for a future Isthmian canal, were likewise defended on these grounds. The proponents of "large policies," such as Henry Cabot Lodge and Theodore Roosevelt, had studied Mahan well.[54]

The interpretation we have advanced here of American foreign policy in the late nineteenth century confirms the Marxian thesis in part in the sense that a faltering, depression-ridden economy turned to commercial expansion as a means of relieving the glut of goods and alleviating the associated unemployment and social discontent. Policy, it should be noted, took this direction because a *laissez faire* capitalism without acceptable means to stabilize the economy by monetary, fiscal, or other techniques, was powerfully drawn toward a foreign solution of its basic problem, that of maintaining adequate stability and growth. The implication of this view for future national policy is clear: given new means and conceptions of controlling the domestic economy, the alternatives facing the makers of foreign policy would not be so limited. The test of this proposition, whether capitalism in the United States could survive without wars and commercial rivalry with other nations, was deferred to the next century. Meanwhile, the Republic, which in its youth had been urged by Washington to avoid foreign entanglements approached the close of the nineteenth century with all the power and responsibility that went with an overseas empire. The international entanglements and the growth of the

---

[54] See LaFeber, *The New Empire*, pp. 407ff. and *passim* for a cogent treatment of these matters.

military institution necessary to defend the new empire were all as yet shrouded by the veil of the future. The economy had, in Rostovian terms, completed the drive to maturity domestically, but it still faced great trials of its political adulthood in the broader arena of international affairs.

Part 7

THE ORGANIZATIONAL REVOLUTION IN AMERICAN ECONOMIC AND POLITICAL LIFE, 1897–1918

INTRODUCTION: THE VEBLENIAN THEORY
OF ECONOMIC DEVELOPMENT

The growth of large-scale enterprise begun in late nineteenth century America continued in the twentieth; indeed, the tempo of the movement seemed to accelerate rather than diminish. Not only did business organizations grow larger, but labor and farmers, small businessmen and professionals turned increasingly to organizations and associations as the solution for their economic problems. The role of government in the economy also grew much larger in this period so that in retrospect there was much truth in Kenneth Boulding's view that America was in the midst of a continuing Organizational Revolution.[1] This whole development involved the substitution of collective effort and decision-making for individual choice and activity. One of the first American economists who emphasized the significance of this large-scale corporate capitalism and who sought to analyze its dynamics rather than the perfect competition of numerous, small individual enterprisers was Thorstein Veblen, whose life (1857–1929) spanned the years of this remarkable economic transformation. As Paul Sweezy has noted, "Veblen treated the United States as the prototype of an advanced capitalist society, just as Marx, writing earlier, had assigned that role to Great Britain."[2]

Thorstein Veblen made his reputation at the University of Chicago where he published his first book, the celebrated *Theory of the Leisure Class* in 1899. Thereafter he published a series of books that rocked the academic community and made his name a by-word among the intelligentsia of his day. *The Theory of Business Enterprise* (1904), *The Instinct of Workmanship and the State of the Industrial Arts* (1914), and *The Engineers and the Price System* (1921) were some of the more important ones. Even the titles of his books were different from the staid *Principles* of his colleagues.

Veblen's work has very often not been seen in true perspective, even by his fellow economists. His thought, scattered as it is over several key volumes and essays, has a unity easily missed by the casual or unsympathetic reader. Veblen was trying to forge an integrated system of economic theory along the lines of what today we would call a cultural or behavioral science. His involved literary style and his penchant for satire undoubtedly have left many readers mystified or simply amused at his lampooning of our economic and social practices. Veblen's phrases—and he was an incomparable phrase-maker—and the broad portrait he sketches, in acid, of late nineteenth century society conceal in some ways a very significant view of economic and social

[1] K. E. Boulding, *The Organizational Revolution* (New York: Harper & Row, 1953).
[2] P. H. Sweezy, "Veblen on American Capitalism," in D. F. Dowd, ed., *Thorstein Veblen: A Critical Appraisal* (Ithaca: Cornell University Press, 1958), p. 177, footnote 1. The standard and most complete biography is that of J. Dorfman, *Thorstein Veblen and His America* (New York: The Viking Press, 1934).

life. Veblen disagreed with his fellow economists as to the proper focus for their investigations. He was especially critical of the neo-classical conception of the economic problem, which tended to view it as one of making the best use of the resources already at hand within the existing framework of social institutions. The emphasis on the analysis of stationary price equilibria, as in Marshall's great work, seemed to Veblen to need supplementation with more dynamic, evolutionary studies. To him, economics was simply the study of how far and by what means society had solved the problem of scarcity; the problem, therefore, that most deserved attention was one of constructing that set of institutions that would be most effective in overcoming scarcity.

Thorstein Veblen (1857–1929) was born on a Wisconsin farm of Norwegian parents. He studied at Carleton College, Johns Hopkins, and Yale where he received a PhD. in 1884. Subsequently, he taught economics at Chicago, Stanford and Missouri Universities and at the New School for Social Research in New York City.

Underwood and Underwood

Economic growth, Veblen insisted, must be understood as a developmental process of human action, shaped by the ever-changing institutional patterns of society. He believed that anthropology was destined to revolutionize the political and social sciences as radically as bacteriology had revolutionized medicine.[3] He consequently made the anthropologist's concepts of culture and cultural change and diffusion central ideas in his interpretation of economic behavior. Rather than isolating and abstracting economic behavior from its cultural context, Veblen argued that economic phenomena are not "neatly isolable" from the culture as a whole. Economic practices and institutions must be studied as integral parts of an emerging, cultural entity. This aspect of Veblen's thought has led some writers to dub it a "holistic" approach, employing a word used by Jan C. Smuts in a book on evolution.[4]

[3] T. Veblen, "Why Is Economics Not an Evolutionary Science?", *Quarterly Journal of Economics* (July, 1898), reprinted in *The Place of Science in Modern Civilization and Other Essays* (New York: Huebsch, 1919), p. 56.

[4] This feature of Veblen's work was not fully developed by him. Since his time the emergence of the "field" and Gestalt approach in psychology has added support to his view of social life. See A. G. Gruchy, *Modern Economic Thought* (Englewood Cliffs, N.J.: Prentice-Hall, Inc., 1947), p. 18.

When Veblen formulated his socio-psychological analysis of modern capitalism, some notable advances were being made in anthropology and psychology, which he incorporated into his theories. For example, in the early nineteenth century psychologists relied heavily upon a subjective, introspective method of interpreting human nature; they over-emphasized reason to the neglect of instinctual, impulsive, and unconscious behavior; they failed to see the intimate links between the individual and the society of which he was a part. Veblen was aware of a school of German anthropologists who were laying the foundations for what they called "folk psychology." This approach pictured the behavior of primitive people as being greatly influenced by cultural factors as well as by those of the individual organism. In later years, in the United States and elsewhere, this point of view has come to be widely accepted as the basis of social psychology.

Veblen was particularly dissatisfied with the individualistic, rationalistic concept of human nature that underlay marginal utility economics. Essentially, he held, this school of thought conceived of man as a calculator of pleasure and pain, a theory that in his mind had become outmoded for several generations. This "hedonistic man is not a prime mover," wrote Veblen. In other words, he sought a view of human nature that would take account of man's active nature. He thought he had found it in the then current theory of instincts. According to this theory, the individual is born with a vaguely defined set of tropisms (innate reactions) and instincts. The instincts differ from the tropisms in that they involve an element of intelligence; they are modifiable by experience, by learning. What modifications the instincts will undergo depends on the human environment and, more particularly, on the institutions or socially accepted habits of mind that happen to prevail in a society. In other words, these institutions provide the proximate or immediate ends that guide the individual.

To Veblen, man is a bundle of instincts in addition to possessing intelligence and a capacity for developing habits. These instincts are purposive and make man active rather than passive. He emphasized four major instincts in his work: the parental bent, or concern for the welfare of others, the instinct of workmanship, the acquisitive instinct, and the instinct of idle curiosity. These are viewed as having been shaped and conditioned by the cultural or institutional environment of man's past, ranging all the way back to the savage era and down to the present epoch of machine industry. To illustrate, during the handicraft era of the early middle ages (to go back no further with Veblen in his speculative cultural history of man), the parental bent and the instinct of workmanship dominated the acquisitive urge. This was the period of the doctrine of "just price" and the philosophy of "live and let live." The medieval, communal ethics controlled economic behavior and inhibited the acquisitive tendencies of man.

With the development of private property in land, money lending, the hiring of workers, and large-scale trading, absentee ownership develops. Certain men, as the division of labor develops, are concerned more with money-making than with the direct production of goods. They become habituated to the pecuniary calculus and view the outcome of the economic process in terms of the essentially metaphysical concepts of profits, legal rights, and private property. In an impersonal pecuniary society such men seek to satisfy their need for self-regard, for status, by excelling in the accumulation of wealth. Others, however, who are more closely involved in the matter-of-fact work of industrial production become habituated to looking at things in terms of physical productivity, engineering efficiency, mechanical cause and effect. Serviceability to the community tends to be their criterion of social status. In other words, an advanced capitalistic society such as that of the United States at the end of the nineteenth century tended, according to Veblen, to be divided into classes: one, the businessman concerned with finance and money-making; the other, workers and engineers whose main daily occupation was in making goods. But in the ordinary run of things, as Veblen characteristically expressed it, business considerations took precedence over industrial, matter-of-fact ones.

Veblen was fascinated with the massive process of technological change that the western world was undergoing in moving from the handicraft age to the era of machine industry. Technological change of this character was a cumulative process, and he therefore analyzed the modern economy in terms of cumulative causation rather than in those of a moving equilibrium of prices or a dialectic of economic forces. Modern machine industry, looked at from the standpoint of the whole economy, was becoming increasingly intricate and interdependent in its functioning and close-knit articulation of processes; its concatenation of processes, as a consequence, was easily disrupted. In his view, business transactions served only in the work of interstitial adjustment among these technical processes. But as he was wont to say, industry (i.e., the technical processes) is carried on for the sake of business, and not conversely.

Veblen's theory of economic development is a long term interpretation of the impact of scientific and technological change and of capital accumulation upon capitalist institutions and attitudes.[5] Rather than limiting his analysis of economic development to the study of the path of stable growth upon the basis of fixed assumptions about the supplies of productive factors and of the character of the underlying institutions, he concerned himself with the "feedback" between the changes in the institutional structure of the economy resulting from its functioning and the consequences of these changes for the subsequent pattern of growth. In other words, to Veblen economic growth is a developmental process in which the institutional framework of the economy itself undergoes change; in this respect, his approach resembles that of Marx.

In Veblen's view, economic growth is not only a matter of increased output.

[5] A. G. Gruchy, "Veblen's Theory of Economic Growth," in Dowd, *Thorstein Veblen* . . ., p. 156ff. is very helpful on this subject; it has been relied upon in much which follows. Veblen set forth many of his basic ideas on economic growth in *The Theory of Business Enterprise* (New York: C. Scribner, 1904). They were elaborated on and somewhat modified in his later works. Gruchy regards his *The Vested Interests and the State of the Industrial Arts* (New York: Viking Press, 1933) as an especially valuable statement of his mature theory of capitalist development.

The *composition* of the output is very important because sustained growth depends upon the production of growth-stimulating kinds of products. Fundamentally, Veblen holds that the pace of economic development depends upon what he terms the "net product of industry." This is what remains after deducting the actual subsistence of the workers (the goods and services they consume during the year) and the yearly depreciation allowance on the nation's plant and equipment from the annual gross output. The net output is a "disposable excess of the yearly output over cost." Since this excess may be allocated either to improving the consumption and therefore the efficiency of the working population or to new capital formation, its size plays a crucial role in the expansion of the nation's total output of final goods and services. Actually, Veblen believed that too much of this net product went into wasteful, conspicuous consumption by the vested interests or "kept classes," leaving comparatively little for private or public net investment. Even the actual subsistence of the working population in the United States at the time he wrote was regarded by Veblen as excessive because it included "consumer superfluities" that were not necessary for subsistence.[6]

Whereas economic growth is the result of the combined use of the productive factors, there was no doubt in his mind that under modern conditions of machine industry capital equipment is the strategic factor. In his view capital equipment is basically an embodiment of science or technology or, as he expressed it, "capital equipment has an unique position since it embodies the community's joint stock of technological knowledge." Thus, the capital stock is the "decisive factor" determining the rate of growth of the nation's economic surplus.

In the light of this relationship between technology and the nation's capital equipment, it is important to emphasize that Veblen believed that technological change was a cumulative process that showed no sign of abatement in its rate. In 1923, he wrote that "there has been a progressive mechanization of the ways and means of living as well as of the ways and means of productive industry, and this mechanization has in recent times been going forward at a constantly accelerated rate, and it is still in progress, with no promise of abatement or conclusion."[7] He described technological growth as one of "unremitting proliferation," a kind of blind process of cultural elaboration, the outcome of which was quite unpredictable in any precise way.

Veblen pointed to four major consequences of this process of incessant technological change: first, the character of capital itself changes as industrial processes and the related capital equipment become more specialized and more standardized, raising the general efficiency of the industrial system. In this process, capital is increasingly substituted for labor, as technological progress spurs the mechanization of industry.

The second consequence of technological change has to do with the size of

---

[6] See below, p. 549.

[7] T. Veblen, *Absentee Ownership and Business Enterprise in Recent Times* (New York: Viking, 1938), p. 251.

the firm and the scale of operations. Technological progress results in a "continuous advance in the scale and articulation of the industrial process at large," he writes. As the firm's scale of operations enlarges, the productivity of the combined inputs of manpower and equipment rises; in the long run, and by that term Veblen means a period long enough to permit improvement in science and technology, the marginal productivity of capital rises. In the Veblenian view there are organic forces that favor the supremacy of the large plant and the large firm.

The third consequence of the unrestrained technological change of the modern era is that it tends to collectivize the economic system. In 1904 when Veblen published his *Theory of Business Enterprise,* the most complete statement of his evolutionary analysis up to that time, the United States was in the midst of what economic historians have come to call the "first merger movement." Veblen sought to explain this revolution in corporate organization, which was radically transforming individual decision-making and enterprise into a regime of collective action. In his presentation, the earlier industrial history of the nation, say from 1830 to 1880, was dominated by "captains of industry," hard-driving entrepreneurs who conducted their own firms either as proprietors or in partnership, performing many functions themselves, often acting as engineers as well as businessmen. By the 1880's, as we have seen, these captains of industry had already begun to be replaced by "captains of finance," i.e., bankers who substituted corporations for the smaller, private enterprises of the past. (Later on Veblen pictured "captains of solvency" replacing the smaller financial promoters and bankers as holding companies took the place of the single corporation.)

Veblen pictured these early combinations as being motivated largely by considerations of pecuniary advantage in the form of the "deals" or other transactions that enabled their sponsors to exercise pecuniary coercion upon others. ". . . The decisive point is business expediency and business pressure. . . . He [the captain of industry] inhibits as well as furthers the higher organization of industry. Broadly, it may be said that industrial consolidations and the working arrangements made for the more economical utilization of resources and mechanical contrivances are allowed to go into effect only after they are long overdue."[8] Unlike most contemporary economists, Veblen was not disturbed by this consolidation movement; indeed, he thought that its promoters were rendering the community a service. As he wrote in his inimitable style, ". . . it is scarcely an overstatement to say that probably the largest, assuredly the securest and most unquestionable service rendered by the great modern captains of industry is this curtailment of the business to be done,—this sweeping retirement of businessmen as a class from the service and the definitive cancellment of opportunities for business enterprise." Consolidation was justified, Veblen believed, because "So long as related industrial units are under different business managements, they are, by the nature

[8] Veblen, *The Theory of Business Enterprise* (New York: New American Library, 1958), Mentor Books, p. 25.

of the case, at cross purposes, and business consolidation remedies this untoward feature of the industrial system by eliminating the pecuniary element from the interstices of the system as far as may be. . . . The heroic role of the captain of industry is that of a deliverer from an excess of business management. It is the casting out of businessmen by the chief of business-men."[9]

Veblen saw the consolidation movement strongest in certain primary or "key" industries such as those producing capital goods where technological progress and capital accumulation tended to favor the largest concerns. Around this central cluster were the consumer goods industries and agricul-ture, in which mechanization did not as yet play so important a part; these industries tended to have lower degrees of economic concentration. Veblen described the early tendencies toward separation of management and owner-ship in the larger corporations of his day and noted the opportunities for unearned profits in the manipulation of the finances of such companies by "insiders." He analyzed too the pricing policies of these corporations, con-tending that their managers' main interest was in vendibility of their products rather than in the serviceability of their output. "The broad principle which guides producers and merchants, large and small, in fixing the prices at which they offer their wares and services is what is known in the language of the railroads as 'charging what the traffic will bear.' " He anticipated later analysis in showing the use of advertising in building up what he called "differential monopolies," i.e., those based on customer good will and continued patronage. Business in the main, he contended, was motivated by a restrictionist psy-chology, grounded in the metaphysics of natural rights and in the principles of the "simple and obvious system of natural liberty." Faced with the "inordi-nate productivity" of modern industry, businessmen are forced, in effect, to engage in industrial sabotage in order to maintain profits. Generally, he holds, that they are inclined toward a "conscientious withdrawal of efficiency," to quote one of his favorite phrases.[10]

These considerations enter into Veblen's theory of business fluctuations and serve to explain, in part, his view (as stated in 1904) that in the United States since the 1870's chronic depression was the rule rather than the exception. In

---

[9] Veblen, *The Theory of Business Enterprise*, pp. 28–29.

[10] In his later years, after World War I, Veblen grew more pessimistic on this point rather than less. For example, in 1923 he pictured the logic of private enterprise as tending toward a progressive decline of total putput in the following manner: "Under these circumstances it seems reasonable to expect that the systematic retardation and derangement of productive industry which is entailed by the current businesslike manage-ment will work out in a progressive abatement of the margin of net output of the industrial system at large; that this progressive abatement of the net industrial output will presently reach and pass the critical point of no net return . . . and that in the calculable future the industrial system . . . will run on lines of a progressively 'diminish-ing return,' converging to an eventual limit of tolerance in the way of a reduced subsistence minimum." [*Absentee Ownership and Business Enterprise in Recent Times* (New York: Viking, 1923), pp. 421–422 as quoted by Gruchy in Dowd, *Thorstein Veblen* . . ., p. 168.]

a sketchy treatment, Veblen concedes that in an earlier period, say from 1816 to 1873, chronic depression was not a consistent feature of the economy. Rather there was an approximation to a pattern of periodic booms, followed by financial crisis, liquidation, and depression. In this earlier situation, a crisis was an abrupt collapse of capitalized values. The latter usually fell in time below the level of the earning capacity of business investment so that a basis was laid for a resumption of the process of capitalizing the expected profits. But since the close of the 1870's, Veblen argues, the advancing efficiency of machine industry reached such a pitch that the cost of production of capital goods persistently outstripped such readjustments of nominal capitalizations as had been made. Seasons of prosperous business since then have been fairly uniformly traceable to specific extraneous causes, i.e., external to the process of industrial business proper, such as extraordinary crops or war. When a crisis of some severity has come, the persistent efficiency of machine industry has overtaken the decline in capitalization without allowing time for recovery and subsequent boom. "The cheapening of capital goods has overtaken the lowered capitalization of investments before the shock-effect of the liquidation has worn off. Hence depression is normal to the industrial situation under the consummate regime of the machine, so long as competition is unchecked and no *deus ex machina* interposes."[11]

The only remedies for this kind of economic stagnation in Veblen's mind were an increase in the unproductive consumption of goods, as in war or in the form of private waste, or an elimination of the "cut-throat" competition, which tends to keep profits below a "reasonable" level. But neither private initiative in waste nor public enterprise in military ventures seemed to Veblen adequate to offset the surplus productivity of machine industry, particularly when account was taken of the tendency of modern business organization to promote an accumulation of savings in a relatively few hands. The only refuge from chronic depression, barring providential intervention, then, is "thoroughgoing coalition in those lines of business in which coalition is practicable." And even the latter is not too hopefully viewed:

> . . . The great coalitions and the business maneuvers connected with them have the effect of adding to the large fortunes of the greater businessmen; which adds to the large incomes that cannot be spent in consumptive expenditures; which accelerates the increase of investments; which brings competition if there is a chance of it; which tends to bring on depression, in the manner already indicated. The great coalitions, therefore seem to carry the seed of this malady of competition, and this evil consequence can accordingly be avoided only on the basis of so comprehensive and rigorous a coalition of business concerns as shall wholly exclude competition, even in the face of any conceivable amount of new capital seeking investment.[12]

While Veblen thus agrees with Marx about the strong tendencies at work in capitalism making for economic concentration, he holds very different views

[11] Veblen, *The Theory of Business Enterprise*, p. 121.
[12] *Ibid.*, pp. 125–126.

about the increasing misery of the working class from those propounded by the "father of scientific socialism." Indeed, he disagreed with Marx as to the facts about the conditions of the "underlying population" and the ultimate destiny of capitalism. As to the former, writing in 1906–07, he stated:

> . . . the result of the last few decades of our industrial development has been to increase greatly the creature comforts within the reach of the average human being. And, decidedly, the result has been an amelioration of the lot of the less favored in a relatively greater degree than that of those economically more fortunate. The claim that the system of competition has proved an engine for making the rich richer and the poor poorer has the fascination of an epigram; but if its meaning is that the lot of the average, of the masses of humanity in civilized life, is worse today as measured in the means of livelihood, than it was twenty, or fifty, or a hundred years ago, then it is farcical.[13]

While the poor were not absolutely poorer, the existing system according to Veblen, by fostering emulation and "keeping up appearances," does create a subjective feeling on the part of the industrious poor that they are "relatively poor." This unrest, Veblen felt, was inseparable from the institution of private property. The exploitation of the underlying populace in his view takes the form of diverting their energies into irrational, non-economic forms such as wasteful, conspicuous consumption or to patriotic, militaristic objectives. The business interests, he says, urge an aggressive national policy and businessmen direct it. The value of such a warlike business policy in diverting social unrest is very clear because such a policy "makes for a conservative animus on the part of the populace." Such an outcome is not surprising to Veblen because he believed that "representative government means, chiefly, representation of business interests."

The fourth broad consequence of technological change in the Veblenian analysis has to do with its psychological results or what Veblen called the "cultural incidence of the machine process." By this Veblen referred to his theory that the dominant influence on people's values and attitudes are the habits of mind induced by their daily employment. Thus, he believed that the workers, engineers, and physical scientists were developing technological habits of mind growing out of their matter-of-fact manipulation of nature and industrial processes markedly different from those of persons engaged in pecuniary employments. Whereas the latter tend to think in terms of the archaic business metaphysic of private property, natural liberty, etc., the technicians are allegedly more inclined to conceptualize in more scientific, cause-and-effect terms and are more concerned with productivity than with profit. We see this aspect of Veblen's thought emphasized in his remarks about the trade unions when he says, "The pervading characteristic of the trade-union animus is the denial of the received natural rights dogmas wherever the mechanical standardization of modern industry traverses the working of these received natural rights. . . ." While the trade unions show

---

[13] *The Place of Science in Modern Civilization* (New York: B. W. Huebsch, 1919), p. 391.

many survivals of the pecuniary habit of thought, significantly they tend, he thinks, to meet their problems by "extra-legal methods" because they are endeavoring under the compulsion of the machine process to construct an institutional scheme consonant with the exigencies of that process.

So too he attributes the "socialistic disaffection" of modern times to the discipline of the machine process, particularly as it affects those who are selected because of mechanical aptitude or training to work in the more mechanized industries or employments. At the turn of the present century, Veblen pictured "modern Christendom" as being at a crossroads between two conflicting cultural destinies, the one embodying the cultural discipline of the machine process, which tended toward a socialistic republic, the other leading in the direction of a warlike, dynastic state based on status, fealty, and arbitrary command. Aware as he was that past societies had often collapsed under the weight of "imbecile institutions," Veblen was usually reluctant to predict the outcome of the process of cultural drift. Yet, in the closing passage of *The Theory of Business Enterprise*, he clearly indicated his belief that the unregulated capitalism of the last quarter of the nineteenth century could not endure: ". . . It seems possible to say this much, that the full dominion of business enterprise is necessarily a transitory dominion. It stands to lose in the end whether the one or the other of the two divergent cultural tendencies wins, because it is incompatible with the ascendancy of either."[14]

Veblen's general theory of the economic process, as delineated in *The Theory of Business Enterprise*, contains several themes and types of analysis. It will serve our purposes in this Part to concentrate our evaluation of the validity of his theory upon his main hypotheses about the causes and consequences of capitalistic economic growth as set out in that work:

1. The inadequacy of the "net product of industry" for the purposes of capital formation; his basic conception of the growth process.
2. The nature of the movement toward economic concentration; its irresistible tendency.
3. The tendency toward "chronic" depression.
4. The nature of labor unrest and of the trade-unionism and socialism growing out of it.
5. The tendency of business politics to promote patriotism and militarism as a solution of the "social problem."
6. The reasons for the transitory character of "the full dominion of business enterprise."

After surveying the main directions of economic growth during these years in the next chapter, we shall consider the first three hypotheses above in Chapter 21 and the last three in Chapter 22.

---

[14] Veblen, *The Theory of Business Enterprise*, p. 189.

Chapter 20

MAJOR DIMENSIONS OF ECONOMIC GROWTH, 1897–1918

THE CONTINUING ORGANIZATIONAL REVOLUTION

The two decades after 1897 saw a continuation of the trend toward the consolidation of business which had started with the trust movement of the 1880's. It witnessed as well other major structural changes in the economy which substantiate the view that America was coming of age industrially in these years. In Rostow's terms, the economy was entering the post-maturity stage in the sense that a period of massive capital formation during the preceding years had given the nation an increasingly productive capital plant and an incomparable national railroad network which enabled the American businessman to operate on a continental scale. Technological changes holding forth the promise of economies of scale, further development of the capital market, the appearance of aggressive financial promoters, and a favorable political climate facilitated and induced the consolidation of business on a national scale. The first merger movement of the years 1897–1904 reflected the buoyancy and confidence that characterized America at the turn of the century. When the consolidation movement so conspicuous in the opening years of the century had run its course, the structure of the national economy was radically transformed. Corporate capitalism was greatly advanced, and the position of the small, independent businessman irrevocably changed. President Woodrow Wilson, later in the period, expressed the significance of this corporate revolution in the following manner:

> Yesterday, and ever since history began, men were related to one another as individuals. To be sure there were the family, the Church, and the State, institutions which associated men in certain wide articles of relationship. But in the ordinary concerns of life, in the ordinary work, in the daily round, men dealt freely and directly with one another. Today the every day relationships of men are largely with great impersonal concerns, with organizations, not with other individual men.
>
> Now this is nothing short of a new social age, a new era of human relationships, a new stage setting for the drama of life. . . .[1]

[1] W. Wilson, *The New Freedom* (Garden City, N.Y.: Doubleday, Page and Co., 1918), pp. 6–7.

These years were not only to see the emergence of larger business firms but also to witness the organization of more workers in trade unions and of farmers in marketing cooperatives. Businessmen cooperated in new ways through the trade associations that came into existence in larger numbers during the years of World War I. Before and during those hostilities the federal government began to intervene in the economy in new and different ways. Over these same years, our cities were growing in population much more rapidly than the countryside, so in many respects the American way of life was becoming a more collective one than it had been in the more individualistic, free and easy years of the early nineteenth century.

THE GROWTH OF THE GROSS NATIONAL PRODUCT
AND ITS INDUSTRIAL DISTRIBUTION

As in earlier parts of this book, we use the estimates of national income to provide us with an overall picture of the improvement in the nation's material plane of living in these years, keeping in mind the qualifications we have previously mentioned about such statistics. The figures in Table 1 are those of the gross national product as originally estimated by Simon Kuznets, expressed in constant 1929 dollars. The figures of per capita gross national product show an increase over these years from $462 in 1897 to $711 in 1918.

TABLE 1

Gross National Product of the United States, 1897–1918[a]
(Commerce Concept, Derived from Kuznets Estimates)
(Millions of 1929 dollars)

Year	Total GNP	Per Capita GNP	Year	Total GNP	Per Capita GNP
1897	$33,327	$462	1908	$49,790	$561
1898	34,068	464	1909	55,893	618
1899	37,172	497	1910	56,499	611
1900	38,197	502	1911	58,312	621
1901	42,587	549	1912	61,058	640
1902	43,004	543	1913	63,475	653
1903	45,123	560	1914	58,636	592
1904	44,123	537	1915	60,424	601
1905	47,870	571	1916	68,870	675
1906	53,420	625	1917	67,264	651
1907	54,277	624	1918	73,361	711

[a] Source: J. W. Kendrick, *Productivity Trends In The United States* (Princeton, N.J.: Princeton University Press, 1961), pp. 296–297. © Copyright 1961 by the National Bureau of Economic Research. Reprinted by permission of Princeton University Press. Dept. of Commerce, *Historical Statistics of the United States: 1789–1945* (Washington: U.S. Government Printing Office, 1948), p. 26.

On the whole, the increase in GNP was more rapid in the earlier years of the period than in the later years.

Kuznets finds the explanation of this retardation in the rate of increase of the national income, at least tentatively, in the slowing down of the rate of growth of reproducible capital (as compared with the rates of the 1880's and 1890's) and in the lower average rate of utilization of the labor supply as a result of the reduction of working hours.[2] This is, as he modestly says, a subject that deserves further study.

We can obtain some broad picture of the overall changes in the principal sectors of the economy in these years by analyzing the industrial origins of the national income. Martin's estimates of the percentages of private production income originating in the various sectors are set forth in Table 2.

TABLE 2

The Industrial Origins of Private Production Income, 1879, 1900, and 1920, in Percentages[a]

Year	Agriculture	Mining	Manufacturing	Contract Construction	Transport Communication	Trade	Service	Misc., Finan.
1879	21%	2%	15%	5%	14%	18%	17%	9%
1900	21	3	20	4	12	19	12	9
1920	17	4	28	4	13	16	9	9

[a] Source: Calculated from data in U.S. Bureau of the Census, *Historical Statistics of the United States, 1789–1945* (Washington, D.C.: U.S. Government Printing Office, 1948), p. 14. Private production income differs from national income in that it excludes incomes paid by government or earned abroad.

The most outstanding shifts in the sources of private income revealed by this table are the increasing importance of manufacturing between 1900 and 1920 and the continued decline of agriculture as a source of the nation's income. A similar picture emerges from analysis of the distribution of the labor force in 1900 and 1920. In the former year, 49.8 per cent of the total labor force was engaged in agriculture, fisheries, and forestry; by 1920, the percentage so engaged had fallen to 26.3 per cent of the total. The percentage of the labor force employed in manufacturing increased from 21.5 per cent to 26.2 per cent.

As these figures suggest, the United States in the two decades from 1899 to 1919 experienced an impressive growth in its economy, though the rate of increase was not spectacular compared to other periods, if one excepts the war years 1914–19. During these years, Faulkner points out that "the number of wage earners almost doubled, wages increased almost fivefold, and the value of products almost sixfold. . . ."[3] Production, in fact, doubled in volume

[2] S. Kuznets, *National Income, a Summary of Findings* (New York: National Bureau of Economic Research, Inc., 1946), p. 60.

[3] H. V. Faulkner, *The Decline of Laissez Faire, 1897–1917* (New York: Holt, Rinehart and Winston, 1951), p. 115.

over the course of the two decades from 1899 to 1919 and, in fact, increased twice as rapidly as the population.

THE LEADING SECTORS OF GROWTH

While aggregate measures of production indicate the extent of industrial growth, we need to break the totals down to determine the directions of the expansion in more detail. Table 3, which presents the five leading industries as rated by value of product in the years 1900, 1914, and 1919, is instructive for this purpose.

TABLE 3

Rank of Leading Industries, 1900, 1914, and 1919[a]

	Rank	Industry	Value of Product (In thousands)
1900			
	1	Iron and steel, steel works and rolling mills	$ 803,968
	2	Slaughtering and meat packing	790,253
	3	Foundry and machine shop products	644,991
	4	Lumber and timber products	566,622
	5	Flour mill and gristmill products	560,719
1914			
	1	Slaughtering and meat packing	1,651,965
	2	Iron and steel, steel works and rolling mills	918,665
	3	Flour mill and gristmill products	877,680
	4	Foundry and machine shop products	866,545
	5	Lumber and timber products	715,310
1919			
	1	Slaughtering and meat packing	4,246,291
	2	Iron and steel, steel works and rolling mills	2,828,902
	3	Automobiles	2,387,903
	4	Foundry and machine products	2,289,251
	5	Cotton goods	2,125,272

[a] Source: H. U. Faulkner, *The Decline of Laissez Faire, 1897–1917* (New York: Holt, Rinehart and Winston, 1951), Appendix, pp. 416–417.

While statistics of the value of the product show that slaughtering and meat packing was the leading industry after 1904, it is important to note that metal industries by 1919 made up three of the first five. In these years, the nation stepped up the mechanization of manufacturing remarkably and devoted relatively more attention to the processing of raw materials than to their production. The output of manufactured goods increased at a rate almost double that of the production of raw materials. In the years before World War I, growth of production was due largely to the growing exploitation of mineral resources and the increased volume of fabricated goods into which raw mineral products entered. The growing importance of minerals in American industry in these years is reflected in the statistics of the growth of physical output. The following industries grew most rapidly in the years 1899 to 1909 in the order named: iron and steel products, printing and publishing, paper products, petroleum and coal products, chemical products, and tobacco products. Between 1909 and 1919 the fastest growing industries were transportation equipment, petroleum and coal products, chemical products, tobacco products, and printing and publishing. Mills provides us with a more specific list of the most rapidly growing industries for the years 1890–1914: automobiles, including bodies and parts, beet sugar, manufactured ice, manufactured gas, refining of petroleum, fertilizers, explosives, salt, canning and preserving, paper and wood pulp.[4]

The automobile industry was in its great formative period in those years— the heroic age of its founders. Its meteoric rise can be measured in terms of its rank in the value of products of American industry: 150th in 1899, 77th in 1904, 21st in 1909, 7th in 1914, and 2nd in 1919; by 1925, it reached first place in terms of this criterion.[5] Table 4 provides us with the statistics of its output in this period.

Fabricant, noting that the automobile industry increased its output at a phenomenal rate over the years 1899–1937, states that in the latter year its

TABLE 4

Output of the U.S. Automobile Industry, 1904, 1909, 1919[a]
(Quantity in thousands)

	1904	1909	1919
Passenger cars:			
Open	19	117	1,400
Closed			{ 157
Public conveyances	b	5	{ 2
Trucks	0.4	3	120
All other types	2.6	2	209

[a] Source: S. Fabricant, *The Output of Manufacturing Industries, 1899–1937* (New York: National Bureau of Economic Research, 1937), p. 303. © Copyright 1940 by the National Bureau of Economic Research.

[b] Data not available.

[4] S. Fabricant, *The Output of Manufacturing Industries, 1899–1937* (New York: National Bureau of Economic Research, 1937), pp. 60–61; F. C. Mills, *Economic Tendencies in the United States* (New York: National Bureau of Economic Research, 1932), p. 29 as quoted in Faulkner, *The Decline of Laissez Faire*, p. 118.

[5] A. D. Chandler, Jr., *Giant Enterprise, Ford, General Motors and the Automobile Industry* (New York: Harcourt, Brace and World, 1964), p. 5.

output was 1,800 times as great as it had been in the former year. ". . . In the first decade (1899–1909) it increased 3,500 per cent, in the next almost 1,500 per cent, and in the third (1919–1929) about 250 per cent. . . . The speed with which an important industry can attain maturity in our economic system cannot be illustrated more strikingly than here."[6]

Although we know that the automobile industry was one of the fastest growing industries of this period, it is well to see its expansion in the context of the economy's growth as a whole. Fabricant's statistics on the value added by the automobile and the other transportation industries in relation to the total value of manufacturing output in this country for these years is of interest in this connection (see Table 5). It is important to realize that remark-

TABLE 5

Value Added by the Transportation Industries as a Per Cent of the Value Added by All Manufacturing Industries, 1899–1929[a]

	1899	1909	1919	1929
Industry				
Automobiles (incl. bodies and parts)	0.6 %	1.47%	4.88%	6.66%
Carriages, wagons, and sleds	1.31	.78	.16	.03
Cars, railroad (not elsewhere classified)	.70	.61	.81	.35
Locomotives, not elsewhere made)	.33	.21	.36	.10
Totals	2.40	3.07	6.21	7.14

[a] Source: S. Fabricant, *The Output of Manufacturing Industries, 1899–1937*, p. 97. © Copyright 1940 by the National Bureau of Economic Research.

able as the growth of the automobile industry was in the period under consideration, it did not attain its full maturity until the 1920's. The above table prevents us from exaggerating its role in the dynamic growth of the economy in these years; we see that by 1919 the value added by the automobile industry was less than 5 per cent of the value added by all manufacturing industries. Still, we must keep in mind the impetus given by the expansion of the automotive industry and the investment and growth it induced in other sectors of the economy. The increased demand for automobiles provided a derived demand for the raw materials necessary for their manufacture; petroleum, glass, rubber tires, steel, and many other products were greatly stimulated by the remarkable rise of the motor car industry in this period. These secondary effects of the industry's expansion are not reflected, of course, in the statistics of Table 5. It is relevant here to note Schumpeter's judgment of the place of the automobile industry in the dynamics of this period. ". . . This industry," he wrote, "though not a starter, yet one of the most important

[6] S. Fabricant, *The Output of Manufacturing Industries*, p. 301.

carriers of this Kondratieff, revealed its full meaning for the economic process and for civilization—it has altered the style and the outlook on life probably more than any prophet ever did—in the downgrade span after the war [World War I], exactly as cotton textiles asserted themselves fully in the downgrade of their Kondratieff. In the prosperity it did not get so far."[7] Incidentally, Schumpeter's concept of "creative destruction" was beautifully illustrated in the effects of the rise of the automobile industry upon carriage manufacture, as Table 5 indicates. The effect on the manufacture of railroad equipment was not at first so marked, but by 1929 it also had experienced a substantial relative decline.

Among the industries providing raw materials or essential supplementary goods for the automobile, none was affected more than petroleum by the advent of the motor car. The output of the oil industry went from 60 million to almost 356 million barrels between 1897 and 1918, and gasoline, which formerly had been a drug on the market, quickly took the place of kerosene as the industry's most valuable product. The rate of growth of petroleum refining, Fabricant found, was exceeded in the years 1899–1937 only by the automobile and cigarette industries.

Another beneficiary of the auto's rise was the cement industry, because as the nation took to wheels, roads had to be built, and cement production sky-rocketed. Technological innovation aided this industry to capitalize on its opportunity in a very opportune way; the rotating kiln, introduced about 1899, enabled the cheaper, more standardized Portland cement to replace the natural product.

One of the principal growth sectors in the economy in these years was electric light and power. Indeed, Schumpeter regarded this industry as the starter of the third Kondratieff and considered it to be, along with auto-mobiles and chemicals, the backbone of that long wave in economic growth that developed after 1897. The groundwork for the revolutionary expansion of the electric power industry had been laid in the previous decades. It was not until 1882 that Thomas A. Edison built the first central power station in New York, and a few years later Westinghouse, Stanley, and Tesla developed the principle of the alternating current and of a reliable AC motor. Hydroelectric operations had been started on a large scale in 1895 when the Niagara Falls plant went into use. Shortly after George Westinghouse, having purchased the rights from the English inventor of the compound reaction steam engine, began to build steam turbines capable of generating electricity at a low cost. His new turbines made the massive reciprocating engines that had been built for the New York subway system obsolete within three years of their installa-tion. Numerous American municipalities were making the transfer from gas to electricity for illumination in these years. More important, especially in the second decade of the period, was the rapid substitution by manufacturers of purchased electric power for other forms of energy. "In 1899, the amount of

[7] J. A. Schumpeter, *Business Cycles* (New York: McGraw-Hill Book Co., 1929), Vol. 1, p. 415.

power purchased and applied through electric motors represented but 1.8 per cent of the industrial power machinery in the United States; in 1919, the percentage had grown to 31.7. . . ."[8] As a consequence of these developments, the production of electric power by utility companies, public and private, soared from 2,507 million to 25,438 million kilowatt-hours between 1902 and 1917. The number of establishments manufacturing electrical machinery and supplies grew from 851 in 1899 to 1,404 in 1919, wage earners in the industry from 42,013 to 212,374 and capital from $83,660,000 to $857,855,000.[9] Exports of electrical machinery in the years 1904–19 grew almost eightfold.

A related industry making great progress during this period was rapid transit in the form of street railways in the burgeoning cities. Frank J. Sprague had installed the first overhead power wire and trolley in Richmond, Virginia in 1887, and his innovation was widely imitated in the succeeding years. The suburban transit lines being built in these years also made possible another new phenomenon on the American scene—suburbia; Tuxedo, New York was one of the first such communities in the nation.[10]

Still another industry with an above-average rate of growth in these decades was the chemical industry. While it is true that the American industry was greatly stimulated by the take-over of some 4,500 patents of the German dyestuffs industry during World War I, substantial progress had been made in heavy chemicals before 1917, particularly in the manufacture of sulphuric acid, ammonia, and alkalis. The expansion of the Solvay process in the 1890's and the development of the electrolytic process after cheap electric power had become available around 1900 greatly promoted the production of the basic alkalis. Thanks to these and other technical improvements, the aggregate value of the chemical industry's product rose from $48 million in 1899 to $158 million in 1914; the industry's growth up to 1919 was even more impressive. Fabricant's studies show that the chemical industry's physical output increased 69 per cent between 1899 and 1919 and 64 per cent in the following decade.

There were other new industries that emerged in these years but did not reach maturity until after World War I. Among these were aluminum, rayon products, and airplanes. There were still other fields that continued to extend the growth started in earlier years. For example, railroad construction, which had played so crucial a part in the expansive growth of the economy in the late nineteenth century, was decelerating in its rate of expansion. A last installment of some 70,000 miles of track was constructed between 1897 and 1913, but thereafter, though the expenditures of this giant industry for maintenance and replacement of equipment were immense, the industry did not have as great a dynamic influence on the economy as it had in the past. In

---

[8] Faulkner, *The Decline of Laissez Faire*, p. 124.

[9] *Ibid.*, p. 127.

[10] R. C. Wood, *Suburbia, Its People and Their Politics* (Boston: Houghton Mifflin, 1959).

fact, by the 1880's the city had become a more important market for the iron and steel industry than the railroads.[11] In 1887, Andrew Carnegie shifted the production of his Homestead Works from rails to structural steel—a decision symbolic of the change occurring in the demand for the product of this key industry. The cities, with their many new office buildings, skyscrapers, apartments, and factories, required vast quantities of steel as well as of other construction materials. Chandler has estimated that between 1890 and 1910 the size of the urban market doubled.[12] This shift in the geographic pattern of demand necessitated changes in steel and other industries and spurred important developments in the organization and conduct of business in these years.

The iron and steel industry, a great bellwether of the American economy, experienced convulsive changes as well. Its output surged from 7,157,000 tons in 1897 to over 31 million tons in 1913 and then during the years of the first great World War climbed to 44,462,000 tons (1918). Drastic changes in the location of the industry took place as it shifted closer to the source of its ores and came to prefer manufacturing locations in the Ohio valley; equally challenging were the rise of new companies, new technologies, and the innovation of government control during the 1917–18 hostilities. Some of these subjects will be discussed more fully below.

The mining industry also underwent a transformation in this period. Indexes of production indicate that it grew at a more rapid rate than either manufacturing or agriculture. For example, using 1899 = 100, the index for the physical output of metals for 1917 was 259, for fuels, 276, and for other non-metals, 281, resulting in a total index for all mining of 268. The comparative figure for manufacturing was 257 and for agriculture, 124.[13] The explanation for this higher rate of growth in mining is largely traceable to the increased exploitation of petroleum and natural gas and to the larger quantities of building stone and crushed rock used in highway construction. The years after 1897 saw a great increase in the mechanization of mining, a willingness to exploit low grade ores, and a good deal of labor trouble about which more will be said later.

The two decades from 1899 to 1919 were one of the rare periods of prosperity that American farmers have enjoyed. Indeed, these years later came to be regarded as a golden age of American agriculture, and it was not without reason that New Deal farm legislation established its famous parities in terms of farm prices in the years 1909–13. The restoration of prosperity to the farm after the devastating depression of farm prices in the late nineteenth century was attributable to a number of factors, principally the reversal in the trend of wholesale prices attendant upon the increased production of gold, the maintenance of exports, and the increased demand for foodstuffs with the

[11] A. D. Chandler, Jr., "Entrepreneurial Opportunity in Nineteenth Century America," *Explorations in Entrepreneurial History*, Second Series (Fall, 1963), Vol. 1, No. 1, p. 117.
[12] *Ibid.*
[13] As cited in Faulkner, *The Decline of Laissez Faire*, pp. 150–151; H. Barger and S. H. Schurr, *The Mining Industries, 1899–1939* (New York: National Bureau of Economic Research, 1944), pp. 13–58.

growth of the urban population. In any case, there could be no doubting the reality of the change in the farmer's position in these years. Between 1900 and 1920 the value of farms and crops increased fourfold and the prices of farm products almost threefold; on the other hand, crop production during the same period increased less than 50 per cent. Clearly, supply and demand conditions were very favorable for the farmer, and his terms of trade with the rest of the community were decidedly improved. The salient trends in American agriculture for these years are shown in Table 6.

TABLE 6

Trends in American Agriculture, 1899, 1914, and 1919[a]
(1909–1913 = 100)

Year	Land Values	Crop Prices	Livestock Prices	Crop Value per Acre
1899	45	—	95	57
1914	111	101	112	103
1919	202	221	212	323

[a] Source: *Yearbook of the Department of Agriculture,* 1921, p. 787 as presented in Faulkner, *The Decline of Laissez Faire,* p. 322.

Though the improvement in the financial status of the farmer in the pre-World War I years is evident in the above statistics, it is apparent also that the war itself was a great boon to the farm regions. Responding to the slogan that "Food will win the war," American farmers increased the acreage under cultivation by no less than 77 million acres in the decade 1910–20. As the picture, "The Plow That Broke the Plains" so graphically showed, millions of acres of the semi-arid Great Plains were brought under cultivation to produce additional wheat. Urged on by organizations, financial aid, guaranteed prices (e.g., $2.20 a bushel for wheat), purchase of tractors, seed, and standardization of methods, the farmers increased output prodigiously in response to the abnormal wartime demand. It was a fabulous type of prosperity, which too soon after the war turned to deep depression.

The upsurge in farm output in these years was concomitant with further geographic changes in the major belts of production: wheat moved westward into the West North Central states as "dry farming" and hard winter wheat made possible cultivation in drier areas; cotton production expanded further in the Southwest, and the dairy belt began to assume its present location in Wisconsin, New York, Minnesota, and in regions around the main urban centers of the nation. Accompanying these changes was a vast move toward mechanization of farming, spurred on by the shortage of manpower during the Great War and the availability of the versatile gasoline engine. Soon tractors were replacing horses and mules, and automobiles and trucks, as Table 7 shows, were carrying the farmer and his produce to town.

TABLE 7

Power Units on the American Farm, 1910–19[a]

Year	Tractors	Trucks	Automobiles
1910	1,000	0	50,000
1914	17,000	15,000	343,000
1917	51,000	60,000	966,000
1919	158,000	111,000	1,760,000

[a] As adapted by Faulkner, *The Decline of Laissez Faire*, p. 332 from G. Barger and H. H. Lansberg, *American Agriculture, 1899–1939* (New York: National Bureau of Economic Research, Inc., 1941), p. 204.

THE CHANGING STRUCTURE OF PRODUCTION

The economic changes we have been describing in terms of the rise and fall of particular industries reflect a basic change taking place in the American economy in these years toward greater mechanization of production and the output of a larger volume of durable consumer goods. Several statisticians have revealed the main outlines of these shifts. Frederick Mills showed that for the years 1901–13 the average annual rate of increase of the physical output of nondurable goods (raw and unprocessed) was 2.5 per cent, semi-durable goods, 2.6 per cent, and durable goods, 4.6 per cent.[14] Simon Kuznets' figures depict the dawn of the age of consumer goods more clearly, as Table 8 shows. (Kuznets himself, it must be admitted, is cautious about the

TABLE 8

National Income, Percentage Distribution between Flow of Goods to Consumers and Net Capital Formation, 1889–1928[a]
(Percentages based on 1929 Prices)

Decade	Flow of Goods to Consumers	Net Capital Formation
1889–98	83.8%	16.2%
1894–03	85.2	14.8
1899–08	86.4	13.2
1904–13	86.9	13.1
1909–18	87.0	13.0
1914–23	88.6	11.4
1919–28	89.8	10.2

[a] Source: Adapted from S. Kuznets, *National Income, A Summary of Findings* (New York: National Bureau of Economic Research, Inc., 1946), p. 53. © Copyright 1961 by Princeton University Press for the National Bureau of Economic Research.

[14] F. C. Mills, *Economic Tendencies*, p. 23 as quoted in Faulkner, *The Decline of Laissez Faire*, p. 117.

significance of these figures, but he does state that "there was also some tendency toward a rise in the share of consumer durable commodities" as part of the total flow of commodities to consumers.)[15] Shaw's analysis of the changing composition of the value of commodity output for this period is the most satisfactory available. One can see in the statistics of Table 9 that while the consumer durable goods began to grow in importance in the years 1909–18, the biggest gain in their output came in the 1920's. Significant also in this table is the slow but steady rise in the share of producer durable goods

TABLE 9

Value of Finished Commodities in Producers' 1913 Prices[a]
(Percentage shares for each decade)

Commodity Class	1899–1908	1909–18	1919–29
Consumer Perishable	58.7%	55.1%	47.7%
Consumer Semidurable	19.5	19.2	18.9
Consumer Durable	10.0	12.9	20.2
Producer Durable	11.9	12.8	13.2

[a] Source: W. H. Shaw, *Value of Commodity Output since 1869* (New York: National Bureau of Economic Research, Inc., 1947), p. 17. © Copyright 1947 by the National Bureau of Economic Research.

as mechanization increased the complement of capital goods used in the production process.

We gain a very valuable perspective on the whole process of capital formation in these years from some estimates of Simon Kuznets that we have set out in Table 10. These show us the relative part played in this period by the major sectors of the economy in the process of net capital formation. We can see the huge amounts of capital formation involved in urban construction in all its forms, residential and commercial, the large sums too that went into building capital plant in the transportation and public utility enterprises of the day, in addition to the new additions to capital plant, inventories, etc. in the manufacturing and other sectors. The need for such large amounts of capital in this period underscores the importance of the financial institutions that had the task of marshalling the nation's savings and providing the credit for so dynamic an economy; the changes taking place in finance during these years were equally as momentous as those occurring in industry.

[15] Kuznets, *National Income* . . . , p. 54. Kuznets also notes the rise in the shares of producer durable equipment and net additions to claims against foreign countries rose over the period from 1869–78 to 1929–38. On this subject see H. G. Vatter, "Has There Been a Twentieth Century Consumer Durables Revolution?" *The Journal of Economic History* (March, 1967), pp. 1–16.

TABLE 10

Net Capital Formation in the United States for 1900–1912[a]
Sector Estimates (In millions of dollars)

Sector	
Agriculture	$ 4,677
Mining	1,855
Manufacturing	8,133
Non-farm residential construction	14,995
Government construction	6,045
Transportation and other public utilities	12,005
Steam railroads	5,212
Electric railroads	1,995

[a] Source: S. Kuznets, *Capital in the American Economy* Table R–35, pp. 610–611. © Copyright 1961 by Princeton University Press for the National Bureau of Economic Research.

THE RISE OF FINANCIAL CAPITALISM

The financial structure and organizations of the nation at the beginning of this period had been profoundly affected by the railroads. Their financing had contributed greatly to the centralizing and institutionalizing of the investment market in New York City in the late nineteenth century.[16] To the demand for funds of this capital intensive industry were now added the needs of the new consolidations in industry that the financial promoters of the day offered a stock-hungry public. J. P. Morgan and Co. had assumed a new role in control of railroads as a result of the part it played in the refinancing and reorganization of many of the nation's lines in the late 1880's. It and other investment bankers continued to maintain a controlling interest in these notoriously wobbly enterprises and also extended their influence over a host of commercial banks, trust, and insurance companies. The far-flung ramifications of the Morgan, Rockefeller, Kuhn, Loeb, and other major banking firms' influence and control over the American financial structure were so great as to lend support to the view that the financier had supplanted the industrial capitalist as the key decision-maker in many of the nation's most important enterprises.[17] The Pujo Committee of the House of Representatives in 1913 concluded that a "money trust" existed in the nation in the sense that there

[16] A. D. Chandler, Jr. makes this point well in his essay, "Entrepreneurial Opportunity in Nineteenth Century America," *Explorations in Entrepreneurial History*, second series (Fall, 1963), Vol. 1, No. 1, p. 115.

[17] See G. W. Edwards, *The Evolution of Finance Capitalism* (New York: Longmans, Green and Co., 1938), *passim;* L. Corey, *The House of Morgan* (New York: G. Howard Watt, 1930).

was "an established and well defined identity and community of interest between a few leaders of finance" and "a vast and growing concentration of control of money and credit in the hands of a comparatively few men. . . ." Such was the revolution in finance brought about by the emergence of giant railroad and industrial enterprises in late nineteenth century America. But apart from these radical changes in the financial habits of the people, which have received so much journalistic attention, how was the vast expansion in industrial production financed?

As in the past, even in these years there was an immense amount of self-financing of new enterprises and of expansion of those not so new. The early years of the automobile industry offer a prime example of this type of internal financing. Henry Ford, in particular, plowed the greater part of the huge profits of his enterprise back into expansion. The bankers of that day avoided the risks of the "horseless carriage," so the automobile pioneers had to develop a method of sale that minimized their need for credit.

The large-scale urban construction of these years was financed by the capital accumulations of the institutional savers such as the savings banks and insurance companies. In 1900, the former had $2.6 billion and the latter, $1.7 billion in funds available for investment in farm and urban mortgages. The trust companies, organized so feverishly in the first decade of the new century, also played an important part in this type of real estate financing.

The expansion in the banking system in the period 1897 to 1913 is shown in the statistics of Table 11. It will be noted that the national banks doubled in

TABLE 11

Banking Development in the United States, 1897–1913[a]
(Dollar amounts in millions)

	1897		1913	
	Number	Capital, Surplus, Undiv. Profits	Number	Capital, Surplus, Undiv. Profits
National	3,610	$966	7,473	$2,046
State	3,857	331	14,011	768
Trust cos.	251	196	1,515	1,027

[a] Source: W. J. Shultz and M. R. Caine, *Financial Development of the United States* (Englewood Cliffs, N.J.: Prentice-Hall, Inc., 1937), pp. 419, 469.

number and the state banks and trust companies had an even larger growth in numbers. As the figures on capital suggest, however, many of the state banks were small, rural institutions that survived in part because of their correspondent relations with larger institutions in the cities. In this period, the rural banks continued periodically to place their surplus funds with the large banks in New York City where this money was invested in the "call money" market.

This practice contributed greatly to the primacy of New York City as a financial center, but it had serious shortcomings from the standpoint of maintaining financial stability in the economy as a whole. It was to correct this element of instability in the nation's financial structure, among other reasons, that the Federal Reserve System was inaugurated in 1913. In the years 1913–17, the number of banks and the amount of their capital showed little increase, but the loans and deposits of the new Federal Reserve member banks expanded remarkably.

Manufacturing's need for capital was met in part by tapping the free savings of the nation through the stock market in ever larger draughts. As evidence of the trend, note that in 1898 only 20 industrials were listed on the New York Stock Exchange; in 1900, the number was 46 and in 1905 it had reached 85. Also listed were the securities of the new public utility trusts; the shares of the smaller trusts were traded in on the Curb.[18]

Public participation in the stock market during this period reached an all-time high in 1901. The feeling of financial euphoria at the time was commented upon by one commercial journal as follows: "The most serious part of the recent situation lay in its indications that the fever of speculation was spreading to all the ranks of society. It was coming to be believed that the conditions underlying this market movement were so novel and unprecedented that old rules could no longer hold. . . . It is notorious that for weeks the smaller brokers' offices and 'bucket shops' have been crowded with people of moderate means who were speculating with all the money that they could control for a rise in stocks."[19] In more than a metaphorical sense, the frontier had shifted from the dusty horizons of the Great Plains to the rosy horizons of industry.

And there now appeared on the national scene a species of financier who made these horizons rosy indeed. The years 1898 to 1904 were the heyday of the professional promoters, those adept in the art of stock-watering about whom Andrew Carnegie used to say, "They throw cats and dogs together and call them elephants." There was Charles R. Flint, The "Father of the Trusts," with 24 consolidations to his credit; Judge William Moore and his brother James; Henry Rogers, William Rockefeller, Elkins, Widener, "Bet-a-Million" Gates, Reid, Morse, Addicks, and last, but not least, the tycoon of finance, J. P. Morgan. The extent of the consolidation movement in these years was later demonstrated by John Moody in his book, *The Truth about the Trusts;* of the 318 trusts listed by him, 98 with a total capitalization of over $1 billion had come into existence before 1898 and 234 with a capital of $6 billion were organized between 1898 and 1904. It was his estimate that by the latter year the trusts controlled fully two-fifths of the manufacturing capital of the nation. Whatever one's view of the benefit of this accomplishment for the nation,

[18] W. J. Schultz and M. R. Caine, *Financial Development of the United States* (Englewood Cliffs, N.J.: Prentice-Hall, Inc., 1937), p. 441.
[19] *The Commercial and Financial Chronicle* of May 11, 1901, as quoted in F. L. Allen, *Lords of Creation* (New York: Harper and Bros., 1935), pp. 53–54.

there is no denying that it was one of the major financial developments of
these years. We shall be concerned with analyzing the broader significance
and impact of this consolidation movement on the economy in the next
chapter.

TRENDS IN FOREIGN TRADE AND FINANCE

Foreign trade, as our previous chapters have pointed out, played a vital
part in the nineteenth century development of the American economy. Its
growth was rapid; in fact, in the years from 1830 to 1910 it doubled every
twenty years. Remarkable as this rapid growth was, the expansion of foreign
trade in the first two decades of the twentieth century was even more accelerated. Our annual exports of commodities, for example, increased in value
from $1,394,483,000 in 1900 to $2,465,884,000 in 1913—an increase of 76
per cent; imports went from $849,941,000 to $1,813,008,000 over the same
years—an increase of 113 per cent.[20] This more rapid increase in the rate of
imports than exports was primarily due to the development of manufacturing
and to the consequent need for more raw materials from abroad. The expansion of our exports during this period was difficult because of the nationalistic, protective measures of the major European powers who had established
themselves in many foreign markets before our businessmen made the
attempt. But the larger American corporations of this era with their ability to
finance export organizations, branch houses, advertising and the like, were
quite successful in overcoming these obstacles. The federal government was of
assistance in this field also through the enterprise of the State Department's
consular offices and the Bureau of Foreign Commerce, which was first established under its jurisdiction in 1897. The Department of Commerce and Labor
was established in 1903 with the purpose, among others, of promoting foreign
commerce; a separate Department of Commerce was set up by Congress in
1913.

An important change took place in the composition of American foreign
trade during these years. Previously, our exports had consisted to a large
extent of such staples as wheat, cotton, and other agricultural products. Now
with the maturing of American industry, manufacturing goods began to bulk
larger in our export trade. The decline in agricultural exports was particularly
noticeable in these years in foodstuffs. Even though food prices were rising,
food exports declined in value from $545,474,000 in 1900 to $502,094,000 in
1913; percentagewise, they fell from 39.8 per cent of total exports to 20.7 per
cent over the same period. Wheat exports, for example, fell from 102 million
bushels in 1900 to less than 47 million bushels in 1910.[21] The decline of food
exports was such that by 1913, iron and steel products were second only to

[20] Faulkner, *The Decline of Laissez Faire*, pp. 52–53.
[21] Faulkner, *The Decline of Laissez Faire*, p. 55.

raw cotton in value as an export. Over all, we can summarize the trend by noting that in 1900 over 60 per cent of our exports were agricultural; by 1913, however, the products of the farm and factory were about the same in value in our export trade.

An equally important shift was taking place in the United States's position in international finance in the opening part of this period, which resulted finally during the years of World War I in our becoming a creditor nation. Whereas Europe's surplus of savings had formerly financed a substantial part of our capital formation, by the end of the century a large share of European capital was being invested in the exploitation of newer countries, such as the nations of South America and Africa, and in Canada and Australia, where the rate of return was higher than in twentieth century United States. Indeed, by 1899, we were lending money to Europe; our total foreign investments totalled $500 million in that year, mostly in Mexican and Canadian property. In the first decade of the new century, Mexico, Germany, Sweden, and England herself borrowed through the American capital market. The reason for the latter action was that the English security market was temporarily disarranged by the Boer War; the talk of the United States becoming the world's banker proved illusory.

The most important form of American overseas finance in this pre-World War I period was direct investment rather than security purchases. For example, U.S. Steel bought iron mines in Cuba; International Harvester built plants in Canada, Russia, Germany, and France; the Vanderbilts acquired Canadian railroad lines; our oil interests invested heavily in Mexico. As one historian states, "The industrialist, not the investor, was the force behind the nascent dollar imperialism."

By far the most significant financial effect of World War I was the conversion of the United States from a debtor to a creditor nation. In 1914 we were indebted to Europe to the extent of $2–2.5 billion. During the war and for two years after, we loaned some $10,350 million to the Allied Powers. In addition to these inter-governmental loans, our favorable balance of trade in the pre-war years had permitted a considerable repatriation of American securities. With the end of war, London regained her place as a major center of world finance and the financiers and statesmen began to grapple with the complex issue of war indebtedness. The United States was now a creditor nation with all the responsibilities that went with this new financial status.

THE MOVEMENT OF POPULATION

The changes in American population, both quantitatively as well as qualitatively, were especially important for economic growth in these years. In fact, Faulkner states that "It may be safely asserted that no period was more significant in the history of American demography and population movements than the twenty years after 1897. . . ."[22] In these years there was a persistence of certain trends of the past, such as the decline in the rate of growth and a continued movement toward the west and the cities, but these trends now became "so strong as greatly to modify the distribution and the type of the American people." Not only were these population shifts of economic importance, but they aroused considerable political protest because of fears that the dominant ethnic groups in the nation would be submerged or that American labor would be injured.

The major features of the overall increase in the total population for these years are set forth in Table 12. It will be noted that while there is evidence of a declining percentage rate of increase, the decennial increase ran to many millions, with all that this implied for the size of the potential labor force and possible market demand for goods and services.

TABLE 12

Population Growth in the United States, 1890–1920[a]

Year	Population	Decennial Increase	Per Cent of Increase since Preceding Census
1890	62,947,714	12,791,931	25.5%
1900	75,994,575	13,046,861	20.7
1910	91,972,620	15,977,691	21.0
1920	105,710,620	13,733,354	14.9

[a] Source: U.S. Bureau of the Census, *Census Monograph No. 1* (Washington: Government Printing Office), p. 21, as reproduced in Faulkner, *The Decline of Laissez Faire*, p. 93.

The principal causes of this enormous increase in the population were natural growth and the remarkable wave of immigration that reached a high in these years. The total inflow of immigrants was higher than in any other similar period in our history. More than eight million foreigners came to these shores in the years 1900–09 and another five million in the period 1910–14. The peak of the movement was reached in 1907 when 1,385,000 entered the nation. The "new immigration" was so called because so many of the migrants came from southern and eastern Europe rather than from the north or west of that continent, as had been the case for so long before. The Slavs, Poles, Russian Jews, and others, fleeing from political persecution and the low standards of life of the old countries, added to the thousands already in the "ghettoes," the "little Italys," etc. in our growing cities. The greater ease of getting to America, thanks to improved transportation, and the prosperity that prevailed up until 1907 were the chief factors contributing to this massive influx of people. The inducements of employers seeking cheap labor and the offers of land promoters also contributed to the vast migration from the Old World.

[22] Faulkner, *The Decline of Laissez Faire*, p. 92.

Internally, there were continued large movements of restless Americans seeking "greener pastures," as agriculture, industry, and the extractive industries shifted the locale of their activities. One of the most important of these movements was the northward migration of the Negro from the South, especially notable during the years of World War I. Between 1910 and 1920, it is estimated that the Negro migration to the North and West registered a net gain of about 334,000. The cities were the lure for these Negroes, with their opportunities for more gainful employment and reduced discrimination; whereas in 1900, the percentage of urban Negroes was 22.7, in 1920 it was 34.

The urban condition was increasingly becoming the predominant one for all Americans in these years of rapid industrialization. One authority, writing in 1934, contends in fact that "at no time or place in the world's history has the phenomenon of city development been so rapid as in the United States during the last half century."[23] The relative rates of urban and rural growth in these years is clearly shown in Chart 1. In the nation as a whole, it is estimated that the proportion of the urban population to the total increased from 5 to 6 per cent each decade during the years from 1900 to 1920. Cities having populations of from 50,000 to 1,000,000 grew more rapidly than either the very largest or the very smallest. While the large cities expanded, the highest rate of growth seemed to be occurring already in the suburban or satellite communities rather than in the city proper or the central part of the metropolitan areas.

The quality of our human resources was being upgraded substantially in these years as the increasing personal and public investment in education was

CHART 1

*The Growth of Urban and Rural Population
in the United States, 1820–1930*[a]

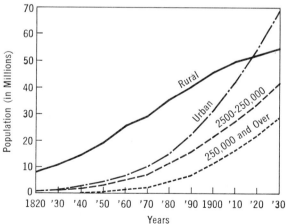

ª Source: Thompson and Whelpton, *Population Trends in
the United States* (New York: McGraw-Hill Book Company,
1956), p. 23.

[23] Faulkner, *The Decline of Laissez Faire*, p. 96.

reflected in the increased size of school enrollments and the degrees earned, as Table 13 clearly shows. Professor Kendrick, a leading student of productivity in the American economy, states with reference to such gains in formal education, "It seems inevitable that this striking advance in the educational attainments of the American people should have increased the skills, efficiency, and inventive potential of the labor force. . . ."[24] Other data reveal that there were marked gains in expectancy of life during these years due probably

TABLE 13

Enrollment and Graduates in Secondary Schools and Institutions of Higher Education, Decennial, 1890–1920[a] *(Per Cent)*

Year	Secondary Schools Enrollment per 100 Persons 14–17 Years Old	Graduates Per 100 Persons 17 Years Old	Institutions of Higher Education Resident Enrollment per 100 Persons 18–21 Years Old	Earned Degrees Per 100 Persons 21 Years Old
1890	6.7	3.5	3.0	1.2
1900	11.4	6.4	4.0	1.9
1910	15.4	8.8	4.8	2.1
1920	32.3	16.8	8.1	2.7

[a] Source: Adapted from J. W. Kendrick, *Productivity Trends in the United States* (Princeton: Princeton University Press, 1962), Table 22, p. 106. © Copyright 1961 by National Bureau of Economic Research. Reprinted by permission of Princeton University Press.

to increased outlays for personal and public health. It is the opinion of experts that the health and efficiency of members of the labor force improved notably during these years.

BUSINESS FLUCTUATIONS IN THE PERIOD

While the years 1897–1918 were not marked by depressions as severe as those of 1873 and 1893, economic growth was hampered by considerable instability. By the end of 1897, the nation was definitely working out of the depression of the nineties. In the closing years of the century we experienced a vigorous expansion, thanks to an enormous demand for American exports (especially for wheat), rising prices, and increased European investment in the United States. In addition, the resumption of large-scale immigration and increasing urbanization opened new markets for industry with the result that boom conditions prevailed until 1903 when, as J. P. Morgan said, "undigested securities" contributed to the so-called "rich man's panic." The forward movement was broken again in 1907 when the instability of the banking system, together with other factors, brought on an acute depression that did

[24] Kendrick, *Productivity Trends in the U.S.*, p. 106.

not end until 1909. The upswing in the latter year was of brief duration. Business was depressed again in 1910–11, underwent a second upswing in 1912, and then slumped in the following year. As Faulkner states, "The upset of 1907 had proved more fundamental than had been supposed. From that year until America felt the impact of war prosperity in 1915, American economic history was largely one of brief spurts and recessions. . . ."[25] Were these the signs that depression was becoming chronic in the American economy, as Veblen contended? In the following chapter, we seek to answer this and other questions related to the organizational transformation experienced by the economy in those changeful years.

[25] Kendrick, *Productivity Trends in the U.S.*, p. 31.

Chapter 21

THE EMERGENCE OF THE ORGANIZATIONAL SOCIETY

THE CHOICES OF A TRANSITIONAL ERA

The decade of the 1890's and the opening years of the new century have generally been regarded by historians as a transitional period. Professor Commager wrote of the former decade as a "watershed" separating the more tranquil society of the nineteenth century from the complex, bustling, and more rapidly changing world of the twentieth.[1] More recently, Rostow has stressed the transitional character of the Progressive era, coming as it did at the close of the drive to maturity and on the eve of the age of high-level mass consumption. In his view, the period was a transitional one because having achieved a measure of technological maturity, the United States was faced with a momentous, three-way choice among alternative uses to which its resources could be allocated. The three choices were: (1) the national pursuit of external power and influence; (2) the development of welfare state objectives, such as the redistribution of income through taxation and protection of the human resources that the free market society had relatively neglected in its drive to maturity; (3) the expansion of consumption beyond the basic requirements of food, clothing, and shelter into the field of the mass consumption of durable consumer goods and services. Rostow argues that each nation that has achieved economic maturity has struck a unique balance among these objectives, reflecting its own peculiar geography, culture, resources, values, and political leadership in the post-maturity phase.[2]

The United States sought its balance among these objectives in a fumbling way in these years, but on the whole after acquiring the Philippines we turned away from the acquisition of empire and devoted our resources increasingly to the acquisition of durable consumer goods and a higher domestic standard of living. The amount of economic resources that went into welfare or social services provided by government continued to be comparatively small in this

---

[1] H. S. Commager, *The American Mind* (New Haven: Yale University Press, 1950), pp. 41ff.

[2] W. W. Rostow, *The Stages of Economic Growth* (New York: Cambridge University Press, 1960), pp. 73–74.

period. What factors during these years led the United States to move predominantly in the direction of the third choice?

It cannot be assumed that a society achieving maturity under predominantly free enterprise auspices, as the United States had, could automatically convert into a mass consumption economy. Besides the technological adjustments and changes in the structure of production that such a conversion required, there were even more difficult institutional pre-conditions that had to be satisfied before the economy could allocate its resources for the production of goods and services for mass consumption. Among these institutional prerequisites for a consumer society were such developments as the organization of business on a national scale with plants sufficiently large to achieve the economies of mass production; the development of the management skills necessary to conduct such large-scale businesses; the determination of consumer wants and the channeling of the increased discretionary income into demand for goods and services that business was ready to produce—the tasks of market research and advertising. In addition, there was the need to adapt tax policies and private financial practices to the objectives of providing mass purchasing power and credit so that the flood of consumer goods could be bought. Our banking system, which had become increasingly unstable and unreliable, had to be reorganized to permit a greater degree of public control over the business cycle and thus achieve more stable economic growth; this was the task confronting the founders of the Federal Reserve System. Finally, government policies, which in the late nineteenth century had reflected the acceptance of a *laissez faire* philosophy, had to be adapted to the service and protection of the consumer and the public interest generally. Thus, the agenda of social and institutional change faced by the Progressive era was a large one; it is no wonder that it was a challenging period of social conflict and controversy. A nation with a democratic heritage was now confronted with reconciling it with what Frederick Allen has called the "dynamic logic of mass production."[3] At the same time, in its cities it faced the task of correcting the evils and inequalities that were the legacy of its over-rapid industrialization. In the arena of world politics, it had to shoulder the responsibilities that came with its newly acquired economic power.

THE CORPORATE THRUST TOWARD THE FUTURE

One institution that was rapidly adapted to the requirements of a mass consumption society was the large corporation. Big business, under corporate auspices, had started with the railroads and developed further in the 1880's with the formation of trusts, principally in the consumer goods industries. A new basis for large corporations was established with New Jersey's legaliza-

---

[3] F. L. Allen, *The Big Change: America Transforms Itself* (New York: Harper and Bros., 1952), p. 109.

tion of the holding company in 1889. As Edwin S. Mead later said, "The little state of New Jersey, containing 2 per cent of the population and 1.3 per cent of the wealth of the United States, by the simple act of amending its corporation law, nullified the antitrust laws of every state which had passed them." With the election of President McKinley and the return of prosperity, there began a new wave of consolidations, many of them holding companies, which lasted until 1903. Many economists refer to the combinations of this period as the first merger movement, and practically all agree that it was perhaps the most important one in shaping the market structures of American industry. In the words of Professor Bain, it represented "a major discontinuity in the concentration of American manufacturing."[4] In fact, the basic pattern of economic concentration it created in many of our industries is still discernible today. It truly was a "watershed" marking the divide between the old individualistic way of life and the new, organizational society into which we have moved. The causes of this corporate revolution were controversial when it occurred, and they have continued to be so until today.

There were several factors that gave the consolidation movement new vigor at this time. Among them were rising prices, the recognition of the possibilities of the holding company device, the speculative fever of the times, and the appearance of the professional promoter of whose activities we have written in Chapter 20. Among the causes of this merger movement that have been given serious attention are the following:[5]

(1) Retardation in the rate of growth of the economy. Myron Watkins sees this movement as a response to the closing of the frontier, the slackening of population growth, the slowing of technological change, and the post-1873 decline in prices. Mergers, it is contended, would preserve profits in the face of slackening demand and greater pressures of competition. Boulding in a provocative article has stressed the idea that the movement was a "defense against deflation."[6] Nelson finds that retardation was generally absent from the industries with the highest merger activity in the decade and a half preceding this merger wave; in his analysis, he used A. F. Burns's production data, but ignored the financial condition of these industries in the depression of 1893 that might have made them receptive to the idea of mergers.

(2) The transportation growth-merger hypothesis. This hypothesis holds that the widening of the market brought about by the completion of the railroad network was a basic cause of the movement. Professor Bain, a supporter of this view, writes: "The unification of local and regional markets

---

[4] J. S. Bain, *Industrial Organization* (Homewood, Ill.: R. D. Irwin, 1959), p. 192.

[5] See R. L. Nelson, *Merger Movements in American Industry, 1895–1956* (Princeton: Princeton University Press, 1959), pp. 71ff, for an up-to-date discussion of the extent and causes of this merger movement. The text treatment above relies basically upon Nelson. A stimulating analysis of the movement will also be found in K. E. Boulding, *The Organizational Revolution* (New York: Harper and Bros., 1953), *passim*; E. Jones, *The Trust Movement in the United States* (New York: Macmillan, 1921) is especially good for descriptions of some of the early combinations.

[6] K. E. Boulding, "In Defense of Monopoly," *Quarterly Journal of Economics* (August, 1945), pp. 524–542.

through completion of the railroad network was bringing into competition with each other firms which had previously been isolated by barriers of distance and transport costs."[7] Professor Markham, another authority on the subject, has also argued that "it can be crudely estimated that the area served by the average manufacturing establishment in 1900 was 3.24 times as large as it was in 1882." Nelson has sought to test the railroad growth-merger hypothesis by correlation analysis and concludes as follows: "The effect of this development on merger activity is hard to assess, however. It probably did place geographically separated firms in more direct competition with one another. On the other hand, mergers occurred more commonly in industries which were geographically concentrated than in those widely dispersed."

(3) The growth of the capital market and the role of the professional promoter. The development of large, vertically integrated enterprises required immense amounts of capital that partnerships and "closed corporations" could not raise. It was therefore necessary to sell stock of the new companies to the public and the investment bankers who had done this for the railroads earlier now applied the same technique to the stock of the new industrial combinations.[8] Many new industrial issues appeared for the first time on the New York Stock Exchange in these years. The profits to be made by the promoters were substantial, the cost of the underwriting often amounting to 20 to 40 per cent of the total value of the stock issued.

Underlying some of the combinations of this period as of those in the 1880's were the possibilities of economies of scale in larger plants. The savings to be attained through vertical integration and the market power this policy often made possible were other powerful incentives to merge. Part of the "urge to merge" was the result of the Napoleonic ambitions of some businessmen with the consequence that combines were often formed that exceeded the optimum size of firm. There was a tendency at the time to believe that the economies of scale were almost unlimited, but later experience was to demonstrate otherwise. In fact, it has been estimated that about half of the chief mergers of the 1890's were ultimately failures.[9] On the other hand, many of the new corporate giants grew up to their size and through the government orders that came to them during World War I became solvent financially.

Ida Tarbell's characterization of the first merger movement as the "nationalizing of business" points to an important feature of these consolidations and sheds light on the aspirations of their founders. The titles that many of the new corporations took reflected their national character: American Sugar Refining, the National Casket Company, Continental Can, the Federal Steel Company, etc. The greatest holding company of them all, the giant United States Steel Corporation, was assembled by the master promoter of that era, J. P. Morgan, in 1901. It was hailed as the first billion-dollar company in the

[7] Quoted in R. L. Nelson, *Merger Movements in American Industry*, p. 95.

[8] T. R. Navin and M. V. Sears, "The Rise of a Market for Industrial Securities," *The Business History Review*, Vol. XXIX, 1955.

[9] Shaw Livermore, "The Success of Industrial Mergers," *Quarterly Journal of Economics*, Vol. 37 (November, 1935), pp. 68–96.

nation's history. The formation of that corporation and of many others like it seems in retrospect to have signalized the close of one era and the beginning of another. With the coming of these huge companies, the old captain of industry went into eclipse. The passing of Andrew Carnegie from the industrial scene as the result of the merger of his company into United States Steel was a milestone in our economic history. It symbolized the end of the regime of the business moguls and the dawn of the age of the managers.

VEBLEN AND THE CONSEQUENCES
OF THE COMBINATION MOVEMENT

There were many liberal critics of the consolidation movement in the Progressive era, but Veblen, we have noted, was not wholly unaware of the possible benefits in such combinations. He pointed out that they were motivated mainly by pecuniary advantage, but his principal complaint was that they went into effect only after they were long overdue. He thought that the forces behind the merger movement made it inevitable. The great attraction to Veblen of such mergers was that they eliminated an excess of business management. ". . . The interstitial adjustments of the industrial system at large are in this way withdrawn from the discretion of rival businessmen, and the work of pecuniary management previously involved is in large part dispensed with, with the result that there is a saving of work and an avoidance of that systematic mutual hindrance that characterizes the competitive management of industry. . . ."[10] While Veblen viewed these coalitions as the businessmen's means to stabilize the economy, he was not optimistic about their success in this effort. In fact, he stressed that the businessmen who headed up the new combines followed restrictionist policies that did not permit the industrial system to produce at its maximum and made it liable to periodic breakdown and depression. In order to appraise this aspect of Veblen's thought we need to examine the changes in business practice and policy promoted by this merger movement.

The most basic change was in the degree of concentration among sellers, i.e., in what the economist calls the structure of the market. While a considerable number of combinations sought for and attained monopoly status, in many industries affected by these mergers the outcome instead was one of oligopoly—competition among a relatively few sellers.[11] The modern theory

[10] Veblen, *The Theory of Business Enterprise* (New York: New American Library, 1958), p. 29. Veblen had no fears about the diseconomies stemming from over-large enterprises, as is evident in his contention that the ore beds of Wisconsin, Michigan, and Minnesota as well as the iron and steel works of the entire country should be managed as one collective enterprise. (See *Ibid.*, footnote 12 to Chap. 3, p. 193.)

[11] G. J. Stigler, J. S. Bain, J. M. Markham, "Survey of the Evidence and Findings on Mergers" in Universities—National Bureau Committee for Economic Research, *Business Concentration and Price Policy* (Princeton, N.J.: Princeton University Press, 1955).

of monopolistic competition suggests that oligopolistic rivalry tends to an avoidance of price competition; oligopolists are prone rather to compete in non-price terms, such as product development, sales, and advertising effort. This is what seems to have occurred in these years as the corporate giants cautiously engaged in quasi-collusive practices such as price leadership in the attempt to avoid destructive competition among themselves. The price leaders in many of the concentrated industries favored policies of price stabilization rather than seeking to maximize profits in the short run. Very often these policies served as a protective umbrella for the smaller followers of the leader so that over time the "independents" who were more efficient and had lower costs tended to gain in sales at the expense of the leading firm.[12] The new practice of price stabilization elicited strong criticism from orthodox defenders of the competitive system, but very often the market stability it provided made for more dynamic competition in terms of product innovation, and for more increases in productivity and output than probably would have been the case under a regime of unrestrained price competition.

The second and equally important change stimulated by the merger movement was the expansion in the administrative structure of the industrial consolidations. As had been the case with railroads earlier, the growing size and complexity of the new corporate structures necessitated larger, more bureaucratic structures in these concerns. Their executives had to improvise and grope toward new ways of delegating responsibility and maintaining control over their immense, far-flung activities.[13] Line officers had to be advised on the innumerable questions of policy by staff men, and increasingly, decisions came to be the result of consultation and committee action rather than depending on the opinion of one man. Even in the earlier companies led by the old "captains of industry," leaders such as Carnegie and Rockefeller had depended heavily on the advice of colleagues. But now, with the problems of administration multiplied manyfold there was a tremendous growth in the number of administrative personnel. The new consolidations could achieve economies in production by mass buying and distribution through their own branches; they could use specialized machinery and skilled managers as well as hire the services of lawyers, accountants, and bankers, but all this was possible only through building up an elaborate administrative organization. The trend toward corporate bureaucracy can be seen in the occupational statistics for these years. The census figures disclose that between 1870 and

[12] For evidence of this tendency in these years, see A. R. Burns, *The Decline of Competition* (New York: McGraw-Hill Book Co., 1936), p. 142. As one economic historian states, "But to maintain any semblance of control over the market, entrepreneurs had to strain toward consolidation for, as soon as the merger movement began to lag, control by the very large firms began to weaken. . . ." (H. E. Kroos, *American Economic Development*, 2nd Ed. (Englewood Cliffs, N.J.: Prentice-Hall, Inc., 1966), p. 171.

[13] See R. W. and M. E. Hidy, *Pioneering in Big Business, 1882–1911* (New York: Harper and Row, 1955) for a detailed analysis of the evolution of Standard Oil's administrative organization. For this development generally, see A. D. Chandler, Jr., *Strategy and Structure: Chapters in the History of the Industrial Enterprise* (Cambridge, Mass.: M.I.T. Press, 1962), *passim*.

1940 managerial employees grew in numbers some fourteenfold, technicians, most of whom were probably employed by corporations, forty times, while the number of independent business enterprises (including self-employed professionals) increased only two and one-half times.[14] Early in the century Max Weber, the German sociologist, had predicted that it was the destiny of industrial man to live in what he vividly called the "iron cage of bureaucracy"; the large corporations were rapidly making a reality in America of Weber's vision of the future.

In these years there was also developing in the large corporations that separation of ownership and control that was to be demonstrated so dramatically later by Berle and Means. Veblen noticed and commented upon the early tendency in this direction in the larger corporations; he stressed the opportunities for quick profits by the managers on the inside, but otherwise regarded the managers merely as the "hired men" of the bankers, or "captains of solvency" as he called them. Veblen's view of this matter was largely justified because most of the managers did not have the degree of autonomy they were to gain later with the decline of banker control. This did not happen until after the passing of J. P. Morgan in 1913 and the development by many giant corporations of a greater degree of financial independence.

Nevertheless, the regime of finance capitalism caused important changes in corporate behavior in this period. In contrast to the usually unrestrained competition of the industrial capitalists, the bankers and their representatives on the boards of the new consolidations had a rather different philosophy. They were not as venturesome and innovative as the older capitalists. They were more interested in stability of capital values and in maintenance of dividends and stable prices. They opposed unrestrained price competition and favored, instead, a policy of "live and let live." For example, Judge Gary, the Morgan-backed board chairman of the United Steel Corporation, was an ardent believer in the policy of price stabilization. He contended that "price should always be reasonable. The mere fact that demand is greater than supply does not justify an increase in price, nor does the fact that demand is less than the supply justify lowering prices. What we want is stability—the avoidance of violent fluctuations."[15] Gary, incidentally, achieved a good deal of stability in steel prices during his leadership of the industry. The published price of steel rails remained firm at $28 per ton between May, 1901 and April, 1916, and at $43 from October, 1922 to October, 1932. Such price stability was remarkable considering the economic fluctuations through which the nation passed during this period; it contrasted sharply with the flexibility of steel prices during the earlier depressions of 1873 and 1893, when the unpredictable Carnegie was a principal factor in the industry.

Gary was of the opinion that price competition in the steel industry tended to be mutually destructive, especially in time of depression. This view rested

[14] J. Burnham, *The Managerial Revolution* (New York: The John Day Co., 1941), *passim*.

[15] I. M. Tarbell, *The Life of Elbert H. Gary* (New York: D. Appleton, 1925), p. 206.

in turn on his belief, which was rather prevalent in the industry at the time, that the demand for steel was inelastic when business was declining. Price cuts, therefore, would reduce profits or add to losses without stimulating additional orders. Furthermore, he realized that in an industry such as steel, which has heavy fixed costs, sellers in time of slack demand may be tempted to sell for less than their total unit costs simply to maintain volume and spread their overhead burden. The pursuit of that policy would mean destruction for all, Gary thought.

When the depression of 1907 set in, Gary began holding his famous dinners, in order, as he put it, "to maintain to a reasonable extent the equilibrium of business, to prevent utter demoralization of business and destructive competition." He exhorted his steel competitors "like a Methodist preacher at a camp meeting" to follow U.S. Steel's price leadership. Thus, Gary inaugurated an era of good feeling and "friendly competition" among steel executives that prevailed until the government brought suit for the dissolution of Big Steel. Thereupon, in 1909 the Gary dinners were abruptly discontinued; however, the steel industry found other means in subsequent years to maintain the policy of price stabilization.

In other industries where concentration had developed there were signs of a lessening of price competition also. In petroleum after the dissolution of the Standard Oil Trust in 1911, a pattern of price leadership developed; in the meat packing industry markets were shared or pooled by the leading companies; price leadership was also prevalent in tin cans, farm implements, cement, and other fields.[16] In addition, in some industries that were not so concentrated, a trade association movement appeared in these years that did much to soften the rigors of price competition. The idea was given much impetus by a lawyer, Arthur J. Eddy, who contended in his book, *The New Competition* (1912), that trade associations were legal under the antitrust laws. Eddy himself was influential in forming "open price" trade associations in which the members shared information about their prices before placing their goods on sale; this technique of doing business, together with the cooperation it engendered among competitors, tended to moderate price competition. In summary, the concentration of industry that followed the merger movement of these years resulted in more uniform and stable prices for many manufactured goods. Instead of prices changing incessantly in response to shifts in supply and demand, they were "administered," i.e., the supply was adjusted to the demand at prices set by the administrative action of the businessmen. However, such price stabilization did not mean the end of all competition; aggressive rivalry among oligopolists still continued in product innovation, service, and sales and advertising effort.

In the light of the preceding we can see that Veblen showed keen insight in recognizing that modern technology tends toward oligopolistic market structures in some industries, but he failed to appreciate the social benefits of

[16] Burns, *The Decline of Competition*, pp. 77ff.

competition. As Dowd states, ". . . but he [Veblen] was just as surely incorrect in assuming that competition served no beneficial function whatsoever, that it was a mere multiplication of money-seekers. Veblen acknowledged the benefits of competition for an earlier period, but he failed to give it credit for the period in which he wrote."[17] This blind spot in his thinking made him unappreciative of the stimulating effects that the ruthless, competitive auto industry had on the economy.

SCIENTIFIC MANAGEMENT AND THE BEGINNINGS OF RESEARCH AND DEVELOPMENT

This dynamic period saw the development of another idea that was to revolutionize American industry and greatly contribute to increased productivity. This was scientific management. The "father" of this movement in this country was Frederic W. Taylor, an engineer, who saw the need for more scientific methods of production while first working in the machine shop of the Midvale Steel Company in 1882–83. Taylor was convinced that the old methods of using force instead of knowledge to increase output were outdated; there was a need to determine the "one best way" to do a job and then set up rules that the workers would follow in order to earn incentive pay for increased productivity. Taylor began to publicize and argue for his methods in 1895, but the response was disappointing until he became president of the American Society of Mechanical Engineers about 1905–06, when they received more attention from progressive executives and engineers. The Harvard Graduate School of Business Administration, which had been established in 1908, accepted his ideas in its work on factory production. But they did not gain wide public attention until Louis Brandeis, the Boston attorney, popularized the term "scientific management" as a result of his calling one of Taylor's followers to testify in a hearing before the Interstate Commerce Commission in 1910. In the following year, Taylor fully expounded his philosophy in a book *The Principles of Scientific Management.*[18] In succeeding years, the Taylor ideas of standardizing products and processes, improving organization, planning and controlling men, machines, and materials, employing time and motion studies, paying incentive compensation, and carefully selecting and training workers were widely adopted, despite the opposition of organized labor. Trade union leaders contended that the "stop-watch" engineers with their confusing pay rates were pitting worker against worker in an inhuman "speed-up." Shorn of some of the excesses in the movement, scientific management went on to contribute greatly to American efficiency and to the development of the assembly line and mass production. The remarkable

[17] Dowd, *Thorstein Veblen* . . ., p. 140.

[18] Among Taylor's disciples were such men as Henry L. Gant, Frank B. Gilbreth, Harrington Emerson, Carl G. Barth, and Henry R. Towne. For a penetrating analysis of the relationships between Taylorism and Progressivism, see S. Haber, *Efficiency and Uplift, Scientific Management in the Progressive Era, 1890–1920* (Chicago: University of Chicago Press, 1944).

increases in productivity we cite below were due in part to this scientific transformation of the nation's industrial practices.

A related development spurred by the formation of large corporations in these years was industrial research, or what we have come to call "R and D"—research and development. Scientific research began to move from the individual workshop to the industrial laboratory as companies developed sufficiently to finance it and appreciate its possibilities. While there had been successful uses of scientists by Carnegie, Edison, the Pennsylvania Railroad, and others somewhat earlier, the credit for the first American laboratory is generally given to the General Electric Company, which established one in 1901. Actually, the federal government had pioneered in creating research laboratories and experimental stations for agriculture under the Hatch Act of 1887. But now private industry began to realize the potentialities in this type of investigation. Bell Telephone, DuPont, and Eastman Kodak were among the first. By 1913, at least 50 companies had set up important laboratories.[19]

Although industrial research advanced in the first decade of the century, it was World War I that gave it its greatest impetus. The Wilson administration established the National Research Council as a clearinghouse of information among scientists in 1916. With the coming of the war, university professors turned to research for industry in a large way. Research in the chemical industry and other fields advanced remarkably in these years. Jewett estimated in 1918 that industrial research had grown ten times between 1915 and the latter year.[20] In 1920, the National Research Council reported that there were more than 300 industrial laboratories in the nation, though many of them were very small. In short, by the end of World War I, industrial research was still in its infancy in the United States, but an auspicious beginning had been made.[21]

THE GROWTH OF OUTPUT AND PRODUCTIVITY

Despite this scientific pioneering in industry, Veblen was critical of the performance of American business enterprise in these years because he believed that the rate of capital formation was too low and that the productive output of the existing capital stock was restricted or sabotaged by the businessmen. How well does Veblen's analysis stand up in the light of our contemporary knowledge of output and productivity trends for this period?

[19] Faulkner, *The Decline of Laissez Faire, 1897–1917* (New York: Holt, Rinehart and Winston, 1951), p. 133.

[20] F. B. Jewett, *Industrial Research* (Washington, D.C.: National Research Council, 1918), p. 2.

[21] In 1920, the National Science Foundation estimated that the nation's expenditures for R and D, $48 million, amounted to .05% of the GNP. By 1960, they had grown to $10,507 million, or 2.08% of the GNP. See H. R. Bartlett, "The Development of Industrial Research in the United States," in National Resources Planning Board, *Research—A National Resource* (Washington, D.C., 1941), Vol. II, pp. 19–42, reprinted in J. T. Lambie and R. V. Clemence, *Economic Change in America* (Harrisburg, Pa.: The Stackpole Co., 1954), pp. 205–245.

At the outset, we must realize that Veblen did not have available the wealth of statistics on these matters that modern economic research has provided. Compared to the studies of the National Bureau of Economic Research and the monumental labors of such scholars as Kuznets, Fabricant, Goldsmith, or Kendrick, his analysis seems overly theoretical and relatively subjective and qualitative in nature. For example, the statistics now available suggest that real capital formation was proceeding at a relatively rapid pace during the years 1899–1919, as displayed in Chart 1. The reader's attention is called to capital input as plotted on this chart, which has a ratio scale; the slopes of the lines indicate the relative rates of change. It will be noted that capital input was at about the same rate during the years 1899–1919 as it was in the

CHART 1

Private Domestic Economy: Real Gross Product and Factor Inputs, 1889–1957
(1929 = 100)

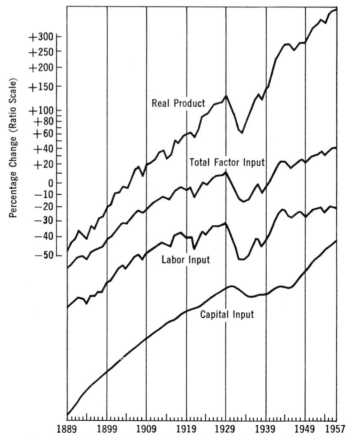

Reproduced from J. W. Kendrick, *Productivity Trends in the United States* (Princeton University Press, 1962), p. 66. © Copyright 1961 by the National Bureau of Economic Research. Reprinted by permission of Princeton University Press.

previous decade. Kendrick's estimates show that the capital stock in manufacturing increased more than threefold over these years and in the electric utility industry the capital input in this period grew about sixfold.[22]

Veblen's criticism was based in part on the reduction in capital formation caused by business depression as well as by wasteful consumption. He did not look at the rate of capital formation in long run terms. Of one thing we can be sure: these were years in which capital was being substituted for labor on an extensive scale, as Chart 2 graphically indicates. With this deepening of capital, there was an increased output per unit of labor, so that efficiency as

CHART 2

Private Domestic Economy: Capital per Unit of Labor Input, by Segment, Key Years, 1889–1953 (1929 = 100)

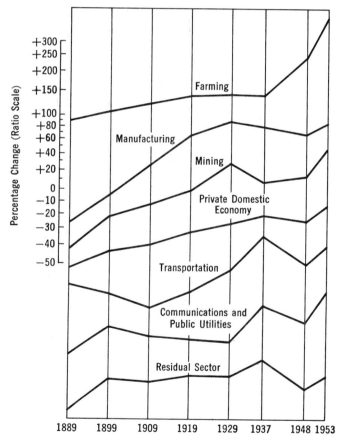

Reproduced from J. W. Kendrick, *Productivity Trends in the United States* (Princeton, N.J.: Princeton University Press, 1962), p. 150. © Copyright 1961 by the National Bureau of Economic Research. Reprinted by permission of Princeton University Press.

[22] J. W. Kendrick, *Productivity Trends in the United States* (Princeton: Princeton University Press, 1961), pp. 464, 590.

measured in these terms was increasing also. It will be noted in Chart 3 that the increase in labor productivity was especially striking in the communications and public utility fields.

In the Introduction to this Part, Veblen's concept of the net product of industry was described and his view stated that too much of this net product went into wasteful consumption, leaving little for capital formation. In the work on productivity cited above, Kendrick develops a very similar conception, which he terms a final "margin for economic progress" and, fortunately for us, he calculates measures of the same for a number of years, including

CHART 3

Private Domestic Economy: Output per Unit of Labor Input, by Segment, Key Years, 1889–1953 (1929 = 100)

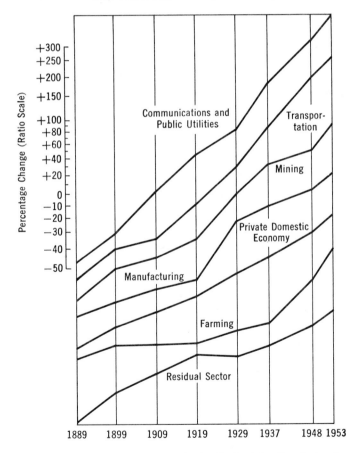

Reproduced from J. W. Kendrick, *Productivity Trends in the United States* (Princeton, N.J.: Princeton University Press, 1962), p. 154. © Copyright 1961 by the National Bureau of Economic Research. Reprinted by permission of Princeton University Press.

the ones we are studying.[23] In Table 1, which is adapted from Kendrick, we see that the margins for economic progress for the years 1899–1919 were substantial and that the amounts devoted to capital formation exceeded that going into new consumption by large sums. Indeed, on the basis of Kendrick's

TABLE 1

Margins over Maintenance of Real National Product, 1889–1929[a]
(Annual averages) (Millions of 1929 dollars)

Period of Average	Real Gross National Product	Maintenance of Population (Consumer and Capital Goods)	National Security	Maintenance of Provision for Growth of Population (Consumption and Capital)	Margin for Economic Progress Consumption	Capital
1889–98	$26,781	$22,264	$ 143	$1,785	$ 314	$ 2,275
1899–1908	42,111	35,180	334	2,906	648	3,043
1909–18	58,937	50,128	1,961	3,544	776	2,528
1919–28	83,181	71,058	1,380	4,284	1,690	4,769
1929–36	84,854	82,862	773	3,002	71	−1,854

[a] Adapted from Kendrick, *Productivity. Trends in the United States* (Princeton, N.J.: Princeton University Press, 1962). Table 19, p. 100. © Copyright 1961 by the National Bureau of Economic Research. Reprinted by permission of Princeton University Press.

estimates, it would appear that the margin for new capital formation in the years 1899–1908 and 1909–18 were, respectively, 7.2 per cent and 4.3 per cent of the gross national product for those years. These rates of capital formation were exceeded in Kendrick's calculations only by that of the period 1889–98, during which the rate was 8.5 per cent.

How can one account for the discrepancy between Veblen's critical view of the rate of capital formation in these years and the statistics we have cited? Veblen could argue in defense of his position that the performance of the economy in this respect could have been greatly improved if more rational methods of planning and social control had been adopted than the contemporary business practices of his day permitted. It certainly cannot be denied that if a greater degree of economic stability had been achieved and the nation's

[23] Kendrick describes this margin of progress as follows: "One helpful way of analyzing the composition of the national product is in terms of the margin that remains after providing for the maintenance of the population of each previous year at the previous years' level of consumption and of net capital stock. This margin for maintenance, in turn, may be broken down into the portions required for national security, for growth of population, and a final "margin for economic progress" that may be invested in increasing the tangible or intangible capital per person. This margin gives us an alternative approach to the measurement of economic growth or progress. . . . (*Ibid.*, p. 99.) This concept, Kendrick states, was developed in a somewhat different form by the late Frederick C. Mills. See the latter's *Productivity and Economic Progress*, Occasional Paper No. 38 (New York: National Bureau of Economic Research, 1952).

economic resources fully employed throughout the period, the actual rate of capital formation, other things being equal, could probably have been exceeded. In this connection, one must recall Veblen's dire prediction of a net deficit in capital formation, which he made in 1923.[24] Table 1 shows that his prognostication of a "progressive abatement of the margin of net output" available for new capital formation was borne out not progressively but in rather catastrophic fashion during the calamitous years of the 1930's.

Veblen, it would seem, did not properly assess the tremendous external economies being developed in the transportation, communication, and public utility industries during these years and did not appreciate that such economies could go far to offset the toll that the captains of finance were imposing on the flow of industry and trade. His restrictionist view of business enterprise emphasized the striving for maximum profit ("charging what the traffic would bear" was his favorite way of expressing it), the price-fixing, etc., but this approach did not sufficiently recognize the concomitant gains in product improvement, innovation, and overall productivity, which the new policies of price stabilization (among other factors) were making possible.[25] Professor Dowd reminds us that Veblen formed his ideas about business during "its most buccaneering period" when the businessmen were on their worst behavior and that he consequently failed to give credit where credit was due.[26] Furthermore, his crucial distinction between industry and business led him to regard the technological evolution of the economy as an impersonal, cumulative process of "unremitting proliferation." He was accustomed to say that industry was carried on for the sake of business, and not conversely. This way of stating the relationship between these two phases of economic activity, though it undoubtedly expressed a partial truth, ignored the important role of business leadership in the process of industrial innovation and change. As Professor Dowd perceptively notes, ". . . The virtues of the American economy Veblen attributed to industrialism as such; the defects he attributed to the aims and techniques of the business community. It seems more accurate to think that there are *some* virtues arising out of business self-seeking and *some* problems arising out of industrialism. . . ."[27]

VEBLEN AND THE DAWN OF THE AUTOMOBILE AGE

Veblen's theories, we have seen, are concerned primarily with the adequacy of the American institutional framework for promoting growth in an economy

---

[24] See footnote 11 in Introduction to this Part.

[25] Schumpeter contended that dynamic competition and product development and innovation require a certain minimum of price stability.

[26] Dowd, *Thorstein Veblen* . . ., pp. 139–140.

[27] Dowd, *Thorstein Veblen* . . ., p. 60. Dowd adds to the above by saying, "Veblen was generally correct, but for purposes of formulating sensible and feasible policies, finer distinctions are required. These in turn require investigations going beyond anything Veblen accomplished or contemplated."

that was, in Rostovian terms, completing the drive to maturity. Our survey of the growth of the economy in the preceding chapter should enable us to examine his theories with some perspective. We have noted his emphasis on the capital goods industries and on the idea that the capital stock is the "decisive factor" determining the rate of growth of the nation's economic surplus. But what is striking, even in his books published after *The Theory of Business Enterprise*, is the relative neglect of the consumer goods industries and the innovations in them that were beginning to play an important part in stimulating capital formation in this period. Having studied the restrictionist maneuvers of the "captains of finance" in the reports of the Industrial Commission, Veblen stressed the sabotage of production involved in high finance and, more particularly, how the concern for the "main chance" and pecuniary considerations tended to keep industrial output far below what was technologically possible. But in all this analysis, he did not develop a theory relating consumption and innovation to the process of capital formation. Consequently, he missed some of the new, emergent elements in the changing economy of his day. Professor Dowd, a most sympathetic student of Veblen's work, has pointed out that ". . . Veblen failed to develop an adequate theory of consumption and investment, the strongest feature of the modern theory of employment. Put differently, Veblen did not systematically examine the reasons why new investment takes place; he asked only why restriction of production from existing investment goods occurs. . . ."[28]

Veblen recognized and described the system of mass production that the automobile industry developed to a high level in these years, but he did not consider the impact of this new industry on the process of capital formation and the growth of the economy as a whole. Of course, when *The Theory of Business Enterprise* was published in 1904, the motor car industry was as yet in its infancy in this country. In that year only 22,130 passenger cars were produced; the most dynamic years of the industry still lie ahead. There is a passage in *The Engineers and the Price System* (published in 1921), which may have reference to the industry. After stressing in his usual fashion the conflict between the engineer and the financier, Veblen makes a surprising admission, saying that in exceptional cases businessmen in America have successfully departed from the conservative principle of "conscientious withdrawal of efficiency" and have actually influenced output by increasing the productive capacity of the industrial system in one way or another.[29] We do not know, however, whether Veblen had the automobile industry in mind when he wrote this.

Actually, the most probable reason for Veblen's neglect of the automobile industry was his view that the investment bankers, by their control of credit,

[28] Dowd, *Thorstein Veblen . . .*, p. 47. Dowd states that Veblen's neglect of the consumer goods industries was "a more reasonable position to take than it is today, because of the lesser role played then by consumer goods (e.g. in the years surrounding 1904, capital goods production was expanding at just twice the rate of consumer goods production)."

[29] T. Veblen, *The Engineers and the Price System* (New York: Viking Press, 1947, p. 10.

controlled the strategic key industries, such as steel and oil, and the latter in turn limited the initiative and discretion of other manufacturing enterprises.[30] As Riesman correctly says, to Veblen men such as Ford were "relics of a more heroic age," i.e., of the earlier stage of industrial capitalism.[31] Nevertheless, Veblen's failure to develop the relationship between the rise of the durable consumer goods industries, especially the automobile, and the demand for new capital was a major one because these industries became one of the most powerful influences in the further growth of the economy.

It may be argued that Veblen may have regarded the automobile as a form of wasteful, conspicuous consumption. While there is an element of truth in that point of view—the horseless carriage was at first a rich man's toy—it was a major innovation and satisfied a pressing national need. Despite the existence of the railroads, which solved the problem of long-distance transportation, and the appearance of the electric trolleys, the nation badly needed a faster and more convenient form of short-distance transportation.

In examining the spectacular rise of the motor car industry, we must consider the conditions required for the mass production of so relatively expensive a product. By the time of its advent, the nation not only had developed the necessary technology and had the available capital, but it had a national market large enough to absorb the product. It soon became clear that mass production required mass consumption. "By 1900 these conditions had been met. Population had grown to 76,000,000, and the purchasing power of the people as a whole was relatively high. It was estimated in 1900 that the per capita consumption of manufactures in the United States was 50 per cent higher than that in Great Britain and twice as great as that in Germany and France. . . ."[32] It is striking to note in this connection the almost incredible fact that Great Britain did not begin to use the moving assembly line in automobile manufacture until 1934.[33]

The horseless carriage made an almost irresistible appeal to Americans from the beginning; we have always been a mobile people, even a restless one. As Henry Ford humorously said, "Everybody wants to be someplace he ain't. As soon as he gets there he wants to go right back."[34] Still, though the United States offered a stronger inducement to mass production of automobiles than existed anywhere else, the opportunities for enterprise in this field had to be appreciated and exploited. The factor of business leadership, in short, was essential; as we shall see, there was no shortage of entrepreneurs in the nation ready to grasp these rich opportunities.

The Americans, however, were not the inventors of the automobile. The British had experimented with steam-powered highway vehicles in the early

---

[30] T. Veblen, *Absentee Ownership and Business Enterprise in Recent Times: The Case of America* (New York: The Viking Press, 1923).

[31] D. Riesman, *Thorstein Veblen* (New York: Charles Scribner's Sons, 1953), p. 207.

[32] Faulkner, *The Decline of Laissez Faire*, p. 121.

[33] J. B. Rae, *American Automobile Manufacturers* (Philadelphia, Pa.: Chilton Co., 1959), p. 202.

[34] Quoted in J. Hughes, *The Vital Few* (Boston: Houghton Mifflin Co., 1966), p. 294.

nineteenth century; the Germans have the best claim to being the inventors of the internal combustion engine, and the French were producing autos in quantity in the early 1890's before we undertook to do so. The distinctive American contribution came in the form of developing the mass production of automobiles and making it into a great modern industry. The pioneers did not usually fit the traditional picture of a mechanical genius building a horseless carriage in his backyard, but more commonly were bicycle manufacturers and carriage and wagon makers. Thus, Colonel Albert A. Pope, the maker of the famous *Columbia* bicycle, was one of the first to attempt auto manufacture as were the Studebaker brothers, the largest producers of horse-drawn vehicles in the world. In addition, there was a wide assortment of engineers and mechanics and producers of many products in New England and the Middle West who were drawn to this fascinating industry. They included some of the historic figures of the industry—Charles B. King, the Duryea brothers, Henry M. Leland, Elwood Haynes, Ransom E. Olds, and a host of others whose names have become part of the American folklore of the motor car. Olds was one of the first to get into quantity production of motor cars, and by 1904 was turning out 5,000 annually. There were a large number of competitors in the first decade of the century in this unpredictable, hazardous industry. Most of them were catering to the demand of the rich with high-priced vehicles, though there were several who favored producing a low-price car. Nearly half of the cars sold in 1906 were priced at between $2,275 and $4,775. The trend after 1903 was toward big, heavy, flashy cars. An interesting indication of the attitude toward the industry at this time was the statement of Woodrow Wilson, then president of Princeton University, "Nothing has spread socialistic feeling in this country more than the automobile," and he added that it offered "a picture of the arrogance of wealth."[35]

Henry Ford, a Michigan farm boy who became an engineer for the Edison Illuminating Co. in Detroit, after holding a variety of other jobs, had begun to experiment with his quadricycle, as he called his first car, in 1896, working on it at night and in his spare time. After the failure of two prior ventures, the Ford Motor Company was incorporated in 1903 with a capitalization of $100,000 (of which only $28,000 was paid in). Ford was backed in this third, successful effort by Alexander Malcomson, a Detroit coal dealer, John S. Gray, a banker, the Dodge brothers, and several others, including the capable James Couzens. In addition, Ford was aided by C. Harold Wills, a remarkable young engineer and metallurgist, who worked on the designs of the original models. Between organizing and making cars as well as racing them, Ford was a busy man. Ford was soon at odds with his shareholders, principally Malcomson, who favored production of the higher priced cars. Ford had noticed that the Model N, a cheap $600 car, was selling better than the more expensive model. By 1906–07, the Ford Motor Company was producing a record-breaking 8,423 cars and it rode out the panic of 1907 with only a slight

[35] F. L. Allen, *The Big Change*, p. 121.

loss in sales. By 1908, the leadership in the industry had passed to the "Big Four"—Buick, Ford, Reo, and Maxwell-Briscoe, which between them produced as many cars as the other manufacturers combined. Ford was making a net income of more than $1 million a year and it was on the eve of its great innovation, the Model T.

Ford had taken a step toward a cheap car with the four-cylinder Model N and with the decision to abandon the higher priced model and concentrate on a single chassis. In the fall of 1908 the Model T went into production, and Ford's vision of a cheap, all-purpose, standardized vehicle was realized; the unforgettable "Tin Lizzie" had been born. Sales of the new model skyrocketed steadily from 10,607 in 1908–09 to 730,041 in 1916–17; the price went down as production stepped up, from $850 for a touring car to $360 in the latter year. Ford's share of automobile production increased from 9.4 per cent in 1908 to 39.6 per cent in 1913 and 48 per cent the following year. In these years the Ford stood practically alone in the cheap car field.

With a growing share of the market, Ford was able to take the steps to achieve mass, assembly line production on a scale that had never been attained before. The Model T had been an ingeniously designed cheap car, sturdy, light, yet powerful. Its planetary transmission, mechanical brakes, magnetic ignition, etc. were the wonder and obsession of millions of Americans for years. The steady reduction of costs and prices was obtained through further integration of manufacturing processes, establishment of branch plants, and an efficient distribution system, but mostly by the development of the assembly line method of production. " 'Born, in 1913, at Highland Park on the outskirts of Detroit, a new world force, the system of mass production, destined to affect all economic and social life'—that, at the time, would have been a bold and incomprehensible announcement. But although the birth of mass production cannot be attributed to a single year or one industrial plant, the statement would have contained enough truth to be arguable."[36] Thus, Allan Nevins describes the Ford innovation of the assembly line. Credit for the conception of the moving assembly line at the Ford plant is a matter of dispute. Charles Sorenson and Clarence Avery, along with Ford himself, claim the momentous innovation. Ford had begun with "stationary assembly," bringing the parts to the worker who then put them together; this had been used years before in the manufacture of watches, sewing machines, guns, and bicycles. Now in the moving assembly line the work was brought to the men, first in the manufacture of smaller parts and then, later, in the production of the chassis. Finally, all the subassemblies were synchronized into one main line where the finished car emerged, the product of thousands of specialized workmen and crews. The assembly line was the capstone of the mass production process, "the payoff of a century of American industrial development."[37]

[36] A. Nevins and F. E. Hill, *Ford: The Times, The Man, The Company*, Vol. 1 (New York: Scribner's, 1954), p. 447.
[37] Hughes, *The Vital Few*, p. 275.

It was the most striking illustration of the cumulative, collective nature of modern machine technology, as Veblen had described it. Its use in the Ford plants cut the production time of the magneto from twenty minutes to five, of the chassis from twelve and one-half to one and a half hours. The assembly line technique was the principal factor behind the sensational reduction in the base price of the Model T.

Behind the achievement of the Ford Company was Henry Ford himself, a folk hero of the American people by 1914, a master mechanic, but many thought an illiterate one, a very complicated man of whose personality even Nevins says, "The creator of the assembly line never quite assembled himself."[38] Ford was the "natural American" who, like his friend Edison, poked fun at the "experts" and from his parochial rural background laughed at city life and its "greenhorns." Out of this rural background, of the *McGuffey Readers* and the other limited reading that Ford did, he distilled "the clearest essence of American puritanism."[39] A maverick businessman, an industrial capitalist in an age of predominantly financial capitalism, he was both a stimulus and a threat to the established order of things. He was Veblen's master technician and as a matter of fact bore a number of similarities in personality and thought to the homespun economist.[40] Ford had an almost paranoid fear of the bankers and in his late years was constantly criticizing their philosophy and influence. "Bankers play far too great a part in the conduct of industry," he would say. In true Veblenian fashion, he said that bankers "want to watch the money, not the efficiency of production. They think of a factory as making money, not goods."[41] His functional view of finance came out in the expression, "Money is part of the conveyor line" or "Money is what we use to keep tally."[42] These skeptical attitudes toward the beneficence of the bankers had some justification as far as the automobile industry was concerned. In its early years the bankers shunned the industry, fearing its instability and forcing the manufacturers to develop rather unique methods of sale. Some of them believed the industry was already over-expanded as early as 1904.[43] Indeed, Wall Street did not take much of an interest in the new industry until the 1920's. When Ford introduced the five-dollar day in 1913, he did not get much support from certain quarters in Wall Street. Ford called the five-dollar a day idea "profit sharing and efficiency engineering," but the government disagreed, and there were many others with critical views of his motives for taking this revolutionary step. The *Wall Street Journal* argued that he was injecting "Biblical or spiritual principles into a

[38] Hughes, *The Vital Few*, p. 581.

[39] Hughes, *The Vital Few*, p. 275.

[40] For an interesting comparison of the two men, see Riesman, *Thorstein Veblen*, pp. 202ff.

[41] Quoted in Hughes, *The Vital Few*, p. 315.

[42] Nevins, *Ford . . .*, p. 575.

[43] R. C. Epstein, *The Automobile Industry* (Chicago: A. W. Shaw Co., 1928), pp. 224–225.

field where they do not belong" (Ford had said that he wanted to help the common man) and said that he was a troublemaker and perhaps a criminal.[44]

COMBINATION AND COOPERATION IN THE
MOTOR CAR INDUSTRY

In the years after 1908 while Ford was creating his industrial empire and piling up fabulous profits, there was a rush of newcomers into the booming industry. Producers of such cars as the Moon (1907), Velie (1908), Auburn, Elcar, and Cole (all in 1909), and the Dort (1910) were among the hundreds of firms that sprang up as assemblers of cars. Some survived for quite a while, others disappeared as quickly as they had started. A total of 181 companies engaged in production between 1903 and 1926; of the 181 concerns in passenger car manufacture over this period, 137 had retired from the business by 1926. The median length of life was 7.10 years.[45] The high mortality rate of the industry was explained by the frequent changes in product, the consequent difficulty of predicting the market, the high unit costs, and the strenuous competition.

It was to avoid these risks through diversification that William C. Durant, one of the industry's most colorful and daring promoters, created General Motors in 1908. There were two ways at that time to achieve the scale of organization necessary to outdistance the horde of competitors. One was by internal growth, the path Ford had taken, the other was to combine existing firms. Durant merged Buick, Cadillac, and Olds with a variety of lesser makes and assorted parts manufacturers to form the biggest consolidation in the industry. Most of these concerns were purchased with GM stock; Durant even attempted to buy the Ford Motor Company, but Ford wanted eight million in cash, which couldn't be raised. In two years, Durant lost control of his shaky, hastily constructed and poorly managed combine to the bankers. He regained control of the company in 1916 by purchasing its shares in the open market with the assets of another of his creations, Chevrolet, only to lose it again and for the last time in 1921.

Other combines, such as the Studebaker-Everett-Metzger-Flanders Co. in 1908 and the United States Motor Co. (1910), had even greater financial difficulties than GM and soon expired. In 1911, the famous Selden patent case was decided, which ended the effort of a Rochester attorney by that name to collect royalties on a patent on an automobile engine (the Brayton 2-cycle type). The courts finally sustained Selden's claims, but held that his patent only applied to those vehicles using his improvements on the Selden engine. Those auto manufacturers who had recognized the legality of the Selden

---

[44] Nevins, *Ford* . . ., p. 536. See Chap. 20 of the same book for a most interesting discussion of the five-dollar day.

[45] Epstein, *The Automobile Industry*, pp. 162–212.

patent had formed an association, a type of patent pool called the Association of Licensed Automobile Manufacturers in 1903; Ford and others refused to join. The legal victory of Ford and Jeffrey in this case ended what some thought had the makings of an automobile trust.[46]

The industry, tired of patent litigation, went on to form a mutual cross-licensing system in 1915 under the supervision of its new trade association, the National Automobile Chamber of Commerce, which had been formed in the previous year. This patent pool facilitated the exchange of technical improvements and modifications among manufacturers (basic inventions were excluded) and thereby proved very beneficial to the young industry.

THE TECHNOLOGICAL REVOLUTION WIDENS

Technological changes came thick and fast in this dynamic, competitive industry after 1907. As cars became more powerful (1–2 cylinder engines gave way to 4 and even 6- to 8-cylinder motors), mass production became imperative, tools and equipment more specialized and expensive. Notable product improvements appeared in these years; one of the most important was the electric starter, which Charles F. Kettering, one of the industry's most prolific inventors, devised for the Cadillac in 1912. Electric headlights, demountable rim tires, and many other innovations were made in these years, as Chart 4 depicts.

The depression of 1907 and the uncertainties of the following years forced the new struggling auto concerns to cut costs and tighten up efficiency in a most Schumpeterian fashion. Improvements in plant layout and design, many of which were traceable to the genius of Albert Kahn, the architect, speeded the flow of product. The technical demands of the auto industry in these years revolutionized the machine tool industry. "As the bicycle industry had come to the rescue of machine tool builders after the panic of 1893, so the automobile sustained their faltering activity after that of 1907. . . ."[47] Veblen's machine industry hummed with the whirl of the new engine and turret lathes, automatic screw machines, vertical millers, and radial drills and resounded with the sound of the monster stamping machines.

The new products and processes of the industry called not only for new tools but for improved raw materials as well. The metal and metal-working industries of the nation, feeling the countervailing buying power of the growing auto industry, responded magnificently. In 1906, Federick W. Taylor, pioneer in scientific management, working with J. Maunsel White at

---

[46] For the details of this historic case, see Nevins, *Ford*, Vol. 1, pp. 284–322, 415–443; for a somewhat different interpretation, see Rae, *American Automobile Manufacturers*, pp. 72–79; for the most extended account, see W. Greenleaf, *Monopoly on Wheels: Henry Ford and the Selden Patent Case* (Detroit: Wayne University Press, 1961).

[47] Nevins, *Ford*, Vol. 1, p. 367.

CHART 4

Trends of the American Automobile for Six Years, Showing Variations of Most Important Factors in Design and Manufacture

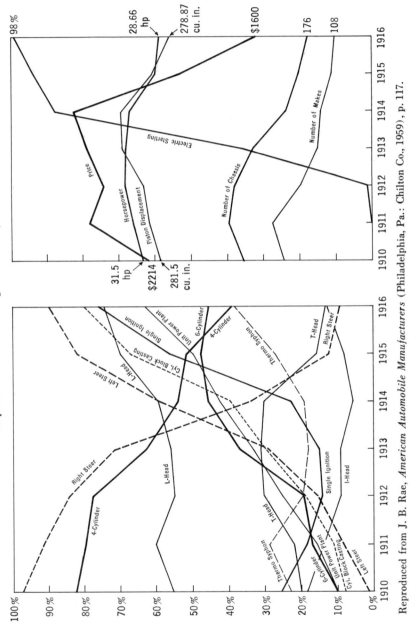

Reproduced from J. B. Rae, *American Automobile Manufacturers* (Philadelphia, Pa.: Chilton Co., 1959), p. 117.

Bethlehem Steel, introduced high-speed carbon tool steel, which more than doubled the productivity of machine tools. After 1910, molybdenum, tantalum, and tungsten-steel alloys were produced by the steel companies. Improvements in the metallurgy of copper, aluminum and other non-ferrous metals were leading in these same years to increased efficiency in their use in the automobile and other industries of the nation.

Better cutting tools made for increased precision and closer tolerances, so indispensable in the technique of interchangeable parts. A related development was the idea of technical standardization of parts, such as spark plugs, wheel rims, and screw heads, which was pushed more rapidly after the formation of the Society of Automobile Engineers in 1910. The smaller members of the industry were at first the most enthusiastic backers of this type of cooperation, but in time even the big companies saw its advantages and joined the association. The standardization the engineers promoted was, of course, essential to the whole idea of mass production and mass distribution of automobiles.

TABLE 2

Output and Labor Productivity in the Motor Vehicle and Equipment Industry, 1899–1919[a]
(1929 = 100)

	1899	1909	1919
Output	0.05	1.8	28.2
Output per Person Engaged	10.0	10.5	35.4
Output per Man-hour	7.8	8.3	33.0

[a] Adapted from J. W. Kendrick, *Productivity Trends in the U.S.* (Princeton, N.J.: Princeton University Press, 1962), p. 482. © Copyright 1961 by the National Bureau of Economic Research. Reprinted by permission of Princeton University Press.

We can form some impression of the influence of these technological developments on the efficiency of the automobile industry from the analysis of J. W. Kendrick. His figures on output and labor productivity for the motor vehicle and equipment industry for the years 1899–1919 are reproduced in Table 2 above. From them it can be seen that the increases in output and productivity for this industry were greatest, as we would expect, in the decade 1909–19. The record of the industry's output per man-hour over the years 1899 to 1954 places it second in a listing of some eighty manufacturing industries. The average annual rate of change in output per man-hour for this industry was 5.0 per cent over these years, second only to the cigar and cigarette industry, which had an average for the same years of 5.8 per cent. The average annual rate of change for all 80 manufacturing industries (simple mean) in Kendrick's calculations was 2.2 per cent.[48] Thus, we can see statistically that this young industry, which had its beginnings in this

[48] Kendrick, *Productivity Trends*, p. 162.

period, became one of the most dynamic in terms of output and productivity of all our great manufacturing industries. Schumpeter was of the opinion that in the period 1909–13 the automobile industry was a primary influence on the prosperity of the nation, though it was supplemented by other industries, some of which were completing developments started earlier.[49] But to appreciate this and other points we have made, we need to look more closely at the economic fluctuations during this period.

BUSINESS CYCLES OF THE PERIOD

Veblen's view that depression was chronic and normal under "the consummate regime of the machine" would seem to have had more validity for the years from 1873 to 1896 than for the period we are considering. In fact, Alvin Hansen, a leading student of business cycles, reverses Veblen's proposition and contends that since 1897 "prosperity has been chronic, so to speak, broken only by temporary periods of depression."[50] Hansen agrees with Veblen that in the long period of falling prices from 1873 to 1897 "depression was chronic in the United States and Great Britain, and to some extent in all countries." In this light Veblen's theory of chronic depression would appear to be a preconception derived from the experience of the late nineteenth century. How relevant and revealing is it during the period of rising prices after 1897? We need to review the principal depressions of this period to answer the question.

The recovery from the depression of 1893 was greatly aided by the increased world production of gold after 1896 that enlarged the monetary base of the international financial structure and contributed to rising prices. Prosperity was stimulated also by the extraordinary increase in European investment in this country and by the sudden increase in our export trade in 1897 and 1898. Thus, exogenous factors such as the poor European wheat crop of 1897 and the stimulus provided by the Spanish-American War in the following year were behind the recovery from the hard depression of the 1890's. With renewed confidence in the stability of the dollar, European investment in the United States skyrocketed. Between 1899 and 1908, foreign investments in this country almost doubled, going from $3,145,000,000 to $6 billion. "This was a more rapid increase than that of the national wealth of the country and more rapid than that at any time except during the 1850's and 1860's."[51] Our favorable balance of trade and the flow of capital into the nation permitted the financial reorganization and rehabilitation of the railroads. Their orders for steel and other goods, together with the growing

---

[49] Schumpeter, *Business Cycles*, Vol. 1, p. 424.

[50] A. H. Hansen, *Cycles of Prosperity and Depression in the United States, Great Britain and Germany* (University of Wisconsin Series in Social Science and History, No. 5, Madison, Wisc., 1921), p. 11.

[51] Faulkner, *The Decline of Laissez Faire*, p. 23.

demand for structural steel in the cities, stimulated the iron and steel industry, and its prosperity, in turn, contributed to a broad economic expansion of the whole economy.

The "rich man's panic" of 1903 was a reaction, fundamentally, to the frantic speculation that had been going on since 1897 in conjunction with the consolidation of business. In the former year some of these trusts failed, and there followed a sharp decline in stock prices. The effect on business activity, however, was slight as the following data indicate. It will be noted that

TABLE 3

Gross National Product and Its Components in the 1903–04 Downturn[a]
(Millions of 1929 dollars)

Year	Gross National Product	Consumption Expenditures	Gross Private Investment New Construction and Equipment	Change in Bus. Inventories	Net Foreign Investment	Govt. Purchases of Goods and Services
1903	$45,123	$32,761	$8,230	$689	$440	$3,003
1904	44,559	33,188	7,761	318	293	2,999
1905	47,870	35,090	8,430	817	310	3,223

[a] Adapted from Table A-II in J. W. Kendrick, *Productivity Trends in the U.S.* (Princeton, N.J.: Princeton University Press, 1962), p. 293; based on the Department of Commerce's concept of gross national product, as derived from Kuznets' estimates. © Copyright 1961 by the National Bureau of Economic Research. Reprinted by permission of Princeton University Press.

consumption expenditures in this recession actually increased; the downturn, it is clear, was mainly associated with the decline in gross private investment.

The boom of 1905 and 1906 was accompanied, as usual, by frenzied speculation on the stock market, despite the unfavorable political conditions. The "muckrakers" had started their exposés of financial skulduggeries and the federal government and the state legislatures were seeking to curb some of these excesses. In 1906, Congress passed the Hepburn Act to tighten the control of the railroads, and the New York State legislature approved the investigation of the life insurance companies by the capable Charles E. Hughes, seeking to correct some of the abuses in that field.

The crisis of 1907 when it came was also at first a rich man's panic, but its results were much more severe. Stock speculation had mounted until the fall of the year, when money rates tightened and confidence in stock prices began to wane. Signs of approaching trouble were appearing in foreign markets. The credit strain on the New York banks and trust companies had become intense in the fall, when finally the over-extended trust companies, notably the Mercantile National and the Knickerbocker Trust Company, were forced to close their doors, whereupon a run on all the trust companies in the city began. J. P. Morgan provided some aid to the solvent banks, the U.S.

Treasury deposited $35 million of the government surplus with the national banks, and clearing house loan certificates were used by the New York City banks to economize on the use of gold.

The downturn in business activity in 1907 was sharp, and though it was followed by a brief recovery in 1909, actually the American economy experienced a series of "recurring depressions" in 1910 and 1911, a second upswing in 1912, and then went into another major depression in 1914. The fluctuations of the gross national product and of its principal components for this peculiar period are shown in Table 4. We can see from this table that the

TABLE 4

Gross National Product and Its Components in the United States, 1907–14[a]
(Millions of 1929 dollars)

| | | | Gross Private Investment | | Net | Govt. |
Year	Gross National Product	Consumption Expenditures	New Construction and Equipment	Change in Bus. Inventories	Foreign Investment	Purchases of Goods and Services
1907	$54,277	$39,702	$10,062	$ 663	$ 210	$3,640
1908	49,790	37,197	8,491	−400	417	4,085
1909	55,893	41,269	9,748	1,395	−276	3,757
1910	56,499	42,034	9,956	875	−264	3,898
1911	58,312	44,064	8,872	706	84	4,586
1912	61,058	45,211	10,027	1,159	73	4,588
1913	63,475	46,701	10,871	1,158	269	4,476
1914	58,636	46,124	7,818	27	−182	4,849

[a]Adapted from Kuznets' estimates as reproduced in Kendrick, *Productivity Trends* (Princeton, N.J.: Princeton University Press, 1962), p. 293. © Copyright 1961 by the National Bureau of Economic Research. Reprinted by permission of Princeton University Press.

depression of 1907 caused a drop of close to $5 billion in the GNP and that the decline in 1908 was mainly in the curtailment of new construction and equipment purchases and a sharp liquidation of inventories. We note also the failure of capital formation in the former category to increase until 1912 and the disinvestment of foreign capital in 1909, 1910, and 1914. Consumption expenditures, on the basis of Kuznets' estimates, continued to rise after 1908 until 1914, but the improvement in this measure of consumer welfare was slower than it had been in the first decade of the century.

The explanation of the slow growth of the economy in the years after 1907 has usually traced the trouble to the "inefficient and inelastic nature of our credit system."[52] Retardation occurred in the growth of banking reserves relative to the financial and industrial development of the country. Further-

[52] W. C. Schluter, *The Pre-War Business Cycle, 1907–1914* (New York: Columbia University Press, 1923), *passim*.

more, the decentralization of reserves, which the old national banking system permitted, aggravated the problem. The inelasticity of the currency was due to the fact that it was secured by the bonds of the federal government; the size of the government's debt bore no rational relationship to the changing need of the economy for a circulating medium. Indeed, in a time of prosperity, the government's debt normally went down, thus shrinking the currency base, and it increased in a depression when usually the need for currency would be less. In short, the national banknotes were "perversely inelastic."

It would appear also that banking capital and surplus as well as the number of banks formed during the years 1907–12 were smaller than in the period 1902–07. Finally, the heavy withdrawal of foreign capital through the selling of securities also resulted in limiting the supply of bank credit.

Apart from the deficiencies of the banking system, the question can be raised as to whether there was insufficient aggregate demand to spur new investment and promote a more rapid rate of economic growth. Professor Hansen at one time believed that there was evidence of our approaching "economic maturity" or stagnation in the creeping depression of the years after 1908.[53] It is of interest to note that Schluter, who is usually cited as offering a bank credit explanation of the slow growth of this period, states that "the expanding volume of industrial production was not accompanied by a corresponding growth in the domestic demand for these products, because of the retarded growth in the consuming power of the agricultural and transportation classes and of the commercial elements allied with the fortunes of these. . . ."[54] He explains further that the retarded purchasing power of the farmers was due to the smaller volume of agricultural production rather than the level of unit prices. (Farm output seems to have increased 20–22 per cent between 1899 and 1913, whereas the output of the manufacturing and mining industries over the same period showed increases of 87 and 127 per cent, respectively.) Schluter found too that the gain in our export trade in these years, though absorbing the increasing volume of mineral and manufactured products, was not sufficient to offset the effects of the retarded agricultural production.

The failure of the new industries of this period, such as the automobile and its ancillary fields, to lift gross private investment to levels that would have made for a faster rate of economic growth needs exploration. There are indications that the growth rate of personal saving was high in these years, and it may be that the automobile industry's tendency toward internal financing prevented some savings from finding outlets in that field. The high cost of living in the pre-war years, attributable in large part to the rise in farm prices, probably dampened the demand for such durable consumer goods as automobiles. Some of these lines of thought are obviously speculative; the available statistics have not enabled scholars to carry out a more satisfactory

[53] A. H. Hansen, *Fiscal Policy and Business Cycles* (New York: Norton, 1939), *passim*.
[54] Schluter, *The Pre-war Business Cycle*, p. 182.

analysis of the economy's performance in these years. The knowledge that we have of the period, however, does not seem to support Veblen's notion of the normalcy of depression. Contrary to his view, great new sources of autonomous investment were opened up for exploitation and development in these years at a time when the railroads and the public utilities were not growing as rapidly as they had earlier. (As noted before, the role of innovations and autonomous investment in the dynamics of economic growth were not adequately treated in the Veblenian system of analysis; he saw technological change as only undermining capitalizations based on older technology.) And yet the investment opportunities created by the innovators in the automobile and its related fields, though they had an auspicious beginning in this period, were to bear their full fruit in the post-war years. But even before the outbreak of the first World War the United States experienced another depression of which some account must be taken.

The recession of 1913, which became a full-fledged depression in the following year (see Table 4) seems to have been related in its origins to the outbreak of the Balkan War in 1912.[55] Following this event, there were the usual effects of war upon the money markets in Europe: sales of securities, rise of discount rates, the hoarding of gold and its importation from the United States. These foreign developments quickly reflected themselves in the American economy. Although there was a return of confidence on the New York and London exchanges in the early months of 1914, commerce and industry in this country did not revive, but rather were adversely affected by additional exports of gold and the decline in foreign trade and commodity prices. The United States sank into another depression with its reduced production and widespread unemployment from which it did not recover until it felt the stimulus of the demand of the European belligerents in early 1915.

THE ECONOMIC IMPACT AND SIGNIFICANCE
OF WORLD WAR I

Though the first effect of World War I on the American economy was a severe financial crisis, in time the enormous demand from abroad lifted national income and employment to new high levels. At first, the effort of European investors and governments to sell their security holdings in this country drove stock prices down so precipitously that the New York Stock Exchange closed its doors on July 31, 1914 and did not re-open them until April of the following year. But soon the doubling of American exports to Europe between 1913 and 1916 caused a boom accompanied by a general price increase. Wholesale prices went up about 22 per cent and consumer prices about 11 per cent within those three years. Industrial employment

---

[55] See A. D. Noyes, *The War Period of American Finance, 1908–1925* (New York: G. P. Putnam's Sons, 1926), Chap. 1 for a competent analysis of these developments.

increased, the number of employed workers jumping from 38.5 million in 1913 to approximately 40 million in 1916. Unemployment, which had been about one million in 1913, practically vanished. Hourly wage rates in manufacturing rose three cents an hour (from 29 to 32 cents) and average annual wages in manufacturing increased from $578 in 1913 to $651 three years later. The impact of the war in these early years on the gross national product and its principal components is shown in Table 5.

TABLE 5

Gross National Product and Its Principal Components, 1915–19[a]
(Millions of 1929 Dollars)

Gross Private Investment

Year	Gross National Product	Consumption Expenditures	New Construction and Equipment	Change in Business Inventories	Net Foreign Investment	Govt. Purchases of Goods and Services
1915	$60,424	$45,322	$7,392	$ 229	$2,466	$ 5,015
1916	68,870	49,408	9,046	1,667	4,016	4,733
1917	67,264	48,342	7,856	486	3,601	6,979
1918	73,361	48,121	6,151	529	2,051	16,509
1919	74,158	50,245	7,869	2,865	3,502	9,677

[a] Adapted from S. Kuznet's *Capital in the American Economy* as reproduced in Kendrick, *Productivity Trends, op. cit.*, p. 293. © Copyright 1961 by the National Bureau of Economic Research. Reprinted by permission of Princeton University Press.

Our entry into the war in April, 1917 accelerated many of the tendencies that had been evident earlier toward a more highly organized economy with an increasing level of mass consumption of durable goods. In addition, the war gave the nation its first experience with comprehensive governmental controls and planning during wartime. While World War II was even more of a total war, in this first international struggle of the twentieth century the entire economic order of the nation was affected and a major segment of it mobilized for war on a vast scale. President Wilson pointed to this fact early in the war when he said, "It is not an army that we must shape and train for war, it is a nation." Howard Coffin, one of the industrial leaders in the mobilization effort, put it more graphically: "Twentieth century warfare demands that the blood of the soldier must be mingled with from three to five parts of the sweat of the man in the factories, mills, mines and fields of the nation in arms."[56]

The effective mobilization of the economy for war soon demonstrated that

---

[56] Quoted in G. B. Clarkson, *Industrial America in the World War* (Boston: Houghton Mifflin Co., 1923), pp. 13–14.

this could not be attained without the imposition of detailed controls on industry, agriculture, and finance and this necessitated the establishment of new, effective bureaucratic structures and a greater degree of governmental intervention in the decision-making process than had ever been the case before. Since organized action along these lines was unfamiliar to the nation, there was the need to improvise these governmental structures almost on a trial and error basis. As illustration, note the following actions. The federal government had set up an advisory Council of National Defense under an act of 1916 to study the problem of industrial mobilization. This body was supplemented in March, 1917, by the General Munitions Board, which had the complex task of coordinating the buying of munitions by the various military services. Still later the Allied Purchasing Commission was established to supervise and avoid competition and conflict between the Allies and U.S. government orders for war matériel. Finally, in July, 1917, the War Industries Board was organized by the Council of National Defense. Its duties were stated in exemplary governmental gobbledygook as follows:

> to act as a clearinghouse for the war industries of the Government, determine the most effective ways of meeting them, and the best means and methods of increasing production, including the creation or extension of industries demanded by the emergency, the sequence and relative urgency of the needs of the different Government services, and consider price factors and, in the first instance, the industrial and labor aspects of the problems involved and the general questions affecting the purchase of commodities.[57]

It was under the War Industries Board directed by its chairman, Bernard M. Baruch, that the nation learned the rationale of national planning, of rationalization of productive methods, of standardization of products, and the importance of conservation of raw materials. The Board's gigantic task is indicated by the estimate that it had to regulate the production of some 30,000 articles. It did this largely through a system of priorities, which gave preference to the production of military goods at the sacrifice of civilian output, enforcing its orders through the government's control of transportation and fuel.

Economy and standardization were the watchwords of industrial mobilization. Thus, in order to save coal, the service of elevators was regulated even to the number of stops and the number of passengers they could carry. The number of colors on typewriter ribbons was reduced from 150 to 5; styles of pocket knives were cut from 6,000 to 144. Even the manufacturers of ladies' corsets were forced to reduce their use of metal. Passenger car production was suspended in order to meet war demands. A major conflict occurred in the iron and steel industry with the "dollar a year men" (businessmen who served without compensation for the duration) over policy, but in the end the government had its way.

The agricultural side of the economy was under the supervision of Herbert

[57] Clarkson, *Industrial America in the World War*, p. 37.

Hoover's Food Administration. It not only fixed the price of wheat at $2.20 per bushel, but it established "wheatless Mondays," "meatless Tuesdays," "porkless Thursdays." The nation experimented with sugarless candy, vegetable lamb chops, whale meat, and shark steak. Brown sugar and oleomargarine were substituted on a large scale for the scarce refined sugar and dairy butter.

The Fuel Administration under Harry Garfield introduced daylight saving and "fuelless Mondays" to save coal; it also banned electric displays and decreed that passenger automobiles should not be operated on Sundays except by doctors, etc.

Early in the war a major bottleneck developed on the tracks of the eastern railroads leading to the coastal ports through which a vast flood of farm and manufactured goods passed. When voluntary efforts to end the congestion failed, the government took over the operation of the railroads in December, 1917, and they were administered by Secretary of the Treasury MacAdoo until March 1, 1920. Under his administration the rail lines of the country were operated as if they constituted a unified system with a single ownership. (Their owners were guaranteed by Congress an income equal to "the average net railway operation income of the three years ending June 30, 1917.") This principle of operation resulted in a sweeping reduction of non-essential passenger train service, common use of terminal facilities and equipment, and other economies. By these means the "traffic blockade" in the East was broken, and the movement of supplies to the battlefront assured. Under the government's operation of the railroads, higher rates and wages went into effect and maintenance of rights of way and equipment were neglected, leading to bitter disputes after the war over the efficiency of government ownership. In addition to the agencies mentioned, the government also organized the Emergency Fleet Corporation to build ships, the War Trade Board to deal in commodities, and the National Research Council to stimulate research, among others.

Apart from the government action in these forms, there was a remarkable increase in collective action among businessmen and workers during the war years. In order to expedite the control of industry, the War Industries Board encouraged the formation of trade associations; Chairman Baruch found it easier to deal with one association representing an industry rather than a host of individual industrialists. As a consequence, trade associations increased from 800 to 2,000 between 1914 and 1919. Justice Hughes stated at the time that "The war has compelled cooperation and the Government, under this compulsion, has fostered what it previously denounced as criminal."[58]

While the leadership of the American Federation of Labor wavered at first with regard to its position on the war, it gradually was won over against a pacifist stance. Later, labor's leaders were represented on some of the govern-

---

[58] *New York Times*, December 1, 1918, section 1, p. 19 as quoted in H. R. Seager and C. A. Gulick, Jr., *Trust and Corporation Problems* (New York: Harper and Bros., 1929), p. 306.

mental agencies, which was another boost to their prestige. With the establishment of the War Labor Board in April, 1918, there was an acceptance of mediation and concilation as a means of settling labor controversies. The Board adopted the principle that there should be no strikes or lockouts; in return, the right of workers to organize was recognized. From about 2.5 million in 1914, union membership grew to a total of close to 3.4 million by the end of the war. The average annual wage in manufacturing has been estimated to have gone from $580 in 1914 to approximately $980 in 1918, but a large part of this gain was cancelled by the increased cost of living.

The financing of the war is a subject that deserves close study because the methods used had wide repercussions in the post-war period; here we shall only be able to sketch the barest outlines of the policies pursued. The cost imposed by this war was staggering from the perspective of pre-war standards. By the end of the fiscal year 1919, the gross federal expenditure was running at the annual rate of close to 19 billion dollars. Yet before the war the federal government had been raising less than $1 billion in taxes. The Wilson administration decided to tax heavily, hoping at first to cover half of the expense by taxation and the rest by borrowing. Eventually, it settled on one-third as the proper proportion of war costs to be borne by taxation.

On the whole, the government borrowed first and formulated its tax program later. Its main reliance was on the income and excess profits taxes, which brought in about three-fourths of its income. Other sources included excises on liquor, soft drinks, tobacco, capital stock, estate, stamp taxes, customs, admissions, and dues. Under the 1918 Act, personal income of $1 million was subject to combined normal and surtax rates of 77 per cent. The magnitudes of the federal government's expenditures and revenues for the fiscal years, 1916 to 1920, are shown in Table 6.

With the large annual deficits of these years, the government's debt mounted extremely rapidly. By August, 1919, its gross total was over $33 billion; after deduction of various credits, such as amounts due from the

TABLE 6

Gross Federal Expenditures and Revenues, 1916–20[a]
(In millions of dollars)

Fiscal Year Ending June 30	Gross Expenditures	Total Revenues	Income and Profits Taxes
1916	$ 724	$ 783	$ 125
1917	2,067	1,124	387
1918	13,771	3,665	2,852
1919	18,952	5,152	2,601
1920	6,140	6,695	3,957

[a] Adapted from W. J. Shultz and M. R. Caine, *Financial Development of the United States* (Englewood Cliffs, N.J.: Prentice-Hall, Inc., 1937), pp. 524, 527.

Allies, surplus supplies and other assets, it was estimated to be $16 billion. This debt had been met during the war by the sale of the popular Liberty bonds and war saving certificates and stamps, but as time passed a large part of the amount outstanding had been bought by the member banks of the Federal Reserve System. By March, 1918, they had over three billion dollars worth of government securities. In retrospect, this large sale of government bonds to the banks was disastrous because it entailed no curtailment of civilian purchasing power. That is to say, if civilians had purchased them, there would have been a corresponding reduction in their purchasing power, but the banks merely had to pay for them by crediting the government with a deposit. This policy served to stimulate the inflation of prices, which was already marked because of the liberal credit program being followed by the Federal Reserve.

The course of the inflation is shown in Table 7 in terms of an index of wholesale prices. As can be seen, by the end of the war the wholesale price level was more than double what it had been in July, 1914. Shortly after our

TABLE 7

Index of Wholesale Prices in the United States, 1914–18[a]

July, 1914	100	Mar., 1917	161
Dec., 1914	98	July, 1917	187
” 1915	106	Dec., 1917	183
” 1916	147	Nov., 1918	206

[a] Source: U.S. Bureau of Census: *Historical Statistics of U.S.*

entry into the war the administration had won the nation over to a patriotic reduction of its purchase of luxuries and even of semi-necessities. For a year, from June, 1917 to June, 1918, this restriction of consumer demand was a fairly adequate offset to the increased war purchases of the American and Allied governments. The government's price-fixing efforts held down the cost of most of the essential goods; the prices of uncontrolled luxuries moved up steadily but not excessively. But in the summer of 1918 price control broke down altogether. "War prosperity" prevailed, and there was an uncontrollable rush to buy. Within three months, prices rose more than they had during the whole of the preceding year.

World War I ended in November of 1918, but its economic consequences were felt by the nation long after that date. The war had produced revolutionary changes in international finance and in many aspects of our national economic life. Even before our involvement in it, the courageous decision of the New York banks to maintain gold payments, even though practically all other nations banned the export of gold, made that city almost overnight the financial center of the world. The subsequent liquidation by Europeans of some three billion dollars in American securities, the massive loans to the

Allies, and the huge favorable balance of trade created by our sale of agricultural and manufactured goods to the belligerents transformed the United States from a debtor to a creditor nation and consolidated New York's position as a center of world finance. But this sudden change in the nation's financial status was to create difficult problems of adjustment in the post-war years. Likewise, at home the war left a legacy of stresses and strains in the form of excess industrial capacity and other distortions in the economy, which were to be persistent problems in the post-war years.

Chapter 22

THE PROGRESSIVE ERA OF POLITICAL AND SOCIAL REFORM

THE PROGRESSIVE RESPONSE TO INDUSTRIALISM

The rapid industrialization and urbanization of the nation, climaxed as it was by the "Organizational Revolution" at the end of the nineteenth century, profoundly transformed the lives of millions of Americans. It not only changed their statuses and roles in society, but it revolutionized their social values and ideologies in a most radical fashion. Of course, the most obvious result of the drive to industrial maturity was the great extremes of wealth and poverty it produced. Henry George as early as 1879 had denounced "the shocking contrast between monstrous wealth and debasing want in the nation," yet the inequalities of income and class status became even greater in the last two decades of the century. But the history of the years 1897 to 1918 was not simply a "popular attack against corporate wealth," as some interpreters would have it. As Samuel P. Hays states, the Populist and Progressive movements of those years were

> something more fundamental and more varied than an attempt by the dispossessed to curb the wealthy. They comprised a reaction not against the corporation alone but also against industrialism and the many ways in which it affected the lives of Americans. The people of that era sought to do much more than simply to control corporations, they attempted to cope with industrial change in all its ramifications. . . .[1]

In this chapter we are concerned primarily with that political movement known as Progressivism, which arose in response to these industrial ills and as a result of the renewed faith in democracy. It sought to solve the social problems of the time by improving democratic political processes. In studying the changes that this movement created in our political mores it will be helpful to keep in mind those characteristics of society that we earlier called "social imperatives" and to note how they were affected by it.[2] The role played by the nation's leadership—political, intellectual, and spiritual—in challenging the dominant ideology of *laissez faire* first claims our attention.

[1] S. P. Hays, *The Response to Industrialism; 1885–1914* (Chicago: University of Chicago Press, 1957), p. 188.
[2] See Chapter 1, pp. 9–11.

However glaring were the evils of the rampant, unchecked industrialism of the late nineteenth century in America and the accompanying social injustices, they were not to be easily corrected. The political corruption and conservatism of the "Gilded Age" stood in the way of adequate reform. And yet after thirty years of almost unchallenged conservative rule, a reaction would seem to have been due. But the political innovations needed to eliminate the nation's social injustices were blocked not only by vested interests, they were inhibited by the even more powerful force of vested ideas. This "steel chain of ideas," as Eric Goldman calls it, was composed of linked conceptions of economics, religion, morals, psychology, and philosophy that denied man's ability to change his society or even to influence his fate. Nineteenth century thought in America as well as in other parts of the western world had become dominated by deterministic ideologies that minimized man's capacity to change his social condition or to shape his future. The mechanistic formulations of the classical economists and of Hegel, Marx, and Spencer taught that man had to conform to the powerful, inexorable forces that determined his destiny. These iron laws of supply and demand, of competition, social evolution, or of the materialistic dialectic influenced the preconceptions and social outlook of many Americans in the late nineteenth century. Thus, the high priest of Social Darwinism in America, William Graham Sumner, stated that "the social order is fixed by laws of nature precisely analogous to those of the physical order" and that, consequently, an ant might as well try to move a mountain as for man to try to modify the unchanging laws of political economy. In a similar deterministic vein, the socialists of the day contended that man was but a creature of his economic class, which was, in turn, determined by the changing technology. Society, in their view, developed strictly according to the "scientific laws of evolution." In 1904, the Socialist Party proclaimed, "The Socialist program is not a theory imposed upon society for its acceptance or rejection, it is but the interpretation of what is sooner or later inevitable."[3]

Fortunately, a new vision of man and his society took shape in the late nineteenth and early twentieth centuries that challenged these deterministic philosophies and beliefs. Influenced by a variety of forces in industry, science, philosophy, and religion, this new conception saw the universe as something that could be changed by man's growing intelligence. In the United States, this outlook was represented by the pragmatism of William James and the young John Dewey, with its emphasis on the openness of a pluralistic universe and the importance of experience, activism, and ideals. Such a philosophy was the negation of the old conservatism and determinism; it was optimistic and held out the hope that the world could be changed for the better by man's creative intelligence.[4]

[3] G. E. Mowry, *The Era of Theodore Roosevelt, 1900–1912* (New York: Harper and Row, 1958), p. 46.

[4] This phase of our intellectual history is competently treated by Morton G. White, *Social Thought in America* (New York: Viking Press, 1949) ; R. Hofstadter, *Social Darwinism in American Thought, 1860–1915* (Philadelphia: University of Pennsylvania Press,

About the same time, the social sciences were becoming more respectable, more independent from the maternal discipline of philosophy, and better established. Professional journals were started, and a group of sociologists, including Lester Ward, Albion Small, Charles H. Cooley, and Edward A. Ross began to attack the dominant thought of the Social Darwinists. Likewise, a revolution in economics started in 1885 with the formation of the American Economic Association. Previously, *laissez faire* was so established a doctrine that, as one university president observed, belief in it was not a test of orthodóxy, "It was used to decide whether a man was an economist at all." Now a group of young rebels, Richard T. Ely, Simon Patten, and Henry C. Adams, challenged this doctrinaire view, asserting in their credo, "We regard the state as an educational and ethical agency whose positive aid is an indispensable condition to human progress."

In jurisprudence, the ideas of Oliver W. Holmes, Jr., as stated in his influential work on the *Common Law* (1881), were gaining a hearing. Holmes, though an avowed conservative, insisted that "The life of the law has not been logic; it has been experience." From this perspective, law was "man-centered, temporal, pluralistic and relative" rather than being the embodiment of absolute, unyielding natural laws. In a notable dissent, which attacked the Spencerian preconceptions, Justice Holmes reminded his fellow jurists that "The Fourteenth Amendment does not embody Mr. Herbert Spencer's Social Statics."

In the 1890's there were also the beginnings of that movement in Protestantism known as the "social gospel." Protestantism had suffered in the late nineteenth century because of its indifference to the plight of labor, its close relationship with the rich among the laity, and its tendency to sanctify the capitalistic ethic. Now, shaken by the discoveries of science and the claims of the New Theology, some ministers, such as Washington Gladden, began to preach a "Christian capitalism." Others, more radical, such as Walter Rauschenbusch and Walter D. Herron, denounced the "unregenerate economic system" and argued that abolition of private property and equal division of wealth were prerequisites for the attainment of real democracy. In 1904, Reform Judaism, recently organized in the United States, also sought through an influential committee to define the missions of Jews in terms basically similar to the Protestant reformers, such as Rauschenbusch. Among Catholics in these years, there was the crusading Father John A. Ryan who sought to apply the humanistic principles of Pope Leo XIII's encyclical, *Rerum Novarum*, to the industrial evils and injustices under unregulated capitalism.

The "new literature," as it was called, also made a contribution to the attack on the old ideas and conventions. The introduction of realism and

1944) ; G. E. Mowry, *The Era of Theodore Roosevelt*, Chap. 2 is a well written analysis of the intellectual tides which influenced the Progressive era. For contemporary European developments, see H. S. Hughes, *Consciousness and Society* (New York: Alfred A. Knopf, 1958), *passim*; for the significance of these trends in sociological thought, see T. Parsons, *The Structure of Social Action* (New York: McGraw-Hill, 1937).

social problems in the novel awakened the social consciousness of the nation and provided potential support for the reforms of the day. Even more effective were the exposés of the "muckraking" journalists, such as Ida Tarbell, Lincoln Steffens, Ray Stannard Baker, which stirred the indignation of the magazine-reading middle class over the "shame of the cities," frenzied finance, and political and economic corruption in all its forms. Even the imperturable Mr. Dooley noticed the change in his magazine fare. . . ."But now whin I pick me fav-rite magazine off th' flure, what do I find? Ivrything has gone wrong. . . . All th' pomes by th' lady authoresses that used to begin: 'Oh moon, how fair!' now begin: 'Oh, Ogden Armour, how awful!' "[5]

The feminist movement had been working to change the status of women since the Civil War, and by 1900 some important gains had been made. Five western states had granted women suffrage; co-education was a reality for those who could afford it. While women and children were still woefully exploited at the beginning of the century, their invasion of the factory and the office and the increased income and independence attending that development, had brought with it many advances in women's social and legal rights. Much, however, remained to be done. Women, especially the middle class ladies with leisure, now began to form clubs, to study social issues, to demand reforms. One of them, just elected president of the General Federation of Women's Clubs in 1904, told her listeners: "Ladies, you have chosen me your leader. Well, I have important news to give you. Dante is dead. He has been dead for several centuries, and I think that it is time that we dropped the study of his *Inferno* and turned our attention to our own."[6] In these years Jane Addams was starting Hull House in Chicago and Florence Kelley and Lillian Wald were establishing settlement houses elsewhere. Among Negroes, dissatisfaction with the gradualist policies of a Booker T. Washington were giving way to demands for immediate political, social, and economic equality. A sign of the new approach was the formation of the National Association for the Advancement of Colored People in 1910. The march of the Negro toward greater freedom and human dignity in the United States was to be a long one, but it had begun.

The "spirit of the times," it is evident, was a reforming one, and the Progressives were at the head of many of the reform movements. Their philosophy, in contrast to that of the conservatives or the socialists, led them to make a generous estimate of man's fundamental character, stressing his essential goodness and nobility. The evil they saw in man's behavior they traced largely to the social environment. In Eric Goldman's perceptive expression, many of them were reform Darwinists, believing that by reordering the social environment they could change human nature. Man was not the mere creature of his milieu, but could choose his course of action, be a prime mover of social change rather than a mere product of it. These convictions were often sustained by a faith and commitment to Christian ethics, even though some of the best Progressives were not churchgoing people.

[5] Goldman, *Rendezvous with Destiny* (New York: Vintage Books, Inc., 1956), p. 135.
[6] Goldman, *Rendezvous with Destiny*, p. 144.

"THE PSYCHIC CRISIS OF THE 1890's"

Understanding the Progressive movement requires an appreciation of what Professor Hofstadter has called "the psychic crisis of the 1890's."[7] The fact is that the depression of 1893 had an unusual emotional impact upon the American people because a number of singular events converged with that depression to heighten its effect upon the public mind. Among these were: (1) the heated campaign of 1896 with its allegedly "radical" agitation for Populist and free silver reforms, which to the middle class mind raised the spectre of social revolution; (2) the development of Big Business and trusts raised the prospect that the old kind of opportunities for the small, free enterpriser were a thing of the past; (3) the closing of the frontier seemed to mean that the land that had absorbed the energies of the American people for three centuries was gone and with its passing the nation faced a strange, new future.

> To middle-class citizens who had been brought up to think in terms of nineteenth century order, things looked bad. Farmers in the staple-growing region seemed to have gone mad over silver and Bryan; workers were stirring in bloody struggles like the Homestead and Pullman strikes; the supply of new land seemed at an end; the trust threatened the spirit of business enterprise; civic corruption was at a high point in the large cities; great waves of seemingly unassimilable immigrants arrived yearly and settled in hideous slums. To many historically conscious writers, the nation seemed overripe, like an empire ready for collapse through a stroke from outside or through internal upheaval. . . .[8]

The emotional crisis of these years revealed itself in two moods: one of sympathy for the "underdog" as shown by the protest and humanitarian reforms already evident in the 1890's (Populism, Socialism, the social gospel, etc.) and the other was power, national self-assertion, aggression. The latter had been displayed in a number of jingoistic episodes in the early 1890's, not to mention others in preceding years. These incidents are relevant to Veblen's contention that business politics promoted patriotism and militarism as a solution of the "social problem." Veblen in his characteristic fashion did not seek to support his view by detailed analysis of specific cases of imperialist or militarist adventure, and we do not intend to do that either. Discussion of these matters would take us too far afield; space will merely permit us to quote Hofstadter who states on this point that "It is hard to read the history of these events [our aggressive diplomatic stance in disputes with Italy, Chile, and the British, the latter over the Venezuela boundary in the years 1891–95] without concluding that politicians were persistently using jingoism to restore their prestige, mend their party fences, and divert the public mind from grave

---

[7] R. Hofstadter, "Manifest Destiny and the Philippines," as reprinted in *American Imperialism in 1898*, edited by T. P. Greene (Boston: D. C. Heath and Co., 1955), pp. 54–70.

[8] Greene, *American Imperialism in 1898*, p. 55.

internal discontents. . . ."[9] This and other interpretations of our foreign policy in these years could be cited in support of Veblen's view of the matter.

It is another story, however, when we turn to the causes of our involvement in the war with Spain over Cuba's freedom. That complex war—complex, that is, as to its causes—cannot, in the light of modern historical scholarship, be simply explained as an instance of business politics diverting the nation's attention from the social problem. Since J. W. Pratt's *Expansionists of 1898* it has been evident that an explanation of our entry into that war in terms of rational economic motives cannot be supported. To regard this as "the newspaperman's war" also ignores the crucial question as to why the public was so receptive to the war propaganda published by the "yellow press." We do know that the underdog elements in American society "showed a considerably higher responsiveness to the idea of a war with Spain than the groups that were more satisfied with their economic or political positions." The war gave these groups, politically frustrated by Bryan's defeat, an opportunity to discharge their aggressions against the Wall Street interests who they felt were coldly indifferent to the fate of both the Cuban insurrectionists and the staple farmers. As Hofstadter puts it, "The primary significance of the war for the psychic economy of the nineties was that it served as an outlet for aggressive impulses while presenting itself, quite truthfully, as an idealistic and humanitarian crusade. . . ."[10]

To place the onus of responsibility for this war upon business politics involves ignoring the key role in the movement for imperialism of that elite group of politicians, intellectuals, and publicists who argued for the "larger view." This group included in its ranks such men as Theodore Roosevelt, Senator Henry Cabot Lodge, John Hay, Senator Albert J. Beveridge, Whitelaw Reid, and others. They were mostly of patrician background, Mugwumps who disdained the corruption of business and domestic politics, and sought a wider sphere of statesmanlike action. Generally they feared that in the new phase of imperialism that was opening up in the western world if the United States did not adopt a policy of expansion and preparation for military conflict, it would be left behind in the struggle for life. Chief among these expansionists was Theodore Roosevelt, who felt that a war with Spain would build up our military and naval forces and would give "our people . . . something to think of that isn't material gain." Roosevelt feared that our power of defense would lag and that we could become "an easy prey for any people which still retained those most valuable of all qualities, the soldierly virtues." In Veblen's view, these men were advocates of dynastic politics, of a reversion to a warlike spirit more appropriate in an earlier age.[11]

[9] Greene, *American Imperialism in 1898*, p. 57.

[10] Greene, *American Imperialism in 1898*, p. 59.

[11] In the war with Germany in 1917–18, Veblen allied himself in sympathy with the Allied cause very early. Nevertheless, he did not regard Germany as a devil among angels. The outbreak of that war was the outcome of longstanding national ambitions and imperialist rivalries.

The war with Spain ended with our annexation of the Philippine Islands, a step that appealed to members of the business and political elite who saw in it the possibilities of increased American power and profits. It was opposed by the anti-imperialists who regarded it as a grave departure from our traditions. In the ensuing debate, the advocates of Manifest Destiny and Duty carried the day. Thanks to Theodore Roosevelt and other statesmen of the "larger view" the annexation of the Philippines was a *fait accompli* before the debate had begun. America acquired an empire in the Far East, but not without fighting a two-year insurrection led by Aguinaldo at a cost of 1,000 American lives and some $170,000,000. The psychic crisis of the 1890's had involved some very unforeseen consequences.

THE CORPORATE REVOLUTION AND PROGRESSIVISM

The Spanish-American War had brought the reform movement of the Populists to an end, but the further consolidation of business and the growth of labor unionism in the opening years of the new century reawakened a broader based drive for social justice, the so-called Progressive movement. Actually, a Progressive movement as such did not exist in the sense of there being a unified campaign for economic, social, or political reform. In the beginning, there was rather a number of movements—for social justice, for political reform in the cities and states, and, lastly, to achieve at the national level more effective control of business and banking and other legislation. Toward the end of this period, there was more unity in the effort because of the interrelationship between local, state, and national politics, though there was always a considerable diversity of ideas and programs.

While there were these differences in the directions of effort among the Progressives, the leaders had many social characteristics in common that give a clue to the nature of their reforms.[12] Generally, they were young and consisted mainly of the generation that had come of age in the nineties. (Theodore Roosevelt, one of the leading Progressives, was the youngest man to rise to the Presidency, and his outlook was symbolic of a generation that felt the need for a new philosophy and a new politics.) The progressives were mainly of American stock, chiefly British in origin; they were predominantly Protestant, with the Quakers, Congregationalists, Unitarians, and Presbyterians constituting the vast majority; Jews were represented among the very wealthy. In terms of social status, the great majority of the Progressive leadership was drawn from the "solid middle class," as it was proudly called. There were some millionaire supporters, but the movement's leaders came largely from the professional and business class. William Allen White,

[12] See A. D. Chandler, Jr., "The Origins of Progressive Leadership," in E. E. Morison and J. M. Blum, *The Letters of Theodore Roosevelt*, Vol. VIII (Cambridge: Harvard University Press, 1954), pp. 1462–1465; G. E. Mowry, *The Era of Theodore Roosevelt*, Chap. 5 and Hofstadter, *The Age of Reform* (New York: A. A. Knopf, 1955), Chap. IV.

surveying the Bull Moose movement of 1912, said it was "in the main and in its heart of hearts *petit bourgeois*": a movement of little business, professional men, well-to-do farmers, skilled artisans from the upper brackets of organized labor . . . the successful middle-class country-town citizens, the farmer whose barn was painted, the well-paid railroad engineer, and the country editor."[13] Professor Hofstadter has advanced the thesis that the Progressive leaders were primarily victims of the status upheaval that had accompanied the corporate, organizational revolution during the late nineteenth and early twentieth centuries; they did not suffer so much economically but from the changed distribution of social deference and power.[14] The new "monied men," self-made captains of industry had bypassed and overshadowed the old Mugwump type, the civic leaders of an earlier era. With the rise of the large corporations, labor unions, and powerful political machines, the unorganized middle class, both old and new, feared that they would be ground between the two extremes of organized power. ". . . The central theme," Hofstadter contends, "in Progressivism was this revolt against the industrial discipline: the Progressive movement was the complaint of the unorganized against the consequences of organization." The Progressive leaders saw themselves as a responsible elite, occupying, as Justice Brandeis put it, "a position of independence between the wealthy and the people, prepared to curb the excesses of either." Harboring a feeling of *ressentiment* against the uncultivated, irresponsible plutocrats, the Progressives directed their middle class moral indignation at the wrong-doings of those whom Roosevelt called "the malefactors of great wealth."

Walter Weyl, a perceptive participant-observer of the Progressive movement, noted many of these features in his *The New Democracy:* "As wealth accumulates, moreover, a cleavage of sentiment widens between the men who are getting rich and the men who *are* rich. . . . The old wealth is not a loyal ally in the battle for the plutocracy; it inclines, if not to the democratic, at least to mildly reformatory, programs. . . ." Weyl noticed the tensions and discontent caused by the blatant, conspicuous consumption of the newly rich. [In Cincinnati a distinction was drawn between the "stick-ems" (the actual pork-packers) and the "stuck-ems."] ". . . Our overmoneyed neighbors cause a relative deflation of our personalities. . . . Our jogging horses are passed by their high-power automobiles. We are obliged to take their dust." The frantic competitive consumption, with its infinite graduations, was increasing the general social friction and producing "an acute social irritation." ". . . We are developing new types of destitutes—the automobileless, the yachtless, the Newport-cottageless: the subtlest of luxuries become necessities, and their loss is bitterly resented. The discontent of today reaches very high in the social scale. . . ."[15]

[13] W. A. White, *Autobiography* (New York: The Macmillan Co., 1946), pp. 482–483.
[14] *The Age of Reform*, pp. 135, 213–214.
[15] As quoted in Hofstadter, *The Age of Reform*, pp. 146–148. Thorstein Veblen had satirized the wasteful consumption of the plutocracy in an unforgettable manner in his classic, *The Theory of the Leisure Class* (New York: The New American Library, Mentor Book, 1953).

Some students detect in the Progressive make-up a certain anti-urban bias, or at least a lack of sympathy and fear of the city with its millions of strange, uncouth immigrants who seemed so difficult to assimilate to the standards of Anglo-Saxon culture. But usually this was offset by either a sense of guilt for the condition of the underprivileged or a heightened sense of moral responsibility and determination to cope with the new conditions of urban, industrial life. Suffusing Progressive thought was the theme of restoring a type of economic individualism and political democracy believed to have existed before the rise of the great corporation and the corrupt political machine. With this restoration would come a kind of morality and civic purity, which, it was believed, the nation had lost.

The Progressive reform movement was unusual because it flowered during a period that was, on the whole, one of relative prosperity. The explanation would seem to be found in the rising cost of living in these years. Between 1897 and 1913 the cost of living rose about 35 per cent. This inflationary trend was particularly a source of discontent to the middle class because it was associated in its mind with the trustification of American industry and the relatively sudden advances made by the young but vigorous labor movement. The pocketbook of the average middle class citizen was pinched. As a result the antitrust movement took on new political appeal, and consumer consciousness, vague though it was, became much more important politically because it provided a least common denominator among people who had little else to unite them on public issues. This concern for that "forgotten man," the consumer, provided the Progressives with a powerful mass appeal that was irresistible.

THE PROGRESSIVE MOVEMENT IN THE CITIES
AND THE STATES

The crusade for municipal reform was the first expression of the Progressive impulse. It began sporadically in the 1890's with the overthrow of Tammany Hall in New York City in 1894 and took form elsewhere in the establishment of civic leagues. The "shame of the cities," as Lincoln Steffens, the muckraker, termed it, went back to the post-Civil War years. The fact was that the organization of city government in the U.S., with its dispersal of power and responsibility among a mayor, council, and numerous independent boards and commissions, was an invitation to machine politics. City governments lacked the cohesion and concentration of authority to govern. Furthermore, even when the forms of municipal government were changed, the machines survived because they were performing social services for the immigrants in the slums that the latter could not get otherwise. Of course, the price was the votes the immigrant masses delivered to the "bosses," but the friendless newcomers were not interested in honesty and efficiency. The machine survived also because it was based on patronage and loyalty. It provided jobs that many of the immigrants could not otherwise get, and in its hierarchical structure it stressed a kind of loyalty and obedience that some of them had known in the folk societies of the Old World. Finally, and perhaps most important, the growth of the cities created a host of business interests who wanted contracts, protection, and exemptions of various sorts. Franchises were needed for the new railway lines, for sewer, gas, and other public utilities, and the bosses had the disposal of these valuable rights; the business-men were willing to pay for them. This was the "system" that the muckrakers exposed in city after city at the turn of the century.

Actually, the city reformers appeared on the scene before the muckrakers had publicized the widespread graft and corruption. In Chicago, the Munici-pal Voters' League in 1895 began a non-partisan move to clean up the graft; similar moves were made in New York City by Seth Low in 1901. At this time there appeared a group of colorful tribunes of the people, men like "Golden Rule" Jones in Toledo, Thomas L. Johnson of Cleveland, and others, who lead successful fights against "the interests." Jones and Johnson were persuasive advocates of municipal ownership of public utilities as a means to curb corruption; the "gas and water socialism" of these years familiarized many Americans with the advantages of limited public ownership. In their efforts the reformers soon discovered that it was not sufficient to throw the rascals out and establish a program of decent government. The city bosses were usually part of the state "rings," and when they lost control of the municipalities they could retire to their state strongholds and await their return to power. For this reason the city reformers joined hands with other reform groups to improve the mechanisms of popular government by advocating the direct primary, the short ballot, the initiative, referendum, and recall. At the same time they sought greater "home rule" for their cities to free them from the corrupting influence of the state legislatures.

The truth was that practically all the states around the turn of the century were under the domination of the corporation-machine alliance, and corrup-tion prevailed in them for pretty much the same reasons that it reigned in the cities. A French map in 1905 depicted the extent of the political corruption in each of the forty-five states. It showed six states as being free from corruption, thirteen as partially corrupt, and twenty-five as wholly corrupt. While there were a few indignant replies to this French charge, there were no blanket denials because most informed Americans admitted the general truth of the allegation. It was facts such as these that justified Veblen's flat assertion made time and again in *The Theory of Business Enterprise* that "representative government means, chiefly, representation of business interests."

The pressure of the corporate interests for legislation was so great that it made the boss almost a necessity as a broker among their conflicting demands. Very often a powerful U.S. Senator became the arbiter and representative of the corporate interests, as did Matthew Quay in Pennsylvania and Thomas C. Platt in New York. In New Jersey, the public utility, railroad, and insurance interests divided the control of the state among themselves. Thomas N.

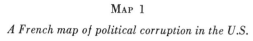

MAP 1

A French map of political corruption in the U.S.

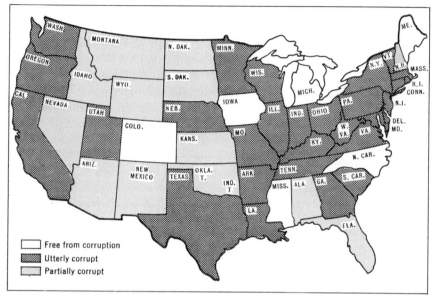

Free from corruption
Utterly corrupt
Partially corrupt

Source: From G. E. Mowry, *The Era of Theodore Roosevelt* (New York: Harper and Row, Publishers, 1958), p. 67. Reprinted by permission of Harper and Row, Publishers, Inc.

McCarter, president of the New Jersey Public Service Corporation, was frank to admit, "We've got everything in the state worth having, except Trenton street cars and Elizabeth gas. . . ." In the Middle West, corporate control was dominant also. In Wisconsin one of the corporation lobbyists boasted that "no bill had passed for sixteen years without their approval." In Missouri, the "boodle" system worked with amazing efficiency in the interests of the railroads and corporations. In the Far West, where one or two railroads commanded vast assets, the state capitals became sort of ancillaries of the main business offices of these firms. Collis P. Huntington, president of the all-powerful Southern Pacific Railroad, complained that politics took more of his time than railroading, remarking that if a man wanted to become constable, he would think that he had first to consult him. Years later Hiram Johnson, one of the great Progressives, won the Republican gubernatorial nomination on the slogan, "The Southern Pacific must be kicked out of state politics."

While there were early efforts at state reform, such as those of Altgeld in Illinois, Pingree in Michigan, and Roosevelt in New York (1899–1901), it was not until Robert La Follette defeated the Wisconsin machine in 1900 that the reform movement really got started. His election as governor started a chain reaction of revolt in the Middle West that later spread to the East. The latter region saw the election of such Progressive governors as Charles Evans

Hughes in New York in 1906 and 1908 and two years later of the crusading Woodrow Wilson in New Jersey. The battlecry of the Progressives in the states was "Give the government back to the people"—and they sought to do this by the political devices of more representative government mentioned above as well as by support for direct election of U.S. Senators and passage of corrupt practices legislation to control and limit campaign contributions and expenditures. Wisconsin, under the energetic leadership of La Follette, enacted the most comprehensive reform program of all the states, including control of railroads and other public utilities, conservation and water power legislation, a banking measure, as well as a mass of social legislation concerning women and children. When La Follette went to the United States Senate in 1906, Wisconsin had earned the title that Roosevelt later gave it, "the laboratory of democracy."

Other states also made outstanding progress in these years in humanizing the industrial system and in making government responsive to the needs of the people. After the Supreme Court held the Oregon ten-hour law constitutional, many states prohibited or limited night work and endeavored to protect women from "sweating" and from work endangering their health.[16] Massachusetts passed the first minimum wage law in 1912 and eight other states followed her example the next year. Likewise, New York State passed the first effective compulsory workmen's compensation act in 1910, and although constitutional amendments had to be made to obviate judicial opposition, so many states enacted such laws that by 1921, only six states and the District of Columbia were without them. While the judiciary, basing its decisions on an eighteenth century philosophy, was slow to change, even the state courts began to heed the humanitarian spirit of the age by upholding such laws, though they continued to harass labor organizations with injunctions and by their general interpretations of the law. In summary, we can note that even before remedial action had been taken on the national level, the Progressives had transformed the theory and practice of politics in the states and had given the nation a conception of the possibilities of positive, humane government in an industrial society.

THEODORE ROOSEVELT AND THE PROGRESSIVE MOVEMENT

Despite the gains being made in the states, it was evident even then that many of the maladjustments and evils that beset American industrial society were national in character and could only be corrected by federal action. But the system of corruption and conservative stand-pattism that had for so long permeated the state governments extended to Washington and paralyzed effective action there as well. This was the political situation when the bullet of an anarchist catapulted the man whom Mark Hanna called "that damn

---

[16] *Muller* vs. *Oregon*, 208 U.S. 412 (1908).

cowboy" into the Presidency. The man who did the most in the early years to weaken the forces of complacency and unreasoning conservatism and challenge the hold of *laissez faire* doctrines on the legislative mind has become a legend and, as portrayed by some, a caricature. Obscured by prejudice and preconception, Theodore Roosevelt's role as a professional politician has been neglected or ignored. Yet, in the case of so complex and controversial a personality, this is an aspect of his career that must be seen in the context of the turbulent, transitional age in which he lived and acted.[17]

Roosevelt was the scion of a well-to-do New York family, a graduate of Harvard, yet he chose to be a politician at a time when that calling was hardly considered respectable among those of his class. As a politician Roosevelt was a conservative, but with a difference. He wished to preserve the institutions of democracy that had emerged out of the American past. ". . . But preservation, he realized, depended upon change. 'The only true conservative,' he told a fellow Progressive, 'is the man who resolutely sets his face toward the future.' So he believed in change, but gradual change; change within established institutions; change obtained by adapting, managing, administering; change 'on suspicion.' "[18] Roosevelt had to adapt the office of the Presidency to the new demands of the emerging organizational society in the face of bitter and often blind opposition, but he succeeded. He did so by achieving a practical mastery of all the political devices at his command. At first he cautiously maneuvered with the conservatives who controlled the Party, later he dominated them; at the same time he persuaded and cajoled the people and the Congress to achieve the ends he sought. He mobilized the full powers of his office to mitigate the conflicts and tensions of our growing industrial society. Roosevelt had a morbid fear of revolutionary violence; in 1908 he said that he felt that he was living in an age like that preceding the French Revolution. He believed that American society could be wrecked by the clash between corporate collectivism and the emergent collectivism of the unions and the more radical movements of the time. In his opinion, the rapidity of social change had weakened the traditional political and social practices and thus strained the fabric of personal morality. Since social order could not be attained by individual or group action alone, it was necessary that a disinterested government should define the revised rules under which the new consolidated interests of the nation could resolve their conflicts in an orderly manner.

Roosevelt accepted the tendency toward consolidation as a fact of life and sought to channel and direct it toward the welfare of the whole nation. "This is an era," he said, "of federation and combination. . . ." Anticipating Professor Galbraith's concept of countervailing power, he went on to argue,

[17] John M. Blum in his *Republican Roosevelt* (Cambridge, Mass.: Harvard University Press, 1954) provides a most penetrating analysis of President Roosevelt in these terms. For biographical details and other aspects of the life of this great American, see W. H. Harbaugh, *Power and Responsibility, The Life and Times of Theodore Roosevelt* (New York: Farrar, Straus and Cudahy, 1961) and E. E. Morison and J. M. Blum, *The Letters of Theodore Roosevelt*, 8 vols. (Cambridge: Harvard University Press, 1951–54).

[18] Blum, *Republican Roosevelt*, p. 5.

A simple and poor society can exist as a democracy on the basis of sheer individualism. But a rich and complex industrial society cannot so exist; for some individuals, and especially those artificial individuals called corporations become so very big that the ordinary individual . . . cannot deal with them on terms of equality. It therefore becomes necessary for these ordinary individuals to combine in their turn, first in order to act in their collective capacity through the biggest of all combinations called the government, and second, to act, also in their own defense, through private combinations, such as farmers' associations and trade unions.[19]

In short, Roosevelt envisioned an equilibrium of the consolidated interests of the nation attained through government intervention and direction. His was a philosophy that totally repudiated the doctrine of *laissez faire*.

Upon assuming the Presidency, Roosevelt proceeded cautiously, feeling his way. Hanna controlled the Republican organization, and he had the power to deny him the nomination and to vitiate his program in Congress. Nevertheless, the President immediately began to construct his own personal organization within the Republican Party. In 1902, he took two steps that greatly strengthened his position: he brought the anthracite coal strike to a successful arbitration and he started the prosecution of the Northern Securities Company. Both these actions had immense symbolic importance because they showed the people that the country had a President who was capable of taking strong and independent action on behalf of the public interest. Roosevelt's action against the holding company, which combined three large northwestern railroads, the Northern Pacific, the Great Northern, and Chicago, Burlington and Quincy, had an ulterior motive. Roosevelt had this suit brought, despite the fact that he was opposed to dissolution as a remedy for the trust problem, because the conservatives in Congress had blocked his proposal to establish a Bureau of Corporations in a new Department of Commerce and Labor. Roosevelt nevertheless knew that an attack on the trust problem was an action that would win him the admiration and support of middle class America. The prosecution of this Company, which the farmers of the Northwest opposed, was "good politics," and the decision of the Supreme Court in 1904 served, in the President's mind, to annul the E. C. Knight case and settle the question whether government had the power to control corporations at all. In the general exultation over the Court's decision, one journalist said rather optimistically that there was no longer a question whether the giant corporations controlled the people or the people the corporations.[20]

Apart from the antitrust suit against the so-called beef trust, there were no further suits brought in 1902 and there was a lull in 1903 and 1904, as the election year approached. But after his re-election the antitrust drive was stepped up, suits being brought against some of the leading corporations in the nation, including the Standard Oil Company and American Tobacco. Roosevelt earned the name of "trust-buster," but ironically he had no faith in

[19] Blum, *Republican Roosevelt*, p. 110.
[20] See G. E. Mowry, *The Era of Theodore Roosevelt*, p. 133 for an acute analysis of Roosevelt's motives in this matter. See also, Blum, *Republican Roosevelt*, pp. 119–120.

dissolution as a cure for the industrial problem. Early in his Presidency and indeed throughout his entire administration he indicated his preference for supervision of the giant corporations rather than breaking them up. Thus, in 1902, he said, "The man who advocates destroying the trusts by measures which would paralyze the industries of the country is at least a quack and at worst an enemy to the Republic." During the 1908 campaign he contended that the only effective solution was to increase "Federal control over all combinations engaged in interstate commerce, instead of relying upon the foolish anti-trust law. . . ."[21]

Re-elected in 1904 by the largest popular majority ever given a candidate, after having campaigned on the slogan of the "Square Deal," Roosevelt confidently ordered an investigation of the meat packing industry and asked Congress for stringent railroad legislation, a pure food and drug act, publicity for campaign contributions, and additional conservation laws. The railroad program, which took form in the Hepburn Act, was the President's chief objective. In this he backed the innovation of giving the Interstate Commerce Commission the power to fix maximum reasonable rates.[22] There was strong opposition in Congress and in industry to the idea, but he shrewdly threatened tariff revision to gain support for his railroad legislation; he vigorously carried the fight to the people in numerous speeches; he wheeled and dealed, and at last, the Congress adopted his program for an efficient, administrative control of this key industry.

The depression of 1907 tended to aggravate the rift between the President and the business community and the conservatives in Congress with the result that he moved further to the left politically. While the conservatives were accusing the President of weakening business confidence and thus causing the depression, he upbraided the speculators and charged that "certain malefactors of great wealth" had increased the intensity of the panic "in order to discredit the policy of the government."

In his December, 1907 message to the Congress, Roosevelt recommended adoption of an inheritance and income tax, the national incorporation and regulation of interstate business, the regulation of railroad securities, and a further proposal for the fixing of their rates. When Congress didn't show much interest in these recommendations, he sent it the most radical message of his entire term of office. He included in it the proposals of the previous one and added another demanding federal regulation of stock market gambling. In addition, he blasted big business and the courts (a federal court had just declared unconstitutional a previously passed railway workmen's compensation law) and denounced "predatory wealth" for its opposition to his reform measures. In this address Roosevelt outlined many of the proposals that he was to espouse as a Progressive in 1910 and in his New Nationalism

[21] Theodore Roosevelt, *Autobiography*, p. 469.
[22] The Elkins Act of 1903 had utterly failed to check the rate discriminations which were given by the railroads to large shippers.

campaign of 1912. For the most part Congress ignored his major proposals for the regulation of business and the relief of labor. One of the major domestic accomplishments of the last two years of his administration was the conservation program. Spurred on by Gifford Pinchot, Roosevelt was successful, again over powerful opposition, in expanding reclamation work, extending conservation to include coal, mineral, oil, and power sites, and adding 150 million acres to the government reserves. This far-sighted program together with the White House conferences held on conservation, country life, and inland waterways was statesmanship of a high order, which set the standards and the guidelines for much that was done later.

TAFT, TARIFFS, AND TRUSTS

While Roosevelt went hunting for lions in Africa (with some American financiers mentally backing the lions), William Howard Taft, the chosen successor to T. R., took up the Presidency in a time of trouble within the Republican Party. The Progressives were challenging the Old Guard, and when they sought to unseat the tyrannical Speaker of the House, Joe Cannon, Taft unwisely sided with the conservative wing of his Party. He further alienated the insurgent elements in the Party and the nation by his stand on the Payne-Aldrich Tariff Act ("the best tariff act" ever passed, he called it) and his part in the Pinchot-Ballinger controversy, in which he backed the anti-conservationist position of the latter. On antitrust matters, Taft carried forward the aggressive program of prosecution and publicity initiated by Roosevelt. When Congress refused to pass his regulatory measures, he moved against the combinations in a wholesale manner. He instituted forty-six proceedings for dissolution of combines, but his major suits against United States Steel and International Harvester ended in failure. On the other hand, during his administration the Supreme Court handed down its historic opinions in the cases against Standard Oil and American Tobacco, which Roosevelt had instituted.[23] Since these landmark decisions affected so much that later transpired in this field, they deserve more than mere mention.

The government indictments against these two companies listed a long number of abuses of corporate power. Standard Oil was charged with controlling in 1904 almost 90 per cent of all the refined oil produced in the nation as well as owning all the important pipe lines that delivered the crude oil to the refineries. It had deliberately set out to obtain a monopolistic position and exclude all possible competitors. It had acquired its position by the most flagrant and predatory of methods: espionage, bribery, secret rebates, local price cutting, and charging exorbitant pipe line transportation rates to its

---

[23] *Standard Oil Company of New Jersey, et al.* vs. *United States,* 221 U.S. 1 (1911) *United States* vs. *American Tobacco Company,* 221 U.S. 106 (1911).

competitors. The Court concluded unanimously that it had grossly violated the Sherman Act, and it ordered its dissolution.

The American Tobacco Company was likewise accused of having a monopolistic control over production (86.1 per cent of cigarette output, 91.4 per cent of little cigars, 96.5 per cent of snuff, 76.2 per cent of smoking tobacco, etc.) and that it had used unreasonable restraints, such as price-cutting, buying up independents and yet advertising as if they were free competitors (bogus independents), etc. The company cited the Knight case in its defense, but the Court was unimpressed, holding that its intended purpose was to monopolize the industry. It, therefore, ordered its dissolution, after affirming the "rule of reason" as set forth in the Standard Oil case.

The Court's use of the rule of reason as *obiter dicta* in these cases began a storm of controversy that has continued even until the present. The adoption of this point of view introduced a broader interpretation of the Sherman Act and justified a distinction between "good" trusts and "bad" ones. (The rule of reason turns basically upon whether the practices employed by the accused have the effect of subverting competition. If they do not, they may be considered reasonable restraints). Abuse of power, it would seem, was the essence of illegality, but the court's ruling at this time gave no clue as to how the law would apply where abuse was absent, nor how much power was necessary to constitute a violation of the law. Critics of the decisions, including Justice Harlan who dissented from the Tobacco ruling, contended that the introduction of the rule of reason was tantamount to judicial legislation.

The dissolution plans, which were accepted by the government in these two cases, were prepared by the corporations' lawyers and provided for the reestablishment of the constituent companies of the "trusts" and a *pro rata* distribution of shares in the new companies on the basis of ownership of shares in the old holding companies. In the post-dissolution period, the new companies in time became truly independent, and the extraordinary expansion of the oil and tobacco industries during World War I helped to create a new competitive situation. Price leadership was practiced in these industries for some time, however, after their dissolution.[24] At the time of the original dissolution, many Progressives contended that the decrees were "a sham and a fraud." Despite the limitations of these decisions, the antitrust efforts of Taft and Roosevelt accomplished important objectives. The courts had made clear that the flagrant means used to establish monopolies in the past were prohibited by law, and in this sense the age of single-firm monopolies was over. Large corporations still dominated whole industries, but the oligopolies resulting from the checking of the monopoly drive now had to meet the rivalry of smaller firms. The protection of potential competition and of the efforts of these smaller competitors became an increased concern of the government thereafter.

---

[24] On the sequel of these decisions, see G. W. Stocking, *The Oil Industry and the Competitive System* (Boston: Houghton Mifflin Co., 1925). R. Cox, *Competition in the American Tobacco Industry* (New York: Columbia University Press, 1933).

THE CHANGING FORTUNES OF LABOR

Veblen's analysis of trade unionism in his *Theory of Business Enterprise* was, as he said, "somewhat schematic" and rather general in its conclusions about the future of the movement. He saw the animus of trade union organization as being at odds with the natural rights institutions of property and free contract. But the trade unions, said Veblen, do not overtly seek to dispute the merits of any given article of natural rights doctrine; they attempt rather to "cut into these articles" and modify them where they patently conflict with the conditions of life imposed by the modern industrial system. Trade unions seek revision not in terms of natural rights of property and individual discretion, but in terms of standardized livelihood and mechanical necessity. "Trade unionism is therefore to be taken as a somewhat mitigated expression of what the mechanical standardization of industry inculcates." When trade unionism becomes overtly hostile to the institutions of a natural rights character, it may be said, according to Veblen, to be socialistic, for want of a better term. Socialism was the logical outcome to which the trade union animus tends, but this was an outcome altogether in the future, if it was to be reached at all. The "socialistic disaffection," such as it was, was most notable in the mechanized industries and employments where the daily round of life and intellectual discipline were likely to create a habit of mind critical of the archaic institutional scheme of things and more inclined to view life in materialistic, matter-of-fact terms. These generalizations of Veblen about the labor movement at the opening of this century were discreetly vague and broad; they represented an application of his general sociology of knowledge regarding institutional influence upon the habits of thought of the different elements of American society.

In reviewing the history of the labor unions during this period in order to assess the general validity of Veblen's theories about them, we might well begin by noting the remarkable fact that the American Federation of Labor had successfully weathered the depression of 1893 and had come out of it, in fact, with a membership of about 265,000. This was an achievement, because in all previous depressions of any magnitude the labor unions had been practically wiped out. In the six prosperous years that followed, the A.F. of L.'s membership grew to a total of 1,676,000. In these years of a rising labor market, which has been termed "the honeymoon period between capital and labor," the unions won a number of notable victories. The general strike of the soft coal miners in 1897 under the capable leadership of John Mitchell resulted in recognition of the union, a 20 per cent increase in wages, establishment of the eight-hour day, and abolition of company stores, among other demands. Strengthened by this victory and over 100,000 strong, the United Mine Workers in 1900 turned to the anthracite coal industry in Pennsylvania, which was controlled by nine powerful railroads. Although the union did not win all its demands in this strike, it did accomplish its major objective, that of organization of the industry. Two years later, when the anthracite operators refused to discuss wage rates with the union, a second strike was called. This ultimately resulted in President Roosevelt's intervention and the grant of an arbitration award that was very favorable to the union; the sympathetic attitude of the public toward the workers and the President's independent action in this famous dispute made it a landmark in American labor history.

The leadership of the A.F. of L. in these years was under attack from within and outside the Federation, because among other criticisms, it was held that it was concerned only with the so-called aristocracy of labor, i.e., the craft workers. Gompers, it is true, was an advocate of "business unionism" and of voluntarism—that is that labor should rely mainly on its own efforts and not look to government for aid. The difficulties of organizing the mass production industries was illustrated by the steel strike of 1901. The Amalgamated Iron, Steel, and Tin Workers, a union that included only the skilled workers, had been defeated by Carnegie in 1892. When the United States Steel Corporation was formed, this union with the Federation's backing sought to organize all the workers, both skilled and unskilled alike. A general strike against the Corporation was called in 1901, but though a majority of the workers went out, the result, for a number of reasons, was unconditional defeat for the union. The Steel Corporation in subsequent years instituted a number of welfare activities, such as profit-sharing, safety campaigns, and workmen's compensation, and continued to stand as a bulwark for employers against the unions. In 1909, the American Sheet and Tin Plate Company, the last organized subsidiary of the Corporation, announced an open shop policy and despite the fact that the union struck for fourteen months, it again suffered a total defeat. As a result of its unrelenting warfare against the unions, in which it used industrial espionage, blacklisting of union leaders, and a welfare program, the United States Steel Corporation was able to maintain an open shop in all its operations from 1909 down to 1937.

Though the A.F. of L. was not successful in organizing the mass production industries in these years, a large number of unskilled workers were added to its ranks through so-called federal unions. Cement workers, hod-carriers, maintenance of way employees and others were directly brought under the Federation's control through such unions since they were not eligible for membership in the international craft unions composing the Federation. In this way the Federation's leaders sought to compete with the agitation of the Industrial Workers of the World for "one big union" that would protect all workers, regardless of skill.

The leadership of the Federation was being assailed from within and without in the opening years of the century. The socialists tried unsuccessfully to "capture" the organization in 1902 and 1903. More threatening to organized labor, however, was the counter-offensive, which the employers undertook in these years on behalf of what they called the "American plan"—the open shop. The counter-attack of the employers had started in 1900 in Dayton, Ohio and then spread to other midwestern cities such as Detroit, Chicago, and others. In 1903, the National Association of Manufacturers, which was composed largely of small and medium sized companies, took over the leadership of the open shop campaign. It established the Citizens Industrial Association for the purpose of forming employers' associations throughout the nation. Such powerful trade associations as the National Metal Trades Association and the National Founders began their opposition to unions in the years 1904–05. In 1902, the hat manufacturers of Danbury, Conn. formed the American Anti-Boycott Association. The former group was successful in prosecuting the famous Danbury Hatters' case (1908), which resulted in heavy antitrust fines for the leaders of the union involved.[25] Likewise, in the Buck Stove and Range case, which involved the boycott of this Company by the A.F. of L., a District of Columbia court issued a sweeping injunction against the Federation's leaders. In these years and in the 1920's the injunction was widely resorted to by employers to restrict unions and their activities. The leaders of organized labor assailed the indiscriminate use of this legal procedure by unsympathetic judges, but they did not succeed in curbing its use substantially until the passage of the Norris-LaGuardia Act in 1932.

The A.F. of L. was faced with the threat of "dual unionism" in these years as well. In 1902, the Western Federation of Miners, critical of the Federation's craft emphasis and general philosophy, disaffiliated itself and formed a rival federation, the American Labor Union. Three years later these industrial unionists joined hands with the radical socialists to form the Industrial Workers of the World. Organizationally, the I.W.W. stressed industrial unionism based on the unskilled workers and the idea of "one big union." Politically, they advocated revolutionary socialism, proclaiming that instead of the conservative motto, "A fair day's wage for a fair day's work," their slogan was "Abolish the wage system." They sought to implement their program by avoiding political or parliamentary action, relying instead on the general strike and sabotage as their chief weapons. The I.W.W. was handicapped from the start by factional quarrels; in 1907, the Western Federation of Miners seceded and later rejoined the A.F. of L. The remainder of the I.W.W. split into two camps—the Detroit and Chicago groups. While the dues-paying membership of the I.W.W. was never large (in 1913, they had only 13,000 such members), their non-dues paying enrollment was probably over 100,000. Nevertheless, the appeal of this organization to the "wobblies" (the migrant laborers who cut the timber and followed the harvests) and to other unskilled workers, and its willingness to employ sabotage, gave it a strength in combatting the ultra-conservative employers of the time. The I.W.W. first attracted public attention in the Goldfield, Nevada strikes of 1906–07, and later in its fight for free speech on the Pacific coast. The peak of its power came in 1912 when it organized strikers at Lawrence, Mass., Paterson, N.J., and Little

[25] *Loewe* vs. *Lawlor*, 208 U.S. 274 (1908).

Falls, N.Y. After those struggles, it waned in power, leaving the nation only the memory of its militant leaders, such colorful figures as "Wild Bill" Haywood, Elizabeth Gurley Flynn, and others. In retrospect, it is generally agreed that the effect of the I.W.W. on the A.F. of L. was salutary in that its rivalry stimulated the older organization to form its industrial departments and in that way the need for industrial unionism was partially, but not adequately, satisfied.[26]

Many Progressives were uncertain about the tactics of the labor unions, if not definitely anti-union. While they usually sympathized with the problems of labor, they tended to fear unions as the sole counterweight to organized capital, and where labor was powerful in politics, Progressivism often had an anti-union character.[27] Middle-class Progressives tended to look to the "neutral state" rather than to labor unions to humanize industrial society through law. The legislation these reformers proposed was looked upon by them as preventive social work; in retrospect, now that much of what they fought for has become a legislative reality, we realize that they were laying the foundations of the "welfare state."[28]

Another phenomenon of these years was the growth of what Veblen called the "socialistic disaffection." The principal manifestation of this was the socialist political movement that grew steadily from 1901 to 1920. Organized in the former year, the Socialist Party of America under such leaders as Eugene Debs and Victor Berger offered a radical but non-doctrinaire type of socialism, which gained increased support. Its popular vote increased from about 95,000 in the Presidential election of 1900 to 897,000 in 1912; the latter figure represented 6 per cent of the total popular vote cast and was the highest percentage strength in the Party's history. Debs ran for the Presidency five times between 1900 and 1920; in the latter year, he polled over 900,000 votes, despite the fact that he was in prison during the campaign under sentence for violating the Espionage Act.

This American socialism comprised a wide variety of groups and individuals: western farmers and miners, German and Jewish immigrants, and a wide array of professionals, many old supporters of Edward Bellamy's type of Nationalism. Though diverse, these groups were unified in a third party that registered their dissent and common feeling of alienation from American society as it existed. As Veblen stated, this type of socialism differed rather markedly from the "Scientific Socialism" of Marx and Engels; it represented rather "an animus of dissent from the received traditions."[29] The "threat" of

26 These departments, such as the Building Trades and Metal Trades departments, sought to avoid jurisdictional disputes among the craft unions. The departments were said to represent "craft industrialism."

27 Hofstadter, *Age of Reform*, p. 239; G. Mowry, *The California Progressives* (Berkeley: University of California Press, 1951), p. 295.

28 R. H. Bremner, *From the Depths* (New York: New York University Press, 1956), p. 138.

29 Veblen, *Theory of Business Enterprise*, p. 161. Veblen's speculations as to susceptibility of certain classes in the United States to socialism are suspect. He says that the men in the skilled mechanical trades are peculiarly liable to it and the great body of

socialism, about which much was made in the Progressive period, served to goad the Progressives to find ways to remedy the ills of capitalism and in this way it gave added impetus to the middle class programs of reform.[30]

In the years 1910–16, the trade union movement made a second advance after the repression and employer opposition of the preceding period. The total union membership of the A.F. of L. increased by slightly more than one-third from 1910 to 1913; during the depression of 1914–15 it temporarily halted and then resumed its growth in the following year. The most notable gains were made in the mining and the clothing industries in these years. Especially significant was the increase in the number of women who were organized and who now for the first time began to take an important part in the labor movement. On the whole, the gain in membership was accounted for in part by the more favorable attitude of the middle class toward the unions, thanks to the "muckrakers" and other social reformers who were making the public conscious of the hardships of working class life. The rising cost of living and the progress of social legislation probably also tended to make for a more sympathetic attitude towards the unions.

The advance in the mining industry was the result largely of successful strikes by the United Mine Workers in the expanding but previously unorganized West Virginia soft coal industry and in further gains in the anthracite field. In the face of long, bitter opposition in which there were many violations of civil liberties, resort to martial law, and outright violence, this union finally won the right to organize and other gains in the years 1912–13. The miners were not so successful when they tried in 1913–14 to correct the deplorable conditions in the mining towns of southern Colorado. Here they had to meet the powerful force of the Colorado Fuel and Iron Co., a Rockefeller enterprise, and an industrial despotism that dominated the lives of whole communities. The conflict came to a climax in the pitched battle between the company guards and workers at Ludlow, Colorado in April, 1913, resulting in the death of several men, two women, and eleven children. President Wilson ordered the federal troops into the state to restore order, and tried unsuccessfully to settle the strike; it collapsed after more than a year of economic warfare between capital and labor.

The organization of the clothing workers, one of the great milestones of union progress in these years, was the achievement of the International Ladies Garment Workers' Union and of the Amalgamated Clothing Workers. During that period, immigrant female workers were being exploited in "sweatshops" in New York's East Side and other cities in which they worked for as long as

---

the rural population are immune. This contention must be squared with the fact that the American Party was strongest in Oklahoma (a reflection of the Populist tradition). Veblen spoke slightingly of those neophyte socialists, "especially rural Americans, who are carrying under socialist mottoes the burden of animosities and preconceptions that once made populism. . . ." (*Theory of Business Enterprise*, footnote 18, p. 219 of the Mentor paperback edition.)

[30] Hofstadter, *The Age of Reform*, p. 238.

seventy hours and earned only four or five dollars a week. The plight of these workers was brought to the nation's attention by the tragic fire at the Triangle Waist Company in New York in 1911 in which 148 persons, mostly girls and young men, were burned, smothered, or trampled to death. The New York State Factory Investigating Commission was set up as a result of this fire, and its chairmen, Robert F. Wagner and Alfred E. Smith, disclosed such neglect of safety and sanitary conditions in the state's factories that the legislature passed more than 35 new factory laws within two years' time. In 1909 the Ladies' Waist Makers' Local went out on a general strike and after much violence on picket lines and arrests of many women, the workers won all their demands but the closed shop. The cloak and suit makers shortly afterward struck also to secure the abolition of subcontracting and won most of their demands; most important, they established the machinery for a system of industrial arbitration that made possible a long period of industrial peace. In this same year, 1910, workers in the men's clothing industry under the leadership of Sidney Hillman struck the firm of Hart, Schaffner and Marx in Chicago; this strike encouraged organization of the men in the clothing industry generally and led eventually to the formation of the Amalgamated Clothing Workers of America and one of the most highly successful experiments in industrial government based on equal participation by employer and union. The organization of these unions in the clothing trade had great significance: it placed Jewish and Italian immigrant workers for the first time in the forefront of the labor movement. These workers, with their more socialist, reform ideology, their staunch commitment to the idea of industrial government based on union recognition, and their belief in industrial unionism reinvigorated American unionism as a whole. Indeed, the "new unionism," as the philosophy and program of the clothing workers came to be known, was outstanding for its rationalization and improvement of the process of industrial government by collective bargaining and by its progressive and generous concern for all workers in the industry. These unions later distinguished themselves by their readiness to help other unions and by their interest in general social reform as well as in the advancement of their own organization.

WOODROW WILSON AND THE PROGRESSIVE MOVEMENT

The Progressive movement came to a flood tide in the years 1910–16, and its turbulent course was irrevocably determined by Theodore Roosevelt's decision to bolt the Republican Party and lead a third one. As a consequence of his action, the nation was afforded a choice between two versions of Progressive ideology in the historic Presidential election of 1912: the New Nationalism of Roosevelt and the New Freedom of the Democratic Party's eloquent candidate, Woodrow Wilson. President Taft in running for re-election stood on his conservative Republicanism and the Socialist Party's perennial candidate, Eugene V. Debs, espoused a philosophy rather more radical than that of three main contenders for the office.

Roosevelt had been maturing his program since as early as 1905; Herbert Croly had outlined a similar philosophy in his influential work, *The Promise of American Life* (1909), which the ex-President had read and generally endorsed. Since his second term of office, Roosevelt had been convinced of the need for stronger national government and wider executive powers to promote the nation's welfare. He had come to the conclusion, in short, that the older individualistic version of the American democratic creed was inadequate for an urbanized and industrialized society. *Laissez faire* as a guiding philosophy of government had to be abandoned for a democratic collectivism ready to employ the governmental power to regulate and protect business, industry, and labor. The New Nationalism, Roosevelt said in the course of the campaign, was

> impatient of the utter confusion that results from local legislatures attempting to treat national issues as local issues. It's still more impatient of the impotence which springs from overdivision of governmental powers. . . . This New Nationalism regards the executive power as the steward of the public welfare. It demands of the judiciary that it shall be interested primarily in human welfare rather than in property, just as it demands that the representative body shall represent all the people rather than one section or class of the people.[31]

On the issue of governmental regulation of business, Roosevelt argued that corporate concentration was inevitable in many industries and that the wisest course was to subject the large corporations to comprehensive regulation by the government. At the same time he would have society recognize that women and children in industry were powerless to protect themselves and therefore should be aided by a broad program of state and federal social legislation.[32]

Woodrow Wilson, Roosevelt's Democratic protagonist in this struggle for the leadership of the national Progressive movement, was a professor turned politician—but quite an unusual professor and an extraordinary politician! Born in Virginia the son of a Presbyterian minister, graduated from Princeton and Johns Hopkins Universities, he was successively a lawyer, professor of political science, president of Princeton University, and governor of New Jersey before he was nominated as a Progressive reformer by the astute Democrats. Actually, Wilson was somewhat of a latecomer to Progressivism; in his early years his economic ideas consisted basically of the *laissez faire* concepts of a Manchester liberal, and his politics stressed states rights. He had long been an admirer of the British cabinet system of government and in his

---

[31] As quoted in J. M. Burns, *The Deadlock of Democracy* (Englewood Cliffs, N.J.: Prentice-Hall, Inc., 1963), p. 115.

[32] A. S. Link, *American Epoch, A History of the United States since the 1890's* (New York: A. A. Knopf, 2nd Ed., 1963), p. 120. Professor Link states that the platform of the Progressive Party "erected mileposts that the American progressive movement would follow for the next fifty years. It was, in fact, the most important political document between the Populist platform of 1892 and the Democratic platform of 1936 . . ."

classic work, *Congressional Government* (1885), he had contended that the basic cause for the failure of leadership in this country's national politics was the separation of the executive from legislative responsibility and action. However, in the interim since the publication of that book he had witnessed the Presidential leadership provided by Cleveland and Roosevelt and his own experience as governor had demonstrated to him that the President as party leader could be "the great unifying and energizing force in national government."

In the campaign of 1912 Wilson's program of the New Freedom stressed the need to destroy the Republican system of tariff protection and to restore competition by outlawing unfair trade practices and enforcing the Sherman Act. These ideas were urged on him by Louis D. Brandeis, his chief adviser in the campaign. In general, Wilson attacked the New Nationalism as creating a business government that would enslave the workers and offered instead new freedom for the small man in a system of individual enterprise and destruction of all special privileges. He was vague on social legislation and presented no definite program such as Roosevelt's. Still, his moving oratory and ability to formulate the issues in moralistic terms undoubtedly captured many votes.

Wilson's victory offered him an unusual opportunity to put his conception of Presidential leadership and the strong executive to the test. The election of a Democratic House and Senate gave his Party control of the national government for the first time since Cleveland's second term. As a consequence of their long exile from power, there was no Democratic machine in Congress, so that whereas Roosevelt could only force that body to act by appealing to the nation, Wilson could act as the leader of the responsible party in power. He executed this role in such magnificent fashion that his management of Congress in 1913 and 1914 has been said to stand as "the copy book model of how a strong President drives his program through Congress." He appeared in person before Congress to present his proposals; he conferred with leaders incessantly; he used the caucus and the veto to forward or defeat bills; he articulated his ideas for the public with an eloquence unrivalled since Lincoln.

First on the Democratic agenda for Congress was the revision of the tariff as promised. Wilson called a special session of Congress for the purpose and in surprisingly short order the Underwood-Simmon Act was passed. This Tariff Act represented a real downward revision of the schedules; the general average of its duties was about 29 per cent as compared with 37–40 per cent under the Payne-Aldrich Act. Iron ore, crude iron, steel rails, farm implements, and raw wool were put on the free list. The sugar duty was reduced and provision made for free entry of that commodity in 1916. To offset the anticipated loss of revenue, the Congress adopted a mild, graduated income tax as suggested by Representative Cordell Hull of Tennessee. It was an auspicious beginning, for despite the howls of the special interests and the machinations of the lobbyists, the tariff had been reformed.

Difficult as the tariff revision had been, the banking legislation presented even greater problems. The nation had been suffering for some years from a banking system that was dangerously decentralized and inflexible, despite the increasingly national and complex character of the economy. The National Monetary Commission, established in 1907 and headed by Senator Aldrich of Rhode Island, had recommended a single central bank such as England's, in which the private bankers would play a dominant role. The Democrats had condemned the Aldrich plan in their 1912 platform, but they were hopelessly divided over an alternative. The progressive Democrats, reflecting the views of those who felt that the West and South were the economic victims of the financial imperialism of Wall Street, argued for a reserve system and a currency owned and controlled by the government. The conservative Democrats, on the other hand, fearing a repetition of Bryan's monetary heresies, favored a decentralized system under private auspices, but free from Wall Street domination. With the able assistance of Representative Carter Glass, chairman of the House Banking Committee, Wilson managed to mediate among these conflicting interests and find an acceptable compromise. As finally adopted, the Federal Reserve Act established twelve Federal Reserve Banks owned by the member banks and controlled by directors, the majority of whom were chosen by the latter. Provision was made for a seven-man Federal Reserve Board (now called the Board of Governors) appointed by the President, who was placed at the head of the organization. The new Act also created the Federal Reserve notes, issued by the Reserve banks on the basis of collateral (commercial or agricultural paper) and a 40 per cent gold reserve. This currency was designed to be flexible, that is, it would expand or contract with the needs of trade because it was based partly on commercial paper. Under the law, every national bank was required to become a member of the Federal Reserve bank of its district. Such member banks were given the right to discount their commercial paper at their district bank so that they could supplement their reserves when needed. This system not only provided the nation with a more uniform and elastic currency, but through the discount privilege among member banks and district banks, it mobilized the monetary reserves of the system and enabled it to function, in effect, as a single central bank. The adoption of the Federal Reserve Act represented a historic break with *laissez faire* in monetary matters; later developments in the Federal Reserve System and in the nation's monetary standard permitted it to move toward a philosophy of managed currency that was increasingly necessitated by the demands of a growing organizational economy.[33]

[33] In a provocative article by W. C. Frederick, "Was Veblen Right About the Future of Business Enterprise?" *The American Journal of Economics and Sociology* (July, 1965), pp. 225–240, the author points out that especially since the Great Depression of the 1930's, "the entire money and banking system has been treated less as a sacred repository of property rights and more as a technical mechanism to be so manipulated that it will exhibit the least interference with the industrial system." (p. 233) He asks, with reference to the latter development, "Isn't this what Veblen meant by the 'cultural incidence of the machine process?'" Rather than accepting the inference of the author's rhetorical question, the authors of the present volume are inclined to answer his question in the negative. What he says about the evolution of the banking system since the adoption of

In line with their campaign promises, the Democrats also renovated the antitrust law by passing the Clayton Act and establishing the Federal Trade Commission. In contrast to the punitive Sherman Law, the new legislation of 1914 had a preventive or prophylactic approach to business regulation. The idea was to curb unfair practices and monopoly in their incipiency, and so, as it was said, prevent the "puppies" from growing into the giant dogs of monopoly. The Clayton Act was an omnibus measure, and we shall not enumerate all its provisions, except to note its principal features. First, it banned price discrimination, such as had been practiced in the form of local price wars where the would-be monopolist would lower the price in one area to drive out competitors, while maintaining it elsewhere. It prohibited so-called tying contracts, which had just been upheld in the United Shoe Machinery case.[34] Lastly, it contained a ban on holding companies and interlocking directorates, where "the effect may be to substantially lessen competition or tend to create a monopoly." (This qualifying clause created trouble for the courts and frequently led them to adjudicate in such a way as to defeat the original intentions of the law's sponsors.) The Clayton Act in Section 6 also gave trade unions and farm marketing cooperatives what seemed like a broad exemption from the antitrust laws, but subsequent court decisions whittled away and nullified much of this gain in the case of the former. The Federal Trade Commission, superseding the Bureau of Corporations, was given a broad mandate to prevent unfair methods of competition and granted far-reaching powers of investigation. Unfortunately, the Commission for many years did not fulfill its promise because of poor, political appointments, inadequate financial support, and weakening of its powers by the courts.

The enactment of the antitrust laws in 1914 marked the completion of the limited reform program of the Wilson administration. In earlier actions the President had clearly indicated that he was not willing to sponsor advanced social legislation such as that advocated by some Progressives and other reformers. The New Freedom envisioned government's role as a limited one, and therefore Wilson drew back from support of the child labor bill, the seamen's legislation, and permitted segregation of Negro and white workers in the Treasury and Post Office Departments. But there were signs of a more progressive outlook in the administration's acceptance of the Clayton Act and the revised conception of the Federal Trade Commission.

With the outbreak of the European War and the Republican gains in the 1914 legislatures, Wilson was faced with the prospect that Roosevelt might lead the Progressives back into the Republican Party and defeat him two years later. To lure Progressives into the Democratic ranks, Wilson had to abandon his *laissez faire* and states' rights doctrines and, paradoxically, adopt many of the former's proposals. Among other Progressive steps, he appointed

---

the Federal Reserve Act is unquestionably true, but it seems to be stretching words and their meaning unreasonably to credit Veblen with foreseeing this development under the umbrella concept of "the cultural incidence of the machine process."

[34] *U.S. vs. Winslow*, 227 U.S. 202.

Louis D. Brandeis to the Supreme Court and supported the Child Labor Act of 1916, a workmen's compensation act for federal employees, the Smith-Hughes Act of 1917 providing federal funds for vocational education in public high schools, and the Bankhead Good Roads Act of 1916, providing federal funds for highway construction. While these changes in Wilson's position undoubtedly represented a shift of philosophical conviction on his part, the pressures of the changing political situation compelled the administration to sponsor and enact the most important social and economic legislation in American history before 1933.

The domestic legislative accomplishments of the Wilson administration were impressive, the leadership of the nation in World War I bold and imaginative, the sponsorship of the League of Nations a far-sighted act of statesmanship, but behind the President's tragic defeat in the battle for the League and in some other areas was his uncompromising moralism and his tendency to see politics only as a grand encounter between the forces of light and darkness. National leadership at the top was needed, and this Wilson gave, but there was a need also for reorganization and leadership of the party at the base; this he failed to provide.[35]

VEBLEN AND THE PROGRESSIVE MOVEMENT

Veblen has been called "a Voltaire (or rather a Bernard Shaw) of Progressivism,"[36] yet when we finally appraise his theory of economic growth in its relation to this period, we see how questionable it is to consider his analysis a typically Progressive one. In many respects his was more a Populist critique of the American economy. His juxtaposition of "savagery" and "barbarism," of industry and finance, was largely derived, as David Reisman and others have pointed out, from the Populist atmosphere of the Middle West in the post-Civil War period.[37] This dualistic interpretation of American economic development with its stress on making goods and making money, while it clarified some aspects of the analytical problem, obscured others, as we have observed in the preceding chapter. The irony of history in his case, as in so many others, was that the cultural lag that he saw in the archaic institutional furniture and ideology of his day applied to his own ideas; social change was so rapid that Veblen's conception of reality became obsolete.

As illustration, let us take his prediction in the closing pages of *The Theory of Business Enterprise* that "the full dominion of business enterprise is

---

[35] See J. M. Blum, *Woodrow Wilson and the Politics of Morality* (Boston: Little, Brown and Co., 1956), pp. 197–198; J. M. Burns, *The Deadlock of Democracy*, pp. 146–147; A. Ranney, *The Doctrine of Responsible Party Government: Its Origins and Present State* (Urbana, Ill.: University of Illinois Press, 1954), pp. 44–77.

[36] P. d'A. Jones, *The Consumer Economy* (Baltimore, Md.: Penguin Books, 1965), p. 378.

[37] D. Riesman, "The Relevance of Thorstein Veblen," in *Abundance for What?* (Garden City, N.Y.: Doubleday and Co., 1964), p. 391.

necessarily a transitory dominion." Veblen was arguing here that there were three main forces contending for dominance in America at the turn of the century: the machine process, the business enterprise system, and what he called "dynastic politics." These three cultural features, he contended, were mutually incompatible. While business enterprise controlled industry and sabotaged its operation, it was, he suggested, likely to be undermined either by the "cultural incidence of the machine process" or subordinated to the demands of the dynastic state. "It stands to lose in the end whether the one or the other of the two divergent cultural tendencies wins, because it is incompatible with the ascendancy of either." This was a very dramatic conclusion for a provocative book, but it left something to be desired. Veblen was not very precise about the timetable for this denouement, saying only that "the calculable future" belonged to the one or the other cultural tendency, but not to business enterprise. Some scholars have interpreted Veblen's prediction of the natural decay of business enterprise to refer to the passing of *laissez faire* capitalism and see in the whole movement toward regulated capitalism a fulfillment of his prophecy.[38] Such an interpretation seems to give Veblen credit for developments with which he was not wholly sympathetic. As Professor Dobriansky has observed, Veblen did not approve of regulated capitalism; his ideal society was more like guild socialism. Veblen, with his materialist metaphysic, was inclined to ridicule the moralism and the uplift characteristic of the Progressives and to be more sympathetic toward the socialist view of reality, though he was aware of the vagueness of the socialists' plans for the future.[39] Still, in retrospect, it is clear that the Progressives were largely successful in passing laws that regulated capitalism and, even more significant, in raising the level of human sympathy in the American political and economic system. "The Progressives, by creating a climate of opinion, in which, over the long run, the comfortable public was disposed to be humane, did in the end succeed in fending off that battle of social extremes of which they were so afraid. . . ."[40] This was an accomplishment that Veblen with his peculiar preconceptions and values was not able to recognize.

Nevertheless, Veblen's achievement as a social critic and satirist did much to demolish the faith in the old order of things and provided that indispensable element of skepticism that exploded the received view of knowledge and

[38] Gruchy, in Dowd, *Thorstein Veblen: A Critical Appraisal*, p. 180.

[39] Veblen in a much overlooked footnote in *The Theory of Business Enterprise* (New York: The New American Library, A Mentor Book, 1958) wrote, ". . . The socialists of the line, in so far as there is any consensus among them, profess that the mechanical exigencies of the industrial system, must decide what the social structure is to be, but beyond this vague generality they have little to offer. And this mechanical standardization can manifestly afford no basis for legislation on civil rights. Indeed, it is difficult to see how any scheme of civil rights, much or little, can find a place in a socialistic reorganization." (*Ibid.*, p. 219, footnote 18.) The insights and point of view expressed in the last sentence were never adequately developed by Veblen in his later work. In his concern with productive efficiency, he completely ignored, at least explicitly, the organic relationship between the character of the economic system and the maintenance of basic human rights.

[40] Hofstadter, *The Age of Reform*, p. 238.

social life and thus contributed to the remaking of the status quo. The late C. Wright Mills wrote that Veblen realized that the world he lived in was dominated by what one might call "crack-pot realism."[41] This is a shrewd observation and contains much truth, but one needs to realize that Veblen's work, despite its insights and suggestiveness, was filled also with his own variety of "crack-pot scientism." Veblen has his strengths, but also some very serious weaknesses. He lacked an appreciation of the manner in which competition might contribute to social welfare; he neglected the role of innovation in relation to investment. He did not appreciate the directive function of the price system; by stressing the need for closer articulation of machine industry he slurred over this aspect of the organization of society and the rational utilization of its resources. Further, by oversimplifying the analysis of the future of business enterprise he ignored the influence of democratic, gradualistic reform. (His constant refrain, "A constitutional government is a business government" had more point in the "Gilded Age" than it did in the Progressive era.) Finally, in picturing the future as involving a choice between socialism and the dynastic state (totalitarianism) Veblen probably oversimplified again. He did not perhaps fully anticipate the resurgence of nationalistic militarism that has been so conspicuous a feature of the post-1919 world, nor did he foresee the possible amalgamation of dynastic politics with the machine process—the possible future of which President Eisenhower warned us in his farewell address—the warfare, garrison state which, some fear, already dominates our lives.[42]

---

[41] Introduction to *The Theory of the Leisure Class*, Mentor Edition (New York: The New American Library, 1953), p. vii.

[42] W. C. Frederick in his stimulating article, "Was Veblen Right About the Future of Business Enterprise?" *The American Journal of Economics and Sociology* (July, 1965), pp. 225–240, makes this point among others.

Part 8

THE EMERGENCE AND DEVELOPMENT OF THE "CONSUMER ECONOMY," 1919–1932

Introduction: Theories of Monetary Management and Stable Economic Growth

Economic Outlines of the "New Era" and the "Great Depression," 1919–1932

The Economic Anatomy of Prosperity and Depression

Sociological and Political Change in an Emergent Consumer Society

INTRODUCTION: THEORIES OF MONETARY MANAGEMENT
AND STABLE ECONOMIC GROWTH

Money assumed a new importance in the American economy and in economic analysis in the post-war years. The unusual changes in bank deposits, governmental debts, and in the price level together with the new creditor status of the nation and the inflow of gold emphasized the influence of money upon the economy, especially in a developed country such as the United States where bank credit was so important relative to currency. In this period also, it must be remembered, the Federal Reserve System was still in the experimental stage and numerous proposals were made to have it conduct its operations so as to achieve more stable economic growth. In these years, writes Dorfman, ". . . The conflicting theories of the monetary experts and the measures for solving most of the problems tended to take specific shapes in the continuing discussions about Federal Reserve policy and legislative proposals for limiting or extending the functions of the system."[1]

As a matter of fact, Veblen's emphasis on the importance of pecuniary institutions in the development of capitalism was represented in these years by the work of one of his chief students, Wesley C. Mitchell, whose monumental book on *Business Cycles* did much to shape thinking on the subject.[2] Mitchell had started to write a book on the money economy in which he proposed to analyze the cultural significance of the pecuniary institutions in the broadest fashion, but growing dismayed at the immensity of the subject, he prepared his treatise on business cycles instead. He called the latter a *Voarbeit* (an introduction or preparatory work) to the money economy. In his work on business cycles, Mitchell, after reviewing the variety of theories that had been previously advanced, turned to a systematic examination of statistical data on cyclical fluctuations and distilled from them an "analytical description" of a typical cycle. Mitchell believed that the earlier theories of business cycles were weak because their authors had been intent on determining a "cause" for such phenomena rather than analyzing the "conditions" that collectively produce cyclical movements in the business system.

In describing the many conditions that produce business cycles, Mitchell did not attempt to point out any single cause or any few causes of cyclical movements. By an analytical description of cycles Mitchell meant a systematic account of the processes by which a given phase of business activity turns into another phase. Rather than merely describing concrete events in the manner of some economic historians, Mitchell sought to measure statistically the fluctuations in the various economic and financial activities that in their totality

[1] J. Dorfman, *The Economic Mind in American Civilization*, Vols. 4 and 5, 1918–1933 (New York: The Viking Press, 1959), p. 279.
[2] *Business Cycles* (Berkeley: University of California Press, 1913).

constitute business cycles. Instead of defining a business cycle at the outset of his investigation, Mitchell preferred to concentrate on the facts first and to defer formulation of a theory until a later stage of his study. "An inquiry into business cycles," he wrote, "cannot wisely begin by defining the general concept, and proceed systematically to take up one part of the whole after another. It should begin rather with the individual processes which can be studied objectively, seeking to find what those processes are, how they affect each other, and what sort of whole they make up."[3]

Wesley Clair Mitchell (1874–1948) was born in Rushville, Ill. He received his Ph.D. in economics from the University of Chicago. He taught at the University of California, Columbia, and the New School for Social Research. He also served on many governmental committees.

Wide World Photos

Mitchell, nevertheless, tentatively defined business cycles to be "a type of fluctuation characteristic of economic activities organized in the form of business economy or high capitalism," to use Sombart's term. For the purposes of his analysis he took the larger institutional framework of the business system as a given datum, i.e., as relatively unchanging, and within this framework he developed his conception of a typical cycle. These fluctuations in general business activity had a wave-like pattern with each cycle including a phase of revival, expansion, recession, and contraction. There was a definite tendency for recurrence of cycles because of an "inner mechanism" that caused one phase of the cycle to generate the next; each period of the cycle was thought of as containing the seeds that would inevitably flower and produce the next phase. This has come to be spoken of as Mitchell's self-generating theory of economic fluctuations.

Thus, it can be seen that Mitchell conceived of business cycles as a highly interrelated economic process that operated over the entire length of the typical cycle. As such, these cycles appeared to him to be a most devastating

[3] Quoted in A. G. Gruchy, *Modern Economic Thought, The American Contribution* (Englewood Cliffs, N.J.: Prentice-Hall, Inc., 1947), p. 294.

hindrance to long term economic growth because an economy subject to them would always be liable to either explosive expansions or a dampening series of economic depressions. So long as they occurred without adequate social control or moderation, an economy could never be sure of sustained development. Furthermore, it is to be noted that Mitchell's concept of the self-generating character of cyclical fluctuations fostered the idea that if a depression was to be avoided, the appropriate preventive action would have to be taken in the preceding phase of the cycle.

Mitchell based his description of the main features of the inner mechanism of business cycles upon his careful study of a wide array of statistical time series. He concluded from this analysis that as the business economy operated through time, there was an uneven movement of costs and prices, with a resulting narrowing of profit margins in some sectors of the economy and an increase in others. For example, in the early phase of expansion, he found that retail prices rose less promptly than the wholesale prices of the same commodity. In general, as the expansion phase proceeded, costs of production tended to creep up on selling prices, largely as a result of increased raw material costs, increased unit cost of labor or declining managerial efficiency. Higher costs might be caused also by rising interest rates or higher rentals. As a consequence, severe strain developed in some particular sectors of the economy.

Mitchell found that the limits to business expansion are set by the expansibility of currency and credit and by the rate of long term loans. He noted too that the expansion may end since some firms in this phase of the cycle overstock because of faulty forecasting. The immediate factor causing a crisis, he observed, is the restriction of credit, because increased interest rates make the capitalized value of securities upon which credit rests fall. Liquidation probably begins with those enterprises caught in the cost-price squeeze and then spreads to other firms. The ensuing contraction causes adjustments conducive to revival, but the latter do not themselves bring it about. Revival is aided by the wearing out of consumer durable goods, change in tastes, population increases, or the working off of excess inventories. In his view the various movements of the business system in each phase of the cycle tend to be self-reenforcing rather than self-limiting. These movements proceed until they have gone so far that a reversal of some kind becomes inevitable. Mitchell insisted that the inner mechanism of this self-generating cycle is more important than exogenous factors in producing change.

On the basis of Mitchell's calculations, the average duration of the cycle he described was about 49 months. He recognized, however, that the length of the cycle was affected by secular changes in the economy or gradual changes in its institutions. "The broader changes of economic organization," he wrote,

> . . . are cumulative, like the lesser changes which make each phase of every business cycle evolve upon its successor. And, being cumulative, their dominating influence upon the phenomena of business cycles stand out clearly in the lapse of years. Hence it is probable that the economists of each generation will

see reason to recast the theory of business cycles which they learned in their youth.[4]

The determination of the regular features of business cycles, Mitchell believed, should make their prediction possible. On the whole, he devoted much more of his attention in the early decades of the century to improving his knowledge of business cycles than to suggesting how they might be controlled. In 1913, his suggestions for control included "the reorganization of the banking system, the development of government spending policies designed to concentrate public spending in depressions rather than in periods of prosperity, the stabilization of the dollar, and the democratizing of the knowledge of current business conditions possessed at that time by only a few of the more important business and financial leaders."[5] Again, in December, 1921, at a roundtable discussion surveying the possibilities of controlling the business cycle, he stressed the manipulation of rediscount rates by the Federal Reserve System, the establishment of unemployment insurance schemes, and the long-range planning of capital expenditures by private business enterprises. In these years Mitchell's philosophy concerning the control of business cycles concentrated on certain strategic points in the economy, such as the money market, from which an effort at stabilization could be made. During the 1920's, he was busily engaged in directing the National Bureau of Economic Research, which he had helped to establish and which he believed could carry out the systematic research to cope with the problems of an increasingly collective economy. He made numerous speeches in those years advocating improved economic intelligence in the form of statistics as the way to "lick" the business cycle; but then came 1929, and Mitchell all but stopped making such speeches. Appointed by President Hoover as the chairman of the Research Committee on Social Trends in that year, Mitchell surveyed the trends of the economy in great depth as the depression grew worse and its economic casualties mounted. Reporting in 1933, to the dismay of the President, Mitchell and his distinguished co-committeemen concluded that existing governmental practices were no longer sufficient to cope with the maladjustments resulting from technological change and the recurrent fluctuations of the economy. Organized social intelligence had to be applied to the problems of economic unbalance if they were to be successfully solved. Collective management of the economy would have to be substituted for the faltering, automatic functioning of the system. As the Committee stated, ". . . To deal with the central problem of balance, or with any of its ramifications, economic planning is called for."[6] In succeeding years, Mitchell continued to express his belief in Veblenian phraseology that the nation was "in for more rather than less governmental planning in the calculable future." The economic planning that Mitchell espoused was definitely democratic in its procedure.

[4] Mitchell, *Business Cycles*, p. 583.

[5] Gruchy, *Modern Economic Thought*, p. 303.

[6] President's Research Committee on Social Trends, *Recent Social Trends in the United States* (New York: McGraw-Hill Book Co., 1933), p. xxxi.

The national planning board would have only an advisory capacity and would submit its recommendations to Congress for its approval and action.

The idea that the price level could be stabilized and with it to some degree employment and production was propagated most vigorously in the 1920's by two brilliant economists, Irving Fisher and John Maynard Keynes, the prophets of "managed currency." Fisher, the "bad boy" of American economics, gained wide attention in the profession in these years for his advocacy of the so-called compensated dollar. Under this plan, he would have the government periodically change the gold content of the dollar as variations occurred in an accepted price index. As he stated it, "I aim to replace a gold dollar of fixed weight and varying purchasing power by a dollar of fixed purchasing power and varying gold content."[7] Without going into the details of Fisher's proposal, it must be made clear that its effectiveness rested, among other factors, upon the validity of the quantity theory of money of which he was a prime exponent. In the 1920's, this theory was expressed in terms of the equation of exchange that Fisher had presented in 1911 in his *The Purchasing Power of Money*.[8] His equation of exchange is stated algebraically as follows:

$$MV + M'V' = PT.$$

In this cash-transactions equation, the symbols on the left side of the equation represent money flow, and the symbols on the right, the money value of the flow of goods.[9] The equation of exchange, as stated, was generally regarded by economists as a truism and occasioned little controversy in itself. However, the advocacy of the quantity theory of money was something else again. This theory contended in effect that the general level of prices was determined normally by the quantity of money, changing proportionally with changes in money (M). Fisher, for example, in the work cited, after considering the behavior of the various factors in the equation of exchange, concluded that M' was a function of M, that V and V' were constants like T, and that therefore P varied with M. "One of the normal effects of an increase in the quantity of money," he wrote, "is an exactly proportional increase in the general level of prices. . . . We find nothing to interfere with the truth of the quantity theory that variations in money (M) produce normally proportional changes in prices."

After the depression of 1920–21 Fisher, impressed with the seriousness of unemployment, advocated the proper control of credit as well as of gold. He

[7] I. Fisher, *The Purchasing Power of Money*, Rev. Ed. (New York: The Macmillan Co., 1931), p. 495.

[8] (New York: The Macmillan Co., 1911).

[9] The symbols stand for the following: M is money in circulation, both coin and paper, but excludes bank reserves and money held by the Treasury. V is the velocity of circulation of money. M' represents the volume of bank deposits. V' is the velocity of circulation of bank deposits. P is the general price level prevailing during a given period, as measured, say, by an index number. T represents the total volume of transactions for which money payments are made; it includes goods, services, and securities and is equivalent to the physical volume of trade. *Purchasing Power of Money*, pp. 157, 183.

contended that the variations in the volume of output and employment were fundamentally due to the "dance of the dollar," i.e., to the fluctuation in its value. In 1924, he argued that the world should remain off the gold standard because credit was now controlled by bank policy rather than the gold supply and, furthermore, return to the old standard would entail deflation and unemployment for such countries as Great Britain and others that might follow her lead. The United States, Fisher maintained, was only nominally on the old gold standard because gold imports were being "sterilized" by the Federal Reserve in order to prevent inflation. Fisher's ideas were given wide circulation; they were embodied in bills before Congress in 1922 and 1924, and he continued incessantly to argue the case for managed currency. However, he opposed the attempts of the Federal Reserve to restrain the stockmarket boom, contending that the "new economic era" was soundly based on a tremendous increase in American productivity. He backed his faith in these views by borrowing on his securities to purchase additional common stocks right down to the eve of the "great crash."

Keynes, the British economist, brought all the force of his keen mind and lucid style to the attack on the gold standard and in behalf of managed currency in the 1920's.[10] He maintained that the gold standard in promoting stability of foreign exchange rates limited the discretion and independent action of central banks and governments and kept progressive communities "below the standard of monetary management which they might otherwise attain." He suggested the substitution of an inconvertible paper standard for the costly gold standard, which he regarded as a "vestigial economic institution." He proposed definite manipulation and control of the supply of money and bank credit with a view toward price stabilization, holding that such measures would eliminate the ups and downs of the business cycle. This would be accomplished mainly through the discount and open-market operations of central banks, aided by a coordinated fiscal policy of government borrowing and repayment.

The managed currency proposals of Fisher and Keynes did not go uncontested in these years. In fact, their monetary heterodoxy was competently criticized, and the quantity theory assailed by economists on either side of the Atlantic. In this country, outstanding among such critics were the pungent H. P. Willis of Columbia University, B. M. Anderson, Jr., the capable economist of the Chase National Bank, Oliver M. W. Sprague of Harvard, an international money doctor for many governments, and Joseph S. Lawrence of Princeton. These monetary controversies reached a new pitch in 1926 when bills were introduced in Congress that would give a direct mandate to the Federal Reserve System to maintain a stable price level. The Federal Reserve authorities unanimously opposed any such mandate, holding that it was impossible to execute such a policy and that even if it were possible it would

[10] Notably in such works as *A Tract on Monetary Reform* (New York: The Macmillan Co., 1924) ; *The Economic Consequences of Sterling Parity* (New York: Harcourt, Brace and Co., 1925) ; *A Treatise on Money* (New York: Harcourt, Brace and Co., 1930), 2 vols.

result in unstabilizing the economy in some other vital aspect or in curbing the growth of the economy. The System's principal instruments of credit control in these years were the rediscount rate, open market operations, and least effective, moral suasion or warnings to the member banks on their use of credit. Apart from other problems, the Federal Reserve's task, as we shall see, was greatly complicated by the remarkable growth of credit extended to the stock brokers in the later years of the securities market boom and the development of a new type of credit, installment finance, which experienced a sensational advance after 1919, especially in the sale of automobiles. Public confidence in the Federal Reserve System in the 1920's was high, and in the latter years of the period some boldly maintained that business depressions were a thing of the past because of the new power of monetary management.[11] In the chapters of this section we shall be appraising, as before, the relative validity of these new doctrines of managed currency in the light of the nation's financial experience.

[11] "Monetary policy reached the height of its prestige during the 1920's. Many experts were convinced that the Federal Reserve System, with its ability to expand and contract money and credit, made panics and depressions impossible. But these convictions were proved altogether wrong when the economy collapsed in 1929. . . ." (H. E. Kroos, *American Economic Development*, 2nd Ed. [Englewood Cliffs, N.J.: Prentice-Hall, Inc., 1965], p. 244.)

Chapter 23

ECONOMIC OUTLINES OF THE "NEW ERA" AND THE "GREAT DEPRESSION," 1919–1932

POST-WAR BOOM AND DEPRESSION

The economic events and experiences of the American people in the years 1919–32 have not only been recounted and analyzed by many historians with scholarly care, they have been indelibly etched upon the minds of millions. Many of the latter have looked back with nostalgia to the "Golden Twenties," while others are alleged to suffer still from a "depression psychosis" as a result of their experience in the 1930's. This period was characterized by unusually severe economic storms at its beginning and its end, with an intervening spell of good economic weather in the middle. This cycle of our economic development opened with a wild, speculative boom, followed by one of the most precipitous declines in business activity we had yet experienced, and then entered upon an illusory period of stability, which was marked, nevertheless, by genuine growth in national income and well-being, only to be succeeded by the most disastrous financial crisis and depression in our history.

The signing of the armistice on November 11, 1918 found the nation with four million men in the armed services and about nine million persons, or about one-fourth of the civilian labor force, engaged in war production. Six billion dollars of war contracts were still outstanding; one-third of these contracts had already been completed and more than half of the remainder were cancelled within four weeks after the cessation of hostilities. Amazing as it may seem, two days after the armistice the War Industries Board began to terminate price controls. The dismantlement of the wartime agencies was so rapid that the executives of some of the government organizations had to lend money to their stenographers to enable them to get home![1] Many Americans were exceedingly anxious to get back to business as usual and their peacetime pursuits, but why didn't this "incontinent abandonment" of wartime controls

[1] G. Soule, *Prosperity Decade: From War to Depression, 1917–1929* (New York: Rinehart and Co., 1947), p. 81.

and rapid cutback of military orders produce a major crisis of unemployment?

Actually, there was a minor slump in business in the late months of 1918 and early 1919 with the result that President Wilson appointed a new Industrial Board under George N. Peek to ease the transition of the economy to peace, but before much was done along those lines, production and employment turned upward in the spring of 1919 and a boom developed that lasted until the middle of 1920. The federal and state governments did relatively little to aid industry, agriculture, or labor in adjusting to peacetime conditions. There had been plans to discharge the men in the armed forces on the basis of job availability, but instead the Army was ordered by the Chief of Staff to demobilize whole military units without regard to employment possibilities. The U.S. Employment Service had been given the task of placement of the returned soldiers, but when Congress severely curtailed the funds of that agency in January, 1919, the nation was finally forced to rely on boy scouts to solicit employers to rehire the servicemen.[2]

Some Americans concerned over the prospect of mass unemployment in the reconversion period had advocated a large federal public works program to stimulate an increase in jobs, but neither Congress, nor the state governments whom President Wilson urged to act in this field, did anything. Home-owners were urged to spruce up their homes to make jobs and the Department of Labor publicized a "Build-Your-Own-Home" campaign, but with little success; construction in 1919 was 11 per cent below the pre-war average of 1910–13.

The boom that started in the spring of 1919, facilitating the reconversion of industry and re-employment of the military forces, was based essentially on two factors. One was the fact that the government, though it cut back on its expenditures from the level of 1918, continued to spend much more than it collected in taxes; the federal deficit in 1919 was over $4.5 billion, and the respending of this money undoubtedly had large indirect effects. Furthermore, the U.S. government continued to make loans to the Allies—$1.75 billion in 1919—and these sums, which were largely spent in the United States, spurred our export trade. Our merchandise exports reached $7.9 billion in 1919 and over $8 billion in 1920 with huge sums being spent on American machinery, locomotives, and food to aid in the rehabilitation of the war-shattered countries in Europe. While there was much less spending of pent-up savings than after World War II, the shortage of housing led to a marked recovery in residential building, and there was a noticeable pick-up in the production and sale of automobiles and civilian clothing, which the citizenry had been deprived of to some degree during the war. As the recovery picked up momentum, the nation went on a buying and speculative spree. The ensuing price inflation was fueled by a rapid expansion of bank credit, which rose 40 per cent in the two years after June, 1918. Wartime price control had

[2] Soule, *Prosperity Decade* . . . , p. 83.

broken down in the summer of the latter year and within three months prices bounded up more than they had moved during the preceding year. Businessmen began to build inventories in anticipation of higher prices with the result that the Bureau of Labor Statistics wholesale price index climbed from 206 in November, 1918, to 272 in May, 1920. The increase in value of business inventories during 1919 was $6 billion, an increase almost four times as large as that in any year of the 1920's except 1923. The vicious spiral of inflation caused the cost of living to soar with the result that millions of workers went on strike largely to protect their real wages from further deterioration. It is estimated that about four million workers were involved in more than 3,600 strikes during 1919. Despite such efforts, wage earners are believed to have gained less than 1% in their real annual earnings in that year at which time they stood about 5% above the level of 1914.[3]

This unwholesome inflation and accumulation of inventories was based on the continued expansion of bank loans to business. The Federal Reserve did not put on the "brakes" as early as it might have because it was committed to a policy of "cheap money" to aid the Treasury in floating the final Victory Loan in 1919. "The Treasury considered the marketing of the Victory Loan at 3¾ and 4¾ per cent more important than discouraging inflationary speculation by high interest rates."[4] The Federal Reserve Board warned the member banks against loans for speculation in the stock market in June, 1919 and later the member banks were advised to curtail speculative loans to finance the holding of materials and inventories. But the member banks did not heed this appeal partly because speculation had become accepted business practice and partly because they could not distinguish between the latter type of loan and that needed for production. The inflation of credit was facilitated by the government's bond issues, which could be used as collateral for further loans. It was not until the end of 1919 when the Federal Reserve Board was released from its "serfdom" to Treasury financing that it was able to act, and then it was too late for preventive action. The rediscount rate of the Federal Reserve Bank of New York had been advanced to 5½ per cent in January, 1920 and in June, it was raised to 7 per cent. But, already by the latter month the boom was turning into a precipitous depression. By June, 1921 the index of wholesale prices had fallen to 148 from the high of 272 (May, 1920); the prices of farm products and other raw materials fell considerably more than this with the result that the American farmer entered a depression that dragged on through the whole of the 1920's and grew worse in the following decade.

This sharp decline in prices resulted in cutbacks of production in manufacturing (at the low point in 1921 production was only 2 per cent higher than it had been in 1914), thousands of business failures, and a sudden increase in unemployment. The number of wage earners in manufacturing was reduced by almost one-fourth between 1919 and 1921 and at the low point was almost at the level of 1914. Approximately 4.75 million persons were out of work and

[3] Soule, *Prosperity Decade* . . . , p. 91.
[4] Shultz and Caine, *Financial Development of the United States*, p. 568.

this at a time when there was no unemployment insurance or organized governmental relief. The unemployed had to survive either on their savings or on charity.

The incidence of the price deflation varied from one income group to another. Shareholders in large corporations did not suffer greatly because the bigger companies had accumulated large surpluses during the war and were able to continue dividends with some exceptions. Dividends as a whole fell from $3.2 billion in 1920 to $2.9 billion in 1921, but the total of property income (dividends, interest, and rent) advanced steadily throughout the depression. While farm output scarcely declined, the fall in farm prices caused gross farm income to decline from $17 billion in 1919 to $10.5 billion in 1921. Wage and salary earners suffered a reduction of $9 billion in their collective income.[5]

This sudden reversal in the nation's income and employment was the subject at the time of much controversy. From the vantage point of today, with our improved understanding of the factors determining national income, it is clear that one of the major reasons for the downturn was the sharp change in the government's fiscal policy. The federal government moved within the short period of a year from large-scale borrowing and budgetary deficit to a condition of surplus. In the last half of 1918 the federal government's deficit was nearly $9 billion; in the last quarter of 1919 and the first half of 1920, the Treasury surplus amounted to $831 million. Within this short span of time, the American economy had to withstand a net decline of purchasing power that amounted to close to one quarter of the total national income.[6] This deflationary fiscal situation was exaggerated by the inventory boom and liquidation, which saw business inventories rise $4,313 millions (in 1929 dollars) in 1920 and then swing to a decumulation of inventory at a rate of $122 million in the following year. The shrinkage in the value of inventories was aggravated by the fact that the bank credit to hold such stocks of goods was being withdrawn just at the time when commodity prices began to fall; the consequence was that there were numerous distress sales, resulting in still further reductions in price; this was the price spiral in reverse. The fall in prices was closely related to the decrease in our exports that took place at this time; our merchandise exports fell from $8 billion in 1920 to $4.5 billion the following year. The changes in the chief components of the gross national product over the course of these years are shown in Table 1. From it we can see that the shrinkage of close to $15 billion in the GNP between 1920 and 1921 was due mainly to the sharp drop in consumer expenditures and in inventory investment.

Monetary policy was a much discussed aspect of public policy during the depression of 1920–21. Despite the severity of the economic decline, the

---

[5] S. Kuznets, *National Income and its Composition* (New York: National Bureau of Economic Research, 1941), pp. 137, 147.

[6] P. A. Samuelson and E. E. Hagen, *After the War—1918–1920* (Washington: National Resources Planning Board, 1943), p. 23.

TABLE 1

Changes in Gross National Product and Its Components, 1919–21[a]
(Commerce concept, derivation from Kuznets estimates)
(Millions of current dollars)

	1919	1920	1921
Gross national product	$78,907	$88,856	$73,938
Personal consumption expenditures	54,659	63,671	58,931
Gross private investment	8,313	10,123	7,753
Change in business inventories	4,054	7,361	63
Net foreign investment	3,824	2,844	1,613
Government purchases of goods and services	9,456	5,904	6,301

[a] Source: J. W. Kendrick, *Productivity Trends in the U.S.* (Princeton: Princeton University Press, 1962), p. 297. © Copyright 1961 by the National Bureau of Economic Research. Reprinted by permission of Princeton University Press.

Federal Reserve Board continued its deflationary policies well into 1921, believing that the liquidation of excess inventories was not completed and that gold would be exported, if it raised the rediscount rate. In the early fall of 1921, however, the New York Bank lowered its rediscount rate to 4½ per cent. While the Federal Reserve authorities had prevented the depression from degenerating into a panic, there was much criticism, some of it unfounded, of the System's policies in this depression. In appraising such matters, it must be realized that the Federal Reserve Board at that time did not have complete control of the discount rates of the District banks nor did it have unified direction of open-market operations.

CHANGES IN NATIONAL INCOME, 1922–29

The years 1922–29 have been seen from many different perspectives; during the depression years of the 1930's it was common to see them as a period of political and moral laxity, of nationalistic isolation—a bizarre social era that was but a prelude to the years of crisis that followed. Today, historians are increasingly treating the period against the background of the American past and recognizing that the so-called "new era" was really new in a sense that had nothing to do with the illusory stability of security prices. Thus, Rostow regards the 1920's as the "centre-piece" of the era of high mass consumption, saying that it was the first protracted period in which a society absorbed the fruits and consequences of the age of durable consumer goods and services. A Japanese economist in a perceptive analysis of the period sees it as inaugurating a new phase of capitalism in the form of consumer asset formation. Professor Leuchtenberg in a recent study stressed what the 1929 Report on *Recent Economic Changes* called "optional consumption"—"that

Americans could buy things with their paychecks that they had never been able to get before."[7]

Those who lived in the hectic twenties and analyzed its place in our economic development appreciated that it represented a break-through, a new plateau of economic achievement. For example, the distinguished group of social scientists who wrote *Recent Economic Changes* stated at one point: "Never before has the human race made such progress in solving the problem of production. . . ."[8] And President Hoover in 1928 made a disastrously premature prediction, though one with some basis in fact, when he said, "We in America today are nearer to the final triumph over poverty than ever before in the history of any land." Before dismissing the latter statement as a patent piece of campaign oratory, let us see how far Americans had gotten in the conquest of poverty and the attainment of a higher standard of living for all citizens by 1929.

As usual the aggregate changes in the nation's well-being can be delineated best in terms of the national income statistics, total and per capita, and in indices of industrial production such as those reproduced in Table 2. As shown in the table, recovery from the depression of 1920–21 was marked in 1922, and the economy climbed strongly to unprecedented heights in 1929, with only minor interruptions in the recessions of 1924 and 1927. By 1929 production was one-third greater than it had been in the boom year of 1920;

TABLE 2

Economic Growth in the Years 1921–29[a]

Year	National Income (Billions)	Real Income Per Capita (1929 Prices)	Industrial Production
1921	$59.4	$522	58
1922	60.7	553	73
1923	71.6	634	88
1924	72.1	633	82
1925	76.0	644	90
1926	81.6	678	96
1927	80.1	674	95
1928	81.7	676	99
1929	87.2	716	110

[a] Sources: S. Kuznets, *National Income and Its Composition, 1919–1938* (New York: National Bureau of Economic Research, 1941), pp. 137, 153. © Copyright 1941 by National Bureau of Economic Research. *Federal Reserve Bulletin* (October, 1945), p. 1049.

[7] Rostow, *The Stages of Economic Growth* (Cambridge: Cambridge University Press, 1960), p. 76; H. T. Oshima, "Consumer Asset Formation and the Future of Capitalism," *Economic Journal* (March, 1961), p. 20ff; W. E. Leuchtenberg, *The Perils of Prosperity, 1914–32* (Chicago: University of Chicago Press, 1958), p. 194.

[8] President's Conference on Unemployment, Committee on Recent Social Changes, *Recent Economic Changes* (New York: McGraw-Hill, Inc., 1929), Vol. 1, p. x.

real income per capita rose 37 per cent between 1922 and 1929. These income gains were not, of course, evenly distributed among the industrial sectors and regions of the nation. The farmers especially did not enjoy the much-vaunted prosperity of the twenties; in 1929 the average per capita income of people on farms was only $273 contrasted with $908 for the non-farm population. There were also wide regional differences, ranging from the high of $1,107 per capita in the Middle Atlantic states in 1929 to a low of $344 in the East South Central states.

In the decade of the 1920's the population of the nation grew some 16 million, from 106,466,000 in 1920 to 123,077,000 ten years later. In absolute terms this was a substantial increase in numbers, but relatively it represented an increase of only about 13 per cent, practically half the rate of decennial growth that the nation had in the late nineteenth century. This slowing down in the rate of population growth was due to a falling birth rate and the restrictions on immigration; the restrictive laws of 1921 and 1924 reduced the inflow to a negligible amount. Geographically, this population growth was very uneven; California grew 66 per cent and Florida 52 per cent in the decade, while Michigan, New Jersey, North Carolina, and New York grew more than 20 per cent in the same years. The most striking demographic development of the decade was the movement from the farms to the cities. The farm population proper declined 1,201,000 during the twenties, and the non-farm rural population rose only slightly. On the other hand, the cities with over 2,500 inhabitants gained 14.6 million persons between 1920 and 1930. These were the years when the suburbs of our great cities especially began to grow rapidly; their population in the 1920's rose 44 per cent compared to 22 per cent for the cities proper, and 16 per cent for the nation as a whole. While the upper classes had started the flight to suburbia in the 1890's, the 1920's marked the beginning of a mass movement out of the inner city.

Behind this trend to suburbia and the transformation in the economy it promoted was the remarkable growth of the automobile industry, which vastly increased the mobility of Americans in the 1920's. Accompanying the movement to the suburbs, and indeed part of it, was a great boom in construction, both residential and commercial, which also constituted one of the main prosperity props of that decade. In the cities, giant new skyscrapers arose, symbolizing the optimistic spirit and profitability of business, while out in the suburbs the prosperous middle class erected new homes away from the noise and bustle of it all.

GROWTH INDUSTRIES AND SICK INDUSTRIES

The place of the construction industry as one of the leading durable goods industries in these years is indicated by the fact that construction amounted to more than $7 billion annually, reaching a high point of $11 billion in 1926. The annual rate of increase in construction is estimated to have been 6.7 per cent in the eight years after 1921. Back of this vast program of building were the wartime shortages, the growth of the population, and the migration from farm to city to suburb. By 1929, when the construction boom had already abated, the industry gave employment to some 2,439,000 workers and accounted for nearly 5 per cent of the nation's private production income.

The automobile industry emerged in the 1920's as the nation's largest single manufacturing industry, its value of output exceeding five billion dollars in 1929. Having mastered the technique of mass production, the leaders of the industry pioneered in the mass distribution of consumer durables with extraordinary success. The number of passenger cars and trucks sold more than doubled between 1922 and 1929. Total registrations of all motor vehicles soared from over 12 million to over 26.5 million in the same period of time. The importance of the industry for the economy as a whole was demonstrated by the fact that in 1929 it produced 12.7 per cent of the total value of product of all manufacturing firms; it employed 7.1 per cent of the manufacturing wage earners and contributed heavily to the prosperity of many related industries. For example, in 1929 it was estimated to be using some 15 per cent of the steel produced in the United States and four-fifths of the processed rubber, not to mention its huge consumption of plate glass, petroleum products, lead, leather, and other products. The use of the automobile gave rise to innumerable garages, filling stations, and tourist camps to accommodate the millions of Americans who took to wheels in the 1920's. By 1929, according to one estimate, the industry gave employment, directly or indirectly, to 3,700,000 persons. Concomitant with these changes came major shifts in the industry's structure. Ford, which had gained about 60 per cent of the industry's sales by 1921, had fallen to a 33 per cent share of the market in 1926, whereas General Motors in the same period increased its share of the industry's output from 13 per cent to 28 per cent. A new giant, Chrysler, had appeared in 1927 creating the Big Three and leaving a steadily shrinking share of the market to the so-called "independents."

The twenties saw spectacular increases in the sales of other consumer durables, such as radios, mechanical refrigerators, toasters, flatirons, etc. The Radio Corporation of America had been organized by General Electric and Westinghouse in 1919, and three years later it began to manufacture receivers and parts on a large scale. The nation was fascinated with this new electrical wonder; sales of radios and equipment went from $28.5 million to over $388 million between 1922 and 1929. The first regular broadcasting began over the famous station KDKA in November, 1920, and four years later the National Broadcasting Company was organized to transmit programs over the telephone lines of A.T. and T.; three years later the Columbia Broadcasting Company began nation-wide operations. The story of the refrigerator was somewhat similar, but perhaps not as sensational as that of the radio. Nevertheless, in its case too the 1921 output was but 0.6 per cent of the rate of output in 1929. And this industry still had a vast future before it.

Many of these new electrical industries presupposed, of course, the wide distribution of electrical power for domestic consumption. This industry did not prove a disappointment in this respect; in the years from 1922 to 1929 the kilowatt-hours supplied to residential consumers rose from less than 4 billion to close to 10 billion, and the number of customers nearly doubled. The horsepower available in generating stations went from 20 million in 1922 to 43 million in 1929. This industry was undergoing a tremendous overall expansion in these years in its production of hydroelectric power; "almost as much new hydroelectric power was developed between 1920 and 1930 as in all the years before 1920. . . ."[9] The industry was the scene too of a vast merger movement as financiers planned huge holding company empires. By 1930, the merger movement had been so extensive that ten holding company groups controlled 72 per cent of the nation's electric power.

The chemical industry was another giant that made vast strides in the twenties. Aided by the confiscation of the German dye patents, spurred by the new synthetics developed after the war, and protected by a high tariff, this industry produced a number of new synthetic fibers and plastics that added to the industry's value of product. By 1929 it was close to $4 billion, and the industry's labor force amounted to 280,000 wage earners. Rayon, which had just come on the market in 1914, had a 69-fold increase in its production between that year and 1931. Such products as Bakelite, quick-drying lacquers, cellophane, and celanese were among the principal additions to the industry's growing list of commodities. The petroleum and coal products industry had one of the highest gains in production between 1919 and 1929, 156 per cent, largely because of the use of gasoline and oil for automobiles.

Motion pictures also experienced a spectacular growth in these years. From its start in 1905 with the first "nickelodeon," the film industry expanded so rapidly that by 1930 it had a capital investment of some two billion dollars and 325,000 employees. There were some 23,000 motion picture theaters in the nation, and in the large cities, the "Big Five" of the industry were opening palatial movie houses for first-run exhibitions of their films. "Going to the movies" had become a habit for millions of Americans; by 1930 the average weekly attendance was 100 million. Spectator sports, such as baseball, football, and tennis, also enjoyed a tremendous following in the 1920's in a period that old-timers still fondly speak of as the "Golden Age of Sports." Organized sport had now become big business as the workingman with increased leisure could spend his weekend watching his team or favorite player.

However, while certain industries were basking in the sunshine of a remarkable prosperity, there were others widely considered to be "sick" or at least depressed. Prominent among the latter was agriculture, which suffered from the over-expansion of acreage in the war years and the change in foreign demand; bituminous coal and textiles were also plagued by a chronic lack of balance between their productive capacity and market demand. In addition, with the rapid growth of chain stores and the mail order business, the old line

[9] Leuchtenberg, *Perils of Prosperity*, p. 190.

wholesalers and independent retailers were in difficulty. In short, the prosperity of the country was far from evenly distributed and the deep malaise of certain industries became a matter of considerable political concern.

RAILROADS, TRUCKS, AND SHIPPING

Two other fields that experienced economic difficulties in adjusting to the swift changes of the twenties were the railroads and the merchant marine. The railroads after the war were first involved in sharp controversy over the desirability of returning them to private ownership. After the Plumb Plan of government ownership of the rails, which organized labor backed, had been rejected by Congress in 1919, the Transportation Act of 1920 was passed as a compromise among the many conflicting interests involved. This Act instructed the Interstate Commerce Commission to prepare a plan for railroad consolidation that would strengthen the weak roads and yet maintain competition. The Commission later published a tentative national plan that would have reorganized the railroads into 18 or 20 systems, but it never carried this idea to completion, and in 1927 it asked Congress to be relieved of the duty. Under this law the I.C.C. was also empowered to fix rates that "under efficient and economical management" would yield the railroads a fair return on their investment. The Commission considered 5¾ per cent to 6 per cent as a fair return during this period, but actually the average return on the railroads' investment exceeded 5 per cent only in 1926, when it reached 5.2 per cent. Though many of the rail lines made improvements in their equipment and in their operations, their traffic did not markedly increase, and in fact, passenger traffic actually declined. Railroad passenger-miles declined from 47 million in 1920 to 31 million in 1929. The competition of passenger car and motor bus was already severe, especially over short distances, though the railroads were still holding their own in the suburban traffic of the commuter. Trucking companies, many of which had been started as one man–one truck affairs right after the war, were also beginning to cut into the short-haul business, but they were no match as yet for the railroads on long distance freight service. Late in the period the airlines were started, and they offered greater speed than the railroads could provide. Thus, though the railroads had made substantial improvements in their service and efficiency, their problems were mounting. The former monopoly position they had over transportation in some localities had been broken; the great era of their construction had come to an end in 1916 when extension of their mileage had ceased. The railroads, like many other industries, were to feel increasingly the cold blast of Schumpeter's "perennial gale of creative destruction."

The shipping industry was faced with even greater troubles than the railroads in the 1920's. During the war the federal government had built a large number of ships and continued to do so in the post-war period with the result that the United States in 1921 had 18 million tons of shipping, more than twice the tonnage it had in 1915. The United Kingdom, the other chief maritime power, had also built considerable tonnage, but with the close of the war there was an actual decline in ocean freight so that the industry was saddled with an excess capacity that depressed freight rates and made it unprofitable. In the following years our slow and largely obsolete merchant fleet could not compete with the more economically operated foreign-owned vessels. The consequence was that the percentage of exports and imports carried in American bottoms fell from 43 per cent in 1920 to 34 per cent in 1930. The one phase of the industry that prospered was coastal shipping, from which foreign vessels were banned. The only way the American position in shipping could be maintained at all was through government subsidy. Such subsidies were granted the shipping interests for carrying the mail, and liberal loans were extended for shipbuilding under the terms of the White-Jones Act of 1928. But the controversial subsidy system did not end the losses caused by uneconomical operation; it simply added to the burdens of the taxpayer.

BANKING AND FINANCIAL DEVELOPMENTS

The nation's banking system after the war consisted of a sprawling host of national and state banks, some large and powerful, others small and financially weak. Unlike other industrial nations in which a few strong banks operated, the United States had a unit banking system operated for profit and supervised by government regulators concerned mainly with preventing dishonesty or flagrantly unsound management. The Federal Reserve System was relatively new, and its powers for coordination of the monetary policies of these numerous financial institutions were still largely untested.

In 1921, the Comptroller of the Currency reported that the nation had 30,812 commercial banks and trust companies. Some of these banks were national banks, members of the Federal Reserve System, but the greater number were state banks, many of which did not choose to belong to the System. In addition, there were a large number of savings banks (both mutual and those owned by shareholders), investment banks, insurance companies, building and loan associations, and some cooperative credit institutions. By 1929, the number of commercial banks had been reduced to 25,330, mainly through bank closings and consolidation. Bank suspensions in the eight years 1922–29, numbered 5,211, the range being from 976 in 1926 to a low of 367 in 1922. Most of these bank failures were concentrated among small institutions, especially those operating in agricultural districts that felt the effects of the long post-war farm depression. Nevertheless, the weakness revealed by these failures was a warning, largely ignored, of the vulnerability of such a system in a period of general depression.

The 1920's was a period of active consolidation of banks. Branch banking and mergers among banks were very popular. The number of banks having branches increased from 530 in 1920 to 763 in 1929 and the number of branches from 480 to 3,350 over the same years. The number of Federal Reserve member banks affected by mergers rose from 77 in 1920 to 343 in 1929. State laws were amended to permit branch banking, the argument having been advanced that a consolidation of banks would provide greater safety such as existed in those countries that had only a few large banks. Subsequent experience was to demonstrate, however, that the large banks were no more immune to bad judgment and failure than the smaller institutions.

Banking practices underwent fundamental changes in the 1920's in line with the other institutional shifts taking place in the economy. For example, the short term commercial loan, which had previously been the "cornerstone" of orthodox commercial banking, did not expand very much in these years because the large, profitable corporations were relying on their own surpluses or stock issues for working capital rather than turning to the commercial banks. This change in practice is reflected in the fact that demand deposits, growing out of commercial loans, grew relatively little in the decade. Thus, the demand deposits of the national banks were $8.7 billion in 1921 and $10.9 billion in 1929. The banks, finding that they could not utilize all their resources through commercial loans, expanded their investments in securities and real estate loans. "Member banks of the Federal Reserve System increased their investments by two-thirds between 1921 and 1929, more than doubled their loans on securities in the same period, and expanded their loans on urban real estate about 3½ times. All other loans—mainly commercial— remained stationary in these nine years."[10]

In the 1920's the commercial banks were becoming "department store" banks, i.e., they were beginning to offer their customers a wide range of services—savings accounts, consumer credit, loans on securities, etc. rather than confining themselves to the conventional commercial loan business. One of the most ominous developments along this line, though its dangers were not fully appreciated until it was too late, was the establishment by some of the larger banks of investment affiliates. This opened the possibility of investing their depositors' funds in securities they were underwriting through their investment houses and thus permitted them to act as agents of both seller and buyer. Apart from the ethical aspects of this practice, it had the tendency to obliterate the old distinction between banking that served the short-term needs of business (commercial banking) and investment banking. Thus, it was increasingly possible that demand deposits would be used for long term, not necessarily self-liquidating, purposes.

While these revolutionary changes were occurring in commercial banking, equally important developments were taking place in other types of finance. The life insurance companies, decreasing their holdings of railroad securities and government bonds, expanded their investments in urban real estate

---

[10] Soule, *Prosperity Decade*, pp. 155–156.

mortgages. The newly organized investment trusts (now more familiarly known as mutual funds) had been formed to collect the funds of small, inexperienced investors and purchase stocks and bonds with them. The prosperity of the period supplied a substantial surplus of funds ready for investment and these new institutions, many of them with questionable financial structures, sprang up like daisies in the spring. From about 40 companies in 1920 their number grew to 728 at the end of 1930; by the close of 1929 their aggregate assets exceeded $7 billion. The subsequent collapse in the prices of the securities of these institutions was so great in the years 1929–32 that, by the latter year, the term "investment trust" was an anathema to the average investor.[11] Another remarkable development of the period was the rise of installment credit. This type of credit was extended by finance companies to permit the purchase of such consumer durables as automobiles, radios, etc., and in the minds of its defenders this innovation was a vital factor in making possible mass consumption. It has been estimated that in 1929 installment sales approximated $7 billion.

FOREIGN TRADE AND FINANCE

America's international economic relations were fundamentally changed by the nation's transformation from a debtor to a creditor status as a result of the war, but governmental policies in post-war years were slow to recognize and adjust to this radical alteration of financial relationships. The readjustment to the new condition was complicated by the Allied indebtedness to the United States and the reparations of the defeated powers, all of which were inevitably interrelated so far as settling the international balance of payments was concerned. In 1919, as Table 3 shows, our creditor position was reflected in total net assets on private and government account of $12.6 billion, of which intergovernmental debts to the U.S. amounted to $9.9 billion. By 1929, foreigners owed us on private account some $8 billion, and our net assets on government account came to $11.6 billion, making a total creditor position of close to $20 billion. The table shows us that even if the war debts had not existed, the shift of private investments and indebtedness during the war had been so great that the United States would still have been a creditor nation in 1919 to the extent of close to $3 billion.

The difficulty posed by the nation's new creditor status lay in the fact that if foreign nations were to pay their war debts and American investors receive a return on their net foreign investment, the debtor nations had to earn sufficient dollar exchange with which to make payment. How were they to do this? They could only do so if Americans bought from them more goods and services than the debtor nations bought from the United States, or if we

11 W. H. Steiner and E. Shapiro, *Money and Banking*, rev. ed. (New York: H. Holt & Co., 1941), p. 357.

TABLE 3

International Balance Sheet of the United States, 1914, 1919, and 1929[a]
(Foreign assets and liabilities in millions of dollars)

Items	1914	1919	1929
Assets (private account):			
Securities	$ 862	$2,576	$ 7,839
Direct investments	2,652	3,880	7,553
Short term credits	—	500	1,617
Total	3,514	6,956	17,009
Liabilities:			
Securities	5,440	1,623	4,304
Direct investments	1,310	900	1,400
Sequestrated property and securities	—	662	150
Short term credits	450	800	3,077
Total	7,200	3,985	8,931
Net assets privately held:	−3,686	2,971	8,078
Intergovernment debts:			
To the United States government	—	9,982	11,685
By the United States government	—	391	—
Net assets on government account	—	9,591	11,685
Total net assets on private and government account	−3,686	12,562	19,763

[a] Source: C. Lewis, *America's Stake in International Investments* (Washington, D.C.: The Brookings Institution, 1938), pp. 447, 450, as reproduced in Soule, *Prosperity Decade*, p. 254.

supplied any deficiency arising from trade or services by making additional loans to them or investing abroad. Under the international gold standard, any deficiencies in the balance of payments of a nation would normally be covered by shipments of gold. But in the post-war world there was not sufficient fluid monetary gold in the world to permit the debtor nations to meet the huge payments due the United States. To meet their obligations in this way would have driven them off the gold standard because their gold reserves would thereby be depleted. There was no way for these debtor countries to service their debts to us but by developing an export surplus of goods or a net balance on "invisible" items (shipping, banking services, etc.). One possible "way out" for them would be to continue borrowing from us, but this would only enlarge their debts and compound the initial difficulty.

The United States had run a favorable balance of trade before the war, and there were strong pressures behind our continuing as a huge exporter; we were a major producer of food and raw materials, which were very much in demand abroad; our manufactured goods, especially machinery, commanded wide markets, and we had the credit to finance foreign purchasers. The figures for the 1920's show that we had a favorable balance of trade throughout tne entire period, ranging from a low of $375 million in 1923 to over $1 billion in 1928. Foreigners did not derive from this trade, therefore, any balance of dollars to pay their debts in the United States.

The principal change in our post-war export trade was the decline in the importance of our farm exports and the relative growth in such manufactured goods as automobiles and their parts, farm machinery, cash registers, type-writers, and numerous other types of mechanical equipment. Our import trade consisted mainly of foodstuffs and raw materials, including coffee, tea, rubber, silk. The invisible items in the American balance of payments were also, on a net basis, in our favor. While we paid out substantial sums for shipping services, and foreign remittances and tourist expenditures were even greater, the incoming payments to us for interest and dividends exceeded such outlays. Thus, we never developed the import excess (of both trade and invisible items), which is usually associated with the status of a creditor nation.

We were, as the saying goes, able to "have our cake and eat it, too," only by reason of the huge capital outflow during these years. Between 1925 and 1929 no less than $5.1 billion of foreign loans were sold in the United States, and in addition, American business concerns made approximately $3 billion of direct investments abroad by building branch plants or investing in large organizations owned by foreigners. It was only because of this massive outward movement of capital and credit that we were able to maintain our favorable balance of trade. Once this extension of capital or credit ceased or declined, our export trade was threatened. In the middle of 1928, American foreign lending began to fall off, partly because of the very precariousness of many of the investments and partly, perhaps, because of the attraction of larger profits in our financial markets. When, with the coming of the depression, our direct investments abroad and our imports declined drastically, the whole foundation of international trade was destroyed because of the world-wide "dollar shortage." These developments played a large part in accentuating the devastating deflation and depression that spread over the economy of the United States and most of the world in those tragic years.

THE ILLUSION OF ECONOMIC STABILITY

The eight long years of general prosperity generated a pervasive optimism in the 1920's, especially toward the end of the period, that the nation had reached a permanent plateau of prosperity. Belief in the permanence of prosperity was, indeed, the cornerstone of the "New Era," and there were many signs and signposts pointed to as evidences of the achievement of stability.[12] The popular doctrine of high wages, which stressed the contribution of wages

[12] E. Ginzberg, *The Illusion of Economic Stability* (New York: Harper and Bros., 1939), a most literate and perceptive account of these years is excellent on the psychological climate of the 1920's and the factors contributing to this illusion. See especially, Chaps. 3–6 upon which we have drawn heavily in the following analysis.

to mass purchasing power, was seen as assuring the continuation of prosperity. The stability of the wholesale price level—for seven years, 1922–29, the fluctuations above and below the 1922 base did not exceed 7 per cent—was taken to be another "proof" of the absence of pathological conditions. The success of some industries in stabilizing individual prices or in regularizing seasonal unemployment was also seen as contributing to stability in the economy as a whole. While aggregate profits increased substantially in the twenties, the stability of corporate income to total capitalizations and to sales was reassuring on this score also. The confidence in the Federal Reserve System and the belief that its existence prevented money panics contributed to the "metaphysics" of the stabilization movement.

These economic rationalizations about stability were periodically supplemented by statements of politicians and respected businessmen who offered their reassuring, optimistic comments on the state of the economy. Thus, President Coolidge in his annual message to Congress on the state of the Union on December 4, 1928, less than a year before the stock market debacle, spoke, in part, as follows: "No Congress of the United States ever assembled, on surveying the state of the Union, has met with a more pleasing prospect than that which appears at the present time. . . . The country can regard the present with satisfaction and anticipate the future with optimism." Almost on the eve of the depression, Magnus Alexander, president of the National Industrial Conference Board, an influential employers' research association, asserted, "There is no reason why there should be any more panics." Another businessman, Irving T. Bush, said about the same time: "We are only at the beginning of a period that will go down in history as a golden age."[13]

The speculative fever manifested itself first in real estate; in the middle twenties, there were sensational increases in the prices of land in California and Florida especially. The boom in the latter state collapsed in 1927, leaving thousands of speculators with losses, but it did not seriously affect the economy as a whole. During the twenties the value of urban real estate in a representative sample of cities showed an increase from $42 to $67 billion; the total urban mortgage debt trebled over the same years from about $9 billion to $27 billion. Part of this rise in realty values was undoubtedly due to an increase in real market demand, but in addition there was a substantial capitalization of prospective earnings. As the "New Era" drew to its close, it was, of course, the stock market that reflected the most extreme degree of this bullish optimism. The bull market had begun about March, 1928, and by 1929 had reached unprecedented heights. Price-earnings ratios on stocks mounted as security buyers vied with each other to possess a share in the profits and the capital gains of the market rise. As Ginzberg states,

if new investment was the key to the expansion of the twenties, the capitalization process was its lock. The rise in the value of equities facilitated increases in bank loans and the money supply, so that the funds for new investment did not depend upon a curtailment of current consumption. It was a charmed

13 E. Angly, *Oh, Yeah?* (New York: The Viking Press, 1931), p. 12.

circle: industrial expansion, enlarged earnings, increases in capitalization, facilitation of new investment, more expansion, larger earnings, further increases in the value of securities.[14]

The upward movement of security prices in these years reflected in part the substantial increase in corporate profits taking place. Between 1922 and 1929 the total net income of all corporations grew from $4,700 million to $8,700 million. But as the stock boom mounted, the future was discounted beyond all reason, and speculation became rampant. Whereas in calmer years (for example, 1922) price-earnings ratios, eliminating the extremes, had hovered around 10 times annual earnings, by 1929 the oils were selling at 29 times earnings, electrical equipment at 30, and merchandising at 50! In many cases there was little discernible relationship between the price of a company's stock and its earnings. Over all, the market value of all the shares on the New York Stock Exchange increased from $27 billion on January 1, 1925 to $67 billion on the first day of 1929 and then in the final spurt to the high of September 3rd, it soared almost to $100 billion. With the surplus of savings available for investment as well as huge amounts of credit, the appetite of the stock-buying public was seemingly unappeasable. New securities issued went from $4 billion in 1923 to $10 billion in the last year of the boom and brokers' loans, which financed the purchase of securities on margin, swelled from $6 billion in 1927 to over $9 billion two years later.

Weakness in the stock market first manifested itself in September of 1929, when security prices sagged from their high at the first of the month. This slippage was discounted as being no more than a minor adjustment, but then in October a number of "breaks" occurred in stock prices that culminated in the great crash of October 24th, which became known as Black Thursday.[15]

Though there was some recovery in October, and many of the insiders were reported to be still selling, Irving Fisher, the economist, announced on October 15th that stock prices stood on "what looks like a permanent high plateau" and added that he expected to see the market "a good deal higher than it is today within a few months." Charles Mitchell, chairman of the National City Bank, was similarly encouraging. Despite such reassurances, the next day the market plunged down an average of fifty points and on the following day, the stock exchange became completely demoralized. Almost thirteen million shares were sold, as the market suffered the widest drop in the history of the exchange. The stock ticker lagged hours behind transactions; brokers frantically sent out telegrams to margin traders, demanding that they put up more margin so that their stock could be held. Many of the latter were sold out, nevertheless, in the prevailing confusion before they had an opportunity to reply to the telegrams. On October 29th, an even larger number of shares was dumped on the market, and this time the drop affected even the strongest companies.

[14] Ginzberg, *The Illusion of Economic Stability*, p. 124.
[15] J. K. Galbraith, *The Great Crash, 1929*, 2nd ed. (Boston: Houghton Mifflin Co., 1961) provides a lively and insightful account of this historic financial debacle.

On October 24th a number of leading bankers in New York had met at the office of J. P. Morgan and pledged themselves to support the market. The slump in stock prices was aggravated by the fact that the non-banking lenders in the call money market (the corporations and others with surplus funds) were withdrawing huge sums of credit in order to avoid further loss. The bankers tried to prevent such credit contraction by taking over these loans, and in the last three weeks of October, they advanced over $1 billion to do so. Though their action certainly moderated the rout, when the market fell again on October 29th, the bankers did not intervene or offer support. Although the market rallied periodically thereafter, the general trend of security prices for the next three years was downward; on the average the price of stocks fell about 75 per cent over these years. In dollar terms, this disastrous deflation of security prices represented a fall of all the stocks listed on the New York Stock Exchange from $67.5 billion in 1929 to $22.8 billion in 1933, a decline of almost $45 billion. The average price of securities on this exchange fell from $89.11 per share in 1929 to $17.35 in 1933.

THE ONSET OF THE "GREAT DEPRESSION"

The initial reaction of the political leaders of the nation to the stock market crash was to assure the people that there was no cause for alarm. President Hoover stated in late 1929 that "the fundamental business of the country is on a sound and prosperous basis," and leading businessmen agreed. And, as a matter of fact, employment in November and December of that year did not fall off drastically. Despite his statements of reassurance, the President was apprehensive and felt that there was a need to prevent a general wave of contraction and panic. While his Secretary of the Treasury, Mr. Mellon, was advising that the only thing to do was "Liquidate labor, liquidate stocks, liquidate the farmers, liquidate real estate,"[16] the President saw the necessity of taking positive steps to contain the stock market crash and prevent its effects from spreading to the general economy. With this in view he called a conference of leading businessmen on November 21, 1929 at which promises were solemnly made not to initiate wage reductions or cut employment in order to maintain profits. Two days later he wired the governors and mayors of the nation requesting them to cooperate in a program of public works expansion. But such pledges were of little avail in stemming the powerful forces of contraction and deflation. Businessmen, caught in such a nation-wide deflation, were in no position as individuals or as heads of corporations to operate at full capacity and pay full wages, when others were cutting back and retrenching. Nor did the cities and states undertake programs of public works expansion adequate to offset the drastic decline in private investment and

[16] A. M. Schlesinger, Jr., *The Age of Roosevelt: The Crisis of the Old Order, 1919–1933* (Boston: Houghton Mifflin Co., 1957), p. 163.

employment. In addition to these efforts, the Hoover administration tried to maintain the level of business activity by making Federal Reserve credit abundant; it sought to prop up agricultural prices through the stabilization operations of the Federal Farm Board; and lastly, through upward revision of tariff rates provided by the Smoot-Hawley Act of June, 1930, it tried to protect the American businessman against foreign competition. By such measures President Hoover sought to maintain prices and purchasing power and restore business confidence.

Of course, those at the political helm at the time could not perceive that they were at the beginning of one of the worst depressions in the nation's history; there was hardly an economist of repute predicting a contraction that would merit the term, adopted years later, of the "Great Depression." Since the economic decline did not occur in a straight line, but rather pursued a jagged course, the occasional interruptions in the downward movement of business periodically gave the administration the hope that the worst was over. Thus, in March, 1930, the President stated, "all the evidence indicates that the worst effects of the crash upon unemployment will have passed during the next sixty days." Two months later he was saying, "We have now passed the worst and with continued unity of effort we shall rapidly recover." In June, when a delegation urging an immediate expansion of public works called upon him the President listened impatiently and then said, "Gentlemen, you have come sixty days too late. The depression is over." The President later took the view that the depression had been practically licked on two occasions, only to be set back by other developments: in 1931, when the financial collapse in Europe retarded recovery in the United States; and again in 1932, when the prospect of unsound Democratic measures weakened business confidence. The political statements effusing optimism in the face of the worsening condition of millions made the prediction that "recovery was just around the corner" a subject for widespread derision and humor.

The depression by the spring of 1930 was beginning to reflect itself in the increased number of the unemployed; at least 4 million were believed to be out of work by that time. In March, 1930, it was reported in New York City that the number of families on relief had increased 200 per cent since the stock market crash. All the principal economic indicators showed disastrous declines from 1929 to 1932. The total gross national product (in constant 1964 dollars) was 27 per cent lower in 1932 than it had been in 1929; per capita disposable income fell from $1,273 to $966 over the same years. The Federal Reserve index of manufacturing production fell almost by one-half (from 100 to 52) during the same period. Private capital formation, always a most unstable activity in major business depressions, fell from $16.2 billion in 1929 to $900 million in 1932 (expressed in current dollars). This catastrophic decline in private investment can be measured in terms of the decrease of production of durable goods as a whole (see Chart 1). The reductions in production in key industries were heavy: railroad capital expenditures were cut from $853 million in 1929 to $167 million in

1932; passenger car production slid from 2,799,737 cars in 1929 to 626,513 in 1932; total construction showed a decline from close to $14 billion in the former year to $5,684 million in 1932.

CHART 1

Fluctuations in Durable Goods Production in the U.S., 1929–40

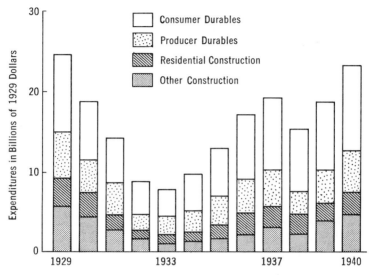

Source: Reproduced by special permission from "Why the Depression Lasted So Long," by G. Burck and C. Silberman, Clifton Line for *Fortune Magazine* (March, 1955), © 1955, Time, Inc.

The impact of the depression on the farm was extraordinarily severe because agriculture had been suffering from low prices throughout the twenties. Whereas many industrialists could reduce production to maintain prices, farmers, not being able to control output, saw no way to maintain their income except by increasing their planting. This, in fact, is what happened during the early years of the depression; total crop acreage rose in 1930 and showed no material decline in 1931. Thus, the burden of agricultural adjustment fell on prices, driving them lower. The contrasting behavior of farm prices and production with those of industry are striking: between 1929 and 1934, farm production declined 15 per cent in volume, 40 per cent in price; industrial production fell 42 per cent in volume and only 15 per cent in price. This relative stability of industrial prices resulted in further deterioration in the farmer's terms of trade; the ratio of the prices the farmer received to the prices he paid fell from 89 to 55 between 1929 and 1932. By the latter year corn was selling for 15 cents a bushel, cotton and wool were down to 5 cents per pound, and beef was at 2.5 cents. "It took 16 bushels of wheat—more than the average yield of a whole acre—to enable the farmer to buy one of his children a pair of $4 shoes."[17] Loaded with fixed costs, such as taxes and debts, which had been calculated in terms of the higher prices of the twenties, the farmer was caught in a price "squeeze," which meant inevitable foreclosure for many. Between 1929 and 1932, in fact, the rate of farm mortgage foreclosures doubled. It was conditions such as these that led Iowa farmers in August, 1932 to strike, refusing to market their products until prices were raised, and dumping the milk and destroying the cargoes of non-cooperating farmers. Others formed the Farm Holiday Association to demand a moratorium on farm foreclosures.

The depression dealt a severe blow to foreign trade as well in these years, exports falling from more than $5 billion in 1929 to $1.6 billion in 1932, while imports shrank from $4.4 billion to $1.3 billion over the same period. As can be seen from these figures, the nation still had a favorable balance of trade in the latter year. It has been explained above that the high level of exports to Europe in the 1920's was maintained through the flow of American loans to some of the leading trading countries of that continent. When this credit was curtailed with the coming of the depression, international repercussions quickly followed. The passage of the Smoot-Hawley Act led to retaliatory protective measures by some nations, thus contributing to the growing economic nationalism, which took the form of import restrictions and exchange controls. These restrictive measures and the quest for liquidity on the part of central banks soon caused the largest bank in Austria, the Kreditansalt, to close its doors on May 11, 1931; the German banks followed suit soon after, and then in September of that year Great Britain itself went off the gold standard. President Hoover sought to meet the international financial crisis in June when he wisely declared a one-year moratorium on intergovernmental debts and worked out a plan to maintain private credits to Germany, which was heavily over-burdened with short-term loans from this country. But these emergency measures did not suffice to shore up the sagging structure of international finance. The disintegration of the web of credit had gone too far to be checked. Nations that had devalued or imposed exchange controls and import barriers were, in effect, seeking desperately to "export their unemployment" to other nations in a suicidal, competitive race—a "beggar-thy-neighbor" policy that could not be reversed by measures such as Hoover's.

As the economy fell to lower and lower levels of production, unemployment, of course, mounted, becoming more and more a mass phenomenon. One of the amazing aspects of the situation was that the nation did not have accurate statistics on the number of the unemployed. By 1932 some estimates put the total of those out of work as high as 20 million, while the conservative "guesstimates" placed the total at about 12 million, or nearly 25 per cent of the labor force. Average hourly earnings did not decline substantially during the first two years of the depression. Average hourly wages of manufacturing labor amounted to 56 cents in 1929; in 1930, they were 55 cents and in the

[17] Schlesinger, *The Crisis of the Old Order*, p. 175.

following year, 51 cents. This relative stability in wage rates probably reflected the results of President Hoover's efforts to maintain income, the power of unions in certain lines to resist cuts, and the persistence of the "New Era" philosophy of increased purchasing power. Still, the maintenance of hourly rates was no consolation to those who were being put on short time or fired altogether because of the lack of demand for their products.

The statistics of unemployment hardly reflected the harsh reality of what the loss of a job meant to a family. In a culture that placed such stress on work and success, a job was an essential attribute of one's identity and status in human society. Arthur Schlesinger Jr. has conveyed as well as words ever can the human significance of unemployment in the first year of the Great Depression in the following passage:

> Across the country the dismal process was beginning, ushering in a new life for millions of Americans. In the twenties wage earners in general had found ample employment, satisfaction in life, hope for the future. Now came the slowdown—only three days of work a week, then perhaps two, then the layoff. And then the search for a new job—at first vigorous and hopeful; then sober; then desperate; the long lines before the employment offices, the eyes straining for words of hope on the chalked boards, the unending walk from one plant to the next, the all-night wait to be the first for possible work in the morning. And the inexorable news, brusque impersonality concealing fear: "No help wanted here" . . . "We don't need nobody" . . . "Move along, Mac, move along."
>
> And so the search continued, as clothes began to wear out and shoes to fall to pieces. Newspapers under the shirt would temper the winter cold, pasteboard would provide new inner soles, cotton in the heels of the shoe would absorb the pounding on the pavement, gunny sacks wrapped around the feet would mitigate the long hours in the frozen fields outside the factory gates. And in the meantime savings were trickling away. By now the terror began to infect the family. Father, no longer cheery, now at home for long hours, irritable, guilty, a little frightened. Sometimes the mother looked for work as domestic, chambermaid, or charwoman; or the children worked for pennies after school, not understanding the fear that was touching them, knowing that they must do what they could to help buy bread and coffee.
>
> As savings end, borrowing begins. If there is life insurance, borrowing on that, until it lapses; then loans from relatives and from friends; then the life of credit, from the landlord, from the corner grocer, until the lines of friendship and compassion are snapped. Meat vanishes from the table; lard replaces butter; father goes out less often, is terribly quiet; the children begin to lack shoes, their clothes are ragged; their mothers are ashamed to send them to school. Wedding rings are pawned, furniture is sold, the family moves into ever cheaper, damper, dirtier rooms. In a Philadelphia settlement house a little boy of three cried constantly in the spring of 1930; the doctor examined him and found that he was slowly starving. One woman complained that when she had food her two small children could barely eat; they had become accustomed to so little, she said, that their stomachs had shrunk. In November the apple peddlers began to appear on cold street corners, their threadbare clothes brushed and neat, their forlorn pluckiness emphasizing the anguish of being out of work. And every night that fall hundreds of men gathered on the lower level of Wacker Drive in Chicago, feeding fires with stray pieces of wood, their coat collars turned up against the cold, their caps pulled down over their ears, staring without expression at the black river, while the automobiles sped comfortably along,

bearing well-fed men to warm and well-lit homes. In the mining areas families lived on beans, without salt or fat. And every week, every day, more workers joined the procession of despair. The shadows deepened in the dark cold rooms, with the father angry and helpless and ashamed, the distraught children too often hungry or sick, and the mother, so resolute by day, so often when the room was finally still, lying awake in bed at night, softly crying.[18]

[18] Schlesinger, *The Crisis of the Old Order*, pp. 167–168.

Chapter 24

THE ECONOMIC ANATOMY OF PROSPERITY AND DEPRESSION

ACCELERATION OR STRUCTURAL CHANGE?

In its generally reassuring report, issued on the very eve of the 1929 stock market collapse, the Presidential Committee on Recent Economic Changes summed up the characteristics of the years after 1922 as follows: "Acceleration rather than structural change is the key to an understanding of our recent economic developments. Gradually the fact emerged during the course of this survey that the distinctive character of the years from 1922 to 1929 owes less to fundamental change than to intensified activity."[1] The advantage of hindsight has enabled economists and economic historians in the years since 1929 to discern more fundamental changes working to disturb the economic equilibrium of the nation than were apparent to the authors of that worthy, but ill-timed report. In this chapter we examine the most important of these changes and consider the efficacy of monetary policy as formulated by the Federal Reserve authorities in maintaining the fabulous prosperity of the twenties and in coping with the Great Depression. In order to understand the functioning of the economy in that period, we need to examine closely the changes in its institutional structure, i.e. the organization of business, of labor unions, farm cooperatives, etc. We shall take especial notice of the changes in the organizational structure of the Federal Reserve System in these years because of their close relevance to the topics under discussion. The sociological pre-conditions for a new era of high-level mass consumption will be examined in Chapter 25. Changes in other aspects of governmental organization and policy will be treated there also.

[1] President's Conference on Unemployment, Committee on Recent Economic Changes, *Recent Economic Changes in the United States* (New York: McGraw-Hill Book Co., 1929), Vol. 1, p. ix. Wesley Clair Mitchell, while not a member of the Presidential Committee on Recent Economic Changes, was a key figure in these years at the National Bureau of Economic Research which conducted the staff investigations for the Committee. His concluding chapter, entitled "A Review," was not as reassuring as the Committee's Report with regard to the prospects for economic stability. See below, pp. 650–651.

THE CHANGING STRUCTURE OF BUSINESS ENTERPRISE

The "Organizational Revolution," discussed in Part 7, entered a new phase in the years 1919–30, which most economists consider to be the second great merger movement in our recent history.[2] This period of business consolidation was less spectacular than that at the turn of the century—certainly it was described in less picturesque language—yet, in absolute numerical terms it was actually larger in size than the so-called first merger movement. Between 1919–30, nearly 12,000 public utility, banking, manufacturing, and mining concerns disappeared; 2,100 mergers occurred, on one count, or about five times the number in the earlier wave. Chart 1 provides a

CHART 1

Number of Mergers and Acquisitions in Manufacturing and Mining, 1919–1961

(ANNUAL TOTALS)

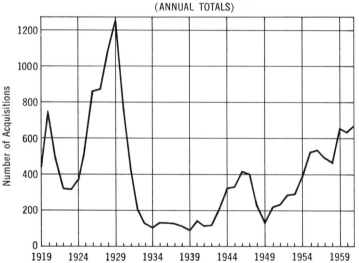

Reproduced from Hearings before the Subcommittee on Antitrust and Monopoly, U.S. Senate, *Economic Concentration* (Washington, D.C.: U.S. Printing Office, 1964), Part I, p. 14.

graphic perspective on the mergers of these and succeeding years. The mergers of these years were especially conspicuous in such industries as iron and steel (which accounted for nearly one-fifth of the total), oil, food, cheese, bakeries, textiles and chemicals, and motion pictures. The public utility field

[2] R. L. Nelson, *Merger Movements in American Industry* (Princeton: Princeton University Press, 1959); J. S. Bain, *Industrial Organization* (New York: J. Wiley and Sons, 1959).

was the scene of one of the most massive merger efforts, with such corporate titans as Samuel Insull and other promoters forming immense holding company empires.

Students of the movement have noted that in many instances the larger horizontal mergers brought together smaller companies and thus enabled them to compete more effectively with the leading giants. The advent of the automobile and the home radio stimulated some mergers in that the former made possible new methods of distribution and the latter opened up the possibility of national advertising via the air waves. Companies such as Standard Brands and General Foods, which were formed during these years, were established to take advantage of such economies in distribution. This merger movement was facilitated by the favorable conditions on the stock market in the late twenties, which enabled the leading investment bankers, such as J. P. Morgan, Dillon, Read and Co. etc., to underwrite the securities of these new combines with little difficulty. The lenient attitude of the Republican administrations in power toward business mergers and the interpretation of the antitrust laws by the Supreme Court in the U.S. Steel case (1920) and subsequent decisions tended to give the process of corporate fusion a "green light."

The effects of this merger movement on market concentration are harder to establish than the extent of the movement itself; an increase in concentration in this sense seems to have occurred more among new and rapidly maturing industries, such as motion pictures, chemicals, and petroleum.[3] One careful student of concentration trends concludes that manufacturing industries "on the average" do not appear to have become either more or much less concentrated over the years from 1905 to 1935; in other words, there was no net trend in market concentration in the manufacturing sector of the economy, despite the number of mergers that took place in the twenties. (It must be kept in mind that the expansion of sales in an industry may outpace the rate of consolidation and thus offset a tendency toward an increase in market concentration due to mergers).

The twenties also was a period of growth for trade associations. These are voluntary, non-profit organizations of the members of an industry that seek to deal with common problems by cooperation. The Coolidge and Hoover administrations encouraged these trade association activities, and the Supreme Court took an ambiguous view of those engaged in price-reporting activities, the latter often resulting in price uniformity.[4] In short, in the

---

[3] By market concentration is meant the percentage of the sales of an industry accounted for by the largest four or eight companies; this is spoken of as the *concentration ratio* of the industry. See J. S. Bain, *Industrial Organization* (New York: Wiley, 1959), pp. 203–206.

[4] *American Column and Lumber* vs. *U.S.*, 257 U.S. 377 (1921); *U.S.* vs. *American Linseed Oil Co.*, 371 U.S. 371 (1923); *Maple Flooring Manufacturers Association* vs. *U.S.*, 268 U.S. 563 (1925); *Cement Manufacturers Protective Association* vs. *U.S.*, 268 U.S. 588 (1925).

twenties many of the trade associations set up during World War I and some new ones experimented with forms of business cooperation and "self-regulation of industry" in the effort to escape from what they regarded as the undesirable excesses of competition.

In 1932, there appeared a study entitled *The Modern Corporation and Private Property*, which presented some striking statistics on the extent of overall corporate concentration as of 1929. The authors of this monograph found that in the latter year the 200 largest non-financial corporations held $81 billion in assets, which represented, on the basis of their estimates, 49 per cent of all corporate wealth, about 38 per cent of all business wealth, and 22 per cent of the entire wealth of the nation.[5] They found that these large, quasi-public corporations were growing much faster than the smaller enterprises, and at their current rate of growth by 1950 they would constitute 65 per cent of the total assets of the American economy. (A prediction, by the way, which was not fulfilled.) They called attention to the immense size of many of these companies, citing A.T. and T. as controlling more total wealth than existed within the boundaries of 21 states. Their analysis revealed that with the diffusion of stock ownership among millions of scattered stockholders and with the development of such legal devices as the holding company, the proxy, non-voting stock, and the voting trust, there was a marked tendency toward separation of ownership and management. To be specific, they found that in 65 per cent of the 200 largest, non-financial corporations, control was possible without having appreciable ownership. Management controlled 44 per cent of these companies without having important ownership of the outstanding stock, and in 21 per cent of the 200 largest corporations, control was accomplished through a legal device (such as the proxy) without important ownership.

The emergence of the salaried manager as the key figure in our large corporations as opposed to the founder or "captain of industry" of the nineteenth century has been well brought out in other studies. In the complex bureaucratic structures of these companies, the professional or salaried administrator was displacing the original entrepreneurs or founders of the enterprises. The former officials, usually having won their posts by advancement within the corporations they headed, had a different occupational experience from their predecessors. Professor Newcomer in a revealing study has demonstrated the "managerial revolution" that was in process in these years; Table 1 summarizes some of her principal findings.

[5] A. A. Berle and G. C. Means, *The Modern Corporation and Private Property* (New York: The Macmillan Co., 1932). Overall concentration or concentration in the large typically measures, say, the percentage of some large aggregate, total non-agricultural employ ment accounted for by the N largest firms in the whole economy. This concept of overall concentration is to be distinguished from that of industry concentration, referred to by Bain *supra*.

TABLE 1

*Principal Occupational Experience of Executives**
(Percentage of executives)

Occupation	1900	1925	1950
Entrepreneur[a]	31.0%	20.2%	9.9%
Capitalist[b]	12.5	6.1	4.9
Banker or broker[c]	7.7	3.7	4.9
Engineer	12.5	15.6	19.3
Lawyer	13.1	13.8	11.9
Other professional[d]	3.8	2.7	7.9
Salaried administrator	19.5	37.7	41.1
Total	100.0	100.0	100.0

* Source: M. Newcomer, *The Big Business Executive* (New York: Columbia University Press, 1955), p. 90.

[a] Many of these might be classified as capitalists. These, however, have established and operated independent businesses at some time, whereas the capitalists have only inherited in or inherited going concerns.

[b] Thirty-five of the 43 capitalists of 1950 inherited the office and the investment from other members of the family, whereas in 1900 this was true for only 11 of the 39 capitalists.

[c] The brokers were 4 in 1900, 1 in 1925, and 5 in 1950.

[d] Includes scientists, physicians, army and navy officers, accountants, and those with degrees from graduate schools of business administration.

MARKET PRACTICES AND PRICE STABILITY

The development of oligopoly (few sellers) in many industrial fields, associated as it was with the rise of these giant corporations, facilitated the efforts of businessmen in these years to escape from price competition. Market control was sought, and a greater degree of price stability attained through a variety of techniques, such as price leadership, basing point systems, patent pools, and trade association activities.[6] The tendency toward the stabilization of industrial prices in our concentrated industries was noted and approved; thus, F. S. Mills, an expert student of price behavior in the report on *Recent Economic Changes* concluded that "Business and prices both become more stable. There is evidence that our economic system is moving in this direction."[7] The effects of this increased price stability in the industrial sector will be discussed further below.

A striking concomitant development of these changes in price competition was the apparently intensified effort to win patronage by non-price competition, such as service, advertising, and new product development. Advertising particularly became big business in the post-war years. By 1927, about $1.5

[6] A. R. Burns, *The Decline of Competition* (New York: McGraw-Hill Book Co., 1936), Chaps. 2–5.

[7] *Recent Economic Changes*, Vol. 2, p. 655.

billion was being spent on all types of media as Madison Avenue sought to replace the anxiety about scarcity with a desire for "luxury consumption of leisure and the surplus product." The older virtues of thrift and prudence were assailed by the sales and advertising man. The dominant psychology, behaviorism, viewed man as being capable of manipulation, and the advertisers overlooked no motive to spur sales. The desire for status, the fear of social ostracism, and the sex drive were used to sell everything from fountain pens to automobiles. Inter-industry competition became more intense as advertising sought to lure buyers from the products of one industry to another, e.g., "Reach for a Lucky instead of a sweet" was a threat to the prosperity of the sugar industry and all its customers. The "new competition," as it was called, involved the promotion of the products of one industry against another— wood against metal, cans versus glass, etc. The attitude of this advertising age reached ludicrous proportions when Bruce Barton, a leading advertising man of the period, wrote a best-seller, *The Man Nobody Knows* (1925), in which he depicted Jesus as a topnotch businessman and an A-1 salesman. His parables, said Barton, were "the most powerful advertisements of all time" and to show His concern for business, he cited Jesus' saying, "Wist ye not that I must be about my Father's business?"

THE CHANGING FORTUNES OF LABOR
AND OF TRADE UNIONISM

The twenties was a period of mixed blessings for workers and their unions. On the one hand, labor's real earnings showed a substantial increase in these years. Average annual earnings in manufacturing rose from $1,158 in 1919 to $1,543 in 1929. Workers' real income, using 1890–99 as = 100, moved from 106 in 1920 to 119 in 1923, and then, after declining slightly in 1924, rose to 132 in 1928.[8] The big jump in real earnings in the earlier part of the period occurred mainly because of the drop in the cost of living. Actually, the movement in real annual earnings did not keep pace with the rise of productivity in these years; the latter rose 40 per cent between 1919 and 1928, while the former increased only 26 per cent. The average work week continued to decline also in these years. From the 60 hours, which was typical in manufacturing in 1890, most manufacturing employees were putting in about 50 hours by 1926. The reduced work week, of course, left more time for leisure and recreation and increased enjoyment of the consumer durable goods for those workers who could afford them. Apart from the severe unemployment of the 1920–21 depression, employment throughout this period was fairly stable, though technological unemployment was beginning to be a cause for concern.

Organized labor suffered serious setbacks during these years. The loss in

[8] P. H. Douglas, *Real Wages in the United States, 1890–1926* (Boston: Houghton Mifflin, Inc., 1930).

trade union membership was especially striking. From its peak of over 5 million members in 1920, the American labor movement lost in excess of two million members by 1933; in the latter year, it touched a low of just under three million.[9] The decline in membership manifested itself first in those industries—shipbuilding and metal working—that had experienced the most wartime growth. The depression of 1920–21 caused a further reduction in membership, so that by 1923, only three years after attaining its high up to that time, the labor movement's loss came to nearly 1.5 million members. Union ranks continued to dwindle in the remaining years of the twenties, and then in the years of depression, 1929–33, the unions lost another half million members. By the latter year, union membership was at a level it had reached in 1916—2.8 million members. For the first time since Samuel Gompers' death a principle he had asserted that labor union membership always gained during a period of prosperity had been breached.

The causes for this weakness in the "House of Labor" during the generally prosperous twenties were multiple. For one thing, not all industries, as we have seen, were doing well; the economic conditions in soft coal and textiles were far from good, and the labor leadership in these industries had failed to organize workers in the South. The migration of enterprise to the unorganized areas and the demise of firms in these fields (i.e., soft coal and textiles) cut into union membership severely. Secondly, there was the failure to organize the mass production industries, such as autos, rubber tires, and steel, where major gains in production were being made. Another factor was the weakness of labor's top leadership. After Samuel Gompers' death in 1924, William Green succeeded to the presidency of the American Federation of Labor. Green was anything but aggressive, but sought rather to achieve greater harmony with industry. He cooperated also with the leaders of the craft unions who dominated the executive board of the A.F. of L., and these men were wary about organizing the mass production industries.

During the twenties, organized labor's leaders had to contend with what was called "welfare capitalism." Many employers in this period sought to counter the attractions of union membership by instituting safety campaigns, group insurance plans, or employee stock ownership (profit-sharing), and by improving factory working conditions. Some, in their effort to avert unionization formed company unions; the number of the latter grew from 145 to 432 between 1919 and 1926. Finally, labor had to cope with employers' associations that fought for the open shop with every weapon at their command. These included the "yellow dog" contract, espionage agents, strike-breakers, company police, and resort to the courts and, especially, to that instrument organized labor hated most, the injunction.

In the face of such repressive measures, the weakened labor movement in the twenties showed relatively little disposition to strike and fight for its

[9] L. Troy, *Trade Union Membership, 1897–1962* (New York: National Bureau of Economic Research, Inc., 1965), Occasional Paper no. 92; L. Wolman, "Labor," in *Recent Economic Changes in the United States*, Vol. 2.

rights. The period had opened with a year (1919) of intense strife between capital and labor in which unrest reached unprecedented proportions; in that year alone there were no fewer than 3,630 work stoppages that involved some 4,160,000 workers. It is estimated that over 20 per cent of the nation's workers were involved in disputes in that year, with the greatest strikes in the steel, coal, and railroad industries. The great steel struggle for recognition and for abolition of the twelve-hour day and other working conditions that labor felt were demeaning to the American worker was a landmark in labor history. After 1909, unionism had been virtually eliminated in the steel industry, but in this period of soaring prices, the A.F. of L. decided to try to organize the big steel companies. Under the able leadership of Gompers, John Fitzpatrick, and William Z. Foster, the effort to organize the steel workers was surprisingly successful; by June, 1919, some 100,000 workers were enrolled. At this point, Gompers asked for a conference with Judge Gary, the chairman of the board of U.S. Steel. Gary refused to negotiate and did not even answer the labor leader's letter. The strike call went out, and about 275,000 workers are alleged to have answered it. Foster claimed that the strike was 90 per cent effective. But many of the skilled workers did not cooperate, and soon the strikers were being called "aliens," un-American, etc.—the United States in that year was in the midst of the Bolshevik hysteria. The steel companies brought in Negro strike-breakers; their detective agencies stirred up enmity between the diverse ethnic groups among the workers; many newspapers were antagonistic to the strike, running headlines about the "failure" of the strike; the financial cooperation of the federated unions was lacking, and soon the different craft unions fell into jurisdictional disputes, before the strike or recognition had been won. One group, the Amalgamated Association of Iron, Steel, and Tin Workers deserted their fellows and went back to work because they had a contract. Finally, Foster, who had played a leading part in the strike, was charged with communism; the Workers' Party had been formed in September of that year and Foster had been actively involved. For these various reasons, the strike failed; organized labor had suffered a major reverse. There was much *post-mortem* discussion of the lessons of the great steel strike of 1919 in subsequent years; but one fact, particularly, stood out—the craft union was ill-adapted to organizing a mass production industry such as steel.

The defeat of the trade unions in the steel and other industries led to a steady decline in the number of strikes during the twenties; the number of workers on strike in 1929 was 62 per cent less than the number in 1923. The unions grew increasingly defensive as their membership and financial resources shrank. The once powerful United Mine Workers was almost moribund by 1926. The flourishing auto industry defied the unions and successfully resisted organization. Efforts were made late in the decade to organize the textile workers in the South, but in a famous incident at Gastonia, North Carolina in 1929, the militia was called out, workers were evicted from company houses, and the strike was defeated. The general inability of organized labor to gain recognition and bargain for higher wages in these years was to play its part in contributing to the economic disequilibrium that finally brought on the Great Depression; this aspect of the matter will be further analyzed below.

THE FARMER TRIES COOPERATION

With farm prices depressed throughout the twenties, it is little wonder that agricultural marketing cooperatives continued to grow in numbers in these years, particularly in the first part of the period. The farmers in many commodity lines had found themselves faced by powerful buyers who were able to bargain to their advantage. Further, farmers in the past had often been forced to sell their crops soon after harvesting in order to get cash; this often led to an over-supply relative to demand with consequent lower prices. Now, the idea of "orderly marketing" was stressed—regulating the flow of the commodity to market to obtain the highest possible price. By organization too, the farmer could obtain a sort of countervailing power vis à vis the large buyers or corporate oligopolies he had to sell to. By 1928 there were more than 150 farmers' marketing associations with an annual business in excess of $1 million each. Some of them, such as Land o' Lakes Creameries, the California Fruit Growers' Exchange, and others were big businesses in themselves. Still, the farm co-ops had their limitations. Only about one-third of American farmers in 1928 were members of such associations. Furthermore, the inability of these voluntary associations to control the production of their members and their general failure to stabilize prices in markets that were international in character ultimately became apparent. While they achieved economies for their members in various ways, they did not solve the problem of chronic over-supply that plagued agriculture in this period. In the effort to cope with the latter problem, the farmers increasingly turned in the 1920's to "bloc politics"; the legislation they were successful in having passed during these years will be analyzed in the next chapter.

THE FORMATIVE YEARS OF THE FEDERAL RESERVE SYSTEM

The general language employed by the drafters of the Federal Reserve Act to assure its passage left the organizers and first officials of the System with the difficult task of completing the legislative process by their interpretations and administrative acts. One of the purposes of some of its Democratic sponsors, we have seen, was to avoid domination of monetary policy by Wall Street; this was the reason for the twelve regional banks and the establishment of the Federal Reserve Board in Washington. Yet, in implementing the Act, the organization that evolved deviated considerably from what one would expect from a chart of the formal structure of the system. To be specific, one might believe that ultimate power rested with the Federal Reserve Board, but in fact for much of the first fourteen years of its existence, the outstanding position of leadership was that of Benjamin Strong, the governor of the Federal Reserve Bank of New York from 1914 until his death in 1928. Professor Chandler in a fascinating biography of this central banker speaks of him as "the dominant personality and *de facto* leader of the entire Federal Reserve System."[10] Strong possessed this status in part because he was the chief executive of the most powerful of the Federal Reserve Banks with a major involvement in domestic and international finance. In addition, he had a persuasive, magnetic personality, an excellent mind, a superior knowledge of central banking, and a dedication to this profession, which was unusual. His pre-eminent role in these years is illustrated by the fact that for many years in the 1920's he was "the principal and almost the only representative of the Federal Reserve System in dealing with foreign central banks."

Strong early asserted his ideas as chairman of the Governors' Conference, an informal organization of the governors of the twelve Federal Reserve Banks, which almost immediately came into conflict with the Federal Reserve Board. He was often the leader in the Conference's criticism of the Board. His power was enchanced in these early years by the fact that the New York Federal Reserve Bank carried out the open-market operations (at that time the purchase and sale of municipal warrants and acceptances), though this was done on a completely free and voluntary basis so far as orders of the different Reserve Banks were concerned. The tension between the Governors' Conference and the Board ended, however, when the United States entered the war; for all practical purposes, effective control passed during the hostilities to the Secretary of the Treasury, who, according to the statute, was an ex-officio member of the Board. The wartime domination by the Treasury grew out of the overwhelming fiscal needs of the federal government and the need to facilitate the sale of its securities and to maintain their prices so that low interest rates could be assured. This meant, in effect, that monetary policy as it affected the private sector of the economy was subordinated to the fiscal necessities of the government. Ironically enough, the effective performance of these latter functions by the Federal Reserve System went a long way to give it a secure place in the nation's financial structure.

By 1920 the period of Treasury domination was ended, but the Federal Reserve officials were not able to undertake a positive control of credit because the gold reserve ratios of the Reserve Banks had fallen so low that they thought they had to maintain high discount rates, regardless of their depressing effect on business and employment. Until early in 1921, these officials

[10] L. V. Chandler, *Benjamin Strong, Central Banker* (Washington, D.C.: The Brookings Institution, 1958), p. 41 and *passim*. Chandler's analysis offers a striking illustration of a point in industrial sociology, namely, that the locus of power in an organization is often different from that indicated by the formal organization. See pp. 41–53 of *ibid.* for Chandler's careful assessment of the factors which made Strong the leader of the system for so long.

believed that they had to operate under the pre-war rules of central banking, i.e., the norms of the international gold standard. Under this regime, the movement of gold into and out of the country influenced the ease or tightness of credit. This conception had unfortunate results for monetary policy in the inflation-deflation cycle of 1919–21. Despite the difficulties of these years, they contributed to the education of the Federal Reserve officials in the difficult art of central banking. In the years 1921–24 especially, there was a faster development of Federal Reserve thinking and policies than in any other peacetime period.[11] The new conditions of domestic and international finance necessitated a thoroughgoing rethinking of policies: the passing of Treasury domination, the absence of an international gold standard, and the large gold inflow into the United States in the post-1921 period with its threat of renewed inflation. By 1924 the Federal Reserve officials had formulated a new set of objectives and policy guides, improved their understanding of the old instruments of monetary policy, and developed an important new one—open-market operations in federal securities. In this period too, these officials were shifting their philosophy of credit regulation from that of passive accommodation to the needs of trade to one of positive regulation,[12] geared to the promotion of high and stable levels of business activity and employment, stable price levels, and European monetary reconstruction.

The recurrent conflict over power and policies between the Federal Reserve Board and the Governors' Conference came to a head early in 1923. While Governor Strong was in Colorado, seeking to restore his health, the Board dissolved the Conference and asserted its jurisdiction over open-market operations. It established a new Open Market Committee, composed of representatives from five of the leading Federal Reserve Banks. About the same time the Federal Reserve Board officials were coming to a new awareness of the potentialities of open-market operations for the purposes of positive credit control. Government securities had never been bought or sold by the Reserve Banks prior to 1922 for the purpose of regulating credit conditions. They had been dealt in, but for other reasons, such as that of earning income to cover their operating expenses and to meet the dividends on member bank stock. Open-market operations in federal securities now provided the Federal Reserve with a powerful instrument of monetary policy. With it the Reserve Banks could inject money into or withdraw it out of the market in such amounts or at whatever time they wished; purchases of government securities tended to create bank reserves and sales had the opposite effect. Used in conjunction with rediscount rate policy, the Board now possessed a means of

[11] Chandler, *Benjamin Strong* . . . , p. 188.

[12] But see M. Friedman and A. S. Schwartz, *A Monetary History of the United States, 1867–1960* (Princeton: Princeton University Press, 1963), pp. 253, 297. Friedman contends that the Federal Reserve Board did not resolve the conflict between the "needs of trade" doctrine (which led to a policy of passive accommodation) and the compensatory concept of credit regulation which sought to offset the extremes of undue expansion or liquidation of inventories.

making its rate "effective." If it wanted to provide more money for bank reserves, it did not have to rely on the initiative of the member banks to borrow more. Through the device of open-market purchases of Treasury obligations it could build up their reserves and, conversely, through sales it could sufficiently deplete their excess reserves to the point where they would need to borrow if they wished to continue lending. By a synchronized use of these techniques of control, the Federal Reserve Board could make its redis-count rate an effective influence on the customers' rate charged by the member banks. Thus, we can see that this new instrument of open-market operations significantly increased the control power of the Federal Reserve authorities.

By 1924 the Federal Reserve officials had also clarified the objectives of their monetary policies and formulated the goals that were to shape decision-making for about a decade. These objectives were: (1) promotion of high and stable levels of business activity and employment, without inflation; (2) the curbing of excessive use of credit for stock market speculation; (3) assistance to monetary reconstruction and maintenance of stability in foreign coun-tries.[13] As Professor Chandler states, all these objectives assumed positive regulation rather than mere passive accommodation of the credit needs of business; they required discretionary action based on judgment rather than action in accordance with a strict formula. Yet it was one thing to state the objectives of monetary policy; it was quite another to cope with the conflicts among these objectives and to manage credit policies so as to achieve them. In the latter part of this chapter, after we have analyzed the functioning of the economy as a whole in the 1920's, we shall examine the implementation of these objectives by the Federal Reserve System and the success or failure of its principal policy decisions. At this point we must turn away from this brief appraisal of some of the salient structural and organizational changes in the economy in the 1920's to consider the functioning of the system. We can profitably begin by looking at the efficiency of the economic machine in that period and the manner in which the fruits of its growing efficiency were distributed.

THE GAINS IN PRODUCTIVITY AND THEIR DISTRIBUTION

There was a remarkable acceleration in manufacturing productivity in the 1920's that must be analyzed in relation to the dynamics of the economy in that period and the 1930 collapse.[14] The facts are indisputable. Kendrick's masterful study of this subject shows us that the output-capital ratio rose from

[13] Chandler, *Benjamin Strong . . .*, p. 199.

[14] By productivity is meant the ratio of output per unit of labor or capital in real terms. Ratios of output to particular inputs are termed "partial productivity" by Kendrick, e.g. output per manhour. Total factor productivity refers to output per unit of capital and labor combined. See Kendrick, *Productivity Trends in the United States* (Princeton: Princeton University Press, 1961), Chap. 2.

an average rate of 0.5 per cent in the years 1889–1919 to 1.3 per cent a year for the period 1919–53.[15] Output per unit of labor jumped from an average annual rate of 1.6 per cent to 2.3 per cent between these same periods. The gains in productivity varied, of course, from one industrial segment to another. Chart 3 (p. 550 above), which shows the changes in output per unit of labor input, is based on a ratio scale; the marked increase in manufacturing productivity for the years 1919–29 is reflected in the steep slope of the curve for that segment. Kendrick notes that the substantial increases in output per unit of input in these years was due in part to the striking increase in non-human energy relative to input, which in turn was promoted by the decline in the cost of energy (electrical power, etc.) as a result of the increased productivity of the energy-producing industries. He also suggests that the change in the productivity trend after World War I was probably attributable to a number of factors: (1) the spread of the scientific management movement; (2) the expansion of college and graduate work in business administration; (3) the increased investment by business in organized research and development. With regard to the latter, Kendrick's data show that expenditures for this purpose more than doubled in the 1920's.[16] In this period too, as some preceding statistics have indicated, the nation was investing more in its human capital as reflected in the increased enrollments in secondary schools and colleges. This enhancement of the skills of the labor force began to pay off handsomely in these years.

This enumeration of factors underlying the increased productivity of the 1920's has not recognized the specific innovations that contributed to the result. The increase in the output-capital ratio is especially striking during the 1920's in such manufacturing industries as transportation equipment (including autos), chemicals, and petroleum; these industries, which were engaged in "capital deepening" in the earlier years of the century, with the result that their output-capital ratios were falling or stagnant, in this period reaped the fruits of this earlier capital formation.[17] Many of the improvements made in this period, such as the perfecting of mass production and flow techniques, were "capital-saving" in nature with the consequence that the output per unit of capital rose.

What disposition was made of the gains resulting from this enhanced efficiency of American industry in the twenties? Such gains, other things being equal, result in lower labor costs. Were these savings offset by higher wages? In manufacturing, average hourly earnings rose 8 per cent between 1923 and 1929 as compared with a gain in product per man-hour of 32 per cent. In railroading, hourly earnings rose 8 per cent as against a 15 per cent gain in productivity. In coal mining, average hourly earnings fell 14 per cent, while productivity (as measured in output per man-hour) rose 4 per cent. In the depressed field of agriculture, farm laborers had no gain in wages.

[15] *Ibid.*, p. 68.
[16] Kendrick, *Productivity Trends in the United States*, p. 109.
[17] Kendrick, *Productivity Trends in the United States*, p. 166.

The above figures clearly indicate that wage earners did not gain in income proportionate to the improvement in productivity in these years. Analysis of the other costs of doing business—raw materials and overhead—does not suggest that they absorbed the gains due to increased efficiency either. Raw material expenditures were not higher in 1929 than they were in 1923, and while overhead costs probably rose, their increase was not sufficient to neutralize the savings made by businessmen on labor and raw materials.

Were the savings growing out of the increased productivity passed on to consumers in the form of lower prices? The statistics of commodity prices for the years 1923–29 do not suggest that, as a whole, consumers were the main beneficiaries of the increased efficiency of industry. Wholesale prices of "all" commodities declined 5 per cent in these years; semi-manufactured goods fell 21 per cent and finished goods 5 per cent, but the cost of living in 1929, while a few percentage points below the high of 1926, was higher than 1923. On the other hand, manufacturing profits rose 38 per cent, while manufacturing output increased 30 per cent—profit per unit was therefore higher in 1929.[18]

THE FAILURE OF INTERNAL ADJUSTMENT

As of 1929 it was authoritatively estimated that American industry as a whole was operating at only 80 per cent of its capacity.[19] Key industries, such as automobiles and construction, were concerned with the market saturation for their products at the existing level of prices and with the prevailing income distribution of the nation. There was an abundance of investment funds, as evidenced by the large amount of new financing and the falling yields on corporate bonds. Under these circumstances, the orthodox economist would expect the prices of consumer goods to fall, thereby stimulating further consumption and restoring the equilibrium between productive capacity and consumption. Such an adjustment had been going on in agriculture and in the cotton textile and bituminous coal industries throughout the twenties, but in industry generally it did not occur. Great gains had been made in productivity, but they had neither been passed on in any substantial way in the form of lower prices to consumers nor had they been shared with workers to a proportionate degree. (No account has been taken in the above analysis of improvement of product attributable to the increased efficiency of industry.) The competitive market mechanism, because of the rigidities in price growing out of quasi-monopoly tendencies in industry, was not achieving those internal adjustments that are necessary to sustain full employment over time. Instead, corporate profits in certain sectors of the economy were registering gains, which produced unsupportable stresses and strains in the aggregative move-

[18] G. Soule, *Prosperity Decade, 1917–1932* (New York: Rinehart, 1947), p. 333.
[19] E. Nourse and Associates, *America's Capacity to Produce* (Washington, D.C.: Brookings Institute, 1934), p. 416.

ments of such key variables as savings and investment. Not only were manufacturing profits 38 per cent higher than in 1923, construction profits were up 56 per cent from that year, though the physical volume of construction was only 27 per cent greater. In the electric light and power industry, profits rose 179 per cent between 1923 and 1929, while output increased 100 per cent. Even railroad profits increased 58 per cent over these years, despite falling traffic. In retrospect, it would seem that the stability of prices, which was considered so widely in the 1920's as a sign of economic health, concealed a "profit inflation" growing out of the reductions in costs due to technological progress and enhanced productivity.[20]

The gains in corporate profits, the total of which went up 62 per cent between 1923 and 1929, served to swell property income disproportionately. Thus, while aggregate wages and salaries increased from 40 to 55 billion dollars between 1922 and 1929, property income payments rose from 6.6 to 11.3 billion dollars. Dividends in 1929 were 65 per cent higher than they had been in 1923 and provision for depreciation and depletion was 67 per cent more than it had been in the earlier year. The large "cash flow" (retained profits plus depreciation and depletion allowances of these years) enabled many large corporations to reduce their current borrowing from the commercial banks and provided many of them with surplus funds, which, in the latter years of the boom, they invested in the call money market, thus enabling more people to buy stock on margin. George Soule later concluded rather plausibly that

A reasonable inference is that the economy would have been in a more wholesome condition if these corporations had followed a policy of raising wages or reducing selling prices more rapidly and if, as a consequence of the enlarged market demand that would thus have been created, they had been led to employ their surplus profits more fully in the expansion of production. Their profits presumably would have been no smaller in the aggregate, if reduced profit margins had led to larger sales.[21]

The disproportionate increase in property incomes aggravated the inequality in the distribution of income over these years, as we could expect, in the light of the fact that approximately 80 per cent of dividends during this period went to the top 5 per cent of the population. The disposable net income of those receiving over $1 million rose 31 per cent between 1923 and 1929, while those with net incomes of $5,000 experienced a 1 per cent increase over the same period. The relative share of income payments going to the highest 1 per cent rose from 12.3 per cent in 1923 to 14.5 per cent in 1929, a 19 per

[20] F. C. Mills, who had considered the stability of industrial prices in the 1920's to be salutary in the report on *Recent Economic Changes* (Vol. 2, p. 655), later wrote, "Many of the troubles arising out of the present world depression, and out of our domestic difficulties, had their origin in the failure of the price system to preserve an efficient adjustment of the working parts of the world economy and of the national economy of the United States, at a time when there were no adequate alternative instruments of coordination." *Economic Tendencies in the United States* (New York: National Bureau of Economic Research, 1932), p. 332.
[21] Soule, *Prosperity Decade*, p. 284.

cent increase. Thus, while the rich were getting richer, the top 10 per cent in 1929 being estimated to receive 40 per cent of the nation's income, 60 per cent of American families in that same year were believed to receive less than $2,000 a year. This increased concentration in the distribution of income increased the funds available for investment and reduced the amount spendable for consumer purchases. These surplus funds flowed into the stock market, and lacking adequate real investment opportunities for their absorption, contributed to the bidding up of the prices of the available securities on the market. They flowed also into foreign investment, a good deal of which was unsound and not likely to yield a return in the long run. There was a great danger in this, both to the individual investor as well as the whole economy, because a large part of our merchandise exports were financed in effect by this capital outflow. Once this foreign investment fell off, as it did, our export trade was bound to be seriously affected.

MITCHELL'S ECONOMICS REVISITED

Wesley C. Mitchell was in a strategic position to appraise the functioning of the economy in that climactic year, 1929. He was a founder and a codirector for the National Bureau of Research, which conducted the principal investigations underlying the report of the Presidential Committee on Recent Economic Changes. Mitchell, indeed, wrote the concluding section of that report in which he carefully reviewed the economic forces at work in the post-war economy, raised the question of whether business cycles had been "ironed out," and finally, assessed the economic situation as of the spring of 1929. It was a momentous opportunity for the world's leading student of the subject, a chance to apply economic knowledge to the diagnosis of business fluctuations on the eve of what turned out to be the most severe depression in the nation's history.

Mitchell's self-generating theory of the business cycle certainly must have made him conscious and alert to the possible elements of instability in the economy that could lead to depression at that particular juncture. However, with characteristic modesty and restraint, he disowned any intent to forecast the future. Nevertheless, while the Committee took a somewhat optimistic view of the economic situation, Mitchell's comments and conclusions were not so reassuring. In what certainly must be one of the most understated estimates of its kind, he said that "recent developments may appear less satisfactory in retrospect than they appear at present."[22] In the body of his review, he concluded that business cycles had not been "eliminated" in the United States, but the amplitude of cyclical fluctuations had been reduced, at least for the years 1924–27 as compared with pre-World War I cycles. He went on to

[22] Mills, *Recent Economic Changes*, p. 909.

warn that "Even on the face of affairs, all is not well." He remarked that the nation had seen "more uniformly good times" and advised that

> if we are to maintain prosperity, we must continue to earn it month after month and year after year by intelligent effort. The incomes disbursed to consumers, and to wage-earners in particular, must be increased on a scale sufficient to pay for the swelling volume of consumers' goods sent to market. The credit structure must be kept in due adjustment to the earnings of business enterprises. Security prices must not outrun prospective profits capitalized at the going rate of interest. Commodity stocks must be held in line with current sales. Over-commitments of all sorts must be avoided. The building of new industrial equipment must not be over-rapid. These and the similar matters which might be mentioned present delicate problems of management which will find their practical solutions in the daily decisions of business executives. Perhaps errors are being kept within the limits of tolerance. Perhaps no serious setback will occur for years to come. But we are leaving 1921 well behind us, and there are signs that the caution inspired by that disastrous year is wearing thin.[23]

It is an instructive commentary on the relative roles of business and government in the economy of the 1920's that Mitchell in the above passage writes of the decisions that would affect the maintenance of prosperity as being "the daily decisions of business executives"; he says nothing of possible preventive or corrective action by government.

The understanding of business fluctuations has a very close relationship to the promotion and attainment of a satisfactory rate of economic growth. The factors responsible for the short term fluctuations we call business cycles are in part separate from the longer term movements of economic growth. But, to an important degree, the two sets of factors are interrelated, and it is difficult to study them in isolation from each other.[24] It is obvious too that frequent or severe depressions will interfere with the attainment of a satisfactory rate of economic growth. Furthermore, from the standpoint of practical policy-making, unless one knows what phase of the cycle the economy happens to be in (and that presupposes knowledge of the cyclical behavior of business as such), it will be difficult to implement monetary or fiscal policies that will be effective in promoting stable economic growth. Granted, then, the importance of a valid theory of business fluctuations for economic growth, how well did Mitchell's analytical description of the cycle meet the challenge of 1929?

In one sense, this is an improper and incorrect question to raise because Mitchell's work on business cycles was largely designed to develop a *theoretical* knowledge of the subject; diagnosing and coping with the problem of stability of the economy in 1929 was a matter of *applied* economics, a much more difficult assignment. Still, it was Mitchell's hope and aspiration that his extensive empirical investigations of this complex phenonemon would provide businessmen and administrators with the economic intelligence they needed to

---

[23] *Ibid.*, pp. 909–910.
[24] R. A. Gordon, *Business Fluctuations*, 2nd Ed. (New York: Harper and Row, 1961), p. 183.

forecast and prevent "booms and depressions." Indeed, there are those who would say that the elaborate studies of numerous statistical series with their lags and leads as possible indicia of the future movement of business activity as a whole had this behavioristic orientation because of Mitchell's desire to be of direct assistance to the businessmen and others responsible for attaining a greater degree of economic stability.

In any case, it is clear that the level of knowledge of business cycles we had in 1929 was not sufficient to aid policy-makers to forestall that great catastrophe. Mitchell was able, as the passages cited from his 1929 review indicate, to point to certain danger signs, to warn of possible errors in business and governmental policy, but he could not diagnose the post-war economic situation with sufficient confidence in his scientific judgment to convince even his peers of the soundness of his analysis. Mitchell stated, in fact, in the review that "The United States has not had a genuine 'boom' in business at large since 1919." His measurements of the so-called short cycles over the years 1885–1927 showed an average duration for the full cycle of 39.3 months. The expansion, which began in January, 1928, on the basis of these studies would, if it conformed to averages for the past, have had a life of 22.8 months; it would, on the basis of the averages, "peak out" in November of 1929. But, as Mitchell said in *Recent Economic Changes*, the fact that business cycles had reverted to type after World War I "does not justify anyone in counting upon 40-month cycles in the near future, for the table of standard reference dates for business cycles shows that cycle lengths are 'subject to change without notice.' "[25] Mitchell's technique of cycle analysis did not enable him, in other words, to predict without reservation that a recession was imminent. Mitchell's reticence about the policies to be followed in 1929 probably reflected the fact that the National Bureau of Economic Research, which he had played so notable a part in founding, aimed to be strictly a fact-finding body. Mitchell probably did not think it proper for him in his role as codirector of the Bureau to make pronouncements on public policy in his concluding chapter of the report on *Recent Economic Changes*. In an earlier book to which he contributed, he had indicated that effective action to prevent depressions had to be taken in the preceding boom. To the objection that we cannot know what is the precise point in the prosperity phase of the cycle to check expansion, he replied that this objection had been "met by the progress of statistical research."[26] From this publication and others, we can see that Mitchell was a pioneer advocate of contra-cyclical policies, even though he was not able to prescribe adequate preventive measures on the eve of the Great Depression.

[25] Mills, *Recent Economic Changes*, Vol. 2, p. 893. The studies of the National Bureau of Economic Research made after the 1929 downturn show the expansion as having ended in August of that year. [G. H. Moore (ed.) *Business Cycle Indicators* (New York: National Bureau of Economic Research, 1964), Vol. 1, p. 670.]

[26] Mitchell, "The Problem of Controlling Business Cycles," in L. Edie, *The Stabilization of Business* (New York: The Macmillan Co., 1924).

In the years since 1929, critics of Mitchell's work on business cycles have contended that it was primarily descriptive and that it failed to explain the causes, the driving forces behind cyclical change.[27] Professor Hansen, in particular, has argued that Mitchell's work sheds light on the sequence of events in business cycles, but does not reveal their innermost nature. He notes that Mitchell's analysis failed to deal with the critical issues involved in the savings-investment process. Professor J. M. Clark in a work based largely on the statistical investigations of Mitchell and his colleagues at the National Bureau of Economic Research draws a distinction between "factors of prediction" and "factors of diagnosis" and persuasively contends that only the latter would serve to discover and reveal at what stage of the cycle a nation might be at any moment and establish some basis for control.[28] Mitchell's "abstracted empiricism" and his pluralistic analysis tended to obscure the search for such basic factors, in the opinion of some of his critics.

THE DIFFICULT TASK OF MONETARY POLICY

Our preceding analysis has described the massive forces that were threatening the stability of the economy as the prosperity of the 1920's came to a head in the great bull market of 1928–29. The shortcomings of the price mechanism in effectuating the adjustments necessary to maintain economic balance have been noted. But it was not the price system as it operated in particular industries in which Americans in the twenties placed their faith. They looked rather to the new Federal Reserve System to preserve the tenuous equilibrium of the economy. Central banking in the United States took on unusual importance in those years because with the gold standard in abeyance in many countries after the war, the checks it normally imposed on domestic monetary policy because of international gold movements were not effective; the financial stability of the nation more than ever before depended on the discretion and wisdom with which credit was regulated. The Federal Reserve System "had to face explicitly the need to develop criteria and standards of monetary policy to replace the automatic operation of the gold standard. One result was a conscious attempt, for perhaps the first time in monetary history, to use central-bank powers to promote internal economic stability as well as to preserve balance in international payments and to prevent and moderate strictly financial crises. In retrospect, we can see that this was a major step toward the assumption by the government of explicit continuous responsibility for economic stability. As the decade wore on, the System took—and perhaps even more was given—credit for the generally stable conditions that prevailed, and

---

[27] A. H. Hansen, in A. F. Burns, ed. *Wesley Clair Mitchell: The Economic Scientist* (New York: National Bureau of Economic Research, Inc., 1952), pp. 304ff.

[28] J. M. Clark, *Strategic Factors in Business Cycles* (New York: National Bureau of Economic Research, Inc., 1935), pp. 160ff.

high hopes were placed in the potency of monetary policy as then administered."[29]

We have already dealt with Federal Reserve policies in the immediate post-war boom and depression of 1919–21; our attention in what follows is wholly with the System's monetary policies in the years 1922–29. While these years were "the high tide of the Federal Reserve System," its managers, faced with exceedingly novel problems, were very definitely forced to feel their way. In the post-war period, though the Federal Reserve Board had won its freedom from Treasury domination, it confronted a number of dilemmas growing out of the multiplicity of its objectives in exercising credit control. If it eased credit in the United States to aid in the restoration of international monetary stability, it ran the risk of stimulating an unsound domestic expansion. If it chose to check speculation on the stock market by tightening credit, it might endanger and discourage general business activity. To make matters worse, there was division of counsel among the System's officials not only with respect to aims, but also as to methods of credit control. Some members of the Federal Reserve Board wanted to regulate the quality of credit (the particular uses to which it was put), but the influential officers of the New York Reserve Bank believed only in quantitative credit control (i.e., the regulation of the total volume of credit and its cost). These divisions of judgment and conflict of objectives made it difficult for the Federal Reserve System to develop a consistent policy in these trying years.

We can follow the main lines of monetary policy in this period by noting the changes in the principal items of Federal Reserve credit outstanding as depicted in Chart 2. With the emergence of the nation from the depression in 1922, the Federal Reserve pursued an easy credit policy by increasing its holdings of government securities. With the inflow of gold, this policy enabled the member banks to pay off their indebtedness at the Reserve Banks and to increase their Reserve balances. The rapid rise in the index of industrial production then led the Federal Reserve to shift from a policy of ease to firm credit control, this being accomplished by heavy sales of government securities by the Reserve Banks. The sale of these securities depleted the member banks' balances, and this led them to increase their rediscounting with the Reserve Banks. (Note the rise in bills discounted in Chart 2 and the decline in government security holdings in 1923.)

When business activity turned down in the recession of 1924, the Reserve Board again began to use some of its newly discovered instruments of credit control. Credit expansion was attempted by increasing purchases of government securities, while the New York Bank lowered its rediscount rate from 4 to 3 per cent. It was charged at the time that this easy money policy was followed in order to discourage gold movements into this country and to aid Germany and Great Britain to return to the gold standard. The Federal

[29] M. Friedman and A. J. Schwartz, *A Monetary History of the United States, 1867–1960* (Princeton, N.J.: Princeton University Press, 1963), p. 240.

CHART 2

*Principal Items of Federal Reserve Credit Outstanding
in the United States, 1916–1932*[a]

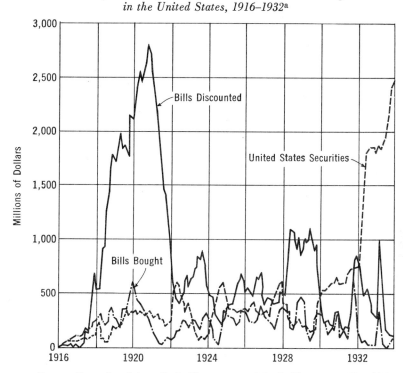

[a] Source: Reproduced from E. D. Kemmerer and D. L. Kemmerer, *The ABC
of the Federal Reserve System* (New York: Harper and Bros., 1950), p. 104,
with the permission of the publisher.

Reserve Board denied that these aims were so controlling in its decision. Whatever the merits of this charge, economic recovery in this country soon followed with the result that the Board again reversed its policies, selling government securities to "mop up" the excess reserves of the member banks, while the New York rediscount rate was raised to 3 per cent in February, 1925.

Similar tactics were followed during the recession of 1927, credit again being eased through large purchases of government securities. Reduction of the rediscount rate at this time was opposed by some members of the Board because of their fear that it would encourage stock market speculation. On the other hand, Governor Strong of the New York Reserve Bank favored a lowering of the rate here in order to aid Great Britain to maintain convertibility of the pound and remain on the gold standard. The outcome was that the Reserve Board, by a bare majority, ordered the Chicago Reserve Bank to reduce its rate to 3 per cent. Immediately a strong protest was made by Senator Glass of Virginia that this action was an illegal usurpation of authority by the Board.

The dispute was finally settled, but it revealed that the ultimate locus of authority on monetary policy within the System was not as yet clearly defined.

While the Federal Reserve authorities were seeking to achieve some coordination of policy within the System, there were others outside the organization seeking to impose one broad and simple objective of credit control upon them. With farm prices far below their pre-war highs, the agricultural interests were especially anxious to reverse the deflation of farm prices and secure some stabilization of prices via monetary means. Thus, after the Goldsborough bill of 1922 embodying Irving Fisher's plan for a compensated dollar[30] had been shelved by Congress, another attempt was made in 1926 to force the Federal Reserve Board to adopt price stabilization as its primary objective. The bill of Representative Strong, introduced in that year, provided, among other things, that "all of the powers of the Federal Reserve System be used for promoting stability of the price level." The Board opposed the bill and Governor Strong of the New York Bank, though sympathetic with its aims, showed that while the System could always influence the volume and cost of credit, this did not give it control over the price level; provisions of this type, he argued, would lead the public to expect too much. The Strong bill was defeated, but similar measures were introduced again in the 1930's. The belief in the panacea of price stabilization via monetary policy was hard to shake.

The most serious challenge to the System came, however, with the rise of stock market speculation in 1928 and 1929. Reserve officials had been concerned about the movement of money from the interior of the country into the New York call money market since 1925. By the end of 1927 the level of common stock prices and the volume of brokers' loans had roughly doubled over their level at the middle of 1924. In the first half of 1928, in the effort to curb speculation, rediscount rates were raised from 3 per cent to 5 per cent and a large volume of government securities were sold. But these measures discouraged stock market speculation only temporarily because as the open market sales of government securities reduced the excess reserves of the member banks, the latter increased them by rediscounting. By the latter part of 1928, stock prices were skyrocketing—quantitative credit control was not working to check speculation. In February, 1929, the Reserve Bank of New York proposed another increase in the rediscount rate in the effort to stem the speculative tendencies, but the Board refused its approval. Instead, it turned to direct pressure or "moral suasion." In a circular issued at that time, it said, "The Federal Reserve Act does not, in the opinion of the Federal Reserve Board, contemplate the use of the resources of the Federal Reserve Banks for the creation or extension of speculative credit. A member bank is not within its reasonable claims for rediscount facilities . . . when it borrows either for the purpose of making speculative loans or for the purpose of maintaining speculative loans." In May, 1929, the Board sent the New York Bank a list of member banks holding a large volume of collateral loans and requested that it

[30] See above, p. 609.

take the appropriate action—i.e., refuse to discount their paper. When the New York Bank refused, it was evident that moral suasion had failed.

The Kemmerers, in their study of the Federal Reserve System, have given us an incisive explanation of the limitations of the Board's policies:

> We must remember that banks were within their legal rights in making loans to speculators provided the loans were well secured. Such loans were merely not eligible for rediscount. Some banks borrowed on eligible paper but used the funds to make loans to speculators. . . . The fundamental difficulty lay in the fact that the Federal Reserve System was founded on the theory that bank credit should grow out of self-liquidating paper. But that was never written into the law for member banks, only for the Federal Reserve Banks. As a result, the Federal Reserve authorities were limited in what they could do about speculative loans.[31]

It must be kept in mind too that the Board at that time did not have any qualitative control over credit (such as control of margin requirements, which it gained in 1934). Its only alternative was to continue to rely on quantitative techniques of regulation. Thus, the Board approved the increases in the rediscount rates of the New York Reserve Bank—from 3 per cent to 4 per cent in February, 1928, to 4½ per cent in May, and to 5 per cent in July of that year. No action, however, was taken along these lines in the latter part of 1928 or in 1929 until August of that fateful year. The System's failure to act more energetically to check the stock market boom during the 1928–29 period is one of the most criticized aspects of its policy-making. When it did approve the increase in the New York rediscount rate to 6 per cent in August, 1929, at the same time it lowered the buying rate on acceptances. The latter action tended to cancel the effect of the former. But by this time it was already too late for preventive monetary action; business activity had begun to decline in midsummer, and the nation was but a few months away from the stock market debacle.

There was a great deal of argument in 1929 and in succeeding years over the wisdom of the Reserve Board's policies in that critical period.[32] The Board itself was divided over policy; the leadership provided by Governor Strong was missing—by the summer of 1928 he was a very sick man and in October he was dead; the dilemma over speculative credit versus credit for business purposes contributed to the indecisiveness of the Board; further, by the spring of 1929, brokers' loans provided by non-banking sources were more important for that type of credit than that provided by the banks. (See Table 2.) This aspect of the credit situation deserves closer analysis at this point. These "loans for others" were provided by corporations with surplus

[31] E. D. and D. L. Kemmerer, *The ABC of the Federal Reserve System* (New York: Harper and Bros., 1950), p. 106.

[32] There is a large literature on this subject. Interesting analyses are to be found in H. Barger, *The Management of Money* (Chicago: Rand, McNally and Co., 1964), pp. 85–96; Friedman and Schwartz, *Monetary History* . . . , pp. 254–266; L. Currie, "The Failure of Monetary Policy to Prevent the Depression of 1929–32," *Journal of Political Economy* (April, 1934); A. C. Miller, "Responsibility for Federal Reserve Policies: 1927–29," *American Economic Review* (September, 1935), pp. 442–458.

funds, wealthy individuals, investment trusts, etc. The funds were drawn into the call money market by the high interest rate on such loans, their liquidity, and their collateral backing. Since these loans did not derive from the banks, they were not subject to control by the Federal Reserve System. Thus, in the late summer of 1929, the Federal Reserve's tight money policy led the banks to reduce their call loans, but the high interest rates induced the "others" to put even more funds into the call money market. Right down to the crash, the Federal Reserve did not succeed in controlling this form of credit.

TABLE 2

Composition of Brokers' Loans, 1926–29[a]
(In millions of dollars)

Date	Funds of N.Y. Banks	For Out-of-Town Banks	"Loans for Others"	Total
Feb. 3, 1926	$1,222	$1,280	$ 590	$3,092
Jan. 4, 1928	1,511	1,371	928	3,810
Nov. 28, 1928	1,235	1,768	2,287	5,290
Apr. 3, 1929	1,021	1,652	2,889	5,507
July 31, 1929	1,205	1,696	3,058	5,960
Oct. 2, 1929	1,071	1,826	3,907	6,804
Oct. 10, 1929	1,834	602	627	3,063

[a] Source: L. Haney, L. Logan, and H. Gavens, *Brokers' Loans*, (New York: Harper & Row, Publishers, 1932), pp. 220–221. Reprinted by permission of the publisher.

In retrospect, it is clear that the Federal Reserve System, hampered as it was by the novelty of its problems and the division of opinion among its officials, was not able to avert the disaster of 1929. As the Kemmerers say, ". . . It would be an historical phenomenon if we could point to this as a case where men in a new position of great authority had exercised a new implement of control with courage and wisdom. . . ."[33] Still, the Federal Reserve authorities did manage to use open-market operations in moderating the minor boomlets and recessions of the period, they aided in the stabilization of foreign currencies, and they succeeded in avoiding the money panics of former years. In meeting the major challenge of 1929, however, their policies of "too little and too late" were grossly inadequate to stabilize the gyrations of so huge and complex an economy as that of the late 1920's. Furthermore, from the vantage point of today, we realize that the depression of the 1930's was the product of much more than a serious stock market collapse. The Federal Reserve authorities might have done much more than they did to moderate the investment boom that came to an end even before the climactic stock market spree, but to do that they would have had to go counter to the "New Era" mania and the powerful economic and political interests that had a

[33] Kemmerer, *The ABC of the Federal Reserve System*, p. 108.

stake in its continuance. Finally, it is to be noted that from the standpoint of modern aggregative economics, the reliance solely on monetary policy to check an investment boom of the proportions of the late twenties is questionable, to say the least.[34]

Hindsight has enabled us to see more clearly the severe limitations under which the Federal Reserve System labored in that period. It has demonstrated too the need for more effective instruments of credit control than the System at that time possessed.

> The experience of 1929 did show . . . that the Board needed to have some more specific controls at its command. Since there was not enough self-liquidating paper in the 1920's, banks made speculative and long-term loans. To handle the speculative situation, the Board needed more power over the stock market. They needed more discipline among the Federal Reserve Banks in carrying out open-market operations. And they needed some additional credit curbs, for open-market operations were not the patent cure-all they had originally been supposed.[35]

The Reserve System was equipped with these more adequate tools of credit control by the Securities and Exchange Act of 1934 and the Banking Act of 1935.

STRATEGIC FACTORS IN THE GREAT DEPRESSION

The stock market collapse in 1929 contributed materially to the decline in business activity that had already started before the avalanche of security prices. It did so because it led to a sharp downward revision of the expectations of business enterprises and consumers. The demand for luxury and

---

[34] The dispute over the monetary policies of the Federal Reserve System during the 1928–29 boom continues among contemporary economists. Witness these two conflicting interpretations of the monetary history of the twenties: Eli Ginzberg in an analysis of that period writes, ". . . the New Era from beginning to end was the beneficiary of an intoxicating monetary flow." [*The Illusion of Economic Stability* (New York: Harper, 1935), p. 132.] In flat contradiction of this view, Friedman and Schwartz conclude their treatment of the same period as follows: "The economic collapse from 1929 to 1933 has produced much misunderstanding of the twenties. The widespread belief that what goes up must come down and hence also that what comes down must do so because it earlier went up, plus the dramatic stock market boom, have led many to suppose that the United States experienced severe inflation before 1929 and the Reserve System served as an engine of it. Nothing could be further from the truth. By 1923, wholesale prices had recovered only a sixth of their 1920–21 decline. From then until 1929, they fell on the average of 1 percent per year. The cyclical expansion from 1927 to 1929 is one of the very few in our record during which prices were a shade lower at the three months centered on the peak than at the three months centered on the initial trough. The stock of money, too, failed to rise and even fell slightly during most of the expansion—a phenomenon not matched in any prior or subsequent cyclical expansion. Far from being an inflationary decade, the twenties were the reverse. And the Reserve System, far from being an engine of inflation, very likely kept the money stock from rising as much as it would have if gold movements had been allowed to exert their full influence." (*A Monetary History of the United States*, p. 298).

[35] Kemmerer, *The ABC of the Federal Reserve System*, p. 109.

durable goods was especially affected because their consumption was of a postponable nature. Once the decline began, it was particularly severe in the durable goods industries. The drastic reduction in the production of the latter type of goods undoubtedly reflected the operation of the so-called acceleration principle.[36] This principle applies to the demand for capital goods, durable goods, and inventories; in all these cases we say that the demand for these goods is a *derived* demand because it depends on the demand for the consumer goods or services that these producer goods make possible. The principle tells us that a change in the demand for the consumer good may bring about a much greater percentage change in the demand for the capital or durable good used in the former's production. The principle operates, with certain qualifications, in both the upswing and recession phase of the business cycle. J. M. Clark, who first stated the concept, described its application to that key durable good, the automobile, in the recession phase of the 1929–33 cycle as follows: "By way of illustrating the operation of these factors, the production of automobiles decreased from 5,621,715 in 1929 to 1,431,494 in 1932, while the number of registrations, taken as an indication of changes in the number of cars in service (though slightly overstating the absolute number) declined from 26,545,281 to 24,136,879. Thus a decline of nearly 75% in annual production corresponded to a decline of only a little over 9 per cent in total number in use. . . ."[37] In this example, Clark is demonstrating the accelerated or magnified change in the rate of production of the consumer goods relative to the relatively small percentage change in the demand for the transportation service provided by automobiles. The decline in the demand for the consumer good itself, the automobile, could be shown to have contributed to a much greater decline in the demand for the capital goods needed to make the former. Furthermore, economists believe that a given decline in investment in new capital goods may induce, via the multiplier, a much larger reduction in the income and employment of a nation because of the secondary effects of the cutback in new investment. Thus, it is possible, as seems to have been the case in the Great Depression, for the acceleration principle and the multiplier to interact to produce a cumulative deflationary spiral.

The severity of the Great Depression has been described in general terms in the preceding chapter, but there are certain details that demand further attention. The downswing of this business cycle continued for longer than any other business contraction since the Civil War, with the exception of that of 1873. According to the National Bureau of Economic Research, the contraction from 1929 to March, 1933, lasted 43 months; the decline after the panic of 1873 went for 65 months. But in terms of the extent of the contraction, the

[36] J. M. Clark, "Business Acceleration and the Law of Demand: A Technical Factor in Economic Cycles," *Journal of Political Economy* (March, 1917), pp. 217–235. The acceleration principle is described and illustrated in most elementary texts of Economics. For example, see P. A. Samuelson, *Economics, An Introductory Analysis* (New York: McGraw-Hill Book Co., 5th Ed., 1961), pp. 295–297.
[37] J. M. Clark, *Strategic Factors in Business Cycles*, p. 36.

amount of distress, the international repercussions, and the slowness of recovery after 1933, there can be little doubt that the depression of the 1930's was "the most severe in our history."[38] Its catastrophic nature can be seen in the fact that per capita real income in 1933 was almost the same as in 1908. "Four years of contraction had temporarily erased the gains of two decades, not, of course, by erasing the advances of technology, but by idling men and machines."[39]

The dynamics of the Great Depression can best be grasped in terms of the behavior of the major components of gross national product, as presented in Table 3. The greatest relative decline over the years 1929–32 took place in

TABLE 3

Major Components of Gross National Product in the United States,
1929–32, in 1963 Prices[a]
(Billions of dollars)

	1929	1930	1931	1932
Gross National Product	$214.2	$194.6	$180.3	$153.8
Personal Consumption Expenditures	145.2	136.6	132.4	120.5
Gross Private Domestic Investment	42.9	29.5	18.4	5.3
Net Foreign Exports	1.0	0.8	0.3	0.2
Government Purchases of Goods and Services	25.0	27.7	29.2	27.7

[a] Source: *Economic Report of the President*, 1964, pp. 208–209.

gross private investment and net foreign exports. The increases in government purchases of goods and services in these years fell far short of compensating for the reductions in these items and in personal consumption expenditures. In economic terminology, the "deflationary gap" produced by these net deficits in investment, consumption expenditures, and net exports go far to explain the nation's failure in these years to attain a recovery to the levels of income and employment in 1929.

The magnitude and the duration of the Great Depression make it impossible to consider it simply as an example of the so-called minor cycle, such as W. C. Mitchell described. As J. M. Clark wrote even in 1935,

> The current depression is more than the end of a business cycle of unusual severity. On the basis of cyclical theory limited to the hypothesis of the type of cycle averaging in this country three and a third years, it is impossible fully to explain all its characteristics—its small rise, enormous decline and long-continued period of prostration. In part it may furnish evidence, of a provisional sort, of the combination of the shorter cycles with a longer cycle of about three times the average duration of the shorter ones. This longer cycle

[38] R. A. Gordon, *Business Fluctuations*, 2nd Ed. (New York: Harper and Row, 1961), p. 430.
[39] Friedman and Schwartz, *A Monetary History . . .* , p. 301.

appears to rest in considerable part on the psychology of speculation, and on the related factors of expansion of fixed capital and of construction.[40]

Studies of the so-called "building cycle" show a peak of activity in 1925 and a trough in 1933.[41] Though their causes are a subject of much controversy, there is evidence to support the view that the Great Depression was fundamentally related to those alterations in the rate of growth that have been called "long swings" or Kuznets cycles (so-called because of his pioneer work on this subject).[42] These long swings, which average about 20 years in duration, show a period of retarded growth from the middle or late 1920's to the middle of the 1930's. While we cannot undertake an evaluation of the relative validity of these various hypotheses as to the causes of the Great Depression at this point, we can indicate our agreement with Professor Clark when he wrote, "A cursory survey of conditions tends to the conclusion that practically all possible factors conspired to do their worst in the present depression (i.e., that of the 1930's) ; especially the non-cyclical factors which appear to have marked this as a phase of post-War dislocation even more than a cyclical decline."[43]

The fall of prices in the early years of the depression undermined the values upon which the banking system was based and contributed seriously to the weakening of the international financial structure. These repercussions, which only were felt as the depression was prolonged, reacted back upon the course of the economy, pushing the marginal efficiency of capital lower, depressing expectations and capital investment in ever-widening circles. As noted earlier, the economy's movements were deceiving; there was an abortive recovery in early 1930, but by the middle of that year the depression was worldwide; the deteriorating condition of the debtor countries led to withdrawal of gold from the United States at the same time that depositors in this country, fearing further bank closings, staged a flight into currency, leading the banks in turn to increase their liquidity by contracting loans or refusing to renew those expiring. There were a series of these liquidity crises—in October, 1930; March, 1931; and in January–March, 1933, the most severe of all, culminating in the national banking holiday. The failure of more than 5,000 banks in the years 1930 to 1932, wiping out more than three billion dollars in deposits, contributed mightily to the deflation of bank credit both directly and indi-

---

[40] Clark, *Strategic Factors*, p. 116. Professor Schumpeter attributed the severity of the Great Depression to the coincidence in time of the depression phases of three separate types of cycles, the 40-month Kitchin, the 9–10 year Juglar, and the 50-year Kondratieff. See J. A. Schumpeter, *Business Cycles*, Vol. 2 (New York: McGraw-Hill Book Co., 1939), Chap. XIV and p. 907. For a brief exposition of Schumpeter's analysis, see Gordon, *Business Fluctuations*, pp. 239–241.

[41] C. D. Long, Jr., *Building Cycles and the Theory of Investment* (Princeton: Princeton University Press, 1940), pp. 135–136.

[42] See M. Abramovitz, statement in *Employment, Growth and Price Levels*, Hearings before the Joint Economic Committee, Part 2, 86th Congress, 1st Sess. (1959) ; *idem.*, "The Nature and Significance of Kuznets Cycles," *Economic Development and Cultural Change* (April, 1961), pp. 225–248.

[43] Clark, *Strategic Factors*, p. 114.

rectly.[44] After the false recovery in the spring of 1931, conditions deteriorated rapidly; wages and other components of aggregate demand declined, and Great Britain's departure from the gold standard in September gave a great impetus to nationalistic measures of economic security.

In summary, it can be concluded that the depression became as severe as it was for the following reasons:

1. The exhaustion of investment opportunities resulting from (a) the working of the acceleration principle in industries approaching maturity and (b) the creation of considerable excess capacity, particularly in residential and commercial building.
2. The financial excesses of the 1920's, which at the same time led to too rapid a rate of real investment in some industries and created a superstructure of inflated capital values the collapse of which weakened the banking system and led both borrowers and lenders to take a pessimistic view of the feasibility of further investment.
3. The unwise lending policies of the commercial banks, which created "frozen assets" on such a scale as to undermine the public confidence in the entire banking system. (This point ignores the unnecessary bank failures caused by the unwillingness of the Federal Reserve authorities to adopt an easy money policy to compensate for the closing of banks in the early period of the depression.)
4. International balance of payments difficulties arising out of (a) the decline in American foreign lending, (b) the erratic movement of short-term capital, and (c) the serious oversupply situation in world primary markets, including some of the principal products of American agriculture.[45]

THE FEDERAL RESERVE AND THE GREAT DEPRESSION

Monetary behavior in this period was extraordinary by any standard of historical comparison. From August, 1929, to March, 1933, the stock of money in the United States fell by over a third, and the velocity of bank deposits by nearly that fraction. This degree of contraction in the money stock was more than triple the largest decline in a historical series extending back to 1867. Such a vast deflation had many consequences, not the least of which was that it "shattered the longheld belief, which had been strengthened during the 1920's, that monetary forces were important elements in the cyclical process and that monetary policy was a potent instrument for promoting economic stability. . . ."[46] Let us examine the evolution of Federal Reserve policy in meeting this great national challenge to the stability of the banking system.

After the stock market crash, the Federal Reserve reversed its policy of restraint and tried to encourage expansion by easing credit. Thus, the New

---

[44] Studenski and Kroos, *Financial History of the U.S.* (New York: McGraw-Hill Co., 1952), p. 370. Friedman and Schwartz, *A Monetary History* . . ., p. 351 stress the role of bank failures in contributing to the severity of the Great Depression.

[45] Gordon, *Business Cycles*, p. 446.

[46] Friedman and Schwartz, *A Monetary History* . . ., p. 300. This work is also the source of the statistics noted above on the monetary stock.

York Bank reduced its rediscount rate from 6 per cent to 4 per cent in November, 1929, to 2½ per cent in June, 1930 and to 1 per cent in May, 1931. The Reserve Banks also eased the position of the member banks by increasing their holdings of government bonds to $600 million by October, 1930. This policy of monetary ease was continued until October of 1931 at which time a sudden change was made. The bank failures in Europe in the summer of 1931 and the closing of many banks in this country led to an external drain of gold abroad and to increased hoarding of currency at home. Both these factors contributed to a decline of our monetary gold stock and a shortage of so-called "free gold," i.e., gold in excess of the legal minimum requirements. The law at that time (1931) required a 40 per cent gold reserve against Federal Reserve notes and 35 per cent against deposits. In addition, the law stipulated that the Federal Reserve notes had to be backed 100 per cent by either gold or eligible commercial paper. If eligible paper fell short of the necessary 60 per cent, gold had to be used to make up the shortage. The "bind" on the Federal Reserve authorities derived from the fact that increased hoarding was demanding a larger circulation of Federal Reserve notes at the same time that the supply of eligible commercial paper was diminishing with the decline of business activity. At the same time, gold exports were running at the rate of $50 million a month. The external and internal drain of gold was the immediate reason for the Federal Reserve's reversal of its cheap-money policy. The rediscount rate of the New York Reserve Bank was raised from 1½ per cent to 3½ per cent in order to maintain the gold reserve ratio, and government bonds were sold on a substantial scale from November, 1931, through February, 1932. This extraordinary restriction of credit during a serious business depression had catastrophic effects because it led to heavy borrowing by the member banks, caused them to be more sensitive about their liquidity, and resulted in a rise in long term interest rates. (Certain long term government bonds rose from 3.3 per cent in September, 1931 to 4.5 per cent in January, 1932; yields of AAA bonds rose from less than 4.4 per cent in the summer of 1931 to 5.3 per cent by the end of the year.) The result, in the opinion of some competent students, was a renewed nosedive in the level of industrial production.[47]

By the spring of 1932, the intensification of the depression had led to a rash of "inflationary" bills in Congress, which prompted the Federal Reserve authorities to undertake a more vigorous open-market policy to head off more radical measures. The 72nd Congress had seen the introduction of more than 50 inflation bills, including free silver, greenback, and land bank proposals. Most seriously considered was the Goldsborough bill of 1932, which proposed to raise prices by broadening the Federal Reserve's open-market operations

[47] See H. Barger, *The Management of Money* (Chicago: Rand NcNally and Co., 1964), p. 101 for a concise and cogent analysis of monetary policy in this period. The gold reserve situation was remedied by the passage of the Glass-Steagall Act of February, 1932 which permitted government bonds to be used as collateral for Federal Reserve notes, among other provisions.

and by devaluation of the dollar. When it passed the House of Representatives in May by a vote of 289 to 60, it contained a provision charging the Federal Reserve System and the Secretary of the Treasury with the "duty" of restoring and maintaining the "average purchasing power of the dollar as ascertained by the Department of Labor in the wholesale commodity markets for the period covering the years 1921 to 1929, inclusive." Conservative forces in the Senate succeeded in shelving the Goldsborough bill, but it and other measures played a part in the renewal of the cheap-money policy via open-market operations. Between March and June, 1932, the Federal Reserve System bought more than one billion dollars in government securities, but this easing of credit failed to stimulate business borrowing. The proceeds were used mainly to reduce the member banks' rediscounts, to cover gold exports, to increase currency in circulation, and to add to excess reserves. The failure of this cheap money policy at this time led many to conclude that this was the final refutation of the quantity theory of money. Others quoted the cliché about the one's ability to "pull a string (tighten credit), but not push one." Some preferred the old adage with reference to the businessmen's failure to borrow, despite the cheapness of credit, about leading a horse to water. Several of our most competent economists have concluded that the easing of credit came too late and that it did not succeed partly because it did not sufficiently lower long term interest rates. It is argued by some that the ineptness of monetary policy in these critical years is traceable to the shift in power within the Federal Reserve System from the New York Bank and Governor Strong's competent leadership to the more divided council of the Federal Reserve Board in Washington.[48] While the Federal Reserve System prevented a money panic such as had characterized other depressions, it failed to avoid a vast deflation of the credit structure in the greatest depression of our history. The relative failure of the Federal Reserve in restoring prosperity during those years contributed, indeed, to a temporary eclipse of monetary policy as a means of coping with cyclical stability and to a faith in the newfound powers of fiscal policy. But that part of our analysis, the rise of the "new Economics," the beginning of the "age of Keynes," belongs to the next Part of this book.

[48] While highly contentious, Friedman and Schwartz provide a most stimulating analysis of this phase of Federal Reserve history. See *A Monetary History of the United States*, esp. pp. 407ff.

Chapter 25

SOCIOLOGICAL AND POLITICAL CHANGE IN AN EMERGENT CONSUMER SOCIETY

THE NEW ERA OF HIGH-LEVEL MASS CONSUMPTION

The 1920's have been regarded by Rostow and others as marking the beginning of high level consumption in the United States. The period can be and has been seen as a new era in this respect as well as with reference to its tragically unstable level of security values. To be understood, the economic growth of these years, as of other periods, must be studied in developmental context; it cannot be appreciated in isolation from the past and future. Indeed, from a sociological perspective, some of the basic social changes that we associate with the 1920's actually occurred during the years of World War I. That war greatly contributed to the change in the temper of American society from the casual voluntarism of the nineteenth century to the more hectic, highly organized industrialism of the twentieth. "In 1916," writes Leuchtenburg, "America still thought to a great degree in terms of nineteenth-century values of decentralization, competition, equality, agrarian supremacy, and the primacy of the small town. By 1920 the triumph of the twentieth century—centralized, industrialized, secularized, urbanized—while by no means complete, could clearly be seen. . . ."[1]

As we have previously noted, the first World War greatly increased the productivity of the economy, and the dynamic technological changes of the post-war decade accelerated this tendency. These gains in productivity with their accompanying increases in industrial capacity created a new concern about the efficient distribution or marketing of goods, as contrasted with their production. In a number of lines after 1919, economists noted a tendency toward a shift from a sellers' market (in which demand tends to exceed productive capacity) to a buyers' market (in which the latter have a relative bargaining advantage because the production potential exceeds the demand). The Committee on Recent Economic Changes expressed the new economic

[1] *The Perils of Prosperity, 1919–32* (Chicago: University of Chicago Press, 1958), p. 43.

imperative in 1929 when it said, ". . . it is not sufficient to be able to produce abundantly; we must also be able to distribute intelligently." In Rostovian terms, with the completion of the "drive to industrial maturity," the nation faced the new challenge of maintaining aggregate demand to match the extraordinary output of goods and services it was capable of producing. For the first time, says one historian, the United States was "confronted with the need to fashion instruments and attitudes appropriate to an economy of abundance."[2]

What are the attitudes appropriate to an economy of abundance or, at least, to one that could produce a wealth of consumer goods never before known? The very nature of this question suggests that the problems posed by the 1920's for Americans were not only technical economic problems of mass distribution, they had to do with some of their most basic social values. Indeed, some have contended that what occurred in these years affected such deep value and attitudinal shifts in the personalities of Americans as to constitute a fundamental characterological change. David Riesman and his collaborators who are the chief representatives of this view as set forth in their now classic work *The Lonely Crowd,* must be incorporated in this presentation by citation; the richness of their provocative analysis of the changing American character can only be fully grasped by reading the book itself.[3] For our purposes it must suffice to note that the type of social character that Riesman terms "other-directed," "moved onto the national stage for the first time in the 1920's."[4] This consumer-oriented type of American, wrote Riesman in 1950, "seems to be emerging in very recent years in the upper middle class of our larger cities," replacing to varying degrees the more work-oriented, inner-directed American. The "scarcity psychology" of the latter was socially adaptive during the period of heavy capital accumulation, but it tended to give way to the "abundance psychology" of the former, who was capable of "wasteful" luxury consumption of the surplus product and of leisure.

Riesman's other-directed man "works" in the environment of the bureaucratized corporation, typically in the middle levels of its hierarchy, and seeks security through cautious interaction with the "others." He is pictured as being most concerned with exhibiting a pleasing personality in contrast to the

---

[2] *Ibid., The Perils of Prosperity,* p. 11.

[3] D. Riesman, in collaboration with R. Denney and N. Glazer (New Haven: Yale University Press, 1950). A most useful review and critique of the Riesman work is S. M. Lipset and L. Lowenthal, eds. *Culture and Social Character* (New York: Free Press, 1961).

[4] Leuchtenburg, *Perils of Prosperity,* p. 278. Carl N. Degler, "The Sociologist as Historian: Riesman's Lonely Crowd," *American Quarterly* (Winter, 1963), pp. 483–497, questions the dating of the appearance of the other-directed American as being in the 1920's and also contends that "rather than a changing American character, the evidence suggests a remarkably stable one, at least since the early years of the 19th century. Degler's analysis, in the opinion of the authors, is vitiated by his failure to note that Riesman is describing "ideal types; he also fails to grasp the psychological difference between "other-direction" and overt conformity. For this and other points, see the perceptive, short treatment in C. Strout, "A Note on Degler, Riesman and Toqueville," *American Quarterly* (Spring, 1964), pp. 100–102.

development of "character" by his inner-directed predecessor. In the consumer phase of his life, the white collar, other-directed man, socialized in the norms of the new, freer ways of consumption by his close association during youth with his peers and by the persuasive mass media, anxiously seeks status and social acceptance by a carefully stylized mode of life in suburbia or in the upper income neighborhoods of the big cities.

Though it is not an aspect Riesman stressed, it is important to note the probable influence of the mobility and anonymity characteristic of the urban way of life upon Americans in the 1920's. During that period many of them were moving from small towns or from the ghettoes to the more impersonal life of middle class neighborhoods in the city or in suburbia. In the latter type of communities the self-image and self-esteem of the other-directed would seem to have been heavily dependent upon the individual's pecuniary status and his ability to display the symbols representative of his social position. In such a rapidly changing, mobile world, many such individuals no longer enjoyed the security and social support offered by stable family or neighborhood life or participated in the community of a meaningful religion. Robert Lynd, the sociologist, in a brief but perceptive analysis of the factors affecting consumption in the 1920's alluded to the stresses and strains of life in that period in the following manner:

> More specific forms of increasing personality unsteadiness are involved in job monotony and pressure in an era of increasing specialization, job impersonality in large offices and industrial units, the often attenuated unsupporting relationship of job and social status in the large city, the weakening of the marriage tie, the new complexities recognized in child rearing, the multiplication of new alternatives to "right" and "wrong" ways of carrying on many homely processes, the weakening consolations of religion in a culture marked by a growing *externalizing of values* in things bought in stores, and so on through a long list of current social changes.[5]

Lynd then went on to call attention to the growing psychological sophistication with which the advertising men of the twenties sought to manipulate the anxious consumer. "During the past decades," he wrote, "the business of selling commercial products as substitutive reactions for more subtle forms of adjustment to job insecurity, social insecurity, monotony, loneliness, failure to marry, and other situations of tension has advanced to a fine art. The tendency of contemporary merchandising is to elevate more and more commodities to the class of personality buffers. At each exposed point the alert merchandiser is ready with a panacea."[6]

The twenties was a period of transition between the values of the older capitalistic culture of the United States and the new demands of the consumer society, between rural and urban ways of living, between native and more alien manners. Characterologically, the society in terms of Riesman's charac-

[5] President's Research Committee on Social Trends, *Recent Social Trends* (New York: McGraw-Hill, Inc., 1933), Vol. 2, p. 867 (our italics).
[6] *Recent Social Trends*, p. 867.

ter types was mixed; the emergent other-directeds found themselves at variance with the more conventional inner-directed Americans and with those who were still tradition-directed. Given these circumstances, it is not surprising that commentators were struck by the conflict of values in the America of that period. Thus, Lynd described these value conflicts as they affected consumption as follows:

> The lingering Puritan tradition of abstinence which makes play idleness and free spending sin; and the increased secularization of spending and the growing pleasure basis of living.
> The tradition that rigorous saving and paying cash are the marks of sound family economy and personal self-respect; and the new gospel which encourages liberal spending to make the wheels of industry turn as a duty of the citizen.
> The deep rooted philosophy of hardship viewing this stern discipline as the inevitable lot of men; and the new attitude toward hardship as a thing to be avoided by living in the here and now, utilizing installment credit and other devices to telescope the future into the present.
> The tradition that the way to balance one's budget is to cut one's expenses to fit one's income; and the new American "solution" by increasing one's income to fit one's expenditures.
> The increasingly baffling conflict between living and making money in order to buy a living; and the tendency, public and private, to simplify this issue by concentration on the making of money.[7]

TWO INSTRUMENTS OF AN ECONOMY OF ABUNDANCE

The shift from an economy with inadequate capacity to satisfy demand to one that increasingly had a surplus of productive facilities created a new social and economic situation in the United States. It meant, in Professor Potter's words, that "the culture must be reoriented to convert the producer's culture into a consumer's culture." Under these new circumstances, the consumer must be educated, and "the only institution which we have for instilling new needs, for training people to act as consumers, for altering men's values, and thus for hastening their adjustment to potential abundance is advertising. . . ." For these reasons, Potter insists that it is "valid to regard advertising as distinctively the institution of abundance."[8] While there is reason to question Potter's emphasis on advertising as the only institution capable of changing men's values and training them as consumers, it cannot be denied that advertising played a major role in the development of high-level mass consumption in the twenties. The statistics of advertising expenditure clearly show the great increases that took place in those years. The total dollar volume of advertising grew from $1,468 million in 1918 to

[7] *Recent Social Trends*, Vol. 2, p. 867.

[8] D. N. Potter, *People of Plenty* (Chicago: The University of Chicago Press, 1954), pp. 173, 175. Potter's Chap. VIII offers a most stimulating analysis of this powerful institution in its relation to the American character.

$3,426 million in 1929.[9] But more important, when we look at such figures in per capita terms and in relation to national income, particularly the former, we see the phenomenonal increase even more vividly. (See Table 1.)

TABLE 1

Volume of Newspaper and Periodical Advertising, Per Capita and as a Ratio of the National Income, 1914–33[a]

Year	Total (In Millions of $)	Per Capita Expenditure	Ratio of Expenditures to National Income
1914	$ 255.6	$2.61	.75
1919	528.2	5.03	.78
1921	676.9	6.26	.83
1923	793.8	7.12	1.17
1925	923.2	8.04	1.27
1927	1,030.2	8.72	1.40
1929	1,120.2	9.22	1.38
1931	868.5	7.00	1.61
1933	569.6	4.53	1.35

[a] Adapted by permission from N. H. Borden, *The Economic Effects of Advertising* (Homewood, Ill.: Richard D. Irwin, Inc., 1942), p. 48. The differences from the figures on the volume of advertising cited in the text are due to the fact that the latter are more inclusive.

From this table, we can see that the per capita volume of newspaper and periodical advertising almost doubled between 1919 and 1929 and that the expenditure figure (again on a per capita basis) was almost quadruple what it had been in 1914. Incidentally, the drastic decline in advertising expenditures in the depression years, 1931 and 1933, reflected the general retrenchment in business spending and the declining faith in that particular way of restoring prosperity. It is of interest to note too that the figures for 1933 represented the low point; after that date there was a slow increase, but the level of expenditures for advertising never regained that of 1929 until after World War II.

Students of marketing, in accounting for the marked growth of advertising in this decade and in the earlier years of the century, cite such factors as these: the widening gap of communication between producers and consumers; the increasing variety of new merchandise on the market; the intensified use of product differentiation as industrialism matured and as "manufacturers had capacity to produce far beyond existing demand"; the development of a competitive battle for control of demand; the widening of retail markets as the means of transportation improved; the effort of manufacturers to bypass middlemen and sell directly to the consumer via advertising; the use of more expensive forms of advertising, such as full-page spreads; the increased recognition by businessmen of the value of advertising as a means of building

[9] *Historical Statistics of the United States, Colonial Times to 1957* (Washington: Government Printing Office, 1960), p. 526.

demand and the vigorous promotion of advertising itself by the various media and the advertising agencies.[10]

Advertising not only increased in quantitative terms in the twenties, it seemed to undergo a qualitative change as well. As suggested earlier, it played upon the emotions, the fears, and anxieties of Americans to a greater degree. Some of the famous slogans of that era were, "Four out of five have it" (pyorrhea) or "Even your best friend won't tell you," etc. The behaviorist psychology of John B. Watson, with its manipulative view of man that was in great vogue in the twenties, was nicely suited to the purposes of mass advertising.

Marketing experts in the twenties were disturbed at the fickleness of consumer demand and the unpredictable nature of the public's reaction to fashions, fads, and frills. One of them, pointing to the bewildering variety of options that the buyer of that period was offered—options among competing makes and brands, among designs and styles, innovations and older goods, and choices between different priced goods—noted that purchasers' decisions were becoming more and more "massed decisions" rather than individual, discriminating choices. He goes on to say,

> If they had been prepared to exercise discriminating taste and judgment, their diversities of individual preferences would have matched the practically unlimited variety of offerings; and in that case multifarious personal idiosyncrasies would have been merged into a harmonious and inherently stable ensemble of demand. But they were not prepared. They were under the sway of forces which herded them into a consuming crowd and transformed their normally diversified consumption into massed demands.[11]

National advertising, this expert contended, since it is designed to appeal to the largest number, inevitably adapts itself to the mentality of the popular audience, i.e., it is demagogic. It employs sophistry and ballyhoo, and hence, "the influence of much current advertising strengthens the tendency toward impulsive, follow-the-crowd decisions." Americans, as a body, in consequence, are made more susceptible to suggestion and to quick, impulsive reactions as consumers.

> These two factors—abnormal susceptibility to suggestion and speed of reactions on a national scale—go far toward explaining the violent, destructive swings of popular favor in consumers' choices among optional offerings. Decisions are less divergent and individualized than in earlier times; they are massed. And massed decisions are unrestrained by the inhibitions of self-reliant individuals. Like the loose gun-carriage in Victor Hugo's "93", they roll with terrifying mass and velocity from side to side of our economic craft.[12]

This analysis of mass advertising and its consequences in the twenties is not that of a sensation-seeking author, but the conclusions of a well-trained

---

[10] N. H. Borden, *The Economic Effects of Advertising* (Chicago: Irwin, 1944), pp. 49–50.

[11] W. H. Lough, *High-Level Consumption* (New York: McGraw-Hill Book Co., 1935), p. 146.

[12] *Ibid.*, p. 148.

business economist. The symptoms he describes remind us, of course, of those delineations of the tendencies toward mass society in America provided by more contemporary authors, such as the late C. Wright Mills.

The automobile industry made especially effective use of advertising and other forms of aggressive sales promotion in the twenties. Its expenditures in national periodicals for this purpose rose from $5 million in 1915 to close to $23 million in 1929; it ranked first among our industries in using this medium in 1915 and 1923; in 1929, it was third in rank. Altogether, over the years from 1915 to 1929, it was first in advertising expenditures in national periodicals, spending over $223 million in this effort alone.[13] In addition, the industry, with General Motors in the lead, started to engage in market research and develop the practice of the annual automobile show and annual models as very effective marketing tools.[14] Indeed, the aggressive sales promotion methods of the auto manufacturers and the appeal of the motor car itself led to significant shifts in demand for other products, leading these industries to turn to sales and advertising effort in self-defense.

Another industry that made extensive use of advertising in changing demand for its products in the twenties was cigarettes. Product differentiation was carried to a new high by the Big Three of this industry (American Tobacco Co., R. J. Reynolds Co., and Liggett and Myers Tobacco Co.) in these years and successful advertising of what an earlier generation had regarded as "coffin nails" contributed to increased smoking by women and millions of others, though other factors as well were involved in this social change. After 1925, George Washington Hill, the astute president of the American Tobacco Company, popularized the slogan, "Reach for a Lucky instead of a sweet" as an appeal to potential women smokers. The sugar industry felt threatened by his sales strategy, and another inter-industry battle for the consumer's dollar was started.

It must be recognized that the stimulation and changes in consumer demand in the twenties were not due wholly to advertising and other deliberate forms of sales promotion. Not to be overlooked was the powerful indirect influence of that other new medium, the "movies," and the experience of urban and suburban life with their greater stress on social distinctions, class, status, and the importance of "keeping up with the (ubiquitous) Joneses."

As the preceding analysis suggests, the conflicts in the American value system of the twenties were especially acute in the area of consumption and thrift. Americans who had been raised on the idea that saving was a virtue were now to be told that it was unAmerican not to spend. In place of the aphorisms of Benjamin Franklin's Poor Richard concerning the prudence of frugality, Americans learned the advertising slogans of their favorite brands of consumer goods. This adjustment in values and ideology was particularly difficult for the bankers, formerly the most symbolic defenders of middle-class

---

[13] *Recent Social Trends*, Vol. 2, p. 874.

[14] "How to Sell Automobiles," *Fortune* (February, 1939), pp. 71–78, 105–109 contains a valuable treatment of the selling methods in the auto industry for these years.

diligence and respectability. They found themselves in competition with the sellers and advertisers of the new consumer goods and with the purveyors of securities. The 1920's was distinctly a "new era of competition for Mr. Average Man's Dollars" and the bankers had no choice but to adjust their ideas of thrift to the consuming and investing habits of the new economic society.[15] Adjusting the traditional idea of thrift to the installment plan was a painful process for some bankers. "Many bankers found it impossible to overcome deeply ingrained beliefs that only the immoral would extend bank credit for the purchase of automobiles, phonographs, radios, washing machines, refrigerators and other luxuries. . . ." Installment selling was high on the agenda of many bankers' conventions about 1926, as its pros and cons were debated. One Pittsburgh banker charged that any businessman, who, lusting for profits, perverted the people's thrift "by unwise fanning of natural desires for possessions [with being] an economic traitor to his country." Another man, a chairman of the National Education Association's committee on thrift education, enumerated the sources of waste in personal budgets, listing goods that have since come to be considered as integral parts of our consumer society: intoxicating liquors, tobacco, jewelry and plate, automobiles, confectionery, soft drinks, tea and coffee, millinery, patent medicines, and chewing gum. It is no wonder that H. L. Mencken described the lot of the conservative banker during the New Era as "the immensely painful one of a good Presbyterian in Hollywood."

Painful as it was, the bankers did succeed in developing new concepts of thrift and spending more compatible with the consumption patterns and needs of the evolving economy. They did so by drawing on the conventional wisdom of the 1920's, which placed much faith in the ideas of scientific management and the gospel of efficiency. According to the latter, resources should neither be wasted nor hoarded, but used in a rationally controlled manner. The new thrift made its peace with the demands of the consumer society by rejecting the thrift of self-denial; paradoxically, it sought to justify thrift by consumption. "Instead of calling for a rejection of luxuries, bankers recommended thrift as the best way to acquire the goods of the new consumer society." Likewise, once the bankers had developed adequate scientific standards for extending installment credit, they began to make loans to consumers and to regulate the flow of credit to the finance companies. A Bridgeport, Conn. bank in 1920 pioneered in making small loans; a Jersey City bank in 1924 opened the first small-loan department in a commercial bank. The new era of consumer finance could truly be said to have arrived with the entry of the giant National City Bank of New York into the business in 1928. Thus, the nation was provided with instruments and attitudes more appropriate to an economy of

[15] A. L. Roe, "Bankers and Thrift in the Age of Affluence," *American Quarterly* (Winter, 1965), pp. 619–633. We have relied heavily on this stimulating and insightful analysis for much in this and the following paragraph. Evans Clark, *Financing the Consumer* (New York: Harper and Bros., 1931) is also useful on the development of installment finance.

abundance. The older ideas about the "immorality of high-level mass consumption" became increasingly obsolete.

Still, in retrospect, the prosperity of the new era, partially based upon the hyper-active use of these instruments of abundance, advertising and installment selling, involved grave perils. Though the urban middle class, on the whole, was infused with a confidence deriving from its new technological and business successes and its "benevolent materialism," how adequate were these sales and promotion policies in stimulating consumption by those who did not have sufficient income to be persuaded to buy? Didn't overcoming sales resistance have limitations in this respect? In seeking answers to such questions, we must remember that these years saw the emergence of a managerial elite in the great corporations; in the opinion of one careful student of the period, the prosperity of the twenties "invested enormous political and social power in a business class with little tradition of social leadership. . . ."[16] How did this elite group see the problem of maintaining sufficient *aggregate* demand to maintain the prosperity? In the following sections of this chapter, we shall examine some of the principal political developments and governmental actions of the period and their relationship to this crucial question.

THE MIXED PATTERN OF POST-WAR POLITICS

Historians have long looked upon the post-war years as a "return to normalcy" under Republican rule and have contended that the war "killed" the Progressive movement. Of late, however, a new interpretation has been advanced that this period was a much more complex one that defies explanation in terms of sweeping generalizations or pat theories.[17] From what we know of the relative power of the different interest groups and the ambivalence and conflicts about values in the post-war era, much can be said for this new view. However, it is indisputable that Progressivism never achieved the status as a national movement that it had in the years 1910–12 or in the early years of Wilson's administration. What seems to have happened was that the business and agricultural wings of Progressivism went their separate ways, with the businessmen winning influence in the executive and regulatory agencies of the government and the Progressive coalitions of farmer and labor groups entrenching themselves in Congress. The result was that for most of these years the nation had conservative political administrations in the federal government confronting Progressive coalitions in Congress. On the state and local levels, Progressivism survived to a surprising degree, concerning itself

---

[16] Leuchtenburg, *The Perils of Prosperity*, p. 9.

[17] See esp. A. S. Link, "What Happened to the Progressive Movement in the 1920's?" *American Historical Review* (July, 1959), pp. 833–851. Also his *American Epoch, A History of the United States since the 1890's* (New York: A. A. Knopf, 2nd Ed., 1963), Chap. 15.

particularly with administrative efficiency and expansion of education and social services.

To understand the political climate of the twenties, we must appreciate the outlook of the urban middle class. Its leaders in business and the professions had led the nation to economic achievements during the war that revealed the tremendous productivity of the economy. The professionalization of business management was going forward, and the emergence of a managerial class exercised a significant effect on political and social ideals. "The urban middle classes were dynamic, expansive, and supremely confident. They knew that they were building a new America, a business civil society based not upon monopoly and restriction but upon a whole new set of business values—mass production and consumption, short hours and high wages, full employment, welfare capitalism."[18] At the same time, the development of the middle and upper middle class suburbs in the twenties tended to diffuse the remaining reform energies of the urban leaders.

With organized labor in retreat and on the defensive and with the radicals practically defunct after the post-war reaction, the Progressive movement consisted mainly of farmers, the railroad brotherhoods, the Democratic organizations in large cities, independent radicals, and social workers. These Progressive elements controlled Congress from 1921 to about 1927 and had near control even during the period of their greatest weakness in the legislative branch, from 1927 to 1930. In these years the farm bloc was the single most powerful interest group in the Congress, and it was able to pass a number of important measures of great benefit to farmers.

In the cities, Progressivism was undergoing an important transition from old style, moralistic reformism to a new approach, which came to be called Liberalism. This new movement was less interested in the moral reformation of man and more concerned with providing specific economic and social benefits through the power of the federal government. It drew its support not from the old middle class of the small towns and cities, but from the urban masses, especially the new immigrant workers in the eastern cities.[19]

The Progressive businessmen, fresh from their labors as "dollar a year" men in the wartime agencies, worked out the most successful accommodation of all these interest groups in coping with the post-war political situation. Instead of frontally attacking the middle-income groups who had challenged them during the Progressive era, the big business leaders gradually neutralized such groups or incorporated themselves in their ranks. Thus, big businessmen in the immediate pre-war years joined such organizations as the National Association of Manufacturers, the U.S. Chamber of Commerce, and the American Bankers' Association, which they formerly had opposed. A permissive federal government served as a "go-between" in working out these compromises and thus, despite sporadic in-fighting among big and small

[18] Link, *American Epoch* . . . , p. 833.
[19] Leuchtenburg, *The Perils of Prosperity*, p. 137.

businessmen, the business community as a whole achieved harmony and something of a united front during the prosperous years of the twenties. Instead of contesting the powers of the new regulatory agencies, many business groups succeeded in capturing the very bodies which had been designed to control them. In this way, businessmen used the federal government as a mechanism for regularizing their affairs.[20] The philosophy of "self-regulation" of business under such benign agencies as the Republican-dominated Federal Trade Commission, Interstate Commerce Commission, etc. was later to flourish as the official doctrine of the New Deal's National Recovery Act.

While a Progressive coalition often held the balance of power in Congress during the 1920's, it was terribly frustrated because it really had no program to present, aside from agricultural aid. It was consequently reduced to sniping at the conservatives, who "knew what they wanted." Thus, since they had no plan for large-scale government spending, the Progressives were finally forced, in the face of large government surpluses, to accept Secretary of the Treasury Mellon's tax cuts. While the Democrats in the northern cities and states had begun to legislate to meet the social and economic needs of the urban masses, an effective political combination of the farmer and urban blocs had to await the coming of the New Deal. Senator La Follette's weak bid for the Presidency in 1924, with its hackneyed oratory about the evils of "monopoly" and its heavy handicap of inadequate grass-roots organization and insufficient financial support, demonstrated the bankruptcy and irrelevance of the old Progressive movement. With southern and northern Democrats disunited in the twenties, a long reign for the Republican Party was almost assured.

These general remarks about the political context of our economic development in the twenties are a necessary background for understanding the action or lack of action taken with respect to some of the major legislative policies and their relation to the adequacy of aggregate demand in maintaining the prosperity of those years.

FEDERAL FARM POLICIES

The post-war farm depression has been referred to in an earlier chapter, but its serious impact on the national economy and on the purchasing power of farmers has not as yet been considered. With the decline in farm prices in the depression of 1920–21, net farm income fell from $9,877 million in 1919 to $8,368 million in 1920 and then to $3,795 million in 1921. It recovered in 1923 and hovered between $5 and $6 billion between that year and 1929. Actually, the prices received by farmers regained levels considerably above

[20] For a penetrating analysis of this aspect of the Progressive movement, see R. H. Wiebe, *Business and Reform: A Study of the Progressive Movement* (Cambridge: Harvard University Press, 1962), Chap. 1 and *passim*. See also his more recent work, *The Search for Order, 1877–1920* (New York: Hill and Wang, 1967).

those of the pre-war years, as Chart 1 shows, but the prices paid by farmers were much higher in the twenties, and they labored especially under a burden of higher interest payments (growing out of the large mortgage debt incurred in the war years) and taxes. The consequence was that the parity ratio (the relationship between prices received by farmers versus prices paid), on a pre-war basis, such as 1910–14 = 100) fluctuated between 80 and 90 for most of the twenties. The depressed state of the farmer relative to others in the nation was shown most graphically in the fact that farmers received 16 per cent of the national income in 1919 and less than 9 per cent ten years later. The farmers resented bitterly that they were not sharing in the urban prosperity of these years; they could not afford the automobiles, radios, electricity, etc. that city dwellers were buying in increased quantities. Bolstering and making effective the farmers' demand and propensity to consume a larger amount of these goods would probably have extended and made the prosperity of those years more stable. Farming in the twenties was suffering from the loss of foreign markets with the resurgence of economic nationalism in Europe after the war and from the changes in domestic demand attendant upon prosperity. Americans ate less wheat and other cereal products and more fresh vegetables and fruit. The result was that farming became more speculative than ever, and as a business, less profitable than other lines of endeavor. When the Great Depression set in, farm prices fell to less than half of what they had been in the late twenties, but the prices the farmer paid declined much less, so that his parity ratio (see Chart 1) slumped to the record low of 55. The farmer and the whole agrarian way of life was seemingly being destroyed by the impact of industrial culture.[21] The farmer was selling, on the whole, in highly competitive markets in which prices were extremely volatile and sensitive to changes in supply and demand, and buying in protected, quasi-monopolistic markets; his market position was a losing one, but, fortunately, the farmer still had considerable political power.

The farm bloc had a commanding position in Congress in the years 1921 to 1924 and during that period it succeeded in enacting "the most advanced agricultural program in American history" up to that time. The three major farm organizations, the Farm Bureau Federation, the Farmers Union, and the Grange, were all backing tariff protection for the farmer. Higher duties on several farm products were provided in the Emergency Tariff Act of 1921, and then, in September, 1922, Congress passed the Fordney-McCumber Act, which, besides providing the highest rates ever for many industrial products, confirmed the protective duties and even raised the duties on such products as wheat, corn, sugar, and wool, among others. Farm implements and fertilizers were put on the free list.

But these protective measures for agriculture were largely futile because the

[21] An excellent analysis along these cultural lines will be found in Theodore Saloutos, "The Agricultural Problem and Nineteenth Century Industrialism," *Agricultural History*, 22 (1948), pp. 156–174, reproduced in J. T. Lambie and R. V. Clemence, *Economic Change in America* (Harrisburg, Pa.: The Stackpole Co., 1954), pp. 313–339.

CHART 1

*Farm Prices of Wheat and Index of Retail Prices of Commodities
Farmers Buy*

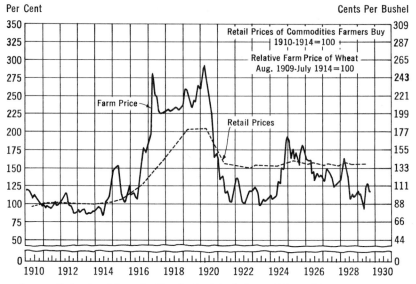

Source: Reproduced from the *Yearbook of Agriculture*, 1930, p. 574.

United States at the time was primarily an exporter of foodstuffs rather than an importer, and since we exported a surplus of most of the protected farm products, their prices were determined in world markets. The only commodities that benefitted in any way from this tariff law were wool and sugar, in both of which we did not have an export surplus. The industries that did benefit handsomely from this law were certain "war baby" manufactures, such as chemicals, which received rates practically excluding any foreign competition.

In these years the farm bloc also pushed through the Packers and Stockyards Act of 1921, which compelled commission merchants and the stockyards to charge reasonable rates and gave the Secretary of Agriculture new powers to preserve competition among the packers. The Grain Futures Act of 1921 gave that same cabinet member control over the grain exchanges. The Capper-Volstead Act of 1922 sought to aid the farm marketing cooperatives by exempting them from the provisions of the antitrust laws. In the next year, the Agricultural Credits Acts established twelve Intermediate Credit Banks to make six-month to three-year loans to groups of farmers.

These farm measures represented valuable, progressive aid to a minority group in distress, but they were based on the assumption, more or less, that farm prices would recover substantially from the lows of the 1920–21 depression. When they did not, the farm leaders moved toward backing more effective forms of government intervention. Specifically, they agreed to support a proposal originally advanced by George N. Peek and Hugh S. Johnson, two Illinois farm implement manufacturers whose business had been hard hit by the post-war depression. These men argued that the export surplus of American farm products, which so depressed the prices our farmers received, should be segregated from the domestic supply and dumped abroad at the prices current on the world market. These ideas were embodied in the McNary-Haugen bill of 1924, which received the massive support of farm interests and the smaller, but even more potent opposition of eastern Republicans and of President Coolidge. When this first measure was defeated in the House in 1924, a revised McNary-Haugen bill was pushed through the Congress in 1927 by a new coalition of southern and western farm interests. President Coolidge promptly vetoed it, denouncing the proposed law as unconstitutional, special interest legislation. Passed again by the Congress in May, 1928, it received a second veto from the President. The eastern business wing of the GOP was adamant in its stand against this form of government aid to agriculture. In retrospect, its stand was probably sound because price-fixing without control of acreage or of production was later shown to be extremely hazardous, if not unworkable.

In the campaign of 1928, Hoover promised the farmers adequate and sane relief, and in redemption of his pledges he called the Congress into special session early the next year. The administration offered two measures to remedy the agricultural malaise, the Agricultural Marketing Act of 1929 and the Hawley-Smoot Tariff bill, subsequently approved in June of the following year with many amendments.

The Agricultural Marketing Act was premised on the idea that the depressed farm prices could be raised by judicious government purchasing to remove the "temporary" surpluses and by aid to farm marketing cooperatives to enable them to engage in "orderly marketing." The latter practice entailed the purchase by these co-ops of the farmers' crops at the harvesting season, when they tended to be in surplus supply, and their gradual sale over the course of the year, as prevailing prices dictated. In this way, it was hoped to prevent the dumping of crops at harvest time by farmers who were hard-pressed for cash. In furtherance of these objectives, the Marketing Act created a non-partisan Federal Farm Board and provided it with a revolving fund of $500 million to finance its so-called stabilization operations. The Board in the years 1929 to 1931 proceeded to organize farmers into cooperatives and bought enormous quantities of wheat and cotton in the effort to lift the prices of these staples. In doing so, it did not know that it was on the eve of a disastrous international depression; the slide of world farm prices to fantastically low levels in 1930 and 1931 as a result of the financial crisis in Europe and the consequent shrinkage of foreign markets for American agricultural products was not foreseen. The consequence was that by the summer of 1932, the Board had lost some $354 million on its stabilization operations. This fiasco in government price-fixing was traceable in part to the Board's lack of authority to compel farmers to limit production as a means of achieving domestic price stability. Though it sought to persuade American farmers to cut back production, its efforts in this direction were futile; in 1930, farm output was only slightly less than it had been the previous year, and in 1931 it actually exceeded that of 1929. The Board in 1932 admitted its failure and urged Congress to establish an effective program for regulating acreage and production. The lesson of this ill-fated experiment in government price stabilization was learned, and under the New Deal the nation advanced to bolder and more stringent policies of agricultural control.

The tariff assistance that President Hoover promised the farmers also backfired and proved disappointing in its results. When the bill came up for consideration in Congress, the lobbies of the manufacturing interests immediately undertook one of their most amazing efforts at pressure politics with the result that the final Act, while containing some 75 increases for farm products, provided no fewer than 925 for manufactured products! This law carried the level of tariff protection to an all-time high, raising the general average of all duties from 33 to 40 per cent. One thousand economists, perhaps more than had ever agreed on a single subject before, urged the President to veto the Hawley-Smoot bill. He rejected their advice, though the sequel was to show that it was sound. The law afforded little extra protection to the farmers, except for those producing meat and dairy products. While its economic effects on foreign trade can be exaggerated, there is little doubt that, psychologically, it gave a great stimulus to economic nationalism and the further strangulation of international trade by restrictive measures. Canada promptly protested our action and retaliated; in 1932, the British broke with long precedent and adopted a system of imperial preference and in the following year, Germany turned to economic autarchy in its severest forms. The Hawley-Smoot Act was one of the most ill-timed measures of tariff protection in the long history of government intervention in this form.

The Republicans' failure to solve or alleviate the farm problem in the twenties was most unfortunate for the stability and growth of the economy in those years. The nation's inability to maintain the purchasing power of this shrinking group of its working population contributed seriously to the imbalance of the whole economy prior to the Great Depression. When that great contraction set in, the declines in farm incomes were major contributors to that insufficiency of aggregate demand that stalled the economic recovery of the country for so long.

FEDERAL FISCAL POLICY IN THE TWENTIES

Businessmen in the twenties were very anxious to achieve a reduction of governmental expenditures and cuts in the high level of taxes imposed during the war years. Such ideas were high on their agenda for a "return to normalcy," and some of them were influential in having Andrew W. Mellon, Pittsburgh millionaire industrialist and banker, appointed by President Harding as Secretary of the Treasury. Mellon was a "seasoned conservative" who believed in low taxes on wealth and reduced governmental interference in business. His first effort to reform the tax laws included repeal of the excess profits tax, reduction of the combined normal and surtax rates from a maximum of 73 per cent to 40 per cent, repeal of the war luxury taxes, a small increase in the corporation tax, and a new federal excise on automobiles. These proposals were submitted to the special session of 1921, but midwestern insurgents in coalition with Democrats in the Senate forced the administration to accept their tax bill instead. The same thing happened in 1924, when the insurgent group again dominated the formulation of fiscal policy, writing a bill more moderate in its tax reduction than the administration favored. A rebellious Congress even passed the Adjusted Compensation bill for veterans (the "soldiers' bonus") over the veto of indignant President Coolidge.

But the business interests seeking tax reduction were not to be put off forever. They poured millions of dollars into the Republican campaign coffers in the elections of 1924 and were successful in electing a Congress that was much more friendly to the idea of drastic tax reduction. When the 69th Congress convened in December, 1925, the administration was in charge of fiscal policy and it succeeded in passing its measure, the Revenue Act of 1926. By that year, the business boom was in high gear, taxes were rolling in, and a substantial surplus in the government accounts was in prospect; surpluses of more than one-half billion dollars had been achieved in each of the years since 1921. (See Table 2.)

TABLE 2

Federal Receipts, Expenditures, and Surpluses or Deficits,
Fiscal Years 1920–32[a]
(In millions of dollars)

Fiscal Year	Receipts	Expenditures	Surplus or Deficit	Surplus or Deficit as Percentage of Expenditures
1920	$6,648	$6,357	$ 291	4.6%
1921	5,571	5,062	509	10.1
1922	4,026	3,290	736	22.4
1923	3,853	3,140	713	22.7
1924	3,864	2,901	963	33.2
1925	3,609	2,892	717	24.8
1926	3,753	2,888	865	29.9
1927	3,992	2,836	1,156	40.8
1928	3,872	2,933	939	32.0
1929	3,821	3,086	735	23.8
1930	4,020	3,282	738	22.5
1931	3,115	3,577	462[d]	12.9
1932	1,924	4,659	2,735[d]	58.7

[a] Source: *Annual Reports of the Secretary of the Treasury on the State of the Finances for the Fiscal Years Ended June 30, 1920–32.*
[d] Deficit.

In the Revenue Act of 1926 Congress followed most of Secretary Mellon's suggestions: it reduced the maximum surtax to 20 per cent (as compared to the 65 per cent rate applicable to 1921 incomes) and reduced the normal rate of the personal income tax 1½ per cent to 5 per cent; it raised exemptions under this tax to $1,500 for single persons and $3,500 for married couples; it repealed the gift tax and reduced the maximum rate of the estate tax to 20 per cent, also raising the exemption to $100,000. The corporation capital-stock tax was abolished, and by way of compensation, the corporate income tax rate was increased from 12½ per cent to 13½ per cent. These lower taxes, on the whole, produced unexpectedly large revenues, as Treasurer Mellon had predicted. Though he and the Congress preferred tax reduction to debt reduction, the federal debt was substantially reduced during these years. The gross debt as of June, 1920, stood at $24,299 million. Through the operation of the sinking fund and repayments out of ordinary and surplus receipts, this debt was reduced to $16,700 million by June of 1929. This reduction was at the average rate of $850 million a year. On a percentage basis, it represented a reduction of 37 per cent in the debt as compared with the 23 per cent reduction that had been achieved over a comparable period after the Civil War. It was an impressive accomplishment, but an even greater dent could have been made in the public debt if Mellon and the Congress had not subordinated debt reduction to tax cuts.

While the federal debt was declining, the state and local governments had launched into capital construction projects on an unprecedented scale, building highways, schools, and other public buildings to make up the deficit of the war years and to meet the public needs of a mobile, demanding citizenry. The aggregate debts of such state and local governments increased by $10 billion, completely offsetting the reduction in the federal debt over the same period. Federal officials such as Presidents Harding and Coolidge bewailed the increase in state and local expenditures, contending that such spending was "a menace to prosperity" and that it could no longer continue "without disaster."[22] Such jeremiads overlooked the benefits of this public spending in building up the public sector of the economy and the contributions it made to the prosperity of the nation as a whole.

The revision of the tax laws in the twenties produced a major transformation in the revenue system of the federal government as compared with prewar practice. Import duties and internal excises declined drastically as sources of revenue, and in their place income and profits taxation assumed vastly new importance (see Table 3). These changes and the attendant experience in government administration of such levies were to prove momentous for the fiscal future of the nation.

The changes in fiscal legislation in the twenties also revolutionized the impact of the income tax on various income groups. Whereas in 1920 those

[22] Quotes are from a speech of President Coolidge on June 11, 1928 as reproduced in part in L. H. Kimmel, *Federal Budget and Fiscal Policy, 1789–1958* (Washington, D.C.: The Brookings Institution, 1959), p. 95.

TABLE 3

Distribution of Tax Receipts of the U.S. Government,
1910–29[a]

Period	Average Annual Tax Receipts (Millions)	Income and Profits (Per Cent)	Customs (Per Cent)	Miscellaneous Internal Revenue (Per Cent)
1910–16	$ 654.4	8.6%	43.5%	47.9%
1917–21	3,906.8	65.7	6.3	28.0
1922–25	3,308.5	55.6	15.2	29.2
1926–29	3,450.7	63.2	17.1	19.8

[a] Source: *Annual Report of the Treasury,* 1929.

receiving less than $10,000 a year were paying collectively 24 per cent of the total income tax, by 1929 their contribution to total receipts had been reduced to 1.4 per cent. Those receiving between $10,000 and 25,000 a year contributed 16 per cent of the total income tax yield in 1920 and only 6 per cent in 1929. Those in the income class, $25,000–$100,000, declined by a smaller percentage, while those in the "over $100,000 category paid in close to 30% of the total receipts in 1920 and over 65% in 1929."[23]

Despite the skill of the Mellon administration in the technical management of the federal debt, the fiscal policies followed in these years have seemed to some experts to have been seriously inadequate. Two of them write,

> . . . Taxes were reduced much too sharply and too rapidly at all income levels, releasing substantial portions of income for added spending, thereby accentuating inflationary pressures and tendencies toward speculation. The rate at which debt was to be retired was set much too low. . . . Instead of seeking merely to achieve budgetary balance inclusive of a small debt amortization, the administration and congressional budgeteers should have sought to achieve an over-balanced budget regularly yielding annual surpluses of a billion dollars or more. Such fiscal policy would have contributed to greater economic stability in the long run.[24]

In recognizing the limitations of the fiscal policies adopted in these years, it is well to remember that in 1929 federal expenditures amounted to less than 4 per cent of the gross national product, and state and local spending came to only 8 per cent. The imbalances that developed in the economy were primarily in the private sector, and it is questionable, given the limited leverage that governmental fiscal policy had on the latter, whether compensatory action along Keynesian lines would have been effective in preventing the collapse of prosperity. Nevertheless, more far-sighted fiscal action might have lessened the burden of the stabilization effort imposed on Federal Reserve policy. Today, we think we know more about the proper "mix" of such policies to promote stability and growth.

[23] Studenski and Kroos, *Financial History of the United States,* p. 314.
[24] *Ibid.,* p. 321.

GOVERNMENTAL POLICIES REGARDING BUSINESS, TRADE UNIONS, AND SOCIAL WELFARE

The 1920's was a trying time for economic liberals interested in the enforcement of the antitrust laws and the maintenance of price competition. While the nation witnessed a massive consolidation movement that was making oligopoly a much more prevalent market structure than single-firm monopoly ever had been, the executive and judicial branches of the federal government exhibited a complacency toward mergers and other big business practices that was shocking to the old-fashioned type of Wilsonian Progressive. The Attorneys General under Harding, Coolidge, and Hoover were relatively lethargic in their enforcement of the antitrust laws; the Supreme Court, dominated by a conservative majority, was disposed to maintain the status quo, if not turn back the clock. The Federal Trade Commission, staffed by appointees who were on the whole friendly to business, sought to encourage the "self-regulation" of industry, which had become the new gospel of progressive businessmen. The twenties was not a time for crusading against big business, but one in which rather the "social intelligence" of business in regularizing its affairs was applauded. Industry had come of age, and the dominant mood was one of living and adjusting to bigness rather than destroying it.

This philosophy was expressed in part in the landmark decision of the Supreme Court in the United States Steel case (1920).[25] In this 4–3 decision, the majority rejected the charge of monopoly levelled against Judge Gary's "good" trust, holding that the corporation did not possess a monopoly, since it did not have greater market power than all its competitiors combined. It was admitted that in its formation, monopoly power had been sought, but it had not been achieved. The Company had not been guilty of abusing its power by predatory means; in this interpretation of the law, the majority in effect was asserting the famous "rule of reason," i.e., that only unreasonable restraints of trade are illegal. "The law," said Justice McKenna, speaking for the majority, "does not make mere size [of combinations] an offense. It, we repeat, requires overt acts, and trusts to its prohibition of them and its power to repress or punish them." The view adopted by the Court in the Steel case was re-affirmed in 1927 in the International Harvester case.[26] While the latter company controlled some 64 per cent of the output of harvesting machinery and was the acknowledged "price leader" in the industry, the Court refused to order its dissolution, stating "The law . . . does not make the mere size of a corporation, however impressive, or the existence of unexerted power on its part, an offense, when unaccompanied by unlawful conduct in the exercise of

[25] 251 U.S. 452.
[26] *U.S.* vs. *International Harvester Co.*, 274 U.S. 693.

its power." "The fact," the Court again stated, "that competitiors may see proper, in the exercise of their own judgment, to follow the prices of another manufacturer, does not establish any suppression of competition or show any sinister domination." This interpretation, in effect, made price leadership even under oligopolistic conditions legal. To some these decisions seemed to exhibit a "double standard" of legality, especially when the leniency toward close-knit mergers was contrasted with the strictness with which price-fixing among independent firms was condemned.[27] Such a schizophrenic policy, it was contended, merely served to encourage the formation of mergers by firms who would be held guilty if they sought the same object of merger via cooperative action among separate firms.

The ambivalence of the Court in these years was seen also in its decisions with regard to "open price" trade associations. In two cases in 1921 and 1923, it held the practices complained of illegal and yet, in 1925, in the *Maple Flooring* and *Cement Association* cases, in the absence of a showing of restrictive effects upon price competition, it upheld the practice of disseminating price information, etc., among competitors.[28]

The Clayton and Federal Trade Commission Acts also suffered such setbacks at the hands of the courts in these years that many spoke of their emasculation. The Supreme Court, on the whole, so interpreted the provisions of the former Act regarding price discrimination, tying clauses, and the prohibitions of mergers by stock acquisitions that the preventative approach to curbing mergers was greatly weakened.[29] At this very time the Federal Trade Commission was encouraging trade practice conferences among domestic competitors and Webb-Pomerene associations among concerns engaged in foreign trade so that some critics felt that the American economy was being cartellized under government auspices. Thus, a conservative Court by decisions of convoluted reasoning and interpretation provided a rationale of sorts for an era of "other-directed," friendly competition. To some, the Court was demonstrating an ingenious ability to "keep up with the times," to others, it was guilty of "judicial legislation."

During these same years, the Supreme Court rendered a series of decisions that shocked organized labor and made it realize that its cherished Magna Carta of labor (its exemption under the Clayton Act section six from antitrust) was an illusion. In 1915, the Court approved the yellow-dog contract;

---

[27] The Supreme Court held in *U.S.* vs. *Trenton Potteries*, 273 U.S. 392 (1927) that price-fixing was a *per se* offense and therefore no rule of reason could apply to this type of business practice.

[28] *American Column and Lumber Co.* vs. *U.S.*, 257 U.S. 377 (1921); *U.S.* vs. *American Linseed Oil Co.*, 262 U.S. 371 (1923); *Maple Flooring Manufacturers* vs. *U.S.*, 268 U.S. 563 (1925) and *Cement Manufacturers Protective Association* vs. *U.S.*, 268 U.S. 606 (1925).

[29] The decisions referred to were, respectively, *Mennen Company* vs. *Federal Trade Commission*, 288 Fed. Rep. 774 (1923) and *National Biscuit Co.* vs. *Federal Trade Commission*, 299 Fed. 733 (1924); *United States* vs. *United Shoe Machinery Co.*, 247 (1926) U.S. 32 (1918); *Thatcher Manufacturing Co.* vs. *Federal Trade Commission*, 272 U.S. 554.

in 1919 it sanctioned the assessment of triple damages against the United Mine Workers under the Sherman Act; in 1921, it declared that a boycott designed by labor to force unionization was illegal and radically curbed picketing. In the next year, in the Coronado case it permitted another union to be sued for damages under the antitrust laws.[30]

In the field of regulation of public utilities where a huge consolidation movement was taking place, the state commissions were often stymied by the endless controversy over "fair value" and the conflicting theories of valuation; the insistence on "due process" often resulted in protracted litigation in rate cases. In railroading, the Transportation Act of 1920 proved disappointing because the major lines did not voluntarily merge into the smaller number of systems, as was intended by the Act. Thus, while the regulated industries were often able to avoid authentic supervision by government, they did exercise a great influence on public opinion through the propaganda disseminated by their public relations bureaus.

While business had relatively little to fear from the courts, the advocates of social welfare legislation suffered heavy setbacks during these years at the hands of a conservative judiciary. For example, in 1918 the Supreme Court in a 5–4 decision held the Child Labor Act of 1916 to be unconstitutional (*Hammer* vs. *Dagenhart*); when Congress passed a law taxing products made by children, the Court declared that Act also to be invalid (*Bailey* vs. *Drexel Furniture Co.* 1922). And again, in 1923 in the case of *Adkins* vs. *Children's Hospital,* the Court found a District of Columbia minimum wage law for women unconstitutional.[31] These decisions frustrated the best efforts of social reformers to protect women and children against inhumane conditions of work. While the twenties were notable for the paternalistic "welfare capitalism" of private business corporations, it was not a decade of great advance for social legislation. The lack of such laws proved to be disastrous with the deterioration of economic conditions during the early thirties. The exposed position of the underprivileged groups in American society to the increased involuntary unemployment of those years, with all its attendant hardship and suffering, revealed how unprepared the nation was to cope with the human costs of private enterprise.

RELIEF AND RECOVERY MEASURES OF
THE HOOVER ADMINISTRATION

The mass unemployment that came with the Great Depression created a relief problem that the voluntary agencies and the local and state governments could not adequately meet. The system existing before the depression was

[30] The cases referred to are, respectively, *Coppage* vs. *Kansas,* 236 U.S. 1 (1915); *Duplex Printing Press Co.* vs. *Deering et al.,* 254 U.S. 443 (1921); and *United Mine Workers* vs. *Coronado Coal Co.,* 259 U.S. 334 (1922).

[31] The citations of the three cases cited are as follows: *Hammer* vs. *Dagenhart et al.,* 247 U.S. 251 (1918); *Bailey* vs. *Drexel Furniture Co.,* 259 U.S. 20 (1922) and *Adkins* vs. *Children's Hospital,* 261 U.S. 525 (1923).

essentially one of local poor relief designed to take care of unemployables— those who could not for physical or mental reasons hold a job. The Hoover administration right down to 1932 opposed federal relief, insisting that the care of the needy was a local responsibility. Many businessmen and conservatives argued that relief was a dole, suitable for the decadent British, but not for responsible, self-reliant Americans. Some businessmen seemed to regard unemployment as a form of malingering. Even President Hoover later wrote that "many persons left their jobs for the more profitable one of selling apples."[32]

But regardless of the position that one took on the philosophical issue of the desirability of federal relief, by 1932 it was clear that the voluntary sources of aid and the localities were at the end of their resources. By that year only about one-quarter of the unemployed were receiving relief, mainly food and a little fuel. In New York City those unemployed who were fortunate enough to get on the relief rolls were averaging $2.39 per family for a week and the City's funds could take care of only about one-half of the unemployed heads of families. Conditions in other cities and towns of the nation were equally as bad as those in New York, or worse. While Will Rogers, the cowboy comedian, tried to lighten the burden of worry and gloom by joking that we were the first nation in history to go to the poorhouse in an automobile, the nation's leaders were hardly living, ideologically at least, in the automobile age; they were agonizingly slow to adjust to the immensity of the crisis.

While President Hoover had earlier, before the depression, espoused the use of public works to relieve unemployment, as the slump deepened and the federal government's revenue fell off, he was faced with a choice between a balanced budget and a public works program. From 1929 to 1932 federal expenditures rose from $3.3 billion to some $4.5 billion, while revenues declined from approximately $4 billion to around $2 billion in the latter year. In his best doctrinaire fashion, Hoover stated in November, 1931 that "Nothing will contribute more to the return of prosperity than to maintain the sound fiscal position of the Federal government."[33] An adequate program of public works clashed with the aim of balancing the budget, so the administration rejected it as an aid to recovery. In fact, in the endeavor to balance the budget, the President and the Congress in June, 1932 approved "the largest peacetime increase of tax rates in the nation's history." The deflationary effects of such a measure were not sufficiently appreciated at the time; from the standpoint of modern aggregative economics, many economists would hold that the government's action under such circumstances prolonged the depression.

The administration's program of recovery in 1932 focussed on maintenance of the gold standard, a balanced budget, and aid to hard-pressed financial institutions and railroads through the agency of the Reconstruction Finance Corporation, which was set up at the beginning of that year to prevent further

---

[32] As quoted in A. M. Schlesinger, Jr., *The Age of Roosevelt: The Crisis of the Old Order*, Vol. 1 (Boston: Houghton Mifflin Co., 1957), p. 241.

[33] *The Crisis of the Old Order*, p. 232.

collapse of key institutions. In July, 1932, this corporation was authorized by the Congress to make loans to the states up to $300 million for relief purposes. In the same month the Home Loan Bank System was established to service banks and other institutions handling mortgages, but this agency did not extend much assistance to such hard-pressed organizations until after the end of the Hoover administration.

The critics of the Hoover program contended that its financial aid was based on the "trickle-down" theory of income distribution and that it did not face up to the need to restore aggregate purchasing power if recovery was to take place.[34] Actually, under the unrelenting pressure of events the President had broken with his ideological convictions in significant ways, but the extent of his departures and the general design of his recovery effort were not sufficient to stem the massive forces of deflation.

The condition of the economy deteriorated further in the latter half of 1932. The nation sadly witnessed the march of the Bonus Expeditionary Force to Washington and the callous evacuation of those unemployed ex-soldiers from Anacostia Flats by the Army under the command of General MacArthur. And then, in October of 1932, almost on the eve of the new administration's office taking, there began in Nevada the bank holiday, which soon spread to Louisiana, Michigan, and many other states. When Illinois and New York declared bank holidays shortly before President Roosevelt's inauguration, no fewer than forty-seven states had closed their banks or placed severe restrictions on their operations. On the very eve of the New Deal, while the bankers were revealing the unsound policies of the New Era that had contributed to the crisis before the Senate Banking Committee, the banking system, the economy's basic means of monetary circulation and credit control, found itself in a state of total collapse. The new administration's first steps were, of necessity, concerned with this financial catastrophe. And so, ironically, an era that had placed such faith in monetary policy as a means to economic stability and growth ended with a nation-wide bank holiday.

In summary, our study of this period has shown us how the values and attitudes of a predominantly rural way of life, a life that stressed the Protestant ethos of work, saving, and self-reliance was profoundly influenced, even in so short a time, by the demands of an increasingly urbanized, surplus economy and an emergent organizational society. The relatively new institutions of national advertising and consumer finance contributed to changes in Americans' conventional notions of consumption and of thrift. The government under the Republican administrations was slow to change its ideology and operating practice in the face of an unprecedented depression, which revealed indisputably the limitations of *laissez faire* in coping with the instability of a mature capitalistic economy. And in the early depression years, in particular, we have observed the failure on the part of government to

---

[34] The trickle-down theory implied that the prosperity of the masses depended upon financial solvency of the rich and that increased income of the latter would be shared by lower income groups.

assure a sufficiently high level of aggregate demand to check the deflation and to stimulate recovery and a return to something like full employment. This governmental task in a full-blown consumer economy was to challenge Americans with growing urgency in the remaining years of the 1930's and in the years beyond.

Part 9

MANAGED CAPITALISM IN PEACE AND WAR, 1933–1945

INTRODUCTION: KEYNESIAN ASPECTS OF THE THEORY OF ECONOMIC GROWTH*

In the recent literature of Economics, there have been many discussions of the significance and influence of the doctrines of John Maynard Keynes. The question has been debated, for example, of whether or not Lord Keynes had developed a general theory of economic growth.[1] Nearly all economists agree that even if his concepts and formulations are not thought to be general enough for a complete analysis of economic development, they form an excellent subtheory to describe the breakdown and cyclical deviation from a "normal" path of economic growth. It is on the basis of a view such as this that we intend to employ the Keynesian model for the insights it can give into this difficult and vital period in American economic history.

John Maynard Keynes, first Baron of Tilton (1883–1946) studied at Cambridge, England. The son of an economist, he himself was a most versatile man. He was a Cambridge don, a banker, journalist, public servant, and patron of the ballet.

Wide World Photos

In order to understand the implications of Keynesian theory for economic growth, it is necessary to be familiar with the economic orthodoxy of the pre-1929 era. Before that date most orthodox economists believed that capitalist economies tended in their functioning toward a condition of full employment

---

* The essential ideas that this Introduction draws on are to be found in J. M. Keynes' *The General Theory of Employment, Interest and Money* (New York: Harcourt, Brace and Co., 1936) and A. H. Hansen, *A Guide to Keynes* (New York: McGraw-Hill Book Co., 1953). Reading Keynes is no easy task for a beginning student in Economics or in Economic History. The difficulties in such an effort are greatly reduced by first reading Hansen's *Guide to Keynes*.

[1] See J. Robinson, "A Generalization of the General Theory," *The Rate of Interest* (London: Macmillan, 1952).

and a level of real income corresponding to that happy state. Growth in real income was expected to be about as fast as capital accumulation, population growth, and the advance in the industrial arts (technology). The idea that aggregate demand might not grow fast enough to absorb the increase in output made possible by growth in resources, technical knowledge, and organization was dismissed as erroneous. The lack of consideration given to the notion of inadequate aggregate demand was firmly based on the classical economic postulate known as Say's Law. Simply put, Say's Law states that "supply will create its own demand."

This equilibrium theory of the classical economists was thought to be correct because of the simplicity of its operation and because the reality of business cycles seemed to conform to its basic premises. The theory's logical simplicity can be easily explained if one considers the so-called circular flow of income. The following chart depicting this flow clearly demonstrates that in order to create a supply of goods or services one must employ persons who, in turn, use their wages and salaries to purchase this supply. There are no "leakages" of income allowed in this circular flow; the wages and incomes business receives will be sufficient, in the aggregate, to purchase the supply created.

CHART 1

The Circular Flow of Income and Goods

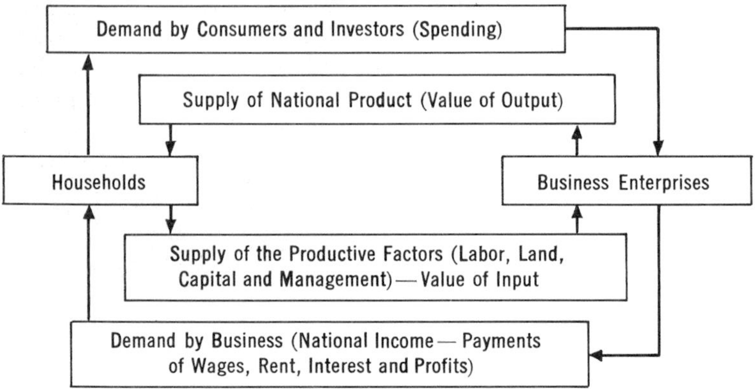

There were certain historical facts in the nineteenth and early twentieth centuries that tended to confirm the classical view of the economic process. Real income in the major capitalist countries seemed to demonstrate a persistent tendency to grow. There was no secular increase in unemployment. Fluctuations in real income were very limited and departures from equilibrium in the path of growth were of relatively short duration in most capitalist countries. In short, the empirical behavior of capitalist societies seemed to support Say's Law. It was not until the great depression of the 1930's that the factual as well as theoretical foundation of the neo-classical position was gravely and irretrievably undermined. The degree to which income losses, mass unemployment, and monetary deflation had developed in the economy was glaringly inconsistent with the normalistic principles of classical theory. Yet such was the hold and impression of such ideas on most decision-makers that they could conceive of no alternative. Keynes later described the potent grip of the "conventional wisdom" upon the great majority of men in these famous, sardonic words: ". . . the ideas of economists and political philosophers, both when they are right and when they are wrong, are more powerful than is commonly understood. Practical men, who believe themselves to be quite exempt from any intellectual influences, are usually the slaves of some defunct economist. . . ."[2]

Something akin to this intellectual situation existed when Keynes wrote his revolutionary work. In the crisis years of the early 1930's the prevailing policy of most capitalist governments on the question of unemployment emanated in part from the thought of the neo-classicists. A. C. Pigou, Keynes's colleague at Cambridge, had put it succinctly as follows: ". . . such unemployment as exists at any time is due wholly to the fact that changes in demand conditions are continually taking place and that frictional resistances prevent the appropriate wage adjustments from being made instantaneously."[3] Pigou therefore urged the orthodox policy; if unemployment exists, it is because wages are too high and "sticky" (i.e., rigid). Full employment can be reached by lowering the wage rate until the quantity of labor supplied is equal to the quantity in demand.

The economic dogma of the time was also able to explain how supply would create its own demand even during cyclical oscillations on the downward side. The classical notion was that the rate of interest could be relied upon to adjust the volume of investment and savings so as to ensure the full use of resources. The rise and fall in the rate of interest would call forth more or less investment as needed. Government policy based on these classical postulates required the state to do nothing except to insure the flexibility of wage and interest rates.

In order to demolish the faulty concepts and conclusions of the classical economics, Keynes proposed his own general theory. In doing so, he formulated some new concepts and general ideas that structure and support his whole, elaborate theoretical system. According to Keynes, a fundamental tautology exists in all economic systems using money and permitting private savings. This tautology can be stated to the effect that national income is equal to consumption and savings. To the businessman the definition is restated to say "national income equals consumption and investment." As a condition of equilibrium it should be pointed out that consumption is the same in both definitions, hence, savings must equal investment. Symbolically, this can be expressed in the Keynesian identity $Y = C + I^*$ and $Y = C + S$, hence, $S \equiv$

---

[2] *The General Theory*, p. 383.

[3] *Theory of Unemployment* (London: Macmillan, 1933), p. 252, cited by Keynes in *Ibid.*, p. 278.

I^* (Y is the symbol of income, C stands for consumption, I^* for investment, and S for savings).[4]

However, before we examine the full import of this tautology, let us make sure that we understand it. Keynes implies that the level of national income, together with its corresponding level of employment, is determined by two variables. They are real investment and consumption. The question then arises, what determines real investment and consumption?

The determinants of consumption will be considered first. What determines the amount of income we spend on consumption goods? According to Keynes, a fundamental psychological law causes consumption to be determined by increases in the individual's income in a certain way. This relationship has been called the consumption function; it reflects a series of objective and subjective factors, which we shall briefly describe. The objective factors determine shifts in the relationship between income and consumption, while the subjective factors such as social practices, psychological influences, and social arrangements determine the mathematical nature of the relationship. To

---

[4] We should distinguish between those identities which involve I^* and equations which contain I, where I is called *ex ante* or planned investment. The Keynesian model argues that the identities always exist, namely aggregate demand is equal to aggregate supply. Aggregate supply is equal to disposable income, but aggregate demand is written as $C + I$ (planned investment). To complete the model, consumption is described as being functionally related to income. From these rather elementary assumptions powerful results are derived.

One concept that is easily derived from the above identity is the multiplier. If we have $Y = C + I$ then a change (signified by $\triangle$) in income must be equal to $\triangle Y = \triangle C + \triangle I$. In order to examine the effects of $\triangle C$ and $\triangle I$ on $\triangle Y$, we eliminate $\triangle Y$ from the equation by dividing by $\triangle Y$ which gives us:

$$\frac{\triangle Y}{\triangle Y} = \frac{\triangle C}{\triangle Y} + \frac{\triangle I}{\triangle Y}$$

$$1 = \frac{\triangle C}{\triangle Y} + \frac{\triangle I}{\triangle Y}$$

These results can be interpreted as follows: $\frac{\triangle C}{\triangle Y}$ is the incremental spending for consumption per increment of a unit of income. This was called by Keynes the marginal propensity to consume. The expression $\frac{\triangle S}{\triangle Y}$ is called the marginal propensity to save. Together the values of these ratios must equal one. Since we are interested in the effect of $\triangle C$ and $\triangle I$ on income, we should isolate $\triangle Y$ on the right side of the equation. First, we bring $\frac{\triangle C}{\triangle Y}$ over to the left side and we obtain $1 - \frac{\triangle C}{\triangle Y} = \frac{\triangle I}{\triangle Y}$. Hence, we have two forms for the marginal propensity to save *(MPS)*—the one on the right side of the equation and the one on the left side. In order to bring $\triangle I$ to the left side of the equation easily we first invert the two fractions which gives us:

$$\frac{1}{1 - \dfrac{\triangle C}{\triangle Y}} = \frac{\triangle Y}{\triangle I} = \frac{1}{MPS}$$

These fractions are called the investment multiplier. Note the three forms. This definition is clearer when $\triangle I$ is moved to the left, giving us:

$$\frac{1}{1 - \dfrac{\triangle C}{\triangle Y}} \times \triangle I = \triangle Y$$

Or in economic terms, the change in income is a multiple of the change in investment.

understand this statement more fully let us examine the following graph
(Chart 2). We have a Cartesian plane with consumption expenditures plotted
on the *y*-axis and income on the *x*-axis.

CHART 2

The Keynesian Consumption Function

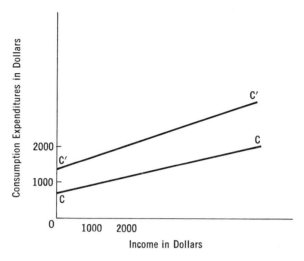

Curve *C-C* shows the different amounts that may be spent on consumption
goods by a hypothetical person out of the varying incomes represented by the
curve *C'-C'*. The former curve has a definite position and slope. From
mathematics we know that the slope can be measured in terms of a change in
the *y*-axis (consumption expenditures) over a given change in the *x*-axis
(income). The slope can, therefore, be written as $\frac{\Delta C}{\Delta Y}$, which is called the
marginal propensity to consume. The curve we have drawn to express the
relationship between income and consumption expenditures is a straight line
that has as its equation *y* (consumption) $= mx$ (income) $+ b$. *m* is the slope
or marginal propensity to consume and *b* is the "*y* intercept" or the amount
of consumption expenditures people will make even if they have no income.
For expository reasons, we have considered the relationship to be linear, but
this does not preclude the possibility of a non-linear relationship (i.e., quad-
ratic, cubic, etc.).

We should further define the relationship between total consumption expenditures and total income, expressed as the ratio $\frac{C}{Y}$, as the average propensity to consume. In other words, the amount of consumption expenditure out
of any given income is called the average propensity to consume. Keynes
asserted that, as a rule, as income increases, consumption expenditures will
increase, but not by as much as income. Hence, it is held that the marginal

propensity to consume (the slope of the consumption income curve) is positive, but less than unity.

Keynes cited several objective factors that could cause a shift in the consumption-income relationship. They are: (1) changes in the wage (price) level; (2) changes in accounting practices; (3) windfall gains or losses; (4) changes in fiscal policy; (5) changes in expectations; (6) changes in interest rates. The first two of these factors can be described as technical rather than behavioral changes. Obviously, if income doubles because money has lost half its value, consumption will increase. In a similar manner, if your assets are conceived to change to half their previous value as a result of a change in depreciation accounting, then your consumption pattern will change. These changes can be overcome by technical means such as using constant dollars in measuring income and consumption or using consistent, unvarying definitions of depreciation; hence, we can dismiss them as unimportant for our present purposes.

Stock market windfall gains or losses, changes in the amount of income taxed or given to the public by government fiscal policy, improvements in the economic outlook, and higher charges for borrowed money would cause changes in the position of the C-Y curve. These represent changes in human behavior and cannot be corrected for by technical means. All these factors, then, constitute the objective determinants of consumption expenditures. Together with the subjective factors, these objective variables compose the determinants of consumption behavior.

Economists term the spending of businessmen for capital goods and inventories *real investment* to distinguish it from financial investment, i.e., the purchase by an individual investor of securities. The latter transaction merely puts funds in the "hands" of the corporation selling the securities; it is its expenditure of such money for real capital goods that provides employment. Our previous study has shown us that business investment (capital formation) is a highly variable element in the functioning of capitalism. When Keynes wrote his *General Theory* he knew this, but he was very dissatisfied with the neo-classical explanation of the process whereby the supply of savings was brought into equilibrium or equality with the demand for capital (investment). By way of providing a better one, he formulated a new theory of interest and a wholly novel theory of national income determination.

In the Keynesian system, the interest rate is held to be determined by two schedules, the liquidity preference and the marginal efficiency of capital schedules. Let us consider the latter first. (Incidentally, we might note that the ideas underlying this bit of theory were not original with Keynes. He borrowed heavily from concepts developed by the Swedish economist, Knut Wicksell, and the American economist, Irving Fisher. However, his adoption of their framework of ideas led him to different conclusions.) The term "the marginal efficiency of capital" is used by Keynes to designate the rate of return (prospective profits) over cost. Keynes defines it rigorously as "the rate of discount which would make the present value of the series of annuities given by the returns expected from the capital asset during its life just equal to its supply price." There are two elements incorporated in this definition that are crucial to its understanding. First, the concept of discount, and second, the concept of depreciation. Keynes would measure return as the rate over and above the cost of replacing the asset and the yield that is indicated as against the going rate of return on investments.

The schedule relating investment and the marginal efficiency of capital is called the investment demand schedule. The investment supply schedule will largely be determined by the interest rate. When the marginal efficiency of capital schedule intersects the investment supply or interest schedule an equilibrium level of investment will be reached.

The other determinant of the interest rate is called the liquidity preference schedule. In explaining the nature of liquidity preference, Keynes distinguishes three motives for holding wealth in a monetary form (i.e., showing liquidity preference). They are: (1) the transactions motive; (2) the precautionary motive; and (3) the speculative motive. Transaction money is funds in circulation; the last two are inactive balances.

The transaction moneys are needed for the day-to-day operation of personal and business exchanges. Precautionary moneys are funds kept in reserve for future requirements or unforeseen contingencies. The amount of cash people will want to hold for transactions and precautionary motives will be determined by their income; only at very high interest rates will the decision to convert these funds into speculative funds be considered. The speculative funds, on the other hand, are needed to take advantage of movements in markets. By holding wealth in liquid form, advantage can be taken quickly of market opportunities with the object of securing a profit. Hence, the supply of money is dependent on the interest rate and income. The demand for money, we have noted, depends on the marginal efficiency of capital schedule, and the intersection of the two will determine the interest rate and the quantity of real investment.

The aggregate of real investment is a prime determinant of the level of national income and employment in the Keynesian system. In Chart 3 below, I-I' represents the aggregate investment function, i.e., it shows the aggregate amount of investment spending that all business firms plan to do at various income levels. The line S-S' represents the aggregate savings function; it shows the total amount of savings at different possible levels of national income. (It will be noted that at low levels of income, negative savings are shown, and as income rises, the total amount of savings increases). In the simple Keynesian model, where the influence of government is ignored, national income will be determined where aggregate investment is equal to total savings, that is, at X. At this level of income, planned savings will be equal to planned investment. Only X is a possible equilibrium level of national income because only at that amount will the investment expenditures of business in the aggregate equal planned savings, thus returning to the businessmen in the form of aggregate receipts what was paid out as compensation of the factors of production and, in turn, expended on consumer goods or saved.

A final task in explaining the Keynesian theory is to relate the consumption sector to the real investment sector. This is done through the mechanism of the investment multiplier. The operation of this mechanism is simple enough to comprehend. Given a certain increment to investment, let us say $2,000, this money will be spent on the production of capital goods. The recipients of the money will be wage earners, landlords, stockholders, and businessmen. To these people the money will represent income, a part of which they will spend on consumer goods and a part of which they will save. The increment to consumption, we have shown, will be determined by their marginal propensity

CHART 3

The Equilibrium Determination of National Income

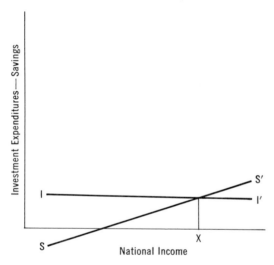

to consume. Suppose their marginal propensity to consume is .90 (it must be less than one); this means $1,800 of the $2,000 will be spent on consumer goods. The recipients of that spending will regard it as income, and they will spend a part and save a part. They will spend $1,620 and save $180, if their marginal propensity to spend is the same as that of the first group. The $1,620 they spend will be income to a new group, and the process continues. The amount of total income created will then be a series beginning with $2,000 + $1,800 + $1,620, etc. The series is an infinite geometric progression (diminishing) and will behave according to the rule $\dfrac{1}{1-c}$ where c is the marginal propensity to consume and $1 - c$ is the marginal propensity to save. The total income created will behave according to the formula $\dfrac{1}{1-c} \times \Delta I = \Delta Y$, or $\dfrac{1}{1-.90} \times \$2,000 = \$20,000$. Hence, we see that small increments in investment may be multiplied by the reciprocal of the marginal propensity to save to yield large increments in income. The multiplier $\dfrac{1}{1-c}$ can be denoted by k, and our formula becomes $\Delta Y = k\Delta I$.

We might at this point ask how the Keynesian theory sheds light on economic growth or the events of the years 1932 to 1945. In short, how does the system operate? At the outset of this presentation we stated that Keynes formulated a bold intellectual challenge to Say's Law. He questioned the fundamental classical premise that the automatic movement of the economy toward equilibrium would lead to full employment. He argued instead that Say's Law might never bring the depressed economy back into full employment equilibrium, except in the very long run and, as Keynes so starkly put it, "In the long run, we are all dead." To understand why the Keynesian system rejects the fundamental mechanism in Say's Law, we must follow its analysis of the functioning of the economy as it moves from prosperity to depression.

When times are good and business cycle conditions are favorable, the tendency is for savings to increase and to be employed as business investment is relatively high. Business expectations, interest rates, and profits are all favorable to the producer. The liquidity preference of businessmen is lower, and the rate of investment higher. Increased investment leads to higher incomes, and hence the multiplier effect exaggerates the movement of the economy upward by the amplification of investment. However, the economy will be in tautological equilibrium via Say's Law with savings equal to investment.

When the economy does go into a downswing, the expectations of investors are lowered, the rate of investment falls off, and interest rates become unfavorable to the businessman. He will react by reducing investment, which will be amplified again by the investment multiplier because consumption will fall as income shrinks. Again, tautological equilibrium might exist at this low level of employment with savings equal to investment. Here is the fundamental problem that Keynes saw in the functioning of an unregulated capitalistic economy. The economy could reach equilibrium at a point far short of full employment because of the failure of aggregate demand to raise it to that level. In short, an unregulated capitalistic economy might remain in a depression for very long periods because inadequate aggregate demand would fail to employ the out-of-work part of the labor force. When such a failure of aggregate demand is coupled with a tendency in the economy toward high, sticky wage rates and rigid prices, economic recovery may be long in coming.

Such an economic stalemate may be protracted because of the individualistic, partial view of the participants in the economic process. The businessman, acting as a single economic unit in such a depressed economy, may not regard it as being in his interest to employ more persons. The net result is that when this attitude is multiplied by many such businesses it adds up to a hopeless depression. The problem is that what may be for the good of a microeconomic unit may not be good for the economic system in the aggregate.

Policies based on this fallacy of composition (what is true for a part is true for the whole) may prolong economic crises and lead to a pessimistic, long-run view that business will decline over time. In an economic climate such as this, the opportunity to invest would probably fall over time, and the resultant falling marginal efficiency of capital could lead to a stagnation in the rate of economic growth.

Keynes's *General Theory* brilliantly showed the perverse error involved in looking at the economy from the standpoint of the norms appropriate to the mangement of one's family budget or those of a private business. As Boulding points out, "The Keynesian Revolution, like the Copernican, involved an abandonment of an 'observer-centered' view of the economic universe."[5] But Keynes was too devoted a liberal and defender of individual initiative and freedom to advocate a wholesale revision of the existing order. Indeed, he wrote of his theory as being "moderately conservative" in its implications, while at the same time pointing out that his proposals were "the only practicable means of avoiding the destruction of existing economic forms in their entirety. . . ."

Keynes did not summarize his policy proposals at one place in his great book, but indicated his position on such questions in the course of his analysis.[6] He admits at one point that "The central controls necessary to assure full employment will, of course, involve a large extension of the traditional functions of government. . . ." His main prescription is clear: it was the task of government to maintain sufficient aggregate demand to maintain full employment. Noting the inadequacy of banking policy in its influence on the interest rate to determine an optimum rate of investment, he advocated a number of policies that have come to be termed compensatory fiscal policy. Thus, in a period of declining business activity and employment, he would have the government inject purchasing power into the income stream through public works expenditures, financed through borrowing, and by appropriate tax measures support and increase the propensity to consume. In the prosperity phase of the cycle, on the other hand, he would dampen the tendency of investment to outrun the rate of savings by reducing public works expenditures and taxing away excessive purchasing power. Keynes would not resort to measures of state socialism, but rather argued that full employment could be attained by "a somewhat comprehensive socialization of [private] investment." This meant, as we can see from his other references to the subject, that Keynes was prepared to have the state directly regulate the volume of investment. He believed that this would be necessary because the avoidance of wide fluctuations in employment would be impossible under existing condi-

[5] K. Boulding, *Principles of Economic Policy* (Englewood Cliffs, N.J.: Prentice-Hall, Inc., 1958), p. 65.

[6] Professor Lowe writes, "The *General Theory* in its entirety is a strange mixture of Pure and Political Economics, with the latter emphasis growing as the argument proceeds. . . ." A. Lowe, *On Economic Knowledge* (New York: Harper & Row, 1965), p. 243.

tions of *laissez faire* and the prevailing psychology of security markets. He concluded, therefore, that "the duty of ordering the current volume of investment cannot safely be left in private hands."[7]

In the following chapter we shall have an opportunity to test the usefulness of the Keynesian concepts and mechanisms in analyzing the disappointing recovery of the late 1930's and the economic impact of World War II. Chapter 27 will be devoted, among other matters, to an examination of the extent to which the Keynesian policy prescriptions were implemented by government action during those eventful years.

---

[7] *The General Theory* . . . , pp. 320, 378, and 379.

Chapter 26

THE GREAT DEPRESSION AND WORLD WAR II

FROM ECONOMIC STAGNATION TO A FULL EMPLOYMENT WAR ECONOMY

The transformation that occurred in the level of income and employment in the American economy in the years between 1933 and 1945 was truly a remarkable one. A Rip Van Winkle who had gone to sleep in the midst of the 1933 despair would hardly believe, on awakening in 1945, that such prosperity could prevail at the height of a terrible, all-out for national survival. In the interim, he would have missed the long, grinding years of depression in the middle and late thirties in which a disappointing recovery failed to restore the nation to full employment. He would not have known, of course, of the stimulus given to the economy and employment by the defense activities that were set in motion after Hitler marched into Poland in September, 1939, inaugurating the unspeakable horror and world-wide economic and human disruption of World War II. Yet, to those who lived through those searing events and even to those who have only read of them, it is clear that they were a watershed in the history of the world, separating the "years of the locust" from the troubled but more affluent post-war period. For the millions who managed to survive the trials of a world-wide depression and total war, there were still the scars, the trauma, the hiatuses left in their lives.

The economy's fluctuations in the years 1933 to 1945 are best described in terms of the major turning points in its movement. National output, employment, and financial activity were at their lowest ebb in 1932 and early 1933. Starting in mid-1933 the economy entered an expansion phase that persisted until May, 1937. In August a sharp recession occurred that in the course of the following nine months saw industrial production fall 30 per cent and employment decline by 23 per cent. After June, 1938, an upturn started again in response to the corrective measures of the federal government; it received a further impetus with the outbreak of hostilities in Europe the following year. From 1939 until the end of the war in 1945, gross national product rose steadily each year, as shown in Table 1; industrial production (as measured by the Federal Reserve Board's index) also rose sharply in these years, but reached its peak in 1943.

TABLE 1

*Total Gross National Product and Industrial Production
in the United States, 1929–45*[a]

Year	GNP (In Billions of Dollars)	Industrial Production (F.R. Board Index, 1957–59 = 100)
1929	$103.1	38.4
1930	90.4	32.0
1931	75.8	26.5
1932	58.0	20.7
1933	55.6	24.4
1934	65.1	26.6
1935	72.2	30.7
1936	82.5	36.3
1937	90.4	39.7
1938	84.7	31.4
1939	90.5	38.3
1940	99.7	43.9
1941	124.5	56.4
1942	157.9	69.3
1943	191.6	82.9
1944	210.1	81.7
1945	211.9	70.5

[a] Source: *Economic Report of the President*, Jan., 1967 (Washington, D.C.: U.S. Government Printing Office, 1967), pp. 213, 250.

The effect of these fluctuations on personal well-being can be partly seen in the changes of per capita disposable income (i.e., personal income after taxes) and in the level of savings during these years (see Table 2 below). The consumer price index, which enables us to obtain *real* per capita income for

TABLE 2

*Per Capita Disposable Income, Personal Savings and the Cost of
Living in the United States, 1929–45*[a]

Year	Per Capita Disposable Personal Income (Current Prices)	Personal Savings (In Billions)	Consumer Price Index, 1957–59 = 100
1929	$ 683	$ 4.2	59.7
1931	516	2.6	53.0
1933	362	– .9	45.1
1935	459	2.1	47.8
1937	552	3.8	50.0
1939	537	2.6	28.4
1941	695	11.0	51.3
1943	976	33.4	60.3
1945	1,074	29.6	62.7

[a] Source: *Economic Report of the President*, Jan. 1967, *op. cit.*, pp. 229, 232, 262.

these years, showed a 14-point decline from 1929 to 1933 and then rose slowly; in the years after 1939 inflation as measured by this vital index was contained surprisingly well, despite the tremendous inflationary pressures created by the war. Real per capita income in the years 1939–45 more than doubled, rising from approximately $750 to well over $1,600. While much of the improvement in personal income during the war years was not reflected in consumption expenditures because of the priorities given to the production of war matériel, it did provide a basis for some of the post-war prosperity. The personal savings of individuals, as we can see from Table 2, rose from less than $3 billion in 1939 to close to $30 billion annually in 1945.

THE CHANGING COMPOSITION OF PRODUCTION
IN PEACE AND WAR

We can obtain an important insight into the underlying dynamics of economic change in these years by examining the structure of output in manufacturing in terms of the distinction between durable and non-durable goods. It has been a commonplace for economists to state that business cycles have largely been fluctuations in the production of capital goods. Chart 1 shows that the manufacture of durable goods was subject to much larger declines than non-durable goods output in the thirties; the former fell to less than one-third of the 1929 level by 1932, while non-durable goods production exceeded the 1929 achievement by 1936. In the war years, on the other hand, durable goods production, which included much heavy matériel, rose by 1944 to an annual rate three times that of 1939; non-durable goods output over the same years increased between 50–55 per cent.

The heavy decline in durable goods production during the thirties and its slow recovery are explained by several factors. For one, durable goods are by their nature more postponable purchases than non-durable goods, such as food and other perishables. Secondly, it must be realized that the economy of 1929 was basically a full employment economy that had built industrial capacity far in excess of the consumer demand of that year in anticipation of a bright economic future. Consequently, with this large "overhang" of idle productive capacity, small changes in ultimate demand did not lead to an expansion of existing capacity, but merely to a higher rate of plant utilization. In technical terms, we would say that under these conditions the acceleration principle does not generate an increase in capital goods production in response to a rise in consumer demand.[1] The steel industry in 1932 offers a good illustration of this condition. In that year, the industry's ingot capacity

[1] This point is emphasized, among others, by Arthur Smithies in his article, "The American Economy in the Thirties," *American Economic Review Supplement* (May, 1946), pp. 11–27.

CHART 1

Industrial Production Indexes, Major Industry's Divisions 1929–1946
(1957–59 = 100)

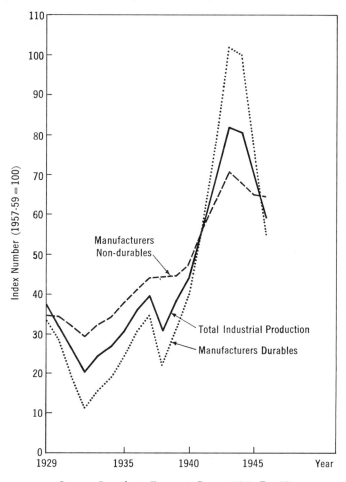

was close to 77 million short tons; actual production was below 14 million
short tons, or less than 20 per cent of capacity. When the demand rose to over
23 million short tons the following year, the industry was easily able to supply
it without adding to its productive capacity because it was still operating at
less than one-third of its full potential. Incidentally, as we shall explain more
fully in the following chapter, the huge increases in durable goods production
during the war years exercised a tremendous multiplier effect on income and
exerted strong inflationary pressure on the economy. The production of war
plant equipment and matériel added to the flow of income but did not augment
correspondingly the output of consumer goods. How the inflationary potential

in that situation was controlled will deserve further examination in the next chapter also.

It may be instructive to survey the contribution of the major industrial divisions of the economy to the nation's income in these years. Table 3 provides us with a panoramic view of the sources of national income for

TABLE 3

Percentage of National Income Generated in Industrial Divisions of the American Economy, 1926–29, 1929–37, and 1937–44[a]

Period	Total National Income (Millions of Current Dollars)	Agriculture	Mining	Mfg.	Transport, Communications, Public Utilities	Trade	Contract Constr.
1926–29[b]	82,818	9.0%	2.2%	21.4%	9.7%	12.9%	4.9%
1929–37	57,460	8.6	1.7	19.6	10.2	13.5	3.0
1929–37[c]	58,763	9.3	2.1	22.8	11.2	16.1	3.1
1937–44	108,684	8.4	2.0	30.6	9.2	15.8	3.5

Period	Finance, Insurance, and Real Estate	Services	Government Federal	Government State and Local	Rest of World
1926–29	17.0%	12.8%		10.2%	—
1929–37	15.7	13.9		13.9	—
1929–37[c]	12.9	11.4	3.7	6.6	0.8
1937–44	8.6	8.4	8.9	4.3	.3

[a] Sources: U.S. Bureau of the Census, *Long-Term Economic Growth, 1860–1965* (Washington, D.C.: U.S. Government Printing Office, 1966), p. 79.

[b] The data used in the first two lines of the table were developed by Simon Kuznets.

[c] Office of Business Economics data. These data have been used in order to make comparisons possible with 1937–44.

1926–29, 1929–37, and 1937–44. What stands out is the continued decline of agriculture in these terms, i.e., of relative income generated, the shrinkage in the manufacturing share during the 1930's, and the increase in the late thirties and war years. Perhaps the most interesting other trend revealed is the rise, as we might expect, in the share of national income contributed by government.

Such analysis of relative shares of national income contributed by industrial sectors should not lead us to overlook significant trends in some of our industries in terms of absolute production. For example, farm output during the depression years did not decline nearly as much as manufacturing production. In fact, it was higher in 1931 and 1932 than in 1929, and after 1936 it was continuously greater than total farm production in the pre-depression year. During World War II, farm output as a whole rose steadily, and in the last three years of the conflict was about 20 per cent higher than the level of output in 1939. The prices received by farmers on all farm products did not attain the 1929 level until 1942. During the war the net income per farm grew threefold over the level of 1939; in real terms, after correcting for changes in the value of the dollar, net income per farm in 1945 was about double that of 1939. The increase in farm output during the war came not so much from increased cultivation of new land, but from higher yields per acre. Agricultural productivity, as measured in output per man-hour, increased about 25 per cent during the war years. The farm surpluses of the depression years helped to feed a nation and a world at war; technological progress made it possible for agricultural employment to be reduced from 11.3 million in 1939 to 10 million in 1945, despite the expansion of output.

An even more dramatic reversal in economic conditions occurred in manufacturing as the nation shifted from an economy of idle men and plants to become the "arsenal of democracy." The "miracle" of wartime production and economic mobilization was aided greatly by the slack in the nation's utilization of its peacetime resources and by the time that elapsed between the beginning of the international crisis in 1939 and our own entry into the conflict as a belligerent. Many of the lessons learned in much shorter first World War were taken advantage of, and excellent use was made of the new technique of national income accounting in allocating resources between "guns and butter." The volume of war matériel of all sorts, which the nation turned out in the years after 1939, was truly astounding; in 1941 the United States produced 12½ per cent of the estimated world output of munitions, the remainder being divided almost equally between the other Allies and the Axis; by 1943, we accounted for 40 per cent of the total, the balance again being divided between the two former groups, so that American output alone exceeded the output of the Axis nations by a third. During the whole war, the United States contributed nearly half of the Allies' total output of munitions.[2] The potential impact of this vast effort on the economy may be judged from the further fact that, whereas war production in 1939 accounted for only 1 per cent of the gross national product, in 1943 it consumed about 40 per cent of that total;[3] in the latter year, our military output was approximately 56 times greater than it had been in 1939.

Yet, despite the massiveness of this military effort, personal consumer expenditures mounted steadily during the war years; it has been estimated that total non-war output was curtailed only about 7 per cent during the years of our active engagement. Consumer durable goods were subject to the greatest amount of retrenchment; the conversion of plants making such products to military items such as bombers, tanks, aircraft engines, machine guns, motorized army equipment, etc., was one of the decisive accomplish-

[2] C. W. Wright, *Economic History of the United States*, 2nd Ed. (New York: McGraw-Hill Book Co., 1949), p. 807.

[3] S. Kuznets, *National Product in Wartime* (New York: National Bureau of Economic Research, Inc., 1945), p. 66.

ments on the home front. The need for additional plant capacity was urgent, but private industry in many instances was fearful that such plant would not be usable for civilian production or would contribute to post-war excess capacity. The federal government, therefore, financed the construction of some $50 billion of new plant and equipment. By 1945, as a result, the manufacturing capacity of the nation was nearly one-half greater than it had been in 1940. This new capacity, combined with the rising efficiency and productivity in the use of capital, made it possible for the nation to more than double its output between 1939 and 1943.

CHANGES IN THE LABOR FORCE AND EMPLOYMENT

The persistence of mass unemployment into the years of the defense effort facilitated the nation's mobilization of manpower for war production, but it did not itself solve the problem. The demands of total war, both on the fighting and the home front, were too insistent and voracious for that. The dimensions of the problem of manpower control can be seen in part by the fact that the draft increased the number of men and women in the armed services from about ½ million in 1940 to a peak of almost 11.5 million in 1945. In addition, military production needed millions of new workers, and while the unemployed in 1940 totalled an estimated 8 million, or close to 15 per cent of the civilian labor force, there was still a need for planning and care in the allocation of the nation's manpower. There was no overall shortage of labor, but there was still the need to assure a labor supply in the proper geographical areas and to recruit a working force with the skills and training required by the new jobs. Fortunately, the labor force demonstrated an enormous capacity for expansion to meet the challenge. Between 1940 and 1944, close to 10 million additional workers were added to the labor force. As a result, as the statistics of Table 4 so clearly indicate, the total civilian labor force in 1945 was less than 2 million short of the comparable figure for 1940, despite the fact that in the former year there were 11.4 million men and women in the armed forces. In the meantime, too, as this table also shows, by 1944 unemployment had shrunk to less than 1 million persons, so that a virtual condition of full employment prevailed.

One of the minor revolutions of the war years, which, in fact, extended a trend long since in process, was the increased employment of women. Women during the war emergency not only worked in offices, but they took over male jobs in munition factories, welding, driving taxis, etc., and did them with a verve and patriotic enthusiasm that was an inspiration to the nation. Female employment increased to the point where fully one-third of the wartime civilian labor force consisted of women.

The failure to achieve full employment in the thirties had a depressing effect on the income of workers in manufacturing and other industries. While

TABLE 4

*The Labor Force, Employment and Unemployment, and the Size of the
Armed Forces in the U.S., Selected Years, 1929–45*[a]
(Thousands of persons 14 years of age and over)

Year	Total Labor Force	Armed Forces	Total Civilian Labor Force		Unemployment as Percent of Civilian Labor Force
			Employed	Unemployed	
1929	49,440	200	47,630	1,550	3.2%
1931	50,680	260	42,400	8,020	15.9
1933	51,840	250	38,760	12,830	24.9
1934	52,490	260	40,890	11,340	21.7
1935	53,140	270	42,260	10,610	20.1
1936	53,740	300	44,410	9,030	16.9
1937	54,320	320	45,750	7,700	14.3
1938	54,950	340	44,220	10,390	19.0
1939	55,600	370	45,750	9,480	17.2
1940	56,180	540	47,520	8,120	14.6
1941	57,530	1,620	50,350	5,560	9.9
1942	60,380	3,970	53,750	2,660	4.7
1943	64,560	9,020	54,470	1,070	1.9
1944	66,040	11,410	53,960	670	1.2
1945	65,300	11,440	52,820	1,040	1.9

[a] Source: *Economic Report of the President*, Jan., 1967 (Washington, D.C.: U.S. Government Printing Office, 1968), p. 236.

average gross weekly earnings rose from their low of $16.65 in 1933, in the remaining years of that decade they did not exceed the 1929 level until 1940. During the war years weekly earnings rose almost 100 per cent, while the consumer price index (of the Bureau of Labor Statistics) increased only about 30 per cent between 1939 and 1945. A good deal of the increase in money earnings was due to a longer work week and to extra compensation for overtime. Regardless of the causes of the increase, there is no doubt of the beneficial effects for workers; their real weekly wages in manufacturing were more than 50 per cent higher in 1944 than they were in 1939. In some lines, such as bituminous coal, where workers had suffered cruelly during the devastating wage deflation and unemployment of the thirties, the recovery in weekly earnings during the war years, thanks to military demand and the strengthening of labor organization, was substantial, and the improvement in wages was relatively greater than in manufacturing as a whole.

There were significant demographic changes in the nation's population and its geographic distribution during these tumultuous years. During the 1930's the population of the United States grew at a substantially lower rate than it had in the previous decade of prosperity. The total increase in the years 1930–40 was 8.8 million, a percentage increase of about 8 per cent, which was half that of the corresponding increase in the preceding decade. The lack of jobs in the cities and the retarded rate of growth in the economy as a whole created serious problems in the way of stranded populations seeking to eke out an existence on marginal land in different parts of the nation.[4] The recovery in business activity in the early 1940's and during our participation in World War II saw renewed population growth, the nation growing in numbers in the years 1940–45 almost as much as it had in the entire period of the thirties. The movement of the people toward the cities, which had slowed down somewhat during the depression years, became marked again; during the years of high employment there was an important movement of Negroes from the South to the industrial cities of the North. The stage was being set for urban developments and problems that were to pose great difficulties and challenges to Americans in the post-war years.

BANKS AND BANK CREDIT IN THE DEPRESSION
AND THE WAR

The continued failure of commercial banks in the early years of the "Great Depression" and the impetus that Great Britain's departure from the gold standard gave to the process of world-wide deflation and economic contraction have been already alluded to. The measures taken by the Roosevelt administration to shore up the banking system and to insure deposits had a very noticeable effect on the number of bank suspensions in the following years. Contrasted with the 4,004 closings in 1933, the number of annual suspensions in the years 1934–40 never exceeded 59, and in the period 1941–45 the maximum number was 9. With the weakest banks eliminated, the administration pursued a vigorous policy of credit expansion through the Federal Reserve, seeking in this way to restore prosperity. While free bank reserves were thus built up to an extraordinary level, as Table 6 shows, business activity under the New Deal did not expand proportionately with the availability of credit. The business loans of all commercial banks increased only from $16.3 billion in 1933 to $18.8 billion in 1940; even during the war years the regular commercial loan did not display any great increase. The "action," rather, during the war years was in United States securities. The banks, as the table shows also, purchased the lion's share of these issues and created demand deposits in favor of the federal government in compensation. With the Federal Reserve committed to a policy of supporting the price of government securities, there was a vast monetization of the growing federal debt. The money supply, defined in this case as demand deposits plus currency outside banks, increased almost threefold in the years of the defense emergency and the war; to be exact, it grew from $33.3 billion in 1939 to

[4] See, for example, C. Goodrich, *Migration and Economic Opportunity* (Philadelphia: University of Pennsylvania Press, 1936).

TABLE 6

Federal Reserve Credit and Bank Loans and Investments, 1929–45[a]

Year	Excess Member Bank Reserves (Averages of Daily Figures, Millions of Dollars)	Member Bank Free Reserves[b]	Total Loans and Investments of all Commercial Banks	Loans	U.S. Government Securities
			(Billions of dollars)		
1929[c]	$ 48	$ −754	$ 49.4	$35.7	$ 4.9
1930	73	−264	48.9	34.5	5.0
1931	60	−703	44.9	29.2	6.0
1932	526	245	36.1	21.8	6.2
1933	766	671	30.4	16.3	7.5
1934	1,748	1,738	32.7	15.7	10.3
1935	2,983	2,977	36.1	15.2	13.8
1936	2,046	2,039	39.6	16.4	15.3
1937	1,071	1,055	38.4	17.2	16.3
1938	3,226	3,210	38.7	16.4	15.1
1939	5,011	5,008	40.7	17.2	16.3
1940	6,646	6,643	43.9	18.8	17.8
1941	3,390	3,385	50.7	21.7	21.8
1942	2,376	2,372	67.4	19.2	41.4
1943	1,048	958	85.1	19.1	59.8
1944	1,284	1,019	105.5	21.6	77.6
1945	1,491	1,157	124.0	26.1	90.6

[a] Source: *Economic Report of the President*, January, 1967, pp. 271, 274.

[b] Excess reserves less member bank borrowings.

[c] The figures of Federal Reserve credit are for December for each year shown.

$94.1 billion in 1945. The inflationary potential in this vast augmentation of the money supply in the war years was reduced somewhat by a decline in the velocity of circulation of money, but after the close of hostilities it contributed importantly to the spiraling of the price level.

Another way to analyze the financial tides and "rip currents" of these treacherous depression years and the hectic war period is to consider the fluctuations in the private and public debt. In 1929, at the peak of peacetime prosperity of this era, the total of individual and corporate obligations was $161 billion; it declined to a low of $124 billion in 1935, hovered in that neighborhood for the remainder of the thirties, and then rose to a top figure of $144 billion in 1944. The public debt, on the other hand, in 1929 stood at a mere $29.7 billion, with the federal government's share coming to $16.5 billion. By the end of the peacetime New Deal, the federal government's debt was $42.6 billion (in 1939) and during the defense build-up and war years proper it soared to a total of $406.3 billion, as of 1945. The state and local governments, meanwhile, increased the level of their indebtedness by about $3 billion from the 1929 figure of $13.2 billion during the depression years of the thirties; they obviously did not go in for "deficit financing" as a way out of the depression. During the war years there was a gradual liquidation of their debt so that by the end of the war the total was only about one-half billion dollars greater than it had been in 1929.[5]

TECHNOLOGICAL CHANGE AND INNOVATIONS

The years of the "Great Depression" did not see the appearance of any major technological innovations that might have offered opportunity for additional private investment. Indeed, the relative dearth of such new industries in those years was one of the arguments advanced by those who believed that the nation was suffering from economic stagnation. There was much talk about the need for "ladder industries" upon which the nation could climb out of the pit of depression. The studies of Simon Kuznets and Arthur F. Burns, published in these years, were demonstrating very clearly that specific industries, after undergoing an initial period of rapid growth, ultimately suffer a retardation in their growth rate.[6] This tendency was especially strong in the early 1930's, and it seemed to lend support to the arguments of the stagnationist school of thought. But others insisted that retardation was but a part of the growth process and that Schumpeter's idea of "creative destruction" demanded that a growing economy must be capable of continuous structural adjustment.

The optimists were sustained by the remarkable technological developments of the World War II period. That war saw technical advances in electronics,

TABLE 7
Average Annual Rates of Change in Total Factor Productivity in the United States, by Industrial Segments, 1919–48[a]
(In per cent)

	1919–29	1929–37	1937–48
Farming	1.2	0.8	2.7
Mining	3.5	4.3	1.0
Manufacturing	5.3	1.9	1.6
Transportation	3.1	4.1	4.7
Communication and public utilities	2.5	3.3	4.3
Total—Private domestic economy	2.0	1.6	2.3

[a] Source: J. W. Kendrick, *Productivity Trends in the United States* (Princeton, N.J.: Princeton University Press, 1962), pp. 136–137. © Copyright 1961 by National Bureau of Economic Research. Reprinted by permission of Princeton University Press.

[5] For these figures, see the *Economic Report of the President*, January, 1967 (Washington, D.C.: U.S. Government Printing Office, 1967), p. 278.
[6] See A. F. Burns, *Production Trends in the United States since 1870* (New York: National Bureau of Economic Research, 1934); S. Kuznets, *Secular Movements in Prices and Production* (Boston: Houghton Mifflin, 1930).

chemicals, and in a host of other fields, which were to have numerous peacetime applications. The greatest innovation of the period was the development
of the atomic bomb, and the nation's hope, even then, was that nuclear energy
could be put to peacetime use.

Later studies have shown that productivity, as in past periods of economic
contraction, declined quite sharply in the early years of the depression, and
only regained the level of the long term trend in the early 1940's (see Chart
2). Actually, the rate of change in total factor productivity varied considerably from one sector of the economy to another over the course of these years.

CHART 2

Private Domestic Economy: Trends in Alternative Productivity Measures, 1919–57

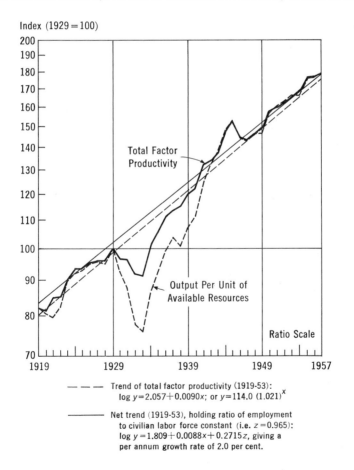

Index (1929 = 100)

Total Factor
Productivity

Output Per Unit of
Available Resources

Ratio Scale

1919   1929   1939   1949   1957

— — — Trend of total factor productivity (1919-53):
          log $y=2.057+0.0090x$; or $y=114.0\ (1.021)^{x}$

———— Net trend (1919-53), holding ratio of employment
          to civilian labor force constant (i.e. $z=0.965$):
          log $y=1.809+0.0088x+0.2715z$, giving a
          per annum growth rate of 2.0 per cent.

Reproduced from J. W. Kendrick, *Productivity Trends in the United
States* (Princeton, N.J.: Princeton University Press, 1962), p. 76. ©
Copyright 1961 by the National Bureau of Economic Research. Re-
printed by permission of Princeton University Press.

As can be seen from the statistics of Table 7, productivity in manufacturing was far below the level of 1919–29 in the depression and war years, whereas it was significantly higher in transportation and communications and public utilities in those periods than it had been in the pre-1929 decade. Farming raised its productivity considerably in the years 1937–48, while in mining in that span of years it was sharply below the levels achieved in the twenties and thirties.

THE REVOLUTION IN GOVERNMENT'S ROLE IN THE ECONOMY

The greatest innovation of the depression years took place not in the field of technology, but in the public sector; more specifically, in the government's relationship to the economy. Whether one regards the governmental measures of the New Deal as revolutionary or not, there is no denying that the Roosevelt era was new because it emphasized, as never before, the dynamic role of the federal government in the economy's functioning.[7] In his inaugural address, President Roosevelt had expressed his hope that "the normal balance of executive and legislative authority may be wholly adequate to meet the unprecedented task before us." He added, however, that it might be necessary that "an unprecedented demand and need for delayed action" will "call for a temporary departure from that normal balance of public procedure. I am prepared under my constitutional duty to recommend the measures that a stricken nation in the midst of a stricken world may require." But, the President warned that if the Congress failed to act speedily on his recommendations, he would ask for "the one remaining instrument to meet the crisis— broad executive power to wage a war against the emergency as great as the power that would be given to me if we were in fact invaded by a foreign foe. . . . The people of the United States . . . have asked for discipline and direction under leadership. They have made me the final instrument of their wishes." These words underlined the gravity of the crisis and made clear the new President's conception of his office.

In the "hundred days" after his inauguration, President Roosevelt sent fifteen messages to Congress and guided to enactment no fewer than fifteen major laws. The bare outline of this remarkable record has been chronicled as follows:

March 9—the Emergency Banking Act
March 20—the Economy Act
March 31—establishment of the Civilian Conservation Corps

[7] D. Perkins, *The New Age of Franklin Roosevelt* (Chicago: University of Chicago Press, 1957); W. E. Leuchtenburg, *Franklin D. Roosevelt and the New Deal, 1932–1940* (New York: Harper & Row, 1963); the works of A. M. Schlesinger, Jr., under the general title of *The Age of Roosevelt* are indispensable for this subject: *The Crisis of the Old Order*, *The Coming of the New Deal*, and *The Politics of Upheaval* (Boston: Houghton Mifflin Co., 1957, 1959, 1960).

April   19—abandonment of the gold standard

May   12—the Federal Emergency Relief Act, setting up a national relief sys-
            tem

May   12—the Agricultural Adjustment Act, establishing a national agricul-
            tural policy, with the Thomas amendment conferring on the Presi-
            dent powers of monetary expansion

May   12—the Emergency Farm Mortgage Act, providing for the refinancing
            of farm mortgages

May   18—the Tennessee Valley Authority Act, providing for the unified
            development of the Tennessee Valley

May   27—the Truth-in-Securities Act, requiring full disclosure in the issue
            of new securities

June   5—the abrogation of the gold clause in public and private contracts

June   13—the Home Owners' Loan Act, providing for the refinancing of home
            mortgages

June   16—the National Industrial Recovery Act, providing both for a system
            of industrial self-government under federal supervision and for a
            $3.3 billion public works program

June   16—the Glass-Steagall Banking Act, divorcing commercial and invest-
            ment banking and guaranteeing bank deposits

June   16—the Farm Credit Act, providing for the reorganization of agricul-
            tural credit activities

June   16—the Railroad Coordination Act, setting up a federal Coordinator of
            Transportation.[8]

Such was the legislative accomplishment of the New Deal during the period of
the administration's "honeymoon" with Congress. Walter Lippmann, the
columnist, expressed best perhaps the effect of these Congressional actions
under the leadership of President Roosevelt upon the morale of the nation as
follows: "At the end of February (1933), we were a congeries of disorderly
panic-stricken mobs and factions. In the hundred days from March to June we
became again an organized nation confident of our power to provide for our
own security and to control our own destiny."[9]

It is not our intention at this point to review the other legislation passed
under the New Deal during the peacetime administration of President Roosevelt; suffice it to say that many of the laws, some of which we shall be
analyzing in the next chapter, increased the degree of governmental intervention in the economy to a peacetime high. It is possible to classify the various
programs of the New Deal, and this suggests the range and nature of the
government's promotional and regulatory activities. Ten classes of programs
have been described as covering most of the New Deal legislation. "They are
(1) money and banking programs, (2) socialization of financial risks, (3)
regulation of business, (4) promoting labor organization and collective
bargaining, (5) relief and public works programs, (6) social security, (7)
promoting agricultural interests, (8) industrial planning, (9) reciprocal trade
policy, and (10) deficit financing."[10]

[8] Schlesinger, *The Coming of the New Deal*, pp. 20–21.

[9] Schlesinger, *The Coming of the New Deal*, p. 22.

[10] G. A. Steiner, *Government's Role in Economic Life* (New York: McGraw-Hill Book
Co., 1953), p. 162.

For the man in the street, the cartoonists, and certainly for many of the New Deal's critics, the government's increased participation in economic life was manifested most conspicuously in the number of governmental agencies that made their appearance in these years. Usually these organizations were designated by some acronym, such as NRA, AAA, etc. The popular impression that the federal bureaucracy was being expanded has been borne out by subsequent academic studies of the subject. One study reveals that of the 88 federal agencies established between the years 1896–1939, 57 came into existence during the New Deal years.[11] The expansion of the federal government's role is reflected, of course, in the number of government workers. While the federal payroll has shown a gradual rise since 1900, the "biggest part of the increase in federal personnel, over two million, came in 1940–49. . . . The next biggest rise, which came in 1930–40, was much smaller, under three-quarters of a million. Nevertheless, more federal workers were added in the 1930's alone than during the preceding decades combined. . . ."[12] These figures suggest clearly that the activities that the New Deal started were "a very substantial factor" in expanding government employment.

The expansion of the government's role in the economy can be measured also in terms of its use of capital resources and its purchases from business. In these respects also, the New Deal years saw an increase in governmental activity. At the beginning of the twentieth century the federal government accounted for only a small portion of the labor and capital resources used for public purposes. Its share rose during World War I, but then during the 1920's its share fell back approximately to the pre-war level, or even lower. During the New Deal it rose again above that level, and with the coming of World War II, it rose still further, so that by the early 1950's the federal government was using half of all the resources (including military equipment) devoted to public purposes. The most patent evidence of the federal government's greater activity is seen in the growth of its budgetary expenditures. In 1929, federal expenditures for all goods and services amounted to $3.5 billion; by 1939 they were $12.5 billion; in 1965 they were approximately $57 billion.[13] Big government in modern times had its beginnings, in large degree, during the years of the New Deal; it has since expanded much more during the hot and cold wars of our troubled era.

The establishment of governmental controls over the economy in World War II, despite the experience that the nation had in mobilizing its resources for the first world conflict, took place haltingly and largely as a result of trial and error. On the very eve of the war in Europe, President Roosevelt in August, 1939 appointed a War Resources Board to aid the military forces in planning the nation's mobilization in the event of war. This agency, which was

[11] Calculated by the authors from data in S. Fabricant, *The Trend of Government Activity in the United States since 1900* (New York: National Bureau of Economic Research, Inc., 1952), Table 17, pp. 69–70.

[12] *Ibid.*, pp. 28–29.

[13] *Economic Report of the President*, January 1966. Figures are in 1958 prices.

not very successful, was abandoned in November of that same year, and in May, 1940 the Office of Emergency Management was established. About the same time the Advisory Commission to the Council of National Defense, a relic of the first World War, was revived. With the fall of France in 1940 and the increased seriousness of the crisis, still another reorganization of our war effort was made—in January, 1941, the Office of Production Management (OPM) was set up under the joint leadership of William S. Knudsen of General Motors and Sidney Hillman, president of the Amalgamated Clothing Workers. Finally, with the attack on Pearl Harbor and evidence of continued delays and shortages, the defense program was overhauled again, and a new agency, the War Production Board, was established. This body, which took over the duties of the OPM and the SPAB (the Supplies, Priorities and Allocation Board), controlled the basic productive effort of the nation for the duration of the war.

The management of this vast enterprise of total war was aided immensely by the numerous businessmen who went to Washington to serve on the numerous other agencies organized to supervise and regulate the nation's industrial effort. Some idea of the proliferation of these agencies can be gathered from the following list of the principal ones.

War Production Board
Office of Price Administration
National War Labor Board
Office of Defense Transportation
Office of Economic Warfare
War Shipping Administration
Foreign Economic Administration
Office of Inter-American Affairs
Office of Economic Stabilization
Office of Scientific Research and Development
Office of War Information
War Manpower Commission
Committee on Fair Employment Practice
Board of War Communications
Petroleum Administration for War
Office of Rubber Administration
War Food Administration
National Housing Agency
Office of Censorship
Selective Service System
War Contracts Price Adjustment Board
Office of War Mobilization and Reconversion

As has been remarked above, the organizational structure of the governmental bureaucracy was subject to considerable reshuffling and improvisation. Thus, to give another example, in May, 1943, the Office of Mobilization was established by the President, and Justice James F. Byrnes resigned from the Supreme Court to head up this new agency. He was given the power as an assistant to the President to coordinate all war programs. Despite the numerous revisions of organization, the nation turned out a prodigious quantity of war matériel, which went far to determine the outcome of the struggle. Not the least of the consequences of this mighty national effort was the assuagement of the conflicts among economic groups, particularly between some segments of the business community and government, which had characterized the preceding depression years. But this development is so important that we shall further examine it in Chapter 28.

Chapter 27

THE GREAT DEPRESSION
AND THE WAR ECONOMY
IN KEYNESIAN PERSPECTIVE

KEYNESIANISM AND THE NEW DEAL

In popular opinion, the New Deal is commonly associated with the doctrines of Keynes. Conservatives especially are prone to conclude that the federal government's failure to solve mass unemployment in the 1930's by deficit spending proved the fallacy of Keynesian public finance.[1] But most economists would now agree that President Roosevelt and his major advisors were not strongly influenced by Keynes until 1938. Indeed, for most of the peacetime New Deal Roosevelt did not sympathize with the philosophy of unbalanced budgets, deficit spending, or a larger national debt. It is true that even in 1932 Keynes and others were calling for increased public expenditures as a means of reducing unemployment. In an open letter to the President in December, 1933, the British economist urged him to start the ball of recovery rolling by increasing national purchasing power by loan expenditure rather than by imposing taxes; the latter, he contended, would not create new aggregate demand but merely transfer buying power from one group to another.[2]

When Keynes and Roosevelt finally met personally for the first time the following year, the reports we have of their talk hardly suggest that the former proved very persuasive to the President. Roosevelt later remarked to his Secretary of Labor, Madame Perkins, "I saw your friend Keynes. He left a whole rigamarole of figures. He must be a mathematician rather than a political economist." And Keynes, apparently equally disappointed, told Secretary Perkins that he had "supposed the President was more literate, economically speaking."[3]

[1] R. Lekachman, *The Age of Keynes* (New York: Random House, 1966), p. 112. Chapters 5 and 6 of this book present a lucid, interesting account of the impact of Keynes on the New Deal and upon the British and American economies during World War II.

[2] *New York Times* (December 31, 1933).

[3] F. Perkins, *The Roosevelt I Knew* (New York: Harper Colophon Books, 1964), pp. 225, 226.

The fact is that a full test of the efficacy of Keynesian fiscal policy did not come until the years of defense spending and World War II, when the enormous military outlays of the federal government so increased aggregate demand that mass unemployment was finally eliminated. In order to comprehend the development of these policies and to analyze their relative failure or success in stimulating recovery, we must study them in their historical context. For example, the New Deal in the course of its evolution underwent a basic change in its direction and objectives, which it is important to recognize.

THE POLITICAL ECONOMICS OF THE FIRST NEW DEAL

A distinction has been made by several historians between the first and second New Deal.[4] This differentiation, although it can be overdrawn, serves the purpose of classifying some of the New Deal legislation in terms of its underlying political philosophy and orientation. In general, the first New Deal, which flourished from 1933 to about the beginning of 1935, espoused a program of structural economic reform; it sought to "reshape American institutions according to a philosophy of an organic economy and a coordinated society." Deriving from the ideas of men such as Professors Raymond Moley, A. A. Berle and Rexford G. Tugwell, original members of the Roosevelt "brain trust," it believed in affirmative national planning in which the government would manage and coordinate "a concert of interests."

Before considering the legislation that reflected this philosophy we should note the nature of some of the first actions taken by the new President in the period of the emergency after the banking holiday. The banking bill that finally resulted in the re-opening of the banks did not reflect any radically new ideas; in fact, in supporting it Roosevelt virtually approved the decisions made by Hoover's fiscal advisers. Rather than nationalizing the banks, as some had urged, the administration's bill extended the government's assistance to the private bankers to re-open their doors. It provided for the operation of banks with liquid assets and for the reorganization of the rest. The House passed this measure practically sight unseen by a unanimous vote; in the Senate, though a small band of progressives objected, its approval was overwhelming. Eight days after his inaugural, the President reassured his listeners in the first of his famous "fireside chats" that it was safe to return their savings to the banks. The next day more people sought to deposit cash than to withdraw it. The banking crisis was over. "Capitalism," Raymond Moley later wrote, "was saved in eight days."[5]

Roosevelt's second message to Congress dealt with government economy,

---

[4] See, for example, Schlesinger, *The Politics of Upheaval*, pp. 385–398; R. G. Tugwell, *The Democratic Roosevelt* (Garden City, N.Y.: Doubleday, 1957), p. 454; W. Leuchtenburg, *Franklin D. Roosevelt and the New Deal, 1932–1940* (New York: Harper and Row, 1963), p. 163 takes a more critical view of this distinction.

[5] Leuchtenburg, *Franklin D. Roosevelt and the New Deal*, p. 45.

and it was even more orthodox in its approach. The President's fiscal ideas were wholly conventional. During the 1932 campaign, at Pittsburgh, he had rather rashly promised to reduce the cost of government 25 per cent, saying that "the one sound foundation of permanent economic recovery [was]—a complete and honest balancing of the Federal budget." In his message to Congress, the President warned that "Too often in recent history liberal governments have been wrecked on the rocks of loose fiscal policy." At this time Roosevelt was following closely the advice of his Budget Director, Lewis Douglas, who was a strong advocate of economy at all costs. The economy bill was adopted by the Congress after only two days' debate; the budget balancers had won a significant victory. Actually, the new administration had begun its efforts at recovery with a policy more deflationary than Hoover had ever attempted. But Roosevelt recognized the deflationary effects of these measures and soon took steps to inflate the price level.

Most of Roosevelt's advisers at this time were stressing the need to "reflate" prices and increase purchasing power if recovery was to be attained. In addition, there was a strong bloc of inflationists in Congress who were urging free coinage of silver and the issuance of greenbacks. To head off these irresponsible actions, the President accepted a qualified version of the Thomas Amendment to the Agricultural Adjustment bill, which was then under consideration. This proposal gave the President permissive rather than mandatory power to issue greenbacks, to remonetize silver, and to alter the gold content of the dollar. The next day the administration definitely abandoned the gold standard, which it had earlier suspended. This action was taken to free the nation to engage in efforts to raise domestic prices. The torpedoing of the ill-fated London Economic Conference in July, 1933 was motivated by similar considerations.

Roosevelt in these difficult times was surrounded by a host of economic advisers, each with his own solution for recovery. One of these was Professor George F. Warren of Cornell University, who argued with an array of charts and graphs that the general price level could only be lifted by raising the price of gold—i.e., by reducing the number of grains of gold in the dollar, which would have the effect of depreciating the dollar in foreign exchange. Roosevelt in the fall of 1933 took up the Warren gold purchase plan for lack of another monetary alternative, and in the succeeding months the price of an ounce of gold went steadily higher. The Warren expectation was that prices would rise in proportion to the devaluation of the dollar, but this did not occur. A monetary debate was started by this policy in which many harsh things were said about the rationality of the administration's actions. Keynes, for one, thought that the Warren theory was "puerile." The fluctuations of the dollar, he said, under the Warren plan "looked to me more like the gold standard on the booze than the ideal managed currency of my dreams."[6] Roosevelt halted the gold-buying program in January, 1934, and under the

[6] Leuchtenberg, *Franklin D. Roosevelt and the New Deal*, p. 81.

Gold Reserve Act of that month, he set the price of gold at $35 an ounce, which involved a reduction of the gold content of the dollar to 59.06 per cent of its pre-1933 level. This monetary experiment had failed; the most that could be said for it was that it contributed to halting the deflationary spiral. Furthermore, it enabled the President to keep monetary policy under his control rather than yielding to the extreme inflationists or the equally fanatic goldbugs.

There were many other measures that the Roosevelt administration persuaded Congress to adopt in the early months of 1933 in response to the pressures of various economic groups and in the effort to reflate the price level. There was relief legislation establishing the Federal Emergency Relief Administration, which provided grants-in-aid to the states, who in turn used these funds for assistance to the unemployed. The Civilian Conservation Corps was set up in 1935, and over 500,000 unemployed young men were engaged in planting trees, reclaiming land, and doing numerous other conservation tasks. The Home Owners' Loan Act provided strong aid to real estate interests and thus indirectly to millions of small home owners. The Securities Act of 1933, followed by another law the following year, which placed the nation's stock exchanges under government control, required full disclosure of information concerning securities in order to protect investors. The Glass-Steagall Act, drawing upon the Pecora investigation of Wall Street practices, compelled the divorce of investment from commercial banking and provided for the creation of the Federal Deposit Insurance Corporation. More radical still, the establishment of the Tennessee Valley Authority fulfilled the dreams of such progressives as Senator George Norris of Nebraska by making possible the planned development of that river valley with multi-purpose dams, capable both of controlling floods and generating electric power. The program also involved reforestation and reclamation of land in the areas affected. The TVA was a pioneer agency in many forms of regional planning. Despite the criticisms of the conservatives, it set an example for many nations of the world and proved to be a resounding success in spurring much private development as well.

But these various laws and programs did not constitute the administration's main attack on economic depression. That was embodied rather in the Agricultural Adjustment and the National Industrial Recovery Acts. The New Deal farm program was a version of the domestic allotment plan as developed by Professor M. L. Wilson of Montana State College, with some assistance from John D. Black and Beardsley Ruml. It was based on the theory that the restoration of farm purchasing power was essential to national economic recovery. "Agricultural adjustment" in this program meant not simply curtailment of output, but an attempt to achieve balance by shifting production out of surplus lines. Production generally was cut back to domestic needs, and reliance was placed on the reciprocal trade agreements to open up foreign markets. Originally, the objective was to raise the prices of seven basic commodities (cotton, wheat, corn, rice, hogs, dairy products, and tobacco) to the level of "pre-war parity"; these "parity prices" measured the ratio of the prices farmers received for the commodities they sold to the prices they paid for industrial goods in the prosperous, pre-war years, 1909–14. (On the basis of parity farm prices in 1929 were 90; in 1933, they were 50!)

Crop curtailment was achieved under the AAA by paying cooperating farmers benefit payments to take the enumerated crops out of cultivation; these payments were made out of the proceeds of certain processing taxes, which were levied on the domestic processors and handlers of such farm commodities. The administration of this program was designed to be decentralized and democratic. A large majority of the farmers growing any crop had to agree by referendum before curtailment could go into effect. Furthermore, the execution of the program was to be as far as possible on a county basis and be controlled by the farmers themselves. Actually, the whole idea of agricultural adjustment and acreage reduction under government supervision was a major innovation in the practice of modern American farming and a drastic departure from the individualism of former days. Henry Wallace, Roosevelt's Secretary of Agriculture, said of it that it was "a contrivance as new in the field of social relations as the first gasoline engine was new in the field of mechanics." And the President himself, in sending a draft message on the program to Congress, warned, "I tell you frankly that it is a new and untrod path, but I tell you with equal frankness that an unprecedented condition calls for the trial of new means."[7]

A month after the passage of the Agricultural Adjustment Act, Congress adopted a supplementary measure—the Farm Credit Act of 1933—which was designed to relieve the heavily mortgaged farmers. Within eighteen months of its enactment, the agency it established had refinanced a fifth of all farm mortgages.

The New Deal farm program was not very long in effect when it became the subject of heated controversy and political debate. Government price-fixing, even when abetted by acreage controls, did pose some difficult problems for its administrators. For example, despite the retirement of more than 10 million acres of land that had been planted to cotton under the program, the production of that commodity in 1933 was some 46,000 bales larger than it had been the previous year. It is true that the price for the 1933–34 crop averaged 11.09 cents as compared with 7.37 cents for 1932–33 and the total income of cotton farmers had nearly doubled. But why had production increased, despite the acreage restriction? The answer was simply that the cotton growers had practiced more intensive cultivation and had obtained larger yields. The average yield on cotton farms in 1933 was 212 pounds, compared with an average for the three previous years of 180 pounds. Acreage control alone, it was evident, had its limitations.

The following year the Bankhead Cotton Control Act sought to avoid this sort of outcome by establishing a compulsory restriction of the cotton crop to

[7] Schlesinger, *The Coming of the New Deal*, p. 39.

10 million bales; quotas were assigned to farmers on the basis of their production in the years 1928–32. Critics pointed out that this type of control involved a "freezing" of cotton production in the established areas of cultivation. New regions of production, it was argued, would not be opened up under such rigid production controls. The question was asked too about quotas for young men coming of age who had not been producing in the base period, 1928–32. An even more serious problem emerged as the higher price of American cotton contributed to increased consumption of foreign cotton. The United States' proportion of world production fell in 1934–35 to 40 per cent, a low level for what had long been one of our great staple exports.

Another consequence of cotton crop control under the AAA that caused much concern was its seeming adverse effects on the condition of the share-croppers of the South. Many of the owners of the land who were receiving benefit payments from the government were adverse to sharing them with their tenants. In fact, it was noticed that under the crop control plan there was a marked displacement of tenants from the farms. The shift from share-labor to the use of wage-labor in growing cotton seems to have added some 700,000 to the relief rolls in the South in the first year of the program. The New Deal later tried to cope with this problem by establishing the Resettlement Administration to take care of those who had been displaced from the land because of crop curtailment or who were suffering economically because of their status as marginal farmers in regions of inferior land.

The National Industrial Recovery Act, the administration's main program for stimulating industry from the doldrums of depression, was hurriedly drafted when Congress showed an inclination to adopt a law that was a more radical and inflexible "cure" for mass unemployment. The New Deal leaders were forced to act by the unexpected passage in the Senate in early 1933 of the Black Bill, which called for a uniform thirty-hour week in industry as a means of spreading employment. Some of the President's advisers met in the office of Senator Wagner of New York to formulate possible alternatives, while others conferred in the office of the Undersecretary of Commerce, John Dickinson. The final draft of a bill, incorporating ideas from both these groups, came from a conference in which Dickinson, Hugh Johnson, Senator Wagner, Rexford Tugwell, Donald Richberg, Secretary of Labor Perkins, and William O. Douglas participated. The provisions of this bill revealed that it had been inspired by a variety of sources—from the nation's experience with industrial mobilization in World War I, from the efforts of the trade associations in the twenties in "self-government of industry," from trade union demands for protection of labor's standards, and the advocacy by certain liberals of national planning in place of competitive *laissez faire*.

The NIRA, as finally approved by Congress, had two main titles. Title I set forth the legislative intent: "to promote the organization of industry for the purpose of cooperative action among trade groups." It provided for codes of fair competition, which were to be exempt from the antitrust laws; it authorized the federal licensing of business, contained the famous Section 7A, which pledged collective bargaining, and made provision for the establishment of maximum hours and minimum wages. Title II called for the establishment of a Public Works Administration with an appropriation of $3.3 billion. The law, it is evident, was an omnibus sort of measure that embodied an eclectic attack on the causes of the Great Depression; because of the broad terms of its provisions, the outcome depended very much on how the law was administered. One thing was clear: the nation was embarked on an unusual peacetime experiment in what the administration liked to call "government partnership with business."

After signing the bill into law, President Roosevelt explained in his simple and effective prose that its purpose was to put people back to work. "It was to raise the purchasing power of labor by limiting hours and increasing wages. It was to elevate labor standards by making sure that no employer would suffer competitive disadvantages as a result of paying decent wages or establishing decent working conditions. . . ." The President, in fact, regarded the NRA as more than a mere program to secure recovery; to him it was "the means for a long-run reform and reorganization of the economy." Recovery, in short, was to be attained through reform. The provisions in the law for an emergency program of public works were not as important to him as those of Title I, and this led him to put the latter under the administration of Hugh Johnson and the public works phase of the Law under Secretary of the Interior Harold Ickes.

Though the National Recovery Act provided for the representation of labor and consumers in the drafting of the industrial codes, the fact was that the employers' trade associations quickly dominated the procedure of code-making. Seeking to protect themselves from further devastating deflation, the businessmen loaded the codes with price-fixing provisions. The price increases caused by these provisions of the NRA soon aroused the ire of consumers; small businessmen complained that they were oppressed by the code provisions favored by the larger corporations. In response to the clamor, the administration established a Review Board under the aged, but still famous Clarence Darrow. Reporting in May, 1934, this body concluded that the NRA had promoted monopolistic exploitation and had caused the oppression of small enterprises, though many were inclined to regard its review as a hasty, dramatic job. Criticism came also from another quarter; other government agencies, such as the AAA, the Federal Trade Commission, etc., felt that the attainment of their recovery objectives was being made more difficult by the price-raising induced by the codes. By 1934, an NRA Policy Board, appointed by the President, recommended drastic changes in the price-fixing and production control provisions of the existing codes. But these recommendations posed a nasty dilemma for the administration. Some 459 industries were already codified, and the industrialists who had gotten what they wanted in the way of "self-government" were reluctant to change their regulations. General Johnson at this juncture assured the businessmen that the new policies would apply only to future codes. Actually, therefore, the

Supreme Court's decision in the Schecter case in May, 1935, removed the administration from an embarrassing position.[8] The Court in a unanimous decision held that the Recovery Act was unconstitutional because it involved too sweeping a delegation of legislative power. Furthermore, it found that the federal regulation of the poultry business of the Schecter Brothers, an intrastate enterprise in its view, was likewise unconstitutional; it had no direct effect upon interstate commerce, so the commerce clause of the Constitution could not be invoked to justify its regulation.

The NRA's effect on recovery naturally became a subject of intense controversy even before its invalidation by the Supreme Court. Attention focused on many of its aspects, including its impact on mass purchasing power and its effect on the level of private investment, which had contracted so disastrously in the depression years. The NRA was an extraordinary peacetime experiment in national economic planning. How effective was it in spurring recovery?

It must be kept in mind that the NRA was supposed to promote recovery by increasing the total real purchasing power of employees. Yet one of the most authoritative studies of this law concluded that average hourly earnings of employees and the cost of living of all employees in the United States rose roughly by about the same amounts from the pre-code to the post-code period. (Both stood 9 or 10 per cent above the pre-code lows.) Between 1933 and 1935 the NRA codes apparently raised living costs concurrently with, or even in advance of, the hourly earnings of labor. Gains in money earnings were largely offset by the effect of the NRA on the prices of the goods and services that labor bought with its earnings. "Average real earnings per hour were but slightly affected."[9]

Similarly, it would seem that the effect of the NRA on the revival of the durable goods industries, which reflect the activity in capital formation and construction, was, on the whole, adverse. The codes resulted in raising the prices of capital goods, and this was hardly conducive to new investment. As the NRA turned out, it became an exercise in the economics of scarcity rather than one of planned expansion of output.

> The practical effect of the NRA . . . was to allow the erection, extension, and fortification of private monopolistic arrangements, particularly for groups that already possessed a fairly high degree of integration and monopoly power. . . . There was little planning of a broad, general nature, either by businessmen or the state; there was merely the half-hearted acceptance of a series of legalized, but generally uncoordinated, monopolistic combinations. The result was no over-all direction, but a type of partial, piecemeal, pressure-group planning, a type of planning designed by specific economic groups to balance

---

[8] 295 U.S. 495 (1935). See Chapter 28 of the Brookings study of the National Recovery Administration [L. S. Lyon et al., *The National Recovery Administration: An Analysis and Appraisal* (Washington, D.C.: The Brookings Institution, 1935], for a convenient review of the mounting criticism of that agency.

[9] Lyon et al., *The National Recovery Administration*, pp. 788–789.

production with consumption regardless of the dislocations produced elsewhere in the economy.[10]

From the Keynesian perspective, the fundamental weakness of the NRA was its failure to perceive that the secret of economic recovery lay not in the level of prices alone, but in the behavior of aggregate demand. Furthermore, the PWA under the slow-moving Ickes did not do enough to counteract or offset the decline in private investment.

At most, so far as its contribution to recovery is concerned, the NRA was "a holding action" rather than a powerful, positive stimulus. In its first year, the shortening of hours and the spreading of work increased employment for about two million workers. The income of the lowest paid groups was raised by its minimum wage provisions, but generally these people were not prosperous enough to spend much of their additional income on durable consumer goods, such as automobiles, which were badly depressed.

The NRA's greatest benefit to the nation lay in the field not of business economics but of social welfare. While organized labor came to be disillusioned with the interpretation of Section 7A, which promoted company unions as well as independent trade unions, there were many enduring social reforms under the Blue Eagle. It established such practices as minimum wages and limitation of hours on a national basis, it abolished child labor, and it went far to destroy the sweatshops. Even in the realm of economic recovery, it must be admitted that the NRA ended the vicious spiral of price deflation and gave the nation a badly needed "shot in the arm." It contributed to the nation's recovery of confidence and its rejection of the economic fatalism that had been hampering recovery. It educated some Americans to think in terms of national policy for business and labor, and it trained many in the responsibilities of public service.

THE SECOND NEW DEAL EMERGES

The death of the NRA, the appearance of radical political threats on the Left such as Huey Long, Father Coughlin, and the Townsend movement, pushed the New Deal in another direction in 1935. The objectives remained the same, but the means employed, the political style, and even the vision itself of the American future seemed to undergo a fundamental change. The first New Deal had accepted the concentration of economic power and had sought to use concentrated political power to control it. The second New Deal sought rather to restore a competitive society within a framework of known rules with provision of a social minimum for all. It showed a partiality for the small businessman, encouraged the counterorganization of the weaker eco-

---

[10] E. W. Hawley, *The New Deal and the Problem of Monopoly: A Study in Economic Ambivalence* (Princeton, N.J.: Princeton University Press, 1966). This competent study is the definitive analysis, thus far, of this aspect of the NRA.

nomic groups, and resorted to partial economic planning in their behalf. Only toward the end of the terrible thirties did this phase of the New Deal turn to deficit finance as a means to economic recovery. It is only with these provisos that we can accept Schlesinger's generalizations: "The second New Deal was eventually a coalition between lawyers in the school of Brandeis and economists in the school of Keynes. . . ."[11] The second New Deal was ideologically more capitalistic than the first because it relied more heavily on competition than central planning. Though generalizations of this type are hazardous, there is some truth in Schlesinger's apt summary: "The First New Deal characteristically told business what it must do. The Second New Deal characteristically told business what it must *not* do."[12]

The shift from the first to the second New Deal was necessitated in large part by the changing historical situation. The crisis of 1932 could only be met by a concerted national effort such as the first New Deal attempted; but once the crisis was averted, the level of cooperation its program entailed could not be maintained; something more realistic and more conservative was called for. The Supreme Court played its part also. By holding so much of the early New Deal legislation unconstitutional, it necessitated the drafting of alternative laws. New faces appeared among the administration's advisers, as the old ones became political liabilities or fell out of sympathy with the direction of policy. Instead of Moley, Tugwell, or Berle, much legislation was now drawn by the team of Corcoran and Cohen,[13] or by other ex-students of Professor Felix Frankfurter of the Harvard Law School who was an especially influential figure in Washington in this period and a capable exponent of the Brandeis philosophy of the evils of bigness in business. Actually, it was not until the battle over public spending in 1937–38 that the second New Deal was fully defined; at that time still other economic advisers rose to ascendancy. But we anticipate our later analysis; let us first examine the character of some of the legislation of the second New Deal.

President Roosevelt experienced a period of indecision in the early months of 1935 when the NRA was in a state of decline and the thunder of various demagogues was building up on the Left. This phase of the New Deal's development ended when a number of measures that were being backed by different advisers met with Congressional favor. One of these was Senator Wagner's labor bill, which had been introduced in 1934, but had not received support from the President. Section 7A of the NIRA had proven disappointing to organized labor because of the ambiguous interpretations of its meaning and the support it had given to company unions. The new labor relations measure proposed to clear up the confusion by establishing a National Labor Relations Board with power to conduct elections to determine the appropriate

[11] Schlesinger, *The Politics of Upheaval*, p. 387.
[12] *Ibid.*, p. 392.
[13] Thomas G. Corcoran and Benjamin V. Cohen were both brilliant students of law from Harvard who framed important legislation for the New Deal in these years. For their backgrounds and careers, see Schlesinger, in *The Politics of Upheaval*, pp. 225–230.

bargaining units; it incorporated the principle that the organization that won the majority of the workers' votes in such elections would be the exclusive bargaining agent. The bill enumerated the "unfair labor practices" of employers that were banned, such as discharging workers for union membership or fostering company-dominated "unions." After the Schecter decision the President included the Wagner measure among his "must" legislation; employer groups resisted it strongly, but it easily won Congressional approval and became law in July, 1935. The Wagner Act was a major innovation in labor relations. It greatly aided the union movement because it put the weight of the government behind labor's right to collective bargaining.[14]

Labor's countervailing power was further strengthened in the following year by the passage of the Walsh-Healey Act. This law repaired in part the damage done by the invalidation of the NIRA. It required government contractors to observe a minimum forty-hour week, prohibited them from using child labor, and compelled the payment of the prevailing wages in the employer's locality. After much delay, the effort to put a minimum floor below which wages could not fall was accomplished with the enactment of the Fair Labor Standards Act of 1938. This law abolished child labor and provided initially for a minimum of 25 cents an hour and a maximum week of forty-four hours, with higher standards for future periods. Actually, this law was the last significant legislative victory of the second New Deal.

Another controversial measure that won legislative approval in the early years of the second New Deal was the Banking Act of 1935. This law was pushed by Marriner Eccles, an unconventional Utah banker whom Roosevelt had appointed as governor of the Federal Reserve Board. Eccles was determined to streamline the organization of the Federal Reserve System, limit the power of the New York City bankers, and increase public control over the monetary system. For example, open-market operations, which had previously been diffused among the Reserve Banks, were to be concentrated in a Federal Open-Market Committee, composed of seven Board members and five representatives of the Reserve banks. This revision of the Federal Reserve's structure met bitter opposition from the bankers, some of whom resented Eccles' Keynesian-like thinking, alleging that he was under the influence of a Keynesian economist on his staff, Lauchlin Currie. One of these bankers derided the bill as "Curried Keynes." "It is in fact a large, half-cooked lump of J. Maynard Keynes . . . liberally seasoned with a sauce prepared by Professor Lauchlin Currie."[15] Senator Carter Glass of Virginia, who believed he was the "father" of the original Federal Reserve Act, also vehemently opposed the measure. Glass won some amendments to the bill, but as passed it was substantially Eccles' proposal. The law gave the Federal Reserve Board greater control over rediscount rates and reserve requirements, expanded the definition of eligible paper, and amended the federal deposit insurance system.

[14] See the next chapter, p. 758–760 for further discussion of the growth of the labor movement in the New Deal years.

[15] Leuchtenburg, *Franklin D. Roosevelt and the New Deal*, p. 159.

This legislation made the Federal Reserve a more effective instrument for the conscious control and management of the monetary mechanism.

The administration found itself in another bitter battle with economic conservatives over the public utility holding companies. The President had strong beliefs about the evils of these holding companies, and he favored the abolition of those that could not be economically justified. Corcoran and Cohen drafted a bill imposing the "death sentence" after January, 1940, on any utility holding company that could not justify its existence. The utility lobby mounted a massive, million-dollar campaign against the measure. After several setbacks and revelations of the corrupt practices of the holding company propagandists, the Congress passed the Wheeler-Rayburn bill. This law compelled the holding companies in this field to register with the SEC, gave it the power to supervise their transactions, and eliminated holding companies beyond the first degree that were not geographically or economically integrated. A powerful blow had been struck against corporate bigness, delighting the Brandeisians and enraging the opponents of corporate reform.

The Social Security Act, which was adopted by the Congress in the same year, stirred another hornets' nest of controversy. The initiative had been taken in this field by Wisconsin, which had enacted the first state unemployment insurance law in 1932. Old age pensions had been pledged by the Progressive platform of 1912, but little had been accomplished in the way of legislation in the interim. The hardships of the Great Depression and the political appeal of the Townsend old age plan spurred the administration to carry out the platform plank of the 1932 Democratic convention. That document had advocated "unemployment and old-age insurance under State laws." The support for this type of legislation at this time did not come from the American Federation of Labor, which under the influence of the conservative craft unions opposed government intervention. Its advocates rather were the liberals, the backers of social welfare legislation, who realized how far the nation was behind other industrialized nations in this respect. After a long debate among the experts over the merits of a state or federal system of unemployment insurance, a law was finally passed that rectified, to some degree, our cultural lag in this field. The Social Security Act established a national system of old age insurance covering most employees and paying retirement annuities at age sixty-five out of revenues derived from taxes on wages and employers' payrolls. The federal government shared equally with the states the care of the indigent aged who could not qualify for pensions. A federal-state system of unemployment insurance was created with a tax-offset feature designed to encourage the states to pass such laws. Finally, national aid was provided the states, on a matching basis, to care for dependent mothers and children, the blind, and other handicapped persons.

This social legislation was a patchwork measure born of compromise and political expediency. Its weaknesses included its failure to set up a national system of unemployment insurance, its reliance on regressive taxation to finance the pension system, and its build-up of vast reserves, which threatened to destabilize further the functioning of the economy. The law unfortunately exempted numerous classes of workers, including some, such as farm laborers and domestic servants, who needed social security most. But these short-comings, some of which have since been corrected, were of no consequence to those who raised the greatest clamor over the passage of this legislation. Many business leaders and most Republican politicians denounced the law as socialistic, contending that it threatened to undermine our national life by destroying initiative, discouraging thrift, and stifling individual responsibility. In retrospect, the Social Security Act of 1935 was a landmark in social legislation, but to the conservative-minded it was a shocking break with their traditional individualism.

The conservatives and the well-to-do received another jolt in 1935 when the administration introduced a radical tax bill that sought to redistribute wealth and power. This measure provided increased taxes on inheritances, imposed new gift taxes, hiked the graduated rates on large personal incomes, and levied a corporation income tax scaled according to the size of corporate income. The wealthy, most businessmen, and the press denounced this "soak the rich" bill, as the Hearst publications termed it. These proposals were opposed also by numerous Congressmen, including the Democratic chairman of the Senate Finance Committee. The debate dragged on during the summer, and a law was passed, much amended, which raised estate, gift, capital stock, and personal surtax rates and even imposed an excess profits tax, which Roosevelt had not sought. This tax bill in its original provisions reflected the Brandeis philosophy that had come into administration favor after the death of the NRA. But after Congressional amendment, it retained little of this character and proved a disappointment in the amount of revenue it raised. It did reap a harvest of bitterness and opposition, however, in the business community.

Thus, 1935, which had begun so dismally for the administration, ended with an extraordinary record of legislative accomplishment. Charles Beard later wrote, "Seldom, if ever, in the long history of Congress, had so many striking and vital measures been spread upon the law books in a single session."[16]

PARTIAL PLANNING IN THE POST-NRA ERA

The dismantlement of the NRA experiment left many industries that had benefitted from its provisions anxious to restore it in some form. One of these was the bituminous coal industry, whose workers had enjoyed the benefits of the soft coal code and whose resuscitated union constituted a strong lobby. In response to pressures from some of the operators and the union, Congress

---

[16] C. A. Beard, "The Labors of Congress," *Current History* (October, 1935), quoted in Schlesinger, *The Politics of Upheaval*, p. 337.

passed the Guffey-Snyder Coal Conservation Act of 1935. This law established a National Bituminous Coal Commission with powers to fix minimum prices on the basis of weighted average costs of production and, if necessary, establish maximum prices. The Commission could approve and enforce trade practice and marketing agreements. Labor's rights to collective bargaining were protected, minimum wages and maximum hours could be established, and a Bituminous Coal Labor Board was given power to adjudicate disputes. This governmentally sponsored cartelization of a basic natural resource industry was declared unconstitutional by the Supreme Court less than a year after the law's enactment, but the damage was repaired in 1937 by the passage of the Guffey-Vinson Bituminous Coal Act of 1937.[17] This new law omitted the provisions to which the high Court had taken objection, but re-enacted most of the other provisions of the 1935 Act.

The petroleum industry was also able to regain some of the advantages of its code through the adoption by Congress, in 1935, of the Connally "Hot Oil" Act. This law supplemented the prorationing laws of various oil states by prohibiting the shipment in interstate commerce of "hot oil," i.e., of oil produced in excess of the state quotas. It was significant that other industries, such as lumber, clothing manufacture, and anthracite coal were unable to secure laws supporting market controls. Generally, these industries lacked either strong lobbies or the right political connections, or were unable to provide a pretext, such as conservation, to justify a departure from the competitive ideal.[18]

The transportation industries were able to lobby for governmentally supported planning in their favor. The Motor Carriers Act of 1935, for example, which put the interstate motor carriers under the regulation of the Interstate Commerce Commission, was favored by the truckers and the railroads because it stabilized the competition among them, even though it meant treating the newer industry as a publicly regulated monopoly. Shipping, another "sick" transportation industry, also received government support. The Merchant Marine Act of 1936 placed the industry under the Maritime Commission and gave the latter power to equalize American and foreign costs by subsidizing American builders and operators. The Commission was given authority to establish an elaborate system of controls over rates, routes, and practices as well as over the industry's wages. Despite this assistance, it was not until the approach of World War II that government investment led to a rapid expansion of our merchant fleet. By the terms of the Civil Aeronautics Act of 1938, aviation too was brought under a system of partial planning, with the Civil Aeronautics Board providing the subsidies, cartel-like regulations, and public control.

Still another group to win partial exemption from the competitive regime was the small merchants. The "Great Depression" had greatly aggravated their

[17] *Carter* vs. *Carter Coal Co.*, 298 U.S. 238 (1936).
[18] Hawley, *The New Deal and the Problem of Monopoly*, p. 224.

struggle with the more integrated distributors—the chains, the department stores and mail order houses—for control over the nation's marketing channels. Wielding their organized political power as a pressure group, they were able to secure passage of the Robinson-Patman Act of 1936, which forbade wholesalers or manufacturers from giving preferential discounts or rebates to large buyers. The local druggists and other independent merchants, having passed resale price maintenance laws (deceptively termed "Fair Trade Acts") in many states, were successful in pressuring Congress and a reluctant President to approve the Miller-Tydings Act of 1937. This enabling law buttressed Fair Trade by legalizing such price-fixing in interstate commerce.

But the partial planning and organization of "countervailing power,"[19] which was involved in most of these measures, proved to be largely ineffective. These forms of state-sponsored cartelization, while they helped to check deflationary forces and provided temporary relief, tended to restrict production, raise prices, and prevent change. In the transportation and distributive industries, the laws often served to protect inefficiency and inhibit desirable technological and organizational innovations. Most serious of all, these efforts at partial planning did not serve to augment aggregate demand or stimulate the depressed capital goods industries to any noticeable extent. Indeed, the disappointment with the results of such laws, so far as stimulating economic recovery was concerned, tended to push some of the planners toward support of public spending as a solution to depression.

RECOVERY AND RECESSION, 1933–1937

In the years 1933–37, a considerable degree of recovery from the low of the great contraction was achieved. National income, which was $52 billion in 1934, had risen to $70 billion by 1937. Other economic indicators, such as corporate profits, trade volume, and wholesale prices had risen considerably from the level of 1933. Employment too had increased close to six million from the depression low of 1933, but the labor force of those willing and able to work had been growing also, so mass unemployment had not been eliminated. It had dropped from 12 million or more in 1933 to 8 million in 1937; in that year an approximate 14 per cent of the labor force was still looking for jobs, before another recession set in.

A good deal of heat and relatively little light was generated in the middle years of the 1930's over the failure of the economy to return to full employment. One school of thought contended that the administration had delayed recovery by accenting reform, weakening business confidence, and engaging, as in the 1936 election, in a political battle with the "economic royalists." Though he did not participate in this controversy in a major way, Keynes

[19] In his *American Capitalism* (Boston: Houghton Mifflin Co., 1952), J. K. Galbraith provided something of a rationale for this type of policy, but he by no means endorsed all the laws passed during this phase of the New Deal.

favored recovery over reform as the first priority for the United States. On one occasion he advised the President as follows:

> Businessmen have a different set of delusions from politicians; and need, therefore, different handling. . . . You could do anything you liked with them, if you would treat them (even the big ones) not as wolves and tigers, but as domestic animals by nature, even though they have been badly brought up and not trained as you would wish. It is a mistake to think that they are more *immoral* than the politicians. If you work them into the surly, obstinate, terrified mood, of which domestic animals, wrongly handled, are so capable, the nation's burdens will not get carried to market; and in the end public opinion will veer their way.[20]

Public spending played an important part in the partial recovery of the years 1933–37, but the New Deal did not employ fiscal policy vigorously enough to attain full employment. As we have seen, the Congress had established the Federal Emergency Relief Administration as early as May, 1933. This body provided grants-in-aid to the states, which then used them for the relief of the unemployed. Harry Hopkins, who headed FERA, explained to Roosevelt the dire need for emergency measures, and the President authorized him to establish the Civil Works Administration. The latter was completely a federal agency; the CWA put the unemployed on the federal payroll and emphasized public works rather than direct relief. By January, 1934, the CWA was employing over four million persons.

> In its brief span the CWA built or improved some 500,000 miles of road, 40,000 schools, over 3,500 playgrounds and athletic fields, and 1,000 airports. . . . The CWA employed fifty thousand teachers. . . . It hired three thousand artists and writers, and used a variety of other special skills . . . The CWA pumped a billion dollars of purchasing power into the sagging economy.[21]

However, Roosevelt, in keeping with his basic philosophy about public spending, ended the CWA as quickly as possible. ". . . He feared he was creating a permanent class of reliefers whom he might never get off the government payroll."[22] Therefore, in the spring of 1934, FERA once again took up the burden of relief. Then in January, 1935, the President launched a massive new program of emergency public employment that was to give work to three and a half million of the jobless. Those so employed would receive more than the relief dole but less than the prevailing wage, so that they would have an incentive to take private jobs if they became available. The remaining million and a half on relief were to be turned over to local charity as unemployables. The President declared, "The Federal Government must and shall quit this business of relief."

Congress authorized nearly five billion dollars for the new program—"the

---

[20] J. M. Blum, *Years of Crisis, 1928–1938*, Vol. 1 of *From the Morgenthau Diaries* (Boston: Houghton Mifflin, 1959), pp. 403–404, quoted in Lekachman, *The Age of Keynes*, p. 122.

[21] Leuchtenburg, *Franklin D. Roosevelt and the New Deal*, pp. 121–122.

[22] *Ibid.*

greatest single appropriation in the history of the United States or any other nation" up to that time. Secretary of Interior Ickes, who had been slow in getting under way the large PWA projects, which he favored as a means of "priming the pump" of private investment, now contested with Harry Hopkins the control of this vast program. Ickes thought Hopkins was an irresponsible spender who was not priming the pump but "just turning on the fireplug." But the President gave the job to Hopkins because his approach would put more men to work quickly. The Works Progress Administration, as Hopkins' new agency was called, could not compete with private industry or regular government work, but it did launch some experimental programs of great imagination, such as theatre, writers', and arts projects and it established the National Youth Administration to provide for unemployed young Americans. The WPA, however, never achieved Roosevelt's goal of giving jobs to all who could work. It cared for no more than 3 million of the 10 million who were estimated at the time to be unemployed. And the unemployables were placed at the mercy of the state governments, which were financially unable, for the most part, to provide for them.

Despite the resort to this program of deficit spending and the other measures of the New Deal, mass unemployment persisted. Table 1 sets out some of the pertinent statistics.

TABLE 1
Federal Deficits and Unemployment in the United States, 1931–40[a]

Year	Deficit (Billions of Dollars)	Unemployment (In Millions)	Unemployed as a Percentage of the Total Labor Force
1931	$ .5	8.0	15.9%
1932	2.7	12.1	23.6
1933	2.6	12.8	24.9
1934	3.6	11.3	21.7
1935	2.8	10.6	20.1
1936	4.4	9.0	16.9
1937	2.8	7.7	14.3
1938	1.2	10.4	19.0
1939	3.9	9.5	17.2
1940	3.9	8.1	14.6

[a] Sources: U.S. Bureau of Census, *Historical Statistics of The U.S., Colonial Times to 1957* (Washington, D.C.: Government Printing Office, 1960).

The deficits are for the fiscal years ending June 30th; unemployment shown is the average for the full calendar year. The deficit figures therefore lead the unemployment data by six months.

Recent analysis of the effects of the fiscal policies of the thirties suggests that they were not as expansionary as some have thought. Since the economy was growing throughout that period, aggregate demand had to be increased at a rate of slightly more than 3 per cent per year in the period 1929–42 to maintain full employment.[23] According to one study, full employment demand, as so defined, was relatively stronger than in 1929 in only two years—1931 and 1936 (see Chart 1). Fiscal policy seems to have been less expansive in this period primarily because of the sharp increase in tax structures enacted at all levels of government. The Federal Revenue Act of 1932 especially had a highly deflationary effect, pushing rates up to almost wartime levels. State and local governments' fiscal policies were expansionary through 1933, but after that year they were almost neutral in affecting full employment demand relative to their influence in 1929 (see Chart 2). ". . . The Federal Government's policies were little more than adequate in most years of the thirties to offset these contractive effects of state and local governments."[24] In this view, then, fiscal policy appears to have been unsuccessful as a recovery device in the thirties—not because it did not work, but because it was not tried. Alvin Hansen reached the same conclusion in 1941: "Despite the fairly good showing made in recovery up to 1937, the fact is that neither before or since has the administration pursued a really positive expansionist program . . . For the most part, the federal government engaged in a salvaging program and not in a program of positive expansion."[25]

From another perspective, the fiscal policies of the years 1933–37 were not effective because of their failure to revive private investment. As Table 2 shows, while personal consumption expenditures staged a good recovery in those years, gross private investment and especially investment in fixed structures, producers durable equipment and housing were slow to return to

TABLE 2

Changes in Some Components of Gross National Product of the United States, 1933–37[a]

(Billions of current dollars)

Year	Total GNP	Personal Consumption Expenditures	Gross Private Domestic Investment	Fixed Investment in Structures	Producers Durable Equipment	Residential Construction
1929	$103.1	$77.2	$16.2	$5.0	$5.6	$4.0
1933	55.6	45.8	1.4	.9	1.5	.6
1934	65.1	51.3	3.3	1.0	2.2	.9
1935	72.2	55.7	6.4	1.2	2.9	1.2
1936	82.5	61.9	8.5	1.6	4.0	1.6
1937	90.4	66.5	11.8	2.4	4.9	1.9

[a] Source: *Economic Report of the President*, January, 1967, pp. 213, 225.

[23] E. C. Brown, "Fiscal Policy in the Thirties: A Reappraisal," *American Economic Review* (December, 1956), pp. 857–879.

[24] Brown, "Fiscal Policy . . .," p. 867.

[25] A. H. Hansen, *Fiscal Policy and Business Cycles* (New York: W. W. Norton & Co., 1941), p. 84; for a contrary view of the effect of New Deal fiscal policy on recovery in the thirties, see A. Smithies, "The American Economy in the Thirties," *American Economic Review, Proceedings* (May, 1964), p. 26.

CHART 1

Effect of Fiscal Policy on Full-Employment Demand[a]
(*All Governments*)

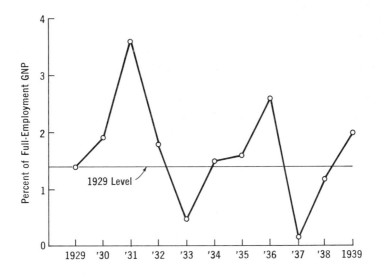

CHART 2

Effect of Fiscal Policy on Full-Employment Demand[a]
(*Federal, State and Local Governments*)

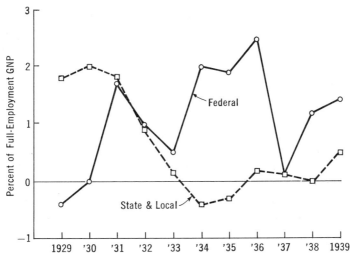

[a] Source: Reproduced from Brown, "Fiscal Policy in the Thirties: A Reappraisal," *American Economic Review* (December, 1956), p. 866 with the permission of the publisher. © Copyright 1956 by the American Economic Review, Stanford.

the 1929 levels. The depression of private investment in these years was reflected very clearly in the volume of new security issues. Domestic corporate issues for new capital had averaged over $5 billion in the years 1926–30; in the years 1933–40, the corresponding annual average was a shocking $644 million.[26]

Critics of the administration argued that the slow recovery was attributable to the policies of the government itself. Tax policy, especially the progressive individual income tax, corporation taxes, and the much denounced undistributed profits tax were alleged to deter individuals and corporations from risking their capital. The security reforms, while improving the quality of issues, probably had an adverse effect on their quantity. Professor Schumpeter at the time contended that the anti-capitalist animus of some of the government's reform measures provided "a chilly climate for innovators." In general, the opposition charged that the mutual distrust between business and government which the administration's measures had created brought on a "strike of capital."[27]

At the beginning of 1937, President Roosevelt indicated in his budget message that he was prepared to turn over the responsibility of continuing recovery to business. The need for further pump-priming was over; the budget could be balanced, as Treasury Secretary Morgenthau had so persistently urged. The budget for the fiscal year 1938 provided for a reduction of about one-third in recovery and relief expenditures; altogether, the curtailment in government expenditures was so drastic that the administrative budget showed a deficit of only $100 million. The cash budget for fiscal 1938 actually showed a surplus. This sharp turn from deficit to surplus financing, coupled with other destabilizing developments in the economy, soon had serious repercussions. The economy had experienced a considerable inventory accumulation in 1937 and then suffered a very rapid liquidation of stocks of goods the following year. The prices of a number of goods had risen in the years 1936–37, partly in response to increased wage costs. Between August, 1936, and May, 1937, the Federal Reserve Board, anxious over the prospect of price inflation, doubled the reserve requirements of the member banks. Signs of trouble appeared first on the stock market; the prices of "industrials" broke in March, 1937 and by late summer the nation was talking about the "Roosevelt recession." The contraction in business activity was one of the sharpest in the nation's recent history. The Federal Reserve Board index of production plummeted eight points in 1938, falling below the level of 1930. Unemployment increased three million within a year. The decline affected consumer goods as well as capital goods production; residential construction was hard hit also. In 1938, the gross national product fell to $84.7 billion

---

[26] S. E. Harris, *The Economics of America at War* (New York: W. W. Norton and Co., 1943), p. 36.

[27] A. Smithies, "The American Economy in the Thirties," *American Economic Review* (May, 1946), pp. 11–27, reprinted in Nash, *Issues in American Economic History* (Boston: D. C. Heath and Co., 1964), pp. 445ff.

from the level of $90.4 billion the year before. Private investment dropped by almost one-half. The impact of this decline in business activity on the nation's morale was grave because it was, in fact, a recession within a depression. In 1937, the unemployment rate (as a percentage of the civilian labor force) stood at about 14 per cent; by the following year, it had risen to 19 per cent of the labor force.[28]

President Roosevelt made a sharp reversal from budget-balancing to further deficit financing in the effort to end the unanticipated recession. In April, 1938, he sent Congress a message entitled "Recommendations Designed to Stimulate Further Recovery." This document was "the first outright recommendation" by the administration of a program to achieve recovery through fiscal policy. In line with it, the Congress approved increased appropriations for WPA, NYA, and other New Deal agencies. The deteriorating international situation provided grounds also for increasing military expenditures. ". . . The net deficit for the last six months of the calendar year 1937 was only $607,000,000, while for the last six months of 1938 it was almost six times as large. . . ."[29]

In 1939, relief expenditures were increased to the unprecedented level of $2.9 billion. This was not the pump priming that had been tried before 1938 when it had been believed that a relatively small expenditure of public monies would stimulate private investment and bring the economy to full employment. Now it was recognized that large and persistent public spending would be necessary. The worsening international situation and the need for enlarged defense expenditures made the nation willing to accept the new deficits, whereas previously it had often been critical of New Deal fiscal policy. Under the changed circumstances, the annual deficit of the federal government went from $3.6 billion in 1939 to almost $5.2 billion in 1941. In seeming response to the fiscal stimulus, gross national product recovered in 1939 to the 1937 level, and private investment also partially revived. Unemployment, however, was more resistant to recovery; in 1939 the percentage unemployed was still 17.2 per cent and in the following year, 14.6 per cent, slightly higher than it had been in 1937.

Despite the administration's resort to fiscal policy in the 1937 recession, it must be recognized that Roosevelt and most of his advisers were still "reluctant Keynesians." As Lekachman says,

Indeed, the Roosevelt administration finally accepted the key public policy conclusion of Keynesian economics: deficits in time of unemployment are fine because they stimulate national income and employment. If deficits are beneficial, it follows that they should be large enough to do their job. Yet the episode was not so educative as it might have been. The President continued to deplore deficits publicly, to yearn privately for balanced budgets, and to

[28] For a detailed analysis of this recession see K. Roose, "The Recession of 1937–38," *The Journal of Political Economy* (June, 1948), pp. 239–248.

[29] B. Mitchell, *Depression Decade* (New York: Rinehart and Co., 1947), p. 44.

promise his constituents that just as soon as possible, fiscal orthodoxy would be restored.[30]

The Keynesian approach had to win academic acceptance and respectability before it could become the basis of consistent fiscal policy-making in the realm of American politics. As a matter of fact, a Keynesian school of thought was just emerging among American economists in the late 1930's. This significant intellectual development deserves our consideration at this point.

THE AMERICANIZATION OF KEYNES

The history of the Keynesian revolution, Galbraith has written, is "perhaps, the worst told story of our era." In his version of that fascinating subject, he further remarks that "As Messiahs go, Keynes was deeply dependent on his prophets."[31] Curiously enough, Professor Alvin Hansen of Harvard, who became Keynes' principal "prophet" and expositor in this country, had originally rejected *The General Theory*, in a rather hostile review, asserting flatly that it did not lay the foundation for a "new economics." But like St. Paul, the critic turned disciple, and in 1938 and the following years he published a number of books and articles that made the new doctrine more concrete and understandable. In the years before 1937, while we had no economists whom Keynes recognized as belonging to "the brave army of heretics" who anticipated his ideas, we did have two government officials who advocated Keynesian-like fiscal policies. Marriner S. Eccles, a Utah banker who became governor of the Federal Reserve Board under Roosevelt, and Lauchlin Currie, a Treasury economist, had been advocating public spending as a remedy for the depression for several years.[32] But Hansen went far beyond mere advocacy; he lucidly expounded Keynesian theory and related it to the American experience. At Harvard and at other academic institutions an increasing number of economists were "converted" to the new theory.

Hansen in these years not only crusaded for Keynesian theory and policy, but he advanced the even more controversial view that the depression was persisting because the economy was suffering from economic maturity or secular stagnation. As he analyzed the situation, the "Great Depression" marked a major break in American economic development. Prior to that time, investment opportunities had been adequate to maintain reasonably full employment, interrupted by periods of depression attributable to special factors. But 1929 represented the end of this era; thereafter, we could expect

[30] Lekachman, *The Age of Keynes*, p. 125.

[31] J. K. Galbraith, "Came the Revolution," *New York Times Book Review* (May 16, 1965), pp. 1ff. A competent, well-written treatment of the Keynesian revolution in the United States is presented by Lekachman, *The Age of Keynes*. Valuable insights can be gained also from S. E. Harris, ed., *The New Economics* (New York: Knopf, 1947). See also A. M. Schlesinger, Jr., *The Politics of Upheaval*, pp. 401–408.

[32] See Schlesinger, *The Politics of Upheaval*, pp. 238–239.

to suffer from a drastic slowing down of the rate of economic growth (secular stagnation) due to a chronic deficiency of investment opportunity. In his presidential address of 1938 to the American Economic Association, Hansen said; "We are passing, so to speak, over a divide which separates the great era of growth and expansion of the nineteenth century from an era which no man, unwilling to embark on pure conjecture, can as yet characterize with clarity or precision."[33]

Hansen offered several causes for this alleged maturing of the economy. Employing contemporary demographic data, he pointed to a slowing down in the rate of population growth—in the thirties the rate was one-half that of the previous decade—and he predicted a further decline in the future. He estimated that the growth of population in the latter half of the nineteenth century was responsible for about 60 per cent of the capital formation in that period. Further, while the extensive population growth of the previous century had both widened and deepened (made more intensive) the use of capital, the prospect of an increasing proportion of elderly people would reduce the demand for housing construction, and the larger proportion of personal services such a group would need would reverse the tendency toward the deepening of capital.

Secondly, it was argued that the absence of a geographical frontier meant reduced investment opportunities and that foreign markets would not provide the outlets for capital that they had in the nineteenth century. Lastly, it was held that a number of "institutional developments," such as "the growing power of trade unions and trade associations, the development of monopolistic competition, of rivalry for the market through expensive persuasion and advertising, instead of through price competition," would dampen investment opportunity. Hansen's pessimistic outlook for the future of the American economy was amplified during the gloom of the 1937–38 recession by a group of Harvard and Tufts economists who asserted that fiscal policy would need to compensate for secular stagnation even more than cyclical depression.[34] In their view, there would have to be a vigorous expansion of the public sector of the economy, more progressive income taxes, and a massive expansion of welfare activities. These bearish diagnoses of the future of American capitalism were rejected by other economists who contended that the persistent depression of the thirties was not irrevocably determined by inexorable secular forces, but was the result of unsound private and governmental policies.[35] The coming of the war economy temporarily ended the economists'

[33] A. H. Hansen, "Economic Progress and Declining Population," in American Economic Association, *Readings in Business Cycle Theory* (Philadelphia: Blakiston, 1944), p. 367.

[34] R. Gilbert, et al., *An Economic Program for American Democracy* (New York: Vanguard, 1938).

[35] See on this topic, G. Terborgh, *The Bogey of Economic Maturity* (Chicago, Ill.: Machinery and Allied Products Institute, 1945); W. I. King, "Are We Suffering from Economic Maturity?" *Journal of Political Economy*, Vol. XLVII (October, 1939), pp. 609–622.

debate over whether the United States was suffering from economic maturity, but it did not reduce the growing influence of Keynesian economic thinking; rather the economic challenges of the wartime economy and the problems of post-war readjustment greatly increased the understanding and appreciation of the "new economics."

THE WAR ECONOMY IN A KEYNESIAN FRAMEWORK

J. K. Galbraith has suggested that the Allies possessed a weapon during World War II that had a greater bearing on their ultimate victory than the atomic bomb. This was the system of national income accounting that had been worked out in this country mainly by Professor Simon Kuznets in the years immediately preceding the war. Its underlying theory of gross national product and its components derived in considerable part from Keynes' seminal work. The national income framework proved indispensable in the Allies' mobilization of their economies. The Germans had not as yet employed the technique and they consequently "mobilized their resources with considerably less skill and boldness than did England or the United States."[36]

In World War II the United States had more time to prepare for total mobilization than it had in the first international struggle, but the task, even allowing for the fact that we started with immense amounts of unemployed resources, was a stupendous and enormously complex one. The financial problems of a government at war—to take just one aspect—are complicated by the fact that the transfer of workers from peace to wartime employment means that those who are engaged in producing war output receive money incomes, but they make no corresponding contribution to the production of civilian goods available for consumption. The danger of inflation is inherent in this very process. It follows that the central task of war finance is to transfer this extra income of workers engaged in wartime production to the government. In a pamphlet that he wrote in 1940 entitled *How to Pay for the War*, Keynes addressed himself to this problem, i.e., that of an economy threatened by wartime inflation rather than depression. Instead of approaching the question in terms of budgetary finance, Keynes employed in his analysis the national income and employment framework of the *General Theory*. In this more holistic analysis of the economy, the problems of war finance were stated in terms of real aggregate demand and real aggregate supply. This technique was superior to the purely financial approach because it dealt with the physical and human resources that had to be allocated between peace and war uses rather than solely with budgetary data. In the book referred to, Keynes shows that the consumption function and the level of war expenditures by the government interact to determine the level of income. The "inflationary gap" is then the difference between what the population will try

[36] J. K. Galbraith, *American Capitalism* (Boston: Houghton Mifflin Co., 1952), p. 80.

to consume out of this income and the amount available for consumption at pre-inflation prices.[37] To cope with such wartime inflation, Keynes advocated limiting the amount of money to be spent on the reduced amount of consumer goods by increasing taxation or through voluntary or "forced" saving; he also approved rationing of scarce materials and goods and price controls, where necessary. Before examining the extent to which such policies were adopted in the United States, we need to consider more closely the impact of the war on the economy.

The outbreak of the war in Europe in September, 1939, had immediate effects on American markets. Memories of the shortages and inflation during the first World War spurred hedge buying. Prices rose precipitately; those of basic commodities rose about 25 per cent in the month of September alone. This price rise in turn stimulated accumulation of inventories that further increased the pressure of demand. A speculative boom was on. Employment in manufacturing increased almost 10 per cent by the end of the year. During the fantastic period of the "phony war" that followed, when some came to believe that the war would not continue, speculation subsided, but resumed when the German armies invaded Denmark and Norway in the spring of 1940.[38]

As the defense program went into gear, government expenditures rose with spectacular effects on production and employment. The fiscal year 1941 was the first full year of the defense effort. In that period the expenditures of the federal government were $12,775 million, of which sum $5,167 million was for defense. The gross deficit in that year was $6,301 million; at the end of the period the public debt was close to $49 billion. "Whereas the calendar years 1938 and 1939 had shown increases in the public debt of about $2 billion, 1940 showed nearly $3 billion, and 1941, to the end of November, over $9 billion. . . ."[39]

After the relatively small "homeopathic" doses of the New Deal, these infusions of public spending had more substantial effects. The American economy responded to this huge new impetus—as the statistics of Tables 1 and 4 in the preceding chapter show; production and employment soared. Between 1939 and 1943, the peak year of war output, the Federal Reserve index of production more than doubled. Increasingly, public works were relegated to the background as the defense spending of the federal government boomed. Once again, Keynes' multiplier theory was evident in the working of the economy. Instead of providing employment for the masses through public works, the government made jobs through its defense expenditures. Once this

[37] To illustrate, the OPA estimated that the income payments for 1942 would be approximately $117 billion, taxes and war savings (in the form of war bonds or stamps) would come to $31 billion, leaving a balance of $86 billion available for spending on civilian goods and services. It estimated that the value of the goods and services produced during that year would come to only approximately $69 billion, thus creating an inflationary gap of some $17 billion. [H. U. Faulkner, *American Economic History*, 8th Ed. (New York: Harper and Bros., 1960), p. 704.]

[38] Mitchell, *Depression Decade*, p. 371.

[39] *Ibid.*, p. 51.

initial step had been taken, the effect of the multiplier was felt, and employment spread to other areas of production. Unemployment rather quickly
shrank to insignificant proportions. As Table 4 of the preceding chapter
indicates, whereas in 1942 the unemployment rate had been 4.7 per cent, by
1943 it was 1.9 per cent and in the following year it reached its wartime low
of 1.2 per cent.

The productive capacity of the economy when maintained close to full
employment levels was remarkable, as the overall statistics of wartime performance demonstrate. "Beside producing $459 billion of war material and
$100 billion of plant, machinery, and other capital goods, we produced in the
five war years $790 billion of consumer goods (1955 prices), or $125 billion
more than in the pre-war five year period."[40] This is, indeed, a striking
measure of the nation's war effort as well as of the terrible economic toll of
the "Great Depression."

As that depression and its accompanying unemployment receded with the
expansion of the war economy, the reverse problem—that of inflation—
became pressing and critical. With production and employment increasing,
the swollen income stream began to exert its inflationary pressure upon the
available supplies of civilian goods. As the money paid out in the defense
effort circulated and multiplied through the economy, the purchasing power of
individuals rose dramatically, and this tended to drive prices up in the classic
fashion of a demand-pull type of inflation.

The previous chapter has described the vast increase in the supply of money
during the years of the defense emergency and the war and has alluded to the
role that the monetization of the debt played in this monetary expansion. The
Federal Reserve could not check the incipient inflation because it did not have
control over government borrowing. Furthermore, one of its principal
weapons of credit control, open-market operations, could not be used for fear
of weakening the government bond market.

Meanwhile, as the government's defense effort accelerated, prices began to
rise rapidly. By the spring and summer of 1941, wholesale prices were rising
at the rate of 2 per cent a month. The Office of Price Administration, which
had been set up in August of that year, had as yet little power. It was still
dependent on voluntary compliance. But after Pearl Harbor and the nation's
entry into the war, the Congress in January, 1942, passed the Emergency
Price Control Act, giving the OPA statutory power to control prices and
rents. This Act was weakened, however, by the exemption of farm prices until
they reached 110 per cent of parity and by the inadequate staff of the agency
and internal conflicts within it. In October, 1942, a reluctant Congress under
administration pressure passed another Stabilization Act, which gave the
President the power to stabilize farm prices at 100 per cent of parity and
directed him to stabilize industrial prices and wages at the level of September
15, 1942. But even the new agency, the Office of Price Stabilization, could not

[40] A. H. Hansen, *The American Economy* (New York: McGraw-Hill, Inc., 1957), p. 26.

stem the inflationary tide; wholesale and consumer prices moved up as much as 4 per cent between October, 1942 and April, 1943.

In the latter month, President Roosevelt issued a new directive to the OPA and the War Labor Board to "hold the line." Ceiling prices were placed on all commodities, and subsidies were used to take care of hardship cases requiring some adjustment. Consumer rationing also helped to check the inflationary pressure. Rationing had been resorted to by the OPA within a month after the war started; in January, 1942, it began by rationing tires, and went on to control fuel oil, sugar, coffee, and a wide variety of canned and packaged goods. By the middle of 1943, rationing applied to as much as 95 per cent of the nation's food supply. This type of control was not completely effective, and there was much grumbling, particularly toward the end of the control period; "black markets" appeared, especially in gasoline and meat. Despite the annoyance and the controversy over these price controls, they finally slowed down the pace of price inflation. From the time of the "hold the line" order to the end of the war, consumer prices rose only 4.2 per cent, and wholesale prices increased less than half this amount. Overall, price control in World War II was much more successful than in the first World War. In the latter conflict, the index of prices (1914 = 100) rose to 162. Yet during World War II, in which our participation was twice as long, the same index, on a base of 1939 = 100, rose only to 133. Despite the difficulties and the slowness in establishing effective price controls, the OPA's record in the war was a remarkable one. The relative success of its effort at price stabilization during the years 1942–45 can be graphically seen in Chart 3.

Price control succeeded to the extent it did because fiscal policy was employed to soak up some of the excess purchasing power created by deficit financing. As Table 3 shows, the size of the federal government's deficit rose

TABLE 3
*Federal Taxes, Expenditures, Deficits and the Public Debt
1939–45*[a]
(In millions of dollars)

Year	Taxes	Expenditures	Deficit	Public Debt[b]
1939	$ 4,979	$ 4,841	$ 3,862	$ 45,890
1940	5,137	9,055	3,918	48,497
1941	7,098	13,255	8,159	55,332
1942	12,547	34,037	21,490	76,991
1943	21,948	79,368	57,420	140,796
1944	43,563	94,986	51,423	202,626
1945	44,362	98,303	53,941	259,115

[a] Source: *The Economic Report of the President*, January, 1965 (Washington, D.C.: U.S. Government Printing Office, 1965), p. 260.
[b] At the end of the year. Includes guaranteed issues. The change in the public debt from year to year reflects not only the budget surplus or deficit but also changes in the government's cash on hand, and the use of corporate debt and investment transactions by certain government enterprises.

CHART 3

Fluctuations in U.S. Wholesale Prices, by Groups, 1939–1948 (1926 = 100)

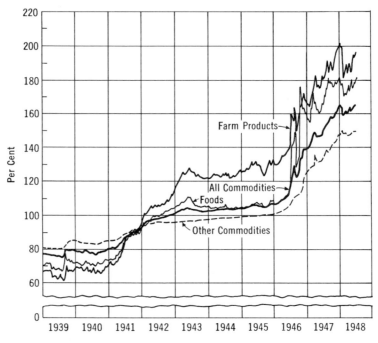

Source: U.S. Bureau of the Census

from less than $4 billion in 1939 to over $57 billion in 1943. Starting with the Revenue Act of 1940, which raised the rates and broadened the tax base, Congress in subsequent legislation succeeded in multiplying tax receipts almost tenfold. In 1943, it instituted the practice of withholding taxes at the source on wages and salaries. Incidentally, the war brought about an amazing revolution in the number of those filing returns with the Internal Revenue Service; in 1939 income taxes were paid by only 4 million Americans, but by 1942 more than 42 million did so. Though there were economists who argued that the government should have taxed more heavily than it did, there was the fear that if rates were pushed up too high, incentives and morale would suffer, and the necessary degree of cooperation would be impaired.

The United States did not embark upon a program of compulsory saving, as Keynes had advocated, but a considerable amount of spending was deferred because of purchases of government bonds by individuals. All together, in its seven War Loans and final Victory Loan, the Treasury sold $156.9 billion of securities between May 1, 1941 and January 3, 1946. Of this amount, about two-thirds was purchased by corporations, one-third by individuals, and the remainder by commercial banks and others. (The failure to remove enough of the excess spending power generated by wartime production made necessary heavier reliance on price and wage control and rationing.)

THE BATTLE FOR PRODUCTION

The nation's remarkable war effort on the home front is not fully understood if presented and perceived only in terms of fiscal policy decisions and Keynesian theory. Equally important were the tough and complex decisions made about plant conversions, material shortages, and the general coordination of the domestic production program. There were major differences of opinion among the policy-makers on these questions and numerous struggles for power behind the scenes among the "war lords of Washington."[41] For example, Bernard Baruch, the venerable czar of the War Industries Board in 1917–18 and a respected adviser to Presidents, had very definite ideas as to how the nation should be mobilized. He held that competition had no place in a war economy. In Baruch's words:

> In war . . . the Government must assume control of the whole supply and ration it—not to the longest purse but to the most necessitous use . . . the distinguishing characteristic of peacetime economic operation is *competition*, and basic prices are largely determined thereby. . . . Under war conditions the entire process is reversed. There is more business than all of the facilities of the country can handle. Competitors must become cooperators in order to meet the very minimum demand for shortage items. Control of this cooperation rests in Government. Thus, because Governmental determination (*and not price*) controls demand, and because only complete cooperation (*and not competition*) can produce supply in sufficient quantity, the law of supply and demand adjourns itself.[42]

President Roosevelt in the early years of the defense effort did not completely accept the Baruch approach. He relied in part on the antitrust activities of Thurman Arnold, the Assistant Attorney General, to prosecute corporations engaged in cartel arrangements with enemy powers or in other practices that restrained trade and hampered the defense effort. Some of our biggest corporations had entered into restrictive agreements with German corporations in the pre-Pearl Harbor years, which seriously jeopardized our technological preparedness.[43] Arnold exposed these cartel affiliations of some of our biggest corporations, but he did not succeed in preventing them from obtaining a preponderant percentage of the prime war contracts. The President threatened many of the big corporate war contractors with antitrust prosecution, but aside from breaking up the cartel agreements, he could do little; the

[41] A most revealing analysis of the intrigue and power struggles among the major officials of the wartime agencies is found in E. Janeway, *The Struggle for Survival* (New Haven: Yale University Press, 1951), *passim*; see also D. Nelson, *Arsenal of Democracy: The Story of American War Production* (New York: Harcourt, Brace & World, Inc., 1946) and B. Catton, *The War Lords of Washington* (New York: Harcourt, Brace and Co., 1948).

[42] Janeway, *The Struggle for Survival*, pp. 156–157. (Italics in original.)

[43] On this subject, see W. Berge, *Cartels: Challenge to a Free World* (Washington, D.C.: Public Affairs Press, 1944).

cooperation of the corporate giants was essential to winning the battle for production.

Meanwhile, the reorganization and realignment of the top administrative agencies continued in the hope that order, speed, and efficiency could be achieved in the management of the vast task of conversion and production for the military effort. When, in January, 1942, the President coordinated the activities of some of the chief agencies under the War Production Board headed up by Donald M. Nelson, it was believed by some that the delays and bureaucratic conflicts that had hampered the program somewhat up to that time were over. That agency did push vigorously the vital task of expanding facilities for the manufacture of arms and ammunitions. When the effort was completed, it was found that most of the war plants had been constructed by the federal government itself through the Defense Plants Corporation.[44] As much as five-sixths of the new construction was done through government financing, so that when the war ended, the federal government owned some of the newest and most efficient manufacturing facilities in the nation. It controlled over 90 per cent of the plant capacity for producing synthetic rubber, planes, ships and magnesium; 70 per cent of aluminum manufacturing facilities; and 50 per cent of the plants suitable for building machine tools. In addition, it had built millions of dollars worth of plants in the steel, high octane gasoline, and chemical industries, as well as thousands of miles of pipe line to carry oil to the east coast. The disposition of these valuable government properties posed major problems of policy in the immediate post-war period.

While this massive construction and conversion of plant for war purchases was carried out successfully, the control of materials flowing into the war machine continued to present problems. Baruch, drawing upon his World War I experiences, had warned that the problem of a wartime economy was priorities. Donald Nelson, the new War Production Board chief, continued to employ the priorities system used by the Office of Defense Management. This soon produced an inflation of contracts and priorities that caused surpluses of output in some lines and shortages in others. In desperation, Nelson in the summer of 1942 adopted a plan called "PRP" (Production Requirements Plan), which allowed each contractor and subcontractor, in effect, to issue priority certificates as fast as he accepted orders. This system dismally failed to solve the problem; in fact, it made it worse as companies scrambled to build up inventories of items in short supply. Production became completely unbalanced; tank treads accumulated without the armor plate, or carburetors and other parts were produced in uncoordinated quantities, and this on the eve of our invasion of North Africa. The President took the situation in hand

---

[44] In addition to such government-built plant private industry was induced to expand its facilities by the device of accelerated depreciation. Under the second Revenue Act of 1940 a contractor who acquired or constructed with his own funds facilities which were necessary to national defense could amortize the cost over a five-year period at a rate of 1⅔ per cent per month. This was in lieu of the ordinary deduction for depreciation based upon useful life.

by appointing James Byrnes Director of Economic Stabilization over Nelson in early October, 1942. By November, Byrnes adoped the Controlled Materials Plan (CMP), which had been proposed by Ferdinand Eberstadt, Chairman of the Army-Navy Munitions Board. CMP ended the crisis by controlling the flow of three essential materials—steel, aluminum, and copper—and permitted orders to be placed only in the quantities needed for producing the finished product. It balanced the input of economic energy with the output of fire power needed on the battle front. By solving the problem of "priorities inflation," Eberstadt, with Baruch's advice, made possible the tremendous output of 1943, which had much to do with ending the war more rapidly than any had dared hope in the previous year.[45]

In mobilizing the economic resources of the nation and winning the battle for production that was so essential to victory, the United States drew heavily on its experience in the earlier world conflict. Though there were inexcusable delays in adopting the financial and economic controls over the war economy, eventually they were put into force, and they made it possible for the nation to harness the domestic front to the shifting, world-wide theater of war more efficiently than it had ever been done before. The nation learned too the amazing capacity of its economy when operated at full employment. It did not learn fully, however, the techniques of implementing politically the essentials of the "new economics."

In our study of the "Great Depression," we have seen the usefulness of Keynes' theory of income and employment in analyzing the fluctuations of that unstable period; we have noted too the limited degree to which Keynesian policies were employed in combatting that depression. In the war years, Keynes' ideas won new converts, but it was not until the post-war period that the "age of Keynes" was truly inaugurated.

---

[45] Janeway's Chap. XI in *The Struggle for Survival* presents a vivid, unforgettable treatment of this phase of the nation's war effort.

Chapter 28

THE POLITICAL ECONOMY OF INTERVENTIONISM

THE GROWTH OF THE WELFARE STATE

The "Great Depression" dealt a fatal blow to the theory of *laissez faire* capitalism in the United States. After that traumatic experience, the American people as a whole no longer seemed willing to accept the idea that unregulated capitalism assures maximum welfare for all or that any attempt to interfere with the private economy would necessarily jeopardize the welfare of the people. The economic security, if not life itself, of workers, the aged, women and children, people of all ranks had been too profoundly threatened by the near breakdown of capitalism in the thirties for them to accept the old dogma. Economists in the United States increasingly rejected the traditional doctrine as they came to recognize the validity of the Keynesian analysis of the possibility of an underemployment equilibrium. Yet, as we have seen in the preceding chapter, it was not Keynesian theory so much that moved the New Deal toward its solutions, but the humane pragmatism of President Roosevelt.

During the first New Deal, the administration's emphasis had naturally been on national unity, and Roosevelt had engaged for this purpose in the conventional politics of organization, dealing with the city bosses of the North and the political barons of the South. The defection of some of these bosses from the New Deal in 1934 gave strength to a new conception of a liberal coalition, based not on the politics of organization but on that of ideology. This new coalition was "bound together, not by habit or by spoils, but by ideas, by a sharp sense of alienation from the business culture and by a belief in positive government as the instrument of national improvement. . . ."[1] The central concern of this new Democratic politics was the urban masses, including labor, the ethnic minorities, women, and intellectuals. These groups were forged into a coalition not by the traditional methods of patronage and handouts, but by the social and ideological programs of the New Deal. As the movement against big business became more pronounced in the summer of

[1] A. M. Schlesinger, Jr., *The Politics of Upheaval* (Boston: Houghton Mifflin Co., 1960), p. 409. Chaps. 22 and 23 of this book are excellent on the politics of the second New Deal.

1935, this tendency was accelerated. The increased concern of the second New Deal with the urban masses "profoundly affected both its politics and its policies."[2] To understand these developments, we need to consider more closely the impact of the depression of the 1930's on the American family.

THE QUEST FOR INDIVIDUAL SECURITY

The depression, according to the Social Science Research Council, "was like the explosion of a bomb dropped in the midst of society." Its studies showed that the insecurity created by the economic collapse caused a degree of alienation, resentment, and anomie toward the American economic system, which was unparalleled in the nation's experience.[3] Perhaps in no other institution of American life was the depression felt more than in the family; fundamental changes in family structure seem to have occurred as a result.

Demographic data for the depression years indicate that fewer families were begun by marriage. As a consequence of fewer marriages, births fell off significantly, and the birth rate registered a new all-time low for the nation. In addition, the number of illegitimate births per thousand increased markedly. Those who married late wed proportionately much less frequently, and many women in the modal marriageable age group found themselves spinsters. The social adjustment of these unwed women became a major social problem; however, they often found it easier to secure employment and make an economic "go" of things than did men of a similar age group. In the marriages that did take place, anticipation of a good future income was a significant factor.

In this period, the American family continued to decline as an economic unit; increasingly, commodities were both produced and consumed from sources outside the family. Many couples, to "make ends meet," resided with the parents of the bride or the husband; as a result, there was somewhat of a return to the extended family. By and large, discord between husband and wife was greater in these years, largely because of financial reasons. Children and the aged could not find employment very easily. With a lack of employment opportunities, youngsters remained with their parents, often continuing their education. In such cases, the result was a lengthened time of parental responsibility and a wider educational gap between parent and child. If the father became unemployed, he frequently found his parental authority over his children seriously weakened. Mixed marriages increased as religious and

[2] *The Politics of Upheaval*, p. 423.

[3] Outstanding among the studies on the depression sponsored by the Social Science Research Council were: S. A. Stouffer and P. F. Lazarsfeld, *Research Memorandum on the Family in the Depression*; D. Young, *Research Memorandum on Minority Peoples in the Depression*; *Research Memorandum on Rural Life in the Depression*; *Research Memorandum on Internal Migration in the Depression*; *Research Memorandum on Social Aspects of Consumption in the Depression* (New York: Social Science Research Council, 1937).

ethnic distinctions seemed to become less important under the stress of economic depression.

World War II did not strengthen social ties either, as families sent children and husbands off to the armed services and took in wives, grandchildren, or friends. The servicemen who were casualties of the war often found their peacetime lives broken or disrupted. In short, the cataclysmic events of these years left the structure of American family life in a weakened condition. It is little wonder that the aged, the very young, the widowed, the unemployed, and the dislocated felt that they were at the mercy of uncontrollable forces and that they looked to the government for support in their distress.

In the "Great Depression," the plight of the unfortunate was brought to the nation's attention by a number of organizations that sprang up to represent them. The Townsend movement publicized the special problems of the aged. The Joe Smith movement reflected the problems of the dislocated and the unemployed. The veterans' organizations spoke for the wounded who returned from the war. President Roosevelt did not disregard these pleas for help nor did he contend that an unregulated capitalism would in its automatic functioning take care of the needy. His New Deal took bold and innovative action to cope with the problems of the unprotected. A national approach was formulated to aid families suffering from a loss of income.

To protect the income of the aged and the survivors of a deceased worker, Old Age Survivors' and Dependents' Insurance (OASDI), was established. Under the provisions of the Social Security Act, protection against presumptive rather than demonstrated need was provided for the aged retired persons and their dependents, survivors of workers, the disabled, and the unemployed; general public assistance was made available for the blind or dependent children.[4]

Old age, survivors', and disability insurance were, in effect, purchased by employer and employee by payroll contributions under the provisions of the Social Security Law. In addition to the OASDI, old age assistance to any needy aged person was provided. Spurred on by the incentive provisions of the Law, many states passed laws to establish protection for the uncovered or to provide a mechanism for matching the federal government's contributions to the needy. Some types of security for the aged, the unemployed, the sick, or the injured required such state matching plans in order to become effective.

Measurement of the social impact of these plans is very difficult. Clearly, in a complex industrial society dominated by large organizations, there was a need for more government protection of the security of the individual. During the "Great Depression," these federal programs alleviated an immediate need. However, of even greater significance was their long run demonstration effect. During World War II, the trade unions were restricted in their negotiation of collective bargaining agreements. Since there were severe limitations on

---

[4] For more information on the Social Security Laws, see W. Haber and W. J. Cohen, *Social Security: Programs, Problems and Policies* (Homewood, Illinois: Richard D. Irwin, 1960).

higher wage packages, many unions turned to the area of security or fringe benefits. Such supplements to the Social Security programs were among the major advances made by the unions during the war. Private pension, medical, unemployment, injury, and job insurance benefits were won in many trade agreements during the war years. For the organized workers, the problem of individual and family security was much improved by these progressive steps. At the end of World War II, the fringe benefits of American labor far surpassed anything enjoyed by workers elsewhere in the world.

BIG LABOR AND THE GOVERNMENT

Under the New Deal the rights and privileges of the American worker were enlarged and protected to an unprecedented degree. In the past, with the exception of the protective legislation passed by the states, it had been an accepted principle of American life that complete equality of treatment under the law for employer and employee, rich and poor, would result in equality of opportunity. Now this philosophy was abandoned, and in its place was substituted the new idea that the less capable groups in society were to be consciously protected. This revolutionary change in the conception of government's function derived in part from the experience of the depression in which the less fortunate often suffered the most. With this changed attitude toward the government's role, there followed a remarkable amount of progressive labor and social legislation. By 1945, after a decade or more of such governmental support, the trade union movement in the United States was literally transformed.[5]

As we have seen, the first major move under the Roosevelt administration to protect the worker was embodied in the National Industrial Recovery Act (the NIRA) of 1933. This law was declared unconstitutional in 1935, but in the immediate period after its enactment it provided for federal regulation of minimum wages and maximum hours. The NRA established codes that covered twenty million workers with a minimum hourly wage of from 30 to 40 cents an hour. The most significant part of the Act for labor was Section 7A, with its strong governmental endorsement of collective bargaining. This concept was again embodied in the Wagner Act of 1935, which is regarded by some authorities as the most important labor law ever enacted.

The Wagner or National Labor Relations Act was essentially based on the philosophy that the failure of employers to accept collective bargaining resulted in industrial conflict. The reasoning underlying this philosophy embraced the idea that there was an inequality in bargaining power between the individual worker and his corporate employer. There was the further

[5] Two excellent works on the subject are C. O. Gregory, *Labor and the Law* (New York: W. W. Norton and Co., 1958) and G. Miller, *American Labor and the Government* (Englewood Cliffs, N.J.: Prentice-Hall, Inc., 1950).

assumption, as stated in the preamble to the Act, that freedom of contract presupposes equality of bargaining power. The sponsors of the Act also believed that this inequality in bargaining power resulted in a reduction of the real wages of workers. By strengthening labor's right to organize it was felt that the purchasing power of workers could be maintained and that this would avoid a condition of insufficient aggregate demand and consequent business depression. Like the NRA, the principal feature of the law was its protection of the right of workers to organize and its guarantee of the workers' right to bargain in good faith with the employer. The key aspects of the law are found in Sections 7 and 8. Section 7 declares, "Employees shall have the right to self-organization, to form, join or assist labor organizations, to bargain collectively through representatives of their own choosing, and to engage in concerted activities, for the purposes of collective bargaining, or other mutual aid or protection."

In order to guarantee the rights of employees under Section 7, a number of unfair employer practices were spelled out in Section 8. Under this law it is an unfair labor practice for an employer:

1. to prevent the employee from exercising his rights under Section 7
2. to dominate or interfere with the administration or formation of a labor union (this clause, in effect, constituted the "death sentence" for the so-called company union)
3. to discriminate in hiring and firing against members of a trade union
4. to discriminate against persons giving testimony under the Act
5. to refuse to bargain collectively in good faith with a recognized trade union

To administer the provisions of the law a three-man National Labor Relations Board (the NLRB) was set up under the Act. The functions of this Board included: (1) to determine whether a union should represent a group of workers for collective bargaining purposes; (2) to prevent unfair labor practices; and (3) to investigate charges arising from the provisions of the Act.

The constitutionality of the Wagner Act was upheld in the landmark Supreme Court case, *NLRB* vs. *Jones and Laughlin Steel Co.*[6] Against the background of the Supreme Court's decisions in the Schecter Poultry case and other adverse rulings against the New Deal and Roosevelt's plan to enlarge the Court, this decision was a historic turning point in the relationship between the New Deal and the judiciary. The National Labor Relations Act had been attacked on three counts:

1. The law sought to regulate labor relations and not interstate commerce.
2. The production workers in the steel plant were not subject to federal control.
3. There was a violation of Section II, Article III of the Constitution (i.e., violations of law must be decided by the judiciary and not the NLRB) and of the Fifth and Seventh Amendments (due process and right to trial by jury, respectively).

[6] 301 U.S. 1 (1937).

In sustaining the NLRA, the Supreme Court held that since a civil suit was not involved, point three of the arguments above was irrelevant. In response to points one and two, the majority decision stated, "Instead of being beyond the pale [of the commerce clause], we think that it presents in a most striking way the close and intimate relation which a manufacturing industry may have to interstate commerce and we have no doubt that Congress had constitutional authority to safeguard the right of . . . employees to self-organization and freedom in the choice of representation for collective bargaining." The Court's view of interstate commerce in this case was at odds with its findings in the Schecter Poultry decision and with previous judicial interpretations of the Constitution as it applied to labor.[7] In retrospect, it is apparent that in the Jones and Laughlin case President Roosevelt won a major victory over the conservatives of the Supreme Court.

While the Wagner Act supported labor's right to form trade unions and the implementation of collective bargaining, it did not fully accomplish all the purposes that had been sought under the NRA. It made no provision for minimum wages, as had the codes of the defunct Blue Eagle; this lack was remedied in 1938 with the passage of the Fair Labor Standards Act.

The early efforts to control wages and hours of work in the area of government contracting had been only moderately successful. The Davis-Bacon Act of 1932 and the Walsh-Healey Public Contracts Act of 1937 had defined a work week and required that prevailing rates of pay for industry should be observed by industrialists with government contracts in excess of stipulated amounts. These acts were not very significant in their effects until World War II vastly expanded the volume of government contracts. The FLSA went beyond these acts in that it covered everyone in interstate commerce who did not belong to one of the following classes: (1) management; (2) retailing or outside sales; (3) seamen; (4) workers covered by the Railway Labor Act; (5) fishing; (6) agriculture; and (7) child acting.

The fundamental provisions of this Act have to do with the establishment of a minimum wage and the definition of a maximum work week for interstate commerce. The passage of the FLSA was intended to raise the legal minimum wage to forty cents per hour by October, 1945 and to discourage employment beyond forty hours per week by October, 1940. If a worker was required to labor in excess of the maximum work week, it was to be at a penalty rate. The Act also provided for constraints on the use of child labor. Any employee under 16 or between 16 and 18 years of age who, in the opinion of the Chief

---

[7] In the Schecter case, a unanimous Court declared in Chief Justice Hughes' words, "It is plain that these requirements of the NRA code for the poultry industry are imposed in order to govern the details of defendants' management of their local business. . . . Stress is laid upon the great importance of maintaining wage distributions which would provide the necessary stimulus in starting 'the cumulative forces making for expanding commercial activity.' Without in any way disparaging this motive, it is enough to say that the recuperative efforts of the federal government must be made in a manner consistent with the authority granted by the Constitution." Schecter Poultry Corp. vs. U.S., 295 U.S. 495, 550 (1935).

of the Children's Bureau of the Department of Labor, was employed in a hazardous occupation made the goods produced illegal for shipment in interstate commerce. Violations of the Act were to be punished by civil and criminal penalties.

The constitutionality of this Act was upheld in the case of *U.S.* vs. *F. W. Darby Lumber Co.*[8] Again, the Supreme Court overturned a precedent established in the case of *Hammer* vs. *Dagenhart,* which had contained similar child labor provisions. This decision marked another step in the acceptance of the social philosophy of the New Deal by the Supreme Court.

The labor laws in effect at the time of the inauguration of the New Deal and particularly those enacted under its aegis created a social environment that was very conducive to trade union organization and the process of collective bargaining. Previous laws had been hopefully termed labor's Magna Carta, but these statutes truly deserved that characterization.

THE RENAISSANCE OF ORGANIZED LABOR

With the passage of the National Industrial Recovery Act in 1933, many in the trade union movement saw the great potentiality of increasing union membership in this country. During the devastating, deflationary years of 1930–32, the unions had been gravely weakened and reduced in size. Under NRA organized labor was now given the right to organize without interference from management, and some of the old, established unions, such as the United Mine Workers, the International Ladies Garment Workers, and the Amalgamated Clothing Workers, were quick to take advantage of the opportunity. However, labor's top organization, the American Federation of Labor, was slow to move in organizing workers, particularly in the powerful, traditionally anti-union, mass production industries. Only after much prodding were union organizers sent into the rubber, automobile, and steel industries. Union leaders such as John L. Lewis of the United Mine Workers were quick to criticize the dominant leadership of the A.F. of L. for not organizing the mass production industries on an industrial rather than a craft union basis.

The conflict with the A.F. of L. over the question of union structure grew to major proportions. The conservative leaders of the Federation were oriented to the skilled, craft unions and were fearful of the effect, on their power and leadership, of enrolling huge numbers of unskilled workers in their organization. The leadership of President William Green was challenged by John L. Lewis at the 1935 A.F. of L. convention. Lewis championed the cause of the industrial unions and demanded charters for these organizations. But the craft unionists, in control of the proceedings, voted down his proposals. Even before the convention had ended, a Committee for Industrial Organization was formed to organize the unaffiliated workers. Lewis, Philip Murray, David

[8] 312 U.S. 100 (1941).

Dubinsky, Sidney Hillman, and others led the United Mine Workers, the International Ladies Garment Workers, Amalgamated Clothing Workers, Typographical Workers, and the Amalgamated Association of Iron and Steel Workers into the new organization. The newly formed body offered the A.F. of L. $500,000 to organize the non-union workers into the Federation. However, the Executive Council of that organization turned down the offer and ordered the CIO to disband or face suspension for promoting dual unionism. The CIO group boycotted the 1936 convention and was expelled by a two-thirds' vote of the delegates present. The "House of Labor" was grievously split at a time of great challenge and opportunity.

Determined to go it alone, the CIO began intensive efforts to organize the steel industry. Steel's management struck back with an entire array of anti-union activities: spying, lay-offs for union men, repression of free speech, mass advertising condemning unionism, and violence. Philip Murray led the union fight, using the tactics developed in past struggles for union recognition, the strike, picketing, boycotts, advertising, and politics. In 1936 the Republicans had nominated Alfred M. Landon for the Presidency. Landon, an independent oil producer of Topeka, Kansas, had been elected governor of that state in 1932, the only elected Republican governor west of the Mississippi, in that year. The CIO aligned itself fully with Roosevelt and the Democratic Party. It provided money, men, and organization to win re-election for the President. The triumph of the Democrats brought new prestige and numbers of new members to the CIO, and in 1937, United States Steel recognized the Steel Workers' Organizing Committee (SWOC) as exclusive collective bargaining agent for the workers. This has been called "perhaps the most important contract in American labor history" because it signified the surrender of a corporation that had taken the lead in the effort to block unionization of the nation's basic industries. Some of the smaller steel companies, collectively known as Little Steel, refused recognition and employed the most vicious anti-union methods in repelling the union, until they were forced by the action of the NLRB to recognize and bargain in good faith with the SWOC in 1941.

A new ally of the CIO in 1937 was the American Communist Party. John L. Lewis had opposed the Communists in the union movement during the 1920's. Now, in order to meet the new organizing commitments of the union he was willing to accommodate himself to his oldtime enemies. The Communist Party members were excellent organizers and membership in the union soared. In the meantime, the radicals used their positions within the unions to create a power base for the Communist Party. Later a split over the inclusion of Communists in union positions appeared within the CIO. David Dubinsky, President of the ILGWU, took his union back into the A.F. of L., charging that Lewis and the Communists were the cause of labor disunity.

In spite of the divisions within the CIO, its organizational drives were extremely successful. In the rubber industry, United States Rubber, Firestone, and Goodrich signed contracts with the union in the late 1930's. The International Union of Mine, Mill and Smelter Workers, the old Western Federation of Miners, also joined the CIO. A new seamen's union called the National Maritime Union was formed. In the automobile industry, under the energetic leadership of the Reuther brothers, the United Automobile Workers organized Chrysler and General Motors employees. By 1937 and 1938 the membership of the CIO had surpassed that of the A.F. of L.

John L. Lewis found himself in 1936 embroiled in another controversy with President Roosevelt. In that year the CIO struck the steel industry, and President Roosevelt failed to support the union in the Little Steel strike as strongly as labor had expected. In addition, Lewis, who was a confirmed isolationist, differed completely with Roosevelt's foreign policy. Encouraged by the Communists, he decided to oppose Roosevelt's third term bid for the Presidency. The Communists at this time also withheld their support from the President because of the Soviet-Nazi Pact and, in fact, promoted strikes to interfere with defense work. Lewis announced his support of the Republican Presidential candidate, Wendell L. Wilkie, and offered to resign from the presidency of the CIO, if the Republicans lost the election. Following the Roosevelt victory at the polls, Lewis duly resigned at the CIO convention and was replaced by Philip Murray. Nevertheless, Lewis continued to dominate that organization until late in 1941 because of Murray's illness and the support of the Communist Party. When the Nazis attacked Russia in June, 1941, Lewis found that his Red support suddenly disappeared; his influence in union politics declined, and in 1943 he took the United Mine Workers out of the CIO.

In these years, despite the internecine warfare within the ranks of labor, union membership grew at an unprecedented rate. Chart 1 shows the rate of growth in trade union membership from 1931 to 1945 and also presents the growth rate of the total civilian labor force for this period. Over these years union membership rose from 6.7 per cent to over 20 per cent of the labor force. The upward trend in the growth of the union movement was profoundly affected by the pro-labor legislation discussed above. Another cause of this growth was the vigorous competition between the A.F. of L. and the CIO. The A.F. of L. had been mainly on the defensive in the early thirties, but with the advent of the CIO and the establishment of the Congress of Industrial Organization as a permanent body in 1938 it found itself competing for members. This competition caused much of the union dues to be channelled into efforts to organize workers. Then, with the involvement of the United States in World War II, another major impetus was given to trade union organization.

In order to prevent industrial conflict during hostilities, the National War Labor Board was established. Management, the public, and union groups were given representation on the Board, with the union representatives evenly divided between the A.F. of L. and the CIO. Cooperation between these two rival federations was comparatively good during the war years and the NWLB achieved a very creditable record for peaceful settlement of industrial disputes. Under the Walsh-Healey Act and other administrative regulations,

CHART 1

*Union Membership in Relation to the Total Civilian Labor Force,
1931–1945*[a-b]

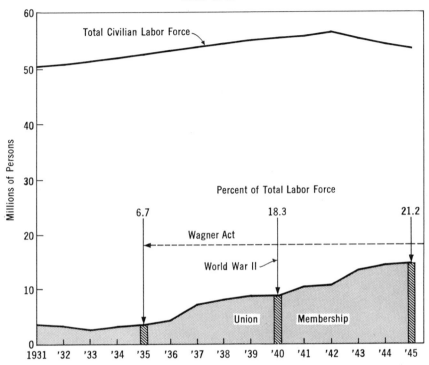

a Source: *Historical Statistics of the U.S., 1789–1945*, p. 72
b Source: *Economic Report of the President* (January, 1967), p. 236

unorganized workers were entitled to choose a collective bargaining agent in firms that had undertaken government contracts. With the nation at war, an ever larger number of producers were working under defense contracts, and they were forced to allow representation elections conducted by the NWLB when their employees requested this. In company after company the workers voted for union representation in collective bargaining. During the hostilities the unions had another advantage under the so-called "maintenance of membership" clause according to which employees who were already union members had to retain their membership for the duration of the contract; this provision, in effect, gave the unions protection against raids by employers or by rival unions. The growth of the unions was also aided in this period by a tight labor market and the expansion of industry.

By and large, the trade union movement was extremely patriotic during the war period. It promoted increased productivity, sold war bonds, encouraged women as workers, and in other ways aided the war effort. Nevertheless, a number of "quickie" strikes combined with a few large ones caused the public to become critical of the movement. Even within the ranks of labor discontent grew because of wartime regulations that prevented labor from gaining increased wages or other benefits. However, even if labor could have increased its wage package, rationing left relatively few consumer goods to buy. With the wages they received, very little expansion of consumption was possible, therefore most increased income went into personal savings of one kind or another.

The war also caused significant changes in the composition of the labor force. With most of the workers between 18 and 35 years of age being drafted into military service, there was a serious labor shortage. The scarcity of labor was overcome through an increased use of women and retired workers as well as by greater reliance on machines and other capital goods. Women showed themselves capable of performing many industrial tasks as well as men. Aged workers also demonstrated that they could produce comparatively well, even though beyond the age of normal retirement. Finally, management made a contribution. A greater degree of rationality was introduced into the productive process, and the efficiency of labor increased significantly.

On the whole, labor's experience from 1939 to 1945 was an economically rewarding one. Average weekly earnings in all manufacturing doubled, with part of the increase coming from overtime pay and part from increased hourly wages. In October, 1942 Congress had frozen wages. However, in succeeding years both wages and the number of strikes rose, despite a no-strike pledge by the unions. Industrial conflict in the coal, steel, aircraft, and other industries brought a rise in wages from sympathetic War Labor Boards and led an across-the-board increase of 15 per cent in 1942. Congress, faced with industrial unrest, passed the Smith-Connally War Labor Disputes Act in that year, giving the President the power to take over an enterprise when a strike threatened the war effort. While this power was used by the President forty times, the general record of labor was very good as demonstrated by the fact that the United States became the "arsenal of democracy" and still maintained civilian production at practically peacetime levels.

In the period 1930 to 1940, union membership increased about 150 per cent and in the latter year reached eight million. Union membership relative to the total labor force rose at almost the same rate, because the number of workers who could be organized was comparatively stable. In terms of potential membership, nearly 24 per cent of all workers who could be organized were in unions, and this share represented more than double the 1930 percentage. During the period of World War II, trade union membership nearly doubled again, rising from close to nine million to nearly fifteen million members. In terms of political advance, membership, and organizational gains, the period 1933–45 could be called labor's Golden Age. However, this remarkable expansion created a giant organization whose problems were in proportion to its newly won size. In 1945, these problems included such questions as the following: (1) How much power should organized labor take from industrial management? (2) Could labor function as a group so as to maintain power and at the same time exercise responsibility in a collective society? (3) Would the unions and their members be able to look beyond their immediate interests and recognize their place in a national community? (4) Could the house of labor be united, thus bringing an end to the internal war between the A.F. of L. and the CIO? (5) Would the trade unions survive the expected post-war economic recession? (6) Having gained an almost exclusive control over the labor supply in various industries, would such organizations recognize in a responsible and democratic way the rights of their members and the public? As World War II drew to a close, the relevance and importance of these questions were not perceived by all union leaders with equal clarity. The euphoria of a Golden Age was soon to be dispelled by the hard decisions of the period of economic adjustment to peace.

THE BUSINESS IDEOLOGY AND CHANGING ECONOMIC THEORY

In a developed economy such as that of the United States, the relationship between business and government is vital for economic growth, but frequently attitudes on the subject have been heavily influenced by ideology rather than by fact. This was never more true than in the controversial years of the New Deal. In the twenties, business, particularly big business, had enjoyed an unusual degree of public approval. Business power and prestige were at an all-time high; a business administration was in the White House, the country had attained a new plateau of prosperity, the stock market was booming, and faith in the self-regulating economy was strong. The Great Crash of 1929, the long, agonizing depression that followed, the revelations by the Senate Finance Committee (the Pecora investigation) of questionable and unethical practices by leading businessmen and bankers dealt a shattering blow to business morale and prestige. Furthermore, when the New Deal agencies began to regulate business in new and unfamiliar ways, the businessmen sensed a shift of power from Wall Street to Washington. And when the second phase of the New Deal began in early 1935, and business, with partial recovery from the depths of the depression, was regaining some of its confidence, the New Deal came under sharp attack from conservative quarters. The National Association of Manufacturers, the American Farm Bureau, and the Liberty League were embattled in the fight to protect the Constitution and American liberties from alleged infringement by the New Deal. Businessmen attacked the Roosevelt administration for its extravagance, the increase in the national debt, and its bureaucratic restrictions on freedom. By 1935, most of the nation's newspapers were on the side of the critics. In the 1936 election with Roosevelt denouncing some of his business opponents as "economic royalists," the atmosphere of business-government relations was that of a feud.

In defending the free enterprise system in these years and during World War II, some spokesmen for American capitalism relied on what has been called the classical ideology.[9] This creed pictures our economic system as unique, based on universal laws of human nature, inherently stable, and unless attacked from without, smooth functioning and socially beneficial. In analyzing the functioning of the economy, this ideology employed a selective and greatly diluted version of the neo-classical theory of perfectly competitive general equilibrium.

The two central elements of this classical explanation are freedom of consumer choice and the conception of the economy as being made up of "a multitude of independent private enterprises striving to meet consumer demands under the stimuli and pressures of profits and losses." According to this ideology, "Competition serves as a regulator and reducer of prices, as an incentive to improved production efficiency, as a guarantee that we shall get what we want, and as a protector of the freedom of opportunity."[10]

Twentieth century academic economics in the United States, prior to 1933, was dominated by the Marshallian (neo-classical) interpretation of the economy. In its analysis of price formation, this system employed two cases, pure competition (the general case) and pure monopoly (the special, rare case). Neo-classical economists admitted that there were frictions (imperfections) in the actual functioning of the economy; it did not completely operate according to the pure competitive model, but tended to do so. Marshallian economics, therefore, was reassuring to businessmen and tended to support the status quo. By the 1920's, however, economists were becoming increasingly uneasy about certain features of Marshallian equilibrium economics. In 1926, Piero Sraffa in a path-breaking article entitled "The Laws of Return under Competitive Conditions," pointed out certain basic flaws in that system.[11] He argued that competitive equilibrium was impossible if external economies governed the flow of product. Furthermore, he stated that the so-called "frictions" of Marshall's bipolar models were more than mere frictions—"they were active forces which produce permanent and even cumulative effects." In the real world, said Sraffa, prices were formed in markets that were intermediate between the two conventional categories of pure competition and pure monopoly. A flood of articles followed Sraffa's essay, and in 1933 two economists, Professors Edward H. Chamberlin and Joan Robinson of Cambridge, Massachusetts, and England, respectively, published book-length analyses that dealt with price behavior intermediate between the polar models of pure competition and pure monopoly.[12] Professor Robinson accomplished this in effect by making monopoly "swallow up" the analysis of competition. All prices were seen as reflecting monopolistic influences to some

[9] F. X. Sutton et al., *The American Business Creed* (Cambridge: Harvard University Press, 1956), pp. 33ff.

[10] Sutton, *The American Business Creed*, p. 164.

[11] *Economic Journal* (December, 1926), pp. 535–550.

[12] E. H. Chamberlin, *The Theory of Monopolistic Competition* (Cambridge: Harvard University Press, 1933); J. Robinson, *The Economics of Imperfect Competition* (New York: The Macmillan Co., 1933).

extent. Professor Chamberlin achieved the same result by viewing most markets as involving a blend of competition and monopoly.

Chamberlin recognized that intense rivalry among sellers would result in efforts to distinguish one product from another by advertising, brand names, patents, and other ways of winning customer loyalty. This "product differentiation" would destroy direct price competition because the competing goods would no longer be homogeneous. Each seller would have, in effect, a monopoly of his own product. The competition among these monopolized products was termed "monopolistic competition" by Chamberlin.

Monopolistic competition would make it possible for such sellers to restrict production to the point at which they would make the maximum profit. When patents, trade marks, brand names, and exclusive designs are employed in business there cannot be, strictly speaking, freedom of entry. Alternative items will only be more or less satisfactory substitutes. The less satisfactory they are, the larger the profit the owner of the partial monopoly may obtain. So, in contrast to the absence of pure profits under conditions of pure competition, there will be monopoly profits scattered throughout the price system, depending on the "gap in the chain of substitutes" for the differentiated products. Professor Chamberlin went on to conclude that "the price is inevitably higher and the scale of production inevitably smaller under monopolistic competition than under pure competition."

Chamberlin and Robinson in their analyses gave a new prominence to the condition of oligopoly (fewness of sellers), a market structure that had become more important because of the merger movements of the past. In analyzing oligopoly, Chamberlin stressed that the results might be little different from those of a pure monopoly. If the oligopolists in setting prices recognized their mutual interdependence, the outcome would be the monopoly one. Further, if an oligopolistic industry practiced price leadership, and the followers accepted the price policy of the leader religiously, the result would be the same as if they were a monopolistic group acting in unison. These striking conclusions were based on a static analysis in which certain factors such as the product, the productive technique, and the scope of the market were taken as given. Theoretical results followed only under the posited conditions. Where oligopolistic sellers, for example, do not take account of their mutual interdependence, where they are uncertain about their rivals' reactions, etc., the outcome, Chamberlin indicated, might be very different.

As compared to the Keynesian impact on economic thought, the new theories of Chamberlin and Robinson were more of a minor revolution, but they won academic acceptance in the United States especially in a remarkably short time. One economist has written of this as follows: "for the historian of economic thought, the most revolutionary feature of the monopolistic competition theories will probably be the unprecedented pace at which they conquered their audience."[13]

[13] R. Triffin, *Monopolistic Competition and General Equilibrium Theory* (Cambridge: Harvard University Press, 1940), p. 17.

The new theories were revolutionary in another sense also; they were a major blow to complacency concerning the outcome of a *laissez faire* philosophy in a highly organized, industrial world. As we have seen, they suggested that where sellers are few and advertising is used to create "brand monopolies," prices will be high relative to what they would be under pure competition, and production will be more restricted. Furthermore, much waste in the form of excess plant capacity and useless advertising may be encouraged. The business world was now seen in a very different light from that which existed when Marshallian economics prevailed—"from a system where nearly everything worked out for the best, economists now found themselves with a system where nearly everything seemed to work out for the worst."[14] The economists who accepted these theories, instead of being staunch allies of the businessman, now often became his severest critic and advocates, as likely as not, of some form of government regulation.

Another economic study appeared in 1932 that had a notable effect on the thinking of economists about big business and the competitive system. This was the influential work by A. A. Berle, Jr., and G. C. Means, *The Modern Corporation and Private Property*.[15] These authors showed how the modern quasi-public corporation was splitting the atom of private property into a passive ownership by the stockholders and an active control by management. They dramatically demonstrated the dominance and swift growth of the nation's two hundred largest non-financial corporations. As of January 1, 1930, they stated that these 200 non-financial corporations controlled 49.2 per cent of all non-banking corporate wealth and roughly 38 per cent of all the business wealth in the country. They estimated that if the 1909–29 rates of growth of these giant corporations were sustained, by 1950 they would control 70 per cent of all corporate activity.[16]

Berle and Means threw doubt upon the relevance of the traditional legal concept of private property and the economists' basic assumption of profit maximization, but they did not offer a detailed analysis of the functioning of modern corporate enterprise. They considered the emerging concept of corporate trusteeship and emphasized the overriding interest of the community. "Neither the claims of ownership nor those of control can stand against the paramount interests of the community. The present claims of both contending parties now in the field have been weakened by the development described in this book. It remains only for the claims of the community to be put forward with clarity and force."[17] In a later government memorandum, G. C. Means advanced the concept of administered pricing by large corporations and

---

[14] J. K. Galbraith, *American Capitalism* (Boston: Houghton Mifflin Co., 1952), p. 51.

[15] (New York: The Macmillan Co., 1932.)

[16] This prediction was not borne out, according to the studies of M. A. Adelman. In 1951, he found indications of an actual fall in the degree of industrial concentration since 1933. See his article, "The Measurement of Industrial Concentration, *The Review of Economics and Statistics* (November, 1951), pp. 269–296.

[17] *The Modern Corporation and Private Property*, p. 356.

argued that relatively rigid industrial prices alongside flexible agricultural prices had a major responsibility for the severity of the "Great Depression."[18] This thesis set off a long controversy about the functioning of the price system under modern industrial conditions.

The Chamberlin-Robinson revision of price theory, we have said, was quickly incorporated into the body of economic doctrine, though not without strong dissent. One of the earliest works to show this influence was A. R. Burns' *The Decline of Competition*, published in 1936. He surveyed current industrial practices from the standpoint of the new theoretical dispensation and concluded that capitalism in the United States had failed to preserve its competitive character; the only recourse was to move toward a more planned, regulated type of economy. This pessimistic view of the future of competitive capitalism was further strengthened by the exhaustive investigation of the concentration of economic power in the United States by the Temporary National Economic Committee, which Congress established in June, 1938. This Committee was formed after a decade of growing hostility to big business. Its formation reflected a suspicion that economic concentration was responsible, in part at least, for the depression. ". . . Following the works of Chamberlin, Robinson, Berle and Means, and Burns, current economic opinion was also predominantly hostile to the monopolistic influences it regarded as pervading the structure of industry. . . ."[19] The TNEC heard over 500 witnesses, compiled a record of 20,000 pages and 3,300 technical exhibits, and sponsored 43 monographs. Though the latter contained much valuable analysis, mainly of a nature critical of big business, so far as the Committee's effort as a whole was concerned, it was pretty much a case of the mountain laboring. . . . The Chamberlin-Robinson price theories were aired, but many of the indictments of big business were weak and poorly substantiated by the voluminous statistical material that was presented to the Committee.[20]

The criticisms of big business that derived from the static analysis of the Chamberlin-Robinson school of thought did not impress Joseph Schumpeter, who had assumed a professorial chair at Harvard. He believed that these theoretical conceptions took too narrow and short-sighted a view of the economic process.[21] In a dynamic analysis, he held that the important factor was innovation over time, and he argued that large-scale free enterprise capitalism had provided an excellent environment for innovation and economic progress. The competition that counts, wrote Schumpeter, is "competition from the new commodity, the new technology, the new source of supply, the new

[18] *Industrial Prices and Their Relative Inflexibility*, Senate Document 13, 74th Cong., 1st Sess., 1935.

[19] W. L. Baldwin, *Antitrust and the Changing Corporation* (Durham, N.C.: Duke University Press, 1961), p. 102; see also D. Lynch, *The Concentration of Economic Power* (New York: Columbia University Press, 1946).

[20] Baldwin, *Antitrust and the Changing Corporation*, p. 110.

[21] Schumpeter's criticisms of this theory will be found in his *Business Cycles* (New York: McGraw-Hill Book Co., 1939), p. 65 and in *Capitalism, Socialism and Democracy* (New York: Harper and Bros., 1942), Chaps. 7 and 8.

type of organization (the largest-scale unit of control for instance)." While he admired the new theories as important contributions to economics, he believed that the results of monopolistic competition would not be so detrimental in the long run because the long run demand curves facing large firms were probably highly elastic. In his opinion, temporary restraints on prices often served to provide insurance against risk and thus induced the businessman to undertake innovations. Some of these same criticisms and doubts about the theory of monopolistic competition were expressed by institutional economists, most notably J. M. Clark and others and somewhat later by J. K. Galbraith.[22] While, therefore, complete consensus did not prevail among economists in these years about the validity of the new theories, they did contribute to weakening the old faith in a *laissez faire* approach to the relationship of government to business.

---

[22] J. M. Clark, "Toward a Concept of Workable Competition," *American Economic Review* (June, 1940), pp. 241–256; J. K. Galbraith, *American Capitalism*.

Part 10

PLANNING FOR ECONOMIC GROWTH AND SOCIAL WELFARE: THE UNITED STATES SINCE 1945

INTRODUCTION: REQUIREMENTS FOR STABLE
AND QUALITATIVE ECONOMIC GROWTH

In our summary of Keynesian economic theory (see Introduction in Part 9), we have seen that the emphasis of the great British economist, in analyzing investment, was on its effects on aggregate demand. This was natural because Keynes' main interest in the depression years was the problem of full employment in the short run; in analyzing that problem he abstracted from reality and ignored the capacity-creating effects of new investment. But in treating the subject of economic growth we cannot neglect this latter aspect for the reason that present investment competes with past and future investment. If new capital is created, but is not utilized sufficiently, will it not discourage future investment and thus cause a further fall in the marginal efficiency of capital? Two economists, one an American, Evsey Domar, and the other a British disciple of Keynes, Roy Harrod, addressed themselves to this question.[1] Though their answers to the questions posed were similar in many important respects, they were not identical.

Domar's response to the question was the conception of the possibility that tomorrow's aggregate demand would not be sufficiently great to absorb the output of the newly created capacity. Although the conditions under which this would occur are extremely rigid and may not be totally realistic, his formulation should be considered. If the symbol σ is used to represent the increment to capacity divided by the increment to capital stock and the marginal propensity to consume (β) is constant, then it is necessary for investment to grow at a constant percentage rate $\beta\sigma$ in order to utilize fully all capacity. This condition is called the equilibrium growth path, or "turnpike" of the economic system. (The economic system we are discussing is represented in the series of equations developed by Keynes and his followers, which provide simple theoretical models of capitalist society.) However, Domar did not state how this condition could be achieved, or explain why the economy did not automatically adjust itself to this condition.

Sir Roy Harrod sought to develop the theory even further. He tried to establish a framework within which the effect of uninterrupted growth could be projected. In doing this, Harrod distinguished between three kinds of growth: the actual rate of growth (G), the warranted rate of growth (G_w), and the natural rate of growth (G_n).

The fundamental identity in the Harrod-Domar growth model is that $G = \dfrac{s}{c}$

In this equation, s represents the average propensity to save, or in other

---

[1] E. Domar, "Expansion and Employment," *American Economic Review* (March, 1947), pp. 34–35 reproduced in his *Essays in the Theory of Economic Growth* (Oxford: Oxford University Press, 1957) and R. Harrod, *Towards a Dynamic Economics* (London: Macmillan and Co., Ltd., 1948).

terms, the ratio of net savings to aggregate income; c is the capital-output ratio. This equation implies that the actual rate of investment must be equal to the actual rate of savings. The warranted rate of growth stands for the rate of growth that is needed for economic advance. In order to sustain an economic advance in steady equilibrium a required amount of capital is needed, called C_r. The conditions for stable economic growth are then given as $G_w C_r = C \cdot c$. It can also be said that in order to achieve a steady rate of growth it is necessary for planned savings to equal planned investment. If G exceeds G_w, this means that the rate of current spending is greater than that needed to call forth the current rate of investment, and investment will increase. Planned investment will exceed planned savings and cause a series of exploding business cycles in the economy.

The natural rate of growth, as the phrase is used by Harrod, can be defined as the potential rate of growth, given full employment, population increase, and technological progress. If the actual rate of growth exceeds the natural rate, a dampened series of business cycles will be set in motion. On the basis of his analysis, Harrod describes the nature of some phases of the business cycle as follows:

1. When the actual rate of growth exceeds the natural rate, this is a recovery or expansionary phase.
2. When the actual rate of growth is equal to the natural rate, this is defined as full employment at maximum economic growth.
3. When the warranted rate of growth exceeds the actual rate, this is defined as a slump or contraction.

In the Harrod-Domar model, the movements of economic phenomena tend to be cumulative, and the differences between the actual and equilibrium rates will lead to severe departures from the path of economic equilibrium. The Harrod-Domar model is more pessimistic in its implications than Keynesian economics about the future growth prospects of mature capitalist economies. It demonstrates that a high investment level is not enough to avoid economic stagnation. To achieve full employment and steady growth in such economies, it argues, the absolute level of investment must become larger and larger in each succeeding period. The situation is like that depicted by the Red Queen in *Through the Looking-Glass*, to stay in the same place you have to run faster and faster.

Many economists have pointed out that without a creative government fiscal policy to insure that the Domar-Harrod condition (i.e., with respect to the output-capital ratio and the marginal propensity to consume) is satisfied, the economy will enter a period of increasing underemployment with each cycle departing further and further from the equilibrium rate of growth. Economists have suggested three policies the government might adopt to avert such semi-stagnation. It can increase public investment to offset the secular deficiency in private investment; it can increase the multiplier by reducing taxes; and/or it can redistribute income from savers to spenders, thus reducing the marginal propensity to save.

The phrase "qualitative economic growth" in the title to this Introduction refers to the question as to the uses to which our wealth, or better, our productive capacity, should be put. As the GNP rose to higher levels in post-World War II America, this issue of the proper allocation of our productive resources between the private and public sectors of the economy became more insistent. Symptomatic of this growing concern were the replies submitted to a 1957 symposium held by the Committee for Economic Development on the question, "What is the most important economic problem to be faced by the United States in the next twenty years?"[2] Of the 48 papers submitted by a dazzling array of internationally known economists, historians, and statesmen, no fewer than six singled out this aspect of the nation's economic life as the most important economic problem of the next generation. In the pithy formulation of sociologist David Riesman, one of the six who stressed this problem, the question was "abundance for what?"[3]

But it was Harvard University's J. Kenneth Galbraith who riveted the attention of the nation on this subject in 1958 with his best-selling work entitled *The Affluent Society*.[4] In this essay, Galbraith noted at the outset that the experience of nations with well-being has been exceedingly brief. But, in the last few generations in parts of western Europe and especially in the United States there has been "great and unprecedented affluence." This state of affluence, he argues, tends to be interpreted with ideas that originated in the prior age of scarcity. These ideas have a most tenacious hold on the minds of men; they constitute the "conventional wisdom," despite their dated and even obsolete character. "The shortcomings of economics," he informs his reader, "are not original error but uncorrected obsolescence."[5]

Galbraith then undertakes what is practically a sociological analysis of knowledge, a diagnosis of the origins and basis of the conventional wisdom in the United States. He analyzes some of the principal values of mid-twentieth century American society and shows how attitudes have changed toward social inequality, economic security, and production of private goods. The latter, he contends, has assumed a paramount position in our value system because it eases the problem of inequality and promotes a sense of economic security. "Production has [thus] become the center of a concern that had hitherto been shared with equality and security. . . ." This has resulted in a disturbance of the social balance between the supply of private and public goods. This social balance is loosely defined as "a satisfactory relationship between the supply of privately produced goods and services and those of the state, . . ."[6] The failure of public services to keep pace with the production of private goods

[2] Committee for Economic Development, *Problems of United States Economic Development*, Vols. I and II (New York, 1958).

[3] The other participants in the symposium who stressed this aspect of the matter were Moses Abramovitz, J. K. Galbraith, Roy F. Harrod, Ralph Hawtrey, and Sumner Slichter. Many of the other contributors showed concern with this question in their essays, but did not single it out as of paramount interest.

[4] (Boston: Houghton Mifflin Co., 1958).

[5] *The Affluent Society*, p. 4.

[6] *The Affluent Society*, p. 255.

has created "an atmosphere of private opulence and public squalor." In a particularly vivid passage, Galbraith describes what this may involve:

> . . . The family which takes its mauve and cerise, air-conditioned, power-steered, and power-braked automobile out for a tour passes through cities that are badly paved, made hideous by litter, blighted buildings, billboards, and posts for wires that should long since have been put underground. They pass into a countryside that has been rendered largely invisible by commercial art. . . . They picnic on exquisitely packaged food from a portable icebox by a polluted stream and go on to spend the night at a park which is a menace to public health and morals. Just before dozing off on an air mattress, beneath a nylon tent, amid the stench of the decaying refuse, they may reflect vaguely on the curious unevenness of their blessings. . . .[7]

In a further analysis of this curious state of social imbalance, Galbraith argues that consumer sovereignty is no longer an adequate doctrine or explanation of the role of the buyer in the functioning of mature capitalism in

John Kenneth Galbraith was born in Canada in 1908. He was educated at the Universities of Toronto, California, and Cambridge. Since 1949 he has been Paul M. Warburg Professor of Economics at Harvard. In a varied career, he has been Deputy Administrator of the O.P.A., a member of the editorial board of Fortune magazine, and Ambassador to India (1961–63).

Used by permission of J. K. Galbraith.

the United States. The wants of the individual consumer are no longer a matter of his autonomous decision, but are dependent on production capacity and are synthesized by modern advertising. This "dependence effect" stimulates consumption because of "the vested interest in output of the important business executive." This cause for social imbalance is abetted by the powerful force of social emulation, which keeps the typical American busy buying private goods to keep up with the ubiquitous Joneses. A third factor enhancing the emphasis on the production of private goods is the truce that has been reached on correcting inequality; rather than opening up this troublesome question of distribution, Americans are pictured as regarding production as a great solvent of the tensions associated with inequality. In short, the argument

[7] *The Affluent Society*, p. 253.

is that a nation that produces a bigger and bigger "production pie," has less reason to squabble over the precise equity with which the slices are cut. Fourthly, Galbraith holds that inflation has caused a deterioration in the quantity and quality of public services because the compensation of public servants has failed to keep pace with the rising cost of living. Lastly, there is the illusion that our national security depends upon the aggregate output of the economy, whereas Galbraith believes that we have probably fought the last of what may be called "gross national product wars." In a thermonuclear war, it is argued, we would not have the time to mobilize and deploy our total economic resources as we did in the two world wars. But here, as in other matters, "attitudes on the relation of production to military power are rooted in the past, hence, the fetishism about production."

In the latter part of The Affluent Society, Galbraith deals briefly with poverty, noting that it can no longer be "presented as a universal or massive affliction," but that it does still survive. The case and "insular" poverty he describes cannot be efficiently remedied by a general advance in income. What is needed rather is more investment in the education of the children of the poor; in short, more investment in human beings. Thus, to Galbraith in this book the elimination of poverty requires to a substantial degree the same steps needed to attain social balance.

Nine years after the publication of his first best seller, Galbraith published another volume that returned to the theme developed in the earlier work.[8] As he stated in the Foreword, "It stands in relation to that book as a house to a window. This is the structure; the earlier book allowed the first glimpse inside. . . ." Actually, in terms of the sociological distinction between the concepts of culture and society, The Affluent Society deals mainly with the culture of an affluent society, whereas The New Industrial State focuses more on the changes in social structure (in the broadest sense of that technical term) growing out of the revolution produced by the maturation of the large corporation in American society. It is a study of institutional dominance, written not by a professional sociologist, but displaying, nevertheless, keen insight into the interrelationships of forces and events in the larger context of social change. This second book hardly provides us with a theory of economic growth in the conventional meaning of that phrase, but it does offer a provocative theory of institutional or social change, especially with reference to the hyper-dynamic society of the United States in the twentieth century.

In this work, which resembles so much the main thrust of Veblen's analysis in some of his earlier books, Galbraith concerns himself mainly with the heartland of the modern economy, with that part of the economy characterized by large corporations.[9] "To understand it," he says, "is to understand that

---

[8] The New Industrial State (Boston: Houghton Mifflin Co., 1967).

[9] Galbraith's treatment of the imperatives of technology, the need for industrial planning, the effects of the industrial system on the policies of the state and the educational establishment are very reminiscent of Veblen's principal contentions. On the growth of what Galbraith calls the technostructure, see J. Gould, The Technical Elite (New York: A. M. Kelley, 1966), passim. On the possible future of the industrial system, Galbraith is

part [of the economy] which is most subject to change and which, accordingly, is most changing our lives. . . ."[10]

Galbraith's vision of the evolution of the industrial system gives a central place to technological and organizational factors in this change. In the transformation of the American economy in the last sixty years, the mature, quasi-public corporation has superseded the entrepreneurial corporation. The large corporation has grown in importance because of the imperatives of technology. Modern technology has tended to lengthen the time span between the beginning and completion of any task, thereby increasing risk and necessitating planning to cope with it. There is a need for much larger sums of capital; the requirement of specialized manpower is constantly growing. And the use of such specialists inevitably means more complex organization. All these factors dictate the necessity of planning. ". . . The size of General Motors," says Galbraith, "is in the service not of monopoly or the economies of scale but of planning. . . ."[11]

The numerous specialists who collect, digest, and aid in the collective decision-making process constitute the "technostructure." It is this organization, Galbraith insists, not the managers, who decide. The effective power of decision in the modern, mature corporation is lodged deeply in the technical, planning staff of specialists. Group decision-making has replaced the classic entrepreneur, Schumpeter's hero.

Corporate planning has as its objectives control of the major unreliabilities of the market (largely accomplished through integration, horizontal, vertical, or conglomerate), control of an assured capital supply, and management of the specific demand and prices of the commodities being sold. With regard to the last, it is to be noted that Galbraith vigorously contends that the corporate oligopolies of the industrial system "manage" demand by the persuasion of advertising and general sales strategy. They do not need to be wholly successful in this; substantial stabilization of the demand for their products is sufficient to facilitate production planning.

The technostructures in their corporate planning need the cooperation of the state. This cooperation takes the following forms: (1) the maintenance of a high level of aggregate demand through fiscal and monetary policy as well as through the measures of a welfare state (social security, unemployment insurance, etc.); (2) the provision of a suitably educated labor force and of replacements for the personnel of the technostructure; (3) the support of technological research and development.

The state, in this view, then tends to provide those needs required by the industrial system, but "the services of the state that are not directly related to

---

more optimistic, shall we say, than the literal technological determinism of Veblen. He seems to hold to a more existentialist interpretation of the movement of events which allows a role for human choice.

[10] *The New Industrial State*, p. 9.
[11] *The New Industrial State*, p. 76.

the needs of the industrial system are much less favored."[12] Such services, most of which fall in the public sector, suffer from a "negative discrimination" as compared with the private goods that the mature corporations have to sell. Furthermore, aesthetic experience and achievement are neglected by the industrial system because they are beyond its reach; the technostructure cannot identify with them. Thus, with a reference to his previous treatment of the subject in *The Affluent Society*, Galbraith explains the "organic tendency to create a natural imbalance between the goods produced and the services supplied by the industrial system and those which are supplied by the state."[13]

This state of social imbalance is further aggravated in the Galbraithian view by the lopsided use of planning. In the private sector of the industrial system extensive use is made of competent planning in the sale of private goods, but in certain areas reliance is still placed on the market. Examples cited are urban and interurban surface transportation and housing; here there are "planning lacunae" and the result is a "nasty mess."

In broad sociological perspective Galbraith sees the state, the university, and the labor union adapting and accommodating themselves as institutions to the needs of the industrial system. "In notable respects," he writes, "the mature corporation is an arm of the state. And the state, in important matters, is an instrument of the industrial system. . . ."[14] Higher education has most extensively and expensively accommodated to the needs of the industrial system, but that "does not necessarily create a primary obligation to the needs" of that system. The educational and scientific estate, Galbraith believes, because of its rapidly increasing numbers and its almost unique role in scientific and social innovation, has the potentiality to become "a decisive instrument of political power" in the evolving industrial state. The labor movement, on the other hand, is seen as faced with the possibility of permanent decline. The overall effect of the rise of the industrial system tends greatly to reduce the union as a social force. The industrial system has largely encompassed the labor movement, dissolved some of its most important functions, narrowed its areas of action, and bent its residual operations largely to its own needs.

The industrial system produces a plethora of private goods and the atmosphere of private opulence for the great mass, but it excludes the unqualified and the unfortunate from its beneficence. It "delivers the goods" to meet man's physical needs, but is it consistent with his liberty? And as the industrial system evolves into "a penumbra of the state" and grows in its powers of persuasion and manipulation, the question of liberty becomes an insistent one. If the goals of the industrial system become coordinate with life, then other dimensions of man's existence that are not compatible with the system are in danger of being neglected and lost. Still, the industrial system in bringing into existence the educational and scientific estate may, in Gal-

[12] *The New Industrial State*, p. 345.
[13] *The New Industrial State*, p. 346.
[14] *The New Industrial State*, p. 296.

braith's mind, have created a community that will reject "its monopoly of social purpose." What the outcome for the nation will be, only the future will reveal. In any case, the relevance of Galbraith's themes to the question of qualitative economic growth is very clear.

In this Part we shall consider the Domar-Harrod theories of economic growth in Chapter 30 and examine Galbraith's main theses in connection with the social and political changes of the period in the last chapter.

Chapter 29

THE CHALLENGE OF ECONOMIC AFFLUENCE

In our economic affairs, as in every other aspect of our lives, ceaseless change is the one constant.

President Lyndon B. Johnson in the 1965
Economic Report of the President

A QUARTER CENTURY OF REVOLUTIONARY CHANGE

As the United States moved into the second half of the twentieth century after World War II, the tempo of change both at home and abroad accelerated. The cumulative growth of technology, so much emphasized by Veblen, catapulted the nation and the world into the awesome age of nuclear power, electronics, and space flight. In international affairs, the end of the war saw the breakup of the Grand Alliance and the beginning of the cold war between the United States and Soviet Russia. The war contributed too to the collapse of colonialism and the emergence of sixty new nations in Asia and Africa. In 1949 the Chinese Communists came to power, and the following year the United States was at war again in Korea. That "police action" was no sooner ended than our tortured involvement in Vietnam began. These cataclysmic changes in the fields of technology and foreign affairs placed enormous pressures on Americans to adapt to the new realities. It is little wonder that this period was spoken of as an "age of anxiety" as well as of change.

The almost exponential acceleration of change in these years was reflected in the increasing speed at which man could travel. In 1945, our fastest airplanes flew up to 470 miles per hour. By 1955, we had passed the 1,500 mph mark, and in the next ten years we raised it to 18,000 mph. In space flight, supersonic speeds were far exceeded.

Another measure of man's "progress" toward possible self-destruction was the acceleration in his ability to create explosive power. In 1945 our airplanes could deliver 6,000 tons of TNT, and an atom bomb was exploded with the power equivalent to 20,000 tons of TNT. Seven short years later we exploded 4 million tons of TNT power and doubled it in 1954 to 8 million tons through the detonation of the hydrogen bomb. (Ironically, the power of the A bomb that ended World War II was used just as the trigger for the H bomb.) By 1961 Russia had exploded a 58 million ton bomb, and today both nations have the capability of delivering 100 million tons of explosive power anywhere in the world or beyond in a single missile. The nation and the world now existed under a precarious "balance of terror" and in an age of "overkill."

The industrial arts underwent spectacular changes in these years. One of the most amazing of these was the development of the digital computer and the whole field of cybernetics it made possible. Here again, the pace of technological change was reflected in the mounting speed of computation. In 1945 we started talking about milliseconds (1/1,000th of a second). During the fifties electronic devices accelerated the process of addition to microseconds (or one-millionth of a second). Then in 1961 a new word had to be coined to keep up with progress, namely, the nanosecond, or one billionth of a second. In 1964, still another neologism was necessary—the picosecond, or one-trillionth of a second. The advance in computers led to their rapid adoption. In the early 1950's it was thought that the nation would need no more than fifteen large computers for a generation or longer. Yet by 1966 nearly 27,000 computers were in operation, and it was estimated that by 1970 45,000 would be in use.[1]

Back of these and other technological innovations we shall discuss was a "knowledge explosion" of stupendous proportions. This manifested itself in a prodigious branching out and further specialization of the established fields of science and also in a new "intellectual technology" such as game theory, decision theory, simulation, linear programming, and operations research. Stimulating as well as reflecting these changes was the whole new emphasis on research and development. While the gross dollar figures require correction for changes in the value of money, they are nonetheless impressive: in 1940, $377 million was spent by government, business, and the universities on research and development; by 1960 the total had risen to $14 billion, and by 1964 the sum was well over $18 billion. The number of persons engaged in R and D also zoomed; in 1940 there were 37,000 so employed, and by 1960 their number had risen to 387,000, a growth rate of more than 10 per cent a year. In the fifties, professional and technical employees were the fastest growing occupational group in the United States. This trend provides the basis for what Galbraith terms the "educational and scientific estate."[2]

The remarkable expansion of research and development in the post-war years owed much to the continuing crisis in international affairs, the consequent increase in defense expenditures, and the rivalry of the major corporate oligopolies for the government and consumer dollars. Without anticipating our later discussion, we can see that much of this unguided and unrestrained

---

[1] Most of the statistics of these paragraphs are derived from an unpublished paper by M. J. Kami, *"Challenge of the Future: 1968 and Beyond,"* no date.

[2] *The New Industrial State,* pp. 282ff.

technological and organizational change had functional as well as dysfunc-
tional effects. The increasing complexity and bureaucratic character of corporate and governmental organizations had both a positive and negative side.
There were great advances in the size of the nation's gross national product in
these years, but also disturbing evidences of personal and social disorganization. The explosion of the metropolis made possible new heights in the
suburban standard of living, but it also created urban sprawl and vast new
ghettoes for the underprivileged and unfortunate. American industry manufactured an unprecedented volume of products, but also an incalculable
amount of by-products in the form of polluted water and air and use of land
that caused much complaint. Internal economies were achieved within firms
through technological and organizational innovation, but the very scale and
unplanned character of these changes produced external dis-economies in the
community. Human relations in industry in these decades made significant
forward strides, but the accompanying demographic and social changes made
the nation increasingly aware of the waste and toll of ethnic discrimination
and exploitation.

This revolutionary era was a time of paradoxes and contrasts. It was an
"age of cold [and hot] war comfort" for some and of violent death and
estrangement for others. Affluence and the new leisure existed side by side
with alienation and the new poverty. The word "gap" increasingly came into
use to describe the lopsided state of national and international society; first,
the term was used by economists as in the phrase the "inflationary gap."
Later, we spoke of the "missile gap," and of the growing gap between the rich
and poor nations. More recently, we have been conscious of the "credibility
gap" and the so-called "generation gap." We do not intend to give credence
to these cliché phrases without careful examination of the relevant facts
related to such alleged discontinuities, but the very prevalence of this mode
of perceiving reality suggests the wide realization of the human and social
costs of unplanned technological and economic change and the apprehension
of the numerous cultural lags it has produced.[3]

POST-WAR TRENDS IN NATIONAL OUTPUT,
EMPLOYMENT, AND INCOME

When we turn from these broad sociological changes to consider the pace of
economic growth in the post-war years, we discover a different picture. After
the process of adjustment to peace in the immediate years after 1945 had been
accomplished without the mass unemployment that many had feared, the

---

[3] Some of these problems will be discussed further in Chaps. 30 and 31. For a broad
prospectus of the changes in the last quarter century, see J. Brooks, *The Great Leap, The
Past Twenty-five Years in America* (New York: Harper and Row, 1966).

economy displayed a sharp upward trend from 1948 to 1956 and then suffered a marked slowing down in its rate of growth from 1956 to 1963. After that date the growth rate improved, and by 1966 the economy caught up with its potential, though there was still considerable unemployment. Over the whole period, 1948 to 1967, though there were minor recessions, there was "a degree of stability and growth rarely, if ever, matched at any time in our history."[4] One of the main reasons for this is that in the post-war period we have not had a truly major depression. Gross national product rose from $208.5 billion in 1946 to $739.5 billion in 1966 (current dollars). Even in stable 1958 dollars, the GNP more than doubled over those twenty years. Per capita disposable income (in 1958 prices) rose from $1,606 in 1946 to $2,294 two decades later.[5] Thus, it was not until the 1950's after the post-war adjustments had been completed and the economy again reached its wartime peak that "the United States truly became the affluent society. . . ."[6]

The economy underwent four recessions in this period, in 1948–49, 1953–54, 1957–58, and again in 1960–61. The 1957–58 recession was the most severe of the post-war cycles, and the disappointing performance of the economy in the years after 1956 produced a national political debate in the 1960 election over the nation's growth rate. A comparison of the growth rate in the period 1948 to 1956 with that of from 1957 to 1963 shows the former to have been dynamic, whereas the latter suggests semi-stagnation. The percentage increases in production, employment, and income in the two periods are shown in Table 1. In the period of the last two cycles covered by the years 1957–63, output, employment, and income dropped substantially below the economy's potential.

In explaining the disparate performance of the economy in these two periods, one should note that there were powerful spontaneous forces at work in the first period, which automatically generated a high level of aggregate demand. These forces were materially weaker in the second period, so that if prosperity was to be attained, it had to be contrived. The favorable factors operating in the first period included the pent-up demand for consumer durable goods caused by the restrictions on purchasing during World War II. In general, the autonomous factors included: (1) the backlog of construction: producers durable equipment and consumers durables left from the second World War; (2) the Korean War and the stimulus provided by the cold war that followed; (3) population increase, urban and suburban growth, and the

[4] A. H. Hansen, *The Postwar American Economy* (New York: W. W. Norton and Co., 1964), p. 5.

[5] *Economic Report of the President* (Washington: U.S. Government Printing Office, 1967), pp. 213, 214, 232.

[6] H. G. Vatter, *The American Economy in the 1950's* (New York: W. W. Norton and Co., 1963), p. 3. Galbraith in *The Affluent Society* had used this phrase largely to contrast the relative affluence of the private sector with the alleged poverty of the public services, but in his first chapter he also emphasized that the American economy of the 1950's was capable of eliminating poverty as a whole and in this sense the nation was affluent.

TABLE 1

*Annual Percentage Increases in Output, Employment,
and Income, 1948–56 and 1957–63*[a]

	1948–56	1957–63
GNP (in constant dollars)	4.7%	3.0%
Industrial production index	5.7	1.0
Total employment	1.2	0.6
Personal disposable income (in constant dollars)	4.6	3.0
Corporate profits before taxes	4.5	2.3
Unemployment rate (average per period)	4.3	5.6

[a] Source: Reprinted from Alvin H. Hansen, *The Postwar American Economy, Performance and Problems.* By permission of W. W. Norton and Company, Inc. © Copyright 1964 by W. W. Norton and Company, Inc.

appearance of new products and techniques developed during the war years, but deferred for later introduction to the consuming public.[7]

The expansionist forces in the years 1948–56 and their weakness in 1956–63 can be clearly seen and measured in the movements of such GNP components as (1) gross private domestic investment; (2) purchases of consumer durables; and (3) defense expenditures. In Table 2 we compare the percentage increases per annum for each of these important aggregates.

TABLE 2

*Annual Percentage Increase in Selected Components of GNP
for the Years 1948–56 and 1956–63*[a]

Factor	1948–56	1956–63
Gross private domestic investment	3.1%	0.4%
Consumers durables	6.8	3.4
Defense expenditures	22.4	2.9
Total	7.3	1.9

[a] Source: Reprinted from Alvin H. Hansen, *The Postwar American Economy, Performance and Problems.* By permission of W. W. Norton and Company, Inc. © Copyright 1964 by W. W. Norton and Company, Inc.

We see that private investment increased at a healthy rate in the first period, but lagged badly in the second. Consumer durables expanded at a tremendous rate in the years 1948–56, but their rate of growth fell to one-half in the second period. In the period that included the Korean War, defense expenditures grew at a remarkable rate, but after that war they receded to turn upward again as we got deeper in the civil war in Vietnam.

[7] Hansen, *The Postwar American Economy,* p. 23.

SECULAR AND OTHER DEVELOPMENTS
IN THE POST-WAR PERIOD

Apart from the forces that reflected cyclical or military events, there were other long-run, secular developments that exercised an important influence on the economy in these years. One of the most surprising of these was the "baby boom," which, starting late in World War II and extending up to 1956 when a peak was reached, reversed previous demographic trends and upset the experts. In the thirties the leading students of population were predicting that the population growth of the United States would slow down and stabilize around 1970. This prognostication was knocked into the proverbial cocked hat by a domestic "population explosion."[8] Live births in 1946 numbered 3.4 million and 3.8 million in 1947 as contrasted with 2.5 million in 1939; the birthrate per 1,000 population went from 18.8 to above 25 over the same period. The nation's total population rose from 139.9 million in 1945 (estimated) to 151.6 million in 1950, 180.6 million in 1960, and 196.8 million in 1966. By the mid-1960's it was clear that the boom was over; the total annual number of live births was running some 300,000 lower than it had been in the peak year 1957. Students of population were not all in agreement as to what lay behind this population burst, some relating it to the improvements of income and others stressing psychological factors, such as a quest for security through having a family in an age of alienation. One of the striking aspects of the phenomenon was that the rise in family size was most pronounced in the middle and higher income strata. One fact was certain in all this: the baby boom would have a decided effect upon the future pattern of family consumption and living and would result in an increased percentage of young adults in the 1960's.

World War II, as we have seen, ended the mass unemployment of the 1930's. In the post-war years there was no recurrence of unemployment for the whole population on so great a scale, but despite the efforts to attain full employment there was a persistent problem of finding jobs for all. On an annual basis, the official figures show unemployment as a percentage of the civilian labor force varying from a low of 2.9 per cent in 1953 to a high of 6.8 per cent in 1958.[9] These figures probably understate the extent of unemployment because part-time workers are not included; nor do they take account of those not seeking jobs because no work was available. Furthermore, these statistics do not reveal the incidence of unemployment among various age and ethnic groups. In the sixties, for example, unemployment of non-whites was approximately twice that of whites. In many American cities in 1967, unem-

[8] J. S. Davis, "The Population Upsurge and the American Economy, 1945–80," *The Journal of Political Economy* (October, 1953), pp. 369ff.

[9] *Economic Report of the President* (January, 1967), p. 236.

ployment among Negroes was worse than it had been in the "Great Depression." Among Negro adolescents, the percentage unemployed reached 25 to 30 per cent.

One of the most striking phenomena of the post-war years, a continuation of a trend begun earlier, was the metropolitan explosion, enlarging suburbia, and creating what came to be called in the sixties the "urban crisis." Metropolitan areas had been growing faster than total population for some time. Between 1950 and 1960 the population of all standard metropolitan areas increased about 24 per cent, while the total population grew about 18 per cent. But to understand what was happening we need to distinguish the suburban part of metropolitan areas from the central cities. When we do this, we find that in the decade of the 1950's, the metropolitan areas outside the central cities increased 47 per cent in numbers, while the population of the central cities grew by only 8 per cent.

To appreciate what this suburban growth meant for the economic growth of the economy we can compare it with the earlier transatlantic immigration. In 1907 when the latter migration was at its peak, 1,200,000 Europeans landed in the United States. Even as of 1953, an average of about 1,200,000 Americans were moving into the suburbs every year; and the movement by no means ended at that time. This mass exodus to suburbia opened up immense, lush new markets for business and created colossal problems for government and society, the dimensions of which we are only beginning to grasp. "This growth accounted for enormous outlays for public services; social overhead capital such as power facilities, highways, streets, sewerage plants, water systems, schools, etc.; housing; transportation equipment; motor fuel; new investment in private industrial and commercial plant and equipment; and a host of private service, maintenance and repair activities. Small wonder that city government expenditures jumped 73% between 1952 and 1959 while GNP rose 40%."[10] The continuation of this "suburban dislocation," to use Riesman's phrase, into the sixties, threatened the nation with an ominous geographical and social polarization of communities into white suburbs and black inner city.[11]

Another aspect of the post-war transformation was the changes in the size distribution of income. Mass consumption requires a wide distribution of income to assure sufficient consumers for the products of our increasingly productive economy; an elite group of consumers would be inadequate for this purpose. Importance attaches therefore to the finding of some economists that in the years from 1935–36 to 1956 there was a movement toward greater equality of income in the United States. Table 3 presents the statistics of one such study. In 1935–36, we see that 20 per cent of the families with the highest incomes earned more than half of all the income. By 1954 their share had fallen by one-seventh, and they received a little less than 45 per cent of the

[10] Vatter, *The American Economy in the 1950's*, p. 23.
[11] National Advisory Commission on Civil Disorders, *Report* (New York: Bantam Books, Inc., 1968), pp. 398, 407.

Table 3

*Distribution of Pre-Tax Personal Income by Quintiles and
Top 5 Per Cent of Consumer Units, Selected Years*[a]
(In percentages)

Quintile	1935–1936	1941	1944	1947	1950	1954	1956	% Change 1935–36 to 1954
Lowest	4.1%	4.1%	4.9%	5.0%	4.8%	4.9%	5.0%	20%
Second	9.2	9.5	10.9	11.0	11.0	11.4	11.3	24
Third	14.1	15.3	16.2	16.0	16.2	16.6	16.5	18
Fourth	20.9	22.3	22.2	22.0	22.3	22.4	22.3	7
Highest	51.7	48.8	45.8	46.0	45.7	44.7	44.9	−14
Top 5%	26.5	24.0	20.7	20.9	20.4	20.5	20.1	−19

[a] Source: S. Goldsmith et al., "Size Distribution of Income since the Mid-Thirties," *Review of Economics and Statistics* (February, 1954), p. 9, as reproduced in R. E. Freeman, *Postwar Economic Trends in the United States* (New York: Harper and Bros., 1960), p. 109.

total. The top 5 per cent of the families had an even sharper decline in their share of the melon. Each of the four lower quintiles increased its share of personal income, though the second highest made a relative gain substantially smaller than the others. This movement toward equalization of incomes seems to have ended by 1947, possibly even by 1944. (A major part of the reason for the equalizing tendency was the increased income deriving from overtime and full employment during the war.) This shift in money income appeared to business as the rise of a new moneyed middle-income class, particularly those family units with cash income after taxes of $4,000 to $7,500.[12]

Finally, another basic identifying feature of the post-war economy that differed certainly from the behavior of the nation in the 1920's was its increased sensitivity to events in the outside world. This took the form of rivalry with the Soviet bloc, increased participation by the underdeveloped nations in international affairs, and new, powerful competition from western Europe and Japan. The "Soviet effect," as it has been called, influenced almost every aspect of American economic life in the 1950's and in subsequent years—"the United States military budget, subsidies to higher education, professional salaries, R & D outlays, tariff policy, foreign aid, and numerous others. . . ."[13] The less developed countries exerted an important influence on American policy also. Their pressing need for development and the financial aid and technical assistance to promote it involved the United States in a rivalry with Soviet Russia and later in the period with the Chinese Communists as well. By 1960, American appropriations for foreign aid were exceeding $4 billion a year; by that time the nation was growing restless with the burden, and the Eisenhower administration urged the German and other

[12] The Editors of Fortune, *The Changing American Market* (Garden City, N.Y.: Hanover House, 1953), p. 52.
[13] Vatter, *The American Economy in the 1950's*, p. 17.

western governments to share in such assistance to the underdeveloped economies of the world. A third external influence was the improvement in the international competitive position of western Europe and Japan. The former area had benefitted greatly in its reconstruction from the $11 billion of aid provided by the Marshall plan; the progress of this area was further promoted in 1958 by the formation of the European Economic Community (the Common Market), embracing Belgium, France, West Germany, Italy, Luxembourg, and the Netherlands. Increasingly, in the 1950's and thereafter, some of these countries and Japan captured a larger share of world trade and even successfully penetrated the American market.[14]

THE CHANGING STRUCTURE OF PRODUCTION
AND EMPLOYMENT

Preconceived notions of the nature of the American economy were of no use in these changing post-war years. The accepted model of the American economy as one of predominantly private enterprise was growing woefully obsolete year by year. Significant changes were occurring also in the very structure of production and in the nature of employment. As the statistics of Table 4 indicate, after 1953–57 the share of income and employment originating in manufacturing began to shrink, while services and the government sector accounted for an increasing percentage of the national income and employment. These trends led some to declare that we were moving into or already were in a post-industrial society. According to the table, the share of services and the government (federal, state, and local) in the national income rose from 19.5 per cent for the years 1948–53 to 24.8 per cent in 1965. The employment provided by these sectors of the economy show comparable gains for the same period.

In the years after 1945, the American economy moved further toward one of high-level mass consumption, but there were significant shifts in the latter part of the period of which we need to take account. The steady rise in personal consumption expenditures is clearly seen in Chart 1. In fact, on an annual basis, aggregate consumption expenditures never declined in amount between 1946 and 1966, despite the intervening fluctuations in GNP. This steadiness in the growth of personal consumption in these years is brought out well in the statistics of Table 5, which show the growth rates of the major components of GNP for the years 1948–60. Aggregate consumption expenditures grew at the same rate as GNP over these years. The table also shows us that personal consumption expenditures were the most stable of the major spending streams; their average deviation from trend was only 1.0. Government purchases of goods and services exhibited an above-average rate of growth in the years 1948–60, but slowed down in the subperiod, 1955–60.

[14] Vatter, *The American Economy in the 1950's*, pp. 17–18.

TABLE 4

Share of Industrial Divisions in National Income and Employment in the United States, Selected Years[a]

(Per Cent Distribution)

Year or period	Total	Industrial divisions								Government	
		Agriculture	Mining	Contract construction	Manufacturing	Transportation, communications, public utilities	Trade	Finance, insurance, and real estate	Services	Federal	State and local
	Millions of current dollars					NATIONAL INCOME					
						Percent distribution					
1926–29[1]	82,818	9.0%	2.2%	4.9%	21.4%	9.7%	12.9%	17.0%[2]	12.8%	10.2%	
1948–53	258,476	7.2	2.0	5.0	31.6	8.5	16.7	9.0	8.8	6.2	4.5
1953–57	330,092	4.8	1.8	5.2	32.1	8.5	15.7	10.3	9.4	6.4	5.3
1957–60	386,032	4.3	1.5	5.1	30.5	8.4	15.7	10.9	10.4	6.2	6.2
1960–65[3]	474,201	3.9	1.2	5.0	29.9	8.3	15.3	11.1	11.2	6.2	7.2
1965	559,020	3.8	1.2	5.1	30.5	8.2	15.0	10.9	11.3	6.0	7.5
	Thousands of persons					PERSONS ENGAGED IN PRODUCTION					
						Percent distribution					
1929[4]	46,216	19.9%	2.2%	5.0%	22.8%	8.8%	16.9%	3.4%	14.0%	6.9%	
1948–53	61,110	10.6	1.6	5.6	26.7	6.9	18.1	3.4	13.1	7.7	6.2
1953–57	64,496	8.8	1.3	5.6	27.0	6.5	18.0	3.8	13.5	8.4	6.9
1957–60	64,798	7.6	1.2	5.5	26.1	6.3	18.6	4.1	15.0	7.6	8.0
1960–65[3]	67,620	6.6	1.0	5.5	25.6	5.7	18.4	4.3	16.1	7.6	9.1
1965	71,248	5.7	.9	5.6	25.9	5.6	18.4	4.3	16.5	7.4	9.6

[a] Source: U.S. Bureau of the Census, *Long Term Economic Growth, 1860–1965* (Washington: Government Printing Office, 1966), p. 79.

[1] Kuznets data.

[2] Kuznets data. This industry also includes income from fisheries, miscellaneous income of private origin, net international transfer of dividends and interest, as well as income from miscellaneous professional occupations, and the hand trades.

[3] Period does not cover a complete business cycle.

[4] OBE data.

TABLE 5

Post-War Growth Rates and Average Deviations from Trend of Major
Components of Real Gross National Product, 1948–60[a]
(*Per cent*)

	Average Annual Rate of Growth	Average Deviation from Trend
Gross national product	3.4%	2.6%
Personal consumption expenditures	3.4	1.0
Durable goods	4.1	5.6
Nondurable goods	2.7	.7
Services	4.2	.7
Producers durable equipment and private nonresidential construction	1.5	4.7
New private nonfarm residential construction	3.9	7.5
Government purchases of goods and services (federal, state and local)		
1948–60	5.1	12.0
1955–60	2.4	1.4

Note.—Rates of growth are based on linear logarithmic regressions using data in 1954 dollars for the period 1948–60.

[a] Source: U.S. Department of Commerce, Office of Business Economics as reproduced in Vatter, *The American Economy in the 1950's* (New York: W. W. Norton and Co., 1963), p. 101.

Averages often conceal more than they reveal. This is one of the limitations of the averages in Table 5, especially the average for consumer durables. The 4.1 per cent average annual growth rate for that category of expenditure does not reveal the sharp contrast in the early and later years of the period under consideration. Expenditure on consumer durables rose at an average annual rate of 6.6 per cent between the second quarter of 1947 and the fourth quarter of 1955, but the rate was only .9 per cent between the fourth quarter of 1955 and the second quarter of 1959. Americans continued, on the other hand, to increase their expenditures on services. Indeed, services as a percentage of total consumer expenditures rose from 31 per cent in 1946 to 41 per cent in 1966. Such a pronounced rate of increase undoubtedly had a stimulating effect on the whole economy, but there were two drawbacks to this: first, this sector was growing at the expense of consumer durables, and, secondly, services have been traditionally a low income and low productivity sector. Consequently, it has seemed to most analysts of the period that the shift of consumer spending to services tended to retard the rate of productivity growth in the economy as a whole. Another unfortunate result, in the opinion of some, was that the shift away from consumer durables, which are capital intensive and more productive relatively of primary wage and salary effects than a dollar spent on services, tended to retard the rate of economic growth itself.[15]

[15] Vatter, *The American Economy in the 1950's*, pp. 103–104.

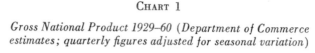

CHART 1

*Gross National Product 1929–60 (Department of Commerce
estimates; quarterly figures adjusted for seasonal variation)*

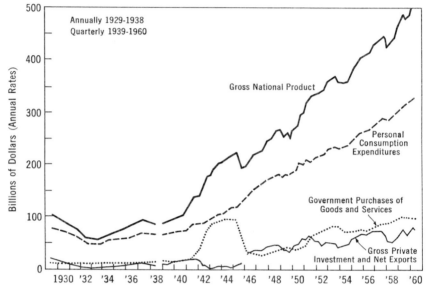

Source: Board of Governors of the Federal Reserve System, Historical Sup-
plement to Federal Reserve Chart Book, September, 1960. Reproduced from
H. G. Vatter, *The U.S. Economy in the 1950's* (New York: W. W. Norton and
Co. Inc., 1963), p. 67, with the permission of the publisher.

THE SHIFTING INDUSTRIAL PATTERN

As one would expect from the foregoing analysis, the pattern of American
industry in the post-war years was a highly dynamic one; some fields were
decidedly growth industries, while others, very often the pace-makers of the
past, lagged in their growth or even underwent absolute declines. Agriculture
continued to shrink as a sector of the economy in terms of both the number of
farmers and the size of the farm population. In 1945 there were 5.8 million
farmers in the United States, and in 1964 there were only 3.1 million—a
decline of over 2.5 million in less than twenty years. The total farm population
fell from 24.4 million in 1946 to 11.5 million, or, expressed as a percentage of
the total population, it went from 17.5 to 5.8 per cent. This amazing transformation in farming was due to a technological revolution that pushed the rate
of increase in farm productivity far above that in manufacturing and made it
possible to grow larger crops with fewer people. The result can be seen in
Chart 2; in 1900 one farm worker's labor fed seven people. By 1950, one farm
laborer fed nearly sixteen people and in 1965, thirty-three!

CHART 2

*People Supplied by One Farm Worker in the United States,
1830–1970*

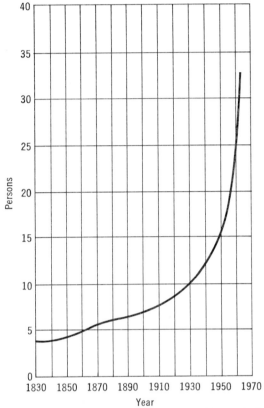

Year

Source: U.S. Department of Agriculture, *Handbook of Agricultural
Charts 1965* (Agricultural Handbook No. 300, 1966).

The total non-farm business population grew only moderately between 1950
and 1961—from approximately 4 million in the former year to 4.7 million
in the latter. The number of manufacturers increased relatively slowly, rising
from 260,000 in 1950 to 311,921 in 1963. The largest number of new entrants
were in the small business fields, such as contract construction, finance, insurance, real estate, and the service activities. The ranks of wholesalers grew
more rapidly than the number of retailers. It will be noted that nearly all these
lines of business are tertiary in character, reflecting the growing service needs
of the mushrooming metropolises.[16]

The leading growth industries were those that availed themselves of high
technology or were beneficiaries of defense needs. In the 1950's these industries could be classified as those having doubled their output in 1960 as

[16] Tertiary industries are usually defined as embracing services, retail and wholesale
trade, finance and government.

compared with that of 1947–49. Table 6 lists the industries that fell in that enviable category.

TABLE 6
Leading Growth Industries of the 1950's
(Based on the Federal Reserve Board's Production Index)[a]
(1947–49 = 100)

Industry Grouping	Annual Average of Index for 1960	Employment 1959 (Thousands)
Total index	164	—
Utilities	287	577
Electric	289	—
Gas	285	—
Electrical machinery	222	1,242
Aircraft and other equipment	368	735
Instruments and related products	221	339
Chemicals and products	255	848
Industrial chemicals	320	611
Rubber and plastic products[b]	200	93
Natural gas and gas liquids[c]	228	32

Item		
Stone and earth minerals (nonmetal)	194	
Equipment, including defense	193	

[a] Source: Reprinted from Harold G. Vatter, *The U.S. Economy in the 1950's.* By permission of W. W. Norton and Company, Inc. © Copyright 1963 by Harold G. Vatter.

[b] Employment total is for plastic products only.

[c] Employment total is for 1958.

The expansion of the electric utilities was tied to the unusually rapid increase in the use of electricity in the home, in industry, and on the farm. Long-distance transmission of gas and new discoveries and technology played a part in the bonanza growth of that field. Perhaps the most sensational new industry of the period was that dubbed "electronics," which was said to have an $11 billion market as of 1960, and created a whole new breed of millionaire entrepreneur. The industry's products consisted mainly of components, such as transistors, electron tubes, resistors, and capacitators, and diverse end products such as computers, television sets, industrial measuring equipment, tape recorders, and hi-fi components, to name a few. This lusty infant owed about two-thirds of its growth to military demand, including the missile race, which began in 1955. The chemical industry, including petrochemicals, was not so dependent on the military for its astounding growth (its output more than doubled in the 1950 decade), yet it dazzled the nation with the variety and ingenuity of its synthetics, plastics, new drugs, etc. in addition to supplying other industries with a vast quantity of heavy chemicals.

Inter-industry competition and the accompanying "perennial gale of creative destruction" were very vigorous in these years and were major factors in accounting for the relatively slow growth of some lines of activity. The principal industrial laggards, judged by their annual production in the 1950's as compared with that of 1947–49, included metal mining, iron and steel, lumber products, textile mill products, leather and its products, and beverages. Coal mining's output declined sharply as compared with the immediate post-war period. The troubles of some of these industries could be traced to the very expansion of some of the growth industries mentioned above. Almost invariably, even though production increased over the decade, these lagging industries showed a decline in employment as well. This tendency was attributable, in the main, to the increases in productivity in these fields.

The steel industry was a particularly striking instance of the difficulties faced by a mature oligopoly in a context of dynamic industrial change. Though it sought to modernize its capacity through large-scale internal financing, it was beset by strenuous competition from substitutes such as aluminum, prestressed concrete, and plastic, and in the later years of the period, by intensified foreign competition. The slowdown in the economy's overall growth in the late fifties also had adverse effects so that an industry that was once in the vanguard of the nation's progress suddenly found itself no longer a leader.

Even the automobile industry, though its sales rose in the fifties to record heights, was faced by serious competition from abroad and by the innovation of the compact car. This mature oligopoly, basically dependent on a replacement market for its product, met these challenges by policies of "planned obsolescence" and increased product differentiation and by heavy investment in the rapidly growing foreign market. In the sixties the "insolent chariots" of affluent America created almost insuperable public problems in the form of traffic congestion, pollution of the air, and safety hazards.

In the late fifties the problems of a high-level mass consumption society such as the United States were intensified by the increasingly high percentage of homes containing such highly prized consumer durables as electrical appliances. By 1959, over 90 per cent of wired American homes had radios, television sets, refrigerators, and electric washers.[17] With the lag in economic growth in the latter part of the fifties some analysts discerned signs of market saturation in the crucial consumer durable industries and speculated that the competition of these fields with the service industries for consumer dollars lay behind the economic slowdown. Generally, however, these problems were overcome by stepping up advertising expenditures and by increased emphasis on styling and engineering changes in products. The nation's "teleconsumers" were growingly conscious, if not critical, of the magnified barrage of words

[17] Cf. figures cited in Vatter, *The American Economy in the 1950's*, p. 175. The percentages of wired American homes with other electrical appliances as of 1959 were as follows: Freezers, 22.1%; vacuum cleaners, 72.5%; dryers (electric and gas) 17.8%; air conditioners, 12.8. These statistics indicate the market which was still untapped in these fields, not to mention the potential demand of the millions whose poverty prevented them from being consumers.

and images to which they were subject in the almost manic effort to sell them more goods and services.

CHANGES IN PRIVATE AND PUBLIC FINANCE

The world of private finance experienced significant changes as the managed economy of the United States became more sophisticated in the post-war years. Thanks to federal deposit insurance and careful regulation, the commercial banking structure was fairly stable, even though the volume of demand deposits and currency swelled from $108.5 billion in 1946 to $168.5 billion in 1966 (as of December). Some of the most decisive changes took place in the capital markets, where despite the continued heavy reliance by corporations on internal financing (retained profits, depreciation, and amortization) from one-quarter to one-third of corporate funds were raised in the decade 1950–60. A marked preference, as much as 70–80 per cent, was shown by corporate fund raisers for debt instruments (bonds, debentures, notes) over equity securities. The most important change in the nation's capital markets in these years was the sensational growth of the financial intermediaries, such as the life insurance companies, mutual savings banks, savings and loan associations, investment companies (mutual funds), and private and government pension funds.

By 1965, life insurance companies had assets of $150 billion, compared with $90 billion ten years earlier. These immensely wealthy organizations invested their funds in mortgages (primarily home), industrial bonds, and public utility bonds, in that order, and in the fifties they were shifting out of railroad and government securities and investing more heavily in industrial and public utility fixed income obligations and in large urban apartment projects. The savings and savings and loan associations also expanded tremendously during the years of the post-war housing boom. By 1965, they had assets, respectively, of $54 billion and $120 billion, most of it invested in real estate mortgages.

The mutual funds grew at a most spectacular rate, adding net about $2 billion a year to their assets. By 1965 their huge purchases of securities on the stock exchanges to keep their $30 billion or more of assets yielding income were of increased concern to the Securities and Exchange Commission. Pension funds, growing at the net rate of $8 billion per year, also posed questions as to how efficient the new institutionalized methods of finance were so far as economic growth was concerned.

The growth of the government sector of the economy in the post-war period explains the expansion in the sphere of public finance. The magnitude of the changes as a whole is brought out well in Table 7. We see that by 1966 a major shift had taken place as compared with 1929. Whereas in the latter

TABLE 7

The Growth of the Public Sector in the United States[a]
(Selected years, in current dollars)

Year	GNP (Billions)	Government Purchases of Goods and Services (Billions of Dollars)		All Govt. Purchases as % of GNP
		Federal	State and Local	
1929	$103.1	$ 1.3	$ 7.2	8.2%
1940	99.7	6.0	8.0	14.0
1960	503.7	53.5	46.1	19.8
1966	739.5	77.0	76.2	20.7

[a] Source: *Economic Report of the President*, January, 1967, p. 213.

year less than one dollar in ten of our national output was attributable to government purchases, in 1966 about one dollar in five of all goods and services was sold to government. This increase in the share of the government's purchasing meant that it could exercise a greater leverage on the national economy and that consequently governmental fiscal policy assumed a new importance in its functioning.

In considering the impact of federal expenditures on the economy, it is essential to recognize how important spending for national defense has become. As can be seen from the data of Table 8, the military budget was cut back severely after the close of World War II, but the outbreak of the Korean War in 1950 sent defense expenditures soaring to a new post-war high of

TABLE 8

Defense and Total Federal Expenditures: Fiscal Years 1946–68
(Administrative Budget in billions of dollars)

Year	Total Federal Expenditures	National Defense Expenditures	Per Cent	Year	Total Federal Expenditures	National Defense Expenditures	Per Cent
1946	$ 60.3	$43.2	71.6%	1958	71.4	44.2	61.9
1947	38.9	14.4	37.0	1959	80.3	46.5	57.9
1948	33.0	11.8	35.8	1960	76.5	45.7	59.7
1949	35.9	12.9	35.9	1961	81.5	47.5	58.3
1950	39.4	13.0	33.0	1962	87.8	51.1	58.2
1951	44.0	22.5	51.1	1963	92.6	52.8	57.0
1952	65.3	44.0	67.4	1964	97.7	54.2	55.4
1953	74.1	50.4	68.0	1965	96.5	50.2	52.0
1954	67.5	47.0	69.6	1966	107.0	57.7	53.9
1955	64.4	40.7	63.2	1967	126.7	70.2	55.4
1956	66.2	40.7	61.5	1968	135.0	75.5	55.9
1957	69.0	43.4	62.9				

[a] Source: Economic Report of the President, January, 1968, p. 262.

$33.6 billion in 1951. From that year to 1966 the United States never had an annual defense outlay of less than $38 billion. This huge yearly expenditure has been the largest single influence on the economy in the post-war era and it has had incalculable effects. Military procurement has been a major prop of what has been called the "underwritten economy."[18] Galbraith writes of post-war business attitudes toward this fiscal development as follows:

> If a large public sector of the economy, supported by personal and corporate income taxation, is the fulcrum for the regulation of demand, plainly military expenditures are the pivot on which the fulcrum rests. Additionally, they provide underwriting for advanced technology and, therewith, security for the planning of the industrial system in areas that would otherwise be excluded by cost and risk. And, to repeat, these expenditures are strongly supported by businessmen. Not for many years has any important business executive condemned the prodigality of expenditures on defense. From all pleas for public economy, defense expenditures are meticulously excluded. . . .[19]

THE GEOGRAPHIC PATTERN OF ECONOMIC CHANGE

The impact of military procurement is especially noticeable in connection with the regional shifts of industry in this period. While industrial location is influenced by many factors, there does seem to be support for the thesis that "the magnitude and . . . the spatial dispersion of economic activity in the 1950's were heavily dependent upon government budgets, particularly the Federal defense budget. . . ."[20] This conclusion is supported by evidence that cannot be considered in detail here, but certain salient facts can be noted. The fastest growing regions in the post-war years were the Southwest, the Mountain states, and the Far West. In terms of regions, as shown in Chart 3, the relative distribution of manufacturing employment fell in the New England, Middle Atlantic, and East North Central states, and rose in the southern Mountain and Pacific states; the region described as West North Central rose slightly in this respect. California, first in the volume of prime defense contracts in 1960, was "the epitome of the state defense economy." The phenomenal expansion of Texas in these years was given strong impetus by large defense allocations; in fiscal 1960, it ranked third in the amount of defense contracts, surpassed only by California and New York. Indeed, at that time it was believed that one-fourth of Texas' annual income was derived from the federal government. The hectic efforts of various states to secure procurement contracts and to attract research and development centers to their environs further confirms the importance attached to defense expenditures in the geography of industrial location.

[18] Vatter, *The American Economy in the 1950's*, p. 221.
[19] Galbraith, *The New Industrial State*, p. 229.
[20] Vatter, *The American Economy in the 1950's*, p. 189.

CHART 3

Geographic Distribution of Manufacturing Employment
in the United States, 1900–64

(In percent)

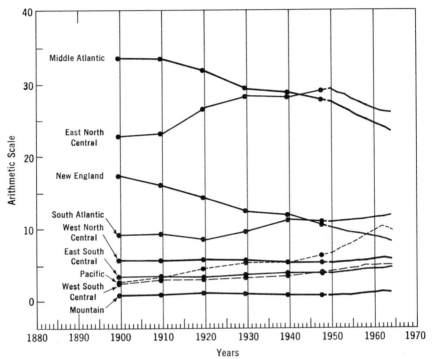

Source: U.S. Bureau of the Census, *Long Term Economic Growth, 1860–1965* (Washington, D.C.: U.S. Government Printing Office, 1966), p. 75.

TRENDS IN INDUSTRIAL CONCENTRATION

Mobilization of the economy for war and the large defense expenditures of this era also had a profound effect on the nation's industrial organization. The concentration of military contracts among the corporate giants during World War II and the substantial increase in their financial liquidity had led to the prediction by one wartime agency that there would be a massive absorption of the weaker firms by the strong after the end of hostilities.[21] This tendency did develop and was strengthened further by the government's maintenance of aggregate demand, largely through defense expenditures, in the post-war years. The condition of protracted prosperity that prevailed in most of these

[21] Smaller War Plants Corporation, *Economic Concentration and World War II*, Senate Document No. 206, 79th Congress, 2nd Session, 1946, passim. On procurement policies in World War and post-war disposal of surplus property in relation to corporate centration, see W. Adams and H. M. Gray, *Monopoly in America* (New York: The Macmillan Co., 1955), Chaps. V and VI.

years, plus fiscal policies augmenting cash flows, created a condition of corporate liquidity that was very favorable for policies of merger and acquisition. Large defense expenditures and huge appropriations for research and development in the aviation, electronic, and aerospace industries, among others, proved to be irresistible to imaginative corporate managers whose own industries were showing signs of maturity and slower growth. At the same time, advances in managerial skills and especially the adoption of the principle of decentralization à la General Motors made possible new ventures in corporate design. The result was the appearance of a larger number of multi-product and multi-national corporations of impressive proportions. This was seen by some perceptive observers as a new evolutionary stage for the major corporations—"the separation of the firm from the mother industry and the domestic economy."[22]

Vast internal growth and numerous mergers transformed the corporate giants of 1939 into super-giants in the post-war years. "Since the end of the second World War," wrote one political scientist, "the corporate form has emerged as the characteristic institution of American society."[23] Certainly, if bigness is the criterion, our corporations increasingly deserved this characterization. Consider that in 1947, there were 113 corporations with assets of $100 million or more; by 1962, their number had more than tripled to 370. General Motors, the nation's biggest industrial company, is bigger today than most nations. In fact, its net operating revenue of $11 billion in 1965 exceeded the 1964 gross national product of all but nine nations of the free world.[24] The increase that took place in overall concentration as accounted for by our largest manufacturing corporations between 1947 and 1962 is shown in Chart 4.

Overall concentration is a global measure; it does not relate the size of companies to the industries in which they operate but to some large aggregate, such as the total value added by all manufacturing. Economists studying market behavior have usually been more interested in concentration by industry. Interestingly enough, despite the growth in size of our leading companies since 1945, the best studies do not show much, if any, increase in industrial concentration in this latter sense. In terms of concentration ratios showing the percentage of sales accounted for by the four largest firms in 400 industries, the results for 1947–58 were as follows:

	Industries Having a Ratio of 75% or More	Industries Having a Ratio of 50% or More
1947	10.0%	23.7%
1954	9.3	24.7
1958	7.9	22.6

[22] R. T. Averitt, *The Dual Economy* (New York: W. W. Norton and Co., Inc., 1968), p. 5 and pp. 184–185.

[23] Andrew Hacker, "Politics and the Corporation," an Occasional paper of the Fund for the Republic (New York, 1958).

[24] "The Massive Statistics of General Motors," *Fortune* (July 15, 1966), p. 298.

CHART 4

*Share of Value Added by Manufacture Accounted for by 200
Largest Manufacturing Companies, 1947–1962*

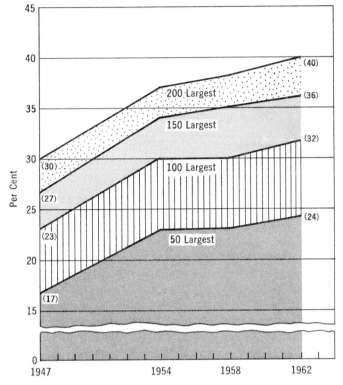

Source: U.S. Bureau of the Census

Summing up a review of statistics of industrial concentration, Dr. John M. Blair, chief economist of a 1964 Senate Committee studying economic concentration stated that ". . . the number of individual industries in which concentration ratios declined between 1947 and 1958 was slightly greater than the number in which it increased. . . ."[25]

How do we explain an apparent increase in overall concentration in the face of little evidence that there has been an increase in the average degree of industrial concentration? There is no denying that we have had a merger movement of significant proportions in the post-war years. Mergers in manufacturing and mining, according to the Federal Trade Commission, fluctuated between 219 in 1950 to 835 in 1959; in the sixties, the annual number moved up from 800–900 to over 1,000 in 1968 (see Chart 5). The explanation for the failure of industrial concentration ratios to rise as an average would seem to

[25] Hearings before the Subcommittee on Antitrust and Monopoly of the Committee on the Judiciary, U.S. Senate, 88th Cong., 2nd Sess., Part I, *Economic Concentration: Overall and Conglomerate Aspects* (1964), p. 105.

lie in the great popularity of conglomerate mergers in recent years. A conglomerate enterprise is one that produces and sells a number of economically
unrelated products. By expanding in a number of industries, some of which
were not so concentrated, conglomerates would tend to hold other industrial
concentration ratios down. This trend toward diversification became very
pronounced after 1954 when Textron, originally a textile firm, started an
acquisition program that led it eventually to collect 70 different firms manufacturing everything from helicopters to watch bracelets. As can be seen from

CHART 5

Mergers in Manufacturing and Mining
1940–1964

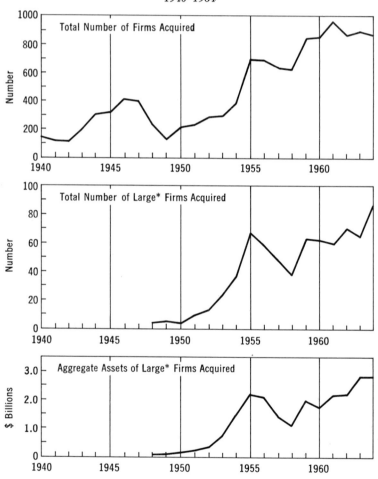

*Large Firms Represent Companies with Assets of $10 Million and Over.

Source: Hearings before the Subcommittee on Antitrust and Monopoly, *Economic Concentration*, Part 2, *Mergers and Other Factors Affecting Industry Concentration* (1965), p. 503.

Table 9, many more companies adopted the conglomerate form in the post-war years. It has become a controversial and challenging type of business enterprise that brings some of the latest managerial techniques to bear in the pursuit of growth and profits. One student, stressing this aspect, has written:

TABLE 9

Distribution of Large Manufacturing and Mining Acquisitions, by Type and by Period of Acquisiton[a]

	1948–1953		1954–1959		1960–1964	
	Number	Per cent	Number	Per cent	Number	Per cent
Horizontal	18	31.0%	78	24.8%	42	12.0%
Vertical	6	10.3	43	13.7	59	17.0
Conglomerate						
Market extension	4	6.9	20	6.4	24	6.9
Product extension	27	46.6	145	46.2	184	52.9
Other	3	5.2	28	8.9	39	11.2
Totals	58	100.0%	314	100.0%	348	100.0%

[a] Source: Hearings on *Economic Concentration*, U.S. Senate, 88th Cong., 2nd Session, Part II, *Mergers and Other Factors Affecting Industry Concentration*, p. 516.

Diversification is one more step in the process of the professionalization of management that has proceeded so rapidly in the United States since the Second World War. It represents the search for a new business structure which will provide a means of survival for the corporation beyond the life cycle of a single industry, just as the corporation form of management provided a means of survival beyond the life cycle of a single family.[26]

The conglomerate is the latest corporate mutation in the continuing "Organizational Revolution" in the United States, which is both challenge and response to the unrestrained technological change of these times. We examine some of the causes and consequences of this and other corporate developments in the following chapters.

[26] S. S. Miller, *The Management Problems of Diversification* (New York: John Wiley and Sons, 1963), p. 136, as quoted in Hearings on *Economic Concentration*, Part 1, *op. cit.*, p. 197.

Chapter 30

THE QUEST FOR STABLE GROWTH AND FULL EMPLOYMENT

THE COMMITMENT TO FULL EMPLOYMENT

At the end of 1946, less than a year and a half after V-J day, the United States completed what the Council of Economic Advisers rather proudly stated was "the swiftest and most gigantic change-over that any nation had ever made from war to peace."[1] The magnitude of that conversion can be inferred from the fact that in 1944, at the peak of the war effort, half of the nation's output of goods and services was devoted to war production and about 45 per cent of its labor force was either so engaged or serving in the armed forces. This vast undertaking was greatly complicated, of course, by the millions of people involved, many of whom would suffer if the job was mishandled. It was obviously imperative that an effective program to restore the nation's peace-time economy be formulated before the conclusion of the hostilities. With such an object in mind, several government agencies in the last years of the war were charged with the responsibility of preparing plans for a smooth and orderly transition to peace.

One of the primary concerns and major objectives of these government programs for demobilization and readjustment was the maintenance of full employment. In his annual message to Congress on January 7, 1943, President Roosevelt had stated: "The men in our armed forces want permanent employment for themselves, their families, and their neighbors when they are mustered out at the end of the war . . . and they will have a right to expect full employment."[2] However, most economists at the time believed that a temporary period of unemployment was unavoidable.[3] Estimates placed the number of temporarily unemployed persons at eight or nine million immediately following the war. It was also recognized that to assure full employment in the post-war period a much higher level of employment, higher than that in any other period in our history, would have to be maintained.

[1] *Economic Report of the President*, January 8, 1947, p. 9.
[2] American Association for the Prevention of Unemployment, *Job Insurance for the Returning Soldiers* (New York, 1943), p. 3.
[3] *Preliminary Statement of the Gray Plan for Post-War Re-Employment* (Connecticut: The Hartford Press, 1943), p. 5.

The conversion from a war to a peacetime economy involved the return of over ten million servicemen to civilian employment and a shift of war manufacturing industry employing over ten and a half million persons to peacetime pursuits. Thus, altogether, over twenty million people were affected. In order to prevent widespread unemployment, which would be the catastrophic consequence of releasing millions of men from the services too rapidly, it was realized that demobilization would have to be as orderly and smooth as possible. It would have to be carried out at a pace that would correspond to the ability of the economy to absorb the discharged men. Even under the best conditions, a substantial degree of unemployment was anticipated. A typical projection of unemployment for this period stated, "We are inclined to believe that even under favorable conditions there would be out of work on the average over a period of years as many as four million. In the best year— under boom conditions—the level might fall as low as three million. Only when the number out of work exceed four million need the employment situation occasion concern."[4]

A principal reason for the expected recession was the reduction in arms expenditure and the attempt by the government to return to a balanced budget. During the war, average yearly expenditures of the government reached $70 billion, and it was anticipated that at the conclusion of the conflict government expenditures would drop by about two-thirds. From a peak annual rate of $91 billion in the first quarter of 1945, a drastic reduction in federal spending brought expenditures to an annual average of $26 billion in the first quarter of 1946. Aggravating the whole difficult process of readjustment was the fact that inflation became serious at the same time. In 1946 President Truman warned that inflation was the nation's greatest immediate domestic problem. The premature lifting of government controls in that year caused prices to soar. Between January and June of 1946 the wholesale price index rose by 5 per cent, and in July it jumped about 10 per cent as retail food prices skyrocketed by 14 per cent.

Labor, forced to accept wage controls during the war, felt it was entitled to compensating increases in income. The rising price level made many in the labor force fear for their real income position, and as a consequence, industrial conflict broke out all over the country. Auto workers, coal miners, rail workers, and others went on strike. The number of man-days lost through labor disputes rose from 38 million in 1945 to 116 million in 1946. Large settlements caused a wage-price spiral to become an active force in the economy. By the end of 1946, wholesale and retail food prices had risen by over 31 per cent.

It was against this background of fear of mass unemployment in a time of rising prices that the federal Employment Act of 1946 was passed. This Act

[4] *The Annals of the American Academy of Political and Social Science, Postwar Jobs for Veterans* (March, 1945), Vol. 238 (New York, 1945), p. 9.

authorized the President to appoint a three-member Council of Economic Advisers to assist and advise him in the development of economic policies that would avoid economic fluctuations, maintain maximum employment, stabilize purchasing power, and foster economic growth. The mechanism by which these objectives were to be achieved included the use of fiscal and monetary policies.

The law as it was finally drafted did not mention the phrase "full employment," but used instead the words "maximum employment," which was not the phraseology that President Truman had desired. Subsequently, the phrases "maximum employment" and "purchasing power" gave rise to a debate about a possible "trade-off" between increased employment and inflation with the central argument being stated as follows, "Was it desirable to have full employment, if it entailed inflation?"

The federal government moved ahead toward reconversion to a peacetime economy in 1945 by the passage of the Revenue Act and the G.I. Bill of Rights. The tax measure was enacted in November of that year, and it provided for major reductions. The excess profits tax was repealed; the corporate income tax was cut from 40 to 38 per cent and the personal income tax levies were also slashed. These revisions of tax rates were helpful in making possible the difficult transition from a war to a peace basis. As can be seen from Table 1, the total gross national product in 1946 was only $3 billion

TABLE 1

Components of the Gross National Product in 1945 and 1946[a]

(Billions of dollars)

	1945	1946	Numerical Increase (+) or Decrease (−)
Total GNP	$211.9	$208.5	− 3.4
Personal consumption expenditures	119.7	143.4	+23.7
Gross private domestic investment	10.6	30.6	+20.0
Net exports of goods and services	− .6	7.5	—
Government purchases of goods and services	82.3	27.0	−55.3
Total federal	74.2	17.2	−57.0
National defense	73.5	14.7	−58.8
Other	.7	2.5	+ 1.8
State and local	8.1	9.8	+ 1.7

[a] Source: *Economic Report of the President*, January, 1967, *op. cit.*, p. 213.

less than it had been in 1945. By the end of the former year the economy had regained its wartime peak, and government planners were astounded. What had caused a seemingly certain economic catastrophe to turn into an economic miracle? In retrospect, it is not difficult to discover the causes of this remarkable economic upsurge. During the war years there was an insufficient supply

of goods to meet the demands of a full employment economy because of the
allocation of the nation's productive resources to the defense effort. With
reduced outlets for the expenditure of income, Americans had increased their
savings tremendously, as shown in Chart 1. These savings had helped to
finance the war, and at its end many were now eager to reallocate such sav-

CHART 1

Changes in Personal Savings in Peace and War,
1939–1947

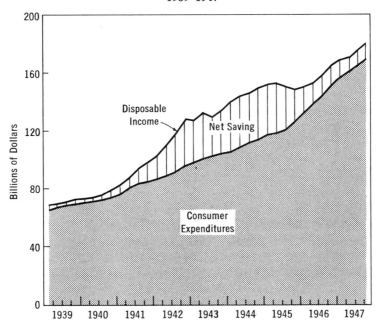

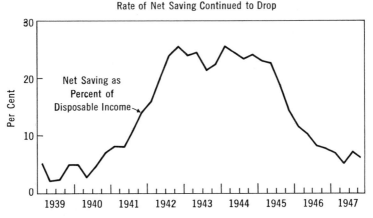

*Seasonally Adjusted Annual Rates

Source: Department of Commerce

ings to the purchase of goods and services. As a result, even with the heavy retrenchment in government expenditure, aggregate demand was sufficient to maintain near-full employment. Since the increase in private investment in the immediate post-war period (see Table 1) did not quickly add to productive facilities, but did augment the flow of income, there was a tendency for aggregate demand to outrun the available supply of consumer goods. The result was, of course, inflation, which became pronounced by the middle of 1946 and by the end of the year had become the major cause of concern in the economy (see Chart 2). From the first quarter of 1945 to the corresponding

CHART 2

The Post-War Rise in Consumer Prices, 1939–1947

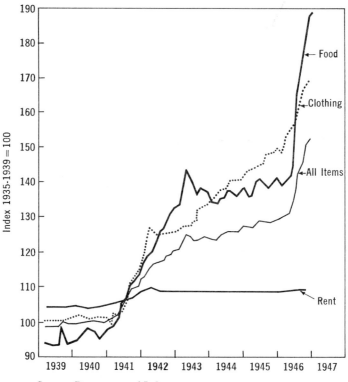

Source: Department of Labor

period in 1946, private spending increased by $40 billion. Compounding this increase in domestic demand there was an enormous jump in American exports as the war-torn nations of the continent sought to reconstruct their economies.

Meanwhile, powerful pressures of a political nature were being exerted for increased federal expenditures. The demands for funds under the G.I. Bill of Rights and the emergence of the cold war were putting new strains on the nation's budget. When the Council of Economic Advisers took office in the fall of 1946, it was confronted by a vigorous inflationary boom characterized by rapidly rising prices, an unprecedented level of investment, a huge volume of exports, and insatiable demand for consumer goods. With the advice of the Council, the Truman administration succeeded in achieving budget surpluses of $13.4 and $8.4 billion in 1947 and 1948, respectively, even though Congress continued to press for tax reduction. This deflationary fiscal policy quickly paid off. Signs of contraction in the economy appeared in 1948, and the dangerous inflation appeared to be in complete control by 1949. Many economists considered the use of fiscal policy in these years as a very creditable accomplishment of the objectives of the Employment Act.

THE POST-WAR RECESSIONS

By 1949 there was clear-cut evidence that the pent-up demand for capital and consumer goods had been satisfied.[5] Industrial production fell by over 10 per cent in the last quarter of 1948, and a mild recession set in. With the increased ability of the economy to supply goods, prices began to fall and expectations for rising profits also deteriorated. Private investment slowed down markedly; the reduction in orders for new plant and equipment placed additional downward pressure on the economy. Finally, a sharp decline occurred in the export surplus. Early in 1948, by way of aiding recovery, Congress reduced tax rates and later adopted the Marshall Plan. Government defense expenditures were stepped up as a countermeasure against the deflationary forces. A spectacular increase in residential construction in the first half of 1949 turned the tide, and by the latter part of that year the downswing had come to an end.

The recession of 1948–49 was relatively mild. It reflected itself in short term changes in business expectations, mainly manifested by the reduced investment in inventories. The long term prospects for economic prosperity were still good. Since wages were rising in the face of falling consumer prices, the economy was basically healthy. But there was one symptom that foreshadowed the difficulties ahead and that was the slowness with which employment was picking up. However, by 1950 the economy had passed its 1948 peak and the beginnings of a major economic expansion were seen. The unemployment rate, which stood at 5 per cent at that time, was a discomfort but was not considered a major economic problem. On January 4, 1950, President Truman reported to the nation that "We have met and reversed the first significant downturn in economic activity since the war."[6]

June of 1950 saw the outbreak of the Korean War and the commitment of

---

[5] D. Hamberg, "The Recession of 1948–49 in the United States," *Economic Journal* (March, 1952), Vol. 62, pp. 1–14; see also W. Lewis, *Federal Fiscal Policy in the Postwar Recessions* (Washington, D.C.: Brookings Institution, 1962).

[6] *New York Times* (January 5, 1950), p. 1.

the United States forces to the defense of South Korea. President Truman felt obliged to request an additional $10.5 billion for defense and a $5 billion increase in taxes. A wave of panic buying by both consumers and businessmen took place with the result that prices rose rapidly during the remainder of 1950 and into early 1951. These inflationary pressures were the result of private sector purchases in anticipation of shortages of goods. Though the President was forced to go to Congress in late 1950 for an additional $20 billion for defense, the resulting substantial increase in government spending did not affect the economy until mid-1951. Late in 1950, the Chinese entered the conflict and again a wave of panic buying hit the economy as firms tried to build up inventories. Prices soared, and the danger of "galloping inflation" confronted the nation's economic planners. They proposed to cope with the threatened inflation by increasing taxes, cutting down on domestic spending programs, such as Social Security, and by a judicious use of price and wage controls.

Fortunately, the panic buying in 1950 had satisfied a great deal of consumer demand and business requirements for inventory so that by 1951 and 1952, despite the diversion of resources to the production of military goods, the economy was still able to meet the aggregate demand for consumer goods. While the fiscal policy of the federal government held the upward inflationary pressures in check, it is clear that the stability in the purchase of consumer goods in 1951 and 1952 was a major contributing factor to the success of that policy.

The inflationary crisis of these years brought about an important change in the role of monetary policy in the management of the economy. Since the New Deal and during World War II and its immediate aftermath, Federal Reserve policy had been largely subservient to the Treasury. From 1946 to early 1951 the Federal Reserve continued the wartime policy of pegging the price of outstanding government securities in order to facilitate and reduce the cost of financing government activities. Since many believed that in a free market economy government bond prices would fall rapidly if a low interest policy were to be maintained, a ready market had to be created artificially, and this could be done only by the Federal Reserve. By its operations in the open market, the Federal Reserve maintained government bond prices and by doing so insured confidence in the Treasury and in the financial institutions that held large amounts of government bonds. The commitment to peg the prices of these bonds by standing ready to buy them tied the hands of the Federal Reserve Board in its use of monetary policy to curb inflation. A commitment to buy government securities meant that the Board could not engage in open-market selling in order to tighten credit. The Federal Reserve Board resented its captive status under the Treasury. At the time, it secured support for its plea for independence from a subcommittee of the Joint Committee on the Economic Report, headed by Senator Douglas of Illinois. After considerable behind-the-scenes negotiation, the Federal Reserve authority finally reached an accord with the Treasury in March, 1951, recognizing its freedom of action; the Board was released from its historic commitment to peg the price of government bonds and was now free to pursue monetary policies in support of economic stability.

The result of this agreement proved to be a surprise to many. Bond prices found their own level, and the capital markets had no great difficulty in handling the Treasury's refunding operations. As time passed, interest rates did rise, but declining bond prices did not threaten the solvency of the nation's financial institutions. The Federal Reserve Board was now free to curb the cyclical influences of inflation and deflation instead of being preoccupied with managing the interest rate on government bonds. During the Korean conflict the Federal Reserve kept a watchful eye over the prices of government securities. Despite the new policy, the private financial institutions were able to finance the national debt without great displacements in the capital markets.

The continued rise in defense expenditures through 1952 kept the economy at a high level of prosperity. However, at the end of 1952 a steel strike, coupled with a prospective fall in military expenditures, created a state of uncertain business expectations. Following this strike, in July, 1952, private demand expanded, accompanied by increased accumulation of inventories. In early 1953 this demand fell off, and retail sales declined again in the face of growing stocks of goods. Businessmen, fearing to be caught holding excessive inventories, cut back on their purchases in 1953 and thus started the process of inventory liquidation. During this recession unemployment rose from approximately 3 per cent to roughly 6 per cent of the labor force; the trough of the business cycle lasted thirteen months. By mid-1954, a rapid but steady expansion had set in.

The mildness of this recession can be explained by the stable performance of disposable income and consumption and the increase in capital flows to the United States from abroad. While utilization of plant capacity was probably at a very low level during the recession, it is clear that productive capacity may have been greater than the ability of labor to utilize it effectively. The long term prospects of the economy were very good, and investment in capital goods with a long period of gestation did not fall off significantly. The severity of the recession was moderated by the continued rise in residential construction and commercial building. It was a period of rapid technological change, which forced businessmen to maintain their investment programs. Finally, spending by the federal and local governments continued to rise steadily.

From late 1954 until early in 1957 the economy went into a strong durable goods boom. This expansion was interesting because many factors that were prominent in previous post-war fluctuations were not present in this upswing. For example, pent-up demand played no role in this upturn in business. The boom was centered rather on durable consumer goods such as automobiles and home appliances. The relative price stability that had prevailed after 1950 now ended, and prices began a slow upward drift. There was also at this time a very pronounced investment boom in the form of expanding plant capacity. Yet unemployment in this whole period of sustained expansion never fell below 4 per cent.

Of all the factors underlying this prosperity phase, the two most important were the demand for durable consumer goods and the tremendous increase in plant capacity. In 1955 automobile sales reached a peak, which surprised even the traditionally optimistic leaders of this dynamic industry. The story was similar in all areas of household appliances. To keep up with the demand for durables, a change in the working force was necessary. More complex technology was introduced into manufacturing processes, requiring the use of more skilled labor. Business machines, computers, electronics, and the construction industries expanded to unanticipated heights. Because of the new technology, businessmen often abandoned serviceable plant and equipment in order to introduce new techniques that lowered production costs, financing them practically out of savings in tax payments. During this period investment funds were generated to a great extent out of such internal sources as depreciation and retained earnings. By 1956 the expansion was so strong that the economy was operating at close to full capacity, yet unemployment remained discouragingly high. The labor force was increasing, and its quality was improving, yet it is evident in the light of present knowledge that not all sectors of the national economy were prospering. Structural problems began to appear in such industries as coal mining and agriculture where incomes and levels of living were not keeping abreast with those in the rest of the national economy.

By the middle of 1957 another downturn occurred. Manufacturers' new orders for durable goods began to decline in response to the softness in the retail markets and the drop in investment. Excess capacity emerged in steel, motor vehicles, appliances, and aluminum. Still the continued expansion in consumer goods expenditures and the relatively high level of federal expenditures kept the bottom from falling out of the economy. The nation was in the midst of another recession, but the administration in power was reluctant to admit it. Private investment in 1958 was off by about 25 per cent from the level of the year before. Unemployment rose from over 4 per cent to over 7 per cent during some months in 1958. Significantly, this recession lasted only about eight months, but even after recovery was under way the level of unemployment remained high.

President Eisenhower's anti-recession program consisted mainly of monetary policy measures to lower interest rates and ease credit.[7] It relied heavily too on such a built-in economic mechanism as unemployment insurance to pull the economy into a new phase of prosperity. The Democrats in Congress had other ideas to counteract the recession; they included accelerating federal spending on authorized projects such as the construction of highways, dams,

[7] Political aspects of President Eisenhower's program are discussed in the following chapter, pp. 844–845.

and military installations, increasing price supports and extending unemployment benefits with state participation. This recession made the nation very conscious of the chronically depressed labor markets, such as those in Appalachia and other states, which failed to enjoy the affluence of the rest of the nation.

The recession of 1957–58 had several residual effects on the economy that became evident even when prosperity returned in 1959. First, in that year the nation incurred the largest peacetime budget deficit in its history; and, secondly, the unemployment rate remained above 5 per cent, even in the relatively prosperous years of 1959 and 1960. Because of these developments a split in policy developed between the Eisenhower administration and the Congress. The President remained concerned with the problem of inflation and through fiscal and monetary measures pursued a tight money policy that caused interest rates to rise from below 5 per cent to 6 per cent. The Congress, under the control of the Democrats, argued that the high unemployment was due to a low rate of economic growth. Several legislators pressed for passage of bills that would aid depressed areas and lift the economy to higher levels of employment, but these steps met some resistance by the administration. In the middle of 1959 the nation endured a 116-day steel strike, but despite the accompanying inconvenience it did not cause permanent damage to the economy. Prosperity persisted into 1960.

The following year President Kennedy took office. In the course of his State of the Union message, he stated: "We take office in the wake of seven months of recession, seven years of diminished economic growth and nine years of falling farm income."[8] The new President sent Congress an anti-recession program in February, 1961 that included increases in the length of unemployment insurance, aid to dependent children, extension of Social Security benefits, an increase in the minimum wage to $1.25 per hour, and a bill for aid to depressed areas. In spite of the enactment of most of these measures, the economy continued to lag in 1962. In order to speed economic growth the President asked for an emergency tax cut. Coupling this action with expansionary fiscal and monetary policies, the administration succeeded in bringing the economic slowdown to an end and, in fact, inaugurated the longest period of domestic prosperity in the nation's history.

THE POTENTIAL PERFORMANCE OF THE ECONOMY

At this point in our analysis, we shall consider the relevance and implications of the Harrod-Domar theory for the experience of the 1950's and 1960's. We must ask some questions that were posed in the Presidential campaign of 1960. "Did the emphasis on policies for monetary stability in the 1950's cost the nation substantial economic growth? Did the multiple recessions of the

[8] *New York Times* (January 31, 1961), p. 1.

post-war period condition the nation to accept relatively slow rates of growth and high levels of unemployment? These questions are partially answered by the Harrod-Domar growth theory. According to this theory, we can only reach full employment growth by expanding and increasing the volume of expenditures. The route to full employment is to increase both private investment and government expenditures. Creative tax policies such as changes in depreciation, depletion, or the treatment of capital gains can be used to control the stream of private investment. However, the quality of such investment remains beyond the cortrol of fiscal policy and is heavily dependent on innovation and investment and their technological application. In the final analysis, the theory holds that only through adequate expenditures in the public sector can the economy be encouraged to reach its potential performance.

Chart 3 below shows that through a large part of the 1950's and 1960's the economy performed well below its full capacity.[9] Between the years 1958 and 1962 the amount of lost output represented by this gap came to $170 billion or nearly $1,000 per person. For example, in 1964 if the economy had achieved its potential performance, it could have increased GNP by an additional $25–30 billion, or more than $300 per family. Unemployment would have fallen by 1 per cent in that particular year and a climate of healthy full employment would have been created. To attain such full employment it is necessary that the private sector invest an amount as large as the public wants to save out of the full employment level of income.

While the economy in the 1950's should have grown at the rate of about 4 per cent a year, its actual rate of growth was 2.5 per cent. What factors explain the loss of this economic potential? First, it would seem that the rate of growth of private and collective consumption did not justify or require the addition of sufficient new productive capacity. Secondly, the monopolistic character of commodity markets and the bureaucratic nature of the corporate hierarchy may have been responsible for ultra-conservative business attitudes so far as plant and equipment expenditures were concerned. Thirdly, the expansion of the service sector of the economy in this period may have been responsible for a relatively low level of private investment; services are not capital intensive, and their quantity can be increased by small amounts of additional investment. Fourth and finally, it is possible that the depressed rate of our exports in these years and the mergers and acquisitions that were so prominent a feature of the period slowed the growth of aggregate demand.

[9] We measure potential GNP as the volume of goods and services that the economy could produce if the unemployment rate were held down to 4%. A potential growth rate of 4% seems to be approximately correct, according to the Kuznets data in *Capital in the American Economy* [National Bureau of Economic Research (Princeton, N.J.: Princeton University Press, 1961), p. 217]. In making the projection of potential economic growth as shown in Chart 3, the President's Council of Economic Advisers used a $3\frac{1}{2}\%$ rate of annual growth for the period from the middle of 1955 to the fourth quarter of 1962 and a rate of $3\frac{1}{4}\%$ thereafter. The Rockefeller Report [*The Challenge to America: Its Economic and Social Aspects* (Garden City: Doubleday and Co., 1958), p. 64] contended that a growth rate of 5% was possible "if we realize[d] fully our impressive opportunities for economic expansion."

CHART 3

Gross National Product, Actual and Potential,
and Unemployment Rate

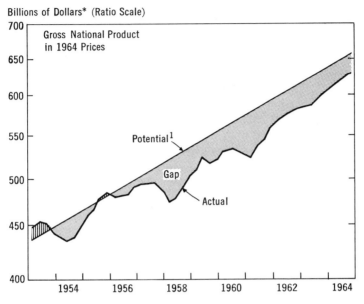

Billions of Dollars* (Ratio Scale)

Gross National Product
in 1964 Prices

Potential[1]

Gap

Actual

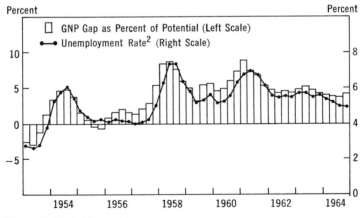

Percent   Percent

☐ GNP Gap as Percent of Potential (Left Scale)
•—• Unemployment Rate[2] (Right Scale)

*Seasonally Adjusted Annual Rates.
[1] $3\frac{1}{2}$ % Trend Line Through Middle of 1955 to 1962 IV; $3\frac{1}{4}$ % Trend Line Thereafter.
[2] Unemployment as Percent of Civilian Labor Force; Seasonally Adjusted.
Sources: Department of Commerce, Department of Labor, and Council of Economic Advisers.

ᵃ Source: *Economic Report of the President*, Jan. 1963, p. 27.

Many economists have concluded that the sluggish performance of the
economy in the 1950's and 1960's was attributable to an excess concern with
price stabilization and insufficient attention to growth. Whatever view or
emphasis is adopted in explaining the disappointing performance of the economy in the late fifties, it can be agreed that the Harrod-Domar theory is

helpful because it indicates the theoretical requirements of full employment and steady growth.

President Kennedy was convinced that if the economy's rate of growth could be accelerated to reach its potential he could acquire the necessary funds to carry out his New Frontier program. In his view, the nation's principal economic priority was to achieve a high rate of economic growth. To accomplish this objective, his administration adopted an expansionary fiscal policy in 1964 as recommended by the Council of Economic Advisers. This policy, in effect, brought the administration's position closer to that of the Rockefeller Brothers' report, which had emphasized the idle plant capacity and high unemployment rate in the economy in the late fifties.[10] From early 1961 to the end of 1966, GNP rose an average of $44 billion a year. Nine billion dollars of this increase was due to the rise of prices; $10 billion of the gain was traceable to putting idle men and machines back to work; and $25 billion came from expanding our production-possibility frontier outward. This achievement was justly hailed as a triumph for positive fiscal policy.

STRUCTURAL VERSUS AGGREGATIVE APPROACHES TO ECONOMIC PROBLEMS

In the post-war debate on economic policy, many economists contended that the aggregative approach to economic development failed to correct structural problems that arose periodically in our various industries. Their point was that aggregative fiscal or monetary policies did not, for example, correct the serious economic problems of American agriculture or the structural maladjustments in the mining areas of Appalachia. A brief examination of the American farm crisis that emerged in this period will serve to illustrate this point of view.

Essentially, five conditions have aggravated the American farm problem in the years since World War II: (1) Productivity has risen about 30 per cent since 1945—the greatest increase in any comparable period of our history. This remarkable surge in productivity has largely been the result of capital accumulated during the war being put to use in modernization and expansion of farms. The size of the average farm has increased 10 per cent since the end of the second World War. (2) The need for agricultural labor has declined faster than the industrial and service sectors of the economy could absorb the surplus farm workers. As machines took over many of the tasks that formerly required manual labor, the demand for farm labor declined as productivity per man-hour increased. While the total resources in agriculture fell by 20 per cent from 1950 to 1960, farm labor declined by 45 per cent on a per unit of output basis. The use of machines has doubled since 1940 and the employment of labor has been halved, ratios of change that reflect the direct substituta-

---

[10] See footnote 9.

bility of capital for labor. Furthermore, the number of people leaving farming has been inversely related to the phases of the business cycle. In other words, in periods of recession when unemployment was highest, the need for opportunities to employ the marginal and displaced farmers and farm laborers has been greatest. The latter's migration from rural to urban areas in the post-war years has contributed greatly to the seriousness of the economic problems facing our cities. (3) The demand for farm goods has not kept pace with rising productivity. This tendency is likely in an affluent society since Engels' Law tells us that as we get richer a smaller proportion of our income goes to purchase necessities such as food. (4) Increasingly, foreign nations have been able to compete with the United States in agricultural production. In addition, some areas such as western Europe have largely closed the market for our agricultural produce by tariffs or have increased their own output. (5) A large decline in farm prices has had little effect on the consumption of agricultural products. While population has increased 15 per cent from 1950 to 1960, food expenditures have gone up only 17 per cent, compared to a total increase in expenditures of 30 per cent. Generally, a 5 per cent decline in prices results in only a 1 per cent increase in the consumption of agricultural products.

The attempts to solve the American farm problem in the post-war period have been largely aggregative in nature. Six basic approaches to a solution were theoretically possible. They were: (1) increase demand; (2) reduce supply; (3) subsidize farm products; (4) allow competition to eliminate the marginal farmers; (5) cut production costs; (6) raise prices by a policy of deliberate inflation.

In the opinion of many students, only the fourth solution is lasting and permanent in its result. Even if the fourth solution is attractive because of its permanency, it is not feasible because it would cause considerable social dislocation and could drive the national unemployment rate up to about 12 per cent.

The fifth solution has resulted in greater efficiency in the form of reduced production costs, but it has also contributed to a greater oversupply because farmers have sought to obtain larger yields at the lower prices.

Inflating the money supply is no longer of benefit to modern farmers because they would have to pay more for farm equipment and other means of production at a time when the increase in productivity has depressed prices. Furthermore, since farm credit is readily available through the various federal agencies, inflation will not have much effect on the cost of the farmer's debt.

Increasing the demand for farm commodities has been a successful part of the contemporary farm program; it has been coupled with foreign aid to spur consumption of our excess farm output and with price supports. Under the "food for peace" program large federal supplies of agricultural commodities have been distributed through "soft money" sales to many of the underdeveloped nations. These countries pay nowhere near the cost of these commodities because the government subsidizes farm prices by paying 85 per cent, on the average, of the ratio of farm prices to U.S. industrial prices for the years 1910–14. (This is the historic parity-price program, which dates back to the New Deal days.) In addition to this program, a certain amount of potential agricultural production is prevented from coming to the market and thus depressing prices by the soil bank plan, which keeps land out of commercial use. This program also has good conservation effects. Wheat, corn, cotton, rice, tobacco, peanuts, and dairy products are subsidized in price, even though United States agriculture is probably the most efficient in the world and its products *sans* subsidy could easily be sold in the unprotected markets of the world. Incidentally, the subsidy program, as it now operates, often benefits the well-to-do farmers more than the low income ones. In 1962, for example, the largest 39 per cent of the farms produced 87 per cent of our total farm output and received an almost proportionate share of the government subsidy to agriculture.

As matters now stand, a vicious cycle exists in American agriculture in its relation to the rest of the economy. The inefficient allocation of resources in agriculture slows up economic growth in other areas of the economy, and this reduces the employment opportunities needed to move the marginal farmers into industry. It is for this reason that the structuralists have argued that the aggregative approach to the solution of this particular problem is inherently ineffective.

A similar type of analysis can be applied to the structural difficulties of the soft-coal mining industry in the Appalachian region. Again, regional stagnation has been rather unresponsive to aggregative attempts to remedy the situation. Because of these structural maladjustments the character of the poverty problem has both a rural as well as an urban aspect. The migration of displaced farmers to the inner cities of the nation in search of economic security comes at a time when our municipalities are faced with staggering financial and social problems. The shrinkage of their tax base, which has accompanied the siphoning of the more affluent middle class to suburbia, reduces the available funds to meet rising welfare and other costs of modern urban government. The interdependence of the problems of rural and urban poverty strikingly illustrates the organic nature of the economy and suggests the need for integral programs to cope with the swiftly changing demands of our complex society.

An attempt to handle these problems on a disaggregated basis was implicit in the proposals of Dr. Walter Heller and Mayor John Lindsay of New York.[11] Dr. Heller's program was advanced while he was Chairman of the Council of Economic Advisers (1961–64). Fundamentally, it takes into account the effect of rapid economic growth on the revenue derived from the federal income tax. Heller pointed out that this tax would yield revenues of $250 billion by 1970 and that in the absence of war such a sum would be in excess of what could be managed soundly by the federal government. He

---

[11] The so-called Heller plan is outlined in W. W. Heller, *New Dimensions of Political Economy* (New York: W. W. Norton and Co., 1967), pp. 145–147. Mayor Lindsay's proposal was set forth in his fiscal message of 1967 to Governor Rockefeller.

proposed to rebate a portion of this tax to the states so that they could more adequately solve their own peculiar structural problems. Mayor Lindsay proposed an analogous program for New York State, arguing that the state income tax should show good growth and that a portion of that tax should be returned to the urban areas so that they could handle their own local problems with these "urban-aid" funds.

THE TRIUMPH OF GUIDED CAPITALISM

During the entire post-World War II period, with the possible exception of the Eisenhower years, there was a broad acceptance of the Keynesian prescription for fiscal policy. The federal government in order to achieve Harrod-Domar steady-state growth has, by and large, adopted the principles of countercyclical policy. The extent to which this is so is roughly shown in Chart 4. Part of this acceptance of Keynesian ideas manifested itself in the use of discretionary fiscal measures and part in the employment of the automatic fiscal stabilizers.

An automatic stabilizer is defined as any device that operates to compensate for changes in the business cycle without waiting for new policy decisions. It tends to produce budgetary deficits in slumps, surpluses in booms, ex-

CHART 4

Business Cycles and Fiscal Policy, 1945–1968

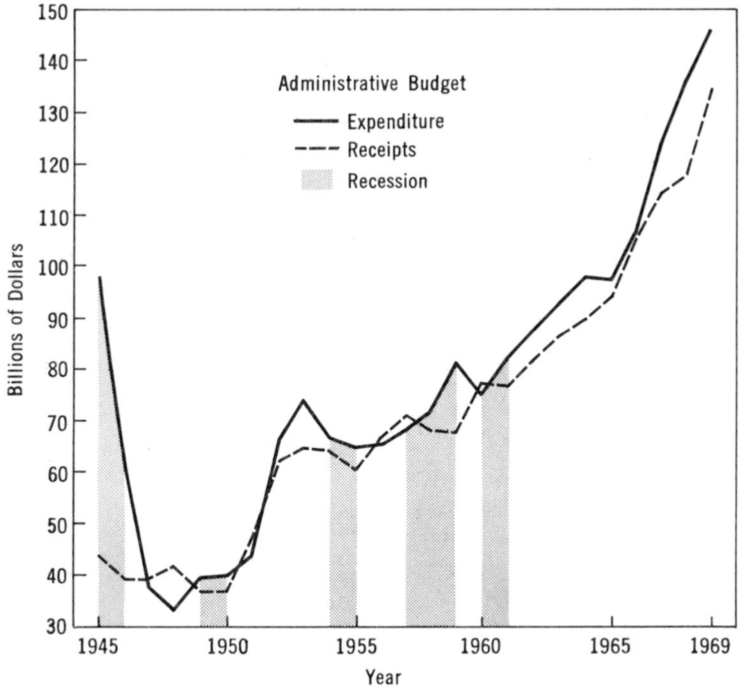

pand the community's stock of wealth, lower cash in slumps, raise it in booms, or any combination of these things. Ideally, these automatic stabilizers should be predictable in their effects, have clearly defined objectives, be free from Congressional control, and contribute to a relatively stable price level and full employment.

The three major sources of the federal government's revenue meet some of these criteria quite well. They are the personal and corporate income taxes and the excises. Clearly when the national income rises the federal government's share increases by a progressive amount. The unemployment insurance and Social Security programs also tend to increase income and lower taxes in recessions and *vice versa* in prosperity; to some degree they operate as automatic stabilizers. Likewise, the federal farm price supports also have this character. These mechanisms go into effect whenever we have a recession or an overheating of the economy, whether or not we recognize or detect these changing business conditions.

On the basis of the post-war experience, it would seem that these stabilizers have reduced the amplitude of cyclical fluctuations. They have also acted to establish upper and lower buffers between which economic activity fluctuates. An attempt has been made to bring these floors and ceilings closer together so that economists can "finely tune" a steady state of economic growth. To a large degree the slowness with which we recovered from the 1949 recession was a result of the lack of power in these stabilizers. The speed with which we recovered from the recessions of 1953–54, 1957–58, and 1960 was also partly traceable to the operation of these automatic stabilizers. They have sharply reduced the secondary repercussions on incomes caused by shifts in inventory accumulation and decumulation, thus assisting in the stabilization of consumer and plant and equipment expenditures. By and large, the functioning of these stabilizers has led to the "socialization" of the investment process with the result that economic planning in the United States is primarily concerned with the aggregate level of consumer expenditures and the related control of the acceleration effect.

Another aspect of guided capitalism that has been much discussed in postwar America is discretionary fiscal policy. Efforts along these lines have not been as easy to implement as the automatic stabilizers because an active fiscal policy requires a knowledge of what phase of the business cycle we are in and a determination of what policies can or cannot be used; in short, there are difficulties because of the timing problem. The complications may be illustrated by what happened in the 1950's in this area of policy-making. In that period the principle was followed in recessions of delaying public works until the downturn in business actually occurred. Once undertaken, these programs often proved to be inflexible because once begun they tended to perpetuate themselves. For example, road building programs were extended beyond the period needed or duplicated other efforts simply because they were supported by Congressmen who wanted "pork barrel" legislation for their constituents.

In 1961, Walter Heller brought a startlingly effective set of ideas about national economic policy to the councils of the Kennedy administration. In general, these policies were supported by the Committee for Economic Development and the majority of Keynesian economists. They were four in number: first, Heller argued that taxes should be related to expenditures, which should have the effect of keeping unemployment at about 3.4 per cent maximum. Secondly, he advocated deficit spending in periods of economic weakness. Thirdly, he called for budget surpluses when unemployment dropped well below 4 per cent in order to prevent rampant inflation. Finally, he urged periodic tax cuts to avoid an excessive tax burden as the economy grew. Three basic concepts underlie Heller's economics: the idea of counter-cylical spending, the assumption that there is a trade-off between inflation and unemployment, and finally, the recognition that "fiscal drag" could be caused by accelerated economic growth.[12]

The successful application of these policies is probably responsible for the growth in personal income from 1961 to 1967 of more than $250 billion. Over the same period unemployment dropped from over 5 per cent to less than 4 per cent, and the number employed went from 66 to 76 million. However, not all economic indicators behaved satisfactorily over these years. The Congress in President Johnson's administration showed a great reluctance to increase taxes to pay for the Vietnam War, and the consumer price index steadily climbed from 104 in 1961 to 118 in 1967. Fiscal policy under the Kennedy-Johnson administrations had achieved economic growth at high rates, but as a whole the problem of price stability was not successfully solved.

A second major tool in combating cyclical fluctuations is monetary policy. We have already pointed out that in 1953 the Federal Reserve Open-Market Committee adopted a policy of limiting their open-market operations to short term Treasury bills, unless unusual developments created disorder in the federal securities market. The Federal Reserve gave as its reasons for this policy its desire for greater stability in bond prices and its reluctance to impose capital losses on holders of long term securities. Thereafter, from 1953 to 1960 the Federal Reserve authorities followed a counter-cyclical monetary policy. In 1953–54, the Federal Reserve eased money to combat the deflationary pressure of the recession. The System tightened money again from 1955 to 1957 to check inflationary tendencies. In the latter year the control of credit was relaxed and then tightened again in 1958 to dampen inflationary forces. Many critics have argued that the Federal Reserve eased credit too much in the recession of 1954 and that the system should have done more credit tightening in 1955 and 1956; in particular, that it should have adopted qualitative credit controls in the latter period. Apparently weary of criticism, the Federal Reserve officials were slow in easing money in 1957 and the tightening up in 1958 was premature and resulted in slowing the recovery from the recession. In 1960 under heavy criticism the System abandoned its "bills only" policy and gave as its reason its desire to ease pressure on the

---

[12] "Fiscal drag" refers to the retarding effect of a full-employment surplus in the federal budget, which siphons too much income out of the private economy and thus chokes further economic expansion.

balance of payments. In fact, the Federal Reserve had found that the long term interest rates did not necessarily follow any change in the short term quotations and that manipulation of the latter did not lead to control over long term rates.

In February, 1961, the Federal Reserve authority announced that it would also purchase long term government securities in order to exercise better control over long term interest rates. For the remainder of 1961 bank credit was expanded as the Federal Reserve sought to ease bank reserves. Short term interest rates rose in 1962 and 1963, as the Federal Reserve continued to supply reserves to the system. The long term rates fell in 1962 and rose in 1963. The Kennedy tax cut in 1964 brought the economy a new level of prosperity, and this fiscal accomplishment caused some to doubt the importance of monetary policy. Professor Milton Friedman of the University of Chicago argued that the Federal Reserve had no way of knowing what open-market purchases or sales did to the money supply and that movements in the rediscount rate or reserve ratio could not substantially affect member bank reserves because of their relative excess.

The power of monetary policy was clearly seen, however, in mid-1966, particularly in the construction industry, when the Federal Reserve tightened money so much that mortgages were nearly impossible to obtain. Savings and loan associations were trapped with a high interest rate to depositors, while housing starts dropped to below one million units. A quick mortgage money expansion saved the economy from a total collapse of construction activity. In still another area monetary policy unaided showed its limitations. Despite all efforts to control the balance of payments by monetary policy, the program was far from successful, and in 1967–68 the international monetary system tottered on the brink of a breakdown.

In short, in these post-war years, monetary policy was open to criticism on the timing of its movement and the inadequacy of knowledge concerning the fluctuations of the economy so that action could be taken at the appropriate time. Both criticisms were somewhat justified, and as a consequence the Federal Reserve began an agonizing reappraisal of its policy.

From this survey of the post-war period, it can be concluded that the management of monetary and fiscal policy has brought us to a point at which the upper and lower boundaries of economic prosperity have been drawn closer together. As a result we tread the complex path of economic growth and development between these narrowed boundaries. This achievement of more stable growth is a triumph of no little consequence for guided capitalism.

THE SOURCES OF ECONOMIC GROWTH

Most economists are in general agreement that the major source of recent growth in the economy has been the increase in productivity. On the average, during the 1950's and the mid-1960's our labor productivity increased by 2.9 per cent a year. Between 1947 and 1964 agricultural real output per man-hour rose by 167 per cent and that of manufacturing by 57 per cent. In general, there have been four principal sources for the increase in our rate of growth in recent years: (1) improved human capital; (2) the economies of large-scale production; (3) the deepening of capital; and (4) technological advances.

Since the end of the second World War and the passage of the G.I. Bill of Rights, the American labor force has consistently enhanced its knowledge and skill through improvement in its educational level. The expansion of higher education and the subsidization of students have led to marked gains in the educational background of workers. Better education for workers has improved the quality of the nation's labor force and this has manifested itself in increased productivity.

A second source of added productivity is the effect of mass production. Here, the "paper revolution" caused by the advent of computers has made it possible to achieve economies of large-scale production even in some white-collar operations. Yet, Dennison estimates that the new economies of large-scale production have added only about 10 per cent to our annual rate of productivity increase.[13]

Deepening of capital has been a third cause of the extraordinary growth of the economy. Since 1947, the average worker has found that the amount of capital aiding him in performing his duties has increased. Large stocks of capital equipment have been accumulated for the worker, and this has made possible increased specialization of function and more productive use of time. The value of the capital stock per worker has been growing at the rate of 2.7 per cent per year since 1947. But the sheer magnitude of this capital increase has not been as important as its qualitative improvement.

This upgrading of capital equipment has been due to advances in technology—the fourth and probably the most important element in recent American economic growth. New products of a demand-creating kind, labor-displacing equipment, research and development, changes in business organization and in the techniques of management have been the principal types of technological breakthroughs in this period. A key factor in increasing technological advance has been investment in research and development; this is the single most important variable in determining technological change. Indeed, the high salaries for scientists and engineers in the United States have led to an influx of foreign scientific talent to this country, which, coupled with existing scientific personnel, has provided a large base for research. Increasingly, the federal government has chosen to underwrite basic research costs in a variety of industries with the net result that there has been a veritable explosion in technology. Without doubt, technological progress has been the most significant factor accounting for American economic growth since World War II.

---

[13] E. F. Dennison, *The Sources of Economic Growth in the United States and the Alternatives before Us*, Supplementary Paper No. 13 (New York: Committee for Economic Development, 1962).

TOWARD FREER WORLD TRADE

At the end of World War II the United States made a historic commitment to the reconstruction of the internal economies of some of the war-devastated nations. In order to do this effectively, American policy in the immediate post-World War II period was grounded on two fundamental ideas. One of these was the establishment of freer trade among the nations of the world. Toward this end, in 1947 the United States signed the General Agreement on Tariffs and Trade (GATT). The other policy which was central to our plans for the restoration of prosperity to a war-torn world was the direct extension of foreign aid to our former allies and to other nations. This aspect of our post-war plans marked a major departure from anything that had occurred in world politics before. The United States as a victor had voluntarily decided to assist her allies and defeated enemies to restore their economic capacities (even though they might eventually compete with us) by a generous program of low-cost loans and outright grants.

In furtherance of this objective, the United States participated in the Bretton Woods Conference in 1944 at which the International Monetary Fund was established. This Fund was to hold on deposit a mixed assortment of gold and currencies of its member nations. These funds were to be used on the international market in order to support the exchange rates of any two countries or to support the exchange rate between a member nation's currency and gold. In this manner it was believed that short term fluctuations in foreign exchange rates could be stabilized. At the same time the International Bank for Reconstruction and Development was formed to provide long term capital loans for reconstruction purposes.

The United Nations Relief and Rehabilitation Administration (UNRRA) had been set up in 1943 to provide immediate relief to the war-ravaged countries by channelling 1 per cent of member nations' national income into the relief of acute economic problems. Over $3 billion in aid was distributed by UNRRA; when it was dissolved in 1947, the remaining relief work was delegated to specialized UN agencies.

In July of 1946 a loan of $3,750 million by the United States to Great Britain was floated over a four-year period. Twenty billion dollars of British lend-lease obligations were cancelled, and $650 million in such obligations were consolidated into a total loan of $4,400 million. The loan was to be paid at 2 per cent interest; first payments started in 1952.

Despite the substantial foreign loans and grants extended under UNRRA and the British loan, the European economic position deteriorated further in 1947. The balance of payments crises throughout Europe and the widespread price inflation, coupled with poor crops in that year, brought many of these nations to a critical juncture. One after another some of the leading nations of eastern Europe had been taken over by Communist governments, and many policy-makers in the United States were convinced that if more was not done to alleviate European economic distress the entire continent might go Communist. It was against this background that Secretary of State George C. Marshall formulated the European Recovery Program. Under this plan substantial grants to the nations of Europe were authorized, with a provision that a proportion of the money should be spent in the United States. This program is credited with starting many of the western European nations on their way to economic recovery.

The total effort made by the United States in the years 1945–51 on behalf of European recovery was truly stupendous in terms of the nation's resources. Table 2 below shows the funds that were advanced by the United States in the

TABLE 2

International Grants and Loans of the United States,
July 1, 1945–December 31, 1951
(In millions of dollars)

	Total	Before E.R.P.	During E.R.P.
Grants			
1. Lend-Lease	$ 1,945	$1,945	—
2. European Recovery Program (mutual security)	12,763	—	$12,763
3. Civilian supplies to occupied areas	5,439	2,412	3,027
4. UNRRA, post-UNRRA, and interim aid	3,443	3,172	271
5. Aid to Philippines	631	130	500
6. Aid to Greece and Turkey	659	165	495
7. Aid to China	243	120	123
8. Other	632	146	485
Receipts	−1,090	−499	−591
Net Total	$24,665	$7,592	$17,073
Loans			
1. British loan	$ 3,750	$3,750	—
2. Export-Import Bank loans	2,937	2,087	$ 849
3. Surplus property (including merchant ships)	1,338	1,236	102
4. Credit-agreement offsets to grants	1,256	1,253	3
5. European Recovery Program (mutual security)	1,277	—	1,277
6. Other	515	362	153
Collections	−1,766	−523	−1,243
Net Total	$ 9,306	$8,165	$ 1,141

Source: W. H. Steiner & E. Shapiro, *Money & Banking*, 3rd Edition (New York: Holt & Co., 1953), p. 629.

form of loans and grants in these years. In 1950 alone the United States' foreign aid contribution to the world amounted to $4.5 billion. An additional

$500 million of private charitable remittances was sent abroad, together with government loans of $150 million and private investments of $1 billion. A grant total of $6 billion represented the American aid and investment package abroad for 1950. These various programs of aid and reconstruction accomplished many of their goals, and by 1951 most of the west European economy was healthy, and the Communist thrust had been repulsed.

In the years after 1958 a general adverse position in the United States' balance of payments provided the world with one billion American dollars. With the expansion of world trade in the post-war period, these funds had become practically necessary for other trading nations because only gold, U.S. dollars, and pounds sterling were used to settle international claims. However, as international trade and finance continued its expansion and the world's gold reserves failed to keep pace, the problem of international liquidity, as it is called, came to the fore. Unless the United States and Great Britain were to run chronic deficits in their balance of payments, the supply of international monies would be insufficient to meet the needs of the world's trade.

In the post-war era, except for 1957, the United States balance of payments was negative, and after 1958 it reached alarming heights. While this almost chronic imbalance in the United States' trade position provided the world with the funds needed for international commerce and finance, foreign nations in the sixties began to question the capacity of this country to meet its financial obligations. The nation's gold stock dwindled, and foreign holdings of dollars exceeded the supply of gold in the Treasury's vaults. In nearly every year after 1960 the free market price of gold was in excess of the United States' pegged price of $35 per ounce.

What were the factors behind these continuing deficits in our balance of payments? They did not originate in the merchandise account because the nation had huge export surpluses during the entire post-World War II period. Nor were there any deficits in the balance on current account, in spite of the sizeable and uncompensated-for tourist and foreign shipping expenditures. In the pre-1955 period, the major source of the imbalance was United States' aid expenditures abroad. After 1955 the main source of difficulties was in the movement of long and short term capital abroad. The formation of the European Common Market had led to the erection by its member nations of a common tariff barrier against the outside world. American manufacturers avoided this protective tariff wall by establishing branch factories within the boundaries of the Common Market. It was the export of American capital to develop these foreign branches and to exploit foreign markets that became the crucial factor in the imbalance in the nation's payments position after the middle fifties.

The attempts to correct the imbalance in the nation's financial position were not at first addressed to its true causes. Initially, Americans were prohibited from buying or selling gold because of the fear that increasing speculation would drain the United States' gold reserves. Then, an act was passed making it illegal for American citizens to own gold in order to limit speculation against the dollar. This was followed by efforts to increase American exports and to limit imports voluntarily. Restrictions on purchases from abroad by tourists caused the untariffed items to fall from $500 to $100 per person. Again, these solutions did not cope adequately with the underlying problem of international liquidity and, hence, were ineffective in reversing the adverse trend of our balance of payments.

In 1960 a debate began on how far the United States should go to correct its imbalance of payments and on the whole question of ways and means. Two camps quickly emerged; one favored direct national action of an emergency sort to curb United States imbalances immediately, and the other advocated strong international measures, with the United States retaining the prerogative of being unconcerned with the entire problem.

Those who favored strong domestic policies to cure the imbalance in our financial position argued that such action was necessary to maintain the competitiveness of the nation in world markets. Individuals of this persuasion favored high interest rates, quotas on foreign investments by Americans abroad, curtailment of the nation's military and foreign aid commitments and domestic deflationary policies to make our goods more attractive to non-Americans. By and large, President Johnson and the Federal Reserve Board accepted many of these recommendations during the late 1960's. However, a group of economists continued to contend that these programs would lead to economic disaster in the long run.

In the entire post-World War II period, the foreign trade of the United States never really accounted for more than an average of approximately 7 per cent of its total commerce. In the light of this fact, many argued that to press forward with drastic domestic reforms to correct the deficit in our balance of payments was tantamount to allowing the tail to wag the dog. Besides, the argument ran, if the fundamental problem was one of international liquidity, these domestic programs would be ineffective in any case. Those holding this view proposed instead the establishment of a central bank for the world with some type of new reserve assets that would be accepted in international trade and could be expanded or contracted to meet liquidity needs. Professors Robert Triffin and Edward M. Bernstein advocated such a program.[14] On the other hand, Milton Friedman and others argued that the needs of liquidity and free trade could only be met through the establishment of freely fluctuating exchange rates rather than holding in the conventional way to stable ratios of exchange. In 1967, the world moved closer to acceptance of the Triffin-Bernstein type of system with accords that in effect gave the International Monetary Fund eventual power over a non-specie adjustable money. The meeting at Rio de Janeiro in September of that year, which constituted an agreement on the establishment of special drawing rights on the

[14] See R. Triffin, *Gold and the Dollar Crisis* (New Haven: Yale University Press, 1961) and by the same author, *Our International Monetary System: Yesterday, Today and Tomorrow* (New York: Random House, 1968); E. M. Bernstein, "The Adequacy of United States Gold Reserves," *American Economic Review* (May, 1961), pp. 439–446.

Fund, was a hopeful step in the evolution of the international monetary system.

At home, even before this momentous agreement was reached, the United States had taken significant action to lower tariff barriers with the Common Market countries. Under the terms of the Trade Expansion Act of 1962, possibly the most important tariff legislation since the Trade Agreements Act of 1934, the President was authorized to reduce any tariff duty in effect as of July 1st of that year by 50 per cent; other provisions of this law made it possible for the President to negotiate a lowering of import duties by bargaining with the other nations of the Atlantic Community. Under the Kennedy Round of tariff negotiations with these countries in 1964 the average level of U.S. import duties was reduced to a century low.

POSSIBILITIES AND PROBLEMS OF A FULL EMPLOYMENT ECONOMY

In 1968 the United States entered the eighth year of an unprecedented period of sustained economic expansion that had begun shortly after the inauguration of the Kennedy administration. This "longest and strongest expansion in our history" was in marked contrast to our earlier cyclical pattern of ups and downs. The longest previous advance was the 80-month expansion that accompanied World War II. Over the nearly seven years of this latest expansion, gross national product, measured in constant prices, increased 41 per cent. The absolute amount of the increase, $231 billion (in 1967 prices) was "greater than the entire real output of the Nation only 30 years ago. . . ."[15] The influence of this remarkable expansion on the components of GNP, personal income, and corporate profits is shown graphically in Charts 5, 6, and 7. The economic performance illustrated by these graphs owed much to the use of discretionary fiscal and monetary policies over the course of these years. To cite just one instance in support of this fact, in addition to our previous analysis, consider what happened in 1967. In the first half of that year a substantial inventory adjustment occurred such as had contributed to the four prior post-war recessions. But this latest inventory liquidation did not lead to a recession. Expansionary fiscal and monetary policies were adopted that caused the expansion to endure.

Like many new powers conferred by the advances of science and technology, our growing ability to stabilize economic growth has potentialities for good or evil. Some opponents of the Vietnam war could rightly wonder, for example, if the nation would have prosecuted that unpopular military effort as long as it has if we had been under the constraint of the principle of an annually balanced federal budget. In any case, in the late sixties as the hor-

[15] *Economic Report of the President*, February, 1968 (Washington, D.C.: U.S. Government Printing Office, 1968), p. 58.

CHART 5

Gross National Product, 1961–67

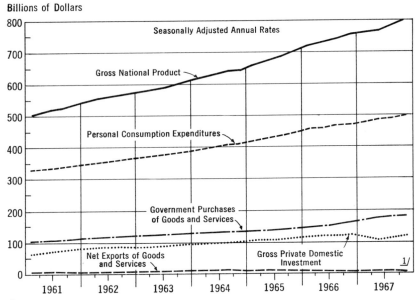

Billions of Dollars

Seasonally Adjusted Annual Rates

Gross National Product

Personal Consumption Expenditures

Government Purchases of Goods and Services

Net Exports of Goods and Services

Gross Private Domestic Investment

1961 1962 1963 1964 1965 1966 1967

¹ Preliminary

Source: Department of Commerce

CHART 6

Personal Income, 1961–67

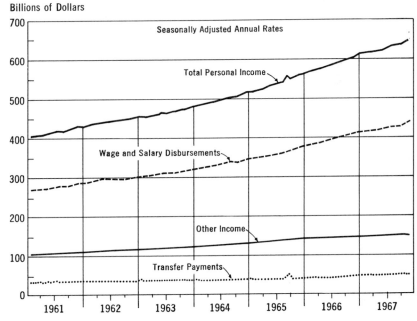

Billions of Dollars

Seasonally Adjusted Annual Rates

Total Personal Income

Wage and Salary Disbursements

Other Income

Transfer Payments

1961 1962 1963 1964 1965 1966 1967

Source: Department of Commerce

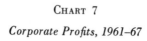

CHART 7

Corporate Profits, 1961–67

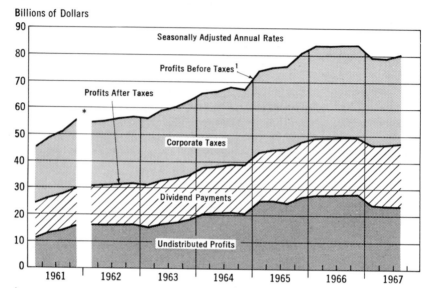

[1] Excluding Inventory Valuation Adjustment.

*NOTE—Data Beginning 1962 Adjusted for Effects of New Depreciation Guidelines ($2½ Billion for 1962) and Therefore Not Comparable with Preceding Data. Data for Alaska and Hawaii Included Beginning 1960.

Source: Department of Commerce

rible little war in that Southeast Asian country seemed to be approaching its end, at least so far as American participation was concerned, there was great national interest about the effects of demobilization on the economy and the possible uses to which the resources so released might be put. Certainly, there was no dearth of private and public wants even in this most affluent of nations. The urban crisis, the ten million families still living in poverty, the vast deficit in housing, the imbalance in social capital goods, and other possible public expenditures with a high social return, all constituted pressing needs that called for solution and action. (Various aspects of some of these problems will be considered further in the following chapter.)

The accomplishments of the "new economics" in the post-war years made many economists confident that the new tools of economic stabilization and growth could readily be applied to solve the problems of peace. It was recognized, of course, that there were serious technical difficulties in the management of a high-level mass consumption society. For example, as the nation approached full employment in 1965, the Council of Economic Advisers acknowledged that "creeping inflation" had set in. In addition, there was the persistent problem of the deficit in our balance of payments that is closely related to and affected by the action taken to promote full employment and price stability. Regardless of such complications, the economy of the late sixties had the ability not only to provide both guns and butter, but, more important, in peacetime it could use Keynesian economics to make possible a more balanced society. The "new economics" represented a historic enhancement of man's economic means and power. By that very fact it magnified the importance of the ends or uses to which the new-found capacity was put. In mid-twentieth century America, as the following chapter reveals, this question of social priorities became more pressing than ever.

Chapter 31

SOCIAL AND POLITICAL CHANGE IN A MASS TECHNOLOGICAL SOCIETY

THE INDUSTRIAL SYSTEM AND THE CHANGING SOCIAL STRUCTURE

In Galbraith's *The New Industrial State*, the phrase, the "industrial system," refers to the "few hundred technically dynamic, massively capitalized and highly organized corporations"[1] in our economy. In his presentation, these giant, mature corporations are treated as the major agents of change in contemporary industrial society. The new relationship of the state to the economy, the further growth of mass advertising, the retardation in the expansion of unions, and the phenomenal increase in the scale of higher education are examined in relation to these dynamic organizations and current technological change. He insists that these changes must be seen not in isolation from each other, but rather in terms of their close interdependence. In its effects on the American economy "this matrix of change has been more than the sum of its parts."[2] In the Galbraithian conception, the imperatives of technology are the fundamental part of this dynamic matrix. They have necessitated the accumulation of huge amounts of capital by the big corporations and forced them to an increased use of planning to avoid market risks and to obtain profit.

Galbraith's analysis should interest the sociologist, for essentially he is considering the effect of change in one part of the nation's social system upon another. In this chapter, in the course of reviewing some of the main social and political changes of the post-war years, we appraise Galbraith's theses about the inter-relatedness of change in our kinetic technological society.

Galbraith's treatment of industrial management and of the repercussions of corporate activities upon the broader society recalls Veblen's earlier work along these same lines as well as that of the institutional economists of the 1920's and the studies of Berle and Means, Burnham, Gordon and Knauth,

---

[1] J. K. Galbraith, *The New Industrial State* (Boston: Houghton Mifflin Co., 1967), p. 9.
[2] *Ibid.*, p. 4.

among others.[3] We mention these earlier analyses not to depreciate the value and insight of Galbraith's book, but to suggest that in dealing with the emergence of the large corporations and the new, powerful role of management he had scholarly predecessors who also recognized the so-called "managerial revolution."

Galbraith contends that today the corporate managers do not make the major decisions. "The effective power of decision," he states, "is lodged deeply in the technical, planning and other specialized staff"—what he calls the technostructure. Whether one agrees with him on this particular point or not, there is no disputing that the degree of management's control in our large corporations has grown since the classic study of Berle and Means. For example, by 1963 there were no privately owned companies among the 200 largest U.S. non-financial corporations. And by that year, the number of management-controlled firms totalled 160 out of the top 200 corporations, a figure almost twice the number so controlled in 1929. In that year, 85 per cent of the assets of the largest 200 corporations were management-controlled, and only five companies of the 200 were controlled through majority stock ownership.[4]

The expansion of these large corporations and the related development of complex technology has had far-reaching effects on our whole occupational structure and, as a consequence, on the nation's social class system. Table 1 shows the sweeping revolution that has occurred in the occupational composition of the labor force in the years between 1900 and 1960.

The high technology that the large corporations have been so eminently able to utilize in their rapid growth has resulted in a massive upgrading of the skills and training required of the labor force. All the so-called white collar groups—professionals, supervisors, technicians, and clerks—have been growing much faster than the blue collar (production) workers. This has been a long term trend, but in 1957 we reached a historic turning point; in that year the white collar group became the biggest single segment of the labor force, outnumbering the blue collar workers for the first time.[5] This change in the occupational structure along with concurrent changes in income distribution and advertising practices in the post-war years went far to widen the ranks of the middle class, or, at least, of those who thought of themselves as middle class.

---

[3] Apart from Veblen's work (see pp. 507–516 above), we refer to A. A. Berle Jr. and G. C. Means, *The Modern Corporation and Private Property* (New York: Macmillan, 1932), J. Burnham, *The Managerial Revolution* (New York: The John Day Co., 1941), R. A. Gordon, *Business Leadership in the Large Corporation* (Washington, D. C.: Brookings, 1945), O. Knauth, *Managerial Enterprise* (New York: W. W. Norton and Co., 1948).

[4] R. J. Larner, "Ownership and Control in the 200 Largest Non-financial Corporations, 1929 and 1963," *American Economic Review* (September, 1966), pp. 775–787.

[5] L. S. Silk, *The Research Revolution* (New York: McGraw-Hill Book Co., 1960), p. 109.

TABLE 1

Occupational Composition of the Labor Force, 1900–60[a]

	Percentage of Labor Force	
	1900	1960
Managerial and professional		
Professional and technical workers	4.1%	11.8%
Managers, officials, and proprietors (nonform)	5.9	10.9
White collar		
Clerical workers	3.1	14.9
Sales workers	4.8	6.5
Blue collar		
Skilled workers and foremen	10.3	12.9
Semi-skilled workers	12.8	18.6
Unskilled workers	12.4	4.9
Household and other service workers	8.9	12.7
Farm		
Farmers and farm managers	20.0	4.2
Farm laborers	17.6	2.6

[a] Source: *Historical Statistics of the United States*, p. 74; *Statistical Abstract*, 1960, p. 216.

The effect of prosperity was greatly to enlarge the middle class. The result was a society in which the great mass of industrial workers and their leaders thought and acted as members of the middle class, not as an impoverished proletariat, and in which the skilled workers often enjoyed higher incomes than teachers and white collar workers.[6]

The research revolution involved a shift from brawn to brains, and this meant that the emphasis upon education became greater. The "baby boom" of the late war and post-war years, the tendency to regard education as the route to success and status, and the increasingly specialized and demanding nature of science, not to mention the influence of Sputnik, created crisis conditions in the educational system, so far as numbers were concerned. Education in the United States truly became a mass phenomenon. Between 1940 and 1960 the number of pupils enrolled in public elementary and secondary schools increased from 25,434,000 to 36,305,000; enrollment in private schools almost trebled. Between the same years the number of college students went from 1,500,000 to 3,402,000. Altogether, between 1940 and 1964 the proportion of high school and college graduates in the labor force nearly doubled. The consequences of this massive and increasingly bureaucratic effort in education for students and their relations with their instructors will be considered below. Here, mention must be made of a development in higher education that was to be of momentous significance. The increased funds available for research, especially for defense-related inquiry, tended to make natural science professors and others more prosperous and often more remote and inaccessible to

[6] A. S. Link, *American Epoch* (New York: A. A. Knopf, 1963), p. 633.

their students. The university's growing obligations to industry, the nation, and the community led one administrator to speak of it as a "multiversity."[7]

Another development not completely related to the gigantic growth of the big corporations in this period, but which reflected the affluence of those fortunate to work for them was the mass exodus to suburbia. This trend, we have seen, had been under way for some time, but in the fifties and sixties it seems to have accelerated. Numerous factors were at work here: the post-war increase in home ownership, the high rate of housing construction, the improving level of living of various social strata, the desire of parents to raise children in less congested environments, and the flight from the migration of Negroes into the inner cities of the nation. While it is only one factor, the prosperity created by the defense industries that frequently themselves located in the suburbs is not to be overlooked. More than one social commentator saw that the new suburbs were "the consumption side of the managerial economy," while "the residual but still immense slums to be found in both country and city are the domestic or consumer side of the low-wage, non-expense-account economy."[8] This emergent "dual economy" with its potential polarization of the nation's metropolises into "lily white" suburbs and black central cities became a matter of increased civic concern after the Negro riots of 1965–67 and the dire warnings of the danger therein by the President's National Advisory Commission on Civil Disorders. Concern was expressed in the fifties also about how the new suburbanites related to politics, some alleging that an apathy and indifference often characterized the political attitudes of the "new middle class."[9] Others pointed out how the churches, especially the Protestant denominations, were becoming the "captives" of the suburbs, leaving the people of the inner cities relatively unchurched and further widening the gulf between the affluent suburbs and the ghettoes of the city.[10]

The relationship of another phase of the nation's social structure, that of the government, was affected in the most dynamic way by the heavy defense expenditures of the post-war period. In the aggregate, national security expenditures in the post-war years may appear to some to be of marginal importance. Certainly, however, relative to the ratio of military expenditures in the federal budget prior to World War II, they were a new phenomenon. From 1931 to 1939, military outlays averaged only 1.3 per cent of GNP. In

---

[7] C. Kerr, *The Uses of the University* (Cambridge: Harvard University Press, 1963). President Eisenhower in his famous farewell speech on the threat of an industrial-military complex to the nation on January 17, 1961 said, "The prospect of domination of the nation's scholars by federal employment, project allocations, and the power of money is ever present and is gravely to be regarded." *New York Times* (January 17, 1961), p. 1.

[8] D. Riesman, "The Suburban Dislocation" in *Abundance for What?* (Garden City, N.Y.: Doubleday and Co., Inc., 1964), p. 231.

[9] On this, see C. W. Mills, *White Collar: The American Middle Classes* (New York: Oxford University Press, 1951).

[10] G. Winter, *The Suburban Captivity of the Churches* (New York: The Macmillan Co., 1962); see also on this subject, H. Cox, *The Secular City* (New York: The Macmillan Co., 1965).

World War II, they reached a peak of 48 per cent, and in the Korean War, at their height they were 12 per cent of GNP. Even in the years of our involvement in Vietnam, the total purchases by the Department of Defense and NASA were about 10 per cent of the total output of the nation.

While national security expenditures, in the aggregate, were limited in the post-war years relative to those of 1941–45, they often had a catalytic role in the American economy for several reasons. First, they utilized a major share of the scientific and engineering talent of the nation. Secondly, because of the specialized nature of defense and space technology, a relatively few durable goods' industries provided most of these needs and, as we have seen, became the leading growth industries of the nation. Thirdly, defense contracting as a consequence became largely independent of the forces producing fluctuations in the private sector of the economy. In the opinion of some students, the government contract has become an increasingly important device of the interventionist state. ". . . The government contract has achieved in two decades a scope and magnitude that rivals simple subsidies, tariffs, taxes, direct regulation, and positive action programs in their impact upon American life."[11]

The United States government in the post-war years was the principal source of funds for research and development. Most of the increase in R and D spending in the two post-war decades resulted from the willingness of Congress to appropriate funds for R and D connected with national defense. In 1959, the federal government provided $7 billion for research—60 per cent of total R and D outlays—and of this total, $6 billion went for research in defense and defense-related industries.[12] These conditions have lent support to Galbraith's view that the line separating the private and public sectors has become fuzzy and ambiguous in these defense industries. Or, as another social scientist writes, "Because of its peculiar and unique ambiguity, R and D has tended to become a central factor in transforming our social and political institutions in ways still dimly perceived. It is something of a cliché to speak of science and technology as frontiers of social as well as technical change; yet it is exactly the reality of what is happening. For government R and D has become a new tool, not merely for carrying out avowed and politically defined public tasks, but also for social and economic management of our national life. For the performer [of such contracts], R and D is not only the means of providing goods and services to government but also the secret of corporate survival and growth as well as the mainstay of community employment and prosperity."[13] These are some facts that tend to substantiate Galbraith's vision of the way in which the mature corporations are transforming American society in our time.

[11] H. L. Nieburg, "Social Control of Innovation," in *American Economic Review, Papers and Proceedings* (May, 1968), p. 668.

[12] Silk, *The Research Revolution*, pp. 172–173.

[13] Nieburg in "Social Control of Innovation," p. 669. For a comprehensive treatment of the impact of the defense establishment on American society, see R. Clapp, *The Weapons Culture* (New York: W. W. Norton and Co., 1968).

ECONOMIC CONCENTRATION AND PUBLIC POLICY

Antitrust has been the historic policy by which the United States has sought to prevent the dominance of the economy and society by the large corporations and to preserve the competitive market. What has happened to the antitrust movement in these years of cold and hot wars and of giant mergers? Paradoxically, it has seemed to one historian that "once the United States had an antitrust movement without antitrust prosecutions; in our time there have been antitrust prosecutions without an antitrust movement."[14] Professor Galbraith goes further than this in his indictment of antitrust policy. He contends that enforcement procedure has ignored entrenched oligopoly and attacked the overt collusion of small businessmen instead. "If a firm is already large, it is substantially immune under the antitrust laws. . . . [It] will not be demerged. But if two medium-sized companies unite to deal more effectively with this giant [corporation], the law will be on them like a tiger. . . ."[15] The antitrust laws, says Galbraith, are a charade that attack the symbols of market power and leave the substance; "in seeking to preserve the market," they "are an anachronism in the larger world of industrial planning."[16]

Galbraith's broad assault on antitrust policy, while it has an element of truth in it, is deficient factually and ignores the stated objectives of the policy as of no consequence. Antitrust officials have clearly stated they are not seeking to dissolve all instances of market power, particularly where such power is justified by economies of scale and is not based on anti-competitive, exclusionary practices. The purpose of the antitrust laws, apart from existing concentrations of economic power, is to "preserve the opportunity for declining concentration in the future as new developments take place—new entry, new products, and the like. . . ."[17] The post-war record of antitrust enforcement in pursuit of this objective and against large corporations has been much more substantial and effective than Galbraith admits. Let us look at the record, so far as space will permit.

Antitrust got off to an auspicious beginning in the post-war period when Justice Learned Hand held in *U.S.* vs. *Aluminum Company of America* (1945) that, contrary to the dictum of the Supreme Court in 1920, size could be a violation of the law; this decision, in effect, condemned the power to abuse, and in so doing, rejected the rule of reason. After protracted litigation

[14] R. Hofstadter, "What Happened to the Antitrust Movement" in E. F. Cheit, ed., *The Business Establishment* (New York: John Wiley and Sons, Inc., 1964), pp. 113–151.

[15] Hearing before Select Committee on Smaller Business, U.S. Senate, 90th Cong., *Planning, Regulation, and Competition*, June, 1967 (Washington, D.C.: U.S. Government Printing Office, 1967), p. 8. This government publication contains a provocative seminar on the antitrust aspects of Galbraith's book.

[16] Galbraith, *The New Industrial State*, p. 197.

[17] Hearing before Select Committee on Small Business, *Planning, Regulation . . .*, p. 30 (statement of Assistant Attorney General Donald F. Turner).

and heavy government subsidy of competitors, the aluminum monopoly was converted into a more workably competitive oligopoly. In 1946, the Court found in a case involving the price-leadership of the American Tobacco Co. in the cigarette industry that collusion could be inferred from the behavior of the oligopolists in that industry rather then being based on overt price-fixing (this is known as the doctrine of conscious parallelism; it was later repudiated by the Court as sufficient in itself to warrant a conviction).[18] In the Columbia Steel case (1948), however, the government suffered a setback; United States Steel's acquisition of the Consolidated Steel Co. was upheld.[19]

In 1950 Congress, believing that it was faced with a giant wave of mergers, passed the Celler-Kefauver Anti-Merger Act. This law was technically an amendment of Section 7 of the Clayton Act, which made it illegal for a corporation to acquire the assets of another company where the effect would be to lessen competition substantially, or tend to create a monopoly in any line of commerce or in any section of the country. Prosecutions under this Act more than doubled in the years 1959–62 over what they had been in the period 1945–48. The actions brought by the Federal Trade Commission and private antitrust suits grew sixfold over the same period.[20] The government was extraordinarily successful in the suits it brought against Bethlehem Steel, Brown Shoe, El Paso Natural Gas, Continental Can, and a number of other corporate giants. Altogether, over the seventeen years from 1951 to 1967, the government challenged about 10 per cent of all large mergers—a percentage that experts would consider large enough to have a deterrent effect. Well over half (61.5 per cent) of the 52 industrial corporations with assets in excess of $1 billion (as of 1965) had one or more of their acquisitions challenged.[21] Suits attacking patent practices and other business methods that impeded entry or restrained competition were frequently successful in their results.[22] Perhaps the most publicized victory of antitrust was that of the 1961 conviction of 29 major electrical equipment manufacturers and 44 of their officers for price-fixing on billions of dollars of merchandise sold to the government. Seven company officials went to jail for 30 days, and the companies paid fines to the government that totalled close to $2 billion. These and other verdicts under antitrust in this period threw doubt upon the correctness of Galbraith's judgment about the fundamental futility of the program. In passing from ideology to a technique, "differentiated, specialized, and bureaucratized," as so much else in our society, antitrust, it is true, has

[18] *American Tobacco Co.* vs. *United States*, 328 U.S. 781 (1946) ; *Theater Enterprises, Inc.* vs. *Paramount Distributing Corporation*, 346 U.S. 537 (1954).

[19] *United States* vs. *Columbia Steel Co.*, 334 U.S. 495 (1947).

[20] J. Markham, "Antitrust Trends and New Constraints," *Harvard Business Review* (May/June, 1963), pp. 84ff.

[21] W. F. Mueller, "The Celler-Kefauver Act: Sixteen Years of Enforcement," mimeographed, available from the Federal Trade Commission, pp. 10, 14.

[22] For a survey of antitrust actions in a wide range of industries which reaches this conclusion, see S. N. Whitney, *Antitrust Policies: American Experience in Twenty Industries*, 2 vols. (New York: Twentieth Century Fund, 1958).

become "the almost exclusive concern of a technical elite of lawyers and economists," but nevertheless, it has not become as ineffectual in maintaining and promoting competition as Galbraith would have his readers believe.

Besides Galbraith, there were others who challenged the liberal economic philosophy underlying the antitrust laws in the 1950's. These so-called economic realists, such as A. A. Berle, Jr. and David E. Lilienthal, argued that bigness in business should be accepted as a twentieth century fact of life, and appropriate positive policies should be adopted to adjust to it.[23] Berle, for example, urged greater reliance on an emerging "corporate conscience" or sense of responsibility in big business. Lilienthal also, in arguing against trust-busting, contended that the nature and scope of the responsibility of big business had changed during the past twenty years, and that we should give more vitality to the almost moribund "rule of reason" in interpreting the antitrust laws.[24] About this same time, Galbraith explained that despite the high economic concentration and market power in the American economy, it worked remarkably well because of the development of "countervailing power" by labor unions, farm cooperatives, chain stores, etc., which offset the market power of corporate oligopoly.[25] Admitting that this concept of countervailing power only functioned to benefit the consumer when there was a relative scarcity of demand, Galbraith offered a new criterion for the government's antitrust policy. He would have the Antitrust Division attack positions of original market power only where these were not effectively offset by the countervailing power of other groups. In this world of power blocs, the government's main function would be to support the weaker economic groups and to operate as a make-weight or balance among the various economic groups of the society.[26]

The critique of the orthodox economic position on antitrust and competition was strengthened by the very noticeable tendency in the post-war years for Congress to narrow the jurisdiction of the competitive principle by exempting industries from the antitrust laws. Thus, in addition to defense contractors, most of whom worked under negotiated contracts rather than having to meet the test of the competitive market, there was a growing list of industries which were immune to antitrust prosecution. Organized labor and farm cooperatives had been made exempt by the Clayton Act and export trade

[23] A. A. Berle, Jr., *The Twentieth Century Capitalist Revolution* (New York: Harcourt, Brace and Co., 1954) ; D. E. Lilienthal, *Big Business: A New Era* (New York: Harper and Bros., 1952).

[24] Lilienthal is not too persuasive in his argument on this score. On one page (p. 30) he states that there is only a trend toward such corporate responsibility, while later (p. 179) he says the change has already taken place. On the evolution of the managerial ideology, see F. X. Sutton *et al.*, *The American Business Creed* (Cambridge: Harvard University Press, 1956).

[25] J. K. Galbraith, *American Capitalism: The Concept of Countervailing Power* (Boston: Houghton Mifflin Co., 1952).

[26] For cogent criticisms of Galbraith's concept of countervailing power, see *American Economic Review, Papers and Proceedings* (May, 1954), pp. 2–34.

associations by the Webb-Pomerene Act of 1918. Now, in the post-war years, the McCarran Act (1945) suspended antitrust against rate agreements of insurance companies for three years and thereafter made them subject to the federal laws only "to the extent that such businesses are regulated by state law." In 1948, the Reed-Bulwinkle Act allowed railroad traffic associations to fix rates subject to review by the Interstate Commerce Commission. Perhaps the most discussed and debated exemption was the legalization of resale price maintenence under the Miller-Tydings Act (1937). When the Supreme Court destroyed the device of the non-signer's clause in Fair Trade agreements by the Schwegmann decision,[27] Congress quickly repaired the damage by passing the McGuire-Keogh Act of 1952 and thus extended the federal exemption to cover the non-signer's clause. Despite that victory, the advocates of Fair Trade suffered serious reverses at the hands of numerous state courts that held the state resale price maintenance laws unconstitutional on one ground or another. By the late fifties, Fair Trade was a dying cause.

One alternative to maintaining competition via antitrust is government regulation of industry. In the post-war period this approach to the social control of industry was extensively applied in the field of public utilities by state and federal agencies and in transport and communications by the federal government. Though there had been great hope for the idea of the independent regulatory commission when it was inaugurated, the limitations of this method of industrial regulation were increasingly recognized. The cumbersome, slow, bureaucratic nature of the process, plus the tendency of the regulated industry to "regulate" the regulators, and other economic defects led many to lose faith in this type of public policy during these years.[28]

LABOR AND LABOR UNIONS IN THE AFFLUENT SOCIETY

Wage earners and trade unions faced difficult problems of adjustment in the post-war decade of cold and hot wars, inflation and rapid technological change. The mechanization of industry and the advance of automation caused powerful unions, such as the United Mine Workers and the United Automobile Workers, to shrink in membership, and grave problems of "structural unemployment" were created for thousands of others by the "manpower revolution" of these years. While women workers entered industry in increased numbers, often to supplement their families' incomes, Negro workers, and especially adolescents, found it increasingly difficult to find jobs because of either discrimination or the upgrading of skills and their inadequate training.

[27] *Schwegmann Bros.* vs. *Calvert Corp.* and *Schwegmann Bros.* vs. *Seagram Distillers Corp.*, 341 U.S. 384.

[28] On this subject, see C. Wilcox, *Public Policies toward Business*, rev. ed. (Homewood, Illinois: R. D. Irwin, Inc., 1960), pp. 760–778.

The labor unions assumed a militant stance in the face of the inflation that set in during the immediate post-war years; these were times that gave some semblance of reality to Sumner Slichter's contention that ours was a laboristic capitalism. Industrial disputes reached a high in 1946 as the unions sought to offset the loss of overtime pay following the end of the war and to meet the spiralling cost of living. In Table 2, we can see that the real average weekly

TABLE 2

Consumer Prices and Average Weekly Earnings of Workers in Manufacturing Industries, Selected Years, 1939–66[a]

	Consumer Price Index (1957–59 = 100)	Net Spendable Weekly Earnings of a Worker with Three Dependents[b]	
		Current Dollars	1957–59 Dollars
1939	48.4	$23.40	$48.35
1944	61.3	43.76	71.39
1945	62.7	42.59	67.93
1946	68.0	42.79	62.93
1947	77.8	47.58	61.16
1948	83.8	52.31	62.42
1949	83.0	52.95	63.80
1950	83.8	56.36	67.26
1951	90.5	60.18	66.50
1952	92.5	62.98	68.09
1953	93.2	65.60	70.39
1954	93.6	65.65	70.14
1955	93.3	69.79	74.80
1956	94.7	72.25	76.29
1957	98.0	74.31	75.83
1958	100.7	75.23	74.71
1959	101.5	79.40	78.23
1960	103.1	80.11	77.70
1961	103.2	82.18	78.87
1962	105.4	85.53	81.15
1963	106.7	87.58	82.08
1964	108.1	92.18	85.27
1965	109.9	96.78	88.06
1966	113.1	99.33	87.82

[a] Source: *Economic Report of the President*, January, 1967, pp. 248, 262.
[b] Average gross weekly earnings less social security and income taxes.

earnings of a worker with three dependents fell about $10.00 from 1944 to 1947 as the consumer price index rose 16 points over the same period. It should be noted that, in real terms, the average weekly earnings of manufacturing workers in 1944 were not surpassed until 1955.

Industrial disputes, many of them of long duration, flared in the years 1946–49. The industries with the most strikes were coal, steel, telephone, automobiles, and meat-packing. While these big strikes filled the headlines, and in 1946 caused the loss of 116 million man-hours, the per cent of the total work time lost—1.43 per cent—was relatively small. Nevertheless, there was much criticism of organized labor, despite the deterioration in labor's real income caused by inflation, and this played a part in Congress' adoption of restrictive labor legislation. After long struggles agreements were finally reached, and more often than not the wage increase would be passed on to the consuming public in the form of higher prices. This wage-price spiral was a subject of wide complaint in many years of the 1950's.

Out of these collective bargaining negotiations there emerged several innovations—pattern settlements, long term contracts, escalation clauses (to protect against higher cost of living during the duration of the contract), fringe benefits, annual improvement adjustments (to share productivity gains with the workers), etc. All these developments testified to the maturing of industrial relations in these years, especially of the relationships between the big, mature corporations, and the unions.

Yet, despite these gains, there was a noticeable loss of élan and drive in the union movement starting about the mid-fifties. The potential for trouble over jurisdictional conflicts between the A.F. of L. and the CIO ended with the merger of the two organizations in December, 1955, but that did not prevent the organizational stagnation that had set in. At the time of the merger, the combined membership of the affiliated unions was over 16 million. But after 1957, total union membership began to fall; in the next five years, the number of union members fell by 1.7 million, despite the fact that the number of workers in non-agricultural employment increased by 4 million. By 1962, the unions had less than 15 million members, and thereafter membership remained fairly stationary.[29]

In explaining the decline or, at least, stabilization in the union movement, Galbraith finds the basic cause in the rise of the mature corporations dominated by their technostructures and in the lessening conflict of interest between the employer and employee. He thinks that the production workers in advanced technology tend to identify themselves with the technostructure. However much truth there is in that, it is to be noted that he also attributes the slowdown of the union movement to adverse technological trends such as automation and the increased numbers of professional and white collar workers who have always been more difficult to organize than the blue collar workers. Others explain the union malaise in terms of the growth of union bureaucracy and a passion for middle class respectability on the part of the union leaders. Other developments that contributed to the weakening of the union movement were the evidences of corruption in unions, as revealed by the McClellan investigation of 1957–59, and the disregard of democratic procedures in union management. The "business unionism" that has for so long dominated the philosophy of the leading unions failed to meet the

---

[29] On post-war union membership, see L. Troy, "Trade Union Membership, 1897–1962," *The Review of Economics and Statistics* (February, 1965), pp. 93–113.

economic and moral challenges of an affluent society. Too many of its leaders were absorbed in enjoying the fruits of affluence to undertake effective organization of the millions of white collar workers, civil service employees, or economically underprivileged, not to speak of the needs of workers in the less developed countries of the world. With certain exceptions, many union leaders, as Galbraith contends, had become part of the business establishment.

In partial modification of this criticism, it must be admitted that the defensive attitude prevailing among union leaders in these years was generated by the anti-union attitudes of certain diehard union opponents in business and in the nation's legislatures. Elements of this type were influential in securing the passage of the Labor-Management Act of 1947, popularly known as the Taft-Hartley Law. This law banned a number of unfair labor practices, such as the closed shop, jurisdictional strikes, secondary boycotts, and strikes by federal employees. The union shop, however, under which workers need not be members of a union to secure employment, but must join within a specified time, was not prohibited. The law placed special restrictions on strikes that were likely to create a national emergency or imperil national health or safety. In such strikes provision was made for a federal injunction to stop the proposed walk-out, followed by a sixty-day "cooling-off" period, intervention by the Federal Mediation and Conciliation Service, a vote by the workers on the employer's final offer, to be certified by the National Relations Board. If all these steps failed to produce a settlement, then the President could report to the Congress his recommendations for appropriate action. The Taft-Hartley Act represented a new high in government intervention in the collective bargaining process and together with the wave of restrictive "right-to-work" laws passed in some eighteen states by the end of the 1950's, drastically changed the concept of the union as a private voluntary association of individuals.

This trend toward converting the union into a quasi-public institution was further advanced by the Landrum-Griffin Act of 1959. With the aim of protecting individual union members from financial exploitation and maintaining union democracy, this law provided for periodic reports to the Secretary of Labor by unions that assumed trustee functions over locals, bonding of union officers, limits on loans by unions to union officers and employees, prohibition of Communists from serving as union officers or ex-Communists or ex-felons from serving in such a capacity until after a lapse of years, and a bill of rights for union members. Under the latter, national and international unions were required to hold elections by secret ballot at least once every five years, and local unions to hold such elections every three years. Extreme measures of this kind were possible to enact because of the malpractices of some union leaders, the disfavor of the public, and the apathy and indifference of large numbers of the rank and file. The latter often displayed a "commodity" orientation toward their union membership—"you pay your dues, and you expect the leaders to deliver the goods." Needless to say, such attitudes and practices were a sad commentary on an acquisitive culture.

GOVERNMENT POLICIES UNDER THE TRUMAN FAIR DEAL

President Harry S. Truman, upon assuming the heavy burdens of office after the sudden death of F.D.R. in 1945, regarded his task as that of continuing the progressive record of the New Deal administration. The jaunty ex-Senator from Independence, Missouri fought a strenuous battle against postwar reaction in his own party and the Republican ranks in a treacherous time of international tension. In his first message to Congress on September 6, 1945, he called for an extension of the Social Security Act, an increase in the minimum wage, a new program of national health insurance, a housing bill, some regional developments similar to the TVA, a full employment bill, government reorganizations, and an extension of wartime economic controls. The fiercest battle was fought between the President and his Republican opposition over the extension of price control under the Office of Price Administration (the OPA). Rather than compromise, Truman vetoed the bill offered by the opposition and so ended price controls on July 1, 1946. All remaining wage and price controls were abandoned on November 9th; the nation soon experienced the most severe inflation it had known since 1942.

In the elections that fall, the Republicans won firm control of the Senate and the House for the first time since 1928. In the ensuing struggles over legislation, Truman took his stand against a Republican bill for tax reduction, but his veto was overridden in July, 1947. In March, 1948, the Republicans were successful in pushing through another tax reduction, again over his veto. This tax reduction providentially strengthened aggregate demand the following year and so cushioned the decline in business activity.

The Democrats continued to suffer legislative defeats on numerous fronts in these years. The Taft-Hartley bill was passed over the President's veto in June, 1947. The broad program of public housing, supported by Senator Taft, the chairman of the Republican Policy Committee in the Senate, was also badly modified, so that the result was not to the President's liking. On farm policy, the Republicans also had their way, continuing support of farm prices at 90 per cent of parity through 1949, but providing for flexible supports after that date.

While the Truman legislative record was thus obviously not very impressive, cooperation with such progressive Republicans as Senator Vandenberg of Michigan and others enabled the Democrats to do better on foreign policy. Outstanding here was the establishment of the Truman doctrine to check Soviet expansion in the eastern Mediterranean and the Middle East, the inauguration of the practical and magnanimous Marshall Plan to aid the reconstruction of western Europe, the lifting of the Berlin blockade, and the adoption of the North Atlantic Treaty, which committed the United States to an unprecedented degree to the military defense of the western European nations.

President Truman's domestic program had been ignored or heavily amended by the Republicans down to the fall of 1948. He campaigned on the slogan, "You never had it so good." Few gave him any chance of re-election in that year, considering the defection of Henry Wallace's Progressives and the opposition of the Dixiecrats. Yet, in one of the most remarkable political upsets of recent history, he defeated the over-confident Governor Dewey and won his right to a second term of office.

The President launched what he called the Fair Deal in his annual message to Congress in January, 1949. In this and subsequent speeches, he asked for many of his past proposals, but again he was successful in getting Congressional approval of only a few. Actually, the Housing Act of 1949 is regarded by some as the only major domestic reform in his second term. In addition, the Fair Labor Standards Act was amended to raise the minimum wage from 40 to 75 cents per hour, and the Social Security Act was extended to 10 million new beneficiaries and the benefits of the retired raised on the average 77.5 per cent. Rent control was prolonged until March, 1951, and after the outbreak of the Korean War, the administration was able in a remarkably short time to institute the price, wage, and fiscal controls, which together with those exercised by the Federal Reserve System, enabled the nation to check inflation during that war.

The Communist victory in China in 1949 was a momentous event that affected the stability of peace in the Far East and potentially the whole balance of power in the world. Its repercussions in this country were soon felt in the form of another Red scare growing out of the contemporaneous revelations of Soviet espionage in connection with the secrets of the atom bomb and the disturbing Hiss case. Senator McCarthy was soon making his wild allegations of Communist subversion and conducting his witch-hunt. These developments were exploited by some Republicans and conservative Democrats and climaxed in the "great debate" over our participation in the defense of western Europe, the recall of General MacArthur from his command in Tokyo, and the Presidential decision to fight a "limited" war in Korea. The frustration of many Americans over the nature of the Korean struggle and the exposé of corruption among Democrats in Washington, including "five per centers" in the Reconstruction Finance Corporation, connections between Democratic city machines, gangsters, and Internal Revenue officials partial to mink coats, sealed the fate of the Democrats in the Presidential election of 1952. Though Adlai E. Stevenson, Illinois' reform governor, waged a hard campaign, he could not counteract the overriding popular desire for peace nor the powerful, highly expensive effort of the Republicans under the banner of General Eisenhower. Stevenson sounded a new note in the rhetoric of Presidential campaigns that had a great appeal to progressives, intellectuals, and youth, but it could not match the moralistic, shrewd public relations approach of his opponent who promised to clean up "that mess in Washington."

THE DYNAMIC CONSERVATISM OF THE EISENHOWER ADMINISTRATION

A conservative, even a modern conservative, in the White House was very much of a novelty after the long Presidential tenure of the Democrats. Still, in electing President Eisenhower, the electorate had put in the office a man whose views were very much in harmony with the temper of the times. The new President described his moderate Republicanism as being "dynamic conservatism"—by which he meant that he was cautious about financial and economic matters, but concerned with human welfare. We need not analyze the implication that these two aspects of social life are independent, but merely note that the emphasis of the new administration, so far as domestic human welfare was concerned, did not lead to a repeal of the social legislation of the New Deal, but rather to its consolidation as part of the modern American way of life. As with the preceding administration, the most substantial achievements of the Eisenhower regime were in the realm of foreign affairs, where the President succeeded in ending the Korean War, maintaining the NATO alliance, and sustaining a semblance of "peaceful coexistence" with the Soviet Communists, as illustrated by the "spirit" of the Geneva conference. He withstood, in the main, the more isolationist and militant elements in the Republican Party and in the nation.

The domestic policy of the Eisenhower administration was dominated by its stress on economy, reducing and balancing the budget, and checking inflation. Since we have dealt with these fiscal aspects earlier and in the preceding chapter, we need not retrace that territory. There is one feature of the conservative Eisenhower philosophy, however, that deserves our attention because of its intrinsic importance and its relation to a basic dilemma faced by the Republicans in power. The Eisenhower Republicans, as Murray Rosant has written, did not represent "merely Hooverism in a soft collar." Yet, they had come to Washington resolved not to expand the functions of the central government and, if possible, to repeal at least some of the legislation of the welfare state. The trouble with this was that most of the problems that the welfare state had sought to grapple with were urban problems—slum clearance, rehabilitation of the handicapped, inadequate schools, a shortage of hospitals, etc. These functions could not be effectively returned to the states, as the conservatives desired, for two basic reasons. The state legislatures were usually dominated by rural interests who had little concern about these problems and wished to economize themselves. Further, with the federal government pre-empting the income tax, the most important source of revenue, the states lacked the tax sources to finance adequate welfare programs. President Eisenhower, seeking to transfer some existing governmental functions to the states, appointed a Commission on Intergovernmental Relations and a special committee of governors to investigate the question, but both these bodies did not recommend much of any consequence.[30] The administration's difficulties were illustrated sharply in 1956 when the national need for more finance for education led it, after much internal conflict, to propose a large program of federal aid for construction of school buildings. The bill became involved in the fight over segregation, in the battle over formulas for assisting the states, and in the economy drive of 1957; with only half-hearted support from the administration, it was defeated in the House in the early summer of 1957. The next year, spurred on by the Russians' success with their Sputnik, a modest program for improving the teaching of science and fostering the education of the brighter children became law. In general, the Republicans did not succeed in transferring many functions of a welfare nature to the states and by failing to meet growing national needs by federal action they contributed to the welfare deficits of the economy.

TOWARD QUALITATIVE ECONOMIC GROWTH

Meanwhile, the surge in consumer spending for automobiles and other durables in the mid-fifties was leading to a concern about balance in the nation's output of goods and services and particularly about the relative neglect of many public needs. In this period of McCarthyism and often flagrant anti-intellectualism, there was a new questioning of the benefits of the bureaucratic, affluent society. David Riesman in a brilliant book, *The Lonely Crowd* (1950), had pictured an America becoming more consumer-oriented and conformist. Later, William H. Whyte, Jr. limned the group-dominated way of life of "orgman" at work and in his homogeneous suburbia in his *The Organization Man* (1958). In the campaign of 1956, Adlai Stevenson, futilely pursuing the Presidential office a second time, introduced a new brand of qualitative liberalism. In one of his speeches, he said:

> But free society cannot be content with a goal of mere life without want. It has always had within it a visionary spark, a dream that man, liberated from crushing work, aching hunger and constant insecurity, would discover wider interests and nobler aims. If quantity comes first so that men may eat, quality comes next so that they may not live by bread alone. Free society in the West has brought most of its citizens to that great divide. The next frontier is the quality, the moral, intellectual and esthetic standards of the free way of life.[31]

After the recovery from the recession of 1954, the automobile industry, competitively seeking to stimulate demand and maintain profits and employment in an economy well-nigh surfeited with cars, pushed its efforts at

---

[30] This aspect of the Eisenhower administration is treated interestingly in E. L. Dale, Jr., *Conservatives in Power* (Garden City, N.Y.: Doubleday, 1960), pp. 157ff.

[31] S. E. Harris *et al.* (eds.), *The New America*, by Adlai E. Stevenson (New York: Harper and Bros.), p. 260. In 1956, Arthur Schlesinger, Jr., chief of Stevenson's brain trust, had written an essay entitled "The Future of Liberalism—The Challenge of Abundance," in which he defined the difference between the "quantitative liberalism" of pre-war America and the "qualitative liberalism" which was possible with America's increasing mastery over production. This distinction was fundamental to the themes of the New Frontier and the Great Society.

salesmanship and planned obsolescence to new heights. The "insolent chariots" became longer and more lavishly ornamented with chrome, tail-fins, and other protuberances. Automobiles, such as the ill-fated Edsel, were designed, in accordance with the advice of motivation researchers, to appeal to deep sexual impulses of their buyers rather than to their need for transportation. The horse-power race among the manufacturers made automobiles ever more powerful lethal instruments. Demand creation in other industries also became frenetic. Some of the affluent found themselves receiving Christmas presents of electric swizzle sticks and other such gadgets. Walter Lippman wrote an article about the triviality of much of this consumption, and the nation's other pundits joined in. The respected Harvard economist, Alvin Hansen, questioned the sanity of the nation's social priorities.[32] "After ten years of almost incredible *output* performance," he wrote, "we need to assess not merely the speed of our growth and progress but also the direction in which we are going. What *qualitative* goals shall we set up? What kind of country do we wish to build? These are matters that we dare not overlook, lest we perish, as a great nation in the midst of material plenty."[33]

It was against this background that J. K. Galbraith published his *The Affluent Society* in 1958. In this book, as we have noted in the Introduction, he attributed the contemporary social imbalance to several elements in American culture—modern advertising, social emulation, the emphasis on production as a means of avoiding the troublesome question of equality, and inflation. In his *The New Industrial State*, on the other hand, he finds the trouble to be the industrial system itself, which practices a negative discrimination against certain public services and inundates us with the private goods it is so capable of producing. Galbraith regards the cultural factors he cites in the former book as complementary to the industrial system in producing the social imbalance.[34] In our opinion, the stress on the cultural factors is more defensible and acceptable than explaining everything in terms of the needs of the industrial system. Furthermore, if the cultural factors are at fault, the correction of the situation will call for rather different remedies than those adequate to reform the industrial system.[35]

From the perspective of the present, ten years after the publication of *The Affluent Society*, when the urban crisis and its relation to the nation's social

[32] A. H. Hansen, *The American Economy* (New York: McGraw-Hill Book Co., 1957), p. 146–151.

[33] *Ibid.*, p. 146.

[34] *The New Industrial State*, p. 346, footnote. It is interesting to note that in *The Affluent Society* education is alleged to be one of the areas of the public sector which is neglected (*ibid.*, p. 355); in *The New Industrial State*, according to the author, education receives the support of the industrial system (*ibid.*, p. 345).

[35] This would seem to be one of the contentions of the late David M. Wright in a review of the *The New Industrial State* entitled "To Hell with It All," *The Intercollegiate Review* (November/December, 1967), pp. 49ff. He wrote, "My major technical criticism is that Galbraith has the cart before the horse. Growth is not something imposed upon us by a corporate elite, but an expression of the deepest aspirations of our culture. . . ." See also C. R. McConnell, "Social Imbalance: Where Do We Stand?" *Quarterly Review of Business and Economics* (May, 1961), pp. 6–23.

imbalance are widely recognized, the question of the existence of this condition will appear to some as very academic. Nevertheless, at the time of the book's appearance, many took issue with the thesis, either denying its existence or challenging the causes advanced by Galbraith.[36] One of the more objective studies provided statistical support for the latter's view.[37] Contrasting government's non-defense purchases of goods and services with the size of the non-defense GNP over a period of years, Bator sought to measure the share of the public sector, so defined, in the civilian GNP. According to his analysis, the government's non-defense expenditures as a percentage of non-defense GNP rose from 7.5 per cent in 1929 to 13.4 per cent in 1939 and then declined to 10.3 per cent in 1957. On a per capita basis, evidence of a deficit in the public sector was even more pronounced. Per capita real non-defense spending by government was approximately the same in 1957 as it had been in 1939 ($234), despite the fact that total real civilian output per head increased from $1,514 to $2,281 over the same period. Aggregative statistics on a national basis are hardly adequate to measure the Galbraithian social imbalance. In the suburbs, many would say that there was little evidence of social imbalance in the 1950's, but in the inner cities and ghettoes there were incredible contrasts of private affluence alongside public squalor and individual poverty.

Galbraith's work called attention to what institutional economists term the social costs of capitalistic progress; he made wide sections of the public and some of its leaders aware of the fact that the unplanned process of economic growth was causing serious external diseconomies detrimental to national well-being. He showed too that the problems of the new poor could not be met except by proper attention to the public sector of the economy. His analysis did not have the technical elegance of a Pigou, but as economics, in the broader humanist tradition, it had a cogency, a relevance, and an impact on the national consciousness that was extraordinary.[38]

TO MOVE A NATION: THE NEW FRONTIER AND THE GREAT SOCIETY

John F. Kennedy campaigned for the Presidency on the slogan "get the country moving again." Considering the slowdown in the nation's growth in the late fifties that was natural enough, but it is important to realize that the

[36] For some of these criticisms, see E. S. Phelps, ed., *Private Wants and Public Needs* (New York: W. W. Norton and Co., Inc., 1962).

[37] F. M. Bator, *The Question of Public Spending* (New York: Harper and Bros., 1960).

[38] For a later study that reaches conclusions similar to Galbraith's on social imbalance, see E. J. Mishan, *The Costs of Economic Growth* (New York: Frederick Praeger, Inc., 1967); a modern critique of economic growth along philosophical and psychological lines is W. A. Weisskopf, "Economic Growth versus Existential Balance," *Ethics* (January, 1965), pp. 77–86. See also H. Marcuse, *One Dimensional Man*, Studies in the Ideology of Advanced Industrial Society (Boston: Beacon Press, 1964).

young Presidential candidate was interested in more than movement for itself; the direction of the nation's progress was of great consequence to him also. In this sense, Kennedy was, as Arthur Schlesinger contends, "the heir and executor of the Stevenson revolution." He too was convinced that affluence was not enough for the good life and certainly not for a nation that still had 35 million people in poverty and lived under the threat of thermonuclear war. So, as we know, he was able to repudiate the spirit of the 1950's, the concern with security and one's advancement, and declare in his Inaugural: "Ask not what your country can do for you—ask what you can do for your country." He was able to call for sacrifice and elicit the response of the young and sensitive in spirit because he was not simply an intellectual, but as Stevenson expressed it after his assassination, he was the "contemporary man." His youth, his vitality, his pragmatic modernity, and most of all, his example, moved the nation and led to changes that are by no means complete today.

Kennedy was a pragmatic President. By that we mean he eschewed the doctrinaire ideas of the past and looked for new options in thought and action. On one occasion he said, "Liberalism and conservatism are categories of the thirties, and they don't apply any more. . . . The trouble with conservatives is that so much of their thinking is so naive. As for the liberals, their thinking is more sophisticated; but their function ought to be to provide new ideas, and they don't come up with any."[39]

Unfortunately for the new President, his victory over Richard M. Nixon was terribly narrow. Kennedy was a minority President, and the control of the Democrats in the Congress was so slim that any cooperation between the southern wing of the party and the Republicans could defeat a measure. While Kennedy secured the passage of certain economic proposals with some degree of consensus during the administration's "honeymoon" period in the spring of 1961—wages and hours extension, social security and public housing—when he asked for bold new steps, to "get the country moving," he encountered a Congressional stalemate. The President lost on major tax reforms, establishment of a Department of Urban Affairs, federal aid for education, medicare, aid to higher education, long term financing of foreign aid, farm legislation, and civil rights. The only outstanding administration victory in 1962 was the foreign trade bill. "Consolidation of the New Deal and the Fair Deal proceeded steadily; innovation on the New Frontier faltered."[40]

On the economic front, as we have seen, he was more successful. By 1963, GNP had risen about $100 billion in three years, a substantial increase that did not, however, succeed in solving the unemployment problem. Kennedy at first was disappointing to liberals, because, surprisingly enough, he was seeking to gain the support of the business community. He was resistant in the first year and a half of his administration to the new fiscal policy ideas. Spending

[39] A. M. Schlesinger, Jr., *A Thousand Days* (Boston: Houghton Mifflin Co., 1965), p. 739.

[40] J. M. Burns, *The Deadlock of Democracy* (Englewood Cliffs, N.J.: Prentice-Hall Inc., 1963), p. 311.

for welfare clashed with the heavy burden of security; also, expansionary fiscal policy, it was feared, would aggravate the deficit in our balance of payments. He rejected a tax cut in 1962 because he thought Congress would oppose it. But after the stock market collapse of May, 1962, the clash with the steel industry over price policy and its sequel, the President moved toward an advanced fiscal position. In his famous Yale University speech in June, 1962, he attacked economic mythology. The fact was that the President had to develop not only what was economically workable, but extend the boundaries of what was politically marketable. In short, he had to educate the public to the value of modern fiscal policy. After favoring business with the investment tax credit and liberalized depreciation policies in 1961 and 1962, the administration finally advocated an expansionary tax cut in January, 1963, along with a number of tax reforms. The President rejected spending as a means of stimulating the economy and meeting the deficits in the public sector, as espoused by Galbraith, and supported the more palatable idea of the tax cut. This bill, shorn of the tax reforms, became the Tax Act of 1964. It was justly hailed as a great triumph of Keynesian economics, even though it reflected the "commercial Keynesianism," which is more acceptable to businessmen, despite the fact that such a policy does not wholly solve the problem of unemployment nor that of social imbalance.

That Kennedy was not unaware of the latter problem was very clear from one of his last speeches, made at Amherst College to honor Robert Frost. In that address he gave his vision of a more fulfilling society which could lie beyond private affluence:

> I look forward to a great future for America, a future in which our country will match its military strength with our moral restraint, its wealth with its wisdom, its power with our purpose.
> I look forward to an America which will not be afraid of grace and beauty, which will protect the beauty of our natural environment, which will preserve the great old American houses and squares and parks of our national past, and which will build handsome and balanced cities for the future.
> I look forward to an America which will reward achievement in the arts as we reward achievement in business and statecraft. . . .
> I look forward to an America which commands respect throughout the world not only for its strength but for its civilization as well. And I look forward to a world which will be safe not only for democracy and diversity but also for personal distinction.[41]

Despite President Kennedy's great appeal to the nation generally, he was never able to win the support of a majority of the business community.[42] In the 1960 election, for example, one survey showed him receiving the votes of only one out of every five businessmen. Though Kennedy strenuously courted the businessmen and gave them several tax favors, after the controversy over

[41] As quoted in Schlesinger, *A Thousand Days*, pp. 1015–1016.
[42] The relations of the Kennedy and Johnson administrations with business are capably analyzed in H. Rowen, *The Free Enterprisers: Kennedy, Johnson and the Business Establishment* (New York: G. P. Putnam's Sons, 1964).

the roll-back on steel prices, the rift between business and the administration still remained wide. President Johnson was more sympathetically viewed by the businessmen, and in the 1964 election in which a majority of business executives favored the conservative Senator Goldwater, one out of three businessmen supported the Democratic candidate. "The business executives who expect to cast the first Democratic Presidential vote of their lives are nearly all affiliated with large companies," reported a *New York Times* correspondent. Big and small businessmen were split on the issue of a purposeful government deficit, such as the 1964 tax cut involved; the latter upheld the conventional view, while the managers of the large corporations approved the use of fiscal power by the federal government to underwrite mass consumption. This political realignment of a substantial number of businessmen with the Democratic Party was a phenomenon of much interest. It demonstrated that business was not monolithic in its Republicanism and that the Democrats under President Johnson's shrewd leadership had established themselves as the center party of the nation. The result, in the opinion of some commentators, was that the New Deal and welfare liberalism now occupied the center in the spectrum of national politics.[43]

The Goldwater movement in the '64 election had challenged the liberal consensus on domestic policies, urged a more militaristic foreign policy, and espoused conservatism generally. The Arizona Senator raised ethical questions as to the future of freedom in the nation and the quality of its life, but he was overwhelmed by the Johnson landslide. The President's plurality of close to 17 million was "the greatest vote, the greatest margin and the greatest percentage (61%) that any President had drawn from the American people. . . ."[44]

With substantial business support and the new seats the Democrats had captured in that election, President Johnson was able to achieve a remarkable legislative record on domestic matters. Apart from the epoch-making tax cut, he had three major achievements to his credit: passage of the Medicare bill, the Education Act of 1965, and the Civil Rights Law of that same year. These legislative accomplishments of the Democrats on the home front were overshadowed, however, by the agony of the protracted struggle in Vietnam. The burden of that undeclared war made the Johnsonian War on Poverty a relative skirmish, and the administration's expenditures for urban renewal were also shockingly inadequate. The President, like his predecessor, had set forth his vision of the nation's future in his "Great Society" speech at the University of Michigan in May, 1964: "The challenge of the next half century is whether we have the wisdom to use our wealth to enrich and elevate our national life—and to advance the quality of American civilization—for in our time we have the opportunity to move not only toward the rich society and

[43] The significance of the political realignment in 1964 is analyzed brilliantly in D. Bazelon, *Power in America: The Politics of the New Class* (New York: New American Library, 1967), Chap. 4; see also M. Harrington, *Toward a Democratic Left* (New York: The Macmillan Co., 1968).

[44] T. H. White, *The Making of the President 1964* (New York: Atheneum Publishers, 1965), p. 400.

the powerful society but upward to the Great Society." The discrepancy between the idealism of that address and the harsh realism of the administration's commitment of the nation and the universities themselves to the prosecution of the Vietnam War illustrated the tensions and conflicts under which the people labored.

A CRISIS OF VALUES

In President Johnson's second term, these conflicts and divisions in the nation came to a head and resulted in his unexpected decision not to run for re-election. American society was confronted with a crisis of values, with a hard choice among social priorities. In the fifties and sixties as the nation became more industrialized, more highly organized and bureaucratized, more urbanized and militarized, as the cold war and the shooting war in Vietnam continued, there were mounting signs of social disorganization and aliena-tion.[45] The problems of American economic growth could no longer be conceptualized in the narrow, technical terms of allocating scarce resources to achieve given ends; the very ends or goals of the society were being called into question more insistently.

The rebellion of the dispossessed and the alienated escalated from protest to revolt. The Negroes, victims of a blatant racism in the South and of a more subtle variety in the North, moved from the Montgomery, Alabama bus boycott in 1963 to mass marches upon Washington, to riots in the cities, and from a policy objective of integration with white society to a fearless confrontation of the establishment by "Black Power."

A new generation of students, rejecting the silence of the fifties and the conformity of the McCarthy era, produced powerful and articulate minorities who boldly criticized their university and in some instances occupied its buildings and defied its administrators. These advocates of student power, militantly idealistic, scored the universities for becoming "super-service stations for government and industry" and in the process becoming impersonalized knowledge factories, woefully lacking as communities of scholarship. These critics saw the university as training and conditioning people for specialized, robot roles in a mass society that was itself out of control. As one

---

45 Two eminently worthwhile studies of this phenomenon are R. McGee, *Social Disorganization in America'* (San Francisco: Chandler Publishing Co., 1962) and K. Keniston, *The Uncommitted* (New York: Harcourt, Brace and World, Inc., 1965). These and other works that could be cited suggest that Galbraith's analysis of education and emancipation (from the dominance of the industrial system), the political lead to be taken by "the educational and scientific estate" in countervailing the power of the techno-structure (Chaps. 33–34 of *The New Industrial State*) may portray our future history in overly rational terms. The psycho-dynamic forces underlying social change are relatively neglected; in this sense, Galbraith's treatment is practically pre-Freudian. "If history is the return of the repressed," the reformation of the values stemming from the Puritan ethic may be a more revolutionary process than the closing chapters of his book suggests.

such critic bitterly expressed it, "That the universities should encourage social acceptance is only natural; they are, of course, only acting *in loco* middle-class *parentis*."[46]

Rejection of the values of a middle class business civilization was nothing new in America. Nineteenth century Transcendentalists such as Emerson and Thoreau had questioned the domination of life by industry. Writers and artists in the twenties had ridiculed the Babbitry of that day. And in the fifties the Beatnik rebellion erupted as a condemnation of "the square" and his hyper-repressed pursuit of success. In 1964 certain elite groups among the students had challenged the University of California at Berkeley in the Free Speech movement. Four years later the campus revolt became almost nation-wide in its proportions. Now, while the objectives and complaints vary from situation to situation, there is usually an underlying protest against the "establishment," the administration of student affairs from the top down. The rebelling students want to be "committed" to some positive cause beyond private, selfish interest. "They are looking for an idealism they too seldom find in the authorities in their universities. Their dissatisfaction is, finally, not so much with their curriculum as with the state of America, whose military and business interests the universities have been serving too faithfully and uncritically."[47] Students who have felt powerless in the face of massive forces threatening them with a draft for a war they reject or for careers in which they find little meaning or challenge have become alienated. Radicals among such student groups have sought to "radicalize" the community and use the university as a springboard for wider social revolution. In their employment of direct action, such groups, despite their voicing of Marxist slogans, have seemed almost anarchist. Stressing "participatory democracy," they have been decentralist, anti-police, and anti-bureaucratic and find direct action their most powerful weapon in disrupting the established society. Often confused and divided among themselves, they add to the chaos and disorganization of the contemporary American scene.

The discontented and rebellious of our complex industrial society are a symptom of its malfunctioning. They serve to remind us that men are not satisfied with economic rewards alone; they want to be free and to enjoy meaningful work, play, and community with their fellows. They need a bit of beauty in their lives and everyday surroundings. For many, our affluent society still does not fulfill these basic needs.

[46] T. Hayden, "Student Social Action—From Liberation to Community," reprinted in *The New Student Left*, edited by M. Cohen and D. Hale (Boston: Beacon Press, 1967), p. 280.

[47] H. J. Muller in *The New York Times* (June 22, 1968), p. 18.

SELECTED REFERENCES

The following brief list of selected references consists of books only. Relevant periodical articles for topics in each of the major Parts of this book will be found in the anthologies listed below.[1]

Chapter 1

Baldwin, R. E. and Meier, R. H., *Economic Development*, New York: Wiley, 1957.

Berkhofer, R. H., *A Behavioral Approach to Historical Analysis*, Glencoe, Ill., The Free Press, 1969.

Goldschmidt, W., *Man's Way*, New York: Holt, Rinehart and Winston, 1959.

Higgins, B., *Economic Development*, Rev. ed., New York: W. W. Norton Co., Inc., 1968.

Rostow, W. W., *The Stages of Economic Growth*, Cambridge: Cambridge University Press, 1960.

Supple, B., *The Experience of Economic Growth, Case Studies in Economic History*, New York: Random House, 1965.

Introduction to Part 1

Hagen, E., *On the Theory of Social Change*, Homewood, Ill.: Dorsey Press, 1963.

Hoselitz, B., *Sociological Aspects of Economic Growth*, Glencoe, Ill.: The Free Press, 1960.

[1] See pp. 869–871.

Tawney, R. H., *Religion and the Rise of Capitalism*, New York: Penguin Books, 1947.

Weber, M., *The Protestant Ethic and the Spirit of Capitalism*, New York: Scribner, 1948.

Chapter 2

Bailyn, B., *The New England Merchants in the Seventeenth Century*, Cambridge: Harvard University Press, 1965.

——, *Education in the Forming of American Society*, Chapel Hill: University of North Carolina Press, 1960.

Beard, C. and M., *The Rise of American Civilization*, New York: The Macmillan Company, 1935.

Boorstein, D. J., *The Americans: The Colonial Experience*, New York: Random House, 1958.

Bruchey, S., *The Colonial Merchant, Sources and Readings*, New York: Harcourt, Brace and World, 1966.

Morgan, E. S., *The Puritan Family;* Essays on Religion and Domestic Relations in 17th Century New England, New York: Harper and Row, 1966.

Morris, R. B., *Government and Labor in Early America*, New York: Columbia University Press, 1946.

Nettels, C. P., *The Roots of American Civilization*, New York: F. S. Crofts, 1938.

Parrington, V. L., *Main Currents in American Thought*, Vol. I, The Colonial Mind, New York: Harcourt, Brace and World, 1927.

VerSteeg, C. L., *The Formative Years, 1607–1763*, New York: Hill and Wang, 1934.

Chapter 3

Dickerson, O. M., *The Navigation Acts and the American Revolution*, Philadelphia: University of Pennsylvania Press, 1951.

East, R. A., *Business Enterprise in the American Revolutionary Era*, New York: Columbia University Press, 1938.

Gipson, L. H., *The Coming of the Revolution, 1763–1775*, New York: Harper and Row, 1954.

Jensen, M., *The New Nation: A History of the United States during the Confederation, 1781–1789*, New York: Knopf, 1950.

Sachs, W. S. and A. Hoogenboom, *The Enterprising Colonials*, Chicago: Argonaut, 1965.

Schlesinger, A. M., *Colonial Merchants and the American Revolution, 1763–1776*, New York: Facsimile Library, 1939.

Chapter 4

Beard, C. A., *An Economic Interpretation of the Constitution of the United States*, New York: The Macmillan Company, 1913.

Brown, R. E., *Charles Beard and the Constitution*, Princeton, N.J.: Princeton University Press, 1956.

Gummere, R. M., *The American Colonial Mind and the Classical Tradition*, Cambridge: Harvard University Press, 1963.

McDonald, F., *We The People: The Economic Origins of the Constitution*, Chicago: University of Chicago Press, 1958.

Nettels, C. P., *The Emergence of A National Economy, 1775–1815*, New York: Holt, Rinehart and Winston, 1962.

Introduction to Part 2

Ginzberg, E., *The House of Adam Smith*, New York: Columbia University Press, 1934.

Smith, A., *An Inquiry into the Nature and Causes of the Wealth of Nations*, New York: The Modern Library, 1937.

Lowe, A., *On Economic Knowledge*, New York: Harper and Row, 1965, pp. 168–179.

Viner, J., "Adam Smith and *Laissez-Faire*," *The Long View and the Short*, Glencoe, Ill.: The Press, 1958.

Chapter 5

Martin, R. F., *National Income in the United States, 1799–1938*, New York: National Industrial Conference Board, 1939.

National Bureau of Economic Research, *Trends of the American Economy in the Nineteenth Century*, Princeton, N.J.: Princeton University Press, 1960.

North, D. C., *The Economic Growth of the United States, 1790–1860*, Englewood Cliffs, N.J.: Prentice-Hall, 1961.

Smith, W. B. and Cole, A. H., *Fluctuations in American Business, 1790–1860*, Cambridge, Mass.: Harvard University Press, 1935.

Chapter 6

Dorfman, J., *The Economic Mind in American Civilization, 1606–1865*, Vol. 2, New York: A. M. Kelley, 1966.

Miller, J. C., Alexander Hamilton, *Portrait in Paradox*, New York: Harper and Row, 1959.

Mitchell, B., *Alexander Hamilton, The National Adventure, 1788–1804*, New York: The Macmillan Company, 1962.

Morison, S. E., *The Maritime History of Massachusetts*, Boston: Houghton Mifflin Co., 1921.

Chapter 7

Balinky, A., *Albert Gallatin, Fiscal Theories and Policies*, New Brunswick, N.J.: Rutgers University Press, 1958.

Beard, C. A., *Economic Origins of Jeffersonian Democracy*, New York: The Macmillan Company, 1936.

Sears, L. M., *Jefferson and The Embargo*, Durham, N.C.: Duke University Press, 1927.

Introduction to Part 3

Clemence, R. V. and F. S. Doody, *The Schumpeterian System*, Reading, Mass.: Addison-Wesley, 1950.

Hirschman, A. O., *The Strategy of Economic Development*, New Haven: Yale University Press, 1958.

Innis, H., *The Fur Trade in Canada: An Introduction to Canadian Economic History*, 2nd Ed., Toronto: University of Toronto Press, 1956.

Schumpeter, J. A., *The Theory of Economic Development*, Cambridge, Mass.: Harvard University Press, 1934.

———, *Business Cycles: A Theoretical, Historical, and Statistical Analysis of the Capitalist Process*, 2 Vols., New York: McGraw-Hill, 1939.

———, *Capitalism, Socialism and Democracy*, Rev. ed. New York: Harper and Row, 1947.

Chapter 8

Goodrich, C., *Canals and American Economic Development*, New York: Columbia University Press, 1961.

———, *Government Promotion of American Canals and Railroads, 1800–1890*, New York: Columbia University Press, 1960.

National Bureau of Economic Research, *Trends in the American Economy in the Nineteenth Century*, Princeton: Princeton University Press, 1960.

North, D. C., *The Economic Growth of the United States, 1790–1860*, Englewood Cliffs, N.J.: Prentice-Hall, 1961.

Taylor, G. R., *The Transportation Revolution, 1815–1860*, New York: Holt, Rinehart and Winston, 1951.

Chapter 9

Albion, R. G., *The Rise of New York Port*, New York: Charles Scribner's Sons, 1939.

———, *Square Riggers on Schedule*, Princeton: Princeton University Press, 1938.

Gates, P. W., *The Farmers' Age: Agriculture, 1815–1860*, New York: Holt, Rinehart and Winston, 1960.

Gibb, G. S., *The Saco-Lowell Shops, Textile Machinery Buildings in New England, 1813–1949*, Cambridge: Harvard University Press, 1950.

McGrane, R. C., *The Panic of 1837*, Chicago: University of Chicago Press, 1924.

Smith, A. G., Jr., *Economic Readjustment of an Old Cotton State, South Carolina, 1820–1860*, Columbia: University of South Carolina Press, 1958.

Smith, W. B., *Economic Aspects of the Second Bank of The United States*, Cambridge: Harvard University Press, 1953.

Smith, W. B. and A. H. Cole, *Fluctuations in American Business, 1790–1860*, Cambridge: Harvard University Press, 1935.

Chapter 10

Hammond, B., *Banks and Politics in America*, Princeton: Princeton University Press, 1957.

Handlin, O. and M. F., *Commonwealth, A Study of the Role of the Government in the American Economy; Massachusetts, 1774–1861*, New York: New York University Press, 1947.

Schlesinger, A. M., Jr., *The Age of Jackson*, Boston: Little, Brown and Co., 1950.

Tocqueville, A. de, *Democracy in America*, New York: Oxford University Press, 1947.

Wade, R. C., *The Urban Frontier, The Rise of Western Cities, 1790–1830*, Cambridge, Mass.: Harvard University Press, 1950.

Ward, J. W., *Andrew Jackson; Symbol for an Age*, New York: Oxford University Press, 1955.

Introduction to Part 4

Rostow, W. W., *The Stages of Economic Growth*, Cambridge: Cambridge University Press, 1961.

Rostow, W. W., ed., *The Economics of Take-Off into Sustained Growth*, New York: St Martins Press, 1963.

Chapter 11

Gray, L. C., *History of Agriculture in the Southern United States to 1860*, Vols. I and II, Magnolia, Mass.: Peter Smith, 1958.

North, D. C., *The Economic Growth of the United States, 1790–1860*, Englewood Cliffs, N.J.: Prentice-Hall, 1961.

Rogin, L., *Introduction to Farm Machinery in its Relation to Productivity of Labor in Agriculture in the United States during the Nineteenth Century*, Berkeley, Calif.: University of California Press, 1931.

Temin, P., *Iron and Steel in Nineteenth Century America, An Economic Inquiry*, Boston, Mass.: M.I.T. Press, 1964.

Chapter 12

Fishlow, A., *American Railroads and the Transformation of the Ante-Bellum Economy*, Cambridge, Mass.: Harvard University Press, 1965.

Fogel, R. W., *Railroads and American Economic Growth: Essays in Econometric History*, Baltimore: The Johns Hopkins Press, 1964.

National Bureau of Economic Research, *Trends in the American Economy in the Nineteenth Century*, Princeton: Princeton University Press, 1960.

Rostow, W. W., ed., *The Economics Of Take-Off into Sustained Growth*, New York: St Martins Press, 1963.

Smith, W. B. and A. H. Cole, *Fluctuations in American Business, 1790–1860*, Cambridge, Mass.: Harvard University Press, 1935.

VanVleck, G. W., *The Panic of 1857*, New York: Columbia University Press, 1951.

Williamson, J. G., *American Growth and the Balance of Payments, 1820–1913*, Chapel Hill: University of North Carolina Press, 1964.

Chapter 13

Bruchey, S., *The Roots of American Economic Growth*, New York: Harper and Row, 1965.

Habakkuk, H. J., *American and British Technology in The Nineteenth Century*, Cambridge: Cambridge University Press, 1962.

Handlin, O. and M. F., *Commonwealth: A Study of the Role of Government in the American Economy, Massachusetts, 1774–1861*, New York: New York University Press, 1947.

Hartz, L., *Economic Policy and Democratic Thought; Pennsylvania, 1776–1860*, Cambridge: Harvard University Press, 1948.

Strassmann, W. P., *Risk and Technological Innovation*, Ithaca, N.Y.: Cornell University Press, 1959.

Turner, F. J., *The Frontier in American History*, New York: Henry Holt, 1921.

Ware, N. J., *The Industrial Worker, 1840–1860*, Boston: Houghton Mifflin, 1924.

Weinberg, A. K., *Manifest Destiny: A Study of Nationalist Expansionism in American History*, Baltimore: Johns Hopkins Press, 1935.

Introduction to Part 5

Higgins, B., *Economic Development*, Rev. ed., New York: Norton, 1968, pp. 227–41, 274–77.

Myrdal, G., *Rich Lands and Poor*, New York: Harper and Row, 1957.

Chapter 14

Andreano, R., *The Economic Impact of the American Civil War*, Cambridge, Mass.: Schenkman Publishing Co., 1962.

Fite, E. D., *Social and Industrial Conditions in the North during the Civil War*, New York: Macmillan, 1910.

Gilchrist, D. T. and W. D. Lewis, *Economic Change in the Civil War Era*, Greenville, Del.: Eleutherian Mills-Hagley Foundation, 1965.

Russel, R., *Economic Aspects of Southern Sectionalism, 1840–61*, Urbana, Ill.: University of Illinois Press, 1924.

Chapter 15

Conrad, A. H. and J. R. Meyer, *The Economics of Slavery*, Chicago: Aldine, 1964.

Eaton, C., *A History of the Southern Confederacy*, New York: Macmillan, 1959.

Elkins, S. M., *Slavery, A Problem in American Institutional and Intellectual Life*, New York: Grosset and Dunlap, 1963.

Genovese, E. D., *The Political Economy of Slavery*, New York: Pantheon Books, 1965.

Woodman, H. D., *Slavery and the Southern Economy, Sources and Readings*, New York: Harcourt, Brace and World, 1966.

Chapter 16

Barnes, G. H., *The Antislavery Impulse, 1830–1844*, New York: Harcourt, Brace & World, 1964.

Cash, W. J., *The Mind of the South*, New York: Knopf, 1941.

Frederickson, G. M., *The Inner Civil War*, New York: Harper & Row, 1965.

Nevins, A., *Ordeal of the Union*, Vol. II, New York: Scribners, 1947.

Nichols, R. F., *The Disruption of American Democracy*, New York: Macmillan, 1948.

Stampp, K. M., *The Peculiar Institution: Slavery in the Ante-Bellum South*, New York: Knopf, 1956.

Introduction to Part 6

Higgins, B., *Economic Development*, Rev. ed., New York: W. W. Norton, 1968, Chap. 4.

Lowe, A., *On Economic Knowledge*, New York: Harper and Row, 1965, Chap. 7.

Marx, K., *Capital*, New York: International Publishers, 1947.

Sweezy, P. M., *The Theory of Capitalist Development: Principles of Marxian Political Economy*, New York: Monthly Review Press, 1956.

Chapter 17

Fels, R., *American Business Cycles, 1865–1897*, Chapel Hill: University of North Carolina Press, 1959.

Kirkland, E. C., *Industry Comes of Age, Business, Labor, and Public Policy, 1860–1897*, New York: Holt, Rinehart and Winston, 1961.

Kuznets, S., *National Income, A Summary of Findings*, New York: National Bureau of Economic Research, 1946.

Cochran, T. C. and W. Miller, *The Age of Enterprise*, New York: Macmillan, 1943.

Chapter 18

Fogel, R. W., *Railroads and American Economic Growth*, Baltimore, Md.: Johns Hopkins Press, 1964.

Friedman, M. and A. J. Schwartz, *A Monetary History of the United States, 1867–1960*, Princeton, N.J.: Princeton University Press, 1963.

Ginger, R., *Age of Excess*, New York: Macmillan, 1965.

Noyes, A. F., *Forty Years of American Finance*, New York: Putnam, 1909.

Tarbell, I., *The Nationalizing of Business, 1878–1898*, New York: Macmillan, 1936.

Chapter 19

Buck, S. J., *The Agrarian Crusade*, New Haven: Yale University Press, 1921.

Clark, T. D., *Frontier America: The Story of the Westward Movement*, New York: Scribner, 1959.

Donald, D., *The Politics of Reconstruction, 1863–1867*, Baton Rouge: Louisiana State University Press, 1965.

Franklin, J. H., *Reconstruction: After the Civil War*, Chicago: University of Chicago Press, 1961.

———, *From Slavery to Freedom: A History of American Negroes*, 3rd ed. New York: Knopf, 1967.

Hays, S. P., *The Response to Industrialism, 1885–1914*, Chicago: University of Chicago Press, 1957.

Hicks, J. D., *The Populist Revolt*, Minneapolis: University of Minnesota Press, 1931.

Jones, M. A., *American Immigration*, Chicago: University of Chicago Press, 1960.

LaFeber, W., *The New Empire: An Interpretation of American Expansion, 1860–1918*, Ithaca, N.Y.: Cornell University Press, 1963.

McKelvey, B., *The Urbanization of America, 1860–1915*, New Brunswick, N.J.: Rutgers University Press, 1963.

Parrington, V., *Main Currents in American Thought*, Vol. 3, New York: Harcourt, Brace & World, 1930.

Pollock, N., *The Populist Response to Industrial America*, Cambridge, Mass.: Harvard University Press, 1962.

Randall, J. G. and D. Donald, *The Civil War and Reconstruction*, 2nd ed., Boston: D. C. Heath, 1961.

Sharkey, R. P. *Money, Class and Party*, Baltimore, Md.: Johns Hopkins Press, 1959.

Stampp, *The Era of Reconstruction, 1865–1877*, New York: A. A. Knopf, 1965.

Unger, I., *The Greenback Era, A Social History of American Finance, 1865–1879*, Princeton University Press, 1964.

Ware, N. S., *The Labor Movement in the United States, 1860–1893*, New York: D. Appleton and Co., 1929.

Introduction to Part 7

Dorfman, J., *Thorstein Veblen and His America*, New York: The Viking Press, 1934.

Dowd, D. F., ed., *Thorstein Veblen: A Critical Appraisal*, Ithaca: Cornell University Press, 1958

———, *Thorstein Veblen*, New York: New York University Press, 1900.

Boulding, K. E., *The Organizational Revolution*, New York: Harper and Row, 1953.

White, M., *Social Thought in America*, Boston: Beacon Press, 1957.

Chapter 20

Barger, H. and S. H. Schurr, *The Mining Industries, 1899–1939*, New York: National Bureau of Economic Research, 1944.

Barger, H. and H. H. Lansberg, *American Agriculture, 1899–1939*, New York: National Bureau of Economic Research, 1942.

Chandler, A. D., Jr., *Giant Enterprise: Ford, General Motors and the Automobile Industry*, New York: Harcourt, Brace and World, 1964.

Corey, L., *The House of Morgan*, New York: G. Howard Watt, 1930.

Faulkner, H. W., *The Decline of Laissez-Faire, 1897–1917*, New York: Rinehart, 1951.

Kendrick, J. W., *Productivity Trends in the United States*, Princeton: Princeton University Press, 1961.

Paxson, F. L., *American Democracy and the World War*, 2 Vols., Boston: Houghton Mifflin Co., 1939.

Chapter 21

Burnham, J., *The Managerial Revolution*, New York: The John Day Co., 1941.

Chandler, L. V., *Benjamin Strong, Central Banker, Washington, D.C.:* Brookings, 1958.

Hidy, R. W. and M. E., *Pioneering Big Business, 1892–1911*, New York: Harper and Row, 1955.

Hughes, J., *The Vital Few*, Boston: Houghton Mifflin, 1966.

Nelson, R. L., *Merger Movements in American Industry, 1895–1956*, Princeton: Princeton University Press, 1959.

Noyes, A. D., *The War Period of American Finance, 1908–1923*, New York: G. P. Putnam's Sons, 1926.

Schluter, W. C., *The Pre-War Business Cycle, 1907–1914*, New York: Columbia University Press, 1923.

Chapter 22

Blum, J. M., *Republican Roosevelt*, Cambridge, Mass.: Harvard University Press, 1954.

———, *Woodrow Wilson and the Politics of Morality*, Boston: Little, Brown & Co., 1956.

Hays, S. P., *The Response to Industrialism, 1885–1914*, Chicago: University of Chicago Press, 1957.

Hofstadter, R., *The Age of Reform*, New York: Knopf, 1955.

Link, A. S., *Woodrow Wilson and the Progressive Era, 1910–1917*, New York: Harper and Row, 1954.

Mowry, G. E., *The Era of Theodore Roosevelt*, New York: Harper and Row, 1958.

Wiebe, R. H., *The Search for Order, 1877–1920*, New York: Hill and Wang, 1968.

———, *Business and Reform: A Study of the Progressive Movement*, Cambridge: Harvard University Press, 1962.

Introduction to Part 8

Dorfman, J., *The Economic Mind in American Civilization*, Vols. 4 and 5, 1918–1933, New York, Viking, 1959.

Fisher, I., *The Purchasing Power of Money*, New York: Macmillan, 1911.

———, *Stabilizing the Dollar*, New York: Macmillan, 1911.

Keynes, J. M., *Monetary Reform*, New York: Harcourt, Brace, and World, 1924.

Mitchell, W. C., *Business Cycles, The Problem and Its Setting*, New York: National Bureau of Economic Research, 1927.

Chapter 23

Ginzberg, E., *The Illusion of Economic Stability*, New York: Harper and Row, 1939.

Kuznets, S., *National Income and Its Composition*, New York: National Bureau of Economic Research, 1941.

Leuchtenberg, W. E., *The Perils of Prosperity, 1914–1932*, Chicago: University of Chicago Press, 1958.

Lewis, C., *America's Stake in International Investments*, Washington, D.C.: The Brookings Institution, 1938.

Samuelson, P. A. and E. E. Hagen, *After the War—1918–1920*, Washington, D.C.: National Resources Planning Board, 1943.

Schlesinger, A. M., Jr., *The Crisis of the Old Order*, Boston: Houghton Mifflin, 1957.

Soule, G., *Prosperity Decade, 1917–1932*, New York: Rinehart, 1947.

Chapter 24

Berle, A. A. and W. C. Means, *The Modern Corporation and Private Property*, New York: Macmillan, 1932.

Burns, A. R., *The Decline of Competition*, New York: McGraw-Hill, 1936.

Clark, J. M., *Strategic Factors in Business Cycles*, New York: National Bureau of Economic Research, 1934.

Douglas, P. H., *Real Wages in The United States, 1890–1926*, Boston: Houghton Mifflin, 1930.

Friedman, M. and A. S. Schwartz, *A Monetary History of the United States, 1867–1960*, Princeton, N.J.: Princeton University Press, 1963.

Kemmerer, E. D. and D. L., *The ABC of the Federal Reserve System*, New York: Harper and Row, 1950.

Presidential Committee on Recent Economic Changes, *Recent Economic Changes in the United States*, New York: McGraw-Hill, 1929.

Chapter 25

Allen, F. L., *The Big Change: America Transforms Itself, 1900–1950*, New York: Harper and Row, 1952.

Benedict, M. R., *Farm Policies of the United States, 1796–1950*, New York: Twentieth Century Fund, 1953.

Boulding, K., *The Organizational Revolution*, New York: Harper and Row, 1953.

Potter, D. N., *People of Plenty*, Chicago: University of Chicago Press, 1954.

Taft, P., *The A.F. of L. in the Time of Gompers*, New York: Harper and Row, 1957.

————, *The A.F. of L. from the Death of Gompers to the Merger*, New York: Harper and Row, 1959.

Introduction to Part 9

Hansen, A. H., *A Guide to Keynes*, New York: McGraw-Hill, 1953.

Keynes, J. M., *The General Theory of Employment, Interest and Money*, New York: Harcourt, Brace and World, 1936.

Lekachman, R., *Keynes' General Theory: Reports of Three Decades*, New York: St Martins, 1964.

Robinson, J., *The Rate of Interest and Other Essays*, London: Macmillan, 1952.

Chapter 26

Mitchell, B., *The Depression Decade, from New Era Through New Deal, 1929–1941*, New York: Rinehart, 1947.

Schlesinger, A. M., Jr., *The Coming of the New Deal*, Boston: Houghton Mifflin, 1958.

Shannon, D. A., *The Great Depression*, Englewood Cliffs, N.J.: Prentice-Hall, 1960.

Wilson, T., *Fluctuations in Income and Employment; With Special Reference to Recent American Experience and Post-War Prospects*, London: Pitman, 1948.

Chapter 27

Chandler, L. V., *Inflation in the United States, 1940–1948*, New York: Harper and Row, 1951.

Hansen, A. H., *Fiscal Policy and Business Cycles*, New York: W. W. Norton, 1941.

Harris, S. E., *The Economics of America at War*, New York: W. W. Norton, 1943.

Hawley, E. W., *The New Deal and the Problem of Monopoly: A Study in Economic Ambivalence*, Princeton, N.J.: Princeton University Press, 1966.

Janeway, E., *The Struggle for Survival*, New Haven: Yale University Press, 1951.

Lekachman, R., *The Age of Keynes*, New York: Random House, 1966.

Tugwell, R. G., *The Democratic Roosevelt*, Garden City, N.Y.: Doubleday, 1957.

Chapter 28

Averitt, R., *The Dual Economy, The Dynamics of American Economic Structure*, New York: W. W. Norton, 1968.

Baldwin, W. L., *Antitrust and the Changing Corporation*, Durham, N.C.: Duke University Press, 1961.

Cohen, W., Jr., *Social Security: Programs, Problems and Policies*, Homewood, Ill.: Irwin, 1960.

Galbraith, J. K., *American Capitalism: The Concept of Countervailing Power*, Boston: Houghton Mifflin, 1952.

Schlesinger, A. M., Jr., *The Politics of Upheaval*, Boston: Houghton Mifflin, 1960.

Sutton, F., et al., *The American Business Creed*, Cambridge: Harvard University Press, 1956.

Introduction to Part 10

Domar, E., *Essays in the Theory of Economic Growth*, New York: Oxford Press, 1957.

Galbraith, J. K., *The Affluent Society*, Boston: Houghton Mifflin Co., 1959.

———, *The New Industrial State*, Boston: Houghton Mifflin Co., 1967.

Harrod, R., *Towards a Dynamic Economics*, London: Macmillan and Co., 1948.

Chapter 29

Brooks, J., *The Great Leap: The Past Twenty-Five Years in America*, New York: Harper and Row, 1966.

Hansen, A. H., *The Postwar American Economy*, New York: W. W. Norton, 1964.

Slesinger, R. E., ed., *National Economic Policy: The Presidential Reports*, Princeton, N.J.: D. Von Nostrand Co., 1968.

Vatter, H. G., *The American Economy in the 1950's*, New York: W. W. Norton, 1963.

Chapter 30

Dennison, E. F., *The Sources of Economic Growth in the United States and the Alternatives Before Us*, Supplementary Paper No. 13, New York: Committee for Economic Development, 1962.

Kuznets, S., *Capital and the American Economy*, New York: National Bureau of Economic Research, 1961.

The Rockefeller Report, *The Challenge to America: Its Economic and Social Aspects*, Garden City, N.Y.: Doubleday, 1958.

Triffin, R., *Gold and The Dollar Crisis*, New Haven: Yale University Press, 1961.

————, *Our International Monetary System: Yesterday, Today and Tomorrow*, New York, Random House, 1968.

Chapter 31

Bazelon, D., *Power in America: The Politics of the New Class*, New York: American Library, 1967.

Berle, A. A., Jr., *The Twentieth Century Capitalist Revolution*, New York: Harcourt, Brace & World, 1954.

Dale, E. L., Jr., *Conservatives in Power, A Study in Frustration*, Garden City, N.Y.: Doubleday, 1960.

Erikson, E. H., ed., *Youth: Change and Challenge*, New York: Basic Books, 1963.

Goldman, E. F., *The Crucial Decade: America, 1945–1955*, New York: Knopf, 1956.

Harris, S. E., *The Economics of the Political Parties, With Special Attention to Presidents Eisenhower and Kennedy*, New York: Macmillan, 1962.

Heller, W. W., *New Dimensions of Political Economy*, New York: W. W. Norton, 1967.

Jacobs, P. and S. Landau, *The New Radicals: A Report with Documents*, New York: Vintage Books, Random House, 1966.

Keniston, K., *The Uncommitted*, New York: Harcourt, Brace & World, 1965.

————, *Young Radicals, Notes on Committed Youth*, New York: Harcourt, Brace and World, Inc., 1968.

Kimmel, L. H., *Federal Budget and Fiscal Policy, 1789–1958*, Washington, D.C.: Brookings, 1959.

Koenig, L. W., ed., *The Truman Administration: Its Principles and Practice*, New York: New York University Press, 1956.

Lerner, M., *America as a Civilization: Life and Thought in the United States Today*, New York: Simon and Schuster, 1957.

Mills, C. W., *White Collar: The American Middle Classes*, New York: Oxford University Press, 1951.

———, *The Power Elite*, New York: Oxford University Press, 1956.

Newfield, J., *A Prophetic Minority*, New York: New American Library, 1966.

Nieburg, H. L., *In the Name of Science*, Chicago: Quadrangle Books, Inc., 1966.

Phillips, C., *The Truman Presidency: The History of a Triumphant Succession*, New York: Macmillan, 1966.

Schlesinger, A. M., Jr., *A Thousand Days: John F. Kennedy in the White House*, Boston: Houghton Mifflin, 1965.

KEY TO READINGS
ON AMERICAN ECONOMIC
DEVELOPMENT

There is a large body of excellent periodical literature on American economic development. Some of the best of these articles have been published in anthology form. Several such books, listed below, are keyed to the principal Parts of this text:

Andreano, R., ed., *New Views on American Economic Development*, Cambridge, Mass.: Schenkman Publishing Co., Inc., 1965.

Chandler, A. D., Jr., S. Bruchey, and L. Galambos, eds., *The Changing Economic Order*, New York: Harcourt, Brace and World, Inc., 1968.

Coben, S. and F. G. Hill, eds., *American Economic History, Essays in Interpretation*, Philadelphia: J. B. Lippincott Co., 1966.

Cochran, T. C. and T. B. Brewer, eds., *Views of American Economic Growth*, 2 Vols., New York: McGraw-Hill Book Co., 1966.

Nash, G. D., ed., *Issues in American Economic History*, Boston: D. C. Heath and Co., 1964.

Robertson, R. M. and J. L. Pate, eds., *Readings in United States Economic and Business History*, Boston: Houghton Mifflin Co., 1966.

Scheiber, H. N., ed., *United States Economic History,* New York: A. A. Knopf, 1964.

INDEX